Data Protection Law and Practice

Fourth Edition

Data Protection
Law and Practice

Fourth Edition

Rosemary Jay

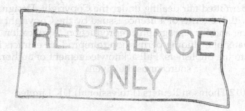

SWEET & MAXWELL

 **THOMSON REUTERS**

Second Edition   2003   by Rosemary Jay
Third Edition   2007   by Rosemary Jay

Published in 2012 by Sweet & Maxwell, 100 Avenue Road, London NW3 3PF part of
Thomson Reuters (Professional) UK Limited (Registered in England & Wales, Company No
1679046.
Registered Office and address for service: Aldgate House, 33 Aldgate High Street, London
EC3N 1DL)

For further information on our products and services, visit *www.sweetandmaxwell.co.uk*

Typeset by Letterpart Ltd, Reigate, Surrey

Printed and bound in Great Britain by CPI Group (UK) Ltd, Croydon CR0 4YY

No natural forests were destroyed to make this product; only farmed timber was used and
re-planted.

A CIP catalogue record of this book is available for the British Library.

ISBN: 978-0-41402-496-0

Preface

I am delighted to have been asked to write a preface to this new edition, the fourth edition, of *Data Protection Law and Practice*.

Looking back to the date of the first edition in 1999 it is striking to realise the extent to which digital possibilities have transformed the way we organise our lives, at work and at leisure. As this has happened, more and more personal information is generated—and needs to be safeguarded. Businesses, public bodies, charities, local councils and organisations, government departments, schools and hospitals all hold and process our personal information. In this environment Rosemary Jay's updated and revised text is greatly to be welcomed

It is also welcome that the text covers the practical implementation of data protection rules in many areas, for example data sharing, the use of data for research or the extent to which criminal records can be accessed. Good data protection practice can often be an enabler not an inhibitor—provided solutions are properly thought through at the outset. The smart use of data, within the rules, opens up possibilities for innovation and growth. To deliver these benefits users have to know and understand the rules and be able to apply them. Tools to help foster that knowledge and understanding are essential and the text provides clear explanations and assistance in many areas. Data protection now touches every area of our lives; if data protection was ever merely of interest to legal specialists that is certainly no longer the case

One of the many changes in the legal landscape since the last edition of this guide concerns the powers of the Information Commissioner himself. The ICO now has the power to impose significant penalties for the most serious breaches of the law. Civil Monetary Penalties have a major reputational impact and are helping to focus minds. The clear explanations of these new powers in the revised text should prove a useful guide both for data controllers and those advising them.

The text helpfully flags the current proposals from the EU and, looking ahead, one can see that a fifth edition will be needed once the shape of the new EU data protection regime is settled. The same drivers that have forced change over the past six years will undoubtedly continue their dynamic effect.

As we look forward we can also see that the cost of getting things wrong will continue to increase—both for individuals and for organisations—as our dependence on digital services grows. For the data subject, breaches of privacy, identity theft and intrusion are serious threats. Individuals are increasingly aware of, and concerned about, their information rights. Data Controllers will face challenges as they consider how well they are responding to this changed environment. Canny organisations will stay ahead of their customers' data protection concerns, since good DP practice will increasingly be expected—and sought out.

This book clearly represents a massive investment of work and time: an investment from which I am sure others will greatly benefit. The Duke of Gloucester's remark to Edward Gibbon comes to mind. 'Always scribble, scribble, scribble'. But Rosemary Jay has done more than scribble. This 'damn thick square book' is a significant achievement, covering the entire range of the topic and it is to be hoped that it will keep many a data controller from a data protection decline and fall.

Christopher Graham
Information Commissioner
November 2012

Introduction and Acknowledgements

It is a pleasure to see this 4th edition finally launched. It has been rather a long time in the making and there have been a lot of changes since the last edition. As a result there are several new chapters, including one on the Commissioner's enforcement powers which have increased significantly. The chapter on the European databases has been removed and much of the material incorporated into the chapter on the EU and international background. This is to give a better background to the section on proposals from the EU Commission that are being debated at the time of writing. Security now has a chapter of its own and the case law of the CJEU features in its own section. Most of the case studies have gone because the Commissioner's Office now produces material which is illuminated by case studies so the justification for having them in the text has diminished.

Given the many changes and the increased complexity of the area, completion of this edition has been a major task and thanks are due to many for their assistance.

In preparing this edition it has been particularly enjoyable to work with three fellow lawyers who have taken over responsibility for specific chapters. The book is much richer for their contributions. Sue Cullen, a Director of specialist training company Amberhawk, has re-written and much improved the chapter on the Freedom of Information Act 2000. Sue has particularly illuminated the development of the case law and its contribution to our understanding (or lack of it) of the term "personal data". William Malcolm, Privacy Counsel at Google UK, has contributed the chapter on Overseas Transfers, bringing to the topic the expertise of a lawyer in a global company intimately concerned with the processing of personal data. Ellis Parry, Global Lead Data Privacy BP, has very generously taken on two chapters, Research Exemptions and Subject Access. His expertise and contribution, particularly on the difficult area of research, is reflected in the real improvements to those chapters. Sue and William are ex-colleagues and I would like to also particularly acknowledge the contribution of another ex-colleague, Chris Pounder, also a Director of Amberhawk. Chris has been a staunch friend throughout the process. He has unearthed cases, provided material on security that I would never have found, had long discussions with Sue about the proper interpretation of specific provisions and, as if that was not enough, peer reviewed at least three chapters and greatly improved them in so doing. Special thanks also to a current colleague, Naomi McBride, for her work on the exemptions for legal proceedings and the material that she contributed to it.

Thanks must also go to all the other peer reviewers whose comments and contributions have been so helpful. To Anne-Christine Lacoste of the Office of the European Data Protection Supervisor for her comments on the chapter on the European background, Dr David Erdos of Oxford University for his on the privacy chapter, Eric Metcalfe of Monckton Chambers who commented on the Interception chapter and Robin Callender-Smith, a deputy chair on the First-Tier Tribunal (Information Rights), who commented on the Tribunals chapter.

Special thanks must go to the ex-colleagues from the Office of the Information Commissioner who were kind enough to review chapters and make expert suggestions or comments; David Smith, Jonathan Bamford, Phil Jones (now of Promontary), Julia Parr and Dave Evans. Also to Jonathan Holbrook for his kind assistance with some quirky queries.

I am also grateful for the support of current colleagues at Hunton & Williams who reviewed and improved chapters, Anita Bapat, Bridget Treacy and Richard Thomas. Thanks also to Jaymini Philps who came in at the last minute to review some final crucial changes in one chapter.

No acknowledgement would be complete without a thanks to the editor, Anthony Brady, who has been endlessly patient and helpful.

As ever my personal thanks to my family, George, Laurence and Lizzie for putting up with me over the last 18 months.

There have been huge changes since the first Data Protection Act was passed in the UK in 1984. We stand on the threshold of another momentous change if the current proposed Regulation is passed. As such it would be nice to be able to fully acknowledge all those who have contributed to the development of the text over the years, as well as all those who have helped and inspired me in working in this challenging area. That of course is impossible; all I can do here is make a nod to all the contributions, support, help and encouragement received over the years I have worked in data protection and on this and previous editions. There are too many to mention individually but Shelagh Gaskill, an ex-colleague who died some years ago, should be mentioned by name for the seminal work that she carried out on understanding and applying data protection through the 20 years after the passage of the first Act in 1984. I have never dedicated the text to anyone before but would like to dedicate this, probably the last edition of this text on the 1998 Act and the Directive on which it is based, to her memory in recognition of her contribution in this field.

Rosemary Jay
October 2012

TABLE OF CONTENTS

CONTENTS

CONTENTS

CONTENTS

CONTENTS

CONTENTS

CONTENTS

CONTENTS

CONTENTS

CONTENTS

CONTENTS

CONTENTS

CONTENTS

CONTENTS

CONTENTS

CONTENTS

CONTENTS

CONTENTS

CONTENTS

CONTENTS

CONTENTS

20. Civil Enforcement Powers Of The Commissioner

CONTENTS

CONTENTS

CONTENTS

CONTENTS

CONTENTS

CONTENTS

CONTENTS

CONTENTS

CONTENTS

CONTENTS

PAGE

APPENDICES

xiii

TABLE OF CASES

TABLE OF CASES

TABLE OF CASES

TABLE OF CASES

TABLE OF CASES

TABLE OF CASES

TABLE OF CASES

TABLE OF CASES

liv

TABLE OF CASES

TABLE OF CASES

TABLE OF STATUTES

TABLE OF STATUTES

TABLE OF STATUTES

TABLE OF STATUTORY INSTRUMENTS

TABLE OF STATUTORY INSTRUMENTS

TABLE OF EUROPEAN LEGISLATION

Conventions and Treaties

Regulations

Decisions

CHAPTER 1

Background, History And Context

INTRODUCTION

In the late 1970s and early 1980s the explosion of information power brought about by computing raised fears that the technology might undermine individual human rights and led to pressure for the adoption of protective measures. The possibility that such measures might restrict the movement and use of data gave rise, in its turn, to fears of a different kind; fears that trade would be fettered if information could not flow freely. The development of standards for the use and dissemination of personal data, or data protection standards, proved to be the response to these fears. The standards are now embodied in enforceable laws throughout Europe and in many other parts of the world.

1–01

Since the first edition of this text was published in 1999, information law has come of age. In each successive edition we have noted the range of relevant legal developments. In 2003 we commented:

1–02

"While data protection instruments, at both international and national level, were probably the earliest legislative responses to the information age, since then the field of information law has matured. There is a host of European legislation either in force or in preparation dealing with what can broadly be described as information law issues; numerous UK statutes cover or include information provisions and the courts are increasingly called on to decide cases concerned with information."

In 2007 we said that:

"The law affecting personal information has become a field in its own right. Practitioners can no longer consider data protection, privacy or rights of access as being specialist or niche areas; as information has become ever more necessary to commercial and public life, the laws governing its use have become equally significant."

Since then we have seen the increased spread of data protection laws throughout the world; the development of a new international instrument in the Asia Pacific Economic Cooperation (APEC) Guidelines, work on international standards for data protection and the inclusion of data protection as a fundamental right in the EU Charter of Fundamental Rights. As this edition is being completed, the EU is working on its proposal to replace the current Directive with a Regulation and the patchwork of provisions applicable to the areas of police and criminal justice with an accompanying Directive. When the law is moving and developing so fast it can be tempting to focus only on the immediate issues; however, sometimes a wider perspective can be useful. In this chapter we review:

- the background to the 1998 Data Protection Act, its national and international context. This is not merely a historical exercise; the older instruments may still impact on interpretation or approach, for example Treaty 108 of the Council of Europe continues to bind the UK, and that Treaty together with Recommendation No.R(87)15 Regulating the Use of Personal Data in the Police Sector remains relevant in rules relating to the exchange of personal data for the purposes of policing and anti-terrorism activities[1];
- the implementation of the Directive by the Data Protection Act and changes to the Act post-implementation;
- the action by the Commission against the UK;
- the European background to the regulation of data protection in Europe covering the development of the Union and the changes in the scope of Union competence as it has developed. We have tried to cover this as succinctly as possible but recognise that it is a complex area. Nevertheless, without an understanding of this European background, it is difficult to make sense of the current proposals for two data protection instruments rather than one and to appreciate the importance of the changes brought by the Treaty of Lisbon and the Charter of Fundamental Rights;
- the relationship with the development of EU law in this area covering data retention and the regulation of electronic communications;
- other European data protection transfer arrangements, such as the transfer of Passenger Name Records and work on the Terrorist Tracking Finance Programme; and
- the current proposals for change from Europe.

1–03   **The nature of informational privacy**   In addressing the background to the data protection regime, the broader context of privacy rights cannot be ignored. Data protection was developed to protect personal information held primarily in electronic form. The UK has been slow to recognise the importance of privacy rights and to protect them in law, although there has been a significant development of the law of privacy in relation to the publication of information by the press in the UK since the implementation of the Human Rights Act 1998 in 2000.

It is a matter of some regret that the Data Protection Act has been little more than an "also ran" in this developing case law on privacy. That is partly because much of the case law has been developed in the context of the use of personal data by the media and in that domain the breadth and procedural difficulties of the exemptions in the Act have hindered its use. In addition the UK courts, including on occasions the First Tier Tribunal (Information Rights), have tended to a particularly narrow view, for example in relation to the use and retention of

---

[1] See paras1-35 onwards. Framework Decision 2998/977/JHA governs the exchange of personal data between competent authorities for the purposes of police and judicial cooperation. National standards are still required to meet R(87)15 under art.25 of Council Decision 2008/615.

DNA or records of criminal convictions.[2] Despite this there are some encouraging comments in judgments for example Lord Nicholls commented in *Campbell v MGM*:

> "The importance of freedom of expression has been stressed often and eloquently, the importance of privacy less so. But it too lies at the heart of liberty in a modern state. A proper degree of privacy is essential for the well-being and development of an individual. And restraints imposed on government to pry into the lives of the citizen go to the essence of a democratic state".[3]

There has been recognition of the importance of data security since the loss of disks containing the entire child benefit database by Her Majesty's Revenue and Customs (HMRC) in November 2007 and the imposition of high fines on financial institutions which suffered similar losses.[4] There has also been some scaling back of the database culture since 2011.[5] On the other hand, the security agenda continues to drive the state towards increased surveillance and data exchange, and developments in technologies continue to increase the opportunities for data collection.[6]

Whether we are achieving a proper balance between privacy protection and social needs for data therefore remains a moot point. A report funded by the European Commission Special Programme for Fundamental Rights and Citizenship in 2011[7] assessed the countries of the EU for the level of protection provided for human rights and privacy. In relation to the UK it singled out the extensive use of visual surveillance and the extensive DNA database as particular problem areas. In relation to Europe generally it pointed to the influence of the security agenda in developments such as the imposition of requirements to retain data from electronic commuincations, an increase in the information made available to the police and other agencies and the mandatory inclusion of biometrics in passports.

Internationally there remains a lively debate about the level of protection or freedom from intrusion to which individuals may be entitled in their day-to-day lives, their work places and in cyberspace, as well as the most appropriate tools for achieving such protection.[8] Although the US has traditionally been considered to have less regard for the importance of personal privacy than Europe, it is often forgotten that it has had a Privacy Act regulating government departments and agencies since 1974 and most US States now have data breach notification laws. In 2010 the FTC issued a preliminary report on consumer privacy. The final report "Protecting Consumer Privacy in an Era of Rapid Change: Recommendations For Businesses and Policymakers," issued in March 2012, sets out

1–04

---

[2] For example in the case of *Efifiom Edem v Information Commissioner* EA/2011/0132 the Tribunal managed to decide that the names of individuals did not amount to personal data about them. Not surprisingly, the decision is being appealed to the Upper Tribunal.

[3] Lord Nicholls, para.12.

[4] Security is now covered in a separate chapter: see Ch.7

[5] See Ch.25 for a full discussion of data sharing.

[6] See the discussion of geolocation data and its uses in Chs 22 and 23.

[7] European Privacy and Human Rights conducted by Privacy International, the Electronic Privacy Information Centre and the Center for Media and Communication Studies.

[8] See the discussions on the scope of the proposed draft regulation at para.1–69.

recommended best practices for businesses in relation to privacy and also recommends the passage of general privacy, data security and breach notification, and data broker legislation.

The recommendations include ones that are familiar to anyone dealing with data protection and include privacy by design, security obligations, collection limitation and quality standards, greater transparency and more options for individuals, including the right not to be subject to advertising based on profiling.

In February 2012 President Obama issued a proposal for legislation on consumer privacy.[9] The proposal would entail the creation of a core set of fair information principles which would be fleshed out by codes of practice for specific sectors and enforced by the Federal Trade Commission (FTC). The core principles reflect those in the OECD Guidelines (covered below) and, to that extent, no doubt will be regarded as insufficient by more hard-line European regulators. However the initiative shows the increased importance attached to the protection of privacy and its relationship with commercial activity.

There remain serious differences between the European approach and that of much of the rest of the world. The US approach to regulation in this area appears to be pragmatic and the proposed US models are closer to the APEC standards and the OECD Guidelines that the European model. By contrast, the EU approach is increasingly doctrinaire and inflexible, with expansive view being taken by the Article 29 Working Party in many of its Opinions and a bureaucratic, process-driven approach adopted in the draft Regulation. There is no sign of any change to the EU focus on blocking transfers of data to countries without equivalent laws, irrespective of the level of risk posed by the transfer. It is therefore difficult to see how there can be a convergence of norms but it is to be hoped that at some point a global standard will eventually triumph over regional differences.

NATIONAL AND INTERNATIONAL CONTEXT OF THE DATA PROTECTION ACT 1998

United Kingdom developments between 1960 and 1972

1–05   In the United Kingdom, the late 1960s and early 1970s saw a commitment to individual rights which resulted in the passage of the Sex Discrimination Act 1975 and the Race Relations Act 1968. It also manifested itself in a concern for personal privacy. The Consumer Credit Act 1974 included provisions to allow individuals to have sight of their credit "files"[10] together with a mechanism for inserting Notices of Correction on those files where the individual disagreed with the information recorded by the credit reference agency. Various privacy Bills were introduced into Parliament during the 1960s and early 1970s.[11] Although the Bills had no real hopes of success they had produced sufficient impetus by May

---

[9] "Consumer Data Privacy in a Networked World: A framework for protecting privacy and promoting innovation in the global digital economy".

[10] Consumer Credit Act 1974, ss.158 and 159.

[11] 1967: Mr Lyon; 1969: Mr Walden; 1968: Kenneth Baker; 1969: Mr Huckfield; 1971: Lord Manocroft.

1970 to persuade the then Labour Government to appoint Kenneth Younger to chair a Committee on Privacy which reported in 1972.[12] As part of its work the Younger Committee undertook a survey of public attitudes to privacy which highlighted a high level of concern regarding the possibility of widespread availability via computers of information about individuals. Younger looked at both physical privacy, that is freedom from intrusion in one's home and family life, and informational privacy. It is in the latter area that his report impacted on subsequent data protection developments.

The Younger Report

The *Report of the Committee on Privacy* (the "Younger Report") was restricted to considering computing in the private sector. It formulated 10 principles which it recommended should apply in the handling of personal information where computers are used. Many of these principles have a familiar ring today and were largely embodied in the legislation in 1984. It is interesting to note that they concentrate particularly on security and access to data rather than issues arising from dissemination of information. This is not surprising given the nature of computing at the time, when communication between computers had yet to become a significant feature of ordinary computing.

1–06

The Younger principles were:

(a) The purpose of holding data should be specified.
(b) There should be authorised access only to data.
(c) There should be minimum holdings of data for specified purposes.
(d) Persons in statistical surveys should not be identified.
(e) Subject access to data should be given.
(f) There should be security precautions for data.
(g) There should be security procedures for personal data.
(h) Data should only be held for limited relevant periods.
(i) Data should be accurate and up-to-date.
(j) Any value judgments should be coded.

Younger recommended that these principles should form the basis of a voluntary code of practice which could be adopted by computer users. Younger also recommended the setting up of a Standing Committee to consider the use of computers and their impact on individuals.

Three years after the Younger Report the Government published two White Papers, one entitled *Computers and Privacy*[13] in which it announced its intention to consider legislation, and the other, *Computers: Safeguards for Privacy*,[14] which dealt with computer use in the public sector. Following the publication of these two White Papers in December 1975, the Government announced the setting up of a Data Protection Committee under the chairmanship of Sir Norman Lindop in July 1976.

---

[12] Cmnd.5012, July 1972.
[13] Cmnd.6353.
[14] Cmnd.6354.

The Lindop Report

1–07   The Lindop Committee's remit was to advise the Government on the best way forward, following the Younger Report's recommendations, to ensure appropriate privacy safeguards in the operation of computers in both the public and private sectors and to look for the establishment of such safeguards in some permanent form.

Lindop reported in December 1978. In his *Report of the Committee on Data Protection*,[15] he recommended legislation covering both public and private sectors. He further recommended that the legislation should be supervised by an independent data protection authority. The report proposed that principles for information use be adopted, as articulated by the Younger Report, covering broadly the same areas and in particular:

(1)   in the interests of data subjects:
    (a)   data subjects should know what personal data relating to them are handled, why those data are needed, how they will be used, who will use them, for what purpose, and for how long;
    (b)   personal data should be handled only to the extent and for the purposes made known when they are obtained, or subsequently authorised;
    (c)   personal data handled should be accurate and complete, and relevant and timely for the purpose for which they are used;
    (d)   no more personal data should be handled than are necessary for the purposes made known or authorised; and
    (e)   data subjects should be able to verify compliance with these principles.
(2)   in the interest of users:
    (a)   users should be able to handle personal data in the pursuit of their lawful interests or duties to the extent and for the purposes made known or authorised without undue extra cost in money or other resources;
(3)   in the interests of the community at large:
    (a)   the community at large should enjoy any benefits, and be protected from any prejudice, which may flow from the handling of personal data.

Lindop further recommended mandatory registration for computer users and the development and adoption of codes of practice to develop compliance with these principles. Such codes of practice would have the force of law. This concept was not adopted in the United Kingdom. Nevertheless, codes and other types of "soft" law have proved to be an enduring mechanism in data protection regimes and continue to have an important place. Several different kinds of codes can be produced under the Directive and the 1998 Act, although none of them have the force of law.

---

[15] Cmnd.7341.

It was several years before the Lindop Report's recommendations were taken further. However, in the interim there were also developments on the international front.

International developments 1978–1982

Over the period in which the United Kingdom was commissioning and considering national reports, the inter-relationships of computers, freedom, privacy and trade were also topics of concern among international organisations. The right to a private domain was recognised in art.12 of the Universal Declaration of Human Rights adopted by the United Nations in 1948 and the right to private and family life is one of the fundamental rights guaranteed by the European Convention on Human Rights and Fundamental Freedoms adopted in 1950 by the Council of Europe. Work carried out during the 1970s by the Organisation for Economic Co-operation and Development (OECD) and the Council of Europe came to fruition in two significant international instruments. On September 23, 1980 the OECD adopted guidelines governing the protection of privacy and transborder flows of personal data and on January 28, 1981 the Council of Europe opened Treaty 108 for signature, that is, the Convention for the Protection of Individuals with regard to Automatic Processing of Personal Data. Both instruments remain applicable today and may, in some instances, be relevant to assist in understanding or even interpreting the law. For that reason they are described in some detail in this chapter.

1–08

While the impetus at national level for law in the area of computerised information was concern for personal freedom and privacy, an equally important impetus for the international instruments was concern for the maintenance of free trade.

There were rumblings from some of those states which had adopted data protection controls in the 1970s which suggested that they might seek to restrict the movement of data about their citizens, to ensure that such data remained within jurisdictions in which the legal systems provided protection for their subjects' "informational freedoms". While the threats envisaged to the liberties of their subjects by the transfer of data might not have been completely clear, the rhetoric was chilling enough to be treated seriously. In a world where global trade was coming to depend on the use of computers and where the movement and manipulation of information was necessary for the healthy expansion of the global economy, threats to restrict data exchange on the grounds of concern for personal privacy were taken extremely seriously. International organisations moved to deal with these problems and develop instruments designed to reconcile the twin aims of respect for personal privacy and the need to ensure free trade between nations.

OECD GUIDELINES 1980

Summary of content

1–09   The OECD is an international organisation, two of whose primary aims are to foster economic stability and encourage trade and development. Like the Council of Europe it owes its existence to the vision of a post-war Europe rebuilt on a new model. It originated in 1948 as the Organisation for European Economic Co-operation, with the aim of co-ordinating national economic policies in Europe and liberalising European trade. In 1961, as other European institutions took responsibility for co-operation in economic and trading areas, it metamorphosed into its present being as the OECD. It adopted a new Convention and refocused its activities, working to foster economic stability and trade. It has 34 Member States, including the founding Western European countries, Canada and the United States plus Japan, Australia, New Zealand, Finland, Mexico and now a number of former Eastern bloc states.[16] The OECD is therefore an international body, not a European one. The membership of the United States and its contribution to its working gives the OECD a powerfully persuasive voice. In 1978 it drew up Recommendations and Guidelines in relation to data protection which were adopted by the Council of the OECD in 1980. The preamble to those Recommendations emphasises the concern that the moves to protect privacy might create unjustified obstacles to trade and recommends that Member States take account of the Guidelines in their domestic legislation in order to overcome the possibility of the growth of trade barriers. The Guidelines apply to data held in both public and private sectors:

> "which, because of the manner in which they are processed, or because of their nature or the context in which they are used, pose a danger to privacy and individual liberties."

Exceptions are provided for where appropriate and a list of governing principles with which data processors should comply is set out. They are:

(a)   personal data should be collected fairly and lawfully;
(b)   personal data should be relevant, and kept up to date;
(c)   personal data should be used only for purposes specified at the time of collection or compatible purposes unless under legal authority or with the consent of the individual;
(d)   personal data should be protected by adequate security;
(e)   there should be transparency in personal data use; and
(f)   there should be subject access to personal data.

They recommend that transborder data flows should not be restricted to other member countries. There is no formal process for Member States to ratify or adopt OECD guidelines. On adoption the Australian, Canadian, Irish, Turkish and UK governments abstained. However the guidelines were accepted by the United

---

[16] Czech Republic, Hungary, Poland and the Slovak Republic. In 2010 Chile, Estonia, Israel and Slovenia joined the OECD (source *www.oecd.org* May 2012).

States which did not abstain. Since the adoption of the Guidelines the OECD has continued to work in the area of data privacy and information security. In 2010 the OECD marked the 30th anniversary of the Guidelines, hosting a number of conferences and delivering a report on "The Evolving Privacy Landscape". The Guidelines are currently being reviewed by an OECD Working Party on Information Security and Privacy (WPISP) to determine whether they need to be revised or updated to address the current environment for privacy and transborder flows of personal data.

The OECD website explains that an expert group is currently

"addressing a number of issues bundled around the following themes:

- The roles and responsibilities of key actors
- Geographic restrictions on transborder data flows
- Proactive implementation and enforcement."

The expert group has been asked to make recommendations for consideration by OECD members by October 2012. The WPISP will then make a determination about how to act on the options presented.

The relevance of OECD material in interpreting the Data Protection Act 1998 is covered in Ch.3.

COUNCIL OF EUROPE CONVENTION 1981

Summary of content

The Council of Europe is a pan-European intergovernmental organisation. Like the OECD it developed from the post-war vision of a reconstructed and peaceful Europe. It was formed in 1949 with the aim of bringing political co-operation for the advancement and protection of individual rights and freedoms throughout Europe. It is responsible for the European Convention for the Protection of Human Rights and Fundamental Freedoms (the Human Rights Convention) and for administering the Court of Human Rights at Strasbourg. Unlike the OECD, the Council of Europe has a formal mechanism for adoption of its instruments.

1–10

In 1973 and 1974 the Council issued two early Resolutions concerning data privacy issues,[17] which it followed up by work on a more substantial legal instrument.

Spurred on by concerns for trading freedoms and individual rights similar to those that motivated the OECD, the Council of Europe drew up the Convention for the Protection of Individuals with regard to automatic processing of personal data (Treaty 108) over the same timescale.

In 1981, the Council of Europe opened the treaty for signature. The preamble makes it clear that its aim is to reconcile the need for privacy embodied in the Human Rights Convention right to private life with free trade as follows:

---

[17] Resolution (73)22 on the protection of privacy of individuals vis-à-vis electronic databanks in the private sector and Resolution (74)29 on the protection of individual vis-à-vis electronic databanks in the public sector.

"Recognising it is necessary to reconcile the fundamental values of respect for privacy and the free flow of information between peoples".

Treaty 108 covers both public and private sectors and allows for exemptions. Like the OECD Guidelines, it contains a set of principles to govern data processing. Its main principles are as follows:

(a)   fair and lawful obtaining and processing of personal data;
(b)   storage of data only for specified purposes;
(c)   personal data should not be used in ways incompatible with those specified purposes;
(d)   personal data should be adequate, relevant and not excessive in relation to the purposes to which the data are stored;
(e)   personal data should be accurate and where necessary kept up-to-date;
(f)   personal data should be preserved in identifiable form for no longer than is necessary;
(g)   there should be adequate security for personal data; and
(h)   personal data should be available to be accessed by individuals who have rights of rectification and erasure.

States should not restrict transborder data flows to other states which have accepted these standards and signed the Treaty. States may not sign the Treaty until they have national law in place guaranteeing compliance with the standards set out in it. Until states can give such guarantees they run the risk of trade barriers being erected against them or alternatively of becoming "data havens" for those who wish to avoid control of data processing.

While concern about personal privacy might not have been sufficient to produce domestic legislation from a UK government (of whatever political persuasion), the threat of trade barriers galvanised the government of the day into action. In 1984 the United Kingdom passed the Data Protection Act. In 1985 it signed Treaty 108, which entered into force, as far as the United Kingdom was concerned, in January 1985.[18]

Council of Europe conventions are binding on states which become signatory to them. Adherence to a convention may have different effect in different states' legal systems. In some cases the convention itself may be self-executing, that is "absorbed" into the national law. This is not the case in the United Kingdom. A convention will be of interpretative force and the UK courts will be bound to seek to interpret any national instrument passed in order to apply the convention in conformity with it.[19]

Following adoption of Treaty 108, the Council of Europe set up a Committee of Experts on Data Protection which has worked on a number of recommendations to Member States on various aspects of data protection. Those

---

[18] In 2001 the Treaty was amended to bring its provisions into line with Dir.95/46 ([2005] OJ L281/31).
[19] *Garland v British Railway Engineering Ltd* [1982] 2 All E.R. 405; *R. v Secretary of State for the Home Department Ex p. Brind* [1991] A.C. 696.

recommendations have been adopted by the Council. These are available on the Council's website and, although advisory only, give useful policy background in particular areas.[20]

Amendments to Treaty 108

Amendments adopted in June 1999 provide for the European Communities to accede to the Convention. The amendments also allow the Committee of Ministers to invite non-Member States of the Council of Europe to accede to the Treaty; however, such an invitation will require a unanimous vote of the Committee. There are associated provisions dealing with territorial coverage and voting rights. The amendment provides for states to apply the Convention to non-automated data and to records relating to legal persons as well as living individuals. States may also disapply the Convention but not to files which would be covered by national data protection laws.[21] As at the time of writing[22] 43 states have signed and ratified the Convention; however all are Member States of the Council. The state of Uruguay is the only non-Member State listed on the website but does not appear to have signed or ratified yet.

1-11

Additional Protocol to the Convention

An additional protocol was agreed on November 8, 2001, which explicitly requires:

1-12

- the creation of independent supervisory authorities with powers of investigation and power to bring legal proceedings; and
- that personal data shall not be transferred to states which are not party to the Convention unless the state affords an adequate level of protection for the intended data transfer.

The latter provision alters the burden in relation to transborder data flows from that originally included in the Treaty and is an example of the strengthening of data protection rules since the inception of Treaty 108.

The new provisions are to be regarded as additional articles to the Convention and are opened for separate accession.

At the International Conference of Data Protection and Privacy Commissioners in 2010 it was announced that the Council of Europe would be embarking on a programme to update the Convention and would involve its many stakeholders in the process. The consultation was opened on January 28, 2011 and posed a list of 30 questions on possible areas for change. Responses were required by March 2011. The first modernisation proposals were put forward by a document

1-13

---

[20] It should be noted that there has been a tendency to look to the Recommendations by the courts when deciding cases on difficult issues of policy. The ECtHR did this in *Z v Finland* (1998) 25 E.H.R.R. 371. In another use of soft law, the High Court in *Campbell v Mirror Group Newspapers* [2002] EWCA Admin 499 referred to Recommendations 1/97 of the Article 29 Working Group on Data Protection and the Media.

[21] Art.1 amending paras 2, 3 and 6 of Art.3 of the Convention.

[22] May 2012: *www.conventions/coe.int* [Accessed September 6, 2012].

prepared by the Consultative Committee in November 2011.[23] This Report recommended a number of changes including the inclusion of a breach notification provision. The aims of the review have been seen as bringing the Convention nearer to Directive 95/46/EC together with a commitment to ensure that the Convention remains technologically neutral and to ensure that it remains an open convention. Two further reports have been issued on January 18 and March 5, 2012 with the latter report setting out all the proposed changes for public consultation. Responses were requested to enable them to be considered and the final proposals submitted to the Committee in June. It was hoped that the changes as proposed would become effective by the end of 2012; however the procedure has been delayed and work is also taking place on coordination between the EU and the Council so the date of agreement and implementation may be some time away.

IMPLEMENTATION OF THE DATA PROTECTION ACT 1984

1–14   In April 1982 the Government produced a White Paper on data protection: *The Government's proposals for legislation*.[24] This was followed by the Data Protection Bill in December 1982. The Bill was introduced into the House of Lords but its passage was brought to an end by the 1983 General Election. In July 1983 a further Bill was introduced in the House of Lords which was to become the Data Protection Act 1984.

The 1984 Act drew on both the OECD and Council of Europe principles and the earlier work carried out by Younger and Lindop. It set out eight principles for data handling, largely drawn from the two international instruments. To the *Lindop Report* it was indebted for the concept of mandatory registration of data users. It also provided for appropriate exemptions from the rigours of regulatory control but did so largely by an unwieldy amalgam of registration and the duty to comply with the requirements of the Principles. The scheme of the Act was to require those data users who were not exempt to register with the Data Protection Registrar and only those data users who actually registered were then subject to the Principles.

Thus users who failed to register, and it was estimated that many thousands who should have done so did not do so, could not be required to comply with the Principles.

The Data Protection Principles were taken almost directly from the Council of Europe Convention. They required that:

(a)   personal data shall be obtained and processed fairly and lawfully;
(b)   personal data shall be held only for specified and lawful purposes;
(c)   personal data shall not be used or disclosed in a manner incompatible with those purposes;
(d)   personal data shall be adequate, relevant and not excessive in relation to those purposes;
(e)   personal data shall be accurate and where necessary kept up-to-date;

---

[23] T-PD-BUR (2011) 27: *www.coe.int*.
[24] Cmnd.8539.

(f)   personal data held for any purpose or purposes shall not be kept for longer than necessary for that purpose or those purposes;

(g)   an individual shall be entitled to subject access; and

(h)   there shall be appropriate security measures for personal data.

In one significant aspect the 1984 Act turned its back on its roots. Although the Younger and Lindop reports were fuelled by concerns over the loss of personal privacy in the computer age, and although both the OECD Guidelines and Treaty 108 specifically relate to the importance of privacy protection, basing their position on the right to private life in the Human Rights Convention, the 1984 Act remained resolutely silent on the point; it pointedly ignored any questions of privacy. The long title of the 1984 Act was:

"An Act to regulate the use of automatically processed information relating to individuals and the provision of services in respect of such information."

This had the curious effect of removing considerations of individual privacy from the interpretation of the 1984 Act except in so far as its genesis via Treaty 108 could be prayed in aid. A similarly obscure refusal to acknowledge its privacy roots can be seen in the 1998 Act which, despite the clear provisions of the Directive relating to private life, equally refuses to acknowledge it.

The long title of the 1998 Act is:

"An Act to make new provision for the regulation of the processing of information relating to individuals, including the obtaining, holding, use or disclosure of such information."

DIRECTIVE 95/46/EC AND UK IMPLEMENTATION

Directive 95/46 of the European Parliament and of the Council of October 24, 1995 on the protection of individuals with regard to the processing of personal data and on the free movement of such data ("the Directive") ("Directive 95/46 EC")

Data protection laws had already spread through Europe before 1981. After the adoption of Treaty 108 they became even more widespread. However, although these laws had a common root, they did not follow the same pattern. The generality of the standards set by Treaty 108 allowed for considerable divergence within the Convention norms. This provoked concern at Community level, resurrecting fears of the erection of trade barriers based on differential privacy protection in Member States. Although the European Commission had earlier hoped that questions of harmonisation of personal privacy protection could be addressed by ratification of the Convention by Member States, and in 1981 issued a recommendation to Member States to ratify Treaty 108,[25] the divergence of the laws adopted by different countries coupled with the failure of some states to legislate at all prompted the Commission in 1990 to address the issue of data

1–15

---

[25] Commission Recommendation 81/679

protection with the aim of harmonising Community law in this area. In 1990, the Commission issued a number of related draft measures covering this area including:

(a) a Directive on the protection of individuals with regard to the processing of personal data and on the free movement of such data (to become the general Directive 95/46);

(b) a Directive concerning the processing of personal data and the protection of privacy in the telecommunications sector (to become the Telecommunication Directive 97/66 later replaced by Directive 2002/58);

(c) a proposal that the Commission adopt a data protection policy; and

(d) a proposal for a Framework Convention on all Title VI agreements (e.g. police activities).

It took 18 years to achieve all four with the final piece, Council Framework Decision 2008/97/JHA, being a Decision rather than a Framework Convention. Out of these, the first two have had direct legislative impact in the United Kingdom. The general Directive was implemented by the Data Protection Act 1998. Directive 2002/58/EC concerning the processing of Personal Data and the Protection of Privacy in the Electronic Communications Sector was implemented by the Privacy and Electronic Communications (EC Directive) Regulations 2003 made under s.2(2) of the European Communities Act 1972. They came into effect on December 11, 2003. The Regulations are covered in Ch.22.

The Commission proposed a Regulation to protect personal data within EU institutions and bodies in July 1999. This was required by new art.286 introduced into the EU Treaty post Amsterdam. This took effect by virtue of Regulation No.45/2001 on the protection of individuals with regard to the processing of personal data by the Community institutions and bodies and on the free movement of such data. The instrument requires the Community institutions to comply with data protection principles and establishes the post of European Data Protection Authority with supervisory powers over Community institutions in the same way as national supervisory authorities. The proceedings of the Committee set up under art.31 of the Directive became subject to amended Conciliation Procedure under art.251 of the Treaty from November 20, 2003.[26]

The last proposal in the list, for a Framework Convention, was implemented by a Framework Decision on the protection of personal data processed in the framework of police and judicial cooperation in criminal matters.[27] It is not the only relevant instrument setting out data protection standards in the area as there remain a number of significant separate conventions and other instruments on Title VI matters. These instruments and the European background to them are described in outline below.

1–16 The first draft of the general Directive appeared in 1990, followed by second and third drafts in 1992 and 1993. Intense negotiations over the terms took place. The UK Conservative Government, intent upon following a deregulatory

---

[26] Regulation (EC) No.1882/2003 of the European Parliament and of the Council of September 29, 2003 adapting to Council Decision 1999/468/EC the provisions relating to committees which assist the Commission in the exercise of its implementing powers laid down in instruments subject to the procedure referred to in art.251 of the EC Treaty ([2003]OJ L284, p.1).

[27] Council Framework Decision 2008/977/JHA.

strategy, did not see the need for a data protection Directive at all and opposed the initiative throughout its European progress. Their opposition succeeded in bringing a number of changes to the detail of the draft but not in defeating the move to adopt a directive, and finally a common position was reached by the Council in February 1995 with the Directive being adopted in October 1995. Significant amendments were made to the Directive as it moved through the agreement process.

The Directive is reproduced in full at Appendix B and in each chapter reference is made to the relevant Articles and paragraphs of the Recital.

The focus of the Directive is on reconciling privacy protection with the free flow of trade. Article 1 sets out the object of the Directive as follows:

"In accordance with this Directive Member States shall protect the fundamental rights and freedoms of natural persons, and in particular their right to privacy with respect to the processing of personal data.

Member States shall neither restrict nor prohibit the free flow of personal data between Member States for reasons connected with the protection afforded under paragraph 1".

The Directive marked a step forward from the earlier thinking on data and privacy. It had a number of significant features which separate it from the previous UK law and from some of the other earlier instruments as follows:

(i)   it applies to some manual files;
(ii)   it sets out requirements for the legitimacy of processing as threshold requirements;
(iii)   it requires that specific controls be afforded to sensitive data;
(iv)   it provides for extensive individual rights, not only the rights of access and rectification;
(v)   it restricts transborder data flows outside the Community to those states without adequate protection;
(vi)   it provides exemptions for journalistic, literary and artistic purposes; and
(vii)   it significantly strengthens the security requirements for processing.

In other aspects, the Directive reproduced features of earlier instruments, providing for notification of processing on public registers and re-affirming the core Data Protection Principles.

Implementation in the UK

Directive 95/46/EC was implemented in the UK by the Data Protection Act 1998   **1–17**
and came into force in March 2000. The UK enacted generally applicable primary legislation, although this was not required by the Directive. Under the Scotland Act 1998 Sch.5 Pt II B2, the DPA is a reserved matter: that is, it is a matter which it is not within the power of the Scottish Parliament to influence or affect. It is also a reserved matter under the Northern Ireland Act 1998 Sch.3 para.40.

The Data Protection Act 1984 was repealed in full when the 1998 Act came into force (Sch.16) and most of the 1998 Act took effect immediately, however, some requirements were delayed by "transitional relief". The rules governing the application of transitional relief were complex. This complexity reflected the constraints imposed by the Directive itself and the Government's commitment to adopt an approach which would make the burden of compliance with the new requirements the least onerous possible. The Act also contains savings provisions to deal with those cases where actions were started under the 1984 Act but not completed before repeal. The aim of the transitional provisions was to allow for a smooth and gradual movement from the 1984 regime to the 1998 one. The transitional period for all data expired in October 2007. In earlier editions of this book the transitional provisions were covered in full but these have been omitted from this edition as they are now of historical interest only. Insofar as they have any remaining effect they are covered in the relevant chapters; for example the special provisions for data held for research purposes after 2001 are covered in Ch.18, which deals with the exemptions affecting personal data used for research.

The details of the implantation package and the passage through Parliament are covered in Appendix 1 in some detail. An excellent introductory overview of the Act is available on the website of the Information Commissioner so we have not included one in this text. There is a growing body of law dealing with information, and personal information in particular. Increasingly specific data protection provisions appear in legislation or other provisions and affect how the DPA applies in particular cases. Where possible we have tried to refer to these in the text but a practitioner researching a particular area should be careful to check for any specific rules.

1–18   **Subsequent amendments to the Act**   Major changes to the DPA were made by the Freedom of Information Act 2000 (FOIA). The relation between the FOIA and the DPA is covered in Ch.26. However, in summary:

- The responsibilities of the parties where data controllers receive a subject access request but need more information to find the information the subject seeks was clarified.
- The definition of personal data was extended in relation to information held by public authorities. Personal data falling in the extended definition became open to subject access and the remedies for inaccurate data apply to it but not the other data protection principles.
- Personnel records falling within the extended definition became eligible for a new exemption from subject access.
- Public authorities were required to include a statement in their notification to the effect that they are public authorities subject to the FOIA.
- A new offence of destroying records in respect of which an access request has been made, is created. This applies whether the access request was made under the DPA or the FOIA.
- The Data Protection Commissioner became the Information Commissioner.

The Act has subsequently been amended several times to extend the powers of the Commissioner. It was amended by the Coroners and Justice Act 2009. This gave powers to enable the Commissioner to carry out mandatory assessments of public bodies to check compliance with the legislation.[28] It also provided for a mandatory code of practice on data sharing.[29] The Act was also amended by the Criminal Justice and Immigration Act 2008 to increase the powers of the Commissioner to impose fines for serious breaches[30] and to provide for a term of imprisonment for the offence of unlawfully procuring the disclosure of personal data without the consent of the data controller, although this provision is not yet in force at the time of writing. The fees regime has also been changed by secondary legislation in 2009 and there have been a number of statutory instruments which have extended the grounds for the processing of sensitive personal data.[31]

UK reviews

There have been a number of reviews of the Act or its workings since implementation. In autumn 2000, even before the first transitional exemptions had expired, the Home Office undertook a post-implementation appraisal. This was partly in order to allow the United Kingdom to contribute to the European Union review required by art.33 of the Directive. Article 33 requires the Commission to report on the implementation of the Directive to the Council and the Parliament at regular intervals starting not later than three years after October 1998.[32] The post-implementation appraisal was stated to be undertaken,

1–19

"to assess the new regime's immediate effect, focussing in particular on those provisions which are new to UK data protection law".

The specific issues covered in the document and on which comments were invited covered:

- definitions of controller and processor and scope of manual records covered;
- conditions for processing and collection notices;
- sensitive data;
- arrangements for subject access and exemptions from it;
- revised notification scheme, particularly the exemptions;
- international transfers; and
- new technology.

The consultation evoked a range of responses however the recurring themes appeared to be the cost of complying with subject access requests and the difficulty of providing notices to data subjects in all cases. The response by the Home Office was fed into the early review of the Directive by the Commission (see below).

---

[28] The powers are covered in Ch.20.
[29] See Ch.25 on Data Sharing.
[30] See Ch.20.
[31] See Ch.10 for the notification regime and Ch.5 for the grounds for processing sensitive personal data.
[32] Arts 33 and 32.1.

1–20   A range of issues over the years have been raised by Commissioners and other in reports and papers and a number are referred to where relevant in the text; however it is worth singling out two issues which have recurred and given rise to a number of enquiries and publications. They are:

- the behaviour of the press in relation to personal information; and
- the sharing of data and its security.

One of the recurring themes arising from the reviews and reports was the absence of strong powers in the hands of the Information Commissioner. The sequence of reports and reviews was influential in bringing about the strengthening of the Commissioner powers. In 2006 Richard Thomas issued two reports, "What Price Privacy?" and "What Price Privacy Now?" revealing the trade in personal information and the use of private investigators by the press. Subsequent inquiries and reports in this area are still continuing with the results of the Leveson Enquiry not expected until at least October 2012. The reports by the Commissioner however were one of the first in this area which exposed this aspect of unacceptable behaviour by the press.

In 2007/2008 several reports were issued, sparked partly by the HMRC loss of data and partly by proposals to increase the powers of government to share personal data more widely. In 2008 the House of Lords and House of Commons Joint Committee on Human Rights produced a report on Data Protection and Human Rights, the Poynter report on the HMPC data losses was published and Richard Thomas and Mark Walport produced their joint report on Data Sharing.

The Commissioner's Office has also taken its part in the review of the European instruments. In 2008/2009 the Commissioner's Office sponsored a report into the Directive which was carried out by the Rand Europe and was intended to be a contribution to the debate on the future of the Directive.

Transfer of responsibility for data protection

1–21   After the passing of the 1984 Act, data protection remained the responsibility of the Home Secretary, latterly as part of the (unlikely sounding) Liquor, Gambling and Data Protection Directorate. In preparation for the implementation of Freedom of Information, responsibility was transferred to the Lord Chancellor's Department in autumn 2001.[33] Responsibility remained with the Department when it was renamed the Department for Constitutional Affairs in June 2003. It currently rests with the Ministry of Justice where it was transferred from May 2007.

COMMISSION ACTION AGAINST THE UK

1–22   In 2004 the Commission opened infringement action against the UK for failure to properly implement the Directive into UK law. The action against the UK has been shrouded in mystery despite the valiant efforts of some, including in

---

[33] The Transfer of Functions (Miscellaneous) Order 2001 (SI 2001/3500) made under the Ministers of the Crown Act 1975 came into effect on November 26, 2001.

particular those of an ex-colleague, Dr Chris Pounder of Amberhawk Training, to understand the reasons for the action. The grounds for the Commission's actions were finally set out briefly by the Commission to Dr Pounder following intervention by the European Ombudsman after his initial request for information in 2007 had been repeatedly refused.[34]

The grounds set out in a letter to Dr Pounder dated December 2010 cited the failure to properly implement the following articles on the following grounds:

Article 2 – a failure to implement the definition of "relevant filing system" as the interpretation applied in the case of Durant v FSA[35] by the Court of Appeal appears to be narrower than is required by the Directive;

Article 3 – the inclusion of "recreational purposes" within the exemption for personal and domestic use appears to be wider than the provision in the Directive which covers "household purposes";

Article 8 – there appears to be a concern that the UK law treats data on criminal offences differently to other categories of sensitive personal data;

Articles 10 and 11 – these cover the information to be provided to data subjects where information to be contained in personal data is collected from them or from a third party. The concern of the Commission is the exemption from these requirements where the information is to be made public under a statutory provision;

Article 12 – under this article data subjects have the right to check the accuracy and currency of personal data about themselves and have it updated, rectified, erased or blocked where it is deficient. The UK law gives courts a discretion in awarding remedies for these rights;

Articles 22 and 23 – in relation to the rights to judicial remedies and the award of compensation the DPA only provides limited rights to compensation for non-material damage;

Article 25 – there is a concern that the UK does not monitor the making of assessments of adequacy by data controllers in relation to overseas transfers; and

Article 28 – there is a concern that the Commissioner has inadequate investigative powers.

Leaving aside arguments as to the merits, for example how compensation for moral rights is are required by the Directive,[36] it seems surprising that threats of action before the ECJ have been raised against the UK as a result of this list of (in

---

[34] For more details (and indeed for one of the most entertaining, knowledgeable, thoughtful and refreshingly non-legal blogs around on the topic of data protection) see *www.amberhawk.com* [Accessed September 12, 2012].

[35] [2003] EWCA Civ 1746.

[36] The issue is discussed in Ch.14.

this commentator's opinion) largely minor issues but that nevertheless is the case. Exactly how the powers of the Commission have been used remains largely a matter of conjecture. The process is for the Commission to write to the Member State sending a Letter of Formal Notice of the alleged infringements after seeking any information required from the Member State. If there is no resolution then the Commission issues a Reasoned Opinion. It appears from information on the Commission's website that 90 per cent of cases are resolved and agreed at this stage but if not then the case goes to the CJEU for decision. The most recent information about the action against the UK which is publicly available appears to be a press release on the Commission's website.[37] This stated that the Commission had "worked with" UK authorities to resolve a number of issues but that several remained outstanding including limitations on the UK Information Commissioner's powers and "other" (undefined or explained) short-comings. The limitations on the Commissioner's powers were stated to be:

- the Commissioner cannot monitor whether the data protection laws in third countries are adequate and this should be done before international transfers of personal data are allowed;
- the Commissioner cannot perform random checks on data controllers or impose penalties after such checks;
- the Courts can refuse to enforce rights to have personal data rectified or erased; and
- the right to compensation for moral damages is restricted.

The current position is unknown as no further information appears to be publicly available. Given the timescales and the current focus on the draft Regulation and Directive it seems unlikely that this action will be pursued by the Commission but the possibility cannot be ruled out.

DATA PROTECTION IN THE EUROPEAN ORDER

1–23   There can be a mistaken view that Directives 95/46 and 2002/58 comprise the totality of European legal instruments regulating the use of personal data. This is a misconception. A whole range of European legal instruments include data protection provisions which govern arrangements for sharing information and are supervised in different ways. This fragmentation is a result of the history of, and the current arrangements for, co-operation between Member States of the Union in matters relating to immigration, border control, customs, justice, and home affairs. These arrangements are complex and continue to evolve at a rapid pace. The complexity arises partly from the mismatch between the fast pace of policy and practical initiatives for co-operation in these areas and the slow pace of developments in the EU legal regime. This has resulted in a patchwork of different initiatives and arrangements for co-operation which have evolved over a period of time.

---

[37] IP/10/811 June 24, 2010.

In order to understand the different data protection instruments in effect and the EU actions in this area and to appreciate the reasons for the 2012 proposals from the Commission it is therefore necessary to appreciate this background. This is set out below as briefly as possible.

Scope and application of Directive 95/46/EC

A directive is a secondary method of Community legislation. Authority for a directive must be found within the Treaties. It goes without saying that a directive, as with any other legislative act of the Community, can only cover those matters within Community competence. Directive 95/46 is a harmonisation measure. The Directive was passed as part of the Community's internal market legislation under art.95.[38] Article 95 provides that, in order to achieve the objectives set out in art.14, that is to create an area without internal frontiers in which the free movement of goods, persons, services and capital is ensured, the Council may adopt measures

1–24

"...for the approximation of the provisions laid down by law, regulation or administrative action in Member States, which have as their object the establishment and functioning of the internal market" .[39]

In Directive 95/46/EC the exclusion of those areas outside competence is made explicit in art.3(2) which provides that the Directive shall not apply to the processing of personal data:

"in the course of an activity which falls outside the scope of Community law, such as those provided for by Titles V and VI of the Treaty on European Union and in any case to processing operations concerning public security, defence, State security (including the economic well-being of the State when the processing operation relates to State security matters) and the activities of the State in the area of criminal law."

The basis of a directive may impact on the powers of the institutions of the Community to take action under it. The basis of Directive 95/46 as a single market measure led to a number of cases before the ECJ. In *Osterreichischer Rundfunk*[40] and in *Lindqvist*[41] the CJEU has held that the legal basis of the Directive as an internal market measure does not mean that there must be an actual link with free movement in every situation governed by the Directive. The same reasoning was applied in the challenge to the Data Retention Directive examined below. However, in the case of the agreements made with the US in relation to the use of Passenger Name Records (PNR) the Court ruled that the agreement was outside the scope of art.95. In view of the significance of the case in respect of the basis of the Directive we have dealt with it here.

1–25

---

[38] The basis of the Directive was specifically accepted in the Opinion of the Advocate General in cases C-317/04 and C-318/04 at paras 185–187.
[39] Title VI art. 95 Common Rules on Competition, Taxation and Approximation of Laws Ch.3 Consolidated Treaty on European Union.
[40] [2003] ECR 1-0000.
[41] See Ch.3 for a full description of the case.

1–26   The background is that, after the terrorist attacks in 2001, the USA had passed legislation providing that air carriers operating flights to, from or through US territory must provide the US customs authorities with electronic access to the Passenger Name Records data contained in their automatic reservation and departure control systems, PNR. The ruling would affect all EU air carriers and there was no clear mechanism to guarantee the lawful transfer of the relevant personal data about passengers to the US. The Commission purported to use its powers under art.26(6) of Directive 95/46/EC to determine that any PNR personal data transferred to the relevant part of the Department of Homeland Security (CBP) would be adequately protected. The Commission agreed terms with the US and made a formal determination on May 14, 2004 that the transfer of the PNR to the CBP on the terms agreed would provide an adequate level of protection for the personal data. This was followed swiftly, on May17, by a Decision by the Council using its powers under art.95 of the Treaty, which had the effect of implementing the terms of the agreement.[42]

1–27   As will be realised from the discussion above, given the legal basis of the Directive as an internal market measure, and the scope of the Directive as set out in art.3(2), this mechanism had an element of the fig leaf, if not the Emperor's clothes, about it and its success depended on the acceptance by all those affected that:

(a)   the Agreement with the CBP was related to the functioning of the internal market and could thus be made as an internal market measure by the Council within art.95; and

(b)   the processing involved, being the transfer of the PNR data to the US, was within the scope of the Directive so that the Commission was entitled to make a finding of adequacy in relation to its transfer under art.25.

Unfortunately for the Council and the Commission neither the European Parliament nor the European Data Protection Supervisor were willing to accept the view of the Council or the Commission as to the extent of their authority in this area.

1–28   The Court dealt with the cases as joined and gave judgement in May 2006 annulling the two instruments. In essence the Court ruled that the Agreement was outside the scope of art.95, thus the Council's purported Decision was a nullity. In the judgment it stated that art.95 EC, read in conjunction with art.25 of the Directive, "cannot justify Community competence to conclude the Agreement".

The Agreement related to the transfer of data for the purposes of preventing and combating terrorism and other serious crimes. As such the processing operations were excluded from the scope of the Directive and the Decision could not have been validly adopted on the basis of art.95 EC. Secondly, the transfer of personal data for the purposes of security was not covered by Directive 95/46/EC and thus the Commission had no power to make a finding of adequacy in respect of it.

The Court did not immediately nullify the adequacy finding but preserved it for a period of 90 days, until September 30, 2006. The 90-day period was selected as the termination period allowed for in the Agreement.

---

[42] See fn.33 above.

On October 16, 2006 the European Union entered into a replacement interim agreement with the United States Government on the basis of a Decision of the Council based on arts 24 and 38 of the Treaty.[43] Article 38 provides that agreements between the EU and states outside the EU may be made for the purpose of police and judicial co-operation in criminal matters. Article 24 allows the Council, acting unanimously, to conclude agreements with other states. Such an agreement will not be binding on a Member State where its own constitution would be breached. The case illustrates the importance of the basis of a Directive.

1–29

EUROPEAN BACKGROUND

The European Community was founded under the Treaty of Rome in 1958 (now referred to as the Treaty establishing the European Community or TEC) with the objective of establishing a common market without barriers to promote trade between Member States. At its inception its remit only covered economic matters, so foreign and security matters, justice and home affairs, and immigration control, were outside the scope of Community competence. It will be appreciated that data protection and privacy are relevant in all of these areas. Since its foundation the Community has moved towards economic and social integration. In 1987 the Single European Act came into force. Its aim was to remove the internal barriers within the Community to the free movement of people, goods, services and capital, creating a single internal market. As noted above Directive 95/46 was introduced as an internal market measure.

1–30

Schengen Accord

In a parallel development the "Schengen Accord" was adopted in 1990 outside the framework of EU law between those Community countries which agreed to abolish border controls between themselves (starting with the Benelux countries). The removal of border controls required consistency between the participating countries in the exclusion of those regarded as undesirable, the treatment of aliens and asylum seekers, documentation for those who entered the area and policing of borders. If an individual had been expelled from one state or was regarded as an undesirable entrant the individual should not be able to enter via the territory of another participating state. The Schengen Agreement or Accord was important in establishing the framework in which the free movement of people between the continental states could be achieved and now largely removes the internal barriers to the movement of people around much of Europe. A core element in making the agreement workable was the agreement to share information and institute an "alert" system which would pick up any attempted entry by anyone in the categories regarded as a threat or undesirable. This was achieved by the pooling of information between the participating countries via the Schengen Information System (SIS). Supervision of the Schengen system and the personal data involved are governed by specific rules in the Schengen Convention.

1–31

A second generation, more sophisticated, version of the SIS will cover all participating states. The SIS has developed to cover a wider range of security and

---

[43] Agreement—[2006] OJ L298/29 and Council Decision 2006/729/CFSP/JHA of October 16, 2006.

related issues than its original function of supporting border control. As the Schengen system has evolved a body of related rules, instruments and agreements has developed, referred to as the Schengen *acquis*.

Treaty of Maastricht 1991

1–32   After the Single European Act the next stage in the movement towards European unity was the Treaty on European Union (TEU) negotiated at Maastricht in December 1991. The Treaty had to be ratified by all the Member States before it could come into force. This process was completed by November 1993. It should be noted that Maastricht introduced a wholly new treaty and to the present there remain two separate treaties both having the same legal rank.[44]

The Treaty on European Union (TEU) (Maastricht Treaty) changed the role of the Community in three ways:

(a)   The areas of Community competence were extended, for example, two of the new areas of competence were public health and consumer protection. The new areas were absorbed into the existing framework of Community institutions, referred to as "first pillar" matters.

(b)   Agreement was reached on moving to intergovernmental co-operation in foreign affairs and security matters, referred to as "second pillar" matters. This co-operation between governments did not involve the institutional framework of the Community i.e. the Commission and the Parliament.

(c)   The Treaty laid the foundations of a "third pillar" of the Community, co-operation in justice and home affairs. This co-operation was also intergovernmental and did not involve the institutions of the Community. It required unanimous agreement between all the governments of the Member States to institute relevant measures. Areas included in the third pillar were asylum, immigration from third countries, and co-operation in combating drug addiction, fraud and terrorism. The third pillar also included policing and co-operation in judicial proceedings in criminal matters.

The background to the introduction of the third pillar lies in the growth of separate initiatives outside the structure of the Community to deal with co-operation in matters outside Community competence such as justice and criminal areas. These had given rise to a complex set of co-operative arrangements between Member States. The introduction of arrangements under the third pillar in the Maastricht Treaty were intended to simplify and streamline co-operation in these areas. Following Maastricht a number of third pillar conventions were adopted. These resulted in the development of large databases operated on a super-national basis and in respect of which data protection arrangements had to be made. In addition, art.30(1)(b) of the Treaty which deals with common action in the field of police cooperation included a provision on the collection, storage, processing, analysis and exchange of relevant information which was to be subject to "appropriate provision on the protection of personal data". This was the legislative basis a number of subsequent provisions inserted in specific instruments and subsequently Framework Decision 2008/977/JHA. It

---

[44]   TEU art.1.

should be noted that it did not require that the provisions should meet the standards laid down in Directive 95/46/EC.

Europol

Under the third pillar the development of a European police information unit was agreed at art.K.1 thus:

> "police co-operation for the purposes of preventing and combating terrorism, unlawful drug trafficking and other serious forms of international crime, including if necessary certain aspects of customs co-operation, in connection with the organisation of a Union-wide system for exchanging information within a European Police Office (Europol)."

1–33

This was originally the legal basis of Europol. It is now an EU Agency having been established as such by a Council Decision in 2009 which has been in force since January 2010.[45] The primary role of Europol is the exchange of information. Europol is not an operational unity. Since it was established the role of Europol has grown from the initial exchange of information about organised drug trafficking, to cover illicit trafficking in radioactive substances, clandestine immigration networks and illicit vehicle trafficking and trafficking in human beings. Like the Schengen Information System Europol was governed by a specific convention, the Europol Convention, which included specific data protection safeguards and rules however the relevant provisions are now set out in the Council Decision.

Customs Information System

There had been co-operation between Customs authorities throughout Europe since the 1960s but the development of the shared Information System was agreed under art.K3(2)(c).

1–34

Like the Schengen and Europol systems it is governed by its own convention, the Convention on the use of information technology for customs purposes. This came into force in the first half of 1999. The Convention has separate specific rules for the supervision of personal data.

The infrastructure of the CIS system is also used for the exchange of information at Community level about "frauds and irregularities in the customs and agricultural domains" (Regulation 515/97). The provision for common usage is made by Commission Regulation 696/98 of March 27, 1998 implementing Council Regulation 515/97 on mutual assistance between the administrative authorities of the Member States. The use of a common infrastructure means that this element of the system falls within Community competence and is therefore a first pillar matter. The CIS is therefore now supervised jointly by the EDPS and Member States as post-Amsterdam the first pillar matter became the responsibility of the new European Data Protection Supervisor.

Each of these is subject to supervision by Joint Supervisory Authorities. There are three separate Authorities for Schengen, the CIS and Europol. Since 2000

---

[45] Council Decision establishing the European Police office April 6, 2009 2009/371/JHA.

they have shared a Joint Secretariat.[46] There is also "co-ordinated supervision" by the EDPS and national data protection authorities with regard to Eurodac.

The Treaty of Amsterdam

1–35   The spirit of co-operation in third pillar areas was taken further by the Amsterdam Treaty signed on October 2, 1997 and which entered into force on May 1, 1999 having completed the processes of ratification in Member States. Title IV of the Treaty covered visa, asylum, immigration and other policies related to the free movement of persons. These provided that, within the five years following the entry into force of the Treaty, measures in relation to external border controls, asylum and immigration were to move to the first pillar. Over the five-year transitional period the Council had to act unanimously to introduce measures in any of these areas. This Title was subject to a Protocol on the position of the United Kingdom and Ireland. By this Protocol none of the provisions of Title IV or measures adopted pursuant to it are binding on or applicable to the United Kingdom or Ireland. However, they may choose to participate in any such measures and there are provisions dealing with the procedures to be adopted should they chose to do so. The issues of visas, asylum, immigration and judicial co-operation in civil matters are now therefore part of the first pillar but the UK and Ireland retain their opt-out.

1–36   Co-operation in policing and judicial co-operation in criminal matters remained as third pillar matters and were dealt with in Title VI of the Treaty. Title VI sets out steps for co-operation in these areas. Article 29 recites that one of the "objects of the Union" is to provide for its citizens

> "a high level of safety within an area of freedom, security and justice by developing common action among Member States in the fields of police, judicial co-operation in criminal matters and by preventing and combating racism and xenophobia".

Fighting crime encompasses fighting drugs, terrorism and organised crime. Policing and judicial co-operation in criminal matter remained areas of inter-governmental activity.

Article 34 sets out the mechanisms which are available to the Council to take action in these areas. These are the adoption of common positions, framework decision, decisions, or conventions.

Common positions define the approach of the EU to a particular matter. Framework decisions are formal instruments which are intended to achieve harmonisation of the laws of Member States. They do not have direct effect but Member States must ensure that the results required by the decision are achieved in national law. Decisions are instruments which apply to the EU itself but do not impact on the laws of Member States. Conventions are separate legal instruments which are recommended to Member States and to which Member States may adhere. The Court of Justice can rule on the validity and interpretation of decisions, framework decisions and the interpretation of conventions.

Under the Amsterdam Treaty, the Schengen *acquis* was incorporated into the EU's institutional framework, with the Schengen Secretariat integrated into the

---

[46] Council Decision October 2000: 2000/641/JHA.

General Secretariat of the Council. However the Treaty did not alter the legal structure of conventions already in force, therefore the Schengen, Europol and Customs Conventions remained in place.

Post-Amsterdam changes

The growth of the European databases continued post-Amsterdam, including a new Visa Information System. The Treaty of Nice amended Title VI to include an obligation on the Council to encourage co-operation in the investigation and prosecution of criminal matters through Eurojust, and Eurojust was established following a Council decision in February 2002. Once the five-year transitional period was over the functions of Schengen related to border control were integrated into the first pillar however, as part of the function of the SIS is to maintain public security, amendments to the Schengen *acquis* continued to have to be achieved by parallel instruments based on the different pillars. The functions of the SIS were extended by a Council Regulation (EC) No.871/2004 of April 29, 2004 and a Council Decision 2005/211 of February 24, 2005 both concerning the introduction of some new functions for the Schengen Information System, in particular in the fight against terrorism. These instruments illustrate the growth in the role of the information systems. The amendments to the Schengen Convention included:

1–37

- giving access to the SIS to Europol and the national members of Eurojust;
- giving access to the SIS to national authorities responsible for the investigation and prosecution of crime; and
- requiring Member States to record all transmissions of personal data and extent the period for which records are kept to three years.

European Data Protection Supervisor

Article 286 of the Treaty of Amsterdam dealt with data protection in the Community. It was incorporated to remedy the much-criticised failure of the Community to apply data protection standards and supervision to its own processing or that of organisations under its control. Article 286 states that Community Acts (i.e. data protection directives) on the protection of individuals with regard to the processing of personal data and the free movement of such data shall apply to the institutions and bodies set up by or on the basis of the Treaty. It also requires the Council to establish an independent supervisory body responsible for monitoring the application of the Acts to Community institutions and bodies. Accordingly post-Amsterdam the Directive has been applied to Community processing and compliance with it is now supervised by the European Data Protection Supervisor. The proposal for the post of European Data Protection Supervisor was adopted in November 2000 and established by Regulation of the Council in December 2000.[47] The Regulation also provides for the data protection standards, derived from Directive 95/46/EC, which apply to the EU institutions and bodies.

1–38

---

[47] Reg. 45/2001 of December 18, 2000.

27

This was confirmed and supplemented by a Decision of September 13, 2004. The supervisory role covers all Community institutions and bodies and applies to the processing of personal data carried out in the exercise of their activities all or part of which fall within the scope of Community law. The European Data Protection Supervisor has three main tasks:

- to monitor the EU administration's processing of personal data;
- to advise on policies and legislation that affect privacy; and
- to co-operate with other similar authorities to ensure consistent data protection.

The post-holder is appointed by the European Parliament and the Council for a period of five years. He has a position and independence equivalent to that of a judge of the Court of Justice of the European Communities. The Supervisor can receive complaints, conduct enquiries and is entitled to access rights to enable him to do so. In applying the requirements of Regulation 45/2001 to the institutions of the Community each institution and body must appoint an internal Data Protection Officer responsible for maintaining a register of processing operations. Systems which pose a special risk are notified to the Supervisor for prior assessment. The Supervisor is responsible for the data protection supervision of Eurodac, the database of fingerprints of illegal immigrants and asylum seekers in the EU as part of co-ordinated supervision with national data protection authorities. In addition he carries out Privacy Impact Assessments on new or proposed legislation and delivers formal Opinions on significant issues. He can order the rectification, blocking, erasure or destruction of all data processed in breach of the standards, impose a temporary or permanent ban on processing and warn or admonish the data controller.

CO-OPERATION OVER POLICING AND ANTI-TERRORISM

1–39   The events of September 11, 2001 brought a new impetus to cooperation over policing and anti-terrorist activity in Europe. The bombings in Madrid and London in 2004 and 2005 only served to reinforce the determination of policy-makers in the EU to ensure that Europe was armed against terrorist attack. Throughout the first decade of the 21st century the Council continued its work to strengthen freedom, security and justice in Europe. A significant part of that work involved the sharing of information for law enforcement purposes. The "principle of availability" was adopted as part of the Hague Programme that is that information needed for law enforcement should be available throughout the Union. In pursuance of this it adopted a number of instruments. The corollary was that no more large databases should be set up unless there was a clear justification for the initiative so there is now more focus on sharing national information. There was also a focus on setting up new arrangements for this enhanced sharing under Framework Decisions of the Council rather than separate agreements or conventions.

Numerous instruments have been adopted relating to cooperation in the areas of justice and policing since 1995. Early instruments were Council Acts or Joint

Actions but post-1999 they are Decisions or Framework Decisions. A document produced by the think tank Open Europe in January 2012 lists a total of 133 instruments adopted[48] by the EU in this area.

Many of the Decisions and Framework Decisions relating to policing and intelligence involved the exchange of personal data in some form. The two major instruments are:

- 2006/960/JHA of December 18, 2006 on simplifying the exchange of information and intelligence between law enforcement authorities of Member States allowed for the exchange of information for the purpose of criminal investigations or criminal intelligence operations; and
- Council Decision 2008/615/JHA on the stepping up of cross border cooperation, particularly in combating terrorism and cross border crime. This replaced the Prum Treaty, which had been entered into between a number of Member States wholly outside the framework of the Community and incorporated it into the EU framework as a third pillar instrument.

One of the recurring issues in this area has been the absence of consistent data protection standards in the instruments.

Background to the Framework Agreement on data protection

The absence of data protection rules and supervision in some of the data sharing arrangements and the lack of democratic accountability and transparency even where such rules exist have been constant refrains. In resolutions of March 27, 2003 and March 9, 2004 the European Parliament called for the creation of uniform data protection rules across the third pillar to provide equivalent standards to those in Directive 95/46/EC. The European Data Protection Authorities in their spring conference in 2005 called for the adoption of a legal framework for data protection applicable in third pillar activities and the European Parliament called for a more radical solution, the abolition of the third pillar and the transfer of all functions to the first pillar to enhance democratic accountability.[49] As Peter Hustix the EDPS put it:

1–40

> " ... the present general framework for data protection in this area is insufficient. In the first place Directive 95/46/EC does not apply to the processing of personal data in the course of activities which fall outside Community law, such as those provided for by Title VI. Although in most Member States the scope of the implementing legislation is wider than the directive itself requires and does not exclude data processing for the purpose of law enforcement, significant difference in national law exist. In the second place the Council of Europe Convention No 108 by which all the Member States are bound, does not provide for the necessary preciseness in the protection as has been recognised already at the time of the adoption of Directive 95/46/EC. In the third place neither of these two legal instruments takes into account the specific characteristics of the exchange of data by police and judicial authorities".[50]

---

[48] "An Unavoidable Choice: More or less EU control over EU policing and criminal law", Open Europe, January 2012.
[49] CAVADA Resolution June 8, 2005.
[50] 2006/C 47/12 para.4.

A form of general supervision was finally reached in the Council Framework Decision 2008/977/JHA on the protection of personal data processed in the framework of and police and judicial cooperation in criminal matters which was finally agreed in November 2008. While the Framework covers only a narrow area and has been the subject of continued criticism for its lack of scope it does at least put in place consistent standards to govern the initiatives such as the exchange of information extracted from criminal records and for the purpose of arrest warrants.

Council Framework Decision 2008/977/JHA

1–41   The Framework Decision was made under arts 30, 31 and 34(2)(b) of the TEU. It is one of the instruments in respect of which the UK Government had an opt-out right. The UK decided to opt into the Framework out of concerns that failure to do so could make it more difficult to share information with other EU countries for the purposes of combating crime.

The Decision does not impact on the use of personal data in national policing; it covers only the protection of personal data where that information is or has been:

- transmitted or made available by the competent authority of another Member State;
- transmitted or made available by Member States to authorities or information systems established on the basis of Title VI of the TEU (such as Europol); or
- transmitted or made available to the competent authorities of the Member States by authorities or information systems established on the basis of the TEU (such as Europol which falls under the third pillar) or the TEC (such as the Schengen System, the CIS or EURODAC or others which now fall into the first pillar).[51]

It does not cover information exchanged for the purposes of national security. It does not cover the exchange of personal data between Member States and third countries such as the US although it would restrict the transfer of data received from another Member State to a third country, and it does not affect the existing arrangements for data protection in existing Title VI instruments. This is dealt with at Recitals 39 and 40:

"Several acts, adopted on the basis of Title VI of the Treaty on European Union, contain specific provisions on the protection of personal data exchanged or otherwise processed pursuant to those acts. In some cases these provisions constitute a complete and coherent set or rules covering all relevant aspects of data protection (principles of data quality, rules on data security, regulation of the rights and safeguards of data subjects, organisation of supervision and liability) and they regulate these matters in more detail than this Framework Decision. The relevant set of data protection provisions of those acts, in particular those governing the functioning of Europol, Eurojust, the Schengen Information System (SIS) and the Customs Information System (CIS), as well as those introducing direct access for

---

[51] Council Framework Decision 2008/977/JHA art.2.

the authorities of Member States to certain data systems of other Member States should not be affected by this Framework Decision. The same applies in respect of the data protection provisions governing the automated transfer between Member States of DNA profiles, dactyloscopic data and national vehicle registration data pursuant to Council Decision 2008/615/JHA on the stepping up of cross border cooperation particularly in combating terrorism and cross border crime. . . .

In other cases the provisions on data protection in acts, adopted on the basis of Title VI of the TEU are more limited in scope. They often set specific conditions for the Member State receiving information containing personal data from other Member States as to the purposes for which it can use those data but refer for other aspects of data protection to [Treaty 108] or to national law. To the extent that the provisions of those acts imposing conditions on receiving Member States as to the use or further transfer of personal data are more restrictive than those contained in the corresponding provisions of this Framework Decision, the former provisions should remain unaffected. However for all other aspects the rules set out in this Framework Decision should be applied".

Instruments not affected by JHA 2008/977

The Framework Decision therefore only applied where other specific data protection supervisory arrangements are not part of the instrument. The following is a summary of the major instruments with supervisory arrangements over specific databases which are not impacted by the Framework Decision. It should be noted, as described earlier, that the supervisory arrangements are not the same for all of these databases.

1–42

- the Schengen Convention, which governs the Schengen Information System;
- the Europol Decision, which establishes information sharing arrangements for policing intelligence purposes;
- the Convention on the use of Information Technology for Customs Purposes;
- the Council decision setting up Eurojust,[52] which established Eurojust as a body of the European Union aimed at improving judicial co-operation and which includes provisions on data-sharing and supervisory arrangements;
- the Convention establishing EURODAC (the Dublin Convention). EURODAC is an information system holding data about requests for asylum made in different Member States and on illegal immigrants. Supervision of the EURODAC system is co-ordinated supervision between the national data protection authorities and the the European Data Protection Supervisor but the rules applied to it remain those in the Dublin Convention;
- Council Decision of June 2004[53] setting up the Visa Information System (VIS), a central information system on visa applications with an interface in each Member State.

---

[52] 2002/187/JHA OJ L063 06/03/2002.
[53] 2004/512/EC.

Obligations in Framework Decision JHA 2008/977

1–43   As noted above the Framework Decision is not applicable to a considerable number of arrangements. For those to which it is applicable it uses the same definitions as the general Directive with some additions, for example "to make anonymous" is defined as being to "modify personal data in such a way that details of personal or material circumstances can no longer, or only with disproportionate investment of time cost and labour, be attributed to an identified or identifiable person".

It includes :

- the principle that processing must be lawful;
- a requirement that processing of sensitive personal data is only permitted where "strictly necessary" and subject to adequate legal safeguards;
- purpose restriction subject to processing for compatible purposes being permitted where there are lawful grounds and the processing is necessary and proportionate;
- requirements that data should not be excessive and should be relevant and adequate to the purposes;
- requirements of transparency and rights of subject access, although these are heavily qualified by exemptions;
- rights of rectification, requirements for erasure when no longer required for the purpose and compensation for damage caused by unlawful processing; and
- restrictions on automated decision making.

Where data are transmitted to another Member State the transmitting State may restrict the time for which they are retained, must verify data quality before transmission and must log and document all transmissions. The use of received data is restricted to use for the purposes of policing or associated purposes, although this can be widened with the consent of the Member State which provided the information. Transfer to authorities in States is subject to safeguards and transmission to private bodies is restricted. There are stringent requirements in respect of the security of processing and requirements for the appointment of supervisory authorities. The Decision had to be implemented in Member States by November 2010.

Legal effect of third pillar instruments

1–44   Third pillar instruments, even ratified conventions, have an anomalous position in terms of European Community law. There is no recourse to the European Court as a matter of Community law, other than on interpretation or the validity of implementing measures, although one may be provided for under the particular instrument. There will be no direct effect stemming from a Decision, Framework Decision or Convention as it is not part of Community law. Neither Framework Decisions nor Conventions are directly applicable in UK law. The UK government has an obligation to implement them via appropriate national legislation. In the case of any ambiguity the UK courts will strive to interpret the law in accordance with the UK's international obligations (see Ch.3 for a discussion of this point).

Implementation of Framework Decision JHA 2008/977 in the UK

The UK did not pass any further legislation to implement the decision and reported to the Commission by November 2011 that its national legislation already covered the areas required. Some Member States reported problems with implementation due to problems in distinguishing which data uses were cross border and which were domestic and the application of different sets of rules on data protection.[54] This was one of the reasons given by the Commission for the proposal to introduce a directive covering data protection in the area of policing.

1–45

LISBON TREATY AND CHARTER OF FUNDAMENTAL RIGHTS

Proposed Constitution

After the Treaty of Amsterdam the next stage in European integration was anticipated to be the replacement of the existing treaties with one simplified and reorganised instrument. It was proposed that the document should be a constitution for the Union. The Constitution would, among other measures, have abolished the third pillar and brought the arrangements for police and judicial co-operation in criminal matters under the first pillar. The terms of the Constitution were agreed after much negotiation and the Constitution was signed in October 2004. However, it was subject to referenda in several Member States. Once France and Holland voted against adoption the process of adoption ground to a halt, despite the fact that a number of the governments in other Member States had agreed to the terms. Since then the growth of the EU by accession has meant that any re-negotiation of the terms of the Constitution would be even more difficult.

1–46

Charter of Fundamental Rights

Odd as it sounds, when the decision to draw up a Charter on Fundamental Rights in the European Union was taken there was no agreed view as to what its eventual legal form would be; whether it would become binding or be declaratory. A decision was taken in 1999 that a charter was needed and should be drawn up. The European Council stated:

1–47

> "There appears to be a need, at the present stage of the Union's development, to establish a Charter of Fundamental Rights in order to make their overriding importance and relevance more visible to the Union's citizens".

---

[54] House of Commons review of the Report of the Commission. European Scrutiny Committee Fifty ninth report of session 2010–2012.

There was also an aim to allow the EU itself to accede to the European Convention on Human Rights.

The charter aimed to cover rights of liberty and equality, economic and social rights, civil and political rights, and rights of citizens of the Union, bringing together the fundamental rights as recognised in the Community treaties, in the constitutional principles common to the Member States, in the European Human Rights Convention and in the social charters of the EU and the Council of Europe.

The European Parliament favoured enshrining the Charter in the treaties in order to make it legally binding on the Community and to allow those with rights under it to be entitled to take cases before the EU Court of Justice.

The Charter was signed at Nice in December 2000. It was incorporated into the proposed Constitution and would have become part of the legal order of the Union. Once the Constitution had been abandoned the position of the Charter remained legally ambiguous, although it was regarded as persuasive. It was subsequently adopted as part of the package agreed with the Treaty of Lisbon (see below).

The Charter incorporates a specific right to the protection of personal data as a fundamental right, in addition to the right to respect for family and private life. Article 8 reads:

"1.   Every person has the right to the protection of personal data concerning him or her

2.   Such data must be processed fairly for specified purposes and on the basis of the consent of the person concerned or some other legitimate basis laid down by law. Everyone has the right of access to data which has been collected concerning him or her, and the right to have it rectified.

3.   Compliance with these rules shall be subject to control by an independent authority".

The impact of the Charter on the interpretation of the Directives and the UK law is covered in Ch.3.

The Treaty of Lisbon

1–48   The Treaty of Lisbon was the most recent development in the maturing of the Union. It was signed on December 13, 2007 and entered into force on January 1, 2009. It did not replace the earlier treaties (TEC and TEU), which remain in force, but amended them. The Treaty makes the Charter of Fundamental Rights legally binding but does not incorporate the Charter into the Treaties. It remains a separate instrument but now has direct legal force. The UK negotiated a specific protocol on the Charter[55] but the effect of the protocol appears to be unclear.[56]

Under Lisbon the Treaty Establishing the European Community (Rome) is renamed the Treaty on the Functioning of the European Union (TFEU). The

---

[55] Protocol on the application of the Charter of Fundamental Rights to Poland and to the United Kingdom Declarations 61 and 62.

[56] The wording of the protocol is to the effect that it only applies to Poland or the UK to the extent that the rights and principles that it contains are recognised in the laws and practices of the Poland or the UK. It is therefore far from being a general opt-out. As data protection is recognised in the law and practice of the UK, art.8 is therefore presumably applicable and justiciable.

Treaty on European Union (Maastricht) is not renamed. The TEU has more constitutional provisions but the divide in not wholly clear-cut. Under the TFEU the areas covered by the previous third pillar, police and judicial cooperation, have been merged with the provisions on immigration, asylum and civil law. These now come under the heading of the Area of Freedom, Security and Justice, new Title V. Subject to transitional provisions, the opt-in agreements with some Member States including the UK, and some restrictions in relation to reviewing policing and law and order issues, these areas all become subject to the jurisdiction of the CJEU. The Common Foreign and Security Policy remains subject to a separate set of rules and executive authority on these areas continues to lie with the Council and the European Council.[57] The role of the CJEU in these areas remains limited.[58]

There is a clearer statement of competences setting out where competence is exclusive to the Union and where shared with States or supporting States.[59] Qualified majority voting becomes the norm in the Council, lessening the power of Member States to exercise a veto although these provisions do not come fully into force until 2017.[60] The Treaty also brought about institutional reforms. A president of the European Council is established. The Commission still retains the power to bring forward legislative initiatives with initiatives by Member States possible in some areas but the Parliament and the Council take a more active part in passing legislation. The standard procedure for legislation is to be the co-decision procedure. The Commission has acquired more power to take "delegated acts", which are a form of delegated legislation. An EU legislative act can delegate power to the Commission to enact non-legislative acts of general application to supplement or amend certain non-essential elements of the legislative acts.[61] The objectives, content, scope and duration of the delegation must be explicitly defined in the legislative act. Either the Parliament of Council may revoke the delegation or the delegated act enters into force if no objection has been raised by the Parliament or Council in the time specified.[62]The Treaty also provided that the Union should accede to the ECHR.[63]

Data protection provisions in the Treaty of Lisbon

In the TFEU art.16B replaces art.286 which was the basis of the appointment of the EDPS and provides a clear basis for the Commission to bring forward legislation for the express purpose of the protection of personal data, rather than as a single market measure.

1–49

"1.   Everyone has the right to the protection of personal data concerning them.
2.   The European Parliament and the Council, acting in accordance with the ordinary legislative procedure, shall lay down the rules relating to the protection of individuals with regard to the processing of personal data by

---

[57] TEU art.24.
[58] TEU arts 9 and 11.
[59] TEU art.8 and TFEU art.17.
[60] TEU art.9 and TFEU art.205.
[61] TFEU art.290.
[62] TFEU art.209(2).
[63] TEU art.6(2).

Union institutions, bodies, offices and agencies and by the Member States when carrying out activities which fall within the scope of Union law, and the rules relating to the free movement of such data. Compliance with these rules shall be subject to the control of independent authorities.
The rules adopted on the basis of this Article shall be without prejudice to the specific rules laid down in Article 25a of the Treaty on European Union".

TEU art.25a inserted in the provisions dealing with common foreign and security:

"In accordance with Article 16B of the Treaty on the Functioning of the European Union and by way of derogation from paragraph 2 thereof the Council shall adopt a decision laying down the rules relating to the protection of individuals with regard to the processing of personal data by Member States when carrying out activities which fall within the scope of this Chapter and the rules relating to the free movement of such data. Compliance with these rules shall be subject to the control of independent authorities."

In respect of the areas of common foreign and security policies therefore the Council would only be able to adopt a Framework Decision, similar to the one which currently applies to policing; however, in other areas it can propose a generally applicable law. In fact the Commission proposals for the reform of the data protection laws made in January 2012 were for a draft Directive for policing and cooperation on judicial matters relating to crime and a draft Regulation for all other areas. Further declarations on the protection of personal data in the fields of judicial cooperation in criminal matters and police cooperation and national security are appended to the Treaty, setting out a recognition of the need for specific rules in these areas.

"The Conference acknowledges that specific rules on the protection of personal data and the free movement of such data in the fields of judicial cooperation in criminal matters and police cooperation based on Article 16 of the TFEU may prove necessary because of the specific nature of those fields ...
The Conference declares that, whenever rules on protection of personal data to be adopted on the basis of Article 16 could have direct implications for national security, due account will have to be taken of the specific characteristics of the matter. It recalls that the legislation presently applicable (see in particular Directive 95/46/EC) includes specific derogations in this regard."[64]

Existing legislation, Directive 95/46/EC, and the regulation setting up the office and role of the EDPS is preserved and Protocol 10 also states that the legal effects of the Framework Decision on policing will be preserved until it is annulled repealed or amended.

There has been no proposal for a framework decision in respect of foreign and security matters.

The position therefore is that, as the Treaty is primary legislation, art.16 will have direct effect in Member States, and under the Charter the right to data protection becomes a fundamental right. Whether and to what extent this will have an impact beyond the terms of the specific EU rules in respect of data protection it is not yet possible to assess.

---

[64] Declaration 20.

TFEU art.218 establishes the need for the consent of the Parliament in all fields where the ordinary legislative procedure applies. Thus the agreements over Passenger Name Records (PNR) required the consent of the Parliament. The Parliament has already made clear that it will not easily accept instruments which it regards as deficient in providing adequate protection for privacy. It initially refused to consent to the Terrorist Finance Tracking Programme (TFTP).

UK opt-in to the Title VI instruments

The UK has preserved and extended its opt-in/opt-out provisions in respect of the Title V instruments. In essence, until December 2014 the UK has to opt-in to any new measures in this area and as at December 2014 has to decide whether to opt-out completely of all the measures or accept them all. There remains, therefore, considerable ground to cover and a degree of uncertainty on the road to harmonisation in this area. The UK has opted in to the introduction of a proposed Directive on data protection in the areas of policing and criminal justice which is covered further in para.1-70.[65]

1–50

ASSOCIATED AREAS

In addition to the general directive and the development of instruments covering data protection and cooperation in criminal justice and policing there have also been EU developments in the areas of regulation of privacy in electronic communications and in the retention of data in the electronic communications sector.

1–51

Directive 2002/58 concerning the Processing of Personal Data and the Protection of Privacy in the Electronic Communications Sector

Directive 2002/58 replaced Directive 97/66 concerning the processing of personal data and the protection of privacy in the telecommunications sector. The 1997 Directive was part of the package referred to in para.1–15 above. It applied to personal data processed in telecommunications systems. A Common Position was agreed on Directive 97/66 in December 1997 and national implementing legislation should have come into effect at the same time as for the general Directive by October 1998. It did not do so in the UK. The implementing legislation came in three stages. Some provisions, those dealing with direct marketing, came into effect in May 1999 in the Telecommunications (Data Protection and Privacy) (Direct Marketing) Regulations 1998.[66] These Regulations were then repealed and replaced by others which implemented all the requirements of the Directive bar art.5. The replacement regulations were the Telecommunications (Data Protection and Privacy) Regulations 1999 which came into effect in March 2000 with the main Act.

    Article 5 which covers security of communication and interception of telecommunications was implemented by the Regulation of Investigatory Powers

1–52

---

[65] *Hansard* April 2012.
[66] SI 1998/3170.

Act 2000 and regulations made under it, the Telecommunications (Lawful Business Practice) (Interception of Communications) Regulations 2000.[67]

Directive 97/66 was subsequently reviewed and replaced by Directive 2002/58. The new directive was required in order to deal with the never-ending increase in communications technologies including developments in digital mobile networks and email and deal with inconsistencies of interpretation of 97/66 in different Member States. It was implemented in the UK by the Privacy and Electronic Communications (EC Directive) Regulations 2003 (PECR) which came into force on December 11, 2003.

Directive 2002/58 was subsequently amended by Directive 2009/136 on November 25, 2009.[68] The amendments:

- strengthen the obligations of security imposed on providers of electronic communications services ("service providers")[69];
- impose an obligation on service providers to notify the regulator of personal data breaches and in some cases also to notify subscribers and users[70];
- require service providers to maintain an inventory of personal data breaches[71];
- strengthen the rules in relation to the use of "cookies" for non-essential purposes so they can only be used in cases where the subscriber or user has given a positive consent[72];
- require service providers to obtain prior consent to marketing for the purpose of value added services[73];
- extend the protection against unsolicited marketing by automated systems, fax and e mail to individual users as well as subscribers[74];
- require Member States to ensure that any person adversely affected by unsolicited electronic communications should have a remedy in legal proceedings[75];
- require service providers to maintain records of access requests to data for security and policing purposes and for the information to be available to the regulatory authority[76];

---

[67] SI 2000/2699.

[68] Directive 2009/136/EC of the European Parliament and of the Council of November 25, 2009 amending Directive 2002/22/EC on universal services and users' rights relating to electronic communications networks and services, Directive 2002/58/EC concerning the processing of personal data and the protection of privacy in the electronic communications sector and regulation (EC) No.2006/2004 on cooperation between national authorities responsible for the enforcement of consumer protection law.

[69] Art.2 amending art.4 of 2002/58.

[70] Art.2(c).

[71] Art.2(c).

[72] Art.2(5) amending art.5(3) of 2002/58.

[73] Art.2(6) amending art.6(3) of Directive 2002/58.

[74] Art.2(7) amending art.13 of Directive 2002/58.

[75] Art.2(7) amending art.13(6) of Directive 2002/58.

[76] Art.2(9) amending art.15 of Directive 2002/58.

- require that the national regulatory authority be given powers to enforce these provisions including powers of audit and criminal penalties as appropriate[77];
- encourage the adoption of measures to ensure effective cross-border enforcement;[78] and
- make a number of drafting clarifications.[79]

The changes were to be implemented by Member States by May 2011. Regulations amending PECR were introduced on the May 4, 2011 and came into effect on May 25.[80] PECR is dealt with in full in Ch.22.

DATA RETENTION DIRECTIVE

Directive 2006/24 on the retention of data generated or processed in connection with the provision of publicly available electronic communication services or of public communications networks and amending Directive 2002/58 EC

The details of Directive 2006/24 are dealt with in Ch.23 on Interception. It amended arts 5, 6 and 9 of Directive 2002/58/EC which cover the privacy of communications and retention of traffic and location data to require Member States to ensure that providers of publicly available electronic communication services retain certain categories of data and allow access to such retained data by competent national authorities.

1–53

Directive 2006/24/EC is a further example of the fine lines that have had to be observed in producing Community legislation dealing with data protection and law enforcement matters. The political reality is that a number of governments have wished to enforce the retention of communications data by service providers and to have access to it by law enforcement agencies since September 11, 2001 and earlier. However the retention was forbidden by 1997/66 and then 2002/58, which required the erasure of communications data once it was no longer needed for the purpose of the services. In any event the provision of access to the data would be out with Community competence. The position was finally dealt with in 2006/ 24/EC.

As we have seen above no directive can cover matters outside Community competence and Directive 2006/24/EC explicitly states (Recital 25) that issues of access by law enforcement agencies to data retained pursuant to implementing national provisions are outside the scope of Community law, and hence the Directive; although they may be covered by national law or action under Title VI of the Treaty. Directive 2006/ 24/EC was made under art.95 of the Treaty as a single market measure on the basis that a number of Member States had exercised powers under art.15(1) of Directive 2002/58, which allows Member States to

1–54

---

[77] Arts 2(4) and 2(10) amending Directive 2002/58 by the addition of new art.15a.

[78] Arts 2(4) and 2(10).

[79] Art.2.

[80] The Privacy and Electronic Communications (EC Directive) (Amendment) Regulations 2011 (SI 2011/1208).

provide derogations from the rights in arts 5, 6, 8 and 9 of 2002/58, to require service providers to retain data for the purposes of law enforcement. It goes on to explain that:

> "The legal and technical differences between national provisions concerning the retention of data for the purpose of the prevention, investigation, detection and prosecution of criminal offences present obstacles to the internal market for electronic communications, since service providers are faced with different requirements regarding the types of traffic and location data to be retained and the conditions and periods for retention."[81]

Accordingly the retention of data under the Directive was justifiable as a single market measure. The Directive is applicable to the data retained by service providers as they are not part of the State or acting for the State in the retention following *Lindqvist*. This would appear to be an arguable, if bold, position although one has to wonder what justification could have been found if there had been no contradictory national law to pray in aid. However the Directive also deals with ensuring that the retained data are "... available for the purpose of the investigation, detection and prosecution of serious crime". It would be difficult to justify this as a single market measure (to put it mildly) and the justification is not at all clear (at least to this commentator) Recital 9 states that the Directive is necessary to provide a lawful basis for the retention given the requirements of art.8 ECHR but does not set out the single market justification. A challenge was mounted to Directive 2006/24/EC in the European Court by Ireland and Slovakia which was unsuccessful however there have remained problems with implementation throughout the EU as in Romania, Germany and the Czech Republic the transposing laws were annulled as unconstitutional by the respective Constitutional Courts. The directive was implemented fully in the UK under the Data Retention (EC Directive) Regulations 2009 and is covered in Ch.24.

REVIEW OF DIRECTIVE 95/46—EUROPEAN COMMISSION

1–55   Developments in the area of data protection continued in parallel to the major changes taking place in the Union. In 2002 the European Commission embarked upon a review of the implementation of the Directive. In its Report following the review it explained that it had not only carried out the review of implementation but conducted an open public debate on the area, which was justified, not only by the nature of the Directive, but the rapid pace of technological change and other international developments since the Directive was finalised in 1995. In carrying out the review the Commission sought a wide range of views including Member State governments, supervisory authorities citizens and data controllers.

---

[81] Recital 5.

Commission position

The Commission issued its Report in May 2003.[82] It concluded that it was not appropriate to make amendments to the Directive in the immediate future because:

1–56

- the delay in implementation meant that there was inadequate experience of the current Directive on which to make sound decisions;
- it considered that many of the difficulties which had been identified in the review could be resolved without amendment as they arose because of the implementation by Member States or the application of the margin of appreciation rather than the requirements of the Directive;
- some proposals for amendment, which were aimed at reducing the burdens of compliance for controllers, would have the effect of reducing the protection of individuals. This would not be possible as those protections are guaranteed by other binding legal instruments such as Treaty 108.

However the Report made clear that there remained work to be done, in particular it expressed concerns at the divergence between the legislation in Member States, particularly on the rules relating to transfers to third countries, and at the problems with weak enforcement, low levels of awareness of rights among data subjects and patchy compliance by data controllers. The Commission indicated that it would be prepared to use its powers under art.226 of the Treaty to enforce compliance but would prefer to proceed by discussion with Member States.

As a result of the review the Commission set out a work programme to address the perceived problems which it then sought to address over the following years.

Follow up programme

In 2007 the Commission published a report on the follow-up of the Work Programme,[83] which set out progress to date. The Action Points from the earlier report are set out below together with a short explanation of the perceived problem giving rise to the need for the action point and a commentary on progress since 2003 and the follow-up Report.

1–57

Commission's initiatives

Action 1: Discussion with Member States and Data Protection Authorities
This was to address any changes needed to national legislation to bring it fully into line with the Directive; to consider strengthening enforcement and discuss improving resources where necessary. Work would also include discussions by the Article 29 and 31 Working Parties and discussions at other meetings with Member States. In 2007 the Commission simply reported that a "structured

---

[82] Report from the Commission First report on the implementation of the Data Protection Directive (95/46/EC) Brussels May 15, 2003 COM(2003) 265 Final.
[83] Com(2007) 87 Final

dialogue" had been in process with Member States with the aim of bringing all the national legislation fully into compliance.

Action 2: Association of the candidate countries with efforts to achieve a better and more uniform implementation of the Directive   The Commission committed to bilateral discussions and possibly peer review to continue up to and beyond accession to ensure alignment of the laws of the accession countries with the Directive. On this the 2007 Report stated that the Commission has been working closely with Authorities to ensure proper alignment with the *acquis*.

Action 3: Improving the notification of all legal acts transposing the Directive and notifications of authorisations granted under art.26(2) of the Directive   The Commission determined to continue to collect data on implementation and exhorted Member States to notify national authorisations for transfer granted under Article 26(2). It committed to the creation of a new web page on work progress on the work plan. In 2007 it reported that there had been an increase in notifications from some Member States and some key national papers, policies and other documents had been put onto the Commission's website.

Action 4: Enforcement   The Article 29 Working Party was asked to consider enforcement practices and compliance guidance for sectors. In 2007 it reported on a Declaration on Enforcement in which the Article 29 Working Party agreed on the criteria for identifying issues for EU wide investigations. In March 2006 the Data Protection Authorities launched a joint investigation on the processing of personal data in the health insurance sector.

Action 5: Notification and publicising of processing operations   There was criticism of divergent notification requirements and the Article 29 Working Party was asked to put forward proposals for simplification and co-operation mechanisms. In 2007 the Commission reported that the Working Party had produced the Report requested and made similar recommendations to those made by the Commission.

Action 6: More harmonised information provisions   This addressed the "fair processing notice" requirements which vary from State to State. The Commission proposed to address this with Member States in so far as it results from inadequate transposition and also called on the Article 29 Working Party to search for a more uniform interpretation. The 2007 Report referred to the work of the Article 29 Working Party and the guidance on multi-layered privacy notices as well as the PNR data notice guidance.

Action 7: Simplification of the requirements for international transfers
This was perhaps the most forceful action point. The Article 29 Working Party was asked to raise discussions about simplification and harmonisation of practices. The Commission stated its intention to make use of the powers under arts 25(6) and 26(4) to make further findings of adequacy or settle agreed contractual clauses respectively; to work on the development of binding

corporate rules and seek a more uniform approach nationally to art.26(1) on adequacy. In the 2007 Report it refers to its further findings on adequacy, the Safe Harbor review, the increase in transfer clauses, Binding Corporate Rules and the Opinion of the Working Party on Article 26.[84]

Other initiatives

Action 8: Promotion of Privacy Enhancing Technologies   The Commission reports on its existing work in this area and commits to further work and consideration of the promotion of PETS by mechanisms such as seals or certification systems. The 2007 Report promises a forthcoming Commission Communication on this.

1–58

Action 9: Promotion of self-regulation and European Codes of Conducts The Commission expressed disappointment at the dearth of Community Codes presented by industry groups. It encouraged the development of such codes. It voiced a hope that an EU instrument on employment and personal data would be possible. The Report in 2007 welcomed the acceptance of the FEDMA code[85] and regretted that it had not been possible to reach agreement on the employment code.

Action 10: Awareness raising   The Commission announced its intention to launch a Eurobarometer survey along the lines of the 2002 consultation. The 2007 Report stated that the survey had been conducted and had shown "that people are concerned about privacy issues, but not sufficiently aware of the existing rules and mechanisms to protect their rights"

In its Overview in the 2007 report the Commission accepted that Member States had transposed the Directive although there remained some concerns at incoherent or inadequate transposition. Overall they concluded that the Directive had succeeded in its aims and did not require amendment. There remained however the continuing problems arising because of the separation of Third Pillar matters and the need to address that.[86] It concluded that the Commission would keep the Directive under review and continue to work with Member States to achieve better harmonisation.

2009 Review

The Commission's next review was conducted in 2009. The review was launched at a conference in May 2009 with the aim of considering the future of the legal framework and how to respond to the challenges of technological change and globalisation. The Commission launched further studies and a public consultation. The Information Commissioner commissioned a report from the Rand Group on the future of the Directive as a contribution to the debate.[87] The Commission review found, in summary, that the core principles of the Directive

1–59

---

[84] See Ch.8 for a full exposition of the rules governing transfers of personal data outside the EEA.
[85] Federation of European Direct Marketing Associations.
[86] [2003] EWCA Civ 1746.
[87] Available from the Commissioner's website at *www.ico.gov.uk* [Accessed September 12, 2012].

remained valid and its technologically neutral character should be preserved. However several issues were identified as being problematic as follows:

- a need to ensure that the principles of privacy protection are applicable and applied to new technologies such as cloud computing, geolocation services and tracing technologies;
- a need to increase harmonisation between Member States to assist business;
- a need to address the globalisation of data transfers and the growth in outsourced processing with the aim of making transfers simpler and less burdensome;and
- a need to improve the coherence of the data protection framework given the fragmentation in instruments which are applicable to different sectors and activities.

The Commission set out its aim to address these issues bearing in mind the revised foundation for data protection in the Union and the impact of the entry into force in 2009 of the Lisbon Treaty and the Charter of Fundamental Rights. The Treaty gave a strong foundation for legislation in the area of data protection and the Charter affirmed its importance as a fundamental right.[88] In November 2011 the Commission launched its work programme to review the legal framework in the area with a communication setting out the next steps. The communication is considered at para.1–68 below. Before considering the communication however it should be set in the wider context of the work on the Stockholm Programme.

STOCKHOLM PROGRAMME POST-2010

1–60   Post-Lisbon, the EU launched an ambitious programme based on the concept of an area of freedom, security and justice serving the citizen, the Stockholm Programme.[89] The programme has a five year life span until 2014. Its overall political aim is to produce a Europe where the rights of citizens are protected but at the same time a Europe which remains and becomes increasingly secure. It therefore covers a wide range of activities. Data protection is included as priority. In relation to data protection in the programme the Council invited the Commission to:

- evaluate the way that the data protection instruments in force are functioning and where necessary seek to further the effectiveness by legislative and non-legislative instruments to maintain the effectiveness of the core principles of data protection;
- propose a Recommendation for negotiations on data protection and where necessary data-sharing agreements with the US for law enforcement purposes building on the work carried out by the High Level Contact Group already working in this area;

---

[88] See above for an explanation of the importance of the Treaty and Charter provisions.
[89] Communication from the Commission to the European parliament and the Council COM(262) Final. [2010] OJEU C115/1.

- consider the core elements for data protection agreements with third countries for law enforcement which may include where necessary privately held data, based on a high level of data protection;
- improve compliance through the application of new technologies;
- examine the introduction of a European certification scheme for "privacy aware" technologies, products and services; and
- conduct information campaigns including raising awareness among the public.

In addition the EU is encouraged to be in the forefront of the development and promotion of international standards based on Treaty 108 and the existing EU standards.

The first and second elements of this programme have been the focus of activity by the Commission. In the following section we cover the work on establishing arrangements for data sharing with the US and then cover the work programme leading to the launch of the draft regulation and Directive.

Negotiations on data sharing agreement with the US for law enforcement purposes

The second area in which the Council invited the Commission to take action in the Stockholm Programme was in relation to the sharing of data with the US for the purposes of law enforcement. Statewatch[90] reports that there are currently seven separate agreements between the US and the EU which deal with the sharing of personal data in the areas of justice and home affairs. Data is shared from the Europol and Eurojust databases. Passenger Name Data (PNR) is disclosed. Data is also disclosed for the purposes of extradition and mutual assistance in criminal matters, as part of the Container Security Initiative (CSI) and financial transactions are disclosed under SWIFT. The main sharing arrangements are under SWIFT and the PNR agreements.

1–61

SWIFT[91]/Terrorist Finance Tracking Program (TFTP)[92]

SWIFT is a financial messaging service used by most of the world's banks. It does not operate financial services such as clearing or money transfer but the transfer of messages and information which inevitably include personal data about the customers of banks, including banks in Europe. SWIFT is European-owned but had a data processing centre in the USA. In June 2006 reports in the New York Times and other US newspapers stated that US agencies were obtaining access to personal data from SWIFT for the purposes of the US program to track financial affairs associated with terrorism. The access had been obtained by way of subpoenas of which the banks themselves were unaware. The access to the personal data of EU customers caused a furore in Europe. The

1–62

---

[90] www.Statewatch.org [Accessed September 12, 2012].
[91] Society for Worldwide Interbank Financial Telecommunication.
[92] Agreement between the European Union and the United States of America on the processing and transfer of Financial Messaging Data from the European Union to the United States for the purposes of the Terrorist Finance Tracking Program, OJ L195/5.

Belgium Data Protection Authority declared that the transfers were in breach of data protection law but no formal action was taken. Negotiations between the Belgian Data Protection Authority, EU and US authorities led to a decision to move the data processing centre to Europe however the US authorities still sought to have access to financial data for the purpose of tracking terrorist finances. Negotiations were then held between EU and US authorities to find a legal solution for the exchange of the relevant personal data. The TFTP Agreement is the result of those negotiations. An interim agreement was signed in November 2009 and in July 2010 the European Parliament approved an agreement to take effect from August 2010 to allow the transfer of data from SWIFT for use in the US Terrorist Finance Tracking Program.[93] The legal basis for the agreement seems to be obscure and it has been criticised by the EDPS[94] and the Article 29 WP.

Under the agreement Europol was charged with checking every data transfer request from the United States. However, under the terms of the Agreement Europol does not see the data or know the amount that has been transferred. A report of the Europol Joint Supervisory Body(JSB) in March 2011 criticised the nature of the requests made stating that they were general in nature and asked for bulk transfers and there was no record of the information provided to back up the requests as it had been provided orally.[95] A further report delivered in March 2012 noted some improvements. The inspection report itself is classified as secret but the JSB has produced a public statement setting out some views. It reports in the statement that the requests were being made in writing however the requests continue to span wide time scales so that essentially they cover a continuous time span. Requests are made by geographic area and by data type. The agreement therefore remains almost wholly secret and no doubt will remain a matter of some political controversy.

PNR Agreements

1–63   Following the decision of the CJEU in 2006 that the original PNR Agreement with the US was outside the terms of Directive 95/46 (covered earlier) the European Union entered into a replacement interim agreement with the United States Government on the basis of a Decision of the Council based on arts 24 and 38 of the Treaty.[96] Article 38 provides that agreements between the EU and States outside the EU may be made for the purpose of police and judicial co-operation in criminal matters. Article 24 allows the Council, acting unanimously, to conclude agreements with other States. Such an agreement will not be binding on a Member State where its own constitution would be breached. The agreement reached allowed the US to continue to access PNR data until July 31, 2007 when the agreement expired. It was extended by mutual agreement in August 2007.

1–64   The Council made a finding of adequacy for the transfer of PNR data to the US in July 2007.[97] The US PNR agreement remained controversial and the

---

[93] June 24, 2010 11222/1/10.
[94] See comments by the EDPS at *www.edps.europa.eu*
[95] Press release European Parliament Committee on Civil Liberties, Justice and Home Affairs March 2011.
[96] Agreement—[2006] OJ L298/29 and Council Decision 2006/729/CFSP/JHA of October 16, 2006.
[97] 2007/551/CFSP /JHA.

revised agreement, which will last for seven years, was not finally agreed by the Parliament until April 2012. The major changes from the earlier version are that data will be "masked out" (i.e. they will remain personally identifiable, but the identity will be hidden unless required) six months after a passengers' flight, EU citizens will be informed about the use of their data, they will be able to request access and request the correction or deletion of their PNR data. EU citizens will, however, have no way of enforcing this right.

PNR agreements have also been entered into with Australia and with Canada. In the case of Australia the agreement has been finalised but must be formally accepted by the Parliament before it can be subject to a Council Decision.[98] In the case of Canada there is an interim agreement in place but negotiations on the final form are still continuing. PNR is increasingly used in other countries therefore there is an increased need for a standard form of agreement covering all PNR transfers. The requirements from a data protection standpoint are set out in a Communication from the Commission on the global approach to transfers of Passenger Name records (PNR) data to third countries[99] This continues to be an area in which the Commission is working to achieve a satisfactory resolution and there is considerable political dissatisfaction with the differences between the Australian agreement and the UA agreement.[100]

1–65

The data sharing arrangements with the US have proved controversial. In each instance the EU has sought to agree with the US rules on the use of the data and arrangements for its protection to at least basic EU standards. However, all of these arrangements are separate and have had to be negotiated on an individual basis. Although the negotiations are not made public the final agreements in some cases have to go to the European Parliament and have been controversial and subject to challenge before the CJEU. The final agreement on PNR data with the US has just been settled at the time of writing.[101] The aim of the Stockholm initiative therefore is to settle one overarching agreement that can be applied to all such exchanges. The Council issued a mandate to the Commission to undertake negotiations. The background is set out in the Explanatory Memoranda to the Commission Mandate.[102]A High Level Contact Group on Information Sharing, Privacy and Personal Data Protection (HLCG) was established in May 2006 and has worked to identify a core set of privacy and data protection principles which should be embedded in any arrangements. The report was delivered finally in October 2009. This was followed by a public consultation in which the options for scope and nature of the agreement were reviewed. Negotiations commenced in March 2011 but have not been concluded at the time of writing. A summary of the progress of the negotiation as at February 2012 is set out in a note from the Commission DG Justice 5999/12 which can be accessed via the Statewatch website; however we have not been able to find a further update.

1–66

There does not appear to have been any major developments in the other areas of the programme, that is improving compliance through the application of new technologies, examining the introduction of a European certification scheme for

1–67

---

[98] 1003/11.
[99] COM(2012) 492 Final.
[100] See debate of European Committee reported in *Hansard* January 24th, 2012.
[101] May 2012.
[102] COM 2012 252/2 Recommendation to open negotiations Annex.

"privacy aware" technologies, products and services, conducting information campaigns including raising awareness among the public and being at the forefront of the development and promotion of international standards based on Treaty 108 and the existing EU standards. The absence of major progress is hardly surprising when one considers the huge effort involved in producing and putting forward the two draft legal instruments. The Commission is due to report on progress on the Stockholm Programme in 2012.

PROPOSAL FOR NEW LEGISLATION

A comprehensive approach to personal data protection in the European Union[103]

1–68   In November 2011 the Commission launched its communication which laid out the Commission's approach to modernising the EU legal instruments for the protection of personal data. The aim of the programme was stated to be to take account of the challenges arising from globalisation and new technology while producing a system which would continue to deliver high standards of protection for individuals. The key aims for the Commission were stated to be to:

- ensure a coherent application of the rules taking account of the impact of new technologies on individuals' rights and the objective of ensuring the free flow of personal data in the internal market;
- increase transparency for data subjects with specific obligations in respect of the personal data of children and standard form EU privacy notices;
- examine the introduction of a general personal data breach notification requirement;
- strengthen individuals' control over their own data including data minimisation, portability, introducing the right to be forgotten and improving the ways that existing rights are exercised;
- increase awareness-raising activities among citizens;
- clarify and strengthen the rules on consent;
- consider categories of sensitive data and whether other categories should be included;
- review sanctions and judicial remedies with a view to strengthening those and extending the powers of individuals and associations to take action;
- seek to increase harmonisation in the internal market;
- consider reducing and simplifying the current systems of notification;
- revise and clarify the rules on applicable law;
- enhance the responsibilities of data controllers by requiring data protection officers, the use of impact assessments and privacy by design;
- encourage self-regulatory initiatives and kite marks or certification schemes;
- consider the application of the rules to areas of police and judicial cooperation in criminal matters;

---

[103] COM(2010) 609 Final.

- review how to deal with, and in the long run align, the different specific rules in the areas of police and judicial cooperation in specific instruments;
- improve and streamline the procedures for overseas transfers including the use of binding corporate rules and the assessment of adequacy;
- work with other international and standards bodies to achieve high levels of protection, reciprocity and the development of international technical standards; and
- strengthen the powers of supervisory authorities and enhance the methods of working together and consider a mechanism to achieve consistency between authorities.

As its next steps the Commission invited feedback on the proposals and undertook to propose legislation in 2011, to review Regulation 45/2001 and continue to pursue its active infringement policy.

The proposed legislation was slightly delayed however in January 2012 the Commission issued two draft legal instruments.

Proposal from the Commission January 2012

On January 28, 2012 the Commission issued its proposals for the wholesale reform of the data protection structure.[104] This consists of two draft legislative instruments together with Explanatory Memoranda and supporting materials. The two legislative instruments proposed are:

1–69

- a proposal for a Regulation of the European Parliament and of the Council on the protection of individuals with regard to the processing of personal data and on the free movement of such data (General Data Protection Regulation) ("the draft Regulation")[105]; and
- a proposal for a Directive of the European Parliament and the Council on the protection of individuals with regard to the processing of personal data by competent authorities for the purposes of prevention, investigation, detection or prosecution of criminal offences or the execution of criminal penalties, and the free movement of such data (Police and Criminal Justice Data Protection Directive)("the draft Directive").[106]

The draft Directive would apply to all processing of personal data by relevant authorities for the purposes of policing and criminal justice, including the transfer of information between authorities in the EU for these purposes. Competent authorities for this purpose are any public authorities

"competent for the prevention, detection and investigation of criminal offences, authorised by law to process personal data for the purposes of the prevention, investigation, detection or prosecution of criminal offences or the execution of criminal penalties".[107]

---

[104] COM(2012) 11/4 draft and Version 34 (2011-11-29).
[105] COM(2012) 11/4 Draft.
[106] Version 34 2011-11-29.
[107] Draft Directive art.4.

Framework Decision 2008/977 would be repealed (see above for an explanation of this instrument), but the draft Directive excludes processing for activities which fall outside Union law such as national security or foreign policy nor does it apply to processing by Union institutions, bodies, offices and agencies which are subject to Regulation (EC) No.45/2000 or other specific legislation. There is no list of such legislation but Recital 78 states:

"Specific provisions in acts concerning police cooperation and judicial cooperation in criminal matters which are adopted prior to the date of the adoption of this Directive regulating the processing of personal data between Member States or the access of designated authorities to information systems established pursuant to the Treaties should remain unaffected".

It appears from this that Europol, Schengen and others such as VIS and Eurojust are not affected and the specific rules in their governing instruments would continue to apply. The Recital also states that the Commission should evaluate these instruments to assess the need for "alignment of specific provisions with the Directive."

It also excludes the processing of personal data of judicial authorities acting in a judicial capacity.

The draft Regulation applies to all processing of personal data save:

- processing covered by the draft Directive or excluded by the draft Directive; and
- processing of personal data for exclusively personal or domestic use with no commercial aspect.

For many public authorities in the UK with investigative and prosecution functions therefore both instruments will be relevant. Assuming that both become law the Regulation will be directly applicable whereas the Directive will have to be implemented by means of national law. In addition, specific aspects of the Regulation, such as exemptions, will require national implementation.

The two instruments are very similar in structure, approach and specific provisions. There are two elements of difference in the current drafts: firstly substantive provisions which are relevant to one sector but not the other, such as grounds for processing or the application of Binding Corporate Rules which are wholly explicable and secondly a number of drafting differences in specific provisions which appear to be where last minute changes were made to the draft Regulation as a result of internal consultation among the Directorates at the Commission. Corresponding changes have not been made to the Directive. We have largely ignored these differences in the brief analysis below and concentrated on the major differences between the instruments.

Legislative process

1–70   Article 294 of the Treaty sets out the ordinary legislative procedure of co-decision. The Commission submits a proposal to the European Parliament and the Council. It is then considered by the Parliament which adopts its position at first reading and communicates it to the Council. If the Council approves the

European Parliament's position, the act is adopted with any amendments made by the Parliament. However, if the Council does not approve the European Parliament's position, it takes its own position at first reading and communicates that to the European Parliament accompanied by a full statement of its reasons. If the Parliament either approves the Council's position or takes no action within three months then the instrument is adopted with the Council's amendments. However if the Parliament rejects the Council's position it is not passed. If the Parliament then proposes amendments those are forwarded to the Council and to the Commission, which deliver further opinions on the amendments.

If, within three months of receiving the European Parliament's amendments, the Council, acting by a qualified majority, approves all those amendments, the act in question is adopted. If the Council does not then the President of the Council, in agreement with the President of the European Parliament, must convene a meeting of the Conciliation Committee.

The Conciliation Committee is composed of the members of the Council or their representatives and an equal number of members representing the European Parliament. Its task is to reach agreement on a joint text and they have a period of six weeks in which to do so. If they do so then the text goes to both the Council and the Parliament which have a period of six weeks in which to adopt the act in question in accordance with the joint text. If they fail to do so, the proposed act shall be deemed not to have been adopted. The time periods can be extended at the initiative of the European Parliament or the Council but only by a few weeks.

It is anticipated that the two proposed instruments will be the subject of considerable debate and proposals for change during this process. It is generally anticipated that it will be at least two years before the final text of the instruments is settled, assuming that they are agreed. As only the first drafts are available at the time of writing therefore it would not be appropriate to undertake a detailed textual analysis. We have therefore set out the broad areas of coverage, similarity and difference between the two instruments in this section. At the end of each chapter we have added a very brief description of the corresponding provisions in the draft Regulation.

1–71

The aim of the approach is to give a general understanding of the main changes proposed and alert readers to those areas in which it may be prudent to start planning for the future. Readers should however bear in mind that this analysis is based on the draft instruments as published in January 2012 and review any current drafts or final instruments.

Elements applicable to both instruments

The draft Regulation and Directive build on the existing Directive and many aspects will be familiar. The structure of having a set of fundamental principles, supported by individual rights and enforced by independent supervisory authorities remains, however there are many significant changes. Overall the new regime will be more restrictive and appears on careful analysis to be significantly more onerous for both controllers and processors.

1–72

Notification is removed and as a result there will be no public registers of processing. The element of transparency which a public register provides is therefore removed. The replacement provisions are a requirement for internal monitoring and record keeping including for most controllers a mandatory data protection officer.[108] This is accompanied by a complex provision requiring the completion of a mandatory Data Protection Impact Assessment before carrying out certain types of processing and the submission of the Assessment to the supervisory authority in specified cases.[109] In some cases there must be consultation with or prior approval of the supervisory authority and there is a power for supervisory authorities to determine those additional cases in which DPIAs are required.[110]

The core principles are retained but are divided up in different ways. The principles[111] cover fair and lawful processing, purpose limitation, obligations in respect of accuracy and in respect of ensuring that personal data are adequate, relevant and limited to that necessary for the purpose. They also include two new specific obligations, the first to ensure that data are kept in a form that identifies data subjects only for as long as is necessary for the purpose and the second an obligation to ensure that all personal data are processed under the "responsibility and liability of the controller" who shall "ensure and demonstrate for each processing operation the compliance with the provisions of this Regulation". The import of this is not apparent. It may mean no more than that a controller must remain responsible for processing and keep appropriate records but there are specific record keeping obligations which would suggest that it requires something in addition.

The concept of grounds for processing and, in the case of the draft Regulation additional grounds where sensitive data are involved, remain. There are new provisions in the draft Regulation which deal with the basis for processing the personal data of a child below the age of 13 where the consent of the parents or guardians must be obtained. Otherwise the grounds for processing both personal data and sensitive personal data are largely unaltered although there are "quality of law" provisions which apply where personal data are to be processed under the powers of the State. The law must continue to respect the rights to data protection and be proportionate. Under the draft Regulation consent remains a ground on which processing can be legitimised however new provisions around the use of consent are imported. When consent is obtained it must relate to specific instances of processing. There is also a provision that a data subject can always withdraw consent. Consent is not a ground for processing under the draft Directive.

Security and the control of overseas transfers are covered in separate articles. The security obligations are increased and include breach notification obligations both to notify the supervisory authority in the case of every breach and to notify individuals in those cases where they may be subject to harm as a result of the breach.[112] Data processors are required to notify data controllers. The relation between data controllers and processors remains one of contract as between the parties but the terms of the contract are set out in far more detail. Data processors are also made subject to some obligations and liable to stringent penalties if they

---

[108] Draft Directive art.20 and art.22 in the draft Regulation.
[109] Draft Regulation art.33 and draft Directive art.31.
[110] Draft Directive arts 31 and 32 and draft Regulation arts 33 and 34.
[111] Draft Directive art.4 and draft Regulation art.5.
[112] Draft Directive arts 29 and 30 and draft Regulation arts 31 and 32.

fail to comply. Unfortunately the extent of obligations on processors is very unclear [113] but there is no doubt that processors will risk significant liability under the new provisions.

Overseas transfers are covered in Ch.V of both instruments and on the face appear to be familiar. The Commission may make adequacy findings and existing findings are preserved. The derogations remain largely the same and model contracts will continue to be available as a mechanism to enable transfers. Transfers by way of Binding Corporate Rules will be recognised under the draft Regulation however BCRs have to be approved via the consistency mechanism which means that they are not likely to be the straightforward mechanism once hoped for. Processors may also enter BCRs but the detail of how this will work is not spelt out. Where a data controller makes a decision that it can transfer based on an adequacy assessment it must notify the supervisory authority.

The rights of individuals are re-cast and now include the right to receive a privacy notice or statement. The detail of the contents of the notice is set out at length and will have an impact on privacy notices. The right of subject access remains a key right and has been supplemented in the draft Regulation by a new "right to be forgotten",[114] which supplements the right to have information erased. It appears to provide for a right to "trace" any publication of personal data but it is extremely difficult to disentangle the meaning of the provision or be sure whether there is one right or two. The right to object to automated decision making has become a ban on profiling without positive consent in the draft Regulation and a ban without legal authority in the draft Directive. There are rights to rectification of personal data in both. The draft Regulation includes the right to object to direct marketing and to other types of processing. It also includes a new right to data portability but again the extent and nature of the right is difficult to understand.

Supervisory authorities are given greatly increased powers and have obligations of mutual assistance and co-operation under both instruments. Under the draft Regulation they are able to levy significant fines of up to 2 per cent of worldwide turnover. The draft Regulation also imposes a complex set of arrangements under which they must co-operate with one another[115]and a consistency procedure which will apply where there is overlapping jurisdiction or a need to co-ordinate action among such authorities.

Individuals are given rights to take action in both instruments but in the draft Regulation they may take such action in their own State irrespective of the location of the controller and there are also rights to representative actions (although the relation between the provisions in the two instruments in not wholly clear).[116]

The Commission also has obligations to report after a time on the progress of the two instruments.

In both instruments a large number of measures are reserved to the Commission to lay down further rules and make further provisions by delegated legislation. This follows the increase of the powers of the Commission to pass

---

[113] Ch.IV of both draft instruments.
[114] Ch.III of both draft instruments.
[115] Ch.VI of both draft instruments.
[116] Chs VIII both draft instruments.

delegated legislation post-Lisbon. The reservation of these powers introduces a level of detailed rule-making some of which appears to be inappropriate, for example the exact content of notices to data subjects; in addition there are so many of these that it will take years before they can be brought in thus importing a level of uncertainty into the new regulatory scheme as well as a long time scale.

Elements present in the draft Regulation

1–73   Provision is made in the draft Regulation for various matters which are then made applicable to the draft Directive, for example the provisions setting up the European Data Protection Board and the making of findings of adequacy are in the draft Regulation although both will be equally applicable to the draft Directive. There are, as can be seen from the review above, significant areas of difference between the two instruments. The grounds for processing in the draft Directive are restricted to legal grounds linked to the relevant functions or processing which is necessary to protect the vital interests of the data subject,[117] whereas the grounds in the draft Regulation have largely the same span as the current Directive. Obligations to apply privacy by design and default apply in the Regulation but do not appear in the draft Directive.[118] As noted earlier the rules around Binding Corporate Rules which would not be applicable to bodies engaged in policing and criminal justice[119] are omitted from the draft Directive as are the rights to data portability and the right to object to processing.[120] The draft Directive includes no provision for codes of conduct or certification seals.[121] The exemptions are also different and there are no special provisions for employment, freedom of expression, health or churches in the draft Directive.[122] Further the draft Directive does not include provisions on territorial scope, establishment or sanctions (other than to provide that the Member State must set appropriate sanctions for breach) or the application of the consistency procedure. Most of the differences arise from the different nature and scope of the instruments and this can be seen particularly when the provisions specific to the Directive are reviewed.

Elements applicable to the draft Directive only

1–74   The draft Directive covers following matters which are not covered in the draft Regulation:

- the principles related to personal data processing include a restriction on processing personal data originally obtained for other purposes and require that all processing has a legal basis and is proportionate. Requests for such information must be in writing and may be subject to other safeguards such as judicial authorisation[123];

---

[117] Art.6; compare art.7 of the draft Directive.
[118] Art.23.
[119] Art.43.
[120] Arts 18 and 19.
[121] Arts 38 and 39.
[122] Ch.IX arts 80–85.
[123] Draft Directive art.4.2.

- all processing of personal data must have a legal basis which meets specified standards including setting out the purposes of processing, procedures to be followed and categories of staff authorised to carry out the processing[124];
- data relating to different categories of data subjects must be distinguished within the personal data held, between those suspected of carrying out crimes, those convicted or those who are victims or third parties[125];
- there must be systems to mark the accuracy and reliability of data[126];
- the grounds on which processing may be carried out are restricted[127];
- there are restrictions on the processing of genetic data[128];
- provision is made for the exercise of subject access rights through the supervisory authority[129];
- some of the exemptions are set out specifically rather than in the more general form as in the Regulation[130];
- specific record keeping obligations are imposed requiring that audit trails be kept[131];
- the security requirements and standards are spelt out rather than being left for the controller to determine[132];
- impact assessments are required for specific processing such as biometric data[133];
- the grounds for transfers outside the EEA appear to be more restrictive than in the Regulation[134]; and
- there is a ban on transmission of personal data to other authorities or private parties which appears to operate as a ban on all transfers to bodies which are not subject to the Directive although the provision is not clear and the heading suggests that it is a ban on transmission within the EU only.[135]

Given the magnitude of the review and the changes made it is inevitable that there are areas of uncertainty and debate in the current drafts. A recurring criticism is an absence of clarity in the drafting but it is likely that some of these problems will be ironed out as the legislation is debated and amended. There are, however, a number of structural problems which look set to remain and we would single out four in the draft Regulation which seem likely to be the source of disputes and difficulties of interpretation if they remain as currently drafted:

1–75

- It is stated to apply to all processing conducted from outside the EU which involves personal data on EU citizens. As a result any kind of non-EU web-based service which collects any personal data about users in the EU

---

124 Draft Directive art.4.3.
125 Draft Directive art.5.
126 Draft Directive art.6.
127 Draft Directive art.7.
128 Draft Directive art.10.
129 Draft Directive art.16.
130 Draft Directive art.13.2, for example.
131 Draft Directive art.26.
132 Draft Directive art.28.
133 Draft Directive art.31.2(b).
134 Draft Directive Ch.V.
135 Draft Directive art.60.

will be impacted. This is not likely to be popular with other countries and raises practical problems in ensuring compliance, for example how the organisation is to know that the user is an EU resident. It is made rather more difficult by the lack of clarity around the position of a representative. A controller with no establishment in the EU is required to appoint a representative in the EU which can be subject to notices, penalties and actions, in addition to actions taken against the controller. However, there is no corresponding obligation on the supervisory authorities to deal with the representative[136] so the position is left ambiguous.

- The approach to establishment and implementation of a "one stop shop" for data controllers has not been effectively carried through. The aim was that one entity which operated in several jurisdictions should be able to work with the supervisory authority in the place of main establishment to provide for a streamlined system. However, the provisions do not apply to subsidiaries which are separate legal entities, thus excluding most large corporates from the possibility of using this mechanism. In addition there is no process to select and agree the main establishment with the supervisory authorities. This is likely to lead to difficulties at a later date.[137]

- The third criticism is the level of administrative fines which are extremely high, determined by worldwide turnover and which can apply for relatively minor breaches of procedural obligations.[138]

- The last point we would single out for concern is the consistency procedure under which an action by one supervisory authority which may impact on the work of another supervisory authority or citizens in more than one Member State must be referred to the European Data Protection Board. While the concept is sound the process is overly complex and many relatively small matters risk being referred. Moreover if there is no resolution at the end of the process the matter is determined by the Commission with no rights of appeal being given to those impacted.[139]

1–76   One cannot avoid the conclusion that regulators appear to have had a disproportionately strong influence on the drafts and have been unwilling to relinquish any of their existing powers or controls. As a result there is no effective mechanism to deliver the benefits of the "one stop shop" and the position of data controllers and processors may be made extremely difficult. However, the draft does have some new and welcome provisions and it is to be hoped that the current weaknesses will be addressed as it moves through the legislative process.

---

[136] Draft Directive art.25.
[137] Draft Directive art.4 for the definition of main establishment and art.51.2 for supervisory powers of the authorities.
[138] Draft Directive art.79.
[139] Draft Directive Ch.VII.

Additional materials

Websites

There are now many sites which provide information on data protection and privacy.

The sites maintained by the main regulatory organisations or government bodies are as follows:

- The Ministry of Justice is at *www.MoJ.gov.uk*. There is a separate (and most useful) section on data-sharing.
- The Information Commissioner's site is *www.ico.gov.uk*. It contains the Commissioner's published guidance. The register can be accessed from the site. It also has a useful index of other links and sites.
- The European Union site is at *www.europa.eu*. Data protection information is found under Justice, Freedom and Security. The entry includes references to other useful European sites including the European Data Supervisor.
- Recent UK case law is available on *www.courtservice.gov.uk*.
- Information on Safe Harbor at the US Department of Commerce site *www.ita.doc.gov*.
- Council of Europe at *www.coe.int* where data protection will be found under the Legal Affairs section.
- The Criminal Records Bureau is at *www.crb.gov.uk*.
- The European Court of Human Rights is at *www.echr.we.int*. This site includes judgments on cases on the art.8 right to private life other convention rights.
- Legislation is found at *www.opsi.gov.uk*. This site includes the Data Protection Act and the statutory instruments.
- OECD is at *www.oecd.org*. This site contains material generated by the OECD.

The *Encyclopaedia of Data Protection* (Sweet and Maxwell) contains a wealth of source materials and background papers.

Statutory instruments

The bulk of the statutory instruments made under the Act came into effect on commencement on March 1 2000. The commencement order for the Act was made in January 31, 2000.

- SI 2000/183: The Data Protection (Commencement) Order
- SI 2000/184: The Data Protection (Corporate Finance Exemption) Order
- SI 2000/185: The Data Protection (Conditions under paragraph 3 of Part II of Schedule 1) Order
- SI 2000/186: The Data Protection (Functions of Designated Authorities) Order
- SI 2000/187: The Data Protection (Fees under section 19(7)) Regulations

1–77

1–78

- SI 2000/188: The Data Protection (Notification and Notification Fees) Regulations
- SI 2000/190: The Data Protection (International Cooperation) Order
- SI 2000/191: The Data Protection (Subject Access) (Fees and Miscellaneous Provisions) Regulations
- SI 2000/206: The Data Protection (National Security Appeals) Regulations
- SI 2000/413: The Data Protection (Subject Access Modification) (Health) Order
- SI 2000/414: The Data Protection (Subject Access Modification) (Education) Order
- SI 2000/415: The Data Protection (Subject Access Modification) (Social Work) Order
- SI 2000/416: The Data Protection (Crown Appointments) Order
- SI 2000/417: The Data Protection (Processing of Sensitive Personal Data) Order
- SI 2000/418: revoked by SI 2000/1864
- SI 2000/419: The Data Protection (Miscellaneous Subject Access Exemptions) Order
- SI 2000/1864: The Data Protection (Designated Codes of Practice) (No.2) Order
- SI 2000/1865: The Data Protection (Miscellaneous Subject Access Exemptions) (Amendment) Order
- SI 2002/2905: The Data Protection (Processing of Sensitive Personal Data) (Elected Representatives) Order 2002
- SI 2005/467: The Data Protection (Subject Access Modification) (Social Work) (Amendment) Order 2005
- SI 2006/2068: The Data Protection (Processing of Sensitive Personal Data) Order 2006
- SI 2005/14: The Information Tribunal (Enforcement Appeals) Rules 2005 [revokes SI2000/189 and 2002/20002] [now revoked]
- SI 2005/13: The Information Tribunal (National Security Appeals) Rules 2005 [revokes SI 2000/206] [now revoked]
- SI 2005/450: The Information Tribunal (Enforcement Appeals) (Amendment) Rules 2005 [now revoked]
- SI 2001/3500: Transfer of Functions (Miscellaneous) Order 2001
- SI 2003/1887: Secretary of State for Constitutional Affairs Order 2003
- SI 2008/1592: The Data Protection (Commencement No.2) Order 2008
- SI 2009/1677: The Data Protection (Notification and Notification Fees) (Amendment) Regulations 2009
- SI 2009/1811: The Data Protection (Processing of Sensitive Personal Data) Order 2009
- SI 2010/ 2961: The Data Protection (Processing of Sensitive Personal Data) (Elected Representatives) (Amendment) Order 2010
- SI 2010/910: The Data Protection (Monetary Penalties) Order 2010
- SI 2011/1034: The Data Protection (Subject Access Modification)(Social Work) Amendment Order 2011
- SI 2012/1978: Data Protection (Processing of Sensitive Personal Data) Order 2012

PROPOSAL FOR NEW LEGISLATION

- SI 2010/192: The Protection of Vulnerable Groups (Scotland) Act 2007 (Prescribed Manner and Place for the Taking of Fingerprints and Prescribed Personal Data Holders) Regulations 2010

CHAPTER 2

Privacy Rights Under The Human Rights Act 1998 And Remedies For The Misuse Of Private Information

INTRODUCTION

Since the implementation of the Human Rights Act 1998 (HRA) the law has developed to provide remedies where the private information of individuals has been or is threatened to be misused. This is a right independent of those guaranteed by the Data Protection Act 1998 (DPA) and, although the information covered by the remedy is not as broad as that covered by the DPA, is a significant addition to the protection of privacy in the UK. The essence of the development of the law in this area was captured by Lord Hoffman in 2004 in *Campbell v MGN Ltd*,[1] explaining where the law stood as well as looking forward to the questions yet to be addressed.

2–01

> "In recent years there have been two developments of the law of confidence....One has been an acknowledgement of the artificiality of distinguishing between confidential information obtained through the violation of a confidential relationship and similar information obtained in some other way. The second......has been the acceptance of the privacy of personal information as something worthy of protection in its own right ...
>
> "What human rights law has done is to identify private information as something worth protecting as an aspect of human autonomy and dignity. And this recognition has raised inescapably the question of why it should be worth protecting against the state but not against a private person.... I can see no logical ground for saying that a person should have less protection against a private individual than he would have against the state for the publication of personal information for which there is no justification ...
>
> "The result of these developments has been a shift in the centre of gravity of the action for breaches of confidence when it is used as a remedy for the unjustified publication of personal information ... Instead of the cause of action being based upon the duty of good faith applicable to confidential personal information and trade secrets alike, it focuses upon the protection of human autonomy and dignity—the right to control the dissemination of information about one's private life and the right to the esteem and respect of other people ...
>
> "These changes have implications for the future development of the law. They must influence the approach of the courts to the kind of information which is regarded as entitled to protection, the extent and form of publication which attracts a remedy and the circumstances in which publication can be justified."

---

[1] [2004] UKHL 22.

As foreseen by Lord Hoffman, over the last eight years the courts have been asked to consider the kind of information which requires protection as well as rights to anonymity, prior notice of intended publication and how the balance between individual privacy and public interest in publication should be achieved. The new rights to take action are welcome. It has to be recognised, however, that cases have been fought tooth and nail by some sections of the press and one senior judge has been subject to personal criticism as a result of his judgments.[2] At the same time the irrelevance of the court system for most ordinary people has been thrown into focus by the revelations about the behaviour of parts of the tabloid press. At the time of writing[3] the question of how journalists can be restrained from making unjustified intrusions into privacy is being canvassed in the Leveson Enquiry into Press Standards.

This chapter describes the development of the law of confidence in the UK, the effect of the HRA, case law from the European Court of Human Rights (ECtHR) at Strasbourg on informational privacy under art.8 of the European Convention on Human Rights (the Convention), the impact of Convention Rights on the interpretation of the data protection directives, and outlines the development of the tort of misuse of private information in the case law in the UK since the implementation of the HRA. It includes an outline of the relevance of art.10, but material on press regulation and some more detailed material will be found in Ch.17 on the exemptions for journalistic and literary purposes. It is recommended that these two chapters should be read together.

2–02   SUMMARY OF MAIN POINTS

(a)   There is no over-arching cause of action in English law for breach of privacy.
b)   The misuse of private information will give rise to a remedy before the courts in certain circumstances. This is equally applicable between private parties. In applying this right the courts will apply art.8 of the Convention rights.
c)   Personal information can be protected where the person had a reasonable expectation of privacy in respect of the information. There is no need for the parties to have been in a prior relationship.
d)   The categories of the information that may be protected are not closed but the essence is that the action protects the dignity and autonomy of the individual. Thus the information may be related to behaviour in public places or information which is known to a limited number of people. Those who are in the public eye or have a public role are as entitled to have their privacy protected as anyone else. Particular care is required to protect the privacy of children and it is recognised that photographs are more intrusive that mere words.

---

[2] The editor of the *Daily Mail*, Paul Dacre, giving the opening speech at the Society of Editors Conference in 2008 criticised the role of Lord Justice Eady in setting significant precedents in privacy cases.
[3] May 2012.

e) The right of free speech is an important human right but it is not paramount. Neither privacy nor freedom of speech are absolute rights, nor is one superior to the other.

f) Where the person who wishes to publish personal information which would affect the privacy of another invokes the right of freedom of speech, the courts must carry out a balancing act between the two rights set out in arts 8 and 10, taking into account the justification for interfering with or restricting each right and applying considerations of proportionality.

g) The right of free speech is one of the most important rights in a democracy and must be fiercely guarded but not all speech has the same value. The right to free political speech is much more important than the right to repeat trivial gossip.

h) Where the disclosure is justified in the public interest, for example to "set the record straight", then it must still be proportionate.

i) There is no legal right to prior notice of intended publication of private information.

j) An interim injunction should not be granted unless the court is satisfied that the claimant is likely to obtain an injunction following trial.

k) Exemplary damages are not recoverable in an action for misuse of private information.

l) In some circumstances the applicant may be entitled to anonymity but the circumstances in which a privacy case will remain unreported ("a super injunction") will be extremely limited and such orders will generally be time-limited.

m) It is no defence to assert that the information is false or inaccurate.

COMMERCIAL EXPLOITATION IMAGE

The law of the UK does not provide a statutory right to prevent the commercial exploitation of the image of the individual. However it appears that the courts will now afford protection for commercial interests in images. Thus photographs resulting from a photoshoot which had been opened to fans to view were protected on the grounds of confidentiality in *Creation Records v News Group Newspapers Ltd*.[4] In making an order to restrain the publication of pictures of a house purchased by a celebrity couple, there was an acknowledgement that the couple had an interest, not only in protecting their privacy, but in the possibility of selling an "exclusive" set of pictures of the property to a magazine.[5]

In some cases where the individual has a commercial interest in the image which the individual could legitimately exploit and which has been unfairly exploited by another party without permission, protection has been provided by the tort of passing off. This is clearly a remedy to protect a commercial interest.

2–03

[4] [1997] E.M.L.R. 444. Case concerned the Oasis photoshoot for a record album cover. A Rolls Royce was put into a swimming pool. Fans were allowed to watch but when one took a photograph and offered it for publication in a newspaper the record company succeeded in restraining the use of the photograph.

[5] *Beckham v MGN* Unreported June 28, 2001, QBD.

Actions can also be taken for breach of confidence where there is a clear obligation of confidence to protect private pictures which have a commercial value.

In *Douglas v Hello! Ltd*,[6] it was accepted that a couple were entitled to protect the exclusive photographic rights to official pictures of their celebrity wedding, to which over 300 guest had been invited, to the extent that they had a legitimate commercial interest in the exploitation of the pictures. In the Court of Appeal it was held that this was a species of property right that could not be passed on to another and hence *OK!* were unable to benefit. However, on appeal to the House of Lords *OK!* succeeded in establishing that the arrangements entered into for the security of the wedding had created a form of confidentiality which protected its interests as well as that of the protagonists and were successful in their action for breach of confidentiality by *Hello!* magazine.

In *Edmund Irvine Tidswell Ltd v Talksport Ltd*[7] a Formula 1 driver was photographed holding a mobile telephone. The image was manipulated so that he looked as though he was listening to a portable radio, which had the words "Talk Radio" on it. The judge held that the photograph amounted to passing-off and acknowledged that celebrities have a property right in their image which is capable of protection. Similarly, the runner, David Bedford, succeeded in a complaint to Ofcom about an advertisement for a directory enquiry service which used "look alikes". He complained of breach of the Advertising Standards Code r.6.3, which provides that living persons must not be portrayed, caricatured or referred to in advertisements without their permission. The advertisements, however, were not banned, despite the finding in David Bedford's favour.

There may be a clear distinction between those cases where the complainant has a commercial interest in protecting an image and those where the complainant is protecting personal privacy, such as JK Rowling's action to restrict the use of images of her children to protect their privacy[8]. In other cases the distinction may be less clear, as in the *Douglas* case where there was both a commercial and privacy interest in images. However the courts have provided remedies for misuse of photographic images in both cases. Images may also be protected where there is neither a commercial interest or a specific privacy interest (see later in relation to the taking and use of photographs).

PROTECTION OF REPUTATION

2–04   The right to the protection of reputation is a right which falls within art.8 as an element of private life (*Re Guardian News & Media Ltd*[9]). The relationship between this aspect of the right and actions for defamation has arisen in a number of cases. In *Jane Clift v Slough BC*[10] Ms Clift brought an action for libel against the Council arising out of the publication of Ms Clift's name on the Council's Violent Persons Register. The Council accepted that the description of her as a person "who posed a medium risk of violence" was defamatory; however, it

---

[6] [2005] EWCA Civ 595, CA; [2007] UKHL 21.
[7] [2002] EWHC 367.
[8] The case law on photographs and privacy is dealt with below.
[9] [2001] UKSC 1.
[10] [2010] EWCA Civ 1171.

defended the publication which was made to a surprisingly wide range of staff and partner bodies on the basis of qualified privilege. It asserted that there was a duty on the Council to protect the safety of its staff and the staff of connected organisations and those persons who received the copy of the Register had an interest in receiving the information.

One of the issues at stake was the very widespread dissemination of the Register. On behalf of Ms Clift it was argued that qualified privilege can only apply where the party publishing has a duty to publish material to those who have a corresponding interest or duty in receiving it. For a public authority this must be consistent with its duties under public law and such duties must be carried out in accordance with the HRA. Therefore if art.8 is engaged by a publication the authority must be able to justify the publication under art.8 and meet the tests of legitimacy, justification and proportionality. The position was accepted by the Court which held that the wide publication failed to meet the test of proportionality:

"Ill considered and indiscriminate disclosure is bound to be disproportionate".[11]

The wide publication breached Ms Clift's art.8 rights and was unlawful. Any argument for a duty to publish fell away and with it the possibility of a defence of qualified privilege.

As an alternative, the Council sought to argue that Ms Clift should have brought an action under art.8 rather than an action in libel. The Court did not accept this and made clear that the complainant was entitled to choose her cause of action.

The relationship between defamation and an action for misuse of private information, however, may be rather more difficult to navigate where a claim is made for injunctive relief and the facts complained of are discreditable but true. It is a complete defence to an action in defamation that the information complained of is true; a court cannot give the complainant any remedy in defamation if the facts complained of are true irrespective of whether there is a public interest in the publication. In addition, the rule in *Bonnard v Perryman*[12] precludes the grant of an injunction to restrain the publication of defamatory material before trial where defendant will claim justification:

2–05

"We entirely approve of, and desire to adopt as our own, the language of Lord Esher, M.R., in Coulson v. Coulson– 'To justify the Court in granting an interim injunction it must come to a decision upon the question of libel or no libel, before the jury have decided whether it was a libel or not. Therefore the jurisdiction was of a delicate nature. It ought only to be exercised in the clearest cases, where any jury would say that the matter complained of was libellous, and where, if the jury did not so find, the Court would set aside the verdict as unreasonable'[13]."

However, in privacy cases publication can be restrained even where the information is true. In addition the threshold for the grant of injunctive relief to restrain publication is not the same. Where an application is made for an

---

[11] [2010] EWCA Civ 1171 per Ward L.J. at para.35.
[12] [1891] 2 Ch. 269.
[13] Per Lord Coleridge C.J.

injunction to restrain publication on privacy grounds pending trial, the test is that the applicant is more likely than not to succeed at trial.[14] In *RST v UVW*[15] an individual applied for an injunction to prevent the publication of information that he had previously paid a lady to provide sexual encounters which took place at his home and had entered into a confidentiality agreement with her under which he had provided consideration for her silence. The claim was advanced in privacy rather than defamation. The courts considered the point that a claimant is entitled to choose his cause of action where more than one is available to him[16]but noted that there is dicta in which it is suggested that, in cases in which it may be an abuse of process, a claimant should not be able to obtain an injunction in privacy where the court takes the view that the real issue is protection of reputation.[17] In that case the interim injunction was granted given the circumstances of the case. However in *LNS v Persons Unknown*[18] the footballer, John Terry, failed in an application for an injunction to prevent publication of the fact that he had had an affair and related personal information.

Mr Terry was married and held a number of apparently lucrative sponsorship deals. Giving judgment, Tugendhat J. noted that there could be an overlap with defamation in a limited number of privacy cases and suggested four broad groups of privacy cases being:

- those where the information complained of cannot be said to be defamatory, such as *Murray* where the law of defamation is irrelevant;
- those where, although the law of defamation overlaps with the privacy claim, the protection of reputation is not in fact the nub of the claim;
- those where the law of defamation overlaps with the privacy claim but the claim relates to conduct which would be unlawful and voluntary, for example financial irregularities, and where it would be unlikely that there would be any inconsistency in the treatment of the cases in relation to injunctions as the remedy would not be available under either head; and
- a limited group of cases where the conduct in question is not unlawful although it involves conduct which is voluntary and discreditable in some way (and by implication the claimant may be protecting reputation as well as privacy or that the protection of reputation may be in reality the nub of the claim).

The judge did not go on to set out in which types of cases claimants would be more likely to succeed, though it is implicit that applications for interim injunctions would be more likely to succeed in the first two types of cases than in the others. He also noted that it was for the applicant to determine which form of action he chooses to bring. However it is implicit that, if an applicant chooses to bring an action for misuse of private information in a case in which he really seeks to protect reputation, the court can weight that in deciding whether to grant injunctive relief. In this particular case the judge declined to make any of the orders sought, which included an injunction against any person who threatened to

---

[14] *Cream Holdings Ltd v Banerjee* [2004] UKHL 44.
[15] [2009] EWHC 2448 (QB).
[16] *Joyce v Sengupta* [1993] 1 W.L.R. 337.
[17] *McKennit v Ash* [2006] EWCA Civ 1714.
[18] [2010] EWHC 119 (QB).

publish the fact of Mr Terry's extra-marital relationship or any details of it. One of the reasons for the refusal was that it was likely that the "nub of the applicant's complaint is to protect [LNS's] reputation in particular with sponsors, and so (a) the rule in *Bonnard v Perryman* precludes the grant of an injunction; and (b) in any event damages would be an adequate remedy for LNS".

BACKGROUND–PRIVACY RIGHTS

As has been explained in Ch.1, the immediate predecessors of Directive 95/46/EC were Treaty 108 and the OECD Guidelines, although those instruments themselves owed their existence to the acknowledgement of the right to respect for private and family life in art.8 of the Convention. Directive 95/46/EC refers directly to art.8. Article I of Directive 95/46/EC states that one of the objects of the Directive is the protection of

2–06

> "…the fundamental rights and freedoms of natural persons, and in particular their right to privacy with respect to the processing of personal data".

While those interpreting the 1984 Data Protection Act tended to look back primarily to its immediate predecessors, particularly Treaty 108,[19] since the 1998 Act came into effect the courts have looked to the Directive and sometimes art.8 directly[20]. At EU level, the importance of informational privacy has been emphasised by the inclusion of data protection in the Charter of Fundamental rights of the European Union. Article 8 specifically covers personal data protection:

> "1.   Every person has the right to the protection of personal data concerning him or her.
> 2.   Such data must be processed fairly for specified purposes and on the basis of the consent of the person concerned or some other legitimate basis laid down by law. Everyone has the right of access to data which has been collected concerning him or her, and the right to have it rectified.
> 3.   Compliance with these rules shall be subject to control by an independent authority." [21]

Even before the Charter entered into force the Court of First Instance commented:

> "although [the Charter] does not have legally binding force, it does show the importance of the rights it sets out in the Community legal order".[22]

In the UK the implementation of the Convention rights in the Human Rights Act has brought an increased familiarity and ease with the application of the right to

---

[19] See the judgments of the Data Protection Tribunal (as it was then) in the cases of *Equifax Europe Ltd v Data Protection Registrar* Unreported June 28, 1991.
[20] See *Brian Robertson Reid v Secretary of State for the Home Department* (284/2011).
[21] See Ch.1 para.1-43 for a discussion of the Charter.
[22] *Philip Morris International and others v Commission* [2003] ECR II-I para.122 cited in the Opinion of the Advocate General in the PNR cases C-317/04 and C-318/04 at para.23.

respect for private life which is increasingly reflected in the case law. That case law has gradually moved the UK towards the development of a privacy right which would have been unthinkable only a few years ago.

UK background

2–07   The Younger Committee discussed the idea of privacy in its report[23] in 1972 and reviewed the various efforts over the years to define it.

David Calcutt, Q.C. in the *Report of the Committee on Privacy and Related Matters* in 1990,[24] after rehearsing the difficulties in coming to a satisfactory definition, posited a working one as:

> "the right of the individual to be protected against intrusion into his personal life or affairs, or those of his family, by direct physical means or by publication of information",

and concluded that:

> "a natural person's privacy shall be taken to include matters appertaining to his health, personal communications and family, personal relationships and a right to be free from harassment or molestation."

Other analyses echo the themes of the right to choose to be alone or seek companions of one's choice, to control the information publicly known about oneself, to seek seclusion and to be free from outside interference in one's own domain.[25] In the context of the Convention, it is part of a package of rights which overlap and intersect, but all of which support the same core values to assert and protect the autonomy and dignity of each human-being.

CONFIDENTIALITY—BEFORE OCTOBER 2000

2–08   The Younger Committee did not consider that a general protection should be afforded to private life but recommended some new remedies to deal with areas of specific mischief. It also commented on the development of the law of confidence, which it thought provided a basis for developing privacy protection. It recommended that the Law Commission should reconsider the action for breach of confidence with a view to such further development.[26] The Law Commission duly reported in 1981 and recommended codification of the law of confidence. The report was never acted on and in 1998, in answer to a Parliamentary question,[27] the Lord Chancellor, Lord Irvinge of Lairg, stated that the report, Breach of Confidence (Law Commission Report No.110), would not be implemented given that the development of the case law had clarified the scope and extent of the breach of confidence action since its publication.

---

[23] The Younger Committee Report, Cmnd.5012 July 1972.

[24] Cmnd.5012.

[25] See Westin and others.

[26] See Toulson and Phipps, *Breach of Confidence* (Sweet and Maxwell, 1996), p.112, para.9.01.

[27] (*Hansard*, March 19, WA 213) Jul 29, 1998: col.WA202.

In the next section we trace that development of the tort of misuse of private information from the law of confidence however it should be recognised that the case law has not developed a general law of privacy. The cases examined in this chapter examine only the area of informational privacy. Other areas of law are related to privacy protection, trespass, nuisance, action for harassment, or defamation, but we are still a long way from a general privacy right.

The tort of misuse of private information has been developed from the law of confidence. In *A v B & C*,[28] which is described below, Lord Woolf L.C.J. said that, in cases on art.8, citation of authorities which relate to the action for breach of confidence prior to the coming into force of the 1998 Act "are largely of historic interest only". Nevertheless, anyone advising in this area will find it helpful to understand the evolution of the current cases.[29]

Development of jurisprudence on confidentiality

The case usually cited as the first major case in the area of personal confidentiality is *Prince Albert v Strange*.[30] When the facts are considered it seems but a short distance to *A v B & C* and surprising that it took 153 years to make the journey (*A v B & C* was decided by the Court of Appeal in March 2002). In the former case, Prince Albert had made some private etchings which he wished to have copied. He placed them with a printer in Windsor to have copies made. An enterprising employee took extra copies which were then offered for sale to the public via a sale catalogue in which they were described, not pictured, and which gave the impression that they were being published with consent. The Prince took Mr Strange, the publisher of the catalogue, to court to stop publication and succeeded.[31] The Prince had no pre-existing relationship with Mr Strange. There was no contract between them. The Court held that there was an infringement of the Prince's rights in the material and that there had been some breach of trust. It was suggested in the judgment that the breach of trust or confidence in itself entitled the Prince to a remedy.

2–09

The textbooks report relatively few cases in the same area over the next 100 years. The courts seem to have been little troubled by cases claiming breach of confidence in personal matters, although there seems to have been a gradual recognition of confidentiality in those relationships where sensitive information most commonly passed between two people.[32] The relationships of bankers, doctors, lawyers, clergy or other counsellors as well as other professionals with their clients are all regarded as confidential.

An extra-judicial development worthy of mention is the article published in the *Harvard Law Review* in 1890 in which the authors, Samuel Warren and Louis B. Brandeis, argued vigorously for a law of privacy to restrain the intrusions of the press. It has been much cited since.[33]

2–10

---

[28] [2001] CA 2086.

[29] For the material in the following section I am much indebted to Toulson and Phipps, above, and Francis Gurry, *Breach of Confidence* (Clarendon Press, 1984).

[30] (1849) 1 Mac. & G. 25.

[31] For a discussion of the historical basis of the action and this case in particular, see Toulson and Phipps.

[32] Gurry, above at p.143 onwards.

[33] 4 *Harvard Law Review* 1890.

The next significant case was *Saltman Engineering Co Ltd v Campbell Engineering Co Ltd*.[34] Although this did not concern personal relationships, it confirmed two features of the action for breach of confidence which were essential for its future vigorous development: there did not have to be a contractual relationship between the parties before breach of confidence could be claimed and, where there was no contract, the action could be used to protect a wide range of subject-matter as long as it was not "public property or public knowledge". The generous approach taken to both the relationships and subject-matter capable of being protected meant that confidentiality could be invoked in a range of situations.

2–11   As the action for breach of confidence developed over the next 20 years, most of the reported cases concerned commercial or employment cases. However, in *Argyll v Argyll*[35] the Duchess of Argyll was successful in stopping her husband from disclosing information about the marital relationship. In that case the court confirmed that the doctrine could be applied in personal matters; rejected the argument that confidentiality could only be argued in a limited class of (primarily commercial) cases; and reiterated that this was a broad jurisdiction.

In 1981, the Law Commission produced a *Report on Breach of Confidence*.[36] The report reviewed the development of the law in this area. The review was no easy task. The body of case law on breach of confidence had grown organically. It had taken and used ideas from other areas. It had provided remedies where it thought they were needed. It had been messy, patchy, haphazard, vigorous and unplanned. There was no agreement on the legal basis of the right (a property right, contract, equity)[37]; the nature of the exemptions (are they exceptions to the obligation or defences to a breach?)[38]; the availability of damages (are they available or can only an injunction be issued?)[39]; or the effect on third parties (in what circumstances could they be bound if they came into possession of the confidential material?).[40] Not surprisingly the Law Commission proposed that these uncertainties and anomalies should be tidied up and the action for breach of confidence put on to a statutory footing. The report was never acted upon. If it had been, the privacy jurisprudence of the last decade might not have been possible.

The publication of personal information which has been unfairly obtained was considered in a number of cases over the following years. In *Stephens v Avery*[41] the defendant had betrayed her friendship with the plaintiff by providing a newspaper with details of the plaintiff's sexual life. The plaintiff claimed damages for breach of confidence. In *Francome v Mirror Group Newspapers*[42] a home telephone was bugged and the conversations over it taped by strangers. The resulting information was sent to the newspaper. In restraining publication before the trial, the Court of Appeal recognised that the conversations were confidential.

---

[34] (1948) 65 R.P.C. 203.
[35] [1967] Ch. 302.
[36] Cmnd.8388 (1981).
[37] Gurry, above, Ch.2.
[38] Gurry, Chs 15 and 16.
[39] Gurry, Ch.23.
[40] Gurry, Ch.13.
[41] [1988] 1 Ch. 419.
[42] [1984] 1 W.L.R. 892.

On the other hand, some judges were reluctant to protect information about those whose lives were in the public domain. Plaintiffs failed in *Woodward v Hutchins*[43] and *Lennon v News Group Newspapers Ltd.*[44] In the first case, the *Daily Mirror* wanted to publish material about a number of pop stars and the court refused to restrain the publication as it said that they had already put their lives in the public domain. In the second, the *News of the World* wanted to publish material about John Lennon's first marriage. The Court of Appeal said that the relationship had ceased to be private and refused to stop publication. The two cases have been distinguished in latter cases and can no longer be regarded as sound authority.

In *Attorney-General v Guardian Newspapers Ltd (No.2)*,[45] the *Spycatcher* case, the judges expressed a range of views on the action for breach of confidence and its application to personal information which have been much cited in later cases. A former member of the security services had published a book of memoirs of his time with the service. The government tried to restrain publication of material from the book in the *Guardian* newspaper, even though it had been published outside the United Kingdom and the UK Government had been unable to restrict its publication abroad. The Government claimed that the disclosure of information by the individual was a breach of confidence. Lord Goff, in his judgment, described the position that the law of confidence had reached at the end of the last century, although he disclaimed any intention to produce a definitive description of the area (ineffectually, as every text book cites it).

Lord Goff said that a duty of confidence arises when:

"confidential information comes to the knowledge of a person (the confidant) in circumstances where he has notice, or is held to have agreed, that the information is confidential, with the effect that it would be just in all the circumstances that he should be precluded from disclosing the information to others".

There can be no confidentiality unless the information is "confidential", that is it has not entered the public domain; the duty does not apply to information which is trivial or useless and confidentiality can, in some circumstances, be negated by public interest.

2–12

In the same case, Lord Keith signalled a green light for future privacy cases by accepting that privacy was a right capable of protection by the law of confidence.[46]

It might have been thought that after such encouraging dicta the courts would have moved forward to develop the action for breach of confidence into one which offered a more general protection for personal privacy. However, the decision in *Kaye v Robertson*[47] the following year proved a setback and, although the decision was later criticised, over the decade before the Human Rights Act came into force even the keenest proponents of judicial activism in this area faced difficulties in seeking to develop a more general right of privacy because of the chilling effect of the decision. In this case the subject had been in an accident,

---

[43] [1977] 1 W.L.R. 760.
[44] [1978] F.S.R. 573.
[45] [1990] 1 A.C. 109.
[46] [1990] 1 A.C. 109 at 255.
[47] [1991] F.S.R. 62.

which had resulted in severe injuries. A journalist entered his hospital room without permission and photographed him. The photograph was published. The action was taken against the photographer. Although the entry was wrongful, being a trespass, and the Court of Appeal acknowledged that the publication was an appalling invasion of his privacy, it refused to grant an injunction restraining publication. As a number of commentators have subsequently pointed out, the Court was not referred to the developing cases on confidentiality, presumably because the intrusion was by a stranger. It must also be borne in mind that the case was decided at a time when possible legislation restricting freedom of the press was a live issue.[48] The Court, recognising that a decision to protect the actor's privacy would be going beyond the boundaries of the law of confidence and, presumably, the wider political context, reaffirmed that the UK law knew no right of privacy and that it was a matter for Parliament, not the courts, to develop one. If the Court hoped that this principled abstention from developing the law would stir Parliament into action over press excesses it was to be disappointed. However, the clarity of the judgment was to prove a setback for those who advocated the development of a judge-made right to personal privacy for nearly a decade. In *R. v Khan*,[49] a case which was later considered by the ECtHR,[50] the House of Lords reiterated that in the United Kingdom there was nothing unlawful about a breach of privacy.

Development continued in related areas, and in *Hellewell v Chief Constable of Derby*[51] the court considered the disclosure of personal information which had been obtained under compulsion by a public body. This was partly a response to a wider development of information sharing by the public sector with increased privatisation, moves to partnership workings with the private sector and the disclosure of information between government departments and other public bodies, for example via data matching initiatives. Concern had previously been expressed at such developments and the limitations on the powers of public bodies to use and disclose personal information was emphasised in *Marcel v Commissioner of Police for the Metropolis*[52] by the Vice Chancellor who had memorably commented that: " ... the dossier of personal information is the hallmark of the totalitarian state".

2–13   In a number of cases the courts held that personal information obtained under compulsion would be subject to an obligation of confidence in the hands of the public body.[53] In *Hellewell* the local police force had provided shopkeepers with photographs of a known shoplifter. The photographs had been taken under compulsion when the individual was in custody. The individual complained of breach of confidence. It was held that there was an obligation of confidence owed to the individual as the information had been extracted under compulsory powers and the police were limited in the uses they could make of the information. In the particular case the disclosure of the photograph was justified in the public interest. More importantly for the purposes of the development of a more general

---

[48] See discussion in Ch.17 on the exemption for journalism.
[49] *The Times*, May 5, 1996.
[50] ECtHR report, *The Times,* May 23, 2000.
[51] [1995] 1W.L.R. 804.
[52] [1991] All E.R. 845; [1992] 1 All E.R. 72, CA.
[53] *Alfred Crompton Amusement Machines v Commissioner for Customs and Excise (No.2)* [1973] 2 All E.R. 1169.

privacy right, the judge commented that the law of confidence would be able to protect someone from an invasion of privacy caused by being photographed without consent from a distance.

The comment was obiter and was not followed in *R. v Brentwood BC Ex p. Peck*.[54] In that case the court dismissed a claim that the local council had acted unlawfully in giving the media copies of a CCTV recording of Mr Peck engaged in a suicide bid in a public place. It should be noted, however, that Mr Peck was later successful in his action against the UK in the ECtHR at Strasbourg . He succeeded not only on art.8 but also art.13 as the Court held that he had no effective legal remedy in the UK in relation to the violation of his right to respect for private life.

In *R. v Chief Constable of the North Wales Police Ex p. Thorpe*,[55] the disclosure of information about an individual's previous criminal history of offences against children by a public authority was considered by the court and held to be justified in the circumstances.

Thus, despite the uneven growth of authority in this area, by the time the HRA came into effect the law of confidence had developed significantly in the United Kingdom and there were persuasive dicta that an action for breach of confidence might be employed to protect personal privacy.

The action for breach of confidence offers a useful starting point for the development of a privacy right. There is no absolute right to confidentiality. Confidentiality may be breached where an opposing interest outweighs the obligation. Thus confidentiality will give way to an order of the court, legal compulsion, or a greater public interest in the disclosure. As such it incorporates a balancing test that makes it a malleable tool to apply where balances have to be struck, particularly between art.8 and other rights.

The European Court recognised the development of the law of confidence in the United Kingdom and its growing potential to protect personal privacy in *Wiener v United Kingdom*[56] and *Earl and Countess Spencer v United Kingdom*.[57] In both cases the applicants chose to bring cases in Strasbourg on the grounds that the United Kingdom did not offer the remedies they needed to protect their privacy rather than try to bring actions in the UK courts. In the *Wiener* case various statements had been made about the plaintiff's relations with his wife, not all of which were true. The court held that the UK law afforded sufficient remedies to protect his reputation (including libel, in respect of which he already had obtained a settlement), but said the failure to take action for breach of confidence did not amount to a failure to exhaust his remedies in the United Kingdom due to the uncertainty and lack of clarity in the jurisdiction. In the *Spencer* case, the Earl and his wife had been subject to articles in the newspapers about their marriage and about her health problems and photographs taken without consent. To that extent it was not dissimilar to the situation in which Naomi Campbell later found herself. The Commission declared the complaint to the court inadmissible as the applicants had not exhausted their domestic

2–14

---

[54] [1998] E.M.L.R. 697; *The Times*, December 18, 1997, QBD.
[55] [1999] Q.B. 396.
[56] Application 1087/84; (1986) 48 DR154, EComHR.
[57] Application 28851/95; (1998) 36 E.H.R.R. CD105.

PRIVACY RIGHTS UNDER THE HUMAN RIGHTS ACT 1998

remedies and the extension and development of the law of confidence by the courts meant that they were likely to have found a remedy in the UK courts.

Regulation of the press

2–15 Between 1989 and 2003 a series of Committees considered whether the United Kingdom should regulate the press to protect the privacy of individuals and issued a number of reports. The history is set out in Ch.17 on the exemptions for the special purposes. To an extent, the considerations of the Calcutt Committee and its reports played their part in the development of this area. They may have been an added reason for the exercise of judicial restraint in the case of *Kaye v Robertson* and were instrumental in bringing about the Press Complaints Commission (PCC) Code of Practice. Although decisions of the Commission have been criticised, and it is currently under fierce attack for its failures to restrain the behaviour of the tabloid press, the Code has been a mechanism for bringing some degree of regulation to bear on the behaviour of the press. (For a detailed analysis of the moves to press regulation, see Ch.17 on the special purposes.) The Code, together with the other self-regulatory codes for the media, has a role in the legal framework as both the HRA and the DPA require courts to take relevant codes into account when considering actions which may restrict freedom of expression. The PCC Code is described in Ch.17 on press regulation.

HUMAN RIGHTS ACT 1998 (HRA)

2–16 The European Convention for the Protection of Human Rights and Fundamental Freedoms (now the European Convention on Human Rights) (the Convention) was adopted by the Council of Europe on November 4, 1950 and ratified by the United Kingdom in 1951. The United Kingdom did not incorporate the Convention into domestic law on ratification. The Convention guarantees civil liberties, which include the right to life, freedom from torture, freedom from inhuman and degrading treatment, the right to a fair trial, freedom of religion, expression and assembly. The Convention binds the State and is enforceable against the State. Individuals have been able to take legal action against the United Kingdom in the European Court of Human Rights at Strasbourg in reliance on the Convention since 1966, but its application in the UK courts used to be limited. It could be looked at as an aid to interpretation in the case of ambiguity, as in *R. v Secretary of State for the Home Department Ex p. Brind*,[58] or to influence judicial decisions where there was an element of discretion as in *Attorney General v Guardian Newspapers (No.2)*.[59] However, individuals were not been able to rely on Convention rights directly in the UK courts. The incorporation of the Convention rights in UK law was the central vehicle in the Labour Government's policy commitment to "Bring Rights Home". The HRA did this by imposing specific obligations on courts and public bodies to take account of and apply Convention rights.

---

[58] [1991] A.C. 696.
[59] [1987] 3 All E.R. 306.

74

Interpreting legislation

Section 3(1) of the Human Rights Act provides that, so far as it is possible to do so, primary and subordinate legislation must be "read and given effect in a way which is compatible with the Convention rights". This provision applies to all primary and subordinate legislation whenever enacted. 2–17

Court rulings

Under s.2(1), "a Court or Tribunal determining a question which has arisen in connection with a Convention right must take into account" any judgment, decision or ruling of the European Court of Human Rights or any opinion of the Human Rights Commission or other authoritative precedent material insofar as that is relevant to the proceedings. 2–18

This imposes a duty to consider the Strasbourg jurisprudence on courts and tribunals, although courts are not bound to follow the case law as they would be if these cases were treated as strict precedents. In *Kay v Lambeth*[60] the House of Lords considered the impact of the duty to take Strasbourg judgments and opinions into account and the duty of the courts as public authorities to act compatibly with Convention rights on the rules of precedent. The question which arose was whether existing domestic rules of precedent should be modified as a result of the HRA so that a court which would ordinarily be bound to follow the decision of another court higher in the domestic curial hierarchy should no longer be bound to follow that decision if it appears to be inconsistent with a later ruling of the Court in Strasbourg. The House emphasised the importance of the doctrine of precedent in achieving legal certainty:

> "As Lord Hailsham observed (ibid, p 1054), 'in legal matters, some degree of certainty is at least as valuable a part of justice as perfection.' That degree of certainty is best achieved by adhering, even in the Convention context, to our rules of precedent. It will of course be the duty of judges to review Convention arguments addressed to them, and if they consider a binding precedent to be, or possibly to be, inconsistent with Strasbourg authority, they may express their views and give leave to appeal, as the Court of Appeal did here. Leap-frog appeals may be appropriate. In this way, in my opinion, they discharge their duty under the 1998 Act. But they should follow the binding precedent, as again the Court of Appeal did here."[61]

Lord Bingham went on to explain that this approach accords with the application of the margin of appreciation for the decisions of national authorities. The one exception to the application of the rules of precedent would be in those very exceptional cases where the policy on which earlier decisions had been based had been eroded by the subsequent impact of the HRA, giving as an example the case of *D v East Berkshire Community NHS Trust*[62] in which the Court of Appeal held that the decision of the House of Lords in *X (Minors) v Bedfordshire County Council*[63] could not survive the introduction of the Human Rights Act 1998

---

[60] [2006] UKHL 10.
[61] [2006] UKHL 10 per Lord Bingham at para.43.
[62] [2004] Q.B. 558.
[63] [1995] 2 A.C. 633.

because the effect of the Human Rights Act 1998 had undermined the policy considerations that had largely dictated the House of Lords decision. It pointed out, however, that such a course is not permissible save where the facts are of that extreme character. It follows therefore that, where a UK court has issued a ruling on a Convention right, junior courts must follow that even where there is some conflict with a later Strasbourg ruling.

Incompatibility

2–19   Under s.4(1), where a court determines in any proceedings that a provision of primary legislation is not compatible with a Convention right, it may make a declaration of incompatibility. Similar declarations may be made in respect of secondary legislation. Section 10 provides for a speedy procedure where by Parliament can make appropriate amendments to the law. Where the ECtHR makes a finding of incompatibility the Government is under an obligation in international law to remedy the breach and alter the law to do so. The Court will allow for a reasonable time for amendment on the basis that the Government has evidenced an intention to take appropriate action.[64]

Acts of public authorities

2–20   Under s.6(1) a public authority is bound to act in a way compatible with the Convention rights. If a public authority acts in a way incompatible with the Convention rights the authority will be acting unlawfully unless the governing primary legislation leaves the authority with no choice in the matter. Where there is an unlawful act a person who is a "victim" of the act may use the Convention rights as either a sword or a shield in the proceedings. That is they may either bring proceedings against the authority "in the appropriate court or tribunal" or rely on the Convention rights concerned in any legal proceedings against them. This remedy is only available to a "victim" of the unlawful act.

Where an act by a public authority is unlawful under this provision the court has a wide jurisdiction to grant relief under s.8. The defence of unlawful behaviour by a public authority applies under s.7(1)(b) to any proceedings "brought by or at the instigation of a public authority". A person will only be regarded as a victim if he "would be a victim for the purposes of Article 34 of the Convention". Under s.7(1) a person may only bring proceedings against a public authority or rely on a Convention right in any proceedings brought against him if he "is (or would be) a victim of the unlawful act". The limitation applies to all proceedings, including judicial review in connection with an unlawful act. Under s.7(7):

> "For the purposes of this section a person is a victim of an unlawful act only if he would be a victim for the purposes of Article 34 of the Convention if proceedings were brought in the European Court of Human Rights in respect of that Act".

---

[64] See *Goggins and Others v UK* (30089/04) July 2011 and others. Supervision is exercised by the Committee of Ministers.

Accordingly, one has to look to the Strasbourg case law to establish the meaning of the term victim. A victim must be affected by the act or omission that is the subject of the complaint. An interest group or public defender cannot take action. The person need not actually have suffered in order to take action. It will be enough if the person is at risk of being directly affected.[65]

Human Rights Act 1998 s.12

This section applies if a court is considering whether to grant any relief which, if granted, might affect the Convention right to freedom of expression. In many cases concerned with freedom of expression and privacy, the applicant will be seeking an order that material should not be published and accordingly s.12 will come into play.

2–21

The respondent must be given an opportunity to be present and to speak. The court is not to grant relief unless it is satisfied that the applicant has taken all practicable steps to notify the respondent or that there are compelling reasons why he should not be notified.

The court must not restrain publication before trial unless it "is satisfied that the applicant is likely to establish that publication should not be allowed".

In reaching its decision the court must have "particular regard" to the importance of the Convention right to freedom of expression and, where the proceedings relate to material which is journalistic, literary or artistic, the section specifies a number of matters which must be considered. It will be noted that the same terms for the special purposes are used as in the DPA. The terms are discussed in Ch.17. As in the DPA they are used without any further definition. The matters to be considered are:

- the extent to which the material is already or is about to become available to the public;
- the extent to which publication would be in the public interest; and
- "any relevant privacy code".

The codes are not specified by order as they are in the DPA but it would be reasonable to expect a court to look at the same codes. In cases since October 2000 advocates have cited decisions of the Press Complaints Commission under the Press Complaints Commission Code of Practice.[66]

Section 12 was inserted into the HRA at the pressing of the press lobby to bolster the right to freedom of expression in the face of the potential for the courts to create a right to privacy using art.8. However, the courts have pointed out that, in considering the impact of the section, consideration of art.10 must entail the reservations in art.10(2) as well as the right itself and thus the need to weight competing rights and interests. Regarded in this somewhat elastic manner, it has not proved a dampener on the development of the privacy right. On the contrary it has been used to justify consideration of art.8 in cases between private persons.

---

[65] *Norris v Ireland* (1998) 13 E.H.R.R. 186.
[66] *R. (Persey) v Secretary of State for the Environment, Food and Rural Affairs* Unreported March 15, 2002; *R. (Howard) v Secretary of State for Health* Unreported March 15, 2002.

Effect on approach to interpretation

2–22   When interpreting any matter that involves the Convention rights the courts must take account of those rights. This impacts on the Commissioner's advice and supervisory actions, both criminal and civil actions. The Commissioner is under a duty to interpret the DPA in a manner compatible with the Convention rights. The same obligation applies to any court or tribunal which is called upon to interpret any provision in proceedings before it. In the introduction to the *Guidance* issued on October 28, 2001 the Commissioner said:

> "As I am required to do, I have sought to interpret the Act in the light of the provisions of the Human Rights Act 1998, which came into force on 20 October 2000. This will need to be kept under review. The full effect of the Human Rights Act on our legal system, and on society as a whole, has yet to be felt. It is however, clear that the role of information in our society makes it increasingly important to develop respect among data controllers for the private lives of individuals and to ensure good information handling practice. The Human Rights Act, and in particular Articles 8 and 10 of the European Convention on Human Rights, provide the legal framework within which interpretation of the Act, and the Data Protection Principles which underpin it, can be developed."

This is not repeated in the current Guide to Data Protection but it is submitted that the position remains the same. The obligation to comply with the Convention also affects the actions of the Commissioner as a public authority in taking enforcement and other actions.

THE APPLICATION OF THE CONVENTION RIGHTS

2–23   The rights are referred to in the HRA as the Convention rights. Some Convention rights are absolute, that is they cannot be interfered with or set aside by the State, for example freedom from torture is an absolute right. The provisions of the Convention which are most obviously relevant to the DPA are arts 8 and 10—the right to respect for private and family life, home and correspondence and the right to freedom of expression respectively. However, before considering those two rights in more detail, it must be emphasised that the HRA cannot be read selectively. The qualifications have to be read with the rights[67] and all the Convention rights have to be read as a whole. There are tensions between some of the rights. Where there are conflicts the presumption will be that absolute rights will take precedence over qualified rights[68] but will not always prevail against rights which are subject to limitations[69]; where two or more qualified rights or rights subject to limitations come into opposition the courts have to take account of all. Where art.10 is concerned the HRA contains special provisions requiring the UK courts to weight the issues with particular care before acting to prevent publication of materials.[70] In many privacy cases the courts have had to assess the balance between the right of the public to open justice (art.6), the right to freedom

---

[67] See comments in *Douglas v Hello! Ltd* [2001] 2 All E.R. 289.
[68] *Venables v Newsgroup newspapers* [2001] 1 All E.R. 908.
[69] *Van Mechelen v Netherlands* (1998) 25 E.H.R.R. 647; however this was in the context of art.6.
[70] s.12.

of expression (art.10) and the right to respect for private life (art.8). Article 6 is described as a limited right in that it is subject to limitations so that it may be curtailed to meet one of the specified needs but such curtailments must be proportionate.

The right to private life, which includes a right to a degree of control over or right to restrict the collection, availability or use of information about an individual, is only one aspect of the art.8 right which requires respect for private and family life, home and correspondence. The ECtHR has considered many cases on art.8 but comparatively few concern the use of information. It should be noted that the scope of art.8 and the DPA are not co-terminous and in many cases the DPA will offer protection to a wider range of personal information that the Convention.

Application to private bodies or persons

The Convention rights are primarily the rights of individuals in relation to the State. However, they may affect the relations between private parties in a number of ways:

2–24

- In some cases the state has an obligation to step between two (or more) private parties and protect one against another. As an example, art.3 guarantees the right not to be subject to inhumane or degrading treatment. In order to comply with this right the State must not only restrain from the prohibited acts but it must also protect its citizens from such treatment by any other person. This obligation applies to art.8: *Stjerna v Finland*.[71] In that case, the court said that the boundaries between the state's positive and negative obligations do not lend themselves to precise definition. This aspect of art.8 is important in that it allows for the extension of the Convention right as between private parties and has been relied on by the courts to do so. In the *Hello!* case[72] Brooke L.J. reviewed the Strasbourg cases on this aspect of the Convention rights (in paras 83–86). In doing so he quoted *X v The Netherlands*[73]:

  > "these [positive] obligations may involve the adoption of measures designed to secure respect for private life even in the sphere of the relations of individuals between themselves."

  He then applied it to the facts of the case to decide that he was able to apply the Article in the action between the two competing private parties.
- The courts themselves are public authorities for the purposes of the HRA. As such they may be obliged to interpret any law that they apply so as to conform to the Convention rights. This obligation and its effect on interpretation were recognised by Lord Woolf in *A v B & C*[74] and have been applied by the courts in subsequent cases.

---

[71] (1994) 24 E.H.R.R. 194.
[72] See paras 2–45 onwards.
[73] (1986) 8 E.H.R.R. 235.
[74] [2002] 3 W.L.R. 542.

There is also the more pragmatic point that, as the courts must interpret the law to comply with the Convention when adjudicating in cases concerning public bodies, there will be a tendency to interpret the same legal provisions in the same way for all litigants.

The nature of qualified rights

2–25 Absolute rights cannot be interfered with by the State. Qualified rights can be interfered with by the state but any interference must conform to the following norms:

- The interference must be "in accordance with" or "prescribed by" law. That means that the state must have a legal basis for the interference. The law must be accessible, predictable and not arbitrary.[75]
- The interference must be carried out for one of the prescribed purposes set out in the second part of the relevant article. The list of the prescribed purposes is specific to each Article. The list is exhaustive in each case. As with all exemptions or restrictions it will be narrowly construed compared to the right.[76]
- The interference must be "necessary in a democratic society": that is it must be a reasonable and proportionate response to the threat which justified the interference. The State must not use "a sledgehammer to crack a nut".[77]

When considering the application of a right the first question is whether the right comes into play or is "engaged" by the facts of the case. A minor invasion might not justify engagement.[78] If the right is engaged, the next question is whether the right has been breached by the action complained of. If the right is breached, the court will consider whether the breach has been carried out with a proper legal basis, is in one of the specified interests and was a proportionate response to the problem. Where the interference is an interference by another private party the courts have not considered the lawfulness of the actions of party in the cases heard to date. It appears to have been accepted by the courts that a private person may carry out any action as long as it is not forbidden by the law. The cases have instead focussed on the questions of justification and proportionality.

---

[75] In *Malone v UK* (1984) E.H.R.R.14 it was held that unpublished administrative arrangements governing telephone tapping in the UK we not sufficient to qualify; *Khan v UK, The Times,* May 23, 2000. In *Gillian and Quinton v UK* Application 4158/05 the powers of stop and search under the Terrorism Act 2000(ss.44 and 45) were not sufficiently circumscribed or subject to adequate legal safeguard against abuse and were therefore not in accordance with law.

[76] *Sunday Times v UK* (1979) 2 E.H.R.R. 245 at 281; *Sunday Times v UK* (1980) 2 E.H.R.R. 245.

[77] *Handyside v UK* (1979–80) 1 E.H.R.R. 737.

[78] In *Costello-Roberts v United Kingdom* (1993) 1 E.H.R.R. 1112 the Court held that the corporal punishment involved was not sufficiently serious to bring it within art.8.

ARTICLE 8

This has proved to be a flexible right and has lent itself to cover a wide range of issues in the Strasbourg jurisprudence.[79] It reads:

2–26

"(1)   Everyone has the right to respect for his private and family life, his home and his correspondence.

(2)   There shall be no interference by a public authority with the exercise of this right except such as is in accordance with the law and is necessary in a democratic society in the interests of national security, public safety or the economic well-being of the country, for the prevention of disorder or crime, for the protection of health or morals, or for the protection of the rights and freedoms of others."

In Gillan and Quinton v UK[80] the Court said:

"As the Court has had previous occasion to remark, the concept of 'private life' is a broad term not susceptible to exhaustive definition. It covers the physical and psychological integrity of a person. The notion of personal autonomy is an important principe underlying the interpretation of its guarantees (see Pretty v the United Kingdom). The Article also protects a right to identity and personal development, and the right to establish relationships with other human beings and the outside world. It may include activities of a professional or business nature. There is therefore a zone of interaction with others, even in a public context, which may fall within the sphere of 'private life'. There are a number of elements relevant to a consideration of whether a person's private life is concerned in measures effected outside a person's home or private premises. In this connection a person's reasonable expectations as to privacy may be a significant, though not necessarily conclusive, factor."

Strasbourg cases on the right to private life and information uses

Article 8 offers protection primarily to individuals, not to legal persons. Limited companies cannot have a family life, nor can government departments. This approach is similar to that taken in the UK in relation to the reputation of public bodies, where such bodies cannot sue for attacks on reputation. In *Derbyshire County Council v Times Newspapers*[81] the Council sued *The Times* for libel and the House of Lords held that a local authority cannot sue for attacks on its reputation. Apart from that limitation, however, it has proved to be a wide and elastic right. It covers more than personal privacy. It has been used for purposes as diverse as restricting night flights over Heathrow Airport to mandating the provision of legal support for a woman who needed to escape from a violent relationship.[82] In its judgment in the case of *Pretty v United Kingdom*[83] the Court accepted that art.8 encompassed the right to determine when the quality of life

2–27

---

[79] See Lord Lester of Herne Hill and David Pannick QC (eds), *Human Rights Law and Practice* (Butterworths, 1999).
[80] *Human Rights Law and Practice*. Application no. 4158/05 ECtHR.
[81] [1993] A.C. 534.
[82] *Airey v Ireland* (1979) E.H.R.R. 305.
[83] *R. (on the Application of Pretty) v DPP* [2001] All E.R. 417.

had become insupportable and chose to leave it, although they went on to decide that the state's interference with that right was justified and proportionate.

It has been used to protect personal informational privacy in a number of cases.

Strasbourg jurisprudence

2–28   It is not always easy to distinguish between informational and other aspects of private life, but in this section we have tried to pick out Strasbourg cases that concern the obtaining, use or disclosure of information about living individuals. When considering the cases there are obviously overlaps with the protection of home and family life. When considering the Strasbourg jurisprudence, regard should be had to a number of interpretational approaches taken by the ECtHR. The ECtHR applies a purposive approach[84] and is not bound to follow its own rulings. In addition, the Convention is interpreted as a "living instrument . . . in the light of present day conditions".[85] Therefore earlier decisions may not be as reliable as later ones in an area of social and technical development. In addition the Court has insisted that rights must be "practical and effective", so paper compliance is not regarded as sufficient.[86] It must also be recognised that States have a margin of appreciation in decision-making so there are areas where Strasbourg will decline to interfere with the rulings of national courts or governments because the topic is within the margin accorded to the State.[87] The extent of the margin is a matter of much debate but generally will be found where qualified rights concern the application of social or economic rights.

Consent as a basis for interference

2–29   Article 8 requires "respect" for private life. Not every interference with private life will be a breach of art.8. Importantly, what might otherwise be an unwarranted interference will not be a breach if the act has the consent of the individual. The consent must be true and freely given. Where genuine consent is given it is implicit that sufficient respect has been accorded to the rights of the individual by the provision of choice. It has been held that there was no interference with the art.10 right where the individual had agreed or contracted to limit his freedom of expression.[88] In another case an individual was offered a new contract of employment which entailed working on a Sunday. The applicant claimed that it interfered with her right to practice religion and took action under art.9. The court held that the applicant had a free choice in employment, could have taken another job and thus the right was not engaged.[89] Although the law can be stated simply, there are difficulties in applying it. The Article 29 Working Group,[90] in a paper on the use of personal data in the employment sphere, has

---

[84] Applying art.31 of the Vienna Convention on the law of treaties.
[85] *Tyrer v UK* (1979–1980) 2 E.H.R.R. 1.
[86] *Airey v Ireland* (1979–80) 2 E.H.R.R. 305.
[87] *Friend v UK* App no.16072/06 Dec 2009.
[88] *Vereniging Rechtswinkels Utrecht v Netherlands* 46 DR 1986, EcomHR.
[89] *Stedman v UK* (1997) 23 E.H.R.R. CD168.
[90] The representative group of data commissioners set up under the Directive; see Ch.25 for an analysis of the work of the group.

suggested that true consent can never be given in the employment context because of the imbalance of power between the parties and inevitable pressure that this brings to bear on individuals[91]:

> "An area of difficulty is where the giving of consent is a condition of employment. The worker is in theory able to refuse consent but the consequence may be the loss of a job opportunity. In such circumstances consent is not freely given and is therefore not valid. The situation is even clearer cut where, as is often the case, all employers impose the same or a similar condition of employment."

It is suggested that this goes too far. Consent may be reluctant but still valid. Individuals can waive their rights under the Convention. The question of whether a consent is valid will be a question of fact in all the circumstances. However it should be noted that the draft proposed Regulation issued by the Commission in January 2012 includes a similar provision restricting the use of consent in the context of employment.

Relationship Between the Case Law and Directive 95/46

Article 1 states that the object of the Directive is the protection of: 2–30

> ". . . the fundamental rights and freedoms of natural persons, and in particular their right to privacy with respect to the processing of personal data".

The Directive is not a codification of the case law on informational privacy as developed by the court at Strasbourg; rather the Directive is a working out of the rules governing informational privacy. Some of the Strasbourg cases cover areas covered by the Directive. The match between the two is closer than it used to be as there have been some findings from Strasbourg that reflect obligations imposed by the Directive,[92] but it remains incomplete. Where there is relevant case law it may be taken into account in the interpretation of the DPA either directly, by resolving ambiguities in the Act, or indirectly by influencing the case law under the HRA. For that reason an outline of the Strasbourg cases on personal information is provided below.[93]

---

[91] Opinion 8/2001 on the processing of personal data in the employment context.

[92] See *I v Finland* (20511/03) July 17, 2008 in which the ECtHR ruled that art.8 imposes a degree of responsibility for the security of personal data.

[93] In producing the summary I made use of the following: Lee A. Bygrave, "Data Protection Pursuant to the Right to Privacy in Human Rights Treaties", International Journal of Law and Information Technology, Vol.6; Lord Lester and David Pannick (eds.), *Human Rights Law and Practice* (Butterworths, 1999); Helen Mountfield and John Wadhad, *Human Rights Act 1998* (Blackstones, 1999); Keir Strumer, *European Human Rights Law* (LAG, 1999); and essays published in *Freedom of Expression and Freedom of Information* (Oxford University Press, 2000), particularly those by Michael J. Beloff QC and Professor David Feldman, as well as case reports from *www.coe.org* [Accessed September 10, 2012] which also publishes a series of FactSheets on specific issues which are maintained and provide an excellent starting point for a review of the relevant case law.

ECtHR cases on personal information

2–31   The cases mentioned in this section have been decided over more than thirty years since *Klass v Federal Republic of Germany*[94] in 1978, and over that period the Court has become more willing to protect individuals against breaches of informational privacy, both by extending the category of circumstances in which it will hold that the right is engaged and by subjecting the State's claim to justification to more stringent scrutiny. In earlier cases the Court has proved itself more minded to allow for a wider margin of appreciation, or area of discretion to the State, in cases where the intrusion is justified on the grounds of combating terrorism or serious crime (see the later section for cases in this area). However this appears to be changing; for example in *Gillan and Quinton v UK*[95] the Court found that the stop and search provisions of the Terrorism Act 2000 were not subject to sufficient safeguards and therefore not in accordance with law.

Collection of information

2–32   The collection of personal information without consent, whether under compulsion or from third parties, will be a breach. In *McVeigh v UK*[96] the taking of fingerprints without consent was held to be a breach, but a justifiable one, as it was in *Murray v UK*.[97] While in the later case of *Van Der Velden v the Netherlands*[98] the Court decided that both the taking and retention of DNA samples from a person convicted of serious offences breached art.8.1 but was justified and proportionate. Article 8 has been raised in cases where personal information was obtained via samples taken under compulsion. In *X v Austria*[99] the court considered the taking of a blood test under compulsion in paternity proceedings and held that there was a breach but that it was justified. In *Peters v Netherlands*[100] it considered the compulsory random drug testing of prisoner's urine and held this was a breach but fell within art.8(2). In *S and Marper v UK*,[101] the compulsory taking of DNA samples was justified although the retention of the samples when no charges were brought or charges had been dropped was not.

Covert collection

2–33   Even where the authority has a legal power to collect information, it should not do so in covert ways unless there is a legal basis for the secret collection and the secrecy is justifiable. The collection of a dossier of information about an individual by a public body without the knowledge or consent of the individual will be a breach of art.8, although it may be justified under art.8(2). In *Hilton v UK*[102] information was collected without the individual's knowledge as part of a

---

[94] (1978) 2 E.H.R.R. 214.
[95] See fn.80.
[96] (1983) 5 E.H.R.R. 71.
[97] (1995) 19 E.H.R.R. 193.
[98] Application No.29514/05.
[99] *X v Austria* (1979) 18 D.R. 154 9 (blood test pursuant to court order).
[100] 77 A D.R. 75 1994.
[101] December 4, 2008 30562/04 and 30566.
[102] (1981) 3 E.H.R.R. 104.

security check and the secret collection was held to be a breach. Covert surveillance has been found to be a breach and the collection of personal information by covert methods will be a breach, even if no record is retained. These cases have usually occurred in the context of police investigations into criminal activity as in *Klass v Federal Republic of Germany*.[103] In *Van Vondel v Netherlands*[104] a breach was found where the National Police Internal Investigation Department had provided recording equipment to assist an officer record conversations with an informer in the absence of rules and safeguards.

It follows that the use of covert and intrusive methods of obtaining of information will be a breach, including telephone tapping and covert listening devices. These areas have given rise to particular problems for the United Kingdom given the UK's previous persistent reliance on non-statutory powers in these areas. The United Kingdom was found to be in breach of art.8 in *Malone v United Kingdom*[105] because the police had an insufficient legal basis for tapping telephones. This was remedied by the Interception of Communications Act 1985, which provided for the interception of calls made on public lines. However, it did not cover interception on private lines nor did it cover the use of listening devices, which continued to be used after 1985 on a non-statutory basis. In *Halford v United Kingdom*[106] the Court found the United Kingdom in breach of art.8 again because the police had intercepted calls on a line which had been provided for private use and the UK had no legal basis on which the interception of private lines could be authorised. In *PG v United Kingdom*[107] the UK was found in breach when the police installed a covert listening device in a flat without a legal basis. In *Copland v United Kingdom*[108] the Court held that there was a violation of the art.8 rights of an employee of a further education college where her work e-mails, telephone calls from work and internet usage were monitored without being given warning that such monitoring would take place. This applied equally to the monitoring of the communication data arising from the calls.[109]

This has now been dealt with, under the Regulation of Investigatory Powers Act 2000 (RIPA). In *Govell v United Kingdom*[110] a hole had been drilled into the wall of a living room from the house next door to enable the police to listen in to the conversations in the room. The only regulation of covert listening devices and visual surveillance at the time was in Home Office Guidelines and again the United Kingdom was found in breach of art.8 on the ground that there was no legal basis for the activity. In *Khan v United Kingdom*[111] and *Schenk v Switzerland*[112] the same rule applied to surreptitiously obtained recordings by police. The court has also found that the collection and use of communications data, for example the maintenance of a register of the numbers called from a

---

[103] (1979–80) 2 E.H.R.R. 214.
[104] October 25, 2007.
[105] (1985) 7 E.H.R.R. 14.
[106] (1997) 24 E.H.R.R. 523.
[107] [2001] Po. L.R. 325.
[108] (2006) 43 E.H.R.R. SE5 Application No.62617/00.
[109] See Ch.23 for a detailed analysis of the law relating to the monitoring of electronic communications.
[110] (1998) E.H.R.L.R. 121.
[111] (1998) E.H.R.L.R. 121, n.19.
[112] (1988) 13 E.H.R.R. 242.

particular telephone or their disclosure to the police, for purposes other than the necessary provision of a telecommunications service, is a breach.[113]

The interception and opening of private mail was an interference with correspondence and also an interference with private life in *Hewitt v United Kingdom*.[114] There have been a number of cases in which the Court has ruled on the interception of prisoners' mail.[115]

Maintenance of records

2–34   It appears that the court will treat the maintenance of any dossier or record on an individual by a public body as amounting to a prima facie interference with the art.8 right, even if the record is not particularly sensitive. In *Amman v Switzerland*[116] both the interception of telephone calls and the maintenance of a record relating to the individual by an authority of the State amounted to an interference. A public body must therefore be able to justify the retention of any record under art.8(2). It must be able to point to a specific legal basis empowering it to maintain the record, the record must be justified in one of the specified interests and it must be proportionate to the interest to be protected to retain the record. In *Chave v France*[117] a record was maintained of the fact that an individual had had psychiatric medical treatment. The individual wished to have the record expunged but the court held that the continued registration was justified. In *Kinnuen v Finland*[118] the Commission held that retention of fingerprints did not constitute an interference. However in *S and Marper v UK*[119] the ECtHR rules that the blanket and indiscriminate nature of the powers to retain fingerprints, cellular samples and DNA profiles of persons suspected but not convicted of offences was a disproportionate interference and breached art.8. The House of Lords had ruled that mere retention of DNA samples did not constitute an interference, but even if that were not the case any interference would be justified under art.8(2). In *Marper* the applicants had not been the subject of criminal proceedings. In *Van der Velden v Netherlands*[120] the applicant was convicted of serious offences and his DNA taken and stored. He complained that the retention of the DNA was in breach of art.8 as the DNA had had no part in his conviction. The Court held that, while the view had previously been taken that the retention of fingerprints did not engage art.8[121] given the use to which cellular material could be put in the future, the retention did constitute an interference but was justified and proportionate. In *Shimovolos v Russia*[122] a breach was found because information about a human rights activist had been registered in a secret surveillance database on the basis of a ministerial order which was not published or accessible to the public. The existence of secret datasets has been regarded as

---

[113] *Malone v United Kingdom* (1985) 7 E.H.R.R. 14.
[114] (1992) 14 E.H.R.R. 657.
[115] See *Silver v United Kingdom* (1983) 5 E.H.R.R. 347.
[116] February 16, 2000, ECtHR.
[117] (1991) 71 D.R. 141.
[118] Application No.24950/94.
[119] See [2008] ECHR 1851.
[120] Application No.29514/05.
[121] *Kinnuen v Finland* (24950/94) Commission Decision of May 15, 1996.
[122] June 21, 2011.

a breach in *Rotaru v Romania*.[123] In *Leander v Sweden*[124] the court held that the maintenance of a dossier by the security service was a breach but the applicant was not entitled to access the information complained of. This illuminates another aspect of art.8—the right to access personal information.

Access to information

In some limited cases the right to private life may entail an obligation on the State to disclose information about an individual's past life by the State. In *Gaskin v United Kingdom*[125] the Court held that the right to private life could require a public authority to open its files and provide information to an individual about his past, subject to having a method of making proper decisions to balance this right with the expectations, and public interest in privacy, of others. This may also apply where the disclosure of information is necessary for an individual to protect his family, as in *Guerra v Italy*[126] where the Court held that the individual had the right to find out about an environmental hazard. The same approach was applied in *McGinley v United Kingdom*[127] where the Court held that ex-servicemen were entitled to know of the levels of radioactivity to which they had been exposed. However there is no general right to access information under art.8. Moreover these cases should be distinguished from those in which the existence of the data has been kept secret.

2–35

Photography

A number of cases have concerned the use of cameras and the taking of photographs, not all of them covert. In *Murray v UK*[128] the police in Northern Ireland took photographs and fingerprints at the police station without consent in anti-terrorist operations. It was held to be a breach. In *Friel v Austria*[129] the applicant was photographed taking part in a demonstration. The court held that no breach of his right to private life was involved either in the taking of the photograph or its retention. However, in that case the individual was not identified by name with the photographic record and the photograph had been taken of a public activity in a public place. In *Sciacca v Italy*[130] and *Gurgenidze v Georgia*[131] the Court held that the publication of photographs, taken as a result of investigations, in newspapers in the context of articles about charges breached art.8. In *Reklos v Greece*,[132] the taking of photographs of a new born baby without the consent of the parents at a private clinic and the retention of the photographs was a held to be a breach. In other cases the Court has addressed the protection which should be afforded to private activity in a public space or a

2–36

---

[123] May 4, 2000.
[124] (1987) 9 E.H.R.R. 433.
[125] (1989) 12 E.H.R.R. 36.
[126] (1998) 26 E.H.R.R. 357.
[127] (1999) 27 E.H.R.R. 1.
[128] (1996) 22 E.H.R.R. 29.
[129] (1995) 21 E.H.R.R. 83. 31 January, 1995 Series A no. 305B.
[130] January 2005 (50774/99).
[131] October 2006 (71678/01).
[132] [2009] E.M.L.R. 16.

"semi-private space" such as a restaurant and held that there is a zone of interaction with others which falls within the scope of private life, even where the action takes place in a private place. The question arose in *Von Hannover*[133] and in *Peck v United Kingdom*.[134] The *Von Hannover* case concerned Princess Caroline of Monaco, the eldest daughter of Prince Ranier of Monaco. Despite having no formal public role, she has been of great interest to the tabloid press in a number of European countries. In 1993 and onward several German magazines and newspapers had published articles and photographs of her without her consent engaged in private activities with her family and friends, such as dining in restaurants, shopping, riding or playing tennis. She objected to the publications but the German courts refused to grant her relief because she was regarded as a figure of contemporary society, *Person der Zeitgeschichte,* in the relevant German provisions, and therefore her right to privacy was limited. She was entitled to privacy where her activities were in a "secluded place", that is somewhere clearly meant to be private, but not otherwise. She was partially successful in her appeal through the German courts and succeeded in restricting the publication of photographs of her children but not other photographs. She complained to the Court of Human Rights that the German law did not protect her art.8 rights. The Court held that:

- art.8 has horizontal effect, therefore the State has positive obligations to protect the individual from other private parties;
- the protection of private life has to be balanced against the art.10 right of freedom of expression;
- a fundamental distinction must be made between those matters capable of contributing to debate in a democratic society and those merely satisfying the curiosity of readers about individuals' private lives;
- the protection of private life extends beyond the family circle and applies to activities which are private and personal but which are conducted in public places; and
- there is a particular interest in protecting private life to contend with the new technologies which make it possible to take surreptitious or long distance photographs and make them widely available

The applicant subsequently returned to the Court alleging that the German courts had failed to apply the judgment.[135] Three photographs of the applicant had been published by German newspapers without the consent of the applicant. The court had held that two were not justified but the other was "related" to an article about Prince Ranier and his failing health and was justifiable. The ECtHR held that there was no breach and the decision was within the margin of appreciation allowed to States in the application of the rights.

---

[133] *Von Hannover v Germany* (Application No.59320/00).
[134] *Peck v United Kingdom* (44647/98) 57 ECHR-1.
[135] *Von Hannover (No.2)* February 2012.

The judgment in *Von Hannover* was referred to in the UK case of *Niema Ash v Loreena McKennit*.[136] In the case of *Peck* the Court had held that the dissemination of photographs of Mr Peck taken in a public place breached his art.8 rights.

Disclosure of information

The disclosure, as well as the collection and retention, of personal information has been raised before the court. In at least two cases applicants have complained about the disclosure of sensitive medical information about them. In *Z v Finland*,[137] the fact that a woman was HIV positive was disclosed in court proceedings and her identity was also disclosed in the court judgment. It was held that the disclosure of the HIV information was necessary for the court case but was not required in the record of the judgment. In *TV v Finland*[138] the court held that the disclosure that a prisoner was HIV positive was necessary to protect prison staff.

2–37

In *MS v Sweden*,[139] the disclosure of medical records to a Social Insurance Office for the purpose of compensation assessment was held to be a breach but was justified. It was proportionate as the recipients were only entitled to make a limited use of the data. In *Peck v United Kingdom*[140] a local authority which disclosed film of an individual who had been caught on CCTV carrying a knife (the individual had used it to try to commit suicide not to harm others) was held to be in breach of art.8. The film was released as an example of the usefulness of CCTV; unfortunately the identifying details had not been properly disguised so the individual could be recognised. The Court accepted that the actions of the local authority were lawful and the disclosure of the film was in support of a legitimate purpose but held that the disclosure was disproportionate and hence a breach.

Notice of disclosure

In *Mosely v United Kingdom*[141] the Court held that there is no obligation under art.8 to provide an individual with notice of an intention to publish material about him. The basis of the Court's reluctance to find such an obligation rests in the potential for it to have a chilling effect on freedom of the press; however they also pointed to the practical difficulties which might be involved.

2–38

---

[136] [2006] EWCA Civ 1714.
[137] *Z v Finland* (1998) 25 E.H.R.R. 371.
[138] (1997) 25 E.H.R.R. 371.
[139] (1994) 776 A.D.R. 140.
[140] (1997) B.H.R.C. 248.
[141] May 2011 (48009/08).

Sensitive data

2–39 There has also been confirmation from the Court that the retention and use of some types of personal data in the sensitive data categories requires particularly strong justification, as in *Lustig-Prean v UK*[142] where the information related to sexual life. See also *S and Marper* and the cases referred to in 2-34 above. However it should be noted that the Court's case law does not cover the range of data in the sensitive data categories and it must be doubted that the Court would regard some data falling into those categories as sufficiently connected with private life to merit protection.

Security of data

2–40 In an interesting development in 2008 the Court considered whether a failure to provide adequate security for medical data could amount to a breach of art.8 in *I v Finland*.[143] The applicant, who had been diagnosed as HIV positive, worked as a nurse in a public hospital. She was treated at the same hospital and began to suspect that her colleagues knew of her illness. The hospital restricted access to her records and made other changes. In 1995 she sought access to know who had accessed her confidential records. The director of the hospital's archives responded that it was not possible to find out who, if anyone, had accessed the records as the data system only showed the five most recent consultations, by unit not person, and even this was deleted once the file was returned to the archives. The system was subsequently amended to show an audit trail of access but the applicant instituted proceedings for failure to keep the record confidential. She failed in her action as there was no evidence that the file had been consulted. The Court noted the extent of positive obligations on the State under art.8. It also noted that, under the Finnish Personal Files Act of 1987, a data controller had an obligation to ensure that personal data and information were appropriately secured against unlawful processing, use, destruction, amendment and theft. It considered that the records system in place in the hospital clearly did not accord with these requirements. It emphasised that what is required is that practical and effective protection was required to exclude the possibility of unauthorised use and that such protection had not been provided.

Cases before the European Court

2–41 As well as cases before the ECtHR, cases which involve the application of human rights issues may arise before the European Court. In the PNR cases before the European Court[144] the Advocate General's Opinion covered the question of whether the Agreement with the US Government for the transfer of Passenger Name Records to the US Bureau of Customs and Border Protection (part of the Department of Homeland Security) was in breach of art.8 on the basis that it was neither accessible nor foreseeable, nor was it proportionate to the objective pursued in view of the significant number of data elements transferred on every

---

[142] January 2003 (44647/98).
[143] July 2008 (20511/03).
[144] Cases C-317/04 and C-318/04 of the European Court of Justice.

passenger and the length of time for which the data were retained. The Advocate took the view that the entire Agreement and linked provisions should be examined together. While he agreed that there was an interference with private life by reason of the transfer he considered that the legal basis was made out and was sufficiently accessible to those affected. He was clear that the transfer pursued a legitimate aim and went on to deal with the question of the margin of appreciation,

> "the scope of which will depend not only on the nature of the legitimate aim pursued but also on the particular nature of the interference involved[145] . . .
> "The review of proportionality by the European Court of Human Rights varies according to parameters such as the nature of the right and activities at issue, the aim of the interference and the possible presence of a common denominator in the States' legal systems.
> As regards the nature and activities of the rights at issue, where the right is one which intimately affects the individual's private sphere, such as the right to confidentiality of health-related personal data the European Court of Human Rights seems to take the view that the State's margin of appreciation is more limited and its own judicial review must be stricter.
> However where the aim of the interference is to maintain national security or to combat terrorism the European Court of Human Rights tends to allow States a wider margin of appreciation".[146]

He went on to suggest that the margin of appreciation should be limited to determining whether there was any manifest error of assessment in making the decision. On the facts of the case he did not regard the number of data items required or the retention time as manifestly unreasonable.

Relation with Directive 95/46

Not every aspect of the Directive has been reflected in the cases heard before the ECtHR or the European Court but, as the analysis above shows, a number have. In particular the cases mirror the requirement to have grounds for processing any personal data and the transparency requirements of the Directive. The Court has referred to data protection guidance produced by the Council of Europe (the influence of which is discussed in Ch.3) in *Z v Finland*[147] when considering a case on information about someone who was HIV positive.

2–42

ARTICLE 10

When considering the use and dissemination of information, art.8 cannot be considered in isolation and account must be taken of the art.10 right to freedom of expression. The balance between the two rights has featured in a number of the privacy cases heard by the UK courts since October 2000. One man's right to freedom of expression may have to give way to another's right to privacy, whether as protected by art.8 or by the specific rights and protections offered by

2–43

---

[145] Cases C-317/04 and C-318/04 para.26, citing *Leander v Sweden* ECtHR.
[146] Cases C-317/04 and C-318/04 paras 228–230, citing cases *Z v Finland; Leander; Murray v UK*.
[147] (1999) 23 E.H.R.R. 548.

the DPA. In this section we briefly explain the art.10 rights and touch on some of the main cases at Strasbourg and in the UK courts.

Article 10 provides:

"(1)   Everyone has the right to freedom of expression. This right shall include freedom to hold opinions and to receive and impart information and ideas without interference by public authority and regardless of frontiers. This Article shall not prevent States from requiring the licensing of broadcasting, television or cinema enterprises.

(2)   The exercise of these freedoms, since it carries with it duties and responsibilities may be subject to such formalities, conditions, restrictions or penalties as are prescribed by law and are necessary in a democratic society, in the interests of national security, territorial integrity or public safety, for the prevention of disorder or crime, for the protection of health or morals, for the protection of the reputation or rights of others, for preventing the disclosure of information received in confidence, or for maintaining the authority and impartiality of the judiciary."

Like art.8 this is a qualified right, but the ECtHR seems to set a higher threshold to justify interference with art.10 than with art.8, at least in respect of political speech. In the United Kingdom the freedom of the press was already protected before October 2000. See the comments of Lord Denning in *Schering Chemicals Ltd v Falkman Ltd* referred to in Ch.17.

Article 10 covers the right to hold opinions, to receive information and to pass it on. It does not give a right to obtain information that another party is not willing to disclose. Thus it cannot be used as the basis of a right to freedom of information.[148] The Court has expressly rejected such a development of the Convention rights to date. The UK courts have followed this line in recent cases.[149] The term "expression" extends to words, pictures, or images to express an idea or convey information. All are protected. There is clearly an overlap with the respect for personal correspondence under art.8 but the Court does not seem to have been asked to consider freedom of expression in relation to personal communication under art.10; that has been dealt with under art.8. The Court has considered freedom of expression in relation to political and journalistic materials, artistic expression and commercial communications. All are capable of protection.

Political and journalistic materials

2–44   The right to express political opinions will require a strong countervailing interest to displace it. To that extent it is the most strongly protected form of expression. Freedom of political speech is regarded by the Court as a core right in a democracy. In *Bowman v United Kingdom*[150] the Court held that the penalty enforcing the restriction on spending by candidates imposed by the Representation of the People Act 1983 was disproportionate to the legitimate aim pursued by the section. In *Handyside v United Kingdom*[151] the banning of a book of political

---

[148] *Leander v Sweden* (1987) 9 E.H.R.R. 433.
[149] *R. (on the application of Howard) v Secretary of State for Health* [2002] EWHC Admin 396.
[150] (1998) 26 E.H.R.R.
[151] (1998) 26 E.H.R.R. 1 121; (1995) 19 E.H.R.R. 193.

thought was found to be a breach. The rights of the press and the right of journalists to report freely and comment freely are accorded a similar weight in *Jersild v Denmark*.[152] In several cases the Court has considered the balance between rights of privacy and freedom of expression. Where the publication of private information has merely been for the purposes of amusement and gossip the Court has held that the privacy right was not out-weighted by the art.10 right; however, where the publication of private information served a valid public interest debate, the Court has found a breach of art.10.[153] In *Mersey Care Health Trust v Ackroyd*[154] the UK Court of Appeal protected the source of information about medical records of Ian Brady under art.10 even though the disclosure of those records had breached his privacy. In *Axel Springer v Germany*[155] the Court considered the nature and application of the balancing test to be applied where there is a conflict between arts 8 and 10. In the case in question an actor on German TV had been arrested for possession of a small amount of cocaine. It was a second offence and therefore a fine was imposed. The publication *Bild* reported the event and the actor applied for orders prohibiting the publication of the information on the grounds that it infringed his right to protection of his personality rights which was not proportionate given the nature of the offence. In the judgment the Court considered the case law on the issue and reiterated that art.8 cannot be relied upon to protect loss of reputation where that is a foreseeable outcome of conduct such as a criminal offence. It set out the criteria relevant for the balancing exercise where the art.10 rights of the press and the art.8 rights of the subject are in conflict. The Court explained as follows:

- An initial essential criterion is the contribution made by photos or articles in the press to a debate of general interest. The definition of what constitutes a subject of general interest will depend on the circumstances of the case. This may cover political issues or crimes but also where it concerns sporting issues or performing artists but not the rumoured marital difficulties of a president or the financial difficulties of a famous singer.
- The role or function of the person concerned and the nature of the activities are also important. A distinction has to be made between private individuals and persons acting in a public context. A fundamental distinction needs to be made between reporting facts capable of contributing to a debate in a democratic society, relating to politicians in the exercise of their official functions for example, and reporting details of the private life of an individual who does not exercise such functions.
- Although in certain special circumstances the public's right to be informed can even extend to aspects of the private life of public figures, particularly where politicians are concerned, this will not be the case—even where the persons concerned are quite well known to the public—where the published

---

[152] (1976) 1 E.H.R.R. 737.
[153] See *Von Hannover* and contrast *Plon (Societe) v France* (58148/00) May 18, 2004 in which the Court found that the restriction of the publication of a book about President Mitterand's health during his terms in offices was a breach of art.10.
[154] Court of Appeal February 2007.
[155] ECHR 2012 227 February 2012.

photos and accompanying commentaries relate exclusively to details of the person's private life and have the sole aim of satisfying the curiosity of a particular readership in that respect.

- The conduct of the person concerned or the fact that the photo and the related information have already appeared in an earlier publication are also factors to be taken into consideration. However, the mere fact of having cooperated with the press on previous occasions cannot serve as an argument for depriving the party concerned of all protection against publication of the report or photo at issue.
- The way in which the information was obtained and its veracity are also important factors. The Court has held that the safeguard afforded by art.10 to journalists in relation to reporting on issues of general interest is subject to the proviso that they are acting in good faith and on an accurate factual basis and provide "reliable and precise" information in accordance with the ethics of journalism.
- The way in which the photo or report are published and the manner in which the person concerned is represented in the photo or report may also be factors to be taken into consideration. The extent to which the report and photo have been disseminated may also be an important factor, depending on whether the newspaper is a national or local one, and has a large or a limited circulation.
- Lastly, the nature and severity of the sanctions imposed are also factors to be taken into account when assessing the proportionality of an interference with the exercise of the freedom of expression.

Applying these tests, the court determined that the restrictions on publication and imposition of the fines were in breach of art.10.

Artistic works are protected by the Court but the right to express artistic impulses may be more easily outweighed by other interests, for example those connected with taste and decency (*Wingrove v United Kingdom*[156]).

Commercial speech will also be protected. It follows that the art.10 right applies to legal persons as well as to individuals. As might be expected, in the hierarchy of protection, the right to commercial freedom of speech is more easily displaced than the others (*Colman v UK*[157]).

In *Mosley v United Kingdom*[158] the Court held that art.8 does not require pre-publication notice to be given to those about whom a newspaper intends to publish personal information. While it deplored the conduct of the newspaper, it took into account the chilling effect which such a requirement would risk, the concerns as to whether such an obligation could be practically imposed and policed and the wide margin of appreciation in the area. The Court has also had regard to the chilling effect of possible sanctions imposed post publication. If those are disproportionate then there will be also be a breach. In *Tolstoy*

---

[156] (1995) 19 E.H.R.R. 193.
[157] (1997) 224 E.H.R.R 1.
[158] 10 May 2011 48009/08.

Miloslavsky v United Kingdom[159] libel damages of £1.5 million were too high and interfered with freedom of speech. In *MGN v United Kingdom*[160] the Court considered the effect of the conditional fee arrangements entered into by Ms Campbell in relation to her case in the House of Lords. The conditional fee agreement had provided for an uplift (or success fee) of 95 per cent. The bill in the Lords was £850,000 of which £365,077 was uplift. MGN's challenge to the uplift on grounds of incompatibility with art.10 was rejected by the House of Lords[161] but successful in the ECtHR. It was held that, while the costs had a legal basis and a legitimate aim of widening access to justice, the high level permitted to be recovered amounted to a disproportionate interference with the art.10 rights of the media and exceeded the State's margin of appreciation.

The Court has looked at collateral issues such as the protection of sources for journalists. In *Goodwin v United Kingdom*[162] the Court considered the effect of the Contempt of Court Act 1981 s.10. This allows the UK courts to order journalists to hand over information about their sources if the disclosure is necessary to allow wrongdoing to be traced. In *Goodwin* it was held that the requirement to hand over information about a disloyal employee was not justified. However, s.10 was still valid.[163]

Freedom of Expression–UK case law

In addition to the privacy cases described below, the courts have heard a number of other cases in which art.10 has been raised and in which the importance of the right, particularly where political speech is concerned, has been asserted. The cases reflect the Strasbourg case law in that it is recognised that freedom of expression co-exist with other rights, such as the right to life and security of the person, as well as having to accommodate privacy rights. In *Venables v News Group Newspapers Ltd*[164] an injunction was granted against the whole world restraining the disclosure of any information that could lead to the identification of the murderers of Jamie Bulger after their release from prison. Dame Elizabeth Butler-Sloss held that the law of confidence could cover the information and the possibly fatal consequences for the individuals concerned, who had been the subject of death threats, outweighed the rights of freedom of expression of the press. The UK courts have also maintained the position taken in Strasbourg that the article does not give any right to access to information.[165] A number of cases of the cases in the UK courts dealing with the public interest in freedom of speech are covered in Ch.17 in relation to the statutory exemption to support for freedom of expression in s.32 of the Act. There is also reference to the relation between Freedom of Information Act 2000 and art.10 in Ch.26.

2–45

---

[159] (1997) 18 E.H.R.R.R 119.
[160] 18 January 2011 39401/04.
[161] [2005] 1 WLR 3394 House of Lords.
[162] (1995) 20 E.H.R.R.R 442.
[163] (1996) 22 E.H.R.R.R 123.
[164] For a review of cases on art.10 in the UK courts other than those which have dealt with personal privacy, see Ch.26 on Freedom of Information.
[165] [2001] Fam. 430.

Procedure

2–46   The way the Convention was inserted into United Kingdom law did not give individuals a direct right to take action in the courts for a breach of their privacy under the HRA. The HRA created no equivalent to a statutory tort of infringement of privacy enforceable against the world at large. Consideration was given to the introduction of such a tort in the Law Commission Report in 1981 but the government of the time rejected the proposal. So far the courts have rejected the creation of such a general cause of action for invasion of privacy. If an action of the State infringes the individual's right to private life, the individual will have a cause of action against the arm of the State or a defence based on the same right if action is taken against him. But if the right to private life is infringed by a private party, such as a newspaper, the individual cannot bring an action based directly on art.8. Litigants since October 2000 have dealt with this by bringing actions for breach of confidence and the courts have responded by gradually aligning breach of confidence with breach of art.8. In the following section the development of this approach post-October 2000 can be seen in the case law. .

2–47   The UK cases post-October 2000 are covered in some detail below. In considering the cases the courts have taken into account the development of the law of confidence, the effect of the Human Rights Act 1998 and, to a far lesser extent, the impact of the Data Protection Act 1998. Regrettably there has been a tendency for the courts to regard art.8 and Data Protection as coterminous and focus only on art.8, even in cases where the Data Protection Act may have been able to contribute to a robust solution. Where the cases have involved the balance between freedom of expression, the courts have also had regard to the Press Complaints Code of Practice as required by s.12 of the HRA. It should be noted, however, that there is still no straightforward privacy right in UK law. In 2002 the House of Lords decided in *Wainwright v Home Office*[166] that English law knows no general tort of the invasion of privacy. Buxton L.J. set out the extent of judicial reservations:

> "Since however the protection of privacy has been seen by some as nonetheless a proper field for the exercise of judicial activism, I venture to go further and draw attention to some difficulties that stand in our way.
>
> 'Privacy' covers a very wide range of cases, which are affected by a very wide range of policy consideration. What occurred in our case is perhaps one of the simpler examples. The right not to have another stare at one's naked body, save by consent or in clearly defined situations of necessity, would be unambiguously regarded as a matter of privacy. But what of the obtaining of information that (on the assumptions made to justify the extension of the law of tort into new situations of privacy) is not covered by the law of confidence? What of the maker of true statements about others, hitherto rigorously excluded from the law of defamation? What of the whistle blower? And, indeed, what of a preference to have photographs of your wedding in one publication rather than another?
>
> As is well accepted, in none of these cases can a right to privacy be absolute. But that is only the start. What needs to be worked out is the delicate balance, particularly in the area of publication of information, between the interests on the

---

[166] [2003] W.L.R. 1137.

one hand of the subject and on the other of someone entering his private space, or that of the publisher and the latter's audience . . .

All these considerations indicate that not only is the problem a difficult one, but also that on grounds not merely of rationality but also of democracy the difficult social balance that the tort involves should be struck by Parliament and not by the judges."[167]

Over the past decade the courts have had little choice but to determine many of these issues as they have been raised by litigants, but the position remains that at present the UK offers no general protection of privacy and the action in relation to private information remains an action in confidence. Whether the law will develop to offer wider privacy rights under the rights provided by the EU Charter of Fundamental Rights remains to be seen.

UK CASES

Since October 2000 the courts have been called on to consider the application of art.8 in a wide range of cases from those concerned with flooding to any number of asylum and immigration cases. In this section a number of the most significant cases in which informational privacy has been considered by the courts since October 2000 are reviewed. In all cases the events giving rise to the case took place after October 2000. While the courts have been responsive to the changes brought about by the HRA, they have not been prepared to change the law retrospectively. In *Home Office v Wainwright*[168] the House of Lords restated the position that there is no common law tort of invasion of privacy and the Human Rights Act could not change the law by retrospectively introducing a right of privacy at common law. In that case the events complained of had occurred in 1997. The claimants had visited prison and had been searched for drugs. One claimant brought an action for breach of privacy. The House of Lords rejected the claim on appeal but commented that the position would have been different had the searching occurred after October 2000 as art.8 would have impacted on their judgment.

There has been a mass of case law concerning the publication or disclosure of private information since October 2000. Many of the cases have concerned the publication of private material about celebrity individuals, and many of those are seminal cases. However they do not paint a full picture. In an effort to present the material in an orderly manner we have dealt with the cases in three parts. In the first part we chart the development of the main principles through the most important cases dealing with privacy and press intrusion. In the second part we have described those cases in which the law has been applied in circumstances other than press intrusion (the non-celeb cases). In the third section we have reviewed the case law on injunctive relief, and cases and guidance on anonymity and the use of "super injunctions".

2–48

2–49

---

[167] Text extracted from paras 108–111.
[168] 168. [2003] UKHL 53.

Development of the main principles—cases dealing with privacy and press intrusion

Michael Douglas, Catherine Zeta-Jones, Northern & Shell Plc v Hello! Ltd[169]

Facts

2–50   The first two claimants are a celebrity couple and the third the owners of *OK!* magazine. The first two claimants had agreed an exclusive licence to *OK!* for a 9-month period to publish authorised photographs of their wedding in New York. The wedding was a splendid affair with many guests but throughout the couple had made every effort to preserve the exclusivity of the pictures, banning cameras and requiring guests to sign an agreement that they would not take photographs. Nevertheless, the rival magazine *Hello!* managed to obtain pictures of the event from a paparazzi photographer who had infiltrated the event and took steps to publish them as a "spoiler", that is before *OK!* published the official photographs. Action was taken by *OK!* to stop *Hello!* selling the issue with the photographs. *OK!* were initially successful in obtaining an injunction but *Hello!* were successful in overturning the injunction in the Court of Appeal. The judges agreed that the remedy, if remedy there was to be, would issue in damages. In the High Court a total of £14,600 damages were awarded to the first two claimants, being £7,000 for the inconvenience they incurred in having to expedite the choice of official photographs and £3,750 each for breach of their privacy. *OK!* were awarded £1,033,156 for interference with their contractual rights. The decision was appealed and cross-appealed to the Court of Appeal, which held that there had been a breach of the claimants' right to privacy and the award to them should stand but overturned the judgment in favour of *OK!*[170] On the further appeal to the House of Lords by *OK!*, in which the claimants took no part, the Lords reinstated the award to *OK!*, holding that there was no reason they should not benefit from the rights of confidentiality in the event.

2–51   Following the substantive hearing in the High Court it was held that the claimants succeeded in their confidentiality claim on the basis that the wedding reception was a private event, and *OK!* also succeeded in their claim for a form of commercial confidentiality as being a:

> "case ... of either commercial confidence or of a hybrid kind in which, by reason of it having become a commodity, elements that would otherwise have been merely private become confidential".

The arrangements for the security at the wedding were such that all those attending would know that they were intended to be confidential in nature. The proprietor and others at *Hello!* knew of the confidentiality of the event and were thus bound by an obligation of confidence in respect of the material. The publication of the pictures as a "spoiler" was to the detriment of both the celebrity couple and *OK!* magazine. The judge held that the Data Protection Act applied and that all three Defendants were data controllers. He followed the *Campbell*

---

[169] *No.1* [2001] 2 W.L.R. 992.
[170] [2005] EWCA Civ 595.

decision in holding that the publication of the material in the UK amounted to processing and therefore fell under the Act. The transitional exemptions did not apply to the relevant processing and there had been breaches of the Act in that the processing was both unfair and unlawful as being without justification under Sch.2. Section 32 would not be applicable to the publication as its requirements had not been met. However he only awarded nominal damages under the DPA on the ground that the damage and distress to the claimants was not caused by the breach of the Act. The reasoning behind this last part of the decision (para.239) is not easy to follow. *OK!* had also claimed against *Hello!* on the basis of economic torts but these claims were dismissed.

In the Court of Appeal hearing in 2005 the Court was able to take account of the development of the Strasbourg case law in *Von Hannover* and *Peck*[171] as well as the more recent UK cases. The lengthy judgment covers both the claims in privacy and those related to the torts of economic loss but in this commentary we only describe the privacy issues. For the most part the judgment reflects the growing consensus of the case law in this area but it includes two elements which are particularly interesting: one deals with the commercial interest of the claimants in their private information and the other the actions which should have been taken at the early stage of the case.

2–52

The Court accepted that art.8 has a horizontal effect and in cases such as these must be applied so as to protect one person's right of privacy from the intrusion of another private party. The Court also confirmed that information does not have to be "confided" for the obligation to apply and will be eligible for protection where information which is obviously private comes into the possession of a third party. One of the points raised by *Hello!* was that any intrusion took place in New York and if the photographs could be lawfully published there the law in the UK should not penalise publication here. The Court did not accept that. It ruled that as long as the claimants were entitled to hold their wedding in private in New York, which they were, then the publication of unauthorised photographs of that wedding in the UK would be considered under UK law.

Hello! further argued that once the claimants had agreed with *OK!* to publish some photographs of the wedding, they could not claim that other photographs were private or confidential. The Court accepted that once information is in the public domain it can no longer be regarded as confidential but pointed out that care must be taken in determining whether this is the case; for example the re-publication of a private photograph will be a fresh intrusion and it will be no defence to a re-publication which breaches privacy to say that the photograph has been published before. This was another "important distinction between the law relating to private information and that relating to other types of confidential information".[172] Moreover the photographs were not all of the same nature. In this case the claimants had chosen those official pictures which they wished to disclose and thereby kept the remainder of the wedding as a private affair out of the public gaze.

2–53

On the question of the extent of the commercial interest that the claimants were exercising in the exploitation of the private occasion, the Court determined that, while the happy couple could have a commercial interest in the

---

[171] *Von Hannover v Germany* (59320/00); and *Peck v UK* (44647/98) and see para.2-33 above.
[172] Per Lord Phillips at para.105.

confidentiality of their wedding, they could not transfer that to a third party. It followed that *OK!* had no legal interest which was breached by the taking of the paparazzi pictures or their publication.

The other noteworthy point was the clear message that the claimants should have succeeded in obtaining their injunction against publication with the clear message that similar claimants should receive such relief in the future.

2–54   The House of Lords judgment was delivered in April 2007[173] and did not disturb the findings in relation to the Mr and Mrs Douglas, who had taken no part in the appeal, but reinstated the judgement in favour of *OK!* By a margin of three to two, the House held that *OK!* could benefit from the confidentiality which had been created in the occasion and there was no reason that exclusive coverage of a "spectacle", as the happy event was described in one judgment, could not benefit from the protection of the law of confidence where the parties had deliberately created that in order to protect it commercial value.

Theakston v MGN Ltd[174]

2–55   This case was considered by the High Court before the Court of Appeal had issued its guidance in *A v B*. The claimant was a television personality who had visited a brothel after a night out drinking. The prostitutes involved wanted to sell the story and photographs which had been taken without the claimant's knowledge to the newspaper. The judge held that the fact that the claimant had visited prostitutes for sexual activity could not be regarded as intrinsically confidential, particularly as one of the prostitutes was eager to tell the tale to the newspapers and therefore her right to freedom of expression was engaged. However he ruled that photographs taken in the brothel could not be published as they were taken without his consent and photographs were particularly intrusive. The judge held that not every sexual relation should be regarded as confidential; confidentiality would depend on the circumstances of the case.

A v B[175]

2–56   There were two aspects to this appeal from the High Court: a procedural one and a substantive one. The procedural aspects are not dealt with here. The facts were: A was a footballer with a club in the premier division football league. He was a married man with children. He had affairs with two women, referred to as C and D. C had wished to sell her story of the affairs to a newspaper, B. D took no part in the proceedings.

In September 2001, the judge in the High Court confirmed an interim injunction restraining publication of the "kiss and tell" story. The order restrained the newspaper from publishing anything about the sexual relationships and restrained C from making any disclosure to the media, although she was free to tell others, for example A's wife, should she chose. The newspaper and C appealed to the Court of Appeal. Before dealing with the facts of the presenting case Lord Woolf set out a set of Guidelines for dealing with actions in which

---

173   [2007] UKHL 21.
174   [2002] EWHC 138, QB.
175   Case No. A2/2001/2086, CA.[2002] EWCA Civ 337.

injunctions are sought to protect claimants from the publication of material on the grounds that the publication of confidential material would infringe their privacy.

His starting point was to accept that a court, as a public authority, has an obligation not to act "in a way which is incompatible with a Convention right". When deciding any case, irrespective of whether the parties are public or private bodies, the courts must take account of the Convention rights. Thus a court can deal with a claim that privacy has been infringed by "absorbing the rights which arts 8 and 10 protect into the long-established action for breach of confidence". The HRA does not give a basis for introducing new torts but, in any event, in the case of privacy protection, there is no need to do so as confidentiality can be, (and was), grown to fit the case. There is no need to cite massive amounts of previous authority, and cases on confidence pre-October 2000 are largely of historic interest only. He reviewed the equitable (and elastic) history of the law of confidence to reinforce this position and then set out a series of Guidelines for dealing with such cases in the future. Subsequent case law has further developed many of the themes in the Guidelines and modified some but they remain a useful tool in approaching these cases.

The Guidelines   2–57

- An interim injunction is a discretionary remedy and the judge must exercise his discretion properly only granting it if it is likely that one would be granted after a substantive hearing (see now *Cream Holdings v Banerjee*[176] covered at para.2–89 below).
- The judge must recognise that the interests to be weighted are both significant ones: if the claimant does not obtain his injunction he may be deprived of the only remedy which is of value to him; but granting an injunction will interfere with the defendant's right to freedom of expression, the importance of which has been emphasised by s.12 of the HRA.
- "Likely" means little more than that there should be a real prospect of success and the *American Cyanamid* test remains the relevant test in deciding whether to grant an injunction, although likelihood is a shade stronger and the possibility of borderline cases was preserved. Section 12(3) of the HRA and the Convention are compatible. (The test has been replaced by the approach taken in *Cream Holdings v Bannerjee*.)
- If the grant of an injunction will interfere with press freedom, that is a matter of particular importance. The existence of the freedom of the press in itself is desirable and any interference with it has to be justified.
- The burden is not on the press to show that the publication of the material is in the public interest. There is an interest in press freedom itself beyond the material published in the specific case. (In view of later case law, it is possible that this went too far.)
- Where privacy merits protection, an action for breach of confidence should be capable of providing that protection so there is no need to tackle the question of whether a new tort should be developed.

---

[176] [2004] UKHL 44.

- In cases where privacy is being weighted against freedom of expression there will not usually be much scope for detailed arguments about whether the subject matter is private and worthy of protection. Whether there is a breach of privacy will be a matter of common sense, not fine analysis of previous cases.

- Where there is a public interest in the publication of material it strengthens the case against granting an injunction. Whether there is a public interest will also usually be a matter of common sense and the citation of authority is not likely to be helpful. (An optimistic assertion which, as Mr Justice Eady commented in *CDE v MGN Ltd*,[177] has not been borne out in practice.)

- The legal basis of an obligation of confidence is elastic enough to offer privacy protection, if such protection is merited on the facts. An obligation can be implied/applied wherever the subject can reasonably expect his privacy to be protected.

- The factual basis is simple: "If there is an intrusion in a situation where a person can reasonably expect his privacy to be respected then that intrusion will be capable of giving rise to liability in an action for breach of confidence unless the intrusion can be justified". However, it should not be taken for granted that obtaining information by unlawful means give an automatic right to an injunction, although obviously the other party will then not be coming with clean hands and it will be weighted heavily.

- Where there is no intrusion (and presumably no contract to maintain confidence) but one party to a relationship wants to talk about the other, the art.10 rights of that party have to be taken into account. Where the parties are or have been married, one can restrain the other from disclosing private material, but other relations, including sexual ones, have different degrees of privacy. These have to be considered on their facts but there is no assumption that one party to any kind of relationship can gag the other about it.(It should be noted that in fact a surprising number of public figures have succeeded in obtaining protection for information about extra-marital affairs.)

- People who are public figures have to be realistic in their expectations as to how far their privacy can and will be protected by the courts. They do have a right to privacy but in a society with a free press they will be the subject of legitimate interest and reporting. The higher the profile, the more they are likely to be interesting to the press. If someone has courted publicity then they will have less ground to object to intrusion that may follow. (It should be noted that this has been distinguished and explained further in subsequent cases and may not represent the current position.)

- In balancing the competing interests, the courts should stick strictly to the core question of whether publication should be restrained. They should not be influenced by disapproval of possibly lurid presentations by the press.

- Section 12(4) requires the court deciding a case to consider any "relevant privacy code" and the Press Complaints Commission Code of Practice has helpful material on privacy and harassment to which attention is drawn.

---

[177] [2010] EWHC 3308 (QB).

Such material has to be considered in full and a court can also take into account that there has been a breach of the Code.

- Although the Code is relevant, individual decisions of the Press Commission are not and should not be cited.

On the specific case the Court ruled that A did not have any special rights to confidentiality in his relations with C and D. Outside marriage, the mere fact of a sexual relation did not make the relation a confidential one; regard had to be had to the nature of the engagement. The judge quoted the dicta of the court in *Theakston v MGM Ltd* with approval on this point (see above). Further the fact that C and D did not regard the relationship as confidential and were happy to talk about it was relevant. The rights of C and D to freedom of expression came into play. The judge at the High Court had assumed that the ban was to the benefit of A's wife despite the fact that she was not a party to the proceedings and had not had a say. The court said that it was not for the court to decide what was or was not to her benefit. The question of a public interest in the publication was a difficult issue for the court to come to a view on and the possibility of there being a public interest should not have been rejected. It was possible that there was some aspect of it. The injunction was therefore discharged. In later cases the courts proved more willing to offer protection to applicants (mainly rich men) who had sexual relationships which they wished to keep out of the public eye. The level of popular cynicism about these orders is clear from the number of cases in which such litigants have been "outed" by social media, as in the notorious case of Ryan Giggs. This might be regarded as a result of prurient interest rather than a high minded defence of the right of freedom of expression. Alternatively it might indicate an uncomfortable gulf between what the courts have regarded as legitimately private and what ordinary people regard as legitimately private.

2–58

Campbell v Mirror Group Newspapers

The next case gained popular coverage because the claimant, Naomi Campbell, is a well-known fashion model who has, in the past, denied taking drugs. At the beginning of 2001 she was surreptitiously photographed leaving a London clinic where she had been having treatment for addiction. The *Daily Mirror* published the picture and information about her therapy. After she complained about the disclosures, the *Mirror* published criticisms of her complaint and claim for breach of privacy. She took action against them claiming damages for breach of confidentiality and compensation under s.13 of the DPA. When the case was heard in the High Court[178] Ms Campbell was successful in her claim for breach of confidence and breach of the Data Protection Act, and was awarded damages amounting to £3,500 for distress and hurt feelings. The *Mirror* then appealed to the Court of Appeal and was successful in overturning the award. Miss Campbell in turn went to the House of Lords and emerged the victor in the end.

2–59

---

178 [2002] EWCA Civ 1373.

High Court judgment

2–60   Ms Campbell had accepted that the paper was entitled to publish the basic fact that she was addicted to drugs and was having therapy, but claimed that it was not entitled to use photographs of her or give details of the therapy or from whom she was receiving it. The judge ruled that the details of her attendance at Narcotics Anonymous had the necessary quality of confidence to attract protection and the information giving details of her attendance must have been imparted in circumstances importing an obligation of confidence, even though it was never shown who had provided them. He held that the publication of the details was detrimental to her and applied the Guidelines set out by Lord Woolf in *A v B*. He held that as Ms Campbell was a role model and had made public statements that she was not addicted, the *Mirror* was entitled to disclose that she had lied and did have drug addiction problems. There was a public interest in revealing that she had lied. However, the newspaper was not entitled to go beyond that into material which she had not put into the public domain. The details which were revealed about her treatment amounted to an invasion of her privacy which was not justified by any public interest.

In relation to the Data Protection Act, the *Mirror* had argued that the exemption in s.32 of the DPA applied to the publication and moreover that they not only had the benefit of the substantive exemption once the material complained of had been published but the procedural exemption in s.32(4) continued to apply after publication. Thus the court was precluded from hearing the case until the Commissioner had made a determination under s.45.[179] The court rejected the contention that the procedural provision applied post-publication and went on to consider the application of the substantive exemption. The judge's ruling on the substantive exemption is not wholly clear. He held that the *Mirror* had not complied with the requirements of the Data Protection Act 1998. It had not obtained the photographs fairly and had no grounds on which to justify the holding of the sensitive data. He then considered whether the *Mirror* could claim the benefit of the substantive exemption in s.32. Unfortunately the judgment appeared to suggest that the substantive exemption itself ceased to apply after publication of the material.[180] Nevertheless, he went on to consider the terms of the exemption and decided that as the *Mirror* could not claim that the publication of the photographs and other detailed material was justified in the public interest they could not fall within the exemption. He considered the effect of s.13 and agreed that where the special purposes were concerned the applicant did not have to show actual damage. He awarded damages of £3000 for distress plus a further £1000 for aggravated damages arising from the response of the *Mirror* after Ms Campbell's initial complaint.

---

[179] See Ch.17 for a full description of the exemption for the special purposes.

[180] On this point, the judge referred, among other material, to the relevant chapter in the first edition of this textbook. It was never intended to suggest in that chapter that the substantive exemption ceases to apply after publication, and I did not think I had done so. (It is somewhat discouraging to a textbook writer to be cited in a judgement in support of something they did not intend to support).

Court of Appeal[181]

It was accepted by Ms Campbell that the publication of the fact that she had a drug problem and was receiving treatment for addiction was justified.

2–61

The *Mirror* accepted that the material published on the whole disclosed confidential information but argued the public interest justified the publication of all the material.

Lord Phillips M.R. held that the fact that Ms Campbell was receiving treatment from Narcotics Anonymous could not be equated with disclosure of clinical details of medical treatment and, given that it was legitimate for the *Mirror* to publish the fact that she was receiving treatment, it did not seem significant that the treatment consisted of attending meetings of NA. The publication of the additional details was not sufficient to amount to a breach of an obligation of confidence.

The Court considered that the detail that was provided in the story and the photographs were a legitimate, if not essential, part of the journalistic package putting out the story:

"Provided that the publication of particular confidential information is justifiable in the public interest, the journalist must be given reasonable latitude as to the manner in which that information is conveyed to the public or his Article 10 right to freedom of expression will be unnecessarily inhibited".

The court dismissed an argument that a publisher of information had to act dishonestly before he could be liable for breach of confidence in the case of personal privacy.

In relation to the Data Protection Act, the arguments took on the labyrinthine nature that seems to afflict nearly all judgments on the DPA. In considering the Act they held that MGM was the data controller and had acted through Mr Morgan, the editor, who had taken the decisions in respect of the publication. It was common ground that, unless the actions of the *Mirror* fell within the s.32 exemption, they would be in breach of the DPA.

The Court held that there were three questions to be decided:

2–62

1. Does the DPA apply to publication of newspapers and other hard copies containing information that has been subjected to data processing?
2. Does the s.32 (substantive) exemption only apply up to the moment of publication?
3. Does the s.32 (substantive) exemption apply to publication, insofar as this falls within the scope of the Act?

On question 1 they held that the definition of "processing" covers publication:

"Accordingly we conclude that, where the data controller is responsible for the publication of hard copies that reproduce data that has previously been processed by means of equipment operating automatically, the publication forms part of the processing and falls within the scope of the Act".

---

[181] [2002] EWHC 299.

On question 2 they agreed that the subss.(4) and (5) are purely procedural and are exhausted on publication. They then considered subss.(1)–(3) and took the view that they apply both after and before publication.

On question 3 they held that, as the processing of the data fell within the Act, the exemption would also apply to it and therefore the *Mirror* was entitled to invoke the protection of the substantive s.32 exemption in answer to Ms Campbell's claim.

They went on to consider how the s.32 exemption applied to the facts of the case. It was accepted by all parties that the publication was for the purpose of journalism. The court held that the data controller did reasonably believe that the publication was in the public interest and would not have been able to publish had they sought to comply with the DPA. Accordingly the exemption was made out. Ms Campbell lost the appeal. The judgment on the DPA suggests that the Court thought that the exemption from s.32 would be of wide application to the press and other daily media, saying:

> "... the definition of processing is so wide that it embraces the relatively ephemeral operations that will normally be carried out by way of the day-to-day tasks, involving the use of electronic equipment such as the lap-top and the modern printing press, in translating information into the printed newspaper. The speed with which these operations have to be carried out if a newspaper is to publish news renders it impracticable to comply with many of the data processing principles and the conditions in Schedules 2 and 3, including the requirement that the data subject give his consent to the processing. Furthermore the requirements of the Act, in the absence of section 32, would impose restrictions on the media which would radically restrict the freedom of the press" (paras 123 and 124).

House of Lords [182]

2–63   The House of Lords was split on the decision on the facts but unanimous on the approach to be taken to the case. The House overruled the Court of Appeal by three to two. It held that the publication of the three disputed items of information (1) the fact that Naomi Campbell was receiving treatment at Narcotics Anonymous, (2) the details of the treatment—how long she had been attending meetings, how often she went and associated matters, and (3) the photographs of her leaving the meeting with other addicts, amounted to a misuse of her private information. On behalf of Ms Campbell it had been accepted that the *Mirror* was entitled to publish the fact that she was addicted and was receiving treatment in view of her earlier public assertions in relation to drug use. There were no findings on the Data Protection Act in the judgments of the Lords. It had been accepted that the DPA case stood or fell with the action for misuse of private information. The basis for this is not explained but it is assumed that the Court considered that if it was decided that the publication of the three disputed items was justified and proportionate then the public interest test in s.32(1)(b) would be made out and the exemption for the special purposes would apply to the publication. In the final analysis the House held that the photographs should not have been published and to that extent Miss Campbell's determination to protect her privacy was vindicated.

---

[182] [2004] UKHL 22.

All of the Law Lords accepted that the rights given by art.8 were applicable between the two private parties and the court was obliged to take them into account in determining the case.[183] There was also unanimous confirmation that, in the case of personal information, no requirement for a pre-existing relationship applies.[184] This confirmed the dicta of Lord Goff in *Attorney General v Guardian Newspapers Ltd*.[185] It follows that in future cases a distinction must be drawn between cases of commercial confidentiality where the information must still be disclosed by a party for the obligation to bite and those concerning personal private information.

There was significant debate about the extent of the right to privacy and how the right should be defined. There was agreement that the test of a "reasonable expectation of privacy" was the threshold which should bring the right into play as per Baroness Hale at para.137, Lord Nicholls at para.21. In a recent Australian case the courts have used the formulation drawn from the US Restatement of Torts[186] that the courts should restrain the publication of information which would be "highly offensive to a reasonable person." Lord Nicholls regarded this as setting the bar too high and preferred the formulation of the individual having a "reasonable expectation of privacy" in relation to the information.[187] Lord Hope referred to the formulation used in *A v B* by Lord Woolf that the disclosure of information in that nature would give "substantial offence" to the individual, assuming that the individual was one of ordinary sensibilities. He also referred to the US formulation and quoted William L Prosser that:

2–64

> "the matter made public must be one which would be offensive and objectionable to a reasonable man of ordinary sensibilities, who must expect some reporting of his daily activities. The law of privacy is not intended for the protection of the unduly sensitive".[188]

In relation to Miss Campbell the court had to consider the disclosure of the photographs from her perspective with her vulnerabilities. This approach was also adopted by Baroness Hale who placed a high premium on the nature of the information and its relation to an individual's health and well-being,

> "...the information was of exactly the same kind as that which would be recorded by a doctor on those [medical] notes[189] ...
> People trying to recover from drug addiction need considerable dedication and commitment, along with constant reinforcement from those around them."[190]

The rights of the press and the importance of freedom of speech were considered at length.[191] The importance of the freedom of political speech was emphasised

---

[183] Paras 17, 50, 86, 132, 167 as per Lords Nicholls, Hoffman, Hope, Hale and Carswell.
[184] Paras 14, 48, 85, 134, 166 as per Lords Nicholls, Hoffman, Hope, Hale and Carswell.
[185] No.2 [1990] 1 A.C. 109, 281.
[186] *Australian Broadcasting Corp v Lenah Game Meats Pty Ltd* (2001) 185 A.L.R. 1, 13.
[187] Para.22.
[188] Para.94.
[189] Para.146.
[190] Para.157.
[191] Paras 61–66 per Lord Hoffman, 108 per Lord Hope, 140 per Baroness Hale.

by Baroness Hale but the focus was on the particular facts and it was emphasised that the issue under consideration was the balance and proportionality involved:

> "There are undoubtedly different types of speech just as there are different types of private information, some of which are more deserving of protection in a democratic society than others. Top of the list is political speech. The free exchange of information and ideas on matters relevant to the organisation of the economic, social and political life of the country is crucial to any democracy."

However, she distinguished the particular material under consideration taking the view that the information was highly invasive of her privacy with no corresponding justification for publication.[192]

There was unanimity that the mere fact that an individual is in the public eye for other reasons or as part of that person's role even where the individual has courted and lives by publicity does not deprive the individual of the right to a proper protection of privacy.[193]

In this case the complaint was made of the publication of the photographs and not the taking of them. It was accepted that the mere taking of a photograph of an individual in the street or another public place was not a breach of privacy. The matter would be different if the person were engaged in a private activity but there was a disagreement of fact as to whether the particular circumstances were sufficiently private to render the publication of the photographs a breach. This case was decided before *Von Hannover*

In Lord Nicholl's view the photographs,

> "..conveyed no private information beyond that discussed in the article. The group photograph showed Miss Campbell in the street exchanging warm greetings with others on the doorstep of a building. There was nothing undignified or distrait about her appearance".[194]

Lord Hoffman agreed that the mere taking of the photographs without consent was no breach:

> "The famous and even the not so famous who go out in public must accept that they may be photographed without their consent just as they may be observed by others without their consent"[195]

However he drew the distinction between the taking of the photograph and the publication so that the widespread publication of a photograph which shows someone in a position of humiliation or severe embarrassment may be an infringement of personal information as may the taking of a photograph in a private place with a long range lens. In the present case as there was nothing humiliating about the photograph it was not an infringement of Miss Campbell's right to privacy.

---

[192] Paras 148 onwards.
[193] Paras 28, 57, 67, 81, 144 and 157, per Lords Nicholls, Hoffman, Hope and Hale.
[194] Para.31.
[195] Para.73.

Lord Hope, in his analysis, agreed that the risk of being photographed in a public place was a hazard of living in society, but drew a distinction between the incidental inclusion on a photograph and the deliberate taking of the photographs in this case:

> "Miss Campbell could not have complained if the photographs had been taken to show the scene in the street by a passer-by and later published simply as street scenes. But these were not just pictures of a street scene where she happened to be when the photographs were taken. They were taken deliberately in secret and with a view to their publication in conjunction with the article. The zoom lens was directed at the doorway of the place where the meeting had been taking place".[196]

He agreed that the publication of photographs could raise breaches of the right of privacy and referred to the case of *Peck*

Baroness Hale took the same view, that a photograph, even a covert photograph does not make the information in it confidential, the activity photographed must be private in nature. In this case she considered that the activity photographed was private in nature.[197]

Lords Nicholls and Hoffman took the view that the art.8 rights of Ms Campbell should not weigh sufficiently heavily to out-weigh the art.10 rights of the press in the circumstances. They agreed with the Court of Appeal that too nice a line cannot be drawn between the different types of information. Lords Hope and Carswell and Baroness Hale came down on the other side on the facts and it was this difference that swung the case in favour of Miss Campbell. However the approach of the judges to the assessment of the balance was the same. As Lord Hoffman said:

> "The importance of this case lies in the statements of general principle on the way in which the law should strike a balance between the right to privacy and the right to freedom of expression, on which the House in unanimous".[198]

There is no presumption in favour of one right or another. The question is how far it is necessary to qualify one right in order to protect the other.[199] The main analysis is set out by Lord Hope in paras 105–113. Of particular importance will be the nature of the freedom of expression which is to be protected. The fact that there are different types of freedom of expression is echoed in the judgment of Baroness Hale.

There was agreement that the right of privacy could be overridden by a disclosure made in the public interest and it was common ground in this case that the fact that Ms Campbell had carried through a public deception justified the press in "putting the record straight".

In *A v B* Lord Woolf had acknowledged the importance of the preservation of a vigorous press in a democracy. The point was pursued in only one of the judgments by Baroness Hale who acknowledged the importance of the press as a commercial sector, in addition to the right of freedom of speech:

---

[196] Para.123.
[197] Paras 154 and 155.
[198] Para.36.
[199] Paras 20, 55 , 105–113, 139, 167 per Lords Nicholls, Hoffman, Hope, Hale and Carswell.

"One reason why press freedom is so important is that we need newspapers to sell in order to ensure that we still have newspapers at all".[200]

However, she did not consider that this could justify the intrusion into the particular area of personal privacy in this case which involved running the piece without the cooperation of Ms Campbell.

In the articles published by the *Mirror* there were a number of inaccuracies but it was held that in all the circumstances of this case the inaccuracies were unimportant and made no difference to the privacy claim:

"... there is a vital difference between inaccuracies that deprive the information of its intrusive quality and inaccuracies that do not. The inaccuracies that were relied on here fall into the latter category".[201]

Re S (FC) (a child)[202]

2–65   In this judgment the House of Lords reiterated its view on the proper way to approach cases where the rights of privacy and freedom of speech are to be balanced, but on the facts of the case came to a different view on the balance to be struck. The judgement was given by Lord Steyn who summarised the position following *Campbell* in four propositions:

"Firstly, neither article as such has precedence over the other. Secondly, where the values under the two articles are in conflict, an intense focus on the comparative importance of the specific rights being claimed in the individual case is necessary. Thirdly, the justification for interfering with or restricting each right must be taken into account. Finally, the proportionality test must be applied to each. For convenience I will call this the ultimate balancing test".[203]

In the particular case there had been a question of whether the identity of a child who was not the subject of proceedings or concerned in any proceedings should be protected by imposing restrictions on reporting of a criminal case against his mother. The mother was accused of killing the child's brother. Those responsible for the care of the child had raised concerns that the publicity associated with the case would have a detrimental impact on the child and sought the order to shield him from it. The effect of an order prohibiting the press from publishing any information about the criminal proceedings which might lead to the identification of the child would be to prevent the reporting of the case against the mother.

The Court recognised that art.6 sets a strong prima facie rule in favour of open hearings in criminal trials but the real tension lay between arts 8 and 10. The House was in no doubt that the courts had the jurisdiction to restrain publicity on the basis of the application of the Convention rights but declined to exercise it powers. As Lord Steyn put it:

---

[200] Baroness Hale at para.143.
[201] Lord Hope at para.102.
[202] [2004] UKHL 47.
[203] Para.17.

"The glare of contemporaneous publicity ensures that trials are properly conducted. It is a valuable check on the criminal process".[204]

The inevitable consequences of the grant of an injunction in this case, leading to further restrictions and restricting reporting and debate, were recognised and the impact that such restrictions would have on regional and local as well as national press. For all those reasons the appeal was dismissed.

McKennitt v Ash[205]

This case was heard by the Court of Appeal on an appeal from a judgment of Mr Justice Eady in which he had found in favour of the folk singer, Ms McKennitt.[206] Ms Ash, a former friend and confidant of Ms McKennitt, had written a book about the singer which revealed various material about the singer's life which she regarded as private. Ms McKennitt had taken action to restrain the publication of the book and had succeeded before Mr Justice Eady. If she had hoped that the Court of Appeal would take a more kindly view of her case, she was sadly disappointed. The judgment of the Court was delivered by Lord Justice Buxton. In this case there was no doubt that Ms Ash had been a confidant in the traditional sense of the term as used in actions for breach of confidence so the Court did not have to consider the situation of the stranger who comes into possession of information.

2–66

The importance of the case in the development of this area can be gauged by the interest of the media. A number of media organisations including the BBC and Times Warner sought permission to intervene despite the fact that these were private proceedings and the would-be interveners had no public interest role. The Court dealt with the difficulty adroitly by taking note of the submissions made but did not allow formal intervention.

The Court reiterated that, while generally Convention rights do not create rights between private bodies, art.8 is different. It has long been accepted that an individual can complain to the State about the behaviour of others which impacts on his private life.[207]

The touchstone of whether there is an action is whether the information is private and falls to be protected under art.8. The Court confirmed the view taken in *Campbell* that the test is a broad one. Quoting the speech of Lord Nicholls in *Campbell*:

"in deciding what was the ambit of an individual's 'private life' in particular circumstances courts need to be on guard against using as a touchstone a test which should more properly be considered at the later stages of proportionality. Essentially the touchstone of private life is whether in respect of the disclosed acts the person in question had a reasonable expectation of privacy".

In particular, the book contained information about a property which Ms McKennitt owned. The High Court had held that there was a reasonable

---

[204] Para.30.
[205] [2006] EWCA Civ 1714.
[206] [2005] EWHC 3003 (QB).
[207] *Marckx v Belgiul* (1979) 2 E.H.R.R. 330; *X v Netherlands* (1986) 8 E.H.R.R. 235.

expectation of privacy in relation to its nature and domestic arrangements. Even trivial details could be protected under this approach. This was confirmed by the Court of Appeal, while it accepted that, whereas Strasbourg cases have tended to be concerned with the security or stability of the home, information about an individual's home could still raise a privacy issue.

The Court found that Ms McKennitt was unusual among stars in the entertainment business in that she guarded her privacy carefully and controlled the information about her which was published. It was accepted that she only released information that she "felt comfortable with" and that some of that information, which was of a private nature, was only released as part of her work for a charity to campaign for water safety after she had suffered personal loss. The appellant argued that once Ms McKennitt had disclosed some information about her loss she had thereby opened up all of that area of her life for public scrutiny. The Court did not accept this argument and took the view that Ms McKennitt was entitled to limit publication of information about herself to that which she wished to be published. This was clearly on the basis that there was no other public interest in publication of information. Lord Justice Buxton stated:

"If information is my private property, it is for me to decide how much of it should be published".[208]

2–67   One of the arguments for Ms Ash was based on the arguments which prevailed in *Woodward v Hutchins*,[209] and to some extent in *A v B Plc*,[210] that Ms Ash was entitled to tell her own story and the restriction upon her was a breach of her own rights to freedom of speech. The Court, however, distinguished the cases pointing out that Ms Ash's story was not about herself but was "largely parasitic". In *A v B Plc* there was no relationship that could be characterised as one of mutual confidence. Dealing with *Woodward v Hutchins*, Buxton L.J. pointed out that this was a case prior to the coming into force of the Human Rights Act and therefore had to be treated with caution, but in any event it concerned singers who had sought and welcomed publicity to the extent that the material which they wished to protect no longer enjoyed the protection of confidentiality in the first place.

The Court considered the ruling in *Von Hannover* and whether Ms McKennitt is a public figure. It repeated the distinction made in that case between matters of legitimate democratic debate and mere trivial interest in the behaviour of those who are in the public eye. In the latter case the individual is entitled to respect for privacy unless there is some circumstance which makes the behaviour of the person a matter of legitimate debate. In this case it held that there were no special circumstances which would warrant public interest in Ms McKennitt. It then considered the controversial comments made by Lord Woolf on *A v B Plc* to the effect that mere celebrity would lessen the extent of the private domain to which an individual was entitled, which dicta it accepted are difficult to reconcile with *Von Hannover*. It further noted, as was urged on it on behalf of the appellant, that the court is bound to apply the Convention rights as interpreted in UK law in a previous UK case in preference to Strasbourg jurisprudence on the same point

---

[208] Paras 6 and 55.
[209] [1977] 1 W.L.R. 760.
[210] Case no.A2/2001/2086 CA.

right.[211] At this stage of the judgement it seemed all might have been lost, until Buxton L.J. pointed out that the court had not ruled on art.10 in *A v B Plc* and therefore he was at liberty to apply *Von Hannover*.

The cases of *Von Hannover v Germany*[212] as well as *Campbell* were considered and the court accepted that *Von Hannover* had extended the reach of art.8. In *Von Hannover,* as we have seen earlier, the Court of Human Rights held that the German courts had failed to protect the privacy of Princess Caroline of Monaco by allowing the publication of photographs of her in public places. The Strasbourg court had held that she was entitled to a degree of privacy for her actions even in public places, as:

> "There is ... a zone of interaction of a person with others, even in a public context, which may fall within the scope of 'private life'".

The appellant advanced the argument that the judgment in *Von Hannover* was fact-specific and should not be the basis of a wider application. It was necessary that media intrusion into the Princess's privacy was restrained because of the intrusive nature of the interest shown by the press into her activities and had this not been the case the photography would have been held harmless.[213] However this argument was not accepted by the Court.

As had been accepted in other cases, the rights of individuals under the two articles must be balanced with neither having precedence over the other.[214]

One of the arguments advanced by the appellant was that there was a public interest in the disclosure of the information as it showed Ms McKennitt to be a hypocrite. The court accepted the there is a public interest override to an obligation of confidence or a claim in art.8 but accepted the finding of the High Court that it did not apply in this case. The court recognised the difficult (and occasionally criticised) comments of Lord Woolf in *A v B*, that weight must be given to the commercial interests of the press, but was able to bypass them pointing out that this had no significant impact on the present case.[215]

The appellant claimed that there could be no restriction of the publication of information on privacy grounds where the court has found that the statements were false. On the face of it a strong, if distasteful, argument. Buxton L.J. dismissed the argument on the basis that such information could still infringe privacy depending on the facts of the matter.

HRH Prince of Wales v Associated Newspapers Ltd[216]

This case followed close on the *McKennitt* case. The facts were simple. Prince Charles has for many years been in the habit of producing hand-written journals setting out his thoughts and impressions after overseas visits. On his return to the UK he would have these copied and sent to a list of individual recipients with a signed letter. The envelope was marked "Private and Confidential". The

2–68

---

[211] Applying the judgement in *Kay v Lambeth LBC* [2006] 2 W.L.R. 570.
[212] (2005) 40 E.H.R.R. 1.
[213] Para.41.
[214] *Re S (FC) (A child)* [2005] 1 A.C. 593.
[215] Para.66.
[216] [2006] EWCA Civ 1776.

recipients were friends from different walks of life. Ms Sarah Goodall worked in the Prince's private office between May 1988 and December 2000. She had signed undertakings as to confidentiality on entering her employment. In May 2005 she supplied the *Mail on Sunday* with copies of eight of the journals via an intermediary. In October 2005 she appears to have had a change of mind and confessed her actions to one of her superiors and also approached the *Mail* to ask for the copies back. Although the set was returned, the newspaper retained a copy. Despite threats from the Prince's lawyers, the *Mail on Sunday* went ahead and published substantial extracts from the journals on November 13, 2005. The Prince's lawyers then succeeded in obtaining an interlocutory order to stop the newspaper printing any more of the material. The substantive issues were reserved for the later hearing.

There were some differences of fact between the newspaper and the Prince (as to how many copies of the journal were circulated, how securely they were held and whether, on a previous occasion a journalist writing an authorised biography had been given access to them). In order to avoid a trial on the facts, Counsel for the Prince invited the Court to proceed on the basis that the facts were those least advantageous to the Prince. The Court did so and even on that basis found against the *Mail* on all counts.

It was accepted that no pre-existing relationship is now required for the action for misuse of private information to be established. However, the Court took the view that the existence of a relationship of confidence remains a relevant issue in the new action. The new action is still built on and reflects the old law of breach of confidence. The court may therefore need to distinguish those cases where the information itself is not obviously such as to engage art.8 but has been received in confidence and art.10 rights may well have to give way to confidentiality even where the confidentiality does not protect personal privacy.[217] In this case the court gave weight to the fact that the information was disclosed in breach of a well-recognised relationship of confidence, that which exists between master and servant, and in breach of a contractual obligation.

The Court was in no doubt that the material was confidential, describing the journals as "paradigm examples of confidential documents".[218] In relation to deciding how the right to protection is to be established, Lord Phillips commented:

"It is not easy in this case, as in many others, when concluding that information is private, to identify the extent to which this is because of the nature of the information, the form in which it is conveyed and the fact that the person disclosing it was in confidential relationship with the person to whom it relates. Usually as here, these factors form an interdependent amalgam of circumstances".

On behalf of the *Mail* it had been argued that, as the subject of the journals was in the public domain and there was a circulation of the journals, then the Prince, being himself a public figure who used the media to further his views, could have no reasonable expectation of privacy in them. This submission received short shrift. Lord Phillips pointed out that the question of whether the Prince had

---

[217] See paras 28 and 29.
[218] See para.35.

forfeited any right of privacy was a separate one from whether the right existed in the first place. He was in no doubt that it did.

The right of the Prince to control his own material and private writings was accepted by the court but one of the most interesting comments was in relation to the extent of privacy to which the Prince, as a public figure, might be entitled.

The *Mail* had run the familiar argument that those whose activities and role are in the public domain can have less expectation of privacy, to be met by the endorsement of a view expressed by the judge at first instance and quoted with approval that:

> "Not the least of the considerations that must be weighted in the scales is the claimant's countervailing claim to what was described in argument as 'his private space'; the right to be able to commit his private thoughts to writing and keep them private, the more so as he is inescapably as public figure who is subject to constant and intense media interest. ... The claimant is as much entitled to enjoy confidentiality for his private thoughts as an aspect of his own 'human autonomy and dignity' as is any other".[219]

This seems to suggest that, far from public figures being entitled to less privacy than the ordinary person, they may be entitled to more, or at least to strong protection for that area which is regarded as legitimately private.

In considering the balance between arts 8 and 10, the Court stressed the importance of freedom of expression in a democratic society and considered those cases where the public interest in freedom of expression has prevailed over privacy rights. It treated the balance in this case as a question of whether the art.10 right represented a public interest argument that could override the right of confidentiality.

The weight that should be given to the rights of confidentiality and the relation between the public interest test for breach of confidence and the application of s.8(2) is canvassed at length in paras 50–69. Lord Phillips concluded that the test for the public interest override has changed:

> "Before the Human Rights Act came into force the circumstances in which the public interest in publication overrode a duty of confidence were very limited. The issue was whether exceptional circumstances justifying disregarding the confidentiality that would otherwise prevail. Today the test is different. It is whether a fetter of the right of freedom of expression is, in the particular circumstances 'necessary in a democratic society'. It is a test of proportionality. But a significant element to be weighted in the balance is the importance in a democratic society of upholding duties of confidentiality that are created between individuals. It is not enough to justify publication that the information is a matter of public interest ... The test to be applied ... is whether in all the circumstances it is in the public interest that the duty of confidence should be breached".

One might have thought that with those cases the ground rules had been laid out and the courts would be able to turn their attention to some other topic but the cases have continued to come thick and fast. In the splendidly titled case of *X & Y v The Person or Persons who have offered and/or provided to the publishers of the Mail on Sunday, Mirror and Sun newspapers information about the status of*

2–69

---

[219] Para.70.

the Claimants' marriage,[220] Eady J. in the High Court granted the claimants an injunction to restrain the publication of information about the claimants' marriage. The initial injunction was granted at short notice and in wide terms as the claimants did not know who was peddling the story about their marriage to the press. At the full hearing the judge provided guidance on the approach that should be taken when deciding to grant injunctions in such circumstances. The court will take into account what the parties have put into the public domain. The fact that some material has been put into the public domain does not make all material "fair game" for the press. He drew a distinction between a couple who allow the publication of wedding or honeymoon photographs (as the couple in question had done) and those who speak to the media about the details of their married lives. In a similar way he distinguished between someone being "in the public eye" and being a "publicity seeker". One of the parties in the case was a model who was, of necessity, in the public eye and who had a contractual obligation to give a number of interviews. He drew a distinction between matters which are naturally accessible to outsiders, such as the fact that a couple are living apart, and matters which are private between the parties only. He acknowledged the difficulty for a third party, such as a newspaper, faced with an order not to disclose private information, in deciding what was private and knowing what might have reached the public domain. The solution adopted in the case was to attach to the order a confidential schedule containing the specific allegations which there is reason to suppose may be made public in the absence of an order banning the publication.

CC v AB[221]

2–70   In this case the defendant wished to tell the press about an affair between his wife and the claimant. The claimant wished to restrain the disclosures in order to protect the defendant's wife, himself and his own wife and children from the stress and strain of press intrusion. The defendant was motivated by a mixture of greed and a wish for revenge. The Court recognised that it had to apply the competing rights between the parties and accepted that there is a powerful argument that the conduct of an intimate sexual relationship is one in which the parties would have a legitimate expectation of privacy. The Court did not distinguish here between a marital or other relationship, although the judge acknowledged that a "fleeting one night encounter" might well attract less protection that a genuine relationship. Despite being urged to refuse the protection of confidentiality to an adulterous relationship the judge refused to do so, emphasising that it was not for a judge to take a personal moral view when applying the Convention rights which he described as a "secular code". The judge considered the extent to which the court should restrict the freedom of the defendant to disclose the information and accepted that there existed a range of disclosures which could not be restricted as to his family, lawyer and others of a similar relationship; however selling the story to the tabloid press was another matter. There was no genuine public interest in the disclosure.

---

[220] [2006] EWHC 2783 (QB).
[221] [2006] EWHC 3083 (QB).

It was argued that, as the adulterous couple had stayed in hotels together and been seen in public, although never recognised, that they had put the affair into the public domain, but the argument was not accepted, particularly in the light of the decision in *Von Hannover*.

The claimant succeeded in obtaining an injunction to prevent the defendant from communicating with the media or on the internet about the former relationship.

Murray v Big Pictures Ltd[222]

The particular interest of this case is that it dealt with the taking and publication of pictures of an infant. The claimant was the infant child of Mrs Murray who writes under the name J.K. Rowling. When her son, David, was approximately 19 months old, a number of photographs were taken of him in his pram being pushed by his father on a family walk. The photographs were taken without consent using a long-range camera. Initially there was some publication in the Scottish press and following that Big Pictures, which owned the rights to the pictures, were asked by the family's lawyers to give undertakings to desist from further publication. In April 2005 the *Sunday Express* published one of the pictures. Action was then taken on behalf of David seeking delivery up of the photographs and to prevent further publication. At first instance the judge struck out the claim on the basis (in essence) that the photograph was taken in a public place and was not, of its nature, private. The claimant sought leave to appeal against the ruling and the Court of Appeal found in favour of the claimant. It would appear that the case was then settled. In the judgment the Court applied the ruling in *Campbell*, but in particular to the facts of the case and the position of the child. The Court held that the question of whether there is a reasonable expectation of privacy is a broad question which takes account of the circumstances of the case. In particular the fact that the picture was taken of an infant and the fact of the widespread publication were important issues. In setting out its position, Sir Anthony Clarke M.R., giving the leading judgment, said:

2–71

> "We have reached a different conclusion from that of the judge. In our opinion it is at least arguable that David had a reasonable expectation of privacy. The fact that he is a child is in our view of greater significance than the judge thought. The courts have recognised the importance of the rights of children in many different contexts and so too has the international community: see eg *R v Central Independent Television Plc* [1994] Fam 194 per Hoffmann LJ at 204-5 and the United Nations Convention on the Rights of the Child, to which the United Kingdom is a party."

The judgment referred to the Press Complaints Commission Editors' Code of Practice which states that editors must not use the fame, notoriety or position of the parent or guardian as sole justification for publishing details of a child's private life. While it was acknowledged that there was information to the effect that the Press Complaints Commission had ruled that the mere publication of a child's image could not breach the Code when the photograph has been taken in a public place and is unaccompanied by any private details or materials which

---

222 [2007] EWHC 1908 (Ch).

might embarrass or inconvenience the child, the Court did not regard that as any form of authority and considered that everything must depend on the circumstances.

It was noted that neither *Campbell* nor *Von Hannover* (the two main cases on the use of photographs and privacy) are about a child and there was no authoritative case in England of a child being targeted as David was. The court therefore had to make its determination without guidance from such authority.

It held that David had an arguable case:

> "We do not share the predisposition identified by the judge that routine acts such as a visit to a shop or a ride on a bus should not attract any reasonable expectation of privacy. All depends upon the circumstances. The position of an adult may be very different from that of a child. In this appeal we are concerned only with the question whether David, as a small child, had a reasonable expectation of privacy, not with the question whether his parents would have had such an expectation. Moreover, we are concerned with the context of this case, which was not for example a single photograph taken of David which was for some reason subsequently published.
>
> It seems to us that, subject to the facts of the particular case, the law should indeed protect children from intrusive media attention, at any rate to the extent of holding that a child has a reasonable expectation that he or she will not be targeted in order to obtain photographs in a public place for publication which the person who took or procured the taking of the photographs knew would be objected to on behalf of the child. That is the context in which the photographs of David were taken.
>
> It is important to note that so to hold does not mean that the child will have, as the judge puts it in [66], a guarantee of privacy. To hold that the child has a reasonable expectation of privacy is only the first step. Then comes the balance which must be struck between the child's rights to respect for his or her private life under article 8 and the publisher's rights to freedom of expression under Article 10. This approach does not seem to us to be inconsistent with that in Campbell, which was not considering the case of a child."

2–72   The claim was also made under the DPA and the Court ordered that the DPA claim should stand, making two interesting observations. First they suggested that, if it was found that a breach of art.8 had occurred, it would follow that the processing was both unlawful and unfair and had no legal basis under Sch.2. Second they suggested that the judge had taken too narrow a view of the requirement for damage and construed the term narrowly which might not be appropriate given the backdrop of the Directive.

Regrettably for data protection lawyers, the case settled so these two interesting points were not further canvassed.

Mosley v News Group Newspapers Ltd[223]

2–73   In this case a group of individuals who engaged in consensual sexual behaviour of a somewhat unconventional nature were betrayed by one of their number who secretly filmed and recorded the activities for payment by *News of the World*. As a result Mr Mosley was accused of taking part in a "Nazi orgy" with "hookers" in a screeching edition which featured photographs of the event and invited "readers" to visit the paper's website where film of the event was made available.

---

[223] [2008] EWHC 1777 (QB).

Mr Mosley sought an injunction to have the film taken down from the website but, in view of the wide publication which had already taken place, this was refused. He subsequently took an action for misuse of private information. The newspaper sought to argue that the clandestine filming and subsequent publication of what was clearly private behaviour was justified because the activity had a "Nazi theme" and this reflected on Mr Mosley's international role as president of the FIA. This was somehow linked to Mr Mosley's father's support for Fascism, which was extensively referred to by the paper. There was a central dispute of fact as to whether the event had any Nazi theme. At trial the paper was unable to produce evidence that there was any Nazi theme to the activities which might justify the intrusion.

The judge, Eady J., held that sexual activity engages the rights protected by art.8 and referred also to the line of authority which addresses the question of clandestine recording. He took the view that it was obvious that the clandestine recording of sexual activity on private property must be taken to engage art.8. He also held that the participant who had carried out the filming had committed an "old fashioned breach of confidence". The meat of the judgment reviews the public interest defence mounted by the *News of the World*. Three strands of argument were relied upon. The first was that it was legitimate for the purpose of exposing criminal behaviour. The defence referred to the case of *Laskey v United Kingdom*,[224] in which it was held that consent could not give a defence to extreme sado-masochistic behaviour. The judge distinguished *Laskey* on the basis that in *Laskey* the cruelty was of a different order and there was an issue that some very young people were corrupted or victimised (observing somewhat dryly that this was not the case here). He also pointed out that the question of proportionality would still be involved even if there was minor infringement of the law. The second was that there was a Nazi theme to the party, but the judge found that there was no evidence of imitating, adopting or approving Nazi behaviour and the defence accordingly fell. The third was that the behaviour was immoral, depraved and adulterous and as such there was a public interest in exposing it. He held that, even if this were the case, it did not support a public interest in disclosing it absent serious criminal behaviour:

> "Everyone is entitled to espouse moral or religious beliefs to the effect that certain types of sexual behaviour are wrong or demeaning to those participating. That does not mean that they are entitled to hound those who practice them or to detract from their right to live life as they chose."[225]

The journalists' perception of the public interest justification was considered at some length. The judge had no doubt that the question of public interest must be determined by the judge but the question was as to whether, and if so to what extent, weight might be given to views of the journalists involved if those were seen as falling within "a range of reasonably possible conclusions":

> "There may be a case for saying, when 'public interest' has to be considered in the field of privacy, that a judge should enquire whether the relevant journalist's

---

[224] (1997) 24 E.H.R.R. 39.
[225] Para.127.

decision prior to publication was reached as a result of carrying out enquiries and checks consistent with 'responsible journalism'."

This has some interesting similarities with the test in s.32 that the data controller "reasonably believes" that publication is in the public interest. He then considered whether the decision to publish could be classed as one that could have been taken by a responsible journalist on the information available at the time. On the facts he held that this was not the case and therefore, even if the defence of public interest depended on the reasonable view of the journalists concerned, it would not be made out.

In relation to the award of damages, the judge refused to award exemplary (punitive) damages in the case on the basis that such damages are an anomaly in civil proceedings and there was no authority for such an award in privacy cases. There would also be a concern as to the potential chilling effect of such awards on freedom of expression. In relation to quantum he pointed out that damages have so far been modest in privacy cases. Damages in such cases should include distress, hurt feelings and loss of dignity and be proportionate. He awarded a sum of £60,000.

Mr Mosely did not assert in the case before the UK courts that the newspaper was under an obligation to give him prior notification of the intended publication; however, that was the substance of the case brought against the UK in Strasbourg which was rejected by the ECtHR (see above).

Development of the main principles—cases other than celebrity and press intrusion

2–74   In *Robertson v Wakefield District Council*[226] the High Court was asked to consider whether the sale of names and addresses from the electoral roll breaches s.11 of the DPA, art.8 and art.3 of Protocol 1 in the HRA. It is dealt with in this chapter as it involves the Convention rights, rather than Ch.3.

In order to vote in the UK, citizens must be registered on the electoral roll. Registration forms are sent out annually. It is an offence to fail to return the form duly completed. Electoral Registration Officers (EROs) had an obligation to sell copies of the electoral register to any person who wished to purchase a copy, subject to the ERO having sufficient copies available for sale.

Copies of the electoral register are sold to many organisations as the basis of various commercial products. The commercial products include the sale of data for direct marketing. Mr Robertson objected to the sale of the electoral register, for which he had been forced to provide his name and address for electoral purposes, for uses which might include the sending of unsolicited mail.

The unrestricted sale of the electoral registers and their commercial use, especially for marketing, had been a point of public concern for some time. In 1999, the *Final Report of the Working Party on Electoral Procedures*[227] had dealt with the sale of the registers and noted that the supply of the electoral registers for commercial use had been a source of complaint.

---

[226] [2001] EWCA Civ 2081.
[227] CO/284/2001.

After the HRA came into force in October 2000, Mr Robertson objected to the sale of his name on the electoral roll. The ERO refused to omit his name from the roll, on the basis that the ERO had a statutory obligation to sell the register imposed by the Regulations. Mr Robertson took an action for judicial review of the ERO's decision.

The claimant relied on three grounds:

a)   that there was a breach of his art.8 right by the sale of his name and address by the ERO;

b)   that, as the ERO knew that the register was purchased for commercial purposes which included direct marketing, the ERO was processing his personal data for the purposes of direct marketing, and therefore had an obligation under s.11 of the DPA to stop processing for that purpose on service of a notice by claimant; and

c)   that the sale breached his right to free elections under art.3 of the First Protocol to the Convention as it imposed an unjustifiable restriction by making his right to vote conditional upon the use of his name by commercial organisations.

The Secretary of State for the Home Department, at that time responsible for the Regulations, was joined as a defendant and had the conduct of the case, the ERO taking no further part in the action.

After the proceedings had started the governing law changed. The Representation of the People Act 2000 replaced the 1983 Act. It contained new regulation-making powers which provided for the making of regulations which would enable voters to choose to have their names and address omitted from the copies of the register provided for sale. Although the power to make such regulations was included in the primary legislation, the regulations[228] did not include an "opt-out" provision. They continued to impose an obligation on the ERO to supply a copy or copies of the register to any person on payment of a fee.

The primary legislation did not mandate the inclusion of the requirement to sell the registers in the Regulations.

The claimant succeeded in his claim on all grounds. The judge found breaches of art.8 and Protocol 1 by the sale of the registers without a right of objection to sale on for commercial purposes. The judge interpreted s.11 of the DPA so as to accord with his view of the impact of art.14 of the Directive. He held that the EROs did "process the personal data on the register for the purposes of direct marketing" when they sold them to commercial organisations knowing that the data would be likely to be put to such a use and were therefore obliged to respond to objections to the use for marketing. He went on to find that the EROs had not been complying with the DPA because they had failed to take account of objections raised with them over subsequent uses for direct marketing. He considered the requirement under the Directive. Article 14(b) provides for the Member State to grant the data subject the right

---

[228] Representation of the People Regulations 1986, made under s.53 and Sch.2 of the representation of the People Act 1983.

"to object ... to the processing of personal data relating to him which the controller anticipates being processed for the purposes of direct marketing".

This is implemented in the UK by s.11, which provides individuals with the right to

"require the data controller at the end of such a period as is reasonable in the circumstances to cease, or not to begin, processing for the purposes of direct marketing personal data in respect of which he is the data subject".

2–76   It was argued that the ERO did not process the personal data for the purposes of marketing and that the mere fact that the ERO knew that others intended to do so after they purchased the data did not amount to processing for the purpose. The judge considered that he was under an obligation to interpret the Act so as to conform to the Directive as far as possible, citing *Lister v Forth Dry Dock Co Ltd*.[229] This could be done by taking a wide construction:

"I therefore find that EROs inevitably anticipate that the personal data will be processed by commercial concerns for the purposes of direct marketing".

The judge also found in favour of the claimant on art.3 of Protocol 1. This is expressed in general terms as:

"[States] undertake to hold free elections at reasonable intervals by secret ballot, under conditions which will ensure the free expression of the opinion of the people in the choice of the legislature".

The judge held that the act of making the right to vote conditional upon the provision of the information to commercial organisations, with no right to object, was an unjustified and disproportionate restriction on the right to vote.

In relation to the art.8 claim, he found that the Article was engaged in the matter despite the limited and harmless nature of the information.[230] It consisted of name and address only. Although in the judgment he posited the possibility that a list of the names and addresses of those known to be in a specific group might involve information which merits protection, a proposition with which few would disagree, on the facts of the case the relevant information did not fall into such a category. It consisted of name and address on the public register and involved no further information. Name and address alone do not appear to have been considered confidential in any ECHR or UK cases to date. In a decision on art.8 of the HRA made earlier in 2001, the High Court had declined to protect the address of Heather Mills, then the girlfriend of Paul McCartney, as private or confidential despite the fact that the publication of her address exposed her to detrimental press attention and potential risk simply because of her celebrity status; neither consequences likely to inconvenience Mr Robertson. In the decision of the Data Protection Tribunal in the case brought, in 1998, by the Data Protection Registrar over the use of name and address of customers of British Gas Trading Ltd, the Tribunal made clear that it did not regard customer name and

---

[229] The Representation of the People (England and Wales) Regulations 2001.
[230] [1990] 1 A.C. 546.

address, without more, as being confidential.[231] Nevertheless, the judge decided that the dissemination of name and address from the electoral register could be protected by art.8. Thus the judgment offers significantly more extensive protection to non-sensitive data than has ever been afforded by the UK courts or the Court at Strasbourg under art.8. In none of the cases before the ECtHR have name and address alone been protected. The judge was aware that he was affording a higher level of protection than had been afforded to such information before:

> ". . . I am being invited to go further than the courts have gone before by holding that the sale of the register engages article 8 . . ."

but nevertheless went on to find that the Article was engaged. The case was followed in *R. (on the application of Ali) v Minister for the Cabinet Office*,[232] where the judge noted that:

> "It is common ground that disclosure of personal data in a census form must comply with the DPA 1998. Secondly the defendants accept (as they have to in the light of R (Robertson) v Wakefield MDC and the Strasbourg authorities considered in it) that compulsory completion of a census is a prima facie interference with Article 8(1) and that disclosure of personal information provided on the census form requires very clear justification in view of the strong public interest in the confidentiality of census data."

Having held that the right was engaged by the sale of name and address from the register, the judge considered whether it was justified under art.8.2 and, if so, whether the restriction was proportionate. In considering art.8.2, he decided that there was a legitimate interest in the commercial uses of the register but that the failure to provide an opt-out was disproportionate.

In *R.(on the application of Pamplin) v Law Society*[233] the High Court held that employment, which is part of a lawyer's public life, would not be protected by art.8 to the degree that an individual's private, that is family or home, life would be.

2–77

Cases on policing and security

In *R. (on the application of S) v Chief Constable of South Yorkshire and the Secretary of State for the Home Department* and *R. (on the application of Marper) v Chief Constable of Yorkshire*,[234] the House of Lords was divided on whether the retention of fingerprints, samples, photographs and DNA profiles obtained in connection with the investigation of an offence, from a person who was never convicted, engaged art.8, but held that if it was such an interference it was "very modest indeed" and was a justifiable and proportionate breach.

The applicants argued that a provision in the Criminal Justice and Police Act 2001 which permits the retention of fingerprints and DNA samples, even if the

2–78

---

[231] See the Encyclopedia of Data Protection for cases under the 1984 Act.
[232] [2012] EWHC 1943 (Admin).
[233] [2001] EWHC Admin 300.
[234] [2004] UKHL 39.

person from whom the samples were taken is found not guilty of any offence or is never charged, was incompatible with the Convention. Alternatively they complained that the Chief Constable had acted unlawfully by adopting a general policy of retention, subject only to exceptions where specific grounds could be made out. The DPA does not appear to have been mentioned in this case.

The legislative background is complex, but in summary the rules used to be that such materials had to be destroyed if taken from individuals who were subsequently cleared of any offence. There had been cases where such material had not been destroyed. The police had tried and failed to introduce it into evidence, so the provision had amended the rules and allowed the retention of samples which should previously have been destroyed.

The section provides that, where fingerprints or other samples are taken in the course of an investigation into a crime, they may be retained but may only be used in the future for purposes related to the prevention or detection of crime, investigation of an offence or the conduct of a prosecution. The only cases in which the fingerprints or samples must be destroyed are if fingerprints or samples are taken from a person who is not suspected of an offence, in the course of an investigation of an offence, and there is no conviction following that investigation (see s.64 of the Police and Criminal Evidence Act 1984 as amended by s.82 of the Criminal Justice and Police Act 2001). Otherwise it is up to the Chief Constable to decide whether to retain the materials. However, Chief Constables are likely to follow the ACPO Guidance which advises retention.

The two claimants, S and M, were both of previous good character and were arrested for unconnected offences. Neither was charged and both subsequently requested the destruction of the fingerprints and other materials relating to them. The Chief Constable refused to destroy the material. It was also argued by the appellants that the Chief Constable should consider each case on its merits and the policy of retaining all materials was flawed. The House of Lords did not accept this and upheld the policy as lawful. As noted above, the decision was overruled by the ECtHR and the Government has now taken steps to review and amend the law in the Protection of Freedoms Act 2012. In *R. (on the application of) GC C v Commissioner of Police of the Metropolis*[235] a challenge was mounted to the retention of biometric samples, DNA and fingerprints, for an indefinite period save in exceptional circumstance. The claimants argued that the court should follow the Strasbourg ruling, but the court held that it was bound by the House of Lords decision in *Marper*. Giving the leading judgment, Lord Dyson found that the relevant provisions of PACE were not incompatible with art.8 as they permitted a policy which was not as far-reaching as the ACPO Guidelines which had been applied to permit the retention and could therefore be read to comply with art.8. He granted a declaration that the ACPO Guidelines were unlawful because they failed to comply with the Convention however he made no further orders on the basis that the Protection of Freedoms Bill included proposals to amend the scheme for the retention of DNA and the Government intended to bring the Act into force in 2011.

2–79   In *Wood v Commissioner of Police for the Metropolis*[236] Mr Wood had been photographed leaving a public meeting, an AGM of a company associated with

---

[235] [2010] EWHC 2225 (Admin).
[236] [2009] EWCA Civ 414.

the arms trade. On leaving, Mr Wood was photographed by police for the purposes of intelligence, in case offences were later committed in connection with the protests against the arms trade. Mr Wood, who had no criminal convictions and had never been arrested, claimed that the taking and retention of the photographs was a breach of art.8. The Court of Appeal held that the taking of the photographs in the particular context was capable of amounting to a breach. The activity was in pursuit of a legitimate aim; however the Court determined that the retention was disproportionate and not justified. The judgment was limited to the facts but, in concluding his judgment, Lord Collins of Mapesbury said:

"It is plain that the last word has yet to be said on the implications for civil liberties of the taking and retention of images in the modern surveillance society. This is not the case for the exploration of the wider, and very serious, human rights issues which arise when the State obtains and retains the images of persons who have committed no offence and are not suspected of committing any offence".

In *Commissioner of the Metropolis v Times Newspapers Ltd*[237] the High Court 2–80 considered the balance between arts 6, 8 and 10 specifically in relation to the disclosure of intelligence information to enable Times Newspapers to defend an action against it. The Court ordered the disclosure of certain information despite the opposition of the police organisation.

In *Author of a Blog v Times Newspapers Ltd*[238] the Court declined to protect 2–81 the identity of a police officer who blogged about his work and associated social issues in anonymous form, holding that the activity of blogging was not personal and private but essentially public and he had no reasonable expectation of privacy in keeping his identity a secret. In any event the art.10 rights of the newspaper would outweigh the arguments for maintaining his anonymity.

In *JR 27, Re Judicial Review*[239] the High Court in Northern Ireland ruled that 2–82 police retention of a 14-year-old boy's DNA and photographs were not illegal. It noted that the question of photographs was not specifically canvassed in *Marper*, but given that they were taken in the same circumstances for the same purposes it took the view that the House of Lords decision took precedence despite the fact that, in the view of the Court the retention was disproportionate and in breach of art.8.

"But for [the House of Lords] decision and our analysis of it, we consider that there is substantial force in the view that the retention of the Applicant's photographic images by the Police Service for a minimum period of seven years, which may be extended indefinitely, unconnected in any concrete or rational way with any of the statutory purposes, interferes with his right to respect for private life guaranteed by Article 8(1)."

In *Catv Commissioner of Police of the Metropolis*,[240] the applicant, who was an 2–83 elderly man of good character, failed to have records related to him removed from the National Domestic Extremism Database. Mr Catt had objected to the

---

[237] [2011] EWHC 2705 (QB).
[238] [2009] EWHC 1358 (QB).
[239] [2010] NIQB 143 (December 23, 2010).
[240] [2012] EWHC 1471 (Admin).

retention of records of his attendance at protest meetings in relation to an arms manufacturer. Although many protests were violent and extreme, Mr Catt's behavior was not and he argued that the retention of information about his attendance was a breach. The Court was not prepared to accept that and held that it was justified within art.8.2.

2–84   In *R. (on the application of RMC) v Commissioner of Police for the Metropolis*,[241] the High Court held that the retention of photographs taken of two people arrested but not charged would constitute an interference with the art.8 rights of the applicants and was not proportionate bearing in mind that:

• there was an inadequate distinction drawn between those who are convicted and other categories such as those charged but acquitted;

• retention could be in place potentially for up to 100 years in the case of one of the applicants; and

• the particular concern about the retention of information about minors was not taken into account.

Other cases

2–85   In *R. (on the application of Morgan Grenfell & Co Ltd) v Special Commissioner of Income Tax*,[242] the House of Lords considered the relation between legal professional privilege and art.8. The House held that the privilege is an important component of the art.8 right.

2–86   Privacy rights have however also been protected in other circumstances. In *Brent LBC v N*[243] the Court held that the local authority had no duty to inform natural parents of a foster parent's HIV-positive status as this would be an unnecessary disclosure which would have a significant impact on the private and family life of the foster parent.

2–87   In *Michael Stone v SE Coast Strategic Health Authority*[244] the Court held that the public interest in the publication of a report into the case, treatment and supervision of a man convicted of murder, which included extensive citation from his medical and psychiatric records, overrode the art.8 rights of the individual and involved no breach of the DPA. Mr Stone had co-operated with the inquiry which produced the report and originally consented to its publication. In 2005 he withdrew his consent. It was accepted that he was entitled to withdraw consent and the question facing the Court was whether to sanction publication in the absence of consent. The court applied *Campbell* and *Re S* in seeking the proper balance in the case. On art.8 and the confidentiality arguments it determined that art.8(2) was properly applied and Mr Stone's rights of confidentiality must give way to a greater public interest in publication. In relation to the DPA however the judgement was less satisfactory and did not address issues of either in fairness or compatibility, which might reasonably have been regarded as significant issues. It focused solely on the ground for the processing under Schs 2 and 3. It followed *Campbell* in holding that the publication would involve processing. In relation to

---

[241] [2012] EWHC 1681 (Admin).
[242] [2002] UKHL 21.
[243] [2005] EWHC 1676.
[244] [2003] EWHC 1668 (Admin).

Sch.3 the Court held, not unsurprisingly, that in the circumstances ground 7 applied in that the publication was necessary for the exercise of the functions of the health authority, accepting that the term "necessary" imports a balance reflecting the concepts of proportionality and public interest.

The wholly unexpected and, it is respectfully submitted, wholly erroneous, finding was that ground 8 could be applied—that it, the publication was "necessary" for medical purposes. The judgement is examined in more details in Ch.7 but strengthens the concern that, while the Courts have clearly taken on board considerations of privacy and human rights in terms of art.8, there is still some way to go before DPA rights and constraints are recognised.

In *R. (on the application of Ali) v Minister for the Cabinet Office*,[245] the Court held that the disclosure of information derived from the census under s.39(4)(f) of the Statistics and Registration Act 2007 is not a breach of art.8. That provision allows the disclosure by the Statistics Board of personal information when it is for the purposes of criminal investigation or criminal proceedings (whether or not in the United Kingdom).

2–88

INJUNCTIVE RELIEF, ANONYMITY AND THE USE OF SUPER-INJUNCTIONS

As explained above, a court which is considering granting any relief which might affect the Convention right to freedom of expression is bound by s.12 of the HRA. In particular the court must not restrain publication before trial unless "it is satisfied that the applicant is likely to establish that publication should not be allowed". The impact of the term "likely" was considered in *Cream Holdings v Banerjee*.[246] Ms Banerjee had passed information about Cream Holdings, her former employer, to the *Liverpool Echo* following which the *Echo* had published articles about alleged corruption involving a director and a local council official. The Cream Group sought injunctive relief to restrain the publication of any further confidential information by the *Echo*. It was agreed that the information was confidential and the *Echo* mounted a public interest defence. The judge at first instance granted an injunction and the ruling was upheld by the Court of Appeal. Ms Banerjee and the *Echo* appealed to the House of Lords.

2–89

Lord Nicholls, giving the leading judgment with which all the judges agreed, recalled that in the 1960s the approach adopted by the courts to the grant of an interim injunction was that the applicant had to show that on the balance of probability he would succeed at trial before an injunction would be granted. This was changed by the *American Cyanamid*[247] case in which it was held that as long as the court is satisfied that there is a serious issue to be tried it should apply a balance of convenience test and where other factors appear to be evenly balanced take "such measures as are calculated to preserve the status quo".

He pointed out that HRA s.12(3) was enacted to allay fears that, on the application of the *American Cyanamid* test, orders imposing prior restraint on publication might be readily granted by the courts. The purpose of s.12(3) was to

[245] [2012] EWHC 1943 (Admin).
[246] [2004] UKHL 44.
[247] *American Cyanamid Co v Ethicon* [1975] A.C. 396.

set a higher test than the *American Cyanamid* test. The court, however, rejected the contention that "likely" must mean "more likely than not" in every case, pointing out that this would mean that injunctive relief would not be applicable even in a case where the consequences of failing to grant such relief could endanger life. The circumstances of the case will therefore be relevant,

> "... on its proper construction the effect of section 12(3) is that the court is not to make an interim restraint order unless satisfied that the applicant's prospects of success at the trial are sufficiently favourable to justify such an order being made in the particular circumstances of the case".

While in general it will be necessary to show that the applicant is likely to succeed at trial, there will be cases in which a lesser degree of likelihood will suffice; for example where the consequences of disclosure would be grave or a short-lived injunction is needed to enable the court to give proper consideration to the application.

Anonymity and the development of the "super-injunction"

2–90   Despite the ruling on the meaning of "likely" in s.12(3), there has been a rise in the number of injunctions to restrain publication of private information. These have been accompanied by orders as to anonymity or even secrecy which have given rise to extensive debate in the media and extensive comment (not always particularly informed) in the blogosphere and what, for want of a better term, might be called the "Twittosphere". Anonymity orders are not new. In *AG v Leveller Magazine*[248] Lord Scarman said:

> "If a court is satisfied that, for the protection of the administration of justice from interference it is necessary to order that evidence either be heard in private or written down and not given in open court it may so order. Such an order or ruling may be the foundation of contempt proceedings against any person who, with knowledge of the order, frustrates its purpose by publishing the evidence kept private or information leading to its exposure. The order or ruling must be clear and can be made only if it appears to the court reasonably necessary. There must be material (not necessarily evidence) made known to the court upon which it could reasonably reach its conclusion, and those who are alleged to be in contempt must be shown to have known, or to have had a proper opportunity of knowing, of the existence of the order (see In re F. (orse. A.) (A Minor) (Publication of Information) [1977] Fam. 58)."

Such orders are a deviation from the general rule that hearings are held in open court and judgments are open documents. However it has long been possible to obtain an order that particulars are not disclosed in appropriate cases.

2–91   There are two kinds of order: anonymity orders are ones where the names of the parties, or one of the parties, are removed and substituted by initials only and where other identifying particulars may be omitted; "super-injunctions" are orders under which the court orders that the very fact of the injunction must not be reported at all. The term "super-injunction" has been attributed to Alan Rusbridger, Editor of the *Guardian* newspaper. The *Guardian* found itself unable

---

[248] [1979] A.C. 440.

to report a question asked in Parliament about the alleged dumping of toxic waste by Trafigura, an oil trading company.[249] The ban was subsequently lifted, but the concerns raised by the order persisted.

In *Re Guardian News and Media*,[250] Lord Rodgers commented on the apparent increase in the use of anonimity orders and explained the history of such orders. In relation to the protection of art.8 rights he pointed out that:

"The power to make such orders in appropriate cases was considered in In re S (A Child) (Identification: Restrictions on Publication[251]) In that case, a woman had been charged with the murder of her son. The guardian of her remaining son sought an order restraining the media from identifying the woman and the victim, in order to protect the privacy of her remaining son. The House of Lords held that no such order should be made. But, speaking for all members of the appellate committee, Lord Steyn affirmed, at p 605, para 23, that the court did have jurisdiction to make an order of this kind and that 'the foundation of the jurisdiction to restrain publicity in a case such as the present is now derived from Convention rights under the ECHR.' More recently, in In re British Broacasting Corpn[252] Lord Brown of Eaton-under-Heywood indicated that the powers of the High Court to make such an order 'arise under section 6 of the [Human Rights Act 1998] read in conjunction with section 37 of the [Senior Courts Act 1981]'."

Lord Rodgers raised concerns that such orders were being made in inappropriate cases and refered to a recent "effloresence" of such orders. Lord Rodgers was not able to put figures on the increase in cases where initials or other anonymity safeguards have been used. No figures are currently published however it seems common ground that between 2000 and 2010 the numbers had been steadily increasing. The *Independent* newspaper carried out an "audit" of orders in 2011 and suggested that 333 relevant orders had been made over the previous five years; however, the bulk of these were uncontroversial orders relating to proceedings in respect of children or vulnerable adults. The remaining 69 included 28 to protect privacy in respect of extra-marital affairs as well as a substantial group of orders to grant convicted criminals anonymity. Other orders concerned commercial confidentiality and it seems reasonable to assume that some cases are immigration or asylum cases and some concern control orders. The number of "super-injunctions" in the privacy area appears to be low; nevertheless the fact of their existence raised concerns.

Such orders raise concerns not only as to whether they are in accord with Article 10 of the Convention rights but also Article 6 (1) which provides that:

"(1) In the determination of his civil rights and obligations or of any criminal charge against him, everyone is entitled to a fair and public hearing within a reasonable time by an independent and impartial tribunal established by law. Judgment shall be pronounced publicly but the press and public may be excluded from all or part of the trial in the interests of morals, public order or national security in a democratic society, where the interests of juveniles or the protection of

---

[249] *Guardian*, October 12, 2009.
[250] [2010] 2 W.L.R. 325.
[251] [2005] 1 A.C. 595.
[252] [2009]UKHL 34.

the private life of the parties so require, or to the extent strictly necessary in the opinion of the court in special circumstances where publicity would prejudice the interests of justice."

The removal of material from judgments therefore must be justifiable under art.6. In *LNS v Persons Unknown*[253] (the John Terry case) Tugendhat J. made clear that a balance must be struck between the rights and there is no presumption that derogations from open justice are routine in claims for the misuse of private information:

"Each derogation from Art. 6 and open justice must be justified on the particular facts of the case, in accordance with the intense scrutiny required".[254]

2–92   Following the concerns raised by the *Trafigura* and John Terry cases, a committee was established by Lord Neuberger, Master of the Rolls, in April 2010: the Committee on Super-Injunctions, Anonymised Injunctions and Open Justice. The remit of the committee was:

- to examine issues of practice and procedure concerning the use of interim injunctions including super-injunctions and anonymised proceedings, and their impact on the principles of open justice bearing in mind s.12 of the Human Rights Act;
- to provide a clear definition of the term "super-injunction"; and
- where appropriate, to make proposals for reform and particularly to make recommendations for any changes to the Civil Procedure Rules (CPR) and Practice Directions.

The Committee reported in May 2011. By the time of its report the Master of the Rolls had delivered two judgments in the Court of Appeal, which had the effect of reining in the use of super-injunctions and anonymity orders by providing guidance on how such orders should be handled where the claims is one for misuse of private information. The first was *Ntuli v Donald*.[255] More detailed guidance was given by the Court of Appeal in *JIH v Newsgroup Newspapers Ltd*.[256]

2–93   In the *Ntuli* case a super-injunction had been granted in April 2010 which restrained the defendant from disclosing initimate or personal material, other information about the relationship or the fact that an injunction existed (apart from a carve out for family and friends) but which allowed the defendant to reveal the fact that she had had a relationship with the claimant. The injunction had been issued to a member of a "boy band" to restrain the publication of personal information by an individual with whom he had had a relationship. The form of the order in the High Court satisfied neither party, Ms Nutli accepted that she would not be able to reveal maters of a sexual nature but sought to be able to disclose other aspects of the relationship and Mr Donald thought that she should not even be able to reveal that there had been a relationship. The matter was

---

[253] [2010] EWHC 119 (QB).
[254] Para.108.
[255] [2010] EWCA Civ 1276.
[256] [2011] EWCA Civ 42.

appealed to the Court of Appeal. The Court did not accept that Ms Nutli's art.10 rights should triumph over Mr Donald's art.8 rights and did not consider that the story she wished to sell held any value as part of a debate of general public interest. The Court did not find the super-injunction was justified or necessary in the particular case nor was anonymity required. The Court considered that there was nothing in the judgment that was significantly invasive of Mr Donald's private or family life.

The next case, *JIH v Newsgroup Newspapers Ltd*,[257] concerned a sportsman who has not been named who wished to restrain the publication of information about a sexual relationship. He had sought and obtained an interim injunction and the parties had agreed that a super injunction should be applied until full trial. Clearly such an order is potentially useful to a media organisation as it retains the exclusivity of the story pending a determination of whether it can be published. The judge, however, was not prepared to make such an order without hearing arguments, on the basis that an order for reporting restrictions and anonymity cannot be made simply because the parties consent, as the parties cannot waive the rights of the public that justice should be seen to be done. After hearing matters, the judge was not prepared to grant anonymity to the sportsman. The case was appealed to the Court of Appeal. In giving the leading judgment, the Master of the Rolls gave the following guidance which is now to be followed in all cases of applications for anonymity and super-injunctions:

2–94

> "In a case such as this, where the protection sought by the claimant is an anonymity order or other restraint on publication of details of a case which are normally in the public domain, certain principles were identified by the Judge, and which, together with principles contained in valuable written observations to which I have referred, I would summarise as follows:
>
> (1) The general rule is that the names of the parties to an action are included in orders and judgments of the court.
> (2) There is no general exception for cases where private matters are in issue.
> (3) An order for anonymity or any other order restraining the publication of the normally reportable details of a case is a derogation from the principle of open justice and an interference with the Article 10 rights of the public at large.
> (4) Accordingly, where the court is asked to make any such order, it should only do so after closely scrutinising the application, and considering whether a degree of restraint on publication is necessary, and, if it is, whether there is any less restrictive or more acceptable alternative than that which is sought.
> (5) Where the court is asked to restrain the publication of the names of the parties and/or the subject matter of the claim, on the ground that such restraint is necessary under Article 8, the question is whether there is sufficient general, public interest in publishing a report of the proceedings which identifies a party and/or the normally reportable details to justify any resulting curtailment of his right and his family's right to respect for their private and family life.
> (6) On any such application, no special treatment should be accorded to public figures or celebrities: in principle, they are entitled to the same protection as others, no more and no less.

---

[257] [2011] EWCA Civ 42.

(7)   An order for anonymity or for reporting restrictions should not be made simply because the parties consent: parties cannot waive the rights of the public.

(8)   An anonymity order or any other order restraining publication made by a Judge at an interlocutory stage of an injunction application does not last for the duration of the proceedings but must be reviewed at the return date.

(9)   Whether or not an anonymity order or an order restraining publication of normally reportable details is made, then, at least where a judgment is or would normally be given, a publicly available judgment should normally be given, and a copy of the consequential court order should also be publicly available, although some editing of the judgment or order may be necessary.

(10)   Notice of any hearing should be given to the defendant unless there is a good reason not to do so, in which case the court should be told of the absence of notice and the reason for it, and should be satisfied that the reason is a good one.

Where, as here, the basis for any claimed restriction on publication ultimately rests on a judicial assessment, it is therefore essential that (a) the judge is first satisfied that the facts and circumstances of the case are sufficiently strong to justify encroaching on the open justice rule by restricting the extent to which the proceedings can be reported, and (b) if so, the judge ensures that the restrictions on publication are fashioned so as to satisfy the need for the encroachment in a way which minimises the extent of any restrictions."

2–95   The Committee on Super-injunctions[258] reported in May 2011. Lord Neuberger reported that, since it had been established in April 2010, only two super-injunctions had been granted in privacy cases: *Nutli*, in which the injunction was discharged, and *DFT v TFD*,[259] which was issued for seven days for anti-tipping-off reasons. The Committee also produced draft Guidance and a draft model order for use in future cases. The Committee did not consider that the procedure required change but did propose that the Ministry of Justice should collect data about super-injunctions and anonymised injunctions so that the numbers would be transparent in the future. The report also lists the 18 cases in which injunctions have been granted since 2010 and the nature of the case.

2–96   While the report has laid to rest the spectre of the courts being awash with secret orders and the new guidelines have set out how anonymity and privacy safeguards should be exercised in practice, there remains a strong public appetite to break the privacy of injunction. Ryan Giggs was outed as the applicant for an injunction via Twitter and other media as were Andrew Marr and Jeremy Clarkson. There appears to be a lack of popular sympathy for individuals being able to use the law to hide the fact of extra-marital affairs. There exist websites devoted to listing the identity of individuals who have successfully obtained had injunctions. The accuracy may be doubtful but some are clearly and, given the subject matter of the injunctions, unfeelingly accurate. The appropriate mechanism to protect the position of individuals who are the subject of publication, harassment and other problems by the use of social media, blogs and Twitter remains a vexed problem however the rules on anonymity, and the use of super-injunctions appear to have been clarified.

---

[258] *www.judiciary.gov.uk* [Accessed September 11, 2012].
[259] [2010] EWHC 2335 (QB).

OVERVIEW

In the cases that have come before the courts since October 2000, judges have **2–97** increasingly taken a holistic view of personal information bringing together concepts from the cases on breach of confidence, arts 8 and 10 of the Convention and the self-regulatory regime governing the media and, although regrettably to a lesser extent so far, data protection standards. In this chapter we have considered the sources and examined the material which is now converging.

The convergence is nowhere near complete and it can be said that informational privacy for the 21st century is still a concept under construction.

So far the courts have moved to offer protection of privacy against press intrusion while maintaining the protection given to freedom of speech. In the process there has been a radical development in the law of confidence, comparable to the developments in *Prince Albert v Strange* and *Saltman*. The significant leap made came in the statement by Lord Woolf in *A v B* that an obligation does not depend for its creation on the relationship between two persons or whether information was confided but rather the nature of the information and the circumstances. It has not yet been confirmed that this will not be taken to apply to all types of confidentiality or only in relation to personal privacy. Even limited to the area of personal privacy, it is a radical re-configuring of the law of confidence. It frees it from the constraints of being a right created by the relationship between two parties in the particular case, and changes it to being an obligation which could bind anyone who intrudes on information of a personal nature. In doing so it has opened the doors to allow the development of a specific action to protect personal privacy in a range of circumstances.

In the cases the courts are gradually teasing out the various aspects of privacy protection and placing them into perspective. Much of the attention has focussed on the celebrity cases however we are seeing more cases tackling the difficult issues of State intrusion into personal privacy. In *Marper* the House of Lords accepted a high level of intrusion in the retention of DNA samples which was strongly rejected by the ECtHR. In other cases the ECtHR seems to be less willing to grant a wide margin of appreciation for the State in the areas of policing and national security. There is a view among many who work in the privacy domain that for most of us personal privacy and liberty are more at risk from State surveillance and intrusion than the attentions of the press. Following the decision in *Marper*, we wait to see how far or how boldly the courts will now be prepared to venture into that terrain. The other area of uncertainty remains the "blogosphere" and the area of social media where there are incursions into individual privacy. This is a privacy challenge yet to be tackled.

CHAPTER 3

Interpretation Of The Act And Case Law Of The Court Of Justice Of The European Union

INTRODUCTION

In this chapter we examine the approach to interpretation of the Act, the cases   3–01
considered by the Court of Justice of the European Union (CJEU) and the status
of other instruments as interpretive tools. There have now been a number of cases
on the Directive before the Court and these are the most important interpretive
tools for data controllers. They have been relatively little reported and referred to
in the UK and for that reason we have considered them fully in this chapter. The
case law of the European Court of Human Rights is covered in Ch.2.

SUMMARY OF MAIN POINTS   3–02

(a) The most important influences on the interpretation of the Act are Directive
     95/46 (the Directive) and the rights in the Charter of Fundamental Rights of
     the European Union (the Charter rights) together with rulings of the Court
     of Justice of the European Union.

(b) The Convention rights under the European Convention (incorporated in the
     United Kingdom by the Human Rights Act 1998) and the judgments of the
     European Court of Human Rights are also applicable as the Convention
     rights are regarded as part of EU law.

(c) The rulings of the UK courts of record including the Second Tier of the
     Information Rights Tribunal which is now a court of record are binding on
     data controllers in the UK.

(d) When considering the interpretation of the Privacy and Electronic
     Communications (EC Directive) Regulations 2003,[1] Directive 2002/58/EC
     is the primary influence on interpretation.

(e) Of secondary importance in the interpretation of the Act are decisions of
     the First Tier Tribunal (Information Rights), other international legal
     instruments, cases from other areas and previous court or tribunal decisions
     on the 1984 Data Protection Act.

---

[1] SI 2003/2426.

(f)   The guidance produced by regulators such as the Information Commissioner or Article 29 Working Party is not legally binding and, is at the most, persuasive.

APPROACH TO INTERPRETATION

Impact of Directive 95/46

3–03   A directive is binding on Member States as to the results to be achieved, but leaves the form and method by which it is achieved to national authorities.[2] The obligation of the Member State is to transpose a directive into national law. This obligation informs the actions of every public organisation that deals with a directive. The courts, when construing statutes based on a directive, must seek to construe them in accord with the directive.

The approach to construction is to be purposive, not literal: that is it must seek to give effect to the objects and purpose of the directive. This has been reiterated in the context of Directive 95/46:

> "It must be observed, as a preliminary point, that, according to settled case-law, the provisions of a directive must be interpreted in the light of the aims pursued by the directive and the system it establishes (see, to that effect, Case C-265/07 Caffaro [2008] ECR I-0000, paragraph 14)".[3]

In the case of *Von Colson*,[4] the European Court of Justice (now the Court of Justice of the European Union (CJEU)) laid down that there is an obligation on authorities of Member States and their courts to produce consistent interpretation and to interpret national laws designed to implement a directive in accordance with the terms and the purpose of the directive. Even when a directive is adequately transposed into national law, therefore, it remains relevant as a standard for interpreting the implementing measure. Not only must the national courts apply consistent interpretation to ensure that the directive is complied with, but they must construe the national provisions in the light of the objectives of the directive.

This was applied by the House of Lords in *Campbell v MGN Ltd*[5] where Lord Philip Worth of Matravers said:

> "In interpreting the Act it is appropriate to look to the Directive for assistance. The Act should, if possible, be interpreted in a manner that is consistent with the Directive. Furthermore, because the Act has, in large measure, adopted the wording of the Directive, it is not appropriate to look for the precision in the use of language that is usually expected from the parliamentary draftsman. A purposive approach to making sense of the provisions is called for".

The interpretative approach can only be adopted within the confines of the national provisions and therefore applies "as far as possible". The UK courts have

---

[2] Art.189(3) of the Treaty.
[3] *Tietosuojavaltuutettu v Satakunnan Markkinapörssi* (C-73/07) para.51.
[4] Case 14/83 [1984] E.C.R. 1891.
[5] [2003] EWCA Civ 1373; [2003] 2 W.L.R. 80 at [96].

considered Directive 95/46 in a number of cases including *Campbell*[6] and *R. (on the application of Alan Lord) v the Secretary of State for the Home Department*.[7] The clearest application of a purposive approach to date is probably to be seen in *Robertson v City of Wakefield Metropolitan Council*,[8] in which the High Court applied a purposive approach to the interpretation of s.11 based on art.14.

In order to look at the purpose of a directive the recitals may be relevant. The other background papers which may be of interpretative relevance are the *travaux preparatoire*. These are usually referred to in the opening provisions of a directive. The papers referred to in Directive 95/46 are the original proposal from the European Commission of 1990 and the opinion of the Economic and Social Committee of 1991. The relation between the Directive and the requirements of art.8 of the Human Rights Convention is relevant in this context. This relationship has been considered in a number of cases. As is explained in Ch.2, the Directive is a "working out" of the art.8 right in the area of personal information and in many areas it goes beyond the relatively limited range of ECtHR cases on informational privacy. Regrettably, however, there has been a tendency in some cases in the UK to treat the requirements of the Act as coterminous with art.8. Courts and Tribunal have assumed that as long as art.8 is satisfied there will be no breach of the Act. It is submitted that this approach, although it may have the effect of simplifying issues, is misconceived and potentially undermines the protection provided to individuals.[9]

3–04

Article 8 of the Convention is a qualified right. The interpretation of directives must take account of all the Convention rights and of the fundamental concepts of Community law: equality, legal certainty, proportionality, natural justice, fundamental rights and the protection of legitimate expectations. The rights and interests guaranteed by the Convention constitute general principles of Community law: see the case of *Nold* (C-4/73 [1974] E.C.R. 491) and art.6(2) of the Treaty on the European Union. In the *Rundfunk*[10] case (described in more detail below) the European Court said:

3–05

> "... the provisions of Directive 95/46, in so far as they govern the processing of personal data liable to infringe fundamental freedoms, in particular the right to privacy, must necessarily be interpreted in the light of fundamental rights, which according to settled case law, form an integral part of the general principles of law whose observance the Court ensures".[11]

The art.8 right is echoed in art.7 of the Charter of Fundamental Rights of the European Union and in more recent cases the CJEU has referred to the Charter rights rather than the Convention rights, although they are to the same effect.

In *Lindqvist*[12] the European Court (now the CJEU) held that the authorities and courts of the Member States must interpret their national law in a manner

3–06

---

[6] [2003] EWCA Civ 1373; [2003] 2 W.L.R. 80.
[7] [2003] EWHC 2073 (Admin).
[8] Case CO/284/2001, November 2001; see para.2–40 onwards for a full discussion of the case. See also the decision of the Court of Appeal in *Campbell v MGN* [2002] EWCA Civ 1373.
[9] See for example, the Chief Constables of West Yorkshire, South Yorkshire and North Wales Police v the Information Commissioner *Decision of the Information Tribunal 2006*.
[10] C-465/00; C-138/01; and C-139/01.
[11] Para.68.
[12] EU ECJ [2003] 101/0.1 See para.3–12 onward for a full analysis of the facts.

consistent with the Directive but also make sure that they do not rely on an interpretation which would conflict with the fundamental rights protected by the Community legal order or with the other general principles of Community law such as the principle of proportionality. It would follow therefore that, where there is ambiguity in the Directive, it should not be assumed that art.8 will be the only influence on its interpretation or even that, in any particular case, it will be the predominant influence; other Convention rights will also have to be considered. For example in *Lindqvist* the Court held that the provisions of the Directive do not in themselves bring about a restriction which conflicts with the general principles of freedom of expression or other rights and it is for national authorities implementing the Directive to ensure that a fair balance is achieved when applying the national implementing legislation.

3–07   The Court has developed the doctrine of direct effect as a tool to employ where Member States have either failed to implement a directive or failed to implement one properly. This doctrine allows a claimant to rely directly on the terms of a directive rather than on national law where the national law has not properly transposed the directive. As the United Kingdom had not implemented Directive 46/95 by October 24, 1998, there was some risk of direct effect actions against public bodies on this basis; however, none materialised. There was a further risk in relation to Directive 58/2002 but the UK escaped action. A claimant can only rely on a directive as against organisations or bodies treated as part of the State, not against private sector organisations. The provision in the directive must be clear and must confer an individual right which is capable of being enforced without further elucidation.[13] In the joined cases of *Asociacion Nacional d Estableicimientos Financieros de Credito and Federacion de commercio Electronico y Marketing Directo v Adminitracion del Estado (ASNEF)*[14] the Court held that art.7(f) of Directive 95/46/EC, which sets out the right to process on the basis of the legitimate interest of the data controller, is capable of having direct effect.

The State may also be liable to pay compensation where a claimant suffers damage because of the non-implementation, or insufficient implementation, of a directive. This occurred in the case of *Francovitch*.[15] Compensation can be recoverable in *Francovitch*-type cases where:

(a)   the result prescribed by the directive entails the grant of rights to the person;
(b)   it is possible to identify the content of those rights from the directive; and
(c)   there is a causal link between the breach of the State's obligation and the loss and damage suffered by the injured party.

---

[13] *Marshall and Southampton* (C-152/84) [1986] E.C.R. 723.
[14] Cases C-468/10 and C-469/10.
[15] Case 9/90 [1991] E.C.R. 1-5357.

Directive 2002/58/EC and the Privacy and Electronic Communications (EC Directive) Regulations 2003

These Regulations and the related Regulations which govern the surveillance and interception of communications are dealt with in Chs 22 and 23. The relationship between these provisions and EU law is complex because the UK provisions cover some areas which fall outside Union competence. A full discussion of the relationship between data protection instruments and Union competence is found in Ch.23. This relationship was also the root of the decision of the CJEU in the PNR case which considered the "agreement" by the EU Commission to permit the transfer of passenger name data to the US. The Court decided that the purported agreement was invalid as the basis of the transfer was for purposes falling outside Community competence. For a discussion of this case, see para.3-18 below.

3–08

Relation with the European Human Rights Instruments

As touched upon above, there are two relevant European human rights instruments, the Charter of Fundamental Rights of the European Union (the Charter) and the European Convention on Human Rights (the Convention).

3–09

The background to the Charter is covered in Ch.1. The status of the Charter between 2000 and 2009 was ambiguous. Until it was incorporated as part of the Treaty of Lisbon, it was persuasive only. The Convention Rights have long been regarded as being a part of fundamental Community law and could be used to assist in the interpretation of the Directive.[16] Before the Charter became part of the Treaty the references to rights and fundamental freedoms in the case law of the CJEU cite the Convention. More recent cases of the Court have cited the provisions in the Charter. The Charter has been referred to in the cases of *Volker und Markus ScheckeGbR*[17] and in the *ASNEF* case.

The content of the two instruments is largely the same, but the scope of the Charter is wider than the Convention, covering rights of liberty and equality, economic and social rights, civil and political rights, and rights of citizens of the Union. The Charter incorporates a specific right to the protection of personal data as a fundamental right, in addition to the right to respect for family and private life. Article 8 of the Charter reads:

"1.   Every person has the right to the protection of personal data concerning him or her
2.   Such data must be processed fairly for specified purposes and on the basis of the consent of the person concerned or some other legitimate basis laid down by law. Everyone has the right of access to data which has been collected concerning him or her, and the right to have it rectified.
3.   Compliance with these rules shall be subject to control by an independent authority."

The Treaty of Lisbon has made the Charter legally binding. Although it is not incorporated into the Treaties, it now has direct legal force. As such it will be

---

[16] *Nold* (4-73) May 14, 1974.
[17] C-92/09; C-93/09.

directly relevant to the interpretation of the DPA in the UK.[18] In a case in the High Court ([2010 EWHC 705 (Admin) at para.155), Cranston J. had indicated that the Secretary of State was not bound to act in accordance with the EU fundamental rights protected by the Charter when acting within the scope of the EU law.

The decision of Cranston J. was appealed and, in the Court of Appeal, Lord Neuberger (Master of the Rolls) referred the questions arising in the appeal in relation to EU law to the CJEU. In paras 6 and 7 of the *NS* judgment, the Master of the Rolls confirmed that the Secretary of State

"no longer seeks to support that finding [of Mr Justice Cranston in paragraph 155 above], as is clear from paragraph 8 of the respondent's notice, which states:

'8. Contrary to the Judge's holding, the Secretary of State accepts, in principle, that fundamental rights set out in the charter can be relied on as against the United Kingdom, and submits that the Judge erred in holding otherwise (judgment, paragraphs 155 and 157, first sentence). The purpose of the Charter Protocol is not to prevent the Charter from applying to the United Kingdom, but to explain its effect.'"

The reference made by the Court of Appeal in July 2010 asked about the effect of the UK and Polish Protocol (so-called "opt out") to the EU Charter of Fundamental Rights, the circumstances in which a risk of a breach of the Charter would preclude transfer under the Regulation, and the compatibility with fundamental rights of the UK's third country deeming provision.

The Grand Chamber's ruling was handed down on December 21, 2011 deciding a number of fundamental issues. The Grand Chamber held, inter alia, that:

"Article 1(1) of Protocol (No 30)... does not intend to exempt the Republic of Poland or the United Kingdom from the obligation to comply with the provisions of the Charter or to prevent a court of one of those Member States from ensuring compliance with those provisions".[19]

The Convention remains relevant to interpretation, particularly as Directive 95/46 is stated to be the working out of the application of the right to respect for private and family life in the informational arena and thus the art.8 right will be relevant to the interpretation of the Directive.[20]

---

[18] *R. (on the application of NS) v The Secretary of State for the Home Department* [2010] EWCA Civ 990.
[19] Saeedi NS (C-411/10).
[20] See Ch.2 for an analysis of the impact of art.8.

COURT OF JUSTICE OF THE EUROPEAN UNION—OVERVIEW AND CASELAW

Jurisdiction

The Court of Justice of the European Union (CJEU) (the "Court") cases are of prime importance in interpreting the national law arising from a directive. The Court gives rulings on cases brought before it. Cases may arise from a number of sources. The most common are references for preliminary rulings. National courts refer cases to the CJEU for rulings where the national provisions adopted to comply with a Directive may be argued to be impossible to reconcile with the fundamental principles of Community law. Most of the data protection cases referred by national courts have been cases of this nature.

3–10

The Commission can start proceedings before the Court if it believes that a Member State is failing to fulfil its obligations under EU law. These proceedings may also be started by another EU country. In either case, the Court investigates the allegations and gives its judgment. If the country is found to be at fault, it must put things right at once. If the Court finds that the country has not followed its ruling, it can issue a fine. The Commission has taken action against Germany and Austria in respect of the nature of its supervisory authorities under this power.[21]

The Court may be asked to rule upon the legality of acts adopted by the Council or other institution. Such actions can also be used by private individuals who want the Court to cancel a particular law because it directly and adversely affects them as individuals. If the Court finds the law in question was not correctly adopted or is not correctly based on the Treaties, it may declare the law null and void. In the case of *Volker und Markus Schecke GbR* the Court ruled that the German regulations which had been challenged by the applicant were incompatible with the directive, although the case was on a reference from the German court. In the PNR case[22] the Court was asked to rule on the legality of the agreement with the United States over the transfer of Passenger Name Records (PNR data). The Court held that the actions of the Commission and the Council (making a finding of adequacy and an Agreement with the US to allow the transfer of Passenger Name Records to the US for security purposes) were not justified under the Treaty and were annulled as being ultra vires.

The Court can also make rulings where the institutions of the Community have failed to act where they are subject to a requirement to do so. Individuals and organisations which suffer damage as a result of the actions of the institution or its staff can also use the Court as the forum to seek damages. We have not traced any cases of this nature in which data protection issues have been raised.

---

[21] See Ch.10 on the powers and role of the Commissioner for an analysis of the case against Germany.

[22] *European Parliament v Council of European Union* (C-317/04); and *Commission of the European Communities* (C-138/04).

In addition, the CJEU may rule on the application of the EU regulations applying the Directive to the institutions of the EU[23] and to those giving access to information.[24] This may give rise to relevant case law where the grounds for refusing access are based on the protection of personal data. There have been several cases in respect of access rights and personal data, in particular the *Bavarian Lager* case[25] and *Egan and Hackett v Parliament*.[26] We summarise the points arising from the case law and then cover the cases on Directive 95/46 in more detail below, setting out the specific questions which have been raised in each case.

How cases are heard

3–11   The number of judges sitting will vary depending on the complexity or importance of the case. There may be a panel of 3, 5 or 13 judges, or the whole Court. After a written process and then an oral hearing the Court may ask for an opinion from the Advocate General assigned to the case. Such opinions are only required if the Court believes that the particular case raises a new point of law. The Court does not necessarily follow the Advocate General's opinion. The Court's judgements are majority decisions and are read out at public hearings.

Case law on data protection

3–12   We have not been able to find an authoritative list of cases in which data protection has been considered by the Court. Excluding the actions for failure to transpose directives in the required timescale, to the best of our knowledge the following cases, which impact on data protection issues, have been considered by the Court: *Lindqvist*[27]; *Rundfunk*[28]; *Heinz Huber*[29]; *Rijkeboer* [30]; *Volker und MarKus ScheckeGbR*[31]; *SABAM*[32]; *Satamedia*[33]; and *ASNEF*.[34] A case was taken by the Commission against Germany for failure to maintain independent supervisory authorities.[35] A case is pending in relation to Google[36] in which judgment is expected this year. The Court has considered Directive 2002/58 in the cases of *Promusicae*[37] and *Tele2*.[38]

---

[23] Regulation (EC) No.45/2001 of the European Parliament and of the Council of December 18, 2000 on the protection of individuals with regard to the processing of personal data by the Community institutions and bodies and on the free movement of such data ([2001] OJ L8, p.1).

[24] Regulation (EC) No.1049/2001 of the European Parliament and of the Council of May 30, 2001 regarding public access to European Parliament, Council and Commission documents ([2001] OJ L145, p.43).

[25] C-28/08.

[26] T-190/10.

[27] Case C-101/01.

[28] Cases C-465/00 and C-138/01 and C-139/01.

[29] Case C-524/06.

[30] *College van burgemeester en wethouders van Rotterdam v MEE Rijkeboer* (C-553/07).

[31] Case C-92/09.

[32] Case C-70/10.

[33] *Tietosuojavaltuutettu v Satakunnan Markkinapörssi Oy and Satamedia Oy* (C-73/07).

[34] Case C-468/10.

[35] Case C-518/07.

[36] Case C-131/12.

[37] Case C-275/06.

Overview of case decisions on Directive 95/46 EC and 2002/58

We have covered all of the cases in more detail later but this section provides a high level summary of the decisions.

3–13

- In *Lindqvist* it was argued that, as the Directive was passed to harmonise data protection regimes in order to ensure the functioning of the internal market, national laws based on it are not applicable to activities which are not directly related to supporting the internal market. The CJEU took a robust approach pointing out that recourse to art.100a of the Treaty as a legal basis "does not presuppose the existence of an actual link with free movement between Member States in every situation referred to by the measure founded on that basis ... what matters is that the measure adopted on that basis must actually be intended to improve the conditions for the establishment and functioning of the internal market".[39] The Court ruled that the Directive is compatible with the Convention rights and that it is for the national authorities and courts responsible for applying the legislation implementing Directive 95/46 to ensure a fair balance between the rights and interests in question, including the fundamental rights protected by the Community legal order.

- In *Rundfunk* the Court was asked to consider the boundary between rights of informational privacy for those employed by the State and the disclosure of information about their emoluments as a matter of public interest. The Court refused to make a substantive decision on the proposed disclosure but confirmed that the relevant information should be regarded as personal data, albeit generated in the course of employment and related to the employment of the individuals, but that the question of mandatory disclosure was for the State to decide. The State had to be satisfied that the disclosure would serve a proper public interest and apply proper principles of proportionality. The case seems to have been little regarded in the UK.

- In *Heinz Huber* the Court held that the concept of "necessity" in art.7(e) imports the test of proportionality and this means that a public authority must be able to demonstrate that any processing of personal data based on it is the minimum necessary for achieving the legitimate aim in question. The particular data was held for the purposes of immigration status. The view taken was that retention of the relevant personal data would not be compatible with the concept of necessity unless it could be shown that there was no other way of enforcing the immigration and resident status rules. The facts were remitted to the national court to take a view. This is a distinctly stricter approach to the term "necessary" than has been habitually taken in the UK.

- In *Rijkeboer* the Court held that the deletion of information about disclosures made from data after a short period of time could amount to a failure to meet the obligation to ensure that individuals could exercise rights of access if the deletion meant that individuals would be unable to know to whom the data had been disclosed. The opinion of the Advocate

---

[38] Case C-557/07.
[39] C-465/00, para.41.

General which was not repeated in the final judgment suggested that metadata associated with personal data (that is data about the use of or access to personal data) should also be regarded as personal data.

- In *Volker und Markus Schecke GbR* the Court considered the publication of information about the beneficiaries of aid from the State and held that the publication of such information amounted to an interference with the rights of the beneficiaries of aid. In the particular case, the detail published was not regarded as proportionate and the Regulation under which it was mandated was struck down.

- In *SABAM* the Court held that a wide injunction which would have required an ISP to monitor and filter all internet traffic to find infringing uses would not accord with arts 8 and 11 of the Charter which protect personal data and the freedom to receive and impart information respectively.

- In *Satamedia* the Court held that a wide meaning must be given to the terms "journalistic" activity as the derogation was intended to protect the right to freedom of expresssion.

- In *ASNEF* the Court held that Member States could not either add to or amend the grounds for processing in art.7 of the Directive. The specific question concerned art.7(f), which sets out the legitimate interest ground for processing. The Court also held that art.7(f) could have direct effect.

- In *Promusicae* and *Tele2* the Court ruled that Member States may impose obligations on providers of electronic communication services to disclose personal data relating to internet traffic to private third parties to enable those parties to bring proceedings for infringement of copyright. However Member States must ensure when passing national laws implementing the relevant directives that they rely on an interpretation of those directives which allows a fair balance to be struck between the fundamental rights involved.

ANALYSIS OF CASES ON DIRECTIVE 2002/58 AND DIRECTIVE 95/46

Directive 2002/58

3–14   The cases of *Promusicae*[40] and *Tele2* on Directive 2002/58 concern the obligations which are being imposed on intermediaries to disclose the identities of file sharers. In both cases the Court considered the compatibility of the restrictions on the retention and use of traffic data under Directive 2002/58 with the protective measures being taken to discover the identity of those in breach of copyright. Promusicae is a non-profit-making organisation of producers and publishers of musical and audiovisual recordings. It applied to the Spanish court for an order that Telefónica should provide it with the names and addresses of individuals to whom it provided internet access services, whose IP addresses and date and time of connection were known. According to Promusicae, these were users of the KaZaA file exchange program (peer-to-peer or P2P) which was used to exchange music in which the members of Promusicae held the exploitation

---

[40] C-275/06.

rights. Promusicae claimed before the national court that the users of KaZaA were engaging in unfair competition and infringing intellectual property rights. It therefore sought disclosure of the information in order to be able to bring civil proceedings against the file sharers. The application was successful. Telefonica appealed against the order on the grounds that disclosure could only be authorised in criminal investigations or for the purpose of safeguarding public security and national defence not in civil proceedings or as a preliminary measure relating to civil proceedings. The CJEU was asked to consider whether Directive 2002/58 precludes Member States from making it mandatory for service providers to disclose personal data for the purpose of civil proceedings to deal with infringement of copyrights, and if that was not the case whether there was any obligation on Member States to do. The precise question was:

"Does Community law, specifically Articles 15(2) and 18 of Directive [2000/31], Article 8(1) and (2) of Directive [2001/29], Article 8 of Directive [2004/48] and Articles 17(2) and 47 of the Charter ... permit Member States to limit to the context of a criminal investigation or to safeguard public security and national defence, thus excluding civil proceedings, the duty of operators of electronic communications networks and services, providers of access to telecommunications networks and providers of data storage services to retain and make available connection and traffic data generated by the communications established during the supply of an information society service?"

The Court held that Directive 2002/58 does not preclude the possibility that Member States may lay down obligations to disclose personal data in the context of civil proceedings however neither are such obligations mandated by other provisions. It is for Member States to apply the provisions so as to strike a proper balance.

In *Tele2*, LSG, which is an Austrian collecting society which enforces the rights of recorded music producers, applied under the relevant Austrian law for an order requiring Tele2, an internet access provider, to provide it with the names and addresses of persons to whom it had provided an internet access service and whose IP addresses, together with the date and time of connection, were known. The relevant Austrian provisions allow for the service of such orders on intermediaries. Tele2 argued that it was not an intermediary within the meaning of the relevant provisions and was also unable to retain the relevant data because of its obligations under 2002/58. The Court ruled that 2002/58 does not preclude Member States from imposing obligations on providers of electronic communication services to disclose personal data relating to internet traffic to private third parties to enable those parties to bring proceedings for infringement of copyright. However Member States must ensure when passing national laws implementing the relevant directives that they rely on an interpretation which allows a fair balance to be struck between the rights protected by those interests.

3–15

Directive 95/46/EC

Bodil Lindqvist v Aklagarkammaren i Jonkoping (C-101/01)[41]

3–16   The first case on Directive 95/46 considered by the CJEU (then the European Court of Justice) involved a Swedish defendant who had been prosecuted for posting information about members of a church congregation on a website. It was referred to the ECJ from the Swedish Court of Appeal for a preliminary ruling under art.234 on seven questions on the interpretation of the Directive. The two preliminary questions dealt with the definition of personal data and the scope of the Directive. The preliminary questions were:

> "(1)   Is the mention of a person—by name or with name and telephone number—on an internet home page an action which falls within the scope of the Directive. Does it constitute the processing of personal data wholly or partly by automatic means to list on a self-made internet home page a number of persons with comments and statements about their jobs and hobbies etc.?
>
> (2)   If the answer to the first question is no, can the act of setting up on an internet home page separate pages for about 15 people with links between the pages which make it possible to search by first name be considered to constitute the processing otherwise than by automatic means of personal data which form part of a relevant filing system?".

The Court was quite clear in answering "yes" to the first question in the following terms:

> "The term personal data used in Article 3(1) of Directive 95/46 covers, according to the definition in Article 2(a) thereof, any information relating to an identified or identifiable natural person. The term undoubtedly covers the name of a person in conjunction with his telephone coordinates or information about his working conditions or hobbies".

This response reinforces the widely accepted view that the term "personal data" is intended to have and indeed has a wide ambit. As the question was answered in the affirmative the Court did not go on to consider the second questions. The further questions posed for the Court covered the following points:

(3)   Could the act of loading the information (referred to in the first question) to the web page be covered by any of the exceptions in art.3(2)?[42]

(4)   Was the information about a colleague who had injured her foot sensitive personal data?[43]

(5)   Could the loading of the data on to a web page hosted in Sweden be a transfer of personal data?[44]

(6)   In a case such as this does the restriction in the Directive conflict with the art.10 Convention rights?

---

[41]   November 6, 2003.

[42]   See Ch.16 for exemptions for private use.

[43]   See Ch.7 for sensitive data.

[44]   The judgment of the Court on this point is considered fully in Ch.8 on overseas transfers.

(7)   Can a Member State provide a higher level of protection or extend the scope of the Directive on the issues canvassed here?

The Court answered as follows:

(3)   No. The processing was neither outside the scope of Community law nor carried on only in the course of the private or family life of the individual.
(4)   Yes. The information constituted information about health and was therefore sensitive personal data.
(5)   No. Mrs Lindqvist's actions did not constitute a transfer of personal data. The transfer only took place when it was accessed from a third country.
(6)   No. Nevertheless the national courts applying the Directive must ensure that restrictions are applied in a proportionate manner.
(7)   No. The Directive is a harmonising measure and must be applied in that way nevertheless the Directive allows Member States a margin for manoeuvre in certain areas. Further nothing in the Directive prevents Member States from extending the scope of national legislation to areas not included in the scope of the Directive provided no other Community law provision precludes it.

The judgment is useful in a number of significant areas. However, in the UK it appears not to have been followed in the important case of *Durant v FSA*, considered later in this chapter.

Joined Cases C-465/00 Rechnugshof and Osterreichischer Rundfunk; C-138/01 Christa Neukomn and Osterreichischer Rundfunk; and C-139/01 Joseph Lauermann and Osterreichischer Rundfunk[45]

Austrian legislation required public bodies subject to the oversight of the Austrian state audit body (the Rechnungshof) to provide it with the names and payments details of those who received salaries or pensions of over a specified value. This information was included in an annual report (the Report) which was sent to the upper and lower chambers of the Federal Parliament and the provincial assemblies and subsequently made available to the public. The legislation itself did not specify that the names of the persons concerned and the amount of annual remuneration received must be included in the Report.

3–17

The first case arose because there was a dispute between the Rechnungshof and various public bodies under its supervision as to whether personal data were required to be disclosed by the legislation. Several of these bodies supplied the information in anonymised form and refused to cooperate in providing access to the original documentation on the payments. Proceedings were brought before the Austrian constitutional court seeking a ruling on the interpretation of the provision. The Austrian court in turn referred the point to the ECJ.

The two individual cases arose from proceedings brought in the Austrian courts by individual employees of the Austrian state broadcasting organisation seeking orders preventing their employer from disclosing information about them to the Rechnungshof.

---

[45] 20 May 2003

The same questions were referred to the ECJ in both cases, namely:

"1. Are the provisions of Community law, in particular those on data protection, to be interpreted as precluding national legislation which requires a State body to collect and transmit data on income for the purpose of publishing the names and income of employees of:
    (a) a regional or local authority,
    (b) a broadcasting organisation governed by public law,
    (c) a national central bank,
    (d) a statutory representative body,
    (e) a partially State-controller undertaking which is operated for profit?
2. If the answer to at least part of the above question is in the affirmativeare the provisions precluding such national legislation directly applicable, in the sense that the persons obliged to make disclosure may rely on them to prevent the application of contrary national provisions?"[46]

The question clearly has significance for any jurisdiction which is subject to a statutory access regime.

The Court dealt with the applicability of the Directive (referred to in para.3–11 above) as a preliminary issue. It pointed out that art.3(1) defines scope in very broad terms. It would follow that any processing of personal data other than that which is outside scope because it falls under the exceptions in art.3(2) will be covered by the Directive. It went on to hold that the provisions were not necessarily in breach but the question depended on the justification for them. If the disclosures were not proportionate then the national legislation would be incompatible with both the Convention rights and the Directive. As arts 6(1)(c) and 7)(c) and (e) apply unconditional obligations on Member States and are sufficiently precise to be applied by national courts, they can be relied upon by the national courts to oust national rules which are not compatible with them.

The Court held that the information about the payments to named individuals relates to identified or identifiable natural persons and is therefore personal data. There is no reason to justify excluding activities of a professional nature from the scope of personal data.

Whilst the retention of such data by the employer is not an infringement of art.8 rights, the communication of such data to third parties amounts to an interference, irrespective of whether the information would amount to sensitive personal data.

The provisions of the Directive must be interpreted in the light of Convention rights. Thus, where the Directive permits derogations from rights it provides, and actions carried out in reliance on those derogations would amount to an interference with the art.8 right, the actions must have a legal basis and the interference must be justified and proportionate. This includes the requirement that the law must be sufficiently precise and foreseeable.

Legal commentators in Austria had deduced in the light of the relevant *travaux preparatoires* that the legislation required the disclosure of specific names and payments. It was for the national court determine whether the provisions met the test of forseeability.

---

[46] Para.23—this is the question as phrased in Case C-465/00; the questions as phrased by the other cases were essentially the same (para.30).

The objective of exerting pressure on public bodies to keep salaries within reasonable limits was a legitimate aim which would be capable of justifying interference with art.8.

National authorities enjoy a margin of appreciation in determining the balance between the social needs and the interference with private life in issue. It is for the national courts to ascertain whether the interference is proportional and it could only be satisfied on this point if the wide disclosure of names and income is necessary for and appropriate to the aim of keeping salaries within reasonable limits.

Where the provisions of a directive are unconditional and sufficiently precise they may be relied upon directly by individuals and applied by national courts. The provisions of art.6(1)(c), under which personal data must be adequate relevant and not excessive in relation to the purposes of the processing, and art.7(2)(c) and (e), which set out the grounds for processing applicable to the public sector fall into that category and may therefore be relied upon before the national courts to oust the application of national rules which are contrary to those provisions.

Passenger Name Records (PNR)

Background

The background to the use of PNR is set out in the Opinion of the Advocate General[47] delivered on November 22, 2005 as follows:

    3–18

> "Soon after the terrorist attacks on 11 September 2001, the United States passed legislation providing that air carriers operating flights to, from or through the United States territory must provide the United States customs authorities with electronic access to that data contained in their automatic reservation and departure control systems, known as Passenger Name Records ('PNR'). While acknowledging the legitimacy of the security interests at stake, the Commission of the European Communities informed the United States authorities, from June 2002, that those provisions might come into conflict with Community and Member States legislation on the protection of personal data, as well as certain provisions of the regulation on the use of computerised reservation systems(CRSs). The United States authorities postponed the entry into force of the new provisions but refused to waive the right to impose sanctions on airlines failing to comply with those provisions after March 2003."

The concern of the Commission was that the US ruling would affect all European air carriers. The Directive forbids the transfer of personal data outside the EEA unless it is adequately protected by law or other adequate protection is provided in the receiving country. There are various ways of dealing with this, which are considered in depth in Ch.8, but all except one would be difficult and burdensome for the European air carriers. The one mechanism that was potentially available was for the European Commission to use its powers under art.26(6) of Directive 95/46/EC to determine that any personal data transferred to the Bureau of Customs and Border Protection (CBP) of the Department of

    3–19

---

[47] Joined Cases C-317/04 and C-318/04.

Homeland Security would be adequately protected. Accordingly, the Commission entered into negotiations with the US administration which resulted in an agreement with the US Administration in relation to the transfer of PNR and the treatment of such data by CBP. On May 14, 2004 the Commission made a finding under art.25(6) of Directive 95/46/EC that the transfer of the PNR to the CBP on the terms agreed between the Council and the US would provide an adequate level of protection for the personal data; followed swiftly, on May 17, by a Decision by the Council using its powers under art.95 of the Treaty which had the effect of implementing the terms of the agreement.[48]

3–20   As will be appreciated, given the legal basis of the Directive as an internal market measure, and the scope of the Directive as set out in art.3(2), this mechanism had an element of the fig leaf (if not the Emperor's clothes) about it and its success depended on the acceptance by all those affected that:

a.   the Agreement with the CBP was related to the functioning of the internal market and could thus be made as an internal market measure by the Council within art.95; and

b.   the processing involved, being the transfer of the PNR data to the US, was within the scope of the Directive so that the Commission was entitled to make a finding of adequacy in relation to its transfer under art.25.

Unfortunately for the Council and the Commission, neither the European Parliament nor the European Data Protection Supervisor were willing to accept the view of the Council or the Commission as to the extent of its authority in this area. Neither response came as a surprise; the agreement had been reached in the teeth of opposition from the European Parliament. The Parliament immediately issued proceedings before the European Court of Justice for annulment of the decisions. The European Supervisor was given leave to join the proceedings, broadly supporting the Parliament, while the UK weighed in on the side of the Council and Commission.

3–21   The Opinion of the Advocate General was given in November 2005, followed by the judgement of the Court in May 2006 annulling the two instruments. In essence the Court ruled that the Agreement was outside the scope of art.95, thus the Council's purported Decision was a nullity. In the judgment it stated that art.95 EC, read in conjunction with art.25 of the Directive, "cannot justify Community competence to conclude the Agreement". The Agreement related to the transfer of data for the purposes of preventing and combating terrorism and other serious crimes. As such the processing operations were excluded from the scope of the Directive and the Decision could not have been validly adopted on the basis of art.95 EC.

Secondly the transfer of personal data for the purposes of security was not covered by Directive 95/46/EC and thus the Commission had no power to make a finding of adequacy in respect of it. The Court found that the processing of personal data in the course of an activity which falls outside the scope of Community law was excluded from the Directive. As the decision on adequacy concerned only PNR data transferred to CBP which was to be used strictly for purposes of preventing and combating terrorism and related crimes, other serious

---

[48] See fn.33 above.

crimes, including organised crime, that are transnational in nature, and flight from warrants or custody for those crimes, it followed that the transfer of PNR data to CBP constituted processing operations concerning public security and the activities of the State in areas of criminal law.

The Commission had argued, following *Lindqvist*, that because the PNR data was collected by private operators for commercial purposes its transfer was not an activity of the State or of State authorities. The Court did not accept this. In the Court's view the transfer fell within a framework established by the public authorities that relates to public security. While the Court accepted that PNR data are initially collected by airlines in the course of an activity which falls within the scope of Community law, namely the sale of an aeroplane ticket which provides entitlement to a supply of services, it took the view that the data processing taken into account in the decision on adequacy was quite different in nature. The data processing in question was not necessary for the supply of services, but data processing regarded as necessary for safeguarding public security and for law-enforcement purposes.

The Agreement was replaced by one reached by the Council on the arts 24 and 38 of the Treaty.[49] Article 38 provides that agreements between the EU and States outside the EU may be made for the purpose of police and judicial co-operation in criminal matters. Article 24 allows the Council, acting unanimously, to conclude agreements with other States.

Huber v Germany (C-524/06)

Heinz Huber, the applicant, was an Austrian citizen who was a resident in Germany. German law provided that, while only a relatively limited amount of personal data about German citizens was held in municipal registers, more detailed information about non-German nationals was also held in a central register. The information on that central register is readily searchable by, and easily available to, a range of public authorities. The questions for the Court were whether the register was discriminatory on grounds of nationality or restrictive of freedom of movement and the extent to which it met art.7(e) of Directive 95/46. Article 7(e) states that:

3–22

> "Member States shall provide that personal data may be processed if . . . processing is necessary for the performance of a task carried out in the public interest or in the exercise of official authority vested in the controller or in a third party to whom the data are disclosed".

The case was a reference for a preliminary ruling. The specific questions were:

> "(1)   Is the general processing of personal data of foreign citizens of the Union in a central register of foreign nationals compatible with ... the prohibition of discrimination on grounds of nationality against citizens of the Union who exercise their right to move and reside freely within the territory of the Member States (Article 12(1) EC, in conjunction with Articles 17 EC and 18(1) EC)[?]

---

[49] Agreement—[2006] OJ L298/29 October 27, 2006 and Council Decision 2006/729/CFSP/JHA of October 16, 2006.

(2)   [Is such processing compatible with] the prohibition of restrictions on the freedom of establishment of nationals of a Member State in the territory of another Member State (first paragraph of Article 43 EC)[?]

(3)   [Is such treatment compatible with] the requirement of necessity under Article 7(e) of Directive 95/46 ...?"

The Court ruled that, given that Member States are prohibited from any discrimination between citizens of the Union on grounds of nationality, a centralized system set up for use by the authorities responsible for Union citizens who are not nationals of the Member State to help carry out their functions could only fall within art.7(e) of Directive 95/46, as being "necessary" if it:

• held only the personal data necessary for the application of the relevant law by the authorities; and

• its centralised nature enables that legislation to be more effectively applied.

It referred the questions of fact to the national court. It also held that the holding of personal data containing individualised personal information in the register could not be considered "necessary" for statistical purposes within the meaning of art.7(e) of Directive 95/46. This is a strict view of the term "necessary", although as "necessary" is always a term importing a test of proportionality it is difficult to assess how it might impact in other circumstances.

College van Burgemeester en Wethouders van Rotterdam v Rijkeboer (C -553/07)

3-23   In *Rijkeboer* the Court was asked whether a specific provision of the Dutch law relating to the retention of information by local authorities was in accord with the directive. The question was:

Is the restriction, provided for in the Netherland's law on personal data held by local authorities, on the communication of data to one year prior to the relevant request compatible with art.12(a) of Directive 95/46/EC when read in conjunction with art.6(1)(c) of that Directive and the principle of proportionality?

In effect, the Court said, the question was

"whether an individual's right of access to information on the recipients or categories of recipient of personal data regarding him and on the content of the data communicated may be limited to a period of one year preceding his request for access."

The Court held that the right of subject access is to enable the individual to understand what has happened to the data about him and be put into a position to exercise other rights such as to apply for the blocking of data. The Court considered the relation with art.6(1)(e) under which peronal data must not be stored for longer than necessary for the purpose and pointed out that, where personal data had to be retained for a long time it would be very burdensome on controllers to have to retain full records of all recipients or categories of recipients and the directive does not require this. However a balance must be struck and in the particular case the imbalance between the one year period for the retention of information about recipients and the very long potential storage periods of the personal data meant that the position was unfair. There was also an argument raised that, as individulas are notified of the nature of the recipients of personal data in the fair processing notices, there was no obligation to retain and provide them under art.12; a view which was rejected by the Court.

Joined cases C-92/09 and C-93/09 Volker und Markus Schecke GbR v Land Hessen

In *Volker und Markus Schecke* two applicants, an agricultural business and a farmer, complained about the publication of information about their receipt of agricultural subsidies on the website of the German Federal Office for Agriculture and Food (the Bundesanstalt). This published the names, address and postcode and the monies received. They applied to the Administrative Court to restrain the publication by Land of Hesse of the data relating to them on the grounds that the publication was an unjustified interference with the fundamental right to the protection of personal data. The national court referred the case to the Court of Justice. The questions asked were:

3–24

"1. Are Article [42](8b) and Article 44a of … Regulation … No 1290/2005 …, inserted by … Regulation … No 1437/2007 …, invalid?
2. Is … Regulation … No 259/2008
(a) invalid, or
(b) valid by reason only of the fact that Directive 2006/24 … is invalid?
If the provisions mentioned in the first and second questions are valid:
3. Must the second indent of Article 18(2) of Directive 95/46 … be interpreted as meaning that publication in accordance with … Regulation … No 259/2008 … may be effected only following implementation of the procedure – in lieu of notification to a supervisory authority – established by that article?
4. Must Article 20 of Directive 95/46 … be interpreted as meaning that publication in accordance with … Regulation … No 259/2008 … may be effected only following exercise of the prior check required by national law in that case?
5. If the fourth question is answered in the affirmative: Must Article 20 of Directive 95/46 … be interpreted as meaning that no effective prior check has been performed, if it was effected on the basis of a register established in accordance with the second indent of Article 18(2) of that directive which lacks an item of information prescribed?
6. Must Article 7 – and in this case, in particular, subparagraph (e) – of Directive 95/46 … be interpreted as precluding a practice of storing the IP addresses of the users of a homepage without their express consent?"

The Regulations referred to in the questions are those setting out the obligations to publish information about the recipients of the subsidies. The questions fell into three groups, the first being about the balance between the publication and the right to private life, the second about the impact of registration under the directive, and the final question a very general one about IP addresses. In effect the 6th question appears not to have been answered.

In considering the right to respect for private life with regard to the processing of personal data the Court referred to the Charter and noted that the limitations which may lawfully be imposed on the right to the protection of personal data correspond to those which allow for the interference with the right to respect for private and family life under the European Human Rights Convention.

The Court took the view that the pubication of the information amounted to an interference with the rights of the beneficiaries of aid. In order to be justified, such interference must be

> "provided for by law, must respect the essence of those rights and, subject to compliance with the principle of proportionality, must be necessary and genuinely meet objectives of general interest recognised by the European Union or the need to protect the rights and freedoms of others".

Moreover, "derogations and limitations in relation to the protection of personal data may apply only in so far as they are strictly necessary."

The Land of Hesse suggested that, as the individuals were informed of the publication and made applications for support knowing of the publication, they could be regarded as having consented to the publication. The Court did not accept this and pointed out that the mere notice could not be regarded as a consent. The Court also held that the information about the individuals' professional and business life fell under the definition of personal data and the protection of private life. The Court emphasised that derogations from the right to respect for privacy and exceptions to the protection provided should only apply as far as necessary to achieve another aim and there is no authority that transparency should be regarded as more important than privacy.

As a result, the Court held that the general obligation to publish under Regulations Nos 1290/2005 and 259/2008 without,

> "drawing a distinction based on relevant criteria such as the periods during which those persons received such aid, the frequency of such aid or the nature and amount thereof",

meant that the Council and the Commission had not complied with the principle of proportionality. They declared the measures invalid, one in part and one as a whole but in view of the large number of publications which had taken place prior to the declaration refused to allow any actions to be brought based on the earlier invalidity. In relation to the questions on registration the Court held that there was no obligation on the data protection officer to make an entry in his register before the processig was carried out and no obligation on the Member State to require prior checking of the processing.

Case Tietosuojavaituutettu v Satajunnan Markkinaporssi Oy and Satamedia Oy (C-73/07)

3–25 The Finnish authorities published information about every individual's income and wealth tax which was then used by a marketing company to provide a service by which, in response to a text message showing the name and municipality of the subject, they would send a return text showing the income and assets of that person. The questions considered by the Court were whether this use was to be considered as a processing of personal data; whether such processing of information which has been made publicly available by the State falls outside the scope of the Directive and whether it could fall within the derogation for journalistic activity, even if carried on for a commercial purpose. The questions were:

"(1)   Can an activity in which data relating to the earned and unearned income and assets of natural persons are:
    (a)   collected from documents in the public domain held by the tax authorities and processed for publication,
    (b)   published alphabetically in printed form by income bracket and municipality in the form of comprehensive lists,
    (c)   transferred onward on CD-ROM to be used for commercial purposes, and
    (d)   processed for the purposes of a text-messaging service whereby mobile telephone users can, by sending a text message containing details of an individual's name and municipality of residence to a given number, receive in reply information concerning the earned and unearned income and assets of that person,
be regarded as the processing of personal data within the meaning of Article 3(1) of [the directive]?

(2)   Is [the directive] to be interpreted as meaning that the various activities listed in Question 1(a) to (d) can be regarded as the processing of personal data carried out solely for journalistic purposes within the meaning of Article 9 of the directive, having regard to the fact that data on over one million taxpayers have been collected from information which is in the public domain under national legislation on the right of public access to information? Does the fact that publication of those data is the principal aim of the operation have any bearing on the assessment in this case?

(3)   Is Article 17 of [the directive] to be interpreted in conjunction with the principles and purpose of the directive as precluding the publication of data collected for journalistic purposes and its onward transfer for commercial purposes?

(4)   Is [the directive] to be interpreted as meaning that personal data files containing, solely and in unaltered form, material that has already been published in the media fall altogether outside its scope?"

As would be anticipated, the Court held that it was a processing of personal data, the fact that it had been published by the State did not mean that it fell outside the Directive, and subsequent uses would be subject to the law. In relation to the journalistic exemption it confirmed that journalism could be commercial and held that art.9 must be given a wide meaning because its purpose is to protect another fundamental right, freedom of expression.

It held that, in order to reconcile those two "fundamental rights" for the purposes of the directive, the Member States are required to provide for a number of derogations or limitations in relation to the protection of data and, therefore, in relation to the fundamental right to privacy, specified in Chs II, IV and VI of the Directive. Those derogations must be made solely for journalistic purposes or the purpose of artistic or literary expression, which fall within the scope of the fundamental right to freedom of expression, insofar as it is apparent that they are necessary in order to reconcile the right to privacy with the rules governing freedom of expression. In order to take account of the importance of the right to

3–26

freedom of expression in every democratic society, it is necessary to interpret notions relating to that freedom, such as journalism, broadly and in order to achieve a balance between the two fundamental rights, the protection of the fundamental right to privacy requires that the derogations and limitations in relation to the protection of data provided for in the chapters of the Directive referred to above must apply only insofar as is strictly necessary.

It confirmed that the exemptions and derogations provided for in art.9 of the Directive apply not only to media undertakings but also to every person engaged in journalism. The fact that the publication of data within the public domain is done for profit-making purposes does not, prima facie, preclude such publication being considered as an activity undertaken "solely for journalistic purposes". They also pointed to the evolution and proliferation of methods of communication and the dissemination of information. As was mentioned by the Swedish Government in particular, the medium which is used to transmit the processed data, whether it be classic in nature, such as paper or radio waves, or electronic, such as the internet, is not determinative as to whether an activity is undertaken "solely for journalistic purposes".

The Court held that all activities such as those involved in the main proceedings, relating to data from documents which are in the public domain under national legislation, may be classified as "journalistic activities" if their object is the disclosure to the public of information, opinions or ideas, irrespective of the medium which is used to transmit them. They are not limited to media undertakings and may be undertaken for profit-making purposes.

Scarlet Extended SA v Societe Belge des Auteurs, Compositeurs et Editeurs SCRL (SABAM) (C-70/10)

3–27   SABAM is a management company which represents authors, composers and editors of musical works. Scarlet is an ISP which provides internet access. In 2004 SABAM concluded that Scarlet customers were using its services to run file-sharing of copyright works in respect of which SABAM represented those entitled to royalties. In 2007 the court in Belgium made an order that Scarlet was to put in place a mechanism for filtering all use of its network so that it would be able to block any copyright infringement. Scarlet appealed on the basis that the order imposed on Scarlet de facto a general obligation to monitor its network, and the requirements of the order were in breach of the general Directive and also the secrecy of communications as required by 2002/58. The questions referred to the Court were:

(1)   Do Directives 2001/29 and 2004/48, in conjunction with Directives 95/46, 2000/31 and 2002/58, construed in particular in the light of arts 8 and 10 of the European Convention on the Protection of Human Rights and Fundamental Freedoms, permit Member States to authorise a national court, before which substantive proceedings have been brought and on the basis merely of a statutory provision stating that: "They [the national courts] may also issue an injunction against intermediaries whose services are used by a third party to infringe a copyright or related right", to order an [ISP] to install, for all its customers, in abstracto and as a preventative

measure exclusively at the cost of that ISP and for an unlimited period, a system for filtering all electronic communications, both incoming and outgoing, passing via its services, in particular those involving peer-to-peer software, in order to identify on its network the movement of electronic files containing a musical, cinematographic or audio-visual work in respect of which the applicant claims to hold rights, and subsequently to block the transfer of such files, either at the point at which they are requested or at which they are sent?

(2)   If the answer to the first question is in the affirmative, do those directives require a national court, called upon to give a ruling on an application for an injunction against an intermediary whose services are used by a third party to infringe a copyright, to apply the principle of proportionality when deciding on the effectiveness and dissuasive effect of the measures sought?

Directives 2001/29 and 2004/48 allow for the holders of IP rights to apply for injunctions against intermediaries who are being used to infringe rights. 2000/31 prohibits national authorities from requiring ISPs to carry out general monitoring of the transmission of material on their networks. The Court held that the system being ordered would require active observation of all electronic communications and would thus fall foul of the prohibition in art.15(1) of 2000/31. In addition, it would be a disproportionate response as it would not represent a fair balance between the protection of property rights of the copyright holders and the freedom to conduct business enjoyed by the ISP. Moreover it would infringe the rights of the ISP's customers to the protection of personal data and the right to receive or impart information, safeguarded by arts 8 and 11 of the Charter. It would breach art.8 because it would involve the collection of IP addresses stating: "Those addresses are protected personal data because they allow those users to be precisely identified". Regrettably, the Court did not expand on this and it is not apparent whether the Court regarded them as personal data because the ISP would have the subscribers' details, which of course it would in this case, or because it regarded IP addresses as personal data simpliciter. The answer to the first question was therefore no and the second issue does not arise.

3–28

Joined Cases C-468/10 and C469/10 Asociacion National de Establicimientos Financieros de Credito (ASNEF) and Federacion de Comercio Electronico y marketing Directo (FECEMD) v Administracion del Estado

Article 7(f) of the Directive provides that one of the grounds for the processing of personal data is where the processing

3–29

"is necessary for the purposes of the legitimate interests pursued by the controller or by the third party or parties to whom the data are disclosed, except where such interests are overridden by the interests or fundamental rights and freedoms of the data subject which require protection under Article 191)".

The Spanish data protection law, the Organic Law 15/99, which transposes the Directive into Spanish law, was implemented by Royal Decree in 2007. Under the Spanish law the primary basis for the processing of personal data is consent and the law had implemented art.7(f) of the Directive so that it only applied to information which was held in public sources. The public sources were listed as the electoral roll, telephone directories and lists of people belonging to professional associations. In effect, the Spanish law had added further requirements to art.7(f). The Spanish Supreme Court (Tribunal Supremo) referred the following questions to the Court:

"(1)   Must Article 7(f) [of Directive 95/46] be interpreted as precluding the application of national rules which, in the absence of the interested party's consent, and to allow processing of his personal data that is necessary to pursue a legitimate aim of the controller or of third parties to whom the data will be disclosed, not only require that fundamental rights and freedoms should not be prejudiced, but also require the data to appear in public sources?

(2)   Are the conditions for conferring on it direct effect, set out in the case law of the Court . . . met by the aforementioned Article 7(f)?"

Article 5 of the Directive requires that Member States shall, "within the limits of this Chapter, determine more precisely the conditions under which the processing of personal data is lawful." It was argued that this gave a basis for the Member State to amplify or restrict the art.7 grounds. The Court did not accept this. It explained that the aim of the Directive is to achieve harmonisation at a high level and to ensure the free movement of data through the Union. It follows that art.7 sets out an exhaustive and restrictive list of the grounds for processing and Member States cannot add new principles relating to the lawfulness of processing or impose additional requirements to the grounds. Member States may clarify the requirements but not amend them. It went on the explain that the balancing test must be done on a case-by-case basis and therefore a provision which purported to definitively prescribe the balance for different categories of data must be fundamentally flawed; although there was no barrier in Member States establishing guidelines for the exercise of the balancing test. The answer to the first question was therefore yes. On the question of direct effect, the Court held that the provision is sufficiently precise to be relied upon directly.

European Commission v Bavarian Lager Co Ltd (C-28/08 P)

3–30   This was a case on the right of access to documents of the institutions of the Community under Regulation 1049/2001 and the impact of Regulation 45/2001 on that right. It is a decision of the Grand Chamber of the Court. Although it may be argued to be a very specific decision on the wording of the provisions in 45/2001, it does set a stringent approach to the disclosure of personal data which contrasts with the view taken by the Court of First Instance.

Bavarian Lager is a company dedicated to the import of bottled German beer to UK pubs. The rules around tied houses and guest beers at the time in question made it difficult for Bavarian Lager to market its products and raised concerns about the UK's compliance with EU competition rules. The Commission held a number of meetings with representative groups and some time later Bavarian Lager applied for access to the minutes of the meetings. The right of access applies to the institutions of the Community under Regulation 1049/2001. The material was eventually given but the names of five persons who were from a representative group were omitted. Bavarian Lager applied for the names and was refused. The Commission relied upon art.8 of 45/2001, which sets the standards for data protection for the Community institutions and provides:

> "Without prejudice to Articles 4, 5, 6 and 10, personal data shall only be transferred to recipients subject to the national law adopted for the implementation of Directive 95/46:
>
> (a)   if the recipient establishes that the data are necessary for the performance of a task carried out in the public interest or subject to the exercise of public authority, or
>
> (b)   if the recipient establishes the necessity of having the data transferred and if there is no reason to assume that the data subject's legitimate interests might be prejudiced."

In addition, art.18 of the Regulation gives individuals the right to object to the processing of personal data about them. In the particular case some of the individuals had objected to the release of their names and others could not be contacted. At appeal in the Court of First Instance the Court drew attention to the provision in art.4 of Regulation 1049/2001 concerning exceptions to the right of access which states that:

> "The institutions shall refuse access to a document where disclosure would undermine the protection of:
>
> b)   privacy and the integrity of the individual, in particular in accordance with Community legislation regarding the protection of personal data."

They also drew attention to the fact that under 1049/2001 the applicant does not have to state what he/she wants the information for. The right of access is "applicant blind". They held that while the names were clearly personal data and the disclosure of the names would be processing of the personal data it was not prevented by Regulation 45/2001 as the disclosure of such personal data would only be exempt where the disclosure would cause harm to the individuals or some detriment to their privacy. The Court of Justice however applied the test in art.8 of 45/2001 and held that the applicant had to show the grounds for disclosure of personal data. This had not occurred and there was also no way of ascertaining whether the disclosure could cause any prejudice. The Court also took into account the fact that some individuals had refused consent and ruled that the Commission had been correct to withhold the names.

OTHER INTERNATIONAL INSTRUMENTS AND LAW OF MEMBER STATES

There is a practical difficulty for data controllers and those advising them in even trying to be aware of decisions made by the courts in other Member States but it is a possibility that the law of other states may be directly relevant. This may occur in two circumstances:

3–31

(a)   Where a provision derives directly from a previous provision in the law of a Member State and was incorporated expressly to preserve it. Such decisions are of persuasive value only. In *Pioneer Electronics Capital Inc v Warner Music Manufacturing Europe GmbH*,[50] a section in the Patents Act 1977 had its origin in an article of the European Patent Convention which in turn was based on a provision in German law. The judge took into account of how a term derived from it had been applied by the German courts. This approach had some relevance in the interpretation of the term "relevant filing system" by the Court of Appeal in Durant when the German law provision which was a predecessor of the term in Directive 95/46 was considered. However such examples are likely to be extremely rare.

(b)   Where a court in a Member State rules on a provision common to the laws of the two states both of which derive from a requirement of the Directive. Such decisions will be of persuasive value only and care must be taken in applying them. In *Wagamama Ltd v City Centre Restaurants Plc*,[51] Laddie J. said:

> "In any event the obligation of the English court is to decide what the proper construction is . . . it would not be right for an English Court to follow the route adopted by the courts of another Member State if it is firmly of a different view simply because the other court expressed a view first. The scope of European legislation is too important to be decided on a first past the post basis."

However we have not attempted to survey cases from other EU countries and are not aware of any index or guide to such cases.

Other international instruments

Interpretative Relevance of the Council of Europe Convention for the Protection of Individuals with regard to Automatic Processing of Personal Data (Treaty 108)[52]

3–32   Conventions are binding on states which become signatory to them. Adherence to a convention may have different effect in different states' legal systems. In some cases the convention itself may be "self-executing" or "absorbed" into the national law. This is not the case in the United Kingdom. A convention will be of interpretative force and the UK courts will be bound to seek to interpret any national instrument passed in order to apply the Convention in conformity with it.[53]

In the UK, Treaty 108 fulfilled this function on two occasions when the 1984 Act was under consideration. In *CCN Credit Systems Ltd v The Data Protection Registrar*,[54] decided in February 1991, the Data Protection Tribunal considered Treaty 108 in order to assist in elucidating the meaning of the term "unfairly" in

---

[50] [1995] R.P.C. 486.
[51] [1995] F.S.R. 713.
[52] See Ch.1 for contents of the treaty.
[53] *Garland v British Railway Engineering Ltd* [1982] 2 All E.R. 402; *R. v Secretary of State for the Home Department Ex p. Brind* [1991] 1 A.C. 696.
[54] Reported in the *Encyclopedia of Data Protection* (Sweet and Maxwell, 2012).

Principle 1. The House of Lords in *R. v Brown*[55] sought assistance from it to decide on the difference between "processing" and "use". In both judgments the background of Treaty 108 and its roots in a concern for the right to private life were acknowledged.

The Treaty remains relevant as the UK is still a signatory, although it has been replaced in importance by the Directive. The Treaty has also been amended to reflect the standards of the Directive and is currently under further review.[56]

Recommendations

Following adoption of Treaty 108, the Council of Europe set up a Committee of Experts on Data Protection which has worked on a number of Recommendations to Member States on various aspects of data protection. Those Recommendations have been adopted by the Council. A list of the Recommendations will be found on the Council of Europe website.[57]   **3–33**

Interpretative relevance of the OECD Guidelines[58]

In UK law, the Guidelines are the least influential of the various instruments covered in this chapter. However, in policy and political terms they may be of assistance in elucidating the intention of or approach to specific provisions. They can best be described as having advisory rather than persuasive effect. In data protection terms, the OECD has its main importance as a forum for discussion of data protection issues among the international community. This is derived from the presence of the United States and other non-European members who come together in regular working groups on privacy and data protection issues. The OECD also issues advisory papers, reports and expert materials which can be found on its website.   **3–34**

DECISIONS OF UK COURTS AND TRIBUNALS

Previous decisions on the Data Protection Act 1984

There is relatively little case law under the 1984 Act. It only figured in one House of Lords case[59] and four High Court cases.[60] Even then it was regarded as a difficult statue. As Woolf L.J. (as he was then) opined in the case of *Rowley v Liverpool City Council*[61]:   **3–35**

---

[55] [1996] 1 All E.R. 545.
[56] See Ch.1.
[57] It should be noted that occasionally the courts have looked at the relevant Recommendations when deciding cases on difficult issues of policy. The ECtHR did this in *Z v Finland* ((1997) 25 E.H.R.R. 371). In another use if soft law the High Court considered Recommendation 1/97 of the Article 29 Working Group on Data Protection and the Media in the case of *Campbell v Mirror Group Newspapers* [2002] EWCA Civ 1373.
[58] See Ch.1 for an explanation of the role of the Guidelines.
[59] *R. v Brown* [1996] 1 All E.R. 545.
[60] Listed at the end of this chapter.
[61] *The Times*, October 26, 1989.

"Before the learned judge [counsel] also relied upon the provisions of the Data Protection Act 1984 and it is right to say straightaway that that Act is a complex enactment in which it is difficult to find your way about unless you are very familiar with it indeed."

Not all of those reached the law reports, although all are available in the *Encyclopedia of Data Protection*. All tribunal decisions including those on the 1984 Act are now available at *www.judgmental.org.uk*.

In approaching interpretation where previous statutes cover the same ground a distinction is drawn between codifying and consolidating statutes. Consolidating statutes are more likely to be interpreted in line with previously decided questions on the same words. However, Bennion[62] states that the distinction between the two has a purposive base. It is prima facie presumed that a consolidating statute did not intend to change the law whereas there is no such presumption for a codifying statute. The issue is whether the new provision is intended to achieve the same end in the same way. The 1998 Act is not a consolidating statute and there is no presumption that the law was intended to remain the same as in the 1984 Act. In considering the relevance of decisions on the 1984 Act to the meaning of the 1998 Act, regard must be had to the provenance of the particular provision. The Data Protection Principles are largely unchanging in wording from the 1984 Act. In some cases, expanded interpretations have been provided, in particular by way of additional interpretative provisions and further Schedules adding to the coverage of Principle 1, but these may be regarded as extension rather than changes to the meaning of the core terms "fair and lawful processing and obtaining". Given the common root of the 1984 Act and Directive 95/46 in Treaty 108 and the use of common terms throughout, and given that a number of the decisions on the Principles in the 1984 Act are expressed to be intended to respect and apply rights drawn from Treaty 108 it is reasonable to regard the case law on those provisions as having a continuing persuasive relevance. This appears to have been accepted by the Court in *Lord*[63] in which the Court was directed to the decision of the Data Protection Tribunal in the case of *Equifax v Data Protection Registrar*[64] when considering the application of one of the exemptions. The Court was considering provisions which were "materially indistinguishable" from those which had been considered in the *Equifax* case and took into account the ruling in the earlier case.

However, it must be recognised that there was no binding case law on the Principles under the 1984 Act. There were nine decisions on the Principles adjudicated by the Data Protection Tribunal whose decisions are, in any event, of persuasive force only. Decisions of the Tribunal under the 1984 Act were put forward by the applicant in *Johnson v Medical Defence Union Ltd*.[65] The court appears to have accepted that they could be considered and cited with approval the view of the Tribunal in relation to fairness.

---

[62] Bennion, *Statutory Interpretation* (3rd edn, 1997), p.463.

[63] *R (on the application of Alan Lord) v Secretary of State for the Home Department* [2003] EWHC 2073 (Admin).

[64] Case DA/90 25/49/7 reported in the *Encyclopaedia of Data Protection*.

[65] [2006] EWHC 321(Ch) paras 116–123.

Decisions on the 1998 Act

There have been very few cases on data protection before the Information   3–36
Tribunal. This contrasts with the large number brought under the Freedom of
Information Act 2000. The Commissioner has brought action against a number of
data controllers for sending unsolicited faxes contrary to the Telecommunications
(Data Protection and Privacy) Regulations 2000 but appeals against the notices in
these cases were settled and, although there was an agreed order, gave rise to no
judgments. In the case of *Chief Constable of West Yorkshire v Information
Commissioner*[66] the Tribunal declined to give any general guidance on the third
and fifth principles. In the case of *Scottish National Party v Information
Commissioner*[67] the Tribunal agreed with the Commissioner's view of the
prohibition on marketing without consent. Since the last edition of this text there
have only been two cases heard in the First Tier Tribunal (Information Rights) on
the DPA itself, as opposed to cases on the application of the exemption for
personal data under the FOIA. *The Secretary of State for Communities and Local
Government v IC* which concerned subject access redactions and *the Chief
Constable of Humberside and others v IC* which concerned the retention of
records and was appealed to the Court of Appeal. In the courts the Directive or
the 1998 Act has been considered or referred to in a number of cases which have
given some guidance on different parts of the Act. The decisions which have had
a bearing on the core definitions are the House of Lords in *Common Services
Agency v Scottish Information Commissioner*[68] and the Court of Appeal in the
Campbell case and *Johnson*[69] (on the definition of the term "processing") and the
cases of *Durant v Financial Services Authority*,[70] *Lord*[71] and *R. (Department of
Health) v Information Commissioner*.[72] As we have seen in the previous chapter,
when considering privacy cases the courts have tended to turn to the law of
confidence and the art.8 rights rather than data protection. This development has
left data protection in a surprisingly undeveloped state considering that it has
been on the statute books for over twenty years.

In the case of *Norman Baker MP v The Secretary of State for the Home
Department*[73] a national security certificate under s.28 drawn in very general
terms was successfully challenged and the Secretary of State had to re-issue it in
more limited terms. It is covered in Ch.15 on the exemptions for national security
but does not offer any general guidance on the DPA.

---

[66] [2005] Po. L.R. 337.
[67] Unreported May 15, 2006.
[68] [2008] UKHL 47.
[69] [2007] 1 All E.R. 467.
[70] [2003] EWCA Civ 1746.
[71] See fn.63.
[72] [2011] EWHC 1430 (Admin).
[73] October 1, 2001 reported in Commissioner's *Annual Report* (July 2002) and *Data Protection and
Privacy Practice*.

HANSARD AND EXPLANATORY NOTES

3–37   Although a Directive will be the governing instrument as far as results to be achieved are concerned, there may remain some leeway, within the transposition of a Directive, for national approaches. In some areas the Directive leaves the choice of how matters are handled to the discretion of Member States. Moreover, in other areas the national legislation may cover issues not dealt with by the Directive. Where there is ambiguity in such provisions, the doctrine in *Pepper v Hart* will allow recourse to be had to the *Hansard* record of parliamentary material in appropriate circumstances.

In *Pepper (Inspector of Taxes) v Hart*,[74] the court held that parliamentary material could be looked at in limited circumstances. Where a statutory provision is ambiguous or obscure or where the literal meaning would be absurd, and it can be elucidated by reference to clear parliamentary material emanating from the Minister which sets out why that provision was enacted and the purpose it was meant to achieve: such material may be examined and taken into account in determining the proper meaning of the provisions.

The limits of *Hansard* material should be borne in mind. In resolving ambiguities the courts now look more frequently towards Brussels or Strasbourg than towards Westminster. It has already been noted that where a statutory provision arises from a requirement of a directive, the directive will be the governing instrument. Further, where a provision is derived from or affected by a Convention right, the court will look to the Strasbourg jurisprudence on that right rather than to the views of Parliament. This shift in emphasis was already underway before the Human Rights Act 1998 (HRA) came into force; see *R. v Broadcasting Complaints Commission Ex p. Barclay*[75] in which the court declined to give *Hansard* preference over matters deriving from the ECHR, and has been mandatory since October 2000 when the HRA came into effect.

Nevertheless *Hansard* material may be relevant in some cases. The range of material can be wide. In *Callery v Gray*[76] the Court of Appeal accepted that explanatory notes produced by the Department sponsoring the Act in question constitute "parliamentary material" for the purposes of *Pepper v Hart* and accordingly can be used to interpret an ambiguous provision. However, the courts have tended to limit the occasions when it can be used to cases falling strictly within the test in Pepper v Hart; that is where the ambiguity is in a statutory expression, not a statutory power, and where it is not possible to resolve the ambiguity by any other means.[77] In cases under the 1998 Act, *Hansard* material was considered to resolve ambiguity in the definition of a relevant filing system in Durant.[78] The passage of the Act through Parliament is described in Appendix 1 and there are notes at the end of each chapter flagging where any specific points were considered as part of the Parliamentary process.

Since 1999, Explanatory Notes have been introduced to accompany Bills through their Parliamentary progress. In so far as they cast light on the setting of

---

[74] [1993] A.C. 593.
[75] [1997] Admin L.R. 256.
[76] *Callery v Gray* [2001] 1 W.L.R. 2112.
[77] See *R. v Secretary of State for the Environment, Transport and the Regions Ex p. Spath Holme Ltd* [2000] All E.R. (D) 2177; *R. v Mullen* [2000] Q.B. 520; *Stevenson v Rogers* [1999] Q.B. 1028.
[78] [2003] EWCA 1746.

a statute and the mischief at which it is aimed they are admissible in the construction of a statute.[79] The Act pre-dates the system, but such Notes have been referred to in cases on legislation in the same area such as the *Marper* case on the retention of DNA under the Criminal Justice and Police Act 2001.

Rules of statutory interpretation—general

As can be seen from this chapter, the topic of statutory interpretation is a large one. The emphasis placed on particular aspects of it in this chapter should not be taken to imply that the usual rules for approaching the meaning of statutes in English law do not apply; they will do so in appropriate cases. For example, the rules that exemptions will be construed narrowly,[80] or that ambiguities in criminal provisions must be resolved in favour of the defendant,[81] continue to apply. However, they have to be applied in the context of an Act intended to give effect to a directive. While the hope must be that the rules applied by English law and the purposive approach of Community interpretation will lead to the same end, and indeed draw strength from one another, the possibility of the two approaches producing conflicting results must be acknowledged. Where there is a conflict resulting from the two approaches to statutory interpretation, the Community approach must be preferred and adopted by the court if possible; but if the conflict raises doubts as to the principle of community law to be applied, the court must consider a reference to the CJEU for guidance.[82]

3–38

CODES OF PRACTICE AND GUIDANCE

Codes of Practice

The Act and Directive provide for the preparation and adoption of Codes of Practice, under s.51 and art.27 respectively. These have no formal interpretive status but are likely to be persuasive. The Employment Practices Code has been issued by the Information Commissioner under the DPA, but relevant codes are also to be found under other legislation. The Code of Practice on the Management of Police Information, issued following the recommendations of the Bichard Enquiry, is referred to in Ch.27. However there are many other relevant Codes of Practice, for example in the area of health. When advising on informational issues it is always prudent to review the existence of soft law surrounding the relevant area. The most recent area of code development is the provision for a code of practice on CCTV, the Surveillance Camera Code, to be overseen by a separate Surveillance Camera Code Commissioner, to be made under the Protection of

3–39

---

[79] *R. v Chief Constable of South Yorkshire Police Ex p. LS; R. v Chief Constable of South Yorkshire Police Ex p. Marper* [2004] UKHL 39 per Lord Steyn at para.4.

[80] The principle "expression unius est exclusion alreius". According to Bennion: "Where an Act contains specific exceptions, it is presumed that these are the only exceptions of the kind intended".

[81] According to *Bennion* the principle applies to any form of detriment, although often referred to as though limited to criminal statutes. It was applied in *R. v Bristol Magistrates Court Ex p. E* [1998] 9 All E.R. 789 at 804 per Simon Brown L.J.: "It's a principle of legal policy that a person shall not be penalized except under clear law".

[82] *Rosgill Group Ltd v Customs and Excise Commissioners* [1997] 3 All E.R. 1012.

Freedoms Act 2012.[83] The Code will include material on issues which clearly overlap with the DPA as it must contain guidance about the use or processing of images or other information obtained by virtue of such systems. The Act also provides that the code may include provision about:

- considerations as to whether to use surveillance camera systems;
- the publication of information about systems and apparatus; and
- access to or disclosure of information so obtained.

In this case the statutory code will only apply to "relevant authorities", which are listed as local authorities and police although it can be extended to other persons. It is likely therefore that the two codes, the Commissioner's code on CCTV and the statutory code will apply in parallel with the Commissioner's code providing broader data protection advice and also applying to those who fall outside the statutory code.

Guidance from the Information Commissioner

3–40　　The Office of the Information Commissioner (ICO) is active in issuing guidance to the Act and its application in specific areas. The website lists the guidance material available covering the DPA and PECR. The guidance was previously arranged in three categories: introductory; practical application; and detailed specialist guides. It has now been re-ordered under 25 topic headings. There are around 80 guidance documents listed at the time of writing this in August 2012; some are very brief, practical and specific and others longer or more general. The Legal Guidance, "Data Protection Act 1998—Legal Guidance" was issued in October 2001 to coincide with the ending of the first transitional period. It has been withdrawn, but in November 2009 a replacement Guide to Data Protection was issued by the Office which we have occasionally referred to in the text. Only current guidance is kept on the Commissioner's website but previous copies can be obtained on request. In addition, the National Archives periodically captures a snapshot of the ICO website enabling anyone to see what was on the website (including guidance) at that date.[84] The ICO is currently revising the approach to this guidance with a view to issuing less general material but having a core spine of guides and codes. In the text we refer only to a few of the specific guidance documents. However, for those advising on the Act it is always worth reviewing the website to check for additional specific materials. It is always useful to consider the view taken by the ICO on any topic; however, a few points should be borne in mind:

- The Commissioner will always reserve the right to amend or develop guidance where an area of particular volatility or uncertainty is in question therefore it is generally worth checking the most recent advice on the website or speaking to his Office.

---

[83] The Protection of Freedoms Act 2012 ss.29–36.
[84] *http://webarchive.nationalarchives.gov.uk/*/http://www.ico.gov.uk* [Accessed September 12, 2012].

- The guidance is not authoritative. The Commissioner habitually prefaces publications with the statement that definitive guidance can only be provided by the courts.

It should also be noted that the Commissioner, quite properly, is keen to advocate good practice, which may go beyond the strict requirements of the law and that, where there is any possible ambiguity, the interpretation favoured by the Commissioner is generally the one which takes a broader view of the boundaries of the Act and the protection of privacy. However, as noted above, this may not be the only legitimate approach as other Convention rights may be relevant, and in some cases in this text a slightly different approach to the one taken by the Commissioner is suggested.

Article 29 Working Party

The Article 29 Working Party (Article 29 WP) has produced a significant amount of material. The Article 29 WP is the only pan-EU body to issue opinions on the Directive as the Article 31 WP has never done so. Its papers therefore span a range of material from the practical, such as the material on Binding Corporate Rules, to the political, such as on APNI systems. The papers reflect both WP policy and the WP's areas of specific interest. As a result there are a lot of papers on internet-related and electronic communications issues and far fewer on issues of more everyday interest such as subject access. The Opinions can sometimes be rather academic and in other cases, for example the Opinion on controllers and processors, the WP can appear to have struggled to come to a common view. This is not to dismiss or diminish the many useful Opinions produced but to caution that they are variable and are policy rather than legal documents. The documents that the WP issues have no formal status and no legal authority. In particular the conclusions that they draw on factual situations are not binding or even persuasive. They are the WP views on fact only. Not unnaturally or unreasonably given its composition, the WP always takes a frankly expansive view of the application of the Directive and an openly one-sided view. Its Opinions are not formed in the intense opposing debates of courts or Parliamentary assemblies and can lack the rigour of judgments of the courts. They are always interesting in showing how regulators may respond to situations and can illuminate difficult areas of discussion but in legal terms are advisory at the most.

3–41

Impact of the draft Regulation in brief[85]

The draft Regulation as proposed would not make a significant difference to the approach to interpretation save that the Regulation itself would be the primary instrument of reference.

3–42

---

[85] See Ch.1, paras 1-68 onwards for an overview of the proposal as at January 2012.

ADDITIONAL MATERIALS

3–43   Directive 95/46 (see Appendix B).
        List of cases decided under Data Protection Act 1984:

- *Data Protection Registrar v Amnesty International* [1995] Crim. L.R. 633;
- *Dubai Aluminium v Al Alawi* [1999] 1 All E.R. 1;
- *Griffin v Data Protection Registrar*, February 1993;
- *McConville v Barclays Bank, The Times*, June 30, 1993;
- *McGregor v McGlennan* (1993) S.C.C.R. 852;
- *R. v Brown* [1996] 1 All E.R. 545;
- *R. v Chief Constable of B County Constabulary*, Unreported November 1997;
- *Rowley v Liverpool Corporation, The Times*, October 26, 1987, CA.

Note: The cases which are not reported in law reports can be found in the *Encyclopedia of Data Protection*.

3–44   **Data Protection Tribunal Cases 1984 Act**

- *Rhonalda Borough Council v Data Protection Registrar* 1990;
- *Runneymede Borough Council v Data Protection Registrar* 1990;
- *CCN Credit Systems Ltd v Data Protection Registrar* 1991;
- *CCN Systems Ltd v Data Protection Registrar* 1991;
- *Equitax (Europe) Ltd v Data Protection Registrar* 1991;
- *Infolink Ltd v Data Protection Registrar* 1991;
- *Credit & Data Marketing Services Ltd v Data Protection Registrar* 1991;
- *Innovations (Mail Order) Ltd v Data Protection Registrar* 1993;
- *Linguaphone Ltd v Data Protection Registrar* 1993;
- *British Gas Trading Ltd v Data Protection Registrar* 1998;
- *Midlands Electricity Plc v Data Protection Registrar* 1999.

Decisions of the Tribunal are available on the website of the First Tier (Information Rights) Tribunal: *www.informationtribunal.gov.uk*.[86]

Copies of Council of Europe Recommendations are included in the *Encyclopaedia of Data Protection* or available from the website of the Council at *www.coe.org*.[87]

Copies of OECD papers are available at *www.oecd.org*.[88]

---

[86] [Accessed September 12, 2012].
[87] [Accessed September 12, 2012].
[88] [Accessed September 12, 2012].

CHAPTER 4

Main Definitions, Scope And Territorial Application

INTRODUCTION

In this Chapter we cover the main definitions and the scope of the Act. It should   **4–01**
be noted that territorial scope and the relevant definitions for the Privacy and
Electronic Communications (EC Directive) Regulations 2003 are covered in
Ch.22, not in this Chapter. The territorial scope and the definitions are both
important in assessing the nature and extent of the responsibilities of data
controllers. In considering definitions, one must distinguish between questions of
fact and law. Many of the questions with which practitioners will be faced
concerning the definitions will be questions of fact. In this Chapter we seek to
provide an explanation of the meaning of the main defined terms as a matter of
law. Not all of the defined terms are covered here. Section 71 of the Act lists a
table of defined terms and the relevant section of the Act in which they are
defined or explained. Here we deal with the basic interpretative provisions which
are set out in s.1 of the Act plus three terms which are not included in s.1 but
which were included in the key interpretative provisions in art.2 of the Directive.
They are "third party", "recipient" and "consent". Other definitions are covered
in the specific chapters which cover the topic to which they relate. The territorial
application of the Act is also dealt with here.

It should be noted that the draft Regulation which was issued by the
Commission in January 2012 would make some significant changes to the scope
of the law both in relation to the data covered and the processing within scope.

SUMMARY OF MAIN POINTS   4–02

1) There are a number of key definitions in the Act which effectively define
   the scope of the Act. The most significant are "data controller", "data",
   "personal data" and "processing"
2) The Act applies to all data controllers who are established in the United
   Kingdom and process personal data in the context of their establishment.
3) The Act also applies to data controllers who make use of equipment in the
   UK to process personal data and such controllers must nominate a
   representative in the UK.
4) The Act binds the Crown and the Houses of Parliament but there are limits
   on the Commissioner's powers in respect of such data controllers.

DEFINITIONS

Introduction

4–03   The Consultation Paper issued by the Home Office in March 1996 on the implementation of the Directive raised the question of how the definitions should be tackled. In the summary of responses, published in March 1997, it was reported that a majority of respondents had made clear their preference for precise definitions. There were, however, two views on how those should be approached. Many had suggested that the new legislation should resemble the 1984 Act as far as possible, because users were familiar with that pattern. Others, however, advocated taking definitions from the Directive to ensure that there was no possibility of conflict between the national law and the Directive.

In the 1998 Act an attempt appears to have been made to please both parties. The definitions are a hybrid owing much to both the 1984 Act and to the Directive. This creates some strains, as it is not always apparent how the definitions map on to the Directive. In this Chapter, where there is ambiguity this is pointed out and where possible an interpretation which resolves the strain is suggested. In view of the importance of the core definitions in some cases, the provisions of the Directive are reproduced in the body of the text to compare and assist in elucidating the position.

There is a difference in approach between the Act and the Directive. The Directive sets out a list of definitions then describes the scope of the Directive (in art.3.1). In the Act, the two are rather more entwined. "Relevant filing system" feeds into "data" which feeds into "personal data" which feeds into "data controller". The data controller carries the core obligations set out at s.4(4). Aspects of scope are, therefore, dealt with by definitions. An example of this is the way the concept of data being "processed wholly or partly by automatic means" has been dealt with by inclusion in the definition of data. The use of this technique makes it more difficult than it might otherwise have been to map the Act on to the Directive and be content that the two are mutually coherent.

As noted above, even where definitions owe something to the 1984 Act, the primary reference point for their interpretation is the Directive. Regrettably, there are also some outstanding ambiguities, and one of the Directive's core terms, "consent", is not defined in the Act.

Personal data

4–04   This definition derives from art.2a of the Directive. Article 2a reads:

> "Personal data shall mean any information relating to an identified or identifiable natural person (data subject); an identifiable person is one who can be identified, directly or indirectly, in particular by reference to an identification number or to one or more factors specific to his physical, physiological, mental, economic, cultural or social identity."

The definition in the Directive gives considerable weight to the concept of an "identified or identifiable person". This is reinforced in Recitals to the Directive. Recital 26 reads:

"Whereas the principles of protection must apply to any information concerning an identified or identifiable person. To determine whether a person is identifiable account should be taken of all the means likely reasonably to be used either by the controller or by any other person to identify such person; . . . whereas the principles of protection shall not apply to data rendered anonymous".

This core definition from the Directive has been rendered in s.1(1) as:

"Personal data means data which relate to a living individual who can be identified

(a)   from those data; or

(b)   from those data and other information which is in the possession of or is likely to come into the possession of the data controller,

and includes any expression or opinion about the individual and any indication of the intentions of the data controller or any other person in respect of the individual".

The term has been considered by the European Court of Justice in *Lindqvist*[1] by the UK House of Lords in *Common Services Agency v Scottish Information Commissioner*[2] and the Court of Appeal in the cases of *Michael John Durant v Financial Services Authority*[3] and *Lord*[4] and *R. (Department of Health) v Information Commissioner.*[5] The decision in *Durant* was followed in the further case of *Johnson v Medical Defence Union.*[6] In June 2007, just after the last edition of this text was completed, the Article 29 WP issued an Opinion on the Concept of Personal Data.[7] In August 2007 the ICO issued a Technical Guidance Note which also considers the definition. There are two areas of difficulty in addressing this definition: what does it mean to say that an individual is "identified or identifiable"? And how proximate does information have to be before it "relates" to someone? These are difficult questions and go to the heart of the scope of the law. In most cases organisations seem to have few problems knowing whether they have personal data or not but there are some borderline or difficult cases where the definition requires close analysis.

Data relating to more than one person

Data can of course relate to more than one person: data on a joint bank account   4–05
for example, will relate to two persons. There is no necessary exclusivity about data. Personal data are not limited to private or family data nor is there any particular way in which the data must relate to an individual. It might be in any aspect of their lives, whether their business lives, professional lives or private lives. If an individual is a sole trader then information about his business is likely to relate to him. If he is a partner then partnership data might relate to him, although this may depend upon the size and complexity of the partnership. The

---

[1] Para.3-12 above, case C-101/01.
[2] [2008] UKHL 47.
[3] [2003] EWCA Civ 1746.
[4] [2003] 2 W.L.R. 80.
[5] [2011] EWHC 1430 (Admin).
[6] [2004] EWHC 347.
[7] WP 136.

requirement that data relate to the individual is no different from the definition in the 1984 Act. There is, however, a difficult issue as between the 1998 Act and the Directive over the concept of identification.

Identified or identifiable—current guidance

4–06   Difficulties arise primarily where individuals connect with others by the use of fragmented or partial digital identities, for example IP addresses which are not known to the recipient of the message to be registered to one person. The people behind these fragmented identities can be the recipients of messages and services; with determination information assembled from their use of machines can sometimes be pieced together so the other party can know who they are, but that is not always possible. Indeed the fact that it is difficult to do that in many cases is the reason we have legislation requiring ISPs to disclose the identity of users of their services to enable copyright holders to defend their intellectual property rights against attack. The point at which such people should be regarded as having emerged from the digital shadowlands into the clear light of identifiability has become a much disputed issue.

4–07   The Act and the Directive cover two concepts. The first is the concept of being identifiable; the second is of being identified. This text has consistently taken the approach that an identifiable person is one whose separate identity is ascertainable but who is not necessarily known in person. He or she may be identifiable by virtue of one or more of the list of factors set out in art.2A, that is by identification number or factors specific to the person's physical, physiological or other aspects of his identity. We have consistently suggested that someone is *identifiable* where there is sufficient information available to distinguish the separate fact of his existence, his being as a unique person. The essence of identifiability is that it is known that the one unique person exists. The essential element of this is that it is clear that there is just one person even if the name and address is not known. This appears to be the view adopted by both the Article 29 WP and the Commissioner, both of which refer to the possibility of a person being "distinguished" in a group. The problem arises when one seeks to apply this test to factual circumstances and in particular IP addresses. An IP address with little more is not likely to meet the definition for two simple reasons: an IP address is not necessarily associated with one computer and, even if it were, more than one person can use a computer.

An identified person is one who can be known in the physical world. A person becomes *identified* where there is sufficient information either to contact him or to recognise him by picking him out in some way from others and know who he/she is. In everyday terms, the latter is usually achieved by knowing a name and address but may be achieved by knowing a unique identifier used in a remote relationship. If we return to the IP address it is clear that an IP address plus other information could well tip over into being personal data, for example an IP address plus registration information, where someone has registered for a service, will be personal data.

Information about both identifiable and identified persons is personal data. The Recital is of assistance in explaining how identifiability is to be assessed. Someone is identifiable if their identity can be ascertained from the information held plus the results of reasonable inquiries, whether made by the controller or another. There is no guidance as to how these "reasonable enquiries" are to be assessed. The Commissioner suggests that the standpoint should be that of a person who is determined to make the connection, and gives the example of a journalist but we are doubtful that this is correct and would suggest instead a sort of "officious bystander" test of someone who is nosey but not to the extent of such nosiness being the source of his or her livelihood. We would also suggest that it should not require specific or forensic skills in investigation to make the link. So if a search on Google or few questions in the local pub would elicit the identity those would be reasonable enquiries but if it required specialist knowledge to conduct a search those would not be reasonable enquiries.

The question of whether an individual is identified or identifiable is a question of fact and not always easy to apply. In the Article 29 WP Opinion it makes specific reference to web behavior and suggests that, as a matter of fact, users are identified by their machines, saying:

> "Also on the Web, web traffic surveillance tools make it easy to identify the behavior of a machine and beyond the machine that of its user. Thus the individual's personality is pieced together in order to attribute certain decisions to him or her . Without even enquiring about the name and address of the individual it is possible to categorise this person on the basis of socio-economic, physiological, philosophical or other criteria and attribute certain decisions to him or her since the individual's contact point (a computer) no longer necessarily requires the disclosure of his or her identity in the narrow sense. In other words the possibility of identifying an individual no longer necessarily requires the ability to find out his or her name."

It is submitted that this conflation of the identity of an individual with the identity of a machine does not reflect the terms of the Directive. As a matter of fact there will be cases where an individual is identifiable because of the use of a specific machine but that does not mean that the identity of a machine equates to the identity of an individual.

The view that IP addresses are personal data appears to have become the settled approach of the WP and is reflected in its Opinions. As such data controllers and those advising them should be aware of it and take it into account. Nevertheless it remains in this commentator's view deeply unsatisfactory. We are aware of no independent research on the identifiability of individuals from IP addresses. Moreover the result is unsatisfactory in the application of the law. How can subject access be safely provided if the data controller cannot be sure of the real identity of the data subject? How can the controller be satisfied that its fair processing notices have been properly given? There is no provision in the Directive for a lesser standard of compliance where the controller does not actually know who he is dealing with but this is the only logical outcome of the WP approach. The question of the scope of personal data remains one of the most contentious issues in the draft Regulation and we must hope that at least the new legislation provides clarity on the point.

Common Services Agency v Scottish Information Commissioner[8]

4–08   The House of Lords considered the definition of personal data in deciding whether a request for access under the Freedom of Information (Scotland) Act 2002 for statistical information should be complied with. The interface between the two pieces of legislation is covered fully in Ch.26. For these purposes it is sufficient to understand that information may be withheld from disclosure where it constitutes personal data under the DPA. The request was for details of all incidents of childhood leukemia by year from 1990 to 2003 for all the Dumfries and Galloway postal area by census ward. A census ward has a minimum of 50 residents or 20 households. The request was refused on the basis that, given the combination of low numbers, the specified age group and the small geographic area, it was personal data within the DPA. The regulator agreed that it was but ordered that it be perturbed so as to stop it being personal data and the perturbed figures released. The Common Services Agency appealed the decision through the courts. The House of Lords held that if the figures could be sufficiently perturbed so no individuals could be identified either by the recipient or the data controller from the information disclosed i.e. the actual data was fully anonymised, then access should be given to the perturbed data. It was accepted that the data controller would still hold the personal data from which the anonymised data was derived. The question of whether the data could be so perturbed was a question of fact which was remitted back to the regulator. Lord Roger and Baroness Hale came to the same view by slightly different routes. In all the judgments it was made clear that there could be no risk of identification and the anonymisation must be effective before a disclosure could be made.

R. (Department of Health) v Information Commissioner[9]

4–09   This was another case under access rights in which the applicant had asked for figures on late term abortions. The Department of Health had refused on the basis that (among other grounds) the data would be personal data. Mr Justice Cranston referred to the Opinion of the WP, although nothing turned on it, and followed the judgment of Lord Hope in the *CSA* case in holding that as long as the data was sufficiently anonymised that the identity of individuals could not be ascertained either from the data itself or the data and other information in the hands of the controller or the person to whom it was disclosed, it would not be personal data within the meaning of the definition.

Information which relates to an individual

4–10   The second element of the test is that information should relate to the individual.
        In the UK, before the judgments in *Durant* and *Johnson*, it was generally accepted that the concept of data "relating" to an individual embraced a wide range of data. Post *Durant* the position in the UK became more uncertain. It remains the case that the question of whether or not particular data relate to a particular individual will be a question of fact, dependent largely on an

---

[8] See fn.2 above.
[9] See fn.5 above.

assessment of the proximity of the data and the relevance of the data to him. It is possible however that the information must be more proximate than was previously thought as *Durant* has given rise to a new test. This poses significant problems for data controllers who are uncertain as to where to draw the line, particularly when dealing with subject access requests. (The practical problems in this area are considered in Ch.11 on subject access.)

Following the decision of the Court of Appeal in *Durant* the Information Commissioner issued guidance on the application of the judgment. Both the decision and the subsequent guidance were the subject of criticism from a number of sources, most importantly the European Commission, as being incompatible with the Directive. The guidance was subsequently withdrawn and replaced with a more generous interpretation which appears to have satisfied the Commission. The judgment in *Durant* is good law in the UK and is binding however the view of the Commission is that it is too narrow (a view with which we agree). Data controllers should therefore be aware of this tension and take it into account. In view of the significance of the judgment it is covered in some depth below.

Michael John Durant v Financial Services Authority[10]

Mr Durant had made a subject access request to the Financial Services Authority (FSA) under s.7 of the Act. The FSA held information on Mr Durant because it had investigated a complaint which Mr Durant had made against Barclay's Bank. The Court considered whether the information sought was personal data within the meaning of the Act. The information which Mr Durant wanted was held in a four types of files and covered:

4–11

- documents relating to part of the complaint about the systems and controls which Barclay's bank was obliged to maintain;
- documents relating to his complaint held on a file containing complaints received from customers on Barclay's bank. These were behind a divider marked with his name;
- documents relating to his complaint on a file relating to issues or cases concerning Barclay's Bank; and
- a sheaf of papers held by the Company Secretariat of the FSA relating to Mr Durant's complaint about the FSA's refusal to disclose information about its investigation of his complaint about Barclay's Bank:

> "The FSA has acknowledged in correspondence that each of the files in question contains information in which Mr Durant features, that some of them identify him by reference to specific dividers in the file and that they contain documents such as: copies of telephone attendance notes, a report of forensic examination of documents, transcripts of judgments, hand-written notes, internal memoranda, correspondence with Barclay's Bank, correspondence with other individuals and correspondence between the FSA and him"

Delivering judgment Lord Justice Auld held that none of the information was personal data which related to Mr Durant, rather it was information about his

---

[10] [2003] EWCA Civ 1746.

complaint and the objects of them, the Bank and the FSA. Auld L.J. acknowledged this to be a narrow interpretation of the term personal data.[11] He stated that he drew support for the interpretation from the way it is applied in s.7, that is there is an entitlement to personal data "of which ….[he]is the data subject". However s.7 offers no support as the point is circular; a data subject is simply someone who is the subject of personal data. More tellingly he relied upon the express inclusion in the definition of personal data of expressions of opinion or intention, pointing out that, if the term had been intended as a broader one such provision would have been otiose.[12]

The alternative view is that the words were indeed mere surplusage, having been included because expressions of intention were excluded explicitly from the 1984 Act definitions.

Auld L.J.'s reasoning and explanation were as follows:

"It follows from what I have said that not all information retrieved from a computer search against an individual's name or unique identifier is personal data within the Act. Mere mention of the data subject in a document held by a data controller does not necessarily amount to his personal data. Whether it does so in any particular instance depends on where it falls in a continuum of relevance or proximity to the data subject as distinct, say, from transactions or matters which he may have been involved in to a greater or lesser degree. It seems to me that there are two notions which may be of assistance. The first is whether the information is biographical in any significant sense, that is, going beyond the recording of the putative data subject's involvement in a matter or an event which has no personal connotations, a life event in respect of which his privacy cannot be said the be compromised. The second is one of focus. The information should have the putative data subject as its focus rather than some other person with whom he may have been involved or some transaction or event in which he may have figured or had an interest, for example, as in this case, an investigation into some other person's or body's conduct that he may have instigated. In short it is information that affects his privacy, whether in his personal or family life, business or professional capacity".[13]

The approach of the Court of Appeal can be criticised for failing to take account of the scope of the provision in the Directive on which the definition in the UK Act is based despite the fact that in the judgment the Court expressly acknowledges that it is bound to interpret the law in accord with the Directive[14] and states that is applying *Lindqvist*.[15]

The application of the ruling in *Durant*

4–12   The ruling by the Court of Appeal on the scope of the term personal data has caused a number of problems for data controllers because it is difficult to apply. Most of the information which data controllers hold about other individuals is concerned with the minutae of day-to-day transactions. Moreover it tends to be mingled with other information, in emails, letters, references in reports and so on. Deciding whether such information should be regarded as "biographically

---

[11] Para.29.
[12] Para.29.
[13] Para.28.
[14] Para.3.
[15] Para.28.

significant" on each occasion can be both difficult and time-consuming. The tests are also difficult to square with *Lindqvist* and the Directive. There does not however appear to be any foreseeable resolution to the uncertainty of the current position. We would suggest that data controllers take the wider view of the term personal data applying the Directive as explained in *Lindqvist.* In the Commissioner's guidance one of the tests suggested to determine whether personal data relates to an individual is whether the data controller intends to use information to contact, influence, learn about or impact on the subject. We would agree that this is perhaps the better test to apply when in doubt as to whether information relates to the individual. It does not of course go to the question of identifiability.

In the case of *Lord*[16] the judge appears to have accepted that, even though taken individually items of information would not amount to personal data within the definition as expounded in *Durant,* in the particular case the sum total of the information was such that it amounted to personal data and should be provided to the applicant.

In the case of *Terence William Smith v Lloyds TSB*[17] the applicant who wished to obtain sight of information about himself argued that documents which had been produced by computer fall within the definition of personal data even when no longer held in that manner. In that case it was not disputed that a number of records were held on manual files which would not fall within the definition of a relevant filing system but it was argued that a document which had *at any time* been recorded in electronic form, for example by being produced on a computer, should be treated as a electronic records even though it was no longer held as such. The Court rejected this contention.

Infringement proceedings

In 2004 the Commission opened infringement action against the UK for failure to properly implement the Directive into UK law. One of the questions apparently was whether the UK law meets the definition in the Directive post *Durant*. It is understood that the position of the UK is that the judgment can be read in such a way as to accord with the Directive however, as noted in Chapter 1, as only limited information is available it is difficult to be sure.

The only public statement of which we are aware apart from some press releases is the letter to Dr Chris Pounder dated December 2010 in response to his access requests. It cited the failure to properly implement a number of articles including:

Article 2—a failure to implement the definition of "relevant filing system" as the interpretation applied in the case of *Durant v FSA*[18] by the Court of Appeal appears to be narrower than is required by the Directive.

The most recent information about the action against the UK which is publicly available appears to be a press release on the Commission's website.[19] This stated that the Commission had "worked with" UK authorities to resolve a number of

4–13

4–14

---

[16] See Ch.11 on subject access.
[17] [2005] EWHC 246 (Ch).
[18] See fn.10.
[19] IP/10/811 24 June 2010

issues but that several remained outstanding including limitations on the UK Information Commissioner's powers and "other" (undefined or explained) short-comings. It is therefore not known whether the Commission regards the UK approach to the definition of a relevant filing system to be defective or not.

Processing

4–15   As with the term personal data, the definition of "processing" was not directly transposed from the Directive although again the reasoning behind the decision here is obscure. The definition in the Directive in art.2 starts with a broad inclusive definition of processing:

> "Processing of personal data shall mean any operation or set of operations which is performed upon personal data, whether or not by automatic means, such as collection, recording, organisation, storage, adaptation or alteration, retrieval, consultation, use, disclosure by transmission, dissemination or otherwise making available, alignment or combination, blocking, erasure or destruction."

However, in the Act the definition specifies three particular processing operations and separates them from the concept of carrying out operations.

In s.1(1) the definition reads:

> "'Processing', in relation to information or data, means obtaining, recording or holding the information or data or carrying out any operation or set of operations on the information or data, including:
>
> (a)   retrieval, consultation or use of the information or data;
> (b)   disclosure of the information or data by transmission dissemination or otherwise making available; or
> (c)   alignment, combination, blocking, erasure or destruction of the information or data."

The definition is extremely wide. All manipulation of data is covered by the definition. In particular capturing of information and dissemination or disclosure of information are included in processing. There are further changes between the wording of the Directive and the UK Act. "Collection" has been changed to "obtaining" and "storage" has been changed to "holding". Throughout the definition in the national legislation "processing" is applied both to data and to information contained in the data. This is explicit in the definition of processing and there is a separate provision in s.1(2) in relation to obtaining, recording, using and disclosing which provide that any of those actions include the same action in relation to the information contained in the data.

4–16   In the 1984 Act only personal data "processed by reference to" the individual was caught by the Act. This restricted the scope of the personal data covered by the 1984 Act. However, the term was widely construed under the 1984 Act and the extension of the definition has not had as radical effect as it might otherwise have done.[20] In the case of *Campbell v MGN*[21] the Court of Appeal held that the

---

[20]   See guidelines on the 1984 Act published by the Data Protection Registrar, p.19 (November 1994).
[21]   [2003] Q.B. 633.

publication of material in hard copy, where it had previously been automatically processed, was processing which fell within the Act. Per Lord Worth of Maltravers MR:

"101   The definition of 'processing' in the Directive and the Act alike is very wide.
        ...

103   The Directive and the Act define processing as 'any operation or set of operations'. At one end of the process 'obtaining the information' is included, and at the other end 'using the information'. While neither activity in itself may sensibly amount to processing, if that activity is carried on by, or at the instigation of, a 'data controller', as defined, and is linked to automatic processing of the data, we can see no reason why the entire set of operations should not fall within the scope of the legislation. On the contrary we consider there are good reasons why it should."

In *Johnson*[22] the Court of Appeal overruled a finding at first instance that the selection of material from both computerised files and various manual and microfiche files, which it was accepted were not themselves covered by the Act, and their inputting into a computer amounted to processing within the Act. There was, however, a strong dissenting judgment from Lady Justice Arden.   **4–17**

The main judgment was given by Buxton L.J. The facts were that Mr Johnson had been a member of the Medical Defence Union (MDU) until his membership was terminated. He brought an action against the MDU on the basis that the MDU had unfairly processed personal data relating to him in making the decisions to terminate his membership. The MDU had a system in which they retained records on every complaint or reference about a member. They assessed the risk of a member having a claim against them by reference to the number of records. Where a member was a high risk they might terminate the membership. The records held by the MDU consisted of three files held on computer, 14 hard copy files (not falling within the definition of a relevant filing system) and a summary of each file held on computer. The activity which Mr Johnson asserted amounted to unfair processing was the extraction of the information, the completion of summaries of each record, the addition of observations, and the allocation of scores by an assessor. The process was not automated and there was no automatic decision-taking involved. The information was evaluated by the assessor addressing her mind to the materials. She then captured her assessment on another data set on the computer and it was transmitted to the decision-making committee in electronic form. The Court of Appeal was asked:

1.   Whether this involved the processing of personal data within the Act.
2.   If so, was there any unfairness in the processing?
3.   If the processing was unfair was the unfairness responsible for the MDU's decision?
4.   If the processing was unfair and that unfairness affected the MDU's decision what, if any compensation, would Mr Johnson be entitled to?

At the first instance the judge had decided that there was processing and some unfairness, in that Mr Johnson had not received a fair processing notice in respect

---

[22] [2007] 1All E.R. 467.

of some of the data held. On the question of whether there was processing within the definition the Court of Appeal had to decide whether the selection, analysis and decision as to what went into the final summary fell into the definition. The Court considered the definition of processing both in the Act and the Directive, together with the relevant recitals and the *Lindqvist* case. The appellant had pointed in particular to the provision in art.2b of the Directive, that the Directive covers the processing of personal data "whether or not by automatic means" and argued that the Court should have regard to the entire operation which resulted in the decision impacting on the appellant. The appellant also relied upon Campbell as authority for the proposition that the term could, and properly did, cover the product of processing as well as the automated sequence. Buxton L.J. decided that the activities did not amount to processing. He distinguished the decision in *Campbell*,[23] expressed concern at the possible reach of the Data Protection Act if the wider view was taken[24] and decided that the relevant activities were conducted wholly by the human agent and involved no processing at all which involved automatic means. On this point Longmore L.J. agreed with him but Lady Justice Arden took the contrary view, arguing that manual selection and presenting into automated form was covered as processing includes collection and obtaining of information and rendering it into automated data.[25] She drew attention to the Strasbourg jurisprudence to the effect that the creation and maintenance of a record engages the art.8 right[26]and cited in support the decision in *Campbell*.

Buxton L.J. approached the case with a focus on the privacy of the data subject and commented that this case did not involve Mr Johnson's privacy rather how he had been treated by the MDU. He went on to consider the remaining questions answering them with the robust response of "No", "No" and "Not as much as the judge at first instance would considered appropriate". These other aspects of the judgment are considered in the relevant chapters. Of particular interest are the discussions on compensation and Lady Justice Arden's consideration of the relationship between fairness and contractual obligations.

Comment

4–18   The decision does not seem to have made a difference to the position of many data controllers. The MDU system was an unusual one with an individual taking a central role in the process rather than it being automated. The case does illustrate the slant that has been given to the Act by the focus on its relation with art.8. In the US, equivalent legislation is often referred to as Fair Information Practices legislation and that captures the fact that the regulatory aim of the regime covers more than privacy alone. The appellant in this case complained that he lost his cover because the way in which the respondent dealt with the information relating to him was unfair. However, he was denied the opportunity to actually make that argument because he had to first bring himself within the technical definitions which he failed to do.

---

[23] Paras 38–43.
[24] Paras 44–48.
[25] See in particular para.128.
[26] *Amman v Switzerland* (27798/95) para.97. See Ch.2 for a discussion of the relevant case law.

Data

A definition of "data" does not appear in the Directive. The inclusion of it in the   **4–19**
1998 Act appears to derive partly from the 1984 Act and partly as a method of
setting out the scope of the Act. The Directive applies to "the processing of
personal data wholly or partly by automatic means".

This is not reproduced in terms in the Act but a definition of data is inserted.
The definition has five limbs. The fifth limb was added by the Freedom of
Information Act 2000, which came into force in January 2000. The additional
category covered is all recorded information held by a public authority.[27] Such
data are however only subject to limited aspects of the Act. The definition covers
information held in any of five different forms:

"(a)   [which is] being processed by means of equipment operating automatically in
        response to instructions given for that purpose."

This definition is very similar to the one in the 1984 Act. The extent of automatic
processing[28] means it will apply to all forms of computerised data. The definition
is not technology specific and the use of any form of equipment will be covered:

"(b)   [which is] recorded with the intention that it should be processed by means of
        such equipment."

The record need not be an automated record. The information could be manually
recorded as long as it is intended it should be automatically processed. It appears
the intention to so process must exist at the time of the recording. It does not
appear that the person who recorded it must also process it. It would, therefore,
be possible for one person to record information as long as there was a present
intention that it should be processed subsequently by automatic means. The
record could be manual data even though it does not fall into the definition of a
"relevant filing system". This provision could possibly catch written documents
intended for document image processing:

"(c)   [which is] recorded as part of a relevant filing system or with the intention
        that it should form part of a relevant filing system."

The term "relevant filing system" is a core definition incorporating the manual
data provisions. Again, this appears to apply only where an intention to add
information to a relevant filing system is present at the time of recording. This
interpretation would have the odd effect that unless information is recorded as
part of a relevant filing system or with such an intention at the time of the
recording, it will not be data within the terms of the definition. On this basis, it
could be suggested that if information is first recorded wholly outside the system
with no intention of it becoming part of a relevant filing system, for example on a
separate sheet, but is later incorporated into a relevant filing system, such
information would not be covered by the definition of data. This view appears to
have been espoused by the Minister speaking in Committee in the Commons on

---

[27] See Ch.26 for the changes brought by the Freedom of Information Act.
[28] See the definition of processing, above.

May 12, 1998 but it is suggested that it is not the correct approach. It does not appear to be compliant with the Directive art.3 of which reads:

"(1)   This Directive shall apply to the processing of personal data wholly or partly by automatic means and to the processing otherwise than by automatic means of personal data which form part of a filing system or are intended to form part of a filing system."

From that, it appears that it is intended by the Directive that data should be covered as long as it forms part of a relevant filing system irrespective of how it was first acquired. One must therefore construe it so as to comply with the Directive, despite the fact that this places some strain upon the words.[29]

"(d)   [which] does not fall within paragraph (a) (b) or (c) but forms part of an accessible record as defined by Section 68".

This last provision covers manual information on personal files held for specific functions. Such information was not immediately subject to all the rigours of the Act.

"(e)   recorded information held by a public authority which does not fall into any of the categories (a) to (d)."

This is further sub-divided into structured and unstructured files. It only applies however to public authorities under the Freedom of Information Act.

Relevant filing system

4–20   This term was considered by the Court of Appeal in *Durant*[30]:

"'Relevant filing system' means any set of information relating to individuals to the extent that, although the information is not processed by means of equipment operating automatically in response to instructions given for that purpose, the set is structured either by reference to individuals or by reference to criteria relating to individuals, in such a way that specific information relating to a particular individual is readily accessible".

In the Directive, personal data filing system (filing system) means:

"Any structured set of personal data which are accessible according to specific criteria, whether centralised, de-centralised or dispersed on a functional or geographical basis."

Such files are not subject to the requirement that they must be processed automatically.

Again, the definition adopted in the national legislation is not the same as that in the Directive. In particular, the words "Whether centralised, de-centralised or

---

[29] See discussion of this approach in para.4-02 above.
[30] See fn.3 earlier.

dispersed on a functional or geographical basis" have been omitted and attempts to have them re-inserted during the passage of the Bill failed.

Since this appears to have been an avoidance of doubt provision in the Directive, it may not be a core omission. However, the words should be borne in mind where any question arises on the application of the Act to dispersed data sets.

There must be a set of information relating to individuals. The use of the term set suggests some degree of coherence in content rather than random groupings of information but could be of any size. In the Interpretation Act 1889, the singular includes the plural and vice versa unless the contrary appears from the legislation. There is nothing to suggest other than the usual rule, so it could cover a set of information about one person.

Further the set must be structured, by one of two possible methods, so as to produce a particular result. That result is that specific information relating to a particular individual is readily accessible. This potentially covers a broad scope and it was this ambiguity which gave rise to the arguments canvassed in *Durant*. The concept of reference to individuals or criteria relating to them could be given either a broad or a narrow meaning. The relevant parts of the Directive are art.2(c) and Preamble 27,

> "2(c) personal data filing system ("filing system") shall mean any structured set of personal data which are accessible according to specific criteria, whether centralised, decentralised or dispersed on a functional basis",

are no less ambiguous than the UK provision, although considerably (and one might say commendably) briefer. However, further assistance is to be found in the Preamble.

Recital 27 reads, inter alia:

> "Whereas . . . nonetheless, as regards manual processing, this Directive covers only filing systems, not unstructured files, whereas in particular, the content of a filing system must be structured according to specific criteria relating to individuals allowing easy access to personal data; whereas in line with the definition in Article 2c the different criteria for determining the constituents of a structured set of personal data, and the different criteria governing access to such a set, may be laid down by each Member State; whereas files or sets of files as well as their cover pages, which are not structured according to specific criteria, shall under no circumstances fall within the scope of this Directive".

The preamble can be viewed as containing four separate aspects of guidance, each starting with "whereas". The first makes it clear that it is not intended to cover all manual records. "Unstructured" files are excluded, so we are looking for an approach that achieves the aim of exclusion of some manual records. The second "whereas" reinforces the approach that the structure mechanism is intended to be a clear set of criteria, so a date may not be acceptable. The third "whereas" makes clear the state has a discretion in this area to set out two criteria, for organisation and for access; the fourth "whereas" reinforces the message that only some manual files are intended to be covered.

Further assistance, persuasive only, might be found by looking at the provenance of this aspect of the Directive. It comes from the German Federal

4–21

Data Protection Act under which some manual files are covered, for example structured sets of data such as card indexes, forms and questionnaires or sortable microfiche.

In the Bundesdatenschutzgesetz (BDSG) Federal Data Protection Act 1993, "data file" means:

"(a)   set of personal data which can be evaluated according to specific characteristics by means of automated procedures (automated data file); or

(b)   any other set of personal data which is similarly structured and can be arranged, rearranged and evaluated according to specific characteristics (non-automated data file).

This shall not include records and sets of records, unless they can be rearranged and evaluated by means of automated procedures.

File means any other document serving official purposes; this shall include image and sound recording media. It shall not include drafts and notes that are not intended to form part of a record."

In the Hessian Data Protection Act (1986), "data file" means:

"(a)   any set of data of which use can be made by means of automated procedures (automated file); or

(b)   any similarly structured set of data which can be organised and used according to specific criteria (non-automated file).""Record" means any document serving an official purpose.

As there is a degree of leeway open to the Member State on this issue and there is an ambiguity in the definition it may be relevant to consider the parliamentary debates and here the issue of the coverage of manual data was canvassed.

Speaking in the debate on the Third Reading in the House of Lords in February 1998, Lord Williams made clear that it was the Government's intention that the definition should be restricted so it covered only highly structured records such as files indexed by sections. The Government introduced an amendment at Report Stage in the House of Lords on March 16, 1998 which altered "particular information" to "specific information" to seek to ensure that the term only covered highly structured files:

"The intention of the wording is that it should only catch manual records where the internal content of the record is structured, rather than catching any file simply because it has the name of an individual on the cover. The restrictive meaning would appear to be consistent with the Directive, it is important to realise that it does not have any bearing on the purpose of files but simply to their internal organisation."

4–22   In *Durant*[31] the Court of Appeal considered the four files to which the applicant sought access:

•   Documents relating to part of the complaint about the systems and controls, which Barclay's bank was obliged to maintain which was arranged in date order.

---

[31] See fn.3 above.

- Documents relating to his complaint held on a file containing complaints received from customers on Barclay's bank. These were behind a divider marked with his name but the papers were not internally structured.
- Documents relating to his complaint on a file relating to issues or cases concerning Barclay's Bank. This contained a sub-filed marked with his name and including documents relating to his complaint but neither the file nor the sub-file was indexed in any way save that his name was on the sub-file.
- A sheaf of papers held by the Company Secretariat of the FSA relating to Mr Durant's complaint about the FSA's refusal to disclose information about its investigation of his complaint about Barclay's Bank. This was not organised by date or any other criteria.

The Court considered the provenance of the definition, referring to art.2(c) and, recital 27. The Court also referred to recitals 11 and 15 as support for a narrow meaning of the term. This may be doubtful as recital 11 merely reflects the provenance of the Directive as having its roots in the 1981 Convention and it is suggested that the judicial attempt to narrow the scope of the Directive to the scope of material covered by the Convention was misconceived. Moreover, the natural reading of recital 15 would limit it to sound and image data on identifiable persons.

In any event the Court concluded:

"that 'a relevant filing system' for the purpose of the Act, is limited to a system:

1) in which the files forming part of it are structured or referenced in such a way as clearly to indicate at the outset of the search whether specific information capable of amounting to personal data of an individual requesting it under section 7 is held within the system and, if so, in which file or files is it held; and

2) which has as part of its own structure or referencing mechanism, a sufficiently sophisticated and detailed means of readily indicating whether and where in an individual file or files specific criteria or information about the applicant can be readily located".

None of the files which Mr Durant sought would be covered by the definition.

In reviewing his conclusion, Auld L.J. referred to the analysis in the earlier edition of this text. As noted earlier, it has subsequently become apparent that the narrow interpretation of the term was one of the points on which the Commission considered that the UK law was deficient in its implementation. However the position may have been resolved by the issuing of guidance by the UK Commissioner which recommends a rather less absolute approach than that taken in *Durant*.[32]

---

[32] "What is data for the purposes of the DPA?", v.1, January 28, 2009.

Category (e) data

4–23   This is the new aspect of the defintion inserted by the Freedom of Information Act 2000 (FOIA) and covers recorded information held by a public authority which does not fall within any of paras (a)–(d). Public authority has the same meaning in the DPA as in the FOIA. The impact is covered fully in Ch.26.

Prima facie the amendment makes a massive extension to the personal information covered by the DPA where public authorities are concerned. As long as the information is reduced to some recorded form (s.84 of the FOIA defines "information" for this purpose as "information recorded in any form") then, if it relates to a living individual who can be identified by that data or that and other information in the hands of the data controller, it is covered by the DPA. However the data is exempt from the impact of all the Principles and the remainder of the Act's provisions other than those covering subject access, obligations in respect of accuracy and rights to rectification and compensation.

Data held by the authority

4–24   The new category of information must be "held" by the public authority, whereas for other data within the definition it must be "processed". Although a different term is used there does not appear to be a material difference between the two.

The section provides that the term "held" shall be construed in accordance with s.3(2) of the FOIA. This does not assist as it merely provides that information is held by a public authority if it is held otherwise than on behalf of another person or is held by another on behalf of the authority. It is included to make clear that it is control of and rights to the information that are decisive, not mere custody.

Structured manual data

4–25   Section 69 of the FOIA adds a new s.9A to the DPA which contains special provisions for the exercise of the right of subject access to the new category of information. The intention is to restrict the obligation on public authorities to giving access to that data which can be found with resonable endeavours. Otherwise the general extension of the definition in (e) would have meant that on a subject access request the authority would have to find every single piece of paper on which the individual had ever written, every old letter in which he/she was mentioned or which was copied to him or her, every tattle of information about him or her. The volume of information with an individual's "fingerprints" on it in an organisation where a person has worked for any length of time is inevitable enormous. The public authority would prima facie be required to find and deliver it all. The problem is tackled by:

●   introducing a further sub-division into the new category which divides it into structured and unstructured information; and

●   restricting access to the unstructured information to that which is described by the data subject and falls within the costs limits as prescribed by the Secretary of State.

Somewhat confusingly, s.9A(1) introduces this further division into the categories of personal data by defining "unstructured personal data". It defines "unstructured personal data" by exclusion as:

"any personal data falling within paragraph (e) of the definition of 'data' in section 1(1), other than information which is recorded as part of, or with the intention that it should form part of, any set of information relating to individuals to the extent that the set is structured by reference to individuals or by reference to criteria relating to individuals."

Thus the definition repeats material parts of the definition of "relevant filing system" in s.1(1). That definition has been discussed above. A relevant filing system is ". . . any . . . set of information [which] is structured, either by reference to individuals or by reference to criteria relating to individuals, *in such a way that specific information relating to a particular individual is readily accessible"* (emphasis added).

In effect, therefore, the amendment introduces a new definition of "structured manual data". For personal data to fall into this definition there must be a set of information and thus something coherent or defining about the nature of the data in order to regard it as a set. The information set must relate to living individuals. The set must have an internal structure and that internal structure must be dictated by reference to individuals or criteria relating to them. To that extent it is the same as the definition of a relevant filing system, however there is no requirement that the specific information must be "readily accessible". Thus a file arranged in date order would be covered as long as it had the name of the individual on the cover or was referenced by some criteria relating to that individual.

4–26

Data controller

This definition is divided into two parts. The first part in s.1(1) is:

4–27

"A person who (either alone or jointly or in common with other persons) determines the purposes for which and the manner in which any personal data are, or are to be processed."

The second part is found in s.1(4) and provides that where personal data are processed only for purposes for which they are required by or under any enactment to be processed, the person on whom the obligation to process the data is imposed by or under that enactment is for the purposes of this Act the data controller.

Note that the second part of the definition does not require a specific clause in a statute referring to the technical nature of processing data, but it will apply where the statute or regulation imposes an obligation which involves the use of information which is then processed as data. The obligation may be imposed on either a public or a private body, for example an employer may be required to keep records of employees' tax and national insurance by a statutory provision and this provision would cover such data. If the controller delegates the responsibility for the processing to a third party such as a data processor it will remain responsible as data controller for the processing.

The term "jointly" has come from both the Directive and the 1984 definition of data user. However, the term "in common" does not appear in the Directive and appears to have been derived from the 1984 Act. In the Guide in dealing with the terms jointly or in common, it is said:

> "The term 'jointly' is used where two or more persons (usually organisations) act together to decide the purpose and manner of any data processing. The term 'in common' applies where two or more persons share a pool of personal data that they process independently of each other."

This echoes very closely the guidance given over the same terms used in the 1984 Act. The point has never been tested but it is difficult to attribute any other meaning to the terms and it is suggested this is an appropriate working definition to apply. The Guidance does not however deal with the issue of split determination, for example where one party decides on the purpose of the processing and the other decides on the manner of the processing.

4–28   A data controller determines the purposes for which and the manner in which personal data are processed. The concept of determining purposes is relatively straightforward and the same term is used in the Directive. However, the phrase "the manner in which data are processed" is more obscure. In the Directive, the wording used is "controls the means of the processing". One possibility is that the term refers to the person who has authority over the choice of the particular types of processing, for example whether by erasure or disclosure or otherwise. It does not appear to mean that the controller has to exercise that authority in each instance and he may be able to delegate it within a range of possibilities to the data processor. However, the controller will be the person who retains the ultimate power to determine whether data should be, for example, retained or disseminated. This appears to be the view taken by the OIC. In the Guide it states:

> "... we take the view that having some discretion about the smaller details of implementing data processing (i.e. the manner of processing) does not make a persona a data controller.
> So when deciding who is a data controller we place greatest weight on purpose –identifying whose decision to achieve a 'business' purpose has led to personal data being processed".

4–29   The extent of control over the purpose of processing and the manner will be relevant in determining whether a body is a controller or a processor. In Opinion 10.2006 on the processing of personal data by the Society for Worldwide Interbank Financial Telecommunications (SWIFT) the Article 29 Working Party considered whether SWIFT should be regarded as a processor or a controller under the Directive. It took the view that SWIFT could not be regarded as a mere processor because SWIFT had, "taken on specific responsibilities which go beyond the set of instructions and duties incumbent on a processor". It decided on the location of its facilities, security levels, services offered and standards or processing. It should be noted that this opinion is persuasive at most however the Belgium Commissioner took a similar view. The importance of establishing which party is a controller and which a processor in commercial relationships is covered in Ch.7 in relation to the appointment of data processors.

Data processor

The definition of data processor is in s.1(1) and: **4–30**

> "in relation to personal data, means any person (other than an employee of the data controller) who processes the data on behalf of the data controller."

The Directive provides that a processor, "shall mean a natural or legal person, public authority agency or other body which processes personal data on behalf of the controller". There are some slight changes in the wording in the UK Act but they do not appear to make any material difference. A processor is similar to a computer bureau under the 1984 Act but the 1984 Act covered those who processed "as agent" for the user. This produced a degree of regulatory control over the middleman or broker in information terms. In the 1998 Act only those who either determine the purposes or the manner of processing are covered. List brokers, who were covered by the 1984 Act, are unlikely to be covered. The definition does, however, extend the range of the processor in another area because it includes the person who disseminates information or who collects it. On this basis it might be wide enough to cover electronic publishing and wide enough to cover those who collect information on behalf of another or others. There is no requirement in the definition that a person must have a direct relationship with the controller and it is submitted that where a processor sub-contracts elements of processing to another that other will also be a processor for the data controller. The requirements to impose appropriate obligations on such persons should be dealt with in the agreements between the parties. The line between whether a party is a controller or a processor has become less clear with the development of more sophisticated services in which the party providing the services determines much of the functionality and extent of the service available. The Article 29 WP has issued an Opinion on the determination however it does not always seem consistent. While the parties can (and should) declare clearly in their contracts which is the controller and which is the processor this will not be determinative if in fact the role of the processor becomes so dominant that it effectively takes control of much of the scope of the processing.

Data subject

There is no definition of "data subject" in the Directive, but one has been included in the Act simply as an individual who is a subject of personal data.   **4–31**

Obtaining, recording, using and disclosing

Each of these activities comes within the definition of processing. Processing, in relation to information or data, means carrying out any of the processing activities "on the information or data".   **4–32**

Given the breadth of that definition it is not apparent why the additional provision has been included in s.1(2) which reads:

"In this Act, unless the context otherwise requires:

(a)   'obtaining' or 'recording' in relation to personal data, includes obtaining or recording the information to be contained in the data, and

(b)   'using' or 'disclosing' in relation to personal data, includes using or disclosing the information contained in the data."

Section 1(2) makes clear that the terms include the same actions in relation to information contained in personal data. Possibly this provision was included to ensure that any disclosure *from* personal data would count as a disclosure *of* personal data irrespective of the fact that identifying particulars might not be disclosed. In *Rooney*[33] the Court of Appeal ruled that the disclosure of information contained in personal data did not require that the identity of the individual must be disclosed.

Third party

4–33   A further set of definitions are found in s.70 of the Act. Of these, "third party" is a key definition derived from the Directive:

"In relation to personal data it means any person other than:

(a)   the data subject;

(b)   the data controller or;

(c)   any data processor or other person authorised to process data for the controller or processor."

Accordingly, an employee or an agent will not be a third party. The term "third party" will only refer to those outside the ambit of the data controllers' authority. The definition is taken, unchanged, from the Directive. It is important in relation to the application of the fair obtaining and processing "code" now incorporated in Sch.I, which requires notice to be given to third parties in some circumstances.

Recipient

4–34   The definition of recipient is also found in s.70:

"In relation to personal data [it] means any person to whom the data are disclosed, including any person (such as an employee or agent of the data controller, a data processor or an employee or agent of a data processor) to whom they are disclosed in the course of processing the data for the data controller, but does not include any person to whom disclosure is or may be made as a result of or with a view to a particular enquiry by or on behalf of that person made in the exercise of any power conferred by law."

---

[33] *R. v Rooney* [2006] EWCA Crim 1841.

A recipient is any person who obtains a disclosure of data and includes employees or agents who would not be regarded as third parties. However, it has an exclusion for those who obtain a disclosure because of legal powers. Recipient is a relevant term in relation to notification. If a person is not a recipient within the terms of the definition the notification need not cover them.

The term comes from the Directive, in which

> "recipient shall mean a natural or legal person, public authority, agency, or any other body to whom data are disclosed, whether a third party or not. However, authorities which may receive data in the framework of a particular enquiry shall not be regarded as recipients."[34]

Consent

Consent is not defined in the 1998 Act. In art.2(h) of the Directive, "the data subject's consent" shall mean

4-35

> "any freely given, specific and informed indication of his wishes by which the data subject signifies his agreement to personal data relating to him being processed".

Consent is one of the grounds on which personal data may be processed legitimately under art.7(a) ("the data subject has unambiguously given his consent"), sensitive data held under art.8, ("the data subject has given his explicit consent to the processing of those data") or personal data transferred overseas to a jurisdiction without adequate protection under art.26(1)(a) ("the data subject has given his consent unambiguously to the proposed transfer").

In the Act, the provisions of art.7(a) are enacted in Sch.2 para.1 in relation to the legitimising grounds for processing personal data, as "the data subject has given his consent to the processing". The art.8 provision in Sch.3 para.1, in relation to sensitive data, is rendered as "the data subject has given his explicit consent to the processing of the personal data". The art.26 provision is rendered in Sch.4 para.1 in relation to overseas transfers as "the data subject has given his consent to the transfer".

As the definition in art.2(h) covers all consent, both for legitimising processing and allowing the processing of sensitive personal data, it is perhaps best approached by regarding the art.2(h) standard as the threshold requirement for all forms of consent, and examining the further requirement for "explicit" consent in Sch.3 para.1 in the light of that.

Article 29 Working Party Opinion on the definition of consent[35]

The Article 29 WP issued an Opinion on consent in 2011 which explores the nature and application of consent. Although much of it is useful and unexceptional it continues to maintain a troublingly absolutist approach which does not appear to be consistent with EU case law.

4-36

---

[34] Art.2(g).
[35] WP 187 01197/11/EN.

In earlier papers, the WP has explored the question of the requirements for valid consent and in one paper suggested that free consent means a voluntary decision,

"... by an individual in possession of all of his facilities, taken in the absence of coercion of any kind, be it social, financial, psychological or other".[36]

It has suggested that consent which is required as a condition of employment cannot be a valid consent.[37] In real life, and in the cases before the UK courts and the ECtHR, consent is rarely so pure. Consent may be grumbling or reluctant but still be consent. Parties often achieve consent at the end of negotiation, whether in the social or economic or personal context, in which the resolution is not wholly satisfactory to both but both freely agree that it is the best achievable outcome. Coercion is a vague term and may come in many degrees, from the child pestering for sweets to the violent partner demanding sex; within that range there are examples where consent can be valid and others where it clearly cannot.

Consent has been considered in some cases brought before the European Court of Human Rights under the Human Rights Convention. The Court has held that individuals are capable of consenting to waive qualified rights under the Convention. In *Stedman v UK*[38] a Christian employee had been required to work on Sundays and had been dismissed for refusing to do so. The Court held that she could not claim breach of her rights under art.9 (the right to freedom of thought conscience and religion) where the obligation to work was a contractual obligation and she was free to resign. The Court held that there was no interference as the individual had a choice as to the employment and had chosen that particular job. She had consented to the breach of her rights. Similar reasoning was applied in the case of *X v United Kingdom*.[39]Whether this would represent the position of the Court if it had to decide a similar case today has been flagged by the Equality and Human Rights Commission[40] but it remains the current position. In relation to art.8 it appears that, if true consent is obtained to an action, there will be no breach of the right. The absolutist view of the WP therefore has been difficult to reconcile with the case law and real life. In the Opinion it cites the decision of the European Court of Human Rights in the case of *Pfieffer v Germany*[41] as support for its views; however in that case the Court did not decide that individual consent was invalid or ineffective, rather that a "consent" purported to be given on behalf of employees by the trade union under a collective agreement did not amount to the real consent of the individual worker. The case was on the Working Time Directive and concerned an attempt to undermine the restriction to 48 hours by incorporating a term agreed with the Trade Union into the employment contract.

The Court held that this did not amount to a consent for the purposes of the law, saying:

---

[36] WP 131.
[37] WP 48.
[38] [1997] E.H.R.L.R. 545.
[39] [1981] 22D.R.27.
[40] See submission by the Equality and Human Rights Commission to the ECtHR in *Eweida and Chaplin* in pending applications 48420/10 and 59842/10.
[41] Joined cases C-397/01 to C-403/01.

"81.   In paragraph 74 of Simap , the Court concluded that the consent given by trade-union representatives in the context of a collective or other agreement is not equivalent to that given by the worker himself, as provided for in the first indent of Article 18(1)(b)(i) of Directive 93/104.

82.   That interpretation derives from the objective of Directive 93/104, which seeks to guarantee the effective protection of the safety and health of workers by ensuring that they actually have the benefit of, inter alia, an upper limit on weekly working time and minimum rest periods. Any derogation from those minimum requirements must therefore be accompanied by all the safeguards necessary to ensure that, if the worker concerned is encouraged to relinquish a social right which has been directly conferred on him by the directive, he must do so freely and with full knowledge of all the facts. Those requirements are all the more important given that the worker must be regarded as the weaker party to the employment contract and it is therefore necessary to prevent the employer being in a position to disregard the intentions of the other party to the contract or to impose on that party a restriction of his rights without him having expressly given his consent in that regard. . . .

84.   It follows that, for a derogation from the maximum period of weekly working time laid down in Article 6 of Directive 93/104 (48 hours) to be valid, the worker's consent must be given not only individually but also expressly and freely.

85.   Those conditions are not met where the worker's employment contract merely refers to a collective agreement authorising an extension of maximum weekly working time. It is by no means certain that, when he entered into such a contract, the worker concerned knew of the restriction of the rights conferred on him by Directive 93/104."

It did not, however, say that consent is not possible in an employment context. It follows that we have grave doubts as to whether the Article 29 position actually represents the current state of European law. While it may be challenging to obtain a valid consent in the employment context it appears to be legally possible.

UK case law

Consent is an area in which there is a variety of UK case law, drawn from different areas of law, particularly contract law, criminal law and confidentiality cases. The following principles have been applied in relation to the question of consent.[42] A UK court considering the issue of consent is likely to have regard to this background.

4–37

No one can consent to something of which he has no knowledge.[43] It follows that consent must be given in advance of the action to which the person consents. Subsequent agreement may amount to a later authorization or ratification but cannot be described as consent. Consent may be express or inferred from some relevant action (implied consent) but cannot be inferred from silence[44]:

"Consent involves some affirmative acceptance, not merely a standing by and absence of objection. The affirmative acceptance may be in writing, which is the

---

[42] Some of the cases are taken from the useful discussion of consent in the criminal law in Law Commission Consultation Paper No.139.

[43] *Re Caughey Ex p. Ford* (1876) 1 Ch. D. 521.

[44] *Attorney General v Jonathan Cape* (the "Crossman Diaries") case) [1975] 3 All E.R. 484.

clearest obviously; it may be oral; it may conceivably even be by conduct, such as nodding the head in a specific way in response to an express request for consent. But it must be something more than merely standing by and not objecting".[45]

The case of *Levi Strauss & Co v Tesco Plc*[46] is authority for the proposition that whilst consent cannot be inferred from silence it could be inferred from conduct. In the data protection area consent is often inferred from some action such as the click of a mouse or the return of a form coupled with a full notice brought to the attention of the data subject.

A person cannot consent to a contract if he was incapable of understanding the nature of the contract.[47] A document may be pleaded as not binding a person under the doctrine "non est factum" where he was induced to sign a document containing a contract which is fundamentally different in character from what he contemplated.[48] In *R. v Jheeta*[49] it was accepted that a consent to sexual relations which was brought about by deception practiced on the victim was not a true consent. In this case the victim was not deceived as to the nature of the act and it may be seen as verging on coercion. Mere notice of something in respect of which the individual has no choice and from which they cannot escape is not a consent even if the document signed states that the individual consents.[50]

4–38   Consent obtained by coercion or duress is not true consent and may be set aside. In relation to a criminal charge duress affords a defence which if proved exonerates the defendant altogether but the cases on duress in criminal matters are not likely to be of much assistance with a data protection case. The pressure of undue influence by another may in some circumstances nullify apparent consent in civil claims. The line between duress or undue influence so as to vitiate consent on the one hand and reluctant but genuine consent on the other is a difficult one. In more recent cases the courts seem to have taken a broader view as to what may vitiate consent. In *The Sibeon* the commercial court took the view that commercial pressure could not vitiate consent, however, later cases have acknowledged that economic pressure can amount to duress so as to vitiate consent. In *Pau On v Lau Yiu Long*[51] a dictum indicates that economic pressure can amount to duress so as to vitiate consent:

"There is nothing contrary to principle in recognising economic duress as a factor which may render a contract voidable provided always that the basis of such recognition is that it must amount to a coercion of the will, which vitiates consent. It must be shown that the payment made or the contract entered into was not a voluntary act".

4–39   Reluctant consent may be valid consent as long as it is voluntary; relevant factors to consider will be whether the person protested, or had an alternative open to him, or was independently advised. Consent must be distinguished from

---

[45] *Bell v Alfred Franks & Bartlett Co Ltd* [1980] 1 All E.R. 356; applied in *Trustees of the Methodist Secondary School Trust Deed v O'Leary* (1993) 25 H.L.R. 364.
[46] Case C-415/99 [2002] Ch.109.
[47] *Boughton v Knight* (1873) L.R. 3 P.D. 64.
[48] *Lewis v Clay* (1897) 67 L.J.Q.B. 224.
[49] [2007] EWCA Crim 1699.
[50] *Volker und Marcus Schecke GbR v Land Hessen* (C-92/09) [2012] All E.R. (EC) 127.
[51] [1980] A.C. 614.

acquiescence or submission. *Hirani v Hirani*[52] indicates that the courts have been taking a broader view of the circumstances which can vitiate consent. In this case P, the daughter of Hindu parents, had formed an association with a young Indian Muslim. The parents arranged a marriage for the young woman with a man of their own religion whom she had never met. The marriage took place but was never consummated. P left her husband, R, and petitioned for a nullity on the grounds of duress exercised by her parents, on whom she was wholly dependent and who had threatened to turn her out of home unless she went through with the marriage. The Court of Appeal held that the crucial question was whether the threats or pressures were such as to overbear the will of the individual and destroy the reality of consent. Duress, whatever form it took, was a coercion of the will so as to vitiate consent. This was followed by the factually similar Scottish case of *Mahmood v Mahmood*.[53]

Drunken consent remains valid as long as the person was capable of knowing what they were doing *R. v Bree*[54] (although the possibility that data controllers will start plying reticent data subjects with strong drink in order to persuade them to consent to data processing activities, such as overseas transfers of data, seems remote).

4–40

As far as capacity to consent applies an individual reaches majority at 18 years of age and under the Family Law Reform Act 1969 s.1(1) is presumed to have sufficient maturity to consent to any medical treatment or enter into a legal contract for him or herself, unless he or she suffers from mental incapacity. Young persons aged between 16 and 17 can consent to medical treatment to the same extent as someone of full age.[55] Children may exercise some rights or consent to the exercise of such rights as long as they are capable of understanding the import of the relevant matters and a person with parental responsibility for a child may give consent to a lawful activity for the child provided he or she acts in the child's best interests.

An individual may be enabled to exercise choice and consent on behalf of another under a Lasting Power of Attorney under the Mental Capacity Act 2005. Speaking in the debate in the House of Lords in answer to a question as to why no definition of consent had been included in the Bill, Lord Williams responded that it was not considered necessary in view of the existing approach in the law. It is suggested that this is supported by the range and nature of the cases cited above. As noted above, art.2(h) of the Directive requires that consent must:

(a)   be freely given;
(b)   be specific;
(c)   be informed; and
(d)   consist of any indication by which he [the data subject] signifies agreement.

---

[52] (1983) F.L.R. 232.
[53] (1993) S.L.T. 589.
[54] [2007] EWCA Crim 804.
[55] Family Law Reform Act 1969 s.8(1).

Freely given

4–41   While consent may be free even if it is reluctant, consideration should be given to the degree of choice open to the individual. It is suggested that a standard industry practice for information uses which effectively deprive the individual of a choice may be questionable where such uses are not essential for the purposes of the contract. As the cases illustrate consent may be freely given even where the giver would prefer not to have to give it. As noted earlier the Article 29 Working Party has considered the giving of consent in the context of employment and has suggested that much consent given to uses of personal data as part of an employment contract is not "freely given", although it accepts that consent cannot be completely excluded as a basis for processing. It is suggested that this is going too far. The entire basis of contractual relationships is that the parties give something in order to gain something. Individuals accept the restraints of working life in order to earn money and may consent to data uses within that context. As noted above the ECtHR has confirmed that individuals may choose to consent to waive their rights.

Specific

4–42   It is not clear what this means. It can be argued that it suggests that the consent should be specific to the processing or the purpose. Vague and generalised consent clauses are brought into question by this requirement but it does not mean that consent cannot be obtained to broad purposes or that consent must relate to a short time only. Clauses can be specific in different ways. For example a clause can be specific in terms of duration if it says "two days" or "two years" or "during your lifetime". Each one describes a specific term. It is suggested that consent clauses can be broad as long as they are very clear about all relevant matters. The level of specificity may be related to the degree of intrusiveness of the processing and the nature of the data to be processed; the more intrusive the purpose the more detailed the notice and consent should be.

Informed

4–43   The data subject need not be aware of every detail of the processing but must be aware of the fundamental nature of the processing and any important features which might particularly affect him. The degree of knowledge and understanding necessary to make consent valid was considered by the High Court in *Johnson*[56] and the particular finding does not appear to have been disturbed by the Court of Appeal. Mr Johnson entered into an agreement with the Medical Defence Union for membership by an agreement the consent clause of which included the following words:

> "I agree that by renewing my membership I consent to [XX] processing personal information about me, including sensitive personal data (Personal Data) for administration of my membership, the insurance policy and indemnity claims, risk management, marketing and advisory purposes . . .".

---

[56] See fn.22.

His membership was not renewed because he was regarded as posing a high risk of making a claim on the funds. He argued that he had not been properly told of the use of his personal data for the purpose of assessing the risk. The Court held that the notification in the clause was sufficient. In doing so it appears to have taken into account the nature and state of knowledge of the individual:

> "I consider that the application of any proper consideration by a doctor to the terms of the processing agreement would or should have informed him sufficiently of the likely ambit of the 'risk management' referred to".[57]

Consist of an indication of agreement

Mere passive acquiescence with no indication of response will not be enough. This has not so far rung the death-knell of the "opt-out" approach to "consent" but it is always preferable to seek a positive response where possible. "Opt-out" consent is obtained where a data controller notifies the data subject of a use to be made of personal data on some appropriate vehicle (like a reply coupon) which will be returned to the controller and states that if a particular action is not taken, usually a box ticked, the "consent" of the subject will be assumed. In such a case the argument runs that the data subject has impliedly consented by returning the vehicle with the box unchecked. However, because the subject may not have noticed the box or read the material sentence, it can be argued that there is no clear indication of agreement from the subject. The point has not been determined in any proceedings to date. A similar technique is commonly used on internet sites to obtain "consent" to send e-mail or sometimes other forms of marketing. A consent clause is included as part of the standard terms and conditions for the use of the website. The user must accept the terms and conditions by checking a box before he or she can proceed to use the site. A separate check box "opt-out" option appears on the site which the user can complete. The combination of the two provides a consent mechanism. It would of course be a question of fact and degree whether the consent was valid and freely given in any particular case. Relevant considerations might also be that such "consent" is usually only used for the sending of direct marketing material, and consumers are increasingly aware of the existence of such boxes and tend to look out for them if they have a dislike of such marketing. **4–44**

Unambiguous consent

This is required by art.7(a) under which consent is the basis for legitimising processing. In the 1998 Act the relevant provision is found in Sch.2 para.1: **4–45**

> "The data subject has given his consent to the processing".

It is suggested that the appearance of the adjective "unambiguous" in the equivalent provision in the Directive strengthens the argument that consent must entail a clear indication of the agreement of the individual to the particular processing.

---

[57] Fn.22.

Explicit consent

4–46 This is required by art.8 where consent is the basis for processing sensitive personal data. In the 1998 Act the relevant provision is found in Sch.3 para.1:

> "The data subject has given his explicit consent to the processing of the personal data".

It is not clear whether the term "explicit" applies to the record of the consent or the nature of the consent itself. It can be argued that it requires a written or other permanent record. In either case, it reinforces the need for any consent for the processing of sensitive personal data to be specific and informed. Furthermore, the existence of appropriate consent will be a matter of fact and degree, to be judged in the light of the particular data, the processing at issue and other relevant facts.

APPLICATION TO THE CROWN AND TO THE HOUSES OF PARLIAMENT

4–47 There are specific provisions dealing with the application of the Act to the Crown and the Houses of Parliament. Under s.63 the act binds the Crown and for the purposes of the Act each Government Department is treated as a person separate from each other Government Department. Section 60(3) sets out the relevant controllers for the Crown being in relation to the Royal Household the Keeper of the Privy Purse, in relation to the Duchy of Lancaster such person as the Chancellor of Lancaster appoints and in relation to the Duchy of Cornwall such person as the Duke of Cornwall or the possessor for the time being of the Duchy appoints. Neither Government Departments nor the three data controllers for the Crown can be prosecuted but they are still bound by ss.54A and 55 and the obligations to provide assistance with the execution of warrants.

4–48   The Houses of Parliament are bound by the Act[58] where personal data is processed by or on their behalf. The relevant data controller is the Corporate Officer of the relevant House. The Corporate Officers are not liable to prosecution but are also bound by s.55 and the obligation to provide assistance with the execution of warrants.

TERRITORIAL APPLICATION

4–49 The Directive applies to the 27 Member States of the EU and also to Norway, Iceland and Liechtenstein.[59] Section 5 sets out the limits of processing covered by the UK Act. In doing so it follows art.4 of the Directive and Recitals 18–20. The general rule is that a controller who is established in an EEA state and processes personal data in the context of that establishment must follow the national law

---

[58] s.63A inserted by the Freedom of Information Act 2000.
[59] Decision of the EEA Joint Committee No.83/1999 of 25 June 1999 amending protocol 37 and Annex XI (Telecommunications services) to the EEA Agreement OJ L296/41 of November 23, 2000.

applicable to the place in which he is established. If the controller has relevant establishments in more than one EEA state he must follow the relevant national law applicable to each one for the processing attributable to each one. Under art.17(3) the processor contract required with a data processor must stipulate that the processor shall follow the security obligations required by art.17(1) as defined in the law of the Member State in which the processor is established. It follows that the concept of establishment is important, for example in those countries in which the law imposes specific security obligations on data processors such processors may be subject to different obligations to those applicable to the controller. Section 5(3) sets out those circumstances in which controllers are to be treated as being established in the United Kingdom.

Establishment

Section 5(3) provides that an individual who is ordinarily resident in the United Kingdom is treated as established here. The concept of ordinary residence is found in other areas of law. A corporate body will be treated as established in the United Kingdom if it is incorporated under UK law. In a similar way a partnership or other unincorporated association formed under UK law will be treated as being established in the United Kingdom. Any other person, which term includes individuals and bodies corporate and unincorporate, who does not fall within one of the three categories referred to above will be treated as established if they maintain a "regular practice" in the United Kingdom, or an office branch or agency through which they carry on any activity.   **4–50**

The concept of a "branch" applies in the rules governing the registration in the United Kingdom of companies incorporated overseas. A "branch" in this sense is not the same as the commonly used term of a branch office. It is a term used in Community law for an organisational sub-division of a company which has some degree of both identity and independence. A branch can consist of more than one office. An office is likely to involve a less substantial presence than a branch and an agency may mean that the controller has no employees in the jurisdiction but merely another who acts on his behalf. It is not clear whether the term "agent" here is used in the sense of one who has the power to enter into a legally binding arrangement on the part of his principal, or the broader general sense of one who acts on behalf of another. It is suggested that the latter is the more likely meaning. The Recitals at 19 deal with the concept of establishment:

> "whereas establishment on the territory of a Member State implies the effective and real exercise of activity through stable arrangements: whereas the legal form of such an establishment, whether simply branch or a subsidiary with a legal personality, is not the determining factor in this respect".

Accordingly, the test is not intended to be one of legal formalism and a purposive approach should be taken.

In each case not only must the controller be established in the United Kingdom but there must be data "processed in the context of that establishment".   **4–51**

The term "in the context of" is not further defined. It is taken directly from art.4(1)(a). It suggests that the processing is carried out in the course of the activities and within the control of the relevant establishment. As long as the processing is controlled by the data controller in the context of the establishment therefore it does not matter where the actual processing takes place. The processing of personal data by a data processor in a third country will remain subject to the Act as long as it is in the context of the establishment in the UK. The question of such control will be a question of fact. It would be possible for personal data to be processed in several Member States but processed in the context of only one establishment. In WP paper 179 the example is given of an EU wide direct marketing activity directed from one state. The WP paper suggests that the law of the state of establishment would apply. While this may be technically correct it feels uncomfortable and we would recommend that the data controller should still apply the local law on notice and choice, particularly if stricter than the law of establishment.

The test of establishment should be the same throughout the EEA. However in considering establishment in another jurisdiction is would also be prudent to have regard to any specific rules or interpretation applicable in that jurisdiction.

The High Court considered the territorial scope of the Act in *Douglas v Hello!*[60] This case arose from the dispute between *Hello!* magazine and *OK!* over the publication of the photographs of the wedding of Michael Douglas and Catherine Zeta-Jones. The main judgment is covered in Ch.2. Mr Ramey was a New York based photographer who was alleged to have obtained the photographs of the wedding which later appeared in *Hello!* He succeeded in his application to have service on him set aside arguing that he had no joint liability for the publication of the material and that he was not subject to the Data Protection Act 1998 as, even if he was a data controller within the terms of the Act, he was neither established in the United Kingdom nor did he make use of any equipment here so as to bring him within the Act.

Representatives

4–52   In some circumstances, a controller who is not established in the United Kingdom or another EEA state must nominate a representative who is established in the United Kingdom. This obligation falls on a data controller who uses equipment in the United Kingdom for data processing and is not established in any EEA state; in other words, is responsible for processing of personal data here but is not subject to the Directive. An example would be a US corporation with no office or establishment in the United Kingdom but a server which was serviced by an employee who worked from home. If it purchased marketing lists with the names of United Kingdom consumers and processed those using its server and its own employee in the United Kingdom it would be "using equipment" in the United Kingdom and would have to nominate a representative.[61] The position is not clear where the overseas data controller uses the services of a third party. It can be argued that in such a case they do not "use" equipment in the United Kingdom. They may cause it to be used or it may be used on their behalf but they may not be regarded as using it themselves and thus may not require to nominate a representative however the contrary interpretation is also arguable. The Article 29

---

[60] December 3, 2002.
[61] See the discussion of this point and the meaning of the term "using" earlier.

WP Opinion on applicable law[62] suggests that the data controller does not need to exercise ownership or full control over the equipment in order to fall into this aspect of the definition. It also suggests that "equipment" should be treated as equivalent to "means" which is used in other language versions. As a result it considers that the use of surveys or questionnaires would bring an entity into scope as would the use of outsourced processors in the EEA or the use of cookies placed on the computers of users.

It also considers the extent to which the relevant EU law would apply in such cases, whether only for the periods that the personal data are processed in the EU or throughout its lifecycle and wherever it is. The Article 29 paper takes the broader view but accepts that this has some strange consequences for the scope of the Directive. It is submitted that this goes too far and a less expansive interpretation should apply.

Where a representative is required (and if the Article 29 paper is correct that would be on many occasions) the representative is to be nominated "for the purposes of this Act". The intention appears to be that the nominated representative will be responsible for ensuring compliance with the UK Act for the processing which takes place in the United Kingdom. However the section does not in terms impose any such responsibility, and it is not clear how the Commissioner's powers or the individual rights apply to such a representative.

4–53

The arrangements set out in s.5 are subject to any additional provisions which may be made under s.54 in respect of actions to be taken by the Commissioner at the request of a supervisory authority in another EEA state. For a discussion of s.54 see Ch.10.

Diplomatic arrangements

The Directive also requires that the law shall apply in any place where the national law applies by virtue of international public law. This relates to the laws which apply in respect of embassies or consulates or in relation to ships and airplanes. In general terms embassies and consulates are not subject to the law of the state in which they are situated but to the law of the state which they represent. The structure of the arrangements is set out in the 1961 Vienna Convention on Diplomatic Relations (VCDR) (and the Vienna Convention on Consular Relations 1963—CRA 1968) to which the United Kingdom is a party. The relevant provisions of the Convention are applied in the UK by the Diplomatic Privileges Act 1964 (DPA 1964) s.2.

4–54

The CPS website explains that diplomatic immunity in the UK is conferred on all entitled members of a foreign mission who have been notified to, and accepted by, the Foreign and Commonwealth Office (FCO) as performing a diplomatic function. Immunity is dependent on rank, and ranges from immunity from criminal and civil and administrative jurisdiction to immunity for official acts only.

The DPA 1964 confers immunity from criminal jurisdiction on diplomatic agents and their families. The FCO may request a waiver of a person's diplomatic immunity in order to arrest, interview under caution and, if appropriate, bring

---

[62] WP 179 Adopted December 2010.

charges and if a waiver is not agreed in certain cases the FCO may ask for the withdrawal of the individual and their family or declare them personae non gratae.

While diplomatic premises in the UK are part of UK territory, they may not be entered without the consent of the Ambassador or Head of Mission.[63] Offences committed in diplomatic premises in the UK are triable under the ordinary principles of English law, subject to the principles of diplomatic immunity for those who have it. Those who do not have this status (whatever their nationality) can be prosecuted as normal, as for example happened in the case of the terrorists who seized the Iranian embassy in London in 1980. The effect of the provision in the Directive therefore is that such UK diplomatic premises overseas must be subject to UK data protection law and premises used by other EU/EEA states in the UK will be subject to their national law.

Impact of the draft Regulation in brief[64]

4–55   The first point to make in terms of scope is that the draft Regulation would not apply to the processing of personal data by competent authorities for the purposes of the prevention, investigation, detection or prosecution of criminal offences or the execution of criminal penalties. These would fall under national law based on the proposed Directive. The second point is that the draft Regulation would have a significant impact on the territorial scope of EU data protection law. It would cover not only those data controllers and processors established in the EU but also data controllers based outside the EU who offer goods or services to EU residents or who monitor the behaviour of EU residents. This extra-territorial extension is the source of active lobbying as this is being written. There is also a change in the definition of personal data which would have an impact on scope. Personal data is any information relating to a data subject and a data subject is defined as an

> "identified natural person or a natural person who can be identified directly or indirectly by means reasonably likely to be used by the controller or by any other natural or legal person, in particular by reference to an identification number, location data, online identifier, or to one or more factors specific to the physical, physiological, genetic, mental, economic, cultural or social identity of that person".

This has the effect of incorporating all the more expansive views of the Article 29 WP (a trait common to most if not all of the provisions of the draft). The definition however still leaves open the question of which information could lead to identification and if adopted there will still be scope for intense disagreement on the issue.

The definition of consent is somewhat clarified and there are specific provisions dealing with the way that consent must be obtained in some cases. It is made explicit that data subjects always have the right to withdraw consent. Otherwise the definitions are not substantively different.

---

[63] DPA 1964 s.2(1) and Sch.3.
[64] See Ch.1 paras 1-68 onwards for an overview of the proposal as at January 2012.

ADDITIONAL MATERIALS

- Directive 95/46 (see Appendix B).
- Article 4, Recitals 18, 19, 20 (see also table above).
- Council of Europe Convention of January 28, 1981 for the Protection of Individuals with regard to automatic processing of Personal Data: art.2 defines "personal data", "automated data file", "automatic processing", "controller of the file".
- Data Protection Act 1984: see the table above and ss.38 (application to Government Departments), 39 (data held and services provided outside United Kingdom) and 41 (general interpretation).
- Organisation for Economic Co-operation and Development Guidelines: Annex Pt 1(a) and (b) define "data controller" and "personal data".

Hansard references

Vol.586, No.108, col.CWH5, Lords Grand Committee, February 23, 1998
Meaning of data, discussion of CCTV:

> "There is no doubt in our mind that 'operating automatically in response to instructions given for that purpose' covers text or image and storage and other processing
> (Lord Williams.)"

Vol.586, No.108, col.CWH8–10
Control of purpose and manner of processing, emails and whether service providers can be controllers for message content.
Vol.586, No.108, col.CWH15
Consent to be a matter for the courts.
Vol.587, No.95, col.467, Lords Report, March 16, 1998
Relevant filing system.
Vol.587, No.95, col.500
Consent and the use of tick-boxes.
Vol.587, No.95, col.625
Withdrawal of consent:

> "Any consent given in any part of the Bill may be withdrawn at any time and there is nothing to prevent that
> (Lord Williams)."

Commons Standing Committee D, May 12, 1998, cols 15–19
Personal data and information, meaning of the term information covers encrypted data; intention of the data controller when data is collected is relevant to the inclusion of data within a relevant filing system.
Commons Standing Committee D, May 12, 1998, cols 25–27
Meaning of establishment and territorial scope.
Commons Standing Committee D, May 12, 1998, cols 29–33
Data processor, personal data, processing and relevant filing system.
Commons Standing Committee D, May 12, 1998, cols 57–60
Territorial application.

Commons Standing Committee D, May 21, 1998
Necessary:

> "I shall deal first with the European provenance of the word 'necessary'. The Government accepts that the restrictions that it places on privacy in favour of freedom of expression must meet the European 'pressing social need' test of necessity, which is set out in Articles 8 and 10 of the European Convention of Human Rights. We also accept that the test embodies the European legal principle of proportionality."

Commons Standing Committee D, June 4, 1998, col.310
On consent and withdrawal of consent:

> "Consent that is withdrawn before it is acted on cannot be explicit consent. Consent can be explicit only for as long as the person giving it allows."

Vol. 315, No.198, cols 615–616, Commons Third Reading, July 2, 1998
Relevant filing system:

> "The definition of relevant filing system in clause 1(1) is based on the provisions of the directive. The Government's purpose has been to cover all the manual records that the directive requires Members States to cover, but to go no further than the directive requires."

CHAPTER 5

Grounds For The Processing Of Personal Data

INTRODUCTION

The processing of any personal data about another living individual is an intrusion into the informational privacy of that individual. The Act requires that a data controller must be able to show a legitimate justification for any such processing. In the Directive some categories of personal data are classed as sensitive personal data and specific conditions are attached to processing them. The grounds on which the processing of personal data may be justified are set out in Schs 2 and 3 to the Act. The Schedules are incorporated into the first principle,[1] which provides:

5–01

> "Personal data shall be processed fairly and lawfully and in particular shall not be processed unless:
>
> (a)   at least one of the conditions in Schedule 2 is met, and
> (b)   in the case of sensitive personal data at least one of the conditions in Schedule 3 is also met."

In other words, no processing is permitted unless at least one of the Sch.2 conditions is satisfied and, additionally, in the case of "sensitive personal data", at least one of the Sch.3 conditions. It should be borne in mind that the term "processing" is very broad and covers all operations carried out on personal data. These conditions apply in addition to the requirement that all such processing must be fair and lawful.

In this chapter the conditions for the processing of any personal data and for the processing of sensitive personal data, set out in Schs 2 and 3 to the Act, are considered. The meaning of the term "fair and lawful" is discussed in detail in Ch.6 on the principles.

A data controller must have legitimate grounds falling within Sch.2, and where necessary Sch.3, for the processing of personal data in any particular case; however there is no explicit duty on the data controller to identify or record the grounds for processing personal data. The registerable particulars submitted for notification do not require him to identify his grounds and he is under no obligation to provide information on this point to the data subject in response to a subject access request. The Commissioner could demand a statement of the

---

[1] principle 1 Sch.1.

205

grounds for particular processing in an Information Notice under s.43 but only if he has received a demand for assessment or reasonably requires the information to determine whether the controller is complying with the principles.

If a data controller does not have proper grounds the Commissioner could serve an enforcement notice requiring the controller to rectify matters, whether by establishing proper grounds or ceasing to process the data temporarily or permanently. In an action brought by an individual before a court the court might also order a cessation of particular processing of particular data on the ground that the controller had no proper basis for the processing. In *Law Society v Kordowski*[2] the court held that the processing of the personal data of solicitors on the website "Solicitors from Hell" was unlawful; however it did not go on to consider the absence of specific grounds for processing. In *Murray v Big Pictures*[3] the Court of Appeal recognised if personal data had been processed in breach of art.8 of the Human Rights Act then the processing (in that case the taking and using photographs of a child without consent of the parents) would be unlawful. The Court also appeared to endorse the view of the judge in the High Court that it would follow that the processing was unfair and that none of the conditions of Sch.2 to the DPA (including that in para.6(1)) could be met.

The sets of grounds for processing in the two schedules have some similarities but are not addressed in exactly the same terms. We have therefore dealt with the schedules separately apart from in the section on consent where we consider that the discussion benefits from a review of the nature of consent and explicit consent being brought together.

5–02   SUMMARY OF THE MAIN POINTS

(a)   Schedule 3 sets out the conditions for the legitimate processing of sensitive personal data and the grounds in Sch.3 have been extended by a number of statutory instruments which are listed at the end of this chapter.

(b)   The conditions in Sch.2 largely follow the grounds set out in art.7 of the Directive and in Sch.3 largely follow those set out in art.8.

(c)   The conditions set out in Schs 2 and 3 are continuing conditions; there must be a legitimisation of the processing throughout the processing.

(d)   The existence of conditions for processing is necessary but does not exhaust the obligations of controllers and all the other principles must be complied with.

(e)   There are similarities between the conditions in each schedule but they are not identical.

(f)   The categories of sensitive personal data are fixed and have been examined in a number of cases before the courts.

(g)   The conditions in Sch.3 which relate to legal advice or proceedings, statutory or Crown purposes or the administration of justice and processing for ethnic monitoring are not to be found in art.8. However, art.8 provides that:

---

[2] [2011] EWHC 3185.
[3] [2008] EWCA 446.

"8.4 Subject to the provision of suitable safeguards, Member States may, for reasons of substantial public interest, lay down exemptions in addition to those laid down in paragraph 2 either by national law or by decision of the supervisory authority."

The meaning of the "necessary"

Processing is defined in s.1(1) of the 1998 Act as meaning "obtaining, recording or holding" the data and carrying out various operations with respect to the data including: organising, adapting, altering, retrieving, consulting, using, disclosing, aligning, combining, erasing or blocking the data. In short, almost anything that might be done to or with personal data is covered by "processing". The definition is considered in detail in Ch.4.

5–03

In many of the grounds for processing the provision requires that the processing be "necessary" for the specified reason. The term is not defined but has been considered in case law. In *Huber v Germany*[4] the CJEU held that the concept of "necessity" in art.7(f) imports the test of proportionality and this means that a public authority must be able to demonstrate that any processing of personal data based on it is the minimum necessary for achieving the legitimate aim in question. The particular data was held for the purposes of immigration status. The court held that retention of the relevant personal data would not satisfy the test of necessity unless it could be shown that there was no other way of enforcing the immigration and resident status rules. This is perhaps a rather stricter approach to the term "necessary" than has been habitually taken in the UK.

In the case of *Chief Constable of Humberside v Information Commissioner*,[5] the Court of Appeal accepted that it was common ground that "necessary" within Sch.2 para.6 of the DPA should reflect the meaning attributed to it by the European Court of Human Rights when justifying an interference with a recognised right, namely that there should be a pressing social need and that the interference was both proportionate as to means and fairly balanced as to ends:

"We note the explanation given by the court in *The Sunday Times v United Kingdom* (1979) 2 EHRR 245 paragraph 59:

'The court has already had the occasion …to state its understanding of the phrase "necessary in a democratic society" the nature of its functions in the examination of issues turning on that phrase and the manner in which it will perform those functions.'"

The court has noted that, while the adjective "necessary", within the meaning of article 10(2) is not synonymous with "indispensable", neither has it the flexibility of such expressions as "admissible", "ordinary", "useful", "reasonable" or "desirable" and that it implies the existence of a "pressing social need.""

In *Stone v SE Coast Strategic Health Authority*[6] Mr Justice Davis commented:

---

[4] Case C-524/06 [2009] All E.R. (EC) 239.
[5] [2009] EWCA Civ 1079.
[6] [2006] EWHC 1668 (Admin).

"It is common ground that the word 'necessary', as used in the Schedules to the 1998 Act, carries with it the connotations of the European Convention on Human Rights: those include the proposition that a pressing social need is involved and that the measure employed is proportionate to the legitimate aim being pursued".

It is submitted that, while the element of proportionality in relation to the grounds for processing is correctly stated, it is somewhat misleading to refer to a "pressing social need". The social need is set out in the ground—for example that the parties wish to enter into a contract or that the vital interests of the subject require protection and the processing of the personal data must be for that purpose and be proportionate to the purpose.

In the Guide to Data Protection, the Commissioner has stated:

"Many of the conditions for processing depend on the processing being 'necessary' for the particular purpose to which the condition relates. This imposes a strict requirement, because the condition will not be met if the organisation can achieve the purpose by some other reasonable means or if the processing is necessary only because the organisation has decided to operate its business in a particular way."

It is submitted that this approach comes close to equating the term with "indispensable" and is somewhat stricter than is supported by the case law.

Sensitive personal data

5–04   "Sensitive personal data" are defined in s.2 of the Act as

"personal data consisting of information as to:

(a)   the racial or ethnic origin of the data subject;
(b)   his political opinions;
(c)   his religious beliefs or other beliefs of a similar nature;
(d)   whether he is a member of a trade union (within the meaning of the Trade Union and Labour Relations (Consolidation) Act 1992);
(e)   his physical or mental health or condition;
(f)   his sexual life;
(g)   the commission or alleged commission by him of any offence;
(h)   any proceedings for any offence committed or alleged to have been committed by him, the disposal of such proceedings or the sentence of any court in such proceedings."

5–05   Sensitive personal data is not a new concept. It occurs in art.6 of Treaty 108 and also in the 1984 Act which provided that special provisions could be made for such data although none were ever made. The recognition of the sensitivity of some types of data reflect the case law on art.8 of the ECHRFF in which some categories of information, such as medical records, have been held to be worthy of particular protection from intrusion by the State.[7] Schedule 3, however, does not provide any additional safeguards for such data beyond the requirement to be able to assert one or more of the grounds for processing.

---

[7] See Ch.2 and the cases of: *Z v Finland* (1997) 25 E.H.R.R. 371; and *MS v Sweden* (1997) 28 E.H.R.R. 313.

The terms are quite widely drawn and in some cases are imprecise. "Racial or ethnic" origin covers two distinct concepts, although the two categories can overlap. Ethnic origin is not synonymous with nationality. In *Meister v Speech Design Carrier Systems GmbH*[8] the CJEU appeared to have accepted that the fact that an individual was Russian was information a matter of ethnic origin. Membership of the Roma was regarded as membership of a group of ethnic origin in *Centre on Housing Rights and Evictions v France*.[9] "Political opinions" is not defined. In *National Anti-Vivisection Society v Inland Revenue Commissioners*[10] it was held that where the main object of a society is to alter the law by prohibiting vivisection altogether, that object is political and not charitable. The promotion of the observance of human rights by campaigning to change the laws or policies of a government was a "political object" within the meaning of s.92(2): *R. v Radio Authority, Ex p. Bull*.[11] Under the United Nations Convention Relating to the Status of Refugees (1951), a crime committed with the object of overthrowing or changing the government of a state or inducing it to change its policy is to be regarded as a "political crime" provided the commission of the crime is not too remote from its objective: *R. v Governor of Pentonville Prison Ex p. Cheng*.[12]

"Beliefs of a similar nature" is qualified by but is distinct from religious beliefs. It does not appear to have been litigated but presumably could include humanism or any system of belief by which an individual orders his or her life. In the Equality Act 2010 religion means any religion and includes a reference to a lack of religion. Belief means any religious or philosophical belief and a reference to belief includes a lack of belief.[13] It seems unlikely on the wording that an absence of belief would be regarded as sensitive personal data but the Directive includes "religious or philosophical beliefs" and it would appear that atheism could be regarded as falling under this wording. Physical or mental health or condition appears to be wider than simple health because of the addition of the word "condition". It is not clear how wide the terms is meant to be but must be associated with a state of body or mind, so being pregnant would presumably be a condition although not an illness. It appears to be assumed that biometric data are sensitive personal data. Presumably there is a view that biometric data, particularly genetic data, consists of information as to an individual's "physical or mental health or condition"; however the point may be arguable and in the draft Regulation the definition of sensitive personal data has been extended to explicitly covered biometric information. The growth in the use of biometrics for identification and developments such as the DNA database has meant that increasing amounts of such sensitive personal data are held on individuals with an increasing need for safeguards.

In the case of *Lord Ashcroft v Attorney General*[14] the Court accepted that data from which an implication of criminal conduct could be drawn could count as sensitive personal data on a hearing on an application to amend particulars of

5–06

---

[8] [2012] 2 C.M.L.R. 39.
[9] [2012]54 E.H.R.R. SE 5.
[10] [1974] UKHL 4.
[11] [1997] 3 W.L.R. 1094.
[12] [1973] A.C. 931.
[13] Equality Act 2010 s.10.
[14] [2002] EWHC 1122.

claim. It was claimed that a reference in a leaked document could constitute sensitive personal data because it could be read as bearing the meaning that Lord Ashcroft had allegedly committed a criminal offence. The judgment reads:

> "The objection is taken that the memorandum does not in terms specify any particular offence and so is not caught by section 2(g). I reject that contention. It is in my view at least arguable that the reference in the memorandum to the laundry arrangements of Lord Ashcroft would be understood to be a reference to the criminal offence of money-laundering."

This was a hearing on whether the case was arguable and should not be treated as stronger authority than that but at least the judge considered it sufficiently arguable.

In *Linqvist*[15] the European Court held that information which Ms Linqvist had placed on an internet page stating that a named colleague had an injured foot and was working part time was sensitive personal data about the colleague within art.8(1) of the Directive.

5–07   It should be noted that in the Directive and the Act it is the nature of the data that determines whether it is sensitive and not the context or the use to which it is put. However, in the case of *Campbell v MGM*[16] the court had to consider whether the photographs of Ms Campbell, a model, should be treated as sensitive personal data as they revealed her colour. The Court held that the photographs were not sensitive personal data as that information was not the import or purpose of the photographs. This approach is reflected in the Guide provided by the Commissioner:

> "Religion or ethnicity or both can often be inferred with varying degrees of certainty from dress or name. For example many surnames are associated with a particular ethnicity or religion or both and may indicate the ethnicity or religion of the individuals concerned. However it would be absurd to treat all such names as 'sensitive personal data' which would mean that to hold such names on a customer database you had to satisfy a condition for processing sensitive personal data. Nevertheless if you processed such names specifically because they indicated ethnicity or religion for example to send marketing materials for products and services targeted at individuals of that ethnicity or religion, then you would be processing sensitive personal data."

Despite the decision in *Campbell*, the point was raised in *Murray*[17] in the High Court when the judge suggested that:

> "if a photograph and the information it contains constitutes personal data then it was hard to escape from the conclusion that insofar as it indicates the racial or ethnic origin of the data subject it also consists of sensitive personal data."

However the point was not pursued in *Murray* at the Court of Appeal.

The decision in *Campbell* appears to support the view of the Commissioner the terms should be relatively narrowly defined and that data which would only be sensitive by association or implication should not be treated as caught by the

---

15 See Ch.4 for a full discussion.
16 [2002] EWHC 299.
17 [2007] EWHC 1908.

provisions. Nevertheless it is sensible for data controllers have to be alert to such issues and ensure that data which might be regarded as sensitive personal data are not held unless it is genuinely necessary for the purpose involved.

GROUNDS FOR PROCESSING

Consent and explicit consent

Consent to processing

The meaning of consent and its interpretation is discussed in detail in Ch.4. The condition in Sch.2 requires the "consent of the data subject", whereas the parallel provision in Sch.3 requires the "explicit consent of the data subject". By implication, therefore, some form of consent which is not explicit is sufficient to satisfy the Sch.2 condition however it must amount to a positive indication of the individual's agreement. There is no requirement that the consent be in writing.   **5–08**

Article 7 of the Directive, which sets out the criteria for making processing of non-sensitive data legitimate, refers to the data subject unambiguously giving his consent. The word "unambiguous" is not included in the 1998 Act. Consent may be either express or implied from some relevant action of the data subject. Reference is sometimes made to "opt-out" consent. True consent cannot be obtained by merely presenting an "opt-out" to the data subject after he has provided information however failure to complete an opt-out box on a coupon or other mechanism which is returned to the data controller can be argued to be an action from which consent may be implied. For example a respondent to a mail order coupon may be presumed to understand that his personal data will be processed for the purposes of dealing with the order. However, if the personal data so gathered are intended to be used for another purpose—in particular direct marketing, either by the original data controller or by a third party to whom the data are sold or transferred—then fairness requires that the data subject must give consent.[18] Such consent might be obtained by sending a communication which has to be returned to the data controller and which includes a description of the proposed new use and an opt-out box prominently situated. Returning the communication with the opt-out box unticked would then be argued to amount to an implied consent.

In practice the specified information requirements of the first principle and the consent condition of Sch.2 are generally dealt with in tandem by the adoption of written or spoken procedures which both convey information about intended processing to the potential data subject and obtain his or her consent.

The Act does not define consent but the Directive (art.2(h)) defines the data subject's consent as meaning any   **5–09**

> "freely given, specific and informed indication of his wishes by which the data subject signifies his agreement to personal data relating to him being processed".

---

[18] *Innovations (Mail Order) Ltd v DPR* Unreported September 1993, para.30. See *Encyclopedia of Data Protection*.

Thus "consent" obtained by trickery or under duress would not suffice, but arguably this adds little to the requirement that personal data must be processed fairly in any event. The requirement in the Directive that consent must be informed suggests that there must be some indication that the data subject has understood the nature of the data gathering or other data processing exercise.

Under the 1984 Act the Registrar served an Enforcement Notice on British Gas Trading Ltd with respect to leaflets sent out informing customers that personal data gathered for the purposes of customer administration would be used for the purpose of marketing products not associated with the supply of gas unless the customers positively signified their dissent. The Registrar stated that this amounted to an unfair use of the customer data held by British Gas. The Registrar's views were upheld by the Tribunal in 1998.[19] The Tribunal considered that where personal data were already held by a data user,[20] having been acquired as part of the sale of an essential service from a company with an effective monopoly, then any processing of that data for marketing purposes would be unfair processing unless done with the consent of the data subject.

In considering whether inaction can amount to consent being "signified" common law principles also have to be borne in mind. It is clear from case law that silence cannot indicate consent.[21] This issue is discussed in more detail in Ch.3. In the case of *Stone v SE Coast Strategic Health Authority*,[22] the court appears to have accepted that a data subject could withdraw a consent, although the point was not actually litigated. The Health Authority had originally argued that a consent to publication of information, once given, was irrevocable but did not pursue the claim.

Explicit consent to the processing

5–10 Clearly if explicit consent is established then the parallel provision requiring simple consent in Sch.2 will also be satisfied.

There is no requirement that explicit consent be in writing. Presumably, explicit oral consent will suffice. However, given that "explicit" implies that the consent is unambiguous, in the case of sensitive personal data, data controllers may prefer to adopt the protective stance of ensuring that the information relating to the intended processing (including the "specified information") is set out in writing rather than delivered orally and left open to interpretation and misunderstanding. The Commissioner has stated that the use of the word "explicit":

> "suggests that the individual's consent should be absolutely clear. It should cover the specific processing details, the type of information (or even the specific information), the purposes of the processing and any special aspects which may affect the individual, for example disclosures that may be made."[23]

---

[19] *British Gas Trading Ltd v DPR* [1997–98] Info. T.L.R. 393. See *Encyclopedia of Data Protection*.
[20] The term used for the equivalent of a data controller under the 1984 Act.
[21] *Jonathan Cape v Attorney General* (the *Crossman Diaries* case) [1976] Q.B. 752.
[22] [2006] EWHC 1668.
[23] "The Guide to Data Protection", p.117.

SCHEDULE 2 GROUNDS

The Commissioner's Guide to Data Protection does not cover the Sch.2 grounds in any detail. Although it includes a section on the "legitimate interests" condition and the grounds for sensitive personal data processing otherwise it does not include an analysis of the other grounds.

5–11

Contractual reasons

Schedule 2 para.2 permits processing where it is necessary:

5–12

(a)   for the performance of a contract to which the data subject is a party; or
(b)   for the taking of steps at the request of the data subject with a view to entering into a contract.

Thus if the data subject replies to a mail order coupon, ordering specific goods, processing for the purposes of obtaining payment for the order and to effect the delivery of the ordered goods would be permissible under this provision (although arguably such activities would also be permitted by way of the data subject's implied consent). Ancillary purposes, such as future mail shots from the data controller regarding additional products, would not be permitted under this provision, since such processing would not be in pursuance of the original contract. Such additional processing might be permissible under the legitimate interest ground or under the consent condition if the data subject's implied or express consent had been obtained to such additional processing at the time that the original contract was entered into—one of the best examples being by way of an "opt-in" or "opt-out" box on the original order form. If the data subject had filled in a mail order coupon to order a catalogue it could be argued that the dispatch of subsequent replacement editions of the same catalogue was justifiable under this head.

The second limb of the "contractual reasons" condition appears to be designed to cover, for example, credit reference checking carried out by the data controller prior to entering into a contract. However, if that is the intention of the limb, then the inclusion of the phrase "at the request of the data subject" seems an odd qualification. A credit reference check is not usually a pre-contractual step "requested" by a data subject. The request for a credit reference check invariably comes from the data controller not the data subject, since its rationale is to protect the lender/controller rather than the borrower/subject. Credit reference checks are procedures which data subjects might consent to, which of course would allow the controller to process in pursuance of the "consent" condition, but they are hardly procedures which a data subject requests. An alternative view would be that a credit reference check is such an essential part of any credit agreement that by requesting a credit agreement a data subject would be deemed to be requesting a credit reference check.

The second limb of the "contractual reasons" condition is clearly wide enough to cover other pre-contractual dealings that require the processing of the data subject's personal data. Given that a "request" from a data subject for processing to take place must necessarily involve their consent to such processing, it is difficult to see what situation the second limb is aimed at that would not already be covered by the data controller obtaining the data subject's consent to processing.

Non-contractual legal obligations

5–13   Schedule 2 para.3 permits processing where it is necessary to comply with any legal obligation to which the data controller is subject, other than an obligation imposed by contract. "Necessary" is used again—see the comments above.

This provision can be seen as complementary to the "contractual reasons" condition, and deals with the situation where a controller is obliged by law to process data rather than with an enforceable agreement with the data subject which necessitates the processing of data.

Thus if the law requires the testing of primary school children and the maintenance of individual children's test results, the data controller (head teacher/board of governors) can claim to satisfy this condition. The permission of the data subjects (parents/children) does not additionally have to be sought.

The data subject's vital interests

5–14   Schedule 2 para.4 permits processing where it is necessary to protect the vital interests of the data subject. "Necessary" is used again—see the comments, above.

The difficulty with the phrase "vital interests" is that the word vital has, effectively, two meanings. Vital may mean "necessary to the continuance of life" or "having or affecting life". Alternatively, it may simply mean "essential" or "very important". The Commissioner issued some guidance on the interpretation of "vital interests" in the previous Legal Guidance but it is not covered in the current Guide. In the previous Guidance it was stated:

> "The Commissioner considers that reliance on this condition may only be claimed where the processing is necessary for matters of life and death, for example, the disclosure of a data subject's medical history to a hospital casualty department treating the data subject after a serious road accident."

Support for the interpretation being restricted to matters affecting the survival of the data subject comes from the Directive itself.

Recital 31 states that the processing of personal data must be regarded as lawful where it is carried out in order to protect an interest which is essential for the data subject's life. The emphasis here, therefore, is on matters of life or death. Article 7 of the Directive, upon which Sch.2 of the 1998 Act is closely based, makes use of the term "vital interests" without any further clarification. Reference back to the Recitals in the Directive therefore suggests that "vital interests" should be interpreted restrictively to matters affecting the very survival of the data subject.

Public functions

Schedule 2 para.5 permits processing where it is necessary: **5–15**

" for the administration of justice

- (aa) for the exercise of any functions of either House of Parliament
- (b) for the exercise of any functions conferred by or under any enactment;
- (c) for the exercise of any functions of the Crown, a Minister of the Crown or a government department, or;
- (d) for the exercise of any functions of a public nature exercised in the public interest."

(Note: "Necessary" is used again—see the comments, above.)

It is submitted that the scope of these provisions applies to processing carried out under a discretionary power rather than a legal obligation

Subclause (d) is an open ended "mopping-up" provision. It is submitted that "functions of a public nature" will be those which are capable of judicial review. In *Campbell v MGN*[24] the *Mirror* tried to argue that the publication of material which it described as being in the public interest was the "exercise of a public function". Not unsurprisingly the court held that the *Mirror* newspaper was not a public body operating in the public interest.

It is possible, however, for some private or quasi-private bodies to exercise public functions and therefore rely on this condition. Anybody carrying out a public function will be subject to administrative law.[25]

The data controller's legitimate interests

Schedule 2 para.6 permits processing where it is necessary: **5–16**

"for the purposes of legitimate interests pursued by the data controller or by the third party or parties to whom the data are disclosed, except where the processing is unwarranted in any particular case by reason of prejudice to the rights and freedoms or legitimate interests of the data subject. The Secretary of State may by order specify particular circumstances in which this condition is or is not to be taken to be satisfied."

Note: "Necessary" is used again—see the comments, above.

The term "legitimate interests" is not in any way further clarified. What is clearly required in determining whether this condition has been satisfied is a balancing act—an assessment of both the interests of the data subject and of those of the data controller. The data controller must be able to establish that he has a legitimate interest before he is justified in carrying out any processing. If it would prejudice the interests of the data subject he must then balance the two competing interests.

In the Guide the Commissioner advises that a data controller looking to rely on this provision should review the two requirements and conduct a balancing act

---

[24] [2004] UKHL 22.
[25] *R. v Panel on Take-overs and Mergers Ex p. Datafin Plc* [1987] Q.B. 815; *Melton Medes v Security and Investment Board* [1995] 3 All E.R. 880.

but "where there is a serious mismatch between competing interests the individual's legitimate interests will come first".

It is suggested that the "legitimate interests" of the data controller will be all those commercial freedoms which are promoted or indeed guaranteed by the EU treaties, while the rights and freedoms or legitimate interests of the data subject will be all those rights promoted and guaranteed by the European Convention of Human Rights, the Charter of Fundamental Rights and UK law.

The pursuit, promotion and marketing of a legitimate business are, it is submitted, all "legitimate interests" of a business-based data controller.

5–17   Balancing acts between the rights of organisations and rights of data subjects are not always easy or straightforward. As an example of a balacing act the Commissioner includes an example of the disclosure of personal data about a debtor to a debt collection agency where a customer has moved house without notifying a finance company of his new address and has not continued to repay the loan. It is suggested that this is not a borderline case which requires a balancing act to be conducted and data controllers face more difficulty where the proposed new processing does not involve any fault on the part of the subject but is to the advantage of the business or where the business comes under other pressures. An example of a more difficult balancing act can be seen in the decision to disclose data from the SWIFT database.

In Opinion 10/2006 on the SWIFT processing the Article 29 Working Party considered the application of art.7(f) (the equivalent of Ground 6) to the processing carried out by SWIFT in transferring the personal data of banking customers to the US where the databank would be subject to disclosure to the US authorities under subpoenas. The WP dealt with the balance as follows:

> "It cannot be denied that SWIFT has a legitimate interest in complying with the subpoenas under US law. If SWIFT did not comply with those subpoenas it runs the risk of incurring sanctions under US law. On the other hand it is also crucial that a "proper balance" is found and respected between the risk of SWIFT being sanctioned by the US for eventual non-compliance with the subpoenas and the rights of individuals. Article 7(f) of the Directive requires a balance to be struck between the legitimate interest pursued by the processing of personal data and the fundamental rights of data subjects. The balance of interest test should take into account issues of proportionality, subsidiarity, the seriousness of the alleged offences that can be notified and the consequences for the data subjects. In the context of the balance of interest test adequate safeguards will also have to be put into place. In particular Article 14 of the Directive provides that when data processing is based on Article 7(f) individuals have the right at any time to object on compelling legitimate grounds to the processing of the data relating to them.
>
> SWIFT conducted the processing and mirroring of its data in a "hidden, systematic, massive and long term" manner without having specified the further incompatible purpose at the time of processing the data and without SWIFT pointing this out to the users of its services. The further processing and mirroring for an incompatible purpose could have far-reaching effects on any individual.
>
> The Working Party therefore considers that the interests for fundamental rights and freedoms of the numerous data subjects over-ride SWIFT's interests not to be sanctioned by the US for eventual non-compliance with the subpoenas."

5–18   Even if the condition is broadly interpreted to permit a new element of processing the data controller remains subject to the obligation to process personal data fairly in accordance with the first principle. Thus even though the legitimate processing hurdle is passed a new use may be in breach of principle 1. The "specified information" which must be provided t the data subject includes the purpose or purposes for which the data are intended to be processed. Thus, although a data controller might be able to claim legitimate processing without the consent of the data subject by relying on the "legitimate interests" condition, this does not remove the obligation to notify the data subject of the intended use of the data.

The provision states that the Secretary of State may make an order as to when this condition is or is not to be taken to be satisfied. The "may" clearly indicates that the Secretary of State has a discretion to issue such clarification, not an obligation. No such order has been made to date.

In a series of cases the Information Tribunal, now the First Tier Tribunal Information Rights, held that public bodies process personal data for the purposes of making disclosures under the Freedom of Information Act 2000 on Ground 6. This appears to have been adopted by the High Court in the case of *Proper Officer of the House of Commons Information Commissioners.* However, in the joined cases of *Rechnugshof and Osterreichischer Rundfunk*[26] the European Court held that the grounds for processing on which public bodies must rely are found in art.7(c) and (d). This raises a number of difficult points under the DPA which are canvassed at length in Ch.26. It is submitted that, leaving aside the knotty and unsatisfactory position which arises in respect of the disclosure of personal data under the freedom of information legislation, public bodies or those carrying out public functions should not be relying on Ground 6.

5–19

Ground 6 also allows for consideration to be paid to the legitimate interests to be pursued by a third party to whom personal data are to be disclosed. This would strongly argue that a data controller proposing to make a disclosure of personal data should ascertain the nature and purpose of the processing to be carried out by that third party.

SCHEDULE 3 GROUNDS

We have considered the nature of consent and explicit consent above.

Legal obligations in the context of employment

Paragraph 2 of Sch.3 permits the processing of sensitive personal data where the processing is necessary for the purposes of exercising or performing any right or obligation which is conferred or imposed by law on the data controller in connection with employment. The Secretary of State may by Order specify cases where this condition is either excluded altogether or only satisfied upon the satisfaction of further conditions. No such order has been made or proposed at the time of writing.

5–20

This condition is not exclusive to employers. It can be claimed by those who oversee compliance by employers as long as the oversight is part of a statutory obligation. The concept of "necessity", which appeared so frequently in the

---

[26] C-465/00, C-138/01 and C-139.

conditions for general processing, re-appears here. For a discussion of its interpretation, see earlier. Compliance with many of the conditions under Sch.3 will also entail the satisfaction of the parallel or mirror provision under Sch.2 since the former are in many cases more restrictive restatements of the latter. In the case of this condition, it is submitted that the same facts will be relevant to compliance with Ground 3 in Sch.2 that:

"Ground 3   The processing is necessary to comply with any legal obligation to which the data controller is subject, other than an obligation imposed by contract".

The para.2 provision in Sch.3 covers processing, including disclosures required for statutory purposes, such as disclosures to the Inland Revenue. The Commissioner has accepted that it does not cover some information which an employer may need to hold but to which none of the other conditions apply and for which it may be difficult to obtain the consent of the data subject. An example is the holding of driving or other conviction information about employees where it is necessary for work-related purposes.

5–21   As well as statutory disclosures it will cover employers who wish to monitor the composition or "make up" of their workforce where such monitoring flows from what is necessary for the performance or exercise of any right or obligation conferred or imposed by law.

General statute imposes obligations on employers in relation to discrimination, either direct or indirect, on the grounds of race, sex, disability, age, sexual orientation, gender reassignment or religious belief.[27] An employer may seek to monitor compliance with non-discrimination obligations imposed by legislation by monitoring the make-up of its workforce and, in particular, the relative proportions of sexes, ethnic groupings and so on. Such monitoring can be seen to facilitate compliance with non-discrimination legislation but may not be a matter of legal compulsion. It will be a question of judgment whether it is "necessary" for such compliance. However, a later condition (para.9 of Sch.3) specifically permits the monitoring of racial or ethnic origin (but not other types of sensitive personal data) providing certain safeguards are complied with. A further condition under SI 2000/417 permits processing of other data categories to monitor or promote equal opportunities (see paras 5–32 and 5–44).

5–22   An employer may also have other arrangements for monitoring, for example an employer may have an agreement with staff that it will provide health insurance and health checks for staff. The employer would however not be able to rely on this ground to hold the sensitive personal data arising from such an agreement. Even if the agreement was incorporated into contracts of employment this would not create an obligation "imposed by law". Contractual obligations are obligations voluntarily taken on by free parties which, subject to the legal principles governing the law of contract, may be enforced at law. They are not obligations imposed on an individual vis-à-vis the State. It would not, therefore, be open to a data controller to claim the benefit of this condition because of any contractual obligation.

It is worth noting that Sch.2 para.3 uses the term "any legal obligation to which the data controller is subject". This term clearly potentially includes

---

[27] Equality Act 2010.

contractual obligations and therefore the paragraph specifically has to exclude them from the ambit of the phrase by adding the qualification "other than an obligation imposed by contract". Schedule 3 para.2(1), however, uses the phrase "any obligation . . . imposed by law". This is materially different from the phrase "any legal obligation to which the data controller is subject" and, it is submitted, clearly excludes contractual obligations.

To protect the vital interests of the data subject or another person where consent cannot be given or is withheld

This condition allows the processing of sensitive data where it is necessary: **5–23**

" (a)   in order to protect the vital interests of the data subject or another person, in a case where:
  (i)   consent cannot be given by or on behalf of the data subject; or
  (ii)   the data controller cannot reasonably be expected to obtain the consent of the data subject; or
  (iii) in order to protect the vital interests of another person, in a case where consent by or on behalf of the data subject has been unreasonably withheld."

Again, "necessity" is a requirement. The parallel Sch.2 condition is clearly the one which allows processing in order to protect the vital interests of the data subject.[28]

There is no requirement that the other person must be a living individual. The term "person" coves both an individual and a legal person. It seems strange however that a legal person could have a vital interest in the sense of being a life or death matter. It is also not clear whether there must be another readily ascertainable and distinct person or whether it might include a class or indeed members of the public at large. The distinction may be important, especially in the cases of a data subject who presents a threat to the vital interests of others—for example, through mental health problems or an infectious and fatal disease. In such a situation, will it be necessary to show a threat to a specific person or will it be sufficient to show a general threat to the public? It is submitted that the latter interpretation is more effective.

Atypically, the Sch.3 condition appears to be more widely framed than the parallel Sch.2 condition allowing, as it does, the processing of sensitive personal data when it is necessary to protect the vital interests not just of the data subject but also of "another person".

Thus data controllers need to take care when relying on this Sch.3 condition that they do not assume that the parallel condition under Sch.2 will automatically be satisfied—it may not be. The "vital interests of another person" would appear to allow, for example, the processing of data relating to a data subject's criminal record or mental health where that record discloses offences or behaviour which may put third parties at serious risk. The data subject may have been asked for his or consent to the relevant processing and may have "unreasonably withheld" that consent. The data controller would thus be able to claim the benefit of this Sch.3 condition but not that of the parallel Sch.2 condition, since the processing is not

---

[28] For the discussion on how "vital interests" may be interpreted see para.5-14 above.

to protect the vital interests of the data subject but of another. The data controller may well, of course, be able to bring the processing within one of the other conditions—either the Sch.2 condition that allows processing where it is necessary for the exercise of any functions of a public nature exercised in the public interest where a public body is the data controller or the condition in para.6 of Sch.2 is likely to be applicable where the controller is a private entity. However, the difference between the parallel Schs 2 and 3 conditions remains a curiosity. It is not immediately clear why the Sch.2 "vital interests" condition was not also worded to cover the vital interests of the "data subject or another person".

5–24   The Sch.3 condition deals with three scenarios in which the data subject's consent is not available. If explicit consent is available then of course the data controller need not worry about compliance with this provision at all, since the first Sch.3 condition would then be satisfied.

The three scenarios are:

(a)   Consent cannot be given by or on behalf of the data subject (for example a comatose data subject who requires urgent medical treatment) or a minor who is not competent to give consent.

(b)   The data controller cannot reasonably be expected to obtain the consent of the data subject (this may apply, for example, where a disclosure of a data subject's mental health or previous convictions is necessary to protect a third party but where seeking the consent of the data subject might seriously aggravate the situation or where the data subject cannot be contacted).

(c)   Consent by or on behalf of the data subject has been "unreasonably withheld" (this may apply, for example, where a disclosure of a data subject's mental health or previous convictions is necessary to protect a third party but where sought the data subject's consent is unreasonably withheld).

What is and is not reasonable or unreasonable will have to be evaluated in each individual case. Data controllers should consider the position carefully before adopting blanket policies for dispensing with data subject consent in a class of cases. It would be prudent for data controllers to be able to demonstrate a specific decision-taking process in each case in which consent is dispensed with

This condition introduces the possibility of consent to processing being given by a third party on behalf of, rather than directly by, the data subject himself or herself. The possibility of a third party giving consent is not one that occurs elsewhere in either the Sch.2 or Sch.3 conditions dealing with the consent of the data subject.

This is not to say that the consent of a third party can never satisfy the Schs 2 and 3 conditions requiring the data subject's consent. As is discussed in detail in Ch.6, the general law does intervene in certain limited circumstances to empower a third party to provide consent on another person's behalf—for example, a parent on behalf of a child or a carer with an Lasting Power of Attorney on behalf of a mental health patient. Thus, even the conditions specifically requiring the data subject's consent may be satisfied by consent being provided by a third party. However, these conditions are silent on this possibility, leaving the general law to intervene when required. Conversely, the Sch.3 condition relating to vital interests specifically raises the possibility of consent being given by a third party. Thus the condition implies situations of a third party providing consent which are not routinely provided for by the general law.

The condition acknowledges that third parties not covered by the general law, may be asked to consent to processing necessary to protect the data subject's vital interests—for example, where a man is brought into a hospital in a coma and his wife is asked to consent to the processing necessary to protect her husband's vital interests. The most common circumstances in which next of kin are asked for consent occur in medical emergencies and the General Medical Council's guidance to doctors covers such eventualities. In such cases the wife is not giving consent "on behalf of" her husband. In the scenario just mentioned, where a wife consents to processing, if she did so "on behalf of" her comatose husband, the hospital would not be able to rely upon the "vital interests" condition as this only applies when consent cannot be given on behalf of the data subject. If the wife can give such consent on behalf of her husband the condition no longer applies.

In the aforementioned scenario, it would also be possible for the hospital to claim the benefit of a later Sch.3 condition (see para.7–21, below) which permits processing which is necessary for medical purposes and is undertaken by:

(a)   a health professional; or
(b)   a person who in the circumstances owes a duty of confidentiality which is equivalent to that which would arise if that person were a health professional.

"Medical purposes" includes the purposes of preventative medicine, medical   **5–25**
diagnosis, medical research, the provision of care and treatment and the management of healthcare services.

It is worth acknowledging that there is likely to be an overlap between processing necessary for medical purposes and processing necessary to protect the vital interests of the data subject. This will be so especially if, as is the view of the Commissioner, "vital interests" should be confined to matters of life and death.

It is interesting to speculate on which classes of sensitive data might fall to be processed under this condition. Physical or mental health or condition is clearly going to be the most common type of sensitive data that falls to be processed in accordance with this condition. Racial origin may be relevant to the vital interests of the data subject if it discloses a predisposition to certain health conditions or illnesses (e.g. sickle cell anaemia). Sexual life may be pertinent again to determine susceptibility to or causes of certain illnesses. Information relating to offending and sentencing may fall to be disclosed to third parties to protect their vital interests. Religious beliefs may be pertinent to the acceptability of certain types of medical treatment—for example blood transfusions.

It is difficult to see how information relating to political opinions, or trade union membership might fall to be processed legitimately in accordance with this condition.

By certain non-profit making bodies in respect of their members

5–26   This condition permits processing where it:

(a)   is carried out in the course of its legitimate activities by any body or association which exists for political, philosophical, religious or trade-union purposes and which is not established or conducted for profit;

(b)   is carried out with appropriate safeguards for the rights and freedoms of data subjects;

(c)   relates only to individuals who are either members of the body or association or who have regular contact with it in connection with its purposes; and

(d)   does not involve disclosure of the personal data to a third party without the consent of the data subject.

This is a little like the unincorporated members' club exemption contained in s.33(2)(a) of the 1984 Act which exempted such clubs, which held personal data relating only to members of the club, from the obligation to register and to comply with subject access rights. The exemption could not be claimed unless the members had been asked if they objected and had not done so. The exemption was also lost if there was any incompatible use of the data or disclosure of the data without the data subject's consent. Carrying out the same process of checking whether a member of or person who has regular contact with the association may be a way of data controllers ensuring that the processing is carried out with "appropriate safeguards for the rights and freedoms of the data subjects" under this 1998 Act condition.

Where the information has been made public

5–27   Processing of sensitive personal data is permissible if the information contained in the personal data has been made public as a result of steps deliberately taken by the data subject. At first sight, this seems a straightforward and clear provision. Difficulties arise, however, in determining what constitutes "making public". Clearly, a data subject making a statement about sensitive personal data relating to him or her on television is making that data public. At the other end of the spectrum, disclosing an issue of sensitive data to one's spouse is not making something public. But what of an announcement to a small gathering of 5, 10 or 20 people? And how would the nature of the gathering affect whether a pronouncement constitutes information being "made public"? A disclosure of information at a private dinner party for 20 would be considered by many as a private matter but possibly not an announcement before a public meeting attended by only 8.

It may be helpful to view "making something public" as a disclosure to a random unselected group as opposed to a set or group chosen by or within the control of the publisher.

It is easy to think of this condition as relating only to confidential or hidden information. However, sensitive personal data may be gleaned from the visibly obvious—for example, information about a person's ethnic origin (or even

222

religion on the case of a Sikh wearing a turban) or disability. A question then arises as to whether the "visibly obvious" constitutes information which has been made public. The point was considered in *Campbell v MGN* (discussed at paras 2-59 and 5-07) where the Court held a photograph of Ms Campbell was not sensitive personal data although it showed her colour, as the aim of the processing in question was not related to that information. There must, however, be cases where information which is "visibly obvious" can be regarded as having been made public, for example, if someone is visibly very sick. However, it is submitted that "visible illness" alone would not legitimise the processing of the information that the person was actually suffering from cancer if that had not otherwise been made public but had been gleaned elsewhere.

The requirement of deliberateness also raises some questions. Clearly, this would exclude information gleaned from a private file which is inadvertently dropped in public, but what of the data subject who loses his temper in a public restaurant and shouts something out which he or she otherwise wished to keep private. Is the act of shouting in a public place a "deliberate" disclosure or inadvertent? It is submitted that the approach likely to be taken by the courts is to mirror the approach taken to the cases on private actions in public places described in Ch.2, for example the *Von Hannover* case in which photographs of Princess Caroline of Monaco taken while having a private dinner in a restaurant were regarded as covered by the protection of art.8 of the ECHRFF albeit the activity took place in a place open to the public. On this basis it would generally require a clear public statement or overt activity by the data subject to fulfill the condition.

Clearly each case will have to be judged on its own facts. What must not be overlooked, of course, is that the data controller must still establish one of the Sch.2 conditions for legitimate processing. This particular Sch.3 condition is one of the few that does not have a clear mirror in Sch.2. Any data controllers relying on this condition will not discharge their responsibilities by showing compliance with it alone but must ensure that a relevant Sch.2 condition is also satisfied.

In legal proceedings

This condition allows the processing of sensitive personal data where it:　　　　5–28

(a) is necessary for the purpose of, or in connection with, any legal proceedings (including prospective legal proceedings);
(b) is necessary for the purpose of taking legal advice; or
(c) is otherwise necessary for the purpose of establishing, exercising or defending legal rights.

The term "necessary" makes a re-appearance. There are no qualifications in these provisions tying them to the data subject. For example, the second sub-clause does not say "is necessary for the purpose of the data subject taking legal advice".

Presumably, this condition permits the processing of sensitive personal data relating to a person not actually seeking the legal advice if the processing of that data is "necessary" for the purposes of obtaining legal advice. Thus a solicitor may be sanctioned to process sensitive personal data relating to their client's opponent (as well as their client) if such processing is necessary for the purpose of obtaining legal advice.

There is no clear mirror or parallel condition under Sch.2. The condition that permits processing where it is necessary for the administration of justice does not mirror this condition as the administration of justice is an essentially public activity whereas this condition is concerned with essentially private activities.

Data controllers carrying out the processing of sensitive personal data which satisfies the legal proceedings condition in Sch.3 will have to take care to ensure that the processing is also legitimised by a Sch.2 condition. Where the data controller does not have a direct relationship with a data subject—for example, the scenario outlined above where a solicitor seeks to process sensitive personal data relating to a client's opponent, the data controller is likely to have to rely on the "legitimate interests" condition. It follows that the controller must ensure that the personal data held about the opponent or other third parties is proportionate.

In the case of *R. (on the application of BT Plc) v Secretary of State for Business, Innovation and Skills*[29] the Court of Appeal considered art.8(2)(e) of the Directive on which this ground is based. Although art.8(2)(e) refers to "legal claims" and the UK provision refers to "legal rights" the Court did not consider that this made any difference in the meaning. In the case BT Plc and Talk Talk Telecom opposed the Digital Economy Act on the basis (inter alia) that it did not comply with the requirements of Directive 95/46/EC. The deficiency alleged was that the copyright owners monitoring the use of services could find themselves in possession of sensitive personal data for which they could show no legitimate ground to justify the processing.[30] They argued that, as in many cases the copyright owners would not take legal action against those who they discovered infringing copyright, the ground for the protection of legal claims did not apply. This was not accepted by the Court, which held that, even though in many cases the results of the processing would not result in legal action, nevertheless the data was clearly being held in order to assert the legal rights of the copyright holders and therefore the ground was made out. Lord Justice Richards also criticized the view of the EDPS who had, in an Opinion, thrown doubt on the question of whether this ground could be used as a legal basis for wide-scale investigation.[31]

In the case of *R. (on the application of B) v Stafford Combined Court*[32] the Court held that a witnesses medical records should not have been disclosed to the accused without a hearing in which she was able to be represented. The case focused on the confidentiality of the records and did not address whether the disclosure could be justified under Sch.3.

To carry out certain public functions

5–29   Paragraph 7 of Sch.3 permits processing where it is necessary:

(a)   for the administration of justice;

---

[29] [2012] EWCA Civ 232.
[30] See Ch.23 for a more detailed explanation of the case.
[31] 2012 EWCA Civ 232 paras 75–78.
[32] [2006] EWHC 1645.

(aa)   For the exercise of any functions of either House of Parliament
(b)   for the exercise of any functions conferred by or under any enactment; or
(c)   for the exercise of any functions of the Crown, a Minister of the Crown or
       a government department.

The Secretary of State may by order specify cases where this condition is either excluded altogether or only satisfied upon the satisfaction of further conditions. The ground was amended by Sch.6 of the Freedom of Information Act 2000 to add the ground in 7(aa) that the processing is necessary for the exercise of any functions of either House of Parliament.

The ground is an almost exact duplication of the Sch.2 condition, which permits processing where it is necessary:

(a)   for the administration of justice;
(aa)   for the exercise of any functions of either House of Parliament;
(b)   for the exercise of any functions conferred by or under any enactment;
(c)   for the exercise of any functions of the Crown, a Minister of the Crown or
       a government department; or
(d)   for the exercise of any functions of a public nature exercised in the public
       interest,

save that the final possibility is omitted. Compliance with this Sch.3 condition will therefore automatically result in compliance with the parallel but more widely phrased Sch.2 condition.

In *Stone v SE Coast Strategic Health Authority*[33] the Court held that ground 7 was the basis for the publication of the report of the inquiry under s.2 of the National Health Service Act 1977 and regulations made under it.

For a discussion on the equivalent Sch.2 provisions see above. The parallel Sch.2 condition does not contain the proviso enabling the Secretary of State to restrict the ambit of the condition. No such orders have been made.

Anti-fraud organisations

A further ground was added by Sch.3 by the Serious Crime Act 2007, s.72 of   **5–30**
which adds ground 7a to the grounds in Sch.3 and permits the processing of sensitive personal data where the processing is necessary for the purposes of preventing fraud or a particular kind of fraud and either it is a disclosure made by a person as a member of an anti-fraud organisation or in accordance with arrangements made by such an organisation or is other processing of the sensitive personal data so disclosed. The further processing can be carried out by either the person who made the disclosure or "another person", which presumably means anyone. An "an anti-fraud organisation" means

> "any unincorporated association, body corporate or other person which enables or
> facilitates any sharing of information to prevent fraud or a particular kind of fraud
> or which has any of these functions as its purpose or one of its purposes".

---

[33] [2006] EWHC 1668 (Admin).

The anti-fraud organisation need not be a public sector organisation. It appears that this allows the disclosure of information to the private sector body by a police force or other public body. The amendment supported the provisions in the Serious Crime Act intended to enable public sector bodies to disclose information to private sector anti-fraud organisations, such as the Credit Industry Fraud Avoidance System (CIFAS). The provision came into effect from October 1, 2008.

For medical purposes

5–31   The eighth condition legitimises the processing of sensitive data where the processing is necessary for medical purposes (including the purposes of preventative medicine, medical diagnosis, medical research, the provision of care and treatment and the management of healthcare services) and is undertaken by:

(a)   a health professional; or
(b)   a person who owes a duty of confidentiality which is equivalent to that which would arise if that person were a health professional.

Section 69 of the 1998 Act sets out the definition of "health professional". Subsection 69(1) provides that in the (Data Protection) Act the phrase means any of the following:

(a)   a registered medical practitioner;
(b)   a registered dentist as defined by s.53(1) of the Dentists Act 1984;
(c)   a registered dispensing optician or a registered optometrist within the meaning of the Opticians Act 1989;
(d)   a registered pharmacists or registered pharmacy technician within the meaning of the Pharmacists and Pharmacy Technicians Order 2007 or a registered person as defined by art.2(2) of the Pharmacy (Northern Ireland) Order 1976;
(e)   a registered nurse or midwife;
(f)   a registered osteopath as defined by s.41 of the Osteopaths Act 1993;
(g)   a registered chiropractor as defined by s.43 of the Chiropractors Act 1994;
(h)   any person who is registered as a member of a profession to which the Health Professions Order 2001 for the time being extends;
(i)   a child psychotherapist; or
(j)   a scientist employed by such a body as a head of department.

Subsection 69(2) defines "registered medical practitioner" as including any person who is provisionally registered under ss.15 or 21 of the Medical Act 1983 and is engaged in such employment as is mentioned in subs.(3) of that section.

Subsection (3) of s.69 provides that "health service body" means:

(a)   a Strategic Health Authority established under s.13 of the National Health Service Act 2006;
(b)   a Special Health Authority established under s.28 of that Act or s.22 of the National Health service (Wales) Act 2006;

(bb) a Primary Care trust established under s.18 of the national Health service Act 2006;

(bbb) a Local Health Board established under s.11 of the National Health Service (Wales) Act 2006;

(c) a Health Board within the meaning of the National Health Service (Scotland) Act 1978;

(d) a Special Health Board within the meaning of that Act;

(e) the managers of a State Hospital provided under s.102 of that Act;

(f) a National Health Service trust first established under s.5 of the National Health Service and Community Care Act 1990, s.25 of the National Health service Act 2006, s.18 of the National Health service (Wales) Act 2006 or s.12A of the National Health Service (Scotland) Act 1978;

(fa) an NHS Foundation Trust;

(g) a Health and Social Services Board established under art.16 of the Health and Personal Social Services (Northern Ireland) Order 1972;

(h) a special health and social services agency established under the Health and Personal Social Services (Special Agencies) (Northern Ireland) Order 1990; or

(i) a Health and Social Services trust established under Art. 10 of the Health and Personal Social Services (Northern Ireland) Order 1991.[34]

The definition of "health professional" is thus extensive but does not cover all the persons who might be responsible for providing medical care and treatment, etc., hence the second limb to the provision covering other persons owing an equivalent duty of confidentiality. Counsellors dealing with health care issues might be one example of persons falling within the second limb.

There is no single clear parallel provision in Sch.2 which is likely to be automatically satisfied if this Sch.3 condition is relied on. In many cases where medical care is being dispensed direct to the data subject, he or she will also be providing at least implied consent and possibly explicit consent to the processing of sensitive data and will thus satisfy the Sch.2 consent condition. Medical purposes which are more remote from the data subject such as research or management may fall within the public interest, legitimate interests, legal obligations or functions exercised under an enactment conditions.

In the *Stone* case, referred to above, the court went on to hold that the publication of the report of the inquiry into the care, treatment and supervision of Michael Stone could be sanctioned under para.8 on the basis that the publication was for the "management of healthcare services" and thus within "medical purposes" and the publication would be carried out by persons who owed a duty of confidentiality in respect of the information (albeit that the duty was being over-ridden in the public interest in this instance).

Ethnic monitoring

The processing of sensitive data is permitted where it: 5–32

---

[34] Definition as at January 2012.

(a)   is of sensitive personal data consisting of information as to racial or ethnic origin;

(b)   is necessary for the purpose of identifying or keeping under review the existence or absence of equality of opportunity or treatment between persons of different racial or ethnic origins, with a view to enabling such equality to be promoted or maintained; and

(c)   is carried out with appropriate safeguards for the rights and freedoms of data subjects. The Secretary of State may by order specify circumstances in which such processing is, or is not, to be taken to be carried out with appropriate safeguards for the rights and freedoms of data subjects.

This condition relates only to sensitive personal data relating to racial or ethnic origin and not to any other type of sensitive personal data. Thus if an employer is processing data which records the sexual composition of his workforce or the incidence of disabilities as well as race details then this condition may not be relied on. Other conditions may permit such processing.

This condition is thus narrower than the "employment" condition set out in para.2 of Sch.3. It is also wider in the sense that there is no requirement that the ethnic monitoring be in connection with employment. Thus monitoring in relation to the provision of services (for example, housing) would be covered.

This is a reasonably clear provision although some question may arise as to how the data controller can establish that the data are processed for the purpose of promoting racial equality rather than for another purpose. Presumably, the use to which such data are put should be carefully scrutinized by the data controller.

The concept of "appropriate safeguards for the rights and freedoms of data subjects" reappears. In this condition, however, unlike the fourth condition, the Secretary of State is empowered to direct in which circumstances the "appropriate safeguards" are or are not established. No such orders have been issued. The relevant provisions under Sch.2 which a data controller will most likely seek to rely on if this Sch.3 condition is claimed are the "public interest" or "legitimate interests" conditions.

Order making power

5–33   The final paragraph of Sch.3 permits the processing of sensitive personal data when "the personal data are processed in circumstances specified in an Order made by the Secretary of State. There is no specific parallel power for the Secretary of State in Sch.2, although the final Sch.2 condition does enable the Secretary of State to specify when the "legitimate interests" condition is (or is not satisfied).

The Data Protection (Processing of Sensitive Personal Data) Order 2000[35]

The Order sets out additional grounds on which sensitive personal data may be processed without falling foul of the first principle. As noted above the data controller must also be able to show that a Sch.2 ground applies and must comply with the other principles of his handling of the data.

    Ten grounds are set out in the Order. In most cases the liberty given by the Order only applies where certain protective conditions are met or where the individual does not object. However this is not uniformly the case and para.10 permits the processing of any sensitive data necessary for the exercise of any functions conferred on a constable by any rule of law. This ground has no conditions attached. Each of the 10 grounds is described below.

5–34

Substantial public interest

Under five of the 10 grounds the processing involved must be carried out "in the substantial public interest". This term has been taken directly from art.8.4 of the Directive and should be approached in accordance with the European legal principle of proportionality. It is therefore difficult to offer a precise guide to how it is likely to be applied other than to comment that a personal or private economic/commercial benefit is unlikely to qualify; the detriment if the processing is not carried out must be more than minimal and it must be in support of an interest generally accepted as being of substantial public significance. The test of whether particular processing is in the substantial public interest in any case will be a question of fact and law to be determined in accordance with generally accepted social values and standards. It is not a subjective test for each controller.

5–35

Necessary (for a particular purpose)

In eight of the grounds the processing must meet some form of test of necessity. In most cases it must be necessary for one or more specified purposes. Again we are dealing with a term with a European provenance which will apply in this context (see para.5–03).

5–36

Safeguards

Article 8.4 permits Member States to extend the grounds for processing personal data "subject to suitable safeguards". The Order does not provide for explicit safeguards in most cases. In the cases of insurance, equality of treatment, political registers and research there are various provisos that the processing must not be used to make individual decisions or cause harm to individuals but these do not appear in all the grounds. It might be argued therefore that, as the UK has not provided explicit safeguards for all the grounds, the Order is deficient and does

5–37

---

[35] SI 2000/417.

not fully comply with art.8.4. On the other hand, the processing is restricted in all the cases and the Government would no doubt regard the restrictions in themselves as amounting to safeguards.

Paragraph 1

5–38   Sensitive personal data may be processed where the processing is in the substantial public interest, is necessary for the prevention or detection of any unlawful act and must necessarily be carried out without the explicit consent of the data subject being sought so as not to prejudice those purposes. The term "act" includes a failure to act.

    The act or omission need not amount to a breach of the criminal law as the term "unlawful" covers breaches of both civil obligations and criminal prohibitions. The ground can only be relied on where there would be real prejudice to the purpose if the individual were told of the processing and asked to consent. The effect of reliance on this ground is to deprive the individual of the right to exercise a degree of control over sensitive personal data relating to him or her. As such it is likely to be construed so as to protect the rights of the individual. It will not be available to data controllers who wish to avoid informing data subjects as a matter of convenience or to save them embarrassment.

Paragraph 2

5–39   Sensitive personal data may be processed where the processing is in the substantial public interest, is necessary for the discharge of functions of a particular type and must necessarily be carried out without the explicit consent of the data subject being sought so as not to prejudice the discharge of the function. The functions are any designed for protecting members of the public against dishonesty, malpractice, or any other seriously improper conduct by, or the unfitness or incompetence of any person, or mismanagement in the administration or of failure in services provided by any body or association. The words, "dishonesty, malpractice, or other seriously improper conduct by, or the unfitness or incompetence of, any person" are exactly the same as those used in the exemption provision in s.31(2)(a) and it would therefore be reasonable to expect them to carry the same meaning. The functions are not otherwise limited in any way. Any function which comes within the description will be covered. The function need not be of a public nature, nor carried out by a public body. There must be some ascertainable role or obligation or duty on a body to offer protection to the public from one or more of the ills described but the relevant processing itself need not be carried out by that body.

Paragraph 3

5–40   This ground relates to the special purposes, that is the journalistic, literary or artistic purposes, and in essence allows the disclosure of wrongdoing to or by the media for the purposes of publication where the publication of the information would be in the public interest. Again the disclosure must be "in the substantial public interest". It must be for one or more of the special purposes and be made "with a view to the publication of those data by any person". Paragraph 3(1)(d) goes on to provide that "the data controller" must reasonably believe that such a publication would be in the public interest.

It should be noted that this ground relates only to the disclosure of information or data and not to other forms of processing. This means that it is a limited ground. It cannot be relied on by a data controller to obtain, record or hold sensitive personal data. Therefore a data controller who legitimately holds relevant sensitive personal data may rely on this provision to disclose information to a journalist but the journalist cannot rely on it to retain the information.

The disclosing data controller must anticipate the publication of the actual data. Therefore it will not cover the disclosure of background information which is not itself intended for publication. The disclosing data controller must also have himself considered and taken a view on the question of whether publication will be in the public interest. This is because the disclosing data controller must reasonably believe that the publication would be in the public interest.

The disclosure must be "in connection with" various types of wrongdoing. The disclosure does not have to be information about actual wrongdoing as long as it is made "in connection with" the issue. For example if an individual has claimed to have been involved overseas in a particular meeting on a particular date and has claimed travel and accommodation expenses, disclosure of information showing that he was in fact in another place at another meeting would be "in connection with" dishonesty or malpractice. The types of wrongdoing are:

(i)   the commission by any person of any unlawful act (whether alleged or established);

(ii) dishonesty, malpractice, or other seriously improper conduct by, or the unfitness or incompetence of, any person (whether alleged or established); or

(iii) mismanagement in the administration of, or failure in services provided by, any body or association (whether alleged or established).

In each case "act" includes a failure to act.

There need only be an allegation of relevant wrongdoing and there is no explicit limitation as to the credibility of the allegation or the source of it. For example, there is no requirement that the allegation be based on any substantive evidence or reasonable grounds for suspicion. However, the data controller making the disclosure must be able to assert that the disclosure was made in the substantial public interest and that publication of the information would be in the public interest. A data controller who makes a disclosure of sensitive personal data in connection with a wild or irresponsible allegation may have some difficulty in claiming the public interest grounds successfully.

Paragraph 4

This ground covers the processing of sensitive personal data for the provision of counselling or similar services. It is intended to cover for example the counselling of victims of sexual abuse which may involve the processing of sensitive personal data about the abuser without the abuser's consent. The processing of

5–41

the sensitive personal data must be in the substantial public interest, be "necessary for the discharge of any function which is designed for the provision of confidential counselling, advice, support or any other service" and be carried out without the consent of the data subject where consent is absent on one of three grounds. These are that the processing is necessary "in a case where" consent cannot be given by the data subject; that the processing is necessary "in a case where" the data controller cannot reasonably be expected to obtain explicit consent; and that the processing:

> "must necessarily be carried out without the explicit consent of the data subject being sought so as not to prejudice the provision of that counselling, advice, support or other service".

In the first two grounds there is a requirement that the processing be "necessary". This appears to repeat the requirement set out in para.4(b) and it is not clear whether two different elements are being dealt with here or whether the repetition is merely an unfortunate piece of drafting. Under para.4(b) the processing of the sensitive personal data must "be necessary for the discharge of any function etc…". Under para.4(c)(i) and (ii) the processing of the sensitive personal data must also be "necessary in a case where consent cannot be given…" and be "necessary in a case where the data controller cannot reasonably be expected to obtain the explicit consent of the data subject". A different formulation is then used in para.4(c)(iii), which applies when it would be possible to seek the consent of the data subject, under which the processing "must necessarily be carried out without the explicit consent of the data subject being sought…".

Paragraph 5

5–42   This paragraph and the following one deal with processing necessary for carrying on insurance business. Paragraph 5 potentially applies to all data. In essence it allows insurance companies and pension schemes to hold relevant medical information about the family of the insured person or scheme member for use in insurance decisions as long as it is not used for decisions affecting those family members. The processing of the sensitive personal data must either be necessary for the purpose of carrying on an insurance business or of determining eligibility or benefits payable under occupational pensions schemes under the Pension Schemes Act 1993. "Insurance business" is defined by reference to the Insurance Companies Act 1982 (now replaced by the Financial Services and Markets Act 2000) and covers the provision of life and annuity insurance and permanent health insurance including that effected by local authorities on their members under the Local Government Act 1972. The only data which may be processed under this provision are personal data as to the physical or mental health or condition of a person who is, or was, within one of the specified categories of blood relation to the relevant insured person or the relevant member of the pension scheme. It only applies in a case where:

- the data controller cannot reasonably be expected to obtain the explicit consent of the data subject; and
- the data controller is not aware of the data subject withholding his consent.

This paragraph does not expand on what the position will be if the data subject is aware of the processing and objects to it. However, as this is part of the conditions which must be met before the ground is made out it must be that if the data subject registers any objection with the insurance company they will not be able to continue holding the data under this head. The data subject will not have to serve an objection notice under s.10 of the Act.

Paragraph 6

This deals with the processing of sensitive personal data which were subject to processing already underway immediately before the coming into force of the Order. It covers any type of sensitive data, not merely the limited category of health data dealt with under para.5, above. It must be necessary for carrying on life and annuity and permanent health insurance in a case where the data controller cannot reasonably be expected to obtain the explicit consent of the data subject and the data subject has not informed the data controller that he does not consent. This is intended for those cases where the insurance company has obtained sensitive personal data about others as part of the provision of insurance cover in the past but has no way of contacting those persons. It only applies to the historic eligible data. The same comments about subsequent objections by the data subject apply as under para.5, above, and in the event of an objection the information must be removed.

5–43

Paragraph 7

This is very similar to para.9 of Sch.3 to the Act which permits the processing of personal data relating to racial or ethnic origin for the purposes of equal opportunities monitoring. It permits the processing of additional categories of personal data relating to religious or other beliefs and mental or physical disabilities for monitoring or promoting equal opportunities. A number of specific safeguards are attached to this ground.

5–44

The processing must not support measures or decisions with respect to any particular data subject unless the subject has explicitly consented and must not cause, or be likely to cause, substantial damage or distress to any person. An individual who is the subject of personal data processed by a data controller under this provision may make an objection in writing to such processing. If he does so the data controller must cease processing the data.

Paragraph 8

This reflects the commitment given during the passage of the bill through Parliament to permit political parties to process personal data about the political opinions of individuals even if they do not have the consent of the individuals. The data may only be held by a person registered under the Registration of Political Parties Act 1998. The data controller may only process the data if the processing "does not cause nor is likely to cause, substantial damage or substantial distress to the data subject or any other person". There is a further safeguard provision in para.8(2) under which the data subject may give notice in

5–45

writing to cease the processing within "such period as is reasonable in the circumstances". The question of what is reasonable will be a matter of judgment depending on the particular circumstances.

Paragraph 9

5–46   This covers the processing of sensitive personal data for research purposes. It adopts the definition in s.33 in which "research purposes" include statistical or historical purposes. As noted in Ch.18, this is a wide definition, however, the conditions imposed on the processing are restrictive. To some extent they echo those found in s.33 but there are some differences. Moreover they are more restrictive in so far as para.9 requires that the processing of the sensitive personal data must be in the substantial public interest. Sensitive personal data may therefore only be held on this ground where there is some public interest in the research itself. The processing must also be necessary for the research purpose. The other safeguard conditions are that:

- the processing does not support measures or decisions with respect to any particular data subject otherwise than with the explicit consent of the data subject; and
- the processing does not cause, nor is likely to cause, substantial damage or substantial distress to the data subject or any other person.

The wording has been subtly altered from that employed in s.33. In s.33 the processing must not support measures or decisions with respect to "particular individuals" and the processing must not cause damage or distress to "any data subject".

Paragraph 10

5–47   This permits the processing of sensitive personal data where it is necessary for the exercise of any function conferred on a constable by any rule of law. There is no requirement that the processing be in the substantial public interest however it may be being assumed that the exercise of the powers of constables will be carried out in the public rather than any private interest.

Elected representatives

5–48   The Data Protection (Processing of Sensitive Data) (Elected Representatives) Order 2002[36] provides for the disclosure of sensitive personal data to and processing of sensitive personal data by elected representatives in certain circumstances. The Order was amended by the Data Protection (Processing of Sensitive Personal data) (Elected Representatives) (Amendment) Order 2010[37] with effect from January 17, 2011.

---

[36] SI 2002/2905.
[37] SI 2010/2961.

234

Elected representatives

The following are elected representatives for the purposes of the order: **5–49**

- a member of the House of Commons, National Assembly for Wales, Scottish Parliament or Northern Ireland Assembly;
- a UK member of the European Parliament;
- a mayor or councillor of a local authority or equivalent in the London Assembly, City of London, the Isles of Scilly, Scotland or Northern Ireland.

There are rules as to when terms of office of members end at the dissolution of Parliament or the Assemblies. The Government of Wales Act 2006 changed the relevant provisions for the Assembly and the 2010 amendment Order made the amendments to the 2002 order to accommodate these changes.

Relevant processing

Paragraph 3 permits the processing of sensitive personal data where it is carried **5–50**
out by an elected representative or a person acting with his authority. The processing must be in connection with the discharge of the functions of the elected representative. The data subject must have asked the representative to take action, either on behalf of the data subject or another individual, and the processing must be necessary for the purposes or in connection with the action reasonably taken by the elected representative. As the processing must be about the data subject and the data subject has asked the politician to help it might be thought that this would be covered by ground 1, Explicit Consent. However it may be that in such cases, while the data subject will implicitly have consented to the processing, the consent is thought to be insufficiently explicit to be eligible. It appears to have been passed as a result of difficulties faced by MPs in obtaining information from NHS Trusts about complaints from constituents about healthcare provision.

Paragraph 4 permits the processing of sensitive personal data where it is carried out by an elected representative or a person acting with his authority. The processing must be in connection with the discharge of the functions of the elected representative. The paragraph applies where the request is made by an individual other than the data subject to take action either on behalf of the data subject or another. The processing must be carried out without the explicit consent of the data subject because the processing:

- is necessary in a case where explicit consent cannot be given by the data subject;
- is necessary in a case where the elected representative cannot reasonably be expected to obtain the explicit consent of the data subject;
- must necessarily be carried out without the consent of the data subject being sought so as not to prejudice the actions of the elected representative; or
- is necessary in the interests of another individual where the explicit consent of the other individual has been unreasonably withheld.

Disclosures

5–51 Where an elected representative or someone acting with his authority has been in contact with a data controller at the request of a data subject para.5 permits the data controller to make disclosures of sensitive data where it is necessary to respond to the query.

Under para.6 the response can involve personal data about a person other than the data subject if it is necessary to carry out the processing without the explicit consent of the data subject on the same grounds as in para.4 (listed above).

The Data Protection (Processing of Sensitive Personal Data) Order 2006[38]

5–52 The 2006 Order came into effect on July 26, 2006 and allows personal data about some criminal convictions to be held by financial institutions. The intention is to facilitate the revocation of contracts with credit card holders where those credit card holders have used cards to pay for unlawful images over the Internet.

The Order provides for the processing of sensitive personal data in circumstances where the processing,

"… about a criminal conviction or caution for an offence listed in paragraph (3) relating to an indecent photograph or pseudo-photograph of a child is necessary for the purpose of administering an account relating to the payment card used in the commission of the offence or for cancelling that payment card".[39]

The relevant offences are listed and cover incitement to commit any of the relevant offences. All the crimes relate to indecent images of children. The main legislation is the Protection of Children Act 1978 (PCA), which makes it an offence to take or distribute indecent photographs or pseudo-photographs of children.[40] The Criminal Justice Act 1988 (CJA) renders mere possession (including on a hard disk) of indecent photographs or pseudo-photographs of a child an offence.[41]

A "pseudo photo" is something that "appears" to be a photo and "appears" to show a child—even if it is not based on a child or indeed a real person. In the Order the term is defined to include an image, whether made by computer-graphics or otherwise howsoever, which appears to be a photograph. This means that electronically manipulated or created images will be caught.[42] Where payment has been made using a payment card for such images and the offender has been convicted or cautioned the information may be passed to the financial institution by the relevant policing or prosecution authority and the institution is then authorised by the Order to hold the relevant personal data for the purpose of the account. The motivation is to encourage financial institutions to cancel the cards used in such criminal activity. The card issuer will usually have contractual grounds allowing the termination of the contract where the card has been used for

---

[38] SI 2006/2068.
[39] SI 2006/2068 para.(2).
[40] PCA s.1.
[41] CJA s.160.
[42] PCA s.1(7)–(9).

criminal activity but the use of the termination power raises many difficult questions. If there is another cardholder on the account the termination will presumably have to be explained and may involve a disclosure of data not already known. The termination may also have the effect of depriving the user of the use of a payment card. While it may be reasonable as a preventative measure to revoke the payment means of persistent offenders to stop them re-offending termination in other cases looks suspiciously like a punitive action which would arguably breach the individual's human rights. The power does not yet appear to have been exercised; financial institutions have so far shown little appetite for holding lists of Internet paedophiles, and it is not clear what effect it has had.

Data Protection (Processing of Sensitive Personal Data) Order 2009[43]

This allows: 5–53

> "The processing of information about a prisoner, including information relating to the prisoner's release from prison, for the purpose of informing a Member of Parliament about the prisoner and arrangements for the prisoner's release."

In the Order, "prison" includes young offender institutions, remand centres and secure training centres and "prisoner" includes a person detained in a young offender institution, remand centre or secure training centre.[44]

The notes to the Order state that:

> "In practice information will only be released to an MP pursuant to this Order if they have entered into a confidentiality agreement with the Secretary of State for Justice whereby the MP agrees not to further disclose the information. The information that will be released to the MP will be restricted to certain high risk offenders and will include the name of the prisoner, the offence they committed, details of the release data and details of any licence conditions to which the prisoner is the be subject."

As the MP cannot disclose the information it is not clear what use he or she can make of it.

Data Protection (Processing of Sensitive Personal Data) Order 2012[45]

A further Order has come into effect which will permit the processing of sensitive   5–54
personal data relating to the events that occurred at Hillsborough Stadium in Sheffield on April 15, 1989. Processing will be permitted where that disclosure is necessary to give effect to the protocol on disclosure of information published on 15th December 2009 by the Secretary of State for the Home Department for the purposes of the Hillsborough Independent Panel.

The protocol envisages disclosure of information which relates to that disaster that is held by public bodies. The protocol was prepared by the Home Office for

---

[43] SI 2009/1811.
[44] SI 2009/1811 art.1(2).
[45] SI 2012/1978

the purposes of the Hillsborough Independent Panel, a non-statutory body established in December 2009. The protocol was published by the Home Office.[46]

Safeguards

5–55   The further orders which have been made are pursuant to the provision in Article 8(4) of the Directive which states that, subject to the provision of suitable safeguards, Member States may, for reasons of substantial public interest, lay down exemptions to the prohibition on the processing of sensitive personal data in addition to those specified in 8(2). These may be done by national law or decision of the supervisory authority. While earlier orders specifically referred to substantial public interest and added safeguard provisions, which was presumably done in order to meet the requirements of the Directive, neither the 2009 order nor 2012 order include such provisions. It is assumed in each case that the view has been taken that provisions build into the disclosure schemes behind the orders identify the substantial public interest reasons for the orders and include specific safeguards and there is no requirement to repeat them on the face of the orders. Specifically in the context of the Hillsborough Order, the Hillsborough protocol on disclosure of information contains safeguards for individuals' privacy. Under the Hillsborough Order moreover the processing of sensitive personal data may take place where it is "necessary to give effect to the protocol on disclosure of information" As this imports a test of proportionality in any event an assessment would have to be made in each case about whether each proposed disclosure is justified and proportionate.

5–56   Although there may appear to be a wealth of Sch. 3 grounds the Commissioner acknowledged in the previous guidance on compliance that the absence of an equivalent "catch-all" ground to that found in Sch.2 has caused some problems, although this has not been repeated in the current Guide.

Impact of the draft Regulation in brief[47]

5–57   The draft Regulation maintains the requirement to show grounds for processing and further grounds for processing sensitive personal data. There are additional specific conditions for processing the personal data of a child under 13 where information society services are to be offered to the child. The definition of sensitive personal data is largely the same but includes genetic data and "criminal convictions or related security measures". These are not defined but it is assumed that they are meant to cover measures such as curfews or house arrest. The grounds for processing are broadly the same although there are some slight changes. Where consent is a ground for processing it must be a consent for "one or more specific purposes" under art.6. Where the basis of processing is a legal duty or power it must be provided for in Union or Member State law which reaches specified standards. A specific ground is included for the processing of personal data for statistical, historical or scientific research which refers to safeguard provisions for such data. It also provides that consent cannot be a legitimizing ground where there is a significant imbalance between the power of

---

[46] http://homeoffice.gov.uk/documents/hillsborough-tor.html[Accessed September 13, 2012].
[47] See Ch.1, paras 1–68 onwards for an overview of the proposal as at January 2012.

the controller and the subject. There are specific provisions around the nature of consent. The data controller must bear the burden of proving that there has been a valid consent; consent must be "distinguishable" where consent is obtained for more than one matter at the same time and an individual must always be able to withdraw consent. The grounds for processing sensitive personal data are largely unchanged although one of the major differences is that the processing of data related to criminal convictions will require a legal basis or a legal obligation. There is a specific ground for health purposes and a separate one for historical, scientific or statistical research. In the case of both sensitive data the Commission can lay down further grounds. Overall it is likely that the threshold conditions for processing personal data about convictions outside the public sector will be difficult to meet.

ADDITIONAL INFORMATION

Derivations   5–58

- Directive 95/46 (See Appendix B)
  - (a)   art.7 (criteria for making data processing legitimate); art.8 (the processing of special categories of data);
  - (b)   Recitals 30, 31.33, 34, 35, 36.
- Council of Europe Convention of January 28, 1981 for the Protection of Individuals with regard to automatic processing of Personal Data: art.5 (quality of data); art.6 (special categories of data).
- Data Protection Act 1984: s.2(3) (sensitive data classes).

Hansard references   5–59
Commons Standing Committee D, June 4, 1988, col.307
Ground 6 of the grounds for legitimate processing:

> "The paragraph seeks to reconcile opposing and possibly conflicting interests."

Vol.315, No.198, col.613, Commons Third Reading, July 2, 1998
Political canvassing to be dealt with by orders under para.10.
Commons Standing Committee D, May 12, 1998, col.36
Sensitive data, other beliefs of a similar nature.
Commons Standing Committee D, June 4, 1998, col.301
Failed attempt to have the canvassing of political opinions exempt and discussion of political opinion information.
Commons Standing Committee D, June 4, 1998, cols 314–316
Criminal conviction information held by various organisations, possible exemptions.

Previous case law

None.   5–60

CHAPTER 6

Principles One To Six Including Issues Common To The Exercise Of Individual Rights Under Principle 6

INTRODUCTION

The data protection principles ("the principles"),[1] found in Sch.1, set out the core standards governing the handling of personal data. All data controllers[2] who process personal data must comply with all the principles unless a specific exemption applies.[3] The principles apply irrespective of the notification status of the controller. They derive from the standards originally set out in Treaty 108 in 1981,[4] which were the basis of the Data Protection Act 1984 and were strengthened by the requirements of Directive 95/46. Schedule 1 includes extensive interpretation provisions and the principles are further amplified by three additional Schedules: Sch.2, which sets out the conditions for legitimising processing; Sch.3, which sets out the conditions for legitimising the processing of sensitive personal data; and Sch.4, which sets out the derogations from the ban on the transfer of personal data overseas to jurisdictions which do not provide adequate protection. Schedules 2 and 3 are covered in Ch.5 and Sch.4 in Ch.8. In this Chapter the requirements of Principles 1–6 are considered; Principle 7, which deals with the security requirements, is covered in Ch.7.

6–01

SUMMARY OF MAIN POINTS

6–02

(a) The first principle incorporates a detailed set of rules that apply to the obtaining and processing of personal data.

(b) The requirement of lawfulness in the first principle incorporates considerations of other legal rules and requires data controllers to have regard to other laws in the context of data protection.

---

[1] It was previously the practice of the Registrar and then the Commissioner to capitalise the principles although the capital is not used in the Act. That practice has now altered. As in previous editions, we have followed the practice of the Commissioner.

[2] See Ch.4 for the meaning of "data controller", "process" and "personal data".

[3] See s.4(4). Exemptions are covered in Chs 15–19.

[4] Council of Europe Convention: see Ch.1 for the background to the legislation generally.

(c)   Principle 2 incorporates the finality principle and imposes limits on the processing of personal data for purposes other than those specified by the data controller either at the point of obtaining or on the register of notifications.

(d)   Principles 3–5 are referred to as the "data quality principles" and include standards of accuracy and retention. They are often considered together as the requirements overlap.

(e)   Principle 6 incorporates the rights of data subjects so that the Commissioner is able to deal with breaches of the individual rights by the use of his investigation and enforcement powers.

(f)   There are only limited formal requirements for the service of rights notices and requests and such notices and requests can be served by electronic means.

(g)   Children can exercise the rights on their own behalf if they are of sufficient understanding.

(h)   Individuals may agree to waive their rights but the rights cannot be excluded otherwise.

(i)   Data subjects are able to seek compensation for any breach of the principles which causes them damage; however in most instances data subjects tend to refer breaches of the principles to the Commissioner rather than taking action in court.

(j)   The principles apply to the personal data relating to each separate individual who is the subject of the data so may be breached in respect of one person but not of others.

There have been remarkably few cases directly on the principles. Principle 1 has been considered in cases heard by the Information Rights Tribunal under the Freedom of Information Act 2000. These have taken effect in a very specific context and are covered in more detail in Ch.26. In addition several of the topics covered by them, such as retention and fairness, have been considered in cases under the Human Rights Act 1998 or other areas. In considering the application of the principles in a particular matter the practitioner is recommended to review these cases including any relevant case law from the CJEU and ECtHR. A summary of the relevant case law from the ECtHR can be found in Ch.2 and the ECJ/CJEU cases on data protection in Ch.3. Regard should also be had to any relevant codes of practice plus any guidance from the Commissioner. It may also be useful to consider papers from the Article 29 Working Party but be aware that the Working Party tends to an increasingly expansive view and UK courts have tended to take a more pragmatic approach. In particular sectors additional detailed guidance has been produced on the application of the principles and the way in which they relate to other regulatory regimes. There are a number of statutory codes which cover related areas, for example the new CCTV code of practice under the Protection of Freedoms Act 2012 will cover areas of data protection concern as well as technical standards. In the health sector practitioners should be aware of the Caldicott principles and the NHS guidance on the uses and disclosures of health information; specific guidance is also found in the financial services sector and much of the public sector including policing and central and local government.[5] The courts have occasionally referred to the relevant codes for example the Code of Practice on the Management of Police Information made under s39A of the Police Act 1996 was referred to in the case of *R. (RMC and FJ) v Commissioner of Police of Metropolis*[6] in relation to the retention of information. The Commissioner's codes of practice on employment and on CCTV are largely devoted to the way that the principles apply in those specific areas. The Commissioner has also produced codes of practice on the application of the principles in specific situations such as the use of privacy notices online.

Enforcement

Enforcement of the principles is carried out by the Commissioner using his enforcement powers, including the powers to serve enforcement notices or impose monetary penalty notices. As an example the Commissioner's annual report from 2011–2012 reports on the service of a preliminary enforcement notice in respect of the use of continuous sound recording in taxis which he considered to be unfair and unlawful processing contrary to the first data protection principle. A number of the data subject's rights are also primarily enforced by the Commissioner as principle 6 requires that personal data be processed in accordance with the data subject's rights. This applies particularly to the right of subject access[7] and the right to object to direct marketing.[8] However, the Commissioner has no locus in respect of claims for compensation.[9] In practice also the Commissioner is unlikely to become involved in claims to prevent processing likely to cause damage or distress[10] or to object to automated decision-making. All of the data subjects' rights under the Act can be enforced by data subjects applying for court orders to enforce their rights. In the case of *The Law Society and Others v Kordowski*,[11] the claimants took their own action to enforce their rights after the Commissioner declined to deal with the complaint. They succeeded in claims against the defendant, which included claims for breach of principles 1, 3 and 6. The High Court granted the Claimants injunctive relief to stop the Defendant running his website (enticingly called Solicitors from Hell) or transferring ownership of it or the data overseas. Enforcement is covered in Ch.20.

6–03

THE FIRST PRINCIPLE

This reflects arts 6.1a, 10 and 11 of the Directive. It requires that personal data shall be processed fairly and lawfully and in particular shall not be processed unless at least one of the conditions in Sch.2 is met and, in the case of sensitive

6–04

---

[5] See "Report on the Review of Patient-Identifiable Information" by the Caldicott Committee December 1997 and the NHS Information Centre website at *www.ic.nhs.uk* .
[6] [2012] EWHC 1681 (Admin).
[7] s.7.
[8] s.11.
[9] s.13.
[10] s.10.
[11] [2011] EWHC 3185 (QB).

personal data, at least one of the conditions in Sch.3 is also met. The Sch.2 and Sch.3 requirements are dealt with in Ch.5. The interpretation provisions to the principles lay down a set of rules which apply to the processing of personal data to ensure fairness.

Processing is defined in s.1(1) of the 1998 Act as meaning in relation to information or data, "obtaining, recording or holding" the information or data and carrying out various operations with respect to the data including: organising, adapting, altering, retrieving, consulting, using, disclosing, aligning, combining, erasing or blocking the information or the data. The term "processing" is considered in Ch.4 on the definitions. The breadth of the term was confirmed in *Campbell v Mirror Group Newspapers*[12] when the Court of Appeal confirmed that processing covered all handling of personal data up to the moment of publication in hard copy however the later decision in the case of *Johnson v Medical Defence Union*[13] put a narrower meaning, at least as far as the selection of information from computerized records is concerned. The case also went on to consider the question of fairness. This element is explored further below.

Neither "fairly" nor "lawfully" are defined in the legislation and accordingly must be given their normal meaning. The term "fairly" is subject to extensive interpretation in Pt II of Sch.I.

Lawfully

6–05   The term "lawfully" means that all processing must be in accord with all relevant laws, covering common law, civil law and criminal law. Personal data which are processed in breach of any statutory provision or legally enforceable obligation or restriction will be processed unlawfully. In *Murray v Express Newspapers Ltd* [2007] EWHC 1908 (Ch) Patten J. said:

> "It seems to me that the reference to lawfully in Schedule 1, Part 1 must be construed by reference to the current state of the law in particular in relation to the misuse of confidential information. The draftsman of the Act has not attempted to give the word any wider or special meaning and it is therefore necessary to apply to the processor of personal data the same obligations of confidentiality as would otherwise apply but for the Act".

This was followed in *Law Society v Kordowski* [2011] EWHC 3185 (QB). The term "lawfully" therefore imports more than compliance with the requirements of the Act itself. That possibility has been suggested because the Recitals to the Directive suggest that "lawfully" could be limited to compliance with the national legislation governing data protection rather than requiring compliance with all relevant legal obligations. Recital 28 commences: "Whereas any processing of personal data must be lawful and fair . . ." Recital 30 then continues: "Whereas, in order to be lawful, the processing must in addition be . . ." and then sets out most of the Sch.2 conditions.[14]

This argument, however, ran counter to the stated intent of the Directive, to harmonize data protection at a level which met the best standards of all the

---

[12] [2002] EWCA Civ 1373.
[13] [2007] EWCA Civ 262.
[14] See the arguments put by Professor Liddell Bio-Science Law Review, Vol.6, Issue 6, 2003/2004.

previous regimes "harmonization at a high level". The requirement to process personal data lawfully is found in Treaty 108 and appeared in the text of the first principle of the Data Protection Act 1984 (the UK's previous legal regime). Under that Act the Registrar's views that the term "lawful" required the data controller to comply with all relevant laws affecting the data processing received the support of the Data Protection Tribunal explicitly in the case of ultra vires, and implicitly in the case of confidentiality, in the appeal by British Gas Trading Ltd (BGTL).[15] Therefore the restriction of the term to a self-referential regime would have been a reduction of the level of protection both from Treaty 108 and in the UK and from the previous legal regime and not permissible in terms of the Directive.

Relation with the Human Rights Act (HRA)

Section 3(1) of the Human Rights Act provides that, so far as it is possible to do so, primary and subordinate legislation must be "read and given effect in a way which is compatible with the Convention rights".

Article 8 of the Convention provides:

6–06

"(1)   Everyone has the right to respect for his private and family life, his home and his correspondence.
(2)   There shall be no interference by a public authority with the exercise of this right except such as is in accordance with the law and is necessary in a democratic society in the interests of national security, public safety or the economic well-being of the country, for the prevention of disorder or crime, for the protection of health or morals, or for the protection of the rights and freedoms of others."

The art.8 right is neither absolute nor paramount. The second part of art.8 makes clear that the state can interfere with the right where other overriding interests require. Any interference must be lawful, justified by reference to one or more of the public interests specified within art.8, and proportionate. Furthermore, the right to a private life has to be balanced with other rights specified in the Convention and in particular art.10—the right to freedom of expression, which provides:

"(1)   Everyone has the right to freedom of expression. This right shall include freedom to hold opinions and to receive and impart information and ideas without interference by public authority and regardless of frontiers. This Article shall not prevent States from requiring the licensing of broadcasting, television or cinema enterprises.
(2)   The exercise of these freedoms, since it carries with it duties and responsibilities may be subject to such formalities, conditions, restrictions or penalties as are prescribed by law and are necessary in a democratic society, in the interests of national security, territorial integrity or public safety, for the prevention of disorder or crime, for the protection of health or morals, for the protection of the reputation or rights of others, for preventing the disclosure of information received in confidence, or for maintaining the authority and impartiality of the judiciary."

---

[15] *British Gas Ltd v Data Protection Registrar,* March 1998. *www.judgmental.org.uk.*

An action which fails to respect an individual's right to be treated lawfully and fairly in the informational sphere is likely to be regarded as a breach of the art.8 right.

An example might be the disclosure of personal data consisting of medical records without consent or other lawful justification. This would be both a breach of the obligation of confidence and a breach of art.8 and thus unlawful under principle 1 as well as being unfair. (Note: The impact of the Human Rights Act is discussed in much greater detail in Ch.2.) In cases on information use and privacy since the passage of the HRA the courts in the UK have tended to focus on the application of the HRA and art.8 rather than the impact of the DPA even where the areas covered would fall under both regimes. As an example, in *R. (Wright) v Secretary of State for Health*[16] the House of Lords held that the low standard of proof before an individual could be provisionally included on the lists of those barred from working with vulnerable adults or children (the POVA and POCA lists respectively) and the denial of opportunity to make representations before being provisionally included on the lists meant that the relevant statutes were incompatible with Convention rights. The DPA was not argued in the case but it is submitted that, if it had been, the process of listing could also have been argued to be unfair processing of the personal data of those listed.

6–07   The courts have described the natural meaning of "unlawful" as "something which is contrary to some law or enactment or is done without lawful justification or excuse".[17] The areas of law most commonly engaged in relation to the use of personal information are:

- breaches of the criminal law which involve personal data, not only those which are offences under the DPA, but other offences such as hacking or identity theft;
- civil law breaches, such as breaches of confidentiality where one arises from the relationship between data controller and data subject, breaches of contract or of statutory obligations and tortious acts;
- failure to meet the rules of administrative law restricting the activities of public bodies to those which are within their legitimate powers; and
- breach of art.8 of the Convention rights in the Human Rights Act 1998.[18]

Breach of the criminal law

6–08   The range of criminal offences that may be committed using personal data is wide. Those offences which focus on the use of personal data, apart from offences under the Act itself and those directly concerned with misrepresentation, would appear to be hacking, identity fraud and pornography. It is perhaps unlikely that action would be taken under the DPA where defendants were being charged with the more serious offences however they are dealt with briefly here.

---

[16] [2009] UKHL 3.
[17] *R v R* [1991] 4 All E.R. 481.
[18] For a full analysis of the law of confidence and data protection see Ch.2.

Hacking

The act of unauthorised alteration or destruction of computer-based personal data is unlikely to amount to an offence of criminal damage in contravention of the Criminal Damage Act 1971 because there will generally be no physical damage. However, such actions may be contrary to the Computer Misuse Act 1990 (CMA) as amended by the Police and Justice Act 2006 and the Serious Crime Act 2007.   **6–09**

The CMA as amended creates four basic offences which cover:

- securing unauthorised access to any program or data held on a computer or enabling such access to be secured (s.1);
- securing or enabling such unauthorised access to a computer with a view to committing or facilitating a serious criminal offence (for example, some form of fraud) (s.2);
- carrying out an unauthorised act in relation to a computer which impairs the operation of the computer, any software or the reliability of any data or enabling any of these to be done (s.3); and
- making, supplying or obtaining any articles for use in offences under s.1 or s.3. For these purposes the term "articles" includes any program or data held in electronic form (s.3A).

The offences in s.1 have to be committed deliberately rather than accidentally.[19] Data or programs on a removable storage medium are also covered. "Securing access" or "enabling such access to be secured" is established if a hacker alters, erases, copies, moves, uses or outputs any program or data or carries out acts which enable another to do this whether by means of a program or by human delivery.[20] The offences in s.3 may be committed where the person is reckless as to whether his actions will have the effect of impairing the operation of any computer, preventing or hindering access to any program or data held in a computer or will impair the operation of any such program or the reliability of any such data. The offence of making, adapting supplying or offering an article for use in the commission of an offence in s.3A(1) requires intent however it is also an offence to supply or offer to supply an article "believing that it is likely to be used to commit or assist in the commission of" an offence under ss.1 or 3.[21] This provision gave rise to some concern when it was first introduced from those who work in the area of computer security and provide the tools to test the security of systems that this could criminalise the distribution of programs used by legitimate IT professionals to check whether a network is secure.[22] The concerns however have not been borne out to date and "penetration testing" which is a form of attempted hacking with consent is now an important feature in assessing the security of an organisation's IT systems. The Police and Justice Act 2006 also increased the penalties for offences so that all the offences, including

---

[19] Computer Misuse Act s.1(1)(c).
[20] Computer Misuse Act s.17.
[21] Computer Misuse Act s.3A(2).
[22] Reported at Outlaw 21/11/2006.

the basic offence of securing access or enabling access to be secured, became indictable and punishable by up to two years imprisonment on conviction on indictment.[23]

The strengthening of the provisions was the subject of a campaign by Computer Weekly magazine and others for several years. The revised provisions made clear that "denial of service" attacks are caught by the provisions as well as catching those who provide programs which are made available to assist would be hackers over the internet. There seem to have been relatively few cases of cases under the CMA. There is no central reporting. A table of cases is maintained on a website run by a forensic expert.[24] Some of the cases reported show the overlap with the misuse of personal data, for example the site lists a case in which a Primary Care Trust data manager accessed confidential data relating to female patients. He was sentenced to six months imprisonment suspended for two years. Guidance on prosecutions and the offences can be found at the CPS site on *www.cps.gov.uk*.

Fraud based on identity theft

6–10   The growth of fraud has continued inexorably and identity fraud is part of that picture fuelled by the growth of personal data and the ease with which it can be misused. In 2011 the National Fraud Authority put the total cost of fraud in the UK as £38.4 billion annually. It is acknowledged that the figures are hard to ascertain but they estimated that identity fraud suffered by individuals makes up about £4 billion of that annual amount[25]:

> "Identity fraud occurs when an individual's personal information is used by someone else without their knowledge to obtain, credit, goods or other services fraudulently. Measuring the financial impact from identity fraud is challenging, partly because there is no standard definition of identity fraud but also due to the fact that identity fraud is an enabler rather than a specific type of fraud."[26]

There are a range of initiatives aimed at helping individuals and businesses deal with the problems of fraud. The website *www.identitytheft.org*[27] aims to provide advice to those who become victims of fraud and is sponsored by a range of public and private bodies with an interest in the issue. The control of identity fraud depends on stopping criminals from being able to obtain and use identity documents. This requires cooperation between the private and public sectors so that, for example credit agencies are alerted when documents have been stolen and the police are able to check the records of such use. The Serious Crime Act 2007[28] introduced specific data-sharing provisions allowing for the exchange of data which includes personal data between specified fraud bodies and the public sector as part of the work to tackle this problem. Information may be disclosed

---

[23] Computer Misuse Act ss.1–3.

[24] *www.Computerevidence.co.uk* [Accessed September 13, 2012].

[25] Annual Fraud Indicator 2011 published by the National Fraud Authority: see *www.homeoffice.gov. uk/publications* [Accessed September 13, 2012].

[26] National Fraud Authority Annual Report.

[27] Accessed September 13, 2012.

[28] In force from March 1, 2008.

public bodies of information for the purposes of preventing fraud to any anti-fraud organization. Such disclosures must comply with a Code of Practice.[29] Certain bodies are also authorized to carry out data marching exercises for the purposes of fraud detection.[30]

The Fraud Act 2006 which came into effect on January 1, 2007 includes a range of offences which may be committed by those dealing with personal data. These include the offence of failing to disclose information which a person is under a legal duty to disclose[31] and actively misrepresenting the truth.[32] In each case the offence must be committed knowingly or recklessly and the person must be acting dishonestly and with intent to make a gain for himself or another or cause loss to another or expose another to the risk of loss. In dealing with false representation the Act criminalizes "phishing" and in ss.6–8 also criminalises the production and possession of "phishing" kits. Phishing is the act of setting up a website or sending an e mail to people purporting to come from a financial institution and obtaining the financial details of those individuals to use in fraudulent transactions. It is also an offence to possess the software and tools necessary to launch a phishing attack or to write software knowing that it is designed or adapted for use in connection with fraud.

These changes update the law and address the fact that personal data on a computer does not constitute "intangible property" and is consequently incapable of being stolen. A data thief could only be charged with the theft of a data storage medium. In *Oxford v Moss*,[33] it was held that confidential information per se did not come within the definition of "property" in s.4 of the Theft Act. (A student obtained, read and returned the proof of an examination paper; he was charged with the theft of confidential information but acquitted.)

Obscenity and indecency

A number of statutes deal with indecency of images and personal data. The Obscene Publications Act 1959 makes it an offence to publish an obscene article or have one for publication for gain and includes powers to prevent such articles from reaching the market by seizure and forfeiture.[34] The Act was amended to deal with electronically stored data and the transmission of such data. The Video Recordings Act 2010 also creates criminal offences which may involve personal data held in electronic format. The Protection of Children Act 1978 (PCA) includes provisions which deal with the holding of personal data relating to children and addresses some issues which have a more general application in dealing with personal data. It is an offence to take or distribute indecent photographs or pseudo-photographs of children.[35] The Criminal Justice Act 1988 (CJA) renders mere possession (including on a hard disk) of indecent photographs or pseudo-photographs of a child an offence.[36]

6–11

---

[29] Serious Crime Act 2007 s.68.
[30] Serious Crime Act s.73 and Sch.7.
[31] Fraud Act 2006 s.3.
[32] Fraud Act 2006 s.2.
[33] (19780 68 Cr.App.R.183.DC.
[34] Obscene Publications Act 1959 ss.2 and 3
[35] PCA, s.1.
[36] CJA, s.160.

A "pseudo photo" is something that "appears" to be a photo and "appears" to show a child—even if it is not based on a child. This means that electronically manipulated or created images will be caught.[37] In such a case the data will not meet the definition of personal data and there will be no unlawful processing under the DPA.

In 2002, the Court of Appeal gave more detailed consideration to what amounts to "possessing" such material in the context of individuals who browse the world wide web and encounter indecent photographs but do not deliberately download the images. There are two parts to the judgment in the case of *R. v Smith*.[38] The first "exonerates" an individual who inadvertently stumbles across indecent photos of children whilst browsing with the result that a copy of the image ends up on his or her hard drive. However, those who cause an indecent photo to appear on their computer screen (even though they do not actively download it) providing they hold the necessary criminal intent are regarded as being in "possession" of such material. The court defined the required criminal intent as

> "the act of making should be a deliberate and intentional act with knowledge that the image made is, or is likely to be an indecent photograph or pseudo-photograph of a child."

Not surprisingly the question of whether those persons became data controllers for the data in question did not exercise the Court of Appeal.

Confidentiality

6–12   The relationship between confidentiality and art.8 of the Convention has given rise to significant case law as the courts have developed the tort of misuse of private information. The cases which develop this aspect of personal privacy are covered in Ch.2. The fundamental point however is that where an obligation of confidence applies in relation to personal data any breach of the obligation without justification is likely to amount to unlawful processing in breach of principle 1. In the cases of *A v B*[39] and *Campbell v MGN Ltd*,[40] the Courts held that a duty of confidence can apply even where information is not "confided" in the traditional manner. The obligation of confidence will apply "in any circumstances where an individual has a reasonable expectation of privacy in relation to the information in question."

There are three grounds which will justify the disclosure of confidential information. These are:

(a)   consent of the individual;
(b)   compulsion of law; and
(c)   public interest.

---

[37] PCA, s.1(7)–(9).
[38] *R v. Smith,* [EWCA] Crim 683 2003, *The Times*, April 23, 2002, CA.
[39] [2002] 3 W.L.R. 542.
[40] [2002] EWCA Civ 337.

Public interest will not necessarily justify widespread publication. Even where the public interest means that the obligation of confidence may be set aside the disclosure of confidential information should only be made to the appropriate authorities.

There are a number of cases where the courts have engaged in balancing the obligation of confidence against the wider public interest requiring disclosure.[41] A fuller exposition is found in Ch.2. In many of these cases the disclosure proposed is not a disclosure to the world at large. In *Wakefield v Channel Four Television Corp*[42] the General Medical Council (GMC) argued that they should not disclose information provided by patients in relation to disciplinary proceedings to Channel 4 to enable it to defend itself against a claim by the applicant as they had obtained the documents under compulsory powers and were therefore not entitled to use them for another purpose; they had given assurances that the documents would only be used for the purposes for which they were obtained and it would undermine their investigative function of they were required to disclose. The Court held that the GMC should make the disclosure taking into account the fact that the disclosure to the applicant would not result in wider disclosure of the information and that it was necessary to enable the proceedings to be dealt with. It advised that the GMC should ensure that its undertakings of confidentiality were accurate and not over-stated.

In the *Campbell* case the House of Lords also accepted that there is a public interest in the disclosure of personal information which "sets the record straight" where the subject has misled the public.

The law of confidence applies to public bodies as well as to private persons. The question as to whether a public body will be bound in confidence wherever it obtains information under compulsory powers or only where the information is particularly sensitive is a difficult one and there is no clear authority on the point. Although case law suggests that the former is the case the cases have all concerned information which was sensitive (although not necessarily in terms of the DPA). These issues are touched on briefly below but covered more fully under the topic of data-sharing in Ch.25. The disclosure of information by the police in considered in Ch.27.

6–13

Breach of contract or tortious wrongs

Information obtained (or otherwise processed) in breach of an enforceable contractual agreement will be unlawfully obtained (or otherwise processed). This intersects however with the broader question of whether information to which an obligation of confidence applies can be disclosed as most contractual clauses bind the parties to maintain confidentiality in information which qualifies for protection as such. The question is therefore more usually addressed as a matter

6–14

---

[41] See, for example, *Butler v Board of Trade* [1971] 1 Ch. 680; *Norwich Pharamacal Co v Commissioners for Customs and Excise* [1973] 2 All E.R. 943; *Alfred Crompton Amusement Machines v Commissioner for Customs and Excise (No.2)* [1973] 2 All E.R. 1169; *Marcel v Commissioner for Police of Metropolis*[1992] 1 All E.R. 72; *Lornhop v Fayed (No.4)* [1994] 1 All E.R. 870; *Bank of Crete v Koskotos (No.2)* [1993] All E.R. 748; *Hoechst UK Ltd v Chemiculture* [1993] F.S.R. 270; *Hellewell v Chief Constable of Derbyshire* [12993] 4 All E.R. 473; *Melton Medes Ltd v SIB* [1995] 3 All E.R.
[42] [2006] EWHC 3289 (QB).

of confidentiality. In addition, actions for defamation will involve allegations of the unlawful processing of personal data as can breaches of intellectual property rights. In *Law Society v Kordowski*[43] the High Court held that the maintenance of the website "Solicitors from Hell" was both unfair and unlawful. It was unlawful by virtue of being in breach of the Protection from Harassment Act 1997 as well as libellous. In that case the court granted a perpetual injunction to prohibit the publication of the website or any similar site.

Powers of public bodies

6–15   The public sector does not enjoy the same freedom of action as the private sector. Public bodies are set up and funded for specific purposes, often with restrictions on the ways in which those purposes are achieved. The nature of the way that the restrictions are enforced are different depending on the nature of the public body but whatever the nature of the body the courts have the power to act to ensure that the body acts only within its powers. Where bodies are established under statute, such as local authorities, their powers will be set out in the statute which establishes the body.[44] They have the powers that Parliament granted them in the statute. The body may carry out those things mandated by the statute and those which are reasonably incidental to them.[45] This is called the ultra vires rule as authorities must not act ultra vires or outside their powers. The Crown is different as the Crown has inherent powers and starts with all the powers of a natural person, in other words the Crown can do anything that is not prohibited by the law. However in many areas Parliament has legislated and where there is legislation then the powers of the Crown are limited by that legislation and must be exercised in accord with it.[46] The Crown may also do those things which are reasonably incidental to the relevant functions. However, this does not extend powers. The absence of an express restriction on an activity does not mean that it can be carried out under and ancillary powers.[47]

In carrying out their functions, public bodies of any type must not act unreasonably, unfairly or use their powers for the wrong reasons. If they do any of these things, then they may be subject to judicial review.

Legitimate expectation

6–16   The courts have also developed the doctrine of legitimate expectation which may constrain the actions of a public body. The processing of personal data in breach of a legitimate expectation could therefore amount to unlawful processing of such personal data. The conditions in which a legitimate expectation will arise were explained in *Council of Civil Service Unions v Minister for the Civil Service*.[48] A legitimate expectation may arise either from an express promise given on behalf

---

[43] [2011] EWHC 3185.

[44] See comment of Lord Neill in *Credit Suisse v Waltham Forest* [1996] 4 All E.R. 176 that statutory powers are conferred on local authorities on trust and can only be used in the ways that Parliament is presumed to have intended.

[45] *Attorney General v Great Eastern Railway* [1880] 5 App. Cas. 473.

[46] *R. v Secretary of State for the Home Department Ex p. Fire Brigades Union* [1995] 2 A.C. 513.

[47] *Credit Suisse v Allderdale BC* [1966] 1 All E.R. 129.

[48] [1984] 3 All E.R. 935.

of a public authority or from the existence of a regular practice. The authority must by its words or its conduct have led someone to expect that it will act in a particular way so that the person affected will receive or retain a benefit. The authority may then be held to its promise or made to abide by its practice unless it is lawful for it to resile from its position. In *R. v North and East Devon Health Authority Ex p. Coughlan*[49] the Court of Appeal explained that consideration must be given to the precise terms of the promise, the circumstances in which it was made and the nature of the discretion that was involved. The Court distinguished between those cases where the public authority was only required to consider the promise and weight it fairly; those where the promise imposes a procedural obligation of consultation before a particular course is adopted and those where the promise has induced a legitimate expectation of a benefit which is substantive. Only if the case falls into the last category will it be enforceable against the public authority.

The concept applies not just to the Crown but also to other public authorities.[50]

As has been noted above, the Human Rights Act also imposes on public authorities the obligation to act only in accord with Convention rights. The intersection of these rules on lawfulness on the use that public bodies can make of the personal data which they obtain or generate as a result of their functions has given rise to a number of uncertainties which have yet to be resolved by the courts. In particular there is a lack of clarity over how far information obtained for one function can legitimately be used for other, unassociated, purposes. It is clear that information can always be disclosed for the purposes of the prevention of crime and the protection of the public as long as the disclosures are limited to those who need to know and accompanied by appropriate safeguards. In the case of *Chief Constable of Humberside v Information Commissioner*[51] the Court of Appeal held that police forces were entitled to hold and retain conviction information on the Police National Computer not only for their own purposes of operational policing but also the use for employment vetting and disclosure to the Criminal Records Bureau, disclosure to the Crown prosecution and the courts for records of convictions and use for multi-agency work to co-operate with other agencies such as social services. These are however closely linked purposes and carried out by public bodies with similar aims. The question of additional uses of personal data among public bodies is covered in Ch.25 on data sharing.

6–17

Breach of other statutory provisions or requirements of soft law

In most cases it is unlikely that the Commissioner will regard breaches of other statutes as being his concern, and indeed has made it clear that he does not regard it as the role of his office to police areas other than the core data protection standards. However, there has been an interesting development in the Protection of Freedoms Act 2012 which has dealt with a number of areas in which the Commissioner's Office has been active. In relation to CCTV and to the retention of DNA in the criminal justice system that Act has also set up separate regulators

6–18

---

[49] [2001] Q.B. 213.
[50] *R. v Devon CC Ex p. Baker* [1995] 1 All E.R. 73, and its joint case *R. v Durham CC Ex p. Curtis.*
[51] [2009] EWCA Civ 1079.

to deal with the issues; however in relation to the fingerprints or other biometrics of children this is not the case and it suggested that the ICO might come under pressure to act in this area.

Under the provisions dealing with the biometric information of children (defined as being under 18) any processing of biometric information by the proprietor of a school or governing body requires prior written notice to the parents unless there are good reasons which make this impossible such as mental incapacity.[52] The parent must also be told of the right to object at any time. The biometric information must not be processed if the child refuses or objects, irrespective of the consent of a parent. Otherwise it can take place as long as at least one parent of the child consents and no parent has objected or withdrawn consent to the processing. It follows that the parents are split on the issue the one which lodges the objection (which must be in writing) will prevail. Where there has been an objection to the processing of biometrics the authority must ensure that there are reasonable alternatives to allow the child to carry out the relevant activities, for example to use the school library. Section 27(5) specifically states that these provsions are in addition to the requirements of the DPA. The provisions have no obvious mechanism for enforcement and it seems reasonable to assume that parents or children who are aggrieved by a failure to comply may seek recourse to the Information Commissioner. Biometric information is defined as information about a person's physical or behavioural characteristics or features which are capable of being used to establish or verify the identity of the person and is obtained or recorded with the intention that it be used for the purposes of a biometric recognition system. It may in particular include information about skin pattern and other physical characteristics or features of a person's fingers or palms, information about the features of an iris or other part of the eye and information about a person's voice or handwriting. It also defines a "biometric recognition system" as one in which information is stored and subsequently information is obtained to compare and verify the identity of the individual.[53]

Does unlawful always mean unfair?

6–19   Personal data must be processed both fairly and lawfully. It is difficult, at first, to conceive of "unlawful" processing that might still be considered "fair" however the two may not be co-terminous. Fairness is a concept which is applicable between two or more parties, usually individuals but possibly organisations or statutory bodies. Lawfulness imports a community-wide set of norms enforceable by the intervention of the state or agreements which can be enforced by courts.

An act could be fair between consenting private parties but unlawful by virtue of legal rules, for example, the madam of a brothel who, with the full consent of both her clients and her staff, keeps a computerised list of clients and their particular preferences for the purpose of running the establishment might not be acting unfairly in carrying out such processing but might be acting unlawfully.

---

[52] Protection of Freedoms Act Pt 3 s.26.
[53] Protection of Freedoms Act s.28(3) and (4).

Breach of Article 8

As noted earlier, in an increasing number of cases the courts have been asked to **6–20** rule on the legitimacy of an organisation's actions in terms of art.8 rather than common law or confidentiality terms although there is often a high degree of overlap between the areas. In *Jane Clift v Slough Borough Council*[54] the Court of Appeal considered the relation between the defence of qualified privilege to an action for libel and the application of the individual's rights under art.8 of the HRA. It held that the wide disclosure of information about Ms Clift to employees of the Council who had no need to know it was outside the protection of qualified privilege and disproportionate. The material was clearly defamatory. It held that a breach of art.8 would render the publication unlawful. If the publication was unlawful the defence of qualified privilege would fall away and the Council would be liable to the publication. The case concerned the inclusion of information on Ms Clift on a register of violent people and is considered in more detailed in Ch.25 on data sharing.

In the Guide to Data Protection the Commissioner has made clear that his **6–21** policy remains one of steering clear of taking positions on other areas of law:

> "Although processing of personal data in breach of copyright (for example) will involve unlawful processing, this does not mean that the ICO will pursue allegations of breach of copyright (or any other law) as this would go beyond the remit of the Data Protection Act. Many areas of law are complex and the ICO is not and cannot be expected to be expert in all of them".

It follows that complainants who are raising issues of unlawful behaviour based on laws others that the DPA will therefore be unlikely to rely on the Commissioner to assist and may need to take their own actions.

Fairly

It is submitted that "fairly" must be an objective standard. This was the **6–22** Registrar's view under the 1984 Act. In the publication The Guidelines,[55] the Registrar contended:

> "Standards of fairness and lawfulness must be objectively assessed and applied. To assess the proper standards the Registrar will use the standpoint of the 'common man'. Thus the Registrar may decide that a data user has contravened the [first] Principle even though the data user did not intend to be unfair and did not consider himself to be acting unfairly."

The point is not dealt with in the current Guidance material; however, there is no reason to assume that the Commissioner would take a different view. In the current Guide the Commissioner focusses largely on transparency and notices. In relation to fairness it covers:

- sharing of data between organisations;

---

[54] [2010] EWCA Civ 1171.
[55] 3rd series, November 1994, at p.59.

- use for a new purpose; and
- disclosure to other organisations for their purposes (in respect of which it advises that individuals should generally be given a choice about such disclosures).

Fairness under the 1984 Act

6–23   A number of cases were decided by the Data Protection Tribunal under the parallel provision (the First Principle) of the 1984 Act. In those cases the Tribunal stated that the purpose of that Act was to protect the rights of the individual about whom data are obtained, stored, processed or supplied, rather than those of the data user.[56] The Tribunal took the view that, in deciding whether processing is fair, the most important single consideration would be the interest of the data subject. The Tribunal weighed the various considerations involved in any particular case but ultimately always gave more weight to the interests of the individual.[57]

In earlier Legal Guidance the interests of the data subject were described as being "paramount".[58] Although the Tribunal did use the term in the first credit reference decision, *CCN Systems Limited v The Data Protection Registrar*, it distanced itself from the term in the second decision *Infolink v The Data Protection Registrar*. The cases have been referred to with approval in subsequent cases[59]; however, in a case decided by the Information Tribunal in an appeal under the Freedom of Information Act 2000 (FOIA) decided in January 2007,[60] the Tribunal has indicated that, in deciding whether a disclosure of personal data under the FOIA is fair, the *CNN* and *Infolink* cases can be distinguished. In that decision the Tribunal made clear that the question of the fairness of the processing has to be considered in all the circumstances of the particular case. In the particular circumstances the processing concerned personal data of public officials which was being processed for the purpose of a public function. In that case the interests of the officials were not first or paramount:

> " ... we find that when assessing the fair processing requirements under the DPA that the consideration given to the interests of data subjects who are public officials where data are processed for a public function, is no longer first or paramount. Their interests are still important but where data subjects carry out public functions, hold elective office or spend public funds they must have the expectation that their public actions will be subjected to greater scrutiny than would be the case with their private lives".

In the same vein the Court of Appeal, in *Johnson v Medical Defence Union*,[61] agreed that in assessing fairness the position of the data controller must also be considered. In the Commissioner's current Guide to Data Protection it states that:

---

[56] *CCN Systems Ltd v The Data Protection Registrar* February 1991, para.5. *www.judgmental.org.uk*.
[57] *Infolink Ltd v The Data Protection Registrar* June 1991, para.61.*www.judgmental.org.uk*.
[58] *Legal Guidance* p.31.
[59] [2003] EWHC 2073.
[60] *Corporate Officer of the House of Commons v Information Commissioner* [2008] EWHC 1084 (Admin).
[61] [2007] EWCA Civ 262.

"The main purpose of [the] principles is to protect the interests of the individuals whose personal data is being processed".

In other cases under the 1984 Act, the Data Protection Tribunal found that personal data will not be fairly obtained unless the individual has been informed of any non-obvious purpose or purposes intended by the data controller before the data was obtained.[62]

6–24

The Tribunal also found in a direct marketing context, that where data subjects could have been told but were deliberately not told, at the time the data were obtained, of the proposed use of their personal data for marketing purposes, the data user (the equivalent term for a data controller under the 1984 Act) is under an obligation to obtain the positive consent of the data subjects for the subsequent use of their data for this purpose.[63]

Cases under the 1998 Act

In *Chief Constable of Humberside v Information Commissioner*[64] a question arose as to whether the retention of a record of a reprimand given to a girl aged 13 was fair in circumstances where she had been told that if she kept out of trouble the reprimand would be removed when she was 18. Police policy on weeding old convictions altered in the interim and the force subsequently refused to remove the record. The Court held that there was no unfairness in the retention although Lord Justice Carnwath dissented and would have allowed the record to be removed.

6–25

Interpretation principles in the 1998 Act

The interpretation of the first principle takes up the largest part of the interpretation provisions set out in Pt II of Sch.1 to the 1998 Act. All the interpretation provisions apply to the term "fairly" alone. None relate to the word "lawfully". The first provision[65] establishes that, in determining whether personal data are processed fairly, regard is to be had to the method by which they are obtained, including in particular whether any person from whom they are obtained is deceived or misled as to the purpose or purposes for which they are to be processed. One impact of this provision is that it imposes an obligation to be fair to the source of personal data, even if the actual data is about a third party (e.g. I ask you about Fred Blogs. I have to be fair to you as well as to Fred). The obtaining of personal data, or the information to be contained in personal data, is an act of processing.

6–26

The second part of the paragraph provides that data will be deemed to be obtained fairly if they consist of information obtained from a person who is either authorised by or under any enactment to supply it or obliged to do so either by or under an enactment or an international instrument. This is stated to be subject to para.2, which sets out the information which must be provided to data subjects. The effect of this provision is twofold:

---

[62] *Innovations (Mail Order) Ltd v DPR* September 9, 1993, para.30. *www.judgmental.org.uk.*

[63] *Innovations (Mail Order) Ltd v DPR* para.31.

[64] [2009] EWCA Civ 1079, CA.

[65] Sch.1 Pt II para.1.

(a)   no disclosure of personal data which is required under statute can be restricted on grounds related to the first principle and the person who obtains personal data for a statutory purpose will not be liable for an act of unfair processing in obtaining the data, even if the data subject had not been told of the possible disclosure. It will not, however, offer protection against subsequent unfair use;

(b)   nevertheless the data subject should be provided with the necessary fair processing notice. Therefore a data controller who has obtained personal data for a statutory purpose in reliance on para.1 will nevertheless be bound to provide the data subject with the "specified information".

To some extent the provision covers the same ground as the exemption in s.35(1), which exempts disclosures of personal data from the non-disclosure provisions where the exemption is required by or under any enactment. The exemption allows for the personal data to be disclosed lawfully by the discloser.

The "specified information"

6–27   The Act provides that data are not to be treated as being processed fairly unless the data controller ensures so far as practicable that the data subject is provided with certain information at the time that the data are gathered from him or, if the data are obtained by another route, i.e. not from the data subject either before the "relevant time" or as soon as practicable thereafter.

"Another route" may include purchase or transfer from another data controller or obtaining the personal data from an associate (wife, parent, etc.) of the data subject. In such a case of course the party obtaining the data would still have an obligation of fairness to the associate.

The "relevant time" is defined in para.2(2) as:

"(a)   the time when the data controller first processes the data; or

(b)   in a case where at that time disclosure to a third party within a reasonable period is envisaged:

(i)   if the data are in fact disclosed to such a person within that period, the time when the data are first disclosed;

(ii)   if within that period the data controller becomes, or ought to become, aware that the data are unlikely to be disclosed to such a person within that period, the time when the data controller does become, or ought to become, so aware; or

(iii)   in any other case, the end of that period."

Subparagraphs (a) and (b)(i) are relatively unproblematic. If a data controller is planning on keeping the personal data to himself, so to speak, then the "relevant time" is when processing first takes place. If the data controller is planning to disclose to a third party then the relevant time is when that disclosure first takes place. Subparagraph (b)(ii) deals with the situation where a data controller originally intends to disclose but then for whatever reason changes his mind—in this case, the relevant time is when the data controller changes his mind. Of subpara.(b)(iii), it can be said that it is otiose since all the possible scenarios appeared to be exhausted by subparas (i) and (ii).

What is the specified information?

The information to be provided to the data subject is:

6–28

(a)   the identity of the data controller;
(b)   the identity of any nominated representative;
(c)   the purpose or purposes for which the data are intended to be processed; and
(d)   any further information which is necessary, having regard to the specific circumstances in which the data are or are to be processed, to enable processing in respect of the data subject to be fair.

The Commissioner now refers to such notices as "privacy notices"[66] and we have followed that practice.

"Nominated representative" is not defined in the 1998 Act, although the phrase also appears in the provisions on notification at s.16(1)(b). A representative must be appointed by a data controller which does not have a presence in the jurisdiction.[67] It should be noted that the notice is meant to cover processing which is "intended" which suggests a settled plan and not simply a long list of possible future uses. It should also be noted that the obligation is to be fair to each data subject; therefore if a controller knows that a particular subject to set of subjects have specific needs or vulnerabilities he must ensure that the notice is accessible to all.

The Commissioner has issued guidance on the contents of privacy notices in his Code of Practice which is covered below. The purpose of the provision of information provides transparency to the data subject, which in itself is regarded as a desirable quality, as well as opening the possibility of empowering the data subject to take a range of steps. The Directive deals with the *purpose* of a fair processing notice in general terms in Recital 38 as follows:

> "Whereas, if the processing of data is to be fair, the data subject must be in a position to learn of the existence of a processing operation and where the data are collected from him, must be given accurate and full information, bearing in mind the circumstances of the collection".

The data subject can be empowered in a number of ways by being made aware of the nature of the processing: he may be put on notice that behaviour is being captured or that information may be shared with others, for example on CCTV or in a credit notice, which may forewarn him to alter behaviour appropriately; he may be made aware that a record is held in respect of which he may wish to exercise his rights of access or, if the data are incorrect, correction; he may be able to assess the notice and decide not to enter into the relationship with the data controller, for example if it is a condition of taking advantage of a special offer that the individual consents to receive direct mail, he may decide not to accept the offer. In its Opinion on the provision of information to passengers in the transfer

---

[66] See the Privacy Notices Code of Practice . There is an alternative view, of course, that Privacy Notices are in fact anti-privacy statements which set out all the ways in which the data controller will use, disclose, sell, barter or rent personal data.
[67] DPA s.5(2).

of PNR data to US authorities,[68] the Article 29 Working Party noted that passengers should be made aware of the nature of the processing even if, in practice, the transfer to the US authorities has become a condition of traveling to the US.

The provision of an appropriate notice overlaps with the obtaining of the data subject's consent as one of the ways of legitimising processing under Schs 2 or 3. Data subjects must be made fully aware of the ways in which their data may be processed in order that they can give fully informed consent to legitimise processing, in appropriate cases.

In the Directive art.10, which covers those cases where the data controller collects data directly from the data subject, lists a number of examples of the type of further information which might be relevant to include. These are:

- the recipients or categories of recipients;
- whether the replies to the questions are obligatory or voluntary, as well as the possible consequences of failing to reply; and
- the existence of the right of access to and the right to rectify the data concerning him.

Article 11, which covers those cases where the data are not obtained from the data subject suggests:

- the categories of information concerned;
- the recipients or categories of recipients; and
- the existence of the right of access to and the right to rectify the data concerning him.

As a matter of good practice, it is suggested that data controllers should consider whether to include these in any privacy notice.

Providing the specified information

6–29   The obligation on the data controller is to ensure, so far as practicable, that the data subject either:

(a)   has;
(b)   is provided with; or
(c)   has made readily available to him

the specified information.

The first term "has" seems to be designed to cover a multi-stage data gathering exercise and to enable the data controller to provide the data subject with the requisite information at just one rather than at every stage. Alternatively, it may cover the situation where data are gathered with the specific intention of passing it to a third party. The original data gatherer may know what the third party's purposes will be and can provide the data subject with the relevant specified

---

[68] Adopted February 15, 2007.

information at the time of gathering. The third party would then know that the data subjects already have the specified information.

The last term—"has made readily available to him"—is rather open-ended and ripe for different interpretations. It could be argued that, for example, handing a data subject a notice saying that the requisite information can be obtained by writing to a specified address, would be sufficient. The contrary argument would be that the information was not "readily" available if it was not immediately to hand. In one of the Tribunal cases under the 1984 Act, consideration was given to the stage at which and the manner in which a data subject should be informed of the uses to which it was proposed their data should be put. In *Innovations (Mail Order) v Data Protection Registrar*, the appellants contended that sending a subsequent notice of uses was acceptable. This submission was rejected by the Tribunal. In that case however there would have been no difficulty in providing the information at the point when the personal data were obtained. The data controller wished to use the data for another purpose (the sale of marketing lists to third parties) which was not an necessary adjunct of the main purpose and the data controller deliberately adopted a policy of withholding the relevant notice until the acknowledgement of order was sent and thereby putting the burden of "opting out" of the sale of the names on the data subject. Not surprisingly the Tribunal did not regard this as "fair". However there may well be circumstances in which simply enabling a data subject to access specified information by another means would be sufficient. The development of the internet and the availability of websites with the capacity to include more detailed information on Privacy Statements or their equivalent has led to a significant development in the approach of regulators to the notice provisions with the encouragement of the use of "layered" notices. The Commissioner has issued guidance on this approach and it has been endorsed by the Article 29 Working Party. The Act is not explicit about when the information has to be placed before the data subject. If the data subject is able to make meaningful decisions based on the information, for example not to enter into the relationship, is will be crucial that the relevant information is provided at that time. To achieve this, the material parts of the information should usually be provided before or at the point at which the data are obtained. However the current guidance on "layered" notices appears to accept that more detailed information or information about matters which will not make a material difference to the individual may be provided at a later date if it would be difficult to provide all the information at the point of obtaining.

The question of whether a data controller can gain an advantage by **6–30** deliberately failing to give a fair processing notice arose in the case of *Grow With Us Ltd v Green Thumb (UK) Ltd*,[69] in whch the court made clear that parties cannot use the Act as a vehicle to avoid commercial obligations freely entered into. Green Thumb had a lawn treatment business in which Grow With Us held a franchise. Grow With Us was obliged under the franchise agreement to supply Green Thumb with a list of its customers' and prospective customers' names and addresses. They had persistently refused to transfer the data to Green Thumb. For that, and other reasons Green Thumb refused to renew the franchise agreement and Grow With Us took them to court to require them to do. One of the arguments employed by Grow With Us was that the disclosure of the names and

---

[69] [2006] EWCA Civ 1201.

addresses would breach the DPA because the customers had not had proper notice. They also argued that there was no appropriate Sch.2 ground. In relation to the notice point they raised two arguments:

- that the obligation to provide a fair processing notice required them to have regard to the purposes for which the disclosee was to process the personal data and they were not aware in sufficient detail of those purposes to provide an adequate notice; and
- the data protection notice given by Green Thumb on the prospectus which went to customers had not been sufficient to notify customers of the purposes for which Green Thumb intended to process the data.

The judge in the Court of Appeal, Buxton L.J., did not have to decide these points but went on to consider them holding that the data protection notice provided by Green Thumb was perfectly adequate to give a general indication of the nature of the processing which was intended and, on the first point, that it would be for Green Thumb to give the notice about their own processing, not Grow With Us. The wording of the notice which appeared on the prospectus was as follows:

> "Green Thumb (UK) Ltd and its franchisees take the issue of protecting your personal information seriously and would be grateful if you would take the time to read the following information about our use of your personal information. We will use your personal information to provide and enhance our services to you; deal with enquiries, administration, security and market research".

As far as the appropriate ground for processing was concerned, the Court held that there was no barrier to obtaining customer consent to the disclosure; but in any event Ground 6 was probably available to the controller.

6–31   The level of detail to be provided in a notice was also considered in *Johnson v MDU* in which the Court held that a notice which referred to the purpose of risk assessment in general terms was sufficient to enable the MDU to utilize Mr Johnson's data in order to assess the wisdom of continuing to supply him with services.[70] In that case the Court appears to have taken the nature of the recipient into account, commenting that the notice, which was in general terms, should have been sufficient to alert a doctor such as Mr Johnson to the scope of processing likely to be carried out. In *R. (on the application of Ali) v Minister for the Cabinet Office*[71] it was argued that a general statement by the Statistics Board on its website about the use and disclosure of personal data collected for the census was insufficient to meet the requirements of principle 1. The court held that the information published was sufficient in that it would give a data subject who was concerned about possible disclosure the opportunity to serve a s.10 notices and/or allow the data subject to ask the Commissioner to make an assessment.

In these cases and the House of Commons case the courts and Tribunal have been prepared to accept that data protection notices given in reasonably general terms have provided adequate notice to the individuals of the general use of the

---

[70] See para.3-64 for the notice which was regarded as acceptable by the Court.
[71] [2012] EWHC 1943 (Admin).

information collected. In the *Ali*[72] case there was also a comment about the possibility of further notice in the event that an unexpected disclosure was to be made:

> "Although the precise content of the requirements of fairness at common law are flexible, absent a prejudice to criminal proceedings or some other compelling public interest, complying with the requirements of fairness are likely to include, where practicable, giving a data subject notice of a request for disclosure and an opportunity to make representations or take part in any court proceedings".

In none of the cases have the courts had to deal with the questions which arise where the individual is in a more vulnerable situation or the information is particularly sensitive. In other areas the courts have been assiduous to ensure that in such cases specific notice is provided to the individual in order to protect the interests of that person. In the case of *R. (on the application of B) v Stafford Combined Court*[73] the High Court decided that a 14-year-old girl who had been receiving psychiatric care should have been notified of the request for disclosure of her medical records to the defence and given an opportunity to object. In the case the girl had made allegations of abuse against an individual who was being prosecuted in connection with the allegation. The defence had asked for access to her medical records and these had been provided without notice or opportunity to oppose the application for disclosure. The High Court held that her right to privacy meant that the records should not have been handed over with proper notice. The case resulted in a change to the Criminal Procedure Rules.

As far as practicable

There has also been a potential weakening of the notice obligations following consideration of the extent of the obligation imposed by the requirements of para.2(1) of Pt II to Sch.1 in the case of *Corporate Officer of the House of Commons v Information Commissioner.*[74] The case was an appeal brought under the Freedom of Information Act and the Information Tribunal was considering whether the details of MPs' expense claims should be disclosed. It was argued on behalf of the Commons that the MPs had not been told that the expenses would be disclosed in detail and therefore the Commons would be in breach of the requirements if it made the disclosure. Since the decision to notify the MPs lay within the powers of the Commons the obvious answer would be to disregard the point on the basis that if the Tribunal ordered disclosure it could delay the implementation of the order for 28 days within which the Commons could carry out the notification thereby complying with the requirement. Only if the Commons failed to do so would there be a breach of the DPA and at that stage the Commissioner could take enforcement action if required. However, the Tribunal took the more complex option of holding that the obligation had been met sufficiently. The reasoning is not completely clear but it appears that they accepted that because the MPs were aware of the disclosure of some information under the Publication Scheme adopted by the Commons the further disclosure

6–32

---

[72] [2012] EWHC 1943 (Admin).
[73] [2006] All E.R. (D) 22.
[74] EA/2007/0060–0063, 0122/0123.

was not regarded as another purpose. They also placed reliance on the fact that the obligation on the data controller to provide the information is not absolute but is only to "ensure so far as practicable" that the information is provided or made available. The decision of the Tribunal was upheld in the High Court on Appeal,[75] but the High Court confined itself to the question of the legitimate expectations of the MPs rather than the specific issue of notice. The Tribunal may therefore be prepared to accept a more generous approach to those cases where a data controller has not managed to provide the necessary information than the Commissioner has generally been prepared to do in the past.

Fairness and contract

6–33   The relationship between the obligations to provide fair processing notices and the terms of a contract were considered in Lady Justice Arden in her dissenting judgment in the case of *Johnson v Medical Defence Union*.[76] In that case the appellant argued that, even thought the Medical Defence Union (MDU) had an absolute contractual right to terminate his membership, if the organisation planned to carry out some processing of which he was wholly unaware in order to assess whether they should continue his membership they should have given him notice. The comments were obiter and also seem to have become mixed up with the question of whether his consent was required for the processing (which it clearly was not as Ground 6 of Sch.2 could be argued to apply). Nevertheless, it does set out the general proposition that a party to a contract cannot use an argument based on the absence of specific notice under the DPA to restrict the processing of information which was foreseeable and was permitted by the contract.[77]

Commissioner's Guidance

6–34   In addition to the material published in the Guide to Data Protection the Commissioner has issued a Code of Practice on Privacy Notices. This is a code issued under s.51 of the Act and will therefore carry a degree of weight even though s.51 codes are not persuasive in legal proceedings. It accepts that the law provides a degree of discretion for controllers in providing notices, ranging from actively communicating the notice to making it readily available. By "actively communicating" the Code explains that the view of the Commissioner is that a positive action should be taken to provide the notice, for example by sending a letter, reading a script or distributing an e-mail. This is distinguished from having a privacy policy available on a website which the individual has to click to access. The Code states that if the controller thinks that the data subject would be surprised by the potential use or find it objectionable in some way then there should be active communication. It therefore ties the method of communication to the way that the notice is delivered and suggests that the need to actively communicate is where:

---

[75] [2008] EWHC 1084 (Admin).
[76] [2004] EWHC 347.
[77] Paras 143 and 147.

- sensitive personal data is being collected;
- the use of the personal data is likely to be unexpected or objectionable;
- providing the information to be contained in the personal data or failing to do so will have a significant effect on the individual; or
- the personal data will be shared with another organization in a way that would not be expected.

While this approach accords with the overall obligation of fairness, and indeed with common sense, it may not be a legal obligation. On the wording of the Act, as long as the data subject has the information made readily available to him and is not misled or deceived, then there is no obligation of active communication. On the other hand the data controller has an overriding obligation to act fairly and there may be cases where fairness requires an active communication.

The Code covers the specific areas of use for marketing, selling information and the distinction between notice and consent. It counsels against telling people the obvious but lists the categories of information that may be useful in addition to the statutory requirements. It also gives practical advice on the provision of notices and offers examples of good and bad drafting. In particular it advocates the use of layered notices, where the initial notice includes the headline information and points to subject to the place where more detailed material can be found. Finally it reminds data controllers to keep their notices under review and make sure that they are current.

Article 29 Working Party Paper

Among the papers which have been prepared by the Article 29 Working Party there are a number which deal with the provision of notices. In Opinion 2/2007 on information to passengers about the transfer of Passenger Name Records to US authorities,[78] they gave detailed advice on both the content and the delivery of such notices. They dealt with the question of the obligations of intermediaries and took the view that an intermediary who is obtaining personal data for another should ensure that the individual is provided with clear, accurate and comprehensive information which should be provided before the purchase of a ticket. The fact that the data are to be transferred to US authorities and used and stored for long periods for purposes different to the original one must be included in the notice. The information should be provided both before and after purchase of the ticket to cater for those cases where the ticket is purchased by a third party. The model notices consist of a shorter notice to give passengers summary information about the transfers and offer them the possibility to find out more. It is suggested that this notice would be suitable for a booking by telephone. The longer version includes Frequently Asked Questions and more detail and would be suitable where the booking is over the web or at the premises of a travel agent. In terms of delivery the Opinion advises the provision of paper copies where the parties are face to face or exchange paper, the short notice being read out over the telephone and the individual directed to a place where the longer notice is available and the website notice divided into a short form which will be seen automatically and a longer notice which can be linked and accessed. The Opinion

6–35

---

[78] February 15, 2007.

therefore applied the guidance given in earlier papers and endorsed by the Commissioner in the UK in respect of the use of appropriately "layered" delivery of the relevant information. In its Opinion on the SWIFT system,[79] the Working Party concluded that neither SWIFT itself (which it regarded as a data controller) nor the financial institutions which used its services, had provided notices to comply with arts 10 and 11 of the Directive. The finding is interesting as it might be assumed that a person transferring money overseas would realize that the service would involve some transfer of personal data overseas, although admittedly not the fact that the data would go to the US where the US authorities would access it for investigative and monitoring purposes.

European Court Opinion of Advocate General in *Rijkeboer*[80]

6–36   This case concerned the deletion of meta data by municipal authorities under Netherlands law. The data was deleted after 12 months with the result that an individual seeking subject access was not able to ascertain to whom the data had been disclosed. In his Opinion the Advocate General made a link between the detail of the information provided in the fair processing notice and the proportionality of deletion of the data. He advised that where a full notice had not been given then early deletion would be disproportionate however if the data subject had been fully informed of the potential disclosure of his data, the proposed length of time for which the data would be held and the identities of the potential recipients then a shorter time limit for retention would be acceptable than if he had not been so informed. These aspects of the Opinion were not adopted by the Court in its final judgment but are an interesting sidelight on the reasons for the retention of information. A similar approach to retention was taken in *I v Finland*[81] in which the European Court of Human Rights held that the absence of an audit trail which retained information about access to sensitive medical data was a breach of the individual's right to the protection of her personal data.

Specific exemption in the case of third party obtaining

6–37   There are a number of general exemptions from the obligations to provide notices which are covered in later chapters under the relevant exemptions; however the interpretation provisions also allow a fairly substantial exemption to the general obligation to provide the specified information, although only in the situation where information is obtained other than from the data subject. A data controller need not, in such a situation, provide the specified information where the "primary conditions"—together with certain additional conditions to be specified by the Secretary of State are met.

The primary conditions are:

---

[79] Opinion 10/2006 on the processing of personal data by the Society for Worldwide Interbank Financial Telecommunication.
[80] Case C-553/07.
[81] ECtHR Application 20511/03.

"3(2)(a) that the provision of the specified information would involve a disproportionate effort; or
3(2)(b) that the recording or disclosure of the data by the data controller is
necessary to comply with a legal obligation other than a contractual
obligation."

The additional conditions were specified in The Data Protection (Conditions
Under Paragraph 3 of Part II of Schedule 1) Order 2000 (SI 2000/185). These are
that the data subject has not made any prior request to be provided with the
information for both para.3(2)(a) and (b) and, in the case of para.3(2)(a) that the
controller also records his reason for believing that the effect would be
disproportionate.

In those cases where the data controller relies upon the disproportionate effort
ground he must keep a record of his reasons for believing that disproportionate
effort applies.

"Disproportionate effort" is clearly therefore an important term. It is not
defined in the Act. Neither the Commissioner's Guide nor the Code refer to the
exemption at all. In previous Guidance[82] it was explained that whether or not
something amounts to disproportionate effort will be a question of fact in each
case:

"In deciding this the Commissioner will take into account a number of factors,
including the nature of the data, the length of time and the cost involved to the data
controller in providing the information. The fact that the data controller has had to
expend a considerable amount of time and effort and/or cost in providing the
information does not necessarily mean that the Commissioner will reach the
decision that the data controller can legitimately rely on the disproportionate effort
ground. In certain circumstances the Commissioner would consider that a quite
considerable effort could reasonably be expected. The above factors will always be
balanced against the prejudicial or effectively prejudicial effect on the data subject
and in this respect a relevant consideration would be the extent to which the data
subject already knows about the processing of their personal data by the data
controller".

While this has not been repeated it is suggested that it is the appropriate approach
and would be likely to be followed.

There are a number of exemptions from the requirements of the Principles,
principally from the first principle, which are covered in the relevant chapters on
the exemptions.

General identifiers

Paragraph 4 of the interpretation provisions provides that if personal data include   6–38
a national identity number or other "general identifier" defined by the Secretary
of State, then fair and lawful processing of any such data will additionally require
compliance with conditions to be specified by the Secretary of State. No order
has been made to date although it could have been made in respect of the UK
National Insurance Number (NINO) or National Health Service Number. In
practice, the use of the NINO is regulated by the Department of Work and

---

[82] ECtHR Application 20511/03, p.34.

Pensions which appears to claim intellectual property rights in the NINO and only permits authorized users of the NINO.

Rights to opt-out

6–39   One particular view expounded by the Registrar under the 1984 Act, which is not repeated in the current Guidance but which it is submitted remains relevant in assessing fairness relates to the right to opt-out of non-core uses of data. In the previous Guidance it was explained as follows:

> "Although the Act does not expressly require it, there may be circumstances where fair obtaining requires a data user to give an individual the opportunity to opt out of additional uses and disclosures of the information he or she has provided beyond the primary purpose for which it was supplied. This will be the case where an individual effectively has no realistic choice other than to use the service of a particular data user, for example, where an individual attends an NHS hospital for treatment.
>
> In situations where the individual does have a choice, the Registrar considers that it is good practice to offer such an opt out."

The suggestion is that even where a data subject is informed about possible uses of his or her data this may not always be sufficient to establish fairness. The data subject may additionally have to be given an immediate right to object to certain processing. In the current Guide the position is not taken as strongly but the point is made that a clear notice may allow the individual to "renegotiate the terms of that relationship". In effect however most marketing organisations do offer opt-outs because of the impact of other regulatory and self-regulatory codes.

Special cases—internet, telephone and fax

6–40   Practitioners should bear in mind that even if the requirements of the first principle are satisfied, the collection and processing of personal information may involve other regulation. Where e-mail addresses and fax numbers are being collected and used for direct marketing there are specific rules governing the collection and use. The current rules about email, fax and automated call marketing can be found in the Privacy and Electronic Communications (EC Directive) Regulations 2003. These are dealt with in Chapter 22 on electronic communications. There are also special rules in the Consumer Protection (Contracts Concluded by Means of Distance Communication) Regulations 2000/42 which set out the information which must be provided to consumers in distance sales. The Electronic Commerce (EC Directive) Regulations 2002 contain further provisions regulating transactions conducted electronically. The use of email for sending commercial communications both unsolicited and solicited is dealt with and in addition to the information specified under the DPA, businesses affected by these Regulations must make further information "easily, directly and permanently accessible".

Other requirements of fairness

Athough the interpretation provisions to principle 1 are detailed they only deal with one aspect of fairness—that concerned with the way in which data are obtained. Clearly therefore they do not exhaust the general requirement that the processing of personal data be "fair". The concept of fairness is open-ended and will vary with the circumstances of the case. It would be impossible to list all the implications given the breadth of the term "processing". The courts have considered whether it is fair to disclose photographs of those accused of criminal activities[83] and the question of the fairness of processing for the purpose of risk management was considered in *Johnson v Medical Defence Union*.[84] In the credit reference cases under the 1984 Act the Tribunal ruled that the processing of personal data by means of a system which would retrieve data about unassociated third parties which would then be used for the purpose of assessing whether to offer credit to the data subject amounted to unfair processing. In the British Gas case the Tribunal held that the use of personal data which was obtained when British Gas was a statutory monopoly for the purpose of direct marketing third party products without the consent of data subjects amounted to unfair processing. In *Law Society v Kordowski* the court held that the publication of libellous and harassing false material about solicitors on a website was unfair processing. Much of the detailed guidance produced by the Commissioner's Office deals with the fairness, or otherwise, of processing for particular purposes, for example whether it is fair to retain markers showing that individuals are considered violent on specific records. Fairness overlaps with proportionality and takes into account the extent to which the individual is aware of the processing, the justification for the processing and the potential harmful impact of the processing on individuals.

6–41

Consequences of breach of the first principle for legal proceedings

While the most obvious possible consequences may be the risk of action by a data subject or enforcement action by the Commissioner the issue of unfairly obtained information also arises in court proceedings, often in conjunction with concerns over breach of s.55 (covered in Ch.21 Prosecution). In *St Merryn Meat v Hawkins*[85] breach of the DPA affected the outcome in other legal proceedings. The claimants lost a freezing order on the basis that they had relied upon information obtained in breach of the Data Protection Act 1998 and had failed to make a full and honest disclosure of the fact to the court. The claimants had obtained information about a fraud against them by tapping a telephone. The court had been informed that the telephone was an office, not a home, telephone. On the basis of the evidence they applied for, and were granted, interim freezing and search orders. The defendants applied for its discharge on the basis that it was a private telephone which had been tapped and the claimants had failed to disclose that fact to the court.

6–42

---

[83] *R. (on he application of Ellis) v the Chief Constable of Essex Police* [2003] EWHC 1321.
[84] See fn.77.
[85] LTL 2/7/2000 (unreported elsewhere).

The court accepted the defendants' argument and marked its displeasure by discharging the order even though it accepted that the claimants had a strong case and it was judged likely that the defendants would dissipate the assets before judgment. In the case of *Jones v University of Warwick*[86] enquiry agents acting for the University gained access to Ms Jones home by subterfuge and secretly filmed her using the kettle. The film was then used in evidence to counter her claim for damages against the University arising from an incident in the course of her employment by the University. The claimant sought to have the evidence excluded having been obtained in breach of art.8 (the DPA was not argued although the same arguments would have applied). The court allowed the evidence and held that the fact that evidence had been obtained in breach of some other legal obligation did not render it inadmissible but penalized the University in costs.

The High Court has been asked to order disclosure against third parties (Norwich Pharmacal Orders under CPR 31.16) in respect of whom the applicant has well-grounded suspicions that there has been an unlawful obtaining of information, in order to have the necessary information in order to bring proceedings, in several cases. In *Hughes v Carrutu International Plc*[87] it came to the attention of the claimant that a third party had obtained information on him when he was contacted by the Office of the Information Commissioner who were investigating a private detective agency. It appeared that the agency had obtained information unlawfully on the claimant but the claimant did not know who the investigator's client was. The court granted him an order so that he was able to pursue a remedy. However, the court refused such an order in the case of *Nikitin v Richards Butler LLP*[88] on the basis that the claimant already had enough material to commence proceedings and the purpose of the Norwich Pharmacal relief was not to allow the victim to "fine tune a pleading".

THE SECOND PRINCIPLE

6–43   This requires that personal data shall be obtained only for one or more specified and lawful purposes and shall not be further processed in any manner incompatible with that purpose or those purposes. There are therefore two limbs to the principle. The first limb requires that a data controller have a specific purpose or purposes in mind before processing any personal data and addresses how the data controller specifies these purposes There is clearly an overlap with the other principles including principle 1. The first principle requires the data controller (subject to any exemptions) to notify a data subject of the purposes for which the data are intended to be processed. This is one manner of specifying the purposes. Principle 2 also allows for the possibility that the purpose specification may be contained elsewhere than the notice to the data subject.

The interpretation provisions allow the purpose or purposes for which personal data are obtained to be specified either in a notice given to the data subject to satisfy the "specified information" requirements of principle 1 or by

---

[86] [2003] EWCA Civ 151.
[87] [2006] EWHC 1791.
[88] [2007] EWHC 173 (QB).

notification to the Commissioner.[89] Data controllers which are exempt from the obligation to notify and chose not to do so voluntarily must therefore rely on the notices provided to data subjects. The second limb of the principle requires that, once the purposes have been specified any further processing must be restricted to a manner not incompatible with the specified purposes.

The use of the word "incompatible" suggests a use that is contradictory to rather than simply different from any originally specified purpose or purposes. Synonyms for "incompatible" are "unsuited", "incongruous", "inconsistent", "unsuitable", "opposite", or "irreconcilable". If this is the correct interpretation then it is open to the data controller to contend that processing for a purpose which was not specified at the time of the collection of the data but is not inconsistent with the original specified lawful purposes does not fall foul of this provision as long as it is subsequently specified by the controller and as long as all the other principles are complied with in respect of the processing. For example, a data controller who processes data for the purposes of satisfying a mail order from a data subject might contend that the subsequent and unforeseen use of the data for the purposes of further marketing mailshots by third parties was not "incompatible" although it was unspecified when the data were first obtained. The new use would have to be unforeseen (which might be difficult to assert in the example given here) and the controller could be subject to scrutiny by the Commissioner but as long as it was unforeseen the controller would meet the principle as long as he specified the new purpose in some appropriate manner and notified the data subject in accordance with the first principle. The interpretation provisions also state that a data controller may "in particular" specify the purpose or purposes by either of these methods, which carries the implication that specification of purposes may take place by another method. Section 24 of the Act suggests at least one other method by which purpose specification may take place. Section 24 has to be read in light of the requirements specified in s.17.

Section 17(1) of the Act prohibits processing of personal data unless the data controller has "notified" the Commissioner. Section 17(2) and (3) set out limited exceptions to this basic prohibition. These are, first, where the relevant data are not information which is being processed by means of equipment operating automatically in response to instructions given for the purpose nor information which is recorded with the intention that it should be processed by means of such equipment.[90] In other words the data is information falls within the categories of manual data including that which forms part of an accessible record as defined by s.68.

6–44

Secondly, the prohibition in s.17(1) does not apply where the Secretary of State has exempted particular processing on the basis that it is unlikely to prejudice the rights and freedoms of data subjects.[91] The exemptions from notification are covered in the Notification Regulations.[92]

If either of these exemption applies then a data controller may, nonetheless, give a notification to the Commissioner under s.18. If a data controller chooses

[89] See Notification in Ch.9.
[90] 1998 Act s.1(1)(a) and (b).
[91] 1998 Act s.17(3).
[92] The Data Protections (Notification and Notification Fees) Regulations 2000 (SI 2000/188).

not do so, then any person may still request the "relevant particulars" from the data controller. Under s.24, the data controller is under a duty to supply the particulars in writing within 21 days and free of charge.[93] These particulars are the equivalent of the information which must be notified to be Commissioner. Any data controller who fails to provide the relevant particulars commits an offence.[94]

Thus s.24 "relevant particulars" may be a further route by which a data controller may specify purposes.

6–45   The interpretation provisions also provide that in determining whether any disclosure of personal data is compatible with the purposes for which those data were obtained, regard is to be had to the purpose or purposes for which the "disclosee" intends to process the data. This provision may put a data controller at risk of enforcement action if he or she discloses to another party who subsequently uses the data for a purpose incompatible with the data controller's original specified purpose. Thus data controllers who disclose to others should identify the purpose or purposes for which the relevant data was originally obtained and impose on the disclosees, by way of contract, obligations to use the data only for compatible purposes, unless an exemption applies. The other option would be to revert to the data subject and obtain his or her sanction for any processing for a new and incompatible purpose. It is not specified to what extent the controller has an obligation to enquire into the detail of the purposes of the disclosee, although they must make sufficient enquiry to be satisfied that the purposes are not incompatible with the original purposes. In the *Green Thumb* case referred to earlier the Court appeared to accept that the data controller need only have a general understanding of the purposes of the disclosee. It is submitted that this is the appropriate approach.

Alternatively, data controllers may seek to obtain personal data from data subjects for a very wide range of specified purposes, so as not to inhibit the purposes for which the data may be passed on and used by subsequent recipients. Such blanket notices are not favoured by the Commissioner although he has recognized that notices may need to be drafted so as to accommodate reasonable changes in business practices:

> "A privacy notice can provide for reasonable evolution in the use of information. However you should not draw up a long list of possible future uses if, in reality, it is unlikely that you will ever use the information for those purposes."

As far as we are aware there have been no challenges in the UK to notices on the basis that their inherent uncertainty or open-ended nature will inevitably lead to unfair processing. At the time of writing the French data protection authority, the CNIL, is making enquiries of Google Inc about the relationship between its statements made in its revised privacy policy and its processing and used of personal data but no decision or resolution to this is currently publicly available.

As noted earlier there must always be a specified purpose for all personal data held. It is not lawful to hold personal data in the hope that it may come in useful sometime. Where it has not been practicable to specify the purpose in the notices

---

[93] 1998 Act s.24(1).
[94] 1998 Act s.24(4).

given when data are obtained or where the exemption to the first principle that has been outlined above applies—i.e. where a data controller who does not gather personal data directly from a data subject decides that providing the specified information would involve a disproportionate effort, the controller still has a responsibility for specifying the purposes of processing in accordance with principle 2.

Commissioner's view

The Commissioner's Guide equates compatibility with fairness in the following extract: 6–46

> "An additional or different purpose may still be compatible with the original one. Because it can be difficult to distinguish clearly between purposes which are compatible and those that are not, we focus on whether the intended use of the information complies with the Act's fair processing requirements. It would seem odd to conclude that processing personal data breached the Act on the basis of incompatibility if the organisation was using the information fairly".

Use for a new purpose: is consent always required?

There will be circumstances where a data controller wants to use personal data for a purpose not specified to the data subject at the time the data were obtained. It will be a question of fact as to whether it is genuinely a new purpose of which notice could not be given at the point of obtaining. Here we consider a case in which the personal data were obtained fairly and lawfully and in accordance with the first principle for a particular purpose, giving all the specified information relevant to that purpose. It does not apply where a controller is merely seeking to avoid his responsibilities to inform data subjects and give them proper choices. The controller must consider the impact of the second principle and decide whether the new use is compatible with that for which the data were obtained. If it is compatible he may use the data for the purpose as long as he complies with principles 1 and 2. Thus he must provide the data subject with the relevant information in accordance with the first principle. If he cannot do that because it is not practicable he must specify the new purpose in some other appropriate way, presumably by including it on the register of notifications.   6–47

The controller must ensure that he has appropriate grounds on which to process the data and if sensitive personal data are involved those grounds must extend to the sensitive data. He must also ensure the fairness and lawfulness of the processing. These may require that the data subject be asked for positive consent or be given an "opt-out". The requirements of fairness in particular will vary with the circumstances of the case. In practical terms it is likely that the cumulative effect of these requirements means it is prudent to obtain positive consent of the data subject but it is not necessary as a matter of law and there must be cases where consent is not necessary. The Tribunal considered the impact of the second principle briefly in the *House of Commons* case described earlier and decided that the disclosure of the travel details to the public in that case was not a use for a new purpose and was not incompatible. It also noted that data controllers comply with this principle at least in part by means of notification which is done under broad headings.

THE THIRD PRINCIPLE

6–48   This requires that personal data shall be adequate, relevant and not excessive in relation to the purpose or purposes for which they are processed. This substantially repeats the fourth principle under the 1984 Act. There are no provisions on interpretation for this principle. As with all the principles it is submitted that the data controller's subjective views as to adequacy and relevance should not be the governing criteria and an objective view should be applied as far as possible. Where different data controllers process data for the same purpose, or where a Code of Practice exists in a particular field of activity, the Commissioner may be able to have regard to the level of information generally found to be necessary to achieve the data controller's purpose in considering whether or not the principle has been breached. However where the purpose is a specialized one it may be more difficult for the Commissioner to take an independent view of what data would be adequate, relevant and not excessive for the particular purpose. In the cases dealing with the retention of conviction data described below, the Court of Appeal endorsed the view first expressed at the Bichard enquiry following the deaths of Holly Wells and Jessica Chapman, that once the police had taken the view that data was relevant for policing purposes, it was not for the Commissioner to impose his view instead. It is not clear how comfortably this sits with the obligations under the Directive which require an independent supervisory authority with appropriate powers. On the other hand it can be distinguished as only applying to the purpose of policing and there is no suggestion that the Courts or the Tribunal would apply the same leeway to any other type of body.

Interpretation under the 1984 Act

6–49   Because of the similarity between the third principle and the fourth principle under the 1984 Act it may be useful to look at decisions under that Act. It must be emphasised however that the decisions of the Tribunal under the 1984 Act are at best persuasive.

In the Tribunal case of *Community Charge Registration Officer of Runnymede BC v Data Protection Registrar,*[95] the Tribunal was asked to consider whether the holding by community charge registration officers of information about property types (i.e. whether the property was a flat, bungalow, caravan, etc.) as part of the community charge register was in breach of the principle. The Tribunal found it was. They found this be the case even though there was unlikely to be any prejudice to the data subjects. They took the view that public bodies which had the power to oblige people to provide personal information were under a

---

[95] Case DA/90, 24/49/3, October 27, 1990. *www.judgmental.org.uk.*

particular onus to ensure that the information demanded was always adequate, relevant and not excessive. The Tribunal also endorsed the approach recommended by the Registrar:

> "We were referred in the course of the hearing to the Guideline booklet Number 4 issued by the Data Protection Registrar entitled The Data Protection Principles. Paragraph 4.2 relating to the 4th Principle advises that data users should seek to identify the minimum amount of information about each individual which is required in order properly to fulfil their purpose and that they should try to identify the cases where additional information will be required and seek to ensure that such information is only collected and recorded in those cases. We endorse this general guidance for those wishing to have a test to apply to answer the question whether personal data is adequate, relevant and not excessive for the purposes for which it is held."

In *Community Charge Registration Officer of Rhondda BC v Data Protection Registrar*,[96] the Tribunal upheld a similar approach taken with respect to the holding of dates of birth. It was accepted, however, that the holding of dates of birth would be relevant in respect of those persons who would shortly become eligible to vote at the age of 18.

Thus, the position under the 1984 Act was that, where a data controller holds an item of information on all individuals which will be used or useful only in relation to some of them, the information is likely to be excessive and irrelevant in relation to those individuals in respect of whom it will not be used or useful and should not be held in those cases. This was repeated in the advice of the Commissioner in 1998. (Subject to the caveat that it would be acceptable to hold information for the purpose of a particular foreseeable contingency which may never occur, for example, where a data controller holds blood groups of employees engaged in hazardous occupations.) In the most recent Guide however the Commissioner has included a specific reference to groups of individuals.

What is meant by "adequate, relevant and not excessive"?

The Data Protection Act does not define these words. Clearly though they need to be considered:

6–50

- in the context of the purpose for which you are holding the personal data; and
- separately for each individual you hold information about or for each group of individuals where the individuals in the group share relevant characteristics.

It is inevitable that, in applying the principle in practice, data controllers have to make decisions based on groups or classes of people. However, if the class is too widely drawn it will effectively undermine the protection provided by the principle.

In the decision of the Court of Appeal in relation to the retention of conviction data described below the Court determined that conviction data as a class could

---

[96] Case DA/90, 25/49/2, October 11, 1990.*www.judgmental.org.uk*.

be retained on every person who has had a criminal conviction, warning or caution irrespective of the age of the conviction. The same approach was taken in the PNR cases[97] in which it had been argued that the amount of personal data which was to be provided by the airlines to the US Customs Bureau was excessive for the purpose for which it was to be held. A total of 34 data elements were listed which were to be provided for each passenger. The point is dealt with in the Opinion of the Advocate General who held that, given the purpose of the processing of the personal data, the total of the data items was not excessive. In reaching his view he made clear that the term "necessary" in the Directive should carry the same meaning as in the European Convention, that the question be weighted as one of proportionality saying:

> "I am of the opinion that, in adopting the list of 34 personal-data elements as attached to the decision on adequacy, the Commission did not agree to a manifestly inappropriate measure for the purpose of achieving the objective of combating terrorism and other serious crimes. First the importance of intelligence activity in counter-terrorism should be stressed, since obtaining sufficient information may enable a State's security services to prevent a possible terrorist attack. From that point of view, the need to profile potential terrorists may require access to a large number of pieces of data. Second the fact that other instruments relating to the exchange of information within the European Union provide for disclosure of less data is not sufficient to demonstrate that the amount of data required in the specific counter-terrorism instrument constituted by the PNR regime is excessive".[98]

Both of these cases concerned sets of personal data held for the purposes of policing and security and could perhaps be distinguished on that basis.

6–51   As the cases on the retention of conviction data raised principle 3 issues as well as principle 5 the cases are covered below. There were two relevant cases; a case which went to the Information Tribunal in 2005 and was not appealed and a later case which went to the Tribunal in 2007 and was then appealed to the Court of Appeal. The reason for the burst of case law around the retention of old conviction data on the Police National Computer (PNC) has been the increased availability of records of criminal convictions as a result of Criminal Records Bureau checks (CRB checks) and the change in police policy to increase retention of records of old convictions which took place in 2003 following the Bichard enquiry. Many more individuals have found old conviction information disclosed to potential employers as a result of these changes and have accordingly raised their concerns. In view of the importance of this area the nature of conviction and intelligence records and the rules relating to CRB checks are covered fully in Ch.27. In the cases the Commissioner held that the retention of the old records engaged and breached both principles 3 and 5 as information which was excessive for the purpose would also be retained longer than necessary. The cases are covered below but the findings relate equally to principle 5.

6–52   The first case which came to the Tribunal was *Chief Constable of West Yorkshire v Information Commissioner* in 2005. The Information Tribunal found that principle three overlaps with principle five and that information which would be in breach of principle 3 would also be likely to be excessive in relation to the

---

[97] See Ch.3 for a full discussion of the cases.
[98] Case DA/90, 25/49/2 para.238.

purpose. They took the view that conviction information which was retained in accord with the Association of Chief Police Officers Guidelines remained adequate, relevant and not excessive for the purposes of policing, which it considered included the administration of criminal justice, even when it related to very old convictions. The Tribunal did state, however, that some older conviction information should not be used for CRB checks associated with employment vetting. Instead the information should be retained for the use of the police only and "stepped down" from use by the Criminal Records Bureau.

Although the Tribunal stated (at para.201) that the judgment was not meant to be a precedent for other cases on conviction data and was being decided on the facts of these cases, the Tribunal treated the conviction information as a class of information in respect of which the retention decisions were to be made. The core elements of the decision, that conviction data can be regarded as a class and a judgment made on all data in that class for the purposes of the relevant principles and that it is for the police to determine whether records should be retained, and not the Commissioner, was later affirmed by the Court of Appeal.

In this case the Commissioner argued that a balance must be struck between the needs of the purpose and the impact on the individual. Chief Constables must exercise discretion when determining whether to remove or "weed" old convictions. Where a data subject requests that the data be reviewed the Chief Constable should review the data and consider the purpose for which the conviction data are held and the likelihood of the particular data being useful for each aspect of the purpose. If the data would not be useful for those purposes he should exercise his discretion to remove the data. Applying that approach to these cases it was the Commissioner's view that the data should be removed and that failure to remove the data breached principles three and five. The Chief Constables argued that such a policy would be unfair to those who did not ask for removal of records but primarily that the purpose is paramount and as long as some justification can be shown for the continued retention of data of that type the controller is entitled to retain it. It was also argued that conviction data is useful in operational policing, in particular in investigative work. It is required for employment vetting for certain occupations and there is a statutory obligation under the Police Act 1997 to supply it for those purposes. Consistency in the retention of conviction information is essential and selective erasure would undermine that consistency. Moreover, the imposition of such a discretion would place an unreasonable burden on the police.

It is not wholly straightforward to discern the findings of the Tribunal which relate to the Act as the judgment covered areas related to the governance of personal data held for the purposes of policing more generally however it is suggested that the following list represents a fair summary of those points relevant to the DPA:

6–53

- There is a significant degree of overlap between principles 3 and 5, so that data which has been kept for longer than is necessary for the purpose is likely also to be excessive in relation to the purpose.
- The question of whether data are relevant to the purpose for which they are processed will depend largely on the nature, content and quality of the data;

- In order to determine whether it is "necessary" for a data controller to keep particular data for a particular purpose the controller should apply a test of proportionality. If the data are potentially embarrassing or damaging to the data subject he may have to undertake a balancing exercise between the importance of retaining the data for his purposes and the negative impact on the data subject.

- The purpose of policing covers operational policing, assisting the courts in the administration of justice and some employment vetting where such vetting is for the prevention or detection of crime or the apprehension or prosecution of offenders (para.179) even though the standard purpose description in the registerable particulars does not include this (para.134).

- A Chief Constable as data controller can only justify retention of data on the Police National Computer for the purposes of employment vetting insofar as the vetting is for the purpose of the prevention or detection of crime or the apprehension or prosecution of offenders (para.183).

- Conviction information may remain relevant for the element of the policing purpose related to the administration of justice even when it is no longer particularly relevant for operational policing (para.185).

- Retention of information involves less interference with the right to private life than using information. (para.72 quoting Bichard 4.45.1).

- In considering whether there is a breach of the third and fifth principles the critical issue is whether or not the purpose for which the data are processed is no longer justified (para.88) (again applying Bichard).

In addition the Tribunal supported the approach taken in the Bichard Report to the role of the Information Commissioner in relation to data held by the police for policing purposes (para.72). This is that it is for the police to decide whether information is required for operational purposes and the role of the Commissioner is limited to a supervisory role similar to that of a court exercising a judicial review function: "If a reasonable and rational basis exists for a decision that should be the end of the story". We would submit that this is not a proper approach and would not accord with the Directive, particularly post Lisbon.

6–54   On the broader issues the Tribunal accepted that a breach of art.8 would inevitably involve a breach of the principles; however it appears to have regarded art.8 and the principles as coterminous.

As noted above, one of the outcomes of the case was the proposal that conviction information should be "stepped down" and old material not made available to the CRB for checks. However it quickly became clear that the proposed "stepping down" of the conviction information was not possible for both legal and practical reasons.

6–55   In the next joined cases to reach a differently constituted Tribunal resulted in a different decision in which the Tribunal ordered the deletion of five old convictions[99] by five forces in England. The Tribunal held that, as the data controllers for the relevant data were the Chief Constables of the forces, the questions of whether information was excessive or was being kept for longer than necessary was to be assessed in the light of the "core" purposes of policing. The fact that the data was used for the purposes of other parts of the criminal justice

---

[99] EA/2077/0096.98.99,108,127.

system and for criminal records checks did not alter that assessment. The Tribunal also held that the question of whether particular data is relevant and not excessive for a purpose is a question on which the Commissioner, and the Tribunal on appeal from the Commissioner's decision, is entitled to make a determination. The Tribunal heard extensive evidence on the relevance and use of old conviction data for operational policing. In its judgment it determined that the old convictions in questions were excessive and irrelevant to the core purpose of policing and should be deleted. The Chief Constables appealed and the case was heard by the Court of Appeal. All of the judges appeared to draw some comfort from the provision in art.8.5 of the Directive that "a complete register of criminal convictions may be kept only under the control of official authority" and argued that this showed that such a complete register was therefore wholly acceptable under and anticipated by the Directive. We would submit that this was a misguided reading. Such a register is not required by the Directive, nor by UK law, and the judges ignored the fact that the Directive also provides for a clear right to individuals to object to the processing of personal data about them by public authorities where the data is processed under a discretionary power as here.

Giving the leading judgment, Waller L.J. held that as long as a purpose is lawful it may be registered with the Commissioner (para.31) and the registered purpose of the Chief Constables was sufficient to cover the use of the data to supply accurate records of convictions to the CPS, the Courts and the CR, saying:

> "'Rendering assistance to the public in accordance with force policies' clearly covers the roles the police seek to perform in those areas and if there was any doubt about it the recipients include 'employers', 'the courts' and 'law enforcement agencies'" (para.35).

Applying the test of whether data is excessive or being retained longer than necessary for those purposes, he said:

> "...there is, it seems to me, only one answer, since for all the above a complete record of convictions spent and otherwise is required".

In relation to the role of the Commissioner and the Tribunal in relation to assessing whether particular data or classes of data are relevant or excessive or held longer than necessary, he rejected the contention that it was their task to apply a test of necessity or proportionality. He cited with approval the extracts from the Bichard Report dealing with the role of the Commissioner:

> "The police are the first judge of their operational needs and the primary decision makers; the Information Commissioner's role is a reviewing or supervisory one... His office will give considerable latitude to the police in their decision making. If a reasonable and rational basis exists for a decision that should be the end of the story".

He went on to say:

"It seems to me that the approach described is the correct approach. If the police say rationally and reasonably that convictions however old or minor, have a value in the work they do that should, in effect, be the end of the matter".

In relation to art.8, he was not persuaded that the retention of the conviction record engaged art.8, but if it did so considered the retention to be within the purlieu of art.8.2.

Carnwrath L.J. was less comfortable that Waller L.J. that the registered purpose could be said to cover the wider purposes; however he said that the inadequacy or obscurity of the purpose specification did not justify the Tribunal's approach. He commented that if the Commissioner considered that the purpose specification was inadequate he could have taken action under principle 2, but in any event the deficiency could be easily remedied by lodging a more detailed statement.

In relation to the purpose of the processing, he described it as "the purpose of maintaining a complete record of convictions" and said:

"The purpose of maintaining a complete record of convictions is not negated by showing in an individual case that one or more particular pieces of information is of no identifiable utility".

Carnwath L.J. also agreed with Waller L.J. that the Commissioner was acting outside his remit in reviewing the decisions of the Chief Constables in respect of retention.

Hughes L.J. echoed the earlier judgments in a succinct summary (para.104), including the finding that the proper purposes of the police in managing the PNC plainly included the retention of information for provision to others who have a legitimate need for it, including (but not limited to) provision under the statutory duty created by the Police Act 1997.

6–56   We would submit that this rendering of the concept of purpose is simply wrong. It is not the case that all convictions are recorded on the PNC. Each Chief Constable as a data controller has the purpose of maintaining a record of the convictions for which his force has been responsible. No Chief Constable has the purpose of maintaining a complete register nor do they collectively have such a purpose.

It would follow that it must be in accord with the Act and the Directive, that if it is shown in an individual case that a record is irrelevant or excessive it could (and should) be removed. We would also, as noted earlier, suggest that the approach to the powers of the Commissioner does not accord with the Directive which requires that there be an independent regulator with appropriate powers over all data controllers.

THE FOURTH PRINCIPLE

6–57   This requires that personal data shall be accurate and, where necessary, kept up-to-date. A definition of inaccuracy appears at s.70(2) of the Act:

"For the purposes of this Act data are inaccurate if they are incorrect or misleading as to any matter of fact."

Thus a mere opinion, which does not purport to be a statement of fact, cannot be challenged on the grounds of inaccuracy.[100]

It is worth noting that the first part of the principle is unqualified—"personal data shall be accurate". The second part, however, is qualified—data need only be kept up to date where "necessary".

The purpose for which the data are used will clearly be relevant in deciding whether updating is necessary. For example, if the data are intended to be used merely as an historical record of a transaction between the data controller and the data subject then, updating would be inappropriate. In other cases updating will be crucial—for example, if the data are used to decide whether to grant credit.

The interpretation provisions allow that there will be no breach of the accuracy requirement where the data are, in fact, inaccurate but where the data controller has accurately recorded the information from a data subject or third party and:

(a)   has taken reasonable steps to ensure accuracy (having regard to the purpose or purposes for which the data were obtained and further processed); and
(b)   has recorded the data subject's view as to inaccuracy within the relevant data, where such views have been conveyed.

The requirement on the data controller to record accurately information obtained from the data subject or third party presumably means that the data controller cannot claim the benefit of this exemption where the data controller himself is responsible for the inaccuracy but only where the controller accurately records erroneous information where the error originates from the data subject or the third party. The requirements in the exemption to record a data subject's view as to inaccuracy and to "take reasonable steps" mirror the provisions in s.22 of the 1984 Act as to inaccuracy. However, under the 1984 Act, the controller could rebut an allegation of inaccuracy either because he could show he had taken reasonable care or by including the data subject's views. Under the 1998 Act, the controller must leap over both hurdles.

The requirement to take reasonable steps "having regard to the purpose or purposes for which the data were obtained and further processed" is presumably an acknowledgment that inaccuracies in certain types of data (e.g. as to creditworthiness) may have more severe consequences than in others, and that consequently more stringent accuracy checks would be required. What constitutes "reasonable steps" is not, defined, but it is submitted that at the very least the controller would have to show a formal procedure for checking accuracy and correcting errors where required.

In *Law Society v Kordowski*[101] the High Court issued an injunction to stop the defendant from further publication of a similar website to the "Solicitors from Hell" site that he published on the grounds (inter alia) that the personal data published on the site was inaccurate.

6–58

---

[100] The issue of accuracy is also to be discussed in greater depth in Ch.14 on Remedies.
[101] See fn.11, above.

The Commissioner's powers to take enforcement action for a breach of the Fourth Principle are supplemental to the data subject rights to apply for the rectification, blocking, erasure or destruction of inaccurate data.[102]

THE FIFTH PRINCIPLE

6–59   This requires that personal data processed for any purpose or purposes shall not be kept for longer than is necessary for that purpose or those purposes. Personal data which is kept for longer than necessary is always excessive. The discussion of the cases on the third principle above should also be considered when reviewing the application of principle 5. We have not repeated that discussion here.

The increase in the capacity of electronic systems to retain vast amounts of personal data and the ease of retrieval has changed the landscape in this area and it has become increasingly difficult for individuals to leave the past behind. As a result there are several important cases around these issues as the retention of personal information has proved to be extremely controversial. The cases are discussed below. It will be noted that, while the Commissioner was not successful in attacking the prolonged retention of police records using the Data Protection Act, applicants have been far more successful in doing so using their rights under art.8 of the Human Rights Convention.

The principle is based on art.6.1(e) of the Directive, which requires that personal data must be

"kept in a form which permits identification of data subjects for no longer than is necessary for the purposes for which the data were collected or for which they are further processed."

The principle also appears in Treaty 108.

6–60   It should be borne in mind that the principle can be complied with by the removal of all identifiers from the data and not only by deletion. The UK provision does not reflect this reference to the anonymisation of personal data. Anonymisation can, however, be very difficult to achieve in practice. The topic is discussed in Ch.18 on exemptions for research.

There are no interpretation provisions for the fifth principle.

6–61   Retention of information in databases is seen as a hallmark of the surveillance society. It is an issue of concern for the Commissioner. In his annual report for 2011–2012 he refers to a complaint by Privacy International into the amount of data held at the police's National Automatic Number Plate Recognition Data Centre (NADC) and reports that the as a result of the Commissioner's "compliance concerns" each police force had to make changes to their systems resulting in the deletion of some 6.7 billion records. The Commissioner also reports that he was asked by the The House of Lords European Union Committee to review the operation of the Serious and Organised Crime Agency's (SOCA) suspect financial transaction database. Again his review resulted in recommendations to implement a shorter retention period which has resulted in the deletion of

---

[102] See s.14 of the 1998 Act and Ch.14.

over half a million records. On the other hand, decisions on retention may require a balancing act to be carried out as controllers must also be alert to their responsibilities to preserve information.[103] In 2004 Philip Morris was sued for $2.75 million for destroying potential e-mail evidence in a civil racketeering action against the tobacco industry. The firm's policy was to delete all email which was over 60 days old but this was no defence as the court found that the policy should have been suspended once legal proceedings were contemplated.

Deletion and rights of subject access

In the *Rijkeboer*[104] case the Advocate General explained that the importance of the right of subject access should be taken into account in setting the times for the deletion of personal data. The argument being that, as subject access is an essential part of the fundamental right of data protection, it should not be thwarted by the adoption of an artificially short retention period which might prevent the data subject from being able to exercise the right to know what information is held and to whom it has been disclosed. It is suggested that the import of the decision is that the right of access should be taken into account in setting retention periods and they should not be artificially curtailed in a way that undermines the right of access, not that personal data must be retained simply for the sake of providing access.

6–62

Setting the standards for retention

Setting and implementing the standards for retention and removal of personal data is part of the broader task of managing records within an organization and practitioners may wish to seek specific guidance from the various records management standard available. A checklist of the most important stages of a records management policy is included in the practical tools at the end of the chapter. The principle relates the period of time for retention to the purpose of the processing. It is therefore essential that controllers adopt policies taking into account the reasons they are holding the personal data and the likely uses of it. The most common way to do this is to have a general Records Management Policy with a section on retention and destruction supported by retention schedules, which may be in different levels of granularity. It is always helpful if external standards can be adopted to assist with setting the retention periods. Some statutes set time-limits for the retention of data and if these are part of the controller's purposes these can be adopted, for example the Companies Act 1985 requires the retention of accounting records for a period of three years from the date on which they are made for a private company and six years for a public company.[105] Codes of Practice may also include relevant provisions. In relation to the public sector the Code of Practice on Records Management issued under s.46 of the Freedom of Information Act is the first resource to consider when setting

6–63

---

[103] The Institute of Chartered Secretaries and Administrators (ISCA) publishes an excellent book which sets out the recommended retention times for different categories of information held by businesses. It is available from their website. The Chartered Institute of Personnel and Development Professionals (CIPD) publishes a similar set of recommendations in respect of employee data.

[104] See fn.81.

[105] Companies Act 1985 s.222.

records standards. There are also recommendations in other Codes of Practice for example the CCTV Code. For the rules on the retention of traffic data under Directive 2006/24, see Ch.23. The Code of Practice for Information Security Management ISO 17799 sets out suggested rules on the keeping of documents electronically.

Commissioner's guidance

6–64   The Commissioner's Guide deals with some common queries on setting retention schedules, for example the case where a relationship has ended:

> "If personal data have been recorded because of a relationship between the you and the individual, you should consider whether to keep the information once the relationship ends.
> You may not need to delete all personal data when the relationship ends. You may need to keep some information so that you can confirm that the relationship existed – and that it has ended- as well as some of the details".

The Commissioner advises that if the data have only a short-term value it may be appropriate to delete them within days or months. He also reminds controllers that, where exemptions such as the exemption for use of personal data for research apply, data may be kept beyond the initial period of its use.

The Guide makes no special mention of the problems caused by e-mail, but it can be useful to point out the clients that e mail is not a special case and the question of retention rests on the content and purpose of a communication, not its format.

Applying the standards

6–65   Once retention standards have been set they should be complied with. The Guide suggests that controllers should review their personal data regularly and delete the information which is no longer required for the purposes and adopt a systematic policy of deleting data. At the end of the standard retention period the record should be reviewed and deleted unless there is some special reason for keeping it.

Case law on retention of personal data

European case law

6–66   In the PNR cases[106] the question of whether the PNR data would be held for excessive periods was considered in the Opinion of the Advocate General, it having been argued that the periods anticipated were unnecessarily generous. In the Opinion he accepted that the normal period of three years and six months was not manifestly excessive nor was the longer period of eight years for that data which had been accessed in the initial period. Again the Advocate General took

---

[106] Joined Cases 317/04 and 318/04.

account of the nature of the purpose for the processing and determined that the State had a wide margin of appreciation in a case of this nature.

In the case of *Marper*, the ECtHR rejected the argument that personal data could be retained indefinitely for the purposes of policing, overturning a decision of the UK House of Lords.

Marper v United Kingdom[107]

In *Marper v United Kingdom* the Grand Chamber of the European Court of Human Rights in Strasbourg, delivering its judgment in December 2008, unanimously held that the UK's policy and law on the retention of DNA had breached art.8 of the Convention rights. In reaching that conclusion the Court considered, among other things, the Data Protection Directive and the EU Council Framework Decision on the processing of personal data in the framework of police and judicial cooperation. The difference between the approach of the UK courts to the questions posed in *Marper* and the approach of the ECtHR indicates a worrying gap between UK judges and their EU counterparts in attitudes to privacy of information in the hands of the State.

6–67

The UK law on the taking and retention of fingerprints and DNA is in the Police and Criminal Evidence Act 1984 (PACE) as amended. Under the Police and Criminal Evidence Act 1984 (PACE), the police have wide powers to take photographs, fingerprints and body samples of persons without their consent where they had been charged with, or convicted of, a recordable offence. Previously, fingerprints and DNA samples taken would have to be destroyed in the event of the person being acquitted, or if the charges were dropped or not pursued. Following amendments to PACE, the police were given powers to retain fingerprints and DNA samples lawfully taken from any person, irrespective of whether or not they are subsequently convicted of an offence. The police policy has been to keep the fingerprints, photographs and samples for the rest of the life of the individual, and only destroy them in exceptional circumstances. The retention was challenged in 2004 by two individuals who pursued cases to force the removal of fingerprints, cellular samples and DNA profiles from police databases. In 2001 one of the two had been arrested, tried and acquitted of a criminal offence; the other had been arrested and charged but the charges had been dropped. The first applicant was only 11 when the samples were taken and the second was in his twenties. The case reached the House of Lords (*R. (on the application of S) v Chief Constable of South Yorkshire Police*[108]), which held that there was no breach of art.8 of the HRA in the retention of the materials (Baroness Hale dissenting in part). The applicants took the case to Starsbourg and the ECtHR found against the UK, finding that the retention of these records was a clear violation of art.8 as being wholly disproportionate:

> "In conclusion, the Court found that the blanket and indiscriminate nature of the powers of retention of the fingerprints, cellular samples and DNA profiles of persons suspected but not convicted of offences, as applied in the case of the present applicants, failed to strike a fair balance between the competing public and private interests, and that the respondent State had overstepped any acceptable margin of

---

[107] ECtHR Applications 30562/04 and 30566/04.
[108] [2004] 1 W.L.R. 2196.

appreciation in this regard. Accordingly, the retention in question constituted a disproportionate interference with the applicants' right to respect for private life and could not be regarded as necessary in a democratic society. The Court concluded unanimously that there had been a violation of Article 8 in this case."[109]

UK case law

6–68   In *Chief Constable of Humberside*[110]the Court of Appeal held that the police forces were entitled to retain all information about convictions, however minor and however old, for the purposes of operational policing and to supply to the CPS and use for multi-agency working. In *R v Chief Constable of the Greater Manchester Police Ex p. Christopher John Coombs*[111] the High Court considered whether the Data Protection Act 1984 was breached by the retention of personal data about the defendant. The police were entitled to retain records of alleged paedophilia where a conviction was dismissed on appeal because the judge in the original case had misdirected on corroboration. In the case of *Pal v General Medical Council*[112] the claimant had brought a claim in defamation and under the Data Protection Act. She claimed that personal data on her was being kept for longer than was necessary. The GMC had applied for summary judgment on the basis that the records complained of could not be destroyed as the GMC was in the process of reconsidering its policy on retention of data and it would be premature to require the deletion of the record complained of. The GMC did not succeed. The court held that it would not be open to the GMC to arrive at a records retention policy that did not comply with the Data Protection Act and there was no justification for striking out the claim on the basis that its policy was not yet settled.

6–69   The UK has now dealt with the decision in *Marper* in the Protection of Freedoms Act 2012, although the relevant provisions are not yet in force. Until the UK law has been changed, however, the House of Lords decision remains binding on courts in the UK.[113] Where there is a conflict between relevant decisions of the House of Lords and the Strasbourg Court in a human rights case the lower court is bound by the decision of the House of Lords. This has meant that where the facts of a retention case can be clearly distinguished from those of *Marper* the courts have been able to follow the Strasbourg ruling, but in cases where the information disputed falls clearly into the categories considered or under issue in *Marper* they have allowed retention in line with the decision of the House of Lords. In *R. (on the application of GC) v Commissioner of Police of the Metropolis*,[114] a challenge was mounted to the retention of biometric samples, DNA and fingerprints, for an indefinite period save in exceptional circumstance. The claimants argued that the court should follow the Strasbourg ruling but the court held that it was bound by the decision of the House of Lords in *R. (on the application of S) v Chief Constable of the South Yorkshire Police; R. (on the*

---

[109] Extract from the press release issued by the Court.
[110] See discussion above.
[111] LTL 24/7/2000 (unreported elsewhere).
[112] [2004] EWHC 1485 (QB).
[113] *Kay v Lambeth Borough Council* [2006] 2 A.C. 465—see discussion in Ch.2.
[114] [2010] EWHC 2225.

application of Marper) v Chief Constable of the South Yorkshire Police.[115] Giving the leading judgment, Lord Dyson found that the relevant provisions of PACE were not incompatible with art.8 as they permitted a policy which was not as far-reaching as the ACPO Guidelines and could therefore be read to comply with art.8. He granted a declaration that the ACPO Guidelines were unlawful because they failed to comply with the Convention however he made no further orders on the basis that the Protection of Freedoms Bill included proposals to amend the scheme for the retention of DNA and the Government intended to bring the Act into force in 2011. The ECtHR was asked to consider the continued retention of fingerprints and samples in *Goggins v United Kingdom*[116] after the decisions in *Marper* and *GC* but before the UK had passed Protection of Freedoms Act. The actions were struck out.

In *JR 27, Re Judicial Review*[117] the High Court in Northern Ireland ruled that police retention of a 14-year-old boy's DNA and photographs were not illegal. It noted that the question of photographs was not specifically canvassed in *Marper*, but given that they were taken in the same circumstances for the same purposes took the view that the House of Lords decision took precedence despite the fact that, in the view of the Court the retention was disproportionate and in breach of art.8:

> "But for [the House of Lords] decision and our analysis of it, we consider that there is substantial force in the view that the retention of the Applicant's photographic images by the Police Service for a minimum period of seven years, which may be extended indefinitely, unconnected in any concrete or rational way with any of the statutory purposes, interferes with his right to respect for private life guaranteed by Article 8(1)."

In *R. (Wood) v Metropolitan Police Commissioner*[118] the Court of Appeal held the retention of photographs of a protester taken by the police in a public place as part of an intelligence gathering operation infringed his right to respect for private life guaranteed by art.8(1). By a majority they held that, having regard to the narrow and time limited purpose for which the photographs had been taken, their indefinite retention by the police was disproportionate.

Per Dyson L.J.:

> "The retention by the police of photographs taken of persons who have not committed an offence, and who are not even suspected of having committed an offence, is always a serious matter ...
> The retention by the police of photographs of a person must be justified and the justification must be the more compelling where the interference with a person's rights is, as in the present case, in pursuit of the protection of the community from the risk of public disorder or low level crime, as opposed, for example, to protection against the danger of terrorism or really serious criminal activity."

6–70

6–71

---

[115] [2004] 1 W.L.R. 2196.
[116] Applications 30089/04 and others, July 19, 2011.
[117] [2010] N.I.Q.B. 143 (December 23, 2010).
[118] [2009] 4 All E.R. 941.

Lord Collins of Mapesbury agreed that there was justification for the taking of the photos, but not for keeping them, making the general point that the balance to be struck between the operation of state surveillance and the privacy rights of citizens, was an ongoing task:

> "It is plain that the last word has yet to be said on the implications for civil liberties of the taking and retention of images in the modern surveillance society. This is not the case for the exploration of the wider, and very serious, human rights issues which arise when the State obtains and retains the images of persons who have committed no offence and are not suspected of having committed any offence".

6–72   The retention of photographs has most recently been considered in *R. (on the application of RMC) v Commissioner of Police for the Metropolis*.[119] In this case the High Court was asked to consider two cases in which individuals had been arrested and had fingerprints, DNA samples and photographs taken. One was a child of 12 at the time, the other a middle-aged woman of good character. The CPS decided not to prosecute the woman and a decision to take no further action was made in respect of the boy. Both applied to have the DNA, fingerprints and photographs destroyed and were refused. The court did not allow appeals in respect of the DNA or fingerprints as the points had already been adjudicated in *R. (GC)* but granted permission in respect of the retention of the photographs and also some PNC data retained in relation to the boy. The photographs were retained under s.64A of PACE, which set no guidelines for retention. The guidelines were set out in the Guidance on the Management of Police Information (the MoPI guidance), which was produced by the National Policing Improvement Agency (NPIA) to support the Code of Practice on the Management of Police Information made under s.39A of the Police Act 1996. Richards L.J. held that the court should follow the decisions of the Strasbourg court unless such a course was precluded by domestic authority. Having reviewed the cases he held that the retention of the photographs would constitute an interference with the art.8 rights of the applicants. In considering the legal basis for the interference he was critical of the "confused picture" around the status of the various pieces of guidance but, in view of the fact that such defects were capable of easy remedy, focused on the question of proportionality. In assessing the proportionality of the retention he held that:

- there was an inadequate distinction drawn between those who are convicted and other categories such as those charged but acquitted;
- retention could be in place potentially for up to 100 years in the case of FJ (one child); and
- the particular concern about the retention of information about minors was no taken into account.

He held that the retention of the photographs was an unjustified interference with the art.8 rights of the individuals. In relation to the record on the PNC in relation to FJ he did not agree that it was disproportionate and dismissed the claim.

---

[119] [2012] EWHC 1681 (Admin).

Current position on DNA retention

The last Labour Government had included provisions on the retention of fingerprints and DNA profiles in ss.14–23 of the Crime and Security Act 2010. These were never brought into force. The new provisions are contained in Chapter 1 Part1 of the Protection of Freedoms Act which received Royal Assent on May 1, 2012. The provisions are not in force at the time of writing and the Home Office website simply states that commencement orders will start to be brought into effect from July 2012.

    Part 1 amends PACE to produce a comprehensive regime for dealing with DNA. It establishes the office of Commissioner for the Retention and use of Biometric Material who will be responsible for keeping under review determinations made by chief officers of police and others that the fingerprints and DNA profiles of individuals are to be retained for national security purposes and the use to which material so retained are put.[120] The appointment of a specialist Commissioner is likely to lessen the influence of the Information Commissioner in the regulation of this area. The National DNA Database is also put on a statutory footing[121] as is the National DNA Database Strategy Board. The Board must issue guidance to chief officers on the circumstances in which DNA samples and profiles should be removed immediately from the Database and chief officers will be obliged to follow the guidance.[122] As there are over 6 million records on the DNA Database including just over 1 million relating to unconvicted persons it also provides for the Secretary of State to make orders prescribing the manner and timing of the destruction programme of samples which will no longer be permissible. The retention regime excludes those persons whose fingerprints are held under immigration powers. Biometric data held under the Terrorism Act 2000 is also excluded but becomes subject to an equivalent regime.

    Under the new provisions there are different rules for samples and the profiles derived from them. All DNA samples must be destroyed once a DNA profile has been derived from the sample and a search has been concluded on the database for a match. The purpose of the search is to check for any matches which would indicate that in fact the person had a connection with a crime scene or another identity. Where it appears to the responsible chief officer of police that the material was taken unlawfully or following an unlawful arrest or as a result of mistaken identity the sample and the profile must be destroyed once the search has been concluded. All other profiles can be retained for a variety of lengths of time. Where the material was given voluntarily it must be destroyed as soon as it has fulfilled its purpose.[123] This will usually be the case with material taken from witnesses. However material which falls to be destroyed can be retained as long as the person consents to retention.[124] Material taken in connection with the investigation of an offence may always be retained until the conclusion of the

6–73

---

[120] Protection of Freedoms Act s.20.
[121] Protection of Freedoms Act s.24.
[122] Protection of Freedoms Act s.63AB(3).
[123] Protection of Freedoms Act s.10.
[124] Protection of Freedoms Act s.11.

investigation by the police or where legal proceedings are instituted against the person the conclusion of those proceedings.[125]

Material which would otherwise fall to be destroyed can also be retained for up to two years where the responsible chief officer of police determines that it is necessary to retain it for the purposes of national security.[126]

In relation to those arrested or charged or served with penalty notices the period of retention varies with the age of the individual i.e. whether they are a juvenile or an adult, whether they are arrested, charged or convicted, the existence of any previous convictions and if so the nature of the offence for which they were previously convicted, and the nature of any relevant offence for which they are arrested or charged and the sentence attached to the offence. Retention periods range from indefinite retention where serious crimes are at issue to a two year period where a fixed penalty has been issued.

The new regime was broadly welcomed by the Human Rights Joint Committee but there remain concerns at some areas and it remains to be seen how it will work in practice.

THE SIXTH PRINCIPLE

6–74 This requires that personal data shall be processed in accordance with the rights of data subjects under the Act. This replaces and extends the seventh principle under the 1984 Act which required compliance with the data subject's access rights. Subject access rights are, of course, a part of the 1998 Act[127] but data subject rights also include the right to prevent processing likely to cause damage and distress,[128] the right to prevent processing for the purposes of direct marketing[129] and rights in relation to automated decision-taking.[130]

The interpretation provisions rather obviously and rather unhelpfully simply state that any breach of the data subjects rights set out in ss.7 and 10–12 will also constitute a breach of the sixth principle. The Commissioner's powers to take enforcement action against a data controller for breaching the sixth principle are thus supplemental to the right of a data subject to seek specific remedies including compensation, under s.13, for damage or distress suffered as a result of a breach of the data subject rights set out in ss.7–12 of the 1998 Act or to have inaccurate personal data blocked, erased or destroyed.

In *Law Society v Kordowski*[131] the High Court made an order in defence of the rights of data subjects under section 10 of the Act which included the issue of an injunction to stop the defendant from further publication of a similar website to the "Solicitors from Hell" site for which he was responsible.

An interesting sidelight on the case was that, in response to a request from the Law Society to consider enforcement action under the Act, the Information Commissioner had written to the Law Society suggesting that the exemption

---

[125] Protection of Freedoms Act s.2.
[126] Protection of Freedoms Act s.9.
[127] 1998 Act s.7.
[128] s.10: see Ch.12.
[129] s.11: see Ch.12.
[130] s.12: see Ch.13.
[131] See para.6-41.

under s.36 might apply to the postings and his office would not become engaged as the DPA "is simply not designed to deal with the sort of problems you have brought to my attention". Tugendhat J. expressed his strong disagreement with this stance pointing out that there was no doubt as a matter of law that the processing was unlawful in the particular case. The individual rights are dealt with separately in Chs 11–14. In this section we review the points common to the exercise of all the rights.

INDIVIDUAL RIGHTS–GENERAL ISSUES

This section deals with points common to the individual rights For example, four of those rights must be exercised by notice in writing. This gives rise to questions as to how the notices must be served. Other common points are whether they can be handled by agents; the exercise of the rights by children; and whether the individual rights can be waived by individuals for example under a contract.

6–75

FORMALITIES OF NOTICES

The Directive does not specify how requests to exercise individual rights have to be made, but under the 1998 Act all rights are to be exercised by a notice or request in writing to the data controller.

6–76

Address for service

The Act does not specify any formalities as to service of notices or requests by individuals. The provisions relating to service in s.65 only relate to the service of notices by the Commissioner. A subject access or any other rights request can be made at any valid address for the data controller. Many large organisations have data protection officers and rights requests can be directed to them. When dealing with a large organisation it may be preferable for data subjects to direct requests to the head office of an organisation rather than to a branch office. Many organisations have standard procedures for dealing with rights requests and it is worth making inquiries as to those procedures before making the formal request.

6–77

Notice in writing

Although notices must be in writing, there are no other formal requirements as to presentation or content. Clearly a request has to be intelligible for the controller to understand it but there is no legal requirement for it to mention the Data Protection Act. Generally, the more relevant information the individual supplies to help the data controller understand and deal with his request the better. In particular, in making a subject access request, the provision of information by the data subject will help the controller find the information sought. Where a controller cannot find the information requested without further assistance from the data subject the obligation to respond is deferred until it has been supplied. Data controllers should ensure that staff are trained to be able to recognise Data

6–78

Protection Act requests and notices. A data controller may find it useful to have standard forms for individuals to complete when requesting subject access or raising objections to particular types of processing to ensure that all the information he needs to deal with the request properly is collected. However, he will not be able to insist that individuals use the form.

Service by electronic means

6–79   Under s.64 any of the individual notices or requests can be served by electronic means as long as the notice is received in legible form and is capable of being used for subsequent reference.

EXERCISE OF RIGHTS BY MINORS OR ON BEHALF OF OTHERS

Exercise of individual rights by children

6–80   The main right provided by the 1984 Act was the right of subject access. The capacity of children to exercise that right on their own behalf was a difficult area because of the difference between the provisions applying in Scotland and other areas. Under Scottish law a child was not able to make an application for subject access on his or her own behalf until the age of 16. Until then the right of subject access had to be exercised by the parent or guardian acting on behalf of the child. In England, Wales and Northern Ireland a parent could make an application on behalf of a child until the child reached an age when he was able to decide for himself whether or not to make the application. The guidance generally followed has been that by the age of 12 a child can be expected to have a sufficient understanding to decide whether or not to make a request. A child may of course achieve that capacity earlier; that will be a question of fact in the particular circumstances. Under the 1998 Act children have all the individual rights and the same guidance should apply to the exercise of all those rights. The position in England, Wales and Northern Ireland remains the same as under the 1984 Act but s.66 has brought the position in Scotland nearer into line with the rest of the UK. Section 66 provides that a child of 12 years or over will be presumed to have sufficient age and maturity to exercise any right conferred by the Act. In other cases a child under that age will still be able to exercise any such right where he has a sufficient general understanding of what it involves.

For children under 12, rights notices or requests will usually be made by parents or guardians acting on the child's behalf. In considering any such request the data controller must give careful thought as to whether he should accept the request. If he has any doubt for example as to whether the parent making the request is entitled to do so in a case where parents are estranged, it will be prudent to refuse access and leave the issue to be decided by a competent court which can weigh what is in the best interests of the child.

In relation to subject access rights the ICO says to take into account the following and there is no reason to restrict to SARs. When considering borderline cases, you should take into account, among other things:

- the child's level of maturity and their ability to make decisions like this;
- the nature of the personal data;
- any court orders relating to parental access or responsibility that may apply;
- any duty of confidence owed to the child or young person;
- any consequences of allowing those with parental responsibility access to the child's or young person's information. This is particularly important if there have been allegations of abuse or ill treatment;
- any detriment to the child or young person if individuals with parental responsibility cannot access this information; and
- any views the child or young person has on whether their parents should have access to information about them.

Exercise of rights by agents

There is no bar on the exercise of the individual rights, for example an application for subject access, being carried out on behalf of another person. An individual can appoint an agent to act in the exercise of his rights for him. However, where someone holds himself out as acting on behalf of another the controller should check that proper authority is held. How the controller does this will depend on the particular circumstances. In some cases it can simply be done by asking the person to confirm in writing that he or she has the appropriate authority. This may be sufficient where the controller is dealing with a solicitor or other professional adviser representing the data subject. In cases where the agent is acting under a formal power the controller may wish to have sight of that power. When the agent is neither a professional adviser nor acting under a formal power the controller should ask for sight of the authorisation provided by the individual, and some proof that it has come from the subject should be obtained. If the controller makes a disclosure to a person without the subject's authority he may be liable for a breach of the Act.

6–81

Exercise of rights on behalf of persons with disabilities

The legislation governing the protection of those with mental disabilities in England wales and Northern Ireland is the Mental Capacity Act 2005 which came into force on the October 1, 2007. It replaced the Enduring Powers of Attorney Act 1985, repealed Pt 7 of the Mental Health Act 1983 and provided for the replacement of the Court of Protection by a new Court with broader powers. In Scotland the relevant law is the Adults with Incapacity (Scotland) Act 2000. Neither law mentions data protection specifically. However, there is no reason to regard data protection rights as different from other powers and a properly appointed agent using powers under those laws will be able to exercise the rights of individuals under the Data Protection Act. The same applies to a person appointed to make decisions about such matters:

6–82

- in England and Wales, by the Court of Protection;
- in Scotland, by the Sheriff Court; and
- in Northern Ireland, by the High Court (Office of Care and Protection).

The Mental Health Act 2005 introduced Lasting Powers of Attorney (LPA). There are two types of such powers, a property and affairs LPA and a personal welfare LPA. It is assumed that data protection rights could potentially be exercised using either type of LPA depending on the nature of the information sought or the right being exercised. In cases where the person is acting under a power of attorney it will be prudent for the controller to ask to see the power and to check that it is sufficient to provide authority for the action sought. If the request is made under an enduring power of attorney the controller will also need to be provided with evidence that the power has been registered with the Court of Protection.

6–83   The MCA created a new Court of Protection to oversee actions taken under the Act and to resolve disputes that involve mental capacity matters. The Court has the same authority as the High Court and appeals can be made against its decisions, with permission, to the Court of Appeal. Section 15 of the MCA gives the Court certain powers, such as the power to make declarations as to whether a person has or lacks capacity to make a particular decision and to rule whether an act that is being proposed in relation to a person is lawful or not. Section 16 gives the Court power to make decisions and appoint deputies to make decisions on a person's personal welfare as well as on property and affairs.

It is assumed that the Court could exercise its powers to make a specific order for any of the individual rights to be exercised in a particular case. The Court is able to appoint deputies as substitute decision makers where a person loses capacity and has not completed an LPA. Deputies are able to take decisions on health and welfare as well as financial matters. Deputies have to make decisions in the person's best interests and allow the person to make any decisions that he or she still has capacity to make—they do not have power to make all of the person's decisions just because they have been appointed. The provision for deputies replaced and extended the old system of receivership for dealing with property and financial matters. Receivers who were appointed and in place before the MCA came fully into force on October 1, 2007 automatically became deputies from that date. Where a notice is received from a deputy or under a LPA the data controller should exercise caution to ensure that he sees evidence that the appointment has been properly made however, save in obvious cases, the data controller is unlikely to be able to make an independent assessment of whether the power is being properly used and will have to rely on the deputy or holder of the LPA. Deputies should follow the Code of Practice issued under the MCA and if in doubt it may be prudent to refer to the Office of the Public Guardian which his responsible for the oversight of deputies.

Litigation

6–84   A child or a person incapable of managing his or her own affairs will not be able to bring court proceedings to enforce the individual rights in his or her own name, but must act by a litigation friend in the usual way.

Disability discrimination

Under the Equality Act, it is unlawful for service providers to treat people less favourably because they are disabled. The Commissioner advises that this may impact on how responses to the exercise of individual rights are handled. In relation to subject access the guidance on the website advises:

6–85

> "If a disabled person finds it impossible or unreasonably difficult to make a subject access request in writing, you may have to make a reasonable adjustment for them under the Disability Discrimination Act 1995 [now the Equality Act 2010]. This could include treating a verbal request for information as though it were a valid subject access request. You might also have to respond in a particular format which is accessible to the disabled person, such as Braille, large print, email or audio formats. If an individual thinks you have failed to make a reasonable adjustment, they may make a claim under the Disability Discrimination Act. Information about making a claim is available from the Equality and Human Rights Commission."

This would apply equally to the exercise of other rights such as the right to object to processing.

CAN THE RIGHTS BE EXCLUDED?

The general rule in UK is that a party may contract out of a statutory protection which is intended to be for private benefit, but he may not contract out of a statutory protection which is intended to serve the public interest *Johnson v Moreton*.[132] In some Acts, there are specific provisions governing this point but the Act does not deal with the possibility of an individual contracting out of the individual rights. At EU level the point is not dealt with in the Directive. Under the Charter the right to data protection has now become a fundamental right however the right of an individual to autonomy and freedom of choice is also a right recognised in the EU. The first point to be made is that any decision to contract out of the rights under the Act would have to be a genuine free choice for the individual if it were to be recognised by a court.

6–86

The data protection principles and the individual rights

Applying the general rule, in the first instance a distinction might be drawn between the data protection principles and the individual rights. On this basis the courts might be prepared to accept that an individual could enter into a contract in which he waived his rights to access or compensation under the Act, but might not countenance a contract under which he purported to waive the application of the data protection principles to the data about him. The reasoning being that the individual rights are for the sole benefit of individuals whereas the principles set the general standards. However, this application of the general rule does not necessarily stand up on closer examination. The individual rights and the principles are closely entwined. Principle 4 requires that personal data shall be accurate and, where necessary, kept up to date; s.14 provides for individual

6–87

---

[132] [1980] A.C. 37: see Ch.11.

remedies in respect of inaccurate data. Principle 6 requires that personal data shall be processed in accordance with the rights of data subjects under the Act; s.13 gives a remedy in compensation to a data subject who suffers damage by reason of any contravention of the Act. In addition individuals have the right to ask the Commissioner to assess the lawfulness of processing, thus invoking the supervisory jurisdiction of the regulator.

6–88   An alternative approach would be to take the view that not all of the principles set out general standards. On this basis, principle 6 could be distinguished from the others as it simply reinforces the importance of the individual rights, rather than setting a general standard. Equally, not all the matters which give rise to individual remedies would be regarded as being solely for the benefit of the individual. Thus the "right" to request an assessment of processing, which involves the role of the supervisory authority might be seen as a different sort of right. Following this thinking, a set of individual rights could be distinguished, being the rights found in ss.7 (subject access), 10 (objection to processing), 11 (objection to direct marketing), 12 (rights relating to automated decision-taking), 13 (rights to compensation) and 14 (remedies for inaccuracy). These would be regarded as the individual rights which could be waived by the data subject. However, although an individual could enter into a contract to agree that the rights did not apply to him, he could not disapply the powers of the Commissioner to take enforcement action in an appropriate case. Principle 6 may be enforced by the Commissioner.

It might be argued that while the individual could not successfully waive his rights under those sections, he could agree not to assert his remedies in the courts. Thus the rights would continue to apply and the powers of the Commissioner would continue to apply but the individual would agree, by an appropriate contract clause, not to seek to exercise his rights or enforce them in court or make a request to the Commissioner for assessment. It is suggested that this is the better view.

Effect of the Directive and the Human Rights Act 1998

6–89   The relevant requirement of the Directive is found at Art.22, Remedies:

> "without prejudice to any administrative remedy for which provision may be made, inter alia before the supervisory authority referred to in Article 28, prior to referral to the judicial authority, Member States shall provide for the right of every person to a judicial remedy for any breach of the rights guaranteed him by the national law applicable to the processing in question".

It could be argued that it is sufficient for the State to ensure that a remedy is available in the law. There is no requirement that the State restrict individuals from contracting out of the exercise of that remedy.

However, this raises the question whether the national law can allow an individual to contract out of an aspect of those fundamental rights which the State has a duty to maintain.

6–90   The right to data protection is now one of the rights guaranteed by the Charter. This raises the question of whether their waiver in a contract would be compatible with the Convention rights.

In relation to Convention rights an individual can consent to acts which would otherwise be a breach of the qualified rights. The consent must be freely given and genuine. In considering whether the consent met those standards a court would be likely to take into consideration the nature and relationship of the contracting parties. Clearly it would not be acceptable for a public authority to require an individual to waive his statutory rights under the Act in order to obtain a State benefit but the position of private parties is not the same as the State.

Position of private bodies

Where the other party is a purely private body, exercising a purely private function, an individual should be entitled to contract out of any or all of the rights to take action under the DPA 1998. Leaving aside the question of the terms of the contract and the issues of fairness, which are dealt with below, it could be argued that there is nothing in the Charter, the Directive, the general law, the Human Rights Act or the Convention to forbid such an agreement, and it is therefore within the powers of a private body and a private individual to enter an agreement that the individual would not take court action to enforce certain of his individual rights under the Data Protection Act.

6–91

It is suggested that it would be lawful for an individual to agree to waive his or her rights to enforce the remedies granted for breach of the individual rights in ss.7, 10, 11, 12, 13 and 14, subject to the requirements that the consent is genuine, freely given and the contract fair and not in breach of the Unfair Terms in Consumer Contracts Regulations 1999. It would not be lawful for anybody to seek to exclude the powers of the Commissioner or the right to complain to the Commissioner.

Contract terms

The intersection of contract terms and fairness in obtaining and processing information exercised the Registrar considerably under the 1984 Act. In the 1998 Act the requirements to achieve fairness in both obtaining and processing are explicitly set out in Sch.1 Pt II paras 2 and 3. A data controller wishing to exclude the individual rights would have to ensure that the clause and its effects are clearly explained to the individual. An exclusion clause would have to be part of a contract agreed with an individual. The data controller cannot unilaterally seek to disapply individual rights. The individual would have to agree and some consideration would have to pass between the parties. To satisfy principle 1, the information about the exclusion terms would either have to be imparted or made readily available before the information is provided by the individual or before the first processing or the first disclosure. It would also fall within the scope of para.3(d) of Pt II being:

6–92

> "further information which is necessary, having regard to the specific circumstances in which the data are or are to be processed, to enable processing in respect of the data to be fair."

Moreover, to satisfy the requirements of contract law the terms of a contract must be available to the individual before or at the point of entering the contract. If a clause is included in the contract which is an unusually wide exclusion or onerous term or involves giving up a right provided by statute the explicit attention of the individual may have to be drawn to it: *Interfoto Picture Library Ltd v Stiletto Visual Programmes Ltd.*[133] It would not be sufficient therefore to seek to give information about exclusion of rights clauses after the data have been obtained.

The Unfair Terms in Consumer Contracts Regulations 1999 (SI 1999/2083)

6–93   Under the Unfair Terms in Consumer Contracts Regulations 1999 (SI 1999/2083) a contract term may not be binding if, having regard to the relative bargaining position of the parties, it is an unfair term. The Regulations apply to any term in a contract concluded between a seller or supplier and a consumer where the term has not been individually negotiated (reg.3). An "unfair term" is any term which, contrary to the requirement of good faith, causes a significant imbalance in the parties' rights and obligations under the contract to the detriment of the consumer (reg.4(1)). In assessing a term the circumstances of the contract are taken into account (reg.4(2)) and in assessing good faith regard has to be had to a specified list of matters (reg.4(3)). These are: the strength of the bargaining position of the parties; whether the consumer had an inducement to agree to the term; whether the goods or services were to his special order and the extent to which the seller or supplier had dealt fairly or equitably with the consumer (Sch.2). Accordingly the relationship of the parties, the nature of the contract, the relative bargaining position of the parties and the nature of the supply (for example, if it is an essential service) will all be relevant in deciding if the exclusion clause is valid. Sch.3 of the Regulations contains an indicative list of terms which may be regarded as unfair, one of which is a term which has the object or effect of excluding or hindering the consumer's right to take legal action or exercise any other legal remedy (Sch.3 para.1q). Thus a contract clause in an agreement covering the use of personal data under which the individual waived his individual rights under the Act would run a significant risk of falling foul of the Regulations.

The Regulations are primarily enforced by the Director General of Fair Trading but the Commissioner may also bring proceedings in respect of unfair terms.

Impact of the draft Regulation in brief[134]

6–94   The draft Regulation includes a list of principles at art.5, which largely cover the present principles 1–6. The detail of the notice provisions however is moved to art.14 and categorised as a right of the data subject. The revised principles require that personal data are also processed "in a transparent manner" and this is reinforced by a specific requirement for transparent and easily accessible policies and communication in art.11. There is more emphasis on data minimization with the third principle requiring that personal data shall only be processed if the purpose could not be fulfilled by processing non-personal data and the fifth principle referring specifically to limits on storing data "in a form which permits

---

[133] [1987] EWCA Civ 6.
[134] See Ch.1, paras 1–68 onward for an overview of the draft as at January 2012.

identification". There is a new addition which makes it explicit that personal data must be processed under the responsibility of a controller who must ensure and demonstrate for each operation the compliance with the Regulation. The new information right requires the provision of very detailed notices although the underlying requirements remain the same.

Records management process

A good records management system will include processes that broadly correspond to those listed here: **6–95**

1. Information capture—the process of acquiring or recording/creating information.
2. Registration—recording the existence of a record and capturing metadata (data about the data) that can be used to uniquely identify a record and locate it.
3. Classification—categorizing information on the basis of business needs which will also inform retention decisions.
4. Access and security levels—determining who within an organisation will have access to information and what measures will be taken to ensure the security of the information.
5. Life expectancy of the record—determining retention and disposal arrangements whether via archive or destruction.
6. Use and tracking of records —the process of using information, retrieving information, tracking location, amendments, version control, distribution of copies.
7. Destruction and disposal—the process of destruction and the retention of a record of the nature and time of the destruction or disposal.

See also ISO 15489, the international standard for records management.

ADDITIONAL INFORMATION

Derivations **6–96**

- Directive 95/46 (see Appendix B):
  (a) arts 6 (principles related to data quality), 10 (information in cases of collection from the data subject), 11 (information where data have not been obtained from the data subject),
  (b) Recitals 28, 38, 39, 40, 46, 56, 57.
- Council of Europe Convention of January 28, 1981 for the Protection of Individuals with regard to automatic processing of Personal Data: art.5 (quality of data).
- Data Protection Act 1984 s.2 and Sch.1 (the Principles).
- Organisation for Economic Co-operation and Development Guidelines: Annex, Pt 2 (Basic Principles of National Application 7, 8, 9, 10, 11).

Hansard references

6-97 Vol.586, No.108, col.CWH 21, Lords Grand Committee, February 23, 1998:
Principle 1, fair collection, meaning of as soon as practicable.
Vol.587, No.127, col.1127, Lords Third Reading, March 24, 1998:
Principle 6, para.8, Pt II, Sch.1.
Commons Standing Committee, June 4, col.304:
Principle 6.

CHAPTER 7

Security Obligations And The Use Of Data Processors

INTRODUCTION

In this chapter we review the legal obligations towards the security of personal data arising from the Act. A legal text is not the place to provide practical advice on how to achieve the best security practice; such advice must be sought elsewhere. We have however pointed to the main standards in para.7–15 below.

It is self-evident that the risk of security breach to business and to public bodies may be significant. Breaches of security can cause financial loss and lead to regulatory action and loss of customer confidence. Since 1991 the Department of Trade and Industry, now Business, Innovation and Skills (BIS), has sponsored research every two years into information security breaches to help UK businesses understand and deal with the risks that they face. The 2012 survey was conducted by Inforsecurity Europe and the results complied by PriceWaterhouse-Cooper.[1] The report is compiled from responses for around 500 organisations of different sizes, around 20 per cent of which are public bodies. This year's report indicates that 93 per cent of large organisations surveyed and 76 per cent of small businesses had had a security breach in the preceding 12 months with the main cause, particularly for large businesses, being an increase in cyber attacks. Within those figures, 45 per cent of large organisations responded that they had had breaches of data protection laws, although they do not give figures for the percentage of these reported to the Information Commissioner. The largest number of monetary penalty notices served by the Commissioner has been in relation to breaches of security (often after the breach has been reported to the Commissioner). In this chapter we review the relevant provisions of the Act and how those interact with other obligations in relation to security of personal data, assess the extent and nature of obligations to notify of breaches and examine the rules relating to the appointment and use of data processors. The provisions dealing with security breach notification obligations in respect of providers of electronic communication services are covered in Ch.22.

7–01

---

[1] *www.pwc.cp* [Accessed September 14, 2012]: Information Security Breaches Survey 2012.

7–02 ## SUMMARY OF MAIN POINTS

(a) The data controller must guard against any risks to the security of personal data throughout its lifecycle.

(b) The security measures must cover both the organizational and the technical aspects of security.

(c) The risks to be assessed are the risks of harm to individuals caused by loss or destruction of the personal data not the risk to the organization of other consequences of a breach of security such as loss of intellectual property.

(d) The measures must be proportionate to those risks and may take account of the cost and the nature of technology available to protect the personal data.

(e) There is no obligation to notify the regulator of a breach of security under the Act but there are such obligations in other instruments and data controllers should be aware of those obligations.

(f) If a data processor is used the data controller must enter into a written contract which provides specific guarantees of security and control.

ANALYSIS OF THE PRINCIPLE

7–03 Principle 7 of Sch.1 requires that appropriate technical and organisational measures shall be taken by the data controller against unauthorized or unlawful processing of personal data and against accidental loss or destruction of, or damage to, personal data.

It is supplemented by significant interpretation provisions in Part II of the Schedule which require the data controller to ensure a level of security appropriate to:

(a) the nature of the data to be protected; and

(b) the harm that might result from unauthorised or unlawful processing or from accidental loss destruction and damage of the personal data, having regard to the state of technological development and the cost of implementing security measures.

As the seventh principle refers to unauthorised or unlawful processing of personal data, it follows that the obligations towards security must cover all personal data for which the controller is responsible at all times. It must therefore apply throughout the lifecycle of any personal data, including when it is stored or archived, when it is being disclosed and when it is being destroyed. It must cover personal data in any manual systems held as relevant filing systems. It applies to any unauthorized or unlawful processing of personal data. Given the wide scope of the definition of processing this means that it applies to information intended to be contained in personal data as it is being collected and as it is being used. The requirements cover both technical measures such as firewalls and encryption and organisational measures such as policies, procedures and controls towards, for example, access to premises or personal data. The risks that must be guarded against can be broken down into different categories. The first area of risk is the risk of unauthorised processing. This would cover, for example, processing by a member of staff for a purpose which has not been authorised by the data controller. This is supported by the requirement in the Directive that

"any person acting under the authority of the controller or of the processor who has access to personal data must not process them except on instructions from the controller",

which has been omitted from the UK Act. However it is possible that "unauthorised" could be taken to mean processing unauthorised by the data subject. It may be arguable that, where a data subject has specifically entrusted personal data to a data controller for a limited purpose, and the data controller processes the personal data for purposes outside that authorization the processing is unauthorised.

Unlawful processing may as a matter of fact overlap with unauthorized processing but will cover actions which are in breach of either criminal or civil law. There is no reason to give the term "unlawful" any meaning other than that given by the courts in case law to date (see *Murray v Big Pictures*[2]). There is also an argument here that unlawful processing includes any processing in breach of the DPA and that the 7th principle therefore imposes an obligation to take technical and organisational measures to protect against inaccuracy, excessive retention etc. and not just traditional security. The next categories of security breach refer to "accidental" loss, destruction or damage. This might suggest that unlawful or unauthorized processing must be in some way deliberate or at least involve a degree of intent. In any event, taken together, with the wide definition of processing, the provision appears to be sufficient to cover almost any breach of security of personal data. The obligation to take adequate security measures against these risks is absolute however the level of the security required must be a matter of judgment for the data controller. It is arguable that the obligation imposes a strict liability rule in respect of security. It is not clear whether and to what extent a data controller who carries out a proper risk assessment will be responsible for a completely unforeseen breach of security and the point has not been considered in any cases of which we are aware.

The security must be appropriate to the nature of the personal data and the harm that might ensue if any of the specified risks materialised. The nature of the personal data implies that consideration should be given to data in the sensitive categories to assess whether enhanced security is required; but it is submitted that non-sensitive categories of data may also give rise to specific types of harm, for example financial data may be used to facilitate identity theft. In order to make a proper assessment of the potential detriment caused by a security breach the data controller must be aware of the nature of the personal data he holds and assess the potential harm. Harm is not defined and it is submitted that a broad approach to the term should be taken covering physical, financial or emotional harm to data subjects.

7–04

The data controller is also entitled to take into account the types of technological measures which are available and the cost of measures. With increasing technological developments it is highly likely that a data controller will be expected to consider a range of technical security measures such as

7–05

---

[2] [2007] EWHC 1908.

firewalls (systems designed to prevent external agencies hacking into a private network) and encryption. Encryption should not, however, be seen as a panacea since its use can in itself lead to security problems. There are risks in allowing employees a free hand in encrypting data and communications. Loss of a private key to encrypted files through either malice or carelessness could expose a company to the risk of serious damage if for example, the personal data are "lost" or unavailable at the material time they were needed. If such files contain personal data then the loss of an encryption key may be the equivalent of the accidental loss of the data.

7–06   The interpretation provisions also require the data controller to take reasonable steps to ensure the reliability of any employees who have access to the personal data. "Reasonable steps" is, as before, not defined but it is submitted that written recruitment, training, performance monitoring and vetting procedures will be a minimum requirement. Although what constitutes "reasonable steps" is not made explicit, it will also depend on the nature and sensitivity of the personal data concerned. In the PWC report referred to in para.7–01 above it was reported that the root cause of security breaches was often a "failure to invest in educating staff about security risks" which is only recognised after an organisation has had a security breach. It is notable that in the cases in which monetary penalty notices have been served for breach of security many are attributable to staff behavior not to technical security breaches. The obligations imposed by the seventh principle are reinforced by the obligation to notify the Commissioner of the security measures in place as part of the notification process.

Relation with the Directive

7–07   Principle 7 reflects art.17 of the Directive, but there are a number of differences between the requirements in the Directive and these provisions of the Act:

(a)   The Directive requires controllers to ensure a level of security appropriate to the risks represented by the processing rather than the harm that might result from a breach and the nature of the data—which is what the Act requires.

(b)   The Directive's emphasis on the need for security "in particular where the processing involves the transmission of data over a network" is omitted from the Act.

(c)   The Directive's requirement that "any person acting under the authority of the controller or of the processor who has access to personal data must not process them except on instructions from the controller", is also omitted, although s.12(a)(ii) imposes a general obligation to ensure that a data processor acts only on instructions from the controller. It is submitted that a court considering the provisions in the Act would seek to construe them in accord with the Directive and would therefore apply a broad approach.

RELATION WITH OTHER INTERNATIONAL INSTRUMENTS[3]

The importance of security has been a constant theme in all of the international instruments on data protection. Treaty 108 deals with data security as follows:

7–08

> "Appropriate security measures shall be taken for the protection of personal data stored in automated data files against accidental or unauthorised destruction or accidental loss as well as against unauthorised access, alteration or dissemination."[4]

The OECD Guidelines on the protection of privacy and trans-border data flows include a Principle on Security Safeguards as follows:

> "Personal data should be protected by reasonable security safeguards against such risks as loss or unauthorised access, destruction, use, modification or disclosure of data".[5]

The detailed comments in Pt B of the OECD Guidelines explain the OECD position as follows:

> "Security and privacy issues are not identical. However, limitations on data use and disclosure should be reinforced by security safeguards. Such safeguards include physical measures (locked doors and identification cards, for instance), organisational measures (such as authority levels with regard to access to data) and, particularly in computer systems, informational measures (such as enciphering and threat monitoring of unusual activities and responses to them). It should be emphasized that the category of organisational measures includes obligations for data processing personnel to maintain confidentiality. Paragraph 11 has a broad coverage. The cases mentioned in the provision are to some extent overlapping (e.g. access/ disclosure). 'Loss' of data encompasses such cases as accidental erasure of data, destruction of data storage media (and thus destruction of data) and theft of data storage media. 'Modified' should be construed to cover unauthorised input of data, and 'use' to cover unauthorised copying."

The OECD has also issued Guidelines for the Security of Information Systems and Networks,[6] which should be considered together with the privacy Guidelines. Neither Treaty 108 nor the OECD Guidelines deal with the use of out-sourced processors. The Directive goes significantly beyond the earlier instruments in that area. It is also a mark of the continually developing position that the draft Regulation focuses on the role of processors in more detail and imposes significant direct responsibilities on them.

---

[3] See Ch.1 for an explanation of the nature and impact of these instruments.
[4] art.7.
[5] Para.11: Security Safeguards Principle. art.11.
[6] Adopted as a Recommendation July 5, 2002.

European case law

7–09   None of the cases before the CJEU to date have dealt with security obligations.[7] The European Court of Human Rights has considered an aspect of security management in the case of *I v Finland*[8] and held that a failure to provide effective security for personal data is a breach of art.8. The applicant was a nurse who was diagnosed as HIV positive and received treatment from the hospital in which she worked. She became concerned that her colleagues were aware of her illness. At the time hospital staff had free access to the patient register which contained patient information. Once she had raised this the register was amended so that only those treating the patient would have access to a patient's records. In 1996, after she had left her job at the hospital, she sought information as to who had accessed her records. She was informed that it was not possible to provide this information as the system in use only recorded the five last occasions of access and even this information was deleted when the case returned to the archives. The applicant then sought redress through the Finnish courts for the alleged failure to keep her patient record confidential. Her case went on appeal to the Court of Appeal which considered her a credible witness but did not find firm evidence that her patient record had been unlawfully consulted. She was refused leave to appeal to the Supreme Court and took her case to Strasbourg.

The Court reiterated the positive obligations imposed by art.8, which may involve the adoption of measures designed to secure respect for private life even in the sphere of relations between individuals themselves.[9] The Court pointed out that:

> "The protection of personal data, in particular medical data, is of fundamental importance to a person's enjoyment of his or her right to respect for private and family life."

The Court concluded that there had been a breach of art.8 because of the failure of the hospital to protect her personal information. The Court found that the decisive issue was that the hospital had failed to meet the legal requirements set out in s.26 of the Personal Files Act 1987, which required that personal data should be secured against, among other things, unlawful access. It went on to say:

> "The Court notes that the mere fact that the domestic legislation provided the applicant with an opportunity to claim compensation for damages caused by an alleged unlawful disclosure of personal data was not sufficient to protect her private life. What is required in this connection is practical and effective protection to exclude any possibility of unauthorized access occurring in the first place".

---

[7]   See Ch.3 for a review of the cases which have been considered by the CJEU.
[8]   Application No.20511/03 July 2008.
[9]   *X v Netherlands* judgment of March 26, 1985 Series A no.91; *Odievre v France* [GC] n.42326/98 ECHR 2003-III.

SECURITY OBLIGATIONS UNDER OTHER PROVISIONS

Financial services

Security obligations will apply under other legislation in addition to the DPA. In particular financial services organisations are subject to legal duties under the Financial Services and Markets Act 2000 (FSMA). The Act established the Financial Services Authority (FSA) a body corporate limited by guarantee, which came into operation on December 1, 2001. Under s.19 of the FSMA, any person who carries on a regulated activity in the UK must be authorised by the FSA or exempt. Breach of s.19 may be a criminal offence and punishable on indictment by a maximum term of two years imprisonment and/or a fine.The bodies which are subject to FSA regulation are set out in the Financial Services and Markets Act (Regulated Activities) Order 2001 (RAO).The RAO sets out the specific activities which firms must receive FSA permission (known as a Pt IV permission) to carry on and cover all the vast range of financial services including accepting deposits, insurance, investments, pensions, Lloyds market activities, e-money, mortgages, share dealing, securities. The FSA is responsible for authorising firms and supervising their activities and has an important rule-making function. Under s.138 of the FSMA:

7–10

> "(1) The Authority may make such rules applying to authorised persons—
>
>   (a) with respect to the carrying on by them of regulated activities, or
>   (b) with respect to the carrying on by them of activities which are not regulated activities, as appear to it to be necessary or expedient for the purpose of meeting any of its regulatory objectives.
>
>   (1A) The Authority may also make such rules applying to authorised persons who are investment firms or credit institutions, with respect to the provision by them of a relevant ancillary service, as appear to the Authority to be necessary or expedient for the purpose of meeting any of its regulatory objectives".

The rules must be published[10] and are published in the FSA Handbook. The Handbook is divided into sections. The first part sets out the 11 general Principles for Business which are the underlying set of core responsibilities of all businesses which are subject to the Rules. There are then a series of more detailed specific Rules. Most important in the context of security are the Senior Management Arrangements, Systems and Controls (SYSC). These outline the FSA's management requirements for the firms which it regulates. SYSC focuses on the responsibilities of directors and senior management to ensure that the firm has appropriate control, supervision and accountancy systems in place, including appropriate operational risk systems and controls. The FSA has a wide power to interpret and apply the Principles. Where there is a difference between the detail of any of the Rules and the Principles the FSA accepts that the detailed Rule will apply but where there are customer complaints, it is not enough for firms to ensure that they comply with all the specific Rules; a complaint may be upheld on the basis of a breach of the Principles: *British Bankers Association v Financial*

---

[10] FSMA s.153.

Services Authority.[11] The FSA's powers to impose financial penalties is significant. Under s.206, if the Authority considers that an authorised person has contravened a requirement imposed on him by or under the FSMA it may impose a penalty, in respect of the contravention, "of such amount as it considers appropriate".

7–11   The relevant Principles which cover the security obligations are:

Principle 2: A firm must conduct its business with due skill, care and diligence.

Principle 3: A firm must take reasonable care to organise and control its affairs.

Principle 6: A firm must pay due regard to the interests of its customers and treat them fairly.

The relevant SYSC requirements are:

Rule SYSC 3.2R: A firm must take reasonable care to establish and maintain effective systems and controls for compliance with applicable requirements and standards under the regulatory system and for countering the risk that the firm might be used to further financial crime.

Rule SYSC 3.2.6A: A firm's relevant systems and controls must be comprehensive and proportionate to the nature, scale and complexity of their operations.

In a report published in 2008,[12] the FSA made clear that the safekeeping of data was a crucial responsibility for firms and it would take appropriate action against firms that did not comply.

7–12   The Report followed a spate of security breaches in the financial services sector. In 2007 the ICO threatened to take enforcement action against a number of banks and other financial institutions unless they improved the security of their processing. There had been repeated media stories that customer records were being left in dustbins outside bank premises, although there were also strong suspicions that the material was only been acquired by dint of positive efforts by those wishing to produce a story. Whatever the background the result was several financial institutions provided the Commissioner with undertakings to abide by and apply proper security procedures in the future. The FSA fined the Nationwide Building Society £980,000 in February 2007 after a laptop computer was stolen from the home of one of the Nationwide's employees in August 2006. The laptop contained customer information which could have been used to further financial crime. The FSA held that the Nationwide had not had had an adequate risk management strategy as it had been possible to download large amounts of customer data on to portable devices. The FSA found that the way that the information security procedures were structured and made available as well as the absence of training and controls were in breach of the Principle 3 requirements to take reasonable care to organize and control the affairs responsibly and effectively with adequate risk management systems. The highest fine which has

---

[11] [2011] EWHC 999.
[12] Data Security in Financial Services April 2008

been levied by the FSA for breach of security is £2,275,000. The fine was imposed on the UK branch of Zurich Insurance Plc (Zurich UK) for failing to have adequate systems and controls in place to prevent the loss of customers' confidential information. The failings came to light following the loss of 46,000 customers' personal details, including identity details, and in some cases bank account and credit card information, details about insured assets and security arrangements. Zurich UK had outsourced the processing of some of its general insurance customer data to Zurich Insurance Co South Africa Ltd (Zurich SA). In August 2008, Zurich SA lost an unencrypted back-up tape during a routine transfer to a data storage centre. As there were no proper reporting lines in place Zurich UK did not learn of the incident until a year later.

Government Security Review and requirements

In October 2007 the National Audit Office asked for a copy of the Child Benefit Database from HMRC. The database was copied on to two disks which were put in the post to the NAO but did not arrive. They had been sent by a post system which did not have a tracking facility. When the disks did not arrive, replacements were sent, but the NAO raised concerns at the loss of the earlier copies. The disks contained 25 million records and have never come to light. The issue became public in November 2007 and was followed in January 2008 by the news that an unencrypted laptop which had 600,000 individual records on it had been stolen from a Royal Navy recruiter. For the next few months the press was awash with pieces about the loss of personal data records and a raft of reviews and reports were commissioned. The most influential was the report prepared by Sir Gus O'Donnell, Data Handling Procedures in Government.

7–13

Data Handling Procedures Report/Security Policy Framework

The Data Handling Procedures Report (DHP Report) was published in June 2008 and mainly covered the security procedures that Government Departments, Non-Departmental Public Bodies (NDPBs) and private sector contractors who work for Government would have to apply in the future when handling information about identifiable individuals. These covered:

7–14

- a set of core security and management measures (the mandatory minimum security measures) across government, including encryption and compulsory testing by independent experts of the resilience of systems to deliver consistent protection;
- a change in attitudes fostered by mandatory annual training and the use of Privacy Impact Assessments for new initiatives;
- accountability for the information in the possession of the Department by the standardisation of data security roles within departments to ensure clear lines of responsibility; and
- transparency and scrutiny with a requirement for Departments to report on their performance under the scrutiny of the National Audit Office and the right of the Information Commissioner to perform spot checks of Departmental data handling.

The Report was followed by a programme of information assurance (most notably the CESG's IAMM—see below) implemented across Government and the public sector.

These requirements are now in place and are implemented by reference to "the HMG Security Policy Framework" (SPF). This Framework sets out a detailed implementation of the requirements identified in the DHP Report. The SPF is regularly updated, and can be found on the Cabinet Office website together with associated documentation on special aspects of security.

In summary, the SPF describes the standards, best practice guidelines and approaches that are required to protect UK Government assets (people, information and infrastructure). It is based around the ISO27002 Code of Practice on Information Security Management (see later) and focuses on the outcomes that are required to achieve a proportionate and risk managed approach to security that enables government business to function effectively, safely and securely. It applies to suppliers (e.g. data processors contracted to a Government Department) and Government Agencies.

Security in Government Departments and the wider public sector also falls within the remit of CESG, part of GCHQ (one of the Government's main agencies dealing with national security). CESG (which now prefers not to use the full historic name of the Communications-Electronics Security Group), is responsible for advising Government and the wider public sector on how to implement the SPF. CESG is responsible for the Information Assurance Maturity Model (IAMM) which assists Government bodies to implement the National IA Strategy (from commencement to maturity). It focuses on the mandatory and other measures set out in the DHP Report and the SPF. CESG has produced specific unclassified guidance on data protection in the context of the SPF ("HMG IA Standard No.6 Protecting Personal Data and Managing Information Risk") and has produced other security documentation (e.g. on security risk assessment) and an IAMM toolkit.

All the documents associated with the SPF and IAMM are relevant to all Government departments and bodies, subject to central government control and have been cascaded down to contractors working for such bodies. The Local Government Data Handling Guidelines, first published in November 2008 and revised and reissued in August 2012, set out similar guidance for local authorities.

All data asset classifications are set out in Appendix 1 of the SPF. Personal data can of course fall into any of the security classifications, depending on its nature and context. There is also a specific "Protect" classification for personal data which merits protection which includes those data that:

> "cause distress to individuals; breach proper undertakings to maintain the confidence of information provided by third parties; breach statutory restrictions on the disclosure of information; cause financial loss or loss of earning potential, or to facilitate improper gain; unfair advantage for individuals or companies; prejudice the investigation or facilitate the commission of crime; disadvantage government in commercial or policy negotiations with other".

It should be noted that these requirements include an obligation on public bodies to notify the Commissioner's Office of material breaches of security. This and the other requirements have not been incorporated in legislation but are Government policy. When considering compliance with the seventh principle it is very likely that a failure by a public body to which they apply to meet these standards would be regarded by the ICO as evidence of a failure to apply appropriate security.

Security standards

Whereas the SPF is focused on the public sector and in particular central Government Departments, the text in the SPF is based on a set of standards collectively known as ISO27k. The important member of this set of standards (ISO/IEC 27002) started life as BS 7799 which soon became an international standard ISO/IEC Standard 17799, which was then reclassified as ISO/IEC 27002. ISO/IEC 27002 contains the detailed security controls that make up the "Code of Practice for Information Security Management".

7–15

Other members of the ISO27k series of standards include ISO/IEC 27005, dealing with information security risk management. It is clear that the ISO27k set is increasing in size and is intended to become the focal point for standardising best practice in any field of security. For instance, ISO/IEC27018 is planned to deal with Cloud Computing whereas ISO/IEC27043 is planned to deals with the security techniques associated with digital evidence investigation principles and processes.The ISO27k set is supported by an accreditation scheme which might become more important in the context of data processor contracts (including those with data processors outside the EEA) as the ISO27k set of standards will be international standards.

Other important standards that impact on the security area are: ISO/IEC 15408 (Security Product certification); ISO/IEC 9000 (Quality Management in general); ISO/IEC 24760 (Identity Management); and BS 25999 (Business Continuity Management), the latter soon to become an ISO standard. The British Standards Institute Code of Practice for Legal Admissibility and Evidential Weight of Information Stored Electronically PD 008 gives guidance to the quality required to ensure that evidence can be used in legal proceedings. BS 4783 Storage Transport and Media Maintenance contains useful guidance on solutions to reduce the chances of damage to data.

It is very likely that the ICO will be guided by these standards when assessing best practice in the security of personal data

Guidance from the Commissioner on Security

Security safeguards are one of the pieces of information which must be provided to the Commissioner on notification. These do not appear on the public register. They enable the Commissioner's staff to make a basic level check that the data controller has some security measures in place but are not reviewed or assessed by the Commissioner to any depth. In the Guide to Data Protection the Commissioner identifies what he considers to be the main points in relation to security and provides details of other sources of advice and information. He does not provide any in-depth guidance on security standards but does produce a Practical Guide to IT Security which it suggests is particularly useful for small businesses. The Commissioner has not mandated many specific actions other than

7–16

the encryption of portable devices and laptops but his approach to security can be seen in the areas in which he has imposed monetary penalty notices for breaches of security. Thirteen notices have been served in 2012 to the time of writing (July 2012). The penalties have ranged from £60k to £325. Some of the breaches are technical ones such as the loss of back-up tapes containing personal data or the sale of old equipment with personal data still on hard drives; some have been more organizational such as the failure to keep archived records secure but many have come to light as a result of the behavior of individuals included sending sensitive medical details to the wrong address and the inappropriate disclosure of sensitive personal data. The Commissioner has taken the view that in these cases there has been a lack of technical or organisational measures such as training that have left the data controller unduly vulnerable to human error rather than just to the particular human error that took place.

It should also be noted that the Commissioner pays particular attention to security when carrying out both mandatory and voluntary audits. The Assessment Notice Code of Practice states that audits will cover:

"b.   The provision and monitoring of staff training and awareness of data protection requirements, relating to their roles and responsibilities.

c.   The processes in place to ensure adequate security is applied to the 'data controller's' IT systems, including portable and mobile devices, to ensure the appropriate storage and use of personal data.

d.   The processes in place to ensure adequate physical security is applied to the storage and use of manual files, both inside and outside the 'data controller's' premises."

Guidance from the Article 29 Working Party

7–17   There is useful guidance from the Article 29 WP both on security and the contractual safeguards required in the controller to processor relationship in its Opinion 05/2012 on Cloud Computing.[13] Although the Opinion focuses on cloud computing the material on security requirements and the appropriate areas to be covered in contracts are more generally useful. In relation to security it focuses on the core security objectives of availability, confidentiality and integrity. For example in relation to availability it emphasises the risks arising from potential loss of connectivity and failures of network infrastructure or hardware. It advises that appropriate diligence should be applied to check that there are adequate mechanisms to deal with these risks.

SECURITY BREACH NOTIFICATION TO REGULATORS AND INDIVIDUALS

7–18   Over the last decade there has been an increased focus on making those organisations which suffer a security breach involving personal information report the breach to the regulator or to individuals who may be affected. Security breach notification is required in most US States. At the time of writing the US Senate is considering a new federal privacy breach notification law, entitled The

---

[13]   01037/12/EN WP 196 adopted July 1, 2012.

Data Security and Breach Notification Act of 2012, which would replace the patch-work of state laws dealing with privacy breach notification. There are difficult questions over the extent of notification and how far the duty to notify regulators or individuals should extend. In 2011 the European Network and Information Security Agency (ENISA) produced a study on data breach notifications in the EU[14] in preparation for the introduction of the breach reporting obligation in Directive 2002/58/EC. It identified the need for an element of proportionality in any breach reporting, pointing out that notifications to individual should only follow breaches of personal data that are likely to cause harm to data subjects or to violate their rights. Issuing notifications for breaches that pose no risk will be redundant. The draft Data Protection Regulation includes wide breach notification provisions however the extent to which they are required under current UK law varies depending on the nature of the information disclosed and the circumstances of the case. Where organisations are subject to FSA regulation then there is an obligation to report breaches to the FSA. For other organisations the position varies.

In *R. (Chris Bryant, Brendan Montague, Brian Paddick and Lord Prescott) v Commissioner of Police of the Metropolis*,[15] the applicants obtained leave to bring a judicial review of the Metropolitan Police in relation to its conduct of the 2005/2006 investigation of the *News of the World* phone hacking activities. The applicants claimed that the failure of the Metropolitan Police to notify them that their details had been found among those of the private investigator Mr Mulcaire had been a breach of their art.8 rights. The applicants argued that the positive obligations imposed by art.8 in certain cases extended to an obligation to notify them that their details had been found among those in possession of the private investigator and therefore their privacy was at risk of being compromised. If they had been warned they would have been able to take appropriate action to guard against invasions of privacy. Leave to bring a judicial review was given on appeal having been initially refused. The case is not authority for the proposition that there is such an obligation as the cases then settled but the judge clearly regarded it as an arguable position.

7–19

The courts have held that individuals are entitled to be notified when disclosures of information are to be made about them. In *Woolgar*[16] it was indicated that in ordinary circumstances where confidential information is to be disclosed the person to whom the information relates should be informed in advance if possible. In the case of *General Dental Council v Savery*[17] the issue of notice was considered. The judge recognised that such prior notice had not been said by the ECtHR in either *MS v Sweden* or *Z v Finland* to be essential before disclosure of information but commented that

7–20

> "there may be scope for development of the law in this area and for a greater focus on the safeguards for patients where confidential medical information about them is to be used for other purposes."

---

[14] Available on *www.enisa.europa.eu* [Accessed September 13, 2012].
[15] [2011] EWHC 1314 (Admin).
[16] [2001] 1 W.L.R.
[17] [2011] EWHC 3011.

It seems a logical step that where confidential information has been disclosed, whether by accident or design, then an individual who may be detrimentally affected by the disclosure is owed a duty to be put on notice.

In many cases data controllers do notify individuals in case of breaches where the breach has given rise to some threat to the privacy of the individual.

Security breach Notification to the Commissioner

7–21   As is noted above, one of the outcomes of the Data Handling Review has been a commitment that government departments and those directly subject to government should notify the Commissioner of breaches of security which are over a certain degree of seriousness. The Commissioner encourages all organisations to notify him of breaches and there is a sense that those in the public sector, including local government, feel under more pressure to notify the Commissioner of breaches than those in the private sector. There have certainly been more actions for breach of security taken by the Commissioner against public sector bodies than private sector ones. This may be partially because there is more breach reporting by the public sector and the Commissioner is able to take action against public bodies because he is informed of the breaches. In addition, the private sector arguably holds more sensitive information than the public sector so there are more opportunities for breach. It may be that the public sector simply does not have the same security controls as the private sector but without detailed research this is largely speculation. The Commissioner produces Guidance on data security breach management and Guidance on when he considers that security breaches should be notified to his Office; both are available on the Commissioner's website. These should be reviewed and considered whenever there is a security breach.

Handling a breach of security

7–22   For most organisations a breach of security raises practical issues around handling the breach as well as legal risk. Organisations are often placed in a difficult position wishing to be open and transparent and at the same time protect the reputation of the organization. If disclosure is to be made to the regulator it is important that it is a full and honest disclosure and this often means that a proper report cannot be provided until the facts have been thoroughly investigated. It is useful to have a breach response plan in place as part of proper management of personal data so that in the event of a breach the organisation knows who should be involved and how it will be managed. Interestingly the Guide to Data Protection published by the Commissioner includes a requirement to be ready to respond to any breach swiftly and effectively. The scope of such plans usually covers the following areas:

- Membership of the core team including communications staff, IT specialists and lawyers as well as managers.
- Contingency to contain and deal with the breach if it is a continuing one.
- Planning for forensic and investigative actions as required.
- Arrangements for continuity, security of compromised data or systems.

- Review of insurance arrangements.
- Consideration of urgent legal actions such as orders for the recovery of data stolen and any contractual or other liability.
- Risk assessment of impact.
- Coordination of communication with stakeholders, police, individuals, regulators and others as required.
- Evaluation and responses.

DATA PROCESSOR APPOINTMENTS

The second group of requirements of principle 7 focus on when a data controller makes use of another party i.e. someone who is not an employee, to carry out processing for him. A data processor is defined in s.1a: **7–23**

> "data processor, in relation to personal data, means any person (other than an employee of the data controller) who processes the data on behalf of the data controller."

The term "processes" covers a wide range of activities and therefore any other party who assists with the handling of personal data will be covered by this definition. It is critical that, when parties cooperate in any activity which requires the processing of personal data in any way, they are clear between themselves as to which is the controller and which is the processor for specific processing operations performed on personal data. It should also be noted that where any processing is to take place outside the EEA measures are taken to ensure that the transfer of the personal data is lawful. The law on trans-border data flows is covered in Ch.8; however it should be noted that if a territory or country outside the EEA offers inadequate protection for personal data then the requirements of principle 7 are unlikely to be met.

The interpretation provisions to principle 7 require that the data controller   **7–24**
must, in order to comply with the 7th principle, choose a data processor providing "sufficient" guarantees with respect to the technical and organizational security measures governing the processing to be carried out and must take "reasonable steps" to ensure compliance with those measures. This requires the controller to carry out due diligence in relation to the choice of processor bearing in mind the nature of the personal data to be processed. The wording of the provision suggests that the controller should have made the risk assessment described in the preceding provisions and apply the results to the level of security required of the processor. The terms reflect a far simpler relationship with data processors than is often the case today when services are commoditised and offered remotely as "cloud" services. In reality sophisticated data processing services offered to many customers will provide a pre-determined level of security. It would not be possible for the service provider to change the nature of the security for each customer. The role of the data controller will be to assess whether that pre-determined level meets his requirements. This is often done by accepting good evidence that the processor meets any relevant ISO/BS/SPF standards. However, the data controller remains under an obligation to assess the security, including the level of staff training, and ensure that it is appropriate for the

relevant personal data. The requirement to take reasonable steps to ensure that the security standards are met may be provided for as part of performance monitoring. It may also be met by the imposition and exercise of an audit right given to the data controller however, again in the case of sophisticated services, the data processor may be reluctant or unable to offer audit rights to every customer and the customer may have to accept undertakings to provide proof of independent audits.

7–25   The relationship between the controller and the processor must be governed by a contract "which is made or evidenced in writing". The requirement could therefore be satisfied by an oral agreement which is recorded in writing but most controllers deal with the provisions by entering into standard contract terms with the controller. The contract must impose obligations equivalent to those imposed by the seventh principle on the data controller. In some cases one sees contracts which require the processor to comply with the Data Protection Act. Such clauses are nonsensical in contracts which apply in the UK as the processor is not directly bound by the Act in any way. The Act imposes all of the obligations on the data controller and the data controller must in some way set out the standards of security and other matters such as staff training which it considers appropriate and bind the controller to meet those. The contract must also provide that the processor may only act on instructions from the controller. There is no requirement that the instructions should be in writing or detailed. The question of the extent of the detailed control required by this provision is contentious. There seems no reason in law why the instructions should not be given in general terms, so as to limit the purposes for which personal data should be disclosed and the nature of disclosures but leave much of the day-to-day decision making with the processor within the scope of that set of instructions. However, the view of the Article 29 WP has inclined to a more restrictive view.[18] It should be noted that in the Directive there is a requirement that the contract must provide that the processor shall be bound to comply with the security requirements of the law of the Member State where the processor is established. This has not been transposed into UK law, presumably because, as a matter of law, a processor established in another jurisdiction would be required by that law to comply with the local provisions. In general this is dealt with in UK contracts by including a requirement that the processor shall comply with any relevant provisions of local law but with no specific procedures to resolve the matter in the case of a difference between the requirements of the data controller and the local law.

7–26   The role of processors has changed and developed with the advent of more sophisticated out-sourced services and the development of cloud services. In the case of SWIFT,[19] the capacity in which the service provider handled personal data was considered by the Belgium data protection regulatory authority and the Article 29 Working Party, although no action was taken. SWIFT is a financial messaging service used by most of the world's banks. It does not operate financial services such as clearing or money transfer but the transfer of messages and information which inevitably include personal data about the customers of banks, including banks in Europe. SWIFT is European-owned but had a data processing centre in the USA. SWIFT and its customers had considered itself to

---

[18] See WP paper on controllers and processors.
[19] See Ch.1 for an explanation of the SWIFT case.

be a processor and the legal agreements with SWIFT reflected that understanding. In June 2006 reports in the *New York Times* and other US newspapers stated that US agencies were obtaining access to personal data from SWIFT for the purposes of the US program to track financial affairs associated with terrorism. The access had been obtained by way of subpoenas of which the banks themselves were unaware. The access to the personal data of EU customers caused a furore in Europe. The Belgium Data Protection Authority declared that the transfers were in breach of data protection law but no formal action was taken. The activities of SWIFT also attracted the attention of the Article 29 Working Party, which characterised SWIFT as a joint controller with the individual financial institutions which it served. The analysis of the Article 29 WP pointed to several factors which it considered characterised SWIFT as being beyond a mere processor. They were:

- SWIFT took on specific responsibilities which, by their nature and scope, went beyond the usual set of instructions and duties for execution by a processor.
- SWIFT's management was able to determine the purposes and means of processing by developing, marketing and altering SWIFT's services (e.g., by determining the form and content of payment orders).
- SWIFT provided additional value to the processing.
- SWIFT's management had the autonomy to take decisions (e.g., determining the security standard to be applied to the data and the location of the data centres).

The SWIFT Opinion was followed by an Opinion on the role of processors in which the WP develops the argument, in essence, that the more sophisticated the services offered the more likely it is that a party will be a joint controller rather than a processor. This view should be taken into account when entering into arrangements with data processors to ensure that the roles of the parties are clear. It should also inform the behaviour of the parties as the contract services are being provided in particular as services are added or the processor takes on more tasks or roles.

Impact of the draft Regulation in brief[20]

Under the draft Regulation security is no longer one of the principles for data processing set out in art.5. It is covered by arts 30–32. The core obligation is largely the same however the obligation is imposed on both processors and controllers. The Commission is also empowered to enact delegated legislation setting out the levels of security required in particular cases. The big changes proposed are in the security breach obligations which are very demanding and in the role of processors more generally. A processor will be covered by the law of the Member State where it is established. If it has more than one establishment in

7–27

---

[20] See Ch.1 paras 1–68 onwards for an overview of the draft Regulation issued in January 2012 by the Commission.

the Union the place of main establishment will be the place of its central administration in the Union. A number of obligations would apply to processors including:

- the obligation to document processing activities;
- the obligation to cooperate with supervisory authorities;
- the obligation to implement security measures and report breaches of security to the data controller;
- obligations in relation to prior authorisation for overseas transfers in some cases; and
- an obligation to appoint a data protection officer.

The individual rights appear not to be applicable as against processors but in some cases the processor may be forced to give subject access. The processor may also be liable to the same level of fines as data controllers. Controllers and processors would become jointly and severally liable for damage caused to data subjects as a result of unlawful processing activity. If a processor acts beyond a controller's authority it would become a joint controller. It is also possible for controllers to enter into Binding Corporate Rules. As a result of these changes there would be significant shift in the relationship between controllers and processors going well beyond the responsibility for security. It would require the re-working of contracts between controllers and processors and a wholesale re-evaluation of the relationship.

Processor contract clauses

7–28   There are a number of standard and precedent contract clauses covering data process or obligations. The EU Model Contracts for data controller to data processor transfers of personal data include security and control clauses which cover the requirements of the seventh principle (see Ch.8 for a review of those clauses). In the UK the Security Policy Framework (SPF) for Government requires those bodies subject to it to ensure that adequate security, information assurance and business continuity requirements are specified in contracts with third party suppliers, and that all contracts involving the handling of personal data adhere to the Office of Government Commerce (OGC) model terms and conditions. The OGC clauses cover the responsibility of data processors and also compliance with Freedom of Information requirements. The precedent provided below is a generic precedent we have drafted for the purposes of illustrating the types of clauses required in data processor contracts. It has no formal status and if model clauses are required or the organisation is subject to the SPF the appropriate models should be followed.

This precedent can be used as the starting point for the production of an appropriate clause whether as part of a larger contract or a stand-alone agreement. Not all of the provisions may be required in a simple agreement.

Data controllers must bear in mind that the contract terms are not a substitute for an assessment of the security standards of the processor as required by principle 7. Before entering into the contract the data controller must have assessed the level of technical and organisational security measures which are required to protect the personal data which are to be processed and have assured himself that the processor chosen is able to provide that level of security. In some contracts the level of security required is captured in schedules and it may be appropriate to refer to those in the clause. In any event if the contract includes such provisions care must be taken to ensure that the clause is consistent with them. Care must also be taken to ensure that the clause is consistent with any confidentiality clause and in particular that the personal data covered by the processor clause is satisfactorily defined. The personal data may be a sub-set of the information which is agreed to be covered by the confidentiality clause.

The contract itself must also capture the specific services to be provided to the specified levels (the time frames and nature of services) as well as the way that instructions must be given to the processor. These will usually be found in the Service Level Agreement and be supported by penalties for non-performance.

It should be noted that other provisions may be required for specific contracts such as provisions setting out the level of employee vetting required or dealing with intellectual property rights. This precedent does not go through all possible scenarios and individual circumstances must be considered before using it.

Precedent data processor contract clauses

Definitions

All terms used in this clause which appear in the [Data Protection Act 1998] [Data Protection Legislation] have the meaning set out in that [Act] [legislation].   7–29

Data Protection Legislation means the Data Protection Act 1998, [the Privacy and Electronic Communications (EC Directive) Regulations 2003].

Notes—in some precedents the terms are listed individually and a number of additional statutory provisions are listed such as the Regulation of Investigatory Powers Act 2000.

It is usually straightforward to state who the parties are and which one is the **Data Controller** *and which is the* **Data Processor.** *For the purposes of this precedent it is assumed that the Parties have been defined and we refer to the Parties here as* **Client** *and* **Supplier**.

It can be more complex to capture the **Personal Data** *which is the subject of the* **Controller/Processor** *obligations. In some cases the parties will know in advance the categories and types of personal data which will be processed. In others they will not necessarily know this in advance.*

Where the categories are known, then they can be set out by reference to the types of data subject, the types of processing and any other known factors. This approach is taken in the Model Clauses for overseas transfers. The relevant personal data which is the subject of the contract is described in a separate schedule. The Model Clause formulation includes a description of the data subjects, the types of personal data processed and the nature of the processing.

[Relevant Personal Data][Client Personal Data] means

(a)   the Personal Data described in Schedule X

However in other cases there is less clarity about the relevant personal data which will be processed as a result of the contract and another method of defining it must be used.

In some cases the contract will have schedules setting out the services to be provided and the data that will be handled by the service provider. In such a case the clause can be drafted by reference to the services provided under the agreement. It will be clear what personal data will be involved, for example if the supplier is providing HR services.

(b)   [the Personal Data processed by the Supplier on behalf of the Client in the delivery of the Services this Agreement]

Where the contract is a straightforward outsourcing of an IT function and the **Data Processor** *will be receiving the personal data from the* **Data Controller** *then it can be described in those terms.*

(c)   [the Personal Data received by the Data Processor from the Data Controller for the purposes of the Services]

In other cases, the personal data with which the parties are concerned will also be generated by the **Data Processor** *or may be received from others. In this case contracts sometimes use a formulation which tries to capture the relevant personal data using formulations like* **Personal Data processed by the Data Processor in connection with this Agreement** *but this may be too wide, for example potentially it captures the personal data about the employees of the* **Data Processor** *who are employed to work on the contract. This should be considered when deciding which approach to use.*

(d)   [the Personal Data processed by the Data Processor in connection with this Agreement]

A general formulation which can be used refers to the **Personal Data processed by the Data Processor in connection with this Agreement in respect of which the Client is the Data Controller** *however, unless this class of information is described or can be ascertained from some other provisions (for example the description of the services as noted above), the question of whether or not particular data are caught by the provision will be a matter of fact to be ascertained during the lifetime of the contract. The parties will not therefore have the certainty that other methods can provide.*

(e)   [Personal Data processed by the Data Processor in connection with this Agreement in respect of which the Client is the Data Controller].

The Parties acknowledge that Client is a Data Controller for the [Relevant Personal Data] [Client Personal Data].

Client appoints the Supplier as a Data Processor to process the [Relevant Personal Data][Client Personal Data] on his behalf.

Supplier's obligations

The Supplier shall process the [Relevant Personal Data][Client Personal Data] only in accord with the instructions of the Client [as given from time to time].

The Supplier shall process the [Relevant Personal Data][Client Personal Data] only for the purposes of the Agreement in accord with the instructions of the Client.

Notes—these provisions are required by paragraph 12 (a) (ii) of Part II of Schedule 1.

The Supplier agrees and warrants that [having regard to the state of technological development and the cost of implementing any measures (a)] and having regard to:

(i)   the nature of the [Relevant Personal Data] [Client Personal Data] and the harm that might result from unauthorised or unlawful processing or accidental loss, destruction of or damage to the [relevant Personal Data] [Client Personal Data] [in particular where the processing involves the transmission of the [relevant Persona Data][Client personal Data] over a network(b)].

(ii)   it has in place appropriate technical and organisational measures to protect the [Relevant Personal Data] [Client Personal Data] against accidental or unlawful destruction or accidental loss, alteration, unauthorised disclosure or access and all other forms of unlawful processing in accord with the requirements of the Data Protection legislation [law of] [name of Member State in which the Data Processor is established if not the UK (c)] which implements Article 17 of Directive 95/46/EC on the protection of individuals with regard to the processing of personal data and the free movement of such data] [including without limitation the minimum provisions set out in [Scheduled Policy or standards or reference to ISO or other standards].

Notes—these provisions are required by paragraph 12 (b). The first set of words in square brackets (a) are not necessary but repeat the provision in principle 7. The second set of words in square brackets (b) which refer to networks are not necessary but reflect the wording of Article 17. Where the processor is established in the UK then the third set of words in square brackets (c) are not necessary however where the processor is outside the UK consideration should be given to including them as Article 17.3 of the Directive requires that the processor shall be required to undertake the security obligations set out in Article 17.1 "as defined by the law of the Member State in which the processor is established".

The Supplier agrees and warrants that it will [take all steps which are necessary to ensure compliance with those measure] [take reasonable steps to ensure compliance with those measures].

The Supplier agrees and warrants that it will take reasonable steps to ensure the reliability of any employees or agents of his who have access to the [relevant Personal Data][Client Personal Data] and in particular will ensure that such persons receive training in data protection, security and the care of personal data.

Notes—the clauses set out above are mandatory for principle 7. The following clauses set out a number of practical measures to go with them and specific remedies for the data controller. The term Relevant Personal Data is used for the rest of the precedent.

The Supplier shall provide the Client with a statement of the technical and organisational measures adopted in order to meet the Supplier's obligations in respect of the Relevant Personal Data together with a statement of the steps taken to ensure the reliability of any employees or agents who will have access to the Relevant Personal Data [before commencement of any processing operations involving the Relevant Personal Data].

The Supplier shall not be entitled to commence processing operations involving the Relevant Personal Data until [the Client has notified the Supplier of its acceptance of the statement] [other trigger event].

If at any time the Supplier becomes aware of a breach of the required standards or is not able to deliver compliance with the required standards he shall promptly inform the Client of the fact and the Client shall be entitled to suspend the processing of the Relevant Personal Data by the Supplier.

The Supplier will indemnify the Client against all costs, claims, damages expenses or proceedings which the Supplier may incur arising from a breach of the Supplier's obligations in respect of the Relevant Personal Data.

The Client may inspect the Supplier's facilities for the processing of the Relevant Personal Data and may audit the Supplier's procedures to ensure that they meet the standards set out in the accepted statements. The Client shall give reasonable notice of such inspection or audit.

At the termination of this Agreement for whatever cause the Supplier shall immediately stop processing the Relevant Personal Data and shall return the relevant Personal Data to the Client.

The Supplier shall comply with any requirement imposed on the Client by any relevant regulator in respect of the Relevant Personal Data and shall comply with any reasonable requirement of the Client in order to ensure compliance with the Data Protection Legislation.

The Supplier will not transfer any of the Relevant Personal Data outside the European Economic Area without the consent of the Client.

The Supplier will not disclose any of the Relevant Personal Data to any person other than for the purposes of this Agreement otherwise than in response to a legal requirement.

Notes—These are all biased towards the data controller. They do not include all the possible arrangements that may be made, for example it may be agreed that the data will be destroyed at the end of the contract; the parties may wish to agree who pays for any audit of the processing; the parties may wish to add more detail to the overseas transfer provisions or those dealing with third party disclosures.

The following may also be useful to include.

The Supplier may appoint other contractors to process the Relevant Personal Data as further Data Processors on behalf of the Client [with the consent of the Client which shall not be unreasonably withheld] provided that the other contractors are appointed on written term that require equivalent protections for the Relevant Personal Data as are required of the Supplier by this Agreement and provide the Client with equivalent rights against the other contractors.

Sometimes contracts permit data processors to sub-contract as long as the terms are equivalent to the main contract and do not require that the sub-contractor enters into a relationship with the data controller. This clause requires the data processor to ensure that the data controller has rights against the sub-contractor There is an argument that if a data controller allows sub-contracts to which he is not a party or cannot enforce the contract he is in breach of principle 7. Where a data processor appoints a sub-contractor the sub-contractor is arguably still a data processor for the data controller because as a data processor is "any person (other than an employee of the data controller) who processes the data on behalf of the data controller" (section 1(1)) principle 7 applies where processing of personal data is carried out by a data processor on behalf of a data controller. The better approach therefore is to ensure that the data controller has the benefit of a written appointment.

The Supplier will, unless prevented by law, promptly inform the Client if it receives any requests in respect of the Relevant Personal Data whether from data subjects or the Information Commissioner or any other persons.

The Supplier will promptly provide the Client with any information which the Client requires in order to comply with any subject access request in relation to the processing of the Relevant Personal Data or to respond to any enquiry by any relevant regulator.

The Supplier will promptly [within x time] notify the Client about any matter which may cause the Supplier to become non-compliant with [this Agreement] [any relevant legislation applicable to the Processing of the Personal Data] and provide such information about remediation as the Client shall reasonably require. Client may require the Supplier to suspend the processing until the breach is remedied to the satisfaction of the Client.

The Supplier will provide the Client with a schedule of the location of the Processing of the Personal Data by country.

Notes—the parties may wish to ensure that data subjects are able to benefit from the clauses but if they do not then the rights of third parties under the Third Parties (Rights in Contracts) Act.

ADDITIONAL INFORMATION

Derivations

7–30

- Directive 95/46 (see Appendix B):
  - (a) Recitals 16 and 17 (confidentiality and security of the processing);
  - (b) Recitals 28, 38, 39, 40, 46, 56, 57.
- Council of Europe Convention of January 28, 1981 for the Protection of Individuals with regard to automatic processing of Personal Data: Art 7 (data security).
- Data Protection Act 1984 s.2 and Sch.1 (the Principles).
- Organisation for Economic Co-operation and Development Guidelines: Annex, Pt 2 (Basic Principles of National Application 7, 8, 9, 10, 11).

Hansard references

7–31

Commons Standing Committee, June 4, col.304:
Principle 6.
Commons Standing Committee, June 4, cols 304, 305:

Principle 7 arm/risk.
Vol.315, No.198, col.611, Commons Third Reading, July 2, 1998:
Principle 7 and Year 2000.

CHAPTER 8

Overseas Or Cross-Border Transfers Of Personal Data

William Malcolm

INTRODUCTION

The aim of the relevant provisions on cross-border flows of personal data in the Directive is to ensure that personal data transferred outside the EEA countries are handled in accordance with the data protection principles. The transfer of personal data outside the EEA is prohibited, save for those cases where the exceptions or derogations can be claimed, unless the destination country (which is also taken to include the country of eventual destination if more than one data movement is contemplated) has an adequate level of personal data protection.[1] Although the derogations seem reasonably wide, they cannot be used in all cases. Some data controllers (particularly international businesses) have long expressed concerns that the exceptions and derogations are inflexible and bureaucratic. This has been the source of continued friction since the Directive was passed and is now a source of intensifying debate as businesses across the EU look to adopt cloud based services and as the EU Commission looks to reform the Directive. Indeed the "location of data processing" was one of the key themes of the July 2012 Opinion of the Working Party on Cloud Computing,[2] which acknowledged that "...the traditional legal instruments providing a framework to regulate data transfers to non-EU third countries not providing adequate protection, have limitations"[3] in a cloud context. Some have expressed concern that some Member States have taken too relaxed a view of the prohibition and regulatory authorities in at least one jurisdiction have been challenged before the courts for taking too strict a view of the rules banning transfers.[4] In non-EEA countries the provision has been seen as a way for Brussels to extend the impact of the Directive beyond the borders of the EU and ensure that others adopt a system of regulation similar to the EU model.

The Commission has the capacity to make findings of adequacy in relation to third countries. The standard it has applied for making such findings in respect of a country is that the country has generally applicable law equivalent to EU regimes. In respect of the United States, although there has been no general finding of adequacy, Safe Harbor has made transfers possible to a limited number

8 01

---

[1] Dir.95/46 art.25.1.
[2] Working Party Opinion 05/2012 on Cloud Computing 01037/12/EN WP 196 July 2012.
[3] Ref.2, p.17.
[4] [Reference case against Spanish data protection supervisory authority].

of organisations that have agreed to meet standards similar to those found in the Directive. The "Safe Harbor" agreement with the US reached in July 2000 came into effect in November 2000. This only applies to certain US organisations; there is no concept of a Safe Harbor in any other jurisdiction.

Another possible solution to the problems caused by the approach of the Directive to overseas transfers is the adoption of contractual solutions. Contracts have long been considered as potential vehicles to deliver data protection solutions. Work was carried out on contracts by the Council of Europe in the 1980s and has continued, with an increasing degree of sophistication, ever since; although some still argue that the current contractual standards are not fit for the modern cloud based environment.

8–02   A further possible route to enable transfers to countries without adequate protection is the development of Binding Corporate Rules (BCRs), under which a global company is empowered to establish its own scheme of binding internal contracts which commit the organisation to adhere to an appropriate data protection standard. The scope of BCRs has been extended recently to include processers and the mutual recognition procedure covering most of the EU has made adoption faster. However, notwithstanding these developments, take up of BCRs has been somewhat limited in the context of the overall volume of international data transfers and some question whether this solution (which requires heavy input from national supervisory authorities) is scalable for the modern cloud. Despite these concerns, BCRS are, at the time of writing, being touted as a central plank of future data protection law reform in this area.

8–03   A fundamental difference in attitudes to overseas transfers between the approach of regulators and the pragmatism of business has gradually emerged since 1998. The Directive (and hence the laws of all Member States) allows the export of data where one of the derogations apply. Therefore businesses tend, not unreasonably, to consider the possibility of using one or more of the derogations as the first option when faced with a transfer to a non-EEA country with no finding of adequacy. Generally, it is only if none of the derogations apply, that businesses look to whether contracts, Safe Harbor or BCRs, or a combination of such measures, offer an acceptable solution. Regulators, on the other hand, are keen to emphasise that derogations should be the last option and only relied upon where no way of providing adequate protection can be found.

8–04   ## SUMMARY OF THE MAIN POINTS

a)   The eighth data protection principle[5] provides that:

> "Personal data shall not be transferred to a country or territory outside the European Economic Area unless that country or territory ensures an adequate level of protection for the rights and freedoms of data subjects in relation to the processing of personal data."

b)   The interpretation provisions for the eighth principle[6] provide an interpretation of the phrase "adequate level of protection".

---

[5] As set out in Sch.1 Pt 1 para.8 of the 1998 Act.
[6] As set out in paras 13–15 of Pt 2 of Sch.1 para.13.

c)   There are a number of exemptions[7] to the restriction in the eighth principle.

d)   Where a "Community finding" has been made in relation to a particular kind of transfer then any question as to an "adequate level of protection" must be determined in accordance with that finding.

A "Community finding" is a finding of the European Commission,[8] that a country or territory outside the European Economic Area does, or does not, ensure an adequate level of protection within the meaning of Art.25(2) of the Directive.

e)   Transfers to non-EEA countries are included on the data controller's register of notification, but this can be done in very general terms.

f)   A transfer is a processing operation in itself and the data controller must also be able to rely on one of the grounds for processing in order to validate any overseas transfer.

g)   Failure to comply with the principle is not an offence but may be subject to enforcement action by the Commissioner.

h)   As well as complying with the eighth principle an overseas transfer must comply with the other principles and issues of fairness, transparency, lawfulness and security of the transfer must be considered.

i)   Common ways for business to comply with the rules on international transfers include use of Model Contractual Clauses (MCCs), Safe Harbor (for transfers to certain US companies), BCRs or transfer to a country "approved by the EU Commission".

WHAT IS A CROSS-BORDER DATA TRANSFER?

No definition of a transfer is provided in the Directive or the 1998 Act. Clause 1 of the Data Protection Bill contained a definition of what constitutes a transfer, but the proposed definition did not survive into the final Act. The clause would have provided that:

> "A person who:
>
> a)   discloses data to a person in a country or territory; or
> b)   otherwise makes the information contained in the data available to a person in a country or territory,
>
> is taken to transfer the data to that country or territory."

This was a broad definition of a "transfer". It would clearly have covered personal data being communicated over the telephone (the "push" transfer) and might have been wide enough to cover the provision of access rights to a third party outside the EEA or placing of material on a website which would potentially be available to persons outside the EEA (the "pull" transfer).

The definition was dropped during consideration of the Bill. In the absence of such a definition it was not clear whether personal data made available for access or posted on an Internet site from where it could be accessed would involve a

---

[7] Para.14 contains a reference to Sch.4 to the 1998 Act.
[8] Under the procedure provided for in art.31(2) of the Data Protection Directive.

transfer outside the EEA. However, the point was decided by the European Court in the *Lindqvist*[9] case, resulting in the decision that the former clearly is a transfer but the later will not necessarily be and may depend on where the server used is situated. The Guide available from the Office of the Information Commissioner[10] distinguishes between transfer and transit as follows:

"A transfer is not the same as transit of information through a country. The eighth principle will apply only if the information moves to a country, rather than simply passing through en route to its destination".

The Act provides that the transfer of information in a form in which it would not fall under the UK Act, for example on a paper copy outside the definition of a "relevant filing system", which is intended to be held as data in the overseas jurisdiction, will still be regarded as a transfer.[11]

A data controller may still retain control over the relevant personal data even if it (or a copy) has been transferred overseas. Control may, for example, be retained by way of strict contractual terms between a transferor and transferee.

8–05   In *Lindqvist*,[12] Mrs Lindqvist had placed personal data on to a website which was hosted within the EEA. The European Court decided that she had not transferred personal data outside the EEA. There is no transfer to a third country within the meaning of art.25 of the Directive in such circumstances, notwithstanding that it thereby makes the data accessible to anyone who connects to the internet, including people in a third country.[13] The Court explained that, if the Directive were interpreted to mean that there was a transfer whenever personal data were loaded on to a website that could be accessed over the internet, then if the Commission found that even one country did not have adequate protection the Member States would be obliged to prevent any personal data being placed on the internet.

This leaves open the question of who is responsible for the "transfer" when such personal data are accessed from a non-EEA. The UK Commissioner has considered the intention of the person uploading the data to be a material consideration:

"Putting personal data on a website will often result in transfers to countries outside the EEA. The transfers will take place when someone outside the EEA accesses the website. If you load information onto a server based in the UK so that it can be accessed through a website, you should consider the likelihood that a transfer may take place and whether that would be fair for the individuals concerned. If you intend information on the website to be accessed outside the EEA, then this is a transfer".[14]

While the decision in *Lindqvist* is wholly understandable, it leaves a possible lacunae in control. As noted from the quotation above the Commissioner seeks to deal with this by pointing out that, even where there is no intention to transfer, the

---

[9] See Ch.3 for a full explanation of the case.
[10] The Guide to Data Protection.
[11] DPA s.1(3).
[12] *Lindqvist* ECJ Case C – 101/01.
[13] Ref.10.
[14] Ref.10.

very fact that the data controller has made the data so widely accessible raises the question of whether the processing is fair.

Onward transfers

The Directive does not deal specifically with onward transfers. It simply requires that one of the elements to be taken into consideration when determining adequacy is the "country of final destination", a phrase which is repeated in the UK provision.[15] The question of how far the recipient organisation in a third country is able to make further transfers and to what extent the original exporting data controller should be held responsible for such transfers is an unresolved question. As might be anticipated, the Working Party and the Commission have been quick to emphasise to data controllers that, in the view of the Working Party and Commission, the onward transfers of personal data to recipients outside the EEA are equally governed by the prohibitions on transfer.

8–06

Adequate protection

The core of the provisions relating to cross-border transfers is the assessment as to whether the foreign country offers an adequate level of protection for the rights and freedoms of data subjects in relation to the processing of personal data. Guidance on assessing whether a foreign country offers adequate protection has been produced by the Article 29 Working Group and the UK Commissioner.[16] In this chapter the guidance from those sources is considered but, however persuasive such guidance may be, it is not in itself law.

Provisions in the Act

The Act itself sets out a number of criteria in Sch.1 Pt 2 para.13 to which any data controller must have particular regard in assessing adequacy.

8–07

The first of these criteria requires a data controller to have regard to the nature of the data. The clear implication here is that there will be more or less sensitive data (sensitive both in the sense defined by the Act as well as in its more general meaning), which will require correspondingly more or less protection. This is, of course, a parallel of the provision in the interpretation of the seventh principle on security measures which requires consideration to be given to the nature of the data to be protected in assessing the "appropriateness" (as opposed to "adequacy") of the relevant security system. It is interesting that the two sets of interpretative provisions on two consecutive principles should utilise two different concepts—"appropriateness" and "adequacy". It is submitted that the concept of "adequacy" could easily have been utilised in both sets of provisions and would have provided thereby at least the security of familiarity.

---

[15] DPA Sch.1 Pt II para.13.
[16] See ICO website section on Sending Personal Data Outside the EEA. The topic is covered in the Guide to Data Protection and four specific notes on Assessing Adequacy, Model Contract Clauses, Binding Corporate Rules and Outsourcing. These have replaced the Commissioner's earlier Guidance.

No further guidance is given in the legislation as to how "adequacy" needs to be balanced against the nature of the data, but clearly the minimum requirement is for a data controller to be able to show a rational decision-making process along the lines of,

> "I considered the level of protection, which involves A, B and C, to be offered by country M to be adequate, given that the data we transferred contained details of X, Y and Z."

The second and third criteria to be considered are the country or territory of origin of the information contained in the data and the country and territory of final destination.

8–08   The implication seems to be that if data were gathered in a country with an "inadequate" system of data protection then a transfer to a country with a similarly inadequate system might be acceptable or at least transfer back to the country of origin. The fourth criterion requires consideration to be given to the purposes for which and the period during which the data are intended to be processed. This is a consideration which goes hand in hand with the requirement that, in assessing adequacy, regard must be had to the nature of the data. A data controller thus must look not only at the nature of the data to be processed but also at the nature of the processing to be carried out in the foreign territory or country and the time when that processing is planned to take place.

Thus the controller will ask the following questions:

(a)   What is the nature of the data?
(b)   What will be done with it?
(c)   For how long will it be used?

Again no further guidance is given in the legislation as to what types of processing will require more or less protective regimes. But, as with the criteria obliging consideration of the nature of the data, it is submitted that the data controller must be able to demonstrate a rational decision-making which takes into account all these factors.

The fifth to eighth criteria require a data controller to consider the details of the data protection regime or regimes in place in the country of destination and specifically:

(a)   the law in force;
(b)   the international obligations adhered to;
(c)   relevant enforceable codes of conduct or other rules; and
(d)   security measures taken in respect of the data.

The last provision requires the data controller to consider what security measures are to be taken with respect to the specific data to be transferred, whereas the first three require consideration to be given to the generality of the regimes in place.

The eighth principle commences by stating that:

"An adequate level of protection is one which is adequate in all the circumstances of the case, having regard in particular to ... ",

before reciting the eight criteria to be considered. Thus the eight criteria are not exhaustive of the matters which a data controller may have to consider in assessing adequacy.

Adequacy assessment

Help in assessing adequacy has already been provided at both an EU level and at a national level.

8–09

EU level

At the EU level there have been a number of formal decisions as to countries and territories which offer an adequate level of protection.[17] The decisions are "Community findings" under the Directive. The interpretative provisions on the eighth principle specifically provide for "Community findings" to be taken into account in deciding adequacy.[18] Such findings on particular types of transfer are binding on data controllers and the national data protection enforcement agencies. A "Community finding" is defined as a finding of the European Commission, under the procedure provided for in art.31(2) of the Data Protection Directive, that a country or territory outside the European Economic Area does, or does not, ensure an adequate level of protection within the meaning of art.25(2) of the Directive.[19] The decisions have been issued as Commission Decisions which operate as Community legal instruments and are directly applicable without the need for further implementing provisions however the UK has chosen to have a formal adoption mechanism.

8–10

The Commission is also empowered to decide that certain standard contractual clauses offer sufficient safeguards in relation to transfers to countries with data protection regimes providing otherwise inadequate protection[20]. This is discussed more fully below.

Article 29 Paper

The Article 29 Working Party[21] produced some helpful guidance on the interpretation of arts 25 and 26 of the EU Directive (the Articles covering cross-border transfers)[22] in July 1998, which has subsequently been relevant in making adequacy assessments and is referred to in later Commission decisions.[23] Although the Working Party has issued a wide range of opinions on international

8–11

---

[17] See *http://ec.europa.eu/justice/policies/privacy/thridcountries/index_en.htm* [Accessed September 16, 2012] for a full list.
[18] DPA Sch.1 Pt 2 para.15.
[19] For an explanation of the art.31 procedure, see Ch.10.
[20] The Directive art.26 paras 2–4.
[21] See Ch.23 for the constitution and work of the Article 29 Working Party.
[22] "Transfers of personal data to third countries: Applying Articles 25 and 26 of the EU data protection directive" DG XV D/5025/98.
[23] See recital 3 of Council Decision 2001/497/EC.

transfer issues, this paper remains the only paper covering the full framework of arts 25 and 26. It is also the most helpful and significant.

The guidance suggests that any meaningful analysis of "adequate protection" must comprise two basic elements: an assessment of the content of the rules applicable and an assessment of the means for ensuring their effective application.

The Working Party also submits that:

> "Using Directive 95/46/EC as a starting point, and bearing in mind the provisions of other international data protection texts, it should be possible to arrive at a 'core' of data protection 'content' principles and 'procedural/enforcement' requirements compliance with which could be seen as a minimum requirement for protection to be considered adequate."

Those principles and requirements, the Working Party suggests, are as follows.

Content Principles

8–12   The basic principles to be included are the following:

(a)   The purpose limitation principle—data should be processed for a specific purpose and subsequently used or further communicated only insofar as this is not incompatible with the purpose of the transfer. The only exemptions to this rule would be those necessary in a democratic society on one of the grounds listed in art.13 of the Directive.[24]

(b)   The data quality and proportionality principle—data should be accurate and, where necessary, kept up to date. The data should be adequate, relevant and not excessive in relation to the purposes for which they are transferred or further processed.

(c)   The transparency principle—individuals should be provided with information as to the purpose of the processing and the identity of the data controller in the third country, and other information insofar as this is necessary to ensure fairness. The only exemptions permitted should be in line with arts 11(2)21 and 13 of the Directive.

(d)   The security principle—technical and organisational security measures should be taken by the data controller that are appropriate to the risks presented by the processing. Any person acting under the authority of the data controller, including a processor, must not process data except on instructions from the controller.

(e)   The rights of access, rectification and opposition—the data subject should have a right to obtain a copy of all data relating to him/her that are processed, and a right to rectification of those data where they are shown to be inaccurate. In certain situations he/she should also be able to object to

---

[24] Art.13 permits a restriction to the "purpose principle" if such a restriction constitutes a necessary measure to safeguard national security, defence, public security, the prevention, investigation, detection and prosecution of criminal offences or of breaches of ethics for the regulated professions, an important economic or financial interest, or the protection of the data subject or the rights and freedoms of others.

the processing of the data relating to him/her. The only exemptions to these rights should be in line with art.13 of the Directive.

(f) Restrictions on onward transfers—other transfers of the personal data by the recipient of the original data transfer should be permitted only where the second recipient (i.e. the recipient of the onward transfer) is also subject to rules affording an adequate level of protection. The only exceptions permitted should be in line with art.26(1) of the Directive.

Examples of additional principles to be applied to specific types of processing are:

8–13

(a) Sensitive data—where "sensitive" categories of data are involved (those listed in art.8 of the Directive22), additional safeguards should be in place, such as a requirement that the data subject gives his/her explicit consent for the processing.

(b) Direct marketing—where data are transferred for the purposes of direct marketing, the data subject should be able to "opt-out" from having his/her data used for such purposes at any stage.

(c) Automated individual decision—where the purpose of the transfer is the taking of an automated decision in the sense of art.15 of the Directive, the individual should have the right to know the logic involved in this decision, and other measures should be taken to safeguard the individual's legitimate interest.

Procedural and enforcement mechanisms

In Europe, there is broad agreement that data protection principles should be embodied in law. There is also broad agreement that a system of "external supervision" in the form of an independent authority is a necessary feature of a data protection compliance system. Elsewhere in the world, however, these features are not always present.

8–14

To provide a basis for the assessment of the adequacy of the protection provided, it is necessary to identify the underlying objectives of a data protection procedural system, and on this basis to judge the variety of different judicial and non-judicial procedural mechanisms used in third countries.

The objectives of a data protection system are essentially threefold:

(a) to deliver a good level of compliance with the rules. (No system can guarantee 100 per cent compliance, but some are better than others.) A good system is generally characterised by a high degree of awareness among data controllers of their obligations, and among data subjects of their rights and the means of exercising them. The existence of effective and dissuasive sanctions can play an important part in ensuring respect for rules, as of course can systems of direct verification by authorities, auditors, or independent data protection officials;

(b) to provide support and help to individual data subjects in the exercise of their rights. The individual must be able to enforce his/her rights rapidly and effectively and without prohibitive cost. To do so, there must be some sort of institutional mechanism allowing independent investigation of complaints; and

(c)   to provide appropriate redress to the injured party where rules are not complied with. This is a key element which must involve a system of independent adjudication or arbitration which allows compensation to be paid and sanctions imposed where appropriate.

Thus to ensure "adequacy" a data controller should consider whether the regimes in the country of transfer provide the elements of protection outlined above.

The Working Party has emphasised that these are minimum requirements. It is clear, therefore, that data controllers may need to consider additional aspects of the data protection regimes in place in the country of transfer depending on the nature of the data to be transferred, and the nature and length of the intended processing.

Adequacy through self-regulation

8–15   Paragraph 13 of the interpretation paragraphs states that an adequate level of protection is one which is adequate "in all the circumstances of the case". Specific reference is made to "any relevant codes of conduct or other rules which are enforceable in that country or territory".

Thus account may be taken of non-legal rules that may be in force in the third country in question, provided that these rules are capable of enforcement. The Working Party emphasises that the mere capacity for the rules to be enforced will not be sufficient—what must be demonstrated is that the rules are complied with.[25] It is in this context that the role of industry self-regulation falls to be considered.

The Working Party suggests that a self-regulatory code (or other instrument) should be taken to mean:

> "any set of data protection rules applying to a plurality of data controllers from the same profession or industry sector, the content of which has been determined primarily by members of the industry or profession concerned."

This would encompass, at one end of the scale, a voluntary data protection code developed by a small industry association with only a few members to, at the other end, the kind of detailed codes of professional ethics applicable to entire professions, such as bankers and doctors, which often have quasi-judicial force.

Evaluation of a Self-Regulatory Code

8–16   The Working Party suggests that evaluation should take the following form

(a)   Evaluate the content of any code—

---

[25] "Transfers of personal data to third countries: Applying Articles 25 and 26 of the EU Data Protection Directive" DG XV d/5025/98, Ch.3.

    (i)   does it comply with the "content principles" (above, para.8-14)?

    (ii)   is it in plain language?

    (iii) does it prevent disclosure to non-members not governed by the code?

(b)   Evaluate the prevalence of any code in the relevant industry—the Working Party suggests that industry- or profession-wide codes will be preferable to those developed by small groupings of companies within sectors, because:

    (i)   consumers will find fragmented industries, characterised by rival associations each with its own code, confusing; and

    (ii)   it creates uncertainty as to which rules apply if data are passed between different companies within one industry, e.g. direct marketing.

(c)   Evaluate the effectiveness of any code—does it achieve:

    (i)   a good level of compliance?

- How is the code publicised?
- Is it voluntary or compulsory?
- How do members demonstrate compliance?
- What auditing mechanisms apply?
- How are breaches dealt with—are sanctions punitive or merely remedial? (The latter, the Working Party suggests, are likely to be inadequate.)

    (ii)   support and help for data subjects?

- Is there a complaints investigation system and does it have adequate powers?
- How are it and its decisions publicised?
- How are alleged breaches adjudicated—is adjudication independent and impartial? Impartiality might be achieved by using an external adjudicator or by having consumer representatives on any adjudication panel.

    (iii) (crucially) appropriate redress, including compensation?

Adequacy through contract

As stated above, contractual "solutions" are possible where the level of general legal compliance with data protection norms would otherwise be deemed inadequate. The Working Party paper reviews the role of contracts in achieving or contributing to adequate protection. The Working Party took a reasonably positive view of the possibility of contractual terms ensuring adequate safeguards for the rights and freedoms of data subjects:

8–17

> "For a contractual provision to fulfil this function, it must satisfactory compensate for the absence of a general level of adequate protection, by including the essential elements of protection which are missing in any given particular situation."[26]

After acknowledging the difficulties in using contractual terms to provide redress, support and help to data subjects and delivering a good level of compliance, the Working Party draws a number of conclusions, including:

---

[26] "Transfers of personal data to third countries: Applying Articles 25 and 26 of the EU Data Protection Directive" DG XV D /5025/98, Ch.4.

(a)   The contract should set out in detail the purposes, means and conditions under which the transferred data are to be processed, and the way in which the basic Data Protection Principles are to be implemented. Greater legal security is provided by contracts which limit the ability of the recipient of the data to process the data autonomously on his own behalf. The contract should therefore be used, to the extent possible, as a means by which the entity transferring the data retains decision-making control over the processing carried out in the third country.

(b)   Where the recipient has some autonomy regarding the processing of the transferred data, the situation is not straightforward, and a single contract between the parties to the transfer may not always be a sufficient basis for the exercise of rights by individual data subjects. A mechanism may be needed through which the transferring party in the Community remains liable for any damage that may result from the processing carried out in the third country.

(c)   Onward transfers to bodies or organisations not bound by the contract should be specifically excluded by the contract, unless it is possible to bind such third parties contractually to respect the same Data Protection Principles.

(d)   Confidence that Data Protection Principles are respected after data are transferred would be boosted if data protection compliance by the recipient of the transfer were subject to external verification by, for example, a specialist auditing firm or standards/certification body.

(e)   In the event of a problem experienced by a data subject, resulting perhaps from a breach of the data protection provisions guaranteed in the contract, there is a general problem of ensuring that a data subject complaint is properly investigated. EU Member State supervisory authorities will have practical difficulties in carrying out such an investigation.

(f)   Contractual solutions are probably best suited to large international networks (credit cards, airline reservations) characterised by large quantities of repetitive data transfers of a similar nature, and by a relatively small number of large operators in industries already subject to significant public scrutiny and regulation. Intra-company data transfers between different branches of the same company group is another area in which there is considerable potential for the use of contracts.

(g)   Countries where the powers of state authorities to access information go beyond those permitted by internationally accepted standards of human rights protection will not be safe destinations for transfers based on contractual clauses.

    In the UK there is no legal barrier to a data controller making its own assessment of the adequacy of protection in the receiving country and this is acknowledge by the Commissioner in his Guide. If the controller proceeds in this way he does not need to make any submission to the Commissioner. The Guide advises that the controller should look at, in particular:

    "the extent to which the country has adopted data protection standards in its law; whether there is a way to make sure the standards are achieved in practice; (for example, whether there are any enforceable codes or conduct or other rules); and whether there is an effective procedure for individuals to enforce their rights or get compensation if things go wrong."

The Guide provides a number of examples where a decision on adequacy may be made without a detailed analysis, for example the transfer of academic biographies of staff by a university or the transfer of information on telephone lists used by a global company. Data controllers who wish to rely on their own view that a country provides an adequate standard of protection will have to be able to demonstrate a rational decision-making process to show an assessment of adequacy.

COMMUNITY FINDINGS—STATES

At the time of writing, the European Commission has issued decisions recognising Andorra, Argentina, Canada, Faroe Islands, Guernsey, Isle of Man, Israel, Jersey and Switzerland[27] as providing adequate protection for personal data on the basis that those countries have generally applicable data protection law which follows the same approach as the Directive; although with respect to Canada this is not a finding for the jurisdiction as the Canadian Act, the Canadian Personal Information Protection and Electronic Documents Act, which came fully into force on January 1, 2004, do not cover personal data held by public bodies or by private organisations and used for non-commercial purposes. Accordingly where the data transfer is to a public body or to a private body for a non-commercial purpose, adequacy will have to be achieved by some other mechanism. There are also data protection laws in a number of States which should be taken into consideration. The Commission also made an adequacy decision with respect to Hungary in 2000, but Hungary has since joined the EU.

8–18

SAFE HARBOR

The US approach to the protection of personal privacy is different from the EU one. The US has a number of statutory protections but these are piecemeal and specific to sectors or particular problems, for example the Children's Online Privacy Protection Act 1998 (COPPA). Otherwise regulation is based on self-regulatory mechanisms and consumer action. This is very different from the EU approach of universally applicable law. The US Administration was concerned that personal data would stop flowing to the US after implementation of the Directive and accordingly the Safe Harbor Agreement was negotiated. The Safe Harbor Agreement is only one possible mechanism to allow data export to the US; reliance can be placed on any of the derogations, such as consent, or a contractual solution adopted. The Safe Harbor agreement has not been

8–19

---

[27] For a full up to date list of Adequacy decisions see *http://ec.europa.eu/justice/policies/privacy/thridcountries/index_en.htm*.

universally popular. On the European side the Parliament expressed reservations about it as did the Article 29 Working Party. Nevertheless it is a significant initiative.

The details of the Safe Harbor Agreement are found in the Commission Decision of July 27, 2000 pursuant to Directive 95/46/EC of the European Parliament and of the Council on the adequacy of the protection provided by the Safe Harbor Privacy Principles and related Frequently Asked Questions issued by the US Department of Commerce.[28] The papers consist of:

- the Decision itself;
- the Privacy Principles;
- the Frequently Asked Questions;
- a list of the US Statutory Bodies recognised by the EU as being able to deal with complaints and offer redress;
- correspondence from those authorities (the Federal Trade Commission (FTC) and the US Department of Transportation (USDoT)) to the Commission;
- a memorandum outlining the authority of the FTC; and
- a statement of the US law on damages for breach of privacy and explicit authorisations in US law.

The materials can be found on the EU website or the US Department of Commerce website, www.export.gov/safeharbor,[29] or www.ita.doc.gov[30] where a list of those companies which have decided to adopt the Safe Harbor Principles can also be found. The material recital in the Commission decision is (5) which reads:

"The adequate level of protection for the transfer of data from the Community to the United States recognized by this decision, should be attained if organizations comply with the Safe Harbor Privacy Principles for the protection of personal data transferred from a Member State to the United States (hereinafter 'the Principles') and the Frequently Asked Questions (hereinafter 'the FAQs') providing guidance for the implementation of the Principles issued by the Government of the United States on 21.07.2000. Furthermore the organizations should publicly disclose their privacy policies and be subject to the jurisdiction of the Federal Trade Commission (FTC) under Section 5 of the Federal Trade Commission Act which prohibits unfair or deceptive trade acts or practices in or affecting commerce, or that of another statutory body that will effectively ensure compliance with the Principles implemented in accordance with the FAQs."

This encapsulates the requirements of the Safe Harbor.

Overview

8–20   Participation in Safe Harbor is voluntary. It is only open to organisations which are subject to either s.5 of the Federal Trade Commission Act (FTCA) or the authority of the US Department of Transportation under Title 49, United States

---

[28] Decision 520/2000/EC.
[29] Accessed September 16, 2012.
[30] Accessed September 16, 2012.

Code, Section 41712. Section 5 of the FTCA does not apply to banks, savings and loans and credit unions, telecommunications and interstate transportation common carriers, air carriers and packers and stockyard operators. Most of these are therefore excluded from Safe Harbor unless covered by the Department of Transportation. This covers the travel industry and airlines. In order to join the Safe Harbor a US organisation must do one of three things: develop its own self-regulatory privacy policy which complies with the Principles[31]; participate in an industry self-regulatory programme which meets the Principles, for example the TRUSTe or BBBOnline programmes; or comply with sector-specific regulations that meet the Principles. The organisation must then certify to the Department of Commerce (or its designee) that it is operating in compliance with the Principles. The certification must include specific information including a statement that the organisation has a privacy policy, which is available to the public, and which complies with the Principles. The notification lasts 12 months and the organisation must make an annual return to the Department confirming its continued compliance. This is called a verification and may be based upon a self-assessment or a compliance review by an outside body. Participants have to have effective enforcement and dispute resolution mechanisms which can be delivered either by a private sector organisation such as BBBOnline or by committing to cooperate with EU data protection authorities. The co-operation option must be chosen where the data controller in the EU plans to transfer personal data about employees in the EU. Where the cooperation option is chosen the company works with a panel drawn from the supervisory authorities in the EU. Failure to comply with the self-regulatory standards must be actionable under s.5 as an unfair or deceptive act or some other statutory mechanism. The organisation only has to apply the standards to data which it receives by way of transfer from the EEA after the adoption of the Safe Harbor. The standards are not applicable to manual information which falls outside the Directive but can be applied if the organisation chooses. If an organisation wishes to include human resources data in the Safe Harbor it must indicate that fact specifically in its certification. An organisation can decide to leave Safe Harbor but the personal data which it received from the EU during its membership must continue to be treated in accordance with the Principles.

Safe Harbor—the Privacy Principles

The seven Privacy Principles are issued by the US Department of Commerce under its statutory duty to foster, promote and develop international commerce. In view of their importance they are set out in full below:

8–21

"• Notice
An organization must inform individuals about the purposes for which it collects and uses information about them, how to contact the organization with any enquiries or complaints, the types of third parties to which it discloses the information, and the choices and means the organization offers individuals for limiting its use and disclosure. This notice must be provided in clear conspicuous language when individuals are first asked to provide personal information to the organization or as soon thereafter as is

---

[31] In this context "Principles" means the Safe Harbor Privacy Principles.

practicable, but in any event before the organization uses such information for a purpose other than that for which it was originally collected or processed by the transferring organization or discloses it for the first time to a third party.

- Choice

An organization must offer individuals the opportunity to choose (opt out) whether their personal information is (a) to be disclosed to a third party or (b) to be used for a purpose that is incompatible with the purpose(s) for which it was originally collected or subsequently authorized by the individual. Individuals must be provided with clear, conspicuous, readily available and affordable mechanisms to exercise choice.

For sensitive information (i.e. personal information specifying medical or health conditions, racial or ethnic origin, political opinions, religious or philosophical beliefs, trade union membership or information specifying the sex life of the individual), they must be given affirmative or explicit (opt in) choice if the information is to be disclosed to a third party or used for a purpose other than those for which it was originally collected or subsequently authorized by the individual through the exercise of an opt in choice. In any case, an organization should treat as sensitive any information received from a third party where the third party treats and identifies it as sensitive.

- Onward transfer

Where an organization wishes to transfer information to a third party that is acting as an agent, as described in the endnote, it may do so if it first either ascertains that the third party subscribes to the Principles or is subject to the Directive or another adequacy finding or enters into a written agreement with such third party requiring that the third party provide at least the same level of privacy protection as is required by the relevant Principles. If the organization complies with these requirements, it shall not be held responsible (unless the organization agrees otherwise) when a third party to which it transfers such information processes it in a way contrary to any restrictions or representations, unless the organization knew or should have known the third party would process it in such a contrary way and the organization has not taken reasonable steps to prevent or stop such processing. If the entity in Safe Harbor discloses other than to an agent the onward transfers may only be made in accordance with the Notice and Choice Principles. That is to say that onward transfers are only permitted where the data subjects have been notified about the types of third parties to whom the data are disclosed and offered the possibility to opt out of such third party disclosures. It is therefore only possible to rely on Safe Harbor for onward transfers in these circumstances where data subjects are notified and offered opt-out choices.

- Security

Organizations creating, maintaining, using or disseminating personal information must take reasonable precautions to protect it from loss, misuse and unauthorised access, disclosure, alteration and destruction.

- Data integrity

Consistent with the Principles, personal information must be relevant for the purposes for which it is to be used. An organisation may not process personal information in a way that is incompatible with the purpose for which it has been collected or subsequently authorized by the individual. To the extent necessary for those purposes, an organization should take reasonable steps to ensure that data is reliable for its intended use, accurate, complete and current.

- Access

Individuals must have access to personal information about them that an organization holds and be able to correct, amend or delete that information where it is inaccurate, except where the burden or expense of providing access would be disproportionate to the risks to the individual's privacy in the case in question, or where the rights of persons other than the individual would be violated.

• Enforcement
Effective privacy protection must include mechanisms for assuring compliance with the Principles, recourse for individuals to whom the data relate affected by non-compliance with the Principles, and consequences for the organization when the Principles are not followed. At a minimum such mechanisms must include, (a) readily available and affordable independent recourse mechanisms by which each individual's complaints and disputes are investigated and resolved by reference to the Principles and damages awarded where the applicable law or private sector initiatives so provide; (b) follow up procedures for verifying that the attestations and assertions businesses make about their privacy practices are true and that privacy practices have been implemented as presented; and (c) obligations to remedy problems arising out of failure to comply with the Principles by organizations announcing their adherence to them and consequences for such organizations. Sanctions must be sufficiently rigorous to ensure compliance by organizations."

Comment

The Privacy Principles do not meet all the requirements of the Directive. In particular the individual rights to object to some kinds of processing and the ban on automated decisions are absent. Moreover there are no specific rules governing telecommunications as there are in Europe under Directive 2002/58. Otherwise the Principles are close to the requirements of the Directive.

The Frequently Asked Questions (FAQs)

There are 15 FAQs. The FAQs relate to: sensitive data; journalistic exemptions-;secondary liability; investment banking and audits; the role of data protection authorities; self-certification under the Safe Harbor; verification of compliance with Safe Harbor; the access principle; personal data used for human resources; processor contracts; dispute resolution and enforcement; timing of opt outs; travel information; pharmaceutical and medical products; and public record and publicly available information. The FAQs amplify the Principles and deal with the practical points relating to the working of the Safe Harbor.

8–22

US regulatory bodies and correspondence from them

The basis of Safe Harbor is that the organisation "signs up" to a publicly stated privacy policy that incorporates the standards set out in Principles and the FAQs. Failure to comply with that privacy policy can be the subject of regulatory action. So the policy becomes enforceable by an independent regulator. The two bodies which exercise relevant regulatory powers are the Federal Trade Commission (FTC) and the US Department of Transportation. Enforcement will take place in the US. The Department of Commerce maintains the public list of subscribers which anyone wishing to export personal data to the US may consult. The list also shows the enforcement body for the subscriber so it can be used by anyone

8–23

wanting to make a complaint. Enforcement action by the regulator may result in the subscriber being struck off the list and losing Safe Harbor status. If a company loses Safe Harbor status that will be made clear in the list. The FTC has undertaken, in the correspondence with the EU, to give priority to referrals of non-compliance with Safe Harbor received from privacy programmes or EU data protection authorities.

Financial services

8–24   As such services are not subject to s.5 of the Federal Trade Commission Act they are not able to take advantage of the Safe Harbor. Discussions are continuing between the EU and the US over bringing financial services into Safe Harbor but have not yet reached fruition at the time of writing.

Can data processers join the Safe Harbor?

8–25   The Department of Commerce (DoC) has accepted Safe Harbor self-certifications from a number of organisations in respect of their activities as data processors (see, for example, the Hewlett-Packard self-certification). However the application of the Safe Harbor Framework to a data processor is not wholly straightforward. The position of processors in Safe Harbor is explicitly covered in the FAQs under the title "Article 17 Contracts". The question and answer are set out:

> "When data is transferred from the EU to the United States only for processing purposes, will a contract be required, regardless of participation by the processor in the safe harbor? Yes. Data controllers in the European Union are always required to enter into a contract when a transfer for mere processing is made, whether the processing operation is carried out inside or outside the EU. The purpose of the contract is to protect the interests of the data controller, i.e. the person or body who determines the purposes and means of processing, who retains full responsibility for the data vis-à-vis the individual(s) concerned. The contract thus specifies the processing to be carried out and any measures necessary to ensure that the data are kept secure. A U.S. organization participating in the safe harbor and receiving personal information from the EU merely for processing thus does not have to apply the Principles to this information, because the controller in the EU remains responsible for it vis-à-vis the individual in accordance with the relevant EU provisions (which may be more stringent than the equivalent Safe Harbor Principles). Because adequate protection is provided by safe harbor participants, contracts with safe harbor participants for mere processing do not require prior authorization (or such authorization will be granted automatically by the Member States) as would be required for contracts with recipients not participating in the safe harbor or otherwise not providing adequate protection".

It appears from this FAQ therefore that, under US law, a US entity which is enrolled in Safe Harbor is not required to comply with the Safe Harbor Privacy Principles where it is acting as a mere processor for an EU controller. However under Commission Decision 2000/520/EC art.2, an EU data controller may only transfer data to the US where the recipient U.S. organisation has "unambiguously and publicly disclosed its commitment to comply with the Principles implemented in accordance with the FAQs" in respect of "each transfer of data". On the face of it this would suggest that the entity must comply with the Principles even if it is a processor. It should be noted that the obligation is to comply with the Principles implemented in accordance with the FAQs, not the Principles simpliciter. The view may therefore be taken that the response to the FAQ quoted above alters the usual position and a processor who applies the line taken in the FAQ will be meeting the Principles implemented in accordance with the FAQs. It has to be said that this is not a wholly satisfactory position. While compliance with some of the Principles, on the face of it, lies in the gift of the controller rather than the processor, such as Notice and Choice, at least some of the obligations in the Principles can, and should, be complied with by the processor such as security principles. Equally a processor could enter into a contract with the controller under which the controller could deal with those aspects of the Principles which are clearly within his gift, such as notice and choice to data subjects. The position is less certain re the access Principle. A controller could authorise the processor to respond to subject access requests as its agent subject to appropriate limits however it might be preferable for the parties to agree that, if an access request is received by the processor, the controller will deal with it. The effect of the contract would be to ensure that the Safe Harbor Principles are met even if not directly by the processor.

Safe Harbor and the Cloud

The Working Party have stated that " ... sole certification with Safe Harbor may not be deemed sufficient in the absence of robust enforcement of data protection principles in the cloud environment."[32] The Working Party encourages customers to obtain evidence that the Safe Harbor principles are being complied with; although no practical guidance is provided about what additional information beyond a certification should or must be sought. Notwithstanding these reservations national data protection authorities have not suspended data flows to a Safe Harbor-certified organisation and notifed the Commission accordingly. They are entitled to do so if there is substantial risk that the Principles are being violated; there is a reasonable basis for believing that the enforcement mechanism concerned is not taking or will not take adequate and timely steps to settle the case at issue; the continued transfer would cause an imminent risk of grave harm to data subjects; and the competent authority has made reasonable efforts under the circumstances to provide the organisation with notice and an opportunity to respond. It therefore seems reasonsonble to conclude that a transfer to a Safe Harbor certified organisation is an acceptable way to achieve adequcy which respect to that transfer and any onwards transfer that falls withth the Safe Harbor framework; although the cloud customer must of course also compy with the other requirements of Directive 95/46/EC in relation to the transfer and subseqent procesing.

8–26

---

[32] WP Cloud Opinion, p.17.

CONTRACTUAL CLAUSES APPROVED BY THE COMMISSION

8–27   Individual contracts or sets of contractual clauses do not, of course, provide an adequate level of protection for an entire country. Thus contractual clauses are a way of complying with an exemption to the Eighth Principle rather than complying with the Principle itself.

The provisions in the Directive have not been translated directly into the 1998 Act. Instead the exemptions set out in Sch.4 provide that the Eighth Principle does not apply where:

> "The transfer is made on terms which are of the kind approved by the Commissioner as ensuring adequate safeguards for the rights and freedoms of data subjects."[33]

Thus, there is no specific reference to contractual terms or clauses.

There is no barrier to individual data controllers agreeing contracts with third parties for the export of personal data on terms negotiated between the parties. In many EU countries such contracts have to be submitted to the national supervisory authority for approval. The United Kingdom and Ireland are exceptional in that the regulators have not required the submission of contracts. Where contracts have to be submitted the national authority will usually review the terms to ensure that certain standards are met and if it considers the contract to be deficient may require amendments. It can take several months for contracts to be approved. Standard form clauses are intended to shorten the process as the national regulatory authorities have to accept contracts drawn up in accordance with the standard.

Three sets of clauses are currently approved by the European Commission for use; two sets of controller to controller clauses and one set of controller to processor clauses. The standard form contracts are very similar even though the legal relationships between the parties are very different. The contracts have been approved under art.26.2. They are not mandatory (at least not in theory) —controllers may still use their own contracts—but where the standard forms are used, in most cases, the national regulators have to accept them as producing adequate protection.

Controller to controller contract

8–28   On June 15, 2001 the Commission approved a standard set of contractual clauses to cover the situation where a data controller in the EU sends personal data to a controller outside the EEA to a jurisdiction which does not offer adequate protection for the personal data.[34] The Decision took effect in September 2001. The UK Information Commissioner authorised transfers made using the model clauses under para.9 of Sch.4 on December 21, 2001. The standard contract has been criticised as it imposes onerous obligations, particularly on the recipient. If a data controller uses the clauses then the contract should be accepted by data

---

[33] Sch.4 para.8.
[34] Commission Decision 2001/497/EC of June 15, 2001 on standard contractual clauses for the transfer of personal data to third countries under Dir.95/46.

protection authorities in all the Member States as providing adequate protection. The contract is intended to take effect under the law of the exporting Member State so the contract has to be altered at least so as to accommodate any legal requirements to comply with contract law in the Member State.

The standard clauses offer a number of options to reach a standard of adequacy. The contract can incorporate standards equivalent to the data protection law of the sending country; or (if the importer is US based and does not already subscribe to Safe Harbor) the Safe Harbor Principles; or the Principles set out in the standard form contract.[35] The data exporter agrees that the transfer complies with the national law and is liable for compliance with the national law up until the export[36] and remains liable for continued compliance with the Principles jointly with the importer.[37] The individual data subjects are entitled to copies of the contract and to have their queries answered by both parties.[38] They must be told of any sensitive data export[39] and be able to enforce rights under the contract.[40] In England and Wales this can now be done by virtue of the Contracts (Rights of Third Parties) Act 1999. The importer agrees to abide by rulings of the national supervisory authority in the exporting jurisdiction and to submit to audit by the exporter.[41]

The contract has appendices in which the parties set out the categories of data subjects about whom data are being transferred, the purpose of the transfer, the categories of personal data being exported, the recipients of the data, the storage limit, i.e. the length of time for which the data will be held, and where sensitive data are involved, the types of sensitive data.

The Commission has published a set of FAQs on the standard clauses which is also available on the Commission website and which covers:

8–29

- whether the clauses are compulsory;
- whether companies can rely on contracts approved at national level;
- whether Member States can block or suspend transfers where the standard clauses are used;
- whether the clauses can be used as part of a wider contract;
- the relation between the Principles and any derogations to those imposed by the importer's national law;
- the burden of joint and several liability;
- the relation with the "safe harbor"; and
- whether those who are not members of the "safe harbor" can use the "safe harbor" aspect of the standard.

The adoption of the clauses was preceded by correspondence with the US interests represented by both the US Departments of Treasury and Commerce (April 2001) and an Opinion prepared by the Article 29 Working Party on January

---

[35] cl.5b.
[36] cl.4a.
[37] cl.6.2.
[38] cll.4c and 5c.
[39] cl.4b.
[40] cl.6.1.
[41] cl.5c and d.

26, 2001. The documents, which are available on the Commission website, show the divergence of positions between the Americans and Europeans over the privacy debate.

Contracts (Rights of Third Parties) Act 1999—England & Wales

8–30   Under the law of England and Wales, a person who is not a party to a contract may enforce a term of a contract if either the contract expressly provides that he may, or the term purports to confer a benefit on him, unless it is clear from the contract that this was not intended by the parties.[42] The third party has to be expressly identified in the contract, either by name or as a member of a class or answering a particular description.[43] This can easily be achieved in overseas transfer contracts by a description of the beneficiaries as employees or some other category. Such a clause will cover future members of the class as well as those in the class at the time the contract is entered into.[44]

The third party's rights apply under the contract so any exclusions or limitations in the contract will apply to him and he will only be able to exercise the remedies that apply under the contract.

Once a third party has become the beneficiary of a contract term his position is protected. The main parties cannot alter the term, or rescind the contract altogether, without the third party's agreement if it would disadvantage the third party because the third party has relied on the term.[45] Otherwise parties could enter into contracts which confer benefits on third parties to allow them to achieve some end, for example make an overseas transfer, and then rescind the contract once the transfer had been made, leaving the third party with no redress. A court, however, can dispense with the agreement of the third party in some cases.

The implementation of the third party rights has made contractual solutions an option for UK data exporters, who wish to contact under the laws of England and Wales. Scots law has always provided for third party rights.

Amendment of controller to controller clauses

8–31   The first set of controller to controller Commission approved contracts were not popular with business. The US Department of Commerce and the Department of the Treasury indicated their disagreement with aspects of them, as well as US business organisations. A more business friendly proposed standard contract was prepared by an alliance of business organisation including the International Chamber of Commerce and was accepted by a decision amending the original Commission decision on December 27, 2004.[46] These were authorised by ICO on May 27, 2004. There are now two sets of model controller to controller clauses, Set I and Set II. Data controllers may choose either set but may not amend the

---

[42] Contracts (Rights of Third Parties) Act 1999 s.1.
[43] 1999 Act s.1(3).
[44] 1999 Act s.1(3).
[45] Contracts (Rights of Third Parties) Act 1999 s.2.
[46] Commission Decision of December 27, 2004 amending Decision 2001/497/EC as regards the introduction of an alternative set of standard clauses for the transfer of personal data to third countries (2004/915/EC).

clauses or the sets. Each set is designed to achieve a balance of protection but does so by the use of different mechanisms. In each case the national supervisory authority in the exporting Member State may prohibit the data flows where certain conditions are satisfied. Set II does not include the joint and several liability clauses as between the importer and the exporter, the parties are liable for their own breach. However the exporter has an obligation of due diligence to determine that the data importer is able to satisfy its obligations under the contract and must agree to submit to data audits on reasonable request of the exporter. Where Set II has been adopted the rights of individuals to enforce for breach of the required standards is directed in the first instance to the exporter and only arises against the importer where exporter has refused to enforce the contract. Set II allows for rather more flexibility over agreements between the parties as to which one should deal with subject access requests. Under Set II rights of termination for breach of the contract are explicitly covered.

Controller to processer contract

On December 27, 2001 the Commission approved a set of model clauses to be used where a data controller in the EU sends personal data to a processor outside the EEA in a jurisdiction which does not offer adequate protection for the personal data.[47] The decision took effect on April 3, 2002. The UK Commissioner issued an authorisation in respect of contracts made using this model. The standard contract is designed to give enforceable rights to data subjects. This involves the exporter "agreeing" with the importer that his actions comply with the requirements of the Directive[48] although this seems unnecessarily complicated as the data subject would have a remedy under national law in any event if the exporter had failed in his compliance. The importer agrees to an audit of his processing if required,[49] to only process on the instructions of the processor and to implement the technical security measures which are set out in the Appendix to the contract.[50] The data has to be described in a similar way to the controller to controller contract.[51] Where data subjects suffer damage in the first instance they must seek any remedy against the exporter of the data[52]; however, if the exporter has disappeared or become insolvent the importer agrees that a claim may be made against him.[53] The contract provides for the return or destruction of the data at the termination of the contract.[54]

8–32

---

[47] Commission Decision of December 27, 2001 on standard contractual clauses for the transfer of personal data to processors established in third countries under Dir.95/46/EC.
[48] cl.4.
[49] cl.5f.
[50] cl.5a, b, c.
[51] Appendix 1.
[52] cl.6.1.
[53] cl.6.2.
[54] cl.11.

Amendment of controller to processer clauses

8–33   New model clauses were approved in February 2010 for data controller to data processor transfers and came into effect from May 15, 2010.[55] These replace the 2001 clauses for new contracts rather than providing a second option, as with the controller to controller transfers. The main difference between the new clauses and the previous version is that the new clauses take account of the expansion of processing activities and deal with the situation where there is further outsourcing of processing to sub-processors. A definition of sub-processors has been added. This extends not just to someone acting as a sub-processor to the main processor (data importer) but to sub-processors engaged by sub-processors—so the requirements flow all the way down the chain. A data importer must not subcontract without the prior written consent of the data exporter and then only by way of a written agreement imposing the same obligations on the sub-processor as the model clauses impose on the data importer (the model clauses suggest that this could be satisfied by the sub-processors co-signing the contract between the data exporter and the data importer). The data importer remains fully liable for the activities of its sub-processors. The data importer is required to send a copy of any sub-processing contract to the data exporter. The data exporter is required to keep a list of the sub-processing agreements which have been concluded and update this at least once a year. This should be available to the data exporter's supervisory authority, in the UK the Information Commissioner.

Contractual clauses for international transfers and the cloud

8–34   "Cloud computing consists of a set of technologies and service models that focus on the Internet-based use and delivery of IT applications, processing capability, storage and memory space".[56]

Cloud is not new but the pace of adoption and the range of cloud services have increased dramatically in recent years. As the Working Party acknowledge cloud based services can bring economic benefits in that on-demand services can be set up, scaled and accessed quickly and easily. However these flexible new computing solutions must operate within the existing data protection framework, including the rules on international transfers. There has been a wide range of debate about whether the existing legal structures are fit for the modern cloud.

8–35   In most cloud arrangements, but not all, the customer will be the data controller and the cloud provider a data processor; as in traditional outsourced relationships. This means that use of the controller to processer clauses may provide a way of achieving compliance if the cloud provider has part of its operations in a third country. However in some cases the cloud provider may undertake activities akin to those of a data controller and in those situations the data controller to data controller clauses or some other mechanism may be more appropriate. Customers will want to assess the status of the parties carefully

---

[55] Commission Decision of February 5, 2010 on standard contractual clauses for the transfer of personal data to processors established in third countries under Directive 95/46/EC of the European Parliament and of the Council (notified under document C(2010) 593).

[56] Working Party Opinion 05/2012 on Cloud Computing 01037/12/EN WP 196 July 2012.

before deciding which adequacy mechanism is the most appropriate. Customers should undertake that assessment with care. Modern cloud providers often offer standard packaged services which cannot be varied or made bespoke to customer requirements. However, standardisation should not be confused with a lack of control. Customers can choose to use a service or not. As the Working Party states:

> "...clients of cloud computing services may not have room for manoeuvre in negotiating the contractual terms of use of the cloud services as standardised offers are a feature of many cloud computing services. Nevertheless, it is ultimately the client who decides on the allocation of part or the totality of processing operations to cloud services".[57]

On the other hand some services may mean that an element of control is lost over how data are processed and customers need to consider the status of the parties against that backdrop.

Cloud services often involve a number of contracted parties that act as data processors. Sometimes these third parties are within the cloud provider's group of companies, sometimes not. The Working Party point out that although sub-processing is permitted under the controller to processer clauses, this must be with the prior written consent of the controller.[58] Many cloud providers require this consent to be provided upfront as part of their terms and conditions of service, pointing out that it would be unreasonable to expect them to collect consent on a case by case basis from every customer given the complexity and rapidly changing nature of the cloud environment. The Working Party has acknowledged that this is acceptable practice provided the processer has a right to terminate if unhappy with any change.[59] This latter requirement has proved controversial and such a right remains by no means uniform in many cloud contracts.

8–36

In addition to sub-processing issues, use of MCCs for cloud services can give rise to a range of other practical issues including provision of audit rights to customers (which may not be practical for security and scalability reasons), detailing the location or locations data are processed (which again is not always practical for security reasons) and deciding on the right contract structure where often the group structures of both the customer and cloud provider are complex.

8–37

BINDING CORPORATE RULES

Although the Directive does not provide any mechanism for the Commission to approve group wide codes of conduct as an acceptable mechanism to deliver adequacy, such codes have been increasingly used.[60] They offer global businesses, which may be subject to a large number of different privacy laws, a

8–38

---

[57] Ref.52, p.8.
[58] Ref.52, p.10.
[59] Ref.52, p.10.
[60] The code developed by Shell for its global business was the starting point for the ICX draft code which was considered by the IPSE initiative under the work carried out by CEN. See *www.cenorm.be* [Accessed September 16, 2012] for a Report on the IPSE work.

method of standardising compliance levels in the business. There was some interest in the possibility of developing a standard form code which could be adopted by business and used as a tool to enable the transfer of personal data intra-group.[61] It gradually became clear that one code would not be able to deal with the vast range of data processing activities but the way forward would be for global companies to develop individual "codes" which meet the necessary standards. These codes are called Binding Corporate Rules. In outline a company works with a national supervisory authority to adopt a binding internal code which the supervisory authority then approves under the national implementing provisions of art.26(2). Article 26(2) allows Member States to authorise transfers to countries which do not ensure an adequate level of protection where the controller,

> " ... adduces adequate safeguards with respect to the protection of privacy and fundamental rights and freedoms of individuals as regards the exercise of the corresponding rights".

The scheme put forward for approval must therefore be able to deliver guarantees of compliance and rights of redress for non-compliance. The relevant national supervisory authority is responsible for liaising with the other relevant data protection authorities in other jurisdictions to obtain the agreement of all.

Originally BCRs could only be used for controllers (i.e. covering "your own data"). More recently the concept has been extended to cover data processors. (i.e covering "third party data").[62] WP 195 sets out the main elements that the Working Party would like to see included in processor BCRs; taking existing criteria for the approval of a BCR and translating what that might look like in a processor BCR. BCRs for processors do not stand alone and must be linked to an Service Level Agreement with the data controller.

Article 29 Working Documents on Binding Corporate Rules[63] (BCRs)

8–39   The field of BCRs has become increasingly complex and it is difficult to summarise the myriad of Working Party guidance in this short chapter. Those considering BCRs are advised to review the full set of Working Party papers[64]; in particular WP 74, WP 108 and WP 155.

8–40   The Working Documents makes it clear that BCRs should not be regarded as having superseded contractual solutions; such solutions are being used in increasingly sophisticated ways, for example by having standard clauses with many parties to the contract. It is emphasised that BCRs may be used with contractual solutions, for example the initial transfer may be made under BCRs and further onward transfers to other recipients than the data importer under separate contractual arrangements. Such contractual solutions can allow for further transfers where the data subjects have given unambiguous consent (where

---

[61] See the work carried out by the Initiative for Privacy Standardisation in Europe Report at the CEN website *www.cen.be* [Accessed September 16, 2012].
[62] WP 195.
[63] WP 195.
[64] WP74, WP108, WP133, WP153, WP154, WP155 and WP195.

sensitive data are concerned) or in other cases been given the opportunity to object. The various documents which set out the standards which must be reached to produce BCRs use slightly different terminology and sequence. In this section we examine the topic by reviewing the substantive content required and then the procedure for authorisation.

The application follows a two stage process. Before embarking on the BCR process proper organisations need to make an initial application to obtain the co-operation of the supervisory authority with which the organisation wishes to work and ascertain that it has the jurisdiction to approve BCRs. As WP 108 makes clear the BCR process is not mandated by the Directive and the participation of supervisory authorities is therefore not required under EU law. WP 108 states that: "The participation of data protection authorities in the approval of binding corporate rules is entirely voluntary". While this is accurate in general terms the UK Commissioner has set out the terms and process on which his office will work with organisations in this area. If he failed to honour those public statements without some good reason an aggrieved applicant might have public law remedies.

8–41

Jurisdiction

A corporate group which wishes to pursue the BCR approach must select the lead data protection supervisory authority using the criteria set out in the guidance. The initial application is made to the selected lead data protection supervisory authority showing the nature and general structure of the processing activities in the EEA/EU with particular attention to:

8–42

- the place where decisions are made;
- the location and nature of affiliates in the EU;
- the number of employees or others concerned;
- the means and purpose of the processing;
- all the places from which the transfers to third countries take place; and
- the third countries to which data are transferred.

The recipient authority will forward the information to all of the supervisory authorities which have a supervisory role for the processing described with a statement as to whether it is prepared to be the lead authority. The authorities will agree among themselves within a period of approximately two weeks as to whether the choice of the lead is appropriate. Once the lead authority has been agreed that authority will work with the applicant to agree the substantive provisions and prepare the deliverables for submission. The lead authority is responsible for circulation of the BCR to other DPAs under the mutual recognition or co-operation procedures. Under the original co-operation process all DPAs have the opportunity to make comments on the draft BCR; which can be time consuming. Under mutual recognition once the lead authority considers that the BCR meets the requirements the draft BCR is circulated to other mutual recognition countries. The DPAs under mutual recognition accept this opinion as sufficient basis for providing their own national permit or authorisation. Over 20 countries are currently signed up to the mutual recognition procedure.

Substantive Provisions

Data Protection Lead

8–43   The corporate must identify a member of its corporate structure within the EU which will be the lead for the purposes of data protection compliance. Either this will be the corporate headquarters or the member of the group which has delegated data protection responsibilities for the group. This entity works with the supervisory authority for the Member State in which it is situated to achieve the BCR approval. WP108 sets out a set of criteria for choosing the correct entity and jurisdiction if the parent or operational headquarters is situated outside the EU. The chosen corporate entity must be appointed by the parent with data protection responsibilities for the corporate group to ensure that the chosen corporate can impose data protection compliance standards on members of the group outside the non-EEA, have authority to work with the chosen data protection authority and takes responsibility for the payment of compensation for damages resulting from a breach of the BCRs by any liable member of the corporate group.

Description of processing and data flows

8–44   The documents submitted for BCR approval (and there may be a suite of such documents—there is no requirement that applicants submit one compendious document) must identify the nature of the data, for example the rules may only relate to one kind of data such as human resource data, the purposes of the transfer, and the extent of the inter-group transfers. The description of the transfers must cover those within the EEA and those outside the EEA and any onward transfers to third parties from those outside the EEA. The level of detail may mirror a detailed notification.

Data protection safeguards

8–45   The data protection compliance standards adopted in respect to the data must be set out. These must comply with the law of the Member State where the responsible corporate is situated and be consistent with the Directive. These rules are to be applicable to all of the defined personal data transferred through the defined corporate group. It should be noted that there may be different standards of enforceability (see later). The OIC notes that this should be more than a restatement of the DPA and contain some "added value" for example practical guidance to staff. The Rules must address:

- transparency and fairness to the data subject;
- purpose limitation;
- ensuring data quality;
- security;
- individual rights of access, rectification and objection to processing; and
- restrictions on onward transfer out of the multinational company covered by the rules.

Legally binding measures

The crux of the mechanism is that the rules must be "binding" both within the corporate and for the benefit of individuals. There is a certain inevitable elasticity to the term "binding". Inevitable because to quote WP74 BCRs are intended to be available to a range of organisations "on the basis of different legal and cultural backgrounds and different business philosophies and practices". Although the term "binding" appears at first sight to be synonymous with "legally enforceable" a closer reading of the material suggests that BCRs may be acceptable if they are enforced in practice even if the organisation is not been able to offer a mechanism which is entirely legally enforceable.

Binding within the organisation

The rules may be made binding by contracts within the group or as corporate codes adopted by a group. WP 74 notes that:

Under international corporate law affiliates may be able to enforce codes of conduct against each other based on claims of quasi contractual breach, misrepresentation or negligence.

The effect may also be achieved by unilateral undertakings given by the parent company and which are binding on members of the group; by the adoption of codes which are capable of having a regulatory effect within an existing legal framework or by incorporating the rules into the general business principles of the organisation backed by appropriate policies, audits and sanctions. This last possibility appears in WP 108 but not in the ICO Guidelines. This may be because such rules would not be enforceable under UK law.

Binding on employees

Employees must be bound to take account of the rules and this may be achieved by including requirements in contracts together with the provision of appropriate training backed up with sanctions for non-compliance.

Binding on sub-contractors

This may be achieved by the incorporation of suitable clauses into contracts.

Binding for the benefit of individuals

It is only mandatory that those data subjects whose personal data emanates from the EU have the right to enforce the BCRs, although the extension of the benefit to others will be welcomed by supervisory authorities. This entails both that individuals are able to pursue a judicial remedy and that the data protection lead corporate is subject to and accepts the supervision of the data protection supervisory authority. Individuals must be able to take lodge their complaints with the member of the group at the origin of the transfer (within the EU) or the group member which is the data protection lead. The lead corporate must demonstrate that it has sufficient financial resource to deal with any claim. The rules must become binding for the benefit of the data subjects by some legal mechanism such as by acquiring third party rights under inter-group contracts. WP 74 notes that in some jurisdictions unilateral declarations by corporates may be sufficient to be the origin of third party rights but in other legal systems this is not the case. The Guidance from the UK Commissioner focuses on the practical steps which must be open to complainants but does not explore the enforceability of the rules by data subjects. WP 74 notes however that all the data subjects will have rights under the data protection laws of the country where personal data relating to them was processed. The remedies available must be equivalent to those mandated by the Directive.

Compliance audit & training, and complaints

8-46   The WP attaches significance to the verification of compliance. The rules must provide for audit by either internal or external auditors or a combination. The supervisory authority is entitled to call for the audit programme to be provided to it. The supervisory authorities will be expected to undertake to only have regard to the material relating to the data protection audit and not to other matters of corporate governance. It is important to include a description of the audit system and a commitment to share audit results with the board of the parent. There should be a commitment to provide training on the requirements of the BCR as well as a detailed explanation of the training programme. A mechanism for complaints handling should also be detailed.

Mechanism for recording and reporting change

It is recognised in WP 74 that "... corporate groups are mutating entities whose members and practices may change from time to time..." and thus the deliverables must include processes to deal with such change. These must ensure that:

- no transfer is made to a new member of the group until the new member is bound by the rules and able to deliver compliance with them;
- an updated list of the group members, the rules and any update to the rules is maintained and made available to the supervisory authority on request; and
- updates and changes are notified to the data protection authorities annually

Procedures and deliverables

8-47   The lead corporate works with the supervisory authority to ensure that its submission reaches the proper standard. It must submit:

- a background paper setting out how the required substantive elements of the BCR structure have been met;
- the set of materials which comprise the rules which are to be adopted by the group; and
- the contact details of a responsible person in the organisation.

This material, referred to in WP108 as a "consolidated draft", is distributed among the relevant supervisory authorities for comment. The period allowed for comment is usually one month. The lead authority will transmit the comments to the applicant and, where necessary there will be further work and discussion to deal with any unresolved problems. Once the lead authority considers that the material is satisfactory it will invite the applicant to send a final draft which can be circulated to all the relevant supervisory authorities for confirmation. The formal approval for the BCR will issue from the lead authority but the confirmation from the relevant supervisory authorities acts as authorisation for the transfer arrangements at each national level. Once approval is granted the Chairman of the Article 29 Working Party will notify all supervisory authorities.

COMMISSIONER'S GUIDANCE

Section 51(6) imposes the following relevant obligation on the Commissioner: **8–48**

"The Commissioner shall arrange for the dissemination in such form and manner as he considers appropriate of:

(a) any Community finding as defined by paragraph 15(2) of Part II of Schedule 1;

(b) any decision of the European Commission, under the procedure provided for in Article 31(2) of the Data Protection Directive, which is made for the purposes of Article 26(3) or (4) of the Directive; and

(c) such other information as it may appear to him to be expedient to give to data controllers in relation to any personal data about the protection of the rights and freedoms of data subjects in relation to the processing of personal data in countries and territories outside the European Economic Area."

The "Community findings" referred to in subs.(a) have been discussed in para.8–20, above. Subsection (b) refers to procedures set out in the Directive for approval of standard contractual clauses which have been discussed above.

Under the previous Commissioner, Elizabeth France, the approach to cross border transfers differed from that of some national supervisory authorities. It has been noted earlier that the UK Commissioner has not sought to approve transfers made under the derogations nor individual contracts made between controller and controller. The Guidance issued by the Commissioner also accepted that where a transfer was made from a controller to a processor it was regarded as sufficient to achieve compliance if the parties had entered into a contract which met the requirement of principle 7. When the guidance was re-issued by Richard Thomas in June 2006, there appears to have been some stepping back from this generous view. The current Guidance consists of the Guide to Data Protection plus material on the website issued in summer 2012 which consists of an overview and four specific topic guides. This suite of guidance replaces the earlier guidance on the eighth principle and international transfers. One of the topic guides covers outsourcing.

The outsourcing guide covers international outsourcing to data processors **8–49**
located in a third country. It emphasises the requirement to satisfy the eighth as well as the seventh principle. It rehearses the basic requirements of principle 7

355

and emphasises that, where processing of personal data is outsourced to a processor, the data controller remains responsible for compliance with the Principles. This includes the obligation on the controller to ensure that the processor provides appropriate security and is bound by a contract made or evidenced in writing. It suggests that an appropriate way of achieving compliance with both principles is the use of the model contract for processor or controller to processor transfers. However it recognises that this is not the only way to satisfy principle eight and other methods of establishing adequacy may be acceptable.

8–50   Interestingly, the Commissioner does not wholly close the door on the use of contracts which satisfy principle 7 although it is clear that the controller who wishes to use such a contract as the basis of the outsourcing transfer must also be able to show that they have satisfied all of the adequacy requirements. The relevant paragraph from the Outsourcing Guide states:

> "You do not necessarily need to use the model contract clauses when entering into an international outsourcing arrangement if you have found an alternative means of complying with, or using an exception to, the Eighth Principle. For example, ensuring compliance with the security requirements of the Seventh Principle will go some way towards satisfying the adequacy requirements of the Eighth Principle (given the continuing contractual relationship between you and your processor and your continuing liability for data protection compliance under the Act)."

In the Sending Personal Data Outside the EEA Guide itself it accepts that a transfer can be made to a processor in reliance on a combination of an adequacy assessment and an appropriate contract:

> "In some cases you might reasonably decide there is adequate protection without a detailed assessment. A common situation is where you transfer personal data to a processor acting on your instructions under contract. You are still legally responsible for making sure the data is processed in line with the principles. In particular, personal data can only be transferred if there is a contract requiring the processor to have appropriate security and act only on your instruction. So individuals' information should continue to be protected to the same standard as in the UK and they will have the same rights they can exercise in the UK. This is because you remain liable for ensuring that the processing complies with the data protection principles. When selecting a processor, you need to satisfy yourself that it is reliable and has appropriate security.
> However, the level of protection is unlikely to be adequate if:
> - the transfer is to a processor in an unstable country; and
> - the nature of the information means that it is at particular risk".

It also explains that data controllers can use their own contracts "to help ensure adequacy for a transfer or set of transfers" where the contract is used to "plug gaps". It notes that contracts can also be used where the data controller is not in a position to judge adequacy and advises that the contract should be comprehensive. It warns that if a data controller uses contract provisions which are different from the model clauses it risks a future challenge to the adequacy of the level of protection provided by the contract.

Fair processing and overseas transfers

The provision of information to a data subject about the implications of any cross-border transfer of their personal data is likely to be part of the provision of the "specified information" required by the fair processing code.

8–51

The first principle provides, inter alia, that data are not to be treated as being processed fairly unless the data subject is provided with certain information at the time that the data are gathered from him or, if the data are obtained by another route (presumably purchase or transfer from another data controller), either before the first processing or disclosure or as soon as practicable thereafter.

The information to be provided to the data subject is as follows:

(a) the identity of the data controller;
(b) the identity of any nominated representative;
(c) the purpose or purposes for which the data are intended to be processed; and
(d) any further information which is necessary, having regard to the specific circumstances in which the data are or are to be processed, to enable processing in respect of the data subject to be fair.

The "any further information" requirement would appear to encompass providing the data subject with information about any non-obvious country to which his/her personal data may be transferred and the implications of such a transfer, although it is not clear or established as a matter of practice just how much information should be provided in order to make the processing fair; especially in the cloud context where data processing location may vary after the date on which data subject is notified. It is submitted that a general statement that that processing may take place outside the EEA (with safeguards) is sufficient; unless the particular risks mean that the data controller has assessed that normal safeguards do not sufficiently manage or mitigate risk to a level that the data subject is likely to find acceptable.

In cases where the consent condition of Sch.4 is being relied upon it is likely that the specified information requirements of the First Principle and the consent condition of Sch.4 will be dealt with in tandem so that data controllers develop specific written or spoken procedures which both convey information about any intended overseas transfer to the potential data subject and obtain his or her consent. This might be achieved, for example, by providing the data subject with a written notice in duplicate detailing the specified information and asking for the return of one copy signed to indicate consent.

EXEMPTIONS OR DEROGATIONS

Schedule 4 to the 1998 Act, following art.26(1) of the Directive, sets out a limited number of situations in which an exemption from the "adequacy" requirement for third country transfers may apply. The interpretative provisions in Pt 2 of Sch.1 indicate that the eighth principle simply does not apply to transfers covered by one or more of the criteria set out in Sch.4.

8–52

These exemptions, like most of the exemptions to general principles in the 1998 Act, are tightly drawn. Broadly speaking, they cover three situations—first, where the risks to the data subject are relatively small secondly, where other interests (public interests) override the data subject's rights, and thirdly where the transfer benefits the data subject.

There are many similarities between the exemptions set out in Sch.4 and the conditions for processing set out in Schs 2 and 3. In some cases, the provisions are identical.

The interpretative provisions[65] reserve the right of the Secretary of State to make orders directing that transfers prima facie falling within the list of exemptions may still be governed by the eighth principle.

The first of the exemptions in Sch.4 covers cases where the data subject gives his/her consent to the proposed transfer.

Article 26(1)(a) of the Directive refers to the data subject giving his/her unambiguous consent. The word "unambiguous" does not appear in the relevant provision in Sch.4 to the 1998 Act. Article 2(h) of the Directive, which contains the definition of consent, states that it must be freely given, specific and informed. The requirement that consent is informed may be particularly significant as it may mean that the data subject must be properly informed of the particular risk arising from his/her data being transferred to a country lacking adequate protection. The Commissioner points in the Guide to the definition of consent in the Directive and states that consent will not be valid if the individual has no choice but to give consent.

There are clearly "grey areas" relating to consent and the extent to which it is "freely given", "specific" and "informed". A job applicant, for example, applying for a job with a multinational company and being asked for consent to the transfer of his/her personal data overseas to a country with an "inadequate" data protection regime is not readily going to refuse such consent, and both the Article 29 Working Party and the UK Commissioner in guidance on employment matters have indicated their view that such consent may not be "freely given".

The Working Party suggests that the "consent" exemption could be useful in cases where the transferor has direct contact with the data subject and where the necessary information could be easily provided and unambiguous consent obtained.

CONTRACTUAL REQUIREMENTS

8–53   A number of the exemptions require that the transfer be "necessary" for the relevant reason or purpose. It must be borne in mind that the term imports a test of proportionality. The use of the term and its importance are considered in Ch.5 on the grounds for processing. The second exemption covers transfers necessary for the performance of a contract between the data subject and the controller (or the implementation of pre–contractual measures taken in response to the data subject's request).

---

[65] Sch.1 Pt 2 para.14.

Thus a data controller relying upon this condition to will only also be able to do so transfer personal data overseas if the contract relied upon is between the data controller and data subject.

The third exemption covers transfers necessary for the conclusion or performance of a contract concluded in the interest of the data subject and entered into at the request of the data subject between the controller and a third party.

The second and third exemptions appear potentially quite wide, but their application in practice is likely to be limited by the "necessity test": all of the data transferred must be necessary for the performance of the contract. Thus if additional non-essential data are transferred or if the purpose of the transfer is not the performance of the contract but rather some other purpose (follow-up marketing, for example) the exemption will be lost. With respect to pre-contractual situations, this would only include situations initiated by the data subject (such as a request for information about a particular service) and not those resulting from marketing approaches made by the data controller.

In spite of these caveats, these second and third exemptions are not without impact. They are applicable, for example, to those transfers necessary to reserve an airline ticket for a passenger or to transfers of personal data necessary for the operation of an international bank or credit card payment. Indeed, art.26(1)(c) of the Directive provides that the exemption for contracts "in the interest of the data subject" specifically covers the transfer of data about the beneficiaries of bank payments, who, although data subjects, may often not be party to a contract with the transferring controller.

Substantial public interest

The fourth exemption permits transfers which are necessary for reasons of substantial public interest. **8–54**

The Working Party suggests that this may cover certain limited transfers between public administrations, although they warn that care must be taken not to interpret this provision too widely. A simple public interest justification for a transfer does not suffice, it must be a question of substantial public interest.

Recital 58, upon which the exemptions are based, actually provides that there should be an exemption:

> "where protection of an important public interest so requires, for example in cases of international transfers of data between tax or customs administrations or between services—competent for social security matters."

This clearly suggests, therefore, that data transfers between tax or customs administrations or between services responsible for social security will generally be covered. Transfers between supervisory bodies in the financial services sector may also benefit from the exemption.

The fourth exemption contains a provision for the Secretary of State to specify by order when relevant transfers are and are not to be taken as necessary for reasons of substantial public interest.

The Immigration and Asylum Act 1999 provides that, for the purposes of para.4(1) of Sch.4, the provision of identification data under s.13 is a transfer of personal data which is necessary for reasons of substantial public interest. The section applies where a person is to be removed from the UK to a country of which he is not a national or a citizen, but will not be admitted unless identity data relating to him is provided by the Secretary of State. This appears to be the only time the power has been exercised. The Home Office discussion documents on subordinate legislation did not contain any proposals for such orders.

Legal proceedings

8–55   The fifth exemption covers transfers which are necessary in connection with legal proceedings, for obtaining legal advice, or for establishing, exercising or defending legal rights.

This exemption is identical to the sixth condition for the legitimate processing of sensitive data. Its terms are discussed at Ch.5. Clearly, again, the satisfaction of this condition for the legitimate processing of sensitive data will also permit the cross-border transfer of such data without consideration of the restrictions in the eighth principle.

The data subject's vital interests

8–56   The sixth exemption concerns transfers necessary in order to protect the vital interests of the data subject. An obvious example of such a transfer would be the urgent transfer of medical records to a third country where a tourist who had previously received medical treatment in the EU has suffered an accident or has become dangerously ill.

It should be borne in mind, however, that the phrase "vital interests" is not without problems. This exemption is of course identical to the fourth condition for legitimate processing contained in Sch.2. Its terms are discussed at Ch.5. Yet again, the satisfaction of this condition for the legitimate processing of sensitive data will also "passport" the cross-border transfer of such data without consideration of the restrictions in the eighth principle.

In the Guide the Commissioner emphasises the view that this exemption may only be relied on where the data transfer relates to matters of life and death.

Public registers

8–57   The seventh exemption concerns transfers made from registers intended by law for consultation by the public, provided that in the particular case the conditions for consultation are fulfilled. The Working Party suggest that the intention of this exemption is that where a register in a Member State is available for public consultation or by persons demonstrating a legitimate interest, then the fact that the person who has the right to consult the register is actually situated in a third country, and that the act of consultation in fact involves a data transfer, should not prevent the information being transmitted to him.

Recital 58 of the Directive qualifies the exemption in the following manner:

"where the transfer is made from a register established by law and intended for consultation by the public or persons having a legitimate interest; whereas in this case such a transfer should not involve the entirety of the data or entire categories of the data contained in the register and, when the register is intended for consultation by persons having a legitimate interest—the transfer should be made only at the request of those persons or if they are to be the recipients."

Thus the Directive makes it clear that entire registers or entire categories of data from registers should not be permitted to be transferred under this exemption. Given these restrictions, this exemption should not be considered to be a general exemption for the transfer of public register data. For example, it is reasonably clear that mass transfers of public register data for commercial purposes or the trawling of publicly available data for the purpose of profiling specific individuals would not benefit from the exemption.

The authority of the Commissioner

The eighth and ninth exemptions empower the Commissioner to authorise or approve certain types of cross-border transfers of personal data. The exemptions permit such transfers when:

8–58

(a) the transfer is made on terms which are of a kind approved by the Commissioner as ensuring adequate safeguards for the rights and freedoms of data subjects; or

(b) the transfer has been authorised by the Commissioner as being made in such a manner as to ensure adequate safeguards for the rights and freedoms of data subjects.

The Commissioner issued formal approval of the EU approved contractual terms under para.8. It is also possible for data controllers to seek such approval of contractual terms or authorisation for particular transfers by application to the Commissioner as well as for the Commissioner to issue such approval or authority on his own initiative after conducting his own investigations.

The Commissioner must consider any applications made by or on behalf of exporting controllers for approval or authorisation under paras 8 or 9, respectively, of Sch.4 of the Act. However, exporting controllers should note that in the past such references have not been not encouraged for individual contracts although consent will be given to the adoption of Binding Corporate Rules under this power.

Contract clauses and authorisations

Any approvals or authorisations by the Commissioner must be referred to the Commission and other Member States for EU-wide approval or rejection in accordance with paras 2–4 of art.26 of the Directive. Section 54(7) of the 1998 Act provides:

8–59

"The Commissioner shall inform the European Commission and the supervisory authorities in other EEA States:

(a) of any approvals granted for the purposes of paragraph 8 of Schedule 4.

(b) of any authorisations granted for the purposes of paragraph 9 of that Schedule."

Accordingly the UK Act does not require that data controllers who make their own assessment of adequacy or establish their own set of contractual protections submit anything to the Commissioner for authorisation. This contrasts with the position in many other Member States. As noted earlier the Commission has raised the question of whether the UK is meeting its obligations under the Directive given the reluctance of the regulator to approve individual contractual arrangements.

The basic prohibition on transfer to third countries which do not provide an adequate means of protection is found in art.25(1). Article 25(2) sets out the considerations which are relevant to a finding of adequacy. The remainder of the Article provides for determinations of adequacy by the Commission or Member States. It is silent on the question of whether a data controller is entitled to make its own determination on the issue. Article 26 provides for derogations, among them art.26(2) which provides that:

> "Without prejudice to paragraph 1, a Member State may authorise a transfer or set of transfers of personal data to a third country which does not ensure adequate protection within the meaning of Article 25(2), where the controller adduces adequate safeguards with respect to the protection of the privacy and fundamental rights and freedoms of individuals and as regards the exercise of the corresponding rights; such safeguards may in particular result from appropriate contractual clauses"

Member States must inform the Commission of any such authorisations. Although the Commission has criticised those countries which accept self assessment of adequacy by controllers and lamented the generally low level of authorisations notified to it, it has stopped short of threatening infraction proceedings.

ENFORCEMENT

8–60   Enforcement of the provisions relating to cross-border transfers is by way of the Commissioner serving an enforcement notice in accordance with s.40 of the 1998 Act. For a detailed discussion of the Commissioner's powers of enforcement, see Ch.20.

Impact of the draft Regulation in brief[66]

8–61   Under Ch.V art.40, any transfers of personal data which are undergoing processing or intended for processing after transfer to third countries or international organisations, are prohibited unless the conditions laid down in the Chapter, including onward transfers from one third country or international organisation to another, are met (plus the other provisions of the Regulation) by the controller and processor.

8–62   The conditions for transfer are a Commission adequacy finding; the controller or processor has adduced appropriate safeguards which include Binding Corporate Rules (BCRs) or can rely on a derogation. An adequacy finding may

---

[66] See Ch.1 paras 1-68 onwards for an overview of the draft Regulation as at January 2012.

relate to an international organisation, third country, or particular territory or processing sector within a third country (art.41). Member States may no longer make adequacy findings. Existing decisions made under Directive 95/46/EC remain in force until amended, replaced or repealed. In determining adequacy the Commission must take account of legislation and the "rule of law", including public security, defence, national security and professional rules, and security measures as well as the existence of supervisory authorities and effective redress and enforceable rights of individuals and the international commitments the third country or international organisation has entered into. Where a decision on adequacy is made the Commission must specify its geographical and sectoral application and, where there is an independent authority, the identity of that authority. The Commission may also decide that a country or territory does not offer an adequate level of protection but in such a case the data controller may still rely on the provisions in arts 42–44 to make transfers.

Article 42 sets out five appropriate safeguards which can be relied upon by a controller or a processor where there is no finding of adequacy: (i) BCRs in accord with art.43; (ii) standard contractual clauses adopted by the Commission; (iii) standard contractual clauses adopted by a supervisory authority in accordance with the consistency mechanism which have been declared valid by the Commission; (iv) individual contractual clauses authorised by the supervisory authority; and (v) individual authorisation by the supervisory authority. Where supervisory authorities seek to adopt standard clauses they must go through the consistency mechanism and also be approved by the Commission. In effect, this allows supervisory authorities to introduce standard clauses for consideration. Although the wording of art.42(1) states that processors or controllers may only transfer if appropriate safeguards are adduced in a "legally binding instrument", in fact art.42(5) allows for transfers to be approved where there is no legally binding instrument in place.

Where controllers or processors rely on BCRs or Commission adopted or approved standard contractual clauses (authorised clauses), no further authorisations (such as permits) are required for transfers to take place. In the cases in which the controller or processor wishes to use contractual clauses other than authorised clauses they must be submitted to the supervisory authority for prior authorisation. If the transfer is based on such contractual clauses and

8–63

> "related to processing activities which concern data subjects in another Member State or other Member States, or substantially affect the free movement of personal data within the Union",

the consistency procedure is set in motion. If the contractual clauses do not affect data subjects in another or other Member States or free movement they can be approved by the supervisory authority to which they are submitted. In the absence of a legally binding instrument, the controller or processor may obtain prior authorisation for the transfer or set of transfers from the supervisory authority "or for provisions to be inserted into administrative arrangements providing the basis of such transfer" under art.34. If the transfer is "related to processing activities which concern data subjects in another Member State or other Member States, or substantially affect the free movement of personal data within the Union",

the consistency procedure is set in motion.

8–64   Article 43 sets out the provisions on BCRs. BCRs that meet the requirements of art.43 may be approved by a supervisory authority but must first pass the consistency procedure. The Commission has reserve powers to make delegated acts in relation to BCRs to specify the criteria and requirements and also the criteria for approval. BCRs may be adopted by processors.

8–65   Where no adequacy decision exists and appropriate safeguards have not been adduced, art.44 sets out eight permitted derogations:

(i)   informed consent;
(ii)   necessary for the performance of a contract between the data subject and the controller, or pre-contractual steps taken at the data subject's request;
(iii)   necessary for the conclusion or performance of a contract between the controller and a third party, concluded in the data subject's interest;
(iv)   necessary on important public interest grounds;
(v)   necessary for the establishment, exercise or defence of legal claims;
(vi)   necessary to protect the vital interests of the data subject or of another person, where the data subject is incapable of giving consent;
(vii)   the transfer is made from a public register; or
(viii) necessary for the purposes of the legitimate interests pursued by the controller or processor which involve transfers which cannot be qualified as frequent or massive, and the controller or processor has assessed all the circumstances surrounding the transfer and where necessary adduced appropriate safeguards.

The derogations reflect those permitted under Directive 95/46/EC; however, they add the provision that a transfer may be made where it is necessary for the purposes of the legitimate interests pursued by the controller or processor, as long as these transfers are infrequent and not massive and safeguards have been adduced for the transfer. This is, however, very constrained as the controller must document the assessment as well as the safeguards and also notify the transfer to the supervisory authority. Public bodies cannot rely on the derogation on contractual grounds for transfer or legitimate interest. There are also restrictions on the use of the public interest test which must be "recognised in law" of the Union or the Member State. The Commission has the power to further specify what falls within this criteria. As it restricts the public interest ground to matters which are specified in the law of the Union or Member State a legal obligation in another jurisdiction is not sufficient to provide a ground for transfer. There is therefore a significant extension from art.25 of 95/46/EC in that the restriction on transfers will cover international organisations which will include ones based in the EU; the conditions will cover onward transfers of personal data; and data processors will be covered by the prohibition.

Additional materials

Directive 95/46/EC art.25 (transfer of personal data to third countries).   **8–66**

Hansard references   **8–67**
Vol.586, No.108, CWH 25, Lords Grand Committee, February 23, 1998:
Adequacy, proposal that contracts should be included as part of programme to
achieve adequacy rejected.
Vol.586, No.110, col.124, Lords Grand Committee, February 25, 1998:
Derogations.
Vol.586, No.110, cols 129, 130:
Data matching codes and preliminary assessment.
Commons Standing Committee D, June 4, 1998, col.317:
Transfers for reasons of substantial public interest.
Vol.315, No.198, col.576, Commons Third Reading, July 2, 1998:
Partial definition of transfer and a provision setting out the geographical scope of
provisions in cl.5 withdrawn.

Case law   **8–68**
Lindqvist (C-101/01) [reference]:
reference to the European Court under art.234.

CHAPTER 9

Notification

INTRODUCTION

Transparency, or openness about the uses of personal data, is a key element in data protection; this is reflected in the right of subject access and the importance of the fair processing notice rules. The public register of data controllers contributes to the transparency of data processing. The system of notification also provides funding for the Office of the Information Commissioner. Until October 2009 this was achieved by way of a flat fee however since that data a two tier arrangement has been introduced and larger data controllers now pay a fee of £500. Notification does not have a regulatory aspect, unlike registration under the 1984 Act. Registration under the 1984 Act could be refused where the Registrar believed that the applicant would not comply with the principles. Under the 1998 Act the Commissioner cannot refuse to place any entry in the register, as long as the application is properly made.

The details of the notification scheme do not appear in the primary legislation. The 1998 Act sets out only the outline provisions. The detail is to be found in a number of statutory instruments and administrative arrangements made by the Commissioner. The relevant SIs are the Data Protection (Notification and Notification Fees) Regulations 2000, the Data Protection (Notification and Notification Fees) (Amendment) Regulations 2001 and the Data Protection (Notification and Notification Fees) (Amendment) Regulations 2009.[1] The administrative arrangements are set out in the *Notification Handbook: A Complete Guide to Notification*.[2] The Regulations include some central aspects of the system, for example some of the exemptions from the obligation to register.

9–01

SUMMARY OF MAIN POINTS

9–02

(a) Notification is not a control mechanism; the Commissioner cannot refuse a notification and exemption from notification confers no exemption from other aspects of the Act.

(b) The information to be notified covers the data, the purposes of processing, data subjects, recipients, and overseas transfers but does not include sources of the data.

---

[1] SI 2000/188, SI 2001/3214 and SI 2009/1677.
[2] July 2010 edn, available from the ICO website.

(c) An entry on the register lasts for one year and must be renewed annually. An annual fee applies which is set as £35 for data controllers in tier one and £500 for data controllers in tier two. The tier is determined by the number of staff and turnover.

(d) Security information must be notified to the Commissioner but does not appear on the public register.

(e) There is a provision for some processing to be designated "assessable processing". Such processing must be notified to the Commissioner before the commencement of the processing for the Commissioner to assess. No categories of processing have been designated as assessable processing to date.

(f) Manual data does not have to be notified unless it falls into an assessable processing category.

(g) There are a number of exemptions from the obligation to register, some of which are set out in the Act itself and others of which are set out in the regulations.

(h) Those who are exempt from making an entry on the public register must still be able to provide an inquirer with information equivalent to that contained in the register; alternatively, voluntary notification is allowed if the data controller wants to make a public statement of processing available.

(i) Only one register entry per data controller is permitted and purpose titles may usually only be used once.

(j) Public authorities must state their status on the register following an amendment introduced by the Freedom of Information Act 2000.

(k) Data processors are not required to notify, unlike computer bureau which were required to register under the 1984 Act.

THE DUTY TO NOTIFY

9–03   Section 17(1) provides that personal data must not be processed unless an entry in respect of the data controller is included in the register maintained by the Commissioner. Under s.21(1) the data controller is guilty of an offence if such processing takes place.

Scope of duty

9–04   The duty is imposed on all data controllers unless an exemption can be claimed. Controllers do not have to notify if:

(a) the personal data are exempt from Pt III of the Act. This applies to data held for personal, domestic and recreational purposes under s.36 or if the purposes of national security require that the personal data should not be registered (i.e. should not be put into the public domain).[3] Personal data which are exempt from Pt III are also exempt from prior assessment;

---

[3] s.28.

(b)   the sole purpose of the processing is the maintenance of a public register under s.17(4). In theory such processing may still be subject to prior assessment but in fact this would be most unlikely;

(c)   the data are manual data covered by the Act. This exemption is provided by s.17(2). Such data may still be subject to prior assessment; or

(d)   the data fall under one of the exemptions to the duty to notify in the notification regulations.

A data controller is entitled to choose the purposes for which he is registered and as long as those are lawful purposes the Commissioner cannot interfere with his choice or restrict the nature of the purpose.[4]

Processing exempt from notification

Exemptions under the Act

These cover: 9–05

(i)   any personal data if the exemption is required for the purpose of national security (s.28 (1));

(ii)   personal data processed by an individual only for the purposes of that individual's personal, family or household affairs (s.36);

(iii) processing whose sole purpose is the maintenance of a public register (s.17 (4)). "Public register" is defined in s.70 as any register which is open to public inspection or open to inspection by any person having a legitimate interest either by or under an enactment or in pursuance of any international agreement;

(iv)   Manual data which fall within the definition of a "relevant filing system".

The exemptions will be narrowly construed. In the case of *Bodil Linqvist v Alklagarkammaren I Jonkoping*[5] the European Court considered the relevant provision in the Directive and held that posting information about members of a congregation on a website would not be covered by the exemption for personal or domestic processing.[6] In the Notification Handbook the point is made in respect of the exemption for public registers that the exemption only applies to the information held on the register and not ant information required to compile it.

Other exemptions

Further exemptions may be prescribed by the Secretary of State but only in cases   9–06
where it appears to him that the processing is unlikely to prejudice the rights and
freedoms of data subjects. In order to comply with art.18(2) of the Directive
which sets out the circumstances in which exemptions from notification may be
permitted the Secretary of State must specify:

---

[4] *Chief Constables of Humberside v Information Commissioner* [2009] EWCA Civ 1079.
[5] [2003] E.C.R I-1297.
[6] See Ch.3 for a full discussion of the *Linqvist* case.

(i)   the purposes of the processing;
(ii)   the data or categories of data undergoing processing;
(iii) the category or categories of data subject;
(iv)   the recipients or categories of recipients to whom the data are to be disclosed; and
(v)   the length of time the data are to be stored.

9–07   Five exemptions from notification are contained in notification regulations. A data controller must comply with the remainder of the Act even if he is exempt from notification. Moreover, if requested he must be able to produce a description of his processing in accordance with s.24. The exemptions will not apply if the processing is assessable processing,[7] although no categories of assessable processing have been declared.

The categories of exempt processing set out in SI 2000/188 are:

- processing for staff administration;
- processing for advertising marketing and public relations;
- processing for accounts and record keeping; and
- membership processing of membership information by non-profit making bodies.

The first three together are sometimes referred to as the "core business purposes" and mean that a small business may be exempt from the requirement to notify as long as the processing remains strictly within those limits. In each case the nature of the processing, the data held and the range of acceptable disclosures are described in the Regulations and the data controller must stay within those bounds to be able to claim the exemption. In each case the exemption is not lost where disclosures are made under the non-disclosure exemptions or where they are required by any enactment, rule of law or order of the court.[8]

For each exemption the purpose of the processing, the types of personal data, the types of data subject, the nature of the permitted disclosures and the length of time for which the data are to be held are set out. If the data controller processes outside these parameters he will lose the benefit of the exemption. However, where the data are required for research and fall within the research exemptions it would presumably be possible for the data controller to continue to hold the data for research purposes within the terms of that exemptions. In such a case a notification covering the research purpose would be required. In addition disclosures may be made under the non-disclosure exemptions. This means that in each case the data may also be disclosed where the particular conditions are fulfilled in the following cases:

- where there are statutory requirements or court orders;
- for the purposes of national security;
- for the purposes of the prevention or apprehension of offenders, prevention or detection of crime, assessment or collection of any tax or duty;
- for journalistic, literary or artistic purposes;

---

[7] SI 2000/188 reg.3.
[8] SI 2000/188 reg.3(b).

- for the purpose of or in connection with any legal proceedings or for the purpose of obtaining legal advice or establishing legal rights; and
- where the data controller is obliged to make the data public.

Staff administration

This is described as processing for the purpose of: **9–08**

> "appointments or removals, pay, discipline, superannuation, work management or other personnel matters in relation to the staff of the data controller".[9]

The data subjects may be past, present or prospective members of staff. Staff includes employees, office holders, workers under a contract for services and volunteers.[10]

The exemption therefore extends to not-for-profit organisations, such as charity shops, which use volunteers. Information may also be held on other data subjects where it is necessary for the data controller to process personal data about them for the exempt purpose. Thus data about the nearest relations of employees might be held for contact purposes or in connection with pensions.

The exemption only applies to data held about the staff of the data controller. So an organisation which handles pensions matters on behalf of a data controller could not rely on the exemption.

The personal data which may be held are limited to name, address, identifiers and information as to qualifications, work experience and pay or "other matters the processing of which is necessary for the exempt purposes".[11] Potentially this covers a wide range of information. Information about health matters, criminal convictions, trade union membership and other sensitive data are often held in relation to personnel and superannuation matters. The disclosure limitation is that the data may only be disclosed to third parties either where it is necessary to make the disclosure in order to carry out the exempt purpose or where the disclosure is made with the consent of the data subject.

The data must not be kept beyond the ending of the relationship between the data subject and the controller unless and for so long as is necessary for the exempt purpose.

Advertising, marketing and public relations

This is described as processing for the purpose of: **9–09**

> "advertising or marketing the data controller's business, activity, goods or services and promoting public relations in connection with that business or activity, or those goods or services".

The data subjects may be past, existing or prospective customers or suppliers or any other person in respect of whom it is necessary to process personal data for

---

[9] Sch.1 para.2(a).

[10] Sch.1 para.1: "workers" has the meaning given in the Trade Union and Labour relations (consolidation) Act 1992.

[11] SI 2000/188 Sch.1 para.2(c)(iii).

the exempt purpose. This would allow, for example, the processing of personal data about contacts for the purposes of public relations. It is not apparent on the face of it why suppliers have been included as data subjects. Organisations do not usually market to their suppliers as such (unless they hope to convert them to customers) but if the intention is to cover such eventualities they would be covered as prospective customers. The term "prospective" is a wide one; however, it is difficult to see how a narrower term could have been used. The point in made in the *Notification Handbook* that a data controller can buy or rent a third party list for marketing purposes without losing the benefit of the exemption but if the controllers sells or rents his own contact or customer list he will lose it.

The personal data are limited to name, address and other identifiers or information which it is necessary to process for the exempt purposes. The purpose description is therefore the main restricting factor on the processing which may be carried out under the exemption.

Disclosures are limited to those where the disclosure is necessary for the exempt purposes or is made with the consent of the data subject but includes savings for disclosures made under enactments and the non-disclosure exemptions (see above).

The limitations on retention of data are the same as for staff administration as described above.

Accounts and records

9–10   This is described as processing for the purpose of:

> "keeping accounts relating to any business or other activity carried on by the data controller, or deciding whether to accept any person as a customer or supplier, or keeping records of purchases, sales or other transactions for the purpose of ensuring that the requisite payments and deliveries are made or services provided by or to the data controller in respect of those transactions, or for the purpose of making financial or management forecasts to assist him in the conduct of such business or activity".

The data subjects may be past, existing or prospective customers or suppliers or any other person the processing of whose data is necessary for the exempt purposes. As noted above the term "prospective" is a wide term.

The data may consist of names, addresses and other identifiers together with information as to financial standing or other data which it is necessary to process for the exempt purposes.

Remote credit checks

9–11   The regulation provides that information relating to the financial standing of customers, suppliers or others does not include personal data processed by or obtained from a credit reference agency. This means that a data controller who carries out remote credit checks from a credit reference agency will not be able to claim the exemption even if he contributes no information and never downloads or otherwise retains the data. The fact that in such cases he does not become a data controller for the credit reference agency data was confirmed by the decision of the Court of Appeal in *Johnson v Medical Defence Union*.[12] In *Johnson* the member of staff employed by the MDU consulted the computer records of references to Mr Johnson and summarised the material on hard copy before entering it into the computer again. The Court of Appeal held that there was no "processing" involved in the activity of reading the material and summarising it. This would appear to be on all fours with the situation of one who consults a credit reference agency in this way. In previous Guidance the Commissioner argued that the user of the credit reference agency services did become a controller but in the current edition the Handbook simply states that:

> "[This exemption] includes processing relating to deciding whether or not to do business with a particular customer or supplier but specifically excludes personal data processed by or obtained from a credit reference agency".

The rules relating to disclosures under the accounts exemption are the same as for the other exempt categories; that is disclosures can be made where necessary for the exempt purpose, with the consent of the data subject or under the non-disclosure exemptions.

The data must not be retained after the end of the relationship or so long as is necessary for the exempt purpose.

Processing by non-profit making organisations

This is described as processing carried out by a body or association which is not established or conducted for profit and is

9–12

> "for the purposes of establishing or maintaining membership of or support for the body or association or providing or administering activities for individuals who are either members of the body or association or have regular contact with it".

The data subjects may include not only the usual categories of past, existing or prospective members and persons in respect of whom it is necessary to process personal data for the exempt purpose but also any person who has regular contact with the body in connection with the exempt purposes. Accordingly, charities are able to keep records of regular beneficiaries without losing the exemption. Interestingly, this appears to mean that the body will lose the benefit of the exemption if it retains records of those contacts who only donate or assist on a "one off" basis.

The personal data may consist of names, addresses and identifiers, information as to eligibility for membership and data necessary for the exempt purposes.

As in the other exemptions disclosures are limited to those made with consent, those necessary for the purpose or those made under the non-disclosure provisions.

The data must not be retained beyond the ending of the relationship except so far as is necessary for the exempt purposes.

---

[12] [2007] 1 All E.R. 467.

Processing for judicial functions

9–13   A further exemption was added by SI 2009/1677 and came into effect on July 31, 2009.[13] The terms of this exemption are not in the same format as the others and it is not clear that they meet the requirements of art.18(2) of the Directive which specifies the level of detail required for an exemption from notification (see para.9–06 above). The category of data controllers and the purpose of the processing are specified but not the data or categories of data, the recipients or categories of recipients or the length of time that the data are to be stored for. It is possible that these may have been specified in some administrative form by the Court Service however we have not been able to trace any relevant documents at the time of writing.

9–14   The exemption applies to the processing by a judge or a person acting on the instructions or on behalf of a judge. A judge includes:

- a justice of the peace or a lay magistrate in Northern Ireland;
- a member of a tribunal; and
- a clerk or other officer entitled to exercise the jurisdiction of a court or tribunal.

A tribunal means any tribunal in which legal proceedings may be brought. The processing is exempt if it is,

> "for the purpose of exercising judicial functions including functions of appointment, discipline, administration or leadership of judges".

There is no further gloss to this description which appears to cover a wide scope.

THE REGISTER

Contents of the register

9–15   Section 16(1) sets out the particulars which the data controller must specify in the public register. The particulars set out in s.16(1) are:

- name and address of data controller;
- identity of a representative (if any);
- description of the personal data being processed and the categories of data subjects;
- description of the purposes of the data processing;
- description of the recipient or recipients of the data;
- names or description of the territories outside the EEA to which the data are to be transferred; and
- statement of exempt processing.

---

[13] SI 2009/1677 reg.2, amending SI 2000/188.

Section 71 of the Freeedom of Information Act 2000 added a provision which requires public authorities to also include a statement of the fact that they are public authorities for the purpose of the FOIA.   9–16

Name and address of data controller

Under s.16(3), the address given for a registered company must be that of its registered office. The address of any other person carrying on a business must be that of his principal place of business in the United Kingdom. The name should be the name by which the person is legally known: in the case of a registered company, its registered name rather than a trading name; in the case of an organisation other than a registered company, its full name as set out in its constitution or other formal document; and in the case of an individual, the name by which he is usually known.   9–17

Name and address of nominated representative

The previous registration system also included a non-statutory, contact name for use by the Registrar's office. A data user could choose to have correspondence about his entry sent to a nominated contact. This was a useful service for some data users. There is now a provision allowing a controller to include the name and address of a representative where he "has nominated a representative for the purposes of the Act". This is a new provision. It is not amplified in any other part of the Act. There is a requirement in s.5 that a person established overseas without a branch or agent in the jurisdiction who processes personal data in the United Kingdom other than merely for transit must nominate a representative. This appears to contemplate that a data controller may nominate a representative within the jurisdiction to deal with all or some of his data protection matters. Presumably the representative need not be an employee and might be a professional or specialist adviser who deals with data protection matters on behalf of clients. The inclusion of a named representative is not a substitute for the name of the data controller. It cannot be used as a method of avoiding the name appearing on the public register. It is to be included, if at all, as an additional piece of information.   9–18

Recipients

In the 1984 Act, both sources and disclosures of personal data had to be registered. Sources no longer figure on the register and disclosures have been replaced by recipients. These are persons to whom data are disclosed other than in pursuance of a legal obligation.   9–19

Form of notification

The Regulations provide that the form of giving notification shall be determined by the Commissioner. Thus the detail of the data subjects, data classes, purposes, recipients, overseas transfers and security measures are determined by the Commissioner. The Commissioner also determines how changes in notification   9–20 under the Act are to be presented. Information about the notification scheme is available in the *Notification Handbook* from the OIC website. The introduction makes clear that notification is not intended to be a detailed system:

> "It is not however intended and (nor is it practicable) that the register should contain very detailed information about a data controller's processing. The aim is to keep the content at a general level, with sufficient detail to give an overall picture of the processing. More detail is only necessary to satisfy specific statutory requirements or where there is particular sensitivity".

The system remains purpose led, as it was under the 1984 Act. The system is template based. When notifying online, the controller selects the business type which most nearly matches his business from a list and an application template comes up which includes those purposes most commonly used by businesses of that type together with the data classes, subjects and recipients most commonly used in connection with each purpose. The controller can amend the template by adding or removing purposes or adding or removing other categories of information. Telephone applications follow the same pattern. If the application is made on an application form the controller may chose purposes and other categories from the standard lists. There are a number of standard purposes, data subject classes, data classes and recipients. If none of the standard purposes fit the applicant should describe the purpose in his own words.

As will be appreciated from the standardised nature of the system the descriptions are presented in broad terms. The controller must specify the final destination of personal data if they are to be transferred indirectly through an EU state. The description of overseas transfers is the broadest of all. The applicant has a choice of registering either:

- none outside the EEA;
- worldwide; or
- naming up to 10 individual countries.

Statement of exempt processing

9–21   Where applicable, a notification must contain a statement that the controller also processes or intends to process personal data covered by a notification exemption or personal data which are part of a relevant filing system s.16(1)(g). This reflects the fact that not all personal data have to be included on the public register. Section 17(2) exempts from notification manual data which are otherwise covered by the Act, that is data held as part of a relevant filing system or manual data otherwise held as part of an accessible record. Further exemptions are made in the notification regulations. A data controller may choose to include any of these categories of exempt data in his register entry on a voluntary basis (see section on voluntary notification below) but if he is registered and decides not to include them his entry must state that he has not done so. The statement of exempt processing on the register is:

> "This data controller also processes personal data which are exempt from notification".

Additional information in the Register

Under s.19(2)(b) of the Act the Regulations may authorise or require the Commissioner to include other information in the register. Regulation 11 provides that the Commissioner may include: **9–22**

- the registration number;
- the date the entry is treated as starting (which will be the date of receipt of the application);
- the date the entry expires; and
- contact information for the data controller.

These are all to be included. Data controllers are also asked to provide a company registration number, however this is not a requirement of the Regulations.

SPECIAL CASES

Under s.18(4), the Act allows special provisions to be made "in any case where two or more persons are the data controllers in respect of any personal data". Such provisions have been made in two cases, for schools and partnerships. **9–23**

Schools

The Government was committed to dealing with the situation in which local authorities, governors of schools and head teachers all registered separately under the 1984 Act. This arose because the statutory provisions dealing with education impose separate legal obligations on the local education authority, the governors and the head teacher. Similar incidents of separate legal responsibility imposed on office holders occur in other areas of the public sector; for example, electoral registration officers were required to register separately from the local authority which employs them. It is not a universal pattern and some office holders on whom statutory duties are imposed registered under the name of the employing body. In many cases they were allowed to register under the name of the office, although the office did not have a legal personality of its own. These anomalies arose over the years, particularly as individual responsibilities were increasingly imposed on individual office holders by statute. Most of these have not been affected but special provision has been made for schools. Regulation 6 provides that in those cases where the head teacher and the school are both data controllers for the same data one notification may be given in the name of the school. **9–24**

Partnerships

Although it is not expressly stated, the presumption appears to be that generally partners will be data controllers jointly or in common for data used by the partnership. The 1984 Act made no special provision for the registration of partnerships or indeed for any form of joint registration. This caused practical **9–25** problems for the Registrar's office. In the early years of the office, a pragmatic approach was adopted to allow partnerships to register under the partnership name, subject to providing the names of the current partners. However, the basis for this was not clear given that a partnership, in England and Wales at least, has no legal personality. It could give rise to problems where partnerships split up or where a small partnership was dissolved and one partner wished to carry on the business as a sole trader. In the former case, as long as the partnership name was retained, the Registrar's office allowed the registration to be maintained by the element of the former partnership which had retained the name; in the latter case the individual was required to re-register. Under the 1984 Act, the Registrar made administrative arrangements under which partners registered jointly for the personal data used in the partnership. Those arrangements were formalised and reg.5 provides that where persons carry on a business in partnership they may register jointly in the name of the partnership for personal data used for the purposes of the firm. The name and address to be specified is the firm's principal place of business. The names of the partners need not be supplied.

Groups of companies

9–26   No special provisions have been made for groups of companies. If companies in the same group are data controllers they must each notify separately. Trading names may be included in the register but not the names of other legal entities.

FEES

9–27   The Secretary of State is under an obligation, when setting fees, to have regard to the desirability of securing that the fees payable to the Information Commissioner are sufficient to offset the expenses of the Commissioner under s.26(2) and the expenses of the Secretary of State so far as attributable to the Commissioner's functions. The fees are no longer related to the cost of the Tribunal since it became part of the General Regulatory Chamber.[14] The fees are not retained by the Commissioner but nevertheless the amount brought in by the fees must be evaluated in the light of the costs of the Office. The fee for notification was previously set at £35 for all data controllers. This was changed by the Data Protection (Notification and Notification Fees) (Amendment) Regulations 2009.[15] These changed the fee regime with effect from October 1, 2009. New notifications and renewals after that date have been subject to the new fees. The change is a response to the long-standing concern that the fee structure did not reflect the allocation of resource used by the Commissioner's Office. Large organisations in the public and private sector generally process far more information, and more sensitive information, than small and medium-sized enterprises. The tiered notification fee structure is intended to reflect the cost of the resource spent on regulating data controllers of different sizes. The House of Commons Justice Committee Report Protection of Private Data, published on January 3, 2008, noted that it was an anomaly that the same basic registration fee

---

[14] The Transfer of Tribunal Functions Order 2010 (SI 2010/22), amending s.26(2)(a).
[15] SI 2009/1677.

of £35 was paid by data controllers, irrespective of size. The Committee considered that a "graduated rate would be more appropriate, more likely to reflect actual costs, and more suited to providing an adequate income for the policing of data protection".

Between July 17 and August 27 2008, the Ministry of Justice ran a public consultation covering the fee change. It also held a stakeholder event on August 28 2008. The ICO reported that respondents to the consultation and attendees at the stakeholder event were overwhelmingly in favour of a tiered notification fee structure.[16]

There are two tiers of controller: tier one controllers who pay a fee of £35per annum, and tier two controllers who pay a fee of £500. A data controller is in tier two if it has been in existence for over one month and is either: **9–28**

- a public authority with more than 250 members of staff; or
- is not a public authority, has a turnover of £25.9 million or more in the relevant financial year and 250 or more members of staff.

Public authorities are as defined in the Freedom of Information Act 2000 and the Freedom of Information (Scotland) Act 2003. Charities and small occupational pension schemes fall into tier one if they are required to notify, .i.e. are not exempt from notification. Notification regulations may prescribe the information about the data controller which is required for the purpose of verifying the fee payable for notification.[17] The power has not yet been exercised as the 2009 Regulations do not provide specifically for the provision of information to the Commissioner to verify the fees. The Regulations provide that where a data controller has been in existence for more than 12 months the "data controller's financial year" is defined as the most recent financial year ending before the notification fee is sent to the Commissioner in the case of a new notification or the date on which the entry expires in the case of a renewal.[18] The financial year in relation to a company is determined in accordance with s.390 of the Companies Act 2006 and for a limited liability partnership with that section as applied by the Limited Liability Partnerships (Accounts and Audit) (Application of Companies Act 2006) Regulations 2008.[19] If the data controller has been in operation for less than 12 months, the turnover is assessed on the basis of the period for which it has been in existence on the date that the fee is sent to the Commissioner. The term "turnover" is not defined in the Regulations but the document "Notification Fee Changes—What You Need to Know", which is available on the ICO website, states that turnover,

- "• in relation to a company, has the meaning given in section 474 of the Companies Act 2006;
- in relation to a limited liability partnership, has the meaning given in section 474 of the Companies Act 2006 as applied by regulation 32 of the Limited Liability Partnerships (Accounts and Audit) (Application of Companies Act 2006) Regulations 2008; and

---

[16] "Notification Fee Changes—What You Need to Know 2009", available from the ICO website.
[17] ss.16(h) and 18(5A) added by Coroners and Justice Act 2009.
[18] reg.3 inserting new s.7A(3) into SI 2000/188.
[19] SI 2008/1911.

- in relation to any other case, means the amounts derived by the data controller from the provision of goods and services falling within the data controller's ordinary activities, after deduction of: trade discounts, value added tax, and any other taxes based on the amounts so derived."

It advises that groups of companies will need to assess the numbers of members of staff and turnover for each separate company in the group, not the overall group figures.

The SI sets out that numbers of staff are calculated by ascertaining the total numbers of people who have been members of staff of the data controller for each month of the relevant financial year, adding together the monthly totals and dividing by the number of months in the controller's financial year. The term "staff" will cover employees, office holders, and workers under a contract for service, partners and volunteers under the Schedule to SI 2000/188. Where information is provided to the Commissioner in order to enable him to verify the fee payable it will not appear on the public register.

9–29   There are specific provisions to deal with the special cases of registration for partnerships and schools (see above). In relation to a partnership registered jointly in the name of the partnership under reg.5 the turnover and members of staff are taken to be of the firm as a whole, which presumably includes the partners themselves. In relation to a notification in the name of a school under reg.6, the members of staff include the staff of the governing body and of the school. A charity in England and Wales has the meaning given by the Charities Act 2006 s.1; in Scotland means a body entered into the Scottish Charity Register maintained under s.3 of the Charity and Trustee Investment (Scotland) Act 2005; and in Northern Ireland has the meaning in s.1 of the Charities Act (Northern Ireland) 2008. Small occupational pension scheme is not defined in the Regulations but the ICO guide states that it has the meaning given in reg.4 of the Occupational and Personal Pension Schemes (Consultation by Employers and Miscellaneous Amendment) Regulations 2006.

9–30   No VAT is chargeable on the fee. Change to entries on the register of notifications is free. Over the last few years there have been a number of "scams" where organisations using similar sounding names to the OIC duped businesses into sending them money to register. A number have now been prevented from trading.

Fees cannot be returned once they have been paid except in exceptional circumstances. Any application for a refund should be made to the OIC setting out the grounds of the application.

GENERAL PROVISIONS

Number of entries permitted

9–31   The Commissioner must maintain a public register of those who give him notification of relevant data processing. He can only allow one entry in the register for each data controller, as under s.19(1)(b) he must make an entry following a notification from any person ". . . in respect of whom no entry as a data controller was for the time being included in the register".

Therefore, if a controller already has an entry in the register and purports to make a further application the Commissioner is under no obligation to accept it. Presumably the Commissioner will reject such a purported application as invalid. In the 1996 consultation paper, the Registrar recommended that each data user should only be able to make use of each standard purpose once and this has been put into effect, although the *Handbook* states that in exceptional circumstances the Office may allow the use of a purpose more than once "where we believe that it will aid transparency".

Refusal of a notification of entry

The Commissioner is given no specific power to refuse an application for notification as long as it is made in the prescribed form. The restriction of applications to the prescribed format should presumably ensure that he is able to treat a purported application for notification which is scurrilous, vexatious or incomprehensible as invalid on the ground that it is not presented in the prescribed form, but does not allow the refusal of any application in the prescribed form however unlikely its contents may be.

9–32

Duration of a register entry

An entry in the register lasts for 12 months or such other period as may be prescribed by the regulations, and different periods may be prescribed for different cases. The entry may be renewed on payment of the relevant annual fee. Fees may be paid by cheque, direct debit or BACS. If an entry is not renewed within the 12-month period it lapses and cannot be renewed. The data controller must make a new application. The practice of the OIC is to send a reminder to data controllers before expiry of the entry, although there is no statutory duty to do so. Where a controller pays by direct debit the entry will be automatically renewed as the fee is taken.

9–33

Public access to the register

The Commissioner must provide facilities for making the contents of the register available for inspection free of charge by members of the public at all reasonable hours. This is a mandatory requirement. The register is kept in electronic, not paper, format. In order to fulfill the requirement physical inspection was available by access to a computer terminal connected to the live register at the Commissioner's Wilmslow office; however this no longer appears to be the case. A copy of the register which is updated daily is available over the internet. The Commissioner may also provide such other facilities for making the information contained in the register available free of charge. This is a discretionary power. From August 2012 the copy of the register will be available in a DVD in reusable format as a result of the Open Government initiative.

9–34

Certified copies

9–35   The Commissioner must supply certified copies of the particulars contained in the register to any member of the public who requests one. A fee is payable for such a copy. The fee remains £2.

APPLICATIONS FOR REGISTRATION

Method of application

9–36   No particular method of application is prescribed by the Act. There is no requirement in the Act that an application must be in writing. The provision in s.64 that notice in writing is to be taken to include electronic form only applies to notices under Pt II, that is those relating to individual rights. Notification regulations may provide for the registrable particulars to be specified in a particular form. This could be in writing but could equally be used to permit applications to be made in electronic form, whether online or by disk. Applications for notification can be made online and over the telephone as well as by completing a form but in each case the applicant has to sign and return a paper form containing a declaration before the transaction is completed.

Security numbers

9–37   The OIC issues each applicant with a "security number" which should be quoted on any application to alter an entry on the register. This replaces the data user number which was issued under the previous system.

Accuracy of applications

9–38   There is no provision dealing with the accuracy of information to be supplied to the Commissioner. In the 1984 Act, it was an offence to knowingly or recklessly provide false information on an application for registration. Separately, the Registrar had a power to refuse an application on the grounds that the information provided by the applicant was insufficient.

The Registrar took the view that inaccurate information could not be regarded as sufficient and was prepared to refuse applications on such grounds. In the absence of either provision, it appears that the Commissioner would have to accept an entry then take action under s.21(2) if he had sufficient evidence it was false. Section 21(2) makes it an offence for a controller to fail to comply with the duty to keep particulars up to date as required under notification regulations.

Removal of an entry

9–39   The data controller can have an entry in the register removed on application to the OIC as long as he can cite the security number.

Assignment of register entry

It appears that the benefit of a register entry cannot be assigned or transferred. This is inconvenient where the data controller undergoes a change of legal personality, for example where a sole trader sets up a limited company to carry on the same business the register entry cannot be transferred. The new company must make a fresh application for notification in its own right.

9–40

Changes

In any case where a controller notifies, he must maintain the entry as an accurate record. The extent of the obligation to notify changes, irrespective of whether the notification is voluntary or mandatory, is set out in the Regulations. The purpose is to ensure, so far as is practicable, that at any time the entry contains:

9–41

(a) the controller's current name and address; and
(b) a description of the controller's current processing practices or intentions,

and that a description of the current security measures is lodged with the Commissioner. Failure to keep the entry up to date in accordance with the notification regulations is an offence under s.21(2). The offence is one of strict liability although a defence of due diligence is available. Application for changes to the entry must be made in writing and accompanied by the security number. Where the data controller either:

● alters his processing to the extent that the application or entry no longer accurately or completely reflects his activities; or
● changes the security arrangements which he has submitted to the Commissioner;

he must notify the Commissioner of the alteration at the latest within 28 days of its taking place, and amend his entry or statement to reflect the current situation.

Obligations of Commissioner

A data controller is deemed to be notified from the date on which the correctly completed application form together with the fee is received at the Commissioner's office. If the application is made by registered post or recorded delivery the period of notification begins on the date on which the application was posted. The Commissioner must inform applicants for notification when he has included an entry in the register as soon as practicable and within at least 28 days of receipt of the application. A copy of the entry is sent to the controller when it has been added to the register.

9–42

Notification of security provisions

9–43   The 1998 Act requires a data controller to notify the Commissioner of the security arrangements which the controller has in place to protect the personal data. Under s.18(2)(b) a notification must not only specify the registerable particulars in the form determined by or under the regulations but also include "a general description of the measures to be taken for the purpose of complying with the seventh data protection principle".
The seventh data protection principle requires that:

> "Appropriate technical and organisational measures shall be taken against unauthorised or unlawful processing of personal data and against accidental loss or destruction of or damage to, personal data".

This security information does not appear on the public register. It is held, and presumably assessed or considered, by the Commissioner.
The seventh principle is accompanied by interpretation provisions covering the matters to be taken into account in deciding if security measures are appropriate. Broadly these cover the nature of the data, their possible uses, and the practical and financial impact of achieving effective security for the data including:

(a)   standards in handling employees who have access to personal data; and
(b)   standards in appointing data processors with access to personal data.

They also require a data controller who is using a processor to process personal data for him to bind the processor by a contract made or evidenced in writing to apply the same standards.

9–44   The security requirements imposed by the seventh principle are thus specified in some detail. However the actual security technique chosen need not be supplied to the Commissioner in that degree of detail. Under s.18(2) the data controller need only supply "a general description" of the security measures.
The Regulations provide that this shall be determined by the Commissioner. These are dealt with by applicants for notification being asked to respond to a list of questions as follows:

> "Do the measures taken by you include
>
> • adopting an information security policy;
> • taking steps to control physical security;
> • putting in place controls on access to information;
> • establishing a business continuity plan;
> • training your staff on security systems and procedures; and
> • detecting and investigating breaches of security when they occur?"

The form previously asked whether the data controller had adopted the ISO Standardon Information Security Management, ISO 17799, but no longer does so. The Commissioner's staff do not assess the level or type of security the controller has in place but simply check that there are some security standards.

ASSESSABLE PROCESSING

Section 22 sets out the power of the Secretary of State to determine the categories of assessable processing for the purposes of the Act. No determination has been made so these provisions have not been activated. Section 22 derives from art.20 of the Directive under which Member States shall:

> "determine the processing operations likely to present specific risks to the rights and freedoms of data subjects and shall check that these processing operations are examined prior to the start thereof".

9–45

The Directive does not state how the checks are to be done. In the 1998 Act, the checks are to be carried out following receipt of a notification of assessable processing. It might reasonably be assumed that, following those checks, the supervisory authority would have some appropriate range of responses available to it to deal with cases which did show serious risks to individual rights and freedoms, possibly including the imposition of conditions before the start of processing or even forbidding processing altogether in the most extreme case. While this may appear to be the spirit of the Directive, it does not in terms require that any particular powers are to be available to the supervisory authority if a check shows that the processing would cause serious detriment to the rights and freedoms of any individual. Section 22 follows the letter of the Directive. If a notification reveals to the Commissioner that the assessable processing is unlikely to comply with the Act he must inform the controller of his opinion. The Commissioner has no power to forbid the processing or require it to be amended until the controller actually carries it out. The Commissioner will then be able to take enforcement action under his enforcement powers. However, it is possible that by such time the breach may be irretrievable and the damage done.

The assessable processing provisions therefore cannot be used to initiate the Commissioner's enforcement powers. They could be a catalyst for the exercise of individual rights in an appropriate case if the Commissioner were free to inform individuals who are potentially affected by assessable processing of the imminent risks. This would enable such individuals to take injunctive action or lodge notices of objection to the processing in an appropriate case. This seems an unlikely outcome, however, and as it stands s.22 appears to be little more than a formal nod towards the implementation of art.20.

Types of processing

Types of assessable processing may be specified by the Secretary of State by Order. To be specified, processing must appear to him to be particularly likely to:

9–46

(i)   cause substantial damage or substantial distress to data subjects; or
(ii)   otherwise significantly to prejudice the rights and freedoms of data subjects.

No further assistance is given as to what amounts to substantial damage or substantial distress. It is not clear whether the test is intended to be subjective or objective.

Three types of processing were canvassed in the consultation in August 1998. They were:

(i)   the processing of genetic data;
(ii)   data matching; and
(iii) processing by inquiry agents.

Each of these had given rise to concern in the past, as reported in the Annual Reports of the Registrar. They continue to be among the most controversial areas of data processing but none have been designated as assessable processing.

Time-limits

9–47   Where a controller carries out processing in an assessable categories he must not start processing until he has sent a notification to the Commissioner and either the Commissioner has responded or the time-limit for the Commissioner's response has elapsed. If he does start processing, he is guilty of an offence under s.22(6).

The time-limits for response by the Commissioner are extremely tight. Where the Commissioner receives a notification which shows that assessable processing is being carried out he has 28 days from the date of receipt of the notification to give a notice to the controller stating the extent to which he considers that the processing is likely or unlikely to comply with the provisions of the Act. He may extend that period of 28 days for up to a further 14 days by reason of special circumstances on one occasion only, by giving notice to that effect to the controller. The nature of what might amount to special circumstances is not specified in the Act.

The controller must not start to process until he receives the Commissioner's response or until the end of the 28 days or the extended period if the Commissioner has extended it.

VOLUNTARY NOTIFICATION

9–48   The concept of an openly available opportunity to make a public statement of processing is taken to its logical extreme by s.18(1), which allows,

> "any data controller who wishes to be included in the register maintained under section 19 to give notice to the Commissioner for inclusion in the register."

Applying this, it is possible for controllers who are entitled to claim exemption from the duty to notify to choose to do so voluntarily. If such a controller does notify he is subject to the full rigours of the notification requirements; he must pay fees and becomes subject to the obligation to maintain the entry up to date. The possible motive for taking on this obligation is to be found in the s.24 duty to make information generally available described below.

The option of notifying voluntarily is only open to controllers who are exempt from notification by reason of s.17, or regulations made under s.17. It is not available to those who are exempt under any of the exemptions found in Pt IV.

Thus the option of voluntary notification is not available to those who:

(a)   hold personal data only for personal, family or household affairs; or

(b)   hold personal data where the national security exemption comes into play.

This is because, by virtue of s.27(1), such data are not to be treated as personal data for the purposes of Pt II (notification).

Those controllers who will be able to notify voluntarily will be those who:

(a)   hold manual personal data including accessible records;

(b)   are exempt by virtue of regulations; and

(c)   hold personal data for the purposes of maintaining public registers.

There appears to be no provision allowing a controller who has voluntarily notified to cancel or withdraw a notification, although as notification is renewed annually it will be open to such a controller to choose not to renew the notification at the expiry of the entry.

DUTY TO MAKE INFORMATION AVAILABLE

Section 24 implements the requirement of art.21(3) of the Directive that: 9–49

> "Member States shall provide, in relation to processing operations not subject to notification, that controllers or another body appointed by the Member States make available at least the information referred to in Article 19(1)(a) to (e) in an appropriate form to any person on request."

The information specified in art.19(1)(a)–(e) is, as may be anticipated, the contents of the register entry. This provision is again based on the belief that all processing should be transparent and information on it freely available. Therefore, even in those cases where a controller does not have to provide a public statement on the register, he must be able to provide the the equivalent information to an inquirer.

The art.21 requirement has been enacted as imposing an obligation on those who process manual data and those who are exempt by virtue of notification regulations and who have decided not to notify voluntarily, to respond to requests for information about their processing.

Under s.24(1) the request must be made in writing. This includes sending the notice by legible and preservable electronic means by virtue of s.64(1)(b). On receipt of the request the controller has 21 days in which to make the relevant particulars available in writing to the inquirer. The response must be made free of charge. It does not appear to impose a duty to send a copy to the inquirer and presumably therefore the controller may insist that the inquirer attend his office to view a copy of the written statement of the particulars. The particulars consist of those set out at paras (a)–(f) of s.16(1), that is all the registration details except the security statement. Failure to provide the statement on request is an offence of strict liability although there is a defence of due diligence.

Provision is made in s.24(3) to allow exemptions from this obligation in the notification regulations.

OFFENCES

9–50   Offences are dealt with in detail elsewhere in the Act. In brief, the offences relating to notification are:

(a)   processing without notification (unless exempt)—s.21(1);

(b)   failure to notify changes in accordance with regulations—s.21(2); and

(c)   carrying out assessable processing when no notification has been given to the Commissioner—s.22(6).

DATA PROTECTION SUPERVISORS

9–51   Section 23 contains a novel provision which there appears to be no intention to use. It allows the Secretary of State to establish conditions under which controllers may appoint data protection supervisors who will be responsible for monitoring the controller's compliance with the provisions of the Act. The monitoring must be carried out in an independent manner. Accordingly the data supervisor would have to have a sufficient degree of independence from his employer or any other influence in relation to his data protection duties. Although the compliance in question is not limited to compliance with notification requirements, the potential exemption applies only to notification. The order may provide that where a supervisor is appointed in accordance with the order and specified conditions are complied with, the provisions of Pt II, that is those dealing with notification, are to have effect "subject to such exemptions or other modifications as may be specified in the order".

Such an order may impose duties on the supervisors in relation to the Commissioner, for example some form of supervisory role might be given to the Commissioner. It may also confer functions on the Commissioner in relation to supervisors.

Impact of the draft Regulation in brief[20]

9–52   Notification or registration does not appear in the draft Regulation and the removal of the obligation to notify has been put forward as a major reduction in bureaucracy by the Commission. There are, however, formal record keeping obligations instead. Under art.22 the controller must adopt policies and implement measures to ensure and be able to demonstrate that the Regulation is being complied with. Article 28 sets out a list of internal documentation which must be maintained unless the organization is exempt. covering:

- the name and contact details of the controller;
- the name and contact details of the data protection officer;
- the purposes of the processing including the nature of the legitimate interests involved where the controller is relying on the legitimate interests ground;
- a description of the categories of data subject and the personal data;

---

[20] See Ch.1 paras 1–68 onwards for an overview of the draft Regulation as issued in January 2012.

- the recipients or categories of recipients;
- transfers to any third country identifying the country and in some cases the safeguards that have been applied to the transfer;
- a general indication of the retention periods for different categories of data; and
- a description of how the controller verifies and checks that it is compliant e.g. its arrangements for data protection audit.

It can therefore be seen that this is a far more onerous obligation than notification. This information must be made available on request to the supervisory authority. Exempt organisations are organisations which have fewer than 250 employees and for whom the processing of personal data is "an activity ancilliary to its main activities".

Data controllers must implement data protection by design and default to ensure that they meet the Regulation and access to personal data is limited. They must undertake mandatory data protection impact assessments in defined cases and the supervisory authority may list further types of processing which are to be subject to mandatory data protection impact assessments. In some cases the processing operations will be subject to prior consultation with the supervisory authority or prior authorisation. Unless exempt a data protection officer must be appointed. Exempt organisations are those with fewer than 250 employees unless the organisation is in the public sector or its activities involve regular ad systematic monitoring of data subjects. The data protection officer must hold a two year appointment and art.37 sets out the allocated tasks of the officer which include monitoring and maintaining the documentation referred to earlier and acting as a contact point with the supervisory authority and data subjects. The identity of the data protection officer must be notified to the supervisory authority.

ADDITIONAL INFORMATION

The regulations are made under the following sections of the Act: 9–53

- s.17(3) (provision of exemptions from notification on the ground that the processing is unlikely to prejudice rights and freedoms);
- s.18(2)(b) (registerable particulars and security measures);
- s.18(4) (joint notifications by partnerships and joint data users);
- s.18(5) (fees provisions);
- s.19(2) (contents of entry including such other material as may be authorised);
- s.19(3) (start date of register entry, i.e. "deemed notification" provision);
- s.19(4) (fees for renewals of entries);
- s.19(5) (time for retention of entries 12 months or otherwise);
- s.20(1) (duty to notify Commissioner of changes to entry);
- s.26(1) (power to vary fees for different cases);
- s.67(2) (general order making powers); and

- Sch. 14, para.2(7) (power to modify the application of s.20(1), i.e. duty to notify of changes in the case of anyone who has an entry in the register on the basis of a previous register entry under 1984 Act).

HISTORY OF REGISTRATION/NOTIFICATION

9–54   The concept of a public register of processing operations was a central recommendation of the Lindop Report in 1978 (Report of the Committee on Data Protection—Cmnd.7341). At that time, computing was confined to a few large powerful organisations. It was judged that such powers should not be wielded in secret. The obligation for such organisations to have their processing "vetted" then made public through the system of registration was seen as a bulwark against the encroachment of Big Brother. This thinking persisted throughout the genesis of the 1984 Act. Accordingly, when the 1984 Act was introduced, the registration provisions were seen as a core element of the regime. Those provisions required each data user to provide descriptions of the purposes of his processing, the data held for those purposes, the sources of the data, disclosures made from the data, and any overseas transfers made. Much of the early work of the Registrar's office was devoted to the development of a comprehensive system of registration in which this information was provided by way of standard descriptions. The aim was to produce a system of registration which was capable of compressing the detail of every conceivable computing usage into a standard format for publication. That aim was to some extent successfully accomplished in the early years of the Registrar's office. But the fact that registration became a legal obligation just as the availability of the personal computer was changing the landscape of computing forever meant that the exercise had a Canute-like quality from the beginning.

By the time the second Registrar, Elizabeth France, was appointed in 1995, the registration system had come to be widely regarded as burdensome, bureaucratic and unnecessarily detailed. The problems of the registration system in terms of content and penetration were widely acknowledged. Estimates of the numbers of those who should have registered but never did so varied, but ranged from 250,000 to over 1 million. The application forms for registration were complex and detailed for data users to complete and difficult for data subjects to follow. In fairness, it must be recognised that no registration system could have kept pace with the rate of change in computing over the relevant period.

9–55   The Registrar's office made efforts to ameliorate the problems with the introduction of a telephone application system based on the use of "templated" applications. In 1996, the Registrar produced detailed proposals for a radical simplification of the registration system but pending the change in the law decided not to implement major changes to the system. The Government was determined to produce a system as simple as possible commensurate with compliance with the Directive. After the 1998 Act came into effect a new system was adopted with the old system being gradually phased out. The two systems, the new and the old, ran in parallel until March 2003 when the last register entries under the old system finally disappeared.

Derivations   9–56

- Directive 95/46 (see Appendix B):
  (a)   arts 18 (obligation to notify the supervisory authority), 19 (contents of notification), 20 (prior checking), 21 (publicising of processing operations);
  (b)   recitals 48, 49, 50, 51, 52, 53, 54.
- Council of Europe Convention of January 28, 1981 for the Protection of Individuals with regard to automatic processing of Personal Data: s.8a (additional safeguards for the data subject).
- Data Protection Act 1984: ss.4 (registration of data users and computer bureau); 6 (applications for registration and for amendment of registered particulars); 7 (acceptance and refusal of applications); 8 (duration and renewal of applications); 9 (inspection of registered particulars).
- Organisation for Economic Co-operation and Development Guidelines: Annex, Part Two (Basic principles of national application 12).

***Hansard* references**   9–57

Vol.586, No.108, col.CWH 58, Lords Grand Committee, February 23, 1998:
Preliminary assessments, extention of time in special circumstances.
Commons Standing Committee D, May 19, 1998, cols 145–167:
Voluntary notification, shared notifications, additional material, schools notification, annual fees, publicly available, preliminary assessments, information made generally available.
Commons Standing Committee D, May 19, 1998, col.175:
Notification fees.
Vol.315, No.198, Commons Third Reading, July 2, 1998:
Preliminary assessment procedure.

Previous case law

None.   9–58

CHAPTER 10

The Commissioner

INTRODUCTION

On March 1, 2001 the Data Protection Registrar became the Data Protection   **10–01**
Commissioner and then on January 30, 2002 the Information Commissioner.[1] The
Commissioner has a broad remit to educate and inform the public about data
protection as well as specific regulatory powers. This chapter covers his general
role and those of his powers under the Data Protection Act 1998 (DPA) ("the
Act") and the Privacy and Electronic Communications (EC Directive) Regulations 2003 (PECR) which are not dealt with in other chapters. The Commissioner's powers and role are set out in Pt VI of the Act. The Commissioner's powers
under the Freedom of Information Act 2000 (FOIA) and the Environmental
Information Regulations 2004 (EIRs) are dealt with in Ch.26 in so far as they
affect his role as data protection regulator. This book does not cover the
Commissioner's general role under the FOIA although it should be recognised
that many of the roles overlap. For example, the Commissioner's obligation to
promote good practice in data protection is mirrored by an equivalent obligation
under s.47(1) of the FOIA. In addition the Commissioner has a limited role to
hear complaints under the INSPIRE Regulations.[2] These Regulations give access
to spatial datasets (mapping data). The Commissioner's role under these
Regulations is equivalent to his role under FOIA or the EIRs, that is to hear
complaints where requests have been refused on the grounds of exemptions/
limitations which closely mimic those in the EIRs.

SUMMARY OF MAIN POINTS

(a)   The Commissioner has a regulatory role and can serve enforcement and   **10–02**
      information notices, monetary penalty notices and bring prosecutions.
(b)   The enforcement powers apply equally to breaches of the Privacy and
      Electronic Communications (EC Directive) Regulations 2003, with some
      amendments, and to breaches of the Freedom of Information Act 2000,
      again with some amendment, as to the provisions of the Data Protection
      Act.
(c)   The Commissioner has mandatory audit functions in relation to Govern-
      ment Departments but may only audit other organisations with consent.

---

[1] ss.18(1) and 87(2)(a) of the Freedom of Information Act 2000.
[2] The Infrastructure for Spatial Information in the European Community Regulations SI 2009/3157
passed in order to meet the requirements of Directive 2007/2/EC.

(d)   The Commissioner has a role in European co-operation and oversight of associated obligations under related conventions.

(e)   The Commissioner may assist individuals in special cases under the provisions dealing with journalistic, artistic or literary purposes.

(f)   The Commissioner's staff and the Commissioner are subject to criminal penalties if improper disclosures of information given to them are made.

(g)   The Commissioner has an explicit role in encouraging good practice and codes of practice. A formal procedure is introduced for settling codes of practice.

(h)   Codes of practice may be made at EU level by the Article 29 Working Party.

NATIONAL ROLES

10–03   The Commissioner operates from four offices. Although originally the Commissioner's office was based only in the North West and the Wilmslow office remains the Commissioner's Headquarters, since 2003 there have been offices in Northern Ireland, Scotland and Wales. The addresses and contact details are given on the website at *www.ico.gov.uk*.[3]

Promotional work

Good practice

10–04   Under the 1984 Act the Registrar had an obligation fulfil his statutory roles so as to "promote the data protection principles". A similar provision occurs in s.51(1) but applies beyond the principles to cover not only all aspects of the Act but also the promotion of good practice. This emphasises that the Commissioner's job in carrying out promotional work goes beyond promoting the legally enforceable standards in the Act. This is explicit in the definition of good practice in s.51(9), where it is described as meaning:

> "such practice in the processing of personal data as appears to the Commissioner to be desirable having regard to the interests of data subjects and others, and includes (but is not limited to) compliance with the requirements of this Act."

"Good practice" may cover a range of activities including practices aimed at achieving compliance and practices which support standards beyond legal compliance.

For example, under this heading the Commissioner may promote the adoption of Privacy Enhancing Technologies although he might not be able to require data controllers to adopt them under the current legislation.

---

[3] Accessed September 17, 2012.

Information and advice

The Commissioner has an obligation to disseminate information to the public   **10–05**
about both good practice and other matters under the Act. He is not restricted as
to the means used to fulfil his statutory duty or as to the extent of the information
he provides. The obligation is simply to disseminate "in such form and manner as
he considers appropriate" such information "as it may appear to him expedient to
give to the public". The Commissioner also has a power to provide advice to any
person on matters under the Act.

The Commissioner's office is active in the provision of advice on all aspects
of the legislation including via webinars, blogs and student packages. The Office
has also initiated online seminars, an online newsletter and produced a CD-ROM
for schools. Since 2004 the Commissioner has focussed on producing practical
guidance and the website lists a range of Good Practice Notes on a range of issues
in the index of data protection guidance materials. While the commitment of
successive Commissioners to provide guidance, and indeed the range of guidance
available, is welcome, it has sometimes been difficult to keep track of where
guidance has altered or developed or how authoritative it is meant to be as there
are different types of guidance (introductory, practical application, and detailed
specialist guides) and the date is not always given on the document. In the Annual
Report for 2011–12 the Commissioner announced a review of the guidance. His
Office has produced a central guide, the Guide to Data Protection, which will act
as the "spine" or basis for more specific guidance. It should also be noted that
extensive guidance is produced by European bodies on specific issues as noted
below.

Charges

Under s.51(8), the Commissioner may charge for relevant services provided   **10–06**
under these provisions. These are defined in s.51(8A) added by s.107 of the
Protection of Freedoms Act 2012. They cover the provision of copies of
published materials, in hard copy or other media which would involve some cost
to the Commissioner or the provision of training or conferences but not the
provision of audit. When it comes into force this provision will allow the
Commissioner to provide wider information and educational services. It is to be
noted that as the relevant services omit audit services the Commissioner is not
able to charge for such services.

International information

The Commissioner is not limited to the dissemination of information about   **10–07**
national issues. The information provided must include material about data
protection in other countries outside the European Economic Area and any
findings made under the provisions of the Act of adequacy or inadequacy of
protection in third countries.

Codes of Practice

Background and general comments

10–08   Codes are generally intended to include practical guidance on the application of the legislation. They may be either sectoral, for example covering policing or direct marketing, or functional, covering for example employment. There can also be general codes. There is no definition of what counts as a code and they vary widely. The concept of codes of practice has been an enduring one in data protection terms.

The Younger Report recommended the adoption of codes of conduct in 1972. Under s.36(4) of the 1984 Act codes of practice could be adopted and one of the tasks of the Registrar was to promote the adoption of such codes. There was a flurry of code-related data protection activity in the years immediately after the passage of the 1984 Act; however, codes were not being widely used in the United Kingdom between 1986 and 2000. The Directive includes provision for both national and European codes and in the Act s.51(3)–(5) sets out a procedure for the formulation and determination of codes. Codes vary in usefulness and relevance. They may simply repeat the standards set out in the legislation, adding no particular value, or they may provide detailed and helpful guidance. Codes may provide something of a subsequent embarrassment where the regulator's thinking moves on if he has agreed to a generous provision in a particular code. For that reason regulators' endorsements of codes of practice are often hedged about with cautious provisos. Codes may have a legal effect, that is they may be taken into account by a court or tribunal, or may have persuasive force only, that is they can be referred to but the court does not have to follow them. Even if they are of persuasive value only they are likely to be considered by a court or tribunal when assessing matters of judgment such as fairness.

Statutory codes under the DPA

10–09   The Commissioner has a duty to produce two codes under the Act. These are the Data Sharing Code 2011[4] and the Assessment Notices Code 2010.[5] The Data Sharing Code is admissible in evidence in legal proceedings and its provisions must be taken into account where relevant. The Code therefore has a stronger element of statutory force than other codes. Previously approval of the Secretary of State was required for these codes but this will be removed by the Protection of Freedoms Act. The procedure for these codes is specified in the relevant provisions. The codes are covered in detail in Chs 25 and 20 respectively.

10–10   There are other codes of practice which are made under statutory provisions which are closely linked to codes made under the DPA and will apply in parallel to them. Examples of such codes are the Criminal Records Bureau Code of Practice made under s.122(2) of the Police Act 1997, which covers the handling of Standard and Enhanced Disclosure and the position of registered bodies or the Code of Practice for Surveillance Camera Systems which is to be prepared the Protection of Freedoms Act 2012. Codes of this type overlap with the work of the

---

[4] DPA s.52A.
[5] DPA s.41C.

Commissioner. The Commissioner's approach appears to be to seek to establish working arrangements and agreements with other regulators on how the overlap should be handled.

Secretary of State sponsored codes under the DPA

The Secretary of State has a potential role in code development and may direct the Commissioner to create a code of practice. This is done by an order of the Secretary of State. Such an order must describe the personal data or the processing to which the code is to relate and may also describe the persons or classes of persons to whom it is to relate. Those classes need not be types of data controllers but might be classes of data subject. For example, the Secretary of State could require the Commissioner to prepare a code relating to the processing of personal data about children by internet users.

10–11

Where the Secretary of State has ordered the production of a code under s.52(3) the Commissioner must lay the completed code before Parliament either alone or as part of an annual or special report. The provision dealing with Secretary of State sponsored codes was inserted during the Committee Stage in the House of Lords, following amendments proposed by Baroness Nicholson of Winterbourne. The amendments followed concerns about the absence of control of data matching exercises being carried out by central government agencies and local authorities. The provision potentially it allows the Secretary of State a considerable power to direct the use of the Commissioner's resources but has not been used. In fact the Data Sharing Code was made under specific powers added to the DPA.

Other codes

The Commissioner may prepare codes where he considers it appropriate to do so. In any case where a code is to be prepared the procedure to be followed is the same. The Commissioner must engage in a consultation with trade associations, data subjects or persons representing data subjects "as appear to him to be appropriate". Trade associations are defined in s.51(9) as including anybody representing data controllers. They may therefore cover representative bodies from public sector organisations which would not normally be described as trade associations, for example, the Association of Chief Police Officers. The aim of the codes is to provide "guidance as to good practice".

10–12

Current codes

The Commissioner has issued codes of practice on Employment Practices (2004 and revised 2011), CCTV (2008), the fair processing of telecommunications directory information, Privacy Notices (2010) and Personal Information On line (2010). The Office is currently working on a code on anonymisation. The fact that there are very few codes reflects the time and effort that the production of a code can take. The procedural route to produce a code can be difficult. Work on the Employment Practices code started in 1999 but was not completed until 2004.

10–13

This reflects in part the fact that some of the issues in the Code, in particular the guidance on the monitoring of employees, were contentious.

Commissioner approved codes

10–14   Codes may also be produced by trade associations themselves. The Commissioner may encourage such associations to prepare codes of practice and has specific responsibilities if presented with a code prepared by such an association. If such a code is submitted to him he must consider it and notify the association whether, in his opinion, the code promotes the following of good practice. Before reaching his conclusion the Commissioner must carry out consultations with data subjects, or persons representing them, as he considers appropriate. There have been approved codes in the past, for example a code produced by the Association of Chief Police Officers. At one point the Commissioner's office produced guidance on how to produce codes however there are no current approved codes listed on the website and the guidance is no longer available. It appears that the Commissioner has taken a view that approved codes are not a preferred option.

Non-statutory relevant codes

10–15   The fact that the Commissioner is not taking an active role in code development of approval by third parties does not mean that codes have stopped being important. In many areas codes are the backbone of the compliance structure. The NHS Confidentiality Code of Practice is the main compliance mechanism for delivering confidentiality protection in the NHS and is an important part of NHS Governance. The Advertising Codes written by the advertising industry through the Committee of Advertising Practice (CAP) and the Broadcast Committee of Advertising Practice (BCAP) are also influential. There appears to be no central resource setting out the codes and standards which have a relevance to data protection issues however practitioners are recommended to review the application of any codes in specific areas or sectors when advising.

Audit powers

10–16   In addition to the powers to carry out statutory audits s.51(7) provides for a power to audit with consent. Section 51(7) provides that the Commissioner may "with the consent of the data controller, assess any processing of personal data for the observance of good practice". The scope and practice in the area of audits is covered in Ch.20.

Reports to Parliament

10–17   Section 52 re-enacts the report provisions in very similar form to those found in the 1984 Act. The Commissioner is required to lay an annual report before Parliament. The report must deal with the exercise of his functions under the Act. The Commissioner's annual report has traditionally been laid in mid-July. Annual reports contain useful case studies and position papers on current issues. The Commissioner may also lay other reports on functions as he thinks fit. The

Commissioner used this power to raise the problems associated with the unlawful trade in personal data in the reports *What Price Privacy?* and *What Price Privacy Now?* delivered to Parliament in 2006.

Funding for assistance in special cases

The Commissioner's powers to fund individual action in some cases are dealt with at Ch.17. In summary, the Commissioner is given a role under s.53 and Sch.10 to provide financial assistance to an individual who brings proceedings in the civil courts for enforcement of his individual rights in a case where the special purposes (that is journalistic, artistic or literary purposes) are involved. The assistance may only be granted where the Commissioner considers that the case involves a matter of substantial public importance. Supplementary provisions cover the Commissioner's duty to notify the parties affected and the procedure which must be followed in such cases. Giving evidence in the Leveson enquiry in 2012, the Commissioner, Christopher Graham, revealed that his office had only ever received one application for assistance under this provision; that application was refused.

10–18

Disclosure of information to the Commissioner

Section 58 allows any person to disclose information to the Commissioner or Tribunal where it is necessary for the discharge of their functions under the DPA or the FOIA, together referred to as "the information Acts". Such a disclosure may be made irrespective of any enactment or rule of law prohibiting or restricting it. This allows for example a solicitor who is bound by client confidentiality to disclose information to the Commissioner in pursuance of the Commissioner's inquiries. Section 58 does not require the disclosure of information and cannot be used to demand information, although the Commissioner may demand information by service of an information notice in an appropriate case under both sets of legislation. Section 58 simply ensures that the person who discloses information in appropriate circumstances has a defence against a prosecution for unauthorised disclosure or an action for breach of confidence or any other legal action based on the disclosure. The equivalent section under the 1984 Act was never litigated and the precise effect of this provision is not clear. It could be viewed as a complete bar to any proceedings for breach of the prohibitory rule or as a defence to any such proceedings.

10–19

Controllers who wish to rely on s.58 are advised to obtain a written record from a duly authorised official employed by the Commissioner stating that the information in question is necessary for the discharge of the Commissioner's functions. It may even be prudent to ask the Commissioner to specify which functions are involved. In cases where data controllers are asked by police forces to release data under the s.29 exemption, the regulator has suggested that users request information about the reason for the disclosure to be provided to them as an additional safeguard to ensure the non-disclosure exemptions are not abused. It might therefore be prudent for controllers to apply the same approach as representing best practice in these circumstances.

If a controller has adopted best practice by making appropriate inquiries and obtaining full authority from the Commissioner's office he should be in a strong position to defend himself from any proceedings brought as a result of a disclosure although, where time permits, it would of course always be preferable to be made subject to a formal notice or a court order before disclosing confidential information.

Disclosures of information by and to the Commissioner

10–20 Section 76A added by the Freedom of Information (Scotland) Act 2002 allows disclosure to the Scottish Information Commissioner of any information obtained or furnished as mentioned in s.76(1) of this Act if it appears to the Commissioner that the information is of the same type that could be obtained by, or furnished to, the Scottish Information Commissioner under or for the purposes of the Freedom of Information (Scotland) Act 2002. Section 76 of FOIA provides for the disclosure of information by the OIC by a number of other bodies where the officials would otherwise be precluded from making disclosures. Section 76 provides for the disclosure of information "obtained by or furnished to" the Commissioner for the purposes of the FOIA or the DPA to a list of Ombudsmen. Schedule 7 provides for disclosure by the Commissioner by the Parliamentary Commissioner for Administration, the Scottish Parliamentary Commissioner for Administration, the Local Commissioner for Administration, the Health Service Commissioners for England and Scotland, the Scottish Public Services Ombudsman, the Commissioner for Local Administration in Scotland, the Public Services Ombudsman for Wales, the Northern Ireland Commissioner for Complaints, the Assembly Ombudsman for Northern Ireland and the Commissioner for Older People in Wales. Schedule 7 also provides for the disclosure to the Commissioner of information by the Parliamentary Commissioner for Information, the Commissions for Administration in England and Wales, the Health Service Commissioners, the Welsh Administration Ombudsman, the Northern Ireland Commissioner for Complaints, the Assembly Ombudsman for Northern Ireland and the Commissioner for Local Administration in Scotland.

INTERNATIONAL ROLE

General

10–21 Directive 95/46 has a life beyond implementation. In particular it provides for:

(a) the continued involvement of the European Commission in the regulation of personal data in Europe;

(b) continued co-operation between Member States in this area; and

(c) continued co-operation between the supervisory authorities of Member States.

In addition, the United Kingdom has entered into a number of third pillar agreements, which involve data protection co-ordination. These are dealt with in Ch.1. The Commissioner has a role in all of these areas.

Community Codes of Conduct

Article 27.1 of the Directive provides that both Member States and the Commission shall encourage the:

10–22

> "drawing up of codes of conduct intended to contribute to the proper implementation of the national provisions adopted by the Member States pursuant to this Directive, taking account of the specific features of the various sectors."

The provisions dealing with national codes of practice have been implemented in s.51 (described above) but there is no provision in the 1998 Act for the adoption of Community-wide codes. Article 27.3 appears to envisage such Community codes as specific instruments applicable throughout the Community and as such one would have expected some mechanism for national adoption. Such a mechanism appears to be absent. Article 27.3 provides that draft Community codes and amendments or extensions to existing Community codes may be submitted to the Article 29 Working Party. The Working Party must consider whether the codes are in accordance with the national provisions adopted pursuant to the Directive. Presumably this means all 27 sets of national provisions. It further provides that "the authority" may seek the views of data subjects or their representatives on such draft codes. It is not clear which authority is meant here but it seems reasonable to assume it covers either a relevant national authority or the Commission itself. Once codes are approved by the Working Party the Commission may ensure appropriate publicity for them.

The codes must be sectoral and formulated by an industry or other representative group. Production of a code and Working Party approval is time-consuming. The Working Party published a procedure for the submission and approval of codes in September 1998. The procedure is for:

- submission of the code and agreement by the Working Party to accept it for consideration;
- preparation of a written opinion of the Working Party; and
- publication of the opinion and communication to those concerned.

Draft codes must have been prepared "by an organization representative of the sector concerned and established or active in a significant number of Member States". Preferably data subjects should have been involved in the preparation. It must clearly define the sector or organisation to which it is intended to apply. Draft codes must be sent in a Community language accompanied by a translation in English and French. Premature drafts or drafts which do not meet these criteria will not be considered. The draft will usually be considered by a sub-group or task force of the Working Party which will prepare a Report. They will consider whether or not the draft:

"is in accordance with the Data Protection Directives and, where relevant, the national provisions adopted pursuant to those Directives and is of sufficient quality and internal consistency and provides sufficient added value to the Directives and other applicable data protection legislation, specifically whether the draft code is sufficiently focused on the specific data protection questions and problems in the organization or sector to which it is intended to apply and offers sufficiently clear solutions for these questions and problems."

Codes have been put forward by the Federation of European Direct Marketing Associations (FEDMA) and the International Travel Agents Association (IATA). The dialogue with FEDMA resulted in the approval of the Code and a further addition to deal with on line marketing[6]; the IATA proposal was submitted to the Article 29 Working Party in 1997 but it did not meet the requirements of the sub-group set up to consider it and it did not prove possible for the parties to resolve their differences. In October 2000 the IATA passenger service conference adopted the proposal as a Recommended Practice but it has not become a Community Code.

The Working Party itself cannot issue codes. This means it does not have an obvious vehicle on which to issue policy statements similar to the Recommendations formulated by the Council of Europe on specific topics which set out ways of handling issues like the development of genetic databases. It has overcome this by issuing Opinions and Working Papers (for which see below).

Article 29 Working Party

Constitution

10–23   The Directive provides for two separate representative groups to be set up: a group of representatives of the Member States, which is attended on behalf of the United Kingdom by an official from the sponsor department now the Ministry of Justice: and a group of representatives of the supervisory authorities of the Member States, which is attended on behalf of the United Kingdom by the Commissioner. These are the Article 31 Committee and the Article 29 Working Party respectively.

Under s.54(1)(b) of the Act the Commissioner is the designated supervisory authority in the United Kingdom for the purposes of the Directive. This entails his attendance at the Article 29 Working Party. Under art.29.1, the Working Party is to have advisory status and must act independently. Its advice is meant to be aimed primarily at the Commission but may go to Member States, to the Article 31 Committee and presumably also to data controllers and subjects where appropriate. Although it acts independently its members under art.29.2 consist of representatives of the supervisory authorities, a representative of the "authority or authorities established for the Community institutions and bodies", that is the European Data Protection Supervisor, and a representative of the Commission. As well as its representative members the Working Party has accepted observers from Iceland and Norway but it is not apparent from the Europa website whether this remains the case. The remainder of art.29 outlines the constitution of the Working Party which is then left to settle its own rules of procedure. The Working

---

[6] *www.fedma.org* [Accessed September 17, 2012].

Party elects a chairman and deputy who hold office for two years. The agenda is formulated from items listed by the chairman either at the request of the supervisory authority or the Commission or at the chairman's own behest. Article 29 provides that decisions are to be taken by a simple majority of the representatives of the supervisory authorities, so the Commission and the supervisory authority for the Commission do not have votes. The Secretariat is provided by the Commission. The relevant Directorate of the Commission for data protection matters is Directorate General Justice. Data protection originally feel under of DG XV as part of the internal market and financial services. It moved to the Directorate for Justice, Freedom and Security which was split into two directorates on July 1, 2010. The Justice Directorate has four units covering, criminal law, civil law, fundamental rights and union citizenship and equality. Data protection falls under fundamental rights and union citizenship.

Role

The role of the Working Party is to consider the implementation of the Directive in the Member States and to provide information, advice and recommendations to the Commission on matters arising from their considerations. They are charged with four specific areas: 10–24

(a)   considering questions of harmonisation within the Union;
(b)   advising on levels of protection within the Union and in third countries;
(c)   advising the Commission on any proposed changes to the Directive or related or additional Community measures affecting data protection; and
(d)   giving opinions on Community-wide codes.

Under art.15 of Directive 2002/58 the Working Party must also carry out the tasks laid down in art.30 with regard to matters covered by that Directive, namely the protection of fundamental rights and freedoms and of legitimate interests in the electronic communications sector.

The Working Party has various functions and obligations arising from these considerations. It must draw up an annual report on data protection in the Community and in third countries which must be made public. The Working Party was set up after adoption of the Directive in 1995 and has met regularly since then. The first annual report was issued in June 1997 and consisted of a summary of developments in the Union, the Council of Europe, third countries and in other international fora such as the International Labour Organisation.

Papers and opinions produced by the Article 29 Working Party

The Working Party has a general role to make recommendations on "all matters relating to the protection of persons with regard to the processing of personal data in the Community". It has produced a very large number of papers. Many are routine or administrative, that is annual reports, implementation reviews, procedural documents for codes of practice and opinions on other instruments. The work on substantive topics has focused on: 10–25

- overseas transfers and the adequacy of protection in other jurisdictions;
- internet and electronic communications issues including search engines;
- PNR data;
- new technologies, such as RFID and geolocation;
- security;
- core definitions, such as consent and data controller/processor; and
- the application of data protection rules in specific situations such as employment or in relation to the protection of children.

There are also Opinions or other papers on a range of other issues such as data protection and the media, whistleblowing, public sector information and marketing.

A list of the papers produced by the Article 29 working party is included on the website at *www.europa.eu/justice/dataprotection*.

The Working Party has a duty to inform the Commission if it discovers divergences in data protection between Member States which are likely to affect the achievement of equivalent protection throughout the Union. The Working Party's opinions and recommendations must be forwarded to both the Commission and the Article 31 Committee. This triggers an equivalent obligation on the Commission (but not the Article 31 Committee) to produce a report informing the Working Party of the actions the Commission has taken in response to their opinions and recommendations. Such a report must also go to the European Parliament and the Council. Although the Working Party's advice and recommendations do not have to be made public the Committee's report does. It does not appear that any such formal reports have been made.

Article 31 Committee

10–26   The Article 31 Committee is composed of representatives of Member States and chaired by a representative of the Commission. Its role is to assist the Commission in drafting Community implementing measures for data protection. The measures in question will be those allowed for under the Directive to supplement or extend the existing provisions. The Commission is not given a free-standing remit to propose major changes to the Directive. The relevant provisions appear in arts 3, 25 and 27. Article 33 requires the Commission to report on the implementation of the Directive to the Council and the European Parliament at regular intervals starting in the year 2001, that is three years after implementation throughout the Community. In particular the Commission must report on the data processing of sound and image data and shall submit

> "any appropriate proposals which prove to be necessary, taking account of developments in information technology and in the light of the state of progress in the information society".

The various reports and reviews carried out by the Commission are covered in Ch.1. Article 27 has been covered above and deals with Community codes of conduct and the introduction of such codes. Article 29 covers the assessment of adequacy and findings of adequacy of protection in third countries in connection with data transfers. The Commission has the power to make formal findings that particular third countries either do or do not ensure an adequate standard of equivalent protection. Such findings must then be acted on by Member States. The findings of the Commission can only be made following the procedure set out in art.31 involving the Article 31 Committee.

The art.31 procedure is for the Commission's representative to submit a draft of a proposed measure to the Committee which must then give its opinion on the proposal within a timescale which is to be set down by the chairman of the Committee, taking into account the urgency of the matter. The voting on the proposed measure is by qualified majority measure in accordance with art.148(2) of the Treaty of European Union. The chairman does not have a vote in this process.

In the event of a dispute between the Commission and the Committee the proposed measure must not be adopted for three months and in that time it must be submitted to the Council of Ministers for a decision. This procedure allows for any particularly thorny questions of third country adequacy to be resolved at the highest political level. If a proposal is approved by the Committee it can be adopted immediately by the Commission.

The decisions taken by the Commission on adequacy under art.25 are binding on the UK Commissioner by virtue of s.54(6), which provides that where the Commission makes a decision on adequacy or otherwise of a third country under the art.31(2) procedure the Commissioner "shall comply with that decision in exercising his functions" in determining questions of adequacy relating to transfers from the United Kingdom.

Convention co-operation

The Commissioner has obligations to co-operate with other supervisory bodies under two international instruments. The Convention for the protection of individuals with regard to automatic processing of personal data (Treaty 108) to which the United Kingdom remains a signatory and the Directive.

10–27

Section 54(1) replaced s.37 of the 1984 Act. Under s.54(1) the Commissioner continues to be the designated authority for the purposes of art.13 of Treaty 108. Article 13 deals with mutual assistance between contracting states. Signatories to Treaty 108 agree to designate a national authority which will be obliged to co-operate with other designated national authorities to provide general information on law and administrative practice in the field of data protection in their jurisdiction and particular information in specific instances. Section 54(2) allows the Secretary of State to make provision for the functions to be discharged by the Commissioner. Provision was made by the Data Protection (Functions of Designated Authority) Order 2000.[7] It specifies the actions required of the Commissioner as designated authority. In particular, the Commissioner must provide information to foreign authorities if requested. He must also proffer assistance to individuals in the United Kingdom to exercise their rights in other convention countries and assist individuals in other convention countries to exercise their rights in the United Kingdom.

---

[7] SI 2000/186.

Directive co-operation

10–28   Article 28(6) requires supervisory authorities in different Member States to co-operate with one another to the extent necessary for the performance of their duties, in particular, by the exchange of useful information. This is implemented in the United Kingdom by s.54(3). Under this the Secretary of State may make provision by order as to co-operation by the Commissioner with the European Commission or other supervisory authorities.[8] Such co-operation in particular can extend to the exchange of information and the exercise of the Commissioner's powers in respect of processors whose processing is carried out in the United Kingdom but who are subject to the law of another Member State. This can occur under the application of the territoriality provisions found in s.5 of the 1998 Act.

Informal co-operation

10–29   The Commissioner's role in working with other supervisory authorities overseas is not limited to fulfilling his statutory obligations. The Commissioner undertakes a considerable amount of additional co-operative work. His staff attend meetings of some OECD working parties and the Council of Europe Committee of Experts. Since 1984 Commissioners from privacy and data protection supervisory authorities throughout the world have met for an annual international conference to discuss issues of mutual concern. In addition, there are ongoing and informal contacts between supervisory authorities.

Colonies

10–30   Section 54(5) provides for the Secretary of State to direct the Commissioner to assist with the exercise of data protection functions in any UK colony. The terms as to such assistance may include terms as to payment. This provision was inserted in the Act to allow dependencies to rely on expertise and services provided by the Commissioner's office. As far as can be ascertained at the date of writing no formal arrangements have been made under the provision.

European supervisory bodies

10–31   There is a brief provision in s.54(4) behind which lurks a major area of work carried out by the Commissioner. Section 54(4) simply provides that:

> "the Commissioner shall also carry out any data protection function which the Secretary of State may by order direct him to carry out for the purpose of enabling Her Majesty's Government in the United Kingdom to give effect to any international obligation of the U.K."

The UK has entered into a number of international treaties which include obligations to co-operate in data protection areas. A full description is to be found in Ch.1. This power enables the Secretary of State to direct the Commissioner to be the supervisory authority for the purpose of such instruments. There was

---

[8] The Data Protection (International Cooperation) Order 2000 [190].

initially some lack of clarity as to the extent of the powers of the Commissioner to carry out the function of supervisory authority as required by specific provisions of the conventions; however those were resolved by the addition of s.54A which was added by the Crime (International Cooperation) Act 2003 and provided that the Commissioner may inspect any personal data recorded in:

- the Schengen information system;
- the Europol information system; and
- the Customs information system.

These powers are exercisable only for the purpose of assessing whether or not any processing of the data has been or is being carried out in compliance with the Act. Before exercising his power the Commissioner must give notice to the data controller except in a case of urgency. He may also test, inspect or operate equipment being used for the purpose of the processing. It is an offence for a person to intentionally instruct someone who is exercising the power or inspection or to fail to give such a person any assistance he may reasonably require. This offence, as with the related offence in respect of obstructing a warrant under the Act is summary only.[9]

Adequacy

As well as implementing Community findings under art.25, s.54(7) requires that the Commissioner must inform the Commission where he approves contractual terms under para.8 of Sch.4 and where he authorises transfers under para.9 of the same Schedule. This has been done in the case of the Commission—approved contract clauses for the export of personal data to countries which do not offer adequate protection.

10–32

OFFICE OF THE COMMISSIONER

Appointment and tenure

The formal provisions dealing with the Commissioner's appointment and tenure are set out in s.6 and Sch.5, as amended by the Protection of Freedoms Act 2012.[10] Under s.6 the office of the Data Protection Registrar was to continue but under the new name of Data Protection Commissioner. It became the Information Commissioner under Sch.2 of the FOIA in January 2002. The Commissioner is appointed by Letters Patent. The Commissioner is not a Crown servant. He is an independent official answerable directly to Parliament and not answerable to a Minister. He exercises legal powers which are vested directly in him and are not delegated by a Minister. He has legal personality as a corporation sole. This is a little used form of corporate personality employed where powers and responsibilities are vested in an individual office-holder. The usual example of a corporation sole is of a bishop. The Commissioner must be selected on merit on

10–33

---

[9] s.60(3) inserted by Crime (International Cooperation) Act 2003.
[10] The provisions are not in force at the time of writing [Ocober 2012].

the basis of fair and open competition and holds office for a period not exceeding seven years but may not be re-appointed at the end of his term. The Commissioner can seek to be removed from office at his own choice but can only be forced to go by the Queen in pursuance of an address from both Houses of Parliament. This requires a report to be presented to Parliament stating that the Minister is satisfied that one or more of the statutory grounds is made out. The statutory grounds are:

- failure to discharge the functions of the office for a continuous period of at least three months;
- failure to comply with the terms of appointment;
- a criminal conviction;
- bankruptcy or sequestration in Scotland and no discharge, or an arrangement or composition with creditors; or
- the Commissioner is otherwise unfit to hold office or unable to carry out its functions.

The Commissioner's salary and pension are to be determined by Parliament. In practice the Commissioner's post is treated as equivalent to that of a senior member of the civil service.

INDEPENDENCE OF THE SUPERVISORY AUTHORITY

10–34   The arrangements for the appointment of the Commissioner are intended to ensure his independence, an independence. The importance of this can be seen when it is contrasted to the position of the supervisory authorities in the German Lander which was the subject of an action by the Commission against Germany for a failure to implement the Directive properly. Article 28 of the Directive requires that Member States must provide that one or more public authorities are responsible for monitoring the application of the provisions. It states that: "These authorities shall act with complete independence in exercising the functions entrusted to them". In Germany the legal system distinguishes between the supervision of bodies in the public sector which are subject to federal data protection law and federal and regional authorities which are answerable to Parliament, and the supervision of bodies in the private sector. Such bodies are subject to Lander data protection laws and, while the supervisory arrangements vary somewhat between the Lander, the authorities are responsive to scrutiny by the administration.

The Commission supported by the EDPS, argued that the requirement that the supervisory authorities exercise their functions "with complete independence" must be interpreted as meaning that a supervising authority must be free from any influence, whether that influence is exercised by other authorities or outside the administration. The Federal Republic of Germany proposed that the term meant that the supervisory authorities must be independent of bodies outside the public sector which are under their supervision.

The Court considered the role of the supervisory authorities and held in favour of the Commission pointing out that it was important that the authorities should also be seen to be free of the possibility of inappropriate influence.[11]

Staff

The Commissioner may employ such staff as he considers appropriate and must determine their salary and terms of service. In making appointments he must have regard to the principle of selection on merit on the basis of fair and open competition. In practice his staffing levels, the terms of appointment and pension arrangements are equivalent to those of civil servants. He must appoint two statutory deputies who fulfil the functions of the Commissioner during any vacancy in that office or if the Commissioner is unable to act for any reason. Apart from the statutory delegation to the deputy the Commissioner has a general power to authorise officers and staff to perform any of his functions on his behalf.

10–35

Staff confidentiality

The DPA contains a provision at s.59 which creates a criminal penalty for the Commissioner and his staff of knowingly or recklessly disclosing information without lawful authority. The prohibition covers information obtained under both the DPA and the FOIA,[12] current and past Commissioners, members of the Commissioner's staff and agents of the Commissioner. They are precluded from disclosing information which is not already in the public domain, which relates to an identified or identifiable individual or business and which has been provided to the Commissioner for the purposes of the Act. This prohibition applies in everything other than six prescribed circumstances. Those circumstances are:

10–36

(a) the disclosure is made with the consent of the individual or business;
(b) the information was provided for the purpose of being made public;
(c) the disclosure is necessary for the exercise of the Commissioner's functions under the Act;
(d) the disclosure is necessary for complying with Community obligations;
(e) the disclosure is made for the purpose of any proceedings; or
(f) the disclosure is necessary for reasons of substantial public interest having regard to the rights and freedoms or legitimate interests of any person.

This provision has been included to implement the art.28(7) requirement that Member States shall provide that members and staff of the National Supervisory Authority are to be subject to a duty of professional secrecy with regard to confidential information to which they have access.

The Directive's requirement only applies to confidential information whereas the s.59 prohibition applies to any information about an individual or business which comes into the possession of the Commissioner. It is not clear why the art.28(7) prohibition has been so transposed or why a criminal penalty has been attached. There are also a number of ambiguities with this provision. The term

---

[11] Case C-518/07.
[12] See Freedom of Information Act 2000 s.68(2)(b) and (5) and Sch.11.

"business" is defined in s.70 which states that "business includes any trade or profession". This would appear to exclude public functions. It is clear, however, that some information provided by public bodies would be confidential in the ordinary use of the term and it would not be open to the Commissioner to disclose without good cause.

FORMALITIES AND FINANCE

10–37 The Commissioner has a seal which is authenticated by his signature or that of another person duly authorised for that purpose (para.6 of Sch.5). There is a presumption of authenticity for documents purporting to be issued under the Commissioner's seal and signed by or on behalf of the Commissioner and they are to be received in evidence and deemed to be authentic unless the contrary is shown (para.7 of Sch.5).

Financial provisions and accounts[13]

10–38 All receipts by the Commissioner must be paid to the Secretary of State, except in so far as the Secretary of State with the consent of the Treasury so directs. This provision allows for the introduction of a financial regime under which the Commissioner may retain some moneys derived from the exercise of his functions. The Commissioner receives the income from notification fees paid by data controllers. This represents around three-quarters of the ICO's income. The income from these fees is used to fund the data protection work of the Office. Grant in aid is received from the Ministry of Justice for the freedom of information responsibilities. The accounts must show the two sets of income separately although overheads can be apportioned between the two sides of the office. Small amount of income are also received from legal costs and miscellaneous items such as payment for certified copies of entries in the public register. Where the Secretary of State receives monies from the Commissioner he must pay those into the Consolidated Fund.

   The Commissioner is under an obligation to keep proper accounts which must be provided annually to the Comptroller and Auditor General and laid each year before Parliament.

Impact of the draft Regulation in brief[14]

10–39 The draft Regulation sets out the provisions on the nature of the supervisory authority in Ch.VI. Article 46 provides that there must be a supervisory authority for monitoring the application of the Regulation which must cooperate with other authorities and the Commission. The authority must be independent. The members of the authority must not take any conflicting roles during the term of office and must exercise integrity and discretion on taking up subsequent appointments. The appointment must be made either by Parliament or Government. A member may be dismissed or deprived of a right to a pension if

---

[13] Sch.5.
[14] See Ch.1 paras 1-68 onwards for an overview of the draft Regulation issued in January 2012.

the person is guilty of serious misconduct. Each Member State must make provision in national law for the detailed rules of appointment including the term of office which must not be less than four years. The authority must be provided with adequate staff and resources and the staff must be subject to obligations of secrecy. The authority must present an annual report on its activities.

ADDITIONAL INFORMATION

Derivations

10–40

- Directive 95/46 (See Appendix B):
  (a) arts 27 (codes of conduct), 28 (supervisory authority), 29 and 30 (working party);
  (b) recitals 61, 62, 63, 64, 65.
- Council of Europe Convention of January 28, 1981 for the Protection of individuals with regard to automatic processing of personal data: art.10 (sanctions and remedies).
- Data Protection Act 1984: s.3 and Sch.2 (the Registrar), s.36 (general duties of Registrar), s.37 (co-operation between parties to the Convention).
- Organisation for Economic Co-operation and Development Guidelines: Annex, Part Five (International co-operation).

Hansard references

10–41

Vol.586, No.110, col.89, Lords Grand Committee, February 25, 1998:
Audit powers of Commissioner.
Vol.586, No.110, cols 120, 121:
Good practice, compliance duties, codes of practice.
Vol.586, No.110, col.123:
Power to assist in special cases.
Vol.587, No.122, cols 509, 510, Lords Report, March 16, 1998:
Information and audits.
Vol.587, No.122, col.524:
Assistance to Gibraltar.
Vol.587, No.122, col.531:
Duty to consult on codes of practice.
Commons Standing Committee D, June 2, 1998, col.252:
Encouraging codes of practice.
Commons Standing Committee D, June 2, 1998, col.258:
Assistance in special cases.
Commons Standing Committee D, June 2, 1998, col.256:
Reports to Parliament and international co-operation.
Commons Standing Committee D, June 2, 1998, col.268:
Confidentiality requirement.
Vol.315, No.198, cols 602, 603, Commons Third Reading, July 2, 1998:
Confidentiality requirement for Commissioner's staff.

Article 29 Working Party Papers

10–42 Reference should be made to the website.

CHAPTER 11

Subject Access

Ellis Parry

INTRODUCTION

When Sir Norman Lindop reported on data protection in 1978, "the right to know" had proved a controversial topic among those who gave evidence to his committee:

> "This principle of subject access is a prominent feature of much of the legislation abroad, and it was emphasised in all the submissions of those bodies that were primarily concerned with the interests of the data subject ... For users, however, this objective proved to be highly controversial; many expressed outright disagreement with it (and these included several government departments), and many more expressed grave doubts and reservations".[1]

11–01

Despite the reservations of data users, however, the right of access to computerised information passed into law in 1984, albeit with a number of wide exemptions. Its inclusion was in part attributable to the importance accorded to the right in the Convention for the Protection of Individuals with regard to Automatic Processing of Personal Data which had been adopted by the Council of Europe in 1981 and which provided the impetus for the passage of the 1984 Data Protection Act (the 1984 Act) in the United Kingdom.

Over the 34 years since the Lindop Report, information reflecting every aspect of our lives has been captured at an exponentially increasing rate. As the extent of that information capture has also increased, it has become correspondingly even more important for individuals to be able to find out who holds information on them, to learn what that information is and to understand how it may be used by the data controller. Armed with such knowledge the data subject may check its accuracy, challenge its use and even, under prescribed circumstances, demand its deletion.

The 1984 Act was one of the first laws to empower individuals to see the information others held about them. However, it was limited in scope, covering only computerised information. Other broadly equivalent rights of access were given by particular statutes, e.g. s.158 of the Consumer Credit Act 1974. A number of these broadly equivalent access rights were consolidated in the Data Protection Act 1998 (the DPA) and are now subject to broadly the same regime. The DPA sets out a framework of rights in relation to personal information and subject access may be regarded as the enabler for the exercise of those rights.

11–02

---

[1] Lindop, *Report of the Committee on Data Protection,* Cmdn.7341 (1978), paras 5,45–5,46.

Unless the individual can learn what personal data are held about him and what will happen to them, his rights to correct or challenge their processing may become valueless.

In *Durant v Financial Services Authority*,[2] Auld L.J., in the leading judgment, commented on the purpose of the subject access provision:

> "In conformity with the 1981 Convention and the Directive, the purpose of section 7, in entitling an individual to have access to information in the form of his "personal data" is to enable him to check whether the data controller's processing of it unlawfully infringes his privacy and, if so, to take such steps as the Act provides, for example in sections 10 to 14, to protect it".

This approach, of considering the purpose of the access right and linking it specifically to privacy infringement, is perhaps a more restrictive approach than earlier commentators had tended to take, but does represent the law as interpreted by the Court of Appeal. Pending a superior court's judgment in this matter, data controllers concerned by the cost of responding to subject access may seek to rely upon this case's dicta in order to set boundaries around the otherwise daunting task of satisfying a data subject's right of access. This more restrictive approach is mirrored in the approach taken by the same court to the definitions of "personal data" and "relevant filing system"[3] in the context of a subject access request. These are discussed later in this chapter and in more depth in Ch.3 on the definitions. However, at the same time as these more restrictive interpretations have gained credence under the common law, more general statutory rights of access have increased significantly, particularly for information held in the public sector with the implementation of the Freedom of Information Act 2000 in January 2005.

11–03 SUMMARY OF MAIN POINTS

a)   Subject to the correct application of any exemptions, the requester's personal data (which, if one follows the dicta in *Durant v Financial Services Authority*,[4] is information which is capable of affecting the requester's privacy, which is biographical about him in a significant sense and has the data subject as its focus) must be provided to the individual within 40 days. The information which must be disclosed is not limited to computerised information but includes personal information contained in sufficiently sophisticated manual filing systems too. Information about the processing must also be provided, not just a copy of the information itself. Data which relate to other individuals who can be identified from those data, including those which identify them as the source of information constituting the requester's personal data must also be provided in appropriate circumstances and a set of rules deals with when that is appropriate.[5]

---

[2] [2003] EWCA Civ 1746, para.27.
[3] See Ch.3 for a full examination of the decision on the definitions.
[4] [2003] EWCA Civ 1746, para.28.
[5] DPA s.7(4).

b)   Access rights which were previously exercised under the Consumer Credit Act 1974, the Access to Health Records Act 1990 and the Access to Personal Files Act 1987 are now exercisable under the data protection regime.

c)   Where the access request is made to a public authority, the right of access extends to all recorded information, with special rules for access to unstructured personal data.

d)   A flat rate fee of £10 is payable on most requests, although credit reference searches cost only £2. The £10 fee must be paid before the data controller has to start searching for the personal data. Access to paper-based health data (previously covered by the Access to Health Records Act 1990) may cost a requester up to £50.

e)   Where unstructured manual information is requested from a public authority, the public authority's obligation to locate, retrieve and extract the information is restricted by the imposition of a cost ceiling (which may, therefore, limit the amount of information which is retrieved).

f)   There are a number of exemptions from the obligation to provide access.

g)   The Information Commissioner can serve an enforcement notice on any data controller who fails to give subject access. Further, he has powers to serve information notices in order to inspect data, to check whether the data controller's exercise of any exemptions is justified and to call for further details from the data controller if he is not satisfied with the explanations given.

h)   Individuals can assert their rights in court and seek court Orders to be provided with their personal data without first consulting the Information Commissioner.

Requirements for requesting information

The Directive does not specify how requests for information have to be made. **11–04** However, under s.7(2), requests do not give rise to a duty to respond unless they are made in writing—data controllers are under no obligation to respond to oral requests. There is no rule preventing a data controller giving information in response to an oral request, but it may be a security risk to do so unless the data controller is already sure of the identity of the person making the request.

The advice of the Information Commissioner is that, where an accidental disclosure would not be expected to cause damage or distress, the data controller may rely on the usual signature of the data subject and dispatch his response to the address recorded by the data controller as the data subject's address. However, better security precautions should be adopted if the information is such that:

> "...its accidental disclosure to an individual impersonating the data subject would be likely to cause damage or distress to the real data subject".[6]

---

[6] Office of Information Commissioner, *Legal Guidance* (October 2001), p.49. It should be noted that this may also involve an offence under s.55 by the person who attempts to procure the information.

The Information Commissioner's Legal Guidance suggests that the data controller may check the identity of the requester by:

- asking the individual to verify his or her identity by providing information which only s/he would know or by producing documents which only s/he would have; or

- asking for the requestor's signature on the access request to be witnessed by a person who is over 18 years of age and is not a relative of the requester.

Address for service

11–05   The DPA does not designate any particular address at which the data controller should expect to receive subject access requests (e.g., its registered company address). Therefore, a subject access request may be sent by a requester to any valid address for the data controller. However, when dealing with a large organisation it may be advisable for a requester to send his request to the data controller's head office or administrative centre rather than to any local office which may or may not have an association with the requester. Further, it would appear only sensible that where an organisation has a data protection officer the request be marked for their attention.

Requests in writing

11–06   Once a data controller has received a written request together with the appropriate fee, he is under an obligation to respond to it unless:

a)   it is not sufficiently clear to enable him to find the information requested[7]; or

b)   he has already complied with an identical or very similar request within a reasonable timescale.[8] The DPA does not indicate what qualifies as a "reasonable interval" between requests but the Legal Guidance from the Information Commissioner suggests that the following factors should be considered:

c)   the nature of the data;

d)   the purpose for which the data are processed; and

e)   the frequency with which the data are altered.

Clearly a request has to be intelligible in order for the data controller to understand and respond to it and the more information the requester gives to help the data controller find the relevant information, the better. If the request does not enable the data controller to identify the person making the request or locate the information sought he is not obliged to comply with the request, provided he has made reasonable enquiries to the requester and has not received the further information that he requires.[9] An individual who wants to ask for subject access should write to the data controller in clear terms explaining what information s/he

---

[7] DPA s.7(3).
[8] DPA s.8(3).
[9] DPA s.7(3).

wants. Although the requester is under no obligation to mention the DPA in the written request, it is usually helpful to data controllers if s/he does so.

Data controllers should ensure that all their staff are trained to recognise and respond to subject access requests, particularly those who work in the headquarters or any central mailroom. Such training may be difficult to devise because requests do not have to be provided in a particular form in order to be valid. This means that staff should be trained to understand the nature and existence of the subject access right, not simply to recognise a standard form request. A data controller may, however, find it useful to have a standard form on which to ask individuals to provide details to help find the information requested. This is particularly the case where a data controller is a large organisation and holds large amounts of data as such forms can help to narrow down the numbers and identities of data repositories which will have to be searched to satisfy the request. Although such a standard form may prove useful to the data controller, the DPA does not oblige the requester to co-operate by completing and returning it to the controller.

Obligations of public authorities under the Freedom of Information Act (the "FOIA")

Section 68 of the FOIA amends s.1 of the DPA by the addition of a further category (category (e)) to the definition of "data" to include "recorded information" held by a public authority which does not fall within categories (a)–(d). Category (e) data is therefore all recorded information held by a public authority other than that: 11–07

a)   held on computer;
b)   recorded with the intention that it should be held on computer;
c)   held in relevant filing systems; or
d)   held in accessible records.[10]

This category (e) is further broken down into "structured" and "unstructured data" [11] Structured personal data are manual data which are part of a set of data relating to individuals where the set is structured by reference to individuals or criteria relating to them but in which specific information is *not* readily accessible. Thus a file with the name of an individual on the cover where the contents are in date order will be covered by this definition. By contrast "unstructured personal data" will be information that is held outside any structured manual filing mechanism, for example references to an individual in diaries or in loose papers.

All of the requirements of s.7 apply to the new category (e) data. However, where unstructured personal data are concerned the public authority is not under an obligation to provide the information unless "the request under that section contains a description of the data" (s.9A(2)). There is no further assistance provided on the level of detail at which the description is to be provided by the requester. While no one would expect the data subject to have to provide an exact

---

[10] For a detailed analysis of the provisions see Chs 3 and 4, Interpretation and Definitions.
[11] DPA s.9A, inserted by s.69(2) of the FOIA.

location within the public authority, it might be reasonable to ask him for an approximate date when the information may have been generated, the subject matter, the type of information sought, e.g. social service files, or letters to the planning department, etc.

Fees for subject access

11–08 The fee is prescribed in regulations (described in the next section) made by the Secretary of State. The Secretary of State may prescribe cases in which *no* fee will be payable, but this power has not been used as at the date of printing. Other than the cases where access rights appeared in predecessor legislation the fee for subject access is now £10.[12] This makes access cheaper than it was under the 1984 Act. Under the 1984 Act, the data user could have as many entries as he wished on the public register, a fee of £10 being payable per entry. The effect of s.7(2)(b) of the DPA is that the fee must be paid before the data controller is under any obligation to start looking for the personal data. This meets the data controllers' concern that individuals might abuse the access provisions by making extensive access requests and then fail to pay the applicable fee. The fee entitles the requester to receive copies of all the responsive data (except in the case of unstructured personal data where the request is made to a public authority).Where the request is made to a public authority which has an obligation to also provide category (e) data, any unstructured personal data will be subject to the appropriate limit prescribed under the FOIA. Therefore, even where the data subject has been able to provide a proper description of the unstructured information,[13] the public authority is not under an obligation to provide it, or to provide any of the information required by s.7(1):

> "if the authority estimates that the cost of complying with the request so far as relating to those data would exceed the appropriate limit".[14]

This has to be read with the next subs.(4) which provides that subs.(3) does not exempt the pubic authority from the obligation to inform the requesterwhether his personal data are being processed. There is no exemption from this part of the subject access obligation unless the estimated cost of complying with that aspect of it alone in relation to the unstructured personal data would exceed the "appropriate limit". The appropriate limit in these two subsections means the amount prescribed by the Secretary of State and any "estimates" made by the public authority for the purpose of the section must be made in accordance with regulations under s.12(5) of the FOIA. The cost is assessed on a notional basis of staff time at £25 per hour and the public authority is able to take into account the time spent locating, retreiving and extracting the information. The limit is currently set at £600 for central government departments and £450 for the rest of the public sector.

It should be borne in mind that the access provisions to "accessible records" continue in force. Accordingly, the public authority will have to decide when a

---

[12] Data Protection (Subject Access) (Fees and Miscellaneous Provisions) Regulations 2000 (SI 2000/191) reg.3.
[13] DPA s.9A(2).
[14] DPA s.9A(3).

request is received whether the information sought might fall under any of the "accessible records" provisions and if so treat those requests accordingly. Where "accessible records" are concerned the authority has to provide all the information, both manual and automated irrespective of the method of filing, for the statutory fee.

THE DATA PROTECTION (SUBJECT ACCESS) (FEES AND MISCELLANEOUS PROVISIONS) REGULATIONS (SI 2000/191)

The subject access provisions in s.7 of the DPA are supplemented by these Regulations. They make provision for differential fees and time limits for response in relation to access requests in the special cases of credit reference files and education and health accessible records. They also cover a number of miscellaneous points. Regulation 3 provides that the maximum fee for subject access in all but the special cases referred to above will remain at £10.

11–09

Treatment of requests

Section 8(1) allows the Secretary of State to make regulations prescribing cases in which a request for information under one part of s.7 is to be treated as also being a request for the information under other parts of s.7. Regulation 2 prescribes that a request under any part of s.7(1)(a), (b) or (c) is to be treated as covering all three subsections. However, a request will only extend to s.7(1)(d) where it shows an express intention to that effect. The request need not actually mention the subsection but must clearly refer to the requirement to have access to information about the logic of any automated processing operation. Equally a request made under s.7(1)(d) will not be treated as covering the first three subsections unless it shows an express intention to that effect.

11–10

Credit reference agencies

Section 9(2) of the DPA provides that, where access requests are made to credit reference agencies, they are to be treated as being limited to personal data relevant to the financial standing of the requester unless the request shows a contrary intention. Where s.9(2) applies, reg.4[15] makes a number of additional changes to the usual procedure. The maximum fee which the data controller can charge for dealing with the request is set at £2.[16] The data controller must respond within seven working days.[17] "Working days" do not include weekends, bank holidays in the jurisdiction within which the data controller is situated or Christmas day, Good Friday or a United Kingdom Bank Holiday.

11–11

---

[15] SI 2000/191.
[16] SI 2000/191 reg.4(1)(a).
[17] SI 2000/191 reg.4(1)(b).

Educational records

11–12   Accessible records which are education records within the meaning of Sch.11 of the DPA are subject to the provisions of reg.5. This applies to the entire record covering the information held as automated data, information recorded in a relevant filing system and information held in the manual files. A data controller cannot charge a fee for giving subject access to such records[18] although he may recover some of the copying charges as allowed under the next subsection. This subsection provides that fees may be charged for providing the information in hard copy form in accordance with the Schedule to the Regulations. The Schedule sets a maximum fee of £50 where the information is to be provided other than by a copy in writing. Where the request is to be met by providing copies in writing the Regulations set a sliding scale of charges depending on the number of sheets copied. This runs from £1 for fewer than 20 pages to a maximum of £50 for 500 sheets or more. The time for complying with a request for access to education accessible records is set at 15 school days where the data controller is situated in England or Wales.[19]

Health records

11–13   Regulation 6(1) only applies to a limited set of personal data; those which are held in a manual system; that which is a health record within s.68 of the DPA and where the access request was made before October 24, 2001. Where the information was to be supplied in permanent form the maximum fee was set at £50. Unlike the education accessible records provision, this fee was not linked to the number of pages made available. However, where the data subject does not want to be supplied with a copy in permanent form and the data are not automated data but are part of an accessible health record some of which was recorded within the preceding 40 days before the request, no fee may be charged. This is to enable individuals to view recently made health records at no charge. An individual may specify that his request is so limited.[20]

RETRIEVING THE INFORMATION—FINDING WHAT THE DATA SUBJECT WANTS

Authenticity of the request

11–14   A data controller who receives a subject access request may not be completely satisfied as to its provenance. Where he is not sure who the request has come from or what information the requester wants, the data controller is not obliged to provide any information until he is satisfied in these regards. Section 7(3) provides that where a data controller reasonably requires further information (either to satisfy himself as to the identity of the person making the request or to locate the information that the person seeks), the data controller is not obliged to

---

[18] SI 2000/191 reg. 5(2).
[19] SI 2000/191 reg. 5(4).
[20] SI 2000/191 reg.5(4).

comply with the request unless he has informed the requester of his requirements and they have been met. This section was inserted into s.7(3) by Sch.6 para.1 of the FOIA. There is no absolute obligation on the data controller, nor is there a time limit within which he must state his requirements. This point has caused the InformationCommissioner to advise:

> "... a data controller should act promptly in requesting the fee or any other further information necessary to fulfil the request. A deliberate delay on the part of the controller is not acceptable".[21]

The data controller should not, however, provide access where he has legitimate doubts about the authenticity of the request. If a data controller does this he risks falling foul of the security and other requirements of the DPA because it might lead to him making an unauthorised disclosure of personal data. A data controller should, therefore, make further inquiries of the person requesting access where he is unsure on any point, either to satisfy himself that the person making the request is entitled to the personal data or to find the particular information that the individual has requested. Where the data controller does make such inquiries, his obligation to supply the personal data does not arise until he has been provided with satisfactory responses by the data subject.

Does all information have to be given?

In *R. v Chief Constable of B County Constabulary and the Director of the National Identification Service Ex p. R*, Laws J. held that the subject access provisions in s.21(1)(b) of the 1984 Act established: **11–15**

> "a simple duty to supply the data subject with the whole of the information held upon him by way of personal data when he requests it".[22]

The circumstances of the case were that an individual who had a spent conviction for a minor offence committed 10 years earlier required a subject access certificate to submit to the consulate general of a country in which he sought employment. He wanted the Chief Constable to provide the results of the s.21 search, excluding the spent conviction. Laws J. held that the wording of s.21 of the 1984 Act, which read:

> "(1)   an individual shall be entitled ...
>   (b)   to be supplied by any data user with a copy of the information constituting ... any such personal data held by him ..."

did not allow the user to do anything other than supply all the information under the relevant purpose heading.

The rigour of that ruling could have been mitigated by regulations made under s.7(7) of the DPA that:

---

[21] Office of Information Commissioner, *Legal Guidance* (October 2001), p.47.
[22] Unreported, November 1997.

"an individual making a request under this section, may in such cases as may be prescribed, specify that his request is limited to personal data of any prescribed description,"

but, as the analysis of the relevant regulations (above) shows, this has not been done.

In reality, however, both public and private sector data controllers habitually reach agreement with data subjects to limit the information provided in response to a subject access request. In principle this approach is unobjectionable provided it is agreed by both parties and does not involve any connivance in "doctoring" the results of access requests to make them acceptable to third parties, the real mischief involved in the above case.

The recent case of *Keith Martin Elliott v Lloyds TSB Bank Plc*[23] considered the lengths a data controller has to go to when making a *search* for personal data responsive to a subject access request (as opposed to the s.8(2) obligation to *supply a copy* of the information in permanent form). The *Elliott* case cites with approval the High Court case of *Ezsias v Welsh Ministers*.[24] Behrens J. holding:

"… [the Defendants] are only obliged to supply such data to Mr Elliott as is found after a reasonable and proportionate search" .[25]

The Information Commissioner issued Guidance[26] after the *Ezsais* judgment, but before *Elliott*:

"The judgment in the 2007 High Court case of Ezsias v Welsh Ministers is sometimes used to suggest that the term 'disproportionate effort' appearing in section 8(2) DPA may be used more widely than as outlined above to release data controllers from their obligations in relation to subject access requests. Such a wide interpretation of the case overlooks the case-specific aspects of the judgment … a data controller cannot refuse to deal with a subject access request simply because the task of 'locating' the information in the first place would involve considerable effort and expense".

In the *Ezsias* case, the personnel within the Welsh Assembly responsible for dealing with Mr Ezsias' access request had, as the Information Commissioner's Guidance states[27]:

"…made extensive efforts to locate all data that should be provided in response to the subject access request [including]:

- making enquiries of all departments that might reasonably be considered to hold the information requested,
- identifying all the information it held about the data subject,
- reviewing all the documents,
- providing disclosure of all information it felt it was obliged to disclose,

---

[23] EW Misc 7 (CC) (April 24, 2012).
[24] Claim No.6CF90111 (November 23, 2007).
[25] Claim No.6CF90111, para.18.
[26] "Disproportionate Effort—Section 8(2)", p.3.
[27] "Disproportionate Effort—Section 8(2)", p.4.

- identifying those documents it was not obliged to disclose (and noting the reason why the documents were being withheld), and
- providing certain information in the form of documents on which some information had been redacted."

The judge reviewed the data controller's actions and concluded that

"the steps taken by the [data controller] in response to Mr Ezsias's request for access to data – the search, identification and consequent disclosure of information…were eminently reasonable and proportionate".

The practical difference between expending considerable effort and expense to locate personal data but not being "obliged to leave no stone unturned"[28] may be difficult for large data controllers to operationalise successfully. However, any difference between the Information Commissioner's interpretation of the extent of the search obligations placed on large data controllers and that of the court's may mean little in practice, as the Information Commissioner will take into account the size of the organisation and any effect upon the data subject of not being provided with a copy of his personal data when determining whether the data controller's actions are reasonable.[29] It may be of assistance to a data controller struggling to understand the scope of its search obligations to rely upon s.7(3)(a) of the DPA. Pursuant to which a data controller is entitled to ask a requester to furnish it with further information in so far as such further information is reasonably required to help the data controller locate personal data responsive to the subject access request. The data controller is not obliged to comply with the subject access request unless and until its reasonable request for further information has been met.

The Information Commissioner's Guidance examines a data controller's duties to conduct appropriate searches opposite three categories of data and considers each in turn. The Guidance draws a distinction between data which have been:

a)   "archived" to storage;
b)   copied to "back-up" files; or
c)   "deleted".

Where a data controller has actively chosen to archive data electronically (presumably because he believes they continue to be of relevance, otherwise he would have deleted them) those data should be searched in order to respond to an access request. This is the case unless the search mechanisms available to search the archived data are not as sophisticated as those which may be deployed to search live data. In which case the Information Commissioner's Guidance is that:

"…the ability of the data subject to provide detailed location information may have a serious impact on the data controller's ability to find the information".[30]

However, the Information Commissioner goes on to limit this apparent caveat:

---

[28] "Disproportionate Effort—Section 8(2)", p.5.
[29] Office of Information Commissioner, *Legal Guidance* (October 2001), p.46.
[30] "Disproportionate Effort—Section 8(2)", p.8.

"However, as the data controller has decided to retain copies of the data for future reference, if it is able to locate the data (possibly with the aid of location information from the data subject), it is required to provide such information in response to a subject access request".[31]

The Information Commissioner's treatment of "back-up" data is pragmatic in so far as "back-up" data are usually simply copies of the live environment. Therefore, if the live environment is searched suitably the "back-up" copy is unlikely to yield substantially different results if searched:

"… the Commissioner will consider whether there is any evidence that the back-up data differs materially from that which is held on the live systems and has been supplied to the applicant. Where there is no evidence that this is the case the Commissioner would not seek to enforce the right of subject access in relation to the back-up records".[32]

In relation to deleted data, the Information Commissioner's view is equally sensible. As one of the main aims behind the right of access is to allow a data subject to verify the accuracy of the personal data being processed about him and, e.g., have any inaccuracies corrected, the Information Commissioner reasons:

"Where information has been deleted by a data controller it is no longer used by the controller to make decisions affecting the data subject and any inaccuracies in the data can have no effect upon him as the information will no longer be accessed by the data controller or anyone else. Consequently, it is difficult to see why a right of subject access should apply to information that the data controller has decided to delete as neither he, nor anyone else, has any further use for it…The Commissioner does not require a data controller to reconstitute data deleted in accordance with the data controller's retention and deletion policies in order to respond to a subject access request".[33]

11–16   In just one case, the DPA makes statutory provision for a limited search to be undertaken; where the data controller is a credit reference agency, s.9(2) provides that an individual making a subject access request shall be taken to have limited that request to "personal data relevant to his financial standing" unless the request shows a contrary intention. The limitation is a "carry over" from the provision in s.158 of the Consumer Credit Act 1974 (unamended). Under s.158 consumers had a right of access to the "file" of credit information relating to them rather than to *all* the information relating to them which the agency held. The largest credit reference agencies in the United Kingdom handle several million requests for access to credit files every year. For the vast bulk of consumers all the information they wish to see is provided on the credit file. The presumption remains that individuals making access requests to credit reference agencies still want access to their credit files only. However, if a consumer wishes a credit reference agency to make a wider search he is entitled to do so under s.7 of the DPA. The specific rules for access to credit information are covered below.

---

[31] "Disproportionate Effort—Section 8(2)", p.7.
[32] "Disproportionate Effort—Section 8(2)", p.9.
[33] "Disproportionate Effort—Section 8(2)", pp.8 and 9.

What information must be given in response to an access request?

The information that must be given will depend upon:

11–17

a) the extent of the data regarded as falling within the definition of "personal data";
b) the information the subject asks for in the particular case;
c) whether any exemptions apply; and
d) whether any of the special rules made under regulations made by the Secretary of State (described above) apply.

A data controller may have to give up to five different types of information to the requester. In summary the data controller has an obligation to:

a) confirm that processing is taking place, in other words to tell the individual whether the data controller is indeed processing information about him;
b) describe the type of processing by explaining what the purpose of the processing is, what kind of data are being processed and describing the identity of any recipients (or categories of recipients) of the personal data;
c) if available, provide the data sources by providing information either generally or specifically about where the personal data came from;
d) describe the processing logic involved, that is, provide information about the logic involved in any automatic processing (although this only applies in limited circumstances); and
e) provide an intelligible copy of the data in permanent form.

In *Johnson v Medical Defence Union*, the court stated that the primary objective of the subject access right is to make it possible for the data subject to learn what information about them is being processed by others. The entitlement to seek information as to the recipients and sources is an ancillary one:

> "The primary objective of the DPA is to make it possible for a data subject to learn what personal data are being processed by others. The entitlement to seek information as to the recipients of the data and the sources of them is ancillary to that. Accordingly, it seems to me that the words 'sources of that data' in section 7(1)(c)(ii) should be construed narrowly".[34]

By the same logic, therefore, the other ancillary rights would fall to be narrowly construed, although this point was not canvassed in the judgment.

Obligation to confirm that processing is taking place

The first category of information the requester needs to know is whether the data controller is processing personal data about him at all. In some cases individuals make subject access requests under the misapprehension that a particular data controller holds information on them. The data controller should always respond to a request even if only to tell the inquirer that he holds no personal data about

11–18

---

[34] [2004] EWHC 347, para.55.

him. Before making any such response the data controller must ensure that a thorough search of his data is carried out so he can be confident his answer is accurate. A data controller is entitled to ask the inquirer for additional information to help him make this search, particularly in relation to archived data (see above). The data controller's right to seek additional information may be particularly important given the extent and disparate and dispersed nature of some larger data controller's electronic data repositories.

Obligation to describe the processing

11–19   The subject access rights involve describing the type of processing and providing information about data sources. Under the 1984 Act if an individual wanted to research this information he had to go to the public register for it rather than directly to the data user involved. If the data user was a large organisation with many entries on the public register (and some public bodies could have over 90 separate purposes listed) it could be difficult for the individual to decide which purposes related to him and, having ascertained those purposes, to work out which of the listed disclosures might relate to him. The information was inevitably set out in general terms on the register and not targeted at each individual data subject. A further complicating factor for the requester was that the categories of information were not related to one another on the public register.

11–20   Under the DPA the data controller has to provide some of that information directly to the individual if he asks for it. The information can still be provided in general terms but the data controller has to select and supply that which is relevant to the particular data subject. The data controller must provide a description of the type of personal data held on the subject, the purposes for which such are held and the recipients of those personal data. A description of the type of personal data is likely to be acceptable even if given in general terms, although, where sensitive data are involved, a particular description of those data should probably be given. It is not clear at what level of detail the purposes for which personal data are to be held will have to be described. Logically the purpose description might be expected to provide more information than the subject already knows, but in practice it seems controllers are providing it at quite a high level.

11–21   A data controller does not have to list the names of the people to whom he may disclose particular personal data. It is open to him to describe them in general terms instead – such people are described as "recipients" of personal data. The term is defined in s.70 of the DPA and means anyone to whom personal data are disclosed, including an employee or agent of the data controller. It does not, however, include anyone to whom disclosure is made as a result of or with a view to a particular inquiry made in exercise of any power conferred by law. Therefore, the term includes those who process personal data under any authority of the data controller but not public authorities which obtain personal data from data controllers in pursuance of their statutory functions. A data controller, therefore, must describe those to whom he passes information except where it is disclosed in the course of the statutory inquiry or other inquiry made in exercise of a legal power. For example, a data controller would not have to name the Inland

Revenue as a "recipient" if he only made disclosures to it in response to statutory requests for information. This exemption appears in the Directive but the reasoning behind its existence is not apparent; perhaps the drafters were working under the apprehension that it is obvious that data controllers would make such disclosures under such circumstances.

Obligation to provide data sources

Data controllers have to provide "any available information" as to the source of **11–22** the data subject's personal data. Curiously, the obligation is not mirrored by an obligation to retain records evidencing where the information came from– therefore it is up to the data controller to decide how much information he wishes to keep about the sources of his personal data. This, somewhat counter-intuitive position was confirmed by Hickinbottom J. in *Ezsias v Welsh Ministers*:

> "The obligation under Section 7(1)(c)(ii) to supply sources of information is limited. There is no obligation to maintain records of such sources – but only to supply them if they are available in recorded form. There appears to be no evidence that the National Assembly have any such records in relation to the source of the information sought by Mr Ezsias".[35]

Where a data controller has information as to the source of personal data available to him (i.e., it is within his knowledge), even if it is not formally "recorded" anywhere, it may be that a well-governed controller would disclose such information as a matter of course in any event. If a data controller does record such information it will have to be given to the data subject in order to satisfy his subject access request. This applies even if the information about the sources is not of itself held as "data" covered by the DPA as the scope of the obligation is undefined, covering "any *information* available to the data controller". There is no definition as to what counts as "available". In the case of *Johnson v Medical Defence Union* the court held that the data subject's right to be told about the recipients and sources of his personal data was "ancillary" and should be narrowly defined:

> "It does not cover every hand through which the data have passed. It does not include the postman or the secretarial and administrative personnel whose job it is to do no more than assemble or deliver material".[36]

In reality many data controllers retain records of the sources of their personal data and will therefore be obliged to disclose them. However, the DPA does not specify the level of detail at which such information must be given and it may be acceptable to provide it in general terms. The obligation is further tempered by the provisions relating to information about third parties. Where the information about recipients or sources reveals the identity of other third party individuals the rules relating to the disclosure of third party personal information will apply. It should be noted that the requirement to provide available information about

---

[35] Claim No.6CF90111, November 23, 2007, para.78(ii).
[36] [2004] EWHC 347, para.55.

sources in response to a subject access request is not mirrored by a corresponding provision in the notification scheme—sources of personal data do not have to be notified on the public register.

Obligation to describe the processing logic

11–23   If specifically requested to do so, a data controller must inform the data subject of the "logic involved" in any decision-taking where automatic processing has constituted or is likely to constitute the *sole* basis for any decision significantly affecting him. This has its origins in art.15 of the Directive and in order to understand the provision it helps to consider art.15(1):

> "... produces legal effects concerning [the data subject] or significantly affects him and which is based solely on automated processing of data intended to evaluate certain personal aspects relating to him such as his performance at work, creditworthiness, reliability or conduct, etc."

One of the fundamental concerns of those framing the Directive was to ensure that individuals should not become subservient to machines—that human values and judgments should always be paramount. One manifestation of this approach is the provision dealing with automated decisions which affect individuals. Individuals have a right to object to important decisions being taken about them solely by automated means. In support of this right to object, individuals are also entitled to access information about any such processing as part of the subject access right. As is clear from the wording of art.15, the information only has to be given where the processing constitutes, or is likely to constitute, the basis for a decision "significantly affecting" the data subject.

11–24   It is not clear from s.7(1)(d) how detailed the explanation of the logic involved in the decision-making system should be. Data controllers hardly wish to provide details of how their decision-making systems work, particularly where such may be proprietary. Therefore, there is a tendency for data controllers to provide information only in the most general terms. Section 8(5) makes it clear that if the information about the logic involved in the decision-making system constitutes a "trade secret" then it does not have to be provided to the data subject. The DPA does not define "trade secrets", but the Law Commission, in a consultation paper on trade secrets, suggested a provisional definition as covering:

> "... information which is not generally known, which derives its value from that fact and as to which its owner has indicated (expressly or implied) his or her wish to preserve its quality of secrecy".[37]

In a Court of Appeal case[38] in the context of employment law, it was held that a trade secret must consist of specific information used in the business which can fairly be regarded as the employer's property and disclosure of which would harm the employer's business.

---

[37] Law Commission, *Legislating the Criminal Code: Misuse of Trade Secrets* (December 1997), para.1.29.

[38] *FSS Travel and Leisure Systems Ltd v Johnson* [1998] I.R.L.R. 382.

Obligation to provide information constituting the personal data

This is the core informational right, the prospect of which caused such outrage to some of Lindop's witnesses in 1978. The data controller must open his files and provide the individual with access to the information he holds and may only withhold information if he can bring himself within one of the exemptions. **11–25**

The extent of the information which may be involved depends on the view which is taken of the definition of "personal data". Personal data means data:

"which relate to a living individual who can be identified from the data or from that and other information in the possession of, or likely to come into the possession of, the data controller and including any expression of opinion about the individual".[39]

The definition is no longer cut down, as it was under the 1984 Act, by the requirement that the data must be processed by "reference to the data subject" or by the exemption for data used only for text processing. The definition has been considered in the context of subject access requests in the cases of *Durant v Financial Services Authority*,[40] *Johnson v Medical Defence Union*[41] and *Smith v Lloyds TSB Bank Plc.*[42]

In both *Johnson* and *Smith*[43] the applicants were unsuccessful in trying to persuade the courts to take a wide view of the term "data". In both cases the materials which the applicants wanted were held in manual files which would not be covered by the right of access. However, information in those files had originally been produced on a word processor or other computing equipment. In both cases the court rejected the applications and made it clear that the information must be held as "data" at the time the subject request is made – thus dismissing the "once data always data" line of argument submitted on behalf of the applicants.

The term "personal data" has also been narrowly construed by the courts in the United Kingdom. In the *Durant v Financial Services Authority*, Auld L.J. applied a narrow meaning to the term. In doing so he took into account the addition to the definition of the words:

"and includes any expressions of opinion about the individual and any indication of the intentions of the data controller or any other person in respect of the individual",

remarking that, if the term "personal data" had the broad construction which the applicant argued for such provision would have been otiose.[44] It is perhaps regrettable that the provenance of the additional verbiage was not drawn to the attention of the court. Commentators had previously suggested that in fact the proviso was otiose, having been inserted as an "avoidance of doubt" provision because the previous definition in the 1984 Act excluded such matters. The court also took into account the practicalities of the matter, arguing that the fact that the

---

[39] DPA s.1(1).
[40] [2003] EWCA Civ 1746.
[41] [2004] EWHC 2509 (Ch).
[42] [2005] EWHC 246 (Ch) (February 23, 2005).
[43] [2005] EWHC 246 (Ch), para.14.
[44] [2003] EWCA Civ 1746, para.29.

data controller has only 40 days to respond to a request and is only paid a fee of £10, emphasises that the obligation on the data controller is to recover data which are kept in such a way that they can be recovered quickly and cheaply. Auld L.J. recognised that it can be difficult to decide what information "relates to" an individual and offered two "tests" to apply when the data controller is in doubt on the point; whether the information is "biographically significant" and has the individual as its "focus", in short information which affects his privacy. In practice these tests can be difficult to apply as they are open to subjective evaluationswhich vary from data controller to data controller.

In *Johnson* the court followed the ruling in *Durant* as far as the evaluation of the term "personal data" was concerned. But it also considered the position where individual paragraphs in a document may not have the requester has their focus when considered in insolation from each other, but when taken together the whole document may be said to constitute the requester's personal data. This deals helpfully with a point that many data controllers wrestle with when dealing with subject access requests; namely at what level of granularity should the rules on whether the information is "personal data" be applied? It also demonstrated the difficulty in applying the "tests" suggested in *Durant*.[45]

Mr Johnson was a surgeon who had had various dealings with the medical defence union who had provided him with professional indemnity insurance. Mr Johnson exercised his right to subject access after the MDU refused to renew his policy. One of the sets of documents the court considered was a summary of the occasions on which Mr Johnson had sought advice or assistance from the MDU in relation to allegations made against him by patients. The totality of the document covered about five pages. Individual entries in the document would précis the date and nature of the advice sought on each occasion. The judge considered one particular entry which recorded the name of the patient and the MDU officer who had dealt with the enquiry and took the view that the entry did not contain Mr Johnson's personal data. The focus was the patient, not the surgeon. On the other hand the totality of the document was about Mr Johnson:

> "The difference between this type of summary and the individual entries is significant. If the individual entries are not personal data, then section 7(1) does not apply and the data subject has no entitlement either to the data or the information about the origin and dissemination of them. On the other hand if the complete summary is personal data, as I think it is, then section 7(1) does apply. Mr Johnson is prima facie entitled to be given a description of that personal data and relevant information about the origin and dissemination of that summary".

It would appear from this that when the data controller considers whether materials meet the criteria for "personal data" he must have regard to the totality of the document and if the document, taken as a whole, can be said to be about the data subject he must provide that document. Following *R. v Chief Constable of B County Constabulary and the Director of the National Identification Service Ex p. R*,[46] information is not to be artificially divided into small tranches in order to avoid disclosure.

---

[45] [2003] EWCA Civ 1746.
[46] Unreported, November 1997.

The data controller must examine all the data held to decide which data are covered by the definition of "personal data". The obligation is, however, to provide the "information constituting" the personal data and not the original documentation itself. In the case of *R v Secretary of State for the Home Department Ex p. Lord*[47]counsel for a Category A highly dangerous prisoner argued that the necessary implication of reading s.7(5) ("and so much of the information sought by the request as can be communicated without disclosing the identity") and s.8(2) ("a copy of the information in permanent form") together is that the data controller *must* disclose the *original* documentation and may not provide a copy. This argument was not accepted by the judge. This finding was confirmed in *Durant*.[48]

11–26

The extent of the obligation to disclose personal data was first considered in *R. v Secretary of State for the Home Department Ex p. Lord*.[49] In that case a Category A prisoner sought subject access to reports prepared by prison staff and other professionals involved in making recommendations re his re-classification to a category less than "highly dangerous". The practice of the prison service was to produce a summary of the content of all the reports—known as the "gist"—and provide only the gist to the prisoner; the reports in their entirety were not provided. A number of issues arose in the case but one of the points made in the judgment was that the gist did not reflect the full content of all of the reports to which the prisoner was entitled pursuant to his s.7(1) application.[50]

Subject access to emails

The obligation to provide all the data subject's personal data includes personal data in emails. This has proved to be a considerable burden for data controllers because of the very nature of email as a medium.

11–27

Emails have a number of specific features which affect the provision of subject access, they:

a)   may have been deleted from live systems but retained as archived material or back-up;

b)   may have been deleted by the sender or recipient but not erased from the system;

c)   may be held locally on stand-alone PCs or laptops and not available to the system administrator;

d)   are likely to contain third party data, at least in the details of the sender or recipient;

e)   may be informal or unguarded in tone and/or content; and

f)   may be "private" to the sender or recipient.

Data controllers can face problems in locating personal data held in emails, in retrieving such data from their systems and in deciding whether any third party data should be provided in response to a subject access request. Another hurdle

---

[47] [2003] EWHC 2073 (Admin) (September 1, 2003).
[48] [2003] EWCA Civ 1746, para.26.
[49] [2003] EWHC 2073 (Admin) (September 1, 2003).
[50] [2003] EWHC 2073 (Admin), para.164.

which data controllers are forced to overcome frequently can be a requester's misapprehension that every email which they have received or sent constitutes their personal data; particularly so in the employment context. Many requesters complain that they have not received all the information that they are entitled to pursuant to a s.7 request when they do not receive copies of every email received or sent as part of the discharge of their job role. Increasingly, data controllers are responding to requesters with a brief summary of what they are (and importantly are not) entitled to receive pursuant to their employer receiving a s.7 request. Some are even going so far as to explain the difference between the right to receive copies of documents under the Rules of Civil Procedure (discovery) and the right to receive "personal data" under the DPA. As Auld L.J. states in *Durant v Financial Services Authority*:

> "[s.7]…is not an automatic key to any information, readily accessible or not, of matters in which he may be named or involved. Nor is it to assist him, for example, to obtain discovery of documents that may assist him in litigation or complaints against third parties".[51]

The Information Commissioner's view in advice given in 2001 (but which no longer appears on the website) was that emails which contain information about identifiable living individuals will be caught by a request for subject access unless they have been printed off, the electronic version wholly deleted and the hard copy version stored in a file which does not fall within the definition of a "relevant filing system". His view was that:

> "even though data may have been 'deleted' from the live system, the emails will be caught if they can be recovered by, say, the systems administrator before their final destruction".

The tone of the advice indicated that the Commissioner was aware of the problems that giving access to emails presents for data controllers. It acknowledged that the Information Commissioner has discretion as to whether to take enforcement action and considered the exercise of that discretion and the matters that would be taken into account before concluding:

> "to summarise, the Commissioner's approach is that where emails are held on live systems and can be located, she [sic] will seek to enforce subject access if this has been denied. Where data are held elsewhere the Commissioner will weigh the interests of the data subject against the effort that the controller would have to take to recover the data and in many instances may be likely to decide not to take action".

The Information Commissioner's stance appears to have hardened somewhat since that Guidance. The current "Disproportionate Effort—Section 8(2) Guidance" specifically draws out emails as an example of "difficult to access personal data":

> "Where a data controller receives an access request that may include personal data held in emails, if the emails have been archived and removed from the 'live' system

---

[51] [2003] EWCA Civ 1746, para.27.

it may be particularly difficult for a data controller to locate personal data in particular messages ... Usually, once the relevant emails have been found, the cost of supplying a copy of the personal data contained within them (the task to which the proportionality test applies) is unlikely to be prohibitive. A data controller cannot therefore refuse to comply with a subject access request on the basis that it would involve disproportionate effort simply because it would be costly and time-consuming to locate the requested personal data held in archived emails".[52]

Both sets of advice acknowledge that the data subject may still seek to take action through the courts should he believe his access rights have not been met, despite the Information Commissioner refusing to take enforcement action because he believes the data controller has acted reasonably:

> "A decision by the Commissioner not to take action against a data controller does not deny the data subject the right to seek access to the information through the courts".[53]

Given their prevalence as the preferred mode of communication in both the business and personal sphere, there remains a compliance risk for data controllers associated with subject access to emails unless their data retention policies are particularly clear and well adhered to. Further, for many data controllers there may be a massive cost in tracing and considering emails pursuant to receipt of an access request. The importance of a robust, clear and consistently enforced email policy as part of a broader policy dealing with electronic communications cannot be stressed strongly enough.

Access to other data

It must be borne in mind there is no distinction between "official" or "business"   **11–28**
data and "personal data". Information about sole traders or partners in a partnership or, in some circumstances, directors of a company may all be personal data and liable to be given in response to a subject access request.

In the same way, subject access requests will cover some forms of manual data. The DPA governs manual data which are held within a "relevant filing system" (s.1(1)). This means:

> "any set of information relating to individuals to the extent that the set is structured either by reference to the individuals, or criteria relating to individuals, in such a way that particular information relating to a particular individual is readily accessible".

The definition was considered in *Durant v Financial Services Authority* in which the Court of Appeal took a narrow approach to the definition which should be applied. A detailed discussion of this provision is found in Ch.2; however, it certainly incorporated sophisticated manual filing systems which meet the criteria laid down by Auld L.J.:

---

[52] "Information Commissioner's Guidance: Disproportionate Effort—Section 8(2)", p.5.
[53] "Information Commissioner's Guidance: Disproportionate Effort—Section 8(2)", p.8.

"... the [1998] Act's extension of its provisions to manual records in the formula in the definition "although the information is not processed by means of equipment operating automatically in response to instructions given for that purpose", indicates that it does so only to the extent that such records are broadly comparable with computerised records in terms of ease of access to and retrievability of data in them".[54]

A further difficult issue for data controllers to resolve in dealing with subject access requests is dealing with third party personal data comingled with the personal data of the requester.

Data about other living individuals

11–29   Just as our lives are rarely lived in isolation so information about us is rarely held in neat discrete packages. One record will often include facts about a range of people. Medical records will show which health professionals have treated a patient; banking records may show which members of staff handled a transaction; local authority housing records will include details of joint tenants at a property and possibly information about others in their households; and police reports will include the identities of the officers who compiled them.

Where an individual asks for access to a record which includes information about others as well as about himself two equally legitimate, but often conflicting, interests come into play; the interest of the requester in having a full and true picture of the information which relates to him and the interest of the other party who features in the record (referred to throughout this section as the "third party"[55]) in maintaining his privacy. There are special rules for the disclosure of third party data where the information falls under the modification orders dealing with social work, education and health records which are covered in Ch.16.

Section 7(4)–(6) of the DPA attempts to set out a code for data controllers to follow to strike a balance between these two competing interests. Unfortunately, some aspects of the code are expressed obliquely. This section explains the background to the provisions and examines how they may be applied in practice.

The United Kingdom used the introduction of the DPA to honour its commitment to incorporate the 1988 decision of the ECHR in *Gaskin v United Kingdom*[56] into its laws. To understand these provisions it is helpful to have an outline of the Gaskin case.

11–30   The plaintiff was in the care of Liverpool City Council during his childhood, which was not a settled one. On reaching adulthood he sought to sue the council for negligence for failing to provide proper care for him as a child. He sought discovery of his personal social work files under the Administration of Justice Act 1970. Initially the council refused to provide them as the records also contained information about third parties such as social workers who had handled his case, doctors, foster parents and others who had been involved in his care. Mr Gaskin took the council to court and after various proceedings and detailed reconsideration of the issues, Liverpool City Council agreed to provide him with

---

[54] [2003] EWCA Civ 1746 (December 8, 2003), para.42.
[55] Not to be confused with the definition of "third party" given in s.70 of the DPA.
[56] [1990] 1 F.L.R. 167.

some of the information he sought. However, in the interim, the Government had stepped in and issued its own guidance on the disclosure of social services records. The Attorney General obtained an injunction to restrain the council from providing all the information sought. Eventually it was resolved that records could be provided, but only with the consent of the third parties. If any of those people either could not be contacted, or refused to give permission then the information would have to be withheld.

Mr Gaskin then took his case to the Court of Human Rights in Strasbourg under arts.8 and 10 of the Human Rights Convention. He claimed that the failure of the State to provide access to his records was a breach of his right to a private life. The court gave its judgment in 1989, holding that he had a right under art.8 to access the records of his childhood as without these he was unable to develop his understanding of himself. However, where information related to others, the public authority should ask such third parties to give permission for the disclosure of their information. If a third party was not available to be asked or unreasonably refused permission, then there should be some provision to allow the case to be reviewed and any third party's refusal to be overridden in appropriate cases. In short, the court took the view that there had to be a mechanism for an independent arbiter to balance the competing rights involved in any individual case.

Is the third party information personal data about the requester?

The data controller only has to undertake the above mentioned balancing exercise   **11–31** where the information relating to the third party forms part of the personal data of the applicant. If it does not do so the question of any balance to be struck never arises.

Who is the third party and what does the requester know about them?

A data controller faced with a subject access request needs to establish whether   **11–32** the records relating to the requester include "third party" data at all. Although this may sound like a simple question, it involves quite a complex test. A "third party" is anyone who the requester is likely to be able to identify. Section 7(4) refers to this as "information relating to another person who can be identified from that information" but it must be read in conjunction with s.8(7) which makes it clear that for these purposes this means that either the:

- information on its own is sufficient to identify the third party to a recipient who does not have any special knowledge; or
- data controller has reasonable grounds to believe that the information is sufficient to identify the third party to the data subject because of knowledge the subject either has or is likely to get hold of.

The data controller is, therefore, faced with considerable uncertainty in those cases where the information about the third party would not on its own be sufficient to identify him, because he must consider what the data subject is likely to know or be able to ascertain about that third party. Accordingly, data controllers have to have regard to what they know about the requester to make a judgment. It is not easy to see how a data controller is able to reach any reasonable assessment in the absence of special knowledge about the requester himself.

If the data are "third party" data, the data controller then has to decide whether or not to disclose them to the requester.

Consent

11–33   There is no statutory obligation on the data controller under the DPA to seek the third party's consent to the disclosure of their personal data to a requester. However, if the third party does grant his consent to the disclosure, then their personal data can always be given to the requester. The form the consent should be given in is not specified in the DPA but the discussion on consent in Ch.3 is relevant here. Data controllers are advised that it would be prudent to obtain clear written consent, particularly before giving information which may prove sensitive if disclosed. Although there is no clear obligation on data controllers to consider whether third party consent should be, or can be obtained, it is suggested that data controllers should do so.

Third party data may be provided to a data subject without the consent of the third party if "it is reasonable in all circumstances" so to do. This is a broadly drawn provision, but the data controller is given some help by s.7(6), which sets out a number of factors to which particular regard should be had in deciding this point. It is clear that the data controller is expected to address his mind to the question of "reasonableness" and not apply a blanket policy of providing or refusing to give third party data.[57] The factors listed are referred to as "particular" factors so are not the only ones to be taken into account and the data controller must consider whether other factors are relevant too. The provisions were considered in *Durant v Financial Services Authority* in which the court took the view that the provisions appear to create a presumption that the information relating to the third party, including his identity, should *not* be disclosed without his consent:

> "...the provisions appear to create a presumption or starting point that the information relating to that other, including his identity, should not be disclosed without his consent. The presumption may, however, be rebutted if the data controller considers that it is reasonable 'in all the circumstances...'".[58]

The statutory factors to which regard must be given are:

a)   any duty of confidentiality owed to the third party;
b)   any steps taken by the data controller with a view to seeking the consent of the third party;
c)   whether the third party is capable of giving consent; and
d)   any express refusal of consent by the third party.

---

[57] *R. v Secretary of State for the Home Department* [2003] EWHC 2073 (Admin) (September 1, 2003).
[58] [2003] EWCA Civ 1746, para.55.

Although the subsection lists the factors to which regard is to be had, it does not say how they are to be balanced or what weight is to be given to each factor. The twin issues which have to be balanced here are "confidentiality" and "consent".

Confidentiality

Some relationships are characterised by confidentiality, for example that between doctor and patient. Where there is an obligation of confidence the party to whom information is confided may not divulge it unless he has legitimate grounds to do so. The grounds on which an obligation of confidence does not apply or can be breached are:

11–34

a)   where the confider consents;
b)   where there is a legal compulsion to make the disclosure; or
c)   where there is an overriding public interest in the disclosure.

An obligation of confidence can arise in any relationship if the right circumstances exist. In order for an obligation to arise, the information must be:

a)   "confidential in nature", i.e., it must not be in the public domain;
b)   substantive, i.e., more than "mere tittle-tattle"[59]; and
c)   imparted, or otherwise coming into the possession of the party, in circumstances which lead to an expectation of confidentiality.[60]

At first sight, the wording of s.27(5) might seem to imply that an obligation of confidence could be overridden by the right to subject access:

> "except as provided by this Part... the subject information provisions shall have effect notwithstanding any enactment or rule of law prohibiting or restricting the disclosure, or authorising the withholding of information".

This subsection, therefore, could be understood to have the effect that an obligation of confidence is simply to be overridden. On the other hand, the wording of s.7(6)(a) that regard shall be had to "any duty of confidentiality owed to the other individual" suggests that the obligation is not overridden.

The position is not clear, but appears to be that confidentiality will not act as a prohibition on disclosure of the third party's information provided the test in s.7(4)(a) is satisfied, i.e., it is "reasonable in all the circumstances to comply with the request without the consent of the individual". In these circumstances, however, the third party might still seek to enforce his confidentiality and argue that the disclosure without his consent was not reasonable. Therefore, a data controller who has to decide whether to give access to third party confidential data always runs the risk of a breach of confidence action brought by the third party where the disclosure is made without his consent.

---

[59] *Coco v Clark (Engineers)* [1969] R.P.C. 41.
[60] See Ch.2 for a discussion of the law of confidence.

11–35   What does s.7(6)(a) therefore involve? Confidentiality is not an overriding consideration which will stop the disclosure of the third party data, but equally the data controller has no guaranteed protection if he does disclose. On the face of it the data controller is left between a rock and a hard place. The answer appears to lie in the subsections which deal with consent. Although the section is worded so that there appears to be no obligation to seek the third party's consent, even where it would be practical to do so, in cases where there is an obligation of confidence and it is possible to seek consent the data controller would be well advised to do so, particularly those data controllers in the public sector who will be subject to public law remedies.

If the data controller obtains the third party's consent he can disclose the data. It seems reasonable to assume that a private sector data controller is entitled to take his own interests into account in determining whether it is "reasonable in all the circumstances" to provide a third party's data, although s.7(4)(a) does not explicitly say so and the contrary might be argued. If the third party refuses to give their consent, the data controller arguably has a legitimate basis on which to withhold the third party's data.

Clearly there may be cases where it is impossible or impractical to obtain a third party's consent. In such cases the data controller must still consider whether it is reasonable in all the circumstances to provide a third party's data. The data controller can, of course, only weigh those circumstances known to him and inevitably his knowledge may be deficient or partial. The sort of considerations a data controller may bear in mind are:

a)   the nature of the data about the third party, in particular whether it might be damaging if disclosed, or cause harm or bad feeling between the parties;
b)   the nature of the third party's role. There will be less justification for withholding information about someone who acted in a formal and official capacity for example a nurse or a lawyer than someone who acted in a private and personal capacity;
c)   whether it is likely that the data are already known to the data subject or are readily ascertainable to him; and
d)   whether the information might be of particular importance to the data subject for example in pursuing some legitimate claim or interest which can be weighed against the competing interests of the third party.

11–36   In *Durant v Financial Services Authority*[61] the Court of Appeal confirmed that much of the balancing test will depend on the nature of the information and its legitimate value to the requester. The point was considered in detail in *Re Lord*[62] where one of the justifications for the disclosure to the prisoner of the "gist" rather than the provision of the reports themselves was to protect the identities of the authors and the opinions which they expressed. The authors of the reports had not consented to their disclosure to the prisoner and "there will, historically, have been some expectation on their part of confidentiality".[63] The argument was made on behalf of the Secretary of State that the mere redaction of the names of

---

[61] [2003] EWCA Civ 1746.
[62] [2003] EWHC 2073 (Admin) (September 1, 2003).
[63] [2003] EWHC 2073 (Admin), (September 1, 2003), para.146.

the authors would not be sufficient to protect their identities as it would be apparent to the applicant which reports emanated from, e.g., a psychologist or his wing manager and that there was a potential risk to the report writers if their contents were disclosed to highly dangerous prisoners.

Giving judgment, Mr Justice Munby did not accept that the balance could be struck by applying a blanket policy of non-disclosure of third party data:

> "The blanket policy of non-disclosure of anything which is not contained in the gist is not, in my judgment, a proportionate response...The Secretary of States' present blanket policy is not, in my judgment, a "necessary measure" to safeguard...the interest of the authors of the reports".[64]

Munby J. accepted that the authors of the reports were themselves data subjects and had important privacy interests which had to be considered in the balancing act. He also accepted that there had historically been some expectation of confidentiality, albeit not absolute. He held that the balance between the legitimate interests of the prisoner and the officials had to be struck on case-by-case basis and the blanket policy of non-disclosure of third party data by the use of the "gist" system could not be justified.

Following this analysis, we can see there appear to be three broad categories of third party information: **11–37**

a)   information where there is no obligation of confidence and no concern or sensitivity attached to disclosure. In those cases it is reasonable to give the information without asking for prior consent, although it would be advisable to notify the third party of the disclosure;

b)   information subject to a clear duty of confidence. The third party's consent should be sought to disclose the information. If consent is given the information should be provided. If consent is not given or cannot be sought, the data controller must undertake a balancing test, but would need strong reasons to disclose the third party's data, thus overriding the obligation of confidence; and

c)   information where there is no clear duty of confidence but disclosure may be sensitive and it would be prudent to seek consent before disclosing the third party's personal data. If consent is obtained the information can be given; if consent is not obtained the data controller must weigh the benefit of providing the information to the data subject against the possible harm to others that might be caused by disclosure.

In *Durant v Financial Services Authority*[65] the court also considered how far   **11–38** an appellate court should be expected to scrutinise the application of the third party rules by the data controller. The court decided not to inspect the material in dispute and took the view that the role of the court is a reviewing one rather than one which assumes the role of primary decision-maker on the merits of the case.

---

[64] [2003] EWHC 2073 (Admin), (September 1, 2003), para.148.
[65] [2003] EWCA Civ 1746, para.60.

Cases where the data controller is not obliged to provide access

11–39   Leaving aside the substantive exemptions, which are dealt with below, data controllers do not have to comply with a request where they have already complied with an "identical or similar request" by the data subject unless a "reasonable interval" has elapsed between the two.[66] Section 8(4) provides that in deciding whether the interval is "reasonable" the data controller should consider:

a)   the nature of the data;
b)   the purpose of the processing; and
c)   the frequency with which the data are altered.

Therefore, where the data are not particularly sensitive and do not need to be updated regularly because they change infrequently it may be that a data controller could refuse to fulfil a second subject access request pursuant to s.8(3) if it was received within a few months of the first. Whereas, where the data are more sensitive, changed frequently and are used to make decisions which have an on-going impact the data subject a data controller would not be able to rely on s.8(3) even where the second request was received weeks after the first.

TIME FOR RESPONSE

11–40   Having received:

a)   written request for subject access;
b)   the appropriate fee;
c)   satisfaction that he is dealing with a legitimate requester; and
d)   sufficient information to find the relevant personal data required,

the data controller then has a maximum period of 40 days within which to supply the information to the data subject.[67] Where any of the data are third party data for which consent is being sought for disclosure a separate 40-day clock ticks for those data only.

The 40-day period is allowed as a "long stop". The data controller's duty under s.7(8) is to comply with a request "promptly". The 40-day period is a prescribed period which may be varied by the Secretary of State by Order made under s.7(11) and different periods may be prescribed for different classes of request.

CHANGES IN THE PERSONAL DATA

11–41   Many data controllers must continue routine processing operations irrespective of receipt of a subject access request and the DPA allows for this. Under s.8(6), the information given must be based on the personal data held at the time the request

---

[66] DPA s.8(3).
[67] DPA s.7(10).

is received. It should be noted this appears to refer to the time of the initial request and not the receipt of the fee if that comes later or the provision of further information from the requester if that is needed to find the responsive data. However, where the data controller would have made amendments or deletions irrespective of receipt of the request these can still be made and the information can still be given based on the personal data as they are at the time of satisfying the request. This provision only allows for routine processing which would have taken place in any event and does not permit the data controller to make other changes to the data.

Offence of altering personal data

The Freedom of Information Act 2000 creates a new offence, which will apply to public sector data controllers only, of altering records after receipt of an access request under either the DPA or the Freedom of Information Act 2000 (see Ch.4 for a discussion of this provision).   **11–42**

HOW CAN THE INFORMATION BE GIVEN?

Under the 1984 Act the data controller was under a straightforward duty to supply a copy of the information constituting the personal data. For some types of data this proved cumbersome, e.g., if the data user had a massive number of records it could involve an enormous amount of work to print out those data. The DPA broadened the scope of how information may be supplied to the requester. While the usual method of dealing with a subject access request remains the supply of a copy of the information in permanent form, this is not necessary if: **11–43**

a)   the individual agrees to accept subject access in another form;
b)   the supply of a copy is not possible; or
c)   the supply of a copy would involve "disproportionate effort".[68]

There has never been a prohibition on supplying information in an alternative form if the requester consents to this. The supply of a copy may not be possible, e.g., where special medical equipment captures an image, subject access may only be possible by giving the patient an opportunity to see the information displayed using such special equipment in situ. Therefore, this provision affords the data controller a statutory basis for restricting the method by which he provides access to personal data in circumstances like these where they cannot be adequately rendered in permanent form. It is more difficult to see the basis for the third provision which allows for information to be given in an intelligible form other than hard copy where the provision of the permanent form would "involve disproportionate effort".

The "disproportionate effort" provision does not release the data controller from the obligation to provide access to the personal data in an "intelligible form", so logic dictates that it applies only to personal data which it is possible to supply in permanent form. It may assist a data controller where a large amount of

---

[68] DPA s.8(2).

information would be difficult to print, but could be transferred easily onto a disk—it may be this circumstance that the provision is intended to cover. The provision to allow a response other than in permanent form only applies to the actual personal data themselves and not to information about the processing or the logic involved in decision-making. The issue of what constitutes "disproportionate effort" was one of the points considered in *R. v Lord* in which the Secretary of State had argued that the work involved in checking an entire file to redact material which should be removed as being third party data or because it is exempt from the obligation to disclose, amounted to a disproportionate effort. The argument was not accepted by the court:

> "Section 8(2)(a) cannot justify withholding from the claimant information in the form in which he would otherwise be entitled to receive it. The administrative burden – light as it is here – has in any event to be assessed in the context of the significance of the information that is otherwise required to be disclosed. Section 8(2)(a) exonerates a data controller from 'disproportionate effort', but in determining what is proportionate one necessarily, as it seems to me, has to have regard to the intrinsic significance of the information whose disclosure is being sought and its importance to the data subject".[69]

The advice of the Information Commissioner is that it will be a question of fact as to whether the *supply* amounts to a disproportionate effort in each case. When making an assessment the Information Commissioner will take into account:

> "… the cost of provision of the information, the length of time it may take to provide the information, how difficult or otherwise it may be for the data controller to provide the information and also the size of the organization of which the request has been made. Such matters will always be balanced against the effect on the data subject".[70]

EXEMPTIONS

11–44   These are fully covered in Chs 15–16. This section includes an outline of the subject access exemptions for convenience only. A data controller may be able to claim exemptions from the obligation to disclose personal data if they fall within the following categories, but in each case there are conditions or limitations attached to the exercise of the exemption. Any exemption applies to all aspects of the subject access rights not just the supply of the personal data.

Subject access is one part of the "subject information provisions" under s.27. The other part of the subject information provisions consists of the rules about providing information to individuals contained in para.2 of Pt II of Sch.1.

National security

11–45   Any personal data or processing can be exempt from the controls in the DPA, including subject access, under s.28 if the exemption "is required for the purpose of safeguarding national security". The judge of whether this exemption applies is

---

[69] [2003] EWHC 2073 (Admin) (September 1, 2003), para.155.
[70] Information Commissioner's Legal Guidance (October 2001), p.46.

a Minister of the Crown who can provide a certificate of exemption. An individual who is refused subject access on the basis of the existence of such a certificate and is therefore directly affected by its issuance can challenge the certificate on the same grounds on which judicial review can be sought. Any such challenge will be heard by a specially constituted Information Tribunal. The Information Commissioner does not have legal standing to challenge a national security certificate, although he may apply to be heard in any proceedings brought by an affected individual.[71]

Hilton v Secretary of State for Foreign and Commonwealth Affairs[72] is one of the more recent cases where an affected individual has sought to challenge a s.28(2) certificate. Mr Hilton sought to exercise his right of subject access against his previous employer, GCHQ, in particular he was seeking information regarding:

> "whether any personal data, sensitive or otherwise, has been transferred to; other parts of the Civil Service, any regional Police Constabularies; the Security service...; the Secret Intelligence Service...; financial regulators such as the Securities and Futures Authority and the Financial Services Authority; my current or previous employers (a list is attached); any organisations outside the United Kingdom".[73]

Initially, GCHQ sought to rely on the s.28(2) certificate in relation to all personal data which it was processing about Mr Hilton except his personnel file, which he was invited to inspect. In respect of any and all other personal data GCHQ issued its standard "neither confirm nor deny" response:

> "Other than the data referred to in (i) above [the personnel file], there is therefore no data to which you are entitled to have access, and you should assume that any data, other than referred to in (i) and (ii) [his vetting file] is or is not held about you".[74]

This standard response was in line with the Respondent's policy of relying upon the s.28(2) certificate to refuse routinely to grant subject access to data other than those constituting personnel files. It is helpful in understanding this case to understand the exact remit of the Tribunal:

> "... the jurisdiction of the Tribunal under section 28(4) of the Act is limited to determining whether the Respondent had reasonable grounds for issuing the Certificate...We are not directly concerned with the issues whether GCHQ's response to the Appellant's request was justified in this particular case".[75]

The Tribunal held that the Respondent had reasonable grounds for issuing the Certificate because, in part, the Certificate requires the GCHQ to exercise their discretion in *every case*. However, such discretion does:

---

[71] The Information Commissioner successfully made such an application in *Baker v Secretary of State for the Home Department* [2001] UKHRR 1275.

[72] In the Information Tribunal (National Security Appeals Panel) (March 7, 2003).

[73] Information Tribunal (National Security Appeals Panel) (March 7, 2003), para.13.

[74] Information Tribunal (National Security Appeals Panel) (March 7, 2003), para.16.

[75] Information Tribunal (National Security Appeals Panel) (March 7, 2003), para.33.

"... permit[s] the NCND [neither confirm nor deny] reply even in a case where a definite response to the particular request would not itself be directly harmful to national security, because of the possible inference that might then be drawn in other cases whether NCND reply was given".[76]

This does not leave an affected individual without remedy, as the Tribunal pointed out:

"the appropriate statutory method of challenging the decision in an individual case is by making a complaint to the Investigatory Powers Tribunal".[77]

Crime and taxation

11–46   Personal data processed for the purposes of the "prevention or detection of crime, the apprehension or prosecution of offenders or the collection of any tax or duty or imposition of a similar nature" are exempt from the right of subject access to the extent that granting such access would prejudice those purposes. This exemption extends to anyone to whom the data are transferred for a statutory purpose. The exemption in s.29 largely reproduces the exemption in its predecessor, s.28 of the 1984 Act, although the DPA extends the provision by including risk assessment information as potentially exempt too. The impact of the exemption and the approach to be taken to it in the context of subject access was considered in *R v Lord*,[78] in which the court confirmed that exemption should not be applied as part of a blanket policy, rather its application must be assessed on a case-by-case basis and the degree of risk evaluated in a realistic manner:

"What section...requires, like section 29(1), is in this context a more selective and targeted approach to non-disclosure, based on the circumstances of the particular case".[79]

Health, social work and education

11–47   Section 30(1) of the DPA provides that the Secretary of State may by Order exempt personal data from the subject information provisions or modify those provisions in relation to personal data consisting of information as to the "physical or mental health or condition of the data subject". The relevant Order is The Data Protection (Subject Access Modification) (Health) Order 2000 (SI 2000/413). The terms of the Order are discussed in full in Ch.16. The presumption, where personal data are governed by this Order, is against disclosure except where medical authorisation has been obtained. The Information Commissioner's Guidance states:

"... the information should not be provided unless the appropriate health professional (also defined) has been consulted. The exception to the rule is where the data controller already has a written opinion from the appropriate health professional obtained within the previous six months that an exemption to the right

---

[76] Information Tribunal (National Security Appeals Panel) (March 7, 2003), para.41.
[77] Information Tribunal (National Security Appeals Panel) (March 7, 2003), para.51.
[78] [2003] EWHC 2073 (Admin) (September 1, 2003).
[79] [2003] EWHC 2073 (Admin), (September 1, 2003), para.49.

of subject access exists because the disclosure is likely to cause serious harm to the physical or mental health of the data subject or any other person".[80]

Section 30(3) provides for the modification of access rights in the case of social work information and s.30(2) for education information. The relevant Orders are the Data Protection (Subject Access Modification) (Social Work) Order 2000 (SI 2000/415) and The Data Protection (Subject Access Modification) (Education) Order 2000 (SI 2000/414) respectively. All three Orders include special provisions dealing with third party data.

Regulatory activity

This exemption applies on a case by case basis where access to information would prejudice any of the wide list of regulatory activities which fall within s.31. In most circumstances only data controllers who have a regulatory function can rely on these exemptions.

11–48

Journalism, art and literature

Subject access is included among the widespread exemptions potentially applicable where processing is undertaken for any of these purposes with a view to publication and where the data controller reasonably believes that the publication is in the public interest and the provision of subject access would be incompatible with these purposes.

11–49

Research, historical and statistical information

Personal data are exempt where they are processed for the research purposes and are not used to make individual decisions provided the processing does not cause damage or distress to the individual and the research itself does not identify any individual data subject (see Ch.18).

11–50

Other available exemptions

11–51

a)   personal data which are publicly available[81];
b)   Crown employment or ministerial appointments where they fall under SI 2000/416;
c)   personal data used only for domestic purposes[82];
d)   confidential references in some cases[83];
e)   personal data relating to the Armed Forces in some cases[84];
f)   personal data relating to judicial appointments and honours[85];
g)   personal data used for management forecasts or planning in some cases[86];

---

[80] Information Commissioner's Legal Guidance (October 2001), p.48.
[81] DPA s.34.
[82] DPA s.36.
[83] DPA Sch.7, para.1.
[84] DPA Sch.7, para.2.
[85] DPA Sch.7, para.3.
[86] DPA Sch.7, para.5.

h)   personal data relevant to negotiations with the requester in some cases[87];

i)   personal data processed in relation to corporate finance under SI 2000/184[88];

j)   examination marks for a period of time[89];

k)   examination scripts[90];

l)   information relating to human embryos, adoption or related matters where they fall under SI 2000/1865;

m)   legal professional privilege[91];

n)   information which would breach the privilege against self-incrimination[92]; and

o)   personnel information about public sector employees held in unstructured manual form.[93]

RELATIONSHIP WITH OTHER LEGAL CONSTRAINTS

11–52   A large number of statutes restrict the disclosure of information about individuals, e.g., s.59 of the DPA itself. Under this section, subject to certain specified exceptions, it is an offence for the Information Commissioner (and past occupiers of the role), his staff or agents to disclose any information relating to an identified or identifiable individual or business which has been provided to the Information Commissioner's office for the purpose of the information acts. In the case of s.59 those exceptions include a provision to allow disclosure with the consent of the individual.

Compliance with a subject access request will often entail the disclosure of information which would otherwise be restricted. The DPA negates the conflict between such restrictions and the right of subject access in s.27(5) which provides that, except as provided by Pt IV of that DPA, the subject access provisions shall prevail over any rule of law or legislation forbidding access. This means that a data controller must give precedence to the right of subject access where there otherwise would be a conflict.

In *R v Lord*[94] the Secretary of State argued that the fact that prisoners could have access to some material under other arrangements in effect displaced the right of access under the DPA. A practice of providing prisoners with information about reports (the "gist") had been instituted following the decision of the court in *R. v Secretary of State for the Home Department Ex p. McAvoy*.[95] The court did not accept that submission—the prisoner's statutory right to apply for subject access was not displaced by the existing administrative arrangements. By the same token, the courts have held that the mere fact that a data subject was unsuccessful in obtaining subject access to personal data under the provisions of

---

[87] DPA Sch.7, para.7.
[88] DPA Sch.7, para.6.
[89] DPA Sch.7, para.8.
[90] DPA Sch.7, para.9.
[91] DPA Sch.7, para.10.
[92] DPA Sch.7, para.11.
[93] Inserted by Freedom of Information Act 2005.
[94] [2003] EWHC 2073 (Admin) (September 1, 2003).
[95] [1998] 1 W.L.R. 790.

the DPA does not debar him from exercising his rights to access information under other regimes, e.g. the Civil Procedure Rules.

In *Johnson v Medical Defence Union*, Mr Johnson sought pre-action disclosure under the Civil Procedure Rules having been unsuccessful in his attempt to gain access to information held by the MDU under s.7. The MDU resisted the application on the basis that the court had already heard and determined Mr Johnson's application for access to information. The attempted defence was rejected by the court, which held that these were two completely separate causes of action and Mr Johnson remained able to exercise his rights under the Civil Procedure Rules despite the failure of his subject access application. Laddie J. held:

> "I have only considered the broad question of principle, namely whether it is open to Mr Johnson to seek disclosure under the CPR notwithstanding the failure of his s. 7(9) application...I have found, there is no fetter on Mr Johnson making his application".[96]

REMEDIES FOR FAILURE TO GIVE SUBJECT ACCESS

The data controller faces the possibility of action by either the Information Commissioner or the individual data subject if he fails to provide proper subject access.

11–53

Data subject remedies

A data subject can apply to a court under s.7(9) for a specific Order to compel the data controller to provide the information which he has failed to disclose. This right exists independently from the general right of a data subject to seek compensation if a contravention of any of the requirements of the DPA has caused him loss or damage.[97] The general compensation right is covered in Ch.14 but it should be borne in mind that if an application is made to court on behalf of the data subject under s.7(9), consideration as to whether any additional loss has been incurred should be taken into account and the possibility of making a s.13 application should be considered at the same time.

11–54

Before making an Order under s.7(9), the court has to be satisfied that a valid request has been made and that the data controller has not provided the information as and when he should have done. The jurisdiction is exercisable by the county court or the High Court in England and Wales or a Sheriff Court in Scotland.[98] In *R. v Lord* the court held that there is no obligation on the data subject to make an application to the Information Commissioner first before being entitled to make an application to the court.

The extent of the discretion available to the court hearing a s.7(9) application has been considered in a number of cases. In *P v Wozencroft (expert evidence: Data Protection)*[99] the court held that it has a discretion as to whether to order the

---

[96] [2004] EWHC 2509 (Ch) (November 9, 2004), para.30.
[97] DPA s.13.
[98] DPA s.15(1).
[99] [2002] 2 F.L.R. 1118.

disclosure of personal data even where as a matter of fact it finds the data controller had withheld them inappropriately. In this case, the applicant argued unsuccessfully that as s.7(1) provides that an individual is "entitled" to his right to access and as the Directive requires that Member States shall "guarantee" every data subject the right to obtain data from a data controller, then the court which finds that an individual has not been given personal data to which he was entitled under s.7(1) *must* order disclosure. This argument was made in the face of the plain wording of s.7(9) which provides that a court which is satisfied that there has been a failure to comply with the obligation by a data controller *may* order him to comply. The discretion of the court was confirmed by the Court of Appeal in *Durant v Financial Services Authority*[100] which went on to consider by what principles a court should be guided in exercising its discretion under s.7(9); Lord Justice Auld commenting that he would agree with the views expressed by Munby J. in *R. v Lord* in which he had held that the discretion was general and untrammelled.[101]

11–55   In order to decide whether the applicant should have access to the information he seeks, a court can require the data controller to produce the personal data withheld from the requester or to the court for its inspection. Curiously, the court does not appear to have the power to require sight of all the other information now covered by subject access, i.e. information as to the sources of the personal data and the purpose behind the processing, etc. Although s.15(2) does provide that the court may require information as to the logic involved in any automated decision-taking be available for inspection. Practically speaking this absence of a statutory power may not prove a difficulty where the action is brought in the High Court (or the Court of Session), because the court may require production of the information under its inherent powers. However, it means that county courts will be limited in their capacity to deal with applications which involve other parts of the information as well as simply the personal data in issue. When personal data are made available for inspection to the court they must not be revealed to the applicant unless and until the case is resolved in his favour.[102]

Where the personal data concern health care, an application to the court can be made by a third party to prevent the disclosure of information to the data subject in certain limited circumstances. See Ch.16 on the effect of the modification Order covering data consisting of information as to the physical or mental health of the data subject.[103]

The Information Commissioner

11–56   Subject access is one of the individual information rights now covered by principle 6 found in Pt I of Sch.1, which requires that:

> "personal data shall be processed in accordance with the rights of data subjects under this Act".

[100] [2003] EWCA Civ 1746.
[101] [2003] EWCA Civ 1746, para.74.
[102] DPA s.15(2).
[103] SI 2000/413.

There is an interpretation provision to this principle in Sch.1 Pt II para.8, which states that failure to supply information which has been duly requested under s.7 will be a contravention of principle 6. In such a case the data subject can apply to the Information Commissioner for an "assessment" of his case under s.42. The nature of assessments and the enforcement provisions are dealt with in detail at Chs 20 and 23. Where the Information Commissioner makes an assessment he may or may not take action. An assessment may involve the service of an information notice or the issue of a warrant or lead directly to an enforcement notice in an appropriate case.

An information notice under s.43 may require the data controller to supply the Information Commissioner with *all* of the information which might be responsive to a data controller's subject access search. An information notice is therefore wider than the s.15(2) power of the court in that regard; however, the powers of the court may be exercised with more expedition. It is an offence for a person knowingly or recklessly to make a false statement in response to an information notice.

11–57

Data controllers have a right of appeal to the Information Tribunal against an information notice.[104] Where an appeal is lodged it may be some time before the issues raised by the notice are resolved. Although in theory a warrant could be used by the Information Commissioner to obtain sight of information requested under subject access, as at the time of writing warrants have never been used by the Information Commissioner for this purpose. This may be because of the difficulty the Information Commissioner would have in executing the warrant, i.e., in finding particular data on any large and complex systems.

Where the Information Commissioner is satisfied that subject access should have been given, he may serve an enforcement notice on the data controller requiring him to give subject access to the personal data. The procedures for service of an enforcement notice are set out at Ch.20. Failure to comply with an enforcement notice is an offence under s.47 of the DPA.

CONSUMER CREDIT ACT INFORMATION

It has been noted above that requests by "consumers" for access to files held by credit reference agencies about them now fall under the remit of the DPA, albeit subject to special provisions. These provisions are contained partly in the Consumer Credit Act (CCA) itself and partly in Regulations made under it. In effect this creates a specific regime dealing with access to and rectification of credit information. Section 62 of the DPA extended the access provisions under s.158 of the CCA with the effect that those provisions now also apply to "partnership or other unincorporated body of persons not consisting entirely of bodies corporate" and not just individuals. Credit reference agencies hold data on consumers covering, among other things, electoral role information, county court judgments, debts and credit card payments. It is important to consumers that such information is accurate as it may affect their ability to obtain credit. Credit reference agencies are regulated by the CCA which deals with licensing and other regulatory matters. Under the CCA, individual consumers and now partnerships

11–58

---

[104] DPA s.48.

and companies have rights to access information held on their credit files under s.158. Agencies are obliged to provide consumers with a copy of the file relating to them on payment of a fee of £2 within seven working days.[105] A "file" is defined in s.158(5) to mean "...all the information kept [about a consumer] regardless of how it is stored". Accordingly, under these provisions, "consumers" (including partnerships, etc.) have access to more information than that covered by the DPA which governs only the treatment of "personal data" as defined.

The Consumer Credit (Credit Reference Agency) Regulations (SI 2000/290)

11–59   The Regulations came into force on March 1, 2000. They deal with the provision of information to consumers by credit reference agencies. Under s.9(2) of the DPA an individual who makes a subject access request to a credit reference agency shall be taken to have limited his request to data relating to his financial standing, i.e. his credit information, unless the request specifies otherwise. Where a data controller which is a credit reference agency receives a subject access request, in addition to the usual subject access response, pursuant to s.158(2) the agency must also give the individual a statement of his rights in the form prescribed under s.159. This sets out the individual's rights to make objections on grounds of inaccuracy and to request the insertion of notices of correction if he considers that the information is incorrect and he is likely to be prejudiced if it is not corrected.

11–60   If the credit reference agency receives an objection from a consumer but does not consider that the information which it holds should be altered pursuant to that objection, the individual may have a notice of correction filed with the information held.[106] If the credit reference agency does not accept the notice of correction then there is a dispute resolution procedure for which the Information Commissioner is the adjudicator.

The Regulations prescribe the equivalent forms to be given under the CCA where searches are made by partnerships and other unincorporated bodies.[107]

11–61   An application for adjudication on a dispute as to accuracy may be made by an agency or the consumer (individual or partnership, etc.) who is the subject of credit data. In each case the applicant must supply the name and address of the credit reference agency and the other party and indicate when the disputed notice of correction was served.[108] Where a credit reference agency is the applicant it must send:

a)   a copy of the file supplied;

b)   a copy of the notice of correction; and

c)   a copy of any related correspondence.

---

[105] SI 2000/290, reg.3.
[106] CCA s.159(3).
[107] SI 2000/290, Schs 2 and 3.
[108] SI 2000/290, reg.5(2).

It must also state the ground on which it considers that it would be improper for it to publish a notice of correction.[109]

An application by an individual or business consumer must give particulars of the entry in the file or the information received from the credit reference agency. He must also explain why he considers the information to be incorrect and why he considers he is likely to be prejudiced if the information is not corrected.[110]

A fee is payable on making the application. The Information Commissioner may make such an Order as he thinks fit. Under s.159(6) of the CCA it is an offence for any person to fail to comply with such an Order in the time specified on its face. **11–62**

Because the CCA covers all records, both manual and computerised, the s.159 rights to removal or amendment of information apply to all information both *manual* and *automated*.

It is important to remember that an individual's rights in respect of inaccurate personal data under the DPA apply only to:

- automated data; and
- manual data falling within relevant filing systems. This was subject to the special transitional provisions in Sch.8 Pt II para.4.

Data about other persons may appear on consumer credit files

The extent to which information about third parties should appear in credit reference agencies' files has, in the past, been a source of disagreement between the credit industry and the Information Commissioner. There is now an industry-wide agreement on the nature and scope of the third party data which are provided in response to a credit search following the resolution of the issue in *Equifax Europe Ltd v The Data Protection Registrar*.[111] Mr Justice Munby summarises the arrangement in *R. v Lord* thus:

> "In the outcome the Tribunal in Equifax substituted for the Registrar's original enforcement notice an amended notice, set out in the Encyclopaedia of Data Protection, Vol IV, paras 6–155 et seq, which in effect prohibited the supply of such third party information unless it was 'reasonable to believe' that the third party had been residing concurrently with the subject at the same address and as a member of the same family as the subject in a single household: even that information could not be supplied if there was information in the possession of the agency "from which it is reasonable to believe that there is no financial connection between" the third party and the subject".[112]

---

[109] SI 2000/290, reg.5(4).
[110] SI 2000/290, reg.5(3).
[111] Case DA/90 25/49/7.
[112] [2003] EWHC 2073 (Admin) (September 1, 2003), para.101.

ACCESSIBLE RECORDS

11–63   Access rights to health records were given under the Access to Health Records Act 1990 (the AHRA). Access rights to personal information held for social work purposes and to personal information held for public sector tenancies were granted under the Access to Personal Files Act 1987 (the APFA). In each case, the access rights given by the particular legislation only applied to information held in *manual form*; access to automated data came under the 1984 Act. This meant that someone wanting access to his or her entire set of records would have to make two applications, one under the 1984 Act for the computerised records and one under the pertinent legislation for the manual information. The rules for applying for information under the different acts were slightly different as were the remedies for non-compliance. The DPA brought all the access rights together by bringing all manual health records into the data protection regime, *including those which do not fall within the definition of a relevant manual filing system*. This was achieved by classifying "accessible records" as data.

"Accessible records" are defined at s.68 as either:

"(a)   a health record as defined by subsection (2); or
(b)   an accessible public record as defined by Schedule 12".

11–64   A "health record" in its turn is further defined as:

"… any record which—

(a)   consists of information relating to the physical or mental health or condition of an individual; and
(b)   has been made by or on behalf of a health professional in connection with the care of that individual".

Apart from in one instance (i.e., music therapists) it is irrelevant whether the health professional was in the public or private sector. Moreover, the health record falls under the auspices of the DPA whenever it was made, the AHRA only applied to records compiled after November 1, 1991 (except insofar as access to the earlier record was required to make intelligible the records to which access was permitted).

Section 69(1) contains a list of categories of medical practitioners who are "health professionals" for the purposes of this section. This section has been updated numerous times by other acts and statutory orders. The current categories include health professionals such as doctors or dentists employed in the public or private sector. However, a "music therapist" will only be covered by these provisions if employed by a "health service body" as defined in s.69(3). The health record must have been made by the health professional "in connection with the care of that individual". In the AHRA s.11, "care" is defined as indicating "examination, investigation, diagnosis and treatment". This definition has not been imported into the DPA, but in a case of ambiguity a court might find it of persuasive assistance. The AHRA remains in force in England and Wales to govern access by personal representatives of deceased patients to a deceased's medical records.

Section 68(1)(c) refers to Sch.12, which contains the provisions which **11–65** originated in the APFA (now repealed). The two sets of records covered are housing tenancy information and social work records. Tenancy information is defined in s.3(3) of Sch.12 as information:

> "... held for any purpose of the relationship of landlord and tenant of a dwelling [house] which subsists, has subsisted or may subsist between [the authority] [or as the case may be Scottish homes] [the Executive] and any individual who is, has been or, as the case may be, has applied to be, a tenant of [the authority] [theirs] [the Exccutive]".

Note: The words in square brackets apply respectively to the positions in England, Wales, Scotland and Northern Ireland because different bodies are responsible for public sector housing in each region but the rights given by the provision and the information covered are the same. It covers information held for "any purpose" of the tenancy or putative tenancy relationship and would cover among others records pertaining to the:

a) allocation of tenancy;
b) conduct of a tenancy;
c) rent payments and arrears;
d) repairs; and
e) termination proceedings.

In England and Wales it is specified that housing action trusts established under Pt III of the Housing Act 1988 are covered. However, it will not extend to housing associations as they are not defined as "local authorities" for the purposes of s.4(e) of the Housing Act 1985. Given that housing associations are publicly funded this may not seem an obvious distinction to have been drawn. It should be noted also that where housing estates have been transferred to the private sector the public sector access rights will not have been transferred.

The social work records to which individuals are entitled to have access are **11–66** those held by a:

a) local social services authority in England and Wales;
b) social work authority in Scotland; or
c) health and social services board in Northern Ireland.

In each case, the records cover information "held for the purpose of any past, current or proposed exercise" of a social services function of one of the defined authorities. The records held by such authorities may cover child care, fostering, adoption, nurseries, special needs, disabilities, or care of the elderly. Again, only information held by public sector bodies is covered.

All of these records, now covered by the term "accessible records", have been brought under the DPA for the purpose of providing subject access and providing rights of correction. While the aim of consolidating the access provisions is welcome the method of doing so is ungainly. The aims of the consolidation appear to have been that:

a) all the records should be covered by the same regime;
b) none of the existing rights should be diminished; and
c) no additional rights should be given unless it was inescapable to do so.

11–67   The provisions in relation to remedies, however, remains slightly varied. While the Information Commissioner's powers to take enforcement action or serve information notices in respect of any breach of principle 6 still apply, the rights of individuals to apply to the courts for specific remedies were reduced until October 2001. The reduced rights are found in s.12A[113]—see later in this chapter. They also applied between 2001 and 2007 to a subset of manual data, that is the manual data held immediately before October 24, 1998 which cannot claim the exemption for historical research.

Although the policy was to seek to maintain the existing rules as far as possible, inevitably, the transition of the access rights to the DPA has resulted in a number of changes. In particular, the exemptions which were set out on the face of the earlier acts have now been transferred to Orders made under s.30 of the DPA—these are dealt with at Ch.16.

EDUCATION RECORDS

11–68   The right of access to education records, which were embodied in the Education (Schools Records) Regulations 1989 made under ss.218 and 232 of the Education Reform Act 1988 and corresponding enactments in Scotland and Northern Ireland have also been transferred to the DPA as "accessible records". In broad terms, the Regulations provided for a right of access to pupil records held by schools. Section 68(1) now covers such records as well as health and social work records.

The relevant records are defined in Sch.11 paras 2, 3 and 4 cover the position in England and Wales; paras 5 and 6 cover the position in Scotland; and paras 7 and 8 cover the position in Northern Ireland. In each case information processed by a teacher solely for the teacher's own use is excluded from the subject access right.

In the case of England, Wales and Northern Ireland the information must:

a) relate to a person who is or has been a pupil at the school;
b) be processed on behalf of a teacher or a governing body at specified types of schools; and
c) have been supplied from "specified sources"

before access to it can be claimed.

11–69   Not all schools are subject to this provision—ordinary private schools are excluded. The access right covers schools funded by education authorities, that is, grant maintained and maintained schools. It also applies to any "special school" as defined in the Education Act 1996 s.6(2).

The "specified" sources of the information are:

a) teachers and other school-related local authority employees;

---

[113] The Data Protection Act 1998 Sch.13.

b)   the pupil to whom the record relates; or
c)   the parents of that pupil.

Information obtained from other sources, e.g. local police liaison officers, will not be covered. In the case of Scotland, the right covers any record processed by an education authority (as defined at s.135(1)) for the purpose of providing education or further education to a pupil within the meaning of the Education (Scotland) Act 1980.

SECTION 12A PENALTIES

Section 12A is found in Sch.13 to the DPA. It entitles a data subject to give notice to a data controller where the subject believes that the data controller is holding personal data which are inaccurate or incomplete or which are being held in a manner incompatible with the legitimate purposes of the data controller.   **11–70**

The notice must be given in writing and state the reasons for the data subject's belief that the contravention has occurred. Where the data subject alleges that the personal data are incomplete or inaccurate he can require the data controller to rectify, block, erase or destroy the data. Personal data are "incomplete" for these purposes if they would be inadequate or are out of date (s.12A(5)).Where the personal data are being held in a way incompatible with the data controller's legitimate purposes he may require the data controller to cease holding the personal data in such a way.

If a court is satisfied that a data subject has given such a notice which is justified, or justified to any extent and that the data controller has failed to comply with it, the court may order the data controller to do so.

IMPACT OF THE DRAFT REGULATION IN BRIEF[114]

The draft Regulation extends the obligations on data controllers in relation to the right of subject access, including by requiring them to: "…establish procedures for…the exercise of the rights of data subjects referred to it Article 15…"[115] in order to facilitate a data subject: "…exercis[ing] this right easily".[116] The maximum time within which a data controller may respond to a subject access request is set at one month, which is less that currently allowed in the United Kingdom. Further, unless a subject access request is "manifestly excessive", the data controller's ability to charge the requester a fee is abolished. Where a data controller can prove a request is "manifestly excessive" the controller has the choice of informing the requester that he is taking no action or charging a fee to satisfy it. The maximum level of the fee which a data controller could charge is not set out in this draft, instead: **11–71**

---

[114] See Ch.1 para.1-68 onwards for an overview of the proposal from the Commission published in January 2012.
[115] Art.12(1).
[116] Recital 51.

"The Commission shall be empowered to adopt delegated acts...for the purpose of further specifying the criteria and conditions for the manifestly excessive requests and the fees".[117]

The Commission also reserves the right to lay down "standard forms" specifying the format in which the data should be disclosed to the requester, in particular where the request is received in electronic form.[118]

ADDITIONAL INFORMATION

Derivations

11–72
- Directive 95/46 (See Appendix B)
  - a)   Art.12 (right of access).
  - b)   Recital 41.
- European Convention for the Protection of Human Rights and Fundamental Freedoms 1950: Art.8 (right to respect for private and family life).
- Council of Europe Convention of January 28, 1981 for the Protection of Individuals with regard to automatic processing of Personal Data: Art.8b (additional safeguards for the data subject).
- Data Protection Act 1984: s.21 (subject access).
- Organisation for Economic Co-operation and Development Guidelines: Annex Part Two (basic principles of national application) 13.

Hansard References

11–73
Vol. 586, No. 108, CWH 44, Lords Grand Committee, February 23, 1998 Trade secrets and whether the term should be widened to cover all intellectual property.
Vol.586, No.110, col.107, Lords Grand Committee, February 25, 1998
Disclosure of references.
Vol.587, No.127, col.1094, Lords Third Reading, March 24, 1998
Subject access general.
Commons Standing Committee D, May 12, 1998, col.20, 23
Accessible records.
Commons Standing Committee D, May 14, 1998, col.69, 70
Consumer credit information requests made to credit reference agencies.
ibid., col.79, 80, 90
Sources of data, the logic of decision making, access to third party data.
ibid., col.108
Reasonable interval.
ibid., col.112
Trade secret.
ibid., col.115
Data to be provided as at the time of the request.
Commons Standing Committee D, June 4, 1998, col.296
Accessible records amendments made.

---

[117] Art.12(5).
[118] Art.12(2).

Vol.315, No.198, col.577, Commons Third Reading, July 2, 1998
Access to decision making logic.
ibid.
Trade credit references.
Vol.591, No.184, col.1477, 1478, Lords consideration of Commons amendments, July 10, 1998
Intention behind provisions dealing with accessible records.
ibid., col.1482
Credit reference searches.
ibid., col.1484
"Trade secret" wide enough to cover credit scoring algorithms.

Previous case law

R. v Chief Constable of B County Constabulary and the Director of the National   **11–74**
Identification Service Ex p. R reported in Annual Report of the Data Protection
Registrar 1997. In this case the High Court held that under the 1984 Act a Chief
Constable did not have discretion to give only part of a record in response to a
subject access request.

CHAPTER 12

Rights to Prevent Processing

INTRODUCTION

The Act contains two distinct rights to prevent processing. Section 11 provides   **12–01**
individuals with a specific right to prevent processing for the purposes of
marketing. Section 10 affords a more general right of objection, but the
circumstances in which it can apply are limited. Both sections are covered in this
chapter. The s.11 right is an absolute right; s.10 is subject to a balancing test.

Section 10 sets out the right to "prevent processing"; however the grounds on
which processing may be prevented have been restrictively transposed from the
Directive. It is not clear that the national provisions adopted are sufficient to
comply with the Directive. The issue is dealt with at the end of this chapter. In
this chapter an interpretation which seeks to accord with the terms in the
Directive has been suggested where possible. Even as curtailed, however, s.10 is
a significant step towards establishing control over one's information. While
individuals cannot stop the tax man calculating what he is owed or the police
keeping records of speeding convictions they can, in some circumstances, stop
particular disclosures or have records to which they object removed.

SUMMARY OF MAIN POINTS   **12–02**

(a)   A specific right is provided in the case of direct marketing. This is not
       subject to conditions.
(b)   A data controller who is aware that a transferee of the data intends to use
       the personal data for direct marketing must take account of any objections
       to the transfer for that use.
(c)   The right of objection applies to all direct marketing, whatever the medium
       used, but there are further restrictions on marketing by telephone, fax and
       email.[1]
(d)   The right to insist that marketing material is stopped applies to a company's
       own marketing to its customers, as well as marketing by third parties.
(e)   There is no right to prevent processing (other than for marketing) where the
       controller relies on one or more of the primary grounds, that is the first four
       grounds of Sch.2, to legitimise his processing.

---

[1] See Ch.22 on Privacy and Electronic Communications for these provisions.

459

(f) The individual must show that the grounds of his objection are made out before the controller is obliged to comply with the objection (other than for marketing).

(g) In deciding whether to accept an objection (other than for marketing) the controller has to balance his reasons for processing against the grounds of objection.

(h) There are no special provisions in relation to sensitive personal data, however:

(i) it is unlikely that sensitive personal data will be available to use for direct marketing as explicit consent would be required;

(ii) the processing of sensitive personal data would be more likely to give rise to damage or distress than non-sensitive personal data so it is more likely that a s.10 notice of objection would succeed where such data are concerned.

(j) The s.10 right can be exercised by an individual who objects to the disclosure of personal data by a public authority under the Freedom of Information Act 2000.

RIGHT TO PREVENT PROCESSING FOR DIRECT MARKETING

12–03 This gives individuals an absolute right to require the controller to stop such processing. It was the only provision in the Bill which was given whole-hearted endorsement by both Lord Williams for the Government and Lord Astor for the Opposition on the First Reading of the Bill in the House of Lords on February 3, 1998.

Direct marketing is defined in s.11(3) as meaning:

"the communication (by whatever means) of any advertising or marketing material which is directed to particular individuals".

It covers processing directly aimed at producing personal mail, fax, telephone calls or any other form of communication. It would also be sufficient to cover host mailings, that is, inserts with other mail or "stuffers" as they are known. Although the point has not yet been tested, it probably extends beyond preventing the receipt of marketing approaches. It may enable an individual to require a controller to cease profiling, screening or data-mining activities even where they do not result in the direct arrival of marketing materials to the individuals. This is because the right in s.11(1) is to require the data controller "to cease, or not to begin, processing for the purposes of direct marketing personal data in respect of which he is the data subject." Data may be processed for the purposes of direct marketing even though the processing does not result in the arrival of marketing material to the individual.

12–04 In the Commissioner's Guide[2] it is stated:

---

[2] OIC, "The Guide to Data Protection", p.146.

"Direct marketing does not just refer to selling products or services to individuals. It includes promoting particular views or campaigns, such as those of a political party or charity. So even if you are using personal data to elicit support for a good cause rather than to sell goods, you are still carrying out direct marketing and would have to comply with a written stop notice."

The broad meaning of this term was endorsed by the Information Tribunal in *Scottish National Party v Information Commissioner.*[3] In that case the Commissioner took action under the Privacy and Electronic Communications (EC Directive) Regulations 2003 (PECR) against the Scottish Nationalist Party. The SNP had made unsolicited automated calls playing a recorded message exhorting listeners to support the Party. They refused to stop despite complaints because they claimed that the message was not a marketing message and therefore did not fall under the rules in the PECR. The Tribunal did not agree and upheld the broad meaning of the term. The right applies in circumstances where the data controller "anticipates" that the personal data will be used for marketing. The effect of this term was considered in the case of *Robertson v City of Wakefield and Home Office* described earlier.[4] Mr Robertson objected to the sale of the electoral roll to third parties who would use it for, among other commercial purposes, direct marketing. The electoral registration officer who sold the roll did not himself use the data for direct marketing. The question for the court was whether the electoral registration officer could be prevented by a notice under s.11 from passing on the data to the third parties. The judge considered art.14(b) of the Directive on which s.11 is based and which provides that the data subject must have the right:

"to object, on request and free of charge, to the processing of personal data relating to him which the controller anticipates being processed for the purposes of direct marketing, or to be informed before personal data are disclosed for the first time to third parties or used on their behalf for the purposes of direct marketing, and to be expressly offered the right to object free of charge to such disclosures or uses."

It was common ground that the United Kingdom had implemented the first **12–05** limb of the Article in s.11. The claimant submitted that domestic law did not meet the requirement in art.14 as the electoral registration officer had a statutory duty to sell copies of the electoral register and there was no provision in the relevant Regulations for individuals to register their rights of objection to the subsequent use of the data for direct marketing.

The judge found as a matter of fact that the register was sold for marketing:

". . . for many years, the data contained in the Register have been purchased by commercial interests and it has been obvious to EROs and to others that the data so purchased have been used for, among other things, direct marketing purposes."

The judge held that s.11 will apply where the data controller "anticipates" that personal data will be processed for direct marketing, even if that processing is carried out by another. He considered that such a reading of s.11 was compliant

---

[3] Available on [2001] EWHC Admin 915.
[4] [2001] EWHC Admin 915. See Ch.2 for fuller discussion.

with the Directive. The judge made clear that he was seeking to establish an interpretation which would accord with the purpose of the provision. He also referred to the construction as being supported by the recital to the Directive, when read as a whole. On the facts he held that the electoral registration officer should have accepted the claimant's objection.

Despite the fact that the finding on s.11 in *Robertson* was potentially wide it does not appear to have impacted on any other public registers.

12–06   The prohibitory notice may cover the marketing of the company's own goods or services, not just the goods or services of others. Thus it will be wider in scope than the addition of a name to the Mailing Preference Service (MPS) suppression file. This is an industry initiative, run by the Direct Marketing Association (DMA), under which individuals who object to the receipt of direct mail may have their names added to a database which is then made available as a tool against which mailing lists are "cleaned."[5] Organisations which are members of the DMA must clean any rented or third party lists against it. They are under no obligation to clean lists of their own customers. Registration with the MPS will stop much direct mail but individuals may also need to contact organisations directly. The MPS is a non-statutory arrangement. The Telephone Preference and Fax Preference Services are statutory. These are covered in Ch.22.

The recommended database management technique to deal with objection is to add suppression markers next to names and addresses where the individuals have objected to the receipt of marketing materials, rather than to erase those names and addresses. This ensures that the names and addresses cannot be added on again from other sources. However, where this technique is adopted, the data continue to be held and processed. If an individual continues to object in cases where a data controller wishes to use suppression markers, the controller may have to argue that processing the data so marked is not processing for the purposes of direct marketing.

12–07   The right is equivalent to a strict liability provision. The formalities for service of the notice are limited. Notice must be given in writing but it need not mention the section. A controller has no obligation to reply to a notice but it would usually be reasonable to expect him to do so. Failure to comply may result in court action by the individual or a complaint to the Commissioner.

The individual must specify the time in which he requires the notice of objection to take effect, which is to be "such period as is reasonable in all the circumstances". This must be a question of fact. It may be appropriate to allow longer to cease existing mailing than it would to not begin new mailing because of the length of time over which mailings may run. The Commissioner indicates in the Guide that he would expect electronic communications to stop within 28 days of receiving a notice and postal communications within two months.

If a controller fails to comply with a notice the individual may apply to court and the court may order a controller to take steps to comply with the requirement as the court sees fit. Failure to comply with an individual's objection may also lead to enforcement by the Commissioner under principle 6.

In the Directive an obligation is imposed on the Member States to take necessary measures to ensure that data subjects are aware of the existence of this right.

---

[5] To register with the MPS, visit *www.mpsonline.org.uk* [Accessed September 18, 2012].

Opt-out boxes and s.11

Opt-out boxes are the little boxes on forms or websites etc., that can be ticked or   **12–08**
checked to signify that the individual does not want marketing material. They
accompany notices which usually explain the various kinds of marketing which
the data controller intends to carry out. They appear on reply coupons and order
forms, any mechanism which the individual has to return to the controller. A
common form wording is:

> "We may pass your details to third parties so they may offer goods and services
> which may be of interest to you. Tick here if you would prefer not to receive such
> offers."

Sometimes the notice and options offered are more detailed. The customer may
be offered options about receiving material from the data controller itself or
telephone contact as well as third party marketing, this may be contributed with
the notices of consent mechanisms needed for e mail or SMS marketing[6];
sometimes an easy opt out from third party marketing, such as a tick box, but a
more difficult mechanism to opt out of the data controller's own marketing, is
offered. The precise content and extent of the collection notice required will
depend on the circumstances in which the data are obtained and what the data
controller intends to do with the information. A discussion of the requirements for
collection notices can be found in Ch.5 in relation to principle 1. In this section
the relationship with s.11 is considered. Section 11 does not make "opt-out"
boxes mandatory, although trade association codes of practice may do so. The
controller must comply with principle 1 and must honour any objections lodged
in accordance with s.11. However, the most commonly accepted way of
providing both notice and choice is to combine notice with an easy option to opt
out on a website or on any collection form which a data subject must return to a
data controller. The opt-out may cover both the data controller's marketing and
the use of the data for third party marketing.

In some forms of trading, particularly mail order trading, it is not realistic to
offer an opt-out from the data controller's own marketing and the opt-out box
may be confined to use for third party marketing or only third party marketing.

The Guide also deals with the possibility of asking data subjects whether they   **12–09**
wish to opt back into receiving direct marketing. It points out that the objection to
processing for the purpose of direct marketing covers the use of the personal data
to persuade people to rejoin the mailing list. However, it goes on to say that:

> "There is some merit in making sure the preferences people have previously
> expressed are up to date, but you should do it sensitively and should certainly avoid
> doing anything that could mean an individual has to inform you that their
> preferences have not changed".

In addition the Guide accepts that it is permissible to remind individuals of their
ability to alter their marketing preferences if it is a minor and incidental addition
to a message being sent out, such as a note on the bottom of a bank statement.

---

[6] See Ch.22 for the rules on electronic marketing.

Commercial considerations and marketing options

12–10 There can be important commercial considerations in the level of opt-in that data subjects have provided and to whom they have provided a consent. It is important to ensure that any commercial agreements include clear explanations and definitions as to the nature of data. In *Playup Interactive Entertainment (UK) Pty Ltd v Givemefootball Ltd*[7] the High Court considered what was meant by a reference to "opted in" users in a commercial agreement. Under a contract, Playup was to pay GMF in return for GMF sending SMS messages and e mails to individuals advertising Playup's interactive gaming service. GMF hosted several websites and users of those websites were able to vote for football-related favourites such as "Player of the Week". Under the agreement GMF agreed that it had to right to licence personal data for use by Playup and that the numbers of data subjects who "have provided the Company [GME] with prior notifications of their consent to receive direct marketing from the Sponsor [Playup]" would reach certain specified levels throughout the term of the agreement. The schedule where the marketing programme was described referred to the numbers of e-mails and SMS messages to be sent to "opted-in" recipients by GMF.

The parties disputed whether it was permissible for GMF to use bought-in lists of data subjects for sending the e mails and SMS messages. Playup said that such lists would not comply with the terms because the bought in data related to those who had not opted-in through the GMF website, the notifications of prior consent by those individuals would not have been provided to GMF and the consents could not have related to the Sponsor. If the opt-ins were in wide terms they would be to companies or organisations associated with the original party which obtained them and not with GMF. The other party, Playup, argued that as long as the data subjects had opted-in to the receipt of e mail or SMS about sport (not necessarily football) they fell within the term. The court had regard to the pre-contractual Sponsorship Proposal in determining the appropriate interpretation. The court held that it was not permissible under the agreement for GMF to use bought-in data and the meaning of "opted-in" in the agreement was meant to cover individuals who had opted-in directly to GMF and given consent to receive direct marketing from a "class of which the Sponsor would be a member".

RIGHT TO PREVENT OTHER PROCESSING

12–11 As is explained in Ch.5 no one can process personal data unless he can justify the processing as being within at least one of the grounds listed in Sch.2. These are divided into the four primary grounds set out in paras 1–4 and the remaining secondary grounds in paras 4–6. In practice it is likely that controllers will seek to rely on more than one of the grounds for any processing. Although technically an individual only has the right to object where the processing is based on one of the secondary grounds, in reality he will usually also be able to object where one of the primary grounds is relied upon, that is the consent ground, because in most cases consent can be revoked. In this context, therefore, consent is dealt with separately from the other three primary grounds for processing.

---

[7] [2011] EWHC 1980.

No right to object

An individual cannot object under s.10 where the processing is carried out with consent or on one of the following Sch.2 grounds: **12–12**

"(2)   The processing is necessary:
  (a)   for the performance of a contract to which the data subject is a party; or
  (b)   for the taking of steps at the request of the data subject with a view to entering into a contract;
(3)   The processing is necessary for compliance with any legal obligation to which the data controller is subject, other than an obligation imposed by contract; or
(4)   The processing is necessary in order to protect the vital interests of the data subject."

The Secretary of State has the power to prescribe additional cases in which individuals will have no right of objection to particular processing.[8] If they wish to escape the possibility of s.10 objections, data controllers will wish to rely on one of the primary grounds for processing. Controllers should consider whether they can bring their processing within one of those grounds. There may also be cases where classes of controllers will wish to lobby the Secretary of State to make s.10(2)(b) orders in order to overcome the possible problems caused by the right to object.

Processing on the basis of consent

Under Sch.2 para.(1) the fact that "the data subject has given his consent to the processing" is a legitimising ground for processing.[9] The consent must apply to the relevant processing. The existence of consent validates processing. A consent once given can be presumed to continue for so long as the particular relevant processing to which it relates continues; however, reliance on consent entails a risk to the controller that the consent may be withdrawn. Data controllers who rely on consent may seek to couple it with an interest or make it irrevocable or only capable of withdrawal upon express notice, in order to lessen this risk. Nevertheless, revocation must remain a possibility. In *Johnson v MDU*[10] there was a brief consideration of the relationship between the terms of a contract and the question of consent to processing. The point is not wholly clear but the view of the judge appeared to be that the data subject could not withdraw consent for the processing of personal data which was necessary for performance of a contractual relationship. The better view might be that the data subject can withdraw consent but the data controller must then rely on another ground to continue processing or treat the contractual relationship as having been terminated by the data subject. **12–13**

If a data subject who has previously consented to a form of processing notifies the controller of an objection to the processing, that objection may operate as a

---

[8] s.10(2)(b)—no orders have been made or proposed up to July 2012.
[9] For a more detailed discussion of the meaning of consent see Ch.4.
[10] [2007] 1 All E.R. 467.

withdrawal of the consent. In determining whether consent has been withdrawn regard will have to be had to the terms of the consent which was originally obtained and any provisions for withdrawal. Once consent to processing has been withdrawn the controller must rely on another ground to continue processing. A private sector data controller may then be forced to rely upon para.6 of Sch.2(1) that the

> "processing is necessary for the purposes of legitimate interest pursued by the controller or by the third party or parties to whom the data are disclosed, except where the processing is unwarranted in any particular case by reason of prejudice to the rights and freedoms or legitimate interest of the data subject".

A public sector data controller would (assuming he was not processing as a result of a mandatory duty, in which case consent would be irrelevant) be forced to rely upon para.5 of Sch.2(1) that the processing is necessary for one of the purposes or functions set out in the ground.

Where these grounds are relied upon, a s.10 objection can be raised to the processing. An individual who wishes to exercise a s.10 right should therefore ensure that any existing consent has been revoked, although it should be recognised that a court may in any event be prepared to treat a s.10 request as a revocation in itself, if it is sufficiently explicit.

On the other hand, controllers will wish to bind individuals to maintain their consent and may look for ways to make consent difficult to revoke even if irrevocability cannot be achieved.

Grounds to which objections may be made

12–14 If the controller bases his processing on Grounds 5 or 6 of Sch.2 then the data subject will have the right to object to the processing. Ground 5 reads:

> "5.   The processing is necessary:
>   (a)   for the administration of justice,
>   (aa)   for the exercise of any functions of either House of Parliament,
>   (b)   for the exercise of any functions conferred on any person by or under any enactment,
>   (c)   for the exercise of any functions of the Crown, a Minister of the Crown, or a government department, or
>   (d)   for the exercise of any other functions of a public nature exercised in the public interest by any person."

In order to establish which activities will be covered by these grounds it helps to look back to para.3 of Sch.2 which covers those cases where processing is "necessary for compliance with a legal obligation to which the controller is subject".

Grounds 3 and 5 must be intended to apply to different circumstances. Any organisation, whether in the public or private sector, which is processing in order to fulfill a legal duty will be able to rely on the para.3 ground. The Inland Revenue is under an obligation to assess the tax liability of citizens. The police have an obligation to keep records of reportable offences; these will process in reliance on Ground 3. It follows therefore that, where data controllers in the public sector are concerned, such controllers will rely on para.5 where the controller is relying on a discretionary power. Applying this approach the individual will be unable to object to processing carried out by a public body where the controller is fulfilling a legal duty but he will be able to do so where the controller is exercising a discretionary power. The right to object to processing in the public sector therefore appears to apply where the controller is carrying out a function on the basis of a power rather than a duty. As a matter of principle this seems to be a reasonable interpretation and one which would accord with the Directive.

In the private sector, Ground 6 may be widely relied upon for marketing and uses of data which are ancillary to the primary relationship. As noted above, it involves balancing the competing interests of the individual and the data controller.

WHICH PROCESSING CAN BE PREVENTED?

Having ascertained whether the right applies to the processing in question, the controller must consider the extent of that right and the grounds on which it may be exercised. The right can perhaps best be regarded as a right to restrict the extent of processing. Section 10 offers the individual a flexible range of requirements which he can seek to impose upon the controller. The individual cannot restrict the processing of data about anyone else, only about himself, although the grounds for restricting it include damage or distress to another. The individual may require the controller to stop processing already under way or to refrain from starting prospective processing. He can seek to restrict the processing by reference to: **12–15**

(a)   the purpose of the processing;
(b)   any particular type of processing; or
(c)   any data held in respect of him.

Processing is defined in s.1 of the Act and covers a wide range of information activities including dissemination of data, alteration of data or their recording. The individual can therefore require that a record should be erased not simply marked; that the controller stop making disclosure of data to others for their purposes; that the controller cease to hold any data about him; cease to disseminate data to particular people; cease to process data for particular purposes; erase particular data fields or make other detailed amendments to his processing. In the notice to the controller the individual must set out the precise processing to which he objects and which he requires to be changed. Despite the right being potentially a wide one there have been very few cases in which it has been raised. It has not been used in the majority of the cases on privacy described in Ch.2 or if cited has not been the main ground relied upon. In several cases the courts have taken the view that a claim under the DPA adds nothing to the rights of the individual under ECHRFF art.8. In both the *Campbell* and the *Douglas* cases, the s.10 right was initially raised but never became part of the final case. It was relied upon in *Law Society v Kordowski*[11] and the court in that case agreed that the objection was validly made out.

GROUNDS OF OBJECTION: WHAT DOES THE INDIVIDUAL HAVE TO SHOW?

12–16   The individual must:

(a)   describe the data involved and the processing to which he objects stating:
    (i)   that the processing in question is causing or is likely to cause substantial damage or substantial distress to himself or another; and
    (ii)   that that damage or distress would be unwarranted; and
(b)   give the reasons why he asserts the processing would cause such distress and would be unwarranted.

Section 10 was amended by the Government during its passage through Parliament. Originally the individual had to show that the processing was unwarranted and was likely to cause substantial damage or substantial distress to him or another. The amendment has reversed the order of the two grounds, and appears to have applied the test of being "unwarranted" to the damage or distress involved. This anticipates that processing could be carried out on one of the secondary grounds, could cause substantial damage or distress to the individual but that damage or distress could be justified by the controller as being "warranted". Each of the elements the individual must cover is dealt with below.

Describe the data and the processing

12–17   A description of the data will be sufficient if it sets out the categories of information involved, for example personnel data, education records, records of insurance contracts; or it may be more specific and relate to particular detailed information, for example the age of the individual.

The individual must describe the processing to which he objects. He can describe it in general terms or he can describe it by reference to a purpose or to a particular activity. Where a description is to be given by reference to a purpose it may be appropriate to consider how purpose is specified in other parts of the Act. Principle 2 deals with the specification of purpose, requiring that: "personal data shall be obtained only for one or more specified and lawful purposes".

Paragraph 5 of Pt II of Sch.1, which gives definitions, states that the purpose or purposes for which personal data are obtained may in particular be specified:

(i)   in a notice given for the purpose of para.2 by the controller to the subject; or
(ii)   in a notification given to the Commissioner under Pt III of this Act.

---

[11] [2011] EWHC 3185.

It is suggested that it will be sufficient for the individual to adopt any of these methods of describing the purpose of the processing as long as the description is sufficient to enable the data controller to pinpoint the particular data involved and to understand which purpose he has in mind. The individual may alternatively describe the processing by referring to the processing activity being undertaken, for example he may refer specifically to disclosure of the data by transmission, dissemination or otherwise making it available or to recording or holding the data.

Once he has described the data and the relevant processing the individual must go on to specify how the processing is causing or is likely to cause substantial damage or distress to himself or another and why that would be unwarranted.

Show substantial damage or distress is likely

The damage or distress has to be related to the processing and not to the nature of the data, although as processing includes the holding of data this may be a meaningless distinction. A likelihood of damage or distress is also required. This appears to be intended to be a stronger test than a mere risk of damage or distress. It is not clear what would constitute substantial damage or substantial distress. The test of substantiality raises problems of construction. Prima facie the test of substantiality must be the same in relation to both damage and distress. The term "substantial" is one of those words, like significant or reasonable, that import the concept of proportionality and thus depend greatly on context. In the Shorter Oxford English Dictionary "substantial" affords a wide range of shades of meaning as:

12–18

(a)   is or exists as a substance, having a real existence;
(b)   (law) belonging to or involving essential right, or the merits of a matter;
(c)   (of food) ample;
(d)   (of structures) solid and workmanlike; and
(e)   of ample or considerable amount, quantity or dimensions.

For the purposes of the Contempt of Court Act 1981, under which penalties may be imposed for activities which create a "substantial risk" of prejudice to a fair trial, it has been held that a substantial risk means a real risk, more than a remote risk,[12] It is suggested that in the context of the Act the test of substantiality should be no more onerous. The Directive refers only to the individual having "compelling legitimate grounds" for his objection. It does not require damage or distress to be involved. It is suggested that it is sufficient that there be a real likelihood of damage or distress arising as a result of the processing.

A further question arises as to how substantial distress is to be ascertained. This could be determined on either a subjective or an objective basis. If a data subject is particularly sensitive to what others think of him he may be prone to extreme distress by knowing that something detrimental is recorded about him. It appears there would be some difficulty in adopting a subjective test. If the test were subjective an individual's rights might vary with the depth of his

---

[12] *Attorney General v Independent Television News Ltd*[1995] 2 All E.R. 370.

sensibilities. It is suggested that the test should be objective. If the individual can show that the processing would be likely to cause distress to a person of ordinary sensibility in the shoes of the data subject the ground should be made out. The Guide published by the Commissioner suggests that substantial distress would be

> "a level of upset or emotional or mental pain that goes beyond annoyance and irritation , strong dislike or a feeling that the processing is morally abhorrent".

This must be distinguished from the evidential difficulty. Clearly if an individual asserts that particular processing is likely to cause real distress the controller is not likely to be in a position to disprove this. Damage will mean actual damage. (For a discussion of what constitutes damage see Ch.14.)

Unwarranted damage and distress

12–19   This appears to entail a balancing test between the reasons of the data controller for the processing and the effect on the individual. The reasons for the data subject's objection need to be set out sufficiently to allow the controller to consider them and decide whether he accepts them. The subject must explain why he considers the processing would cause unwarranted damage or distress. The damage or distress point is a matter for the individual to assert. Then he must show why it is unwarranted. The most likely reasons which may be given as unwarranted are that the processing will amount to a breach of the private or family life of the individual, for example that the data user is holding sensitive personal data which is not justified by the particular circumstances and which may be intrusive, or that the processing amounts to a breach of the principles, for example that the data is being held for longer than is necessary by the data controller.

It is unlikely that inaccuracy of the data would be sufficient to rely upon as there is a specific remedy where data is inaccurate, but a breach of one of the other principles could well give grounds for making an application for objection. The data may be irrelevant to the purpose; they may be excessive or inadequate, may have been held for longer than is necessary for the purpose or may have been obtained by trickery or deception or used in a way which is incompatible with the purpose for which they were obtained.

Formalities of the objection

12–20   A s.10 notice must be given in writing. It does not have to be served at a specific address but it would be advisable to send it to the data controller's head office or administrative centre and it may be helpful to address it to a data protection officer. The request does not have to refer to s.10 or be in any particular form although it will probably be helpful to controllers if it does so.

The notice has to specify a time within which the controller is required to comply. A reasonable time for compliance will depend upon the particular processing involved unless it is essential to comply in a shorter time scale, e.g. to restrain a proposed disclosure but is unlikely to be less than 28 days, which is the equivalent minimum time within which a controller would usually be required to comply with an enforcement notice.

How should a data controller respond?

A data controller must tell the subject, by written notice, whether he agrees to take the action or objects to it within 21 days of receiving the objection notice. In his response under s.10(3) he must state that he has complied or intends to comply with the notice or state his reasons for regarding the data subject's notice as unjustified and the extent (if any) to which he has complied or intends to comply with it. The controller may therefore agree to a request in whole or in part. Alternatively a controller may choose to respond by requesting further information from the data subject to enable the controller to find the particular data or to isolate the processing. Although such exchanges are not required by statute, in any subsequent court hearing a court is likely to consider how the data controller has dealt with the request. Equally, a data controller may wish to enter into negotiations to find an alternative method of dealing with the individual's concerns. The cost of complying with a requisition is not dealt with in the section and it is not clear how far a controller is entitled to take this into account. Cost alone will probably not be a sufficient reason to justify refusal to comply with a requisition, unless the cost is thoroughly disproportionate; it may however be a relevant factor for a court to consider in deciding how an application which it decides is justified should be complied with. The section gives no assistance on this point or on what a controller should do if he cannot comply with the requisition without making major changes to the processing or if he cannot comply with the requisition because the data also relate to a third party. The Act is silent on these points.

12–21

Once a controller receives a request not to process in a specific way, for example by making a disclosure which he plans to make, he is under no obligation to stop the processing involved immediately. Receipt of a requisition does not impose a ban upon processing. However, it is possible that an individual could seek an injunction to restrain the controller from continuing to process, for example from making a specified disclosure. If a disclosure were made without justification after receipt of a s.10 objection which the court later upheld, the individual might subsequently be able to claim damages under s.13 of the Act. Under the Freedom of Information Act 2000 the fact that an individual has lodged a valid s.10 objection which has been accepted by the data controller may be a ground upon which the personal data relating to the data subject may be exempt from the obligation to disclose in response to a request. The provision is dealt with in Ch.26.

Objection to processing after the death of the data subject

The DPA only applies to the living individuals and gives no privacy protection to the dead. This can be a cause of great distress to families. It is not clear whether an objection lodged during the lifetime of the individual can endure after death or if the data controller ceases to be bound by the objection once the individual has

12–22

died. If the objection can endure it would enable individuals to protect the privacy of their personal information after death. This would be of particular interest now that the Freedom of Information Act 2000 is fully in force. If individuals could serve s.10 notices on bodies, such as their GP or the HM Revenue and Customs, who held personal information about them which notices would endure after death, they would be able to preserve at least some of their privacy into the grave.

Relation to the Principles

12–23   Failure to comply with a notice under s.10 may be a breach of the sixth principle by virtue of para.3 of Pt II of Sch.1. Principle 6 requires that "personal data shall be processed in accordance with the rights of data subjects under this Act."

Under para.3 of the interpretation section to this principle, a person is to be regarded as contravening the sixth principle if:

> "(b)   he contravenes section 10 or 11 by failing to comply with a notice duly given under that section."

The wording here suggests that the extent of the obligation under ss.10 and 11 are equivalent but in fact they differ considerably. Where a notice is duly given under s.11 the controller must comply with it and this will be enforced by a court. A s.10 notice, however, requires a balancing exercise to be performed as described above. Where a justified requisition has not been complied with then the Commissioner may serve an enforcement notice under s.40 of the Act in an appropriate case.

Powers of the court

12–24   As well as asking the Commissioner to assess the processing involved an individual may make an application to court for an order that the controller comply with the requisition. The court must be satisfied:

(a)   that the notice has been duly given;
(b)   that the controller has failed to comply with the notice; and
(c)   that the requisition is justified whether in whole or in part.

The court will be required to balance the competing interests of the data controller and the subject. It will have to take into account the grounds on which the controller processes and the respective interests of the parties. This will be similar to the considerations which apply where the processing is based on the Sch.2 para.6 provision—that is,

> "that the processing is necessary for the purposes of the legitimate interests pursued by the controller or by the third party or parties to whom the data are disclosed except where the processing is unwarranted in any particular case by reason of prejudice to the rights and freedoms or legitimate interests of the data subject."

Among the rights and freedoms to be taken into account will be those set out in the Human Rights Convention and in the Charter of Fundamental Rights.

A court may order the controller to take specific steps to comply with the notice and has a wide discretion as to what it may require.

How can an individual use this right?

The right is likely to be most useful where the individual is dealing with specific **12–25** data or specific relationships which are not contractual, for example, data recorded and processed during pre-contractual negotiations. In theory an individual could use his or her rights under the Data Protection Act to conduct a privacy audit by carrying out subject access searches and then raising objections to any processing which he or she considers objectionable. It might, however, take a particularly motivated individual to go to such lengths. To date the author is only aware of s.10 being used to seek erasure of data.

Impact of the draft Regulation in brief[13]

The right to object to processing in art.19 of the draft Regulation is very similar **12–26** to the existing right in the Directive. The general right applies where the controller is processing on the basis of specified grounds being processing necessary to protect the vital interests of the data subject (although why anyone should object to such processing is somewhat baffling), processing to carry out a public task on a discretionary basis and processing on the basis of legitimate interest. The right of the data subject is to object on grounds relating to their particular situation and must be acted on unless the data controller can show that it has compelling legitimate grounds to process which override the rights of the data subject. There is therefore a total reversal of the burden in the current UK provision. The right to object to direct marketing remains an absolute right but in addition the right must be explicitly offered to the data subject in an intelligible manner.

Checklist for data controllers

How to use this checklist

The average data controller may not need to use all the points on this checklist. It **12–27** is suggested he should select those appropriate to his particular circumstances. He may also find it necessary to add further details under some of the headings. The checklist should therefore be used as a starting point in producing a procedure to deal with objection notices.

- Does the objection relate to marketing or another form of processing?
- Does it relate to direct marketing within the definition in the section?
- Is it in writing or sent electronically or oral?
- If it is not in writing or electronic is it appropriate to deal with it as sent or should the individual be required to put it in writing or send it by electronic means?

---

[13] See Ch.1 paras 1–68 onwards for an overview of the draft Regulation as issued January 2012.

- At which branch or office was it received?
- On what date was the request received?
- Has the individual making the request given an intelligible name and address to which the controller can respond?
- When does the 21 days for response expire on a s.10 notice?
- What time scale has the individual specified to stop marketing processing on a s.11 notice?
- What marketing processing is affected?
- Is more time needed to comply with the requirement?
- How is the marketing data held? Is it manual or automated or some of both?
- Does the s.10 objection apply to manual or automated data?
- Has the individual described the data?
- Has the individual described the processing?
- Has the individual explained why unwarranted damage and distress would be caused?
- On what grounds are the data being processed?
- Can one of the primary grounds be claimed?
- Does the notice amount to a revocation of an existing consent?
- Is it possible to comply with the objection?
- Is processing about others affected?
- Would compliance mean system changes?

ADDITIONAL INFORMATION

Compliance with the Directive

12–28   The data subject's general right to object is found at art.14 which states:

> "Member States shall grant the data subject the right, at least in the cases referred to in Article 7(e) and (f) to object at any time on compelling legitimate grounds relating to his particular situation to the processing of personal data relating to him, save where otherwise provided by national legislation. Where there is a justified objection, the processing instigated by the controller may no longer involve those data".

It is dealt with in the recitals by recital 45:

> "Whereas in cases where data might lawfully be processed on grounds of public interest, official authority or the legitimate interests of a natural or legal person, any data subject should nevertheless be entitled, on legitimate and compelling grounds relating to his particular situation, to object to the processing of any data relating to himself; whereas Member States may nevertheless lay down national provisions to the contrary".

The Article and the recital are in almost identical terms. Under art.14 an objection can be made on "compelling and legitimate grounds", which relate to the individual's particular situation. Under s.10, however, the individual must show that the processing is likely to cause or is causing "substantial damage or substantial distress" which would be "unwarranted."

This appears to impose a different, and narrower, test than is imposed by the Directive. For example, it might be argued that a breach of principle by a data controller which affected an individual would give rise to a legitimate ground of objection by that individual. If the effect on the individual was detrimental and not outweighed by any countervailing public interest in the processing being undertaken, it might reasonably be regarded as a compelling objection. However, the individual might struggle to show that he suffered "substantial damage or distress" within the terms of s.10.

As was explained in Ch.3, it is the duty of the Member States to implement a Directive. One of the tools adopted in order to achieve this end is for the courts to construe statutes in accordance with the Directive. It is possible therefore that the courts may be minded to interpret the s.10 rights generously to ensure that they correspond to the rights as set out in art.14. Considerable concern was expressed in Parliamentary debate that the section failed to transpose the art.14 rights adequately. These are reflected in the *Hansard* references cited below.

Derivations

12–29

- Directive 95/46 (See Appendix B):
  (a) art.14 (the data subject's right to object);
  (b) Recitals 25, 30, 45.

Hansard references

12–30

Vol.586, No.108, col.CWH 47, Lords Grand Committee, February 23, 1998:
Whether the term "substantial damage and distress" properly reflects the requirements of the Directive.
Vol.586, No.108, col.CWH 50:
Direct marketing covers not-for-profit mailings.
Vol.587, No.122, col.496, Lords Report, March 16, 1998:
Notices of objection to processing, general objection clause revised.
Vol.587, No.122, cols 500, 501:
Compelling legitimate grounds and substantial damage and distress.
Vol.587, No.127, col.1129, Lords Third Reading, March 24, 1998:
Consent in s.10.
Commons Standing Committee D, May 14, cols 117–121:
Rights to prevent processing, substantial damage and distress.
Commons Standing Committee D, May 14, col.123:
Right to prevent processing to direct marketers, notice to consumers.
Commons Standing Committee D, May 14, col.125:
Emails are covered by the right to object to processing.
Vol.591, No.184, col.1486, Lords consideration of Commons amendments, July 10, 1998:
Right to prevent processing for direct marketing, tick boxes as objections.

Previous case law

None.

12–31

CHAPTER 13

Rights Relating To Automated Decisions

INTRODUCTION

Section 12 allows individuals to insist that some decisions should not be taken by automated means. It also provides that individuals must be specifically informed about some decisions taken on an automated basis and allows them to raise subsequent objections and require those decisions to be reconsidered. It originates from a provision in the French data protection law. It appears to have been little used. The section was significantly changed by Government amendment during the passage of the Bill. In its original form it would have imposed a ban on relevant automated decision-making. As enacted, however, the individual must activate the ban. The equivalent provision in the draft Regulation issued in January 2012 by the Commission operates as a prohibition.

13–01

SUMMARY OF MAIN POINTS

13–02

(a) The right does not affect any use of manual data but only automated processing.

(b) An individual is able either to ban the taking of automated decisions by a data controller or to make a data controller undertake a non-automated review of a relevant decision.

(c) The right does not necessarily allow the individual to have the decision overturned although that may be the effect of a reconsideration.

(d) A significant number of ordinary commercial decisions are exempt from this right, as are those taken under statutory powers. Where data controllers make use of any systems (either their own systems or those provided by others) which are affected by this provision they must take steps to ensure that:

    (i) individuals who have objected are not subject to decisions made by such systems;

    (ii) appropriate notices can be given to individuals where decisions are made by such systems; and

    (iii) they have procedures to take account of any objections raised and to allow decisions to be reconsidered with human intervention.

PROCESSING AFFECTED

13–03   The s.12 rights apply to any:

> "decision taken by or on behalf of the data controller which significantly affects that individual [and which] is based solely on the processing by automatic means of personal data of which that individual is the data subject for the purpose of evaluating matters relating to him such as, for example, his performance at work, his creditworthiness, his reliability or his conduct [except where those decisions are exempt decisions]."

The s.12 rights derive from art.15 of the Directive, which provides that:

> "Member States shall grant the right to every person not to be subject to a decision which produces legal effects concerning or significantly affects him and which is based solely on automated processing of data intended to evaluate certain personal aspects relating to him, such as his performance at work, credit worthiness, reliability, etc."

NATURE OF THE DECISION

13–04   The right of objection applies only where processing is carried out in order to make assessments of, or pass judgments on, individuals. The right applies to the taking of any decisions based on such an assessment without some form of human intervention. The decision may be about anything; however, four specific examples are given, three of them taken from the Directive. The four specific examples are performance at work, creditworthiness, reliability or conduct. It is clear these are not exclusive but they indicate the kind of evaluations which are contemplated by this provision. While the general words are wide enough to encompass a broad range of activities, the examples given are taken from a relatively narrow range.

Significant effects

13–05   In all cases the assessment or evaluation must be capable of resulting in a decision which significantly affects the individual. The term "significantly affects" is not defined. A decision may affect a data subject by causing emotional distress. It does not necessarily have to result in physical damage or financial loss. Nor indeed does the section require that the effect on the individual should be detrimental. On the other hand it would seem unlikely that a data subject will object to receipt of an unsolicited benefit even if it has occurred because of automated processing. The effect need not be a legal effect, for example, an individual may be significantly affected by being stopped or searched or questioned even where he is not subsequently arrested or charged.

The provision is silent as to whether the test of whether an individual is significantly affected by a decision is to be assessed objectively or subjectively. The examples given are ones which would be generally regarded by reasonable persons as significantly affecting someone. On the other hand, an individual may be significantly affected by matters which would not be of concern to others because he or she may have particular sensitivities. On this basis the test could be subjective. The point does not appear to have been litigated to date. It will be for the courts to resolve this issue. It is perhaps unlikely that a court will require a decision to be retaken unless objectively it is seen to have a detrimental effect on an individual.

NATURE OF THE PROCESSING

The prohibition can be applied only where a decision is based solely on automated processing. This suggests that any human intervention, however slight, will be sufficient to overcome the prohibition.

13–06

The decision must be taken "by or on behalf of the data controller". The person who takes the decision is described as the "responsible person" in s.12(9). The responsible person therefore need not be the data controller or the one who carries out the actual processing but must be the one who makes a decision. This opens possible questions about liability for breach where the data controller and responsible person are different persons, although it seems unlikely that such a split would occur in most cases.

The prohibition cannot be applied in a number of cases, described as exempt decisions, which are considered below. There is a possible ambiguity in the drafting of s.12 because the prohibition can only be applied to decisions about a data subject based solely on "the processing by automatic means of personal data in respect of which he is the data subject."

Article 15 of the Directive is not limited to data in respect of which the individual is the sole data subject but simply refers to automated processing of data. The wording adopted in s.12 leaves it open to argument that if the processing is based on personal data about both the data subject and another or others it would fall outside the prohibited category. This would seem to be an absurd result and presumably was not intended. If correct it would significantly undermine the rights given by the section, as many forms of automated decision-making will involve data about others. For example, in a job evaluation scheme a decision may be based on the processing of data about a group of individuals, not just one data subject. In view of the wording of the Directive the better view therefore will be that such processing is covered and that the term "solely" relates only to the automated processing in question and not the data subject.

EXEMPT DECISIONS

Section 12(4) provides that a prohibition notice will not be effective in respect of an "exempt decision". An "exempt decision" is one which meets the criteria in s.12(6) and (7), or which is made in other circumstances prescribed by the Secretary of State.

13–07

No orders prescribing additional circumstances have been made or proposed at the time of writing so the only current exemptions are to be found in s.12(6) and (7). Section 12(6) sets out, (rather wordily) four circumstances in which decisions may be made, and s.12(7) sets out two conditions which can apply to them. This combination gives eight separate circumstances in which decisions will be exempt. They are listed below using the wording taken from the section (which explains the constructions employed).

13–08   **Categories of exempt decisions**

(a)   The decision is made in the course of steps taken for the purpose of considering whether to enter into a contract with the data subject and the effect of the decision is to grant the request of the data subject.

(b)   The decision is made in the course of steps taken for the purpose of considering whether to enter into a contract with the data subject and steps have been taken to safeguard the legitimate interests of the data subject (for example by allowing him to make representations).

(c)   The decision is made in the course of steps taken with a view to entering into a contract with the data subject and the effect of the decision is to grant a request of the data subject.

(d)   The decision is made in the course of steps taken with a view to entering into a contract with the data subject and steps have been taken to safeguard the legitimate interests of the data subject (for example by allowing him to make representations).

(e)   The decision is made in the course of steps taken in performing a contract with the data subject and the effect of the decision is to grant a request of the data subject.

(f)   The decision is made in the course of performing a contract with the data subject and steps have been taken to safeguard the legitimate interests of the data subject (for example by allowing him to make representations).

(g)   The decision is authorised or required by or under any enactment and the effect of the decision is to grant the request of the data subject.

(h)   The decision is authorised or required by or under any enactment and steps have been taken to safeguard the legitimate interests of the data subject (by allowing him to make representations).

It will have been noted that three of the conditions in s.12(6) deal with contractual situations and the remaining one applies where processing has a statutory basis. The conditions in s.12(7) are intended to ensure that the interests of the individual are safeguarded. Therefore either the effect of the decision must be to grant a request of the individual or his interests must have been protected in some way.

The data subject need not know about the automated processing before it takes place, or at all in the case of exempt decisions. However, where the request condition applies there must have been some form of request which can be relied upon and which the data controller is dealing with. On the face of it, the request need not be proximate in time to the automated processing. It is not clear what degree of particularity the request must have. For example it might be argued that a data subject who has ticked an "opt-in" box relating to the marketing of financial products could be described as having "requested" that he be considered for the purpose of considering whether to enter into a contract with the data controller and therefore targeted for the receipt of marketing-material on an automated basis. However this is perhaps a bold construction, and the better view is probably that a request must be a specific request to a specific data controller resulting in a specific case of automated decision-making.

Contractual situations

Where one of the contractual grounds is to be relied upon the contract must be with the data subject about whom the data are processed and not with any other person. The decision need not necessarily be proximate to the pre-contractual considerations. The connection need only be sufficient to fall within the broad parameters of, "in the course of steps taken for the purpose of considering". The processing may take place at a different time or the decision be taken by a different controller to the one who enters into the contract. Example (a) and example (c) in the above list are extremely similar. Possibly the former applies where an application is considered and rejected, and the latter applies when the application is considered and accepted in principle but the automated decision relates to the terms of the offer. The latter appears to be intended to be more proximate to the contract and could possibly cover circumstances where the customer has made an application for credit. Where the decision is taken in the course of performing a contract such automated decisions are therefore permitted. That permission will cease once a contract has been concluded or negotiations have been terminated.

13–09

Statutory authorisation

For a decision to be authorised or required under any enactment, the controller must be able to point to a specific statutory provision. The few remaining government activities which are operated under the prerogative powers, such as the issuing of passports by the Identity and Passport Service, will therefore be unable to rely on this. Although the decision must have a statutory basis the specific authorisation for automated processing need not be found in statute. For example, if the Department of Work and Pensions is empowered to make a statutory determination as to the amount of benefit payable it does not need specific authority to use a computerised system to make the automated decision.

13–10

SAFEGUARDS

Where the effect of processing which falls within one of the exempt processing categories is to grant a request of the data subject, no further action by the data controller is required. It is assumed that the data subject has no cause for complaint. Where the request of the data subject is not granted then the data controller must take steps to ensure that the subject's interests are safeguarded, for example he may provide an opportunity to make representations. This would entail informing the individual of the result of the decision, of his right to make representations and giving a fair hearing to those representations. It is not clear

13–11

how far the subject has to be informed of the nature of the processing or indeed that the decision is as the result of automated processing.

The right to make representations is only one method of safeguarding the legitimate interests of the data subjects. Other methods may be used. Possibly these would include a right of appeal to an ombudsman or an internal review in which the individual is not involved.

The steps taken must safeguard "the legitimate interests of the data subject". Those legitimate interests are not specified. In this context, however, it is suggested that they cover at least the right to respect for private life and family accorded under the Human Rights Convention and the rights guaranteed by the Charter of Fundamental Rights as well as the economic interests of the individual as a consumer or an employee.

When the courts consider whether steps have been taken to safeguard the legitimate interests of the data subjects, they may also take into account whether proper procedures have been followed which ensure that the relevant considerations are weighed in making the decision.

Prohibition notices served by individuals

13–12   Under s.12(1) an individual is entitled to prohibit a data controller by notice from taking any such automated decision at any time in relation to him. The notice must be in writing although the Act does not specify how or where it should be served. The formalities of service set out in s.65 of the Act only apply to service of notices by the Commissioner. A prohibition notice could be served on a data controller at a local office or branch office of a big organisation, although it would perhaps be prudent for anyone serving such a notice to do so at the head office or registered office in the case of a limited company.

A prohibition notice requires the controller to ensure that no decision which falls within the section is taken by or on behalf of the controller. A notice is not time limited; once served it will continue to apply until revoked by the individual. It will only apply to that individual, so for example a prohibition by an employee on the application of an automated assessment system will only apply to that individual and not to the post which he or she holds.

There is no prohibition on the service of a notice on behalf of another, so a solicitor could serve on behalf of a client or a parent on behalf of a child. The same considerations in relation to service of a notice on behalf of another will apply here as in the case of subject access. These are discussed in full at Ch.6.

The notice need not mention s.12(1), but it would be prudent to do so to assist controllers to recognise such a notice.

Obligations of data controllers

13–13   If a s.12(1) notice is not in effect and a controller takes an automated decision which falls within the section, then the controller must, "as soon as is reasonably practicable" notify the individual that the decision was taken on an automated basis and that he is entitled to request that it be reviewed or reconsidered.

It is not clear how far there is a difference between a requirement to reconsider a decision or take a new decision otherwise on an automated basis. Possibly the latter is a requirement to take the decision de novo without reference to the earlier one.

Notification by data controller

The notification need not be in writing (unlike other s.12 notices) although it would be prudent for a controller to commit himself to writing. Nor does the notification have to be given within a specified period (again unlike the other s.12 notices). It must be given "as soon as reasonably practicable" after the relevant decision is taken. It appears that the notice need not be given before the decision is implemented, although controllers would be well-advised to delay implementation of any decision which has a significant impact if it is possible for them to do so. This allows for the possibility of a successful objection by the individual. The alternative might be a difficult process of unpacking the effects of a decision which has been implemented. Moreover, it could be argued that the possibility of making an objection only after such a decision has been implemented is not sufficient to comply with the art.15 requirement that every person "shall have the right not to be subject to such a decision."

13–14

While equally it could be argued that the existence of the initial right of objection contained in s.12(1) implements the prior objection provision of art.15 and the s.12(2) right is additional to that, the point cannot be free from doubt and it is suggested that the better course for controllers would be to notify the individual of a decision and then withhold implementation until any objection can be considered.

Section 12(2)(a) does not specify the level of detail at which the notification must be given. As the decision involved is one which will significantly affect the individual it might be anticipated that the controller is likely to be communicating with the data subject in any event. It is suggested that the controller should inform the individual:

(a)   of the actual decision taken;
(b)   of any effect that the decision will have on the individual;
(c)   of the fact that it was based solely on automated processing; and
(d)   of the individual's entitlement to require the controller to reconsider or take a new decision.

It has to be said that it is not completely clear from the wording that the controller is under an obligation to notify the individual of his right to object, but it is submitted that a public authority would be under an obligation to do so as a matter of good faith and proper conduct as part of its public functions. It is suggested that failure to do so would be maladministration by a public authority and it would be prudent for any data controller to do so.

Data subject response

13–15   Section 12(2)(b) entitles the individual who has received notice of an automated decision from the data controller to serve a counter notice within 21 days of receipt. The counter notice must be given in writing and require the controller to reconsider the decision or take a new decision "otherwise than on" an automated basis. The data subject is not entitled to set any other parameters or conditions, for example he cannot insist on the decision being taken in a particular way or by a particular person. He may, however, be entitled to distinguish between requiring a decision to be reconsidered or taken afresh. It might be expected that a data subject would require decisions to be taken afresh to overcome any possible bias towards the initial decision made by the machine and it would be sensible to request that the person taking the decision on a non-automated basis should not be made aware of the automated decision.

Once a controller receives a valid notice of objection the individual has clearly activated his art.15 right and the controller should not implement the disputed decision even if this causes him inconvenience.

Counter-notice by data controller

13–16   The controller who receives a s.12(2)(b) notice of objection must respond in writing to the individual within 21 days of receipt. In his response he must "specify the steps that he intends to take to comply with the data subject notice". The section does not deal with the level of detail at which the steps are to be specified but as a minimum it might be expected to:

(a)   explain that the controller is going to reconsider the decision or have it taken on a new basis;
(b)   state when this will be done; and
(c)   explain any effects this will have on the individual.

It would also be reasonable for the controller to subsequently inform the individual of the results of the reconsideration or retaking of the decision although again it is not a statutory requirement to do so. However, for a public body it might be maladministration to fail to do so.

BREACH OF S.12

Failure to observe a s.12(1) or 12(2)(b) notice

13–17   Section 12(8) gives the court power to make a specific order to have the decision reconsidered or retaken in cases in which a prohibition notice has been ignored. The data subject must apply to the court for such an order. The section provides that the order be made against "the responsible person", that is "a person taking a [relevant] decision in respect of [a data subject]." This formula may have been used to cover those cases where the decision is taken by another on behalf of the data controller. However, since the data controller is the person ultimately responsible for the processing and notices of objection are to be served on the data controller, to which the controller is responsible for responding, it seems unlikely that the responsible person will be anyone other than the controller in the vast majority of cases. An order under s.12(8) that a decision be reconsidered or retaken shall not affect the rights of any person other than the data subject or the responsible person. This is the effect of s.12(9). Thus if a decision has been implemented so as to affect the rights of another those rights will not be affected even if the decision is reconsidered or overturned. The position of a controller or third party might be affected, but any right to redress, for example in contract, against the responsible person will stand. Otherwise it might be argued that the contract was avoided due to the successful statutory objection. The provision appears to be aimed at ensuring that the responsible person carries the risk of implementing a challengeable automated decision and not any other affected person. This appears to be an equitable position where the affected person is a third party. A person who risks being an affected third party in such a situation should ensure he is covered by an appropriate clause in his contract with the data controller. However the point is less clear where the person affected is himself the data controller.

Compensation

Failure to comply with the s.12 rights will give rise to compensation rights under s.13 if it causes damage. The compensation rights are dealt with in Ch.14.　　**13–18**

Powers of the Commissioner

Failure to comply with the requirements of s.12 may give rise to enforcement action by the Commissioner for breach of principle 6. The powers of the Commissioner are dealt with in Chs 20 and 21.　　**13–19**

Failure to serve a s.12(2)(a) notice

Unfortunately, no specific remedy is provided for the individual in circumstances where a controller takes a relevant automated decision but neglects to inform the individual of his rights. The controller could be subject to enforcement action by the Commissioner and the individual will be able to claim compensation if damage is caused to him. However, a lower court may not be able to order the controller to give the appropriate notice or to reconsider the decision, although the High Court could do so under its inherent powers.　　**13–20**

PRACTICAL TOOLS

Examples of automated decision-making　　**13–21**

(a) A solicitors' firm using an automated debt collection system to despatch final demands, followed by the issue of court summonses without human intervention.

(b) A financial services company using an automated system to target, select and, more importantly, reject customers for particularly good credit offers.

(c) Investigative agencies using a computer programme which profiles information about travellers in order to pinpoint particular travellers who fall within the profile of typical drug smugglers, to stop and search their luggage.

(d) A lottery company selecting name and address by random programme from electoral information and sending one individual a cheque for having won the lottery.

(e) The police issuing a court summons to a person recorded as a vehicle keeper with DVLA on the basis of a police camera record of the vehicle speeding without further investigation or intervention.

Checklist for data controllers: automated decisions

How to use this checklist

13–22 The average data controller may not need to use all the points on this checklist. It is suggested he should select those appropriate to his particular circumstances. He may also find it necessary to add further details under some of the headings. The checklist should therefore be used as a starting point in producing a procedure to deal with objection notices.

Objections under s.12(1)

- Is the objection made in writing or electronically or oral?
- If it is not in writing or in electronic form is it appropriate to accept it or should the individual be asked to put it into written or electronic form?
- At which branch or office was it received?
- On what date was it received?
- Has the individual lodging the objection given an intelligible name and address?
- Is the individual lodging the objection an existing data subject?
- Is the objection lodged by the individual to whom it relates or by another acting on his or her behalf?
- If it is made by another, in what capacity is that person acting?
- Is proof of authority to object on behalf of another required or has it been supplied?
- Is the objection lodged by a child?
- Is it lodged by a child in Scotland?
- What is the child's age?
- If it is lodged on behalf of a child does the person lodging it have locus standi to do so in respect of the child?
- Is a proper record kept of all valid objections lodged under s.12(1)?
- Can all automated decision-making within s.12(1) be recognised by the organisation?
- Is all such processing checked to see if one or more of the exemptions apply to it?

- Is the personal data to be subject to non-exempt automated decision making checked against the s.12(1) record of objections before the process is run?

Procedures to be followed under s.12(2)

- Is a record kept of each incident of non-exempt automated decision-making processing?
- Is there a proper system for notifying individuals significantly affected by such decisions?
- Has the date of the non-exempt processing been recorded?
- When was the data subject notified of the non-exempt processing?
- Has the decision been implemented or suspended pending a response from the data subject?
- Has a response been received from the data subject within the time allowed?
- What does the data subject notice require?
- How is the response to be handled?
- Has the data subject been notified of the final decision?

Impact of the draft Regulation in brief[1]

Article 20 prohibits measures based on profiling. The prohibition does not apply where the measure is:

13–23

- carried out with the consent of the individual in accord with the Regulation (art.7 includes provisions on consent);
- expressly authorised by Member State or Union law which also lays down safeguard measures to protect the interests of the individual; or
- carried out in the course of or performance of a contract at the request of the individual and where there are suitable safeguards in place.

Where any of these apply the data controller must include in the fair processing notice provided to the data subjects information about the use of the decision making and the possible effects on the data subject. In all cases automated profiling to reach decisions on individuals may not be made solely on the basis of personal data in the sensitive personal data categories.

Measures based on profiling are measures which produce legal effect or significantly affect a natural person and which are based solely on automated processing intended to evaluate certain personal aspects relating to the person or to analyse or predict "in particular the natural person's performance at work, economic situation, location, health, personal preferences, reliability or behaviour".

---

[1] See Ch.1, para.1–68 onward for an overview of the draft Regulation as issued in January 2012.

ADDITIONAL INFORMATION

13–24   **Derivations**

- Directive 95/46 (see Appendix B):
  (a)   art.15 (automated individual decisions);
  (b)   Recital 41.

13–25   ***Hansard* references**

Commons Standing Committee D, May 19, 1998, cols 137–143:
Exercise of objection rights.

Previous case law

13–26   None.

CHAPTER 14

Accuracy Of Personal Data, Compensation And Individual Remedies

INTRODUCTION

The 1998 Act significantly increased the range of remedies available through the courts (although special procedural provisions were introduced in respect of the special purposes[1]). Since the Act came fully into effect data controllers have faced an increased likelihood of civil action for breach of its provisions. Individuals may not only take action to enforce their individual rights, but also take action for compensation for other contraventions of the Act.

14-01

In this chapter, the remedies available through the courts in such actions are categorised under three headings:

(a)   rights orders;
(b)   accuracy orders;
(c)   compensation and other orders including injunctive relief.

The term "rights order" is not found in the Act; but breaches of the individual rights described in Chs 11–13, that is the right of subject access and the rights to object to the taking of automated decisions, to processing for direct marketing and to other specified forms of processing, are mirrored by specific remedies which can be granted by the courts. These are referred to here as "rights orders". The award of compensation is not limited to cases where there has been a breach of the individual rights. One of the most important provisions in this context is the requirement that personal data shall be accurate. That requirement is dealt with in this chapter. Compensation can be sought for any contravention of the Act which has caused damage to the individual. Where compensation can be claimed the courts can make associated orders, such as orders to rectify the data in question. The courts have also proved willing to allow for Representative Actions and to issue injunctive relief in relation to the unlawful processing of personal data.[2]

"Accuracy orders" is another term not found in the Act. It is used here as a generic term to describe the wide range of actions which a court may take to deal with cases where data are or have been deemed to be inaccurate.

Although the remedies are presented here sequentially, in any particular case it may be appropriate to pursue more than one remedy; for example, it would be

---

[1] See Ch.17 for a full treatment of these special provisions.
[2] See *Law Society v Kordowski* [2011] EWHC 3185.

usual to bring an action both for damages and for rectification where inaccurate data have caused loss and are being maintained on an individual's file. Moreover, it is increasingly the case that actions under the DPA include claims for breach of the Human Rights Act 1998, although not every breach of the individual rights in the DPA will also be a breach of the Convention rights.[3]

14–02   SUMMARY OF MAIN POINTS

(a)   The individual rights are accompanied by a specific remedy for breach of each right.

(b)   Accuracy rights as well as remedies are substantial. A data controller must consider the accuracy of data received from a third party.

(c)   Where data are inaccurate the powers available to the court are both flexible and extensive. In particular the court can order that further inquiries be made, can provide for data to be "blocked" and can require alterations in data to be notified to third parties who had previously received inaccurate information.

(d)   Compensation may be claimed for any contravention of the Act which causes damage and associated distress, or, in some circumstances, which causes distress alone.

(e)   Orders for injunctive relief may also be made and in one case the courts have allowed a Representative Action in a claim involving a DP issue.

(f)   The absence of rights to compensation for pure distress or moral damages in the UK is one of the areas criticized by the Commission although the basis for this remains obscure.

RIGHTS ORDERS MADE BY THE COURTS

Subject access orders

14–03   Under s.7(9), a court may order a data controller to comply with a valid subject access request which has been made to him. In such a case the claimant must satisfy the court that a request has been made under the provisions of s.7 which complied with the requirements of that provision and that the controller has failed to comply with that request.

The court has a discretion as to whether to order the controller to comply. The extent of this discretion has been the subject of consideration by the Court of Appeal in the case of *Durant v FSA*.[4] The existence of a discretion is clear from the use of the word "may" in s.7(9). However, on the face of it there are limits to the court's discretion. In the 1984 Act the factors which the court was to take into account in deciding whether to make a subject access order were described at s.21(8), which provided that:

---

[3] See Ch.2 for a discussion of the HRA and the overlap with the DPA.
[4] [2003] EWCA Civ 1746.

"A court shall not make an order under this sub-section if it considers that it would, in all the circumstances, be unreasonable to do so, whether because of the frequency with which the applicant has made requests to the data user under these provisions or for any other reason."

Therefore, under the 1984 Act, it was clear that the court had a wide-ranging power to consider all the relevant circumstances in deciding whether or not to make the order, and could decline to do so if it considered it unreasonable. The considerations were narrowed in the 1998 Act to those which appear in s.8. These are:

(a)   a discretion as to how the information must be supplied;
(b)   an ability to withhold data in view of the frequency of requests;
(c)   an ability to withhold data if the data constitute a trade secret; and
(d)   an ability to withhold data if the data relate to third parties.

Thus it is clear that the court may still take into account whether the individual has made unreasonably frequent requests. This may provide the data controller with a defence against an application to a court for an order for access. Under s.8(3), a controller who has previously complied with a subject access request does not have to comply with an identical or very similar request until a reasonable interval has elapsed between the two. Under s.8(4), a reasonable interval must be determined taking account of the nature of the data, the purpose of the processing and the frequency with which the data are altered.

The data controller who has determined not to respond to a second or subsequent request on this ground and who is faced with an action against him would be able to apply to strike out the action under the Civil Procedure Rules (CPR) r.3.4 or contest an application for a court order on the ground that he had satisfied the same or a sufficiently similar subject access request reasonably recently. An application to strike out would be made on the basis that the statement of case discloses no reasonable grounds for bringing a claim.[5]   **14–04**

Subject access may also be refused, at least in part, if the logic involved in the relevant decision-making involved constitutes a trade secret. This is found in s.8(5).

Under s.7(9) the court is not, in terms, empowered to order a subject access request to be complied with only in part or refuse because it appears to be vexatious or for any other reason, even if it might seem to be a reasonable and just response. Thus the discretion does not appear to be as extensive as the powers of the court under the 1984 Act. It also contrasts with the power a court enjoys in making an order dealing with an objection to processing under s.10 of the Act, where an order can be made that the individual's request should be complied with "to any extent". However, in *Lord*[6] Mumby J. held that the discretion conferred by s.7(9) is general and untrammeled,[7] a view later supported by the Court of Appeal in *Durant*[8] where the Court held that it has a   **14–05**

---

[5] CPR r.3.4(2)(a).
[6] [2003] EWHC 2073 (Admin).
[7] Para.160.
[8] [2003] EWCA Civ 1746.

general discretion as to the manner of dealing with such cases and the orders which it makes. The question which the Court of Appeal considered in *Durant* was as follows:

"By what principles should a court be guided in exercising its discretion under section 7(9) of the Act to order a data controller who has wrongly refused a request for information under section 7(1) to comply with the request?"[9]

In the particular case it was not necessary to answer the question as the Court found that the data controller did not hold any personal data relating to the requester. In the High Court the judge had added that, even if the applicant had been entitled to the data, he would not have ordered its disclosure for three reasons: that he (the judge) could not see that the information would be of any practical value to the applicant; that the purpose of the legislation was to ensure that accurate records are held and allow the individual to challenge any inaccuracy and in this case the applicant wanted the information in order to take proceedings against Barclay's Bank; and finally that the FSA had acted throughout with good faith. On appeal the applicant had argued that these were not legitimate reasons to refuse to provide access; the subject access right was not limited to checking the accuracy of information and the reason that Mr Durant wanted the data was not relevant to the exercise of discretion under s.7(9). It was further argued that art.12 of the Directive, which requires Member States to "guarantee" every data subject the right to obtain access to their personal data, meant that the Court enforcing s.7 rights was obliged to order disclosure if it was shown that the request under s.7 was otherwise justified. In granting leave for the appeal, Ward L.J. had paid particular attention to the discretion arguments as a ground for appeal. However, the argument that the court's discretion was curtailed in any way did not find favour with Auld L.J. in the Court of Appeal.

14–06   This overcomes the potential problems which could arise if the court had no such discretion For example, if the court had to decide a case in which a subject access request had been made for both archive and live data, which the court considered would require an unreasonably extensive trawl of the archive data held by the controller, if the court could not order compliance in part the only option open to the judge would be to require the request to be complied with in full. In *R. v Chief Constable of B County Constabulary* Unreported November 1997, the High Court held that a data controller could not be required to make a selective response to a subject access request. In that case the data subject wished the controller to omit "spent" convictions from a subject access response. The subject had been required to obtain the subject access information by an overseas government for submission in support of an application for a permit to teach in that country. Applying the case it could be argued that a data subject cannot chose to make a partial access request, nor a controller to grant one. An alternative view of the case is that the parties cannot use subject access to present a falsely partial picture by omitting relevant material from a particular record, but that there would be no difficulty in confining the request and the answer to defined records or data sets. In *Elliott v Lloyds TSB Bank Plc (t/a Lloyds TSB Corporate*

---

[9] Para.20.

Markets),[10] the judge rejected an argument that a request for subject access was an abuse of process where the applicant also had commercial disputes with the data controller. He held that the fact an applicant had mixed motives was no bar to enforcing a subject access request although, following *Durant*, it would be an abuse if the real purpose had nothing to do with the subject's concerns about his personal data.

Under s.15(2), a court considering an application under s.7(9) is entitled to inspect any relevant data or information as to the logic involved in any decision-making in order to determine whether it should be made available to the claimant. However, it must not permit disclosure of such information to the claimant prior to determination of the case.

14–07

Prevention of processing order

Under s.10(4), a court may order a data controller to desist from the processing of personal data to the same extent as an individual could so require under section 10; that is, to cease within a reasonable time, or not to begin, processing or processing for a specified purpose or in a specified manner any personal data. The power is exercisable where a court:

14–08

"... is satisfied, on the application of any person who has given a notice under sub-section(1) which appears to the court to be justified ... that the data controller in question has failed to comply with the notice ..."

The claimant must therefore show that:

(a) he has given notice under s.10(1);
(b) the notice was wholly or partly justified in that the processing has caused or is likely to cause substantial damage or substantial distress to him or another;
(c) that the damage or distress is unwarranted; and
(d) that his notice to desist has not been complied with.

However, his claim will be completely defeated if the processing by the data controller was based on one of the primary grounds for processing set out in Sch.2.[11] It appears that the evidential burden of showing that none of those grounds apply lies with the claimant as the right to serve a notice does not apply where the relevant conditions in the Schedule are met.

If the court is satisfied under these heads, and the respondent does not succeed in dislodging the application, whether by showing that he processed on a primary ground, or disputing the facts, the court may order the controller to take such steps to comply with the notice as it thinks fit.

The order may therefore require partial compliance with the notice. Rights orders will be similar to mandatory injunctions and in all cases orders should be drawn with care to ensure that they are specific and leave the controller in no doubt of what actions are required to comply with the order. Where mandatory

---

[10] Leeds County Court, April 24, 2012.
[11] By this is meant the first four grounds in the Schedule. See Ch.5 for Sch.2.

injunctions are granted, they must be in such a form that the recipient knows what he must do in order to comply: *Redland Bricks Ltd v Morris*[12]; *Video Arts Ltd v Paget Industries Ltd*[13]; *Harris v Harris*.[14] This is particularly the case with orders to prevent processing. The order will need to specify the processing in question, the purposes of the processing, the duration and any other relevant matters. In *Law Society v Kordowski*[15] a s.10 notice was served on Mr Kordowski (the owner of the website "Solicitors from Hell") seeking the cessation of the processing of personal data relating to a number of lawyers and the removal and destruction of the data. Numerous breaches of the Act were also cited. The court made an order requiring that the defendant cease from publishing the website and requiring its removal from the internet. This order was, in part, made in response to the s.10 application.

The direct marketing order

14–09   Under s.11(2), a court may order a data controller to desist from processing for direct marketing to the same extent that an individual might do so—that is to cease within a reasonable time, or not to begin, processing particular personal data for the purpose of direct marketing. The claimant must show that he has given notice under s.11(1) and that the controller has failed to comply with the notice. There is no defence to the application, although the court retains a general discretion as to whether or not to grant the order. It should be noted that the court can order any processing for the purpose of direct marketing to be stopped, not just that which results in the receipt of direct mail. The provision was considered in *Robertson v Electoral Registration Officer for Wakefield*,[16] in which the judge held that such a notice could be served on a data controller who does not himself carry out direct marketing but supplies data to another in the knowledge that the data will be used for the purpose. The order may apply to the use of personal data for any type of marketing including telephone marketing or e mail marketing even those these are specifically regulated by the Privacy and Electronic Communications (EC Directive) Regulations 2003. Regulation 30 of those Regulations provides that a

> "person who suffers damage by reason of any contravention of any requirement of these Regulation by any other person shall be entitled to bring proceedings for compensation from that other person for that damage".

However, there is no provision in the Regulations to exclude remedies under s.11.

Automated decisions orders

14–10   These derive from the individual rights in s.12. There are two separate rights but only one type of order to remedy a breach of those rights. Under s.12(8) a court may order a person who has taken a decision based solely on automated

---

[12] [1969] 2 All E.R. 576, HL.
[13] [1986] F.S.R. 623.
[14] [2001] 3 F.C.R. 640.
[15] [2011] EWHC 3185.
[16] [2001] EWHC Admin 915.

processing to reconsider the decision or take a new one on a non-automated basis. Under s.12(1) an individual may serve notice on a controller requiring him to ensure that no decision within the terms of the subsection is taken in respect of him. If the controller breaches this requirement and takes such a decision the data subject may apply to the court. If he satisfies the court that:

(a)　he has served such a notice; and
(b)　the controller has made a prohibited decision which is not an exempt decision;

the court may order the data controller to reconsider the decision or take a new one not based on such processing. However, it is not apparent how the individual will know that such a decision has been taken, as the controller's obligation in s.12(2) to notify an individual that such a decision has been taken only applies where no notice under s.12(1) has been served. It may have been assumed that, if the processing significantly affects the individual, then he or she will inevitably learn of it, but this cannot be a foregone conclusion. The decision may be one which has no immediate impact, as, for example, an evaluation of work performance which is noted on a record but only to be used when a question of promotion or redundancy is raised. Moreover, the individual will not necessarily know that a decision has been taken on the basis of automated processing even if he is aware of the result of the decision. It is suggested that the provision is unsatisfactory in this regard.

The court may also make an order where the controller has not complied with   **14–11**
a notice served under s.12(2)(b). Under s.12(2) a controller must inform an individual of the taking of a decision within s.12(1) which is not an exempt decision (unless as noted above a s.12(1) notice has been served). In such a case the individual is entitled to serve a counter-notice under s.12(2)(b) requiring the controller to reconsider or retake the decision.

If the controller breaches this requirement and fails or refuses to reconsider or retake the decision the data subject may apply to the court and must satisfy the court that:

(a)　there has been an automated decision within s.12(1) of which he received written notice;
(b)　within the relevant time of receiving notice (21 days) he gave notice in writing to the controller requiring him to reconsider or retake the decision; and
(c)　the controller has failed to comply with the requirement.

If he can show that this is the case the court may order the data controller to reconsider the decision or take a new one not based on such processing. However, it is not clear what routes are open to the individual if the controller fails in his duty to notify the individual but the individual becomes aware of the processing. It is suggested that in such a case the individual should serve the s.12(2)(b) notice, if possible within 21 days of learning of the relevant processing. The data controller should not be able to rely on his own failure to comply with the law to remove the individual's right to object.

It has to be remarked that the procedure set out by the section is unwieldy and unclear. In the Bill as originally drafted it appeared as a relatively straightforward prohibition. It was substantially amended at Report Stage in Parliament. The difficulties described above are largely attributable to the complexity of the amendment. We have not been able to trace any cases in which it has been used by data subjects.

ACCURACY

Accuracy of data

14–12   Under s.70(2), data are inaccurate if they are "incorrect or misleading as to any matter of fact". There appear to be three possible types of inaccuracy:

(a)   a record of an opinion may be inaccurate if it fails to reflect the opinion truly held;

(b)   an opinion itself may be inaccurate, particularly if it is based on an inaccurate assessment of the facts; or

(c)   the purported record of fact may not accurately reflect the reality.

Under s.14(1) an individual will have a remedy against both the holding of inaccurate data and against the record of any opinion which appears to a court to be based on the data held. If an opinion is inaccurate but not related to inaccurate data held there will be no remedy. This can be demonstrated by an example. A data controller may have a record of a worker showing that he or she never turns in for work on a Friday. That record is accurate. The controller may be of the opinion that the worker does not like working on Fridays because he or she is lazy. If the controller adds a note to the record to the effect that in his opinion the worker is not committed because he never attends work on a Friday (which is the firm's busiest day) that opinion will not give rise to any action for inaccuracy. This is the case even if the opinion is misguided because in fact the worker has to go for hospital treatment on a Friday. There will be no remedy, however, because the inaccurate opinion is based on an accurate data record.

Data may be misleading if a material aspect of the information is omitted. On the other hand there is no requirement that data needs to be exhaustive. This point again may be illustrated by a simple example. A man may be called Jacque Marie Ivan Johnson-Court. His name may be recorded in various ways:

(a)   J. Marie I. Johnson-Court;

(b)   J.M.I. Johnson-Court;

(c)   J.M.I. Court.

In the first example, the record is arguably misleading as to a matter of fact (his gender). In the second example, his name has been abbreviated but is not misleading because it gives accurate information about him. In the third example, the data are arguably inaccurate because they omit a material part of his surname. We would suggest that Jacque Marie could have the data in the first and third examples corrected as being misleading and incorrect respectively but could not insist in the second example that all his names were set out in full.

Where data are received from a third party, Sch. 1 Pt II para.7 provides that the fourth principle is not regarded as being contravened where the data "accurately record information obtained by the data controller from the data subject or a third party" and where two conditions are satisfied. Those conditions are (a) that the data controller has taken reasonable steps to ensure the accuracy of the data having regard to the purposes for which the data were obtained and further processed, and (b) if the data subject has notified the controller that he considers the data inaccurate, that the data are marked to indicate that fact. Where these conditions have been complied with the Commissioner cannot enforce principle 4. However, even where the data accurately record information obtained from a third party and the conditions have been complied with the individual may still have a remedy against inaccuracy on an application to the court.

14–13

These provisions are different from the s.22 provisions in the 1984 Act, under which the obligation of the data user was simply to indicate that data had been received from the third party and ensure any such indication was extracted when the data themselves were extracted. In the 1998 Act the controller is under no statutory obligation to mark the data. His obligation is to ensure that they are accurate. The data subject may apply for a remedy for inaccuracy in respect of "personal data of which the applicant is the subject". It does not allow the data subject to apply for the amendment of data which relate to others. The position becomes more difficult where the same data relate to more than one person but only one party claims that the data are inaccurate. In such circumstances it is suggested that the most appropriate remedy may be a supplementary statement rather than any amendment to the data.

ACCURACY ORDERS

Faced with a charge of inaccuracy a court has a wide and flexible range of powers. On an application made under s.14(1), a court may order the data controller to:

14–14

(a)   rectify the data;
(b)   block the data;
(c)   erase the data; or
(d)   destroy the data.

In each of those cases the order may also cover any other personal data which contain an expression of opinion which appears to the court to be based on the inaccurate data. The court may also order:

(a)   verification inquiries;
(b)   supplementary statements; or
(c)   communication orders.

None of the terms used in s.14 for the remedies granted, that is rectification, erasure, blocking or destruction, are defined in the Act. Their meanings must therefore be ascertained by reference to their ordinary meaning in the English language, and any relevant interpretative instruments. They are important terms and their meanings will determine the extent of individual rights under the Act. Each of the terms is considered below.

Rectification orders

14–15   This appeared in the 1984 Act at s.24(1) in a similar context to its current one. Under s.24(1) a court could "order the rectification or erasure of any data". There is no case law on the terms rectification or erasure in this context. They never appear to have been litigated. The term rectification appears in the OECD Guidelines at para.13(d) in relation to individual rights and in Treaty 108 at art.8.d, again in relation to individual rights. In both cases, however, it appears without further gloss.

  In the Directive it only appears in art.32 in relation to the transitional provisions relating to manual data. This Article provides that Member States may allow a transitional period of up to three years for controllers to comply with the requirements for "processing under way" as at October 24, 1998. For manual filing systems the Member States may allow a further period for controllers to comply with arts 6 (data quality), 7 (lawfulness), and 8 (sensitive data). Article 32 then continues:

> "Member States shall however grant the data subject the right to obtain, at his request . . . the rectification, erasure or blocking of data which are incomplete, inaccurate or stored in a way incompatible with the legitimate purpose of the controller."

This provision is, unfortunately, not of much assistance in understanding what the term rectification is meant to entail. It is clear that under the Directive rectification need only be available in these limited circumstances.

  Leases or other contracts which fail to reflect the common intentions of the parties may be rectified by the courts to give effect to the common intentions.[17]

14–16   The Shorter Oxford English Dictionary (OED) meaning of rectification includes:

(a)   to put or set right, to remedy, to correct, amend, make good;
(b)   to restore to a sound and healthy condition; and
(c)   to correct by removal of errors or mistakes.

Setting a record right would usually entail removing or altering an old version and replacing it with a new one. This may be acceptable on a register, however, in terms of handling personal information, this can be a difficult issue as this may destroy the continuity of the record—unless, that is, the record itself shows when it was altered and why. In many cases the preservation of an audit trail is important to show that the security requirements of the Act are being complied

---

[17] *Toronto-Dominion Bank v Oberoi* [2002] EWHC 3216 (Ch).

with, and in *I v Finland*[18] the ECtHR held that there was a failure on the part of the State to secure respect for the private life of the applicant where a hospital failed to keep proper control over access to health records or maintain a log of all persons who had access the applicant's medical file.

It is suggested that, where data are shown to be inaccurate and rectification is chosen as the appropriate route, the data should be "rectified" by a change being made in such a manner that it clearly shows when and why the change was made in order to ensure that an audit trail is kept. It is suggested that rectification is a preferred option to erasure for remedying inaccuracy. If removal of the data is chosen, by whatever method, it may be appropriate to keep a record as to why the data were removed for the purposes of audit.

This may give rise to difficult decisions. For example, if a patient has been wrongly diagnosed as having an illness or condition which is socially sensitive, whether it be a sexually transmitted disease or head lice, he may want the record completely removed. However, the medical record may show that he has been sent for particular tests or given particular treatment. Those parts of the record are not inaccurate but will be difficult to understand or may be open to misinterpretation without the information about the inaccurate diagnosis.

Blocking orders

This term appears in s.1(1) of the Act in the definition of "processing", without further explanation. It is a relative newcomer to data protection legal instruments as it makes no appearance in the 1984 Act or in either the OECD Guidelines or Treaty 108. It appears in the Directive in art.28.3 as an example of the powers of intervention with which a supervisory authority should be endowed and again in art.32 (set out above). No assistance as to its meaning can be drawn from either of those provisions.   **14–17**

The OED entry for "block" is lengthy. Its meanings include:

(a)   to obstruct or close with obstacles;
(b)   to shut up or in by obstructing ingress or egress; and
(c)   to obstruct the course of (something).

If one applies these meanings in the context of data, it appears that a blocking order may require a controller to ensure that particular data, while remaining on the record, are made inaccessible either in general or to particular recipients. The term "recipients", it will be recalled, includes servants or agents of the controller. There is no guidance as to how a controller is to deal with data which have been made subject to a blocking order if the data are subsequently requested under a statutory provision. It is submitted that the best course would be for the controller to make an application to the court to lift the blocking order and allow for disclosure.

In the absence of any definition it is also unclear whether blocking can only restrict disclosure of data or whether the use of the data, either by the controller or by others, can also be blocked. In view of these uncertainties it is

---

[18] ECtHR Application No.20511/03, July 2008.

recommended that anyone applying for a blocking order should specify precisely how the order requested is intended to operate and what it is intended to cover.

A blocking order may be a useful tool to ensure compliance with principle 2 under which personal data are restricted from being processed in a manner incompatible with the purposes for which they were obtained. We are not aware of any cases in which a blocking order has been made by a UK court.

Erasure and destruction

14–18   These terms are dealt with together to cover the point that, in the context of information, they should have the same effect, although they appear to envisage different activities. If actions to erase or destroy information are successful then the information content should no longer exist. The difference between them would appear to relate to the context in which particular data occur. If only the inaccurate data are held on a single medium that medium may be physically destroyed. A disk can be crushed; paper can be shredded; marked cards can be burnt. The data can be destroyed with the medium. On the other hand, if the target data are held in a medium with other data some of which are not inaccurate, for example on a disk with other information or as part of paper records which relate to others, then the medium cannot be destroyed. In such cases, however, the offending data will need to be removed by erasure, leaving the remainder of the record intact.

Erasure

14–19   This appeared in the 1984 Act in s.24, under which a court could order the erasure of data. The term was not defined in the 1984 Act. There is no case law on it. It appears in the OECD Guidelines at para.13(d) in relation to individual rights and Treaty 108 as art.8.d. In both cases it appears without further gloss. In the Directive it occurs in art.28 together with blocking and destruction but no further assistance as to its meaning is to be gained from that provision.

The OED entry for "erase" includes:

(a)   to scrape or rub out, to efface, expunge;
(b)   to obliterate from the mind or memory; and
(c)   to destroy utterly.

A consideration of erasure in relation to data raises a technical point on how data can be erased. On a normal computer hard disk the "delete" command does not actually delete the digitised information. It simply removes the index reference to the file so the file can no longer be retrieved using the computerised index. This frees that part of the disk or other medium for re-use. However the data held in that file have not been erased and will not be removed until they have been overwritten. That may never occur. Accordingly routine deletion will not erase data and specialist assistance may be necessary to comply with an erasure order. Moreover it may be prudent for the order itself to specify that simple deletion from an index will not be sufficient to ensure compliance with such an order.

Destruction

This term appeared in the 1984 Act in s.23 as one of the occurrences which could   **14–20**
give rise to an action against a data user, not as a potential remedy. It was not
defined and there is no case law on it. It does not appear in Treaty 108 or the
OECD Guidelines.

It appears in the Directive in art.28.3 together with blocking and erasure but
not in art.32. Again these Articles give no assistance and neither the recitals nor
the rest of the Directive help us.

The OED definition of "destroy" includes:

(a)   to pull down or undo;
(b)   to lay waste; and
(c)   to undo, break up, reduce into a useless form.

Although in the paragraph above a distinction was drawn between erasure and
destruction it has to be said it is not obvious that the requirement to destroy data
must entail a requirement to also destroy the medium. On the face of it
destruction means no more than erasure. However, there may be cases where
erasure of information would not be practicable, for example where the
information appears on sheets of printed paper and destruction is the only
practicable option.

Bearing these points in mind it is suggested that an order for erasure or
destruction should be framed to cover both possibilities to ensure that any
offending data are effectively dealt with.

Verification inquiries

This term has been used to describe the provision which is found in s.14(2)(b).   **14–21**
Such inquires can be ordered:

(a)   where the controller has obtained personal data from a third party or the
      data subject on trust as to their accuracy; and
(b)   has taken no further independent steps to verify their accuracy or indeed to
      include the data subject's view if the data subject disputes their accuracy.

In such a case, where the data subject disputes the accuracy of the record and
takes the matter to court, under s.14(2)(b) the court can order the controller to
follow the verification requirements which apply to received data and which are
set out in Sch.1 Pt II para.7, that is to take:

"(a)   . . . reasonable steps to ensure the accuracy of the data; and
 (b)   if the data subject has notified the data controller of the data subject's view
       that the data are inaccurate, the data indicates that fact."

Presumably the court can direct that inquiries be made both of the data subject
and of any third party. As the data subject has brought the action inquiries can be
made in the course of the proceedings and his views taken on board. One would
anticipate, however, that the very fact that the data subject has brought

proceedings must mean the data subject disputes the accuracy of the data. Inquiries of third parties may be difficult to make the subject of court orders as, on the face of it, the third parties have no obligation to respond to the data controller. However, this difficulty could be dealt with by calling any third party who supplied the data or who can speak to its accuracy, as a witness, if necessary by issue of a witness summons. An alternative is to seek discovery against the third party under the *Norwich Pharmacal* rules.[19] This enables an application for discovery to be made against one who is not a party to litigation where that party is known to be in possession of relevant information or material. Such applications are governed by CPR r.31.17. The court can then evaluate the evidence of accuracy. The use of *Norwich Pharmacal* orders appears to have increased with the growth of malicious online postings or material. In *G v Wikimedia Foundation Inc*[20] the court made an order requiring the respondents to disclose an IP address of a registered user to allow the claimant to trace a person who had disclosed private material in amendments to an article on Wikimedia's website. The material also concerned a child and the court in that case also allowed a hearing in private to protect the privacy of the child. In the Defamation Bill before Parliament at the time of writing it is proposed to encourage website owners to disclose the identity of those who post statements without the need for a court order by providing the website owner with a defence in libel if they disclose the identity of the person who posted the defamatory material.

Presumably, having directed inquiries and heard evidence, the court can order that the data subject's views should be added to the data record as they could have been by the controller under para.7(b). This is on the basis that the court may "make such order as it thinks fit for securing compliance with those requirements". Although it appears that this would be within the powers of the court it seems more likely that the court would find on the accuracy of the data and order a supplemental statement of the true facts to be added. It may do so under both s.14(2)(a) and (b).

Supplemental statement

14–22 The court may order a supplemental statement both where verification inquiries have been ordered and where the data controller has already complied with the Sch.1 Pt II para.7 requirement. A supplemental statement as to the "true facts relating to the matters dealt with by the data" can only be ordered where the disputed data are "received data". The court can also make rectification, blocking, erasure or destruction orders in respect of such data.

Communication orders

14–23 Where inaccurate data have been ordered to be rectified, erased, blocked or destroyed the court can make a communication order under s.14(3). The order will require the controller to notify third parties to whom the data have previously been disclosed of the action taken. The court can only make such an order if it is reasonably practicable for the data controller to comply with it. In deciding

---

[19] *Norwich Pharmacal v Commissioners for Customs and Excise* [1974] A.C. 133.
[20] [2009] EWHC 3148 (QB).

whether it is reasonably practicable, s.14(6) requires the court to have regard, in particular, to the number of persons who would have to be notified. Clearly this is only one consideration and it will also be relevant to take into account how difficult such communication would be. A controller may have an existing effective method of regular communication even if he has a large number of disclosees, and in those circumstances he should not be relieved from his responsibilities by the weight of numbers. The court will also need to weigh:

(a)   the nature of the inaccurate data;
(b)   the damage it may cause to the data subject; and
(c)   the risk of further damage caused by disclosures if dissemination is not stopped.

The High Court considered the application of s.14 in *P v Wozencroft*[21] and held that an application under s.14 for rectification of an expert report delivered to the court in family proceedings was an abuse of process and should be struck out. P was a litigant in person who was seeking access to a child. Dr Wozencroft was a consultant child psychiatrist who was charged with producing a report for the court in the proceedings. He duly produced a report, of which P was deeply critical. In the family proceedings the judge made an order which followed the recommendation of the expert. P appealed the order unsuccessfully. Several months later P made a subject access request seeking a copy of the report and subsequently challenged the accuracy of the report in an action under s.14. The subject access request was resolved however the rectification application was considered by the court. P asked the court that various statements in the report which related to him be "rectified". It was accepted that the report was personal data within the Act. The question of whether the data controller was CAFCASS, which had commissioned the report, or Dr Wozencroft, who had written it, was not decided. The judge did not rule on the accuracy of the data in the report. He ruled that it would be wholly inappropriate for a court to exercise the discretion to retrospectively amend a report given to a court and therefore it was not necessary to consider the accuracy of the contents:

"In my judgment it is clear that the claimant could never persuade the court to exercise its discretion to make an order for rectification under section 14 of the Act. This forum, is quite simply, wholly inappropriate for articulation of the issues which the claimant raises in relation to the defendant's reports."

He pointed out that a claimant had an opportunity to challenge the report in cross-examination and to appeal the decision and challenges to the accuracy of the contents of the report should have been disposed of in that forum:

"It is entirely inapt that over a year later there should be free-standing proceedings in this court in which the claimant seeks to do what he should have done at the hearing."

The case was dismissed as an abuse of process. It would have been an interesting case had it gone to hearing. It seems highly unlikely that any plaintiff would

---

[21] [2002] EWHC 1724, Fam.

succeed in showing that opinions delivered by an expert were inaccurate in that they were not honestly the true opinion of the expert. It is suggested that had the case gone to hearing, and had the judge been satisfied that any data relating to P were inaccurate it would not be appropriate to alter a report which had been put before the court. The appropriate remedy would be to order a supplemental statement to be held with the original report. However, these can only be ordered where the data are "received" data. Such an order would therefore have to be made on the basis that CAFCASS was the data controller and had "received" the data from the expert.

COMPENSATION AND ASSOCIATED COURT ORDERS

Who can sue?

14–24   An individual who suffers damage by reason of any contravention of the Act is able to sue under s.13. The individual need not be the data subject affected by the processing for these purposes. It is sufficient that a contravention of the Act has caused that person damage. The usual rules as to capacity of parties to take action will apply. For example a child will be unable to bring proceedings in his or her own name even though she or he was competent to make a subject access request or exercise any of the other rights, but must sue by a litigation friend unless the court makes an order permitting the child to conduct proceedings without one under CPR r.21.2.

Representative actions

14–25   The use of representative proceedings was considered in *Kordowski*[22] and it was made clear that the Act is suitable for such actions in appropriate cases.. The Law Society and the other two solicitor claimants sought to represent all those solicitors who were listed on the website "Solicitors from Hell". Not all of those listed had been contacted but under a Representative Order a person may be represented without his consent even where he can be found.[23] Such orders are made under the Civil Procedure Rules.

CPR Pt 19.6 provides:

"(1)   Where more than one person has the same interest in a claim-
    (a)   The claim may be begun; or
    (b)   The court may order that the claim be continued
By or against one or more of the same persons who have the same interest as representatives of any other persons who have that interest.

(2)   The court may direct that a person may not act as a representative".

The three claimants were the Law Society plus two firms of solicitors who had been listed on the site. The judge held that the Law Society could not act in a representative capacity as it was not suing in its own right and did not have

---

[22] See fn.15.
[23] *PNPF Trust Ltd v Taylor* [2009] EWHC 1693 cited in *Kordowski, above.*

sufficient common interest and grievance with law firms. The two firms of solicitors could take representative actions under the DPA in seeking the injunction requested against the website owner. The judge said:

"In my judgment the proceedings by the Second and Third Claimants in respect of the claims for harassment and under the DPA should be continued as they have been begun. Solicitors who have not been named have an interest in the injunction in so far as it is *quia timet*. Consent to be represented is not required, as the authorities show. A class is readily identifiable once persons or firms are named on the Website. An injunction would be equally beneficial to them all.

The common interest arises from the fact that the claim as pleaded is made in respect of a course of conduct, which includes data processing, which is the same or similar in relation to all the Represented Parties. The common grievance arises from the facts pleaded regarding the operation of the Website. There is at least a threat to cause distress to all Represented Parties in circumstances where no defence has ever been raised by the Defendant, nor could be raised by him. The question whether that course of conduct constitutes a breach of the PHA (Protection from Harassment Act) or the DPA is common to all Represented Parties because the same course of conduct is used in respect of them".

In that case, the remedy sought was a permanent injunction to remove the website. There was no claim for damages as the defendant was bankrupt.

Who can be sued?

The controller whose contravention of the requirement of the Act has caused the damage or the distress will be liable. It is possible that controllers may be jointly liable particularly where they share or otherwise pool data. In such a case one would expect the court to apportion liability in accordance with the degree of responsibility. The usual rules as to vicarious liability will apply, with an employer being liable for actions carried out within the scope of his employment.[24]   14–26

DAMAGES

The plaintiff must show that the contravention has caused him to suffer damage. The term "damage" is not defined. In UK law it would cover pecuniary loss such as loss of profits or earnings, and non-pecuniary loss such as pain or suffering and loss of amenity.[25] Damages for pain and suffering depend on the individual's awareness of the pain[26]. Damages for loss of amenity are assessed on an objective basis to calculate for the actual loss.[27] Damage may also consist of damage to reputation.[28] However in the case of *Johnson v Medical Defence Union Ltd*[29] Buxton L.J. rejected the possibility of such a head of claim in a data protection   14–27

---

[24] *Lister v Hesley Hall Ltd* [2001] 2 All E.R. 768.
[25] *Hassell v Abnoof* Unreported July 6, 2001, QBD.
[26] *Lim v Camden Health Authority* [1979] 2 All E.R. 910.
[27] *O'Brien v Harris* Unreported February 22, 2001, QBD.
[28] *Gillick v Brook Advisory Centres* [2001] EWCA 1263.
[29] [2007] EWCA Civ 262.

case where the appellant relied upon assumptions that his reputation had been damaged and a financial value could be put on that:

"I am certainly not prepared to import those assumptions, peculiar to, and in the view of some an unedifying feature of, the English law of defamation into this wholly different chapter of law".[30]

This refusal to countenance damages for loss of reputation appears to have been one of the grounds which the Commission regarded as a failure to implement the Directive properly. The Press Release from Commissioner Reding stated:

"Courts in the UK can refuse the right to have personal data rectified or erased[31] The right to compensation for moral damage when personal information is used inappropriately is also restricted".

The position of the Commission is considered in more detail below under the heading Moral Damage. In the case of *Sofola v Lloyds TSB*,[32] Tugendhat J. was prepared to contemplate that a claim to have been refused banking facilities on the basis of inaccurate data could be argued as damage under s.14, although the point was not determined. In the case of *Pal v General Medical Council*[33] the court accepted that the retention of data in breach of the Act which has an impact on the individual could found an action. In *Murray v Big Pictures*[34] the Court of Appeal upheld the appeal of Mrs Murray against the decision of the High Court to strike out an action for misuse of private information and breach of the DPA in respect of photographs taken and published of her infant son without consent. The Master of the Rolls giving judgment expressed the view that:

"In these circumstances, the issues under the DPA should be revisited by the trial judge in the light of his or her conclusions of fact. Those issues include the other issues considered by Patten J under this head, notably (but not restricted to) those relating to causation and damage. Given that there is now to be a trial, we do not think that the claims under the DPA should be struck out, whatever the conclusions of fact may be. They seem to us to raise a number of issues of some importance, including the meaning of 'damage' in section 13(1) of the DPA. It seems to us to be at least arguable that the judge has construed 'damage' too narrowly, having regard to the fact that the purpose of the Act was to enact the provisions of the relevant Directive. All these issues should be authoritatively determined at a trial".

The point was not, sadly, explored further as Big Pictures were refused leave to appeal to the House of Lords and the case settled. In the High Court[35] the judge had held, following *Johnson v Medical Defence Union Ltd*,[36] that damages were limited to pecuniary damages and could only be claimed for financial loss. The

---

[30] Para.78, above.
[31] Since we have been unable to trace any case law on this, it is not clear why the Commissioner has arrived at this view.
[32] See *Sofola v Lloyds TSB* [2005] EWHC 1335 (QB); and *Pal v General Medical Council* [2004] EWHC 1485.
[33] [2004] EWHC (QB).
[34] [2008] EWCA 446.
[35] [2007] EWHC 1908.
[36] [2007] EWCA Civ 262.

claimant had argued for damages to be awarded on a restitutionary basis by reference to the market value of the data which had been misused.

In general in UK law, damages for distress are not recoverable save in those circumstances in which extreme distress which results in damage may count as actual damage, by causing psychiatric injury.[37]

Damages for distress

There are actions in which damages will issue for distress alone. Some of these are statutory such as actions for unlawful discrimination but a small number have been developed by the courts. There appear to be three categories where this has occurred: claims for spoilt holidays; claims for abuse of State powers such as false imprisonment; claims for misuse of private information. Damages are awarded for distress in contract claims where the object of the contract is to provide relaxation, peace of mind or sanctuary following *Jackson v Horizon Holidays*.[38] In that case Lord Denning M.R. held that as a contract for a holiday is a contract for enjoyment, rest and relaxation if those were not forthcoming the contract had not been fulfilled. Payments will also be made where an individual has suffered from an abuse of State power such as false imprisonment. The payments are made in recognition of a loss of dignity, helplessness and distress. The area of payments in cases of misuse of private information is still not wholly developed. In the case of *Douglas v Hello!*[39] there seemed to be a conflation of the right to privacy with the right to control image and the commercial exploitation of image. There may be a view that the wider the publicity and worse the intrusion the higher the level of damages will be. Under statute there are damages for hurt feelings in cases of discrimination. In such cases an award is not automatic but the tribunal must be persuaded that the applicant suffered anger, distress and hurt feelings.

14–28

Categories of damages

Damages are intended to place the individual in the position which he would have been in apart from the wrong which has been done. Damages are not intended to be punitive. Special damages are awarded in relation to particular heads of loss, e.g. loss of employment. Aggravated damages can be awarded where the behaviour of the respondent aggravates the injury, for example additional injury to feelings and loss of dignity. In the High Court aggravated damages were awarded against the *Mirror* newspaper in the case brought by Naomi Campbell,[40] and Max Mosely also recovered aggravated damages in his action against the *News of the World*. Exemplary or punitive damages can be awarded but are very rare and the court refused them in the *Mosely* case. It is possible that exemplary

14–29

---

[37] *Alcock v Chief Constable at South Yorkshire* [1992] 1 AC 310.
[38] [1975] 1 W.L.R. 1468.
[39] [2007] UKHL 21.
[40] See Ch.2.

damages might be awarded in a sufficiently serious case.[41] Damages may be reduced due to a claimant's own conduct in some cases and all claimants have an obligation to mitigate loss.

Grounds for a claim

14–30   A claim under the DPA will be a claim for breach of statutory duty. The claimant need only show that any of the requirements of the Act have been breached. This is a very broad provision and would cover breach of the notification requirements, failure to honour the individual rights or breaches of the following requirements of the principles:

(a)   personal data shall be processed fairly and lawfully;
(b)   personal data shall only be used for the purposes for which it was obtained or compatible purposes;
(c)   personal data shall be kept up to date where necessary;
(d)   personal data shall be adequate;
(d)   personal data shall be relevant to the purpose or purposes for which it is collected and processed;
(f)   personal data shall not be excessive (in relation to the purposes of the processing);
(g)   personal data shall not be kept for any longer than is necessary for the purpose;
(h)   personal data shall be held and processed securely; and
(i)   personal data shall not be transferred outside the EEA unless there is adequate protection for it in the receiving jurisdiction.

Breach of any of these requirements in a way which causes damage to an individual may give rise to an action by the individual. The security obligation under the Directive is treated rather differently to the other obligations and perhaps it is not correct to characterise it as a data subject right. However, it may also give rise to an action for compensation. It should however be noted that in the Campbell case the Court of Appeal suggested that the exemption for the processing of personal data for the special purposes would usually apply so as to defeat a claim for damages, at least as far as the daily media are concerned. In *Lord Ashcroft v Attorney General*,[42] Lord Ashcroft brought a claim against the Government in respect of the leaking of two documents which he claimed were unlawfully disclosed and the disclosure of which caused him to lose standing and interfered with his private life. Several months after the proceedings had been started he sought to amend his claim to include claims for breach of the Data Protection Act 1984 and 1998. The judge had to decide whether to allow the amendments, the test being whether they showed an arguable case. The judge accepted that Lord Ashcroft could claim for any breach of the 1998 Act which caused damage. He rejected a further (and particularly adventurous) contention that the DPA obliged the Government to carry out adequate inquiries into any

---

[41] *Rookes v Barnard* [1074] A.C. 1129; *Kuddus v Chief Constable of Leicestershire Constabulary* [2001] UKHL 29.
[42] [2002] EWHC 1122 (QB).

allegation of breach of private life, a point contended by the claimant as part of his complaint in respect of the alleged inadequacy of the leak inquiry. He considered the further contention that, while the disclosure complained of pre-dated the 1998 Act and thus could not found an action for breach of Principle under that Act, the documents in issue continued to be held by the Government after the 1998 Act came into force and, as the 1998 Act requires personal data to be relevant and accurate, the continued holding of the data amounted to unfair processing in breach of principle 1 under the 1998 Act. The judge agreed that an arguable case could be mounted along those lines and allowed this part of the pleadings to stand. In the case of *Sofola v Lloyds TSB*,[43] Mr Sofola took action against the bank for damage caused to him by unlawful processing of personal data and inaccurate data. The bank succeeded in having the claim struck out, apparently, in part at least, under the mistaken belief that the bank had deleted the offending record. It transpired that in fact the record had not been deleted and Tugendhat J. took the unusual step of allowed the appeal to be reinstated on the data protection issues. In *Murray* the claimant argued that the fact that the defendant was unregistered "tainted" all its processing with being unlawful and this could assist in a claim for damages. The High Court judge rejected the contention pointing out that in any event there was no causative relationship between the fact of non-registration and the damage alleged.

Section 13(2) provides that an individual who suffers distress as well as damage because of the contravention may claim for that distress. Where processing is for the special purposes, that is journalistic, artistic or literary purposes, distress on its own will be sufficient as a basis of a claim.[44]   **14–31**

Level of payments for distress

There is no guidance available as to the level of payment that may be appropriate in a DPA case when a claimant has suffered distress. There may be a wide spectrum depending on the particular facts of the case, ranging from a limited amount for injury to feeling caused by a minor inaccuracy to substantial damages for intense and justified distress. The nearest analogous areas may be misuse of private information. In the areas where damages are awarded for hurt feelings, (described above) the levels of damages are not particularly high. The courts expect individuals to face life with a degree of stoicism. They are not sympathetic to the idea that any unhappy experience should result in a financial windfall. In *Milner v Carnival Plc*[45] the judge set out the expectations for awards for ruined or unsatisfactory holidays as follows: **14–32**

- Marriage abroad ruined: £4360–£4406
- Honeymoon ruined: £321–£1890
- Special holiday ruined: £264–£1161
- Ordinary holiday ruined: £83–£876

---

[43] [2005] EWHC 1335 (QB).
[44] *Campbell v Mirror Group Newspapers* [2004] UKHL 22.
[45] [2010] EWCA Civ 389.

In the area of abuse of State power, there is guidance from the Judicial Studies Board which advises an award of £500 for the first day of false imprisonment reducing steadily thereafter; £3000 for 24 hours of false imprisonment again reducing day by day thereafter; and around £2000 for a malicious prosecution lasting up to two years.[46] In privacy cases the claimant is often seeking an injunction but there have been a range of awards of damages. Max Mosely received a sum of £60,000, with the court making clear that the intrusion in the particular case was one of extreme seriousness. In *McKennit* the claimant received £5,000. Lady Archer received £2,500 in an action against an assistant for breach of privacy. Naomi Campbell received £2,500 plus £1,000 aggravated damages, and in the *Douglas* case the claimants received £3,750 each for misuse of the private information plus £50 for breach of the DPA. A wide range of levels can apply to cases for injury to feelings arising as a result of discrimination on grounds of sex or race. In *Vento v Chief Constable of West Yorkshire*[47] the court gave guidance on figures, saying that awards for hurt feelings should be constrained but can vary between £500 and £25,000 depending on the individual, the nature of the harm, the behaviour of the parties and the impact on the individual. Three bands of compensation were set for injury to feelings. The top band is between £15,000 and £25,000. Only in exceptional cases should damages exceed £25,000. There is no central record of the number or types of cases brought under the DPA or payments made as a result of breaches. In an unreported case in October 2011 *Grinyer v Plymouth NHS Trust* the judge sitting at Plymouth County Court assessed damages for personal injury under s.13(1) on a conventional common law basis and refused to reduce the level because the damages were statute based. In that case access had been obtained to an individual's medical records unlawfully by the claimant's partner. The claimant's pre-existing medical condition had been exacerbated as a result. He was awarded £12,500 for the exacerbation of his condition and £4,800 for loss of earnings.

Defences to an action for compensation

14–33   In any action for compensation it is a defence to a claim for the controller to prove that he has taken: "such care as in all the circumstances was reasonably required to comply with the requirement concerned". This is found in s.13(3). The obligation on data controllers is to comply with the Data Protection Act. This does not involve any issue of foreseeability of loss to the individual or the person affected. However, the foreseeable risk will be relevant in assessing whether the controller has taken such care as was reasonably required "in all the circumstances". Those circumstances would presumably include matters such as the risk of possible damage to individuals, and the extent of such damage. Properly documented policies and procedures are important in establishing that due diligence was used as one adherence to appropriate standards such as security standards.

---

[46] *www.jsboard.co.uk* [Accessed September 20, 2012].
[47] [2002] EWCA Civ 1871.

Moral damages

One of the grounds on which the Commission argued that the UK had not implemented the Directive correctly was that the UK Act does not provide for "moral damages". The term "moral damages" may be unfamiliar to many UK lawyers. It is a right to compensation for breach of individual rights where the rights are non-pecuniary or non-property based. It covers rights such as business reputation or the right to privacy. There is no reference to moral damages in the Directive. Article 23 provides that Member States shall provide that any person who suffers damage as a result of an unlawful processing operation or of any act incompatible with the national provisions adopted pursuant to this Directive is entitled to receive compensation from the controller for the damage suffered. There is no presumption in EU law that the term "damages" includes moral damages. Nothing in the recital to the Directive refers to moral damage. We have found nothing in Commission or Article 29 WP papers to suggest that the Directive requires compensation for moral damages. As there is no published material setting out the basis for the Commission's view one can only hazard the guess that her view is that "an effective remedy" must include some element of compensation for any breach of the DPA and therefore where a breach has caused a hurt to feelings or dignity but no actual loss a remedy in damages should be provided by the UK courts. On the other hand it can be strongly argued that there is no such obligation as long as the domestic legal system provides an effective set of remedies. Moreover the fact that awards can be made for distress (the moral damage equivalent) where the breach involves the literary, journalistic or artistic purposes would argue that any reputational damage is likely to be covered.

14–34

Associated orders

The court has an additional power to order rectification, erasure, destruction or blocking of the data under s.14(4) where:

14–35

(a) an individual has suffered damage;
(b) in circumstances in which he would be entitled to compensation under s.13; and
(c) there is a substantial risk of further failure by the controller to comply with the Act in respect of that data in the same circumstances.

The claimant does not have to bring an action for compensation under s.13 in order to invoke this provision. However, as the conditions for a s.13 action must be met it is difficult to envisage circumstances in which a claimant would not make such an application at the same time.

In effect, this provision enables the court faced with a s.13 application to make a related order dealing with the data in order to prevent further damage occurring.

Other orders of the court—powers of the court

14–36   The remedies sought will determine the court in which the proceedings are to be brought. Under s.15(1) the jurisdiction conferred by ss.7–14 is exercisable by the High Court or a county court, or in Scotland by the Court of Session or the Sheriff's Court.

Under the CPR, which took effect from April 26, 1999, claims are allocated to three tracks:

- small claims—for claims up to £5000;
- fast track—£5000 to £25,000;
- multi-track—£15,000 plus.

Proceedings under the Act have not been classified as "specialist proceedings" under CPR Pt 49.

It might be expected that claims for compensation will fall under the small claims or fast track procedures.

High Court

14–37   The High Court is not the most obvious venue for a data protection action. The level of damages usually claimed and the nature of the orders sought might seem unlikely to justify the expense for an individual claimant. However, it may be considered appropriate in some circumstances, particularly if the claimant also seeks other orders such as injunctions under the High Court's inherent powers. Lower courts do not have such powers.

Injunctive relief

14–38   Applications for injunctions may be made on an interim (interlocutory) or final basis to the Court for an order that a particular action, in these cases processing of a particular nature, cease. As an injunction is an equitable remedy it is never available as a matter of right and the Court always has a discretion whether or not to grant it. The main consideration in whether to grant an interim injunction (i.e. until trial or further order) is whether the claimant can be adequately recompensed by money for the wrong done. An injunction may be refused where the wrong done is minor and there is no danger that it will be repeated. If he is to succeed in an application for an interim injunction the claimant must show that he has an arguable case, that there is a serious issue to be tried and that he cannot be adequately remedied for any injury done pending trial by money damages. As we have seen in the extensive case law reviewed in Ch.2 there has been a significant development of the jurisprudence over the grant of injunctions in privacy cases since the Human Rights Act 1998 came into effect. In some of those cases the courts have referred to the DPA however the general approach has been to regard the DPA claim as coterminous with the HRA claim and to stand and fall with it. Here however we have considered a few cases in which the injunctive relief has issued primarily to remedy DPA breaches not involving or primarily focusing on the HRA art.8 right. There have been some data protection cases in which injunctive relief has issued. In *Sunderland Housing Company v Baines*,[48] SHC sought relief under harassment, data protection and defamation to have defamatory and harassing material about its staff removed from a website. The order also required the defendant to stop processing personal data about the individual employee and representative parties.

In *Kordowski*[49] the court granted a perpetual injunction in broad terms to require the defendant to stop publishing his website and to remove it from the internet in its entirety, restrained him from setting up another similar one or encouraging others to do so, and to cease to process any personal data in relation to persons in the represented group in the same manner and prohibiting the transfer to any other person. An order had earlier been made to prevent the transfer of the website and the personal data on it to unnamed "experienced owners who operate overseas". The transfer had been blocked by an order prohibiting the Defendant from "disposing of, selling or transferring any or all of the data on the Website to any third party" because it would amount to "unlawful data processing and harassment".

In the case of *Microsoft Corp v McDonald (t/s Bizads)*[50] the High Court granted an injunction as relief for an action brought by Microsoft under reg.30 of the Privacy and Electronic Communications (EC Directive) Regulations 2003. Regulation 30 provides that a

> "person who suffers damage by reason of any contravention of any requirement of these Regulation by any other person shall be entitled to bring proceedings for compensation from that other person for that damage"

The respondent sold lists of e mail addresses for use for unsolicited commercial e mail. The court agreed that Microsoft, whose services were detrimentally affected by the sending of such e mails, fell within the scope of the provision and was entitled to claim damages and granted an injunction under the provisions of the Supreme Court Act 1981.

A permanent injunction can be obtained without interim relief being applied for. An order for a speedy trial can be sought in appropriate case.

County Court

This is the more likely venue for individual claims. Claims for damages below £5,000 will fall within the small claims limit. County courts are creatures of statute and do not have the inherent powers of the High Court. In relation to actions for compensation under s.13 they will be able to issue associated orders under s.14(4). However, their powers will be limited to providing remedies in accordance with the Act. A court order for a money sum will operate as a money judgment to be enforced in the usual way. Where an order to take specific action or refrain from taking specific action has been made by a court and not complied with an action for contempt can be brought and eventually the contemptor be condemned to prison until the contempt has been purged.

14–39

---

[48] [2006] EWHC 2359.
[49] See fn.15.
[50] [2006] EWHC 3410.

FINANCIAL SUPPORT FOR LITIGATION

14–40 Claimants bringing claims under the 1998 Act are not eligible for legal aid. Such claims would be eligible for conditional fee arrangements. Section 58 of the Courts and Legal Services Act 1990 as amended by s.27 of the Access to Justice Act 1999 makes such agreements lawful (provided that they satisfy certain requirements) both when they do not include a success fee and when they do. Such conditional fee agreements are now widely used, however, they only allow for the recovery of costs where costs are awarded. It is therefore unlikely that solicitors will enter into them in small claims where the normal rule is that no costs are awarded.

Access to Commissioner's papers

14–41 Complainants and their representatives sometimes seek to deal with a breach of the Act both by making a complaint to the Commissioner and, in appropriate cases, by taking private action before a court. In order to pursue the private proceedings complainants may seek access to reports or statements arising from any investigation carried out by the Commissioner. However, practitioners should be aware that they cannot rely on evidence from the Commissioner's investigations being made available to them. The Commissioner's powers are regulatory and the Commissioner's papers are rarely made available on a voluntary basis to assist with private actions. The case law on information generated during a criminal inquiry is clear on this point. In the case of *Bunn v BBC*[51] the court held that statements made to the police by an accused person under caution enjoyed confidentiality. This was because it was clearly implicit in the relationship between the police and the accused that the information was only to be used for the purposes for which it was to be provided, although on the particular facts of that case the information in the statements was in the public domain because they had been read in open court. However the same reasoning would apply to statements made under caution to another investigating agency such as the Commissioner. In *Taylor v Serious Fraud Office*[52] the House of Lords held that there was an implied undertaking for material disclosed by the prosecution in criminal proceedings that it should not be used for a collateral purpose. If the circumstances so required, the court could release the undertaking. In other cases the courts have ruled on how far information acquired by a public authority in the course of its functions may be used or disclosed for other purposes.[53] In broad terms a public body will usually only be able to disclose confidential information with the consent of the person who provided it, unless the disclosure is in the public interest.[54] This ruling applies to material gathered during an investigation. It follows that papers generated during an inquiry by the Commissioner, even if not dealing with a possible criminal offence, are unlikely

---

[51] [1998] 3 All E.R. 552.
[52] [1998] 4 All E.R. 801.
[53] *Bunn v BBC* [1998] 3 All E.R. 552; *Woolgar v Chief Constable of Essex Police* [1999] 3 All E.R. 704; *R. v A Police Authority in the Midlands Ex p. LM* (2000) U.K.H.R.R. 143.
[54] *Hellewell v Chief Constable of Derbyshire*[2005] 4 All E.R. 473.

to be available to assist an individual in taking a private action. The Commissioner and his staff are also bound by s.59 of the Act.

Freedom of information

The Information Commissioner is a public authority covered by the Freedom of Information Act 2000 (FOIA), but this does not provide for extended access to case papers. The FOIA includes exemptions for information which is subject to an enforceable obligation of confidence and which is subject to a statutory barrier on disclosure. Moreover, there are exemptions for information relating to the investigation and prosecution functions of bodies carrying out law enforcement and regulatory activities, such as the enforcement work of the Commissioner.[55]   **14–42**

Obligations on the Commissioner to disclose information

The Commissioner only has a limited obligation to disclose the results of his consideration of an assessment where he has investigated a complaint. Under s.42(4) he need only notify the person who made the request whether an assessment has been made and of any view the Commissioner has formed or action taken as a result of the request. He does not have to provide information about the nature of the assessment, whether any further inquiries were undertaken or provide any finding of fact or evidence.   **14–43**

The Commissioner has powers to require the production of information and evidence from data controllers by the use of an Information Notice, or the issue of a warrant, but again an individual will have no right to access any information obtained by such means. The Commissioner may serve an enforcement notice on a data controller for breach of the Act but an individual has no right to be consulted on the form or effect of such a notice, even where it was provoked by his initial complaint.

Accordingly, although an individual may make a formal complaint to the Commissioner in the form of a request for assessment, once he has made that request the matter is out of his hands and out of his control. The Commissioner does not have the same powers as a court. Moreover, the Commissioner has a regulatory role and while he may actively investigate an alleged breach, which a court cannot do, he will not act on behalf of the complainant in a matter. In addition he has no power to award compensation and his enforcement powers are more limited than the order-making powers of a court. If the complainant is unhappy with the way the Commissioner handles the case his only recourse might be to complain to the ombudsman or seek judicial review of the Commissioner's actions or decisions if he believed the Commissioner had either failed to carry out his obligations or carried them out improperly.

The enforcement and prosecution powers of the Commissioner are treated in full at Chs 20 and 21 respectively.

---

[55] FOIA ss.30 and 31.

Assistance in cases involving special purposes

14–44   The special purposes are treated in detail in Ch.17. However, the assistance provisions are mentioned here as a special case where the Commissioner may act on behalf of or in concert with a complainant.

The powers only apply where the case concerns data processed for the special purposes. Those are defined in s.3 of the Act as meaning any one or more of the following:

> "(a)   the purposes of journalism;
> (b)   artistic purposes;
> (c)   literary purposes."

These terms are not further defined within the Act. A full treatment of the terms will be found in Ch.17. There are exemptions in s.32 for data held and used for the special purposes. Under s.53 an individual who brings any proceedings for:

(a)   failure to provide subject access;
(b)   failure to comply with an objection to processing;
(c)   inaccuracy of data;
(d)   failure to comply with a notice in respect of automated decision-taking; or
(e)   action for compensation,

which relate to personal data processed for the special purposes may apply to the Commissioner for assistance in relation to those proceedings.

This provision is supplemented by Sch.10 to the Act, under which the assistance provided may include the making of arrangements for the Commissioner to bear the cost of legal advice and assistance and legal representation of the applicant in preliminary proceedings or in negotiations. It should be noted that no special provision is included to cover the disclosure of investigative material obtained by the Commissioner during any investigation into a complaint or a request for assessment covering the special purposes, but there would be no bar to the Commissioner making appropriate disclosures in a case where assistance is provided, as long as the disclosures are necessary for the discharge of the Commissioner's functions.

The Commissioner is only empowered to provide assistance if in his opinion the case involves a matter of substantial public importance.

To the extent provided for by s.53 and Sch.10, therefore, the Commissioner may directly assist an individual in bringing his or her case but those provisions are relatively narrow.

Impact of the draft Regulation in brief[56]

14–45   Remedies, liabilities and sanctions are covered in Ch.VIII. Under art.74 both natural and legal persons have the right to a judicial remedy against decisions of a supervisory authority concerning them. In the case of legal persons this will

---

[56] See Ch.1, paras 1-68 onwards for an outline of the draft Regulation proposed by the Commission in January 2012.

presumably be satisfied by a right of appeal against decisions affecting them. Although the decisions are not stated to be ones having legal effect so it is possible that any kind of "finding" in respect of an organisation might give rise to a right of action. Data subjects also have a right to a judicial remedy to oblige a supervisory authority to act on a complaint or in cases where the supervisory authority has not informed the subject of the progress or outcome of a complaint within three months. A data subject who is concerned by a decision of a supervisory authority in another Member State can ask the supervisory authority of the Member State where he has his residence to bring proceedings against the supervisory authority with which he is dissatisfied. Under art.75 every data subject also has a right to a judicial remedy if they consider that any of their rights under the Regulation have been infringed as a result of the processing of their personal data in a way that is not compliant with the Regulation. These proceedings may be brought against either a processor or controller. However, where the obligations are imposed on controllers only then it is assumed that processors will not be at risk of proceedings. Compensation and liability are covered in art.77 which provides that any person who suffers damage as a result of an unlawful processing operation or an action incompatible with the Regulation shall have the right to receive compensation from the controller or processor for the damage suffered. Where there is more than one controller or processor involved they are to be jointly and severally liable but may be exempted if they can show that they are not responsible for the event giving rise to the damage. Article 76 provides that actions can be brought by bodies organisations or associations which aim to protect data subjects' rights and interests as long as they have been properly constituted in accord with the laws of the Member State. Such bodies can bring actions on behalf of one or more data subjects.

ADDITIONAL INFORMATION

Derivations 14–46

- Directive 95/46 (See Appendix B):
  (a) Arts 12(b) and (c) (right of access and rectification), 22 (remedies), 23 (liability), 28 (supervisory authority), 32 (final provisions);
  (b) Recital 55.
- Council of Europe Convention of January 28, 1981 for the Protection of Individuals with regard to automatic processing of Personal Data: art.8c, d (additional safeguards for the data subject).
- Data Protection Act 1984: ss.22 (compensation for inaccuracy), 23 (compensation for loss or unauthorised disclosure), 24 (rectification and erasure), 25 (jurisdiction and procedure).
- Organisation for Economic Co-operation and Development Guidelines: Annex Pt Two (basic principles of national application 13(d)).

***Hansard* references** 14–47

Vol.586, No.108, col.CWH 52, Lords Grand Committee, February 23, 1998:

Power of court to require controller to tell of rectification when correction otherwise than by order of court.
Vol.585, No.95, col.523, Lords Report, March 16, 1998:
Information commissioner must give to individuals following making of assessments.
Vol.587, No.127, col.1095, Lords Third Reading:
Compensation rights.
Commons Standing Committee D, May 14, 1998, col.101:
Scope of requests for assessment to Commissioner.
Commons Standing Committee D, May 14, 1998, cols 126–129:
Damages include compensation for pure financial loss, levels of compensation for distress under special purposes, notices to third parties of orders made.
Vol.315, No.198, col.580, Commons Third Reading, July 2, 1998:
Powers of court to order rectification.

14–48　**Previous case law**
R. v Chief Constable of B County Constabulary Unreported November 1997; *Mayor and City of London Court*, May 11, 1999 (case under s.22 of the DPA 1984).

CHAPTER 15

Exemptions For National Security, The Prevention And Detection Of Crime, Regulatory Purposes And Taxation

INTRODUCTION

The first three aspects of the title of this chapter may appear to form a logical set whereas the last one looks slightly out of place. The exemption for processing for the purpose of the collection of taxes has been included with these provisions because s.29 applies the same exemptions to processing for the purpose of taxation as to crime prevention and the apprehension and prosecution of offenders.

It could be argued that the usual rule, that the Directive is the primary source of interpretation, should not apply to the exemptions for national security and crime control in the same way as to other parts of the Act. Where the function falls outside Union competence it could be argued that the relevant provision does not rely for its interpretation upon the provisions of the Directive. However, in so far as the same exemptions will cover data which are used for some purposes within and some purposes outside Union competence and in so far as the Act was passed to give effect to the Directive this may be a purely academic distinction. It should be expected that the courts will have regard to the terms of the Directive in construing the application of any exemption in the 1998 Act. The point arose indirectly in the case of *R. (on the application of SSHD) v Information Tribunal*.[1] The case is considered in more detail below but it was argued on behalf of the Secretary of State that the impact of art.3 of the Directive, which provides that it does not apply in the course of activities falling outside the scope of Community law, meant that any issues concerned with national security are wholly outside the remit of the Information Commissioner who is not even able to question whether the exemption has been properly applied. This was rejected by the court which held that, while art.3 sets out the general principle, the combination of arts 13 and 28(4) which deal with the application of specific exemptions and restrictions in national implementing provisions and the powers of national supervisory authorities to check whether these exemptions and restrictions are being properly applied respectively, means that the role of the national supervisory authority cannot simply be ousted where exemption on the

---

[1] [2006] EWHC Admin 2958.

grounds are claimed. However, once the exemption is made out it appeared to be accepted that the Directive could have no further impact on interpretation or approach.

All the exemptions in this chapter, except the national security exemption, are to be applied on a case by case basis. The text follows the same pattern for each exemption, describing who can claim the exemption, what the exemption covers and when it can be claimed, followed by specific points relating to the particular sections.

15–02 SUMMARY OF MAIN POINTS

(a) The national security exemption is a class exemption and certificates can have "prospective" effect. There are two limited forms of appeal on specific grounds. There are additional special procedures dealing with such appeals. Appeals will be directed to the Upper Tribunal and not dealt with by the First Tier Tribunal (Information Rights).

(b) The crime and taxation exemptions are to be applied on a case by case basis; they include those who receive information in pursuance of statutory functions and include an additional exemption for risk classification systems.

(c) There is a specific exemption from the subject information provisions for the armed forces.

(d) The exemption for processing for regulatory purposes is widely drawn.

NATIONAL SECURITY

Who can claim the exemption?

15–03 Any data controller may be able to claim the benefit of the exemption because it applies to any personal data where the exemption is necessary for the purpose of securing national security. There is an evidential provision that a certificate by a Minister of the Crown shall be conclusive evidence of that point but the exemption does not depend on that certificate. It is a matter of fact as to whether the exemption is required for the purpose of safeguarding national security.

What does the exemption cover?

15–04 The exemption covers Pts II, III and V of the Act, the principles and s.55, that is the individual rights, notification, the Commissioner's powers of enforcement, compliance with the principles, and restrictions on the unlawful procuring of information. It also may apply to the Commissioner's powers to inspect personal data recorded in the overseas information systems listed in s.54A.[2] The scope of the exemption is set out in s.28(1). If it is necessary for the purpose of safeguarding national security any data may be released from the mechanisms of

---

[2] s.28 amended by the Crime (International Co-operation) Act 2003.

control under the Act. This is the broadest exemption in the Act. The exemption does not however apply to ss.51–54 which include the general powers of the Commissioner in s.51 to " . . . so perform his functions under this Act as to promote the observance of the requirements of this Act by data controllers".

When can the exemption be claimed?

There is no definition in the Act as to what amounts to "safeguarding national security". The website of MI5 explains that:

15–05

> "The role of the Security Service, as defined in the *Security Service Act 1989*, is the protection of national security and in particular its protection against threats such as terrorism, espionage and sabotage, the activities of agents of foreign powers, and from actions intended to overthrow or undermine parliamentary democracy by political, industrial or violent means.
>
> The term 'national security' is not specifically defined by UK or European law. It has been the policy of successive Governments and the practice of Parliament not to define the term, in order to retain the flexibility necessary to ensure that the use of the term can adapt to changing circumstances.
>
> As a matter of Government policy, the term 'national security' is taken to refer to the security and well-being of the United Kingdom as a whole. The 'nation' in this sense is not confined to the UK as a geographical or political entity but extends to its citizens, wherever they may be, and its system of government."

The decision to claim the exemption rests, in the first instance with the data controller, which will typically be a Government Department or other public body.

Certificates and evidence

Section 28(2) provides that a certificate signed by a Minister of the Crown certifying that the exemption is, or at any time was, required for the purpose, shall be conclusive evidence of that fact. The certificate may identify the personal data by means of a general description and may be expressed to have prospective effect. This is contained in s.28(3). A general description presumably means exactly what it says and can be satisfied by a broad phrase, for example "personal data held by the Home Office for the purpose of immigration", although there must be some limit to how general the description may lawfully be. There is some ambiguity in the combination of the provision that the certificate "may be expressed to have prospective effect" and the requirement that the exemption is at any time or was required for the purpose. While the term "prospective" suggests that a certificate may have future effect, the limitation to the exemption being currently required or having previously been required suggests it should not be able to have future effect. The certificates which have been issued and, to the best of our knowledge are currently in force, are expressed in general terms and have prospective effect. The certificates are all in the same form. A copy of one is available on *www.justice.gov.uk* appended to the published decisions.

15–06

The certificate must be provided by a Minister. There is a further provision dealing with evidence which allows a certified copy of a certificate to be received in evidence. This is contained in s.28(9). Section 28(8) provides that a document purporting to be a Minister's certificate shall be received in evidence and deemed to be such a certificate unless the contrary is proved. The relationship between these provisions is not immediately apparent. The copy is not conclusive evidence. It appears that, where the actual certificate is produced, that will be conclusive evidence unless the contrary is proved but where a certified copy of the certificate, which by its very nature cannot be a "document purporting to be a Minister's certificate", is produced then it must be accompanied by evidence to produce it and can be dislodged by contrary evidence.

Nature of appeals

15–07   There was previously a separate National Security appeals panel of the Information Tribunal, members of which were designated and appointed to hear appeals under s.28 of the Data Protection Act 1998. Since the changes to the tribunal structure covered in Ch.28, national security appeals will be allocated to the Upper Tribunal of the Administrative Appeals Chamber, although appeals should be lodged with the First Tier Tribunal in the normal way.[3] A number of those who sit as judges of that Tribunal form the National Security Certificates Judicial Group. The selection of judges will be made from such members. The hearing will be under the Tribunal Procedure (Upper Tribunal) Rules 2008 Sch.2.

These appeals are against a certificate issued by a Minister of the Crown, providing conclusive evidence that the exemptions from the sections of the Data Protection Act 1998 identified in s.28(1), of the Act are required for the purposes of national security. Anyone directly affected by the issue of a certificate may appeal against it. The Tribunal applies the principles of judicial review to the certificate, as to whether the Minister had reasonable grounds for issuing the certificate. In the case of *SSHD*, the Tribunal accepted that the Information Commissioner may be a person directly affected by a certificate as such a certificate is able to oust his supervisory powers.

When personal data are identified by a data controller, and a certificate is issued, an appeal may also be made under s.28(6) of the Act, on the ground that the certificate does not apply to the data in question.

15–08   There are thus two separate appeals provided for by s.28 of the Act. A person "directly affected by the issuing of a certificate" can appeal under s.28(4) to the Upper Tribunal "against the issue of the certificate". A business or commercial or voluntary body could be directly affected and as the term "person" covers legal persons,[4] the appellant might not be an individual. It was held that Privacy International was not a "person directly affected" when it sought to appeal against the issue of a certificate. The appeal will be determined upon judicial review grounds. Section 28(5) provides that where the Tribunal finds that, applying the principles applied by the court on an application for judicial review, the Minister did not have reasonable grounds for issuing the certificate, the Tribunal may allow the appeal and quash the certificate. The Tribunal's powers appear to be limited to quashing the certificate in whole and not in part. The only ground on which it may do this is that that the decision to grant the certificate was *Wednesbury* unreasonable, that is it was so unreasonable that no reasonable

---

[3] Tribunal procedure (First Tier Tribunal) (General Regulatory Chamber) Rules 2009 r.19A.
[4] Interpretation Act 1978 Sch.1.

Minister properly directed could have made that decision.[5] In the case of *Hichins v Secretary of State for the Home Department* the Tribunal pointed out that this would not oust the right of an individual to seek judicial review of a decision to issue a Neither Confirm Nor Deny (NCND) response under a certificate in a particular case but the Tribunal's only role is to determine whether a certificate is valid or not. All the appeals of which we are aware have been brought under this provision.

The other provision for appeal is in s.28(6). This applies where proceedings have been brought under or by virtue of the Data Protection Act 1998, in other words where there are actions for individual rights under Pt II of the Act, actions by the Commissioner under the enforcement provisions or prosecutions brought by the Commissioner or the DPP's office. In any of these proceedings a data controller may claim that a certificate under s.28(2), which identifies the personal data by means of general description in accordance with s.28(3), applies to any personal data. The other party to the proceedings may then appeal to the Tribunal under s.28(6) on the basis that the certificate does not apply to the personal data in question. In any of these proceedings, therefore, the controller may lay claim to the exemption. The other party can, if the certificate is worded in general terms, appeal to the Tribunal on the grounds that the certificate does not cover the particular data.

15–09

On the face of the provisions, although the controller will be a party to the appeal and of course the party who objects to the breadth of the certificate will be the appellant, it is possible that the Minister of the Crown who issued the certificate would not be a party. On the other hand it is difficult to see how the Tribunal could reach a determination as to what data are covered by a certificate in the absence of evidence from or on behalf of the relevant Secretary of State who provided the certificate. In the cases reported the relevant government department has acted under delegated powers in making decisions on the application of certificates to particular cases and has given evidence accordingly. No separate evidence has been called on behalf of the relevant Secretaries of State.

On the hearing of an appeal the Tribunal may determine under s.28(7) that the certificate does not apply to the particular personal data which are the subject of the appeal.

Decisions on national security appeals

As at July 2012, six appeals against the issue of certificates are listed at www.justice.gov.uk. Several of these were heard in private and were not published at the time. They do not appear to have case reference numbers so we have referred to them by name only. We are aware of a further appeal made by Privacy International which does not appear on the website.

15–10

In the matter of *Baker v Secretary of State for the Home Department*[6] the appellant, a Member of Parliament, believed that the Security Service (commonly known as MI5), a data controller under the Act, held personal data about him. He made a subject access application to establish whether or not his belief was

---

[5] *Associated Provincial Picture Houses v Wednesbury Corp*[1948] 1 K.B. 223, CA.
[6] [2001] U.K.H.R.R. 1275.

correct and to require the Security Services to disclose the data to him. The respondent to the appeal was the Secretary of State for the Home Department. He signed a certificate dated July 22, 2000 which purported to exempt the Security Service from complying with the provisions of inter alia Pt II of the Data Protection Act 1998, which includes s.7. The Service responded to the appellant's request in ambiguous terms providing a NCND response. It also relied upon the certificate as conclusive evidence that any data which it held were exempt from the requirements of s.7 of the Act. Effectively what was being sought by the Home Secretary was a blanket exemption for the Security Service in relation to any subject access request.

Mr Baker appealed under s.28(4) as a person "directly affected" by the issue of the certificate. He believed that the Security Service held information about his involvement with ecological and environmental pressure groups in the 1980s and that, although the file on him had been closed, it still existed.

The Home Secretary contended that there were reasonable grounds for authorising the Service to give a non-committal reply to this and other requests, because this was considered necessary to safeguard national security. Much of the evidence was directed towards justifying the NCND policy in relation to the operations of the Service. This evidence was not challenged. The appellant, supported by the Information Commissioner, who intervened in the proceedings, accepted that the NCND policy is justified in relation to s.7(1)(a) requests for information made to the Service, in all cases where the Service lawfully determines that a positive response would be harmful to national security.

15–11 The validity of the certificate in question was disputed, however, on the ground that its terms were wide enough to relieve the Service from any obligation to decide whether or not national security would be harmed by a positive response to the particular request. The appellant and the Information Commissioner contended that the Home Secretary did not have reasonable grounds for issuing the certificate in such wide terms, which could permit the Service to give the NCND reply even in cases where a positive response would not be harmful to national security.

The Tribunal, as it was required to do, addressed only the narrow issue as to whether the Home Secretary had reasonable grounds for issuing the certificate in terms which exempted the Service from the obligation to respond positively to any request made to it under s.7(1)(a) of the Act, regardless of whether or not national security would be harmed by a positive response in the particular case. The Tribunal concluded, applying the principles of judicial review, that the Home Secretary did not have reasonable grounds for issuing the certificate which had this "unnecessarily wide effect". They took into account the need to read the DPA "so far as it is possible to do so" in a manner which protects human rights under the European Convention on Human Rights and the Human Rights Act 1998 and to construe it as far as possible in accord with the Directive. The Tribunal quashed the Home Secretary's Certificate dated July 22, 2000 but acknowledged that this did not prevent the Home Secretary from issuing a fresh certificate aimed at circumventing the Tribunal's criticisms. The Tribunal refrained from attempting to draft the terms in which a valid certificate might be issued.

Following the decision, a replacement certificate was issued on December 10, 2001 which was not appealed by Mr Baker.

Mr Baker subsequently made a complaint to the Investigatory Powers Tribunal **15–12**
(IPT) under s.65 of the Regulation of Investigatory Powers Act 2000. The
preliminary judgment of the Tribunal is publicly available on its website at
www.ipt-uk.com.[7] The site notes that, although r.6 of the Investigatory Powers
Tribunal Rules[8] states that no document or information nor the fact that any
document or information has been provided to it can be disclosed, the IPT has
decided that the Rules do not prevent it from notifying and publishing their
rulings of law on a complaint. The IPT's role in assessing complaints is on the
basis of judicial review of the decision or action of the public body complained
of. It considered as preliminary questions:

- whether, in the absence of any relevant data, a NCND response to a subject
  access request engages the right to respect for private and family life under
  art.8 of the Convention and the Human Rights Act 1998 (HRA); and
- if art.8 is engaged, the approach that the IPT should take to determining
  whether the NCND response was justified.

The Tribunal determined that if no relevant personal data is held by a body and
the body gives an NCND response there is no interference with the art.8 right.
Article 8 does not give a right to peace of mind and it cannot be said that an
inchoate worry that data is held about oneself amounts to a breach of the right to
private and family life. In the event that such data is held the Tribunal determined
that the approach to the exercise of its jurisdiction must be to apply the "intense
scrutiny" which is required in human rights cases. It will not be enough to assert
that national security is involved, the relevant public body must show sufficient
facts and context to satisfy the Tribunal that its conduct has been rational and
proportionate. The Tribunal must then weight all relevant facts including the
context, the nature of the information and extent of the interference in
determining whether art.8(2) is satisfied.

In the case of *Al Fayed v Secretary of State for the Home Department*, the **15–13**
Tribunal considered similar issues to those considered in the *Baker* case. In the *Al
Fayed* case the appellant had made subject access applications to the Security
Service and the Secret Intelligence Service (commonly known as MI6).

A certificate in the same terms as that issued to the Security Service was
issued in respect of the Secret Intelligence Service by the Foreign Secretary. The
Tribunal's decision in *Baker* however had the effect of quashing the certificate
issued by the Home Secretary and the Foreign Secretary conceded, in light of the
Baker decision, that his certificate should be withdrawn. At the hearing on
December 11, 2001 the only contentious issue was that of the Applicant's costs.
The Respondents contended that, as the respective certificates had been either
withdrawn or quashed prior to the hearing, the Tribunal had no power to award
the Applicant his costs. The Tribunal rejected this argument and awarded the
costs.

In the case of *Gosling v Secretary of State for the Home Department* Mr **15–14**
Gosling, a journalist, challenged the replacement certificate which was issued by
the Secretary of State for the Home Department after the first version was

---

[7] Accessed September 20, 2012.
[8] SI 2000/2665.

quashed in the *Baker* case. The replacement certificate was issued on December 10, 2001. Mr Gosling made a subject access request in March 2002. He received a NCND response to his request for his "security service file". In his appeal he argued that the Service had behaved improperly in conducting its activities generally and in particular that there was, in effect, a blanket ban on providing subject access despite the fact that the Service gave evidence that specific consideration had been given as to whether a NCND response should be given in his particular case. The Tribunal considered the revised certificate which set out the different functions of the Service and specified the extent to which each function requires exemption. They noted that the intention was to provide for exemption proportionate to the risk of disclosure in respect of each category of information and that the certificate set out the circumstances in which exemption would be claimed. It was noted by the Tribunal that the decision to give an NCND response in the case was taken by the Service.

The Tribunal considered whether, applying judicial review principles, it was lawful for the respondent, the Home Secretary, to provide in the certificate that the decision on whether to issue a NCND response in each case was wholly within the discretion of the Service. The UK case law was considered in which the courts have consistently accepted that national security is the sole responsibility of the executive and the courts cannot interfere. The Tribunal noted that this approach had not met with complete approval from the ECtHR saying,

"... we discern in the European jurisprudence a broader principle to the effect that claims to national security should, save perhaps in the most exceptional and extreme circumstances, be subject to some form of independent scrutiny".

Accordingly the Tribunal expressed serious doubts as to whether Parliament had intended that the Service itself would exclusively determine the application of the NCND policy without any form of independent scrutiny. However the Tribunal reviewed whether the applicant would have recourse to the IPT to make a complaint about the Service's behaviour and its decision to issue a NCND response. The complaint to the IPT would be that the Service's conduct in giving him an NCND response was unlawful either because it was incompatible with his rights under art.8 or an unjustified decision using its discretion. After discussions with the respondent it was accepted that he would have the right to make such a complaint under s.65 of the Regulation of Investigatory Powers At 2000. The Tribunal concluded that the IPT was best placed to determine the complaints and dismissed the appeal but noted its concerns at the extent and use of the delegated powers.

15–15   A similar case was brought around the same time by a journalist who had been a Marxist activist 30 years earlier but was now a conservative journalist. In *Hichins v Secretary of State for the Home Department* the applicant had made requests which had spanned the two certificates. His appeal against the receipt of a NCND response under the second certificate was heard in March 2003, after the *Gosling* case had been heard. Mr Hichins pointed out that some information about the activities of the Security Services from 30 years earlier had been released into the public domain and in relation to himself there was no reason to regard him as a threat to national security at the time of the request. The Service had, as one of the reasons for the issue of a NCND response, made the argument that if it responded in some cases by acknowledging that it did or did not hold personal data for national security reasons the issue of a NCND response in other cases could indicate that in fact there was information that it did not wish to reveal. The Tribunal found it difficult to accept this absolute position saying that,

"... as a matter of commonsense [there must be] some cases where a definite response would not enable an inference to be drawn in other cases".

However the Tribunal accepted that as long as the certificate was valid it could make no further order. Although it was critical of the fact that the certificate was not accompanied by or included any guidance on relevant factors to be taken into account in deciding whether to issue a NCND response it dismissed the appeal and pointed the applicant to the IPT.

In the case of *Hilton v Secretary of State for Foreign and Commonwealth Affairs* the applicant had worked at GCHQ and the certificate considered was issued in respect of GCHQ and the Secret Intelligence Service (SIS). The hearing was in March 2003. Again the requests had spanned the two versions of the certificate. The GCHQ certificate was in the same form as the Home Office one but was accompanied by guidance on the application of certificate and the considerations to take into account in deciding whether to issue an NCND response. In this case the applicant was provided with his personnel records. He was informed that GCHQ did hold a vetting file on him and information about post-employment monitoring but this would not be disclosed for security reasons. He received a NCND response in relation to any other information. The Tribunal accepted that the certificate was valid and dismissed the appeal. The applicant was referred to make any complaints about the issue of the NCND response to the IPT.

15–16

In the case of *SSHD*,[9] the case was appealed to the High Court which supported the view which had been taken by the Tribunal. The original applicant had sought subject access from the Immigration and Nationality Department (IND) and received a NCND response in the following terms:

15–17

"We have processed your request and enclose copies of all the information which IND is required to supply under the Data Protection Act".

SSHD applied to the Information Commissioner for an assessment and the Commissioner wished to check that the s.28 exemption had been properly claimed. The Commissioner served an Information Notice asking for sight of any information which the Department claimed was covered by the exemption in order to check that the exemption was being properly applied. The Department responded by obtaining a Ministerial Certificate. The form of the Certificate is not set out in the High Court judgment but the Tribunal explained that the certificate was signed on the premise that the Commissioner had no statutory role within the context of the s.28 exemption. The Commissioner then appealed against the Certificate as a person "directly affected". The Tribunal agreed that he

---

[9] See fn.1.

was a person directly affected and had the locus to mount an appeal. It held that the Certificate was liable to be quashed as it had been issued on the basis that the Commissioner had no proper role:

> "As the certificate was signed on the premise that the Commissioner had no statutory role within the context of section 28 exemptions it must follow that the Secretary of State fundamentally misdirected himself as to the law and accordingly did not have reasonable grounds for issuing the certificate. This means that the certificate is liable to be quashed".

The Secretary of State appealed to the High Court which dismissed the appeal and agreed with the Tribunal. The interesting aspect of the case is that, on a reading of the Act, it would appear that the effect of s.28 was intended to exclude the Commissioner from the process. All the regulatory powers of the Commissioner are excluded by s.28. However the High Court followed the Tribunal in finding that the Commissioner's general remit as set out in s.51 was a sufficient basis to allow him to at least make efforts to check the assertions of Government Departments. In doing so they applied an interpretation which accords with arts 13 and 28(4) of the Directive.

15–18   The relevant certificate does not appear to have been altered after the decision. This conclusion is drawn from the fact that the certificate lists premises covered by the certificate and in March 2008 it was amended to include some further premises. The fact that four current certificates are in operation is in the public domain because the statement to this effect appears in a response to a Parliamentary question asked by Lynne Jones MP. The letter from the Home Office Minister in December 2008 lists four certificates as:

- December 2001 in respect of the Security Services;
- March 2008 in respect of the Security Services;
- March 2002 Intelligence and Security Committee and Secretariat; and
- July 2002 Transport for London Traffic Data.

Copies of these certificates were placed in the House of Commons library. In addition it is assumed that the certificate issued in respect of GCHQ remains in operation. We are not aware of any others although it may be assumed that there are further certificates in operation.

15–19   In 2009 the pressure group, Privacy International, brought an action to challenge the TfL certificate, which relates to the use of data collected by cameras that are used to track vehicles for the purpose of the congestion charge. The certificate provides in effect that such data may be withheld on national security grounds. Privacy International argued that it was "directly affected" as the cameras tracked many of its members. The Tribunal however dismissed the applicant and held that it did not fall within the category of persons directly affected by the certificate and had no locus to apply to the Tribunal.

CRIME AND TAXATION

Who can claim the exemption?

Section 29 was amended during its passage through Parliament as a result of **15–20** intense debate. It covers two distinct elements of exemption. The first element, contained in s.29(1)–(3), largely reproduces exemptions which appeared in the 1984 Act. The second element, contained in s.29(4)–(5), deals with systems of risk assessment, and was new in the 1998 Act. The risk assessment exemption is dealt with at the end of this section.

As with national security, and indeed most of the exemptions, the application of the exemptions in s.29(1)–(3) is not determined by the identity of the person who claims them. Anyone who can fulfil the exemption conditions may lay claim to one or more of the exemptions. The exemptions apply to anyone who processes for one of 10 relevant purposes and who fulfils the necessary conditions. The purposes are set out in s.29(1)(a), (b) and (c). Broken down, they cover the following:

(a)   the prevention of crime;
(b)   the detection of crime;
(c)   the apprehension of offenders;
(d)   the prosecution of offenders;
(e)   the assessment of any tax;
(f)   the collection of any tax;
(g)   the assessment of any duty;
(h)   the collection of any duty;
(i)   the assessment of any imposition of a similar nature to a tax or duty; and
(j)   the collection of any imposition of a similar nature to a tax or duty.

The processing must have been carried out for one of these purposes. It is clear that the provision will apply to those bodies for which the investigation of crime or the prosecution of offenders is their primary purpose. It is less clear where the boundaries lie for those who might be described as carrying out such processing for "secondary purposes", that is otherwise than for the core purposes of the organisation. There may be actions by a private body or a public body where a crime is not central to the reason for the processing action or decision but has a relevance to the processing. For example, the investigation of dishonesty in an employee may be investigated primarily as a disciplinary matter by an employer. The employer may choose not to report it to the police. Nevertheless, the actions of the employee were criminal. It is not clear whether the controller could claim the exemption for the apprehension of crime for any processing involved. The heading "prevention of crime" could cover a very wide area. It is suggested that the proper approach is to construe these narrowly as they are exemptions. Prosecution is limited to criminal proceedings and does not cover civil proceedings.

What does the exemption cover?

15–21   The exemption covers the first principle (except to the extent to which it requires compliance with Schs 2 and 3) and the subject access right in s.7 but only in any case to the extent to which the application of those provisions to the data would prejudice the particular purpose. It should be noted that it does not cover Schs 2 and 3 hence the provisions that data processing shall be carried out on legitimate grounds and the requirement for specific additional grounds for holding sensitive data remain. It does cover the requirement that personal data shall be processed fairly and lawfully together with the detailed requirements in paras 1 and 2 of Pt II of Sch. I. The requirements to inform individuals of the identity of the controller and the purposes of the processing, therefore only apply to the extent that they would not prejudice the relevant purpose. The data will be exempt from the right of subject access to the same extent.

The subject access and the fair processing obligation exemptions can also be "transferred" from the person who initially held personal data for one of the 10 purposes which are covered by s.29(1) to another person who processes it for the purpose of discharging statutory functions. Under s.29(2) such data are exempt to the same extent as they were in the hands of the original controller. There is no restriction on the type of statutory function. It need not be one concerned with or connected with the original purpose. The terms "to the same extent" is not explained. It is assumed that it means that the personal data are exempt only to the extent that the disclosure would prejudice the original purpose. For example if the police pass intelligence information to HM Customs and Revenue the Revenue would not have to provide subject access to the extent that the police would have been able to claim a s.29 exemption.

The further element of the exemption is the non-disclosure exemption. In s.29(3) personal data are exempt from the non-disclosure provisions where the disclosure is for one of the 10 purposes and the exemption provisions apply, that is, that compliance with the provision of the Act would prejudice any of those 10 purposes. It should be noted, however, that the non-disclosure provisions cannot be transferred to third parties. The non-disclosure provisions mean the principles, apart from principle 7 dealing with security, to the extent which they are inconsistent with the disclosure in question.

For example, the principles include a restriction on disclosures which are incompatible with the purpose of processing. If the exemption applies a controller may make any disclosure, even if it would otherwise be unfair or incompatible, if it is for one of the crime or taxation purposes and the application of the principle would prejudice any of those matters in relation to that particular disclosure.

When can the exemption be claimed?

15–22   The exemption can only be claimed on a case by case basis. It is not a blanket exemption. In *R. v Secretary of State for the Home Department Ex p. Lord*[10] the Secretary of State sought to argue that review reports on Category A prisoners should never be disclosable in response to a subject access request because the reports were held for the purpose of preventing and detecting crime and

---

[10]   [2003] insert reference

disclosure would prejudice those purposes. It was argued that the disclosure would lead to less frank assessments being made because of the concerns of prison officers for their safety. Further it was submitted that some reports might contain information the disclosure of which would prejudice prison security for example by providing information on prisoners' associates or revealing intelligence information. In effect this was an argument for a class exemption to be applied to the reports. In deciding the point the judge referred to the decision of the Tribunal in relation to the equivalent provision of the 1984 Act in the case of *Equifax Europe Ltd v Data Protection Registrar*,[11] in which the Tribunal had accepted that the term "in any case" meant "in any particular case" and that the test had to be applied on a case by case basis. The judge agreed that the data controller must show that one or more of the statutory purposes would be prejudiced or be likely to be prejudiced by the disclosure of the particular personal data in the particular case. He did however accept that the data controller remains able to take into account the potential consequential effect that disclosure in one case may have in others.[12] This applies equally to data in the hands of the original controller or in the hands of the person discharging the statutory functions to whom they have been passed, and applies to the non-disclosure exemptions as well as to the subject information provisions. Data will only be exempt in a particular case to the extent to which the application of the relevant provisions to the data would be likely to prejudice any of the functions listed in this section.

Whether there is a likelihood of prejudice in a particular case will be a question of fact and judgment. In order for there to be prejudice there must be a positively detrimental effect and likelihood will be judged on the basis of whether it is more likely than not. In *R. v Lord*[13] the court considered the meaning of the term "likely", pointing out that the term has "neither a single nor even a prima facie meaning". He quoted Chadwick LJ in *Three Rivers District Council v Governor and Company of the Bank of England (No.4)*[14] in which he said that,

15–23

> "'likely' does not carry any necessary connotation of 'more probable than not'. It is a word which takes its meaning from context. And where the context is a jurisdictional threshold to the exercise of a discretionary power, there may be good reason to suppose that the legislature—or the rule-making body, as the case may be—intended a modest threshold of probability".

He explained that in *Re H*[15] the House of Lords treated the word "likely" in s.31(2) of the Children Act 1989 as meaning that there has to be a real, substantial, rather than merely speculative, possibility, whereas in the *Three Rivers* case the word imported simply a test that the outcome was "more than fanciful". He summed up the correct approach as follows:

> "I accept that 'likely' in section 29(1) does not mean more probable than not. But on the other hand it must connote a significantly greater degree of probability than merely 'more than fanciful'. A 'real risk' is not enough. I cannot accept that the

---

[11] *Encyclopaedia of Data Protection* reference DA 90 25/49/7.
[12] *Lord*, para.122.
[13] See fn.12.
[14] [2003] 1 W.L.R. 210.
[15] [1996] A.C. 563.

important rights intended to be conferred by section 7 are intended to be set at nought by something which measures up only to the minimal requirement of being real, tangible or identifiable rather than merely fanciful. Something much more significant and weighty than that is required. After all the Directive, to which I must have regard in interpreting section 29(1) permits restrictions on the data subject's right of access to information about himself only (to quote the language of recital (43)) 'in so far as they are necessary to safeguard' or (to quote the language of Article 13(1)) 'constitute a necessary measure to safeguard' the prevention and detection of crime (emphasis added). The test of necessity is a strict one. The interference with the rights conferred on the data subject must be proportionate to the reality as well as to the potential gravity of the public interests involved. It is for those who seek to assert the exemption in section 29(1) to bring themselves within it and moreover to do so convincingly, not by mere assertion but by evidence that establishes the necessity contemplated by the Directive.

In my judgment 'likely' in section 29(1) connotes a degree of probability where there is a very significant and weighty chance of prejudice to the identified public interests. The degree of risk must be such that there 'may very well' be prejudice to those interests, even if the risk falls short of being more probable than not"[16].

15–24   In relation to the equivalent provision under the 1984 Act the view of the Registrar was that the assessment of likelihood of prejudice should be an objective assessment. The question would not be whether the controller believed there to be a likelihood of prejudice but whether in fact there would be prejudice. In the case of *Chief Constable of Humberside Police v Information Commissioner*,[17] a comment was made by Lord Justice Hughes about the application of s.29(1) to the retention of records of convictions in which he suggested that the retention of all conviction records is taken out of the fairness requirement of principle one by s.29(1) on the basis that the absence of a comprehensive record of such matters would be likely to prejudice the prevention and detection of crime and the apprehension or prosecution of offenders. The comment was obiter but we would submit it must be contrary to the fundamental requirement that the exemption be applied on a case-by-case basis.

There have been a range of cases which have considered the disclosure of personal data but most of them have been dealt with as raising questions under art.8 of the Convention rights rather than Data Protection Act issues.[18] It was mentioned briefly in *Re R (A Child)* (2004),[19] but only for the court to comment that the Act neither prevented nor required the disclosure of particular information. In the current Guide the Commissioner states:

"The Act does not explain 'likely to prejudice'. However our view is that for these exemptions to apply, there would have to be a substantial chance (rather than a mere risk) that complying with the provision would noticeably damage one or more of the crime and taxation purpose."

---

[16] Lord, paras 99, 100.
[17] [2009] EWCA Civ 1079.
[18] See the discussion of case law in Ch.2.
[19] [2004] EWHC 2085 (Fam).

Risk assessment classifications systems

Section 29(4) provides for an exemption from the rights of subject access   **15–25**
contained in s.7 for personal data which consist of some risk assessment
information.

The data controller for the personal data must be either a government
department, or a local authority or another authority administering housing
benefit or council tax benefit. It applies where the authority operates a system of
risk assessment in connection with its functions which it applies to data subjects
to evaluate the risk (broadly) of non-payment, non-compliance or fraud. If the
authority had to provide the risk markers attached to particular records in
response to subject access requests it might undermine the operation of the
system. The risk assessment system has to be operated for one of the following
purposes:

(a)   the assessment or collection of any tax or duty or any imposition of a
       similar nature; or
(b)   the prevention or detection of crime, or apprehension or prosecution of
       offenders, where the offence concerned involves any unlawful claim for
       any payment out of, or any unlawful application of public funds; and
(c)   the personal data involved must be processed for one of these purposes.

By virtue of s.29(5), "public funds" includes funds provided by any
Community institution. The subject access exemption is available "to the extent
to which the exemptions [are] required in the interests of the operation of the
system". This provision had a stormy passage through Parliament. The original
version of s.29(4) was the subject of the only defeat for the Government. It
provided for a sweeping exemption which was subsequently significantly
narrowed down to its current limits. The passage of the Bill through Parliament is
dealt with in Annex 1A.

Responding to requests by law enforcement agencies for personal data

It should be noted that s.29 is simply a permissory provision. In relation to the   **15–26**
powers of public bodies s.29 does not provide a power to disclose. Case law
suggests that public bodies may disclose confidential information or personal
data for the purposes of the prevention or detection of crime as being in the public
interest.[20] Equally s.29 cannot overcome any prohibitions on disclosure found in
other provisions. In this it can be contrasted to Pt 3 of the Anti-Terrorism Crime
and Security Act 2001 (ATCSA), which removed statutory restrictions on the
disclosure of information, including personal or confidential information,
contained in around 60 Acts including the restriction on the Commissioner in
s.59(1). It also extended the grounds for some public sector data holders to
disclose personal and/or confidential information for law enforcement purposes.
In general terms, the extended purposes are those of any criminal investigation or
proceedings, whether in the United Kingdom or elsewhere. However, neither s.29

---

[20] See Ch.25 on data sharing for a discussion of the powers of public bodies in this area.

DPA nor Pt 3 of ACSA compel the holders of personal data to disclose such information to the law enforcement agencies. If a data controller is under any such obligation it will be found elsewhere.

15–27   A data controller who is the subject of a request from the police or other law enforcement agency for the disclosure of personal data may therefore find that they have to engage in a difficult balancing act between satisfying the request from the police and acting within the constraints of confidentiality or protecting the interests of their clients or customers. The data controller will have to consider the extent of its powers to make the disclosure requested, any specific legal constraints to which it is subject including the data subject's rights under the DPA and the Human Rights Act 1998 and, in particular the qualified right to privacy established by art.8 of the ECHR and any duty or obligation to provide information to the authorities.

15–28   The case of *R. (on the application of NTL Group Ltd) v Ipswich Crown Court*[21] provides some clarification for a data controller seeking to balance apparently conflicting statutory obligations relating to the disclosure of personal data to law enforcement agencies.

The claimant, NTL, was a telecommunications company which had a computer system which automatically stored emails from the relevant internet provider. Those emails were destroyed one hour after being read by the recipient. Unread emails were kept for a further limited period. The police had good reason to believe that a number of persons were involved in a widespread conspiracy to defraud members of the public. A detective constable served on the claimant a notice of application for the production of special procedure material under s.9 of, and Sch.1 to, the Police and Criminal Evidence Act 1984 (PACE). Paragraph 11 of Sch. 1 provided that where a notice of application for an order had been served on a person, he should not conceal, destroy, alter or dispose of the material to which the application related except with the leave of the judge or written permission of a constable until the application was dismissed or abandoned or he had complied with an order made on the application.

The claimant was of the opinion that the only way to comply with the notice was to intercept the emails by transferring them to a different email address to that intended for the recipient which would involve it in committing an offence under s.1 of the Regulation of Investigatory Powers Act 2000, namely intentionally and without lawful authority intercepting any communication in the course of its transmission. It accordingly wrote to the police constable requesting permission to destroy or dispose of the material to which the application related. That request was turned down and the police force therefore applied to the Crown Court. The judge ruled that the claimant would not be committing a criminal offence once they had received the notice of application.

The claimant applied for judicial review of that decision contending that by preserving the emails it would be necessary to modify or interfere with its telecommunications system or its operation and monitor transmissions made by means of the telecommunication system, the purpose of which would be to make some or all of the contents of the communication available, while being

---

[21] [2002] EWHC Admin 1585.

transmitted, to a person other than the sender or intended recipient of the communication and thus would fall within meaning of interception contained in s.2(2), (7) and (8) of RIPA.

The Divisional Court dismissed the application. Reading s.2(2) in conjunction with s.2(7) and (8) of the 2000 Act, it was clear where an email was preserved by transmitting it to a different address to that of the recipient an offence would be committed. However, it was implicit in the terms of para.11 of Sch. 1 to PACE that the body, subject to an notice of application for special procedure material under s.9 of PACE, had the necessary power to take the action which it had to take in order to conserve communications by email within its system until such time as the court decided whether or not to make an order. No harm would be caused to any third party because unless a judge was prepared to make the order and therefore remove the protection which would otherwise exist for third parties the police would have no right to be informed of the contents of the material retained by the claimant. It followed that the judge had come to the correct conclusion.

A data controller who is approached by a law enforcement agency for disclosure of personal data but who is uncertain about the applicability or ambit of the exemptions in the Data Protection Act 1998 and the legitimacy of the disclosure should exercise prudence. Clearly the data controller will wish to check the bona fides of the requester but in addition it is not wrong to require that the agency obtain an order or warrant under appropriate enabling legislation. At the very least the controller should seek written confirmation from the police stating that personal data are required for a criminal investigation and that seeking the data subject's consent would undermine the investigation. Where the data controller foresees that he may face such requests he should ensure that the initial notice to data subjects makes it clear that personal data will be disclosed to a law enforcement agency where the data controller has reasonable grounds for believing that an unlawful act has been committed.

15–29

15–30

REGULATORY ACTIVITY

Who can claim the exemption?

A range of bodies can claim exemption under s.31 from the subject information provisions to the extent that the application of those provisions would prejudice the proper discharge of the relevant functions. Like the crime and taxation exemption and the national security exemption, it applies to personal data processed for particular functions rather than to specific bodies or organisations. However, in this case it is difficult to find a general term which covers the different categories of functions.

Section 31(2) applies to "relevant functions" which broadly cover regulatory activities of a public nature. The regulatory activity must be carried out by or under any enactment, or by the Crown or a Minister of the Crown or government department or be exercised in the public interest and be of a public nature.

15–31

Although the last category does not limit the nature of the legal persons who can carry it out, it limits the function, in that broadly speaking it must be one which would be judicially reviewable.

The exemption can be claimed where personal data are processed for the purpose of discharging any of the functions specified in s.31(2) as long as those functions are carried out by one of the types of bodies specified in s.31(3).

The relevant functions cover those designed for protecting members of the public from financial loss caused by dishonesty or malpractice of various kinds. They would, for example, cover the functions of the Law Society regulating the conduct of solicitors in so far as they are relevant to providing protection against malpractice, dishonesty or other seriously improper conduct or in relation to the unfitness or incompetence of persons authorised to carry on professional activity. It only applies, however, where the relevant function relates to persons "authorised" to carry on any professional activity. Therefore it would not apply if there was no need for authorisation to conduct the activity. So for example the functions of the Advertising Standards Authority which is a self-regulatory organisation would not be covered because practitioners are not authorised to practise by that body.

The charity and community interest functions relate to those for protecting charities and community interest companies against misconduct or mismanagement in their administration, protecting the property of charities and community interest companies from unlawful misapplication or for the recovery of the property of charities or community interest companies. The provision allowing exemption where recovery of property is involved is wider than any other and extends into an area which is not covered by any other exemption.

There are then further provisions where functions are designed for securing the health, safety and welfare of persons at work or for protecting persons other than persons at work against risk to health or safety arising out of or in connection with the actions of persons at work.

15–32 Section 31(4) applies to a further set of personal data, that is personal data processed for the purpose of discharging the functions of a listed number of public sector ombudsmen designed for protecting members of the public against maladministration by public bodies, failures in services provided by public bodies or failure of public bodies to provide the public services for which they are responsible. The ombudsmen are:

- The Parliamentary Commissioner for Administration;
- The Commissioner for Local Administration in England;
- The Health Service Commissioner for England;
- The Public Services Ombudsman for Wales;
- The Assembly Ombudsman for Northern Ireland;
- The Northern Ireland Commissioner for Complaints; and
- The Scottish Public services Ombudsman.

Insofar as it covers maladministration it is only maladministration by public bodies. Therefore it does not cover the functions of the private ombudsmen who regulate by contractual agreements, as for example the banking ombudsman or the insurance or pensions ombudsmen.

Section 31(4A) covers personal data processed for the purpose of discharging any function which is conferred by or under Pt XVI of the Financial Services and Markets Act 2000 on the body established by the Financial Services Authority for the purposes of that Part. Part XVI of the FSMA establishes an ombudsman scheme—described as a scheme whereby certain disputes may be resolved quickly and with minimum formality by an independent person. The disputes potentially covered relate to complaints of misbehaviour within the ambit of activities regulated by the Financial Services Authority.

Section 31(4B) covers personal data processed for the purposes of any function of the Legal Services Board.

Section 31(5) covers personal data processed for the purpose of discharging **15–33** any function which is conferred by or under any enactment on the Office of Fair Trading and is designed for one of three particular functions. Those functions are, broadly, those of:

(a) protecting members of the public against sharp or improper business behaviour;
(b) regulating anti-competitive agreements; and
(c) preventing abuse of dominant position in the market.

Regulation 29 of the Enterprise Act 2002 (Amendment) Regulations 2006 **15–34** inserted a new s.31(5A) as follows:

"(5A) Personal data processed by a CPC enforcer for the purpose of discharging any function conferred on such a body by or under the CPC Regulation are exempt from the subject information provisions in any case to the extent to which the application of those provisions to the data would be likely to prejudice the proper discharge of that function."

A CPC enforcer is a body which enforces consumer protection law but in this case excludes the Office of Fair Trading.

Under s.31(6), personal data processed for the purpose of the functions of considering a complaint under ss.113(1) or (2) or 114(1) or (3) of the Health and Social Care (Community Health and Standards) Act 2003, or s.s24D, 26 and 26ZB of the Children Act 1989, are also covered by the exemption.

The content of the exemption is relatively narrow. It applies to the subject **15–35** information provisions, namely the first principle insofar as it requires compliance with the fair processing requirements and s.7, that is the right of subject access.

When can the exemption be claimed?

It can be claimed in any case to the extent to which the application of the fair **15–36** processing requirements or the subject access provisions would be likely to prejudice the proper discharge of the particular function. The test of prejudice and likelihood and the provision for a case by case basis are the same as in relation to crime and taxation as above.

The exemption only applies to the extent required for the particular function and the particular exemption. For example, if a function would only be affected by the fair processing provisions the data controller dealing with it may only lay claim to that exemption and not also to the subject access provisions. If he wishes to claim the subject access exemption, that must be justified separately.

ARMED FORCES

Who can claim the exemption?

15–37   This exemption is contained in para.2 of Sch.7. It exempts personal data from the subject information provisions. The exemption can be claimed by any data controller as long as the controller can establish that to comply with the subject information provisions would prejudice the combat effectiveness of the armed forces.

What is covered?

15–38   The exemption covers the subject information provisions, namely, the is the fair processing provisions in para.2 of Pt II of Sch.I and the subject access provisions in s.7.

When can it be claimed?

15–39   It can be claimed in any case to the extent to which the application of those provisions would be likely to prejudice the combat effectiveness of any of the armed forces of the Crown. This will be a question of fact. Presumably the view of a senior officer of the Crown will be decisive in establishing whether there is a likelihood of prejudice. The comments in relation to the extent of prejudice and the nature of likelihood in the section on crime and taxation are equally applicable to this provision.

IMPACT OF THE DRAFT REGULATION IN BRIEF

15–40   The impact of the proposals are complex in this area Any processing of personal data which is outside the scope of Union law or is for the purposes of the common foreign or security policy of the Union is outside the scope of both the Regulation and the Directive. Therefore the proposals do not affect personal data processed for the purposes of national security.

All processing of personal data which is for the purpose of prevention, investigation, detection or prosecution of criminal offences or prosecution of criminal offences or execution of criminal penalties by competent authorities, i.e. public bodies with functions in respect of such activities will be covered by the proposed draft Directive and not the Regulation. Articles 11 and 13 of the draft Directive provide for Member States to apply exemptions from the right to have notice of processing and the right to access where these may be justified and proportionate. The Directive will have to be implemented by national law so the terms of the exemptions will depend on the national law. It may be assumed that the national law adopted to implement the Directive will also be applied to the processing of personal data for the purposes of national security. Private sector bodies processing for the purposes of the prevention or detection of crime will be subject to the draft Regulation as will public bodies carrying out processing for the collection of taxation. Article 21 of the draft Regulation provides for Member States to apply exemptions to the revised set of principles (which exclude security and overseas transfers), the individual rights and the obligation to communicate a data breach to individuals where the restrictions constitute a national and proportionate measure to safeguard any of the following:

- public security;
- prevention, investigation, detection and prosecution of criminal offences;
- other public interests of the Union or Member State in particular and important economic or financial interest;
- prevention, investigation, detection and prosecution of breaches of ethics for regulated professions;
- a monitoring or inspection function in connection with one of the three listed above; and
- the protection of the data subject or the rights or freedoms of others.

It follows that there will be exemptions but they will be for the Member State to determine and we are not able to comment other than to say that the provision appears wide enough to allow for a repeat of the current applicable exemptions covered in this Chapter

ADDITIONAL INFORMATION

Derivations   15–41

- Directive 95/46 (See Appendix B):
  (a)   arts 3 (scope), 13 (exemptions and restrictions);
  (b)   Recitals 13, 43, 44.
- Council of Europe Convention of January 28, 1981 for the Protection of Individuals with regard to automatic processing of Personal Data: art.9 (exceptions and restrictions).
- Data Protection Act 1984: ss.27 (national security), 28 (crime and taxation), 30 (regulation of financial services etc.).
- Organisation for Economic Co-operation and Development Guidelines: Annex Pt One (scope of guidelines).

Hansard references   15–42

Vol.586, No.108, col.CWH 60, Lords Grand Committee, February 23, 1998: Exemptions for national security
Vol.586, No.110, col.67, Lords Grand Committee, February 23, 1998: "In any case".
Vol.586, No.110, cols 70, 71:
Effect on exchanges of information under the Crime and Disorder Bill 1998.

Vol.586, No.110, cols 73, 74:
Exemption from First Principle.
Vol.587, No.127, col.1097, Lords Third Reading, March 24, 1998:
Regulatory bodies.
Commons Standing Committee D, May 19, 1998, col.177:
Extent of the non-disclosure exemption in cl.28.
Commons Standing Committee D, May 19, 1998, col.180:
National security certificates.
Commons Standing Committee D, May 21,1998, cols 184–190:
Extent of s.28 exemptions and relation to data sharing.
Commons Standing Committee D, May 21,1998, cols 192–195:
Insertion of Government amended cl.28(4).
Commons Standing Committee D, May 21,1998, cols 201, 203, 204:
Addition of Ombudsmen to regulatory list.
Vol.315, No.198, cols 586–591, Commons Third Reading, July 25, 1998:
Crime and taxation.
Vol.591, No.184, col.1494, Lords consideration of Commons amendments, July 10, 1998:
Consideration of s.28(4) as amended.

15–43   **Previous case law**
Equifax (Europe) Ltd v Data Protection Registrar (1991) Data Protection Tribunal.
In this case the Tribunal held the exemption in s.28 of the 1984 Act applied on a case by case basis.

CHAPTER 16

Exemptions For Personal And Family Information, Health And Social Work, Employment And Schools

INTRODUCTION

This chapter covers the exemptions which are intended to protect individuals plus those which cover personnel information. Some of the exemptions appear in the body of the Act but the health, social work, education and embryology exemptions are contained in orders made by the Secretary of State. If data are covered by an exemption the data controller will not have to tell the individual that the exemption is being claimed. Thus if information is withheld when a subject access request has been made the controller may not be required to tell the individual of that. As is the case with all exemptions a court will construe them strictly against the party seeking to rely on them. Where the subject access exemption applies to data which are otherwise covered by the Act the courts will have no powers to enforce the subject access rights or to deal with any associated claims for failure to give subject access. The Commissioner will have no power to take enforcement actions. However the other individual rights will continue to apply in respect of the personal data. An individual could, in theory, serve a s.10 notice of objection or a s.12 prohibition in respect of automated decision-making in respect of personal data to which the controller did not have to give subject access. It is not clear how the individual could describe the data or how the controller could respond in such a case. In practice, the other individual rights lose much of their force where the subject access right is removed.

16–01

SUMMARY OF MAIN POINTS

16–02

(a) The health and social work exemptions cover the right of subject access and, in some limited cases, the fair processing obligations found in Sch.1 Pt II para.2.

(b) Even where the exemption covers the fair processing obligations (as described above) it does not exempt the controller from the general duty to comply with the first principle and therefore to process data fairly and lawfully.

(c) An exemption is included for pupil records held in schools, and in Scotland in further education establishments. This reproduces provisions originally found in the Education (Schools Records) Regulations 1989. The exemption mirrors the transfer of the access rights to records previously provided for under these Regulations.

(d)   The health and social work exemptions apply on a case-by-case basis.

(e)   The Freedom of Information Act 2000 introduced a new subject access exemption which applies only to manual data held by public authority and covers personnel records.

PERSONAL AND FAMILY INFORMATION

16–03   Section 36 provides that personal data processed by an individual only for the purpose of that individual's personal, family or household affairs (including recreational purposes) are exempt from the data protection principles and the provisions of Pt II and Pt III. This exemption derives from art.3.2 of the Directive, which provides that the Directive shall not apply to the processing of personal data "by a natural person in the course of a purely personal or household activity". It is very similar in wording to s.33(1) of the 1984 Act, which provided exemption for:

> "Personal data held only by an individual and concerned only with the management of his personal, family or household affairs, or held by him only for recreational purposes."

In the 1998 Act, Pt II covers the rights of data subjects and Pt III covers notification. The exemption therefore covers the individual rights of data subjects but does not disapply the supervisory regime. Thus the Commissioner is able to serve information notices in respect of such data. This was probably not necessary to comply with the Directive but brings the exemption into line with other exemptions under the Act. Section 55 of the Act also applies to the data, so it may be an offence to obtain, disclose or procure the disclosure of such personal data to another without the authority of the controller (who will presumably be the individual him or herself).

16–04   The originating provision in the Directive was considered by the European Court in *Lindqvist*. Mrs Lindqvist had posted information about members of her congregation on a website and been prosecuted under the Swedish legislation for doing so without having notified the processing to the regulator. Article 3.2 includes two exceptions from the scope of the Directive the second of which covers the processing of personal data, "by a natural person in the course of a purely personal or household activity". The European Court held that that exception

> "... must therefore be interpreted as relating only to activies which are carried out in the course of private or family life of individuals which is clearly not the case with the processing of personal data consisting in publication on the internet so that those data are made accessible to an indefinite number of persons."

This decision in effect answers the concerns expressed by the then Commissioner in submissions to the Home Office, made as part of the post-implementation appraisal of the Act (see Ch.1):

"An exemption for domestic purposes is clearly justified but potentially has very wide effect. For example an individual who installs a CCTV camera on his/her house for security purposes can direct it through a neighbour's bedroom window deliberately yet still be exempt from the Act. It is in relation to the Internet that many problems arise. One individual can publish a great deal of offensive and damaging material about others on the world wide web. This involves the processing of personal data but falls outside the scope of the Act if it is only for the individual's personal, family or household affairs (including recreational purposes)."

It appears from *Lindqvist* that a very narrow interpretation should be placed on the exception. It might be argued that *Lindqvist* suggests that the exemption does not apply where information is posted on the internet. However, such an interpretation would mean that users of social network sites who post information about friends would fall outside the exemption, a position which regulators would presumably be reluctant to take. The exemption was considered in *Law Society v Kordowski*.[1] The judge in that case held that the exemption did not apply to the website "Solicitors from Hell". It appeared from a letter read out in court that the Information Commissioner had suggested that the s.36 exemption would apply to the website. The letter was quoted in the judgment. In it the Commissioner had said that the s.36 exemption is

". . . intended to balance the individual's rights to respect for his/her private life with freedom of expression. ... The situation would clearly be impossible were the Information Commissioner be expected to rule on what it is acceptable for one individual to say about another individual. That is not what my office is established to do."

In its judgement the court made clear that it considered the Commissioner's veiw to be wrong. The website was moderated, was run as a commercial venture and clearly included third party material. The position of the Commissioner appears to be that any posting by an organisation or which is commercial will take the material out of the exemption but that an individual can still post personal data about others and fall within the exemption as long as the use is "personal and domestic".

HEALTH INFORMATION

Section 30(1) contains an order-making power for the Secretary of State to exempt from or modify the subject information provisions in relation to personal data consisting of information as to the physical or mental health or condition of the data subject. The Data Protection (Subject Access Modification) (Health) Order 2000 (SI 2000/413) was made under this section and came into force on March 1, 2000 with the Act.

16–05

---

[1] [2011] EWHC 3185.

The Data Protection (Subject Access Modification) (Health) Order 2000 (SI 2000/413)

Introduction

16–06   The 1984 Act contained a similar provision which applied only to the subject access provisions. In the 1998 Act some data may also be exempt from the fair processing obligation to provide privacy notices at the point of collection of information from the data subject. The Order applies to personal data consisting of information as to the physical or mental health or condition of the data subject. There is no definition of physical or mental health or condition but the same approach would presumably be taken to the equivalent categories of sensitive personal data defined in s.2 of the Act. It should be noted that for these purposes the term personal data covers all information about an individual, irrespective of whether it is held in computerised or manual form.[2] The Order does not apply to data which could also fall under an Order made under s.38.

Court proceedings

16–07   Certain personal data falling under the Order which are processed by a court are exempt from both the fair processing obligation in Sch.I Pt II para.2 and the subject access provisions in s.7.[3] In essence this provision preserves the confidentiality of certain reports provided to the court in proceedings concerned with the care of children. In order to qualify for the exemption the information must be related to the physical or mental health of the individual and be supplied in a report or evidence given to the court in the course of specified proceedings relating to the care of children in which the rules of court provide for the contents of the report or evidence to be withheld. The report may be made by a local authority, Health and Social Services Board or Trust, probation officer or other person making a report in the course of the specified proceedings. As with the social work and educational records orders it is not clear whether the exemption only applies when the data are in the hands of the court or when they are in the hands of the supplying person. This part of the exemption is not subject to any test of prejudice nor is it applied on a case by case basis.

Serious harm to physical or mental health

16–08   By para.5 other personal data may be exempt from the s.7 subject access rights in any case to the extent that the application of the subject access rights would be likely to cause serious harm to the physical or mental health or condition of the data subject or any other person. Thus the data subject might not be told that the controller holds personal data on him or her if to say even so much would be likely to cause serious harm. Regulation 7 provides for data controllers to obtain written confirmation from a health professional that information on an individual should be withheld but controllers must not rely on such a statement if it is over six months old or it is unreasonable to do so. The written confirmation may cover

---

[2] See Ch.11 for a discussion of the rights of access to accessible records.

[3] SI 2000/413 reg.4(2).

all the personal data held. However, more commonly, data controllers will only consider the possibility of the exemption when actually faced with a request for access and personal data will only be withheld in part.

A data controller cannot withhold data which he knows has already been seen by the subject or is already within his knowledge no matter how much harm repetition or confirmation of the data might cause.[4] A data controller who is not himself a health professional as defined in the Order must consult the appropriate health professional before withholding data under the provision.[5] The appropriate health professional is defined in para.2. The data controller should refer to the health professional who is currently or most recently responsible for providing care in relation to the matters covered by the request or if there is more than one such professional the one most suitable to advise on the issue. In the event that there is no appropriate health professional to turn to, or in those cases where the data relating to physical or mental health have been processed in relation to benefit claims under Child Support or pensions provisions, then advice should be sought from any health professional with the necessary experience and qualifications.[6]

Access by those acting on behalf of the data subject

As was noted in Ch.6, subject access requests may be made by a third party on behalf of the data subject. The Order deals with the possibility that the data subject may not want the person acting for him to have access to some information. Where the data subject is a child for whom the person with parental responsibility has exercised the subject access right or it has been exercised for the data controller by a person appointed by a court to manage his or her affairs, personal data which fall under the Order will not be disclosed if:

16–09

- the information was provided by the data subject with the expectation that it would not be disclosed to the person making the request;
- the information was obtained as a result of an examination or investigation to which the data subject agreed in the expectation that it would not be disclosed to the person making the request; or
- the data subject has expressly indicated that the information should not be so disclosed.

It is expressly provided that the data subject can alter his other mind and allow access to data which he or she had previously vetoed.[7]

Information about health professionals

Regulation 8 modifies s.7(4) of the Act which deals with access to third party data. The effect of the modification is that information on those who have contributed to the health record as professionals, usually those who have

16–10

---

[4] SI 2000/413 reg.6(2).
[5] SI 2000/413 reg.5(2).
[6] SI 2000/413 reg.2.
[7] SI 2000/413 reg.5.

provided health care to the data subject, cannot be withheld on the basis that it relates to another individual who can be identified from that information.

The court is given power to decide how far a data controller should give or not give subject access to such data which it may either exercise at the request of the data subject or on the application of:

"any other person to whom serious harm to whose physical or mental health or condition would be likely to be caused by compliance with any such request in contravention of those provisions."

This is designed to protect those about whom information would otherwise be given, for example, because they have provided health care.

SOCIAL WORK INFORMATION

16–11 Unlike the health provisions the order-making power in s.30(3) is subject to a prejudice test. There is no apparent reason for this difference. It was not the subject of any Parliamentary debate and appears to have been carried forward from the 1984 Act which made the same distinction. The Secretary of State may only make exemption or modification orders to the extent that he considers the relevant requirements of the Data Protection Act would "be likely to prejudice" the carrying out of social work.

Social work is not defined in the section. The relevant order is the Data Protection (Subject Access Modification) (Social Work) Order 2000,[8] which came into effect on March 1, 2000 with the main Act. The 2000 Order has been modified by the Data Protection (Subject Access Modification)(Social Work) (Amendment) Order 2005,[9] which added the Children and Family Court Advisory and Support Service (CAFCASS) to the list of bodies which are covered by the provisions and the data Protection (Subject Access Modification-)(Social Work)(Amendment Order) 2011 which added data processed by the Welsh family proceedings officers and Welsh Ministers in order to bring the obligations of CAFCASS Cymru into line with its counterpart in England. The Social Work Order will not apply where any of the health, education or miscellaneous subject access exemption orders apply.

Court proceedings

16–12 Under para.4, certain personal data which are processed by a court are exempt from both the fair processing requirements in Sch.I Pt II para.2 and the subject access provisions in s.7. The data must be "processed by a court" but it is not clear whether the exemption only applies to the personal data while they are in the hands of the court or to the same data in the hands of the person supplying it. The data will almost inevitably also be held by another because the data must consist of information supplied in a report or other evidence by a person in the course of legal proceedings dealing with the welfare of children. The proceedings

---

[8] SI 2000/413.
[9] SI 2005/467.

are ones in which the court has the power under the applicable Rules to withhold information from the data subject.[10] The data in the hands of the person supplying it may well be eligible for the more general social work exemption from subject access described below but the exemption from the fair processing obligation to provide privacy notices would not apply.

This part of the exemption is not applied on a case-by-case basis and involves no test of prejudice.

Social work

By para.5, other personal data may be exempt from the s.7 rights, apart from the requirement in s.7(1)(a) that the subject be informed whether the data user holds information on him, but only:

    16–13

> "In any case to the extent to which the application of those provisions would be likely to prejudice the carrying out of social work by reason of the fact that serious harm to the physical or mental health or condition of the data subject or any other person would be likely to be caused."

"Serious harm" is not defined. The order lists activities which are regarded as "carrying out of social work" in para.1 of the Schedule. As the explanatory note states:

> "The Order principally applies to data processed by local authorities, in relation to their social services and education welfare functions, and health authorities to whom such data are passed and by probation committees and the National Society for the Prevention of Cruelty to Children. The Order also applies to data processed for similar purposes by the corresponding bodies in Northern Ireland. Data processed by government departments for certain purposes connected with social work and by officers such as guardians ad litem and (in Scotland) the Principal Reporter of the Scottish Children's Reporter Administration are also within the scope of the Order. Provision is made enabling other voluntary organisations or other bodies to be added to the list of bodies whose data are subject to the provisions of the Order where the data are processed for purposes similar to the social services functions (or in Scotland social work functions) of local authorities.
>
> In the case of social work authorities in Scotland who receive certain data from the Principal Reporter, the Order requires such data controllers to obtain the Principle Reporter's approval before complying with any section 7 request."

Section 7(4) of the Act, which deals with access to third party data, is modified so that information on those who provide social work functions in a professional capacity cannot be withheld on a subject access search.[11]

    16–14

The court is given power to restrain a data controller from giving subject access in breach of the provisions of the Order in respect of such data on the application of

> "any person to whom serious harm to whose physical or mental health or condition would be likely to be caused by compliance with any such request in contravention of those provisions."

---

[10] Sch.1 para.2.
[11] s.7(1)(a) and (2).

The provision is designed to protect those about whom information would otherwise be given because they have provided social work functions. It is not clear how this provision could apply in any other situation. It is not likely that any other person would know that a subject access request which might affect him or her had been made, or be aware that he might be seriously affected by the information to be given on a subject access request.[12]

Access by those acting on behalf of the data subject

16–15   As was noted in Ch.6 subject access requests may be made on behalf of data subjects. The Order recognises that, even in such cases, there are situations where a data subject may not want anyone else to have access to certain information about him or her. Where the data subject is a child for whom the person with parental responsibility has exercised the subject access right or it has been exercised for the data subject by a person appointed by a court to manage his or her affairs, personal data which fall under the Order will not be disclosed if:

- the information was provided by the data subject with the expectation that it would not be disclosed to the person making the request;
- the information was obtained from an investigation or examination to which the data subject had consented in the expectation that it would not be so disclosed; or
- the data subject has expressly indicated that the information should not be disclosed.

It is expressly provided that the data subject can alter his or her mind and allow access which had previously been vetoed.

EDUCATION INFORMATION

16–16   The order-making power in s.30(2) mirrors the health data power in s.30(1). It contains no test of prejudice. It extends to the subject information provisions so it covers both subject access and the fair processing obligations in Sch.1 Pt II para.2. It allows the Secretary of State to exempt data from the subject information provisions or modify them in the case of personal data about pupils. The provisions are slightly different for Scotland, although in relation to primary and secondary schools the effect is the same. The exemption covers personal data which fulfils two conditions:

(a)   the data controller must either be the proprietor of, or a teacher at, a school, or an education authority in Scotland; and

(b)   the data must relate to persons who are or have been pupils at the school or are receiving or have received further education provided by the education authority.

---

[12] s.7(1)(b).

"Proprietor" is defined in s.30(5)(a) at some length. In brief it has the same meaning as in the Education Act 1996 in England and Wales, that is broadly covering the governing bodies of state schools and the equivalent controlling bodies, whether Boards or owners, of the various types of independent schools. The term has the same import in Scotland and in Northern Ireland although the particular arrangements and therefore the detailed list are different.

The Data Protection (Subject Access Modification) (Education) Order 2000 (SI 2000/414)

The Data Protection (Subject Access Modification) (Education) Order (the Education Order) will not apply where the health or miscellaneous orders apply. The exemption order came into force on March 1, 2000 with the main Act. The order applies to personal data in educational records as defined in Sch.11 of the Act.

16–17

Court proceedings

Under para.4, certain personal data which are processed by a court are exempt from the fair processing obligations in Sch.1 Pt II para.2 and the subject access provisions in s.7. The data must be "processed by a court" but it is not clear whether the exemption only applies to the personal data while they are in the hands of the court or to the same data in the hands of the person supplying it. The data will almost inevitably also be held by another because the data must consist of information supplied in a report or other evidence by a person in the course of legal proceedings dealing with education matters relating to children. The proceedings are ones in which the court has the power under the applicable rules to withhold information from the data subject.[13] The data in the hands of the person supplying it may well be eligible for the more general exemption for educational records from subject access described below but the exemption from the fair processing and fair obtaining codes would not apply. This part of the exemption is not subject to prejudice and is not applied on a case by case basis.

16–18

Educational records

By para.5, other personal data may be exempt from the s.7 rights in any case to the extent to which the application of the subject access right would "be likely to cause serious harm to the physical or mental health or condition of the data subject or any other person". "Serious harm" is not defined.

16–19

Personal data may also be exempt even where there is no likelihood of harm if, in certain circumstances it would be in the best interests of the data subject that access should be withheld. This does not apply in Scotland but otherwise applies where a request is made by another person acting for the data subject being either a parent or a person appointed by the court to manage another's affairs. In such a case, personal data "consisting of information as to whether the data subject is or has been the subject of or may be at risk of child abuse" are exempt to the extent to which it would not be in the best interests of the data subject to give the

---

[13] s.4(2).

information. "Child abuse" includes physical injury as well as physical and emotional neglect, ill-treatment and sexual abuse of a child.

16–20   Section 7(4) of the Act, which deals with access to third party data, is modified so that information on those who are employed in providing education services in a professional capacity cannot be withheld on a subject access search. However, such individuals are not left without protection where it is appropriate. The court is given power to restrain a data controller from giving subject access in contravention of the provisions of the Order in respect of such data on the application of:

> "any person to whom serious harm to whose physical or mental health or condition would be likely to be caused by compliance with any such request in contravention of those provisions."

It is not clear how this provision could apply in any other circumstance as it is not likely that any other person would know a subject access request had been made or would know that he or she might be seriously affected by it.

Education authorities in Scotland who receive and detain data from the Principal Reporter in Scotland are required to obtain his opinion on whether the disclosure of the information might cause serious harm to anyone before disclosing it in response to a subject access request.

HUMAN EMBRYOS

16–21   These are dealt with under the Data Protection (Miscellaneous Subject Access Exemptions) Order 2000[14] (amended by the Data Protection (Miscellaneous Subject Access Exemptions) (Amendment) Order 2000.[15]

The Data Protection (Miscellaneous Subject Access Exemptions) Order 2000 (SI 2000/419)

16–22   An order under s.38(1) reverses the general rule, set out in s.27(5), that subject access rights take precedence over other legal prohibitions on disclosure of information. This provides that:

> "... the subject information provisions shall have effect notwithstanding any enactment or rule of law prohibiting or restricting the disclosure, or authorising the withholding, of information."

Section 38(1) empowers the Secretary of State to override this. In effect an order under this section re-imposes the prohibition which is otherwise lifted by s.27(5). The powers prevail so far as is necessary to safeguard the interests of the data subject or the rights or freedoms of any other individual.

The equivalent order-making power was used under the 1984 Act to provide for a raft of subject access exemptions which have been re-enacted under the

---

[14] SI 2000/419.
[15] SI 2000/1865.

1998 Act. The order applied to information held in pursuance of various statutory functions largely concerned with the care of children, for example adoption records and reports.

The s.38(1) Order came into effect on March 1, 2000 with the main Act. It sets out a number of legal provisions which prohibit or restrict the disclosure of information and provides that where they apply the prohibition takes precedence over the subject access rights in s.7. The list comes in three parts covering the Human Fertilisation and Embryology Act 1990 which applies throughout the United Kingdom, provisions relating to adoption records and papers which apply in England and Wales and the equivalent provisions in Scotland. The exemption has no test of prejudice. It is limited to subject access and does not exempt any of the information from the fair obtaining and processing codes.

16–23

Background

The Human Fertilisation and Embryology Act 1990 established the Human Fertilisation and Embryology Authority.[16] It contains detailed provisions under which individuals born as a result of fertility treatment are able to research their genetic heritage. The Authority maintains a register which includes information about individuals who have been born or might be born as a result of fertility treatment.

16–24

The exemption from subject access was inserted to ensure that access by affected individual to such data would be gained under the aegis of the Authority, rather than via a data protection route. The Human Fertilisation and Embryology Act contains safeguards surrounding such access. These deal with the form in which a request for access to the register maintained by the Authority is to be made and sets out the information which may be disclosed.

PERSONNEL RECORDS

Exemption for manual personnel records

A new subject access exemption was added by the Freedom of Information Act 2000 for the purposes of category (e) data only; that is structured or unstructured manual data which is not held on a relevant filing system. The 2000 Act extended the right of subject access to cover such data where it is held by public bodies covered by the 2000 Act. The exemption covers category (e) data which is also data held for personnel matters. The policy behind the new exemption appears to be to maintain parity between employees in the public and private sectors. If the exemption had not been added a public sector employee would enjoy a far wider right of access to his employment records via subject access than an employee in the private sector. It also has the effect of preserving such information from third party inquirers because the existence of a subject access exemption means that the public authority must apply the exemption when dealing with a request for data by a third party.

16–25

---

[16] There is a proposal to transfer the functions of the Authority at the time of writing but no indication that there will be changes to the access provisions.

16–26   The additional subject access exemption is found in s.33A in the DPA inserted by s.70(1) of the FOIA. Section 33A(2) exempts this class of data from all the data protection principles, from the individual rights, from notification and from s.55 (unlawful obtaining of personal data). It is not exempted from the powers of the Commissioner which means that the power of the Commissioner to serve an information notice under s.43 to ascertain whether the DPA applies will still bite. The new exemption applies to:

> "(2) Personal data which fall within paragraph (e) of the definition of 'data' in section 1(1) and relate to appointments or removals, pay, discipline, superannuation or other personnel matters, in relation to—
>
> (a)   service in any of the armed forces of the Crown
> (b)   service in any office or employment under the crown or under any public authority, or
> (c)   service in any office or employment, or under any contract for services, in respect of which power to take action, or to determine or approve the action taken, in such matter is vested in Her Majesty, any Minister of the Crown, the National Assembly for Wales, any Northern Ireland Minister (within the meaning of the Freedom of Information Act 2000) or any public authority."

It should be noted that the existence of an exemption places the authority under no obligation to rely on it and many authorities follow an open records practice for personnel records.

Data covered by the exemption for personnel records

16–27   The line between personnel matters and administrative/management matters may be a grey one. It is possible that the exemption could be used to remove more information than anticipated from the public domain. A similar question arises to that raised in respect of the exemption for journalistic purposes; when does data fall into one category or the other?

The position of contractors in relation to the personnel exemption

16–28   Under s.5(1) of the FOIA, the Secretary of State may designate as a public authority for the purposes of the Act any person who is neither listed in Sch.1 nor capable of being added but who appears to the Secretary of State to exercise functions of a public nature or is providing under a contract made with a public authority any service whose provision is a function of that authority. The order may designate a specific person or office. The order must specify the services provided under the contract to which the designation applies. Only information held in relation to those services will be covered by the designation. The interaction of a designation and the extended right of subject access and new exemption is problematic. For example a contractor may provide facilities management or processing services under a contract. The contractor will have a responsibility for the provision of the services under the contract. As long as he meets the agreed service levels set out in the contract he will fulfil his contractual obligations. The power of the public authority over the detail of how he fulfils those obligations may be limited. The employees who carry out the service will be employed by the contractor, not the public authority. Where the Secretary of State designates a contractor as being one who is providing a service whose provision is a function of the authority and designates the services being carried out under the contract it is not clear whether the contractor will be counted as a public authority for all purposes.

If the result of a designation is to give employees of the contractor the benefit of the extension to subject access it is arguable that the contractor does not recieve the benefit of the exemption. The employees of the contractor do not appear to fall clearly within any of the classes in s.33A(2)(a)–(c). It could be argued that the employment is "service in any office or employment under the Crown or under any public authority" or that it is service

16–29

> "in any office or employment or under any contract for services in respect of which power to take action or determine or approve the action taken is vested in [one of the specified list],"

but either interpretation seems to stretch the wording of the section. If the wording cannot be stretched then the employees of the designated contractor would obtain extended subject access without the employer having the benefit of the exemption. The prudent course might be for those entering into contracts to include a clause making clear, for the avoidance of any doubt that the particular contract, is, for the purposes of the DPA a contract falling in (b) or (c).

Impact of the draft Regulation in brief[17]

Article 2 provides that the Regulation does not apply to the processing of personal data by a natural person without any gainful interest in the course of his own exclusively personal or household activity. The version of the regulation which was circulated within the Commission for comment before the version for publication was agreed included a further proviso that the exemption did not apply where personal data of other natural persons is made accessible to an indefinite number of individuals but this was removed. The personal and domestic exclusion therefore seems little changed.

16–30

Article 21 of the draft Regulation provides for Member States to apply exemptions to the revised set of principles (which exclude security and overseas transfers), the individual rights and the obligation to communicate a data breach to individuals where the restrictions constitute a national and proportionate measure to safeguard any of the following:

- public security;
- the prevention, investigation, detection and prosecution of criminal offences;
- other public interests of the Union or Member State in particular and important economic or financial interest;
- the prevention, investigation, detection and prosecution of breaches of ethics for regulated professions;

---

[17] See Ch.1 paras 1-68 onwards for an overview of the draft regulation issued by the Commission in January 2012.

- a monitoring or inspection function in connection with one of the three listed above; or
- the protection of the data subject or the rights or freedoms of others.

It follows that there will be exemptions but they will be for the Member State to determine and we are not able to comment other than to say that the provision appears wide enough to allow for a repeat of the current exemptions covered in this chapter.

ADDITIONAL INFORMATION

16–31 **Derivations**

- Directive 95/46 (see Appendix B):
  (a) arts 3.2 (scope) 13.1g (exemptions and restrictions);
  (b) Recitals 12, 22.
- Council of Europe Convention of January 28, 1981 for the Protection of Individuals with regard to automatic processing of Personal Data: art.9 (exceptions and restrictions).
- Organisation for Economic Co-operation and Development Guidelines: Annex Pt One (scope of guidelines).

Hansard references

16–32 On May 10, 2012 Mr George Howarth announced that the drafts of six of the statutory instruments, which include the exemption orders for education, social work and embryology, were to be published on the Internet. The Home Office had previously consulted on the form of the orders.

1998—the Home Office issued a consultation paper on proposals for orders to be made under the Act.

Commons Standing Committee D, May 21, 1998, cols 199–200:

Excluded data.

Vol.315, No.198, col.593, Commons Third Reading, July 2, 1998:

Education information exemption.

Previous case law

16–33 None.

CHAPTER 17

Freedom Of Expression And Exemptions For The Special Purposes

INTRODUCTION

The provisions dealing with the special purposes and the exemptions which apply   **17–01**
to those purposes are set out in ss.3, 32, 44, 45, 53, 55 and Sch.10. The reason for
this spread throughout the Act is that the exemptions are complex.
They:

- allow for non-compliance with some of the standards set out in the Act;
- restrict the powers of the court prior to publication of material;
- restrict the power of the Commissioner to take enforcement action both prior to and after publication;
- provide for the Commissioner to fund proceedings where the special purposes are in question; and
- provide a defence to the offence provisions under s.55.

All of these elements are dealt with in this chapter against the background of
press regulation and freedom of expression.

The exemptions amount to a generous implementation of the derogation in
art.9 of the Directive as far as journalistic, artistic and literary works are
concerned. They go beyond what might have been required by art.9. On the other
hand the restriction to three particular areas: journalism, artistic and literary
works could be seen as a narrow interpretation of the right to freedom of
expression. It is now clear however that a broader view should be applied as the
European Court in the *Satamedia* case[1] gave a wide meaning to the relevant
provisions in art.9 of the Directive. It also confirmed a wide meaning should be
given to the term "journalistic activity".

Background

After adoption of the Directive and before the Data Protection Bill was published   **17–02**
there was negative reporting of it in the UK press. One or two pieces suggested
that the Directive would spell the end of a free press as it is known. The Bill was
much delayed in publication. It was to be published in November 1997, then it
was delayed until December 1997 and finally saw the light of day in January

---

[1] *Tietosuojavaituutettu v Satakunnan Markkinaporssi Oy and Satamedia Oy* (62007 CJ0073).

1998. It was clear from the positive response the Bill evoked from the press when it did appear, including the comments from Lord Wakeman of the Press Complaints Commission speaking in the House of Lords in the opening debate, that the time was spent by the Government resolving the differences with press interests. The resulting provisions are intentionally complex. Giving evidence in the Leveson Inquiry the Information Commissioner, Christopher Graham, explained the complexity in relation to his enforcement powers making the point that it was clear that the political intention at the time that the Act was passed was to ensure that the press was not regulated by the Commissioner. He did however appear to suggest that the provisions were such as to allow individuals to take action themselves. In reality the data subject who wishes to restrict publication in reliance under the Data Protection Act faces an equally burdensome task. It is not simply that the provisions are complex, but that the shifts in responsibility and in the burden of proof in crucial points in the proceedings, together with the multiple possible adjudications and appeals before final disposal, make any case difficult to conclude. An individual who wishes to use the Act to take action against the press will need deep pockets, a robust constitution and preferably a favourable life expectancy. The Commissioner, while not seeking any greater role in the regulation of the press did make the point that the provisions are particularly complex and would benefit from simplification.

The emasculation of the Act has not however protected the media from the gradual restriction on intrusive journalism since the implementation of the Human Rights Act 2000 (HRA). Individuals have not sought to use the DPA to restrict publication of material. However, the courts have been prepared to grant injunctive relief to protect individuals' rights to privacy of information using the action for misuse of private information as the concepts of privacy and confidentiality have gradually been aligned in cases brought under the HRA.

The provisions of the HRA, and the relationship between privacy and freedom of expression are covered in more detail in Ch.2 and the material not repeated here, although some cases on art.10 are examined in more detail in this chapter. Any consideration of the exemption for journalistic, literary and artistic material must take into account the developments under the HRA and it is suggested that this chapter should be read together with Ch.2.

Section 32 was considered in the case of *Campbell v Mirror Group Newspapers*,[2] which is discussed in more detail below in respect of s.32 and generally in Ch.2.

The regulation of the press and the balance between press freedom and other rights are extremely topical at the time of writing. However the challenges of finding the right balance are not new. In *Schering Chemicals Ltd v Falkman Ltd*[3] Lord Denning M.R. dealt with the question of the freedom of the press to publish thus:

> "The freedom of the press is extolled as one of the great bulwarks of liberty. It is entrenched in the constitutions of the world. But it is often misunderstood. I will first say what it does not mean. It does not mean that the press is free to ruin a reputation or break a confidence, or to pollute the course of justice or to do anything which is unlawful. I will next say what it does mean. It means that there should be

---

[2] [2002] EWCA Civ 1373; see Ch.2.
[3] [1982] 1 Q.B. 1.

no censorship. No restraint should be placed on the press as to what they should publish. Not by a licensing system. Not by executive direction. Not by court injunction."

It will be interesting to see how far Lord Leveson reflects this view in his eagerly awaited report.

SUMMARY OF MAIN POINTS 17–03

(a) The s.32 exemption for journalistic, literary and artistic works applies on a case-by-case basis; it is not a blanket exemption.

(b) The exemption includes a balancing test, taking into account an assessment of public interest; it is not an absolute exemption.

(c) Protection against court action by individuals is given to journalistic, literary or artistic work prior to publication; once material is no longer being processed with a view to publication that procedural element of the exemption no longer applies.

(d) After the material has been published, individuals can take court action but the publisher may have a defence as the substantive element of the exemption continues to apply.

(e) When the substantive exemption comes into play it is extremely powerful. It can provide both a sword and a shield. It can be used to mount a defence against actions taken against publishers under the Act. The individual rights and the principles, apart from the security principle, give way. Even the rules requiring legitimacy of processing and restricting the use of sensitive data may be overridden.

(f) The powers of the Commissioner to take enforcement action are also restricted in relation to the special purposes.

(g) Private actions involving the special purposes can be funded by the Commissioner where issues of significant public interest arise.

(h) It is a defence to a charge under s.55 of the Act that information was obtained for the special purposes in the reasonable belief that it was in the public interest to do so.

REGULATION OF THE PRESS

Between 1989 and 2010 a series of Committees considered whether the United 17–04 Kingdom should regulate the press to protect the privacy of individuals and issued a number of reports. In 1989 the Government set up a committee under the chairmanship of David Calcutt QC to consider what measures might be needed to protect "individual privacy from the activities of the press". This Committee on Privacy and Related Matters reported in June 1990.[4] Largely as a result of the pressure resulting from its report, the Press Complaints Commission (PCC) was set up in 1991 to replace and strengthen the previous self-regulatory regime. The

---

[4] *Report of the Committee on Privacy,* Cmnd.1102.

press was given "one final chance" to show that legislation was not needed and that voluntary self-regulation could be made to work.

As noted in Ch.2, the possibility of legislative reform and establishment of the PCC may have been one of the reasons for the judicial restraint displayed in the case of *Kaye v Robertson*[5] when the Court reiterated that regulation of privacy was a matter for Parliament. Although decisions of the PCC have been criticised, and it is currently under fierce attack for its failures to restrain the behaviour of the tabloid press, the Code has been a mechanism for bringing some degree of regulation to bear on the behaviour of the press. The Code, together with the other self-regulatory codes for the media, has a role in the legal framework as both the HRA and the DPA require courts to take relevant codes into account when considering actions which may restrict freedom of expression. The PCC Code is described below.

Two years later, Sir David Calcutt QC (as he had then become) was asked to conduct a review of press self-regulation which was presented to Parliament in January 1993.[6] The review recommended that the Government should give further consideration to the introduction of a tort of infringement of privacy and on January 14, 1993 the Government announced that it would consider this proposal.

The issues arising from media intrusion and related privacy matters were also considered by the National Heritage Select Committee which recommended the enactment of a Protection of Privacy Bill.[7]

In July 1993 the Lord Chancellor's Department and the Scottish Office issued a consultation paper entitled Infringement of Privacy seeking responses on the proposal that a civil tort of infringement of privacy should be created. The consultation exercise took some time. In a response published in July 1995,[8] the Government responded to both the consultation paper and the National Heritage Select Committee Report at the same time. The Government concluded that no persuasive case had been made out for statutory regulation of the press and announced that it had no plans to introduce a statutory right to privacy.

The initiatives demonstrate both the depth of concern caused by media intrusion and the strength of the opposition to any government control over its behaviour. The Data Protection Directive and later the UK Bill were strongly opposed by media interests, which, having fought off the various moves to impose statutory regulation, viewed the new law as an attempt to achieve similar ends by the "back door". As was noted above this opposition resulted in the effective emasculation of the Act as a tool for media regulation.

17–05   The knotty question of how to regulate the media has of course continued to vex both politicians and pundits since the PCC came into being. In 2002–2003 the Culture Media and Sport Committee of the House of Commons produced its report on Privacy and Media Intrusion. It recognised the start (as it was at the time) of the judge-made law on art.8 and the route towards a privacy law that it was likely to take. It recommended that, rather than leaving the development to the courts, the Government should bring forward legislative proposals and deliver

---

[5] [1991] F.S.R. 62, CA (Civ Division).
[6] Cmnd.2135.
[7] *Fourth report of the Committee*, March 1993.
[8] *Privacy and Media Intrusion*. Cmnd.2918.

a privacy law to protect individuals from unwarranted press intrusion. This was not acted upon. Other recommendations argued for the strengthening of the PCC, improving its independence and the sanctions available as well as some changes to strengthen the Code itself. The Code was amended in 2004 and there have been further amendments since however it has remained a self-regulatory regime widely regarded as ineffective in controlling the excesses of press behaviour. In May 2006 the Information Commissioner published his report, *What price privacy? The unlawful trade in confidential personal information*,[9] in which he revealed that an investigation by his office into the procuring and sale of private information (Operation Motorman) had shown that there was an active and lucrative trade in personal information with journalists among the keenest customers. Six months later he published a follow up report, *What price privacy now? The first six months progress in halting the unlawful trade in confidential personal information*. In the report he listed the main media users of the services, a list headed by the *Daily Mail*. As a result of these reports the Commissioner pushed for a sanction of imprisonment to be imposed for the offence of unlawfully procuring information under s.55 of the Act.

News of the World convictions

In a parallel development that was to have seismic effects on the newspaper industry in 2007 Glen Mulcaire and Clive Goodman were jailed for six and four months respectively for offences under the Criminal Law Act 1977 of conspiracy to intercept communications in breach of s.1 of the Regulation of Investigatory Powers Act 2000. The circumstances were that Glen Mulcaire, a private investigator, was shown to have hacked into the voicemails of members of the royal family in order to supply Mr Goodman, royal correspondent for the *News of the World* newspaper, with stories. As a result the editor of the paper, Mr Coulson, resigned from his role although insisting that this was simply a case of "one rotten apple". In 2007 a further inquiry into self-regulation of the press by the Culture Media and Sport Select Committee was held as a result of these revelations and the press harassment of Ms Middleton (as she was then).[10] Despite a critical report, particularly in respect of the harassment of Ms Middleton, they concluded that the system of self regulation should be maintained for the press.

17–06

In 2009 the Culture Media and Sport Select Committee reported on "Press Standards, Privacy and Libel".[11] By this stage it had become clear, as a result of enquiries by the *Guardian* newspaper and the payment of damages by the *News of the World* to a number of people whose phones had been hacked, that there had been serious failings at the paper and the royal hackings were not isolated incidents. The extract below gives a flavour of the report:

> "We reopened oral evidence to consider the allegations contained in the *Guardian* in July 2009 that the *News of the World*'s parent company had paid over £1m in damages and costs to settle three civil actions relating to phone-hacking. We took these claims very seriously as they cast doubt on assurances we had been given

---

[9] HC No.1056, May 2006.
[10] HC No.375, July 2007.
[11] Session 2009–2010.

during our 2007 inquiry Privacy and Media Intrusion that the phone-hacking at News of the World had been limited to one 'rogue reporter', Clive Goodman.

We find that it is likely that the number of victims of illegal phone-hacking will never be known, not least because of the silence of Clive Goodman and Glenn Mulcaire, their confidentiality settlements with the *News of the World* and the 'collective amnesia' at the newspaper group which we encountered during our inquiry. It is certainly more than the 'handful', however, cited by both the newspaper and the police.

There is no doubt that there were a significant number of people whose voice messages were intercepted, most of whom would have been of little interest to Clive Goodman as the paper's royal editor. The evidence, we find, makes it inconceivable that no-one else at the *News of the World*, bar Mr Goodman, was aware of the activity. We have, however, not seen any evidence that the then Editor, Andy Coulson, knew, but consider he was right to resign. We find, however, that the newspaper group did not carry out a full and rigorous inquiry, as it assured us and the Press Complaints Commission it had. The circumstances of pay-offs made to Messrs Goodman and Mulcaire, as well as the civil settlements with Gordon Taylor and others, also invite the conclusion that silence was effectively bought.

The readiness of all concerned—News International, the police and the PCC—to leave Mr Goodman as the sole scapegoat without carrying out full investigations is striking. The verdict of the PCC's latest inquiry, announced last November, we consider to be simplistic, surprising and a further failure of self-regulation.

In seeking to discover precisely who knew what among the staff of the *News of the World* we have questioned a number of present and former executives of News International. Throughout we have repeatedly encountered an unwillingness to provide the detailed information that we sought, claims of ignorance or lack of recall, and deliberate obfuscation. We strongly condemn this behaviour which reinforces the widely held impression that the press generally regard themselves as unaccountable and that News International in particular has sought to conceal the truth about what really occurred."

Despite this, the Committee continued to recommend against statutory regulation and remained in favour of self-regulation. Throughout 2009 and 2010 claims emerged of hacking of other individuals' phones and the News of the World settled a number of cases against it. In early 2011 the Metropolitan Police re-opened its investigation into phone hacking at the paper. The final blow for the *News of the World* came in July 2011 when it was revealed that the paper had hacked into the mobile phone of murdered schoolgirl Millie Dowler, allegedly giving false hope that she remained alive. In July the Murdoch Corporation announced that the paper would be closed down. The fall-out continues at the time of writing. A number of arrests have been made in connection with the affair and some individuals have been charged but there have been no further convictions at the data of writing. In the same month as the Dowler revelations David Cameron announced an inquiry to be conducted by Lord Justice Leveson with a remit which included a review of the general culture and ethics of the British media.

Leveson Inquiry

The inquiry is expected to run until at least October 2012. Its terms of reference   **17–07**
were set out in a statement to Parliament by the Prime Minister.[12] They are:

Part 1

1.   To inquire into the culture, practices, and ethics of the press, including:
     a.   contacts and the relationships between national newspapers and politicians, and the conduct of each;
     b.   contacts and the relationship between the press and the police, and the conduct of each;
     c.   the extent to which the current policy and regulatory framework has failed including in relation to data protection; and
     d.   the extent to which there was a failure to act on previous warnings about media misconduct.
2.   To make recommendations:
     a.   for a new more effective policy and regulatory regime which supports the integrity and freedom of the press, the plurality of the media, and its independence, including from Government, while encouraging the highest ethical and professional standards;
     b.   for how future concerns about press behaviour, media policy, regulation and cross-media ownership should be dealt with by all the relevant authorities, including Parliament, Government, the prosecuting authorities and the police;
     c.   the future conduct of relations between politicians and the press; and
     d.   the future conduct of relations between the police and the press.

Part 2

3.   To inquire into the extent of unlawful or improper conduct within News International, other newspaper organisations and, as appropriate, other organisations within the media, and by those responsible for holding personal data.
4.   To inquire into the way in which any relevant police force investigated allegations or evidence of unlawful conduct by persons within or connected with News International, the review by the Metropolitan Police of their initial investigation, and the conduct of the prosecuting authorities.
5.   To inquire into the extent to which the police received corrupt payments or other inducements, or were otherwise complicit in such misconduct or in suppressing its proper investigation, and how this was allowed to happen.
6.   To inquire into the extent of corporate governance and management failures at News International and other newspaper organisations, and the role, if any, of politicians, public servants and others in relation to any failure to investigate wrongdoing at News International.

---

[12] *www.number10.gov.uk/news/leveson-inquiry-panel-terms-of-reference* [Accessed September 21, 2012].

7.   In the light of these inquiries, to consider the implications for the relationships between newspaper organisations and the police, prosecuting authorities, and relevant regulatory bodies – and to recommend what actions, if any, should be taken.

The Inquiry is running in four modules. These are:

- Module 1: The relationship between the press and the public and looks at phone-hacking and other potentially illegal behaviour.
- Module 2: The relationships between the press and police and the extent to which that has operated in the public interest.
- Module 3: The relationship between press and politicians.
- Module 4: Recommendations for a more effective policy and regulation that supports the integrity and freedom of the press while encouraging the highest ethical standards.

In relation to the role of data protection regulation the Inquiry has considered evidence arising from the Operation Motorman exercise by the then Information Commissioner, Richard Thomas, and current Commissioner, Christopher Graham. It is clear from Christopher Graham's evidence that he does not regard the Data Protection Act as the appropriate vehicle to regulate press behaviour and in effect his office has a policy of eschewing action in that area, (a policy which was implicitly criticised by the court in *Law Society v Kordowski*[13]). As will be seen from the analysis below it is incontrovertible that the enforcement provisions are very complex and difficult to use, particularly where the possibility of a defence is raised. Furthermore, there are difficult questions of balance to be drawn and the interface with the role of the PCC is politically sensitive. However, it appears that the Commissioner's "hands off" approach also applies to blogs, posts and other publications which are not within the remit of the PCC's self-regulatory role. These are the areas in which individuals, unless very wealthy, are unable to take action. It is submitted that, certainly in respect of ones which are likely to be taken seriously and have a real impact, the Commissioner should be acting as a regulator in this area. A simplification of the enforcement regime as well as a simplification of the provisions governing actions by individuals would be positive developments.

The Inquiry has heard reams of evidence about the methods used by journalists. These rarely come to the attention of the court although an instructive introduction to the means used to pressurise individuals into agreeing to provide their stories to the press can be found in the judgment in *CDE and FGH v MGM Ltd and LMN*.[14] Such behaviours and worse appear to be ingrained in the culture of the popular press. In March 2012, the PCC announced changes to its structure and approach: whether these will be sufficient to head off the current calls for statutory regulation remains to be seen.

---

[13] [2011] EWHC 3185 (QB).
[14] [2010] EWHC 3308 (QB).

Article 29 Working Party

The Directive set a tougher set of standards than Treaty 108 on which the earlier **17–08** legal regimes in the EU were based. It brought into focus the tension between the right to respect for private life in the information context and the right to freedom of expression. As such it was one of the first issues to occupy the Article 29 Working Party of representatives of supervisory authorities set up under the Directive. In February 1997, the Working Party adopted Recommendation 1/97 Data Protection Law and the Media. In the Recommendation the Working Party acknowledged the tension but took the view it had a positive side:

> "However, the two fundamental rights must not be seen as inherently conflicting. In the absence of adequate safeguards for privacy individuals may be reluctant to freely express their ideas. Similarly identification and profiling of readers and users of information services is likely to reduce the willingness of individuals to receive and impart information."

The paper has been referred to in UK case law (see para.17-32), however it is a useful analysis of the balancing test between the two rights.

WHAT ARE THE SPECIAL PURPOSES?

The special purposes are set out in s.3 of the Act being: **17–09**

"(a) the purposes of journalism;
  (b) artistic purposes; and
  (c) literary purposes."

No further assistance is offered in respect of these definitions. Accordingly the terms must be given their ordinary and natural meaning. As with any provision based on the Directive the courts will take a purposive approach to interpretation, seeking to give effect to the intent of the Directive. This exemption is derived from art.9. Article 9 is headed "Processing of personal data and freedom of expression". It provides that Member States shall provide for exemptions or derogations ". . . for the processing of personal data carried out solely for journalistic purposes or the purposes of artistic or literary expression".

The Directive gives no further assistance in describing what these purposes are. The terms themselves are extremely broad. Journalistic, artistic and literary endeavours are clearly meant to be different matters.

The terms have now been considered in a number of cases. The European Court has considered art.9 of the Directive in the *Satamedia* case, described below, and confirmed that the reason for the derogation is to protect freedom of expression and that the term "journalism" is a wide one. In that case the Finnish authorities published information about every individual's income and wealth tax which was then used by a marketing company to provide a service by which, in response to a text message showing the name and municipality of the subject, they would send a return text showing the income and assets of that person. The questions considered by Court were whether this use was to be considered as a processing of personal data; whether such processing of information which has been made publicly available by the State falls outside the scope of the Directive and whether it could fall within the derogation for journalistic activity, even if carried on for a commercial purpose. As would be anticipated the Court held that it was a processing of personal data, the fact that it had been published by the State did not mean that it fell outside the Directive, and subsequent uses would be subject to the law. In relation to the journalistic exemption it confirmed that journalism could be commercial and held that art.9 must be given a wide meaning because its purpose is to protect another fundamental right, freedom of expression:

"52. ... it is not in dispute that, as is apparent from Article 1 of the directive, its objective is that the Member States should, while permitting the free flow of personal data, protect the fundamental rights and freedoms of natural persons and, in particular, their right to privacy, with respect to the processing of personal data.

53. That objective cannot, however, be pursued without having regard to the fact that those fundamental rights must, to some degree, be reconciled with the fundamental right to freedom of expression.

54. Article 9 of the directive refers to such a reconciliation. As is apparent, in particular, from recital 37 in the preamble to the directive, the object of Article 9 is to reconcile two fundamental rights: the protection of privacy and freedom of expression. The obligation to do so lies on the Member States.

55. In order to reconcile those two 'fundamental rights' for the purposes of the directive, the Member States are required to provide for a number of derogations or limitations in relation to the protection of data and, therefore, in relation to the fundamental right to privacy, specified in Chapters II, IV and VI of the directive. Those derogations must be made solely for journalistic purposes or the purpose of artistic or literary expression, which fall within the scope of the fundamental right to freedom of expression, in so far as it is apparent that they are necessary in order to reconcile the right to privacy with the rules governing freedom of expression.

56. In order to take account of the importance of the right to freedom of expression in every democratic society, it is necessary, first, to interpret notions relating to that freedom, such as journalism, broadly. Secondly, and in order to achieve a balance between the two fundamental rights, the protection of the fundamental right to privacy requires that the derogations and limitations in relation to the protection of data provided for in the chapters of the directive referred to above must apply only in so far as is strictly necessary.

57. In that context, the following points are relevant.

58. First, as the Advocate General pointed out at point 65 of her Opinion and as is apparent from the legislative history of the directive, the exemptions and derogations provided for in Article 9 of the directive apply not only to media undertakings but also to every person engaged in journalism.

59. Secondly, the fact that the publication of data within the public domain is done for profit-making purposes does not, prima facie, preclude such publication being considered as an activity undertaken 'solely for journalistic purposes'. As Markkinapörssi and Satamedia state in their observations and as the Advocate General noted at point 82 of her Opinion, every undertaking will seek to generate a profit from its activities. A degree of commercial success may even be essential to professional journalistic activity.

60. Thirdly, account must be taken of the evolution and proliferation of methods of communication and the dissemination of information. As was mentioned by the Swedish Government in particular, the medium which is used to transmit the processed data, whether it be classic in nature, such as paper or radio waves, or

electronic, such as the internet, is not determinative as to whether an activity is undertaken 'solely for journalistic purposes'.

61. It follows from all of the above that activities such as those involved in the main proceedings, relating to data from documents which are in the public domain under national legislation, may be classified as 'journalistic activities' if their object is the disclosure to the public of information, opinions or ideas, irrespective of the medium which is used to transmit them. They are not limited to media undertakings and may be undertaken for profit-making purposes."

UK case law

In the UK the Supreme Court considered the terms "journalism, art and literature" in *Sugar v BBC*.[15] This was a case brought under the Freedom of Information Act 2000. In that Act the BBC is listed as a public authority for the purposes of that Act "in respect of information held for purposes other than those of journalism art or literature." The BBC held a report, the Balen report, commissioned in 2003 into the approach to the Israeli-Palestinian conflict. The applicant had made a request for this and it had been refused on the basis that the report was still held for the purposes of journalism, albeit it was accepted by the BBC that it was also held for administrative and management purposes. The case was appealed to the Supreme Court. It was noted in several of the judgements that the terminology is derived from the Data Protection Act and the scope of the exemption in s.32 is to protect freedom of expression. The judgment accepted that the terms would cover all the BBC's output but did not examine them in forensic detail. At an earlier stage the Information Tribunal had divided journalistic activity into three types, in essence the collection and writing of materials, the editing and selection and subsequent review of standards. This was not adopted by the majority in the Supreme Court and it is not clear that this rather technical delineation is useful, save that it makes clear that subsequent review and assessment of material and standards is included in journalistic activity. The Shorter Oxford English Dictionary (OED) describes a "journalist" as "one who earns his living by editing or writing for a public journal or journals. One who keeps a journal".

17–10

The first part of the definition suggests that payment of some sort is necessary, however this appears to be an unnecessary restriction. In the Recommendation of the Article 29 Working Party the point is made that it is not the journalist but the freedom to express views which is protected by the exemption:

> "Article 9 of the Directive respects the right of individuals to freedom. Derogations and exemptions under Article 9 cannot be granted to the media or to journalists as such, but only to anybody processing data for journalistic purposes".

It appears, therefore, that a piece written without payment for a parish magazine could count as journalism. Journalism does not appear to be limited to the reporting of fact but may include associated comments on reporting of fact. The medium used is not relevant so the use of a blog or other outlet could be covered. Presumably it is wide enough to include comment irrespective of whether any

---

[15] [2012] UKSC 4.

factual reporting is involved. The work does not have to be done by a journalist as the relevant processing may be undertaken by "any person".[16]

There was some comment on the scope of the term "journalism" in *Law Society v Kordowski*.[17] The case concerned the website "Solicitors from Hell". The Information Commissioner had suggested that the site attracted the exemption for personal and domestic purposes. That view was roundly rejected by the judge however the judge did comment that today anyone with access to the internet can engage in journalism at no cost and if the Defendant in that case had had a public interest defence he could have invoked the protection of s.32.

17–11   The terms "artistic" and "literary" purposes are equally imprecise. Literary works must presumably involve the use of words. In the first edition of this text we suggested that "therefore artistic work, by exclusion, will not do so". However, this is probably too narrow a view. There seems no reason why an artistic work could not include words as well as other material. How a literary or artistic work is to be judged is not clear. If a hopeful would-be author or artist works on a piece which is never finished, or which indeed turns out to have no literary or artistic merit, is he or she within the definitions? In relation to copyright protection under the Copyright, Design and Patents Act 1988 a literary work is any original written material. There is no test of literary merit attached. It is suggested that this is also the correct approach to the concept of literary work in the context of the DPA. This approach is based on the same reasoning as is applied above in relation to journalism, that the purpose of the exemption is to protect freedom of expression.

One may presumably have a work which is both literary and artistic, as in a multi-media presentation. Can a data-base be a literary work? Is a piece of software a literary work? If an inter-active business game is based on real people will that be a literary work containing personal data?

Unfortunately, the Act provides no answers to these questions. One can say that as one is dealing with exemptions from the rigour of the Act the general rule of statutory interpretation is that they will be interpreted strictly against the party seeking to rely on them. On the other hand as the purpose of the exemption is to protect the right to freedom of expression a purposive approach tends towards a generous interpretation of the terms. In any event it is difficult to see how such broad and general terms can be strictly interpreted. As we have noted above the courts have taken a liberal approach to those activities which may give rise to a claim to the exemption. There have been insufficient cases to come to any general conclusions about how the exemption is being applied but it would be reasonable to expect a strict construction to be applied to the terms of the exemption itself. This accords with the general principle that exemptions are to be construed strictly. The Article 29 Working Party put the point thus:

> "Derogations and exemptions under Article 9 must follow the principle of proportionality. Derogations and exemptions must be granted only in relation to jeopardise freedom of expression and only in so far as is necessary for the effective exercise of that right while maintaining a balance with the right to privacy of the data subject."

---

[16] s.32(1)(a).
[17] [2011] EWHC 3185 (QB).

WHAT ARE THE GROUNDS OF THE EXEMPTION?

The exemption can be claimed where personal data are processed only for the special purposes and where three separate conditions are fulfilled. Before considering these three conditions it should be emphasised that the personal data involved must be processed only for the special purposes.[18] It is not clear how proximate the processing must be to the special purposes in order to fulfil this test. One might argue that fulfilling the personnel function or dealing with the accounts of a media business involves processing personal data for the purposes of journalism, but it is suggested that a tighter line should be drawn in this area and that the exemption should be restricted to the processing of matter which is itself intended for publication. This is the approach taken by the Article 29 Working Party in its Recommendation:

17–12

> "Derogations and exemptions may cover only data processing for journalistic (editorial) purposes including electronic publishing. Any other form of data processing by journalists or the media is subject to the ordinary rules of the Directive."

It is clear that personal data processed only for the purposes of delivering invoices and collecting payment is not covered by art.9; however the decision in the *Satamedia* case suggests that even information sold in a marketing context could be covered by the exemption. The question of whether information is held "otherwise than for the purposes of journalism" has been litigated in *Sugar v BBC*.[19] The Supreme Court held in that case that as long as the information in question is held for the purposes of journalism then the exclusion from the Freedom of Information Act 2000 applies. A report which assessed the nature of the coverage in a controversial area was therefore excluded from the right of access. The scope is therefore wide and covers information which is not directly intended for publication. The FOIA test however is different from the DPA test which requires that the data be held only for the special purposes but it is submitted thst a court considering the DPA exemption would take an analagous approach.

There must exist a definable act of processing carried out for the special purposes, not simply an intention to process for those purposes, or processing to which those purposes are incidental. Presumably any processing which fulfils any part of the definition of processing may qualify for the exemption.

With a view to publication

The first test is that the processing is undertaken with a view to the publication by any person of any journalistic, literary or artistic material.[20] Publication is not defined but the term "publish" is defined in s.32(6) as meaning, for the purposes of this Act, as "making material available to the public or any section of the public".

17–13

---

[18] s.32(1).
[19] See fn.7, above.
[20] DPA s.32(1)(a).

Clearly something will be made available to the public if it is published in a newspaper, or on a website, on the internet, or in a book on public sale, or displayed at a public art gallery so that any person may look at it. It is less clear what is envisaged by the term "a section of the public". The same wording is used in the Contempt of Court Act 1981,[21] the Equality Act 2010[22] and in law relating to charities. It appears to cover groups as opposed to individuals but where there is no selection of the membership of such groups. The essential difference seems to be between controlled and public access. The question raised is how far this applies to social media uses where the publication is to a group. It is submitted that there would be a difference between a case in which publication was intended to an open group that anyone could join, such as followers on Twitter, and a closed group such as a limited number of friends on Facebook. However, there is no authority on the point.

The processing must have taken place "with a view" to publication. It is not clear how specific this view must be. Must the material be due to be published within the foreseeable future? It is presumably a question of fact as to whether or not there is a genuine view to publication. As a matter of law it should not be necessary to point to a particular publication date but there must be a genuine aim to publish. This would suggest that data kept on file as background to a potential story would not necessarily be eligible for exemption on this ground.

Publication in the public interest

17–14   The second condition is that the data controller must reasonably believe that, having regard to the special importance of the public interest in freedom of expression, publication would be in the public interest.[23] The provision also requires that the touchstone is that the data controller held the reasonable belief.

Public interest is a notoriously elusive concept. To compound the possible ambiguity the term appears twice in the same subsection. Regard must be had to the specific interest in freedom of expression as part of a broader concept of public interest. Public interest tests arising in other context may be of only limited assistance. Since the Human Rights Act 1998 came into effect the courts have had to weight competing interests in freedom of expression and other areas of public interest in a large number of cases. A selection of the most significant where the protection of personal privacy was given more weight are dealt with in Ch.2. In other cases the courts have determined that the right to freedom of expression out-weighs the right to privacy or that the public interest is not served by restricting the publication of information.

17–15   The test appears to be a two stage test. The data controller must have regard to the special importance of the public interest in freedom of expression which presumably means that he or she must review and consider the guidance in codes and case law and then, applying those to a detailed analysis of the particular facts, must reasonably believe that in the particular case the publication would be in the public interest.[24]

---

[21] Contempt of Court Act 1981 s.2(1).
[22] s.29.
[23] DPA s.32 (1)(b).
[24] DPA s.32(1)(b).

The controller is given additional assistance by s.32(3), which states that, in considering for the purposes of subs.1(b) whether a belief that publication is in the public interest was a reasonable one, regard may be had to his compliance with any code of practice which is relevant to the publication in question and is designated by the Secretary of State by order for the purpose of this subsection. In the next sections a selection of the relevant cases and code of practice are considered.   **17–16**

Cases

In the context of publication by the press, it has been held that public interest is not the same as what is interesting to the public. In *Lion Laboratories Ltd v Evans*[25] the court considered a case in which a newspaper had obtained confidential documents from an ex-employee which disclosed doubts about the reliability of the Lion Intoximeter 3000. The question for the court was whether disclosure of the information in the documents was in the public interest. It was held that it was in the public interest to disclose it, even if the information had been obtained in breach of confidence and there was no wrongdoing on the part of the company. The court held that in deciding whether publication was in the public interest there was no requirement there should be misconduct on the part of the person to be "exposed" but it had to take into account: (a) the difference between what is interesting to the public and what is in the public interest; (b) the fact that the media have an interest in publishing things which will increase circulation; and (c) the fact that the public interest might be best served by someone going to the police not the press. It then had to weigh the nature of the material, the competing interests in confidentiality and whether the publication went to matters of real public concern.   **17–17**

The question of public interest in publication was re-visited by Lord Woolf in *A v B*.[26] The approach taken by Lord Woolf suggested a more generous view of the public interest and in particular acknowledged that there is a broad public interest in the existence of a free and vigorous press. For a full discussion of *A v B*, see Ch.2. The generous view does not appear to have been universally applied in subsequent cases.

In *H (a healthcare worker) v Associated Newspapers Ltd*[27] the Court of Appeal lifted a ban which had been imposed in the High Court to stop journalists from soliciting information which might lead to the discovery of a healthcare worker who had been diagnosed as HIV positive. The court held that this was too wide a restriction to place on the press and was an unacceptable fetter on the right to freedom of expression. In a similar vein the High Court held that an injunction restraining the publication by the BBC of the identity of social workers who had been involved with a celebrated case would be a disproportionate interference with the art.10 rights of the BBC and two children who wished to disclose their own story.[28] Similar decisions were made in *Re Webster (a child)*; sub nom.   **17–18**

---

[25] [1984] 2 All E.R. 417.
[26] [2002] 3 W.L.R. 542.
[27] [2002] EWCA Civ 195.
[28] *BBC v Rochdale Metropolitan Borough Council*[2005] EWHC 2862 (Fam).

Norfolk CC v Webster,[29] in which an interim order restricting access by the media to an interim hearing was held to be too wide and interfered with the art.10 rights of the parents. In that case however the interests of the parents were not the only factor in favour of openness; there were other strong interests, in particular the need to command full confidence in the judicial process. In *Leeds City Council v Channel Four Television Group*[30] the court held that Channel 4 was entitled to screen a documentary including film shot covertly in a local secondary school which showed the disruptive and defiant behaviour of children and the demoralised response of staff. While it was accepted that the disclosures involved an intrusion into the art.8 rights of the children the balance came down in favour of publication in view of the serious issues of public interest raised and the fact that the surreptitious filming appeared to be the only way of exposing the problems In *Venables v News Group Newspapers Ltd*[31] the court had to weigh the art.10 rights against the right to life and security. The case arose as Venables and Thompson reached 18 years of age. There had been injunctions in place banning anyone from disclosing information about them. As they approached 18, applications were made for the injunctions to be maintained against all the world so as to ensure that their whereabouts and current identities were not published. The court held that their rights to security and safety out-weighted the rights protected by art.10. Lifetime protection was also accorded to the woman formerly known as Mary Bell and her daughter in similar circumstances. Mary Bell (as she had been) had been convicted of the manslaughter of two young children when she was herself 11 years old. The court held that in the exceptional circumstances the balance favoured the protection of the privacy of the individual and granted an order *contra mundum*.[32]

17–19   In *Re Attorney General's Reference (No.3 of 1999)*[33] an anonymity order imposed in relation to a defendant accused of rape was lifted to allow the BBC to report on the case. The reporting restriction had been imposed after D was acquitted of rape. He was acquitted because it was ruled that crucial DNA evidence obtained when he was arrested for a burglary was held to be inadmissible. The DNA sample, which matched that from the rape victim, should have been destroyed under the Police and Criminal Evidence Act 1984. The BBC wished to make a programme following the removal of the double jeopardy rule about cases in which there were arguments that a retrial should be held. In order to do so it wished to use D's case and identify D. The court held that, while the information about the acquittal was public, the link of the DNA sample to the rape for which he was acquitted were private information in respect of which D had an expectation of privacy. However, the court held that the BBC's proposed broadcast was in exercise of its right to freedom of expression and the question of the double jeopardy rule was an issue of legitimate public interest. There was no doubt that the balance fell in favour of the BBC's right to freedom of expression.

In *Independent News and Media Ltd v A*[34] the Court considered whether representatives of the media should be allowed to attend a hearing of the Court of

---

[29] [2006] EWHC 2733.
[30] [2005] EWHC 3522.
[31] [2001] 1 All E.R. 908.
[32] [2003] EWHC 1101 (QB).
[33] [2009] UKHL 34.
[34] [2010] EWCA Civ 343.

Protection making decisions about the future care of a severely disabled adult. Under Court of Protection Rules hearings are to be in private although the Court may accept other parties to be present. The individual who was the subject of the case was of intense interest because he is both severely disabled and also a talented pianist who has won international recognition. Accordingly the decisions about his future living arrangements were of interest to the media. It was clear that his art.8 rights were engaged. The judge at first instance had ordered that a limited number of media representatives could attend the private hearing and having listened to the case would be able to make informed submission about what, if anything, it was acceptable to report. There was debate in the judgment about the point at which the media's art.10 rights were engaged in this case however there was no doubt that they were engaged and the appropriate balance was to allow limited representation at the hearing with subsequent control on topics of publication.

In *BKM Ltd v BBC*[35] the BBC was successful in resisting an application for an injunction to stop the broadcast of a programme which included material obtained by surreptitious filming of individuals in a care home. It was made clear that the film would be pixelated to ensure that no individual could be generally identified, although it was accepted that relatives or others who knew that individuals were in the home would be able to identify them. It was also made clear that there would be no film of intimate care or behaviours. The BBC succeeded in the application that its art.10 rights outweighed the privacy rights of the residents taking account of the proportionality of the intrusion. In assessing the balance the Judge took account of the Ofcom Code and the Editorial Guidelines described in para.17-22 and following below.

While in *BKM* the deciding factor to restrain the issue of an injunction was the public interest in *Essex County Council v Stedman*[36] the basis for the refusal of relief appeared to be pragmatic as much as anything else.

The Canute Principle

In the case of *East Sussex County Council v Stedman*[37] the High Court declined to continue and extend reporting orders which had been sought by the local authority. In that case a group of four children became the subject of intense publicity because of a claim that one of them, a boy of 13, was the father of a child born to a girl who was just 15. The case had been brought to tabloid attention by the father of one of the children. It had provoked a huge amount of publicity, much of which was hurtful to the mother. The local authority obtained an order that the girl, the baby and the putative father should be made wards of court and an application was made for reporting and publishing restrictions which were granted. However, there were already many pictures of the children in the public domain and, once DNA tests showed that the 13-year-old was not the father, an article to that effect using existing pictures was published in the *Daily Mirror.*

17–20

---

[35] [2009] EWHC 3152.
[36] [2009] EWHC 935 (Fam).
[37] [2009] EWHC 935 (Fam).

Applications were subsequently made to vary the restrictions to add a ban on preventing pictures which were already in the public domain being reused and prohibiting publication of the DNA tests. The 13-year-old wished to give publicity to the fact that he was not the father. The Court had to weigh the rights of the baby, the mother, the boy and a further named child who was possibly the real father. MGN Ltd sought to report the developments and also opposed the application to restrict the normal public domain exception aspect of the order. Applying the test in *Re S* and considering all the circumstances of the case, King J. refused to extent the reporting restrictions. In doing so she referred to the "Canute Principle", enunciated in the *Mosely* case by Eady J., where information has become so widely available that a restriction on the republication of existing material would serve no useful purpose. She considered that a ban would be disproportionate and futile given the extensive publicity which had already occurred.[38]

In making this decision, the Court applied the approach taken in *Attorney General v Guardian Newspapers (No.2)*,[39] in which the Court held that it was not in the public interest to prevent the publication of the book *Spycatcher* in the UK given the fact that copies were already widely circulating.

Codes of practice

17–21   The code of practice need not necessarily be one made under the Data Protection Act. The designated codes[40] listed in the SI are:

- the Press Complaints Commission Code of Practice, now the Editors' Code of Practice;
- the Broadcasting Standards Commission Code on Fairness and Privacy under s.107 of the Broadcasting Act 1996, the Radio Authority Code under s.91 of the Broadcasting Act 1990,[41] the Independent Television Commission Programme Code under s.7 of the Broadcasting Act 1990. The Radio Authority and the Independent Television Authority ceased to exist from December 18, 2003 and their functions were taken over by Ofcom. The three radio and broadcasting codes have now been superseded by the Ofcom Broadcasting Code which applies to all radio and television broadcasts.
- the British Broadcasting Corporation Producers' Guidelines. These have now been replaced by the BBC Editorial Guidelines.[42]

17–22   Under the Ofcom Broadcasting Code, invasion of privacy may be warranted where it is in the public interest in the particular circumstances of the case:

---

[38] The case brought by Max Mosely against the *News of the World* is considered in Ch.2.
[39] [1990] 1 A.C. 109.
[40] Data Protection (Designated Codes of Practice) (No.2) Order 2000 (SI 2000/1864).
[41] February 28, 2011 drawn up under the Communications Act 2003 and the Broadcasting Act 1996.
[42] October 2010.

"Examples of public interest would include revealing or detecting crime, protecting public health or safety, exposing misleading claims made by individuals or organisations or disclosing incompetence that affects the public".[43]

As described earlier, the Press Complaints Commission (PCC) was established in 1991 following the Calcutt Committee. The Code has been amended several times since then. The Editors' Code covers accuracy; opportunity to reply; privacy; harassment; intrusion into grief or shock; children; children in sex cases; hospitals; reporting of crime; clandestine devices and subterfuge; victims of sexual assault; discrimination; financial journalism; confidential sources; witness payments in criminal trials; payment to criminals; and the public interest test.[44] Out of these topics, several are related to privacy and data protection rights. Several provisions are subject to a public interest test. It applies to editorial content in newspapers and magazines. The Commission will consider complaints of breach of the code from members of the public, either individuals or organisations directly affected by the content complained of. It adjudicates on the complaint and may require a publication to carry a note of rectification or apology but has no power to order compensation. The Code is succinct. The section dealing with privacy reads:

17–23

"(i)   Everyone is entitled to respect for his or her private and family life, home, health and correspondence including digital communications.

(ii)   Editors will be expected to justify intrusions into any individual's private life without consent. Account will be taken of the complainant's own public disclosures of information.

(iii)   It is unacceptable to photograph individuals in private places without their consent.

Note—Private places are public or private property where there is a reasonable expectation of privacy"

The section dealing with clandestine devices and subterfuge reads:

"The press must not seek to obtain or publish material acquired by using hidden cameras or clandestine listening devices; or by intercepting private or mobile telephone calls, messages or emails; or by the unauthorised removal of documents or photographs; or by accessing digitally-held private information without consent.

Engaging in misrepresentation or subterfuge, including by agents or intermediaries, can generally be justified only in the public interest and then only when the material cannot be obtained by other means.

The areas which most intersect with the standards and requirements of data protection are:

- accuracy of information;
- a ban on unfair collection by the use of clandestine listening devices or intercepting private telephone calls; and
- restrictions on the use of data in some of the sensitive categories—sex cases, particularly those involving children, and information gathered in hospitals."

---

[43] r.8.1 .

[44] Editor's Code of Practice, January 2011.

It accepts that members may derogate from privacy standards and some of the other standards where it is in the public interest to do so. "Public interest" is not exhaustively defined but "includes":

"1.   ...
    (i)   detecting or exposing crime or serious impropriety;
    (ii)   protecting public health and safety;
    (iii)   preventing the public being misled by an action or statement of an individual or organisation.
2.   There is a public interest in freedom of expression itself.
3.   Whenever the public interest is invoked the PCC will require editors to demonstrate fully that they reasonably believed that publication or journalistic activity undertaken with a view to publication would be in the public interest.
4.   The PCC will consider the extent to which material is already in the public domain, or will become so.
5.   In cases involving children under 16, editors must demonstrate an exceptional public interest to over-ride the normally paramount interest of the child."

The Code was considered relevant in the case brought by the model, Naomi Campbell, which is described later. Cases decided on the Code are published on the website of the PCC, which also publishes Guidance Notes on issues including data protection.[45]

17–24   Under the BBC Editorial Guidelines the question of an invasion of privacy on the grounds of public interest is covered as follows:

"Private behaviour, information, correspondence and conversation should not be brought into the public domain unless there is a public interest that outweighs the expectation of privacy. There is no single definition of public interest. It includes but is not confined to:

- exposing or detecting crime
- exposing significantly anti-social behaviour
- exposing corruption or injustice
- disclosing significant incompetence or negligence
- protecting people's health and safety
- preventing people from being misled by some statement or action of an individual or organisation
- disclosing information that assists people to better comprehend or make decisions on matters of public importance.

There is also a public interest in freedom of expression itself.
    When considering what is in the public interest we also need to take account of information already in the public domain or about to become available to the public.
    When using the public interest to justify an intrusion, consideration should be given to proportionality; the greater the intrusion, the greater the public interest required to justify it."

---

[45] *www.pcc.org.uk*

It can be seen, therefore, that there is a strong degree of commonality between the formulations in the relevant Codes, although they are not exactly the same. To date, these differences do not appear to have been material in any of the decided cases. In *R. (on the application of Gaunt) v Ofcom*[46] the claimant was found in breach of the Ofcom Code for breaching "generally acceptable standards" by making offensive and insulting remarks to the person being interviewed. The interviewer submitted that the finding breached his Art.10 rights to freedom of expression. The Court accepted that the Ofcom had to act in a way compatible with the Convention rights but found on the facts that the finding did not interfere with the applicant's freedom of expression.

The belief that publication is in the public interest must be held by the data controller for the personal data involved. If the data controller is a corporate entity it would follow that the reasonable belief should be attributable to a responsible individual who acts for the company in this regard and has addressed his mind to the case in question. In *Tesco Supermarkets Ltd v Nattrass*[47] the House of Lords considered the attribution of mental capacity to a corporation in relation to an offence under the Trade Descriptions Act 1968. They held that the mental element required for the offence had to be attributable to a senior official or manager who could be regarded as part of the management of the organisation. This followed the judgment of Denning L.J. in *HL Bolton (Engineering) Co Ltd v TJ Graham & Sons Ltd*[48] in which he likened a company to a human body in which some workers act as the hands and arms of the company but others represent the "directing mind". However *Tesco* was a criminal case and a less stringent approach may be taken outside the criminal context. A court may be prepared to accept that the reasonable belief should be held by a senior journalist with relevant responsibility for the relevant content. It would appear that the same person should also have directed his mind to the third condition, which is the test set out in the following subsection.

17–25

Incompatibility with the special purposes

The third test which must be fulfilled before the controller can claim the exemption is that he reasonably believes that, in all the circumstances, compliance with the relevant provision of the Act is incompatible with the special purposes.[49] It is a question of fact as to whether the controller did reasonably believe that the matters would be incompatible. The term incompatible is used on a number of occasions in the Act and is never defined. It must therefore be given its ordinary meaning. The OED defines incompatible as:

17–26

"1.   Of benefices, etc., incapable of being held together;
    2.   Mutually intolerant; incapable of existing together in the same subject; discordant, incongruous, inconsistent;
    3.   Unable to 'get on' together; at variance;
    4.   Irreconcilable."

---

[46] [2010] EWHC 1756.
[47] [1971] 2 All E.R. 127.
[48] [1956] 3 All E.R. 624.
[49] DPA s.32(1)(c).

This sets quite a high standard and suggests that the controller must reasonably believe that he will be unable to publish either in total or a substantial part of the work if he complies with the relevant requirement of the Act. It does not apply only to the action of publication but may apply to any of the processing leading up to publication and necessary to achieve it, for example the collection of information from an individual without the provision of a collection notice.

WHAT DOES THE EXEMPTION COVER?

17–27 If the test in s.32(1) is met, that is, putting it broadly, that the controller reasonably believes that if he complies with the relevant data protection provision either he will be unable to publish material which it would be in the public interest to publish, or he will be unable to do so effectively or fully, then he is not bound by the particular data protection provision in that case.

The relevant data protection provisions from which he may be exempt are found in the principles (except the security principle) and a number of the individual rights.

The Principles

17–28 The controller may claim exemption from any of the data protection principles, apart from principle 7, which covers the security of data processing. The linked provisions in Schs 2, 3 and 4 are also covered by this exemption. This allows the controller to disregard the prohibition on sensitive data holding, the requirement for legitimacy of processing and the prohibition on overseas transfer where he reasonably believes that the s.32(1) tests are made out. The balancing test involved in assessing whether the publication is in the public interest and whether the relevant data protection provision would be incompatible with publication is likely to be particularly difficult where the data controller seeks to avoid compliance with these fundamental provisions. The courts have to balance these issues when claims for compensation come before them to be met by media claims for exemption. As is seen in the discussion on s.32(4) below this moment is likely to be postponed until after publication of the material.

The exemptions from the principles will come into play pro-actively in that the controller will have to make a positive decision not to comply with the relevant principle(s) in a particular case. The controller will also have to be prepared to defend this position if challenged. It is suggested that those involved in journalistic, literary and artistic areas who are likely to wish to claim the exemption should establish procedures to ensure that clear decisions are made on appropriate grounds where the exemptions are claimed and that a record of the use of the exemptions is retained in case of future challenge.

17–29 Individual rights

(a) The right of subject access—s.7. Where subject access is refused the attendant information rights, for example to a statement of the logic involved in any processing decision, may also be refused.

(b)   The right to prevent processing likely to cause damage or distress—s.10.
(c)   The right to object to automated decision taking—s.12.
(d)   The rectification blocking and erasure provisions dealing with inaccurate data—s.14(1)–(3).

These exemptions will be claimed reactively when an individual seeks to exercise the relevant right. It is suggested that those data users who may wish to take advantage of these exemptions adopt an appropriate system for authorising the exemption claim to ensure that any claim complies with the s.32(1) provisions. The exemptions may either be claimed when the individual request is first made to the data controller and the response refused, or may be claimed in proceedings brought by the individual to enforce his or her rights. Where the exemption is claimed in legal proceedings brought by an individual before publication the issues cannot be adjudicated by the court unless the Commissioner has made a finding that the processing was not taking place only for the special purposes following the procedure which is described later in the chapter.

HOW LONG DO THE EXEMPTIONS LAST?

The policy behind these exemptions is to protect freedom of expression. A major   **17–30**
consideration in formulating the provisions appears to have been to ensure that there can be no prior restraint of publication. The protection afforded against prior restraint accords with the balance between the right to freedom of expression and individual liberties accepted in previous UK case law. In *Schering Chemicals Ltd v Falkman Ltd*[50] Lord Denning M.R. expressly rejected the possibility of prior restraint of the press:

> "It means that there should be no censorship. No restraint should be placed on the press as to what they should publish. Not by a licensing system. Not by executive direction. Not by court injunction."

The accepted restriction on prior restraint accounts for the provision in s.34(4) which is designed to provide for a stay of proceedings where such proceedings are brought prior to publication, and will apply even though there has been one publication in the previous 24 hours. This extension to a previous 24-hour application period is intended to ensure that the daily media cannot be restrained between the issue of editions.

The procedural exemption continues to apply to any processing which is undertaken "with a view to publication". It endures for as long as there is an intention to publish. The exemption may be claimed afresh for each publication but will only apply to that particular publication.

---

[50] [1982] 1 Q.B. 1.

Application after publication

17–31   Once the material has been published it is clear that the prohibitions on court proceedings brought by data subjects no longer applies. This point was considered by the High Court and subsequently the Court of Appeal in the case of *Campbell v Mirror Group Newspapers*. In the High Court the Mirror argued that the Court was wholly prohibited from hearing any case in relation to the special purposes until s.32(5) was satisfied, that is until the Commissioner had made a determination under s.45. The judge ruled against the Mirror on this point and held that he could consider the case. He ruled that the restriction on bringing proceedings in s.34(4) only applied prior to publication and once the material has been published the court could consider the case under the DPA. In relation to the substantive aspect of the exemption the judgment was less clear In the Court of Appeal it was held that the data controller who published material can claim the benefit of the substantive exemption after publication and on the facts of the case the Mirror was entitled to it.

Facts

17–32   The claimant was a well-known fashion model who had denied in public that she had drug problems. She was photographed leaving a clinic where she had been having treatment for addiction. The photograph was published by the *Mirror* newspaper in February 2001 which also published the fact that she was being treated by having therapy. After she complained about the disclosures of the information and the publication of the photograph the newspaper published further material criticising her complaint and claim for breach of privacy. She took action against the newspaper claiming damages for breach of confidentiality and compensation under s.13 of the DPA in respect of the articles and photographs published. The claimant accepted that the paper was entitled to publish the basic fact that she was addicted to drugs and was having treatment, but was not entitled to use photographs of her or give detail of the treatment, i.e. the therapy or the therapist. In the High Court the Judge considered both the claim under the DPA and the application of the exemption for journalistic material. He referred to the background of the DPA in the Directive and to the treatment of the right to freedom of expression under art.10 of the Covention rights in art.9 of the Directive. He also considered the Article 29 Working Party Recommendation 1/97 on Data Protection and the Media. The *Mirror* submitted that the exemption in s.32 applied to the publication and argued that not only did the substantive exemption apply but the procedural exemption in s.32(5) continued to apply post-publication and thus the Court was precluded from hearing the case until the Commissioner had made a determination under s.45. The Court rejected the contention that the procedural provision applied post-publication (citing among other things the first edition of this text) and went on to consider the application of the substantive exemption.

17–33   The Court held that the information about the applicant's drug use and treatment related to her physical or mental health or condition and thus was sensitive data. It held that the photographs of the applicant leaving the clinic were unfairly obtained as they were taken by a photographer concealed in a car at a distance. Ms Campbell had no opportunity to evade the shot or refuse consent. Moreover the fact that the photographs and information were obtained in breach of confidence meant that they were obtained unlawfully. The judge then considered which of the Sch.2 grounds legitimised the processing by the *Mirror*.[51] He rejected the argument put forward by the newspaper that it could rely on ground 5, which relates to processing for the exercise of a public function. He accepted that ground 6 was available to the newspaper, however, he said that some of the material failed the balancing test in ground 6 as the publication of the details of the treatment and the photograph went beyond the legitimate interests of the paper. He then considered the Sch.3 grounds[52] and SI 2000/417 ground 3(1), which permits the disclosure of wrongdoing to the media where publication would be in the public interest.[53] He held that the conditions in ground 3(1) were cumulative. The newspaper had submitted otherwise. He also held that the publication of the nature of Ms Campbell's treatment was not in the substantial public interest. Moreover her actions were not in connection with the commission of offences but with efforts not to commit offences. He concluded that none of the three requirements of the first principle, fair processing, lawful processing, or grounds under Schs 2 and 3, were made out. Accordingly there had been a breach of the DPA. There was no defence that the newspaper had taken reasonable care to avoid such breach, on the contrary it was a deliberate and knowing action. He then considered the effect of s.13 and agreed that where the special purposes were concerned the applicant did not have to show actual damage but was entitled to compensation for distress. The judge assessed the amount of the damages for distress and injury to feelings as £2,500. The claimant had claimed aggravated damages for the behaviour of the *Mirror* after the publication. These, however, could be compensatory only and not punitive. On the aggravated damages issue the judge held that the paper was entitled to assert that the claim against it should not have been made and say so in print. However in this case, in doing so it had belittled the claimant in relation to her claim. He therefore held that she was entitled to aggravated damages as the article "trashed her as a person". The claimant was awarded a further £1,000 in aggravated damages bringing the total damages to £3,500 and £50 for data protection

After a further appeal, Ms Campbell succeeded in the House of Lords. The data protection points were not considered in the Lords but in the Court of Appeal the Court agreed that the publication of the material was processing within the terms of the DPA and did not appear to depart from the reasoning and approach of the High Court to the application of the DPA.

RESTRICTIONS ON INDIVIDUAL ACTIONS

A data controller who processes for one of the special purposes and against whom court proceedings are brought by an individual to enforce his rights under ss.7, 10, 12 or 14 (1)–(3) before publication of the material in question can insist that the proceedings are halted until the Information Commissioner has made a

17–34

---

[51] See Ch.6 for an analysis of the grounds for processing.
[52] See Ch.7 for an analysis of the grounds for processing sensitive data.
[53] See Ch.5 for the grounds for processing.

declaration that the processing is no longer carried out for the special purposes or is not carried out only for the special purposes. In effect this allows the data controller to have proceedings stayed until after publication of the relevant material. This procedure, under which specified issues are transferred from the courts to the jurisdiction of the Commissioner, appears to have no counterpart in other statutes. It applies in addition to the substantive exemption and is a procedural aspect of the exemption. Section 32(4) and (5) provide:

> "(4)   Where at any time ('the relevant time') in any proceedings against a data controller under sections 7(9), 10(4), 12(8) or 14, or by virtue of section 13 the data controller claims, or it appears to the court, that any personal data to which the proceedings relate are being processed:
>
> (a)   only for the special purposes; and
>
> (b)   with a view to the publication by any person of any journalistic, literary or artistic material which, at the time twenty four hours immediately before the relevant time, had not previously been published by the data controller, the court shall stay the proceedings until either of the conditions in sub-section (5) is met.
>
> (5)   Those conditions are:
>
> (a)   that a determination of the Commissioner under section 45 with respect to the data in question takes effect, or
>
> (b)   in a case where the proceedings were stayed on the making of a claim, that the claim is withdrawn."

Under this provision, if the data controller is able to claim that the processing in question is carried out with a view to publication for the first time by that controller, the power of the court to deal with the case is stayed until an external determination is made on whether the exemption applies. A Commissioner's determination under s.45 may only be made to the effect that personal data are not being processed only for the special purposes, or are not being processed with a view to publication by any person of any journalistic, literary or artistic material which has not previously been published by the data controller. The Commissioner may therefore lift the stay on the court proceedings where he is able to make a determination to that effect but otherwise the stay will continue to apply. The matter, however, does not end there. Where the Commissioner has made such a determination the data controller may appeal to the Tribunal against the determination. This gives those who process for the special purposes a potent weapon to resist any interference with publication on data protection grounds.

17–35   It is not apparent why Parliament decided that the determination has to be made by the Commissioner. It would be far simpler for the courts to make appropriate determinations as to whether the processing was being carried out for the special purposes. The court seised of the matter would be able to hear witnesses on the claim and cross-examination on the issue. The Commissioner is not in a position to do this.

It could be suggested that, as the Commissioner has the power to serve a "special information notice" under s.44 of the Act in relation to the special purposes, in which he may require the data controller to furnish him with information for the purpose of ascertaining whether the personal data are being processed only for the special purposes, or whether they are being processed with a view to the publication by any person of any journalistic, literary or artistic material which has not previously been published by the data controller, he has an advantage over the courts in making such a decision. However, a special information notice is limited under s.44. The Commissioner may only serve one either where he has received a request by a data subject to consider any particular processing or has reasonable grounds for suspecting, in a case in which the data controller has made a claim under s.32 in any proceedings, that the personal data to which the proceedings relate are not being processed only for the special purposes or are not being processed with a view to the publication by any person of any journalistic, literary or artistic material which has not previously been published by the data controller.

The effect of this is to place the Commissioner in a difficult position. He may only serve a s.44 notice to enable him to make a determination under s.45 where he has reasonable grounds for suspecting that the claim made by the data controller is not made out, however the data controller may make the claim giving no evidence of grounds. The Commissioner therefore faces an evidential burden before he can even seek information from the data controller whereas the data controller may assert the exemption before a court without showing any grounds. The effect appears to be to allow the case to be prolonged and to make it particularly difficult for an individual to bring any proceedings.

However, eventually publication must take place. The Commissioner will then be able to make the s.45 determination and a court will be able to consider the substantive claim. At that stage the court will have to assess whether the grounds in s.32(1)(b) and (c) were made out at the time the processing took place.

Powers of the Commissioner

These have been referred to above. There are special provisions affecting the Commissioner's powers to deal with personal data processed for the special purposes.
17–36

Special information notices

A special information notice is served under s.44. It can only be served where one of two conditions applies; either the Commissioner has received a request for an assessment under s.42 or, as explained above, a stay has been claimed under s.32 in court proceedings brought against a data controller. In the case of a s.32 claim the Commissioner can only serve the notice where he has reasonable grounds for suspecting that either the data are not being processed for the special purposes or they are not being processed with a view to publication of material which has not been published previously. He must state his grounds for his suspicions in the notice. The notice is limited to ascertaining whether the grounds for a s.32 claim are made out, that is whether the data are being processed only for the special purposes with a view to first publication. The recipient of such a notice may appeal to the Tribunal. The usual provisions as to cases of urgency apply.
17–37

Information notices

17–38   Section 46(3) provides that the Commissioner cannot serve a standard information notice under s.43 with respect to the special purposes unless he has first made a s.45 determination which has taken effect. This means that before the Commissioner can even require any information from a controller about data processed for the special purposes, other than the specific information dealt with by a special information notice, he has to go through a formal process of determining that the exemption could not be claimed and allow for an appeal against that determination.

In the case of either a special information notice or ordinary information notice, if the controller appeals the information need not be furnished pending the determination or withdrawal of the appeal.

Enforcement notices

17–39   Section 46 provides that the Commissioner may not serve an enforcement notice on a data controller with respect to the processing of personal data for the special purposes unless he has made a s.45 (1) determination and the court has granted leave for the notice to be served. This restriction applies even after publication of the material in question.

The relevant court will be the county court or High Court in England and Wales or a Sheriff Court in Scotland. Where the Commissioner makes an application for leave to serve a notice the court shall not grant leave unless it is satisfied that the Commissioner has reason to suspect a contravention of the principles which is of substantial public importance and, except where the case is one of urgency, that the data controller had been given notice in accordance with the rules of court of the application for leave.

17–40   It is not clear, and no assistance is given in the text, as to what constitutes substantial public importance in relation to the contravention of the data protection principles, nor is it clear whether it differs from public interest or if so how. The Commissioner must have grounds to suspect the contravention of the principles and that contravention must be of substantial public importance. The Commissioner must then satisfy the court that he has reasons for this view. It is not clear whether the Commissioner has to satisfy the court that the matters actually are of substantial public importance or simply that the Commissioner reasonably believes that they are.

It could be suggested that examples of issues of particular public importance would be where sensitive data are alleged to have been misused or where processing has been unlawful or where particularly damaging allegations or inaccurate statements have been made about a data subject.

Particular weight may be attached to a breach of the right to private and family life. It could be argued that there is a particular public importance that the Convention rights, as fundamental or higher order rights, be upheld by the courts. On this basis almost any breach of the right to private life could be the basis for enforcement action. The contrary argument would be that the right to freedom of speech is also a fundamental right which must be upheld by the courts. The task for the court is to balance the competing rights in any particular case.

When the Commissioner serves an enforcement notice that notice may also be appealed to the Tribunal.

The relevant time

It is not clear from s.32(4) how the relevant time is crystallised. It appears that the controller must assert his claim in court proceedings, asserting also the date and time of the relevant processing in order to allow the 24-hour countdown. The application presumably will be to the court for a stay, supported by an affidavit.

17–41

Defence to section 55 offences

Section 78 of the Criminal Justice and Immigration Act 2008 inserted a new subsection into s.55 which provides a further defence to a charge under that section. It states that the prohibition on knowingly or recklessly obtaining or procuring personal data without the consent of the data controller is not applicable to a person who shows that he acted:

17–42

- for the special purposes;
- with a view to the publication by any person of any journalistic, literary or artistic material; and
- in the reasonable belief that in the particular circumstances the obtaining, disclosing or procuring was justified as being in the public interest.

It is therefore a specific defence where the special purposes are involved. As there is already a public interest defence in s.55(2)(d) it is not clear what this adds save possible to bolster the position of the media. The provision was added at the same time as the penalties for breach of s.55 were widened to include a penalty of imprisonment (see Ch.21 for details of the provisions). Neither provision has been brought into force at the time of writing.

Provisions relating to monetary penalty notices

Provision has also been made to protect those processing for the special purposes from penalties under the new powers of the Commissioner to serve monetary penalty notices. Section 55E provides that the Secretary of State may make provision that a monetary penalty notice cannot be served on a data controller with respect to the processing of personal data for the special purposes except in specified circumstances. No such order has been made at the time of writing.

17–43

ASSISTANCE OF THE COMMISSIONER

Section 53 provides that an individual who brings proceedings for individual rights which relate to personal data processed for the special purposes may seek assistance from the Information Commissioner. When the Commissioner receives an application for assistance he must consider it and decide whether and to what extent to grant it but he can only grant the application for assistance if in his

17–44

opinion the case involves a matter of substantial public importance. It will be noted that this is the same test which is applied in s.46(2)(a) in respect of an application for leave to the court to take proceedings by enforcement action. Proceedings need not actually be in train, but may include prospective proceedings. If the Commissioner decides to provide assistance he must notify the applicant. If he decides not to provide assistance he must also notify the applicant of that decision and he may provide reasons for his decisions but is under no obligation to do so.

A matter of substantial public importance would appear to denote some degree of public interest or benefit to the public at large or of societal values whether of justice, fairness, privacy or otherwise. The comments above in respect of the relevance of Convention rights will be applicable here also. These provisions are supplemented by Sch.10, which provides that the Commissioner must ensure that the person against whom proceedings are commenced is informed that assistance will be provided in those proceedings. Schedule 10 also provides that assistance may include making arrangements for the Commissioner to bear the cost of advice or assistance or representation or assistance in the proceedings or steps preliminary or incidental to the proceedings.

The reasoning behind the inclusion of this provision may be to ensure that the individual faced by the procedural claims under s.32(4) can obtain a fair hearing in compliance with art.6 of the Human Rights Convention. Legal aid is not available for cases under the Data Protection Act. In the absence of some form of support for litigants it might be argued that the complexity of the provisions means there is an "inequality of arms" between the respondent (which will most commonly be a media organisation) and the individual who seeks to assert his individual rights.

Where assistance is provided it shall include an agreement to indemnify the applicant for costs arising by virtue of any order, subject to any exceptions specified in the notification to the individual. In his evidence to the Leveson Inquiry, Christopher Graham referred to this power and stated that only one application for such assistance had been received by his office but that it had been refused.

Impact of the draft Regulation in brief[54]

17–45   Under art.80 of the draft Regulation, Member States shall provide for exemptions or derogations from the general principles, the rights of data subjects, the obligations on controllers and processors including breach notification, the transfers of personal data outside the EEA, the powers of supervisory authorities and the cooperation and consistency mechanism for the processing of personal data carried out solely for journalistic purposes or the purpose of artistic or literary expression. These are in order to reconcile the right to protection of personal data with the rules governing freedom of expression. The Member State must notify the Commission of the laws which it adopts pursuant to this provision.

---

[54] See Ch.1 para.1-68 onwards for an overview of the draft Regulation proposed by the European Commission in January 2012

The exemptions therefore will vary from State to State. There are no constraints on the nature and extent of the derogations which can be permitted so they may be very wide. As with current provisions therefore we are likely to see wide variations between the extent of the exemptions for freedom of expression between Member States.

PRACTICAL TOOLS

Example of the application of the special procedures applicable before publication—journalistic purposes

Note: This case study differs from others in the book as it does not analyse the legal issues. It is included to illustrate how the special provisions could apply in a practical situation.

A young woman, Anna Brown (AB), was the subject of an article in the   **17–46** *Weekly Wonder Magazine* (WWM) last year. The article dealt with her relationship with her father, who is now deceased. It alleged she had behaved extremely badly to him in his dying years and had extorted money from him in his final illness. AB is suing WWM for defamation in respect of the article about her.

She learns from friends that a reporter with WWM, one David Edwards (DE), has been making inquiries about her relationship with her elderly mother-in-law. AB suspects that DE is making the inquiries for the purposes of defending the defamation proceedings against WWM, although the reason he has given for the inquiries is that he is researching another story about AB.

AB makes a subject access request to WWM under s.7 of the Act. WWM refuses to respond to her request, so AB asks the Commissioner to make an assessment under s.42 as to whether WWM is complying with principle 6 ("personal data shall be processed in accordance with the rights of data subjects under this Act"). At the same time, she makes an application to the county court for an order under s.7(9) that WWM provide subject access to any personal data held about her.

The Commissioner makes further inquiries of both AB and of WWM. He is informed by WWM that the inquiries about AB were made, and the resulting data are held, with a view to the publication of material not previously published about AB. AB, on the other hand, informs the Commissioner of her suspicions that the inquiries are not being made in connection with a further article but in connection with the defamation proceedings. The Commissioner considers whether it would be appropriate to serve a special information notice under s.44. However, before a decision on that is made the proceedings under s.7(9) are listed for trial. At that stage in the proceedings, WWM serves an affidavit from the editor which states that all the personal data held about AB are being processed for the purpose of journalism with a view to the publication of material which has not previously been published by it.

AB believes that most of the data WWM holds are data that were obtained and   **17–47** used in the publication of the previous article. As a result of some comments made by the reporter, DE, during his conversations with her friends, she suspects

WWM does not want to publish the material, or at least that is not its primary purpose, and in fact it wishes to use the information in the defamation proceedings.

The court has no option but to stay the proceedings and AB presses the Commissioner to make a determination relating to the data held by WWM. After considering the information available, the Commissioner decides that it throws reasonable doubt on the assertions of WWM. He serves a special information notice on WWM under s.44(1) stating his grounds for suspecting that the data are not being processed only for the journalistic purposes with a view to first publication. In the notice he asks a series of detailed questions about the data held, the purposes for which they may be used and the publication plans of the WWM.

On receipt of the special information notice the WWM appeals against it to the Information Tribunal and the case goes to a contested hearing. It is several months before the hearing but finally, after a two-day hearing before the Tribunal, it rules that the WWM must respond to the special information notice and allows it 28 days to do so. WWM decides not to appeal the Tribunal decision but to respond to the notice.

The Commissioner considers the response to be equivocal. In the response, WWM states that the data held on AB are being used to prepare for its defence in the defamation proceedings and that much of the data was previously published but that the information is also being held for the purpose of the publication of a second piece to come out after the conclusion of the defamation proceedings. This planned article will contain additional material which has not previously been published.

The Commissioner decides that in those circumstances WWM cannot claim the s.32 stay, certainly not for all the data held, and makes a determination under s.45 that the personal data are not being processed only for the purposes of journalism. He serves notice of the determination on WWM, which appeals the determination to the Information Tribunal. It takes some months for the matters to come to hearing; however, after a three-day hearing before the Tribunal, the Tribunal agrees with the Commissioner's view and upholds the determination.

The Commissioner then considers whether enforcement action is appropriate and decides that he should serve an enforcement notice to require the WWM to give AB access to the data. Before he can do so he must seek permission of the court under s.46. He serves notice on the WWM under s.46(2)(b) that he intends to apply to the court for leave to serve an enforcement notice and makes his court application under s.46(1)(b). The Commissioner argues that the failure to give subject access on the grounds cited by WWM raises an issue of substantial public importance which justifies the court giving leave for service of the notice. The application is contested by WWM and after some months it comes to hearing. After a contested hearing lasting two days the court decides to give leave and the Commissioner serves his enforcement notice under s.40 for failure to give subject access to AB. WWM appeals the enforcement notice to the Information Tribunal on the substantive grounds in s.32(1) that even though the processing is not taking place only for the special purposes eventual publication is still one of the purposes of the processing; it is in the public interest that the article be published and if subject access is given to AB publication will become impossible. It takes some months for the matter to come to a hearing and the contested proceedings last four days. The Tribunal upholds the enforcement notice and orders subject access be given to AB.

Clearly there could be further appeals to higher courts at any stage but even assuming there are no such further appeals it will have taken four contested hearings and probably several years of litigation to secure AB's subject access rights. AB discontinues her action in the court.

ADDITIONAL INFORMATION

Derivations   17–48

- Directive 95/46 (see Appendix B):
  (a)art.9;
  (b)Recitals 17, 37.
- Council of Europe Convention of January 28, 1981 for the Protection of Individuals with regard to automatic processing of Personal Data: art.9 (exceptions and restrictions).
- Organisation for Economic Co-operation and Development Guidelines: Annex Pt 1 (scope of guidelines).
- European Convention for the protection of Human Rights and Fundamental Freedoms: art.10 (freedom of expression).

Hansard references   17–49

Vol.586, No.110, col.90, Lords Grand Committee, February 25, 1998:
Meaning of publishing sufficient to include any media.
Vol.586, No.110, cols 95–97:
Effect of the exemption.
Vol.586, No.110, col.99:
Codes to be designated.
Vol.586, No.110, col.103:
Accuracy exemption.
Vol.587, No.127, cols 1115–1117, Lords Third Reading, March 24, 1998:
Extent of exemption and relation with ECHR.
Commons Standing Committee D, May 12, 1998, cols 53–55:
Definition of the special purposes.
Commons Standing Committee D, May 21, cols 211–229:
Effect of exemption.
Commons Standing Committee D, June 2, 1998, col.249:
Special information notices.
Commons Standing Committee D, June 4, 1998, cols 323, 324:
Effect of information notice on issue of warrants.

CHAPTER 18

Research

Ellis Parry

INTRODUCTION

Research which entails the use of personal data must comply with the Data Protection Act (DPA). Some of the standards required by the DPA and associated legislation may present difficulties in the context of research—these are explored in this chapter.

18–01

The DPA includes only limited exemptions for research so researchers need to understand and apply the data protection principles appropriately particularly in the light of the wider evolving landscape. Policy makers, legislators and the Information Commissioner recognise the benefit of research, but as the Information Commissioner has commented:

> "...the public wants...to see their privacy rights respected too. The risks of anonymisation can sometimes be underestimated and in other cases overstated; organisations need to be aware of what those risks are and take a structured approach to assessing them, particularly in light of other personal information in the public domain".[1]

The nervousness expressed by the Information Commissioner over allowing large administrative datasets gathered for one purpose to be re-used for a secondary purpose, may have its roots in the events surrounding the troubled legislative passage of the Coroners and Justice Bill in 2009. The Bill contained a provision which would have given a "designated authority" powers to make "Information-Sharing Orders" permitting public sector bodies to disclose and use personal data for purposes other than those for which they were initially collected. However, after representations by a range of civil liberty advocates and a softening in the Information Commissioner's support for the provision, the government withdraw the provision from the Bill and replaced it with provisions for a statutory data sharing code[2]—for a fuller discussion of the failed aspects of the Coroners and Justice Bill, see Ch.25. The data sharing code is not itself hard law rather it is persuasive and advisory only although it is admissible in legal proceedings.

The government continues to champion its transparency agenda advocating that public services can be transformed through the realisation of the benefits

---

[1]   http://www.ico.gov.uk/news/latest_news/2012/ico-consults-on-new-anonymisation-code-of-practice-31052012.aspx [Accessed September 21, 2012].
[2] http://www.ico.gov.uk/for_organisations/data_protection/topic_guides/data_sharing.aspx

589

which a society may derive from the analysis of large administrative datasets. There is a body of opinion that believes that these benefits are in danger of not being fully realised because:

(a)   of an over emphasis being placed on individuals' rights to informational self-determination as opposed to the collective good;

(b)   public bodies are unsure about the extent of their statutory and common law powers to share personal information;

(c)   the legal and regulatory landscape is confused and confusing; and

(d)   when in doubt, data custodians tend to be conservative and say "no"—they feel it is more likely to be "wrong" to share personal data than to refuse to do so.

In 2010 the Ministry of Justice issued guidance on data sharing for all public bodies (including data sharing across government). The Data Sharing Protocol (DSP),[3] with its nine annexes, sets itself up as: "practical help when...start[ing] new projects which may involve the sharing of personal data". The DSP is quite high level and may, in order to give good practical advice, have over-simplified some aspects of the law governing public bodies' powers (express or implied) to share personal data and the extent to which individuals' common law rights of confidentiality may be set aside without their consent—see the Guidance section later in this chapter. The importance of striking an appropriate balance between the sometimes competing interests of informational self-determination and societal good has been emphasized in the NHS Confidentiality Code of Practice,[4] the Thomas & Walport Data Sharing Review[5] and the Information Commissioner's Data Sharing Code of Practice.[6]

The practical problems which arise when applying the data protection principles to the use of personal data for research include:

(a)   researchers wishing to use personal data which were originally collected or generated for other purposes when no one was aware of their potential use for research, e.g. medical researchers may wish to refer to records of childhood illnesses or use data generated as a result of treatment;

(b)   researchers wishing to re-use material or information originally collected for a limited or different research purpose, e.g. research into a specific illness;

(c)   the information which may be useful for research may not be needed for the primary purpose of collection, e.g. the investigation of a road traffic accident may not require the age of the driver to be available but it may be useful information for researchers investigating patterns of road accidents;

---

[3] *http://www.justice.gov.uk/information-access-rights/data-protection/data-sharing* [Accessed September 21, 2012].

[4] *http://www.dh.gov.uk/en/PublicationsandstatisticsPublications/PublicationsPolicyAndGuidance/DH_4069253* [Accessed September 21, 2012].

[5] *http://www.connectingforhealth.nhs.uk/systemsandservices/infogov/links/datasharingreview.pdf/view?searchterm=walport*[Accessed September 21, 2012].

[6] *http://www.ico.gov.uk/for_organisations/data_protection/topic_guides/data_sharing.aspx* [Accessed September 21, 2012].

(d)   researchers may wish to retain and use data long after the primary purpose for which the data were collected has expired, e.g. a researcher examining housing needs and provision may wish to access tenancy records long after the tenants have moved away or a house has been sold; and

(e)   it may be difficult for researchers to provide subject access to personal data.

The two codes and the Thomas & Walport Review all put forward suggestions on how a democratic society's legitimate aim to raise standards for everyone may be met without unduly infringing upon individuals' rights; in particular those rights under the common law of confidence and the Human Rights Act 1998 (the HRA). As the Thomas & Walport Review states:

> "Decisions about the extent of data sharing go to the heart of the fundamental democratic debate about the relationship between individuals and society".[7]

Personal data are increasingly important in carrying out research and researchers need to be sure that they are complying with all aspects of the law and relevant ethical standards, placing due weight on professional and regulatory guidance.

Human Rights Act 1998

In Ch.2 the impact of the right to respect for private and family life, home and correspondence under the HRA is explained. This right may also impact upon a researcher's ability to source and use personal data, in particular from public bodies.   18–02

The law of confidence

Principle 1 requires that all personal data be processed "lawfully". Thus, in considering principle 1, legal standards other than those contained within the DPA itself have to be considered. In the context of much research, the law of confidence is the most relevant. In Ch.2 the law of confidence as it impacts on personal information is examined, and in Ch.6 the interface with principle 1 is explained. Although, as will be examined in more detail later in this chapter, there are circumstances prescribed under statute and common law when the obligation of confidentiality owed to one or more confiders may be set aside if the interests of public disclosure outweigh the benefits of maintaining such confidence.   18–03

Ethical and professional standards

Because principle 1 also requires that personal data be processed "fairly", relevant standards of fairness have to be considered when it is applied. Applicable and widely accepted ethical, professional and regulatory standards could therefore be regarded as part of the obligations in principle 1 because to process otherwise than in accordance with them may render such processing "unfair".   18–04

---

[7] *http://www.connectingforhealth.nhs.uk/systemsandservices/infogov/links/datasharingreview.pdf/view?searchterm=walport* [Accessed September 28, 2012], Foreword, p.i.

Where administrative datasets are used for research the researcher should look at all these matters—the flowchart at the end of this chapter may prove helpful in structuring a consideration of these issues. Dealing with this range of legal, ethical, professional and regulatory considerations is not always easy. In addition to the impact of the DPA, researchers and those charged with making decisions on the use of personal data in the research area (such as members of ethics committees) have, in the past, faced uncertainty over the impact of the HRA and the common law of confidence. This has often led to a cautious stance being taken to personal data sharing for the purposes of research.

The use of records relating to individuals—general issues

18–05   Research may be records-based. The nature and extent of the records available for possible research have increased dramatically over the last 50 years. Society is still working towards a satisfactory way of resolving the tension between research needs and individual autonomy in respect of such records. However, the formation of organisations like the Administrative Data Liaison Service[8] may evidence a societal shift in attitude away from the unimpeachable primacy of individual autonomy towards a recognition of the validity of the competing interest of the wider public good.

    Many records are held by the state as a result of the provision of care at the public expense or the exercise of policing functions, these data can be known as "administrative data". The most striking examples are patient records held by the NHS and the national DNA and fingerprint databases held by the police. The secondary use of NHS records and biological samples taken from patients, (sometimes without specific notice or consent) has given rise to controversy in the past. The government has acted to resolve some of the problems by introducing legislation (dealt with later in this chapter). In December 1997 the Caldicott Report[9] (named after its author Dame Fiona Caldicott) identified weaknesses in the way the NHS handled patient data. The report recommended the appointment of Caldicott guardians whose remit would include:

> "…[to] actively support work to facilitate and enable information sharing, and advise on options for lawful and ethical processing of information as required".[10]

GENETIC MATERIAL

18–06   The collection of genetic material gives rise to particular concern because it is a member of the small class of data which is immutable and identifies you uniquely. It may also render other members of your biological family distinguishable as a class; your surrender of a sample of your genetic material may have unforeseen consequences for other people to whom you are related. The United Kingdom now has the largest forensic DNA database in the world.

---

[8] *http://www.adls.ac.uk/about/* [Accessed September 28, 2012].
[9] *http://www.dh.gov.uk/en/Publicationsandstatistics/Publications/PublicationsPolicyAndGuidance/DH_4068403* [Accessed September 28, 2012].
[10] Caldicott Report, para.3.1.

The practice of taking samples from people who are arrested (but not necessarily charged or convicted) and keeping them indefinitely was challenged in the courts,[11] including in the European Court of Human Rights (the ECHR). In December 2008, 17 judges ruled unanimously that there had been a violation of art.8 of the European Convention on Human Rights as the United Kingdom's indefinite retention of the samples of the innocent was not a proportionate response necessary to achieve a legitimate aim of a democratic society.[12]

In 2009 the Home Office initiated a public consultation recommending that samples taken from suspects subsequently convicted of a "recordable offence" should be kept indefinitely; with samples taken from people suspected of committing more minor offences being kept for between 6 and 12 years. In February 2011 the Protection of Freedoms Bill was announced, limiting the scope of the retention of DNA samples to comply with the ECHR's legal ruling. The Bill received Royal Assent and became law on May 1, 2012. The Protections of Freedoms Act 2012 (the PFA) contains substantial amendments to the Police and Criminal Evidence Act 1984 and sets out a complicated retention regime for samples taken at the time of a suspect's arrest. The retention periods differ according to whether the sample was taken before the commencement of the PFA or after. If the sample is taken after the PFA's commencement, the duration of the sample's retention will be dictated by an interplay of numerous factors, including:

(a)   the seriousness of the offence for which the suspect is arrested, charged or convicted;
(b)   the age of the suspect at the time of conviction (i.e., 18 years or less);
(c)   whether or not, upon conviction, a minor was given a custodial sentence of more or less than five years' duration; and
(d)   whether the sample was given voluntarily.

Possibly the most contentious aspect of the PFA is that where a suspect is charged with a serious "qualifying offence"[13] (which includes murder, manslaughter or kidnaping) but is not subsequently convicted of that offence their sample may still be retained indefinitely where they have previously been convicted of a lesser "recordable offence" (which includes non-custodial offences such as failure to provide a breath specimen, taking a pedal cycle without owner's consent, begging and poaching).[14] The PFA also provides for the destruction of samples collected prior to its commencement using a similarly convoluted matrix of influencing factors a precise examination of which is outside the remit of this volume.

In 2002 the Human Genetics Commission published a major report into the storage and use of personal genetic information, "Inside Information—Balancing Interests in the Use of Personal Genetic Data". This contained a number of recommendations which would impose clear limits on the uses of genetic information without consent, including:

---

[11] *R. v Chief Constable of South Yorkshire Police Ex p. Marper* [2004] UKHL 39.
[12] *http://www.bailii.org/eu/cases/ECHR/2008/1581.html* [Accessed September 28, 2012].
[13] *http://www.legislation.gov.uk/ukpga/1984/60/contents?view=plain* [Accessed September 28, 2012], s.65A.
[14] *http://www.legislation.gov.uk/uksi/2000/1139/schedule/made* [Accessed September 28, 2012].

(a)   restrictions on use by employers;

(b)   ring-fencing of research databases so they could not be accessed for other purposes;

(c)   independent oversight of genetic databases; and

(d)   the creation of a criminal offence for testing or accessing genetic material without consent for non-medical purposes.

Not all of the recommendations have been taken forward at the time of writing, but the difficult issues raised by bio-information continue to give rise to concerns.[15] The Human Tissue Act 2004 which came into effect in September 2006 has, however, made it an offence to take a sample with the intent of analyzing the DNA without the individual's consent.[16] Some exceptions to this requirement are contained in Sch.4 Pt II and permit the non-consensual analysis of DNA for the prevention or detection of crime, the conduct of a prosecution and for the purposes of national security.[17] Further, the Secretary of State may by regulations specify the circumstances in which the High Court in England and Wales may order the use of the results of the analysis of DNA for the purpose of research in connection with "... disorders, or the functioning of the human body".[18]

Historical records

18–07   Difficult questions are also raised by the fact that the DPA is only concerned with the living and there is no provision in it to protect the privacy of the dead. Once, when most ordinary people died, the record of their lives died with them. For some there was an inscription on a tombstone or a life event recorded in a parish register; sometimes records of individual lives survived but this was an unusual occurrence mainly associated with the infamous and/or very wealthy. This is no longer the case. The most insignificant of us will leave behind a personal historical record more complete than those left by the emperors of the past. The histories of our childhoods, jobs, pensions, children, health, DNA, finances, on-line browsing and social networking habits will outlive us in one way and another. They may also live on to have an effect on our descendants.

The DPA only applies to personal data about living individuals but should it, or can it already, be used to give us a say in what happens to those records after death? Should individuals be entitled to choose obscurity in death? While a doctor may be bound by an ethical obligation to keep patient information confidential after the patient dies, the more general rights to privacy protected by the DPA will no longer apply. At least one step has been taken in the direction of providing such protection; in the Freedom of Information (Scotland) Act 2002 the exemption for personal privacy extends to the medical records of a deceased person. In a case decided by the Information Commissioner under the Freedom of Information Act 2000 (the FIOA), the Commissioner ruled that the medical

---

[15] See "Forensic Use of Bio-information: ethical issues", Consultation Paper, Nuffield Council on Bioethics, January 2007.

[16] Human Tissue Act 2004 s.45(1).

[17] Human Tissue Act 2004 Sch.4 Pt II s.5(1).

[18] Human Tissue Act 2004 Sch.4 Pt II s.6.

records of a deceased individual did not have to be disclosed and could still be regarded as subject to an obligation of confidence which remained binding on the public authority. While most individuals would welcome these decisions, they complicate further the maze of considerations which researchers have to navigate in order to grant or obtain access to records for the purpose of conducting retrospective records-based research.

Records-based research

Where research is records-based, the researcher will usually not meet the individual whose record s/he peruses. Some of those who are the subject of records may be dead (in which case the DPA will no longer be applicable) but, unless the researcher is dealing with records which are all over a century old, there can be no certainty that all of the individuals on a database are dead. Therefore, in order to protect sufficiently the interests and rights of individuals while simultaneously maximising the benefits that records-based research may yield, researchers should to the greatest extent possible work with data which have been anonymised. This is perhaps the simplest path through "the murky legislative framework".[19]

18–08

Opinion 4/2007 of the Article 29 Working Party on the concept of personal data:

> "Where identification of the data subject is not included in the purpose of the processing, the technical measures to prevent identification have a very important role to play. Putting in place the appropriate state-of-the-art technical and organizational measures to protect the data against [re]identification may make the difference to consider that the persons are not identifiable …".[20]

Therefore, as the Working Party itself concludes:

> "This means that a mere hypothetical possibility to single out the individual is not enough to consider the person as 'identifiable'. If, taking into account 'all the means likely reasonably to be used by the controller or any other person', that possibility does not exist or is negligible, the person should not be considered as 'identifiable', and the information would not be considered as 'personal data'. The criterion of 'all the means likely reasonably to be used either by the controller or by any other person' should in particular take into account all the factors at stake".[21]

The Working Party's approach is endorsed by the Information Commissioner in his "Guidance: Determining What Is Personal Data":

---

[19] Thomas & Walport Data Sharing Review, para.5.27.
[20] *http://ec.europa.eu/justice/policies/privacy/docs/wpdocs/2007/wp136_en.pdf* [Accessed September 28, 2012], p.17.
[21] *http://ec.europa.eu/justice/policies/privacy/docs/wpdocs/2007/wp136_en.pdf*, p.15.

"Therefore, the fact that there is a very slight hypothetical possibility that someone might be able to reconstruct the data in such a way that the data subject is identified is not sufficient to make the individual identifiable for the purposes of the Directive".[22]

The Administrative Data Liaison Service[23] offers researchers a useful disclosure risk analysis service to estimate how re-identifiable particular datasets are. Issues examined include:

(a)   the overall data environment (i.e., what other data are already available which could be cross matched to seek to re-identify individuals);
(b)   how unique the data are (i.e., special uniques which may aid re-identification because of their statistical rarity); and
(c)   scenario analysis (i.e., an assessment of why someone would seek to attack the data with the aim of re-identification).

Where the use of truly anonymised data is not possible, for example, where the research seeks to check correlations between life incidents which are removed in time from one another, a mechanism to allow an individual's data to be correlated over time may be necessary to ensure that the correct records are matched. In such circumstances individuals' data may be pseudonymised in order to obscure the affected individuals' identities while allowing correlation. The NHS "Confidentiality Code of Practice" defines pseudonymised information thus:

"This is like anonymised information in that in the possession of the holder it cannot reasonably be used by the holder to identify an individual. However, it differs in that the original provider of the information may retain a means of identifying individuals. This will often be achieved by attaching codes or other unique references to information so that data will only be identifiable to those who have access to the key or index. Pseudonymisation allows information about the same individual to be linked in a way that true anonymisation does not".[24]

Before data are pseudonymised and made available to the researcher, the original provider will still need to negotiate all aspects of the law, relevant ethical standards and professional and regulatory guidance to ensure such processing complies with the data protection principles. However, in the hands of the recipient researcher, the protective cloak which the pseudonymising technique throws around the identity of the concerned individuals means that the application of the data protection principles is more flexible:

"Retraceably pseudonymised data may be considered as information on individuals which are indirectly identifiable. Indeed, using a pseudonym means that it is possible to backtrack to the individual, so that the individual's identity can be discovered, but then only under predefined circumstances. Although data protection rules apply, the risks at stake for the individuals with regard to the processing of

---

[22] http://www.ico.gov.uk/for_organisations/guidance_index/data_protection_and_privacy_and_ electronic_communications.aspx [Accessed September 28, 2012], "Determining What Is Personal Data", p.7.
[23] http://www.adls.ac.uk/ [Accessed September 28, 2012].
[24] http://www.dh.gov.uk/prod_consum_dh/groups/dh_digitalassets/@dh/@en/documents/digitalasset/ dh_4069254.pdf [Accessed September 28, 2012], "Glossary of Terms", p.5.

such indirectly identifiable information will most often be low, so that the application of these rules will justifiably be more flexible than if information on directly identifiable individuals were processed".[25]

The "predefined circumstances" mentioned by the Article 29 Working Party in this example are those of a pharmaceutical company which has released the pseudonymised results of a clinical trial to a recipient researcher and the recipient researcher's analysis has discovered a danger to one of the participants. By alerting the pharmaceutical company to the danger, the company may arrange for the correct participant to be contacted via the responsible medical professional because that person's identity is ascertainable by the holder of the key code list.

Although there is as yet no further guidance on the exact nature and scope of this "flexibility", it is widely accepted that recipient researchers may process robustly pseudonymised data without the data subject's explicit consent without necessarily contravening the data protection principles; provided suitably worded data use agreements mandating minimum policies and procedures are in place. The data use agreement should set minimum standards in the areas of:

(a)   data and physical security;
(b)   software and hardware security;
(c)   data handling practices;
(d)   staff access protocols, confidentiality agreements and training; and
(e)   adherence to applicable and widely accepted ethical standards and professional and regulatory guidance.

Where the above measures are suitably robust and continually reviewed over time to ensure they keep pace with developments in the power of computing technology and the wider data environment, the Information Commissioner's stance is that:

> "a person who puts in place appropriate technical and organizational and legal measures to prevent individuals being identifiable from the data held may prevent such data falling with the scope of the Directive".[26]

Subject to this recent guidance from the Information Commissioner and the Article 29 Working Party, the DPA has introduced stricter controls over the use of personal data than those previously in force. The transitional reliefs have now expired. This chapter describes the exemptions in the DPA which deal with research involving personal data in the context of the broader issues.

---

[25]   *http://ec.europa.eu/justice/policies/privacy/docs/wpdocs/2007/wp136_en.pdf* [Accessed September 28, 2012], p.18.

[26]   *http://www.ico.gov.uk/for_organisations/guidance_index/data_protection_and_privacy_and_ electronic_communications.aspx* [Accessed September 28, 2012], "Determining What Is Personal Data", p.7.

18–09   SUMMARY OF MAIN POINTS

(i)   "Research" is broadly defined in the DPA and covers statistical and historical studies.

(ii)   The use of personal data for research is subject to the principles, including:

    (a)   the detailed rules governing, fairness, lawfulness and the provision of notice to individuals;

    (b)   the need to show a legal justification for any processing and the more stringent rules for processing sensitive data;

    (c)   the restriction on the uses that may be made of personal data to those for which they were collected or those compatible with the purposes of collection;

    (d)   the quality standards and limitations on retention;

    (e)   the rights of individuals;

    (f)   the security requirements; and

    (g)   the ban on overseas transfers.

(iii)   There are two "safeguard conditions" which researchers must satisfy in order to rely on the applicable exemptions:

    (a)   the research must not be used to make decisions about the individuals to whom the data relate; and

    (b)   the processing must not cause substantial damage or distress to the individuals whose data are utilised in the research.

(iv)   If the safeguard conditions are met, the personal data may be:

    (a)   used for research even if they were not originally collected for a research purpose; and

    (b)   retained indefinitely for the purposes of research.

(v)   If the results of the research are anonymised and the safeguard conditions are met, individual data subjects may be refused their right of subject access to the data.

(vi)   These exemptions can apply to any research, whether carried out in the public or private sector, whether commercial or academic, as long as the safeguard conditions are met.

(vii)   The use of data held prior to October 1998 can continue for research without having to comply with the DPA in full, subject to fulfilling the safeguard conditions.

It follows that researchers can use personal data for research purposes even if the individual has not been told of that specific use, provided that they have a high level awareness that their personal data may be used for the broad purpose of "research". Subject to the two safeguard conditions, researchers may retain the personal data indefinitely, even if to do so would otherwise breach principle 5. However, it is important to note that there are no exemptions from the requirement that data controllers have a legitimate basis for processing personal data or from the fair obtaining and processing codes. It should be further noted that there are only limited grounds for the processing of sensitive personal data for the purposes of medical and other research. Sensitive personal data are data concerned with:

(a)   racial or ethnic origin;
(b)   political opinions;
(c)   religious or similar beliefs;
(d)   trade union membership;
(e)   physical or mental health or condition;
(f)   sexual life; and
(g)   the commission or alleged commission of any offence or any criminal proceedings.

HISTORY

Recommendations R(83)10 and R(97)18

The tension between the needs of the research community for information and moves by international bodies to protect personal data led to an early focus on this area with data protectors holding sway over the debate. The Council of Europe's 1981 Treaty 108 on the "Protection of Individuals with regard to Automatic Processing of Personal Data" specifically refers to the use of data for research. In 1983 the Council of Europe gave further guidance to signatory states on the use of personal data for research in Recommendation R(83)10. This has been replaced by the later Recommendation (97)18 but the description of the issues remains applicable today.

In the Explanatory Memorandum to Recommendation (83)10[27] the problems are explained:

18–10

"Personal data frequently play an important, if not vital, role in research. Sociological studies, with their questionnaires and interviews, are probably the best-known example of interest in personal data, but there are many others. Special studies into cancer incidence or multiple births also demonstrate how greatly epidemiology, for instance, depends on access to named data which can be used for research based on the case histories of individuals. The same is true of psychology and educational research. Thus disciplines may vary but broad areas of research still require information about identifiable persons.

For a long time no particular justification for the use of personal data was necessary. The mere fact that data were needed for research was sufficient, and the few rare criticisms were met by reference to codes of professional ethics. Since the beginning of the 1970s, however, the situation has begun to change as a result of developments in data protection legislation in several member countries. The need for rules stipulating the conditions under which personal data may be collected, stored, transmitted or used in any form is coming to be recognised openly in legislation.

Research is bound by the same fundamental rules as any other activity involving the use of personal data. The laws on data protection do not recognise privilege. They may well adapt their requirements to the particular structure and specific objects of the information process, but they do not allow any exception to the duty to observe the restrictive principles which they lay down.

---

[27] *https://wcd.coe.int/*
com.instranet.InstraServlet?command=com.instranet.CmdBlobGet&InstranetImage=602986&SecMode=1&DocId=680
[Accessed September 28, 2012].

Thus data protection legislation may be clear in its attitude. The consequences are no less so. With or without data protection longitudinal studies on child development demand knowledge of a minimum of personal data. The aetiology of heart diseases and the efficiency of certain forms of treatment cannot be understood without access to information on the behaviour of patients. Any critical analysis of social policy rests largely on the availability of micro-data. No one can seriously claim that research in any of these cases should be abandoned on grounds of data protection".

The Recommendation R(83)(10) sets out a general approach to the use of personal data for research based on the principle of "functional separation". Broadly speaking, exemptions from the standards required by data protection are acceptable as long as the data are not used to make decisions about, or take actions which may affect, the individuals whose data are the subject of the research.

On September 30, 1997 the Committee of Ministers adopted a further Recommendation (97)18 concerning the protection of personal data collected and processed for statistical purposes. The revised Recommendation was considered necessary in the light of the progress which had been made in statistical methods and information technology since 1983. The revised Recommendation closely reflects the provisions of the Directive, now embodied in the DPA. It contains detailed rules governing the fair collection of data and covers questions of trans-border data flows and lawfulness of processing which are set out in the data protection principles. It also strengthens the exhortations to anonymise personal data as soon as it is no longer necessary to retain them in an identifiable form.

In the Explanatory Memorandum to R(97)18 the Committee of Ministers:

"... acknowledge[s] that statisticians themselves were among the first to take privacy into account in the production of statistics based on personal data and that statisticians' concern has been reflected in codes of conduct, basic principles and legal standards ... Article 9 of the 1981 convention in fact gives statistical work the benefit of an exception whereby data subjects' exercise of certain rights is restricted;

d.   the Committee of Ministers states the purpose of the recommendation to be to establish appropriate procedures reconciling the interests of the various parties concerned in the production of statistics: on the one hand, the producers' interest in being able to produce representative statistics and, on the other, data subjects' interest in being protected against unnecessary intrusion into their private lives".[28]

Directive 95/46

18–11   The Directive deals with the tension between the needs of research and the requirements of data protection in similar ways to Recommendation R(83)10, although in considerably less detail. Article 6 contains derogations for the processing of personal data for historical, statistical or scientific purposes which provide that such uses shall not be regarded as incompatible with the original purpose of collection of the data and that data may be kept for longer periods than required for the purposes for which they were collected provided that Member

---

[28]   *https://wcd.coe.int/ViewDoc.jsp?id=589361* [Accessed September 28, 2012], para.45(b).

States provide sufficient safeguards in their implementing legislation. There are further provisions to allow for exemptions from providing information where personal data are shared for the purposes of research and from the right of subject access.

Despite these provisions for derogations and exemptions compliance with the following elements of the Directive gives rise to some difficulties for researchers:

(a)   the right of individuals to know of the use of personal data;

(b)   the primacy accorded to individuals' right to consent to the use of sensitive personal data; and

(c)   the right of individuals to object to the use of personal data in appropriate cases.

CURRENT ISSUES

Despite the efforts to provide protection for the privacy of individuals in the face of data-hungry research, problems were still arising in this area. As the Thomas & Walport "Data Sharing Review" states:

> "We have found that in the vast majority of cases, the law itself does not provide a barrier to the sharing of personal data. However, the complexity of the law, amplified by a plethora of guidance, leaves those who may wish to share data in a fog of confusion".[29]

18–12

Perhaps the best known is the controversy over the Icelandic data bank. Iceland has a small population which has been largely untouched by immigration. Icelanders have a passion for genealogy and the records available allow families to trace their antecedents back through recorded history. Healthcare has been provided by the state since the early years of the last century. The combination of these factors means that Iceland presents a wealth of material which can be mined for genetic research. In 1998 the Icelandic Parliament passed the Health Sector Database Act (the HSDA), allowing the Ministry of Health to grant a licence to a third party to create a database of Icelanders' health data, including genetic and genealogical data. The HSDA did not require consent from individual data subjects before research could be carried out on data relating to them as it was predicated on "presumed consent". In 2000 the Ministry granted a licence to a private company called deCODE, permitting it to cross-reference Icelanders' medical records with their genetic and genealogical data. The licence grant provoked fierce controversy. The pressure group Mannvernd (which means "human protection") successfully campaigned for Icelanders to have the right to opt-out of inclusion in the database. However, the opt-out was only applicable to living data subjects. A case was then brought by one of Mannvernd's supporters, Ragnhildur Gudmundsdottir, on behalf of her deceased father, objecting to the inclusion of data relating to him in the database. Gudmundsdottir was successful in her claim and in November 2003 the Icelandic Supreme Court ruled that she

---

[29]   *http://www.connectingforhealth.nhs.uk/systemsandservices/infogov/links/datasharingreview.pdf/ view?searchterm=walport* [Accessed September 28, 2012], "Foreward", p.i.

had the right to object to inclusion of information about her deceased father in the data bank because information about her could be inferred from the information about her parent.

More latterly the Data Inspection Board (the data protection regulator) in Sweden has also been active in this area. In April 2011 it ruled that the Karolinksa University Hospital's approach to patients opting-out of having their medical data, bio-information and samples shared with third parties (both public and private sector) did not meet the standard of consent required under Swedish law. The hospital was leading Sweden's largest medical research project ever—LifeGene—to study how genes, environment and lifestyle affect health. In response, the Swedish government announced a number of changes to the Swedish constitution and applicable laws to improve conditions for investigative studies with the aim of making Sweden a world leader in data-based research. In a further show of strength, in 2012 the Data Inspection Board ordered the Swedish National Data Service (SND) to stop processing research data because the SND did not give notice or obtain consent from the research subjects. As at the time of writing the University of Gothenburg has lodged an appeal concerning this regulatory action with the administrative court in Stockholm. The appeal appears to hinge on whether or not the SND do, indeed, collect "personal data" as a data controller or whether they are mere processors; the SND arguing that the burden of compliance with the data protection principles lies with the principal investigators who collect the data from the research subjects.

The United Kingdom is not without its own controversy where the state builds large data-banks of genetic material under statutory powers granted to itself (see above).

MEDICAL RESEARCH IN THE UK

UK developments in the use of personal data in the NHS

18–13   In the United Kingdom there has been a significant development in the attitude of the government to the use of personal data for medical purposes, including research. This is attributable, in part at least, to the Alder Hey Inquiry which followed news stories about the widespread removal and retention of organs from the dead, for ill-defined future research purposes, without the full knowledge or consent of the next of kin. Similar stories surfaced in Bristol. These practices—which were not illegal at the time—resulted in the passage of the Human Tissue Act 2004 which regulates the collection of biological samples.

In 2000 the General Medical Council revised its 1995 guidance on confidentiality and in doing so advised a more restrictive view on the use of data for research by clinicians. The current guidance to doctors was issued in 2006.[30] It advises that express consent is usually needed before the disclosure of identifiable information for purposes such as research and epidemiology. If the patient withholds consent or consent cannot be obtained then disclosures may only be made where they are required by law or can be justified in the public

---

[30] "General Medical Council Confidentiality: Protecting and Providing Information".

interest or are covered by a regulation made under s.251 of the NHS Act 2006.[31] For more information on s.251, see later in this chapter.

Human Rights Act 1998

The collection, storage, use and disclosure of directly identifiable patient information by the NHS clearly engages art.8 of the European Convention on Human Rights. Where the information is used in connection with the provision of healthcare its use will be justified by the consent which the patient has given to receive treatment. However, for medical research uses the NHS should be able to point to either a full and informed consent given by the patient or a justification which fulfills the three requirements of art.8(2):

18–14

(a)   pursuit of a legitimate aim;
(b)   which is considered necessary in a democratic society; and
(c)   is proportionate to the identified need.

The NHS "Confidentiality Code of Practice 2003" maintains that:

"Current understanding is that compliance with the Data Protection Act 1998 and the common law of confidentiality should satisfy Human Rights requirements".[32]

It can be argued that this approach appears to conflate three separate branches of jurisprudence, each with their own requirements to be satisfied. Evidently, satisfaction of the requirements of the DPA is not synonymous with compliance with the HRA. Further, the extent to which research re-using administrative data sets may be justified under art.8(2) remains uncertain given that the majority of the relevant ECHR case law has not considered how the interference with the art.8 right to privacy may be justified "for the protection of health or morals".

GUIDANCE

Ministry of Justice's Guidance to all public bodies

The Ministry of Justice's DSP[33] is a useful place to start for all public bodies that wish to share personal data as it assists the responsible person to structure their department's consideration of the relevant issues, including:

18–15

(a)   any express (or implied) statutory power they may have to share personal data;
(b)   any pertinent common law powers they may have;
(c)   the proportionality and necessity of any data sharing in view of the stated purpose behind the sharing; and

---

[31] Replacing s.60 of the Health and Social Care Act 2001.
[32] http://www.dh.gov.uk/prod_consum_dh/groups/dh_digitalassets/@dh/@en/documents/digitalasset/dh_4069254.pdf [Accessed September 28, 2012], para.33.
[33] http://www.justice.gov.uk/information-access-rights/data-protection/data-sharing [Accessed September 28, 2012].

(d) inviting the public authority to consider and enumerate any negative impacts of not sharing.

Of the DSP's nine annexes, we only touch upon one here in any detail—Annex H "Legal Guidance on Data Sharing". Section 1 opens on page two:

> "This document is intended to be a general guide and to offer key information on relevant legal issues on data sharing to lawyers and to other interested professionals working in the public sector…We hope it will increase understanding of the existing legal framework which governs public bodies' rights to share personal data and their responsibility when doing so. It is not intended to be a substitute for specific legal advice on particular issues. Any public body contemplating data sharing should seek its own legal advice".

This caveat is further qualified in the footnote which accompanies it:

> "The guidance is written with reference to the law of England and Wales and the statutory provisions that apply in those jurisdictions. However, certain key statutes (such as the Data Protection Act 1998 and the Human Rights Act 1998) apply equally to Scotland".

Before a public body shares data, it will need to satisfy itself that it has the *power* to do so. Most public bodies are creatures of statute which derive their powers from the written word of the instrument which brings them into being. Section 3 of Annex H reads:

1. A public body may only share data if it has power to do so. The power may derive from statute (expressly or impliedly), or from the common law. Public bodies that are not central government departments headed by a Minister of the Crown…will normally, but not always, derive their powers entirely from statute.
2. There is no general statutory power to disclose, obtain, hold or process data. So when considering whether a body has statutory power to share data, it will be necessary to consider the specific legislation governing the policy or service that the data sharing would support. That legislation may include an express power to share data, or it may do so impliedly.
3. Express powers to share data give the highest degree of certainty, but are relatively rare and tend to be confined to specific activities and exercisable only by named bodies. It will be more common to rely on implied powers.
4. In the case of central government departments headed by a Minister of the Crown, even if a power to share data cannot be reasonably implied from statutory provisions defining the Minister's powers, the minister may still have common law powers to share data.

The distinction between the rarely expressed statutory power to share data and the more common implied one is important because (by their very nature) the scope of implied powers is more difficult to judge. A further complicating factor is that some statutes are only permissive in their language, i.e. they give a public body the ability to share, but they do not mandate such sharing so the legitimacy of relying on such permissive language, in the absence of the affected individuals' consent may be open to challenge.

Section 10 of Annex H on the topic of implied powers states:

"Where no express statutory power to share or receive data exists, such a power may be implicit in the provision defining the relevant powers or functions. Many activities of statutory bodies will necessarily be carried out pursuant to implied statutory powers, given the difficulty of defining expressly all the activities that they may carry out in connection with their day-today functions. The courts will interpret implied powers relatively generously".

The case which the guidance refers to is *Attorney General v Great Eastern Railway Co*. The Lord Chancellor Selborne states:

"whatever may fairly be regarded as incidental to, or consequential upon, those things which the Legislature has authorized, ought not (unless expressly prohibited) to be held, by judicial construction to be ultra vires".[34]

This case was over 130 years ago, over a century before the HRA was enacted. Whether or not its dicta would survive the weight of an examination by the ECHR adjudicating whether public sector data sharing undertaken on an assessment of implied powers had violated unreasonably an individual's right to privacy under art.8 remains to be seen.

In the absence of express or implied statutory powers, government departments which are headed by a Minister of the Crown may be able to rely on their inherent common law powers to share data. However, as the DSP makes clear:

"Ministers' common law powers may be extinguished by statute and may otherwise be limited by the requirements of public law, the law of confidence or by agreement".[35]

Annex D makes it clear that following the 2008 review of data handling procedures within government, it is now mandatory for government departments to undertake Privacy Impact Assessments for certain initiatives:

"… which ensure that privacy issues are factored into plans from the start, and those planning service are clear about their aims".[36]

It is, therefore, recommended strongly that any public body sharing administrative data sets for secondary research purposes under implied powers document the reasoning behind any decisions by completing a Privacy Impact Assessment.

Annex E sets out a stringent hierarchy of access which should be followed when disclosing data. The order of preference is that the recipient should view:

(a) only aggregated data;
(b) only anonymous records;

---

[34] [1874-80] All E.R. Rep. Ext 1459 at 1462.
[35] [1874-80] All E.R. Rep. 1459 Ext, para.15.
[36] [1874-80] All E.R. Rep. 1459 Ext, p.2.

(c)   material from single identifiable records; and

(d)   material from many identifiable records simultaneously.

NHS Code of Practice

18–16   In November 2003 the Department of Health issued its NHS "Code of Practice on Confidentiality" which followed a wide consultation and was endorsed by the Information Commissioner, the General Medical Council and the British Medical Association.

The Code of Practice was the end product of a project to address health information in the wider context of the Connecting for Health programme. In December 2001 the Department of Health issued a policy document "Building the Information Core—Protecting and Using Confidential Patient Information: A strategy for the NHS". The document quoted the Minister for Health speaking to the Commons Committee:

> "Informed consent is crucial to the Government's view of how a modern NHS should work. We simply cannot move to a patient centred service if patients are not informed and consenting participants in the services they receive. But we all know too well that this is not the way the NHS operates at the moment. Much of what is done in the NHS relies upon implied consent. In some cases this is appropriate, for example sharing information within a hospital to ensure a patient receives appropriate care, but in other cases the definition of implied consent is pushed too far".

The Code provides guidance to the NHS and related bodies on confidentiality issues. It states:

> "… information that can identify individual patients must not be used or disclosed for purposes other than healthcare without the individual's explicit consent, some other legal basis, or where there is a robust public interest or legal justification to do so. In contrast, anonymised information is not confidential and may be used with relatively few constraints".[37]

The Code acknowledges that:

> "There are situations where consent cannot be obtained for the use or disclosure of patient identifiable information, yet the public good of this use outweighs issues of privacy. Section 60 of the Health and Social Care Act 2001 currently provides an interim power to ensure that patient identifiable information, needed to support a range of important work such as clinical audit, record validation and research, can be used without the consent of patients".[38]

The Code's definition of "anonymised information" deserves scrutiny in that it appears to set a relatively low threshold to bring de-identified data within the legal safe harbour of anonymity:

---

[37] *http://www.dh.gov.uk/prod_consum_dh/groups/dh_digitalassets/@dh/@en/documents/digitalasset/dh_4069254.pdf*, [Accessed September 28, 2012], p.7, para.11.

[38] *http://www.dh.gov.uk/prod_consum_dh/groups/dh_digitalassets/@dh/@en/documents/digitalasset/dh_4069254.pdf*, p.8, para.17.

"This is information which does not identify an individual directly, and which cannot reasonably be used to determine identity. Anonymisation requires the removal of name, address, full post code and any other detail or combination of details that might support identification".[39]

The National Health Service Act 2006 s.251[40]

Under s.251,[41] the Secretary of State may make regulations to:

"(1) ... make such provision for and in connection with requiring or regulating the processing of prescribed patient information for medical purposes as he considers necessary or expedient

(a)   in the interests of improving patient care, or
(b)   in the public interest".

Any regulations made may:

(a)   not regulate the processing of personal data for the provision of healthcare, nor may they override the provisions of the DPA[42];
(b)   deal with both confidential and non-confidential patient information; and
(c)   provide that where disclosures are made in accordance with the regs. they are deemed to be lawful "despite any obligation of confidence owed".[43]

Therefore, s.251 can be used to provide a secure legal basis for disclosure of confidential identifiable patient information for medical research purposes where:

(a)   the use of anonymised data is impossible; and
(b)   seeking individuals' consent is not practicable when the likely cost is calculated, taking into account the technology available.

Section 157 of the Health and Social Care Act 2008[44] establishes the National Information Governance Board (the "NIGB"). The Ethics and Confidentiality Committee[45] of the NIGB assesses applications for use of patient identifiable information without consent and makes recommendations to the Secretary of State on the use of his powers under s.251. An example of the Secretary of State using these powers (albeit under the previous almost identically worded s.60 of The Health and Social Care Act) are the Control of Patient Information Regulations.

18–17

---

[39] http://www.dh.gov.uk/prod_consum_dh/groups/dh_digitalassets/@dh/@en/documents/digitalasset/ dh_4069254.pdf, p.5.
[40] Replacing The Health and Social Care Act 2001 s.60.
[41] http://www.legislation.gov.uk/ukpga/2006/41/section/251 [Accessed September 28, 2012].
[42] s.251(2)(7).
[43] s.251(2)(c).
[44] http://www.legislation.gov.uk/ukpga/2008/14/contents [Accessed September 28, 2012].
[45] Taking over from the Patient Information Advisory Group.

The Health Service (Control of Patient Information) Regulations 2002[46]

18–18   The Regulations came into effect on June 1, 2002 permitting the processing of confidential patient information relating to patients referred for the diagnosis or treatment of neoplasia for "medical purposes" including research.[47]

The Regulations further permit the Secretary of State to make provision for the processing of confidential patient information for the recognition, control and prevention of communicable diseases and other risks to public health. As set out in the Schedule to the Regulations, the directly identifiable information may be processed with the approval of the Secretary of State in order to:

(a)   anonymise or pseudonmyise it;

(b)   identify geographical locations which may be relevant for research purposes;

(c)   identify and contact patients to approach them to solicit their consent to take part in medical research;

(d)   link or validate data from more than one source; or

(e)   perform a quality audit of the provision of healthcare.

Where the processing is for medical research the research must also be approved by an ethics committee.[48]

Regulation 7(1) sets out the restrictions placed upon the health professional (or person who owes an equivalent obligation of confidence) in possession of the confidential patient information. The processing is limited to that necessary to achieve the purpose for which s/he is permitted to process the information under the Regulations and in particular s/he shall:

(a)   remove identifiers in so far as they are not required for the purpose;

(b)   restrict access to the information to properly trained employees on a need-to-know basis;

(c)   ensure the information is held securely; and

(d)   undertake an annual review of the necessity of holding and continuing to process the information.

18–19   The Regulations apply to all medical information, not merely those categories of information that are subject to the DPA, but the provisions clearly reflect the requirements of the DPA, e.g. the definitions of "health professional" and "processing" are the same. Further, the Regulations are worded so as to ensure conformity with the DPA's legitimate processing grounds and, therefore, do not replace the requirement to have a legitimate ground for processing personal data. However they will, in effect, provide for exemption from the remainder of principle 1.

Pursuant to reg.4, the processing is deemed not to constitute a breach of confidence. The logic is that as all United Kingdom legislative instruments are

---

[46] *http://www.legislation.gov.uk/uksi/2002/1438/contents/made* [Accessed September 28, 2012].

[47] reg.2(1)(d).

[48] reg.2(1)(d).

required to comply with the HRA in order to become law. Therefore, the Regulations as drafted must be taken as complying de jure with the requirement of art.8(2), i.e. that they have been made:

(a) in pursuit of a legitimate aim;
(b) which is considered necessary in a democratic society; and
(c) are proportionate to the identified need.

However, this logic is not immune from challenge: if the Secretary of State exercises his powers under reg.2(4) the fair processing notice (otherwise required under para.2(1)(b) of Pt II of Sch.1 of the DPA) will not have to be provided to affected data subjects. However, the removal of this safeguard might lead to arguments about proportionality under the HRA and therefore risk a challenge in the courts by way of judicial review that the provisions of the Regulations do not satisfy art.8(2) of the HRA after all.

The cancer registries

An application for authorisation to use confidential patient information for the purposes of research (without the affected data subject's explicit consent) was made by the United Kingdom Association of Cancer Registries (UKACR). Cancer registries are responsible for the compilation of national registers of cancer sufferers. These are databases on which clinicians register information about patients diagnosed as suffering from particular cancers. The databases are non-statutory being maintained by cancer charities. The functions of the cancer registries are described as including monitoring trends, evaluating prevention and treatment and investigating causes. Analysis of the registries, which have been kept since 1971, can show survival rates of patients suffering from different cancers in different parts of the country and allow comparison with treatment results in other countries.

18–20

It was likely that disclosure of identifiable patient information to the registries by clinicians (without the patients' consent) was a breach of the obligation of confidence owed to the patient. Assuming that the patient details which were disclosed included personal data, the cancer sufferers should at the least have been informed of the disclosure and given an opportunity to object to it. It appeared that clinicians were not informing patients that their details were being registered on the databases, let alone obtaining the sufferer's explicit consent. The UKACR expressed concerns that patients may object and refuse to be registered, with resulting degradation in the quality of the data or, if they had discovered that they were registered without their consent, would seek to be removed from the registers.

The registries were one of the first research data sets to be submitted as suitable for being the subject of regulations made under the old s.60. After considering the UKACR submission, the Patient Information Advisory Group[49] expressed reservations about the:

---

[49] Now replaced by the National Information Governance Board.

(a)   poor communication with patients concerning the work of the registries using their personal data;

(b)   clinicians' failure to tell patients about the disclosure of their information from the registries to third parties; and

(c)   absence of appropriate retention and disposal policies for the data,

all of which issues it said should be addressed. However, subject to those caveats it went on to recommended that the application be successful and the registries be made subject to a s.60 Order.

The opportunity to have the Regulations deal with Market Authorisation Holders' (MAH) legal requirement to perform pharmaco-vigilance pursuant to Directive 2001/83/EC[50] was missed. In short, a MAH must have systems in place which detect and assess adverse reactions to its products once they are in circulation in the general populace. The aim of these systems is to understand the safety and efficacy profile of marketed pharmaceutical products in order to protect and promote the public's health. However, the 2001 Directive is not prescriptive about exactly what information should be collected in relation to a patient's adverse reaction.

Stakeholders have written guidelines[51] which are no more specific than referring to "Individual Case Safety Reports" collecting information on "identifiable patients" and their health. Collecting identifiable patient information helps identify and deal with duplicate reports and allow for appropriate follow-up with affected patients. However, the guidelines do not have the force of law providing a clearly identifiable legitimate ground upon which the MAH could rely to justify processing identifiable sensitive personal data. Therefore, tension exists between the MAH's obligation to collect, process and disclose such sensitive identifiable health information and the patient's right to medical confidentiality and data protection.

RESEARCH PURPOSES

Data controller

18–21   The definition of a data controller is covered in Ch.3. In any research context, as shown by the Swedish Data Inspection Board's intervention in the SND case, it is important to ascertain the identity of the data controller. In most cases it will be the academic institution undertaking the research but it may be the funding organisation or the head of the research team. In all cases responsibility for compliance with the DPA will rest with the data controller. This appears to be the crux of the SND's appeal to the administrative court in Stockholm against the Swedish Data Inspection Board's recent ruling (see above).

---

[50] http://ec.europa.eu/health/files/eudralex/vol-1/dir_2001_83_cons/dir2001_83_cons_20081230_ en.pdf [Accessed September 28, 2012].

[51] http://ec.europa.eu/health/files/eudralex/vol-9/pdf/vol9a_09-2008_en.pdf [Accessed September 28, 2012].

Definitions

The exemptions apply to personal data used for "research purposes". Section 33 **18–22** of the DPA states that "research purposes include statistical or historical purposes"—none of these terms are further defined. In the *Concise Oxford English Dictionary* "research" is defined as:

> "the systematic investigation into and study of materials and sources in order to establish facts and reach new conclusions."

"Statistical purposes" are presumably aimed at the study of or the production of statistics. "Historical purposes" could reasonably be regarded as covering historical studies. However, these are only specific elements covered by the definition and "research purposes" may be substantially wider than these two. As the exemption does not depend solely on just fulfilling the definition of "research" but is also dependent on satisfying the safeguard conditions it does not appear to be particularly material that the definition of "research" is a broad one. Therefore, "research" may be pure academic or "blue sky" research, targeted commercial research, or anything in between, including market research into consumers' attitudes. In the area of medical research the term will cover epidemiological studies and clinical studies. However, research will only qualify for one or more of the exemptions if it fulfils the safeguard conditions. These vary with the particular exemption involved.

EFFECT OF THE DPA ON RESEARCH

Three provisions of the DPA appear to have most impact on the use of personal **18–23** data for research.

Grounds for legitimate processing

The use of personal data for research is not of itself a legitimating ground for **18–24** processing. The two grounds which might be expected to be relied upon by researchers are: Ground 1, that the data subject has consented to the processing; and Ground 6, that the processing is "necessary" for the purposes of legitimate interests pursued by the data controller or by the third party or third parties to whom the data are disclosed, except where the processing is unwarranted in any particular case by reason of prejudice to the rights and freedoms or legitimate interests of the data subject. In the case of research required by law, for example for pharmaco-vigilance referred to above, Ground 3 may be relevant provided that the personal data collected are deemed to adhere to the data minimisation principle.

The DSP opines on the correct interpretation if the word "necessary":

> "Data sharing may be 'necessary' … if it is a proportionate method of achieving a legitimate objective: it need not be absolutely essentially to the achievement of that

objective. Whether it is 'necessary' will depend on the circumstances of each case, including the sensitivity of the data and the effects that the disclosure may have on the data subjects and third parties."[52]

Whether or not this somewhat generous view of the extent of "necessity" (*R. V Secretary of State for Health, Ex p. C*[53]) would be upheld at the European level remains open to doubt as the DSP appears to truncate the test for assessing the legitimacy of an infringement of an art.8 right:

> "... 'necessary' in this context does not mean 'absolutely essential', and data sharing may meet this condition if it is a reasonable and proportionate way for a public body to give effect to its functions".[54]

The European jurisprudence in this area is more restrictive in its approach to any encroachment on an individual's art.8 right, with the test of "necessity" only arising if the domestic legislation authorising the disclosure of personal data:

> "... contain[s] detailed provisions circumscribing the scope of that power and providing safeguards against its arbitrary use".[55]

The House of Lords and House of Commons Joint Committee on Human Rights, Fourteenth Report, March 4, 2008, continues:

> "The right to respect for private life in Art.8 imposes a positive obligation on the State to ensure that the laws provide adequate protection against the unjustified disclosure of personal data."

If the domestic law does not meet the stringent requirements to ensure against the arbitrary use of personal data, then it cannot be "valid law" as it violates the European Convention on Human Right's requirements ab initio. Whether or not a United Kingdom legislative instrument meets European requirements is not a matter which the United Kingdom may decide solely for itself. In his 2008 article published in the May edition of "data protection law and policy", Douwe Korff, Professor of International Law, London Metropolitan University argues that the ECHR case of *Copland v United Kingdom (App. No.62617/00)*[56] illustrates this. In this case, the government argued that a public authority employer's monitoring of an employee's emails, telephone and internet usage was lawful because it was based on broad powers which authorised the public authority to do "anything necessary or expedient" for the purposes of providing higher education. The ECHR did not agree and held that at the relevant time there had been no valid law in the United Kingdom capable of being relied upon to justify the interference with the employee's art.8 rights. Professor Korff continues his analysis:

---

[52] *http://www.justice.gov.uk/information-access-rights/data-protection/data-sharing* [Accessed September 28, 2012], para.10.

[53] [2000] EWCA Civ 49, paras 16–20.

[54] *http://www.justice.gov.uk/information-access-rights/data-protection/data-sharing* [Accessed September 28, 2012], para 19

[55] *http://www.publications.parliament.uk/pa/jt200708/jtselect/jtrights/jtrights.htm* [Accessed September 28, 2012], p.7, para.11.

[56] [2007] All E.R. (D) 32 (Apr).

"The 'statutory gateway' invoked by the UK Government was thus no gateway at all: it did not provide the legal basis for the interference which the Government claimed it did. The same applies to all similar sweeping provisions currently relied on to legitimize data sharing: such reliance is simply in violation of the ECHR, and thus also incompatible with the Human Rights Act – and with the DPA, since the Act itself stipulates (in accordance with the data protection directive) that all processing (and sharing) of personal data must be 'lawful'."[57]

Where a public body is not able to identify a valid statutory gateway to justify the disclosure of personal data, it should be noted that the author remains sceptical of their ability to rely on Ground 6 of the DPA to legitimate the disclosure, as the author believes that public bodies should be able to show they either have:

(a)   a duty to carry out specific processing (including disclosures)—Ground 3; or

(b)   a power to do so—Ground 5.

Therefore a consideration of Ground 6 may be irrelevant.

Grounds for processing sensitive personal data

Schedule 3 contains a limited provision in Ground 8 for sensitive personal data to be processed for medical research purposes. Sensitive data may be processed for medical research under Ground 8 where: **18–25**

"(1) The processing is necessary for medical purposes and is undertaken by:

(a)   a health professional; or
(b)   a person who in the circumstances owes a duty of confidentiality which is equivalent to that which would arise if that person were a health professional.

(2) In this paragraph 'medical purposes' includes the purposes of preventative medicine, medical diagnosis, medical research, the provision of care and treatment and the management of health care services."

"Health professional" is defined in s.69. Where the research is undertaken by a health professional it appears to be immaterial that no direct obligation of confidence subsists between the data subject and the health professional undertaking the research. Where information is obtained by a third party health professional from a person who is under an obligation of confidentiality to the subject and the information is obtained with knowledge of that obligation, the third party health professional will be equally bound by it. Thus, if information is obtained subject to an obligation of confidentiality it can be transferred subject to the same obligation. Ground 8 may, therefore, offer considerable scope for medical researchers but will not necessarily cover all medical research. The alternatives are Ground 1, the individual has given his explicit consent to the processing of the personal data, or the further ground inserted by The Data Protection (Processing of Sensitive Data) Order 2000 in relation to research. This provides that sensitive personal data may be processed if necessary for research

---

[57] Data protection law and policy, May 2008, p.13.

purposes; provided that the processing is "in the substantial public interest" and the two safeguard conditions are met. It is also possible that research involving ethnic or racial data may be carried out on the limited basis and to the limited extent specified in Ground 9.

Guidance as to what does and importantly does not constitute the "substantial public interest" under the DPA is in short supply. In *Re Madoff Securities Ltd*, Lewison J. simply states in relation to the Sch.4 exemption from principle 8:

> "I am satisfied that it is in the public interest for an alleged fraud on this scale and of this complexity to be investigated, and on the evidence before me I am therefore satisfied that transfers of the information scheduled to the draft order are necessary for reasons of substantial public interest".[58]

The application of the fair obtaining and processing codes

18–26   These require that an individual is told at the time of collection of the data of the proposed uses and disclosures or, if that does not occur, is told before data are processed for the relevant purpose. The application of this principle would require that, where an individual has not been told at the time the data were collected that the information would be used for research purposes s/he should be so informed when they are to be so used and given the identity of the data controller, if that person is different from the controller who first collected the data, or at least should have this information made readily available to him. As far as is practicable, this should be done before the processing for the research starts or, if disclosures are involved, the disclosures are made. The rigour of these provisions may be mitigated in two circumstances, either if the provision of such notice "would involve disproportionate effort" or if the processing is carried out to fulfil a legal obligation, other than one imposed by a contract, and in each case the data controller complies with the further conditions prescribed in The Data Protection (Conditions under para.3 of Pt II of Sch.1) Order 2000. Different conditions are prescribed for each of the two circumstances.

Researchers must also comply with the data quality requirements of principles 3 and 4; the individual rights, apart from in those cases where the limited exemption from subject access may be claimed; the security requirements of principle 7; and the prohibition on overseas transfers to jurisdictions without an adequate system of data protection in principle 8.

Applicable exemptions

18–27   These can only be claimed if the safeguard conditions are met.

Safeguard conditions

18–28   These are twofold. The data must not be processed to:

- "support measures or decisions with respect to particular individuals; and

---

[58] [2009] EWHC 442 (Ch), para.8.

- nor processed in such a way that substantial damage or substantial distress is, or is likely to be, caused to any data subject".

The first condition carries forward the concept of "functional separation" referred to earlier. The prohibition appears to be aimed at the use of particular personal data, not the use of the results of the research. So, research leading to statistical findings, for example that a particular drug has positive effects on a particular type of patient, which are then used as a basis to make decisions about other patients is within the exemption; but research based on personal data, for example on the genetic make-up of members of the same family which are used to take a decision on treatment for a child of that family, is not within it. Thus translational research, that is where the research results may inform the treatment of the study subject, will not be able to claim the exemption. The second element of the exemption, that there must be no damage caused to the data subject, fits in with the approach taken throughout the Directive and in turn in the implementing legislation, of allowing exemptions only in cases where the risk to the rights and freedoms of individuals is low.

Where the safeguard conditions apply the researcher is exempt from three of the requirements of the DPA:

(a)   principle 2;
(b)   principle 5; and
(c)   subject access.

There is a further exemption which applies to "historical research" which is explained below. However, this only applies to a very specific type of data. It is also complicated to apply so it may only be of limited use.

Exemption from Principle 2

Principle 2 requires that personal data shall be obtained only for one or more   **18–29**
specified and lawful purpose(s) and shall not be further processed in any manner incompatible with that purpose(s). The exemption in s.33(2) only applies to the second limb of the principle. The further use for research purposes will not be regarded as incompatible with the purpose(s) for which the data were obtained as long as the safeguard conditions (see above) are complied with. The data must still be obtained in the first instance for a specified and lawful purpose(s). If it is known that data are to be used for research or it is likely this will occur at some later stage, the data controller should notify the individual at the point of collection or otherwise in accordance with the requirements of principle 1.

Exemption from Principle 5

Principle 5 requires that personal data processed for any purpose(s) shall not be   **18–30**
kept for longer than is necessary for that purpose(s). Under s.33(3) personal data which are further processed for research purposes (subject to the safeguard conditions) may be kept indefinitely despite the strictures of principle 5.

Exemption from the right of subject access

18–31   Section 7 provides for individuals to have access to personal data held about them (see Ch.11). Section 33(4) provides that personal data processed only for research purposes are exempt from the s.7 rights if they are processed in accordance with the safeguard conditions and the results are not made available in a form which identifies the data subjects.

Permitted disclosures

18–32   Section 33(5) sets out a list of disclosures that may be made from personal data without risking the loss of any of the research exemptions. These cover:

(a)   disclosure to any other person for research purposes only;

(b)   disclosure to the data subject or to a person acting on his behalf;

(c)   disclosure at the request of a data subject (or someone acting on his behalf) or with his consent; and

(d)   disclosure where the person making the disclosure has reasonable grounds for believing it falls within one of the above.

Exemption for historical research

18–33   This exemption started in 2001. As with the other exemptions, the researcher must comply with the safeguard conditions. The exemption is twofold, the two provisions both applying to personal data processed only for the purposes of "historical research", which term is not defined. The term may have been intended to cover research carried out using pre-October 24, 1998 data. The effect would be that research which involved the use of personal data and which was started before October 1998 (but not concluded by October 2001) would not be jeopardised. It is suggested a broad meaning is justified for the term "historical research" following the logic set out in para.18-22, above. There are two sets of exemptions:

(1)   one applies to eligible manual data and to eligible automated data which are not processed by reference to the data subject; and

(2)   the other applies to eligible automated data which are processed by reference to the data subject.

Therefore, in order to determine which of the exemptions applies in dealing with any particular data set, the researcher will have to consider whether the proposed processing is to be done by reference to the data subject.

Example

18–34   Research programme A is looking at the nature of car accidents which occur at a particular junction. Among the data are personal data about named drivers. The data are searched by reference to the make of car never by reference to the driver.

The identity of the driver is immaterial to the research. These data are not processed by reference to the data subject.

Research programme B is seeking to ascertain which treatment is most successful in treating drug addicts. Most addicts have several attempts at treatment and the research tracks addicts to look at which treatments they received. It requires the personal data to be searched and extracted by reference to the individual addict. These data are processed by reference to the data subject.

The exemption for automated data not processed by reference to the data subject may not prove to be of much practical assistance to researcher B, as it is difficult to envisage a reason for processing data incorporating personal identifiers if it is not processed by reference to the data subject.

Eligible manual data and eligible automated data not processed by reference to the data subject

Eligible manual data is manual data covered by the DPA, which was subject to **18–35** processing already underway immediately before October 24, 1998 and eligible automated data are data falling within s.1(1) (a) or (b) of the DPA which falls into the same historic category. The terms were significant during the transitional period but are now only of relevance in relation to this exemption. Eligible manual data processed only for historical research purposes (subject to the safeguard conditions) are exempt from:

(a) principle 1—the requirement that personal data shall be processed fairly and lawfully and in particular subject to the conditions for legitimacy of processing personal and sensitive personal data, except for the fair obtaining and processing code contained in para.2 of Pt II of Sch.1;

(b) principle 2—that personal data shall be obtained for specified and lawful purposes and not further processed in any manner incompatible with those purposes;

(c) principle 3—that personal data shall be adequate, relevant and not excessive for the purpose for which they are being processed;

(d) principle 4—that personal data shall be accurate and where necessary kept up-to-date;

(e) principle 5—that personal data shall not be kept for longer than is necessary for the purposes for which they were processed; and

(f) the right to accuracy orders granted by the courts under s.14(1)–(3).

Eligible automated data processed by reference to the data subject

Data falling into this category are exempt from: **18–36**

● Sch.2—the requirement that personal data be processed subject to one of the legitimacy conditions; and

● Sch.3—the requirement that sensitive personal data be processed subject to one of the sensitive data conditions.

ANONYMISATION AND PSEUDONYMISATION

18–37   "Anonymisation" and "pseudonymisation" are increasingly popular terms in the data protection arena. The Information Commissioner's "Technical Guidance 2007: Determining What is Personal Data"[59] states:

> "Article 1 of the Directive states that 'personal data means any information relating to an identified or identifiable natural person.' Recital 26 of the Directive states that 'to determine whether a person is identifiable, account should be taken of all the means likely reasonably to be used either by the controller or any other person'. This means that where, though it is conceivable that someone could identify a particular individual or individuals if they devoted sufficient effort and resources to the task, it is unlikely that anyone will do so then the individual(s) are not 'identifiable' for the purposes of the Directive".

Therefore where researchers use truly anonymised data the DPA will not apply. In the recitals to the Directive it is accepted that the use of anonymised data falls outside its remit. Recital 26 states:

> "whereas the principles of protection shall not apply to data rendered anonymous in such a way that the data subject is no longer identifiable".

The exact nature and scope of the processing that personal data would need to go through in order to pseudonymise them successfully is less clear, as is whether the data controller would have the power or permission to lawfully process them into a pseudonymised state in the first place. However, the category of pseudonymised (or "key coded") data is explicitly recognised by the Information Commissioner as existing and as not constituting "personal data":

> "Example: An EU based company carries out pharmaceutical research on identifiable individuals. They remove the obvious identifiers from the individual records (name, address etc) and key code them (that is they assign a unique code such as KLPR767805 to each individual record). They then release the 'anonymised' individual records to another pharmaceutical company which will use them for further research. In the event that the second company identifies that a particular individual might be at risk because of the combination of their illness and the drugs they are using, the second company can alert the first company, 'identifying' the individual in question by means of the code. The first company can then contact the individual. The key question is whether the second company holds the records in question as personal data.
>
> The second company is able to isolate particular records where the medical histories and current medication give cause for concern and 'identify' them by means of the codes. Unless there are exceptional circumstances, for example where an individual has a very rare condition and there has been publicity in the press which named them, it is unlikely that the second company will ever find out the name and address or other information which would enable them to physically find the individual in question. However, by alerting the first company to their concerns they do cause the individual to be contacted and thus their processing has a clear effect on the individual. Nevertheless, because they do not contact the individual

---

[59] *http://www.ico.gov.uk/for_organisations/guidance_index/data_protection_and_privacy_and_ electronic_communications.aspx* [Accessed September 28, 2012], "Determining What Is Personal Data", p.20.

themselves and because they have no interest in the individuals themselves, merely in ensuring that where records give cause for concern the individual is contacted, we consider that for all practical purposes they do not hold the key coded records as personal data. A significant consideration here is that as long as the first company have appropriate security in place there is little or no chance that any other person who might have access to the coded records would be able to link an individual by name and or address to a particular record. In such circumstances the chances of an individual suffering detriment are negligible".[60]

Cases on anonymisation, pseudonymisation and disclosure

While anonymised data fall outside the DPA, the processing required to achieve anonymisation and/or pseudonumsation must entail the use of personal data. There is also the question of whether the use or disclosure of anonymised and/or pseudonymised data breach art.8 of the HRA or any obligation of confidentiality. There have been few cases in which the use or disclosure of anonymised and/or pseudonymised data has been considered.   **18–38**

A Health Authority v X

In this case a Health Authority had sought to obtain disclosure of directly   **18–39**
identifiable patient records in order to consider the compliance of a medical practice with the terms of service of general practitioners. There had been an allegation that the GPs involved had colluded with patients to overcharge the public purse. Two patients had refused to give their consent to the disclosure of their medical records for the disciplinary committee's consideration. The GPs under investigation refused to disclose these patients' records arguing that to do so in the face of their refusal to give consent would involve an actionable breach of confidence. The court ordered that the records be disclosed (subject to certain safeguards), framing the question before it thus:

> "... whether the public interest in effective disciplinary procedures for the investigation and eradication of medical malpractice outweighed the confidentiality of the records".[61]

At an earlier hearing, Munby J. had characterised a doctor's duty of confidentiality very widely. This construction was quoted with approval by Thorpe L.J.:

> "Dr X's ultimate obligation is to comply with whatever order the court may make. But prior to that point being reached his duty, like that of any other professional or other person who owes a duty of confidentiality to his patient or client, is to assert that confidentiality in answer to any claim by a third party for disclosure and to put before the court every argument that can properly be put against disclosure".[62]

---

[60] http://www.ico.gov.uk/for_organisations/guidance_index/data_protection_and_privacy_and_electronic_communications.aspx [Accessed September 28, 2012], "Determining What Is Personal Data", p.20.
[61] [2001] EWCA Civ 2014 (21 December 2001), para 20
[62] [2001] EWCA Civ 2014 (December 21, 2001), para 7

The court considered the ECHR decision in *Z v Finland (Application No.22009/93)*.[63] In this case the ECHR ordered the disclosure of medical records because of "weighty public interest criteria"—i.e., as evidence in her husband's criminal trial for knowingly spreading HIV—subject to certain safeguards, namely the:

- relevant records were examined in camera; and
- case documents were treated as confidential with Z's anonymity being preserved as far as possible.

While prima facie the disclosure of medical records without consent would be a breach of art.8, in this case the disclosure was justified, limited in scope and protected by safeguards against abuse which secured Z's privacy. The safeguards included the anonymisation of the data prior to their release and a further stipulation that the data could not be disclosed more widely than was necessary to assist the trial.

So, it appears that a court may order proportionate disclosure of confidential information where safeguards are put in place to limit the necessary intrusion upon the affected individual's art.8 rights. However, this is not the same as a public body making a decision for itself as to what is/is not a proportionate and necessary infringement, indeed the court in *A Health Authority v X* endorsed the views of Munby J. in the lower court stating that the balance between the private and public interest in whether or not confidentiality should be set aside "required a decision of a High Court judge".[64]

R. v Department of Health Ex p. Source Informatics Limited

18–40   Source Informatics Limited (Source) wished to obtain information about the prescribing habits of GPs, which information they intended to sell to pharmaceutical companies for marketing purposes. Source proposed to obtain this information from pharmacists, who would gather it with the consent of GPs from prescription records. The data would be stripped of patient identifying data and passed on to Source. Both GPs and pharmacists were to receive some small consideration. In 1997 the Department of Health, which was concerned that the outcome would be to increase the NHS drugs bill, issued guidance to pharmacists that patient confidentiality would be breached by the disclosure of the prescription data even though the identifying particulars of the patients were removed. Source sought judicial review of the DoH advice.

The DoH argued that the anonmyisation of the patient identifiable data in order to sell the prescription data was a processing purpose other than the one for which the data had been collected amounting to a misuse of the information and a breach of confidence. Source argued that neither the processing to anonymise nor the disclosure of the anonymous information constituted unlawful processing amounting to a breach of confidence.

---

[63] (1997) 25 EHRR 371, 45 BMLR 107
[64] [2001] EWCA Civ 2014 (21 December 2001), para 14

The Court of Appeal held that, as long as the patients' privacy was not put at risk, there could be no breach of confidence involved in either the processing required to anonymise the data or the disclosure of the anonymised information.

Although the case pre-dates the implementation of the DPA, reference was made to the Directive, with both sides seeking to rely on it. It was argued by the DoH that the processing for the purpose of anonymisation was processing which fell within the Directive and therefore would require the consent of the patient or other grounds in Schs 2 and 3 and by Source that such processing should be regarded as outwith the Directive as it is intended to produce data which are not "personal". Simon Brown L.J. did not have to decide the point but favoured the later view saying:

"Although this is clearly not the appropriate occasion to attempt a definitive ruling on the scope of the directive—and still less of the impending legislation—I have to say that common sense and justice alike would appear to favour the GMC's contention. By the same token that the anonymisation of data is in my judgment unobjectionable here under domestic law, so too, I confidently suppose, would it be regarded by other member states. Of course the processing of health data requires special protection and no doubt the 'erasure or destruction' of such data is included in the definition of processing for good reason: on occasion it could impair the patient's own health requirements. It by no means follows, however, that the process envisaged here should be held to fall within the definition: on the contrary, recital 26 strongly suggests that it does not.[65]"

Various arguments on the extent and nature of implied consent were raised which the judge did not find necessary to determine. However, he did not find acceptable the contention that consent could be implied to a range of uses of which individual patients might not be aware. He thought that the preferable approach was to accept that some of the more innocuous uses of personal information, such as use for stock taking, did not breach any obligation of confidence as the equitable duty of confidence "ought not to be drawn too widely in the first place.[66]"

Common Services Agency v Scottish Information Commissioner (Scotland)[67]

The most recent case to consider the issue of whether directly identifiable personal data may be released to a third party after undergoing processing to anonymise them was decided by the House of Lords in 2008. The case turns on whether or not a statutory body (the Scottish Common Services Agency) was under a duty to anonymise effectively personal data in order to render them disclosable pursuant to a request under the Freedom of Information (Scotland) Act 2002 (FOISA). On behalf of a member of the Scottish parliament, a Mr Collie requested that, pursuant to the FOISA, the Agency release details, by census wards, of all incidents of leukaemia for both sexes, in the age range 0–14, by year, from 1990 to 2003, for all of the Dumfris and Galloway postal area. This followed years of concerns being expressed about the risks to public health in the

18–41

---

[65] [2000] 1 All E.R. 786, p.799 at (b).

[66] [2000] 1 All E.R. 786, p.800 at (h).

[67] [2008] UKHL 47 (July 9, 2008).

area arising from the operations at the Ministry of Defence's Dundrennan firing range, the now decommissioned nuclear reactor at Chapelcross and the nuclear processing facilities at Sellafield.

The Agency declined Mr Collie's request because it believed that the small number of cases in each ward meant that there was a significant risk of the sufferers being capable of being identified by way of the data which it would release (even if stripped of direct identifiers). Therefore, the Agency claimed that any data they would release would be "personal data" and therefore subject to exemption from disclosure as such under s.38(1) of the FOISA. Mr Collie appealed that decision to the Scottish Information Commissioner who agreed with the Agency's reasoning.

However, interestingly the Scottish Information Commissioner went one step further when he went on to hold that the Agency had been in breach of its obligation under s.15 FOISA, which requires a public authority to provide, so far as it is reasonable to expect it to do so, advice and assistance to a person who has submitted a freedom of information request. The Scottish Information Commission held that:

"...the Agency had been under a duty to consider whether information could have been provided to Mr Collie in a 'less disclosive' manner by perturbing the data so that the risk of personal identification would be "substantially removed" and telling Mr Collie what had been done and why. The Commissioner accordingly required the Agency to provide the census ward data for the relevant years in a barnardised form".[68]

Barnardisation is a method used to render data anonymous in so far as is possible.

The Scottish Information Commissioner's attitude in this case is of interest to researchers because it appears that he believes that public bodies governed by freedom of information legislation are under a duty (subject to the statutory time and cost limits integral in such legislation) to perform a processing operation upon directly identifiable data (e.g., by applying the technique of barnardisation) in order to render those data sufficiently anonymous so that they may be released to third parties without contravening the principles. From this, researchers may be able to construct an argument that, subject to sufficiently robust anonymisation or key coding, disclosures may be made from personal data by the original holder without breaching the data protection principles. However, this decision of the Scottish Information Commissioner's was appealed successfully and it does not impact on a public body's identification of a permissive power (express or implied) to disclose personal data or on a consideration of the confidentiality issues (see above).

It was without the House of Lord's remit on this occasion to comment on the particular facts of this case and whether barnardisation of these statistics was sufficient a protective measure to adequately minimise the re-identification risk (widely referred to as the "disclosure risk" by statisticians). The Agency's appeal before the House of Lords was successful and the matter was referred back to the Scottish Information Commissioner:

---

[68] [2008] UKHL 47, para.71.

"... so that he can examine the facts in light of your Lordships' judgment and determine whether the information can be sufficiently anonymised for it not to be 'personal data'."[69]

The Information Commissioner has launched a consultation on a new anonymisation Code of Practice.[70] The outputs of the consultation (which closed on August 23, 2012) will be relevant to any organization that wants to release anonymised data into the public domain, for example under the government's Open Data agenda[71] launched by the Prime Minister in July 2011.

FUTURE DEVELOPMENTS

The area of medical research using personal data is one in which the law is still developing. However, recent developments, not least the recommendations of the Thomas & Walport "Data Sharing Review", appear to be construing any "right to privacy" over administrative data more as a right not to be harmed by their secondary processing; rather than one which bestows an inalienable right to prevent personal data which relate to you being processed in the substantial public interest without your prior, freely given and explicit consent. This approach echoes the DPA's existing s.10 which bestows a right to prevent processing "likely to cause damage or distress". Striking the right balance between an individual's rights and the wider public good is advocated by Thomas & Walport:

18–42

> "Again, the example of medical research is particularly helpful here. Respondents in this sector agreed almost unanimously that a requirement to seek fresh consent for any supplementary use of previously collected personal information would be unworkable and have a severely detrimental effect on the ability to conduct important medical research. The time, money and effort required to do this would all have an adverse impact on research programmes and on patient care. This is an example where the principle of implied consent is valid. An NHS patient agreeing to a course of treatment should also be taken to have agreed that information given during the course of the treatment might be made available for future medical research projects, so long as robust systems are in place to protect personal information and privacy. After all, that patient may be benefiting from research using health information from earlier patients".[72]

Given the above, including the fact that the Thomas & Walport review was co-authored by an ex-Information Commissioner himself, it would not be unreasonable to infer that the courts would be sympathetic towards the view of researchers: subject to suitable safeguards, including compliance with the DPA, where medical research is carried out in the public interest that interest should be capable of encroaching upon personal confidentiality (except in unusual cases) in

---

[69] [2008] UKHL 47, para.44.

[70] http://www.ico.gov.uk/news/latest_news/2012/ico-consults-on-new-anonymisation-code-of-practice-31052012.aspx [Accessed September 28, 2012].

[71] http://www.number10.gov.uk/news/pm-sets-ambitious-open-data-agenda/ [Accessed September 28, 2012].

[72] http://www.connectingforhealth.nhs.uk/systemsandservices/infogov/links/datasharingreview.pdf/view?searchterm=walport [Accessed September 28, 2012], p.34, para.5.18.

so far as such encroachment is in pursuit of a legitimate aim which is considered necessary in a democratic society and is proportionate to the identified need.

Impact of the draft Regulation in brief[73]

18-43   There are no exemptions from the obligation to provide notice to individuals or from the right of subject access where personal data are to be used for research. To that extent the provisions of the draft Regulation are less generous in its provision for research. However, art.83 includes a provision on: "processing for historical, statistical and scientific research purposes" which appears to raise the possibility that a data controller could use personal data for research by creating "Chinese walls" within its own organisation. Article 83 reads:

> "Within the limits of this Regulation, personal data may be processed for historical, statistical or scientific research purposes only if: ... These purposes cannot be otherwise fulfilled by processing data which does not permit or any longer permit the identification of the data subject; [and] data enabling the attribution of information to an identified or identifiable data subject is kept separately from the other information as long as these purposes can be fulfilled in this manner".[74]

This appears to permit the use of pseudonymised data being processed for research purposes.

The Article further provides that bodies conducting historical, statistical or scientific research may only publish or disclose identifiable data with the consent of the data subject or subject to appropriate safeguards.

However, as has been noted in respect of other provisions in the draft the Commission has reserved to itself powers to:

> "... adopt delegated acts in accordance with Article 86 for the purpose of further specifying the criteria and requirements for the processing of personal data for the purposes referred to [above] ...".[75]

The impact of the eventual legal provisions governing the secondary use of administrative datasets is difficult to judge. Although, it should be noted that the Explanatory Memorandum does specifically recognise that:

> "..the right to the protection of personal data is not an absolute right, but must be considered in relation to its function in society".

---

[73] See Ch.1 for an overview of the draft Regulation issued by the EU Commission in January 2012.
[74] art.83.
[75] art.83(3).

PRACTICAL TOOLS

Data protection checklist for researchers

The Administrative Data Liaison Serivce[76] offers resources to the research community, including training which has been endorsed by the Information Commissioner. The ADLS's mission is to:

> "...act as an intermediary between academic researchers and data holding organisations to provide information, aid with communication and promote the use of administrative data".

At present there are no standard procedures for research access to the United Kingdom's administrative data. The ADLS recommends that when a researcher seeks access to data, both the reseacher and the data holder need to identify a clear objective justifying the researcher's access and consider and record the potential benefits and risks of the proposed information sharing.

When making applications for access to personal data, the ADLS recommends a four step approach. The DSP for public bodies contains more detail in its nine annexes, but mirrors closely the approach recommended by the ADLS:

(a) the researcher should seek to ascertain whether anyone has been granted access to the data previously and establish the restrictions which were placed upon the successful applicant. This will give the researcher an insight into the prevailing attitude towards data sharing within the target holding organisation;

(b) a realistic assessment of whether the researcher needs access to directly identifiable data, or whether truly anonymised or pseudonymised data will suffice. Access to individual level data will usually be more difficult to justify and will be subject to lengthier procedures which may well entail ethics approval and more stringent data use agreements;

(c) the researcher should discover whether the data holder has a standard application pack and procedure which should be followed to expedite the process. The ADLS keeps a list of 20 organisations which have standard processes and hyperlinks to them[77]; and

(d) verifiable evidence that the researcher has adequate data security policies and processes in place which will suitably mitigate any disclosure risk. As a minimum, the policies and procedures should address:
  (i) physical (i.e., building), hardware and software security;
  (ii) data handling (including access) practices; and
  (iii) staff training and terms of engagement (e.g., non-disclosure agreements).

18–44

---

[76] http://www.adls.ac.uk/services-for-researchers/ [Accessed September 28, 2012].
[77] http://www.adls.ac.uk/find-administrative-data/by-organisation/ [Accessed September 28, 2012].

Further, the ADLS offers a free and confidential statistical disclosure risk analysis service to data holders to help them to assess the risk of a third party successfully re-identifying the anonymised and/or pseudonymised data it releases.

The Information Commissioner's "Data Sharing Code of Practice" lists the following factors to consider when deciding whether to enter into a data sharing agreement[78]:

> **"What is the sharing meant to achieve?** You should have a clear objective, or set of objectives. Being clear about this will allow you to work out what data you need to share and who with. It is good practice to document this.
>
> **What information needs to be shared?** You shouldn't share all the personal data you hold about someone if only certain data items are needed to achieve your objectives. For example, you might need to share somebody's current name and address but not other information you hold about them.
>
> **Who requires access to the shared personal data?** You should employ 'need to know' principles, meaning that other organisations should only have access to your data if they need it, and that only relevant staff within those organisations should have access to the data. This should also address any necessary restrictions on onward sharing of data with third parties.
>
> **When should it be shared?** Again, it is good practice to document this, for example setting out whether the sharing should be an on-going, routine process or whether it should only take place in response to particular events.
>
> **How should it be shared?** This involves addressing the security surrounding the transmission or accessing of the data and establishing common rules for its security.
>
> **How can we check the sharing is achieving its objectives?** You will need to judge whether it is still appropriate and confirm that the safeguards still match the risks.
>
> **What risk does the data sharing pose?** For example, is any individual likely to be damaged by it? Is any individual likely to object? Might it undermine individuals' trust in the organisations that keep records about them?
>
> **Could the objective be achieved without sharing the data or by anonymising it?** It is not appropriate to use personal data to plan service provision, for example, where this could be done with information that does not amount to personal data".

ADDITIONAL INFORMATION

18–45   *Hansard* references
Vol.587, No.95, col.122, Lords Report, March 16, 1998:
Use of research to trace beneficiaries.
Commons Standing Committee D, May 21, 1998, col.230:
Meaning of research.

---

[78] *http://www.ico.gov.uk/for_organisations/guidance_index/data_protection_and_privacy_and_electronic_communications.aspx#sharing* [Accessed September 28, 2012], p.14.

ADDITIONAL INFORMATION

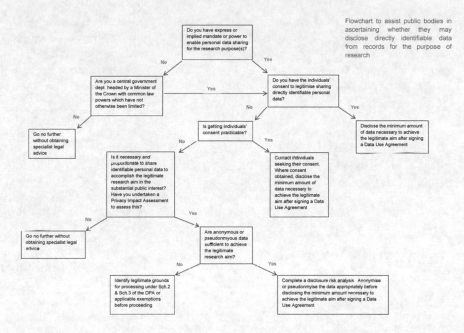

Flowchart to assist public bodies in ascertaining whether they may disclose directly identifiable data from records for the purpose of research

CHAPTER 19

Miscellaneous Exemptions

INTRODUCTION

A review of the remaining exemptions can give the impression that the Act **19–01**
consists more of exemptions than of anything else. The impression would be
unfair but there are a considerable number of exemptions which are difficult to
categorise conveniently and are covered in this chapter.

SUMMARY OF MAIN POINTS **19–02**

(a) There are exemptions for the purposes of business management planning
     and corporate finance.
(b) There is a wide exemption for legal rights which covers almost any
     disclosure of information where there is any possibility of legal
     proceedings at any stage.
(c) Examination scripts have a specific exemption from the right of subject
     access.
(d) In many cases where there is an exemption from subject access there is also
     an exemption from the fair processing obligations to provide notice to the
     data subject set out in para.2 of Pt 1 of Sch.2 ("fair processing
     obligations"), these are together referred to as the "subject information
     provisions".[1]
(e) The Act includes several order-making powers which allow for further
     exemptions to be made.
(f) As with all the exemptions, the fact that an exemption applies does not
     place the data controller under any obligation to take advantage of it.

BUSINESS EXEMPTIONS

Confidential references

Schedule 7 para.1 exempts personal data from the subject access provisions in s.7 **19–03**
if they consist of a reference given or to be given in confidence[2] by the data
controller for one of three purposes. The purposes are:

---
[1] s.27.
[2] For an explanation of the law of confidence, see Ch.2.

(a)   education, training or employment, or prospective education, training or employment of the data subject;

(b)   the appointment or prospective appointment of the data subject to any office; or

(c)   the provision or prospective provision by the data subject of any service.

The exemption applies both before and after the reference is given but it only applies to "the data controller". Hence it appears that the only data controller who can claim the benefit of the exemption is the data controller who provides the reference and not the party who obtains the reference. This seems somewhat illogical but would appear to be the result of a strict reading of the paragraph, although the alternative view is not unarguable. The Directive is of no interpretative assistance as this provision does not derive from the Directive. The Commissioner in the Guide has taken the view that the exemption only applies to the provider of the reference.

The reference must be given in confidence. Controllers who wish to claim the exemption should therefore specify that they intend references they provide to be confidential.

The exemption only applies where the reference is for one or more of the purposes listed above, of education or employment or the provision of services. Therefore it does not apply to those entering into business partnerships and does not appear to apply to bankers' references or credit references or financial assessment. The exemption from subject access is absolute. It is not subject to any test of prejudice. It covers all the aspects of the right of subject access in s.7.

Management forecasts

19–04   Under Sch.7 para.5 personal data processed for the purpose of management forecasting or management planning to assist the data controller in the conduct of any business or other activity are exempt from the subject information provisions in any case, to the extent that the application of those provisions would be likely to prejudice the conduct of that business or other activity.

This exemption applies to all the subject information provisions and therefore covers both subject access and the fair processing obligations. It only applies in an individual case to the extent that giving subject access or giving notification of subsequent uses or disclosures of the personal data would be likely to prejudice the particular business or activity.

The personal data can be processed for one of two purposes, either the purpose of management forecasting or the purpose of management planning. These must be intended to assist the data controller in the conduct of any business or other activity. The exemption is therefore not limited to businesses and may apply to some other form of venture or activity such as a charity or an educational establishment.

The terms "management forecasting" and "management planning" are not defined and therefore should be given their ordinary meaning. There must be some business or venture in the course of operation because the only application of the exemption is "in the conduct" of any business or other activity. The exemption may allow businesses to plan for staff progression; however, in order to claim the exemption the data controller must be able to show that providing subject access or complying with the fair processing obligations would be likely to cause prejudice to the conduct of that business or the activity carried out.

Negotiations

Schedule 7 para.7 provides that personal data which consist of records of the intentions of the data controller in relation to any negotiations with the data subject are exempt from the subject information provisions in any case to the extent to which the application of those provisions would be likely to prejudice those negotiations.   **19–05**

As with management forecasts, this exemption applies to both subject access and the fair processing obligations. It must be applied on a case by case basis and only applies to the extent to which the provision of those individual rights would be likely to prejudice the negotiations. The explanation for the exemption may lie in problems which had been experienced in the insurance industry with individuals seeking subject access to reserve figures held by insurance companies in relation to claims. It is not clear whether the exemption achieves the aim of exempting these figures from subject access, as reserve figures could be argued to be held in connection with financial forecasting rather than negotiation.

It should be noted that the prejudice test applies to prejudicing the particular negotiations. It is not a general prejudice to the position of one party or to the position of the controller. The risk to negotiations is probably that there is a risk of the failure of negotiations. Alternatively it could be argued that the risk may be that the bargaining position of one of the parties would be substantially weaker. The exemption is particularly useful in personnel matters, for example, in employment tribunal proceedings.

CORPORATE FINANCE

Under Sch.7 para.6 there are two exemptions from the subject information provisions. They are primarily intended to ensure that the individual rights given by the Act cannot be employed to affect price-sensitive information in financial markets. They are dependent on detailed conditions being fulfilled and it is not easy to explain them in simple terms.   **19–06**

Financial instruments

Under para.6(1) the exemptions apply in any case in which personal data are processed for the purposes of, or in connection with, a corporate finance service provided by a relevant person and: **19–07**

- there is a financial "instrument" either already in existence or to be or may be created; and
- giving access to the personal data or complying with the fair processing obligations could affect the price of the instrument or the data controller reasonably believes it could do so.

The effect need not be prejudicial, but the presumption would appear to be that any artificially induced price movement would be prejudicial to the functioning of the financial market.

Important interest of the United Kingdom

19–08 Under para.6(1)(b) the second exemption applies to any personal data processed for the purposes of, or in connection with, a corporate finance service provided by a relevant person, where the data are not exempt under the previous provision and:

- giving subject access to the data or complying with the fair processing obligations could affect an important economic or financial interest of the United Kingdom; and
- that interest requires to be safeguarded against such an effect.

The question of whether a particular interest is an important economic or financial one for the United Kingdom which requires safeguarding appears to be a matter for the data controller to determine in the particular case. However, it is not left to the discretion of the data controller. The Secretary of State is empowered to make an order specifying matters to be taken into account in determining whether the exemption is required. He may also specify circumstances in which the exemption is not to be taken to be required. The relevant order is the Data Protection (Corporate Finance Exemption Order) 2000 (SI 2000/184).

The circumstances specified in the Order are where:

- the data controller reasonably believes that giving subject access to particular personal data could affect a decision whether to deal in or subscribe to or issue a financial instrument or cause any person to act in a way that might affect business activity; and
- giving subject access to such data (whether regularly or occasionally) will result in a prejudicial effect on the orderly functioning of financial markets or the efficient allocation of capital within the economy.

The reference to an effect on business activity includes, in particular, a reference to an effect on the industrial strategy of any person, or on the capital structure of an undertaking or on the legal or beneficial ownership of a business or asset.

Corporate finance services

19–09 These exemptions will only apply to a limited range of services. These "corporate finance services" are defined in para.6(3)(a) and (c) to cover underwriting in respect of issues of, or the placing of issues, of any instruments and services relating to such underwriting. An instrument is defined in technical terms as "any instrument listed in section C of annex 1 to Directive 2004/39/EC of the European Parliament and the Council of 21 April 2004 on markets in financial instruments".

The reference to Sch.1 of the Investment Services Regulations 1995 which previously appeared in the definition was repealed by the Financial Services and Markets Act 2000 (Consequential Amendments) Order 2002[3] and the Financial services and Markets Act 2000 (Markets in Financial Instruments) Regulations 2007.[4] The term "price" includes the value of the instrument. The most common instruments to which this applies would appear to be stocks and shares. As well as share issues a corporate finance service covers advice to undertakings on capital structure, industrial strategy and related matters, and advice and services relating to mergers and the purchase of undertakings.[5]

An example of how this applies might be an adviser (who must fall within the definition of a relevant person for these purposes) who is working for a company which is considering a bid for another undertaking and who carries out inquiries into the directors of the target undertaking. If those inquiries were to become known, via response to a subject access request, it could trigger price movements in the shares in the target company. For the purpose of this provision price includes value, thus covering movements in the market value of instruments even when they are not sold.

Relevant person

As noted above, the corporate finance service must be provided by a "relevant person" and six categories of persons are listed as follows:

19–10

(a) any person who, by reason of any permission he has under Part IV of the Financial Services and Markets Act 2000, is able to carry on a corporate finance service without contravening the general prohibition, within the meaning of section 19 of that Act;

(b) an EEA firm of the kind mentioned in paragraph 5(a) or (b) of Schedule 3 to that Act which has qualified for authorisation under paragraph 12 of that Schedule and may lawfully carry on a corporate finance service;

(c) any person who is exempt from the general prohibition in respect of any corporate finance service

   (i) as a result of an exemption order made under section 38(1) of that Act, or

   (ii) by reason of section 39(1) of that Act (appointed representatives);

(cc) any person, not falling within paragraph (a), (b) or (c) who may lawfully carry on a corporate finance service without contravening the general prohibition"[6]; and

---

[3] SI 2002/1555 art.25(2).

[4] SI 2007/126 Sch.6(1) para.12.

[5] SI 2007/126 para.6(3).

[6] Substituted by the Financial Services and Markets Act 2000 (Consequential Amendments) Order 2002 (SI 2002/1555).

(d)   any person who in the course of his employment, provides to his employer a service falling within paragraph (b) or (c) of the definition of "corporate finance service"; or

(e)   any partner who provides to other partners within a partnership a service falling within either of those paragraphs.

LEGAL EXEMPTIONS

Legal professional privilege

19–11   Schedule 7 para.10 re-enacts the professional privilege exemption in s.31(2) of the 1984 Act. However, in the 1984 Act the exemption was limited to subject access whereas in the 1998 provision the personal data are exempt from the subject information provisions. The exemption applies if the data consist of information in respect of which a claim to legal professional privilege, or in Scotland confidentiality as between client and professional legal adviser, could be maintained in legal proceedings. Legal privilege is the privilege of the clients and is limited to legal advice provided by qualified solicitor, barrister or appropriately qualified foreign lawyer. It does not extend to advice received from other professional advisers, such as accountants or consultants.[7] It has been held by the ECtHR to be part of the right to privacy guaranteed by art.8.[8] It is also a right recognised by the CJEU as part of European law.[9] Once information can claim privilege it may last forever.[10] Accordingly where subject access is sought to information which was originally subject to legal professional privilege but where the litigation has been concluded, access to that data can be blocked forever.[11] As the privilege is the client's it is up to the client whether to claim the exemption or give subject access. There is no test of prejudice attached to this exemption.

It is difficult to see how the exemption from the fair collection element of the subject information provisions can apply in practice. It might be argued that it allows a solicitor acting on behalf of a client in legal proceedings to obtain information for use in those proceedings without complying with the fair obtaining and processing code. This seems an unlikely scenario and might not accord with rules of professional conduct.

In *London Borough of Redbridge v Lee Johnson*[12] the High Court considered the position where legal advice which was subject to legal professional privilege was disclosed by mistake in response to a subject access request. An ex-employee of the Borough had made a subject access request and been provided with the legal advice given to the Borough by external solicitors about the ex-employee's case. The Borough sought an injunction to prevent the ex-employee using or

---

[7] *R. (on the application of Prudential Plc) v Special Commissioner of Income Tax* [2010] EWCA Civ 1094; *New Victoria Hospital v Ryan* [1993] I.C.R. 201.

[8] See *Campbell v United Kingdom* (1992) 15 E.H.R.R. 137.

[9] See *AM&S Europe Ltd v Commission of the European Communities* (155/79) [1983] Q.B. 878.

[10] See *Calcraft v Guest* [1898] 1 Q.B. 759.

[11] This has changed for the public sector since the Freedom of Information Act came into effect and the exemption is subject to a public interest test.

[12] [2011] EWHC 2861 (QB).

disclosing the advice. The judge held that in such a case he did not have to conduct a balancing exercise between the position of the parties but that the right to privilege was absolute. As long as the documents have not been tendered in evidence by the recipient the party which disclosed them inadvertently is entitled to an injunction restraining the use or further disclosure of such documents.

Self-incrimination

Paragraph 11 of Sch.7 provides that a person need not comply with a subject access request or order made by a court under that section to the extent that to do so would reveal evidence of the commission of an offence other than an offence under the Act or a number of other listed provisions The provisions listed are:

19–12

- an offence under s.5 of the Perjury Act (false statements made otherwise than on oath);
- an offence under s.44(2) of the Criminal Law (Consolidation)(Scotland) Act 1995 (false statements made otherwise than on oath); a d
- an offence under art.10 of the Perjury (Northern Ireland) Order 1979 (false statutory declarations and other false unsworn statements).[13]

The list mirrors those in ss.43(8A) and 44(9A) in relation to the service of information and special information notices. The effect is that a person who has made a false statement cannot avoid answering a subject access request on the basis that the earlier falsity would be revealed and this open him to possible proceedings.

Paragraph 11(2) provides that information disclosed by any person in compliance with a subject access request, or order made following a request, will not be admissible in proceedings for an offence under the Data Protection Act. The effect is that a person need not give subject access if to do so would reveal evidence of a non-data protection offence which would expose him to proceedings for that offence. It should be noted that it will only apply where he would be exposed to proceedings. Given that subject access overrides other prohibitions contained in statute (see s.26) the usual statutory provisions forbidding the disclosure of information would not expose an individual to proceedings for any of the making a disclosure in breach of those provisions. This exemption applies where the actual content of the subject access reply would provide evidence of another offence.

19–13

Where information which is actually disclosed shows a data protection offence it is not admissible in proceedings against an individual for such offence.

Disclosures required by law or made in connection with legal proceedings, etc.

The "etc." in this heading is fraught with understatement. This is a very wide exemption. The exemption has no test of prejudice nor are its terms limited to a case by case basis. It is divided into three separate provisions. The first covers mandatory disclosures.

19–14

---

[13] Amended by the Coroners and Justice Act 2009 Sch.20 Pt 4.

Mandatory disclosures

19–15   Section 35(1) exempts personal data from the non-disclosure provisions where the disclosure is required by or under any enactment, by any rule of law or by order of the court. An enactment means an Act of Parliament or a statutory instrument. A rule of law will usually be a common law rule and an order of the court will be an order of any court or tribunal having the status of a court.

Elective disclosures

19–16   These are dealt with in s.35(2) which provides for exemption from the non-disclosure provisions where the disclosure is necessary for:

(a)   the purpose of or in connection with legal proceedings (including prospective legal proceedings); or

(b)   for the purpose of obtaining legal advice.

This is a widening of the provision which appeared in the 1984 Act. In the previous provision the disclosure in connection with legal proceedings was only exempted where the person making the disclosure was a party or a witness to the proceedings. This was found to be unnecessarily narrow in practice. It made it difficult for a prospective witness to make appropriate disclosures or for an affidavit to be filed on the basis of which proceedings were to be started, because the exemption only applied where legal proceedings were in existence. The matter could have been dealt with by removing the words "to which the person making the disclosure is a party or a witness", or by adding the words "including prospective legal proceedings". The draftsman chose to do both and the effect was to widen the non-disclosure provision considerably. Prospective legal proceedings may be of any nature. It is not clear how prospective they must be or whether a settled intention to take action is required.

Although the disclosure must be necessary for these purposes it is not necessary to show that the proceedings or the advice will be prejudiced if there is a failure to make the disclosure. Despite the widening of the provision the courts have not treated it as a "get out of jail free" provision. In the case of *Matthew Mensah v Robert Jones*[14] the High Court considered the application of s.35 where a doctor disclosed medical records relating to a patient in order to obtain his own legal advice on a claim that the patient was threatening to bring against him. The patient then claimed that the doctor was in breach of the DPA in making the disclosure as the complaint was in respect of an alleged assault and the disclosure of the medical records was not "necessary" for the purpose of taking legal advice. Lightman J. dismissed the claim stating that it was indeed necessary for the defendant to disclose all the circumstances surrounding the case to his solicitors.

In *R. (on the application of TA) v North East London NHS Foundation Trust*[15] the High Court rejected an argument that the combination of s.35 and provisions in regulations dealing with the handling of complaints against the NHS provided an implied right to access an individual's records without her consent. In *Totalise*

---

[14]   [2004] EWHC 2699.
[15]   [2011] EWCA Civ 1529.

Plc v Motley Fool Limited,[16] the Court of Appeal made clear that there is no obligation on a data controller to make a disclosure on the basis of s.35(2) and a controller is entitled to wait for a court order so it may make a disclosure under s.32(1).

In this case the defendants, the Motley Fool and Interactive Investor Ltd, were **19–17** companies who operated websites, which incorporated discussion forums for various companies including the claimant, Totalise Plc. An anonymous contributor known as Z made numerous entries on each forum, which made wide-ranging defamatory allegations about Totalise. Totalise Plc contacted both website operators and complained that the statements by Z were defamatory and asked that the postings be removed, that Z's rights to post material be withdrawn and that the identity of Z be revealed to them. Both defendants eventually banned Z from their websites and removed all of the items he had posted. However, they refused Totalise's request for Z's details. Totalise brought an application for disclosure of Z's identity. Interactive responded that the combination of their privacy policy and the effect of the Data Protection Act meant that they could not disclose the information requested. Both defendants resisted the application on the basis that their internal policies were not to reveal the identity of their users. Totalise applied to the court for a Norwich Pharmacal order. This is named after the case *Norwich Pharmacal Co v Customs & Excise Commissioners*.[17] It allows disclosure to be ordered by the court against a third party who has become "mixed up" in tortuous activity through no fault of his own. The defendants relied upon s.10 of the Contempt of Court Act 1981 to resist disclosure. This provides that:

> "No court may require a person to disclose, nor is any person guilty of contempt of court for refusing to disclose the source of information contained in a publication for which he is responsible, unless it be established to the satisfaction of the court that disclosure is necessary in the interest of justice or national security or for the prevention of disorder or crime".

The defendants further relied upon the Data Protection Act 1998. They submitted that s.35 of the 1998 Act, which provides that personal data was exempt from the non-disclosure provisions where the disclosure was required by law in connection with legal proceedings, should be given a restrictive interpretation so that the identity of Z in the instant case should be protected by the general principles of the 1998 Act, which prevented disclosure without the consent of the data subject. Totalise submitted that, as operators of a bulletin board, the defendants were not "responsible" for contents placed there by others outside their control, except in the circumstances provided by s.1 of the Defamation Act 1996, upon which no reliance had been placed. Totalise also submitted that there was no justification for a restricted interpretation of s.35 of the 1998 Act and that the established principles in relation to the court's jurisdiction to require a person "mixed up in the tortious acts of others" were preserved and not restricted by the 1988 Act.

The High Court ruled:

---

[16] [2002] 1 W.L.R. 1233, Case No.A2/2001/0558.
[17] [1974] A.C. 133.

(1) Section 10 of the 1981 Act was concerned with protecting journalists' sources and balancing the right of a free press with the legal rights of others. In the instant case, the defendants had no responsibility for and exercised no legal or editorial control over the items on the websites; they merely provided a facility for discussion. They were accordingly not "responsible" for publication for the purposes of s.10.

(2) There was no justification for a restrictive interpretation of s.35 of the 1998 Act: that section clearly preserved and did not restrict the right of the claimant to obtain disclosure of a tortfeasor's identity in accordance with the pre-existing law. In the instant case, it was clear on the facts that Z had defamed Totalise in a very serious manner and as part of a concerted campaign. Z was hiding behind anonymity and Totalise had no other practical means of establishing his identity. The balance weighed clearly in favour of granting the relief sought. If it were otherwise, it would be possible for individuals to defame with impunity on websites such as those of the defendants.

He held that the defendants should have supplied the information requested without waiting for a court order. They would be entitled to make the disclosure applying the exemption under s.35 of the DPA, which exempts disclosures necessary for the purposes of establishing, exercising or defending legal rights and thus should bear the costs of the court order.

Costs were ordered against the two defendants. The second defendant appealed this order to the Court of Appeal which considered the matter in December 2001.

19–18   On appeal against the costs order the Court of Appeal accepted that s.35(2) applied to the disclosure but said that the provision could not be looked at in isolation. The disclosure amounted to a processing operation and thus required the data controller to be able to justify the disclosure on one of the grounds in Sch.2. The court referred to ground 5(a) which allows disclosure for the purposes of the administration of justice but went on to consider ground 6 and whether the disclosure was outweighed by any prejudice to the rights and freedoms of the data subject. It considered that

> "it is legitimate for a party [such as the defendant] who reasonably agrees to keep information confidential and private to refuse to voluntarily hand over such information".

The court held that Interactive should not be liable to pay the costs of the application by Totalise Plc as they were justified in waiting for a court order before disclosing the information.

The court implicitly recognised that the mere existence of a non-disclosure exemption does not impose an obligation on the data controller to make the requested disclosure and the data controller must consider all the circumstances of the case, in particular the privacy rights of the data subject and any undertakings given to him, before making a disclosure. The inference from this decision is that where there is doubt over the legitimacy of a disclosure a party being asked to disclose is not at fault for asking the party seeking disclosure to obtain a court order for disclosure.

It appears to have become common practice in cases in which parties seek   **19–19**
information about those who post material about them on websites for the
website owner to require a court order, although the site owner will rarely oppose
such an order. In *G v Wikimedia Foundation Inc*[18] the applicant mother and child
sought a Norwich Pharmacal order against the respondent to obtain the IP address
of a registered user who had posted sensitive and private information relating to
the applicants. The respondent indicated that it would not oppose the order but
that it would not disclose without an order. The order was duly made.

The approach taken by the court in *Totalise* has much in common with a   **19–20**
number of cases concerned with the disclosure of personal information for the
purpose of other types of legal proceedings. In *Bennet v Compass Group UK &
Ireland*[19] the Court of Appeal decided that defendants in personal injury cases
should not be given authority to have direct access to claimants' medical records.
Whereas it was formerly the practice for the court to order claimants to sign
authorisations allowing direct access to claimants' records, in *Bennet* the Court of
Appeal decided that such orders could infringe the art.8 rights of claimants. In
future such access should be via the claimants' solicitors. The orders for
disclosure should be clear as to the documents to be disclosed. In *Asda Stores v
Thompson*[20] the Employment Appeal Tribunal made an order aimed at preserving
the privacy of "whistleblowers" who made statements in the course of
investigations into a claim of gross misconduct and who were offered
confidentiality. The EAT overruled an order for blanket discovery by the Tribunal
and said that the applicants did not need to know the identity of those making
statements which led to the investigation. *Asda Stores* was applied in *Sago v
Arqiva Ltd*,[21] which held that discovery would only be ordered, notwithstanding
the issue of confidentiality, where necessary to fairly dispose of the proceedings,
as opposed to being merely relevant to the proceedings. In *Sheffield Wednesday
Football Club Ltd v Hargreaves*[22] the High Court similarly held that no order
(whether Norwich Pharmacal or otherwise) should be made for disclosure of a
data subject's identity without first considering the legitimate interests balancing
test as set out in Sch.2 para.6 of the Data Protection Act. That case concerned a
fan website of the first defendant's football club which contained allegedly
defamatory postings regarding the club's directors and chairman. The court
refused to make orders disclosing the identity of users behind posting which were
trivial and barely defamatory. However, disclosure orders were made in relation
to the more serious posting, where the defamatory language outweighed the
users' rights of anonymity and freedom of expression.

An unusual attempt was made to use s.35 in *SM v Sutton London Borough*[23] to   **19–21**
overcome the withholding of personal data about third parties on a subject access
response. The applicant was an estranged parent who was seeking information to
assist her case. The local authority had been asked for subject access and had
redacted some information about the ex partner which had been supplied by third
parties. Under s.7 information does not have to be supplied where it consists of

---

[18] [2009] EWHC 3148.
[19] (2002) L.T.L. April 18.
[20] (2002) I.R.L.R. 245.
[21] [2007] All E.R. (D) 163 (Apr).
[22] [2007] EWHC 275 (QB).
[23] [2001] EWHC 3465.

information about a third party in respect of whom an obligation of confidentiality is owed. The Commissioner had reviewed a complaint by the applicant and decided that the material had been validly withheld. The applicant argued that, under s.35(2), the local authority was able to disclose the information to her in response to her subject access request irrespective of the obligation of confidence owed to the ex-partner because she required it for use in her legal proceedings. The court did not determine the issue but remitted it to the court dealing with the family matters. It is submitted that the exemption in s.35 does not have this effect because the purpose of the subject access request is not the purpose of legal proceedings.

19–22   Non-parties to litigation have been able to obtain a copy of a statement of case or a judgment or order made in public without the court's permission since a change in the Civil Procedure Rules in 2006.[24] Other documents are only available with the court's permission. In *Various Claimants v News Group Newspapers Ltd*[25] the High Court considered the principles governing which court documents are publicly available and held that a statement of case for these purposes includes only the documents expressly mentioned in the definition at CPR 2.3(1) (namely a claim form, particulars of claim, defence, Pt 20 claim, reply to defence, or any further information given in relation to any of them), and amended versions of these documents. In an earlier case[26] it had been held that an acknowledgment of service and detailed grounds in a judicial review claim were available to non-parties without the court's permission under CPR 5.4C.

A court may restrict the access to materials but will only do so on the application of the party. It follows that a party which wishes to protect personal information from disclosure by these means must make a specific application to the court under the relevant provisions.

Legal rights disclosures

19–23   The section includes a further provision which allows the personal data to be exempt from the non-disclosure provisions where the disclosure is "otherwise necessary for the purposes of establishing exercising or defending legal rights".

Clearly in these cases there do not need to be current or even prospective legal proceedings, and it must be wider than obtaining legal advice because that is dealt with in s.35(2)(b). Although on a strict grammatical reading it appears to suggest that the disclosure is necessary to establish the legal right, it may be that the intention was that the disclosure was necessary for the purpose of establishing the existence of a legal right not the legal right itself.

This could allow organisations to carry out wide matching, trawling or tracing activities free from the non-disclosure provisions if they can show that the disclosures are necessary for the purpose of establishing exercising or defending legal rights. For example, the Department of Work and Pensions has a legal right to collect maintenance from absconding or absenting fathers. This provision might enable it to process personal data exempt from the non-disclosure provisions, on the grounds that the disclosure of data to it is necessary for

---

[24] The Civil Procedure (Amendment) Rules 2006.

[25] [2012] EWHC 397.

[26] *R. (Corner House Research) v Director of the Serious Fraud Office* [2008] EWHC 246.

establishing that it has a right to obtain payment from particular parents. It might also apply to insurance fraud databases or other investigative agencies.

The provision exempts personal data from the non-disclosure provisions, namely the principles in so far as those are incompatible with the disclosure, but not from other rights, so an individual may still have a right to prevent processing or to require the blocking of inaccurate data. However, both the principles and any possibility of compensation derived from breach of those principles as far as they affect disclosure, are taken out of the picture. Although the term disclosure in the singular is used, the Interpretation Act 1978 provides that the singular includes the plural unless the contrary is clear from the context.

However, it should be recognised that the disclosure must be "necessary" for the relevant purpose and this imports a test of proportionality[27] which would have to be satisfied in each case.

GOVERNMENT USES

Judicial appointments and honours

Paragraph 3 of Sch.7 provides an exemption from the subject information provision where personal data are processed for the purposes of assessing any person's suitability for judicial office or the office of Queen's Counsel or the conferring by the Crown of any honour. There is no test of prejudice available attached. The exemption does not attach itself to any particular data controller; as long as the controller processes personal data for those purposes exemption may be claimed. The exemption is absolute and does not have to be considered on a case-by-case basis nor does it only apply to the extent of any incompatibility. This is an absolute exemption. It could presumably apply to an employer who provides a reference, or recommendation of a voluntary group that provides a recommendation for the provision of an honour or someone who provides "soundings" for judicial office. The exemption applies not only to the subject access provision but also to the fair processing obligations. **19–24**

Parliamentary privilege

Schedule 6 paras 2–5 inclusive of the Freedom of Information Act 2000 inserted provisions extending the coverage of the Act to the processing of personal data by or on behalf of either of the Houses of Parliament[28] and providing for matching exemptions to preserve parliamentary privilege. In the absence of such provisions legislation does not extend to the Houses of Parliament. **19–25**

The data controllers are to be the Corporate Officers of the two Houses where personal data are processed by or on behalf of the Houses. The Corporate Officers may not be prosecuted but s.55 (unlawful obtaining of data) and para.12 of Sch.9 (obligation to assist with the execution of a warrant) will apply.

---

[27] See *Hansard*, quoted in Ch.3.
[28] Para.3 inserting new s.63A after s.63 of the DPA.

Schedules 2 and 3 of the DPA are amended by the insertion of grounds for processing which cover the exercise of any function of either House of Parliament.

The exemption provision extends to:

- the first Principle (except as far as it relates to Schs 2 and 3);
- the second, third, fourth and fifth principles;
- the right of subject access in s.7; and
- the rights of objection, rectification, compensation in ss.10–14(3),

if the exemption is required for the purpose of avoiding an infringement of the privileges of either House of Parliament.[29]

EDUCATIONAL EXEMPTIONS

Examination marks

19–26   Paragraph 7 of Sch.7 re-enacts the provisions of s.35 of the 1984 Act almost word for word. It amends the subject access provisions in relation to examination marks. The data to which it applies are personal data consisting of marks or other information processed by a controller for the purpose of determining the results of professional, academic or other examinations. Any form of examination, assessment, report or work will be covered as long as it falls within this definition. The definition is contained in sub-para.(5) under which "examination" includes any process for determining the knowledge, intelligence, skill or ability of a candidate by reference to his performance in any test, work or other activity. Clearly there must be a candidate who performs in some way which must be subject to a valuation process producing a result, but it can be any type of valuation process or indeed any type of examination. Playing the piano at a local music festival, a Grade I ballet examination, the completion of a Brownie badge or the primary school, SAT tests, university finals and everything in between falls within this omnibus definition.

The exemption appears to apply to the data consisting of actual marks and marking schemes and to data processed as a consequence of the determination of results. This would appear to cover the pass-mark, the rankings, and any re-marking.

Where the exemption applies the controller may delay responding to a subject access request until the time when he would have given the examination results. The provision is designed to stop students "jumping the queue" to obtain the results of examinations earlier than they would do in the normal scheme of things.

Where the controller receives a subject access request and the appropriate fee before the results are due to be announced then the subject access response time (40 days) either does not start to run until after the exam result is announced or, if that date would be more than five months away, the controller must give the data within the five month period.

---

[29] Para.2.

If the period before giving the response is going to be longer than the usual 40-day period the controller must provide a fuller set of data than usual, being all the changes to the data until the time they are finally provided. This may act as a disincentive to controllers trying to take advantage of the five month maximum.

The five month maximum has presumably been arrived at on the basis of assessments from the start of an academic session onward. Results are treated as given when the candidates are told of them or they are published.

Examination scripts

This was a new exemption to the 1998 Act inserted by para.8 of Sch.7. It provides that personal data consisting of information recorded by candidates during an academic, professional or other examination are exempt from s.7. "Examination" is given the same extended meaning as in the previous provision relating to examination marks.

19–27

There is no test of prejudice and it appears to be an absolute exemption to subject access. It is difficult to ascertain how this can be justified under the Directive or indeed in common-sense terms, given that the personal data would have been provided by the subject directly in the examination. Previously the Commissioner in the Legal Guidance suggested that the exemption does not extend to "comments recorded by the examiner in the margins of the script" which it advises should be given "even though they may not appear to the data controller to be of much value without the script itself".[30] This assumes that the scripts are covered by the Act, however, if they fall outside the definition of a "relevant filing system" they may not be covered.

OTHER EXEMPTIONS

Publicly available information

Section 34 provides a wide exemption for data which consist of information which the data controller is obliged by or under any enactment to make available to the public, whether by publishing it, by making it available for inspection or otherwise whether gratuitously or by payment of a fee. This has the same effect as s.34 of the 1984 Act. The exemption applies to the subject information provisions, the fourth principle (accuracy), ss.14(1)–(3) and the non-disclosure provisions.

19–28

The subject information provisions cover both subject access and the fair processing obligations. The fourth principle deals with accuracy and s.14 deals with the rights of individuals to take action for the correction of inaccurate data. The non-disclosure provisions mean any provisions incompatible with the disclosure required. Schedules 2 and 3, which deal with legitimacy of processing and sensitive data, still apply, as does principle 3, which requires that data should be adequate, relevant and not excessive in relation to the purpose or purposes for which they are processed.

---

[30] *Legal Guidance,* p.72.

The exemption only applies when the data are in the hands of the particular data controller who is under an obligation to make it public. It would not apply, for example, to the electoral roll when it is sold and passes into the hands of another party. In the case of the electoral roll there are provisions enabling individuals to lodge a notice of objection to use by third parties. The objection is lodged with the Electoral Registration Officer. The name of the objector will be removed from what is called the edited register which is sold to the private sector without any restriction on the use of the list. However the objector cannot thereby opt-out of all use of the roll by the private sector. It can still be used for money laundering and credit checking purposes.[31] The exemption only applies to the information that the data controller is obliged to publish not to supporting information in the hands of the controller.

Relation with the Freedom of Information Act 2000

19–29   The range of information which is available in the public domain has been widened since the passage of the Freedom of Information Act 2000 and the Environmental Information Regulations 2004.

As s.34 applies to information which the data controller is obliged to make public there was a concern that the publication or provision of access to information under the FOIA would deprive individuals of the rights they would otherwise have. Thus prima facie, where an authority was willing to give access to personal information to the public under a request for access, the data subject would thereby be deprived both of his individual rights of access and his remedies for wrongful disclosure and inaccuracy. While the former would be of less moment, save where there were disputes about the data covered, as the individual would be able to find the information anyway as a member of the public, the latter would mean that the individual was deprived of one of his rights guaranteed by the Directive. Section 72 of the FOIA deals with this by inserting the words "other than an enactment contained in the Freedom of Information Act" into s.34. Accordingly where the information is disclosed under some other legal provision, e.g. an obligation to publish planning applications, the exemption will still apply but not otherwise.

This appears to apply to s.21 as well as specific disclosures. Section 21 of the FOIA exempts information from FOIA requests if the information is reasonably accessible to the applicant other than under s.1, i.e. other than in response to a specific request. It applies where the public authority is obliged to communicate the information by or under any enactment to members of the public on request or under a publication scheme. Thus it can only apply to personal data that would be freely available to the public. So where personal data are contained in a publication scheme they will be exempt from the individual right of access under FOIA by virtue of s.21.

They would also be covered by the exemption under s.34 of the DPA 1998 but that now excludes the class of information available under FOIA but not under other legislation. So there are:

---

[31] See Ch.2 for an explanation of the relevant regulations.

- personal data which are exempt from access under the FOIA under s. 21 because such data are generally publicly available to anyone, e.g. planning application data. The data are then exempt from subject access, accuracy and the non disclosure bars under DPA 1998 under s.34; and

- personal data, not falling within the above, which are made available under the FOIA or under the Environmental Information Access regulations, thus available under an enactment contained in the FOIA but the amendment to s.34 means that the data are not exempt from subject access or the accuracy rights as far as the position of individuals are concerned.

The Freedom of Information Act 2000 and the Environmental Information Regulations 2004, and the relation with s.34, are explored in detail in Ch.26.

FURTHER ORDERS

Orders under s.38

There are two order-making provisions under s.38. Section 38(1) re-enacts the provision found in s.34(9) of the 1984 Act which allows the Secretary of State to exempt personal data from the subject access provisions if they consist of information the disclosure of which would be prohibited or restricted by or under any enactment. In this case the Secretary of State may order an exemption from the subject information provisions but only if and to the extent he considers it necessary for safeguarding the interests of the data subjects or the rights and freedoms of any other individual, or considers that the prohibition or restriction in the original Act ought to prevail over the subject information provisions. The relevant order is SI 2000/419 (as amended by SI 2000/1865 and is dealt with in Ch.11. The second sub-section of s.38 provides that the Secretary of State may by order exempt from the non-disclosure provision disclosures made in circumstances specified in the order. He may only do this if he considers the exemption necessary for safeguarding the interest of the data subject or the rights and freedoms of any other individual. No such orders have been made as at July 2012.

19–30

Crown employment

Paragraph 4 provides for the Secretary of State to make an order exempting personal data from the subject information provisions where that data are processed for the purpose of assessing suitability for particular public appointments. Those are either employment by or under the Crown or an office through which appointments are made by Her Majesty, a Minister of the Crown or by a Northern Ireland Authority. A Northern Ireland Authority means the First Minister, the deputy First Minister, a Northern Ireland Minister or a Northern Ireland Department. The relevant order is the Data Protection (Crown Appointments) Order 2000 (SI 2000/416). The appointments listed in the order include senior clerical appointments in the Church of England, the Poet Laureate, the Astronomer Royal and the Provost of Eton.

19–31

FURTHER POWERS

19–32   In addition to the exemptions set out in these chapters, there are some specific "exemption possibilities" in other parts of the Act. For example, Sch.1 para.1 has a provision allowing for additional exemptions from the fair processing obligations, and Sch.3 para.9 provides for further exemptions to be made from the sensitive data provisions. Orders under Sch.3 are dealt with in Ch.6.

Impact of the draft Regulation in brief[32]

19–33   Article 21 of the draft Regulation provides for Member States to apply exemptions to the revised set of principles (which exclude security and overseas transfers), the individual rights and the obligation to communicate a data breach to individuals where the restrictions constitute a national and proportionate measure to safeguard any of the following:

- public security;
- the prevention, investigation, detection and prosecution of criminal offences;
- other public interests of the Union or Member State in particular and important economic or financial interest;
- the prevention, investigation, detection and prosecution of breaches of ethics for regulated professions;
- a monitoring or inspection function in connection with one of the three listed above; and
- the protection of the data subject or the rights or freedoms of others.

It follows that there will be exemptions, but they will be for the Member State to determine and we are not able to comment other than to say that the provision appears wide enough to allow for a repeat of the current applicable exemptions covered in this chapter.

ADDITIONAL INFORMATION

19–34   **Derivations**

- Directive 95/46 (see Appendix B):
  - (a)   art.13 (exemptions and reservations);
  - (b)   Recitals 42, 43, 44, 45.
- Council of Europe Convention of January 28, 1981 for the Protection of Individuals with regard to automatic processing of Personal Data: art.9 (exceptions and restrictions).
- Data Protection Act 1984: ss.31 (judicial appointments and legal professional privilege), 34 (other exemptions), 35 (examination marks).

---

[32] See Ch.1 paras 1-68 onwards for an overview of the draft Regulation proposed by the Commission in January 2012.

- Organisation for Economic Co-operation and Development Guidelines: Annex Pt One (scope of guidelines).

Hansard references   19–35

Commons Standing Committee D, May 21, 1998, col.232:
Prospective legal proceedings is not intended to cover purely speculative or fishing expeditions.
Commons Standing Committee D, June 4, 1998, col.320:
Exemption for negotiations should cover intentions in the event of future negotiations (such as insurance budget allocations).
Commons Standing Committee D, June 10, 1998, col.340:
Exemption for corporate financial activities.
Vol.315, No.198, col.595, Commons Third Reading, July 2, 1998:
Publicly available registers.

Statutory instruments   19–36

SI 2000/184: The Data Protection (Corporate Finance Exemption) Order;
SI 2000/416: The Data Protection (Crown Appointments) Order;
SI 2000/419: The Data Protection (Miscellaneous Subject Access Exemptions) Order;
SI 2000/1865: The Data Protection (Miscellaneous Subject Access Exemptions) (Amendment) Order.

CHAPTER 20

Civil Enforcement Powers Of The Commissioner

INTRODUCTION

Powers and policy on enforcement have posed difficult questions for successive   **20–01**
Commissioners, reflecting some uncertainty over the role of the Commissioner
and whether he is primarily an educator or a policeman. Over the quarter of a
century since the first Data Protection Act came into force the enforcement
powers available to the Commissioner have been gradually strengthened.
Successive Commissioners have argued for tougher powers and heavier
sanctions. Richard Thomas, Commissioner between 2002 and 2009, was
successful in obtaining increased powers, helped by the public indignation at a
rash of security breaches in the public sector starting with the loss of 25 million
Child Benefit records by HMRC in November 2007. This incident was followed
by a number of other high profile data losses in both the public sector and the
financial sector. These events highlighted the fact that the Commissioner was not
able to impose penalties on those responsible, in contrast to the data protection
regulators in other jurisdictions and to other regulators in the UK, for example the
Financial Services Authority.

In 2008 the Government amended the Act to give the Commissioner power to
impose monetary penalties for significant breaches. This was extended to breach
of the Privacy and Electronic Communications (E C Directive) Regulations 2003
(PECR) from May 26, 2011.[1] Although the level of the fines was set at a much
lower limit than those which can be imposed by the Financial Services Authority
it marked a recognition that beaches of the Act are serious and can attract real
penalties. An example of the FSA's draconian powers can be seen in the financial
penalty of £2.28 million imposed on Zurich UK in August 2010 for the loss of a
disk containing the records of 46,000 customers (a breach which was
compounded by the fact that Zurich remained unaware of the loss for a period of
12 months).

The power to impose fines was followed by a further amendment in 2009
under which the Commissioner was empowered to conduct mandatory audits of
processing being carried out by government departments. The provisions include
a power for this to be extended to other bodies. Both new powers came into effect

---

[1] Reg.11 of the Privacy and Electronic Communications (EC Directive) (Amendment) Regulations
2011 (SI 2011/1208).

in April 2010. While the new powers are not as extensive as those campaigned for by Richard Thomas[2] they mark a new era in the enforcement of data protection in the UK.

The Commissioner's powers have been further extended in relation to providers of public electronic communications services, largely in order to enforce the new obligations in respect of security and mandatory breach notification which are described in Ch.22. He may also audit measures taken to safeguard security[3]and serve third party information notices against the providers of electronic communication services requiring them to provide the Commissioner with information about a service user in certain circumstances. Most of the new provisions were required in order to implement amendments to Directive 2002/58/EC.[4] They took effect in May 2011.

Whether the Commissioner will be able to take full advantage of these new powers given the constraints on his expenditure and staff numbers remains to be seen at the time of writing The Commissioner has not always made extensive use of his formal powers, for example information notices have rarely been served and we have only been able to trace one use of the powers to take action under the Enterprise Act 2002.

In this chapter we cover the civil enforcement powers of the Commissioner, including those applicable to breaches of the Privacy and Electronic Communications (EC Directive) Regulations 2003 (PECR). The powers to prosecute and apply for warrants of entry are covered in Ch.21. The powers to take action in respect of the special purposes are covered in Ch.17. The powers under the Freedom of Information Act 2000 and the Environmental Information Regulations 2004 are covered in Ch.26. Practitioners should, of course, be alert to the fact that the same problem may give rise to both civil and criminal penalties as well as the possibility of action by individuals.

SUMMARY OF MAIN POINTS

20–02   The Commissioner now has a range of powers and remedies at this disposal:

(a)   the Commissioner has an obligation to make an assessment of processing if a data subject seeks one;

(b)   the Commissioner has powers to require data controllers or persons subject to PECR to provide him with information by means of the service of an information notice;

(c)   the Commissioner has the power to serve assessment notices on certain data controllers requiring them to submit their processing to mandatory audit;

(d)   the Commissioner may serve enforcement notices on data controllers who have contravened or are contravening the principles and persons who have or are contravening the requirements of PECR;

---

[2] See ICO paper *Data Protection Powers and Penalties: the case for amending the Data Protection Act 1998*, December 21, 2007, available at *www.ico.gov.uk* as at September 2011.

[3] *Data Protection Powers and Penalties: the case for amending the Data Protection Act* 1998.

[4] Directive 2009/136/EC amending Directive 2002/58/EC art.2.

(e)   the Commissioner has the power to serve monetary penalty notices on data controllers for significant breaches of the Act or persons subject to PECR for significant breaches of those regulations;

(f)   the Commissioner has the power to serve third party information notices on communication providers to release information held about another person's use of a network or service where he considers the information is necessary to investigate compliance with PECR;

(g)   the Commissioner may require a provider of public electronic services to notify the subscriber or user of a personal data breach;

(h)   the Commissioner may issue a fixed monetary penalty notice of up to £1000.00 on a provider of a public electronic communications service who fails to notify the Commissioner of a relevant security breach;

(i)   the Commissioner has the power to audit the compliance of providers of electronic communications services with their obligations in safeguarding the security of the services and with their obligations in respect of notification and recording of breaches of personal data breaches under regs 5A and B;

(j)   the Commissioner has the power to inspect any personal data recorded in the Schengen, Europol and Customs Information Systems to check compliance with the Act;

(k)   it is intended that the Commissioner may require a communication provider to notify him of the procedures and requests for access to information made for the purposes of national security; however, these provisions have not yet been put in place;

(l)   those served with enforcement, information, third party information, assessment and monetary penalty notices, including fixed monetary penalty notices under PECR, may appeal to the Tribunal;

(m)   the Commissioner may apply to the courts for an enforcement order requiring a person to cease conduct harmful to consumers under s.213 of the Enterprise Act 2002;

(n)   the Commissioner may apply for an injunction to a court under reg.19 of the Unfair Terms in Consumer Contracts Regulations 1999 to prevent the continued use of an unfair contract term; and

(o)   the Commissioner rarely serves information notices and habitually uses non-statutory undertakings rather than serving enforcement notices.

In this chapter the Commissioner's powers under the Act, PECR, the Enterprise Act and the Unfair Terms in Consumer Contract Regulations are covered. The enforcement of the FOIA is dealt with briefly in Ch.26. The Commissioner may also order a credit reference agency to add a "notice of correction" to a consumer's file under s.159 of the Consumer Credit Act 1974; this is covered in Ch.11 as part of the subject access chapter.

ENFORCEMENT POLICY AND STRATEGY

Regulatory policy

20–03   The Commissioner's latest statement of policy on enforcement was issued in March 2010 under Christopher Graham and is called Data Protection Regulatory Action Policy and followed on from a strategy document issued in September 2009. In this document the Commissioner takes a high level view of the approach to be adopted by his office in the exercise of any of his powers. In the guidance on the Commissioner's approach to enforcing PECR following the changes in the Privacy and Electronic Communications (EC Directive) (Amendment) Regulations 2011[5] it is stated that the Commissioner will, subject to the specific provisions in that note, "continue to follow the approach set out in his Data Protection Regulatory Action Policy". The policy document is amplified by more detailed guidance dealing with particular powers and of course some powers, such as prosecution powers, are subject to specific codes. Overall the Commissioner states that the approach will be to

> "take a practical down-to-earth approach—simplifying and making it easier for the majority of organisations who seek to handle personal information well and tougher for the minority who do not".

The focus of the policy is to adopt a targeted approach taking into account the level of data protection risk when evaluating the use of formal powers. The policy lists the types of regulatory action open to the Commissioner in which it includes "Negotiation" with the comment that this can be used to bring about compliance with the Act and explains that a negotiated resolution can be backed by a formal undertaking given by an organisation to the ICO. This is covered in this chapter under the section on the use of undertakings. It also sets out the guiding principles that will be applied, when regulatory action will be initiated, the criteria adopted in making decisions on taking regulatory action and how far the actions will be transparent. It includes some specific statements on the use of the new powers to impose monetary penalties and to carry out mandatory assessments.

Guiding principles

20–04   These are transparency, accountability, proportionality, consistency and targeting. These five principles of better regulation were originally set out by the Better Regulation Task Force in 1997. The Task Force was succeeded in 2006 by the Better Regulation Commission whose remit was to reduce unnecessary regulation and ensure that both regulation and enforcement meet the five principles. In its turn the BRC was replaced by an Advisory Council which has now been wound up but the principles remain the core statement of government policy on effective regulation and enforcement.

---

[5] SI 2011/1208.

Initiation of regulatory action

The policy states that the Commissioner will be selective in pursuing action   **20–05**
taking into account the detriment caused by non-compliance as opposed to
pursuing issues of technical breach. The Commissioner will look at compliance
issues from whatever source they are raised, whether issues giving rise to public
concern, or concern raised by novel or intrusive activities, issues raised by
complaints or issues that the Commissioner's staff become aware of in their
work. In deciding whether to take investigations further however the strategy
states that his staff will select particular areas or sectors for attention taking into
account issues such as numbers of complaints or whether market forces may act
as a regulator. As noted earlier the policy document is couched in very general
terms and this part in particular is phrased in a way to ensure that the
Commissioner retains the widest discretion as to the areas he addresses.

Criteria on taking regulatory actions

Twelve criteria will be used to assess whether to take action, the form of any   **20–06**
action and how far to pursue it. They are:

"• Is the past, current or prospective detriment for a single individual resulting
   from a 'breach' so serious that action needs to be taken?
 • Are so many individuals adversely affected, even if to a lesser extent, that
   action is justified?
 • Is action justified by the need to clarify an important point of law or
   principle?
 • Is action justified by the likelihood that the adverse impact of a breach will
   have an on-going effect or that a breach will recur if action is not taken?
 • Is the organisation and its practices representative of a particular sector or
   activity to the extent that the case for action is supported by the need to set an
   example?
 • Is the likely cost to the organisation of taking the remedial action required
   reasonable in relation to the issue at stake?
 • Does a failure by the organisation to follow relevant guidance, a code of
   practice or accepted business practice support the case for action?
 • Does the attitude and conduct of the organisation both in relation to the case
   in question and more generally in relation to compliance issues suggest a
   deliberate, wilful or cavalier approach?
 • How far do we have a responsibility to organisations that comply with the
   law to take action against those that do not?
 • Would it be more appropriate or effective for action to be taken by other
   means (e.g. another regulator, legal action through the courts)?
 • Is the level of public interest in the case so great as to support the case for
   action?
 • Given the extent to which pursuing the case will make demands on our
   resources can this be justified in the light of other calls for regulatory
   action?"

Transparency

The policy states that the ICO will be open about regulatory action which means   **20–07**
that organisations which breach the law and are the subject of regulatory action

will be publicly exposed. The policy is that monetary penalty notices, enforcement notices, undertakings, assessment notices and the outcomes of prosecutions will be published although confidential or commercially sensitive data will be redacted from the published versions. Data controllers therefore know that once the Commissioner has made a determination on a case the outcome is likely to be published. In some cases however the Commissioner will give publicity to a case during the course of the proceedings as he did when considering the complaints against Google street view.

Working with other regulators

20-08   The role of the Commissioner overlaps with the functions of other regulators in a number of areas. In particular there is an overlap with the Financial Services Authority where those providing financial services are involved, with Ofcom where the misuse of telecommunications is concerned and with the Office of Fair Trading where consumer protection is involved. The Commissioner works with such bodies and has entered into formal memoranda of understanding in relation to enforcement with Ofcom and the Financial Ombudsman Service, although there does not appear to be a formal agreement with the FSA or the OFT.[6] If dealing with a case in which more than one regulator may have an interest it is sensible for the practitioner to check whether any formal agreement applies. While these are not legally binding between the regulators they can be a helpful guide to the way that the case is likely to be handled.

The Commissioner is also party to an international agreement to combat unsolicited e-mail (spam) made between the US Federal Trade Commission (FTC), the Secretary of State for Trade and Industry, the Office of Fair Trading in the United Kingdom and the Information Commissioner in the UK and the Australian Competition and Consumer Commission (ACCC), and Australian Communications Authority in which the parties[7] agree to share information and evidence and cooperate with each other to combat spam.

Joint enforcement action by the Article 29 Working Party[8]

20-09   One of the most interesting developments from the Article 29 WP over the last few years has been its decision to take a role in pan EU enforcement. The term enforcement is a misnomer as the WP has no enforcement powers and in reality the documents it has produced as a result of its "enforcement" initiatives have been reports on levels of compliance in Member States. Nevertheless it demonstrates the interest in pan EU enforcement.

---

[6] Memorandum of Understanding between the Information Commissioner's Office and the Financial Ombudsman service, Letter of Understanding between the Office of Communications and the Information Commissioner's Office (*www.ico.gsi.gov.uk*).
[7] Memorandum Of Understanding On Mutual Enforcement Assistance In Commercial Email Matters Among The Following Agencies Of The United States, The United Kingdom, And Australia: The United States Federal Trade Commission, The United Kingdom's Office Of Fair Trading, The United Kingdom's Information Commissioner, Her Majesty's Secretary Of State For Trade And Industry In The United Kingdom.
[8] See Ch.10 for an explanation of the role and work of the Article 29 WP.

In its First Report on the implementation of the Directive (COM(2003) 265 final) the Commission had encouraged the Article 29 WP (WP29) to consider the question of better enforcement with the Directive and "the launching of sectoral investigations at EU level". WP29 set up an Enforcement Task Force (ETF) in June 2004 and produced a Declaration on Enforcement in November 2004 (WP101), in which it announced a commitment to "developing proactive enforcement strategies [and] increasing enforcement actions".

The first area that it reviewed was private health insurance. It reported in 2007 (Report 1/2007 adopted June 20—WP137). The findings of the report were not particularly riveting. In essence the report found that there was generally a good level of compliance but there were problems in some companies. Those problems identified were referred to the national supervisory authority to take appropriate further action. However, the procedure and the extent of cooperation between the relevant supervisory authorities in the Member States were significant. All the data protection authorities of the 27 Member States took part in the exercise, plus Norway. The report explained that much time was spent agreeing a common questionnaire and approach but it was a process from which lessons could be learnt.

The second joint enquiry was launched in June 2008 to investigate the compliance of service providers with standards for the retention of traffic data in accord with the Data Retention Directive 2006/24/EC. It was a slightly strange choice given that the process of transposition was not over in all Member States however the WP felt strongly that the retention issues raised grave privacy concerns and this was an appropriate topic for a pan-European review. A slightly different procedure was followed in that the questionnaire was followed up by on-site visits. The report set out a series of recommendations which included the enhancement of security measures for retained data and the collection of proper figures on the numbers of requests for access to data. The report (WP172) and its recommendations did not lead to direct enforcement action but have been influential from a policy perspective. A number of the provisions in Directive 2009/136 echo the recommendations made in WP172. The Working Party has also issued an Opinion on compliance in the SWIFT case. In a further development the regulators have agreed between themselves in a number of high profile cases that one authority would take the lead on dealing with an issue which has a pan EU application, as in the Google revised privacy policy where the French authority, the CNIL, agreed to take the lead.

REQUESTS FOR ASSESSMENT

Individual request for assessment

Under s.42, a person may ask the Commissioner for an assessment of any processing by which he believes himself to be directly affected. An assessment in this context means an assessment as to whether it is likely or unlikely that any processing of personal data has been or is being carried out in compliance with the Act. The request can be made by the person directly affected or by another on his behalf and the person must be, or believe himself to be, directly affected by   **20–10** the processing in question.[9] The belief on the part of an individual that they are affected by processing is almost certainly a subjective belief rather than an objectively reasonable belief. The latter could have been established by inserting the word "reasonably" before "believes". The power to request an assessment cannot be used as a general check by someone who is not affected by particular processing.

The request does not have to specify whether the person has any grounds for suspicion that the processing is being carried out in contravention of the Act.

The Commissioner has a duty to make an assessment when requested. This is subject to the Commissioner's being satisfied as to the identity of the person making the request and being able to ascertain the relevant processing which is complained of. Such information may be "reasonably required" by the Commissioner for the purpose.[10]

The qualification is however very limited. If a Mr Smith were to write to the Commissioner stating that he held the [objectively wholly unreasonable belief] that Bloggs supermarket were holding details about him and his family including details of their sex lives and political opinions then, providing Mr Smith identified himself and his concerns accurately, the Commissioner has an obligation to assess the matter.

The Commissioner has a degree of discretion in the manner in which he fulfils his duty to make an assessment.[11] Under s.42(2) he may "make an assessment in such manner as appears to him to be appropriate". This would cover a range of possible options, from a consideration limited to evaluating only the information given in a letter of complaint, to a full-scale investigation by officers of the Commissioner. The former course might be followed for example where a letter of complaint raised a matter already adjudicated by the courts or tribunal and where the judgment could be applied directly to the case; alternatively, a full investigation including interviews and inquiries of the controller, might be the preferred approach in a case alleging breach of s.55 (unlawful procuring of data).

20–11   As the right in s.42 applies to "persons" rather than individuals, it follows that requests for assessment may be made by limited companies and other bodies not just individual data subjects. However, the rights to subject access in s.7 only apply to individuals. Accordingly, it appears that the Commissioner can take into account under s.42(3)(c) whether the complainant is an individual. The list in s.42(3) is clearly not exclusive and other factors may also be relevant to the particular case.

20–12   The Act, whilst denying the Commissioner any discretion over whether to conduct an assessment, does provide a considerable discretion as to the form of the assessment. Section 40(3) allows the Commissioner in determining the appropriate form of the assessment to take into account:

- the extent to which the request appears to him to raise a matter of substance;
- any undue delay in making the request; and

---

[9] s.42(1).
[10] s.42(2).
[11] s.42(2).

- whether or not the person making the request is entitled to make an application under s.7 (which establishes the right of access to personal data—see Ch.11—Subject Access) in respect of the personal data in question.[12]

The basic obligation—to carry out some form of assessment as to whether it is likely or unlikely that the processing has been or is being carried out in compliance with the Act—is not removed, however, just tempered. It would appear that even the most trivial or out of date complaints must trigger some form of inquiry by the Commissioner, if only to assess whether there is any relevant processing. Thus it is presumably not permissible for the Commissioner to respond "Your complaint is now too old to be considered", but it is permissible to respond

> "due to the age of your complaint the only step the Commissioner proposes to take is to pass your inquiry on to the data controller in question and to forward their response".

However, this is still a burden placed on the Commissioner.

Section 42(4) provides that the Commissioner must notify the applicant: **20–13**

(a) whether he has made an assessment as a result of the request; and
(b) to the extent that he considers appropriate, having regard in particular to any exemption from s.7 applying in relation to the personal data concerned, of any view formed or action taken as a result of the request.

Subsection (a) thus implies discretion as to whether an assessment is carried out at all although presumably, given the wording of the rest of the section, this will only be a permissible response where the Commissioner lacks information about the identity of the applicant or the relevant processing.

Subsection (b) allows for the possibility that the Commissioner may, as a result of the assessment, become party to information that the data controller would not be obliged to disclose to the applicant because a subject access exemption applies. In such a case the Commissioner may only provide limited information to the applicant about the results of his assessment. The Commissioner has powers to require the production of information and evidence from data controllers by the use of an Information Notice, or the issue of a warrant, but again an individual will have no right to access any information obtained by such means. The Commissioner may serve an enforcement notice on a data controller for breach of the Act but an individual has no right to be consulted on the form or effect of such a notice, even where it was provoked by his initial complaint.

The Act does not provide any guidance on the form of a request for an assessment. In practice it appears that the Commissioner's office interprets any written reference or complaint as a request for assessments. However, those

---

[12] s.42(3).

seeking an assessment are asked to complete standard forms where possible setting out the history of the matter, including any related correspondence and their dealings with the data controller.

Accordingly, although an individual may make a formal complaint to the Commissioner in the form of a request for assessment, once he has made that request the matter is out of his hands and out of his control. The Commissioner does not have the same powers as a court. Moreover, the Commissioner has a regulatory role and while he may actively investigate an alleged breach, which a court cannot do, he will not act on behalf of the complainant in a matter. In addition he has no power to award compensation and his enforcement powers are more limited than the order-making powers of a court. If the complainant is unhappy with the way the Commissioner handles the case his only recourse might be to seek judicial review of the Commissioner's actions or decisions if he believed the Commissioner had either failed to carry out his obligations or carried them out improperly.

Assessments in practice

20–14   The Information Commissioner's Annual Reports over the years show a steady growth in the number of requests for assessment. In the year 2000/01 the Commissioner's office received 8875 requests for assessment. In 2005/06 the Annual Report provided a figure of 22,059 new cases received. However, over half of these were resolved by providing advice and guidance, which would suggest that the basis for counting a "case" was not necessarily that it raised a substantive issue requiring investigation. By 2011/12 the Annual Report recorded 12,985 data protection complaints received in the the preceding 12 months and 7,095 complaints under PECR. However, in a presentation given at the Data Protection Officer Conference hosted by the ICO in March 2011, "Dealing with data protection related complaints, a revised approach" the spokesman for the ICO stated that around 60 per cent of complaints are resolved at the first contact stage with only a limited number being referred to the complaints resolution teams. He also stated that the ICO dealt with around 6,000 cases involving breaches of the Act and the PEC regulations during the previous financial year. The cases were handled by approximately 30 staff equating to roughly 190 cases per case officer per year. Allowing for some backlogs this would suggest that out of the "cases" received approximately only one-fifth are substantive cases that require specific investigation.

There have been periods during which the Office has had a significant backlog of cases however the 2011 Annual Report showed that the new Commissioner, Christopher Graham, was achieving success in his efforts to bring the backlog down and improve case handling. The average time taken to handle a complaint dropped between 2009/2010 and 2010/2011 from 89 to 60 days. By the Annual Report in 2011/2012 the figure for data protection complaints was that 95 per cent were closed within six months of receipt.

The policy approach explained at the DPO Conference in 2011 appears to have replaced the previous Policy on Handling Assessments the last version of which was January 8, 2003. There is no replacement specific policy available on the website, although the general approach to regulatory action in the Data Protection

Regulatory Action Policy described above would of course be relevant to assessments as to any other route to regulatory action. The 2011 Annual Report does not refer to any replacement policy although it refers to a new operational structure for handling complaints. The main change in the policy and approach since the 2003 document appears to be twofold, a new emphasis on assessing the overall level of compliance by data controllers and the use of information from complaints to build more sophisticated pictures of the way that controllers operate. The difference was highlighted in the Annual Report 2011, as follows:

> "We now expect more from data controllers and public authorities and emphasis the need for them to address the issues properly. For example, as well as asking organisations to explain the circumstances of individual complaints we now ask for information about how they intend to put things right where they have gone wrong. Importantly, we also ask organisations to tell us how they adhere to their general information rights obligations".

The structure for handling complaints is, as noted earlier, to dispose of as many at first contact as possible. These include cases where there has been no response to a subject access request and it may be enough to draw the attention of the controller to its obligations. More complex cases are handed on to the complaints resolution teams which are organised on a sectoral basis. The ICO continues to consider complaints as an effective way of identifying and addressing bigger issues than the individual concerns. It also maintains the view that complainants should be directed to the best place to have their complaints resolved and, if that is not the ICO, they will direct the complainant accordingly. On a practical level the presentation set out a regulator's "wish list" of the type of responses that they like to receive from data controllers runs as follows: **20–15**

> "●   Chronology of complaint (and any relevant history)
> ●   Evidence of attempted resolution—remedy or apology
> ●   Answers all the questions [asked by the case officer]
> ●   Admit to mistakes and ask for help
> ●   Provide full details—and copies of—relevant safeguards
> ●   Explanations of action taken (or timescales for the work)
> ●   Simple language—no need to quote large sections of the DPA or use overly 'legalistic' language
> ●   Even if resolved, an understanding that we still need to assess".

Clearly those advising controllers have to consider the interests of the controller as well as the aspirations of the regulator and there can be cases where it is inappropriate to provide the level of detail the ICO would like or where the case officer has asked irrelevant questions but this is a useful list to be aware of.

Investigation in the absence of a request for assessment

In considering matters of non-compliance or setting in train investigations, the Commissioner is not limited to those cases where he has received a request for an assessment but may use his own discretion to investigate matters of concern. This is explicit in the provisions dealing with information notices and other powers which may be exercised either when he has received a request for assessment or **20–16** if he reasonably requires any information for the purpose of determining whether the controller has complied or is complying with the principles. In a number of cases the Commissioner has set in train projects to investigate particular problems, such as the unlawful procuring of information, without being requested to do so by data subjects.

Enforcement under the Privacy and Electronic Communications (EC Directive) 2003

20–17   Under the Privacy and Electronic Communications (EC Directive) Regulations 2003 (PECR) as amended by the Privacy and Electronic Communications (EC Directive) (Amendment) Regulations 2011,[13] Pt V of the DPA 1998 is applied with appropriate modifications as set out in Sch.1 to the Regulations. In addition, there are several powers which are specific to the PECR. The modifications are covered below. Those enforcement powers specific to PECR are covered separately in this chapter.

Modification of powers in the Act

20–18   The complaint and assessment provisions are worded differently from s.42. Whereas under s.42 an individual who is or believes himself to be affected by processing may make a request to the Commissioner for an assessment of the processing in question, this does not apply under PECR. Instead, under reg.32 either OFCOM or a person aggrieved by an alleged contravention of the Regulations may request the Commissioner to exercise his enforcement functions in respect of a contravention. The Regulations do not in terms impose a duty to consider such a request or make a determination following it but applying the principles of public law the Commissioner will be under an obligation to consider any request properly made to him under the legislation. In order to decide whether to exercise his enforcement functions the Commissioner will have to make a decision on whether or not the processing involved complies with the Regulations. The Commissioner may exercise his enforcement powers where he is satisfied that a person has contravened or is contravening the requirements of the Regulations including the imposition of civil monetary penalties for serious breaches. The Commissioner's powers are therefore not limited to breaches committed by data controllers as under the Act. In deciding whether to exercise his powers of enforcement the Commissioner is not required to consider whether distress has been caused to any person but merely damage. The Commissioner may also service information notices on any person for the purpose of determining whether that person has complied or is complying with the relevant requirements. The provisions in relation to special purposes (including special information notices and determinations in relation to the special purposes) are omitted as are other provisions which are not relevant to PECR.

---

[13] SI 2011/1208.

Information notices

The power to serve information notices and special information notices was new **20–19** in the 1998 Act although in practice it appears to have been relatively little used. The Commissioner may, upon receiving a request for an assessment, or on his own initiative, serve an information notice on the data controller requiring the provision of information to enable the Commissioner to determine whether the data controller has complied or is complying with the data protection principles.[14] Under PECR, the notice may be served on any person to determine whether the provisions of the Regulations have or are being complied with. The notice must state whether the information is sought in response to an assessment request or because the Commissioner is conducting his own inquiry into a possible breach of the principles. In the latter case the Commissioner must also state the reasons for regarding the information sought as relevant.[15] Under PECR the notice must contain a statement that the Commissioner regards the information as relevant in order to make his determination on compliance and the reason he regards it as relevant.[16]

An information notice must set out the rights of appeal.[17]

The Commissioner has discretion over:

- the timescale for compliance with the notice—subject to appeal time limits; and
- the form in which the required information is to be provided.[18]

There is a procedure for urgent information notices.[19]

Timescale for compliance

Subject to the provisions on appeals and urgent notices it is for the Commissioner **20–20** to determine the appropriate timescale. The Commissioner, save in urgent cases, may not require compliance with the information notice before the end of the appeal period. Furthermore, if there is an appeal by the data controller then the need for compliance is suspended until the determination or withdrawal of the appeal.[20]

In urgent cases the Commissioner may require compliance after a minimum period of seven days from the service of the notice. It is for the Commissioner to determine whether the situation is urgent. The Act merely indicates that such a decision may be reached by "reason of special circumstances". Clearly urgent information notices will be relevant when the Commissioner has concerns that something is about to happen vis-a-vis the relevant compliance issues, for example there is about to be a (another) transfer overseas in breach of the principles or there is about to be a (another) disclosure in breach of the Act. In

---

[14] s.43.
[15] s.43(2).
[16] SI 2003/2426 Sch.1, amending s.43 for the purposes of PECR.
[17] s.43(3).
[18] s.43(1).
[19] s.43(5).
[20] s.40(7).

such circumstances he may require the information to be supplied immediately to enable him to take emergency enforcement action.

The word "another" is used in parentheses in the preceding paragraph since the Act only allows an information notice to be served with respect to current breaches—which would appear to exclude anticipated future breaches.

There are exemptions to the general obligation to respond to an information notice in respect of:

- material covered by legal professional privilege in so far as it relates to advice given in relation to the 1998 Act;
- material which would incriminate the recipient of the information notice in so far as it discloses offences other than offences under the 1998 Act or offences under a specified list being:
- an offence under s.5 of the Perjury Act (false statements made otherwise than on oath);
- An offence under s.44(2) of the Criminal Law (Consolidation)(Scotland) Act 1995 (false statements made otherwise than on oath);
- An offence under art.10 of the Perjury (Northern Ireland) Order 1979 (false statutory declarations and other false unsworn statements).[21]

The Commissioner is empowered to cancel but not (unlike enforcement notices) to vary the terms of information notices.[22]

20–21   The Commissioner may also serve special information notice on a data controller in order to investigate suspected breaches or abuses of the "special purposes" exemptions specified in s.32 of the Act. The provisions in respect of special information notices in ss.44–46 do not apply to PECR as there is no equivalent exemption for the special purposes. A special information notice may be served either in response to an assessment request or in certain other limited circumstances. If the Commissioner decides that the exemption has been wrongly claimed then he may issue a determination to this effect.

The ability of the Commissioner to investigate a suspected abuse of the "special purposes" exemption without a request for an assessment is limited to situations where a court has stayed proceedings brought under the Act in response to a claim by a data controller, that the special purposes exemption applies. Any such stay will be for the specific purpose of the Commissioner making a determination as to whether the "special purposes" exemption has been wrongly claimed. The procedure is governed by s.32(4)–(5) of the 1998 Act.[23]

The provisions relating to the mandatory contents of special information notices (SINs), rights of appeal, urgent SINs, cancelling SINs and exemptions for legal professional privilege and self-incrimination are identical to those for ordinary information notices.

The Commissioner may not serve an "ordinary" (as opposed to "special") information notice on a data controller who claims to be processing personal data only for the "special purposes" without first issuing a determination to the effect

---

[21] Amended by the Coroners and Justice Act 2009 Sch.20 Pt 4.
[22] s.43(9).
[23] See Ch.17.

that the "special purposes" exemption has been wrongly claimed.[24] Any such determination, like other notices, must set out the rights of appeal and cannot take effect until the appeal time-limit has passed or, if there is an appeal, until that has been determined or withdrawn.[25] Unlike other notices there is no procedure for urgent determinations.

Third party information notices under PECR

In dealing with abuse of various kinds on the Internet it can be necessary to apply to the courts for orders to require service providers to release the identity of those using their services. The circumstances where this applies include dealing with defamatory sites or those hosting illegal contents where the identity of the site owner is concealed. The new provision in reg.31A of PECR means that, where the Commissioner needs this information to investigate a relevant complaint, he can rely on a statutory notice served on the service provider. The previous information notice powers under Sch.1 of PECR apply where the Commissioner reasonably requires information for the purpose of determining whether a person has complied or is complying with relevant requirements of PECR and enable him to require such information "relating to compliance with the relevant requirements" as is specified in the notice. This is not wide enough to require the service provider to provide information on the identity of the user of a network or service.

20–22

A notice can now be served on a communications provider and require the provider to release information which it holds about another person's use of a network or service where the Commissioner believes that the information requested is relevant information.[26] The term "use" is broad and could cover use for advertising, communications, and collection of data or information.

Relevant information is broadly defined in reg.31A(3) as information that the Commissioner considers is necessary to investigate the compliance of any person with PECR. There is no requirement that the Commissioner's belief should be based on reasonable grounds although the absence of grounds for the belief could clearly give rise to an appeal.

The notice must set out:

20–23

- the information requested;
- the form in which the information must be provided;
- the time limit within which the information must be provided; and
- information about the rights of appeal under PECR.[27]

The notice cannot take effect until the time limit for lodging an appeal (28 days) has passed other than in a case of urgency. In such a case the notice must

---

[24] s.46(3) and s.43(10).
[25] s.45.
[26] reg.31A(1) and (2).
[27] Reg.31A(4).

state that the case is urgent and provide the Commissioner's reasons for reaching that conclusion and must give a minimum of seven days to provide the information.[28]

There is an exemption for legal advice given by a professional legal adviser with respect to the client's obligations, liabilities or rights under the PECR or in connection with or in contemplation of proceedings under PECR including Tribunal proceedings. In the second case the privilege can extend to communications between the legal advisers and other persons, such as expert witnesses, as well as communication with the client.[29]

A communication provider served with a third party notice may appeal to the Tribunal. The appeal can be on fact or law and the usual Tribunal rules will apply.

Jurisdiction

20–24   There is no equivalent to s.5 of the Act in PECR so the normal rules as to jurisdiction will apply. Any provider of communication services within the jurisdiction will be subject to the powers of the Commissioner. There is no limitation on the location of the users of the services in respect of whom information may be required. It follows that the service provider can be required to disclose these even if they are located outside the UK. However, in such a case the powers of the Commissioner to take further action would be constrained by territorial limits.

Enforcement of information notices

20–25   A failure to comply with an information notice, or special information notice can be enforced by prosecution under s.47. In respect of a third party information notice the same provision is applied by Sch.1 of PECR.[30] A person who, in purported compliance with any relevant notice makes a statement that he knows to be false in any material respect or recklessly makes a statement which is false in a material respect is guilty of an offence.[31] It is, however, a defence to show that he acted with all due diligence to comply with the notice.[32]

AUDIT POWERS

Voluntary audits

20–26   The use of compliance audits to assess the extent to which organisations are meeting their obligations under the Act has become increasingly common over the last few years. Audit services are offered by most law firms with specialist practices in the area and also by consultants, both those from the big firms and

---

[28] Reg.31A(5)–(7).
[29] Reg.31A(8).
[30] Privacy and Electronic Communications (EC Directive) Regulations 2003 Sch.1 art.6 amended by SI 2011/1208.
[31] s.47(2).
[32] See Ch.21 for the criminal powers under the Act.

those who work specifically in the privacy area. Audits usually follow a similar pattern. The auditor will review the policies and procedures which the data controller has in place and then visit the organisation to see how these are working in practice. Most audits will focus on the areas of particular risk for that organisation and will result in a report, recommendations and a set of actions to remediate any shortcomings found as a result of the audit. Most are followed by follow-up visits, training or reviews. Audits are a useful way of bringing compliance issues to the attention of relevant staff, transferring knowledge, assessing risk and obtaining backing from managers to put in place a programme of compliance.

Since the Act came into effect the Commissioner has had the power to audit data controllers with their consent. Section 51(7) provides that the Commissioner may "with the consent of the data controller, assess any processing of personal data for the observance of good practice". After the 1998 Act was implemented the Commissioner published an Audit Manual which has been available on the Commissioner's website for others to use. The Audit Manual was widely criticised as unwieldy and overly detailed. More recently the Commissioner has published a short guide on how his staff will carry out an audit and what it covers. This does not refer to the Audit Manual nor does the Assessment Notices Code of Practice. It appears therefore that the Commissioner's Office no longer supports the Audit Manual.

Data controllers in both public and private sector bodies can request a voluntary audit. There is no fee charged by the ICO and accordingly the ICO has to be careful to ensure that it only uses its resources on auditing those organisations where there is a degree of risk. In fact the Commissioner has taken the initiative in respect of the use of audits and is now likely to approach organisations to ask them to undergo an audit when he has determined that there is a compliance risk.

20–27

After the loss of the HMRC disks in 2007, the Cabinet Office imposed an obligation on Government Departments to submit to audit at the request of the Commissioner. As a result there were a number of audits of public bodies. The Commissioner has also audited private bodies by agreement. The summary reports are available on the Commissioner's website. Since April 2010 the Commissioner has been able to undertake mandatory audits following the service of an Assessment Notice on a data controller. The provisions covering Assessment Notices are examined below however it should be noted that in practical terms the Commissioner will apply the same considerations as to whether to approach a data controller with a view to a voluntary or mandatory audit.

Mandatory audit powers following assessment notices

The power to require data controllers to undergo assessments or audits as they are more commonly known was introduced by the Coroners and Justice Act 2009, s.173 of which amended the DPA by the insertion of new ss.41A–C. Under s.41C the Commissioner must prepare and issue a code of practice about the manner in which he will use the power. This provision came into effect on February 1, 2010

20–28

to enable the code to be prepared in advance of the introduction of the substantive provisions.[33] The Code was issued in April 2010.

Who is subject to the power?

20–29   The Commissioner starts the process by the service of an assessment notice on a data controller. The purpose of the assessment is to enable the Commissioner to determine whether the data controller has complied with or is complying with the principles. It therefore cannot be used to check on whether a controller is properly notified or has been subject to s.55 breaches.[34] The only data controllers currently subject to this power are government departments.[35] This is a relatively narrow category of data controllers and excludes many public sector data controllers which hold vast databases of sensitive data such as the police or NHS Trusts not to mention private sector data controllers such as banks or credit agencies.

The scope can be extended as the Secretary of State may designate public authorities or other persons by order for the purposes of this section. A public authority is defined as any body, officeholder or other person in respect of which an order could be made under ss.4 or 5 of the Freedom of Information or the Freedom of Information (Scotland) Acts respectively.[36] There is no specified process for the designation of public authorities under the section. The section however sets out a formal process that must be covered before any private sector organisations may be designated. The first step in the process is for the Commissioner to make a recommendation to the Secretary of State that a category of persons in question should be so designated. Before making such a recommendation the Commissioner must be satisfied that the designation is necessary having regard to: a) the nature and quantity of data under the control of such persons; and b) any damage or distress which may be caused by such persons by a contravention of the principles.[37] It is assumed that the term "necessary" carries the meaning as a term of proportionality that it is reasonably necessary in all the circumstances. It appears, therefore, that the designation could be by reference to any description whether the nature of the business or the nature of the personal data processed or the type of the processing carried out. Before making an order in response to the recommendation of the Commissioner the Secretary of State must also be satisfied that the designation is necessary on these grounds. The Secretary of State must also consult with those who represent the relevant proposed designated data controllers and such other persons as he considers appropriate. It is assumed that the consultations would be carried out once the Secretary of State has formed a preliminary view before it is finally determined. No timescale is provided for the process. There is no equivalent requirement that the designation is judged to be necessary because of the risks involved to data subjects or specified process for the designation of further public authorities under the section however it would be reasonable to anticipate that

---

[33] SI 2010/145 as amended by SI 2010/186.
[34] s.41A(1).
[35] s.41A(2)(a).
[36] s.41A(12).
[37] s.41A(10).

similar considerations would be borne in mind and a similar process adopted before any decisions are made to extend the powers to other parts of the public sector.

In all cases of further designations the Secretary of State must reconsider the designation at least every five years and determine whether it is appropriate (in the case of public sector designations) or that it continues to be necessary in the light of the risks to data subjects (in the case of the private sector).

In the code of practice the Commissioner has commented:

"The scope of our extended powers is at the moment relatively modest, as they only apply to government departments. However moving forward it is entirely reasonable to expect that, where the evidence supports it, I will seek to extend my powers to undertake "compulsory" audits in both the public and the private sectors."

Exemptions from coverage

Assessment notices cannot be served on the following:

20–30

- judges, which includes justices of the peace, lay magistrates in Northern Ireland, members of tribunals or a clerk or other officer entitled to exercise the jurisdiction of a court or tribunal[38];
- any body which is a member of the security services as defined in section 32(3) of the Freedom of Information Act 2000[39]; or
- the Office for Standards in Education, Children's Services and Skills in so far as it is a data controller in respect of information processed for the purposes of functions exercisable by her majesty's Chief Inspector of education, Children's Services and Skills by virtue of s.5(1) of the Care Standards Act 2000.[40]

Even where an assessment notice has been served documents dealing with legal advice on compliance with the Act or the conduct or proceedings under the Act are exempt. The material covered is:

- any communication between a professional legal adviser and the adviser's client in connection with the giving of legal advice with respect to the client's obligations, liabilities or rights under the Act; or
- any communication between a professional legal adviser and the adviser's client (which includes references to any person representing a client), or between such an adviser or the adviser's client and any other person, made in connection with or in contemplation of proceedings under or arising out of the Act including proceedings before the Tribunal and for the purposes of such proceedings.[41]

---

[38] s.41B(6).
[39] s.41B(6).
[40] s.41B(6).
[41] s.41B(3).

In the code of practice the Commissioner also states that access will not be sought to information which has a high level of commercial sensitivity and his staff will respond to legitimate concerns about sensitive information such as that relating to international activities.

Content of an assessment notice

20–31   An assessment notice must set out what the Commissioner requires the data controller to do, plus for each requirement, the time at which it must be complied with or the period during which it must be complied with[42].The requirements which can be included are to allow the Commissioner or his officers or staff to:

- enter any specified premises;
- direct them to any documents of a specified description which are on the premises;
- assist them to view any information of a specified description capable of being viewed using equipment on the premises;
- provide a copy of any such documents or (in such form as may be requested) such information;
- direct them to equipment or other material of a specified description on the premises;
- permit them to inspect or examine any of the documents, information, equipment or material;
- permit them to observe the processing of any personal data which takes place on the premises; and
- make available for interview a specified number of persons of a specified description who process personal data (or such number as are willing to be interviewed).[43]

The assessment notice therefore gives the Commissioner wide powers to review the processing carried out by or on behalf of the data controller. Note that the relevant premises need not be the controller's premises and could, for example, be the premises of a data processor which provides services to the controller.

20–32   In the code of practice the Commissioner states that notices will be accompanied by covering letters which will "identify the purposes, objectives and scope of a compulsory audit." Such letters will also identify additional requests for assistance such as the identification of a single point of contact.

Time for compliance

20–33   An assessment notice may require actions to be taken by a specified date or requirements to be complied with during a specified period of time but not until after the period allowed for the data controller to lodge an appeal has expired.[44] Therefore the dates specified or the start of the period specified must be at least

---

[42] s.41A(5).
[43] s.41(a)(3) (a)–(h).
[44] s.41B(1).

28 days after the date of the assessment notice. The Commissioner can require a data controller to comply with an assessment notice requirement as a matter of urgency and in that case the period is reduced to 7 days. The period can only be reduced if "by reason of special circumstances" the Commissioner considers that it is a matter of urgency.[45] It is difficult to conceive of circumstances in which this would apply and it is not anticipated that it would be used very often. If the Commissioner serves a notice as a matter of urgency the notice "may" include a statement to that effect and a statement of the Commissioner's reasons for reaching that conclusion. It is surprising that this appears to be discretionary as it might be expected to be mandatory for the Commissioner to give reasons as to why he was shortening the normal period.

Withdrawal of notices

The Commissioner may cancel an assessment notice. In the code he explains that this may happen if the controller is able to satisfactorily explain why an assessment should not take place or should be postponed for some time. The other situation which may lead to cancellation is where the Commissioner is no longer able to conduct the audit for any reason.

20–34

Code of Practice

Section 41C requires the Commissioner to prepare and issue a code of practice as to the manner in which the Commissioner's functions in relation to assessment notices are to be exercised. The Secretary of State must be consulted on the code[46] before it is issued. The current code was passed before the amendment made by the Protection Of Freedoms Act and was in fact agreed by the Secretary of State. Once issued it must be published in such form and manner as the Commissioner considers appropriate. The code may be altered or replaced and any alteration or replacement must follow the same procedure.

20–35

The code differs from other codes issued by the ICO as it applies to the way that the *Commissioner* behaves, and not to the behaviour of data controllers. Its function as far as data controllers are concerned is to provide comfort and reassurance as to how the Commissioner will behave in an audit.

The Commissioner reserves the right to amend the code to reflect changes in auditing standards. It will be reviewed within two years of publication or if the Secretary of State designates any further bodies as subject to the compulsory audit powers.

The Introduction makes clear that the same broad approach will be covered in the procedure for compulsory and voluntary audits although voluntary audits will consider the following of good practice (as set out in the ICO codes and The Guide to Data Protection) whereas compulsory audits are limited to legal compliance. The Commissioner reserves the right to add other standards documents against which data controllers will be judged. This might suggest such standards as security standards or Business Information Management standards

---

[45] s. 41B(2).
[46] s.41C(7) as amended by the Protection of Freedoms Act 2012 (not yet in force as at October 2012).

could be considered in the future. The code sets out the sources of information that will be used to identify high-risk data controllers who will then be targeted for audit as being:

- business intelligence, such as news items;
- data controllers' annual statements on controls;
- data controllers' information security maturity models;
- information received from other regulators;
- the number and nature of complaints received by the Commissioner; plus
- other (unspecified) relevant information.

The section sets out the specific issues that must be covered by the code. In the section below we have set out each topic which must be covered and then examined the relevant contents of the code.

Factors to be considered in determining whether to serve an assessment notice

20–36 The code states that assessment notices will be served in three categories of cases:

- where there has been a risk assessment which has indicated a compliance risk that would involve a likelihood of damage or distress to individuals and the controller has refused to undertake an audit or allow the ICO to undertake one without due reason. This indicates that purely technical breaches are not likely to give rise to assessment notices. It also suggests that the ICO might accept the data controller having its own audit carried out as opposed to allowing the ICO to conduct one. In such a case it is assumed that the ICO would wish to have sight of any report although there might be more scope for discussion around the extent of access to any report;
- where the Commissioner wishes to check that an undertaking or enforcement notice has been complied with; and
- where the Commissioner has a formal responsibility for scrutiny for example under the Cabinet Office's Data Handling Procedures in Government.

The factors which will be considered in determining risk are listed. They appear to fall into three categories: those related to the data being handled; those relating to the compliance history and behaviour of the controller and those related to the particular facts of the matter.

In relation to the data the code refers to the nature and extent of the data involved and any perceived impacts on individuals. In relation to the compliance history and behaviour the code refers to complaints, self-reported breaches, its own internal audits, reports by whistle-blowers and any existing accreditation. In relation to the particular facts of the matter it refers to new systems being implemented, business intelligence, statements of internal control and notification details.

Descriptions of documents and information that are not to be examined or
inspected in pursuance of an assessment notice

The code explains the exemptions (described at paragraph x above). It further
states that access will not be sought to very sensitive commercial information.
Access to information classified as restricted or above in the government's
security classifications will be limited to staff with Security Check clearance or
better.
    The code must include provisions that relate to documents and information
concerning an individual's physical or mental health and documents and
information concerning the provision of social care as defined in the Health and
Social Care Act 2008. The code states that the confidentiality of such records will
be respected and access limited to the minimum required to carry out the audit.
The content of such records will not be taken off site, copied or transcribed into
notes and will not appear in any report. It is interesting that these are the only
specific categories of sensitive personal data that are specified; however, it is
reasonable to assume that the Commissioner will be sensitive about the
publication of any sensitive personal data about individuals. The code explains
that the Commissioner will listen to representations by controllers about access to
sensitive categories of information.

20–37

The nature of inspections and examinations carried out in pursuance of an
assessment notice

The code explains that the individuals carrying out the audits will either be
employed directly by the ICO or contracted to him and will either have or be
working towards a relevant qualification in both audit and data protection. It also
provides that such staff will be willing to sign confidentiality clauses with the
controllers as long as these do not unreasonably restrict the ICO's functions. It
will be prudent for data controllers to take advantage of this and agree
appropriate confidentiality terms with the ICO. Auditors may also be accompanied by other specialist staff or those with particular knowledge of the work of
the department being audited.
    The audits will be conducted in two stages: a first stage review of policies,
procedures and documents such as training materials and guidance followed by a
site visit to meet staff and observe data-handling in practice.
    The list of documents that will be examined includes the standard information
such as strategies, policies and procedures as well as job descriptions, contract
terms, protocols, privacy statements, and training materials used.
    The on-site inspections and examinations will review the data-handling
practices adopted including logs and audit trails to evaluate the handling through
the data lifecycle from obtaining and storing the data, through retrieving and
using it, disclosing it to destruction and removal. The reviews will also evaluate
security and storage.

20–38

The nature of interviews carried out pursuant to an assessment notice

20–39   In the code the Commissioner explains that interviews may be conducted both with the controllers' staff and with processors and contractors. Staff of the appropriate knowledge and grade will be selected in discussion with the controller. Staff will be made aware of the ground to be covered in any interview in advance. The interviews are intended to be fact-finding and will not normally require a third party present. If any indications of criminality come up during an interview the interview will be terminated.

The preparation, issuing and publication by the Commissioner of assessment reports

20–40   An assessment report is a report which contains a determination as to whether a data controller has complied or is complying with the principles, recommendations as to any steps that the controller ought to take or refrain from taking to ensure compliance with the principles and other matters specified in the code of practice.[47]

The code states that as well as the required determination the report will cover levels of assurance against the prescribed scope of the audit and the identified risks and controls implemented by the data controller. The contents of an audit report will be:

- a summary of findings;
- an audit opinion;
- detailed findings against predefined risks; and
- associated recommendations.

The audit opinion will be based on the assessment carried out and consider the governance and associated controls in place to deal with risk. If the data controller has not met the requirements of the assessment notice, for example by not providing full access to documents, the Commissioner may refer to that in the report if he considers that it was material. The recommendations made to improve compliance (if any) will be rated in terms of risk to identify those needing immediate attention and those which can be subject to a staged programme.

The process will be for the Commissioner's staff to provide a draft of the report to the data controller for consideration and comment before the report is finalised. An executive summary of all reports will be prepared for publication. As with the full report the data controller will be given an opportunity to comment on this in draft before it is finalised and will have a copy before it is published by the Commissioner.[48]

Publication of reports

20–41   The audit reports will not be published. The executive summaries will be made available on the website for 12 months from the data of the audit. Clearly reports

---

[47] s.41C(4).
[48] Code of Practice s.5.1.

- with respect to personal data accurately recording information from a data subject or third party, to incorporate an approved statement of the true facts.[62]

The latter two possibilities obviously envisage a situation where the data controller has accurately recorded inaccurate information from a third party or data subject and the data subject has objected. In addition to the general powers to require rectification, etc., the Commissioner may also require the data controller to take reasonable steps to check the accuracy of the information and/or may require the addition of an approved statement of the true facts. It is the Commissioner rather than any other party who "approves" the statement. These provisions stem directly from the interpretative provisions for the fourth principle set out in para.7 of Pt II of Sch.1.[63]

Any enforcement notice requiring rectification, blocking, erasure or destruction of personal data (i.e. not just an enforcement notice dealing with the fourth principle) may require a data controller, if "reasonably practicable", to notify third parties to whom the data have been disclosed of the rectification, etc. The Commissioner may also require this step to be taken if he is satisfied that data which have been rectified, etc., had been processed in breach of any of the principles.[64]

The Act provides that in determining what is "reasonably practicable" regard must be had, in particular, to the number of third parties to be notified.[65] The insertion of the words "in particular" clearly means that the number of third parties to be notified is not the only matter to be considered when deciding on practicability but it is a major factor. It will be the responsibility of the Commissioner in the first instance to determine what is and is not reasonably practicable. The data controller may challenge the Commissioner's interpretation by an appeal to the Tribunal.

Timescale for compliance

Subjects to the provisions on appeals and urgent notices it is for the Commissioner to determine the appropriate timescale. The Commissioner, save in urgent cases, may not require compliance with an enforcement notice before the end of the appeal period. Furthermore, if there is an appeal by the data controller then the need for compliance is suspended until the determination or withdrawal of the appeal.[66]

20–53

In urgent cases the Commissioner may require compliance after a minimum period of seven days from the service of the notice. It is for the Commissioner to determine whether the situation is urgent. The Act merely indicates that such a decision may be reached by "reason of special circumstances". The word "another" is used in parentheses in the preceding paragraph since the Act only

---

[62] s.40(3) and (4).
[63] See Ch.6, "The Principles".
[64] s.40(5).
[65] s.40(5).
[66] s.40(7).

allows an enforcement notice to be served with respect to current on-going breaches—which would appear to exclude anticipated future breaches.

What must a notice contain?

20–54   The enforcement notice must contain:

- a statement of the data protection principle or Principles which the Commissioner is satisfied have been or are being contravened and his reasons for reaching that conclusion;
- details of the data controller's rights of appeal against the enforcement notice[67]; and
- with urgent enforcement notices, a statement that compliance is required as a matter of urgency and a statement of the Commissioner's reasons for reaching that conclusion.[68]

Cancellation and variation

20–55   The Commissioner is empowered to vary or cancel any enforcement notice.[69] Conversely the subject of any enforcement notice may apply for cancellation or variation but only after the expiry of the appeal time-limit. Under the 1984 Act the Registrar alone was empowered to cancel (rather than cancel or vary) enforcement notices.[70] The power of variation was therefore new in the 1998 Act although it made little practical difference as under the 1984 Act the Registrar could cancel an enforcement notice and then issue a new one containing varied terms.

Enforcement notices served

20–56   Enforcement notices are relatively rare. On the Commissioner's website, 14 were listed in 2010. Since August 2010 those have been moved and a further four were listed up to August 2012. Out of the 14, 13 arose from the issues arising in the construction industry blacklist case. One was a notice served against Marks and Spenser Plc in 2008 in relation to a security breach but our understanding is that it was subsequently withdrawn. It is also known that in July 2004 the Commissioner issued enforcement notices against the Chief Constables of West Yorkshire, South Yorkshire and North Wales Police in relation to the retention of information on criminal convictions. The Commissioner sought the erasure or destruction of old conviction information. On appeal the Tribunal allowed the appeal as far as the retention of the information for policing purposes but not in respect of vetting (see Ch.6 for a detailed analysis of the case). A further notice on the same issues was served in 2007 and was appealed to the Court of Appeal

---

[67] s.40(6).
[68] s.40(8).
[69] s.41.
[70] s.10(8) of the 1984 Act.

which overturned the notice. We are aware therefore of around 20 enforcement notices which have been served since the 1998 Act came into effect but are not aware of a full list of those notices.

PECR—ORDERS TO NOTIFY

These are new types of notices introduced from May 2011. They apply where there has been a breach of security by a service provider which the Commissioner regards as a personal data breach. The nature and impact of personal data breaches are described in chapter Ch.22. In essence the service provider must notify relevant subscribers or users who may be impacted by the breach unless the information was sufficiently securely encrypted to make it inaccessible. If a service provider fails to make the notification in an appropriate case the Commissioner can require the service provider to notify subscribers or users if the service provider has not done so and the Commissioner considers that the likely adverse effects of the breach make it appropriate to do so.[71] There is no formal process for this, such as service of an enforcement notice and it appears that there is no direct appeal against such a determination by the Commissioner, nor is there a direct appeal if a service provider considers that material was properly encrypted but the Commissioner disagrees, although in both cases the Commissioner may be judicially reviewed if his decision is wholly unreasonable. The provisions are enforced by the service of a fixed monetary penalty notice in respect of which the Commissioner must go through a formal process before service and against which there is a right of appeal. As the notice must set out the grounds on which it is served this will presumably operate as the mechanism by which decisions of the Commissioner in this area will be open to challenge.

20–57

Nevertheless this is an indirect mechanism and the Commissioner could impose a very significant notice obligation on a service provider against which the provider will have no direct appeal.

Enforcement of PECR notification requirements

Regulation 5C of PECR sets out the procedure and appeals in respect of the power of the Commissioner to issue a fixed monetary penalty notice of £1000.00 for failure to comply with the "notification requirements of regulation 5A".[72] The term "notification requirements" is not defined. It must cover the obligations to give notice to the Commissioner and to give notice to subscribers and users where appropriate. It is not explicit that it also covers the obligation which can be triggered by a requirement of the Commissioner to give notice but it is submitted that this is the logical and correct reading of the term. Regulation 5C includes detailed provisions dealing with prior notice of intent to serve the fixed monetary penalty notice and a right to appeal to the First Tier Tribunal (Information Rights). As noted in the preceding paragraph this will presumably be the route by which decisions of the ICO on these points will be open to challenge. There is a statutory discount of 20 per cent of the penalty where the amount is paid within

20–58

---

[71] PECR reg.5A(7) as amended by SI 2011/1208.
[72] PECR reg.5C amended by SI 2011/1208.

21 days of receipt of a notice of intent to issue such a notice.[73] It is not clear if this discount is available if the recipient makes representations or subsequently appeals against the notice.

20–59   The procedure is for the Commissioner to serve a notice of intent on the service provider which will set out:

- the name and address of the service provider;
- the nature of the breach;
- the amount of the fixed monetary penalty;
- a statement informing the service provider that it can discharge liability for the penalty if it pays the Commissioner £800 within 21 days of receipt of the notice of intent;
- the date on which the Commissioner proposes to serve the penalty notice; and
- the right to make written representations within 21 days from the date of service of the notice.

The Commissioner cannot serve the final notice until the 21-day period for making representations has expired. There is no restriction on the nature of the representations therefore it is assumed that a service provider could dispute that there has been a relevant breach for example it might submit that the event did not amount to a personal data breach or that, if it did, it was not likely to adversely affect the personal data or privacy of a subscriber or user and notice should not be given or that the data was sufficiently encrypted. The Commissioner must then consider the representations and determine whether to serve the notice.

If he does the notice must state:

- the name and address of the service provider;
- details of the notice of intent served;
- whether there have been any written representations;
- details of any early payment discounts;
- the grounds on which the Commissioner imposes the penalty;
- the date by which the penalty is to be paid; and
- details of and the time limit for the right of appeal.[74]

20–60   The appeal is made to the First Tier Tribunal (Information Rights). The Regulations are silent as to whether there is an appeal on fact or law and therefore the grounds of appeal are both. The procedure for appeals will follow the Tribunal procedure.

The penalty is recoverable by action in the country court or High Court in England, Wales and Northern Ireland or the sheriff court in Scotland "in the same manner as an extract registered arbitral bearing a warrant for execution issued by the sheriff court of any sheriffdom in Scotland".[75]

---

[73] reg.5C(5).

[74] reg.5C(7).

[75] reg.5C(10) and (11).

Can the Commissioner exercise any other powers in respect of breach of the notification requirements?

It appears that the notification requirements and the penalty provisions operate as **20–61** a "stand alone" set of obligations. The provisions in respect of the fixed penalty notices do not include words equivalent to "without prejudice to the exercise of any other powers" which would have made it clear that the Commissioner could also serve enforcement notices or issue civil monetary penalty notices moreover reg.5A is not included in the "enforcement functions" of the Commissioner under PECR as new regs 31A and 31B have been.[76]

One concern might be that a service provider would be willing to pay out the £1,000 on a fixed monetary penalty notice rather than go to the expense of giving notice to many subscribers and users. It is not clear whether the Commissioner could serve more than one notice in respect of the same breach although we would incline to the view that this would not be possible. It is of course unlikely that a service provider would refuse to give notice if a Tribunal had found against it, unless it was appealing on a point of law. It would run the risk of receiving very bad publicity as the Commissioner would no doubt publicise the failure to comply. However, there may be service providers which would be less than scrupulous and unmoved by such publicity. In such cases it is assumed that the Commissioner would seek a mandatory injunction from the High Court on the basis that there was no other way of maintaining the legal obligation.

MONETARY PENALTY NOTICES

Section 55 gives the Commissioner the power to impose monetary penalties, sets **20–62** out the procedures to be followed before imposing the penalties, provides for the issue of guidance by the Commissioner and the making of further and related provisions by order of the Secretary of State. The Secretary of State is responsible, among other things, for setting the maximum level of monetary penalty.[77]

What is a Monetary Penalty Notice?

The notice is a formal notice served on the data controller by the Commissioner **20–63** requiring him to pay to the Commissioner, within the period set out in the notice, an amount determined by the Commissioner.[78] The amount must be set out in the notice. The statutory maximum is £500,000. The notice must comply with the requirements set out in the relevant orders. The Commissioner does not retain the payment. It is paid into the Consolidated Fund.[79]

---

[76] reg.31(2) as amended by SI 2011/1208.
[77] s.67(4)(5)(ca) and ss.55A(5) and 55B(3)(b).
[78] S.55A(4)(5)(6).
[79] s.55A(8).

Background and implementation

20–64 Section 55 was inserted into the Act by s.144 of the Criminal Justice and Immigration Act 2008. Parts of s.144(1) and (2) came into effect on October 1, 2009 to enable work to be carried out on the preparation of the supporting and related guidance and regulations. The maximum level of penalty and details of the procedural requirements were set in the Data Protection (Monetary Penalties)(Maximum Penalty and Notice) Regulations 2010[80] and the Data Protection (Monetary Penalties) Order 2010.[81] Guidance was issued by the Commissioner as required by s.55C in January 2010[82] and the supporting orders came into force on the April 6, 2010. The first penalties issued under these powers took effect in November the same year.

Lord Bach, speaking for the Government in Grand Committee in the House of Lords on the introduction of the order on March 1, 2010 reminded the House that there was widespread support for the introduction of increased powers for the Commissioner:

> "In particular, your Lordships will remember that the Data Sharing Review Report, the Thomas-Walport report, published in July 2008, specifically called for stronger penalties and sanctions and for the Information Commissioner to be given increased powers and resources to carry out his duties more effectively."

He also explained the work which had taken place to set the level of fine:

> "More recently, in November and December last year, we held a public consultation on the Government's proposal to set the maximum amount for civil monetary penalties at £500,000. The large majority of respondents agreed that there was a need for such a power and supported its immediate introduction. In addition, there was cross-party support in another place for the introduction of this power.
>
> Additionally, we have worked closely with the Information Commissioner's Office and involved other stakeholders in the development of this policy. We held two stakeholder events to discuss the new regulations and the commissioner's guidance on civil monetary penalties. The Information Commissioner's guidance was also available for comment on the ICO website."

The consultation was relatively short (six weeks) but had been preceded by a more informal series of discussions with data controllers and other regulators. The Government has undertaken to review the level of the penalty after a three year period.[83]

In the Regulatory Action Policy the Commissioner has stated that the penalties will be used as both a sanction and a deterrent.

---

[80] SI 2010/31.
[81] SI 2010/910.
[82] Information Commissioner's Guidance about the issue of monetary penalties prepared and issued under s.55C of the Data Protection Act 1998. Presented to Parliament an d ordered by the House of commons to be printed January 12, 2010.
[83] Lord Bach speaking on March 1, 2010 Grand Chamber.

The nature of civil penalties

The power to impose civil penalties has become more common among regulators **20–65** in the UK over the last few years. They are something of hybrid between criminal proceedings and true civil enforcement. They are punitive in nature and may often carry very heavy fines. Given these factors it is possible that they would be regarded as equivalent to criminal penalties under the European Convention on Human Rights and the parties subject to them would be entitled to the protection of art.6, the right to a fair trial. The European Court of Human Rights has held that the name given to a sanction by the country imposing it is not the deciding factor in determining whether a sanction is criminal or not, although if it is classed as criminal by the State it will be regarded by the Court as criminal. If a sanction is classed as civil but carries all the hallmarks of being a criminal one then the procedure to convict any person of it must meet the requirements of art.6.[84] As will be seen the procedure to be followed before service of a monetary penalty is a formal one and there is a formal right of appeal. The question of the essential nature of the sanction may also be relevant to the question of whether a data controller will be able to insure against the fines. Increasingly insurers are offering products which will insure against the consequences of breaches for example where a breach of security involves costs of investigation and notification to individuals. Criminal fines are not recoverable from insurance under the maxim *ex turpi causa*, which means a person cannot recover for damage which is the consequence of their own criminal or quasi-criminal act. In *Safeway v Twigger*[85] the Court of Appeal held that fines imposed on Safeway under the Competition Act 1998 could not be recovered against their directors (and thence against the insurers). However, in that case Safeway had accepted that the maxim applied to the fines. It should be noted that if a loss is not directly attributable to a criminal act or if the act is not criminal the loss may be insurable. It is our view, on balance, that monetary penalty will not be insurable losses.

Exemptions

There are two categories of exempt data controller; a few controllers are exempt **20–66** by virtue of their constitutional positions but more importantly for ordinary data controllers, there is an absolute exemption where the contravention has been discovered as a result of an audit carried out by the Commissioner.

In the first category the powers are not exercisable against the Crown Estate Commissioners or any of the persons listed in s.63(3). That section covers the Royal Household, the Duchy of Lancaster and the Duchy of Cornwall. For each of these a designated individual acts as the responsible data controller. In respect of the Royal Household it is the Keeper of the Privy Purse; in the case of the Duchies the person so appointed by the Chancellor of the Duchy of Lancaster and the Duke of Cornwall respectively.[86]

---

[84] *Adolf v Austria*, ECtHR, March 26 1982, Series A no.49; *Engel v Netherlands*, ECtHR, 1976, Series A no.22.
[85] EWCA Civ 1472.
[86] s.55A(9).

In the second category, the Commissioner cannot serve an assessment notice if the breach has come to his attention in connection with an audit which he has carried out, either a mandatory audit or one for which the controller has volunteered.

The wording of the provision is interesting. Section 55A(3A) provides as follows:

"The Commissioner may not be satisfied as mentioned in subsection (1) by virtue of any matter which comes to the Commissioner's attention as a result of anything done in pursuance of—

(a)   An assessment notice;
(b)   An assessment under section 51(7)".

Assessments carried out voluntarily pursuant to s.51(7) under notice have been considered earlier. The effect is not only to exempt the relevant breach from the exercise of the Commissioner's powers but appears to place a wider restrain on the powers of the Commissioner to make negative findings in relation to any breach that comes to light during an audit. It raises the question as to how far the Commissioner is constrained in the exercise of other aspects of his powers. The possibility that the Commissioner would take enforcement action against a data controller as a result of matters that came to light as a result of an audit has always acted as a bar to the up-take of voluntary audits. This section clarifies the point that no penalty notices can be served as a result of contraventions found as a result of such audit but leaves open the question of other action. The provision means that the Commissioner cannot be satisfied that the matters set out in subs.(1) are met. Presumably he could be satisfied that there has been a contravention although one which was neither knowing nor reckless nor of a kind likely to cause substantial damage or distress.

Clearly this is a legal fiction. As a matter of fact there will inevitably be matters which come to the attention of the Commissioner as a result of assessment notices or voluntary audits which are significant and serious contraventions, are knowing or reckless and could cause real damage or distress. Whatever the facts, legally the Commissioner cannot be satisfied that the threshold for his powers to issue penalty notices is met.

20–67   The question must arise therefore as to whether he would be able to use his other powers in such a case, for example to serve an enforcement notice or take any other regulatory action. As an example the Commissioner may serve an enforcement notice if he is satisfied that a data controller has contravened or is contravening any of the data protection principles. In deciding whether to serve such a notice he must consider whether the contravention has caused or is likely to cause any person damage or distress. The material differences between this and the penalty notice provisions are that the penalty notice requires there to be a *serious*contravention and that the damage or distress must be *substantial.*

It is submitted that subs.55A(3A) would not prevent the Commissioner from serving an enforcement notice as the threshold for the service of such a notice is lower however he could possibly be estopped from alleging in any statement of fact in support of such a notice that the facts met the tests required for a penalty notice.

Special purposes

As is explained in Ch.17, the Act includes wide a very wide exemption for the special purposes. Where the conditions of the exemption apply, this exempts personal data processed for those purposes from the individual rights and all the principles except principle 7 (security). It follows that personal data processed for the special purposes will only be at risk of a monetary penalty order either where the conditions of the exemption are not made out or where there is a breach of security. Section 55E provides for the Secretary of State to make further provisions in connection with monetary penalty notices and the notices of intent which must precede them in respect of the special purposes. Section 55E (2)(a) states that an order may provide that a monetary penalty notice may not be served on a data controller with respect to the processing of personal data for the special purposes except in circumstances specified in the order. Given the wide exemption already available for the processing for these purposes it is difficult to see any justification for further restrictions on the Commissioner's powers in respect of them however the power has been provided. The two orders made to date do not include any provisions dealing with the special purposes.

20–68

Further provisions covered by order

Section 55E(2) provides that the orders made by the Secretary of State may also cover:

20–69

- the cancellation or variation of notices;
- rights of appeal to the First Tier Tribunal (Information Rights);
- the procedure for such appeals; and
- further rights of appeal.

These have been covered by orders and the substantive provisions are covered under the relevant headings below.

Power to amend the Act

Section 55E(3) and (4) include the following further provisions:

20–70

"(3)   An order under this section may apply any provision of this Act with such modifications as may be specified in the order,

(4)   An order under this section may amend this Act".

This appears to be limited to the provisions dealing with monetary penalty notices and allows for a power to use secondary legislation to amend the provisions dealing with monetary penalties or to disapply it in any circumstances and for any reason. It is difficult to see why this was required. We can trace nothing in the consultation about the monetary penalty notice provisions which touches on this or in the Commissioner's Guidance or the Government statement when s.55 was introduced.

What is covered by the power?

20–71   A monetary penalty notice can be served for a contravention of s.4(4). This is the provision which requires data controllers to comply with the data protection principles in relation to all personal data with respect to which they are the data controller. As principle 6 incorporates the obligation to respect the rights of data subjects it follows that a penalty notice can also be served for failure to comply with the data subject's rights as well.

Guidance

20–72   Under s.55C, the Commissioner must prepare and issue guidance on how he proposes to exercise his functions in respect of the imposition of monetary penalties. The guidance must deal in particular with the circumstances in which he would consider it appropriate to issue a monetary penalty notice and how he will determine the amount of the penalty.[87] The Secretary of State must be consulted and the Commissioner may lay it before each House of Parliament before being issued.[88] The Commissioner must arrange for the publication of any guidance issued in such form and manner as he considers appropriate and may alter or replace the guidance. If he does so the same procedure must be applied to the replacement guidance.[89] The Commissioner issued his first guidance "Information Commissioner's Guidance about the issue of monetary penalties prepared and issued under section 55C(1) of the Data Protection Act 1998" in January 2010. In the analysis of the new powers below we have referred to the relevant examples from the guidance.

Grounds for imposing a penalty

20–73   A penalty notice is essentially punitive rather than restorative. As with other forms of enforcement the Commissioner has a discretion as to whether to use these powers. A penalty notice may be issued at the same time as an enforcement notice if the Commissioner considers that the controller also needs to take steps to set matters right for the future. He may serve a controller with a notice if he is satisfied on three counts as follows:

1.   That there has been a serious contravention of the principles by the data controller;
2.   The contravention was of a kind likely to cause substantial damage or substantial distress and either
3.   The contravention was deliberate or the data controller knew or ought to have known that there was a risk that the contravention would occur and that if it did occur such a contravention would be of a kind likely to cause substantial damage or substantial distress and failed to take reasonable steps to prevent the contravention.

---

[87] s.55C(2)(a) and (b).
[88] s.55C(5) and (6).
[89] s.55C (7)(8)(3).

As noted above the threshold test is clearly higher than the threshold test for service of an enforcement notice. On the face of the provision therefore it appears that this would only be exercisable in the most serious cases however the examples given in the statutory guidance issued by the Commissioner seems to suggest that he may incline to take a generous view of what amounts to a serious contravention. Clearly it is difficult to provide detailed guidance when the provision is new and data controllers will only really have a guide to the Commissioner's approach when the powers have been sufficiently used and tested. The guidance states that he will approach the question of whether a contravention is serious as an objective test and will "aim to reflect the reasonable expectations of individuals and society and ensure that any harm is genuine and capable of explanation." It also states that it is possible that a single breach may be sufficient to trigger the use of the powers. All of which statements would seem wholly reasonable. However, the examples of possible serious contraventions which are given are as follows:

> "The failure by a data controller to take adequate security measures (use of encrypted files and devices, operational procedures, guidance etc..) resulting in the loss of a compact disc holding personal data.
>
> Medical records containing sensitive personal data are lost following a security breach by a data controller during an office move."

In both of these cases it is possible that the contravention could be insignificant for example, in the first case the personal data on the disk might be limited in scope and amount and in the second records, although lost, may still be somewhere inside the data controller's offices.

The Commissioner makes clear that a range of factors will be taken into account in determining whether a particular contravention is serious as follows:

> "1.   The nature of the personal data concerned.
> 2.   The duration and extent of the contravention.
> 3.   The number of individuals actually or potentially affected
> 4.   The fact that it related to an issue of public importance.
> 5.   The contravention was due to either deliberate or negligent behaviour on the part of the data controller".

The difficulty of separating the relevant factors becomes apparent when one considers this list. While the first four factors would appear to be relevant to determining whether a contravention is serious in any particular case, arguably factor 5, the question of deliberate or negligent behaviour does not of itself relate to the seriousness of the breach but the extent of the data controller's responsibility and is of itself a separate test that must be met before the power is exercisable.

The second test is that the contravention was of a kind likely to cause substantial damage or substantial distress. Note that there is no requirement that such damage or distress must have been caused. The Commissioner will have to make an assessment of likelihood in any given case. The guidance does not provide any detail on the assessment of likelihood and simply states that the Commissioner will consider whether it was "more likely than not" to cause substantial damage or substantial distress. This appears to put the test on the balance of probabilities. It might be argued that the appropriate threshold should be higher and should be require the Commissioner to be satisfied beyond reasonable doubt that such damage or distress could be caused, given the clearly punitive nature of the power.

The assessment of what amounts to substantial damage or distress raises a number of points. The damage or distress need not be suffered by data subjects. It is possible therefore that a financial loss by a commercial organisation could be taken into account. It is also possible that distress might be caused to someone who is not a data subject in relation to the specific controller. The decision as to whether damage or distress is "substantial" is clearly a difficult test. The Commissioner's guidance includes the following section:

> "The likelihood of damage or distress suffered by an individual will have to be considerable in importance, value, degree, amount or extent. The Commissioner will assess both the likelihood and extent of the damage or distress as objectively as possible. In assessing the likelihood of damage or distress suffered by an individual the Commissioner will consider whether the damage or distress is merely perceived or of real substance".

The example provided is of inaccurate personal data held by an ex-employer disclosed by way of an employment reference resulting in the loss of a job opportunity for an individual.

The guidance describes damage as any financially quantifiable loss suffered by an individual such as loss of profit, earnings or other things. The example given is identity fraud following a security breach in which financial data is lost. Distress is described as any injury to feelings, harm or anxiety suffered by an individual and the example given is of worry and anxiety suffered by an individual that details will be made public when medical details are stolen in a security breach even if that eventuality does not occur.

It is noted that the Commissioner states that he will seek to assess likelihood and extent of damage or distress as objectively as possible. In relation to assessment of distress it is assumed that this means he will consider whether an ordinary person of average fortitude would be likely to suffer substantial distress if affected by the relevant circumstances. In relation to damage there will presumably be some notional financial threshold set although none has been included in the current guidance. Interestingly the examples given in the guidance are ones in which damage has been suffered or distress caused, but on the face of it neither of these are examples of substantial damage or distress. It is not clear whether the possibility of a contravention affecting large numbers of people in a relatively limited way could amount to substantial damage or distress.

Mental element

20–74 The third proviso requires that the Commissioner show a mental test attributable to the data controller. This requires either a deliberate contravention or a specific form of recklessness. This raises the question of how that knowledge and responsibility for the action must be shown. It is assumed that the test to be applied will be the state of mind or knowledge and actions of responsible persons employed by the relevant data controller. Where a data controller is an individual the tests will apply to that individual. However, most data controllers are corporate entities or public bodies. Where there is a mental element to a criminal action it must be shown that a person who is a "directing mind" of the organisation has the requisite knowledge or recklessness.[90] (See Ch.21 for a discussion of the point.) The penalty notice is not on the face of it a criminal provision however it is punitive and the procedure has many of the hallmarks of a criminal test (see discussion earlier). The test of the attribution of a directing mind may therefore not be required to meet the standard necessary in a criminal case but some mental element will be required. The level of seniority of relevant staff may perhaps be less important than the degree of relevant responsibility. A similar approach has been taken to prosecution for breach of health and safety legislation.[91]

Deliberate contravention

A deliberate contravention is one which goes beyond simply having knowledge to having some form of specific intent. The term was considered by the House of Lords in *Cave v Robinson Jarvis Rolf (a Firm)*.[92] The House canvassed two possible meanings of the term "deliberate"; the first simply that the relevant action is witting rather than inadvertent and the second that the action must not only be witting but must also require knowledge of the fact that the act amounts to wrongdoing. It is submitted that the term is clearly used in the second sense in s.55A(2). It will not be enough to show that the contravention was as a result of a deliberate act on the part of the data controller; the Commissioner will have to be satisfied that the data controller knew that the act amounted to a contravention and went ahead and did it anyway.

    These sorts of contraventions are likely to be rare among most data controllers; however, it does provide the Commissioner with an additional sanction against those who dishonestly obtain the personal data from a legitimate data controller. The usual circumstances in which this occurs are when a rogue employee copies a database or parts of a database and uses the data for their own purposes. On occasions the purpose may be to try to defraud or trick the data subjects. The Commissioner's guidance on the question of a deliberate contravention includes two examples of deliberate contravention that, on the face of it, appear more properly to fit under the second heading. The cases where:

20–75

> "The data controller was aware of and did not follow specific advice published by the Commissioner or others and relevant to the contravention".

This raises a number of questions. One of the first questions is who are the "others" whose views would be relevant? It may be assumed that this is a reference to regulators for a specific sector such as the FSA which have a statutory remit to consider standards of compliance which interface with data protection such as security. However, it is submitted that the number of "others"

---

[90] *Tesco v Nattrass* [1972] A.C. 153.
[91] *R v British Steel* 1994 CA.
[92] [2002] UKHL 18.

whose advice would be relevant is limited and it would be preferable from the point of view of clarity and certainty for data controllers if the Commissioner were to specify the relevant bodies.

The second question raised is what the position would be if the data controller (acting by its appropriate officer) is unaware of the advice published. The Commissioner publishes a range of advisory materials. The list can be found on the website. The document list is not dated although when you go into specific documents most have a date at the end. The only way that a controller can know that there is new guidance on a specific area is to keep a watching brief on the site. However, unless he or she is aware of the existing material and manages to spot something new it may be missed. It is submitted that if the Commissioner is going to make awareness of his guidance a relevant issue he will have to take more targeted steps to bring it to the attention of data controllers.

The second factor regarded as a deliberate contravention is where

"the contravention followed a series of similar contraventions by the data controller and no action had been taken to rectify what had caused the original contraventions".

This will be a question of fact and there is no guidance on what the Commissioner is likely to regard as "similar" contraventions or the period over which they must occur in order to be taken into account. On the face of it as long as some action was taken the test is not met however again it is assumed that the Commissioner will apply the test in practice as being no proper and effective action was taken to rectify the original contraventions.

The example of a deliberate breach is more straightforward as follows:

"A marketing company collects personal data stating it is for the purpose of a competition and then, without consent, knowingly discloses the data to populate a tracing database for commercial purposes without informing the individuals concerned."

Knew or ought to have known

20–76   The second type of mental state is a form of recklessness. The data controller must either know or should know of the risk of such a contravention and that if it occurred it would be likely to cause substantial damage or distress. The further provision is that the data controller failed to address the risk.

The Guidance lists a number of tests by which it can be ascertained whether the mental element can be satisfied:

"

The likelihood of the contravention should have been apparent to a reasonably prudent data controller.

The data controller had adopted a cavalier approach to compliance and failed to take reasonable steps to prevent the contravention, for example, not putting basic security provisions in place.

The data controller had failed to carry out any sort of risk assessment and there is no evidence, whether verbally or in writing, that the data controller had recognised the risks of handling personal data and taken reasonable steps to address them.

The data controller did not have good corporate governance and/or audit arrangements in place to establish clear lines of responsibility for preventing contraventions of this type.

The data controller had no specific procedures or processes in place which may have prevented the contravention (for example, a robust compliance regime or other monitoring mechanisms).

Guidance or codes of practice published by the Commissioner or others and relevant to the contravention, for example, the BS ISO/IEC 27001 standard on information security management, were available to the data controller and ignored or not given appropriate weight."

Failed to take reasonable steps

The question of what steps would be reasonable will be a question of fact in each case assessing the risks involved. The guidance describes the reasonable steps as follows:

20–77

"The Commissioner is more likely to consider that the data controller has taken reasonable steps to prevent the contravention if any of the following apply:

a) The data controller had carried out a risk assessment or there is other evidence (such as appropriate policies, procedures, practices or processes in place or advice and guidance given to staff) that the data controller had recognised the risks of handling personal data and taken steps to address them;

b) The data controller had good governance and/or audit arrangements in place to establish clear lines of responsibility for preventing contraventions of this type;

c) The data controller had appropriate policies, procedures, practices or processes in place and they were relevant to the contravention, for example, a policy to encrypt all laptops and removable media in relation to the loss of a laptop by an employee of the data controller;

d) Guidance or codes of practice published by the Commissioner or others and relevant to the contravention were implemented by the data controller, for example, the data controller can demonstrate compliance with the BS ISO/IEC 27001 standard on information security management".

In other words the obverse of the factors which will indicate that the data controller knew or ought to have known that there was a risk. The list provides a helpful resource for practitioners who are advising clients on the appropriate steps to put in place to address their compliance programme.

The Guidance also makes clear that:

"This list is not exhaustive and the Commissioner will consider whether the data controller has taken reasonable steps on a case by case basis. In doing so he will take into account the resources available to the data controller but this alone will not be a determining factor."

Taken together however they amount to a positive statement of how data controllers should address the issues of compliance, assessment of risk, introduction of corporate responsibility and governance, implementation of procedures which follow best practice and routine checking or audit to assess whether the procedures are adequately addressing the risks.

The Guidance recognises the questions of proportionality and risk and gives as an example a case where the controller has taken swift and effective remedial action following a breach.

Other considerations

20–78   In the Guidance the Commissioner lists two other considerations which he will take into account in assessing whether a monetary penalty is appropriate. These are:

> "The need to maximise the deterrent effect of the monetary penalty by setting an example, where there are grounds for a penalty to be imposed, to other data controllers where it is necessary so as to counter the prevalence of such contraventions",

and:

> "The data controller had expressly, and without reasonable cause, refused to submit to an Assessment which could reasonably have been expected to reveal a risk of the contravention".

The first deals with the need to set examples so that others are put on notice. In the first cases dealt with the Commissioner has taken action where the contraventions have been the result of clear lack of care or standards which he has required and against controllers with appropriate levels of resource to be able to deal with compliance. The statement appears to simply refer to the appropriate level at which penalties will be set and does not suggest that any particular data controllers will be held up as examples and given higher or harsher punishments than others, an approach which would require some care.

The second consideration may give rise to more debate. There are two provisions which allow the Commissioner to carry out an assessment. One is mandatory which is not applicable here and the other is voluntary. There is no legal obligation on any data controller to submit to a voluntary assessment. In the Guidance however the Commissioner appears to be using the threat of a fine or a higher fine as a lever to persuade data controllers to allow the Commissioner to audit their processing. It is submitted that this would be an irrelevant consideration and one that should not be taken into account in deciding on a fine. While the Commissioner might argue that allowing the Commissioner to audit would have been a reasonable step which could have dealt with a defined risk there is no reason why such an audit should be the remit of the Commissioner. In circumstances in which a data controller had ascertained a risk which it was appropriate to address by going through an audit process it could indeed be relevant that the controller had failed to address it by failing to carry out the audit. However there is no obligation to allow the Commissioner to do that.

Procedure

The procedure is set out in section 55B and the Data Protection (Monetary   **20–79**
Penalties) Order 2010[93] and the Data Protection (Monetary penalties) (Maximum
penalty and Notices) Regulations 2010.[94]

Under s.55B(1) before serving a monetary penalty notices the Commissioner
must serve the data controller with a notice of intent stating that the
Commissioner intends to serve such a notice and informing him that he may
make written representations in relation to the proposal within a specified
period.[95] The notice must contain the following information:

- the name and address of the data controller;
- the grounds on which the Commissioner proposes to serve the penalty
  notice including;
- the nature of the personal data involved in the contravention;
- a description of the circumstances of the contravention;
- the reasons that the Commissioner considers that the contravention is
  serious;
- the reason that the Commissioner considers that the contravention is of a
  kind likely to cause substantial damage or substantial distress; and
- whether the Commissioner considers that the contravention was deliberate
  or reckless within the meaning of s.55A(3).[96]

The notice must also indicate the amount of the proposed penalty and any
aggravating or mitigating factors that the Commissioner has taken into account as
well as the date that the notice is proposed to be served.[97]

The data controller has a right to make written representations to the   **20–80**
Commissioner and the Commissioner must take any representations made into
account before making a final decision.[98] The representations may be in respect
of any aspect of the issues in question so they may deal with the facts, the
judgement as to whether the contravention was serious or might cause significant
damage or distress, the mental elements, the amount of the proposed fines or the
exercise of the Commissioner's discretion.

If the Commissioner decides to serve a notice after considering any   **20–81**
representations the notice must contain the same categories of information as the
notice of intent as listed above, plus details of the notice of intent and whether the
Commissioner received written representations, plus of course the amount of the
penalty including any aggravating or mitigating factors that the Commissioner
has taken into account when settling the amount. In addition it must set out
details of how the money is to be paid, the rights of appeal available both against
the imposition of the penalty and against the amount, and the Commissioner's
powers to enforce payment.[99]

---

[93] SI 2010/910.
[94] SI 2010/31.
[95] s.55B(2).
[96] See above for a discussion of this provision.
[97] SI 2010/31 reg.3.
[98] SI 2010/910 reg.2.
[99] SI 2010/31 art.4.

Timescales

20–82 Once the Commissioner has served a notice of intent he has a period of six months within which to determine the case. If he does not serve a monetary penalty notice within that time it appears that he must re-serve the notice of intent before proceeding.[100] The wording does not appear to preclude the Commissioner from starting the process again by serving a new notice of intent although one would anticipate that he would be subject to serious criticism if this occurred without very good reason. The period specified for the submission of the written representations must not be less that 21 days starting with the day after the date of service of the notice.[101] The Commissioner may not serve a penalty notice until that time has expired.[102] When the Commissioner serves a penalty notice he must specify how long the data controller has in which to pay the amount due. This must not be less that 28 days beginning with the first day after the date of service.[103] The Commissioner cannot enforce the payment of the penalty until that period has expired.[104] Nor can the Commissioner enforce payment until the period allowed for an appeal to the Tribunal has expired whether against the penalty notice or any variation of it.[105] In most cases one would expect that the period within which an appeal could be brought to be the same period of 28 days; however this provision presumably allows for the possibility that the period for appeal may be longer than the 28 day period whether because the Commissioner has allowed a longer period or because the Tribunal has extended the period. There is no specific provision that relieves the data controller from paying the penalty if he appeals. However, as Commissioner cannot enforce the payment until all relevant appeals against the notice or any variation of it have been decided or withdrawn[106] data controllers may decide to withhold payment until after an appeal has been decided. There are no provisions to allocate interest accrued during the period of an appeal and, interestingly, no provisions which state that the Commissioner must repay any penalty paid if his notice is overturned on appeal. It is assumed however that a data controller who has paid pending a determination on appeal would be able to successfully sue for the return of his money if there was any dispute.

Level of penalty

20–83 The penalty has been set at a maximum of £500,000 by the relevant order. The Guidance sets out the issues that the Commissioner will take into account in setting the level of penalties. It also notes that there may be wide variations in the size of monetary penalties. It does not indicate any likely tariffs associated with particular factors however it does state that once precedents are available then the Commissioner will issue further guidance so it appears that tariff guidelines will emerge as the penalties become more common.

---

[100] SI 2010/910 reg.3(2).
[101] SI 2010/910 reg.3(1).
[102] s.55B(4).
[103] SI 2010/910 reg.3(3).
[104] SI 2010/910 reg.6(a).
[105] SI 2010/910 reg.6(c).
[106] SI 2010/910 reg.6(b).

In the introduction, the general point is made that the level must be sufficiently meaningful to act both as a sanction and a deterrent and that the Commissioner will take into account the sector, for example if the controller is a voluntary organisation, the size, financial and other resources of the data controller. It goes on to state that the purpose of the penalty is not to "impose undue financial hardship on an otherwise responsible data controller". As a general rule a data controller with substantial financial resources is more likely to attract a higher monetary penalty than a data controller with limited resources for a similar contravention.

The guidance acknowledges that the factors which will be relevant to the level of monetary penalty are very closely related to those which are relevant to determining whether a penalty should be imposed at all. The guidance lists the nature of the contravention, the effect of the contravention, the behaviour of the data controller and the impact that the fine will have on the controller as relevant factors. The first three have been examined earlier ; the considerations related to the impact on the data controller however are specific to this part of the guidance. These are listed as follows:

> "
> The Commissioner will aim to eliminate any financial gain or benefit obtained by the data controller from non-compliance with the Act;
>
> The Commissioner will take into account the sector, for example, whether the data controller is a voluntary organisation and also the size, financial and other resources of the data controller;
>
> Whether the fine will fall on individuals and if so their status;
>
> The Commissioner will consider the likely impact of the penalty on the data controller, in particular financial and reputational impact;
>
> The Commissioner will take into account any proof of genuine financial hardship which may be supplied. The purpose of a monetary penalty notice is not to impose undue financial hardship on an otherwise responsible data controller. In appropriate cases the Commissioner will adjust the monetary penalty where, for example, a data controller made a loss the previous year".

Penalties must be paid by BACS transfer or cash but if the payment is received within 28 calendar days of the notice being served the Commissioner will reduce the monetary penalty by 20 per cent. This last is apparently standard Treasury policy for the payment of fines. It clearly is used to encourage early payment however there is no statutory basis for it in the DPA. Using the statutory mechanism the only way that it appears it would work would be for the controller to pay the original amount on the basis that the Commissioner would then vary the notice to show a penalty with the 20 per cent reduction and refund the overpayment.

Variation and cancellation

There are specific provisions dealing with variation of notices and cancellation. It is not immediately obvious why the Commissioner would chose to vary or cancel a penalty notice once he has been through the complex procedure for determining

20–84

and serving one (other than to give the 20 per cent reduction described above) but he is empowered to do so and if in varying a notice he reduces the amount payable he must repay any money paid in excess of the new amount.[107] Any variation or cancellation must be done by giving written notice to the person on whom the original penalty notice was served.[108] Where the notice is used to vary the penalty notice it must identify the original notice and state how it has been varied. There is no obligation to explain why it has been varied. The variations cannot make the notice more punitive so the variations cannot increase the specified penalty or reduce the period allowed for payment of the amount.[109] Once a notice has been cancelled the Commissioner cannot take any further action under the monetary penalty provisions in respect of the contravention which gave rise to it.[110] It appears that he would be able to take other actions so there is barrier to his cancelling a monetary penalty notice and taking enforcement action against a data controller instead.

Appeals

20–85 The recipient of a notice may appeal against the issue of the notice or against the amount of the penalty.[111] It is to be expected that appellants will appeal on both grounds. Appeals may also be lodged against a decision of the Commissioner to vary a penalty notice.[112] The appeals are to be dealt with under s.49 in the same way as any other appeals against the use of the Commissioner's powers under the Act.

Enforcement

20–86 If the data controller fails to pay the amount due within the specified period the Commissioner may enforce the payment in the county court or the High Court in England, Wales and Northern Ireland as if the penalty were payable under an order of the relevant court.[113] In other words the court can offer no possibility of the data controller arguing that the amount is not payable. In Scotland it may be enforced in the equivalent manner. It would be enforced as if it were an extract registered decree arbitral bearing a warrant for execution issued by the sheriff court of any sheriffdom of Scotland.[114]

The level of the fines will be reviewed in three years.

---

[107] SI 2010/910 reg.4(6).
[108] SI 2010/910 regs 4(1) and 5(1).
[109] SI 2010/910 reg.4(3) and (4).
[110] SI 2010/910 reg.5(2).
[111] s.55B(5).
[112] SI 2010/31 art.4(5).
[113] s.55D(2)(4).
[114] s.55D(3).

Cases published to date

As at the time of writing in August 2012, 23 penalty notices are listed on the ICO website with fines totally over £2 million since April 6, 2010. Many are for breach of security and include fines against local authorities, NHS organisations and private bodies.

20–87

SERVICE OF NOTICES

Section 64 provides that individuals may serve any of the notices under the Act by electronic means as long as the resulting notice is received in legible form and capable of being used for subsequent reference. This provision does not apply to notices serviced by the Commissioner in the exercise of his regulatory functions. Service of notices by the Commissioner is covered under section 65 which sets out how notices may be served on individuals, bodies corporate or incorporate and partnerships in Scotland. The provisions are without prejudice to other lawful methods of service or giving notice. A notice may be served on an individual by delivering it to him, sending it by post to his usual or last known place of residence or business, or leaving it for him at that place. A notice may be served on a body corporate or incorporate by sending it by post to or leaving it at its principal office addressed to the proper officer. A notice may be served on a partnership in Scotland by addressing it to the partnership and either posting it to or leaving it at the principal office of the partnership.

20–88

RIGHTS OF APPEAL

A person upon whom an enforcement, information, third party information, assessment or monetary penalty notices, including fixed monetary penalty notices under PECR, is given various rights of appeal by s.48 of the 1998 Act. All appeals are to the First Tier Tribunal (Information Rights)(see Ch.28).

20–89

The rights are:

- the right to appeal against any notice[115];
- the right to appeal against the refusal of an application by the recipient to cancel or vary an enforcement notice[116];
- the right to appeal against the decision by the Commissioner to include a statement that the notice is urgent and the right to appeal against any timescale consequently imposed[117]; and
- the right to appeal against a determination made under s.45.

Section 48 needs to be read in conjunction with Sch.6 of the 1998 Act which provides more detail on appeal procedures. The composition and powers of the Tribunal are covered in Ch.28.

---

[115] s.48(1).

[116] s.48(2). The ability to make such an application is set out in s.41(2).

[117] s.40(3). The procedures for urgent notices are set out in ss.40(8), 43(5) and 44(6).

USE OF UNDERTAKINGS

20–90 The use of undertakings has become more and more common and a glance at the Commissioner's website shows that the numbers are increasing steadily. Undertakings are the regulatory weapon of choice and for that reason they are considered here in some detail.

The practice of accepting undertakings is not new. The Commissioner accepted undertakings under the previous Act where he had received representations and was satisfied that no enforcement notice was required. They were however relatively rare and were an outcome of the enforcement process rather than regarded as an end in themselves. It is clear however from the numbers listed on the Commissioner's site compared to the relatively rare appearance of enforcement notices that undertakings are now regarded as the first response of the regulator. The benefit to the regulator of course is that undertakings cannot be appealed to the Tribunal and to the data controller that breach of an undertaking is not itself a criminal offence.

20–91 The change appears to have arisen in around 2007 when the Commissioner accepted undertakings from a number of financial organisations such as banks and building societies in respect of concerns about the security of hard copies of personal data about customers. There had been a lot of publicity about security breaches at various banks and the Commissioner had been the recipient of a number of complaints about such security. The publicity coincided with the campaigns being waged against the imposition of bank charges for unauthorised overdrafts. The Commissioner did not move to enforcement action against the banks but asked for undertakings instead. In the last edition of this text we commented that the existence of the undertakings might owe more to the finance industry's unwillingness to upset the regulator than any real breach of their legal obligations. However, they have since become the first choice for regulatory activity. The website shows that 100 undertakings have been given to the Commissioner since January 1, 2011 to the date of writing (August 2012). The data controller is offered an undertaking where the Commissioner considers that he has sufficient grounds to take enforcement action. If an undertaking is offered and the data controller refuses to agree to give one then the Commissioner will usually move to enforcement. It appears that the Commissioner now ensures that the grounds for an enforcement action are in place before seeking an undertaking but this has not occurred on every occasion in the past. In January 2008, Marks and Spenser Plc suffered the loss of some personal data about staff pensions. The actual loss was the fault of one of their agents who acted as a data processor. The Commissioner sought an undertaking from Marks and Spenser which it was reluctant to provide as it took the view it had taken all due care to select a processor and was not in breach of its obligations. The Commissioner served an enforcement notice however it is understood that the notice had to be withdrawn although there is no information available on the Commissioner's website.

Effect of undertakings

In giving an undertaking the data controller states that it will take certain actions. **20–92**
The question of the status of such undertakings and how they might be enforced
is an interesting one. The traditional view would be that undertakings operate as
binding contractual agreements. In consideration of the regulator agreeing not to
exercise his formal enforcement powers the data controller agrees to take certain
actions to remedy any agreed breaches of the law. If the data controller breaches
the terms of the undertaking the Commissioner could take High Court action
against the controller and seek a mandatory injunction to force the data controller
to comply with his undertaking. However this is not how undertakings appear to
be viewed by the Commissioner, rather they serve as formal public warning
notices to data controllers.

It is unlikely that any of the undertakings listed on the Commissioner's site
could be enforced by an action in the High Court as the Court would only be able
to enforce an undertaking where the terms were clear and the undertaking
specified the actions which had been agreed and which the controller had failed
to honour. A mandatory order would be sought by the Commissioner and the
terms of a mandatory order must be sufficiently clear that a party subject to such
an order can be in no doubt about what is required of him. If the undertakings
which have been given to the Commissioner are reviewed it appears that none of
them would be able to meet the necessary tests of specificity and clarity to be the
basis of a mandatory order. The Commissioner's officers habitually request
undertakings in the most expansive terms. As an example, even if the incident
which has drawn the controller to the attention of the Commissioner's office is a
specific breach of security (such as loss of a set of forms) at a specific site (such
as a particular shop) in a specific business (such as the retail arm of a company)
the Commissioner's office is likely to require the controller to undertake that all
the companies in the group will comply with the seventh principle in respect of
all personal data at all sites in the future. The Commissioner's position is then if
the data controller is responsible for another breach of the principle in respect of
which the undertaking was given the Commissioner will consider taking
enforcement action rather than accepting another undertaking. If the undertaking
is very wide, for example that the controller will comply with the seventh
principle, then this poses a risk for the data controller that a subsequent breach
which is entirely separate from the original breach and concerned with a different
aspect of the Principle could give rise to an enforcement notice.

This approach raises problems for data controllers. When confronted with a
request for a wide undertaking most will seek to have the terms of the
undertaking narrowed down to mitigate the risk of a subsequent breach not
related to the original breach giving rise to formal action against them. On the
other hand data controllers generally do not want the undertaking narrowed to the
point at which the Commissioner could actually enforce it by seeking a
mandatory injunction.

To date there have been no public disputes around this issue between the
Commissioner and any data controllers. One must assume that the Commissioner's staff would recognise the unfairness in penalising someone for a subsequent

breach which was wholly unrelated to an earlier one simply because the controller had been persuaded to give a wide undertaking and that each case would be judged on its merits.

It should be noted that breach of an undertaking cannot of itself lead to a monetary penalty notice or to an enforcement notice. If there is a further occurrence the Commissioner must investigate and may only take action if he is satisfied that there has been a breach and the breach warrants formal action.

POWERS UNDER OTHER CONSUMER PROTECTION LEGISLATION

Enterprise Act 2002

20–93   The Commissioner had powers to require business to cease unlawful activities detrimental to consumers under the Stop Now Orders (EC Directive) Regulations 2001 made under the Fair Trading Act 1973. That Act was replaced by the Enterprise Act 2002 which implemented Directive 98/27/EC on injunctions for the protection of consumers' interest (the Injunctions Directive). Part 8 of the Enterprise Act (EA) deals with the enforcement of consumer protection legislation.

The EA gave stronger powers to the OFT and other bodies responsible for the enforcement of consumer law to seek court orders against businesses which breach certain consumer legislation. It enables injunctive action to be taken against businesses.

Under Pt 8, breaches of legislation are classed as either a domestic infringement or a community infringement. Domestic infringements relate to a wide range of UK laws listed in secondary legislation made under Pt 8. Community infringements are acts or omissions that breach provisions implementing directives which are specified in Sch.13 to the EA as amended by further secondary legislation.

There are three types of enforcers: general enforcers (the OFT and others with general responsibility for consumer protection), designated enforcers (organisations which are designated by the Secretary of State and are responsible for specific consumer protection laws) and a further category of Community enforcers.

An enforcer can be designated in respect of all infringements or only specified ones. The Commissioner is a designated enforcer in respect of Community and domestic infringements of the specified provisions.

The OFT has statutory responsibility for action taken in the UK in respect of either type of enforcement including the responsibility for the coordination of action by all enforcers. Part 8 allows enforcers to apply to the courts for an Enforcement Order to stop a business from breaching certain legislation where the breach harms the collective interests of consumers.

20–94   The predecessor regulations to PECR dealing with the use of telecommunications for direct marketing were specified in the EA 2002 and the ICO was designated as an enforcer in respect of them.[118] This was amended by SI 2005/2418,[119] under which the provisions of regs 19–24 of the Privacy and Electronic Communications (EC Directive) Regulations 2003 in their application to consumers in relation to the use of telecommunications services for direct marketing purposes, were substituted for the 1999 regulations.

It should be noted that the Commissioner is only a designated enforcer for these provisions of PECR and there is no equivalent designation under the DPA. It is understood that the Commissioner took action under these powers in 2007 but no details are available on the website.

Article 3 of Directive 2009/136/EC amended the relevant EC legislation[120] to include the revised provisions of EC 2002/58 art.13 as one of the instruments dealing with consumer protection which should be enforceable by injunctive action. Article 13 deals with the use of telecommunications for marketing and has been implemented by regs 19–26 and 30 and 32 of PECR. Regulations 16 and 17 of SI 2011/1208 implement this change, in effect adding regs 25, 26, 30 and 32 to the relevant provisions infringement of which is a Community Infringement under Pt 8 of the Enterprise Act.

The lead on enforcement is taken by the OFT and the OFT has set out a clear guidance on the taking of actions under these powers. Before taking any action the enforcer must consult the OFT and then give the business time to respond and give undertakings it will amend its behaviour. Proceedings must be brought by the most appropriate body and take into account other powers and regulatory mechanisms.

20–95

Unfair terms in Consumer Contract Regulations 1999 (UTCCR)[121]

The Commissioner is a qualifying body for the purposes of considering complaints and applying for injunctive relief against unfair terms under the 1999 UTCC Regulations.[122]

20–96

The Regulations apply to the terms of contracts entered into between a seller or supplier and a consumer. Terms which are mandated by law are excluded from scope.[123] All contract terms are covered unless they have been individually negotiated. There is little scope to avoid the impact of the Regulations as no pre-drafted term is regarded as "individually negotiated" and even if there is scope for negotiation on specific aspects the Regulations will apply if an overall assessment indicates that the consumer is dealing on a pre-formulated standard contract.[124] If the contract is covered by the Regulations than any term which causes a significant imbalance in the parties' rights and obligations arising under the contract, to the detriment of the consumer, will be regarded as unfair.[125]

---

[118] The Enterprise Act 2002 (Pt 8 Designated Enforcers: Criteria for designation, designation of Public Bodies as designated Enforcers and Transitional provisions) Order 2003 (SI 2002/1399).

[119] The Enterprise Act 2002 (Part 8 Community Infringements Specified UK Laws) (Amendment) Order 2005

[120] Regulation (EC) No.2006/2004 (the regulation on consumer protection cooperation).

[121] SI 1999/2083.

[122] SI 1999/2083 Sch.1.

[123] SI 1999/2083 reg.4.

[124] SI 1999/2083 reg.5.

[125] SI 1999/2083 reg.5.

Schedule 2 contains an "indicative and non-exhaustive list of the terms which may be regarded as unfair". None of the terms in Schedule 2 directly cover the use of information however a number may have relevance where a contract includes provisions dealing with the use of personal data. The list includes:

- terms irrevocably binding the consumer to terms with which he had no real opportunity of becoming acquainted before the conclusion of the contract;
- terms enabling the seller or supplier to alter the terms of the contract unilaterally without a valid reason which is specified in the contract; and
- terms enabling the seller or supplier to alter unilaterally without a valid reason any characteristics of the product or service to be provided.
- The terms in Sch.2 are indicative only. Regulation 6 provides that the unfairness of a contractual term shall be assessed, taking into account the nature of the goods or services for which the contract was concluded and by referring, at the time of conclusion of the contract, to all the circumstances attending the conclusion of the contract and to all the other terms of the contract or of another contract on which it is dependent.

20–97   Regulation 7 provides that a seller or supplier shall ensure that any written term of a contract is expressed in plain, intelligible language and if there is doubt about the meaning of a written term, the interpretation which is most favourable to the consumer shall prevail.

Clearly there are many hurdles to be overcome before the UTCC Regulations might come into play in relation to privacy policies or clauses dealing with the use of personal data, not least that the parties must be in a consumer/supplier relationship. Nevertheless the Regulations do appear to offer some protection from the most egregious of provisions. Privacy policies can be difficult to find on websites, the use of legalistic language which is difficult for ordinary users to understand has been widely criticised and it is common for such policies to state that the supplier may alter the terms of the privacy policy at its total discretion with no notice to the user.

20–98   An unfair term is not binding on a consumer.[126] However, in the arena of terms dealing with the use of personal data the consumer has no real redress as the use of the data is controlled by the data controller or collector of the information. The most potent weapon would be the use of an injunction to stop the seller/supplier using the term. A qualifying body may, with the blessing of the OFT, apply for an injunction (including an interim injunction) against any person appearing to the Director or that body to be using, or recommending use of, an unfair term drawn up for general use in contracts concluded with consumers.

The Commissioner has ancillary powers to obtain information and documents in order to facilitate consideration of a complaint that a contract term drawn up for general use is unfair; or ascertain whether a person has complied with an undertaking or court order as to the continued use, or recommendation for use, of a term in contracts concluded with consumers.[127]

20–99   While the power may appear to be useful it is doubtful whether, in most cases, it would be more effective than an enforcement notice. It is suggested that, if a

---

[126] SI 1999/2083 reg.8.
[127] SI 1999/2083 reg.13.

term is so unfair that it would fall foul of the UTCC Regulations, the collection and use of the relevant personal data under the term would be likely to amount to unfair processing of personal data in any event and it would be open to the ICO to take action under his wider powers. Nevertheless, there may be cases where these powers would be useful. As far as can be ascertained from the publicly available information this power has not yet been deployed by the ICO.

ENFORCEMENT OF DATA SUBJECT'S RIGHTS

The Commissioner may also enforce data subjects' rights as breaches of the principles. These are the rights to subject access[128]; to prevent processing likely to cause damage or distress[129]; to prevent direct marketing[130]; or to object to automated decision-making.[131] This is in addition to the rights of the data subjects to apply for court orders. These rights and their enforcement by the data subjects are discussed more fully in the chapters on data subject's rights (Chs 11–13).

20–100

Impact of the draft Regulation in brief[132]

The draft regulation includes specific powers for supervisory authorities and a complex mechanism to ensure that they cooperate and work together.

20–101

Powers of supervisory authorities

The duties of supervisory authorities are set out in Article 52 and include duties to hear complaints lodged by data subjects. Their powers are set out in art.53, under which the powers include powers to:

20–102

- order data controllers and processors to remedy breaches;
- order data controllers or processors to comply with data subjects' rights;
- order data controllers or processors to provide information;
- carry out prior checks and consultations;
- order rectification, erasure or destruction of data and notice to those to whom data have been disclosed;
- impose a ban on processing; and
- suspend data flows to third countries.

These are very similar to the existing powers of the Commissioner. The supervisory authority will also have investigative powers to access all personal data and information necessary and enter premises. The powers to enter premises must be exercised in accord with Member State law. They may also impose fines for breaches of the Regulation as set out in art.79 and have a power to bring

---

[128] s.41.
[129] s.10(8) of the 1984 Act.
[130] s.42(1).
[131] s.42(2).
[132] See Ch.1 paras 1-68 onwards for an overview of the draft Regulation as issued in January 2012.

matters to courts. The fines are set at very high levels of up to €250,000 or 0.5 per cent of annual worldwide turnover for the lowest level, €500,000 or 1 per cent of worldwide turnover the middle level, and €1,000,000 or 2 per cent of worldwide turnover for the highest level. Any breach of the Regulation can lead to a fine including things such as failing to adopt internal policies or misusing a seal or certificate. The penalty provisions have been widely criticised.

Cooperation with other supervisory authorities

20–103   The provisions for cooperation and achieving consistency between the actions of supervisory authorities are very complex. Supervisory authorities must cooperate with one another and provide mutual assistance under art.55. Mutual assistance includes carrying out prior assessments where requested by another authority. Requests between authorities must be made formally and responded to within one month. They may also carry out joint investigations and where one authority is investigating something which will affect data subjects in the State of another authority there are rights to engage in joint investigations.

There is a complex mechanism to achieve consistency between authorities in taking action in cases that affect data subjects in a number of States where several supervisory authorities may have an interest in the outcome. A European Data Protection Board is to be established and a range of measures must be reported to the Board so that the consistency mechanism can be applied. These measures include agreeing to Binding Corporate Rules, the list of the types of processing that a supervisory authority considers require prior approval and anything where the processing affects data subjects in other Member States. As a result it appear likely that any significant enforcement matter is likely to have to go through the consistency procedure.

ADDITIONAL MATERIALS

20–104   Directive 95/46:

- recital 63—whereas such authorities must have the necessary means to perform their duties, including powers of investigation and intervention, particularly in cases of complaints from individuals, and powers to engage in legal proceedings; whereas such authorities must help to ensure transparency of processing in the Member States within whose jurisdiction they fall;
- recital 55—whereas, if the controller fails to respect the rights of data subjects, national legislation must provide for a judicial remedy; whereas any damage which a person may suffer as a result of unlawful processing must be compensated for by the controller, who may be exempted from liability if he proves that he is not responsible for the damage, in particular in cases where he establishes fault on the part of the data subject or in case of force majeure; whereas sanctions must be imposed on any person, whether governed by private of public law, who fails to comply with the national measures taken under this Directive;

- art.22—Remedies;
- art. 23—Liability;
- art.24—Sanctions.

Directive 2002/58:

- recital 47—whereas where the rights of users and subscribers are not respected national legislation should provide for judicial remedies. Penalties should be imposed on any person, whether governed by private or public law, who fails to comply with the national measures taken under this Directive;
- art.15.2.

Directive 2009/136 (amending 2002/58):

- recital 66—whereas third parties may wish to store information on the equipment of a user, or gain access to information already stored. The enforcement of these requirements should be made more effective by way of enhanced powers granted to the relevant national authorities.
- recital 69—whereas the need to ensure an adequate level of protection of privacy and personal data transmitted and processed in connection with the use of electronic communications networks in the Community calls for effective implementation and enforcement powers in order to provide adequate incentives for compliance. Competent national authorities, and where appropriate, other relevant national bodies should have sufficient powers and resources to investigate cases of non-compliance effectively, including powers to obtain any relevant information they might need, to decide on complaints and to impose sanctions in cases of non-compliance;
- art.2 amending art.4 of 2002/58.

CHAPTER 21

Criminal Offences, Warrants And Prosecutions

INTRODUCTION

The Act imposes a considerable number of obligations on data controllers and provides data subjects with a number of rights. In order to ensure that those obligations are heeded and the rights are capable of being exercised, the Act has to support both with an enforcement framework. That framework has two elements: first, the Commissioner is empowered to take civil enforcement actions against data controllers who are not processing personal data in accordance with the Act and to commence prosecutions in the criminal courts if a data controller or third party commits any one of a number of criminal offences created by the Act; second, individuals have the right to take action in the courts to enforce their rights. This chapter covers the prosecution and warrant powers of the Commissioner. The provisions dealing with the enforcement of individual rights will be found in Chs 11–14. The provisions dealing with the enforcement powers of the Commissioner will be found in Ch.20.

21–01

SUMMARY OF MAIN POINTS

21–02

(a) The Commissioner may seek a warrant of entry to premises where evidence of a contravention of the Act or the Privacy and Electronic Communications Regulations 2003 (PECR) may be found.

(b) The Act imposes a range of criminal sanctions including sanctions for breach of notices, for unlawfully procuring information, for some breaches of the notification requirements and for breach of the confidentiality obligations imposed on the Commissioner.

(c) The offence of procuring information became an imprisonable offence in 2008, but the provision imposing the sanction has not been brought into force at the time of writing (August 2012).

(d) Prosecutions may be brought by the CPS under other provisions in relation to information protected by the Data Protection Act such as misfeasance in public office.

ENTRY AND INSPECTION

21–03 The 1998 Act contains powers for the Commissioner to obtain a warrant for his officers to enter and search premises and to seize evidence where a breach of the legislation is suspected. The powers of entry and inspection are contained in Sch.9. This power applies equally to suspected breaches of the Privacy and Electronic Communications (EC Directive) Regulations (PECR).[1]

For the grant of a warrant a circuit judge (sheriff in Scotland, county court judge in Northern Ireland) must be satisfied of several matters. He must be satisfied by information on oath, supplied by the Commissioner, that there are reasons for suspecting that a data controller has contravened or is contravening any of the principles or that an offence under the Act has been or is being committed[2] or a person has contravened PECR. The power to grant a warrant therefore only applies in respect of past and current breaches of the Act or PECR; it does not apply when it is expected that an offence or contravention will be committed in the future. He must also be satisfied that there is information that evidence of the contravention or offence is at the specified premises.[3] "Premises" include any vessel, vehicle, aircraft or hovercraft.[4] Save in exceptional circumstances, the warrant will not be issued unless the judge is satisfied that the Commissioner has given seven days' notice in writing to the occupier demanding access[5] and:

- access was demanded at a reasonable hour and unreasonably refused; or
- although entry to the premises was granted, the occupier unreasonably refused to comply with a request to permit the Commissioner's staff to exercise any of the rights covered by the warrant[6]: and
- the occupier has been notified of the warrant application and has had an opportunity to make representations to the judge.[7]

Even when satisfied of all these matters, a judge still has a discretion to decline to grant a warrant.[8]

21–04 The exceptional circumstances permitting the grant of a warrant without notice to an occupier are if the judge is satisfied that the case is one of urgency or that compliance with the notice provisions would defeat the object of the entry.[9] "Urgency" is not more precisely defined but in practice the Commissioner must show some evidence or suspicion of an imminent act which could thwart the investigation. The usual argument would be that notice would enable the subject of the investigation to remove any relevant evidence.

---

[1] Privacy and Electronic Communications (EC Directive) Regulations 2003 (SI 2003/ 2426) reg.31 and Sch.1.
[2] Sch.9 para.1(1).
[3] Sch.9 para.1(1).
[4] Sch.9 para.13.
[5] Sch.9 para.2(1)(a).
[6] Sch.9 para.2(1)(b).
[7] Sch.9 para.2(1)(c).
[8] Sch.9 para.1.
[9] Sch.9 para.2(2).

No warrant may be issued in relation to data processed for the "special purposes" unless a s.45 determination by the Commissioner has already been made.[10]

A warrant must be executed within seven days. The warrant authorises the Commissioner or any of his officers or staff to enter the premises, to search them, to inspect, examine, operate and test any equipment found there which is used or intended to be used for processing personal data and to inspect and seize any documents or other material found there which may be evidence of a breach of one or more of the principles or the commission of an offence under the Act or contravention of PECR.

Search warrants under the Act are not limited to premises occupied by data controllers. Other premises may be searched providing the warrant criteria set out above are satisfied.

Reasonable force may be used in the execution of the warrant.[11] The warrant should be executed at a "reasonable hour", unless it is reasonably suspected that the relevant evidence would not be found at such a time.[12] "Reasonable hour" is not more precisely defined. For business premises it is likely to mean ordinary working hours. For domestic premises the term most likely excludes ordinary sleeping hours (23.00–08.00 approximately). The warrant should be shown, and a copy provided, to the occupier of the premises or, if the occupier is not there, then a copy of a warrant should be left in a prominent place on the premises.[13]

If property is seized under the warrant then a receipt must be given if it is requested.[14] The legislation is not specific on when this must be done. The Codes of Practice made pursuant to the Police and Criminal Evidence Act 1984 state that with respect to the seizure of property by the police a list or description of the seized property must be provided to the occupier at the time and to any person with an interest in the property within a reasonable time.[15] The absence of any time limit in the 1998 Act suggests that the receipt must be given on demand, although it might be anticipated that in practice the Commissioner's staff would follow the PACE Code as far as possible.

21–05

The "seizer" of property is empowered to hold it "as long as is necessary" in all the circumstances.[16] In practice this will mean that once property has been eliminated from an investigation then it must be returned forthwith. Property which is the subject of a prosecution or enforcement action may be retained until the end of that action and, if its destruction is not ordered, will have to be returned at the conclusion. In practice there is likely to be a considerable delay with respect to data retained on computer or disk (or other removable storage media) before such property is returned. This is because such property has to be examined with care—in particular to ensure that the examination does not result in an alteration of the data. Typically such forensic examinations are carried out by experts. Even computers and disks which turn out not to contain "offending"

---

[10] Sch.9 para.1(2).
[11] Sch.9 para.4.
[12] Sch.9 para.5.
[13] Sch.9 para.6.
[14] Sch.9 para.7(1).
[15] Code B, para.7.12 .
[16] Sch.9 para.7(2).

material can thus be out of the owner's possession for a considerable period of time whilst undergoing forensic examination.

21–06   The occupier must also be provided with copies of anything seized if they so request and if the person executing the warrant considers that it can be done without undue delay.[17] It would appear therefore that if the occupier, for example, requests copies of any data and if copying facilities are readily available then such copying must be allowed unless undue delay would result. This is a valuable right which should be exercised by all data controllers subject to seizure of their property not least because it will enable them to continue operating pending any decisions or further investigation.

21–07   There are no powers of inspection and seizure in relation to personal data which are exempt to protect national security under s.28 of the Act. These exemptions are considered in detail in Ch.15. Furthermore, the powers of inspection and seizure do not apply to:

- communications between a professional legal adviser and his client with respect to legal advice given about the 1998 Act; or
- communications between a professional legal adviser and his client, or between such an adviser or his client and any other person, made in connection with or in contemplation of proceedings under the 1998 Act.[18]

Anything held by a person other than the professional legal adviser or his client and anything held with the intention of furthering a criminal purpose is excluded from this exemption.[19] "Client" does however include any person representing such a client.[20]

In practice, those professional legal advisers engaged in dispensing advice on the Act would be well advised to implement the practice of marking correspondence as privileged so that any such documents can be readily identified during any search.

21–08   In the case of *R. v Chesterfield Justices Ex p. Bramley*,[21] the High Court considered the responsibilities of the police in relation to material that was claimed to be the subject of legal professional privilege. The facts were as follows.

During the course of a criminal investigation concerning B, the police applied for warrants to search two premises for documents. Under the criteria, a magistrate could issue a search warrant only if he had reasonable grounds for believing, inter alia, that the material on the premises did not consist of or include items subject to legal privilege. However, no reference was made to the possibility that there was material subject to legal professional privilege at the two premises. The magistrates granted the warrants, and the police duly carried out the searches. No one was present at the first site where certain privileged documents were inspected only to the extent necessary to establish their nature. At the other site, a claim by B to privilege in respect of certain documents was rejected and those documents removed from the site, but the police returned them

---

[17] Sch.9 para.7(2).
[18] Sch.9 para.9(1).
[19] Sch.9 para.9(2).
[20] Sch.9 para.9(4).
[21] [2000] 1 All E.R. 411.

without inspection following representations from B's solicitors. B subsequently applied for judicial review of the magistrates' decision to grant the warrants, and of the police's decision to seize privileged documents. In particular, the court was asked to determine whether the police were entitled to remove documents from premises for later sifting, whether they were entitled to remove documents from the premises for sifting elsewhere and whether the police could sift on site documents which were said to be privileged.

The court held (Jowitt J. dissenting):

"(1)   If the officer who made the application did not volunteer information on the specific issue of privilege, the magistrate should ask whether the material sought consisted of or included items subject to such privilege and if there were reasonable grounds for believing that the material sought included items subject to privilege, the targeted material would have to be redefined in such a way as to enable the magistrate to be satisfied that there were no longer reasonable grounds for such a belief, otherwise he could not issue the warrant.

...

(3)   In order to decide how much of the available material fell within the scope of the warrant, the searchers would have to look at the documents, but if there was a lot of material and it was not possible to sort the relevant material reasonably quickly and easily, the statute did not enable the officer to remove all or a large part of the material to sort it out properly elsewhere.

(4)   Whether or not an officer had reasonable grounds for believing an item was not subject to privilege was a question of fact, to be decided in the context of any given case. It was preferable for an agreement to be reached at the time of the search as to what was and what was not subject to privilege, but if that was not possible, the officer conducting the search should package separately for later examination items which were relevant but which he believed might be subject to privilege.

(5)   If there was a difference of opinion which could not be resolved during the search as to whether an item seized was within the warrant or was subject to privilege the issue should be determined preferably by means of an action for trespass to goods, although it would be possible to proceed by way of judicial review."

The decision was distinguished in *R. (on the application of H) v Inland Revenue Commissioners*[22] in which the Revenue seized two computers from the applicant's home having entered his premises under a warrant granted under the Taxes Management Act 1970. The officers could not copy the hard drives in situ so they removed the computers and then copied the hard drives. The court held that a hard drive should be regarded as a single "thing" that could be required as evidence for the purposes of the Taxes Management Act.   **21–09**

There is a significant and potentially material difference between the provisions in the Police and Criminal Evidence Act 1984 and those in the Data Protection Act 1998.   **21–10**

Section 19(6) of PACE provides that:

"No power of seizure conferred on a constable under any enactment (including an enactment contained in an Act passed after this Act) is to be taken to authorise the

---

[22] [2002] EWHC 2164.

seizure of an item which the constable exercising the power has reasonable grounds for believing to be subject to legal privilege."

The Chesterfield Justices cases establishes that whether an officer has reasonable grounds for believing that material is subject to legal privilege is a question of fact to be decided on a case by case basis but if such reasonable grounds for believing are established then any seizure will be illegal.

In the Data Protection Act 1998 Sch.9 para.9(1) simply states that the powers of inspection and seizure conferred by a warrant issued under Sch.9 are not exercisable in respect of material which is the subject of legal privilege.

This, on the face of it, seems to put the Commissioner's investigators in an impossible position since if material is in fact the subject of legal privilege then any inspection and seizure will be automatically unlawful. There is no "reasonable grounds for believing" qualification in the Data Protection Act 1998. Thus if the occupier of premises being searched by the Commissioner's investigators claims legal privilege but an investigator proceeds to check the assertion by an on-site inspection and the material does turn out to be privileged it would appear that the inspection will have been unlawful. Similarly, if the disputed material is removed for an off-site inspection and it turns out that the material is in fact privileged then both the seizure and inspection will be unlawful. It appears that it would not be open to an investigator to claim that at the time of inspection of seizure they held a reasonable belief that the material was privileged.

21–11   If an occupier objects to the inspection or seizure of any material on the grounds that it consists partly of privileged material then he must, if the person executing the warrant so requests, still provide copies of the non-privileged parts.[23]

Warrants must be endorsed and returned to the issuing court after being executed or, if not executed, within seven days. The endorsement must state what powers have been exercised under the warrant.[24]

OFFENCES AND PROSECUTIONS

Application to the Crown

21–12   The 1998 Act creates several criminal offences. Section 63(5) of the 1998 Act provides that neither a government department nor the person who is the data controller for the Royal Household (the Keeper of the Privy Purse), the Duchy of Lancaster and the Duchy of Cornwall shall be liable to prosecution under the Act. However the provisions in s.55 (unlawful obtaining and disclosing of personal data) and the provisions relating to obstructing the execution of a warrant do apply to a person in the service of the Crown as they apply to any other person.

In England, Wales and Northern Ireland the Commissioner and the Director of Public Prosecutions are the only people able to bring proceedings for an offence

---

[23]   Sch.9 para.10.
[24]   Sch.9 para.11.

under the Act.[25] Almost all the offences under the Act are either way offences carrying the statutory maximum financial penalties (£5000 in the magistrates' court and an unlimited fine in the Crown Court). In addition to imposing a penalty on conviction the court may also, for most offences, order that any document or other material used in connection with the processing of personal data and appearing to the court to be connected with the commission of the offence be forfeited, destroyed or erased.[26] A court may not make such an order where a person other than the offender claims an interest in the relevant material unless the person is given an opportunity to be heard.[27]

Defence of due diligence

Section 47 of the 1998 Act creates two criminal offences relating to enforcement and other notices. First, a person who fails to comply with a notice under the legislation commits an offence.[28] It is a defence to show that all due diligence was exercised to comply with the notice.[29]

21–13

The concept of "due diligence" also appeared in the 1984 Act, but there have been very few prosecutions for failing to comply with an enforcement notice and none which have involved an appeal to the higher courts. Therefore, despite the concept of "due diligence" having been in existence in the context of data protection for nearly 30 years, there are no useful authorities on its interpretation in that context. In other contexts it has been held to cover not just the obligation to put in place appropriate procedures but to establish processes to check that they are being adhered to in fact.

Section 47 of the 1998 Act creates a second offence of knowingly or recklessly providing information which is false in a material respect in response to any information/special information notice. The requirement that the information is false in a material respect will exclude trivial or inconsequential falsehoods.

21–14

Admissability of information provided in response to information notices

Sections 43 and 44 cover the admissibility of information provided in response to service of an information notice or special information notice. The provisions are couched in the same terms. Under ss.43(8) and 44(9) a person is not required to furnish the Commissioner with information in response to service of an information notice or special information notice if furnishing that information would, by revealing evidence of the commission of any offence other than an offence under the Data Protection Act or one of the Acts listed in s.43(8A) or s.44(9A) respectively expose him to proceedings for an offence. The offence under the Acts listed are:

21–15

---

[25] Data Protection Act 1984 s.6(5).
[26] s.60(4).
[27] s.60(5).
[28] s.47(1).
[29] s.47(3).

- an offence under s.5 of the Perjury Act (false statements made otherwise than on oath);
- an offence under s.44(2) of the Criminal Law (Consolidation) (Scotland) Act 1995 (false statements made otherwise than on oath); and
- an offence under art.10 of the Perjury (Northern Ireland) Order 1979 (false statutory declarations and other false unsworn statements).[30]

Therefore, if the person has previously made a false statement to the Commissioner that would expose him or her to prosecution under these provisions if it became apparent, the person cannot refuse to answer the information notice or special information notice if to do so would show the discrepancy and thus expose the person to a possible prosecution. A false statement provided by a person in response to an information notice or special information notice can be the subject of prosecution under s.47. However, ss.43(8B) and 44(9B) provide that such statements cannot be used in a prosecution for any other offence under the Act, unless in the proceedings in giving evidence the person provides information inconsistent with the statement and evidence relating to it is adduced or a question relating to it is asked by that person or on that person's behalf.

Knowing or reckless

21–16   The offence of providing false information under s.47 may be committed "knowingly or recklessly". Both terms are well established concepts in criminal legislation. Where the word "knowingly" is included in the definition of an offence, it makes it plain that the doctrine of mens rea applies to that offence. When the term is used the prosecution must prove knowledge on the part of the offender of all the material circumstances of the offence. For example, on a charge of "knowingly having in his possession an explosive substance", the prosecution must prove that the accused knew both that he had it in his possession and that it was an explosive substance.[31] Applying this principle to the offence under s.47 would mean that the prosecution must prove that the provider of the information knew that the information was false in a material respect.

The view of the courts at present is that this is a matter of evidence, and that nothing short of actual knowledge will suffice. See the dictum of Lord Bridge in *Westminster City Council v Croyalgrange Ltd*.[32]

The exclusion of "wilfully shutting one's eyes to the truth" from the ambit of "knowingly" arguably has little impact on the offence under s.47 of the 1998 Act since the offence can be committed "knowingly or recklessly" and it is likely that "wilful eye closure" will be covered by the latter concept.

21–17   In the case of *R v G*,[33] the House of Lords considered the requirement for mens rea in the case of an offence under the Criminal Damage Act 1971. The House departed from the decision in the case of *Caldwell* in which it had held that the defendant would be reckless if a reasonable person would have recognised the

---

[30] Amended by the Coroners and Justice Act 2009 Sch.20 Pt 4.
[31] *R. v Hallam* [1957] 1 Q.B. 569; (1957) 41 Cr.App.R. 111, CCA.
[32] (1986) 83 Cr.App.R. 155 at 164, HL.
[33] [2003] UKHL 50.

risk. The House held that this was capable of leading to obvious unfairness and the need to correct it was compelling. Accordingly a person would be taken to act recklessly within the meaning of s.1 of the Criminal Damage Act with respect to circumstances when he was aware of a risk that existed or would exist and, being aware of the risk it was unreasonable to take it.

The courts had an opportunity to consider the term "recklessly" within the context of the 1984 Act in *Data Protection Registrar v Amnesty International*.[34] The brief facts were that the defendant was a charity which was registered under the 1984 Act. It entered into an agreement with another charity which involved it disclosing its database of supporters to a mailing house so that the mailing house could carry out a mailing on behalf of the second charity. The Registrar alleged that as a consequence Amnesty International had operated outside the terms of their registration entry and had committed offences under s.5(2)(b) and (2)(d) of the 1984 Act. The particular offences were the use of personal data for an unregistered purpose—namely trading in personal information and the disclosure of personal data to a person (the mailing house) not described in the registration entry. One of the consequences of Amnesty's action was that their supporters received mailing seeking contributions to the second charity. One of the recipients complained to the Registrar. The Registrar put the case on the basis that Amnesty International had operated outside the terms of its register entry and had committed the s.5(2) offences recklessly rather than knowingly. It was contended that it had altered the use of the personal data they held without giving any consideration to whether this had implications for their data protection registration.

The stipendiary magistrate dismissed the informations at the conclusion of the   **21–18**
trial. One of the reasons given was that Amnesty's actions had not caused any "serious harmful consequences" as apparently required by the *Lawrence/Caldwell* definition of "recklessness". The stipendiary magistrate took the consequences of Amnesty's action to be the receipt of unwanted "begging" letters by Amnesty's supporters and took the view that this could only sensibly be described as irritating rather than "serious" or "harmful".

The Registrar appealed to the Divisional Court on the basis that the phrase in the *Lawrence/Caldwell* definition "the kind of serious harmful consequences that the section that created the offence was intended to prevent" had to be read in the context of the particular piece of legislation. In the context of the 1984 Act it meant no more than "the kind of consequences (i.e. a data user operating outside the terms of their register entry) that s.5(2) of the 1984 Act was intended to prevent. The words "serious" and "harmful" really only had meaning within the context of the offences that *Lawrence* and *Caldwell* were considering—causing death by reckless driving and criminal damage respectively.

The Divisional Court held that this was the correct interpretation. Amnesty's acquittals however stood as the Registrar did not seek to have the matter remitted to the magistrates' court.

For a consideration of recklessness on the part of a corporation in the context of the Data Protection Acts 1984 and 1998 see the discussion of *Information Commissioner v Islington LBC*,[35] below.

---

[34] [1995] Crim. L.R. 633.
[35] [2002] EWHC Admin 1036; [2002] All E.R. (D) 381.

The two offences under s.47 are either way offences. Both are punishable by a fine—maximum £5,000 in the magistrates' court, unlimited in the Crown Court.

Notification offences

21–19   Under the 1998 Act the system of registration by data users was replaced by one of notification by data controllers. The supporting criminal offences which buttress the requirement of notification are no longer neatly contained in one comprehensible section of the legislation (as they were with s.5 of the 1984 Act).

The requirement to notify the Commissioner is set out in ss.16–20 of the Act. These provisions require data controllers to notify the Commissioner of:

- their name and address;
- a description of the personal data;
- the purpose(s) for which they are held;
- the recipients of disclosures;
- non EEA countries to which the data may be transferred; and
- security measures to comply with principle 7.

For a more detailed consideration of Notification, see Ch.9.

Section 21 makes it an offence to fail to notify the Commissioner of the processing of personal data and also to keep the Commissioner notified of relevant changes (for example as to the address of the controller, or to the intentions of the controller with respect to the processing of personal data, or to the security measures to comply with principle 7).

The failure to "notify" and the failure to notify changes are either way offences punishable with a maximum £5,000 fine in the magistrates' court or an unlimited fine in the Crown Court.

Failure to provide relevant particulars (s.24)

21–20   Section 17(1) of the Act prohibits processing of personal data unless the data controller has "notified" the Commissioner. Section 17(2) and (3) set out limited exceptions to this basic prohibition. These are, first, where the relevant data is not information which is being processed by the means of equipment operating automatically in response to instructions given for purpose nor is it information which is recorded with the intention that it should be processed by means of such equipment.[36] In other words the data is information which is recorded as part of a relevant filing system or which forms part of an accessible record as defined by s.68. These have come to be known as "manual records".

Secondly, the prohibition in s.17(1) does not apply where the Secretary of State has exempted particular processing of the basis that it is unlikely to prejudice the rights and freedoms of data subjects.[37] This power has been used to exempt some forms of common processing from the requirement to notify. The

---

[36] 1998 Act s.1(1)(a) and (b).
[37] s.17(3).

categories of processing which have been determined as falling within this class are set out in the Notification Regulations and are described in Ch.9 on notification.

If either of these exceptions applies then a data controller may, nonetheless, give a notification to the Commissioner under s.18. If a data controller chooses not do so then any person may still request the "relevant particulars" from the data controller. The data controller is under a duty to supply the particulars in writing within 21 days and free of charge.[38] These particulars are the equivalent of the information which must be notified to be Commissioner.

Any data controller who fails to provide the relevant particulars commits an offence.[39] It is a defence for the data controller to show that he exercised due diligence to comply with the duty to supply the relevant particulars. For a discussion of the concept of "due diligence", see above.

Again the offence is an either way offence and punishable with the statutory maximum financial penalty.

Unlawful obtaining and disclosing of personal data

Section 55 of the 1998 Act radically reworked aspects of the equivalent offences in the 1984 Act. It has become one of the most important criminal provisions in the Act. However, it did not appear in the original 1984 Act and does not derive from the Directive. The section addresses the problem of third parties obtaining information by deception, sometimes referred to as "blagging". In this text it is referred to as the practice of obtaining information by deception.   **21–21**

The problem came to prominence with a news story about the (then new) head of British Intelligence Stella Rimington. In 1994 Ms Rimington was the first named head of British Intelligence and the press decided to celebrate this limited openness by seeing what other information could be unearthed about her. "Investigative" journalists therefore set about finding out details about her affairs. This did not result in any major disclosures; the most startling appeared to be that she routinely shopped at Marks and Spencer on a Thursday evening, but it did raise the question of how material about her could be accessed so readily. It transpired that the information had been obtained by deceptive telephone calls to her financial services providers. When a complaint was made to the ODPR it was decided that no prosecution could be brought since the duped data users had not committed any knowing or reckless breach of their register entry.

Clearly this incident alone did not spark the alterations to the 1984 Act—rather it was symptomatic of a general concern about the ease with which private detectives and journalists were apparently able to obtain purportedly confidential personal information. Some private investigators even boasted in advertisements that they could obtain "full financial profiles" of any named individual. The issue was addressed in 1994 by amendments to the 1984 Act introduced by the Criminal Justice and Public Order Act 1994.

The amendments introduced three new offences of procuring the disclosure of personal data, selling or offering to sell it. The offences were fraught with potential difficulties, particularly because the offences were linked to registration,   **21–22**

---

[38] s.24(1).
[39] s.24(4).

that being the fundamental concept under the 1984 Act. There were a number of successful prosecutions but they were difficult to bring home and the wording of the provision was revised in the 1998 Act.

21–23   Under the 1998 Act it is an offence knowingly or recklessly:

- to obtain or disclose personal data or the information contained in personal data; or
- to procure the disclosure to another person of the information contained in personal data,

without the consent of the data controller. For a discussion of "knowingly or recklessly", see above.

The obtaining/disclosing/procuring without the consent of the data controller will not be an offence if the perpetrator can prove on the balance of probabilities that the obtaining, disclosing or procuring:

- was necessary for the prevention or detection or crime;
- was required or authorised by or under any enactment, rule of law, or court order;
- the "obtainer or procurer", etc. acted in the reasonable belief that he had a right in law to act as he did or that he would have had the consent of the controller if they had known of the particular circumstances;
- that he acted for the special purposes with a view to the publication of literary, artistic or journalistic material and in the reasonable belief that in the particular circumstances it was justified in the public interest; or
- it was, in the particular circumstances, justifiable as being in the public interest.

In any criminal proceedings the onus will initially be on the relevant person to raise one or more of these issues as a defence. If that initial onus is satisfactorily discharged then the onus will shift to the Commissioner to prove beyond reasonable doubt that the defence claimed does not apply.

The requirement that the "obtainer", etc. held a reasonable belief imposes an objective standard. In other words it will not be sufficient for the "obtainer" to hold an honest belief about particular circumstances if that belief was objectively unreasonable. The defence based on the reasonable belief that the obtainer, etc., had in law the right to obtain, etc., obviously undermines the basic proposition that ignorance of law is generally no defence. Such defences are not, however, unknown in the criminal law. For example, under s.2(1) of the Theft Act 1968 a person is not to be regarded as dishonest "if he appropriates the property in the belief that he has in law the right to deprive the other of it". The defence which relates to the use for the special purposes was added by the Criminal Justice and Immigration Act 2008 and is not in force at the date of publication (December 2012).

21–24   In many prosecutions under s.55 the fundamental allegation is that the data controller has been duped into disclosing personal data. It could be contended that although the controller was deceived the disclosure was not without their consent. The most common type of deception employed on a data controller by those seeking to obtain personal data unlawfully is a deception as to their identity. Typically they pretend to be the data subject or someone authorised to act on the subject's behalf.

However, the courts have addressed this issue in the law on consent in other contexts and case law has held that a mistake as to the identity of the person carrying out an action will vitiate apparent consent as will a fraud as to the nature of the act *R. v Linekar*.[40]

It is also an offence to sell or to offer to sell personal data that has been unlawfully obtained/procured/disclosed. An offer to sell includes an advertisement indicating that personal data are or may be for sale. The offences do not apply to personal data where an exemption is necessary for the purposes of national security (see s.55(8)). Thus such deceptive means of obtaining information may continue to be used by those concerned with national security where it is necessary for the purpose. Nor does s.55 apply to the new category of recorded information added by the amendments in the Freedom of Information Act 2000. These offences again are either way offences and again attract the statutory maximum financial penalties

21–25

In November 2002 one of the first prosecutions under s.55 came to trial before the Kingston Crown Court. In *R. v Codrington* (Unreported), C was an employee of the Benefits Agency who had abused his access to the Agency's computer equipment to look up personal data relating to friends and family. He was prosecuted by the Commissioner under both s.5(6) of the Data Protection Act 1984 and s.55 of the Data Protection Act 1998 since the alleged behaviour occurred both before and after March 1, 2000. The matter was contested but C was convicted of all matters.

21–26

In the course of the trial the trial judge was asked to direct the jury on the meaning and ambit of the term "knowingly or recklessly" in the context of s.55. The trial judge agreed with prosecution counsel's submission that the term applied both to the lack of consent of the data controller and to the "obtaining", "disclosing" or "procuring".

The trial judge in *Codrington* considered that "knowingly or recklessly" had to apply to the lack of consent of the data controller as otherwise the phrase would have appeared after "without the consent of the data controller".

Thus the prosecution in *Codrington* had to demonstrate knowledge or recklessness on the part of the defendant in respect of the lack of the consent of the Benefits Agency and the obtaining of the personal data. Of course most "obtaining" of personal data is going to be with knowledge but it is clearly possible to envisage a reckless "disclosure" of personal data.

In the case of *R v Rooney*[41] the defendant was charged with having knowingly or recklessly obtained and disclosed personal data relating to her sister's estranged partner. The defendant was an employee of Staffordshire police in the HR department. She accessed the computer records of the address of her sister's ex-partner on several occasions and following the last occasion she disclosed to her sister that the officer had moved to "an address in Tunstall." She was convicted of having disclosed personal data and appealed on the grounds that the information disclosed did not fall within the definition of personal data as no one

21–27

[40] (1995) 2 Cr.App.R. 49, CA.
[41] [2006] EWCA Crim 1841.

could be identified from it. The appeal was dismissed on the grounds that it was sufficient that she had disclosed information contained in personal data and it was not an essential component of the offence that the identity of the individual be disclosed.

21–28   The mischief addressed by the section has grown as more and more parties seek to access information about others, often for journalistic purposes but occasionally for other reasons such as the collection of debts. The Information Commissioner has been active in pursuing such offences. In May 2006 he presented a report to Parliament under his powers in s.52(2) of the Act[42] in which he set out the problems arising from the illicit trade in personal data and made an argument for significantly increasing the penalties available for the offences. The core recommendation of the report was that the Government should raise the penalty for conviction on indictment for s.55 offences to a maximum of two years imprisonment or a fine or both and for summary conviction to a maximum of six months imprisonment or a fine or both. The report included a number of other recommendations as follows:

- Businesses buying information should only buy information which they are confident has been properly obtained.
- The Security Industry Authority should include a caution or conviction for a s.55 offence among the grounds for refusing or revoking a licence for a private investigator.
- The Association of British Investigators should include explicit reference to the offences in its training standards.
- The Press Complaint Commission should take a stronger line to address the use of such tactics by the press.
- The Office of Fair Trading should amend its debt collection guidance to condemn s.55 offences.

The Commissioner also signalled that he would continue discussions with all the relevant parties, seek further evidence from the public and publish a follow-up report in six months time.

21–29   The follow-up report was duly published in December 2006[43] and Richard Thomas was able to report on six months of effective progress. In particular, he welcomed the decision of the Department of Constitutional Affairs to launch a public consultation on the possibility of increasing the penalties for deliberate and wilful misuse of personal data.[44] The consultation document proposed an increase in the criminal sanctions in line with the ICO recommendation. The consultation had closed in October 2006. Other parties had also responded positively to the recommendations in the report which has received a very broadly positive response.

On February 7, 2007 the Government announced its intention to increase the penalties as sought by the Commissioner when a suitable legislative opportunity presented itself.

---

[42] "What price privacy? The unlawful trade in confidential personal information", May 10, 2006, HC 1056.
[43] "What price privacy now? The first six months progress in halting the unlawful trade in confidential personal information", December 13, 2006, HC 36.
[44] July 24, 2006.

The opportunity arose with the passing of the Criminal Justice and Immigration Act in 2008. Sections 77 and 78 of that Act provide powers for the Secretary of State to provide for custodial sentences for breaches of s.55 and a new defence for journalism respectively.

The provisions came into force on May 8, 2008 but no order was made. In September 2009 the Information Commissioner called for an order to be made to introduce the provisions before the Culture, Media and Sport Select Committee inquiry "Press standards, privacy and libel" and in October 2009 the Ministry of Justice published a consultation document (CP 22/09) on the introduction of orders. Despite the consultation to date no such orders have been made under the section. Under s.77 the Secretary of State may, by order, provide that a person who is guilty of an offence under s.5 may be liable to imprisonment as well as a fine or both. On summary conviction in the Magistrate's court he may specify a fine of up to the statutory maximum and a maximum period of imprisonment of up to twelve months, although in the case of punishment for an offence which took place before the commencement of s.283(1) of the Criminal Justice Act 2003 (the point at which the sentencing powers of the Magistrates' Courts increased from 6 months to 12 months) any order must provide that the period would be read as a reference to a maximum of six months. In the Crown Court he may specify an unlimited fine and a term of imprisonment of up to two years.

Before making such an order the Secretary of State must consult the Information Commissioner, such media organisations and other persons as the Secretary of State considers appropriate. The section also provides that an order under the section may amend the Date Protection Act.

An additional defence was at the same time added to s.55, which it is intended **21–30** should come into effect at the same time as the custodial sentence. The defence is that the accused acted for the special purposes, with a view to the publication by any person of any journalistic, literary or artistic material and in the reasonable belief that in the particular circumstances the obtaining, disclosing or procuring was justified as being in the public interest.

The consultation on the introduction of the section ended in January 2010. **21–31** Four questions were asked in the consultation:

1. Should the provision be introduced?
2. If introduced should the sentences be set at the maximum levels of six months and two years respectively?
3. If introduced should that be in April 2010 when the additional powers of the Information Commissioner to impose monetary penalty notices was to come into force?
4. If introduced should the defence of acting for the special purposes be introduced at the same time?

Before the response was published the general election intervened and no formal response has ever been published on behalf of the Government. In October 2011 the Justice Select Committee called for the powers to be implemented swiftly, noting that the current fines were an "inadequate deterrent" to breaches, but the call did not evoke a positive response from government and at the time of writing there is no indication of a date for the provisions to be brought into effect. This is despite repeated calls from the Information Commissioner for their introduction and the furore that has arisen from the evidence coming to light as a result of the News of the World phone hacking cases and the Leveson enquiry.

21–32   As a result of the absence of effective penalties under the DPA there has been a tendency for prosecutions to be brought under other provisions which do carry powers to imprison instead of the DPA. Prosecutions have been brought against police officers who disclosed information from the Police National Computer under the common law offence of misfeasance in public office. In the case of *Attorney General's Reference (No.1 of 2007)* sub nom. *R. v Hardy*, the Attorney General referred a sentence of imprisonment which had been suspended and a requirement to undertake 300 hours unpaid work to the Court of Appeal as being unduly lenient. The Court held that on the facts the officer's misconduct had required a sentence of immediate imprisonment and the minimum sentence for the offence should have been 18 months. The journalist Clive Goodman and private investigator Glenn Mulcaire were jailed in 2007 for four and six months respectively for offences under the Criminal Law Act 1977 of conspiracy to intercept communications in breach of s.1 of the Regulation of Investigatory Powers Act 2000. In March 2012, four private investigators received jail sentences for obtaining data by deception having been prosecuted under the Fraud Act 2006 by SOCA. The four men accepted "commissions" to obtain information by deception from organisations such as banks or building societies on particular targets.

The reasons for using alternative offence provisions can be seen when the sentences are compared with those under the DPA. Information available from the ICO website on s.55 prosecutions includes:

- a bank cashier who accessed the accounts and banking records of a woman who had accused the cashier's husband of sexual assault was fined £800, made to pay £400 costs and a £15 victims' surcharge Brighton Magistrates Court in September 2011;
- an employee of a personal injury claims company who had obtained information on NHS patients from his former girlfriend (who worked at an NHS hospital), which he used to generate leads for personal injury claims, was fined £1,050 and made to pay £1,160 towards prosecution costs in July 2011;
- two T Mobile employees who stole and sold customer data were given a conditional discharge in June 2011, although they were ordered to pay a total of £73,700 in confiscation costs under the Proceeds of Crime Act 2002;
- one of the two former members of the BNP who posted the party membership list on the internet in November 2008 was fined £200;
- two private investigators who unlawfully obtained personal information from BT for a client who was trying to trace her partner were fined £400 and £500 respectively; and
- a London estate agent who attempted to access the account of a benefit claimant over the telephone was fined just £200 in March 2012.

Offences in connection with warrants

It is an offence under para.12 of Sch.9 to intentionally obstruct the execution of a warrant or to fail, without reasonable excuse, to give reasonably required assistance for the execution. Examples of the latter type of obstruction might be the refusal to give a password to access a computer system or the refusal to unlock a filing cabinet.

The most common form of obstruction in the criminal justice system is the obstruction of a police constable in the execution of his duty.[45] A defendant obstructs a police constable if he makes it more difficult for him to carry out his duty.[46] No physical act is necessary to constitute obstruction. Simple refusal to answer questions does not constitute an obstruction.[47] Answering questions incorrectly may, however, amount to obstruction.[48] A person may obstruct by omission but only if they are under an initial duty to act.[49] There is also a common law offence of refusing to aid a constable who is attempting to prevent or to quell a breach of the peace and who calls for assistance.[50]

Thus it can be seen that the obligation to assist a person executing a warrant under the 1998 Act is an extension to the usual concept of "obstruction" and a potentially onerous obligation. There may be situations where the obligation clashes or appears to clash with a suspect's right against self-incrimination as stated in the European Convention on Human Rights.[51] For example, if an occupier is asked to provide a password to a computer system which the occupier knows contains incriminating information, does the obligation to assist imposed by Sch.9 breach the right against self-incrimination?

Unlike other offences under the 1998 Act this obstruction offence may only be dealt within the magistrates' court and is punishable with a maximum fine of £5,000.

Enforced subject access

This subject is more fully discussed in Ch.27. However, it is worthwhile in this section highlighting the offence created by s.56(5). This makes it an offence for a person in connection with:

- the recruitment of another person as an employee;
- the continued employment of another person; or
- any contract for the provision of services to him by another person,

to require that other person or a third party to supply him with a "relevant record".

Similarly, it is an offence for a person concerned with the provision of goods, facilities or services to the public or a section of the public to require, as a

---

[45] Police Act 1996 s.89.
[46] *Hinchcliffe v Sheldon* [1955] 1 W.L.R. 1207.
[47] *Rice v Connolly* [1966] 2 Q.B. 414.
[48] *Green v DPP* (1991) 155 J.P. 816.
[49] *Lunt v DPP* [1993] Crim. L.R. 534.
[50] *Waugh, The Times,* October 1, 1986.
[51] European Convention on Human Rights art.6.

condition of providing such goods, etc., to another person, that other person or a third party supply him with a "relevant record".

"Relevant record" is given a lengthy and specific definition in s.56(6) and this is discussed in detail in Ch.27.

Liability of directors

21–35   Section 61 provides that where an offence has been committed by a body corporate and is proved to have been committed with the consent or connivance of or to be attributable to any neglect on the part of any director, manager, secretary or similar officer or any one acting in such capacity that person shall be guilty of the offence as well as the body corporate and liable to be proceeded against and punished in the same way. Offences by bodies corporate which require mens rea can only be successfully prosecuted where a senior officer of the body corporate or a "directing mind" can be shown to have the necessary mental element. This is an additional provision that enables the prosecutor to seek a penalty against the individual in his or her own right arising from that person's engagement in the offence. It is a pre-condition that the prosecution prove the offence against the body corporate. Section 61 is essentially parasitic. The standard required to be shown in respect of the senior officer is relatively low; the offence need only be with their consent, connivance or even attributable to neglect.

Where a body corporate is managed by its members, then the section applies equally to members who hold management positions and in a Scottish partnership (which is an entity with separate legal personality from its partners) to partners in the same position.

Prosecutions and penalties

21–36   In addition to the penalties by way of fine and costs the prosecution may, in the case of some offences and an appropriate case, apply for an order of the court dealing with the prosecution that any document or other material used in connection with the processing of personal data connected with the offence be forfeited, destroyed or erased.

The relevant offences are failure to notify, failure to keep a notification up to date, the unlawful procuring of data, enforced subject access and breach of an enforcement notice. Where a person (not the offender) claims to be the owner of or otherwise a person interested in the material in question the court must give them an opportunity to be heard and explain why such an order should not be made.

Unlawful disclosure by the Commissioner's staff

21–37   Section 59(3) makes it a criminal offence for the Commissioner, his staff and agents to disclose information obtained in connection with the Act unless disclosure is made with lawful authority.

The information must relate to an identified or identifiable individual or business and must not already be in the public domain.[52]

A disclosure will only be with lawful authority if:

- it is made with consent;
- the information was provided for the purpose of being made public in accordance with the Act;
- the disclosure is required by the Act or any Community obligation;
- disclosure is for the purpose of any civil or criminal proceedings;
- disclosure is in the public interest having regard to the rights and freedoms or legitimate interests of any person.[53]

Assessable processing

"Assessable processing" is defined in s.22(1) as processing specified in an order made by the Secretary of State as appearing particularly likely to cause substantial damage or distress to data subjects or otherwise significantly to prejudice the rights and freedoms of data subjects.

21–38

The Commissioner is placed under an obligation by s.22(2) on receiving notification to consider whether any of the relevant processing is assessable processing and, if so, whether it is likely to comply with the provisions of the 1998 Act.

If the Commissioner decides that assessable processing is involved then within 28 days of receiving notification (the period may exceptionally be extended by up to 14 days) the Commissioner must give notice to data controller of the decision and the opinion as to whether the processing is likely or unlikely to comply with the Act. This provision does not give the Commissioner the power to prohibit processing—only to give an opinion. If the Commissioner wishes to prohibit processing then he must use the enforcement notice procedure.

No assessable processing, in respect of which a notification has been given to the Commissioner, may be carried on unless:

- the 28 day period (or exceptionally extended period) has expired; or
- before the end of that period the data controller has received the notice of the Commissioner's opinion.

If a data controller breaches this requirement then an offence is committed[54]. There is no statutory defence of being able to show due diligence. It is an either way offence punishable with the maximum financial penalties. However, no orders have been made and no processing is currently classed as assessable processing nor do there appear to be any proposals to change this.

---

[52] s.59(1)(a).
[53] s.59(2).
[54] s.22(6)

Procedural issues and delay

21–39   Investigations conducted by the Information Commissioner's office are often quite prolonged—for a variety of reasons including staffing levels. There have sometimes been substantial delays between the receipt of a complaint of an alleged offence and the commencement of a prosecution. However, the current position under UK law would appear to be that the courts are rarely concerned, in relation to art.6 rights, with the delay between the start of an investigation and the commencement of a prosecution unless the defendant can show "material prejudice" prior to being summonsed. It is difficult to envisage "material prejudice" occurring during an investigation conducted by the Information Commissioner since the Commissioner's investigators have no power of arrest and detention and cannot even insist on an interview taking place. It is just about possible to imagine "material prejudice" occurring if the alleged offender is in a business where the secure processing of personal data is crucial and details of the investigation become widely known.

Rather the courts' concern in relation to delay is what happens post charge or summons. There are rarely significant delays attributable to the Information Commissioner in DPA prosecutions post summons. Thus, although abuse of the process arguments based on art.6 rights and delay have been threatened and indeed presented in DPA prosecutions in the past, none have been successful.

PROSECUTIONS UNDER THE 1984 ACT

21–40   There were a number of problems with the offence provisions of the 1984 Act. There was also a period of some uncertainty after the implementation of the Act in March 2000 in relation to offences committed before implementation. These were covered in earlier editions of this textbut are now of historical interest only.

There were six cases where the courts have considered the interpretation of the 1984 Act. These are:

- *R. v Brown* [1996] 1 All E.R. 545;
- *R. v Chief Constable of B County Constabulary* Unreported November 1997;
- *Rowley v Liverpool Corp, The Times,* October 26, 1987, CA;
- *Amnesty International (British Section) v Data Protection Registrar* Unreported November 1994;
- *Griffin v Data Protection Registrar* Unreported February 1993; and
- *Information Commissioner v Islington LBC* [2002] EWHC Admin 1036; [2002] All E.R. (D) 381.

Of these, the unreported case of *R. v Chief Constable of B County Constabulary* relates to the issue of data subject access and is not, therefore, directly relevant to issues of enforcement and prosecution. It is discussed in the Ch.11 on Subject Access.

Amnesty International is a case on the meaning of recklessness within the Data Protection Act 1984. It is discussed earlier in this chapter. It is submitted that the decision may still be relevant to the concept of recklessness under the 1998 Act.

Impact of the draft Regulation in brief[55]

There are no specific criminal provisions in the draft. Under art.53 the supervisory authority must have the power to access all personal data and all information necessary for the performance of its duties and be able to access any premises including data processing equipment where there are reasonable grounds for presuming that an activity in violation of the Regulation is being carried on. These must be exercised in conformity with Union and Member State law so it will be necessary for the warrant and entry powers to be specified in some other instrument. The power to fine will rest with supervisory authorities and not the courts.

21–41

There is no equivalent in the draft Regulation to s.55. If the Regulation becomes law no Member State will be able to "gold plate" the rules by adding further requirements however this may not impact on the s.55 offences which can reasonably be regarded as having more in common with Computer Misuse Act offences that "pure" data protection ones.

Derivations

Directive 95/46:

21–42

- Recital 63—whereas such authorities must have the necessary means to perform their duties, including powers of investigation and intervention, particularly in cases of complaints from individuals, and powers to engage in legal proceedings; whereas such authorities must help to ensure transparency of processing in the Member States within whose jurisdiction they fall;
- art.23—Liability;
- art.24—Sanctions.

---

[55] See Ch.1, paras 1-69 onwards for an overview of the draft Regulation proposed by the EU Commission in January 2012.

CHAPTER 22

Electronic Communications And The Privacy And Electronic Communications (EC Directive) Regulations 2003

INTRODUCTION AND BACKGROUND

Developments in electronic communications over the past three decades have been dynamic and extensive. The digitalisation of networks and availability of broadband have extended the modes in which information can be transmitted; services and service providers have multiplied and media channels have converged. These developments have given rise to powerful pressures on personal privacy, for example mobile services based on location data allow the tracking of users, social media sites involve the widespread sharing of personal information, mobile devices offer a vast range of uses while "cookies"[1] and similar technologies can be used to track web usage and target consumers. The passage of a specific sectoral directive in 1997 (Dir.97/66/EC) relating to data protection and telecommunications, reflected the significance of the growth of the telecommunications sector at the end of the last century. This Directive was repealed and replaced within a mere five years by Directive 2002/58 of the European Parliament and the Council of July 12, 2002 concerning the processing of personal data and the protection of privacy in the electronic communications sector (the Privacy and Electronic Communications Directive or Directive 2002/58). In the replacement Directive, the term "telecommunications" was replaced by "electronic communications" throughout; evidence of the importance to the Commission of achieving a "technology neutral" regime. Some aspects of Directive 2002/58 were contentious and it was finally agreed under the art.189b co-decision procedure introduced after Maastricht.

22–01

Many of the provisions of Directive 2002/58 were unchanged from Directive 97/55. The main areas of change were:

22–02

- the references to "telecommunications" were altered throughout to "electronic communications";
- the definitions became both tighter and more extensive;

---

[1] Cookies are small text files used in the delivery of internet communications. A webserver can send these bits of code to a user's computer when a user visits a website. They are used, for example, to enable the website to recognise the visitor on a subsequent occasion. They can be used for tracking and web usage. For more information about how cookies work and are used, visit *http://computer.howstuffworks.com/cookie.htm* [Accessed October 4, 2012] or see *www.aboutcookies.org* [Accessed October 4, 2012].

- the coverage of traffic data was extended;
- the restriction on service providers using personal data about users to market only their own services was lifted;
- notice of the use of "cookies" was required, with users having the option to decide not to accept cookies, except where the cookie was essential to deliver contracted services;
- a set of rules governing the uses of location data was included;
- emergency services were given the right to access location data;
- the rules relating to directory information were changed to deal with developments in the use and availability of directories; and
- it was made explicit that marketing to individual subscribers by e-mail (which includes SMS) requires consent save in certain cases where the marketer has an existing trading relationship with the subscriber.

22–03   Directive 2002/58 was implemented in the UK by the Privacy and Electronic Communications (EC Directive) Regulations 2003 (PECR) ("the Regulations").[2] Directive 2002/58 has subsequently been amended by Directive 2009/136 on November 25, 2009.[3] The amendments:

- strengthen the obligations of security imposed on providers of electronic communications services ("service providers")[4];
- impose an obligation on service providers to notify the regulator of personal data breaches and in some cases also to notify subscribers and users[5];
- require service providers to maintain an inventory of personal data breaches[6];
- strengthen the rules in relation to the use of "cookies" for non-essential purposes to cases where the subscriber or user has given a positive consent[7];
- require service providers to obtain prior consent to marketing for the purpose of value added services[8];
- extend the protection against unsolicited marketing by automated systems, fax and e mail to individual users as well as subscribers[9];
- require Member States to ensure that any person adversely affected by unsolicited electronic communications should have a remedy in legal proceedings[10];

---

[2] SI 2003/2426.

[3] Directive 2009/136/EC of the European Parliament and of the Council of November 25, 2009 amending Directive 2002/22/EC on universal services and users' rights relating to electronic communications networks and services, Directive 2002/58/EC concerning the processing of personal data and the protection of privacy in the electronic communications sector and Regulation (EC) No.2006/2004 on cooperation between national authorities responsible for the enforcement of consumer protection law.

[4] Directive 2009/136/EC art.2 amending art.4 of Directive 2002/58.

[5] Directive 2009/136/EC art.2(c).

[6] Directive 2009/136/EC art.2(c).

[7] Directive 2009/136/EC art.2(5) amending art.5(3) of Directive 2002/58.

[8] Directive 2009/136/EC art.2(6) amending art.6(3) of Directive 2002/58.

[9] Directive 2009/136/EC art.2(7) amending art.13 of Directive 2002/58.

[10] Directive 2009/136/EC art.2(7) amending art.13(6) of Directive 2002/58.

- require service providers to maintain records of access requests to data for security and policing purposes and for the information to be available to the regulatory authority[11];
- require that the national regulatory authority be given powers to enforce these provisions including powers of audit and criminal penalties as appropriate[12];
- encourage the adoption of measures to ensure effective cross-border enforcement[13]; and
- make a number of drafting clarifications.[14]

The changes were to be implemented by Member States by May 2011. The Department for Business, Innovation and Skills (BIS) consulted on implementation in September 2010.[15] The consultation only reviewed the areas of PECR which required substantive amendment, namely the introduction of the personal data breach provisions, the strengthening of the enforcement powers of the Information Commissioner and the changes to the rules on cookies. Regulations amending PECR were introduced on the May 4, 2011 and came into effect on May 25.[16] The revised PECR do not include all the changes required by Directive 2009/136; some minor changes to give users as well as subscribers rights to agree to the receipt of marketing appear to have been omitted. These are noted in the text where relevant. In this chapter we cover the rules on marketing and the use of cookies, restrictions on the use of traffic data, the new breach obligations and the powers of the Commissioner.

SUMMARY OF MAIN POINTS
22–04

(a) The Regulations apply in addition to the Data Protection Act 1998.

(b) The Regulations apply to those who use and provide electronic communications services; it follows that those subject to the Regulations may not be data controllers for the purposes of the Data Protection Act 1998.

(c) The use of electronic communications services (including e-mail) for direct marketing is regulated.

(d) The sending of unsolicited faxes for direct marketing to individual subscribers is banned; such faxes can only be sent with consent.

(e) The sending of unsolicited faxes for direct marketing to corporate subscribers is permitted but the sender must stop sending them if the subscriber objects either directly or by electing to be included on the fax preference list.

(f) Unsolicited marketing telephone "calls" to individual subscribers are still allowed but there is a "stop list" of numbers of subscribers who do not want

---

[11] Directive 2009/136/EC art.2(9) amending art.15 of Directive 2002/58.

[12] Directive 2009/136/EC art.2(4) and (10) amending Directive 2002/58 by the addition of a new art.15a.

[13] Directive 2009/136/EC art.2(4) and (10) amending Directive 2002/58.

[14] Directive 2009/136/EC art.2.

[15] Implementing the revised EU Electronic Communications Framework BIS September 2010.

[16] The Privacy and Electronic Communications (EC Directive) (Amendment) Regulations 2011 (SI 2011/1208).

such calls and corporate subscribers are permitted on the list. Calls must not be made to those numbers on the list or the numbers of those who have objected directly to the caller.

(g)   The use of automated calling systems for direct marketing without consent is banned whether the marketing is to individuals or other subscribers.

(h)   Direct marketing is widely defined and includes advertising even if nothing is being offered for sale.

(i)   Service providers are required to safeguard the security of their services.

(j)   Service providers must maintain an inventory of personal data breaches and notify the regulator of personal data breaches and in some cases also notify subscribers and users.

(k)   The use of cookies or equivalent tools for non-essential services is not permitted without the consent of the subscriber or user.

(l)   Limits are placed on the retention of traffic data and the purposes for which they can be used.

(m)   Limits are placed on the processing of location data.

(n)   Callers must be able to block the presentation of their calling line identification; equally those receiving calls where the CLI has been blocked must be entitled to refuse to accept such calls.

(o)   Individuals are given the right to limit the information about them which is published in directories or available from directory enquiry services and may go ex-directory free of charge.

(p)   Service providers will have to maintain records of access requests to data for security and policing purposes and make the information available to the regulatory authority.[17]

(q)   Subscribers may opt to receive non-itemised bills.

(r)   The Information Commissioner may serve third party notices on service providers.

(s)   The Information Commissioner has extensive audit powers in relation to the personal data breach obligations.

(t)   Breaches of PECR may lead to monetary penalty notices as well as other enforcement action by the Commissioner.

IMPLEMENTATION OF DIRECTIVE 2002/58

22–05   Implementing legislation was required by October 31, 2003. In the UK the timetable lagged slightly. In March 2003 the DTI issued a Consultation Document, *Implementation of the Directive on Privacy and Electronic Communications*, which reviewed the options for implementing those changes required by the Directive. Following the consultation the Privacy and Electronic Communications (EC Directive) Regulations 2003[18] (PECR) came into force on December 11, 2003. PECR replaced the Telecommunications (Data Protection and Privacy) Regulations 1999 (TDPP Regulations). The Regulation of Investigatory Powers Act 2000 (under which art.5 of both Directive 2002/58 and its predecessor

---

[17] This provision has not yet been applied but is referred to for completeness.
[18] SI 2003/2426 amended by the Privacy and Electronic Communications (EC Directive) (Amendment) Regulations 2004 (SI 2004/1039).

provision in 1997/66 had been implemented) was unaffected, and the Telecommunications (Lawful Business Practice) Regulations 2000 were subject to minor amendment only. A further development occurred in June 2004 when PECR was amended by the Privacy and Electronic Communications (EC Directive) (Amendment) Regulations 2004 to allow corporate subscribers to register with the Corporate Telephone Preference service. PECR was further amended in May 2011 to implement the changes required by Directive 2009/136.

Article 29 Working Party

The Article 29 Working Party has a continued interest in electronic communications and associated matters and has issued a range of Opinions on these issues since the implementation of 2002/58/EC:

22–06

- Opinion 13/2011 on Geolocation on smart mobile devices;
- Opinion 2/2010 on online behavioural advertising;
- Opinion 1/2009 on the proposals amending Directive 2002/58/EC on privacy and electronic communications;
- Opinion 2/2008 on the review of Directive 2002/58 on privacy and electronic communications;
- Opinion 1/2008 on data protection related to search engines;
- Opinion 8/2006 on the review of the regulatory Framework for Electronic Communications and Services with focus on the ePrivacy Directive;
- Working Document on data protection and privacy implications in ecall initiative (September 26, 2006);
- Opinion 5/2005 on the use of location data with a view to providing value-added services; and
- Opinion 5/2004 on unsolicited communications for marketing purposes under art.13 of Directive 2002/58/EC.

As early as February 2004 the Working Party was expressing concerns that, despite the fact that Directive 2002/58 introduced a harmonised regime for marketing using electronic communications, some of the concepts used in the Directive "appear to be subject to differences of interpretation". Those concerns, including the level of consent required under the Directive, have continued to recur. The various Opinions of the WP are covered under the relevant sections below.

REGULATION OF ELECTRONIC COMMUNICATIONS

The rules regulating electronic communications derive from a number of interlinked EU Directives. The main ones being:

22–07

- Directive 2002/19 on access to and interconnection of electronic communications networks and associated facilities (Access Directive)[19];

---

[19] [2202] OJ L108/7.

- Directive 2002/20 on the authorisation of electronic communications networks and services (Authorisation Directive)[20];
- Directive 2002/21 on a common regulatory framework for electronic communications networks and services (Framework Directive)[21];
- Directive 2002/22 on universal service and users' rights relating to electronic communications networks and services (Universal Service Directive)[22]; and
- Directive 2002/58 concerning the processing of the personal data and the protection of privacy in the electronic communications sector (Privacy Directive).[23]

22–08   The objectives of the EU Commission are to:

- promote competition within the telecommunications market, in part by ensuring that access to telecommunication services and the services themselves are interoperable, thus providing a greater choice for consumers;
- develop the internal market and in particular the harmonisation of EU regulations relating to the provision of telecommunication services; and
- promote the interests of EU citizens.

The aim is for all legislation flowing from the Directives to be technology neutral.

Communications Act 2003

22–09   The Directives were implemented in the UK by the Communications Act 2003. Even though the Communications Act 2003 has over 400 sections and 19 schedules, it provides the United Kingdom with a light touch regulatory regime. The Office of Communications ("Ofcom") is the national regulatory authority for the United Kingdom and represents the United Kingdom in Europe. It is the single regulator for the entire communications sector and has taken over the roles of the five previous regulators. The provisions of earlier legislation and the licences granted thereunder are still in force but now are regulated by Ofcom. The previous licensing regime was replaced with a general authorisation regime under the Communications Act. This means that, provided a service provider complies with the obligations imposed by a set of general conditions and with any specific conditions imposed on it by Ofcom, there is a general permission to provide electronic communication services or to operate electronic communication networks (see definitions below). However, certain areas such as broadcasting are still subject to licensing regimes set out in the Broadcasting Act 1990.

As part of its function, Ofcom is required to undertake market reviews of the various communications markets. Following these reviews it determines whether any organisation has a significant market power and is required to establish

---

[20] [2002] OJ L108/21.
[21] [2002] OJ L108/33.
[22] [2002] OJ L108/51.
[23] [2002] OJ L201/37.

conditions which may be imposed ex ante to ensure that the service providers within that market segment provide a competitive offering. Such conditions and the market itself are monitored by Ofcom. Any conditions imposed by Ofcom are subject to periodic review in light of changes in the market. Ofcom is also the enforcement agency in relation to the regulation of the communications sector and acts as a dispute resolver for both communication service providers and their customers, apart from those matters regulated by the ICO.

Payphone Plus

The provision of premium rate services (such as television votelines, competitions, mobile ringtones, interactive TV games, adult entertainment, information (weather, traffic, etc.) and directory enquiry services) is regulated by PayPhonePlus, which replaced the Independent Committee for the Supervision of Standards of the Telephone Information Services (ICSTIS). The Communications Act gives Ofcom the power to approve a Code to regulate premium rate services.[24] Certain providers, which provide "controlled premium rate services", are required under the conditions of their licenses and s.120(3)(a) of the Communications Act to comply with the Code; for other suppliers the code is voluntary. Ofcom has delegated its powers as the enforcement authority for the premium rate sector and ultimately enforces any sanctions that PayPhonePlus may impose. PayPhonePlus issues the Code supported by non-binding guidance available on its website. The role of PhonePayPlus is important in dealing with the problems caused by silent calls from the use of "power diallers". The issue is dealt with below.

22–10

DIRECTIVE 2002/58

Scope of the Directive

Directive 2002/58 applies in addition to the general Directive 95/46. It applies irrespective of whether personal data are being processed. Where personal data are involved the data controller must comply with the rules in the Data Protection Act 1998 and PECR.

22–11

Technical features and standardisation

One of the reasons for a specific directive on personal data and electronic communications is a concern that different data protection rules arising from different national applications could undermine technical and legal harmonisation in this area. This is reflected in arts 14a, 14 and 15a(4) which are not implemented in PECR because the obligations which are imposed rest upon Member States.

22–12

Article 14 requires that, in implementing Directive 2002/58, Member States must not impose any mandatory technical requirements which could impede the free market in telecommunications equipment. Where provisions of the Directive

---

[24] Communications Act 2003 s.121.

can only be implemented by requiring that telecommunications equipment has specific technical features, Member States have to inform the Commission (art.14(2)) and the Commission will consider the reference in the light of its powers to impose common standards.

Under art.14a provision has been made for the Commission to adopt pan-European measures which concern the security of processing, and the requirements for notification and the provision of information in the event of security breaches. These may be developed under a form of delegated power under which the Commission may adopt implementing measures which do not affect the substantive provisions of the relevant directives (2002/22/EC Universal Services Directive and 2002/58 Directive on Privacy and Electronic Communications).

Article 15 provides that the national regulatory authorities may adopt measure to ensure effective cross-border co-operation in the enforcement of national laws and create harmonised conditions for the provision of services involving cross-border data flows. However, before any such measures are adopted the authorities must supply the Commission in advance with a summary of the rationale for the action, the envisaged measures and the proposed actions. The Commission shall, after consulting the European Network and Information Security Agency (ENISA) and the Article 29WP, be able to make comments or recommendations in particular "to ensure that the envisaged measures do not adversely affect the functioning of the internal market". National regulatory authorities are to "take the utmost account" of the Commission's comments.

Services (digital and analogue exchanges)

22–13   Article 3 states that the Directive shall apply to the processing of personal data in all publicly available electronic communications services in public communications networks in the Community. However, whereas arts 8, 10 and 11 apply to subscriber lines connected to digital exchanges, they only apply to such lines connected to analogue exchanges where it is technically possible to apply them and where it does not involve a disproportionate economic effort to implement those standards. Member States should inform the Commission of those cases in which it is not possible to implement the provisions of these Articles for those reasons. Articles 8 and 10 cover Calling and Connecting Line Identification and art.11 covers automatic call-forwarding. PECR include provisions to reflect this by imposing the requirements on prevention of calling line identification only where the facility is available.

Method of implementation of the Directive

22–14   Directive 2002/58 was implemented by regulations made under s.2(2) of the European Communities Act 1972. This means that the Regulations do not apply to matters outside Community competence. This was used as the basis for the retention of communications data for an extended period of time for the purposes of crime prevention. In all other ways, however, the interpretation of the Regulations should be approached as the main Act. A full description of the approach is set out at Ch.3. In particular a purposive approach must be taken to interpretation bearing in mind the aims of the Directives.

ARE COMMUNICATION SERVICE PROVIDERS PROCESSORS OR CONTROLLERS?

One of the first questions posed in the data protection and privacy context is the extent to which those who provide communication services do so as data controllers or as data processors. Although this may be regarded as a fundamental question about the way that electronic services work it is only obliquely addressed directly in the legislative scheme. The Article 29 Working Party in Opinion 2/2006 refers to recital 47 in the general directive, 95/46/EC, which states:

> "whereas a message containing personal data is transmitted by means of a telecommunications or electronic mail service, the sole purpose of which is the transmission of such messages, the controller in respect of the personal data contained in the message will normally be considered to be the person from whom the message originates, rather than the person offering the transmission service; whereas nevertheless, those offering such services will normally be considered controllers in respect of the processing of the additional personal data necessary for the operation of the service".

The question of who is regarded as the "person from whom the message originates" is left unanswered as is the question of control of any communications data. We would submit that this is ultimately a question of fact but the presumption in the case of public telecommunication systems should be that where the user is an individual user or subscriber, that individual user or subscriber should be regarded as the data controller; in the case of organisations or businesses the subscriber should be regarded as the legal entity and not the individual employee or users. In all, even if the controller is exempt from the DPA, as they are using the personal data for personal, domestic and recreational uses, the service provider will be subject to the requirements of Directive 2002/58, which imposes limits and restrictions on the use of the traffic and billing data, as well as security obligations. This ensures that the subscriber or user's data is protected even though the public electronic communications service provider may not be not subject to a data processor contract.

However, where an electronic communications service is provided on a private system to an organisation then the organisation will also have access to communications data arising from the use of the system. The service provider will not be subject to Directive 2002/58 in respect of that data. We would suggest that the provider should be treated as a normal processor and required to enter into a processor agreement which restricts the rights of the processor as to the data generated as a result of the service and requires the provision of appropriate security controls.

22–15

GUIDANCE FROM THE INFORMATION COMMISSIONER

22–16 The Information Commissioner has issued detailed guidance on the PECR Regulations. Version 3 was issued in May 2004.[25] It was updated slightly in 2007 and a new version issued in July 2011 to take account of the changes made in May 2011. Unless otherwise stated, any references in this chapter to the Commissioner's Guidance refer to the Guidance published in 2011.[26] The Guidance is divided into two sections: the first section covers marketing and the second section covers the remainder of the regulations. The Guidance is particularly detailed and useful in relation to marketing and is supported by a series of Frequently Asked Questions which cover points in considerable detail.

DEFINITIONS AND OTHER GENERAL PROVISION

22–17 Article 2 of Directive 2002/58 provides a number of specific definitions. It also provides that where terms are not specifically defined then the definitions in Directive 95/46/EC (the data protection general directive) and Directive 2002/21/EC (the Framework Directive for telecommunications) apply. As noted earlier the Framework Directive was implemented in the UK by the Communications Act 2003. PECR therefore adopts definitions from the following sources:

- the Communications Act 2003;
- the Broadcasting Act 1990; and
- the Electronic Commerce (EC Directive) Regulations 2002.

The definitions imported are:

- "communications provider";
- "electronic communications network";
- "electronic communications service";
- "information society services";
- "programme service";
- "public electronic communications network";
- "public electronic communications service";

PECR definitions

22–18 The material definitions are as follows[27]:

- Bill—includes an invoice, account, statement or other instrument of similar character and 'billing' shall be construed accordingly.

---

[25] Guidance to the Privacy and Electronic Communications (EC Directive) Regulations 2003.

[26] The Guide to Privacy and Electronic Communications, Version 1, July 9, 2011.

[27] Note that some other terms are in the list such as Ofcom and individual but are not covered here.

- Call—a call is specifically a connection established by means of a telephone service available to the public allowing two-way communication in real time.
- Communication—means any information exchanged between a finite numbers of parties by means of a public electronic communications service but is distinguished from a broadcast. Thus a distinction is drawn between SMS, e-mail and other methods of asyncratic electronic communication and telephone communication. Electronic mail is a form of communication which has a separate definition.
- Electronic mail—means any text, voice, sound or image message sent over a public electronic communications network which can be stored in the network or in the recipient's terminal equipment until it is collected by the recipient and includes messages sent using a short message service.
- Location data—means any data processed in an electronic communications network or by an electronic communications service which shows the geographical position of the user of terminal equipment, who is using a public telecommunications service. Location data includes not only immediate location but also the direction of travel and the time the location was recorded. The words "or by an electronic communications service" were added by the Privacy and Electronic Communications (EC Directive) (Amendment) Regulations 2011 implementing art.2(2) of Directive 2009/136. The aim of the amendment was to ensure that all location data is covered whether in the hands of a network provider or a service provider.
- Subscriber—means a person who is party to a contract with a provider of public electronic communications services for the supply of such services. The subscriber is the legal being who enters into the contract to pay for the services. It should be noted that the Regulations distinguish between individual subscribers and others in respect of the protection afforded; the extent of the protection depends on the category into which the subscriber falls, whether as an individual or a corporate subscriber. In an ordinary household the subscriber will be the person whose name is on the bill and who signed the original agreement. In a company it will be the name of the corporate entity which enters into the legal agreement. Some rights given by the Regulations have to be exercised by or in the name of the subscriber. The subscriber is usually the person whose name appears in any directory.
- Corporate subscriber—means a subscriber who is an incorporated company, a partnership in Scotland, a corporation sole and any other body corporate or entity which is a legal person distinct from its members. This will include bodies in the public sector such as local authorities or government departments. Unincorporated bodies are not defined but will be treated in the same way as individual subscribers. The definition of an individual in art.2(1) specifically includes an unincorporated body of such individuals. Accordingly organisations such as local groups and societies will have the wider protection given to individuals. This may be particularly useful where the secretarial functions for such groups are exercised, as is often the case, by an individual member from his or her home address. An individual subscriber is a living individual.

- Traffic data—means any data processed for the purpose of the conveyance of a communication on a network or for the purpose of billing for the communication and includes data relating to the routing, duration or time of communication.
- User—means any individual using a public electronic communications service.
- Value added service—means any service which requires the processing of traffic or location data beyond that necessary for the transmission of the communication or the billing in respect of the communication.

Guidance issued by the Office of the Information Commissioner ("the PECR Guidance")[28] includes "caller" in the section on definitions stating:

"'**Caller**'— this means the instigator of a call. This is usually a legal person. The call would not be made or the fax/email/text/picture message would not be sent unless the caller paid for it to be made or sent".

However, there is no legal definition of the term "caller" and in the Regulations a distinction appears to be drawn between the person who physically makes the call and the instigator.

Communications Act definitions

22–19   The defined terms are to be found in ss.32, 151 and 405 as follows:

"1)   "Communications provider" (s.405) means a person who (within the meaning of s.32(4)) provides an electronic communications network or an electronic communications service;

2)   "Electronic communications service" (s.32) means a service consisting in, or having as its principal feature, the conveyance by means of an electronic communications network of signals, except in so far as it is a content service;

3)   "Content service" in sub-s.(2) means so much of any service as consists in one or both of the following:
   (a)   the provision of material with a view to its being comprised in signals conveyed by means of an electronic communications network;
   (b)   the exercise of editorial control over the contents of signals conveyed by means of a such a network;

4)   "Electronic communications network" (s.32) means:
   (a)   a transmission system for the conveyance, by the use of electrical, magnetic or electro-magnetic energy, of signals of any description; and
   (b)   such of the following as are used, by the person providing the system and in association with it, for the conveyance of the signals—
      (i)   apparatus comprised in the system;
      (ii)   apparatus used for the switching or routing of the signals; and
      (iii)   software and stored data;

5)   "Public electronic communications network" (s.151) means an electronic communications network provided wholly or mainly for the purpose of making electronic communications services available to members of the public;

---

[28] Guidance to the Privacy and Electronic Communications (EC Directive) Regulations 2003 Pt1, "Marketing by Electronic Means", Version 3, May 2004.

6) "Public electronic communications service" (s.151) means any electronic communications service that is provided so as to be available for use by members of the public."

Broadcasting Act definitions

Section 201 of the Broadcasting Act 1990 defines programme service as follows: **22–20**

"'programme service' means

(1) In this Act 'programme service' means any of the following services (whether or not it is, or it requires to be, licensed under this Act), namely—

    (a) any television broadcasting service or other television programme service (within the meaning of Part I of this Act);

    (b) any sound broadcasting service or licensable sound programme service (within the meaning of Part III of this Act);

    (bb) any digital sound programme service (within the meaning of Part II of the Broadcasting Act 1996);

    (c) any other service which consists in the sending, by means of a telecommunication system, of sounds or visual images or both either—

        (i) for reception at two or more places in the United Kingdom (whether they are so sent for simultaneous reception or at different times in response to requests made by different users of the service); or

        (ii) for reception at a place in the United Kingdom for the purpose of being presented there to members of the public or to any group of persons.

(2) Subsection (1) (c) does not apply to—

    (a) a local delivery service (within the meaning of Part II of this Act);

    (b) a service where the running of the telecommunication system does not require to be licensed under Part II of the M1Telecommunications Act 1984; or

    (c) a two-way service (as defined by section 46(2)(c))."

Electronic Commerce (EC Directive) Regulations definition

The definition of "information society services" is summarised in the Electronic **22–21** Commerce (EC Directive) Regulations 2002 by reference to the original EC Directive as follows:

"'information society services' (which is summarised in recital 17 of the Directive as covering 'any service normally provided for remuneration, at a distance, by means of electronic equipment for the processing (including digital compression) and storage of data, and at the individual request of a recipient of a service)' has the meaning set out in Article 2(a) of the Directive, (which refers to Article 1(2) of Directive 98/34/EC of the European Parliament and of the Council of 22 June 1998 laying down a procedure for the provision of information in the field of technical standards and regulations, as amended by Directive 98/48/EC of 20 July 1998)."[29]

---

[29] The full definition is set out in a subsequent amendment (Directive 98/48/EC of July 20, 1998).

The use of remuneration captures both subscription services and those sites that derive revenue from other sources, for instance advertising. The requirement that the services are provided for remuneration is very broad and includes sites which are established solely to promote a business and from which there is no direct revenue. The former DTI's guidance notes[30] indicate that the definition catches all e-commerce sites including those of businesses providing free information on a website as well as all on-line ads, e-mail etc. This means that virtually all business websites are caught. Best practice is to assume that any form of commercial website is caught by the definition of information society services.

Public electronic communications network and services

22–22   The series of definitions in the Communications Act 2003 which apply in PECR distinguish those services that provide the public with the ability to communicate, in essence the communications networks and services, from the content and information services that are transmitted over them. It is clear that a network provider such as BT is covered. The term "service provider" also clearly applies to those who do not supply the infrastructure but act as sellers of services. Any party from which electronic communications services are purchased will accordingly be covered. It is not clear however how far those organisations that make connectivity available to members of the public, usually at no charge, such as some coffee shops, are covered. Are such entities providing a service to those that use it or is the service actually being provided by another to the coffe shop and the coffe shop is merely letting the user take advantage of that service? On balance we would suggest that the latter is the case but the point is not settled.

The definition of "public electronic communications network" refers to a network which is made available to the members of the public. Equally, the definition of "public electronic communications services" refers to services available for use by members of the public. In neither case is there any further explanation as what is meant by making the network or use of the services available to the public. Accordingly, the words must be given their ordinary meaning. It follows that Directive 2002/58 does not cover private branch exchange systems (PBX systems), for example those used by large companies for their workplaces or universities for their students and staff, despite the fact that these systems may have a large number of users. These are covered by the provisions of the DPA 98 but not by PECR.

22–23   Regulation 27 states that any provision of a contract between a subscriber and service provider or a service provider and a network provider which would be inconsistent with the Regulations shall be void.

Accordingly it is clear that subscribers cannot contract out of the protection of the Regulations. While the position in the main Act is not completely clear (see detailed discussion at Ch.6), the position in the Regulations is made explicit in reg.27.

---

[30] Available in November 2011 from the National Archive website.

DIRECT MARKETING

Who is covered?

In most cases the rules are of general application and apply to any person.   **22–24**
"Person" includes any legal entity, a corporate entity or individual and includes
any body of persons (Interpretation Act 1978). Some provisions only apply to
subscribers, and the provisions in reg.24 which deal with the information that
must be given by those carrying out marketing apply to persons "using" the
service or "instigating the use of the service".

It appears that the "instigator" may be a different person to the caller, and the
caller need not necessarily be employed by the "instigator". Clearly the term
"instigator" would apply to an employer whose employees make calls in the
course of employment; therefore if a marketing business employs staff to make
telephone sales calls the employing organisation will be responsible for
complying with the Regulations and open to penalties for non-compliance. The
term "instigate", however, is wider than "require" or even "cause". It would
appear to be sufficient to cover an organisation which encourages individuals
who are ostensibly self-employed and acting on a commission sales basis to carry
out electronic direct marketing. It is probably wide enough to apply to charitable
organisations which encourage volunteers to use their home telephones to make
calls recruiting helpers to sell raffle tickets or conduct house-to-house collections
for the charity. There is no requirement that the "instigator" should have a
financial relationship with the caller. In the Guidance the Commissioner makes
clear that, where a service provider is used, any enforcement action would be
taken against the employing entity rather than the provider unless the two parties
had connived to breach the Regulations:

> "If we were to take enforcement action we would usually take it against you not your
> subcontractor. You should check you have appropriate contracts to guard against
> such failures."[31]

A person need not be a data controller or a data processor to be caught by this
aspect of the Regulations. He or she does not need to have a computer or to
process personal data. All the caller has to do is use the telephone for direct
marketing and the relevant provisions will apply.

Direct marketing

This is not defined in either Directive 2002/58 or Directive 95/46. The definition   **22–25**
which applies in the Regulations is therefore the same as that in s.11 of the DPA
98. Under reg.21(2), any reference to direct marketing is a reference to the
communication of any advertising or marketing material on a particular line. It
should be noted that any reference to line shall be construed as a reference to
anything that performs the functions of a line and the term "connected" in
relation to a line is to be construed in the same way.[32]

---

[31] The Guide to Privacy and Electronic Communications, ICO, Version 1, July 9, 2011, p.8.
[32] reg.2(4).

Marketing has been given a broad definition under the Data Protection Act 1998 by the Information Tribunal. In the case of *Scottish National Party v Information Commissioner*[33] the SNP argued that the playing of pre-recorded telephone messages from Mr Alex Salmond and Sir Sean Connery before the election to encourage voters to support the party should not be regarded as marketing. The Tribunal held that the activity constituted direct marketing and not-for-profit organisations such as political parties were not excluded from the ambit of the Regulations. The Tribunal supported the broad view which has been adopted by the Commissioner. The advertising need not be of a commercial product, nor need anything be offered for sale. This fits with the commonly used sense of the term. In Recommendation R(85)20 of the Council of Europe on the Protection of Personal Data used for the purposes of Direct Marketing, for the purposes of the Recommendation "direct marketing":

"comprises all activities which make it possible to offer goods or services or to transmit other messages to a segment of the population by post, telephone or other direct means aimed at informing or soliciting a response from the data subject as well as any service ancillary thereto."

Under the Distance Selling Directive (97/7), direct marketing is not specifically defined but advertising is. The term advertising

"is to be taken to include all forms of direct marketing communication, including any sales promotion or fund raising, whether or not it contains an offer or an invitation to treat."

22–26   In Recommendation (95)4 it is made clear that direct marketing includes not only commercial marketing, but also political marketing and approaches made by trade unions, charitable organisations and others.[34]

The Federation of European Direct Marketing, which represents the direct marketing sector at European level, issued its view of the meaning of direct marketing in its response to the Council of Europe Privacy Guidelines on the Internet in July 1998 thus:

"Direct marketing is a series of marketing strategies, using various delivery techniques designed to provide the receiver (consumers and companies) with information at a distance. Direct marketing is principally but not exclusively database, one-to-one relationship marketing. Direct marketing is not a homogenous marketing discipline but rather a series of different strategies using different means of approach (e.g. broadcasting, printed press, mail, telephone, on-line services). It is used to sell products, to deliver information, public announcements, and for after sales services, customer care services, charity and political appeals."

In its Code of Practice on data protection approved by the Article 29 Working Party Direct marketing is defined as:

---

[33] Appeal EA/2005/0021 Information Tribunal.
[34] Explanatory Memorandum, para.85.

"The Communication by whatever means (including but not limited to mail, fax, telephone, on-line services etc..) of any advertising or marketing material which is carried out by the Direct Marketer itself or on its behalf and which is directed at particular individuals".

The Article 29 Working Party confirmed that, in its view, art.13 covers

"... any form of sales promotion, including direct marketing by charities and political organisations (e.g. fund raising etc.)."[35]

The ICO Guide make it clear that the Commissioner takes the view that the term covers a wide range of activities including the promotion of an organisation's aims and ideals. While these are not legal definitions for this purpose they show that the term has been given a wide meaning and this has been followed by the Tribunal.

Automated calling systems

Regulation 19 bans the use of automated calling systems for direct marketing without the prior consent of the subscriber. This provision affords equal protection to individuals and corporate subscribers. The subscriber must have previously notified the caller or the instigator of the call that he consents to receiving calls via an automated call system for the time being. The term "automated calling system" is defined as a system which is capable of automatically initiating a sequence of calls to more than one destination in accordance with instructions stored in that system and transmitting sounds which are not live speech for reception by persons at some or all of the destinations called. This is a restricted meaning of the term "call" and excludes any form of communication other than voice. The systems were described in Recommendation (95)4 at para.95 as:

22–27

"robotic dialling devices [which] allow for the random dialling of pre-recorded marketing messages. They feed on lists of numbers which are dialled over and over again until the subscriber replies."

The essence of such a system is not only that the calls are dialled automatically but that the same message is given automatically to all recipients. Thus automatic dialler devices which allow human operators to have numbers dialled for them and then be ready to pick them up when someone answers the telephone are not caught: see para.22–26, below, in respect of such systems. The Commissioner's Guidance states that automated calls are caught even if one of the recorded options is to press a digit and speak to a live operator. In addition the person "using or instigating the use of the system" must ensure that the name of that person and either an address or telephone number at which he can be reached is provided with the communication. This means that the automated call must include this information. The relevant provision in Directive 2002/58 was amended by 2009/136 to require that automated calling systems may only be

---

[35] Opinion 5/2004 on unsolicited communications for marketing purposes of the Article 29 Working Party 11601/EN WP 90, para.3.3.

used where the users, as well as subscribers, have given consent. In effect this requires a system to be introduced to allow users to give consent to the receipt of automated calls. The UK provisions are that such calls cannot be made without the consent of the subscriber. The UK has therefore (technically) failed to implement the provision.

Automated diallers and silent calls

22–28   The use of automated diallers has given rise a problem of subscribers receiving silent calls. The problem does not arise from automated calling systems but from ones where the organisation uses staff to speak to customers or targets. It arises because the organisation wishes to maximise the number of contacts that staff can make. Therefore they use a programme which dials numbers automatically before there is an operative ready to pick them up. If no member of staff is ready to take another call the recipient picks up the telephone to find no one on the other end. These silent calls can be extremely worrying for recipients.

In an early version of the Guidance the ICO took the view that such calls do not fall under the PECR, because no marketing material was actually conveyed by the call.

However, the subscriber who is troubled by such calls is not left without a remedy because Ofcom has taken action to restrict the impact of these systems in relation to silent calls. Ofcom is under a duty, under s.131 of the Communications Act 2003, to publish a policy on enforcement and to have regard to its policy in taking action. In September 2008 Ofcom revised its policy statement to make clear that it regards abandoned or silent calls as an example of persistent misuse of an electronic communications network or service. In June 2010 it consulted on a further revision and in September 2010 published a revised document, "Tackling abandoned and silent calls: statement". In September 2010 the maximum penalty available to Ofcom to punish persistent misuse was increased from £50,000.00 to £2 million. Ofcom has acted against organisations which have failed to deal with systems which resulted in silent calls to subscribers.

E-MAIL MARKETING

22–29   The term "spam" or "spamming" is popularly used to describe unsolicited commercial e-mails sent over the Internet. This may be on an individual basis or take the form of unsolicited bulk email. In some cases email addresses are "harvested", that is gleaned by automated programmes which pull addresses out of newsgroups and web pages. Some users deluge the networks with spam using automated sending facilities. Service providers strive to filter out spamming and once a service provider is alerted to the practice it will usually terminate the user's account, but by that time the damage may have been done.

22–30   The use of spam to mount Denial of Service (DOS) attacks is now an offence under the Computer Misuse Act 1990 (CMA). The aim of a DOS attack is to deny genuine users access to specific computing resources. Such attacks can be mounted by the use of software that automatically sends e-mails to nominated e-mail servers. The volume of e-mails overwhelms the server, in essence preventing it from sending or receiving e-mail. The CMA was amended after a case in which a former employee deluged his former employer's systems with e-mail using a mail bomb program. Mr Lennon used software to send in the region of 5 million e-mails to a server belonging to Domestic and General Group Plc (his former employer). In the first instance, the judge in the Youth Court held that there was no case to answer on the basis that the employer's e-mail system had been set up to receive e-mail and so there was an implied consent to send e-mail to it. Even if such implied consent did not extend to sending multiple e-mails to the e-mail address, it was not possible to determine at what point such implied consent came to an end and so no offence could have been committed. The case turned on the wording of s.3 of the CMA and whether there had been a modification to the employer's systems. Not surprisingly the prosecution appealed the decision and the matter was considered by the High Court.

In the High Court, Jack J. held that a denial of service (DOS) attack amounted to a breach of the CMA. he found that the receipt of emails by the email server was an "unauthorised modification" for the purposes of the CMA on the basis that the implied consent could not be considered to extend to the sending of malicious e-mails, purportedly from another user, with the express intent of overwhelming the e-mail system.

Under PECR the Commissioner can take enforcement action to restrain the spammer if he can be found, culminating if necessary in prosecutions. Clearly this depends on being able to trace those responsible and the efficacy of the remedy will also depend on where the actions are deemed to be carried on. As much spam originates outside the United Kingdom, the relevant territorial provisions will be important. It is now also possible for a person who suffers damage because of the effect of unsolicited direct marketing to bring an action for compensation under reg.30 (see para.22–120 below for an examination of this provision).

Relevant provisions in Directive 2002/58

Under art.13(1) the use of electronic mail for the purposes of direct marketing 22–31 without the consent of the recipient is not permitted. The term "recipient of the electronic mail" is clearly wide enough to cover both subscribers and users. The UK provision therefore meets the revised requirement of art.13(1) of 2002/58 as amended by 2009/136 which requires both subscribers and users to be covered. Electronic mail is widely defined and the definition is sufficient to cover messages left as voicemail calls on telephone systems as well as text messages to mobile telephones.

Scope

Marketing messages sent by SMS to mobile telephones are also covered. It was 22–32 not clear whether email and SMS were covered by the TDPP Regulations however since PECR the position has been clear. In the Guidance the Commissioner deals with scope as follows:

"In other words, email, text, picture and video marketing messages are all considered the be 'electronic mail'. Marketing transmitted in WAP messages is considered the be electronic mail. WAP Push allows a sender to send a specially formatted SMS messsage to a handset which, when received, allows a recipient through a single click to access and view content stored online, through the browser on the handset.

We consider that this rule also applies to voicemail and answerphone messages left by marketers making calls that would otherwise be "live". So there are stricter obligations placed on you if you make live calls but then wish to leave messages on a person's voicemail or answerphone".

Individual and corporate subscribers

22–33   Regulation 22 of the PECR implements the provisions covering unsolicited communications for direct marketing email in art.13. The opt-in rule is incorporated in reg.22(2), which applies to the transmission of unsolicited communications by means of electronic mail to recipients. Where the subscriber to a line is an individual subscriber the rights apply to those who receive electronic communications using that line. Such persons are referred to as recipients. The term recipient is not defined in the PECR. It is defined in the Act in relation to personal data only however the provisions of reg.22 apply irrespective of whether the messages contain personal data. The better view therefore is that the technical definition in the Act will not apply but may be of persuasive value. This leaves open the question of whether a recipient can be a legal person as well as a natural person. It could be argued that, as the term recipient in the Act would cover legal as well as natural persons, where the subscriber is an individual who allows a legal entity to use the relevant line the legal entity itself could be regarded as a recipient. However, reg.22(1) restricts the provisions to the transmission of unsolicited communications to individual subscribers so the better view is probably that the term recipient in the Regulations should not be regarded as covering corporate bodies. It also follows that where an individual subscriber allows several other individuals to use a facility such as a PC each individual will be a recipient and be able to make his or her own choices about the receipt of e-mail marketing. This leads to an interesting issue where the subscriber is a large partnership which would more usually be regarded as the equivalent of a corporate entity. The ICO Guide accepts however that in such a case the wishes of the subscriber should over-ride the choices of the employees, using the example of an employer who wants an employee to keep in regular contact with conference organisers, an obligation which means the employee has to accept the receipt of marketing materials.

The provision does not apply where the subscriber is a corporate body and therefore does not cover spam aimed at individuals at their corporate e-mail addresses or mobile telephones, although where personal data are involved, such marketing will be covered by the provisions of the Act.[36]

22–34   Under reg.22(2):

"a person shall neither transmit, nor instigate the transmission of unsolicited communications for the purposes of direct marketing by means of electronic mail

---

[36] The ICO Guidance notes that the Committee of Advertising Practice Code restricts the sending of individual marketing e-mails to corporate addresses.

unless the recipient of the electronic mail has previously notified the sender that he consents for the time being to such communications being sent by or at the instigation of the sender".

There are a number of potential ambiguities in this regulation: the meaning of the term "unsolicited"; the distinction between that and "consent"; and the duration of "the time being".

The obligation to comply falls on the person who transmits or instigates the transmission of the e-mail. In most cases the subscriber whose line is used for the transmission of the marketing material will be responsible for this. However, if the subscriber allows another person to use his line it appears that he would only be responsible if he was involved in the transmission. It would be prudent, however, for any person who acts as an agent for others, or provides marketing services or allows others to use his lines for e mail marketing to ensure that the rules are being followed.

When is an e mail "unsolicited"?

The regulation covers "unsolicited" direct marketing communications by e mail but does not define the term "unsolicited". The ICO Guidance describes an unsolicited marketing communication as one

> ". . . that they have not invited but that for the time being they do not positively object to receiving".

The use of the word appears to add nothing to the provision as consent is required before e-mail marketing can be sent. Therefore the individual must have done something from which the marketer is able to infer consent to the marketing. In relation to the meaning of the term "consent" the Guide points out that where personal data are concerned the definition in the main directive, Directive 95/46, continues to apply. The consent must therefore be freely given, informed and signified to the recipient.[37] Where consent is being obtained online, it need not be restricted to a tick-box but may be some other mechanism such as clicking on an icon or sending an e-mail. It is crucial, however, that some clear action is taken by the subscriber. One of the repeated questions from marketers is whether notice coupled with a failure to register an objection, i.e. an "opt-out" mechanism, is sufficient to be regarded as a consent. The ICO makes clear that such a mechanism alone will not be sufficient but may be combined with other mechanisms to achieve a sufficient consent:

> "However, in context, a failure to indicate objection may be part of the mechanism whereby a person indicates consent. For example, if you receive a clear and prominent message along the following lines, the fact that a suitably prominent opt-out box has not been ticked may help establish that consent has been given: e.g. "By submitting this registration form, you will be indicating your consent to receiving email marketing messages from us unless you have indicated and objection to receiving such messages by ticking the above box".

22–35

---

[37] For a full discussion of the meaning of the term see Ch.3.

For a consent to be informed, the collector of the e-mail address must have given a proper notice of the intended use. The consent is specific to the "sender" of the e-mail marketing but there is no restriction on the beneficiary of the marketing. In other words the sender may obtain consent to market goods being sold by third parties but may not pass on the names and e-mail addresses for others to carry out the marketing themselves unless he has obtained a consent which applies directly to the third party. For example, a company may seek an individual's consent on behalf of itself and all its affiliated companies. The question of whether such a consent is valid and effective will depend on the facts of the case and particularly the level of detailed information provided to the recipient. The ICO Guidance accepts that a positive response to a question phrased in general terms will be sufficient, for example:

> "We'd like to pass your e mail address to other companies so that they can send you online offers too. If you agree to this, tick here [box]"

would be sufficient to obtain a consent for the third parties as long as it evoked a positive response.

However, the Guide cautions that care should be taken by those buying in lists for e mail marketing to ensure that the consents being relied on are valid.

For the time being

22–36   The phrase is used in regs 20, 21, 22, 25 and 26. Subscribers may notify the holders of the preference service lists or marketers that they do not "for the time being" wish to receive unsolicited communications or may notify the senders of marketing materials by facsimile or e mail that they "consent for the time being" to receiving such communications, or, in reg.20(5), "do not object for the time being" to unsolicited facsimiles. The term is not derived from the Directive. It must therefore be given its usual meaning subject to the obligation to apply a purposive approach to achieve the aims of the Directive. Under the Directive the provisions on unsolicited communications are dealt with in art.13. The material section is s.13(3), which provides that Member States

> "shall take appropriate measures to ensure that, free of charge, unsolicited communications for the purposes of direct marketing, in cases other than those referred to in paragraphs 1 and 2 [Note: these deal with consent and the exception for similar goods and services in the case of e mail marketing] are not allowed either without the consent of the subscribers concerned or in respect of subscribers who do not wish to receive these communications, the choice between these options to be determined by national legislation."

It is extremely difficult to work out what, if anything, the phrase "for the time being" adds. Perhaps the simplest approach is that it makes explicit that contributors are always able to change their minds and therefore neither a consent nor an objection is an eternal choice. The Directive makes clear that some forms of marketing require consent and for others marketers may be made subject to an opt-out regime. Consent must be given its normal meaning and the question of whether a consent continues to apply should be determined on the basis of the evidence available. It is suggested therefore that the term adds nothing of value to the concept of consent.

It appears from the ICO Guidance that it has been suggested that the addition of the term "for the time being" to the requirement for consent suggests that consent must inevitably lapse after a certain period. However, we would suggest that whether consent exists or not must be a question of fact. The Guidance takes what appears to be the same view and suggests that an initial consent will remain valid:

> "... [w]here there are good grounds for believing that the recipient remains happy to receive the marketing communications in question, for example where the recipient has responded positively (i.e. other than to object) to previous recent marketing e mails".

The Regulations came into effect on December 11, 2003. The transitional provisions in Sch.2 provide that consent obtained before the commencement endures.

"Soft opt in"

The restriction to only sending marketing e-mails with consent is subject to the proviso in art.13(2) of the Directive that, where e-mail addresses have been obtained from customers in the context of the provision of goods or services with full notice, they can be used for the marketing of similar products or services, subject to the subject being given the opportunity to object free of charge and in an easy manner to such use when the data are collected and to there being a consistent opt-out message on every subsequent communications. This has been implemented in reg.22(3), under which a person may

22–37

> "send or instigate the sending of electronic mail for the purposes of direct marketing where—
>
> (a) that person has obtained the contact details of the recipient of that electronic mail in the course of the sale or negotiation for the sale of a product or service to that recipient;
> (b) the direct marketing is in respect of that person's similar products and services only: and
> (c) the recipient has been given a simple means of refusing (free of charge except for the costs of the transmission of the refusal) the use of his contact details for the purposes of such direct marketing, at the time when the details were initially collected, and, where he did not initially refuse the use of the details, at the time of each subsequent communication".

The particular issues to be considered are: what amounts to the course of negotiations for the sale of a product and how similar products and services should be interpreted. The PECR Guidance accepts that where a person has actively expressed an interest in purchasing a company's products and services and not opted out of further marketing of that product or service or similar products or services when their details were collected then the marketer can continue to use their details for his own marketing. It makes clear that the similar products and services must be those of the entity which had the contact and does not cover other companies in a group. In relation to similar products the Guide refers to promotional material that the individual would "reasonably expect". The Article 29 Working Party in its Opinion 5/2004 took a more stringent view and suggested that the exemption for similar products and services should be narrowly interpreted.

Means of refusing

22–38   Regulation 22(3)(c) requires that the recipient must have been provided with a simple means of refusing the use at the point of initial collection of his contact details and at the time of each subsequent communication. While this is relatively straightforward on websites and e-mails, being achieved by the use of the "unsubscribe" option, it can present practical problems where the marketing is being sent by SMS. The ICO comments that the practical limitations of standard mobile screens do not mean that marketers can ignore the rules about giving proper initial notice and advocates the provision of information via advertise-ments or websites where individuals sign up for services. The ICO is more sympathetic to the difficulties caused in providing the subsequent notice. In the Guidance it is explained that the Commissioner had originally considered that opt-out notices should provide a postal or e-mail address, but after further consultation with the industry has agreed that a short code can be used as long as the sender has been clearly identified, the short code message is not a premium rate charge and the short code is valid.

E-mail marketing by charities

22–39   The use of the soft opt-in is restricted to those cases where the e-mail address has been obtained "in the course of a sale or negotiation for the sale of a product or service". Thus this is only available where the e-mail address of the target has been obtained in a commercial relationship. It is common for charities and not-for-profit organisations to obtain contact details in an environment which is initially non-commercial but to later want to use those e-mails for contact which will include marketing, for example contact by a university with its alumni. Strictly such users cannot take advantage of the soft opt-out and require positive consent to send such e-mails. In practice, however, the ICO has recognised this anomaly, and comments in respect of charities:

"We recognize that this disadvantages you".

The Guidance suggests that charitable organisations might address the problem by looking at the wording of their data protection and privacy statements to supporters and try to word them so that supporters actively agree to receiving marketing by e-mail.

22–40   A further area where there is a perceived gap in the provisions dealing with e-mail marketing is the sending of e-mails to individuals at their corporate addresses or text, pictures or other marketing to mobile phones which are supplied to employees by corporate subscribers. The Guidance explains that the e-mail rules simply do not apply to corporate subscribers and the Commissioner's powers to enforce PECR do not extend to these. There is no equivalent of the fax or telephone preference services for e mail so even the use of a preference service is not available to individuals at corporate addresses.

ICO Guidance

In addition to the issues canvassed above in relation to e-mail marketing the ICO Guide covers viral marketing and the implementation of pan-European marketing campaigns by e-mail. On viral marketing it points out that a marketer which encourages recipients to pass on material will be an "instigator" of electronic mail for direct marketing purposes and remain responsible under the Regulations. This is particularly the case where the marketer offers a reward of some form for sending on the material. Where a marketer encourages recipients to pass the names and contact details of friends they must not use the details unless satisfied that the individuals know and have consented. In relation to pan-European campaigns it simply notes that some jurisdictions have taken a more stringent line on e-mail marketing than the UK and marketers should take legal advice and ensure that they comply with all relevant laws if carrying out a pan European campaign. Interestingly in the Article 29 Working Party Opinion on applicable law the WP takes the view that the law of the Member State where the marketer is based would be the relevant law for a marketing campaign into other Member States and there would be no obligation to comply with the law of the individual Member States.

22–41

Concealing the identity of the sender

Regulation 23 prohibits "any person" from transmitting or instigating the transmission of a communication for the purposes of direct marketing by means of electronic mail where the identity of the person on whose behalf the communication has been sent has been disguised or concealed or where a valid address to which the recipient of the communication may send a request that such communication cease has not been provided. A "valid address" must be provided. The ICO accepts that in the online environment this could be an e-mail address and in text messages a short code could amount to a valid address. As good practice however it recommends a website address or PO Box number should be included. This imposes an obligation on the person "on whose behalf" the marketing is sent to ensure that there is no deception.

22–42

There is no positive requirement in relation to electronic mail in the PECR that the sender must include the identity of the organisation responsible for the marketing. This contrasts with the obligations imposed by reg.24 on those who make telephone calls, use automated calling systems of market by fax.

However, reg.7 of the Electronic Commerce (EC Directive) Regulations 2002 requires the originating party to be identified where any "commercial communications" (see definition below) are made on its behalf. In addition any such communication should clearly identify:

- that it is a commercial communication and the person on whose behalf it is made
- any promotional offers;
- any promotional competitions; and
- in an accessible, clear and unambiguous way the terms and conditions surrounding any promotional offer or competition.

Regulation 2(1) defines "commercial communication" as

"a communication, in any form, designed to promote, directly or indirectly, the goods, services or image of any person pursuing a commercial, industrial or craft activity or exercising a regulated profession, other than a communication—

(a)   consisting only of information allowing direct access to the activity of that person including a geographic address, a domain name or an electronic mail address; or

(b)   relating to the goods, services or image of that person provided that the communication has been prepared independently of the person making it (and for this purpose, a communication prepared without financial consideration is to be taken to have been prepared independently unless the contrary is shown)".

In addition, reg.8 requires service providers to clearly identify unsolicited commercial communications sent by electronic mail so that it is clear to the recipient, upon receipt, that the communication is unsolicited.

TELEPHONE MARKETING

22–43   Regulation 21 covers unsolicited telephone calls for direct marketing purposes. A person must not use, or instigate the use of, or permit his line to be used for such marketing where an objection has been lodged by the subscriber for the line in question. An objection can be lodged either by the subscriber notifying the caller that unsolicited calls should not "for the time being" be made on the line or by the subscriber listing the line number on the stop list kept by Ofcom. The provisions protect both individual and corporate subscribers. Since June 2004 corporate subscribers have also been able to register with the Telephone Preference Service (TPS). The protection applies to subscribers and not to recipients of calls therefore if the subscriber for a line has registered an objection, either directly or on the TPS, unsolicited calls cannot be made on that line. Solicited calls are not affected and therefore if a user of the line who is not the subscriber has agreed to receive marketing calls this is still permissible.

Unsolicited

22–44   As in reg.22(2) this is not defined This does not mean, as a matter of law, that any call should be treated as unsolicited unless the subscriber has explicitly agreed to accept direct marketing from or at the instigation of that particular caller. It is possible that a call could be treated as not unsolicited in other circumstances but in most cases a call will be unsolicited if the subscriber has not clearly agreed to the caller, or someone acting at his behest, contacting him via the telephone (see para.22-35, above, for a discussion of the term as used in reg.22(2)).

Regulation 21(4) provides that the fact that the subscriber registers with the telephone preference service will not automatically override a notification of non-objection to the receipt of calls. Such calls may be made by the caller on the line even though the number is registered with the TPS. It is not completely clear from the wording whether this is meant to apply to prior or subsequent notification however the Information Commissioner takes the view in the Guidance that where the subscriber has previously agreed to receive calls from a specific organisation a general registration on the TPS does not override that consent. In practice, in most cases therefore, where a subscriber has notified a caller that he does not object to receiving direct marketing calls, the caller may rely on this until it is specifically revoked, usually by the caller being directly advised otherwise. Clearly the question of whether a consent remains valid will be a question of fact and it may not be wise for an organisation which has not made marketing calls to a particular subscriber for some time to rely on an "old" consent in relation to a subscriber who has registered on the TPS in the intervening period.

22–45

Subscribers who register on the TPS should therefore specifically notify organisations which they have previously agreed could call them, if they wish to stop future calls. A notification does not have to be made in writing but it may be prudent for evidential purposes to give a written notice and retain a copy. Subscribers should allow 28 days for the TPS registration to take effect. A call within the first 28 days of registration will not breach the Regulation.[38]

MARKETING BY FAX

Rights of individual subscribers

Regulation 20 deals with unsolicited direct marketing faxes. Such faxes are prohibited without consent "for the time being". The prohibition covers a person transmitting or instigating the transmission of such faxes or a subscriber permitting his line to be used for their transmission. In the case of a subscriber who permits others to use a line for which he is the named subscriber the regulation is not specific as to the extent of knowledge required before he is held responsible for permitting the use. In *Sweet v Parsley*[39] it was held that the term "permit" connotes actual knowledge or grounds for suspicion that the prohibited act is going on and an unwillingness to act to prevent it. This was a case under the Dangerous Drugs Act 1965 in which the occupier of premises was charged with permitting premises to be used for drug taking. This was confirmed in *R. v Souter*.[40] The knowledge or suspicion must go to the relevant aspects of the prohibited activity. If actual knowledge is required the subscriber would have to be aware that the user of the line was undertaking the prohibited acts before he

22–46

---

[38] reg.21(4).
[39] [1969] 1 All E.R.347.
[40] [1971] 1 W.L.R. 1187.

could be held to have "permitted" them. Alternatively it may be argued that, as in *Sweet v Parsley*, suspicion coupled with turning a blind eye may be sufficient.

Consent

22–47   An individual subscriber must have

> "previously notified the caller that he consents for the time being to such communications being sent by or at the instigation of the caller".

The consent must be provided to the caller before the fax is sent. Applying general principles consent may be implied from a relevant action but cannot be implied from inertia or silence (see discussion of consent in Ch.4). The consent must be explicit as to the particular kind of marketing ("such communications"), so a general consent to the receipt of marketing materials will not be sufficient to cover fax marketing. It must also be specific to the caller in question ("notified the caller"), so a general consent to receive fax marketing will not suffice. The consent must emanate from the subscriber for the line, not merely from one of the household. It is not clear how a marketer is meant to distinguish individual subscribers in all cases. Clearly a number may be allocated to a named individual and shown so in the directory. Equally the directory entry may show the name of a limited company. It will be apparent from those that the subscriber is an individual or a corporate subscriber respectively. However, in some cases a trading name may be used and it may not be clear whether the subscriber is an individual or a corporate entity. In the case of a corporate entity the caller does not need prior consent but only to respond to an objection if notified (see below). The fact that there may be some possible confusion in some cases should not, in the long term, be a detriment to the individual subscriber as he may also make use of the fax preference service designed for corporate subscribers. If an individual subscriber's line continues to be used for marketing faxes, possibly because it appears from directory information to belong to a corporate entity, then the individual can also exercise the rights described below. It does however have the effect of reducing the effective level of protection to opt-out in such cases. This is borne out by the agreement reached by the regulator in a case brought in 2000.

22–48   In January 2001 the Information Commissioner settled enforcement cases against two companies, Second Telecom Ltd and Top 20 Ltd, for sending unsolicited faxes, by an agreed enforcement notice which imposed obligations on the companies to routinely screen their existing databases against list of residential subscribers so as to exclude those who appeared on such databases from their marketing lists. The agreed notice was accompanied by an order of the Tribunal, which imposed obligations on both companies not to send faxes to anyone who had opted-out of receiving faxes either by notifying the Commissioner or the companies themselves or who appears on the Fax Preference service stop list.

22–49   Because of the definitions used for corporate subscribers and individual subscribers, partnerships, whatever their size, fall to be treated as individual subscribers unless they are limited liability partnerships. Partners are persons who carry on business together with a view to profit (Partnership Act 1890). A partnership, apart from a limited liability partnership or a partnership in Scotland, is not a corporate entity with a legal personality of its own and therefore does not fall into the definition of corporate subscriber in reg.2(1). While it may seem strange that some of the very large accountancy or legal partnerships are entitled to be treated as individual subscribers that is the case.

A caller may rely on a previous consent until he is notified that it no longer applies. Where a subscriber who has consented to the despatch of marketing faxes is no longer the subscriber for that line, it will be helpful to his successor to the line if he either tells those to whom he has given the consents of the change, or leaves his successor a list of those to whom he has given consent. However, this is perhaps asking a lot and it may not be a common occurrence.

A subscriber who has given consent may withdraw consent at any time.[41]

Rights of corporate subscribers

Although this section is headed the rights of corporate subscribers, in fact, as explained above, individual subscribers are also able to take advantage of the stop list. Under reg.20(1)(a) transmitting, instigating the transmission of or permitting the use of a line to make unsolicited direct marketing faxes is not allowed where either:

(a) the called line is that of a corporate subscriber who has previously notified the caller that such unsolicited communications should not be sent on that line; or

(b) the number allocated to the subscriber is on the stop list run by OFCOM.

In the first case, the notification must have been made to the caller, not the person whose line is being used. The notice need not be in writing. The notice must have told the caller that unsolicited faxes for marketing should not be sent on that line.

A 28-day period of grace applies to the fax preference service stop list as to the telephone preference service list. Under reg.20(5), where a subscriber who has registered on the stop list "has notified a caller that he does not for the time being object to such communication being sent by that caller on that line" such communications may continue to be sent notwithstanding the appearance on the stop list. This point has been discussed earlier.

Directive 2002/58 was amended by 2009/136 to provide that the use of facsimile machines for marketing (inter alia) may be allowed only in respect of individual subscribers and users who have given prior consent. The effect would appear to be that users as well as subscribers should be able to consent to the receipt of marketing faxes however no change has been made to PECR.

INFORMATION TO BE PROVIDED ON MARKETING

Certain information must be provided on all direct marketing sent using public electronic communication services by virtue of reg.24. The name of the person using or instigating the service must be given for all calls whether fax, telephone

22–50

22–51

22–52

---

[41] reg.20(6).

or an automated call. In relation to fax and automated calls the address of the person or a telephone number at which he can be reached free of charge must be provided. In the case of other direct marketing that information must be communicated if the recipient of the call so requests. It should be noted that the request may be made by the recipient of the call. It need not be made by the subscriber. The information must therefore be available when the call is made. It will not be sufficient for a caller to say it will be sent by post or is available in some other place.

STOP LISTS

22–53   Regulations 20 and 21 refer to the stop lists for both fax and telephone lines. A telephone preference service and a fax preference service were previously run by the direct marketing industry. These were replaced by the statutory arrangements under PECR In essence these set up "stop" lists of those who have stated that they do not want to be subject to fax or telephone marketing; both allow individuals and business to register. The responsibility for the lists rests with Ofcom under regs 25 and 26 although Ofcom has delegated the tasks to a third party. The arrangements for each list are similar.

Fax Preference Service (FPS) and Telephone Preference Service (TPS)

22–54   Any subscriber, whether a corporate subscriber or an individual, can notify Ofcom that he or she does not wish for the time being to receive unsolicited direct marketing faxes on a particular line.[42]

Any subscriber may notify Ofcom that they do not want for the time being to receive unsolicited direct marketing calls.[43] Until June 25, 2004, the right to register with the TPS was restricted to individual subscribers however this was altered by the Privacy and Electronic Communications (EC Directive) (Amendment) Regulations 2004,[44] which permitted corporate subscribers to register. Corporate subscribers can register numbers allocated to particular lines by notice in writing to Ofcom The term corporate subscriber also covers schools, hospitals, government departments and other public bodies.

The notices do not have to be in writing, apart from the notices provided by corporate users of the TPS, although clearly it will be helpful if subscribers put their objections in writing. Ofcom must maintain and keep up to date a list of all the fax numbers notified to them in this way and a list of the telephone numbers notified to them. If Ofcom has reason to believe that the subscriber who notified the objection is no longer the holder of that particular line number they must remove the number from the stop list.

Ofcom has corresponding duties under regs 25(3) and 26(3) to make information from the stop lists available to any person who wants to send unsolicited direct marketing faxes or make calls for unsolicited direct marketing.

---

[42] reg.25.
[43] reg.26.
[44] SI 2004/1039.

Thus the marketer will be able to check that none of the numbers which he intends to contact belong to those who have objected. Ofcom must also make information from the records available to subscribers who want to check whether their number is on the list and have it removed. Ofcom can charge fees for making the information available and may charge different fees for providing different information, subject to an overriding duty to ensure that the systems pay for themselves.

The Regulations do not set out how the stop lists are to be run. Ofcom may keep the records in electronic or in printed form. Ofcom is permitted to make arrangements with another or others to provide the stop list mechanisms, but not the power to set the fees for use.

28-day time delay

A 28-day time delay is built in from the time that a number appears on the list to allow for those mounting marketing campaigns to apply the list. If a subscriber registers with a preference service just after the marketer has received his copy of the stop list the marketer may (quite innocently) telephone or fax that subscriber despite the fact that he has objected. Regulations 20(4) and 21(3)deal with this situation by providing that the caller will not be held to have contravened if the number was not on the list within the preceding 28 days before the call. In effect callers will not be able to rely on copies of the stop lists any older than 28 days.

22–55

SECURITY OF ELECTRONIC COMMUNICATIONS

Those providing public electronic communications services have significant obligations both to ensure proper security for the systems and also to give notice to subscribers and users of any breach of security which is likely to adversely affect the personal data or privacy of a subscriber or user. The security breach notice obligations were introduced by Directive 2009/136 amending 2002/58 and are the first generally applicable obligations of their kind at EU level. The background can be seen in the recitals to the relevant articles in Directive 2009/136. Recital 52 reiterates that, where providers of services are data controllers they have security obligations under the general directive, for example to stop unauthorised access or resist "denial of service" attacks. However many electronic communication services are now provided by those who are not themselves data controllers and the protection of consumers should not depend on whether the service providers are controllers:

22–56

> "It is necessary to ensure that consumers and users are afforded the same level of protection of privacy and personal data, regardless of the technology used to deliver a particular service".

Interestingly the recitals then go on to make clear the views of the Commission that notification of security breaches "reflects the general interest of citizens" and urges mandatory notification to be extended to all sectors as soon as possible.

The effect of the extended security and new personal data breach obligations is to impose direct obligations on one category of data processors and, in respect of the personal data breach obligations, obligations on one category of data controller beyond those imposed on others.

Enhanced obligations of security

22–57   Regulation 5 is based on art.4 of Directive 2002/58 and imposes an obligation on providers of public electronic communications services ("service providers" or "the service provider") to take "appropriate technical and organisational measures to safeguard the security of that service". Providers must also alert users to particular security risks involved with the service. The general obligation is not limited to the protection of personal data and applies to the entire service provision. Therefore if the communication service has links to non-personal information, for example information about things, that must also be secured. Recital 55 specifically refers to the use of Radio Frequency Identification Devices (RFID) and states that:

> "where such devices are connected to publicly available electronic communications networks or make use of electronic communications services as a basic infrastructure the relevant provisions of Directive 2003/58 including those on security, traffic and location data and on confidentiality should apply".

The general security obligation was extended and made more specific in relation to any personal data processed in the provision of the service by Directive 2009/136.[45] It now provides that:

> "... the measures referred to in paragraph 1 shall at least:
> ensure that personal data can be accessed only by authorised personnel for legally authorised purposes,
> protect personal data stored or transmitted against accidental or unlawful destruction, accidental loss or alteration, and unauthorised or unlawful storage, processing, access or disclosure, and,
> ensure the implementation of a security policy with respect to the processing of personal data".

It follows, therefore, that the relevant personal data in respect of which this obligation applies will be personal data processed by the electronic communications service provider in the course of delivering that service. The obligation will not therefore apply to other personal data held by the service provider, for example personal data relating to the employees of the service provider. The provisions are applicable to any service provider and apply irrespective of whether the provider is a controller and/or a processor. Therefore the subscriber and location data held by a provider will be covered. It also appears that personal data processed in the course of transmission may be covered. The point is considered further below. These new requirements are more prescriptive than the existing obligations imposed on data controllers by principle 7.

The new provisions will require the service provider to have a security policy which covers all the relevant personal data, a method of implementing that policy and a system of providing for authorization of staff who access the personal data.

---

[45]   Art.2 Directive 2009/136 implemented by SI 2004/1039 reg.5(1)(a) in force from My 2011.

The obligation is mirrored by the notification obligations sparked by a **22–58** "personal data breach" and the two lay the foundation of a raft of other obligations, breach of which can lead to a range of actions by the Commissioner.

The definition of a personal data breach which has been included in the definitions in reg.1 of PECR has been replicated from Directive 2009/136 and reads as follows:

> "'Personal data breach' means a breach of security leading to the accidental or unlawful destruction, loss, alteration, unauthorised disclosure of, or access to, personal data transmitted, stored or otherwise processed in connection with the provision of a publicly available electronic communications service in the Community".

Although the two provisions work together a breach of the security obligations will not always amount to a personal data breach, for example the service provider must ensure that personal data is only accessible by authorised personal for "legally authorised purposes" however access for a purpose which is not legally authorised while it might be a breach of principle 7 would not, of itself, be classed as a personal data breach. In the same way the service provider must protect against "unlawful storage, processing, access or disclosure" but unlawful storage, processing access or disclosure would not, of itself, necessarily amount to a personal data breach. It would seem to follow that processing personal data without an appropriate ground for processing or without a proper notification, would not be counted as a personal data breach although it would breach the security obligation if it were regarded as unlawful storage or processing.

Extent of the obligation

The extent of the obligation is not as clear and the recitals are little help in **22–59** resolving this. The security obligation in reg.5(1)A(b) applies to personal data "stored or transmitted" in connection with or in the course of delivering the service. These are two distinct activities and it might be suggested that other types of processing (if any are carried out in connection with the provision of the service) are therefore not covered by the specific obligation. However, reg.5(1)A(a) and (c) have no such limitation. Given this and the fact that reg.5(1)A starts with the words "in particular" and that the linked personal data breach provisions apply to personal data "stored, transmitted or otherwise processed" in connection with such provision it is submitted that this would be a misreading. The obligation applies to all personal data processed in connection with the provision of the service; storage and transmission are merely the most typical processing activities associated with such provision. It is clear that the obligation covers some types of information. Subscriber information such as name and address, and communications data such as time of call, nature of call and duration of call, are covered where the information is personal data (usually this will be the case when the provider knows that a subscriber is an individual subscriber). However, it is not clear exactly how the personal data breach obligations will apply to a breach involving the content of communications between users where these include personal data and if they do apply how the service provider is meant to deal with the problems that this presents. This is considered in more detail below.

Inventory of security breaches

22–60   Directive 2009/136 also requires that competent national authorities should have the necessary means to perform their duties including having information about security breaches which can then be monitored. This has been implemented by the imposition of a requirement on service providers to retain inventories of security breaches.

The service provider must maintain a record of any personal data breaches, called an "inventory" of such breaches which must include information on:

- the facts surrounding the breach;
- the effects of the breach; and
- remedial action taken.

There is no provision for the Commissioner to determine the level of detail to which these records are to be kept. However, the provisions dealing with pan-EU harmonisation allow for the possibility of common standards on information notification and security requirements being settled at EU level (see para.22-12). No actions to implement this have been taken at the time of writing.[46] The regulation states that the inventory shall "only include information necessary" for the purpose of enabling the Commissioner to verify compliance with the provisions covering personal data breach. The Commissioner will clearly be able to have access to the inventory as he is empowered to audit the service provider's compliance with the personal data breach provisions.[47] It is likely therefore that the Commissioner will issue guidance to service providers setting out the information that should be recorded in the formal inventory.

The obligation to maintain an inventory falls on all service providers. If there are any public sector providers therefore it appears that the inventory could be a target for requests under FOIA although it might be assumed that public bodies would seek to maintain the confidentiality of such an inventory on the basis that disclosure could undermine the security of the service by showing areas of weakness.

Audit powers of the Commissioner

22–61   The Commissioner may audit the service provider's compliance with its security obligations. He may also audit the inventory. This is a separate audit power to the general power to audit the security of the service however in practical terms it seems likely that the Commissioner would be likely to exercise both together. See Ch.20 for an examination of the powers of audit.

The primary obligation to take appropriate technical and organisational measures to ensure the security of the service falls on the service provider, but the

---

[46] December 2011.
[47] PECR reg.5B as amended by SI 2011/1208.

network provider also has an obligation to respond to any reasonable request made by the service provider for security purposes. It is not clear whether the network provider can be liable to enforcement action if he fails to comply with the reasonable request of the service provider, but it appears that he has a mandatory duty to take security measures in conjunction with the service provider and accordingly could be liable if he fails in that duty.

Where there is still a significant risk to the security of the service despite the efforts of the service and network providers, then the service provider is under an obligation to provide a number of relevant pieces of information to the subscriber. No explanation of what constitutes a "significant" risk is provided. The Directive uses the term "particular" risk. A risk might be regarded as significant if it affects a large number of users, to the extent that even though the effects of the breach of security might be minor the risk of it happening to any subscriber is high. To take a simple example, there might be a risk that snatches of conversations could be picked up by others occasionally. However, they would never be more than a few words and not in a way that would show the identity of the speakers. Alternatively a risk might be relatively unlikely but if it did occur could involve a major loss of privacy. For example, there might be a risk that someone using a mobile telephone in the vicinity of a public address system point could find the entire conversation picked up and broadcast over the public address system. The risk might be relatively remote but if it did occur it could mean a major breach of privacy. Both could be regarded as significant risks. It is suggested that, given the use of the word "particular" in the Directive it would be more prudent to take a broad view of the word significant and regard both as falling within the category.

The obligation of the service provider is to inform the subscriber of: **22–62**

(a)   the nature of the risk;
(b)   any appropriate measures that the subscriber may take to safeguard against the risk; and
(c)   the likely costs involved in taking such measures.

The factors which determine whether measures are appropriate are the cost of implementing the solution and the state of the technology. These have to be measured against the risks against which the data is being guarded. The service provider is not under an obligation to proffer advice on untested expensive new solutions for problems, but to give mainstream advice on reasonably costed remedies. The information must be provided free of charge.

PERSONAL DATA BREACH OBLIGATIONS

A personal data breach means a breach of security leading to the accidental or **22–63** unlawful destruction, loss, alteration, unauthorised disclosure of, or access to, personal data transmitted, stored or otherwise processed in connection with the provision of a publicly available electronic communications service.[48] Although

---

[48] PECR reg.5A inserted by SI 2011/1208.

there is some difference of wording between this and principle 7, it is submitted that any differences are merely in expression and there is no difference in substance.

Two conditions must be satisfied before there has been a personal data breach:

- there must have been a loss, alteration or one of the other consequences in respect of relevant personal data; and
- it must have been occasioned by a breach of security.

It is possible, therefore, that there could be a loss, etc., which caused serious harm but was the result of some wholly unlikely combination of circumstances which was not part of, and could not reasonably have been expected to be part of a security plan or system. It must be expected however that such cases will be rare.

In the event of a personal data breach, the primary obligation is to notify the breach to the Commissioner.[49] The notification must contain at least a description of:

- the nature of the breach;
- the consequences of the breach; and
- the measures taken or proposed to be taken by the provider to address the breach.

This is not quite the same wording as is used in respect of the inventory of a data breach which must include the facts surrounding the breach, the effects of the breach and remedial action taken. However it is submitted that there is no real difference in meaning and it would be usual for a provider to use the same format to record information in the inventory and to submit material to the Commissioner. At the time of writing the Commissioner has suggested that service providers should follow the existing guidance on voluntary reporting of data breaches which is explained in Ch.7.

The notification must be given "without undue delay". In considering whether there has been undue delay the nature of the detail required in the notification will be relevant. For example it may not be possible for a service provider to set out the measures to be taken for example until there has been at least an initial investigation and response plan put in place.

Notification to subscribers and users is not always required. There are two provisions dealing with such notification, in reg.5A(3) and in reg.5A(6). It is not wholly clear how the two fit together.

Notification of breach

22–64   Regulation 5A(3) imposes an obligation to notify a subscriber or user if a personal data breach is likely to "adversely affect the personal data or privacy" of the subscriber or user. As with the duty to notify the Commissioner there is no set

---

[49] PECR reg.5A inserted by SI 2011/1208.

timescale but the notification must be made without undue delay.[50] Directive 2009/136 provides some assistance in considering what might be regarded as an adverse impact. Recital 61 states that:

> "A breach should be considered as adversely affecting the data or privacy of a subscriber or individual where it could result in, for example, identity theft or fraud, physical harm, significant humiliation or damage to reputation in connection with the provision of publicly available communication services."

Therefore the adverse effect may not be limited to physical or financial loss but could cover damage to reputation.

The obligation appears to be one of strict liability. It is not limited to those cases where the service provider knows there has been a breach. Clearly the service provider cannot notify of something of which it is unaware however it may be argued that the nature of the obligation means that service providers must have appropriate mechanisms to become aware of any breaches of security to ensure that they are able to comply with their notification obligations. Therefore if a third party service provider is used it would be advisable to impose a duty on that third party to notify of any breach by them.

The service provider will have to take a view on the question of whether a breach is likely to adversely affect the personal data or privacy of a subscriber or user.

Contents of a notification

A notification to the subscriber or user must include at least: 22–65

- a description of the nature of the breach;
- information about contact points in the service provider's organisation from which more information may be obtained; and
- recommendations of measures to allow the subscriber to mitigate the possible adverse impacts of the breach.[51]

Although the regulation refers to contact points in the service provider's organisation it is not uncommon for call centres to be used for this purpose where there has been a major breach and it is submitted that this should be acceptable as long as the organisation used is engaged under proper terms ensuring appropriate security.

The sort of measures that are generally considered useful to data subjects are credit monitoring services which help individuals see whether there have been any false applications for credit in their name.

Encrypted information

The notice to subscribers or users is not required if the service provider has   22–66
demonstrated to the satisfaction of the Information Commissioner that it has
implemented appropriate technological protection measures which render the

---

[50] PECR reg.5A(3) inserted by SI 2011/1208.
[51] PECR 2003 reg.5A(5) amended by SI 2011/1208.

data unintelligible to any person not authorised to access it and that those measures were applied to the data concerned in that breach. This is not a point for the service provider to decide. The provider must prove this to the satisfaction of the Commissioner who will then presumably make a formal decision on the point.

It will be important therefore that, where relevant, service providers make available sufficient information, whether within the formal notification to the Commissioner or as additional material, to enable the Commissioner to take a view on whether the information was properly encrypted to the extent that it cannot be read without the relevant keys.

How do the obligations apply to personal data which is part of the content of communications?

22–67   It is not clear how far these obligations apply to the content of communications (as well as the identities of those communicating and linked communications data). The recitals are not explicit and the guidance issued by the ICO in May 2011 did not deal with the extent to which the content of communications is covered. The application of the obligation to the content of communication appears to pose many problems for service providers however the provisions relating to encryption strongly indicate that contents are intended to be included in scope.

As both the security and the personal data breach obligations are specific to personal data the initial question must be in whose hands the material must be personal data. As a service provider is a data processor for the contents of communications presumably one possibility is that it would merely have to be personal data in the hands of a relevant data controller and need not be personal data in the hands of the service provider. However this runs directly counter to the fundamental principle that any person should be able to know whether and to what extent they are subject to the law.

The service provider cannot know in relation to any transmission of a communication what the nature of the communication may be or whether it includes personal data or not. The service provider cannot access the contents of communications in order to check whether they include material that might be personal data and then check with the relevant sender or recipient to assess whether the UK definition applies to the particular data.

The difficulties can be seen by considering two examples. On the one hand, if there is an exchange of e-mails between subscribers which are limited companies about a wholly commercial matter where none of the information is "about" a living individual there would be no personal data involved. An interception by a third party could not amount to a personal data breach. On the other hand if the exchange of e-mails between the two included information "about" living individuals for example employees, then personal data will be involved and an interception could be a personal data breach.

22–68   The service provider appears to be placed in extremely difficult position. In the first place there will be uncertainty whether the content of a communication will be information "about" an individual "identifiable" to a data controller (applying the UK's restricted statutory definition and subsequent interpretation by the courts). In the second place, even if there is a transmission of material which could meet these tests, some will be transient and it will be difficult to show that personal data was involved. Voice telephony will be transient and only recorded if captured as voicemail, although e mail, Twitter or other media will be recorded.

It should be noted that the obligation to notify is not restricted to notification to subscribers who are themselves data subjects affected by a personal data breach. On the face of it, therefore, if there has been a security breach involving the contents of communications which contain personal data, the service provider should presumably give notice to the subscriber even if that subscriber is not an individual affected. For example if the subscriber was an organisation providing services to individuals which involved personal data, for example health services or counselling, a breach of security on the public side of the communication network used by the organisation giving rise to the disclosure of personal data relating to users of the service could amount to a personal data breach. The communication service provider would not be able to notify the individuals as it would not know who they are but would have to notify the subscriber in such a case. There is no obligation on the subscriber to notify the individuals nor can the Commissioner require the subscriber to do so.

As noted earlier there is nothing specific in the Directive or its recitals which addresses these difficulties. However, recital 62 appears to recognise that there are potential problems with the provisions and introduces a specific reference to fundamental rights:

> "When implementing measures transposing Directive 2002/58/EC (Directive on Privacy and Electronic Communications), the authorities and courts of the Member States should not only interpret their national law in a manner consistent with that Directive, but should ensure that they do not rely on an interpretation which would conflict with fundamental rights or general principles of Community law, such as the principle of proportionality".

It would clearly be disproportionate and a breach of the right to privacy of correspondence for service providers to be able to access the content of communications in order to determine whether there is personal data in those communications. In order to achieve compliance one option would be to require the service provider to notify every subscriber of every data breach because the service provider cannot know whether there is personal data involved and, if so, whether the breach would trigger the notification obligation. However this also seems extremely onerous and disproportionate. It is submitted therefore that the test must be whether the service provider has reasonable grounds to believe that a communication in the course of transmission includes personal data. It is assumed that service providers will have to make some broad assumptions as a basis for adopting policies on when they will notify of personal data breach.

One possible approach would be to start from the assumption that any communication from or to an IP address or number of an individual subscriber will always involve personal data. This would be a very "broad brush" approach but it is possible that it may have been in the mind of the Commission taking account of recital 52, which provides:

"Developments concerning the use of IP addresses should be followed closely, taking int o consideration the work already done by, among others, the Working Party on the Protection of individuals with regard to the Processing of Personal Data … and in the light of such proposals as may be appropriate."

Even if this view is taken, the service provider would then have to consider whether it would regard any breach of security of any communication from or to such an IP address or number as a personal data breach or whether it would only regard one as a personal data breach (and therefore notifiable) where the service provider knows or has reason to believe that the breach would adversely affect the privacy or personal data of the subscriber or user. In cases where the subscriber is not an individual it is suggested that the service provider might only consider the question of a personal data breach where the service provider has reason to know that the content of communications is likely to include personal data. Altogether the provisions are not clear, and pose a number of difficult questions for service providers, the difficulties were not canvassed in the consultation prior to implementation; however, it did propose that the implementing regulations should provide for the ICO to issue guidance in relation to the notification mechanism. This was not included in the Regulations. In his Note on the new provisions issued in May 2011 the Commissioner wrote:

> "The Commissioner does not consider that service providers need a lengthy period in which to implement the new breach notification requirements. Following consultation with service providers he will be issuing guidance on their detailed application but the basic requirements are clear from the 2011 Regulations. They are also in line with the voluntary breach notification system currently operated by the Commissioner".[52]

It is submitted that, while the basic requirements are clear, their detailed application in this area is not. This is an area where it would be useful to have a view from the Commissioner and possibly Ofcom.

Provision of information on access

22–69   The drafters of the amending regulations intended to give police and security services rights to access the personal data of users of services. This is intended to be supported by an obligation on service providers to establish and maintain procedures for recording such access for scrutiny by the Commissioner.

Regulation 10 has provided for the establishment and maintenance of the internal procedures and the scrutiny by the Commissioner but omitted the substantive power to be given to police and security services. It is understood that this will be added when legislative opportunity permits.

The scrutiny provisions are that communication service providers shall on demand provide the Commissioner with the following information:

- the procedures established for dealing with these requests;
- the number of requests received;
- the legal justification for the request; and

---

[52] See Ch.7.

- the service providers response.[53]

COOKIES AND CONFIDENTIALITY OF COMMUNICATIONS

Regulation 6 was amended from May 2011 by SI 2011/1208 to make it clear that the insertion of any device used to store information or gain access to information stored on a user's terminal equipment requires consent save in very limited cases. This is the result of a long-running, and often impassioned, debate between regulators, industry, government and civil society organisations about the use of such technologies. Despite the amendment the debate continues as the use of browser settings to provide consent is canvassed. In this section we set out a very broad description of the type of technologies at issue, including the nature of cookies, explain their use (focussing on their role in delivering advertising), review the revised provisions in the Directive and explain how they have been implemented in the UK. It should be noted that the description of the technology is very "broad brush" and for a proper understanding the reader should refer to a specialist technology text or website.

22–70

Devices used to store information or gain access

There are many ways of remotely obtaining information over an Internet connection about the uses that have been made of a computer or other device, for example by looking at the URLs which have been visted by that computer over the recent past. Some methods are more "underhand" than others and some may be carrried out for sinister reasons. The fact that such enquiries are being made is not apparent to the average computer user, hence there has always been a requirement to make such collection apparent to the user.

22–71

The provisions of the Directive and PECR are not technology specific and apply to any technology that can be used to store information or gain access to information stored on a user's computer. The best known example of such technology is probably the use of "cookies" and the term has become a shorthand for a range of technologies that work in similar ways. Cookies are very small text files, that can be inserted into the memory of one computer by another. Cookies are the programmes most commonly stored by or on behalf of legitimate businesses on users' computers. The genesis of the technology was to help the interaction between websites and users; so far so innocent. However, the technology also allows for the collection of information about the user's on line behaviour and, in turn, the delivery of content (usually advertising) selected by the site owner and not by the user. Once websites started to use the technology in this way (essentially for the benefit of the business or other site owner rather than at the request of the user) the battle lines were drawn between privacy activists and EU regulators.

When a user visits a website that uses cookies the webserver associated with that site sends the cookie text file to the user's computer where it is lodged in the memory. The cookie text file can then be read by any webserver programme that knows what to look for. So when the user re-visits the website that was

---

[53] reg.29A inserted by SI 2011/1208 reg.10.

responsible for the delivery of the cookie, or any other site that can also recognise the cookie, the webserver or servers being used know that the same computer is being used. Cookies are described by ENISA as follows:

> "Cookies, also known as HTTP (Hypertext Transfer Protocol) cookies, are generated and modified by the server, stored by the browser and transmitted between browser and server at each interaction."[54]

Cookies can be persistent i.e. remain stored in the memory after the visitor leaves the website or may only last for the browsing session. Other similar technologies are gifs or web beacons which are used in e-mail marketing campaigns as tracking devices to assess how many people opened a marketing e-mail.

Use of cookies to deliver advertising

22–72   The growth of the internet has been fuelled by marketing and the delivery of advertising. The development of advertising has given rise to huge profits for those in the business; in October 2011 the Guardian newspaper reported that Google had generated $1.05 billion from online and mobile advertising in the UK in the previous three months. It has also kept the costs of internet access low worldwide and consumers take for granted that most internet services are free at the point of delivery. Much of that advertising depends on the use of cookies and it is the use of cookies, particularly third party cookies as they have developed to deliver behavioural advertising, that has caused most concern among privacy activists and regulators. In Opinion 2/2010 the Article 29 Working Party set out its views as to the applicability of Directives 2002/58 and 195/46 on the development of behavioural advertising. It described such advertising as:

> "advertising that is based on the behaviour of individuals over time. Behavioural advertising seeks to study the characteristics of this behaviour through their actions (repeated site visits, interactions, keywords, online content productions etc..) in order to develop a specific profile and thus provide data subjects with advertisements tailored to match their inferred interests".

The Opinion sets out the role of the parties involved in delivering behavioural advertising. In outline it works as follows: advertising network providers agree with web site publishers that ad network cookies will be delivered to visitors to their sites. These cookies can then be recognised by others in the network. This allows a picture of the sites visited from an individual computer to be built up. Web pages have spaces for advertising which they provide to the ad network so the advertiser has a range of websites on which to deliver advertising. The ad network agrees with businesses that they will advertise particular goods or services to those who appear to have an interest in them. When a visitor goes to one of the ad delivery sites the visitor's browser is checked to see if they have any ad network cookies and if they are recognised that information is linked to any information about relevant browsing activity or interests. An appropriate advertisement is then displayed on the web page being visited. This happens by

---

[54] *Bittersweet Cookies: Some Security and Privacy Considerations,* European Network and Information Security Agency.

the user's browser being directed to the webserver which delivers the ad in the slot on the web page. So, for example, if a user has visited holiday sites for a particular destination then it is likely that ads relating to that destination or similar ones will be displayed next time the individual visits a site in the advertiser's network.

The ad provider may know the identity of the individual user of a computer because he or she has registered for a service, in which case it is clear that the provider is processing personal data relating to the individual. In other cases the ad provider may have a picture of the individual user built up through activity plus an IP address, in which case the question of whether the information is personal data is rather more difficult,[55] but in either event the cookies are used to deliver the advertising.

The Internet Advertising Bureau Europe describes OBA as follows:

> "OBA means the collection of data from a particular computer or device regarding web viewing behaviours over time and across multiple web domains not under common control for the purpose of using such data to predict web user preferences or interests to deliver online advertising to that particular computer or device based on the preferences or interests inferred from such web viewing behaviours".[56]

Provisions in Directive 2009/136

Under Directive 2002/58, art.5.3 required Member States to ensure that the use of electronic communications networks to store information or to gain access to information stored in the terminal equipment of a subscriber or user was only allowed on condition that the subscriber or user was provided with clear and comprehensive information about the purpose of the processing in accordance with Directive 95/46/EC and offered the right to refuse such processing by the data controller.　　　　　　　　　　　　　　　　　　　　　　　　　　**22–73**

This was implemented in PECR by reg.6 which prohibited the use of an electronic communications network to store information or gain access to information stored in the terminal equipment of a subscriber or user unless that person was provided with clear and comprehensive information about the purposes of the storage of or access to that information and had been given an opportunity to refuse the storage or access. The prohibition is not applicable where the sole purpose of the device is to carry out or facilitate the communication itself or is strictly necessary for the provision of an information society service which the subscriber or user has requested. An information society service is given the meaning that it has in the Electronic Commerce (EC Directive) Regulations 2002. This is,

> "any service normally provided for remuneration, at a distance, by means of electronic equipment for the processing (including digital compression) and storage of data, and at the individual request of a recipient of a service".

Therefore a service such as online shopping will be an information society service as long as it has been requested by the recipient of the service, is carried

---

[55] See Ch.4 for a discussion of IP addresses and personal data.
[56] IAB Europe EU Framework for OBA April 14, 2011.

out electronically at a distance and is one normally provided for remuneration. The terms of the two exceptions from the prohibition are narrow. In the case of facilitating the communication itself the device must be used for that sole purpose. In the case of the provision of an information society service the device must be "strictly necessary". As the term "necessary" is a term implying a balance the addition of the term "strictly" here means that test here is specific and strict. In his Guidance on the new rules on cookies the Commissioner emphasises that the service must have been requested by the user, stating:

"Indeed the relevant recital in the Directive on which these Regulations are based refer to services "explicitly requested" by the user. As a result our interpretation of this exception has to bear in mind the narrowing effect of the word 'explicitly'".

Interestingly, the UK implementation of art.5.3 meant that the rules on the use of cookies applied irrespective of whether the information to which access was being gained was personal data whereas the wording in the Directive implied that the prohibition only applied where the person setting the cookie or other technology was a data controller, in other words that the person held personal data on the subscriber or user.

Control of cookies

22–74   Cookies can be deleted from the browser of a computer by the user. However, the user has to find the list of cookies and take the necessary technical action to delete. In addition browser settings can be used to control cookies by accepting or rejecting them. In some cases, if a cookie is rejected, the website may not run as well but that is the user's choice. Not all cookies are easily deleted. There are some types of "supercookies" such as Flash cookies which may not be deleted by the usual browser deletion. They can be used to back up ordinary cookies and therefore, in effect, override the user's decision to delete cookies. Such cookies can be controlled but it is not as easy as for ordinary cookies.

Browser settings as consent

22–75   Because most cookies can be rejected by using appropriate browser settings on a computer the question arose as to whether it was sufficient to comply with reg.6 to notify users of the use of cookies through the website privacy policy and provide the opportunity to refuse storage by directing the user to the possibility of using his/her browser settings to delete cookies. This use of browser options was accepted by the Commissioner, although in the Guidance he stressed that the notice had to be

"sufficiently full and intelligible to enable individuals to gain a clear appreciation of the potential consequences of allowing storage and access to the information collected by the device should they wish to do so",

and the opportunity to refuse had to be clear and the mechanism for refusal "prominent, intelligible and readily available to all, not just the most computer literate or technically aware". He also advised that, where the refusal mechanism was part of the privacy policy, this should be signposted and easily accessible within the policy.

As the regulation simply required that the information "be provided" it could also be provided using a third party. The Interactive Advertising Bureau (IAB) is an industry body which has a website which explains the functions of cookies at www.allaboutcookies.org. Many website owners simply linked to that site to provided information about cookies and how to refuse them.

A general practice therefore developed of giving notice of cookies in privacy policies and offering browser controls as the mechanism for refusal. Some notices were clearer than others. An example of a clear notice being the wording used by Google:which is as follows:

> "**Cookies**—When you visit Google, we send one or more cookies to your computer or other device. We use cookies to improve the quality of our service, including storing user preferences, improving search results and ad selection and tracking user trends, such as how people search. Google also uses cookies in its advertising services to help advertisers and publishers serve and manage ads across the web and on Google services. ...
>
> Most browsers are initially set up to accept cookies, but you can reset your browser to refuse all cookies or to indicate when a cookie is being sent. However, some Google features and services may not function properly if your cookies are disabled."[57]

Since the passage of Directive 2002/58/EC, however, there has been a massive growth in the use of behavioural advertising, much of it led from the USA. Moreover few average computer users appear to actually use the browser setting options to reject or control cookies, whether through lack of understanding or apathy or choice. As noted earlier the use of cookies to deliver such advertising and the gradual building of profiles of individuals as a result of the collection of information about their browsing habits and interests has caused real concern among privacy activists and some regulators in the EU. There has equally been a fierce resistance to tighter control of cookies from a range of companies but largely led by those companies that deliver advertising or carry out analytics that depend on the use of cookies.

Amendments to the cookie rules

In Directive 2009/136 the balance was altered in relation to the acceptance of cookies and the relevant article amended to make clear that consent is required to set non-essential cookies. The amendment was a last minute change by the European Parliament and had not been proposed by the Commission nor apparently particularly sought by regulators. The Directive also includes a reference to the use of browser settings as a possible mechanism to obtain consent in the relevant recital. As a result those whose businesses rely on the use of third party cookies and for whom consent could pose significant problems have remained fervent in their view that the use of browser settings will remain possible as the mechanism to deliver choices over the use of cookies, despite the

22–76

---

[57] Google Privacy Policy October 2011.

clear wording of the requirement in the Directive. The issue proved so controversial in the UK that the Department for Media Culture and Sport (DCMS) which took over responsibility for this area part way through the implementation process felt compelled to issue an open letter about the Government's approach in May 2011 in which it fiercely denied that it had "gold-plated" the Directive.[58]

Revised Article 5(3)

22-77 This now reads:

> "Member States shall ensure that the storing of information or the gaining of access to information already stored, in the terminal equipment of a subscriber or user is only allowed on condition that the subscriber or user concerned has given his or her consent, having been provided with clear and comprehensive information, in accordance with Directive 95/46/EC, inter alia, about the purpose of the processing. This shall not prevent any technical storage or access for the sole purpose of carrying out the transmission of a communication over an electronic communications network, or as strictly necessary in order for the provider of an information society service explicitly requested by the subscriber or user to provide the service".

It will be noted that the revised article no longer refers to the clear and comprehensive information being given by *the data controller*, although it still refers to notice being given in accord with Directive 95/46/EC (the general data protection directive). It is submitted that the reference to notice being given in accord with Directive 95/46/EC suggest that the provisions in 2002/58 (as amended) were drafted so as to apply where personal data is being processed. Article 1 of 2002/58 also refers to the aim of the Directive as being to

> "ensure an equivalent level of protection of fundamental rights and freedoms....with respect to the processing of personal data in the electronic communication sector"

in setting out the scope and aim. The UK provisions however do not limit the control of cookies to those cases where personal data is being processed and there is no doubt that in the UK the rules apply to any cookies being placed or used. The position however may not be as clear in other Member States. The relevant recital is recital 66 of Directive 2009/136. As this is such an area of debate it is set out here in full so that the reference to the use of browser settings can be seen in context:

> "Third parties may wish to store information on the equipment of a user, or gain access to information already stored for a number of purposes, ranging from the legitimate (such as certain types of cookies) to those involving unwarranted intrusion into the private sphere (such as spyware or viruses). It is therefore of paramount importance that users be provided with clear and comprehensive information when engaging in any activity which could result in such storage or gaining of access. The methods of providing information and offering the right to refuse should be limited to those situations where the technical storage or access is strictly necessary for the legitimate purpose of enabling the use of a specific service

---

[58] *http://www.dcms.gov.uk/images/publications/cookies_open_letter.pdf* [Accessed October 4, 2012].

explicitly requested by the subscriber or user. *Where it is technically possible and effective, in accordance with the relevant provisions of Directive 95/46/EC, the user's consent to processing may be expressed by using the appropriate settings of a browser or other application.* The enforcement of these requirements should be made more effective by way of enhanced powers granted to the relevant national authorities".

The reference in this recital to the relevant provisions in Directive 95/46/EC can only be to the definition of consent which provides that consent must be a freely given, specific and informed indication of his wishes by which the data subject signifies his agreement.[59]

The reference to the use of browser settings is, therefore in effect, otiose. Even in the absence of the recital there would seem little doubt that consent could be given by the use of a form of technology as long as it is a genuine and informed consent in which the user unambiguously indicates agreement.

It is impossible to see how any use of browser settings as they currently apply could meet the standard for consent required by the law, nevertheless a version of the sentence has made its way into the UK implementation (see further below).

UK implementation

The UK amendments came into effect on May 25, 2011. The use of cookies is covered in the Guide to PECR. In addition the Commissioner issued two papers, *Changing the rules on using cookies and similar technologies for storing information*[60] and *Enforcing the revised Privacy and Electronic Communications Regulations (PECR)*[61] after the new provisions came into effect. Regulation 6 now provides that a person shall not use an electronic communication network to store or to gain access to information stored in the terminal equipment of a subscriber or user unless they are provided with clear and comprehensive information about the purposes of the storage or access to that information and "has given his or her consent".

22–78

It will be noted that the provisions which require the giving of information are not altered. The information need only be given once. The regulation does not say who has to provide the notice. It might be thought that it is implicit in the provision that the person responsible for inserting the device should give the notice however the Guide suggests that a third party might have the responsibility in some cases:

"The Regulations do not define who should be responsible for providing the information and obtaining consent. Where a person operates an online service and any use of a cookie type device will be for their purposes only it is clear that the person will be responsible for complying with this Regulations".[62]

---

[59] Directive 95/46/EC art.2(h).
[60] Version 1, May 9, 2011.
[61] Version 1, May 25, 2011.
[62] ICO Guide, September 7, 2011, p. 44.

Timing of consent

22–79   On the face of the provision one would expect that the notice must be given and the consent obtained *before* the cookie is inserted. It is a norm of obtaining consent that the person obtains consent before the action is taken, as otherwise the action is taken without consent. Prior consent does pose a problem for users of cookies as the existing practice is to set the cookie as soon as a user visits a website. In its open letter the DCMS suggested that prior consent might not be required but consent could be given during or after the processing. This seemed to be based more on practicality than law and it is submitted that in order to be a valid consent in law the consent should be provided before the action to which the consent relates is taken. Therefore to comply with new regulation 6 consent should be obtained before the cookie is set.

The Regulation has also been amended to include the reference to the use of browser settings as follows:

> "...consent may be signified by a subscriber who amends or sets controls on the internet browser which the subscriber uses or by using another application or programme to signify consent".[63]

As with the provision in the recital this does not appear to add anything of substance. It is difficult to see this as anything other than a sop to lobbying. At best it is an "avoidance of doubt" provision. It must be the case that consent could be signified by the use of a programme or technology as long as the use of the technology met the necessary tests to be a valid consent. The only oddity is that it refers to "subscriber" but not "user". In its open letter (see para.2–72 above) the DCMS stated that "subscriber" was meant to cover "user" (although quite how this mysterious duality was meant to occur was not explained), but in any event it would look at the provision again to see whether reference to a user should also be added.

Who must obtain consent?

22–80   The Regulations are silent as to who is responsible for obtaining the consent from the user. As the consent of the user is required for both storing and gaining access to information stored, clearly in the first instance it must be obtained at the point at which the cookies is first delivered to the user's browser. There is no reason why a process could not be appropriately structured to obtain consent on behalf of the others who will later gain access to the cookie. However, as the consent must be based on a full notice, this would require a full explanation of the other persons who would later be able to gain access to read the cookie. If a consent which covers subsequent access by others is not obtained when the cookie is first set then it must be sought on subsequent occasions before the advertiser accesses the cookie to check whether it can deliver the advertisement.

In Opinion 2/2010 the WP also refers to the responsibilities of the various parties involved in the delivery of behavioural advertising to give notice. It stated that it is clear that the party that allows the advertiser to collect the IP address and

---

[63]   PECR reg.6(3A).

details of the user's browsing will have obligations to provide notice to the user, particularly where there is any personal data of the user involved. It takes the view that the advertising network which delivers the cookies will be responsible for obtaining the consent of the user. The Opinion also suggests that the publishers of the advertisements should take responsibility for giving notice to users of the relevant processing. It also draws attention to the responsibility of advertisers where the user clicks through on an ad and visits the advertiser's website. The provision of notice and obtaining of consent in the current model of delivery is clearly an area that poses practical difficulties. Both the Commissioner and the Government have called on industry to suggest new ways of dealing with the requirement for consent. The regulation does not distinguish between the subscriber and the user. These may be different people. The consent of both is required so even if a subscriber gave a consent if the organisation which is placing or using the cookie can distinguish that the equipment is being used by a different person the consent of that person is also required.

Information Commissioner's policy on enforcement

During the consultation on the implementation of the revisions to Directive 2002/58, the Government expressed its awareness that the changes which would be required as a result of the new cookie rules would be difficult for many businesses. While it expressed sympathy for the difficulties faced by business it stated clearly that, given the substantive changes to the wording of the Directive, the current use of browser settings "as a form of consent" (sic) was not consistent with the revised wording. It did not accept that it was the role of Government to mandate a technical solution stating that any technical solutions should be developed by industry. It did however agree to work with browser manufacturers and with the industry initiative on the use of third party cookies in behavioural advertising.[64]

22–81

After the provisions came into effect on May 25, 2011, the Commissioner issued two papers, Changing the rules on using cookies and similar technologies for storing information[65] and Enforcing the revised Privacy and Electronic Communications Regulations (PECR).[66] In the first paper the Commissioner reviewed the ways in which consent might be obtained, accepting that a valid consent can be gained by the use of a consent clause in the terms and conditions of web use but emphasising that this must be a positive consent (such as a tick box) based on appropriate information. In the second paper he set out the approach his office would take to enforcement over the next 12 months and stated that, although he could not issue a dispensation from the new requirements he would "allow a lead in period of 12 months for organisations to develop ways of meeting the cookie related requirements of the Regulations". The lead-in period was due to end in May 2012. This would allow the work to go ahead on the development of technical solutions as encouraged by the Government. The paper did however make clear that the Commissioner expected businesses to be

---

[64] Government response following the consultation on implementation of Directive 2009/136, paras 311–325.
[65] Version 1, May 9, 2011.
[66] Version 1, May 25, 2011.

working towards a solution and making appropriate preparations. Post-May 2012 there has to date been no sign of enforcement activity. On August 14, 2012 Privacy Laws and Business reported on a response to a Freedom of Information request that although the ICO had received tips about over 300 websites which were possibly non-compliant the team who are to deal with the cookie compliance programme was not yet in place and the information had yet to be analysed.

Current initiatives in online behavioural advertising (OBA)

22–82   As was noted in the opening paragraphs of this section the issue which has caused most concern to regulators has been the growth of third party OBA, where advertisements shown on a website are not from or for that website but have been selected to be targeted at the individual browsing the site on the basis of information inferred or gathered as a result of surveillance of that individual's previous on line activities. The growth of third party OBA has also been of concern to regulators in the US and since 2009, spurred on by the Federal Trade Commission, the industry in the US has adopted a self-regulatory code based on the concepts of notice, display of a standard icon (the AdChoice icon) and the ability to opt-out of further OBA.

A similar self-regulatory scheme was launched in Europe by the Interactive Advertising Bureau in April 2011.[67] Those organisations which sign up to it should have mechanisms to deliver compliance with the scheme in place by June 2012. Given that the scheme is based on consumers mainly opting out from the collection and use of data for OBA it will not be sufficient to ensure compliance with the law in the UK; however, it may have more relevance in any EU or EEA country that has limited the requirement for consent for the use of cookies to those cases where the advertiser is using personal data.

There are six principles covering, notice, choice, data security, sensitive segmentation, education and compliance and enforcement programmes. Notice of the use of OBA must be given by both third parties which use OBA and web site operators that deliver OBA in their privacy policies. Where the organisation collects and uses data which has been harvested from most or all of the URLs visited by a particular computer across multiple sites then explicit consent of the user is required, as is the use of sensitive personal data to segment for the purposes of OBA. In other cases users must be given clear notice and choice to refuse the collection of data for OBA. The programme will eventually also use an icon to alert users to the fact that advertising is OBA. The remainder of the provisions deal with restriction on the creation of segments for children under 12, the delivery of compliance which requires audit, dealing with complaints and consumer education.

Comments

22–83   As will be appreciated from this section the current position is far from satisfactory. It remains to be seen whether there will be a "solution" using browser settings, however such a solution looks very unlikely given the current

---

[67] IAB Europe EU Framework for Online Behavioural Advertising, April 27, 2011.

practical problems. As there is currently no way to distinguish cookies used for the delivery of advertising and all other cookies the only way to safely say that consent had been obtained by the use of browser settings would be for all browsers to be set to a default to reject all cookies and for users to alter their settings to accept essential cookies (whether generally or on a specific basis) as well as non-essential cookies. Further many users have old browsers and any technical solution would have to be somehow rolled out to those old browsers in order to be used.

TRAFFIC, BILLING AND LOCATION DATA

Electronic communications generate vast amounts of information about users. Directive 97/66 started from the basis that those users have rights to privacy in respect of that data; rights which do not amount to ownership of the information but restrict the uses that service and network providers could make of the data generated in providing telecommunications services. The approach reflects that taken over 15 years ago in Recommendation (95)4 at para.2.1 of the appendix to the Recommendation which stated:

22–84

> "Telecommunications services, and in particular telephone services which are being developed, should be offered with due respect for the privacy of users, the secrecy of correspondence and the freedom of communication".

This recognises that the rights of individuals to use communication services can be seen as an aspect of the right to freedom of expression. So, for example an Internet service provider should not be able to sell lists of subscribers who have visited particular sites or otherwise exploit the data about subscribers arising from his control of the service provision. The uses of such data are restricted. In this respect the rights of corporate subscribers are protected as well as those of individuals. This part of the Regulations deals with the uses which can be made of the data generated in the running of the services either with or without the consent of the subscriber. In broad terms the uses are restricted to those which are necessary to run the services. The subscriber may be asked to consent to some wider uses but even those are restricted in scope. The restrictions specify and make explicit the purpose specification restrictions imposed by the main Act. Despite these controls the privacy of use has come under intense pressure with the development of technical innovation and new services and continues to do so. In particular services are now provided by organisations which do not fall within the definitions of providers of electronic networks or services because the technology employed is not covered by the Directive. The stresses being imposed on the legal framework by these developments are considered below.

Meaning of the terms traffic data, location data, and value added service

"Traffic" data are the data which are produced from the running of the network. "Traffic" data are defined in reg.2(1) as

22–85

"any data processed for the purpose of the conveyance of a communication on an electronic communications network or for the billing in respect of that communication and includes data relating to the routing, duration or time of a communication".

Traffic data are distinguished from "location data". There are specific rules for the two sets of data, although the end result is very similar. Traffic data may only be used for the provision of value added services with the consent of the subscriber or user. "Value-added service" means any service which requires the processing of traffic or location data beyond that which is necessary for the transmission of a communication or the billing in respect of that communication. Hence the term is capable of covering a whole range of services such as navigation and breakdown services based on location.

Traffic data do not have to be personal data to be covered by the definition, although the restrictions imposed only apply to traffic data relating to subscribers or users which are processed and stored by a public communications provider. It follows that anonymised traffic data which can no longer be said to "relate" to a subscriber or user are outside the specific restrictions imposed by reg.7. There is no separate definition of billing data (although the term "bill" is defined). If the data fall within reg.7 the basic rule is that they should be erased or, where the identifying data relates to an identifiable individual or corporate entity, anonymised, when no longer required for the purpose of the transmission of a communication. The rules on erasure were modified by Directive 2006/24 on the retention of data generated or processed in connection with the provision of publicly available electronic communications services or of public communications networks. Directive 2006/24 is dealt with in Ch.24. Regulation 7(1) requires that personal data should be modified so that it is no longer personal data and, in relation to corporate subscribers "modified so that they cease to be data that would be personal data if that subscriber was an individual". This, rather horrid, definition in respect of corporate subscribers absorbs the elements of the definition of personal data so presumably, in UK terms, data will be relevant data for these purposes about a corporate subscriber if they relate to that corporate subscriber, and the corporate subscriber can be identified from that information or that and other information in the possession of the telecommunications service provider. Presumably a corporate subscriber will be identified by its legal name and address or identifying number such as a company registration number, but it is possible that a trading name would be regarded as sufficient. However of necessity providers are entitled to use the data to send bills to customers and a number of other legitimate uses of the data are permitted.

Applying the definition of "bill" in the general definitions, in which bill includes an invoice, account, statement or other document of similar character, billing data will be any information relating to invoices, accounts, statement or other instruments of the like character.

Permitted uses of traffic data

Billing

Predictably enough traffic data held for the purposes of assessing and levying   **22–86**
charges by a subscriber or in respect of interconnection payments may be
processed and stored until the payment has been completed. Interconnection
payments are the amounts one provider charges to another for the use of
connections. The data can continue to be processed until the debt in respect of
which they are processed becomes time-barred or until any proceedings,
including appeals, arising from non-payment are concluded (reg.7(5)–(6)). It
appears that they should then be erased. The OIC advises in the Guidance on the
Regulations that such data should not be routinely retained for the maximum
six-year period but should only be retained as long as they are actually needed.
The subscriber or user must be told what types of traffic data are to be processed
for this purpose and how long the processing will last, although prior consent is
not required (reg.8(1)).

Authorised activities

Under reg.8(2) the only processing of traffic data which may be carried out is that   **22–87**
which is required for one or more of a restricted list of purposes and even then
subject to a range of conditions. The purposes are:

- the management of billing and traffic;
- customer enquiries;
- the prevention or detection of fraud;
- the marketing of electronic communications services; or
- the provision of value added services

In all cases the activity may only be carried out by the provider or those acting
under his authority. Accordingly a provider cannot sell or disclose the traffic data
to third parties to use for their purposes without a limitation on use (reg.8(2));
however, it is not clear how far a provider could agree a use by a third party and
authorise that use. It is suggested that as long as the third party is acting "under
the authority" of the provider this would be possible.

Marketing and value-added services

Under reg.7(3) traffic data relating to a subscriber or user may be used for   **22–88**
marketing telecommunications services or the provision of value-added services
to that subscriber or user with the informed consent of the subscriber or user. The
services marketed or the value-added services may be supplied by a third party.
The subscriber or user must have been provided with information about the types
of traffic data which are to be processed and the duration of the processing before
the provider seeks consent. It is not explicit how the consent of a corporate
subscriber is to be given. Presumably the service provider can rely on the consent
of anyone who holds himself out as being able to give consent on behalf of the

company. As in all other cases where consent is required it must be real consent. The wording of reg.7(3)(b) was amended by SI 2011/1208 to read "the subscriber or user to whom the traffic data relates has *previously notified the provider that he consents*". The new formulation therefore clearly requires prior consent which involves some form of notice to the provider. The effect may be to make implied consent inadequate (for a full discussion of consent see Ch.4). The ICO Guide makes clear that the subscriber or user should be given enough clear information to ensure that they have a broad appreciation of how the data is going to be used and the consequence of consenting to the use. It goes on the say:

> "In the light of this, the service provider will not be able to rely on a blanket 'catch-all' statement on a bill or a website but must get specific informed consent:
>
> - for each value-added service requested; and
> - to market their own electronic communications services.
>
> If, for example , a communications provider offers a value-added service using a third party, then in the interests of transparency the person who will be regarded as responsible for providing that service should get the consent to process for that purpose."[68]

There are no special rules for marketing the services and the marketing may involve any form of marketing initiative but must of course comply with specific rule on telephone, fax, etc.

Under reg.7(4) subscribers must be able to withdraw their consent at any time.

Dispute resolution

22–89   Regulation 8(4) states that nothing in the Regulations shall prevent the disclosure of traffic data to a competent authority for the purposes of the settlement of disputes by any statutory mechanism. This is not dissimilar to the non-disclosure exemption for legal proceedings in the DPA 98.

Customer inquiries

22–90   No further definition is included of what customer inquiries covers. It could be that the inquiries must be made by customers but equally it could be argued that they need only be about customers. If they are restricted to inquiries by customers it is not clear whether they must be about the customer's own particular account or whether the provider can give information in response to one customer's inquiry about another's account. The OIC view in early guidance was that the inquiries are limited to those made by customers about their own accounts however the point has not been covered in more recent guides.

Prevention or detection of fraud

22–91   This only covers fraud. It does not cover the detection of other criminal activity such as offences against the person or drugs offences. Although on the words the

---

[68] ICO Guide to Privacy and electronic communications, September 7, 2011, p.48.

fraud does not appear to have to be directed against the service operator or the provider this appears to be the reason for the specific provision. It is not clear whether it applies where the fraud is perpetrated against another customer, for example by making dishonest use of his line. Where other criminal activities are concerned there are exemptions in reg.29 from restrictions on processing where it is carried out for the prevention or detection of crime. Fraud has now been defined in the Fraud Act 2006, which came into effect in January 2007. An offence of fraud may cover a wide range of activities.

Management of billing or traffic

Again no definition is included so the term "management" has to be given its ordinary meaning. The management purposes must be the purposes of the provider, not the purpose of others.

22–92

Restrictions on the processing of location data.

Regulation 14 specifically covers location data. It does not apply to traffic data. Location data is a defined term and means any data processed in an electronic communications network or by an electronic communications service[69] indicating the geographical position of the terminal equipment of the user of a public electronic communications service including data relating to the latitude, longitude or altitude of the terminal equipment, the direction of travel of the user, or the time the location information was recorded. Recital 55 of 2009/136 states that information from RFID should also be regarded as covered by the rules relating to location data. However under the current definition this can only be the case where a "user" or "subscriber" is associated with the RFID application, for example an electronic service provided to an individual wearing a badge with RFID capacity.

22–93

The use of location data allows for a range of services but also allows for significant surveillance and intrusion. The regulation provides that location data relating to a user or subscriber of a public electronic communications network or service cannot be processed for anything other than the provision of value added services and even then with consent. The prohibition does not apply if the data have been successfully anonymised so that the user or subscriber cannot be identified (reg.14(2)). In relation to obtaining consent for the use of location data the Commissioner takes the view that the service provider will not be able to rely on a blanket "catch all" statement on abill or a website but must get

- "● specific informed consent:for each value-added service requested; and
- ● to market their own electronic communications services".[70]

The consent must be fully informed, in that the provider must have told the user or subscriber the types of location data that will be processed, the purposes and duration of the processing and whether the data will be passed to a third party for the service to be provided (reg.14(3)). The user or subscriber has a right to

---

[69] As amended by SI 2011/1208 implementing art.292 of 2009/136.
[70] p.50.

withdraw consent and there must be a continuing right of opt-out on a transaction basis. In other words, at every point of connection or each transmission to be given the right to opt-out "using a simple means and free of charge". Services based on the use of location data such as advertising sent to mobile devises when a potential customer is near a restaurant or retail outlet therefore require positive informed consent if they are based on the use of information about that user or subscriber generated by an electronic communications network or service. If the location information is generated from another source the provision does not apply.

The processing must be restricted to that necessary for the purpose of providing the value-added service. There are also restrictions on the persons who may carry out such processing. These are restricted to the provider in question or someone acting for him and under his authority, or the third party provider of the services or those acting for him and under his authority (reg.14(5)).

However, there is no restriction on the processing of location data by the users of the Emergency numbers, 999 and 112.[71] This means that emergency services can always trace the location of callers to these numbers.

GEOLOCATION

22–94   At the time of writing there continues to be significant debate around the privacy questions and challenges asociated with geolocation services. In this section we have briefly set out the issues in a simplified form. In essence the Directives (both 95/46/EC and 2002/58) have been outpaced by both technology and the market:

- The scope of Directive 2002/58 is limited to public electronic communicatons and services. However increasingly electronic communication devices, such as smart phones, can make use of signals that are not generated or sent by those who provide electronic communications services to the public, notably individual WiFi installations and the use of GPS (Global Positioning satelites).
- Many of the businesses that make use of the new possibilites of geolocation information are suppliers of information society services and are outside the scope of Directive 2002/58, for example a mapping service that shows a user where they are on a map on a smartphone is a content provider.
- These businesses can gather a significant amount of information about the users, for example that the user spends time each week at the location of a massage parlour.
- Despite having a potentially tasty mess of information about the user however the providers of such location services may well be unaware of the terrestrial identity of the user, the name and address, which means that (in practical everyday terms) there is an argument that the information is not personal data.

---

[71] reg.16(1)(c).

- It is practically difficult to explain to users how these services work, where the data is coming from and how it may be used so as to gain meaningful consent.
- These are the fastest growing areas of many economies, consumers like the new services and there would be little political will to stifle development by regulation that would irritate consumers and could provide a barrier or blockage to developments.

The Commission did not seek to further regulate this developing area in the review of 2002/58. There are different views from different regulators in the EU on the extent and nature of regulation applicable and necessary in this domain and work has been carried out by the Article 29 WP. There is no material from the ICO on this issue, accordingly we have reviewed the most recent opiniion of the WP on this topic, Opinion 13/2011 on Geolocation services on smart devices. [72] The Opinion takes an extremely expansive view and one would not expect its more ambitious assertions to find favour in the UK. Nevertheless there must be sympathy for the concerns of the WP given that the alternative approach is that this developing area, with its capacity for significant intruion, is left without targetted regulation.

Opinion 13/2011

This is the second Opinion from the Article 29 WP on location data. The first was in 2005. Even in 2005 the WP took the view that location data will always be personal data in the hands of the application provider, stating that: "Since location data always relate to an identified or identifiable person" they are always personal data under 95/46/EC. This assertion has been repeated in Opinion 13/2011. This assertion depends on the assumption that mobile devises are intimately connected with their individual users, are so constantly in use that they show information about the users activities in some way and these are specific enough to lead to an actual identification of the user. In some cases these assumptions will be valid however in many others, particularly for older users of the technology, they will not. The question of whether data are personal data or not in any particular case will be a question of fact. Therefore while some location data in some cases will clearly be personal data, the same arguments that apply to IP addresses will apply here and in some cases the location data will not be personal data. As an example a smart device equipped with a location application which is provided by an employer to an employee will not necessarily give rise to personal data in the hands of the application provider. Both Opinions appear to recognise this tension and advise that, in any case where the party processing the location data knows that some of the data is personal data they should treat it all in the same way as subject to the legislation.

In Opinion 13/2011 the identity and position of WiFi access points of individual subscribers are also asserted to be personal data about those individual subscribers. WiFi access points operated by providers of public electronic communications services are regarded as part of the service provision and subject to 2002/58. WiFi access points provided by businesses or other corporate

22–95

22–96

---

[72] 881/11/EN.

subscribers are not discussed but it must be assumed that the WP would accept that this is not personal data. Again the assertion depends on the association of a WiFi point with a geographic area, and the association of that area with individuals at particular addresses whose details can be ascertained from other sources. Again these assumptions are open to serious question.

The Opinion illustrates very starkly the breath of the scope that is being given to the definition of personal data in the WP.

In considering the applicable grounds for the processing of location data it asserts that consent should be the applicable ground as "location data from smart mobile devices reveal intimate details about the private life of their owner". There is no proper explanation of the suggested link between sensitive personal data and location data and it must be questioned how location data can show ethnicity, race, religion, philosophical beliefs, physical or mental health or sexual life in other than very specific and individual cases. The examples given are that the location of an individual can be pinpointed at the address of a place of worship by the application provider however there is the counter argument that, unless the worshipper is engaged in solitary prayer or contemplation, it is highly likely that others will be present and there is no way of knowing from the location alone, which worshipper the information is actually about without linking it to any other information. However the WP argues that specific informed consent must be obtained for the use of location data and it is not sufficient to include a consent provision that in the terms and conditions for the location service. They also advise that:

- by default location services must be switched off;
- special care must be taken with information about children and employees with reliance on consent questionable; and
- consent should be renewed annually.

In relation to the WiFi points these are used by providers of geolocation services to assist with mapping and make location more precise. The WP accepts that these can be collected on the basis of the legitimate interst of the controller collecting them but that individual must be given the option to opt-out of the WiFi address and location being captured. Interestingly as part of the settlement reached with the French regulatory authority for data protection, the Commission Nationale des Informatiques and des Liberties (the CNIL), over the Streetview case in which Google inadvertently collected information from WiFi points Google agreed that they would not capture the MAC address of WiFi points which had amended settings to opt out of inclusion on its mapping by showing a "Nomap" response.

Other location technologies

22–97   The WP Opinion looked specifically at technologies based on mapping using base data, WiFi and GPS. However, location is also captured by a range of other technologies including automatic numberplate recognition, e-tickets such as Oystercards, CCTV and toll systems. Information can also be transferred by devices that use other technologies such as BlueTooth. These raise the same problems as to whether the data captured in any particular case is personal data, whether all such data should be treated as personal data, if it is clear that some will inevitably fall into that category and how notice can be provided and whether consent is necessary before processing.

Radio Frequency Identification Devices (RFID)

In this context mention should also be made of the questions which are raised by the increasing use of RFID and, as with geolocation, the development and use of RFID technology has exercised the Article 29 WP. In 2005 it issued a Working Document on Data Protection Issues related to RFID technology. Most recently it has issued a paper setting out the process for conducting a PIA on RFID applications. RFID applications do not necessarily involve peronal data, although particular applications may be linked to individuals. RFID applications will also be separate from an electronic communications system. In this context it is difficult to understand what is meant by Recital 55 of revised 2002/58 which specifically refers toRFID and states that

> "where such devices are connected to publicly available electronic communications networks or make use of electronic communications services as a basic infrastructure the relevant provisions of Directive 2002/58 including those on security, traffic and location data and on confidentiality should apply".

It is submitted that the provisions of 2002/58 are not applicable to the information generated by the RFID although if there is associated personal data that would be subject to 95/46/EC.

BILLING

Itemised billing

Regulation 9 deals with itemised billing. Regulation 9 provides that any subscriber, not only individual subscribers, shall be entitled to require the communications service provider to submit to him bills which are not itemised. The intent of this is to preserve the privacy of members of a household. In Recommendation R(95)4 the potential privacy problems in itemised billing were described thus:

> "Nevertheless urgent data protection problems are raised by the provision of itemised bills to subscribers, as well as by the retention by the network operator of the service data on which the bill is based . . . the provision of an itemised bill to a subscriber enables him or her to examine the telephone use of other people living in the household. In particular it allows the principal subscriber to identify the co-respondents of the co-users."[73]

Regulation 9(2) imposes a general duty on Ofcom to have regard to the needs to reconcile the rights of subscribers to receive itemised bills and the privacy rights

22–98

22–99

---

[73] Explanatory Memoranda para.99.

of callers and recipients when exercising various powers under the Communications Act 2003 it draws attention to the possibility of using privacy-enhancing methods of communication or payment. The sort of facilities considered may be cash payphones or anonymous pre-paid telephone cards.

Call forwarding

22–100   Call forwarding is the term used for diverting calls. For a description it is helpful to turn again to Recommendation R(95)4:

> "Call forwarding allows a user to re-route his incoming calls to the terminal of a third party. This service is not dependent on the digitalisation of the network since it has always been available in the analogue system."[74]

Regulation 17 requires a service provider to remove a divert at the request of the subscriber to whose line calls are being diverted where the divert is "as a result of action taken by a third party". Presumably if the divert has been requested by the subscriber himself then the right of removal does not apply (although it seems unlikely that a service provider would insist on retaining a divert the subscriber did not want). The divert has to be removed without any charge and must be removed without any avoidable delay. The subscriber's service provider may have to ask other network or service providers to assist in achieving this and they in turn are subject to duties to comply with any reasonable request made by the subscriber's service provider for the purpose of achieving this end.

Calling or connected line identification

22–101   Calling line identification (CLI) was seen as a highly privacy-invasive feature when introduced and there was concern that callers should be able to protect anonymity of calls by blocking in-coming CLI. Recommendation R(95)4 set out the potential problems with calling line identification (CLI) in terms that seem almost quaint:

> "The digitalisation of networks has made possible this new service feature in voice telephony. With the aid of a display unit on a subscriber's terminal, it is now possible to identify the source of incoming calls, that is the identity of the calling party....
>
> This new service feature brings with it many advantages for subscribers. First, it allows them to be in control when the telephone rings. With the incoming number displayed even before the communication takes place, the subscriber is in a position to decide whether or not to speak to the calling party. Secondly, the new service feature is a useful tool to combat abusive or malicious calls since those responsible for them will no longer be able to conceal their identity (provided of course that they are telephoning from a terminal connected to the ISDN network). Thirdly, the display of the incoming number on the called party's terminal presents obvious advantages for emergency services such as police, ambulance and fire brigade....
>
> The perceived advantages indicated in the preceding paragraph need to be evaluated in the light of a number of possible privacy problems which have been identified by the data protection community. First, the service feature may possibly

---

[74] Explanatory Memoranda paras 107–110.

undermine the anonymity which is guaranteed by ex-directory facilities. Secondly, calling line identification constitutes an obstacle to the freedom of communication of individuals contacting help line services, such as Alcoholics Anonymous, advice centres or the Samaritans.... Thirdly the release of a telephone number to a commercial or marketing agency as a result of a telephone enquiry regarding a particular product or service may give rise to unwanted calls of a commercial or marketing nature."[75]

CALLING LINE IDENTIFICATION

The Regulations cover calling or connected line identification in relation to both in-coming and out-going calls. The rules on the use of CLI are set out in regs 10–13. Information about the identity of the calling line may be available to the subscriber or end user in two ways; either from a display on the telephone equipment in use or from a call return service. The identity of the calling line is always known to the service provider. In the United Kingdom CLI has been available through a call return service by dialling 1471 since 1994. The services are governed by the Code of Practice for Network Operators in relation to Customer Line Identification Display services and other Related Services.[76]   **22–102**

Publicity

CLI is perceived as a service to consumers which may be of benefit to them and which they should be entitled to use. Accordingly, where CLI services are available any public electronic communications service provider who offers those facilities must provide information to the public about the service and the options open to users and subscribers.[77] However, CLI is not always to be available and may be overridden in some particular circumstances.   **22–103**

Malicious and nuisance calls

The provisions allowing callers to withhold numbers cannot be used as a cloak by nuisance callers. Under reg.15(1) a communications provider can override anything which is done to prevent the presentation of CLI where it is necessary or expedient to trace the source of malicious or nuisance calls on a subscriber's line. The subscriber has to apply to the service provider to trace the source of such calls. This right will override any contract term to the contrary. Moreover the provider may let any person with a legitimate interest know the identity of the subscriber for the line from which the nuisance calls have been made. Clearly a person with a legitimate interest would cover the police or another enforcement agency, but it also appears wide enough to cover the subscriber who is receiving the nuisance calls. It will not necessarily identify the actual caller, particularly where it is a line to which a number of people have access, but will pinpoint the physical location of the calls.   **22–104**

---

[75] Replace old 22.
[76] Both available from *www.ofcom.org.uk*.
[77] reg.12.

Emergency number calls

22–105 The other circumstance in which CLI will not be available is on calls to emergency services. CLI cannot be blocked for calls made to either 999 or 112 (the European emergency number). As noted earlier location data may also be processed in relation to calls to the emergency numbers.

Apart from these special cases subscribers are to be able to exercise several choices over the presentation of identity and acceptance of calls from others without identifying information. Where a subscriber has more than one line the rights apply separately to each line so a subscriber might have a different policy on accepting calls on different lines.[78]

Preventing out-going presentation of CLI

22–106 Regulation 10 sets out two choices for blocking presentation of identity; per call blocking by users and per line blocking by subscribers. Anyone using a telephone line which offers the technical facility for blocking must be able to prevent the presentation of the identity of the line he is using on a call by call basis (per call blocking). Any subscriber, that is the one who has a contract with the service provider, must be able to block any CLI presentation for all calls on the line (per line blocking). These facilities must be provided by a simple mechanism and must be free of charge by the service provider.

Third country calls

22–107 In art.8(5) the Directive requires that the blocking of CLI must apply to calls originating in the Community and made to third countries. The only way this can be achieved, other than by agreements between service providers in Europe and third countries, is by the service provider marking such calls as CLI unavailable. No specific provision in the Regulations deal with this requirement; no such duty is imposed on service providers. The Guide notes that it is still not possible to block CLI individually on some in coming international calls so any block will have the effect of cutting off all such calls.[79]

Presenting in-coming presentation of CLI

22–108 At first sight it is not easy to see why a subscriber would want to disable CLI presentation but it can occur where a help line wishes to guarantee anonymity of calls made to it or to preserve individual privacy in a shared household. To deal with such cases reg.11(2) provides that where CLI is available the subscriber whose line is being called can prevent the CLI of the caller being made available to him. This is a self-denying ordinance. It applies to the line and not to individual calls.

---

[78] reg.10(3).
[79] ICO Guide to Privacy and electronic communications, September 7, 2011, p.54.

Preventing outgoing presentation of CLI

Regulation 11(4) is intended to allow a subscriber to prevent the presentation of the "real" number being called from being made available to a caller where he call comes through a connected line. This will apply where a caller is ringing a number and the call is being forwarded on to another number. For example a GP may have his calls routed through the surgery number but actually be taking them at home. He may not want his home number presented to calling patients. This provision allows him to block the presentation of the number of the connected line, that is the home number.

22–109

Refusing calls without CLI

If CLI is available to the person being called before the call is taken and the caller has blocked the CLI of the call, then the person being called will be able to see that is the case before he takes the call. Regulation 12(3) provides that where a person being called is aware that CLI has been blocked on a call he must have a simple means to reject the call or all such calls. It need not be a free service. The right to refuse to take a call on which the number has been blocked is contained in art.8(3) of the Directive.

22–110

The appropriate way to deal with this has been a matter of some debate. The problem is that, while fixed networks can offer a service called Anonymous Call Rejection (ACR), there is no direct equivalent on mobile networks. Where ACR is available calls without CLI are not delivered to the subscriber, and the subscriber gets a message explaining why the call has been rejected and how to overcome the rejection, by releasing the CLI.

22–111

On mobile networks however this facility is not available. However, the current Guidance from the Commissioner's Office seems to accept that this is not a significant problem.. The Guidance states that:

> "The Commissioner's current understanding based on Ofcom advice is that as the relevant regulation applies to the automatic rejection of voice calls only, automatic call rejection can be implemented relatively simply using a recorded voice message".

In other words mobile users should record a voicemail message explaining to callers that their calls may have been rejected because of the absence of CLI, then press the busy button when presented with a call without CLI that they do not want to accept and divert to voicemail.

Co-operation by providers

Regulation 13 requires all communication service providers to comply with reasonable requests made by others to give effect to the CLI rights of subscribers and users.

22–112

DIRECTORIES

22–113 Regulation 18 covers any directory of subscribers. The term "subscriber" is defined as meaning a person who is a party to a contract with a provider of public electronic communications services for the supply of such services. The directory may be in printed or electronic form but must be made available to members of the public or a section of the public including by means of a directory enquiry service. It follows that directories may cover fax numbers, email numbers, or mobile telephone numbers and this is how the Information Commissioner has interpreted the provision.[80] They are not limited to directories of telephone numbers. It does not matter who compiles them or offers the directory service, nor does the form of the directory matter, whether on CD-ROM or paper or given over the telephone in response to a request. The provisions do not apply to any editions of directories published before December 11, 2003 when the Regulations came into force.

22–114 Subscribers have rights to have details relating to them to be omitted from further editions of directories; they cannot require existing or previous editions to be amended. Whenever a revised version of a directory is issued it is deemed to be a new edition.[81]

22–115 Obligations are laid upon both those who "collect" personal data and those who "produce" directories. Neither of these terms are defined and therefore must be given their natural meaning. The rights to be notified of the inclusion in the directory and to withdraw rest with the subscriber rather than the user. The Regulation appears to be based on the assumption that the subscriber will be the user of the telephone. It is not clear how it applies in other cases, for example where parents subscribe to mobile telephones for use by children.

Individual subscriber entries

22–116 Before details relating to an individual subscriber are included in a directory he must be told by the person who collects the personal data that it is intended for inclusion. He must be given the opportunity to have particular information omitted from a directory but cannot insist that specific information is included. There is no specific requirement that the subscriber provides prior consent to inclusion, an opt-out appears to be sufficient. In the Guide the Commissioner refers to these provisions as reflecting the transparency requirements of the first data protection principle and emphasises that the nature of the directory product and potential use should be considered. In particular the more information is to be included in a directory and the more sophisticated the product, the more information should be provided to the subscriber:

> "... those collecting information from subscribers will need to ensure subscribers understand appreciate that
>
> • their information will be made available via a variety of directory products and services; and

---

[80] Guidance to PECR.
[81] reg.18(7).

- this will enable those who know their name and address to get their phone number.

Where there are a range of ex-directory options the subscriber should be told about all of them."

An individual subscriber can also "verify, correct or withdraw" his entry without charge at any time.

Corporate subscriber entries

Corporate subscribers have the right to be omitted from a directory where the corporate subscriber has notified the producer of the directory that it does not want "its" data to be included. This would presumably allow a corporate subscriber to require that all its direct dial numbers should be omitted from a directory.[82]   **22–117**

Directory inquiries

The rules about directories appear to apply equally to directory inquiry services.   **22–118**

Reverse searching

The Regulations include provisions which deal with directories which offer reverse searching, that is the provision of the name and address from the telephone number. This was not covered under the previous Regulations but the OIC took action against providers who offered this service without the consent of the subscriber as being unfair processing. Subscribers must be expressly informed and give express consent before their details can be included in a directory which allows reverse searching of facsimile or telephone numbers.[83]   **22–119**

It should be noted that directory services are treated as a mandatory service to subscribers under other telecoms provisions. Ofcom states on its website that it must ensure that: **22–120**

- at least one comprehensive directory and directory enquiry services (DQ) exists and that end-users have access to them;
- subscribers have the right to be listed in directories and DQ services; and
- communication providers which assign telephone numbers provide "all relevant information" on fair, objective, cost-oriented and non-discriminatory.

---

[82] reg.18(4).
[83] reg.18(3).

EXEMPTIONS

22–121 As noted above, specific exemptions are included in relation to the use of traffic data. There are also more general exemptions in regs 28 and 29 relating to national security and law enforcement.

These exemptions apply to the specific requirements of PECR.

Relationship between the exemptions in the Regulations and the DPA 98

22–122 The DPA 98 sets out a regulatory regime for personal data and allows some disclosures to be made outside that regime or some of the rights to be abrogated where there is a strong countervailing interest such as the prevention of crime. The exemptions in the main Act apply to the requirements of the main Act. The exemptions in the PECR apply to the requirements of the Regulations only, not to the requirements of the DPA 98. The two are without prejudice to one another so the same facts would be able to give rise to an exemption claim under s.28 of the DPA 98 and under reg. 29 of the PEC Regulations but each would apply separately to the processing involved.

National security

22–123 This is dealt with by way of a general exemption from the Regulations in reg. 28 if such an exemption is required in order to safeguard national security. This is followed by detailed provisions under which conclusive evidence of the requirement for the exemption is to be provided by a certificate signed by a Minister of the Crown and for appeal to the Tribunal on limited grounds. The provisions relating to the certificates, the rights of appeal and the constitution of the Tribunal are the same as those in the main Act, which are dealt with fully at Ch.15 and are not repeated here.

Legal proceedings and law enforcement

22–124 Under reg.29 none of the provisions of the Regulations shall require a communications provider to do anything or stop him doing anything:

(i) inconsistent with any requirement imposed by or under an enactment, or order of a court; or

(ii) likely to prejudice the prevention or detection of crime or apprehension or prosecution of offenders.

The communications provider will also be exempt from any requirement of the Regulations if exemption is required for the purpose of legal proceedings, including prospective legal proceedings:

(iv) necessary for the purpose of obtaining legal advice; or is

(v) otherwise necessary for the purpose of establishing or exercising legal rights.

This is similar to the legal proceedings exemption in the DPA 98. There is no exemption for the collection of tax or duty.

In the Directive exemptions are dealt with in art.15, which includes a requirement that any exemptions must meet the standards of proportionality required for any breach of art.8 of the ECHRFF. It also includes a specific provision for communications data:

> "... Member States may inter alia adopt legislative measures providing for the retention of data for a limited period justified in grounds laid down in this paragraph. All the measures referred to in this paragraph shall be in accordance with the general principles of Community law".

The topic of retention of communications data is covered in Ch.24.

ENFORCEMENT AND INDIVIDUAL RIGHTS

This area is covered fully in Chs 20 and 21 on enforcement and prosecution and Chs 11–14 on individual rights.

Compensation

Regulation 30 provides that a person who suffers damage by reason of any **22–125** contravention of any of the requirements of the Regulations by any other person shall be entitled to bring proceedings for compensation for the damage. There is no compensation for associated distress in these cases, unlike the provisions in respect of the main Act. Damage means actual damage (see discussion of what constitutes damage in Ch.14). It is difficult to envisage what actual damage is likely to be caused by unsolicited telephone calls, although in the case of fax messages and spam email there is a cost to the subscriber associated with the receipt of the messages. The cost is extremely small and it might be thought that it would hardly be worth seeking monetary compensation but it would enable an individual to bring an action before the courts. The court would then be able to use any other powers at its disposal to deal with the case. It appears however that an enterprising data subject has succeeded in an action in the Edinburgh Sheriff Court against Transcom for the damages associated with receipt of an unsolicited email. It is reported on a website[84] that he was awarded damages of £750 plus costs of £617 (the court having lifted the usual cap on costs in a small claims action) against Transcom for sending an unsolicited email to his personal email address.

In *Microsoft v McDonald*[85] Microsoft took action under reg.30 against a spammer who had used their network services. Regulation 30 allows "any person" who has suffered damages as a result of breach of the regulations to seek compensation. The Court held that Microsoft was within the class of persons entitled to claim under reg.30. In the case Microsoft sought an injunction to

---

[84] *http://scotchspam.org.uk* [Accessed October 4, 2012].
[85] [2006] EWHC 3410.

restrain the spammer from repeating his actions. The High Court granted the injunction under its powers under the Supreme Court Act 1981.

If proceedings for compensation are brought under this regulation it is a defence for the defendant to prove that he had taken such care as in all the circumstances was reasonably required to comply with the requirement. It is suggested that, as far as the marketing aspects are involved, this would cover giving proper training and instructions to staff; making sure proper stop lists are maintained of those who notify objections to direct marketing by these methods; ensuring regular use of the current stop lists; ensuring the relevant information is given and available when requested; ensuring notifications given are passed on expeditiously to OfCom or the persons running the stop lists on his behalf.

The Government clearly considered that the rights to take action under reg.30 are sufficient to comply with the requirement of art.13(6) of 2002/58 as amended by art.2(7) of 2009/136 that any person adversely affected by unsolicited electronic communications should have a remedy in legal proceedings. However, the fact that actual damage must be shown before any action can be taken may argue against this and it may be suggested that some action should be open to individual consumers without proof of damage to satisfy the new requirement.

Enforcement

22–126   The enforcement provisions are drafted by reference to the DPA 1998. Part V of the DPA 1998 is applied with appropriate modifications set out in Sch.1. These powers are covered in Ch.20. The complaint and assessment provisions are worded differently from the DPA 98. Under s.42 of the DPA 98 Act an individual who is or believes himself to be affected by processing may make a request to the Commissioner for an assessment of the processing in question. The Commissioner then has obligations to make the assessment and respond to the individual. Under reg.32 either Ofcom or a person aggrieved by an alleged contravention of the Regulations may request the Commissioner to exercise his enforcement functions in respect of that contravention The Regulations do not in terms impose a duty to consider such a request or make a determination following it but applying the principles of public law the Commissioner will be under an obligation to consider any request properly made to him under the legislation. In order to decide whether to exercise his enforcement functions the Commissioner will have to make a decision on whether or not the processing involved complies with the Regulations.

Assistance of Ofcom

22–127   Under reg.33 Ofcom has a duty to provide technical advice to the Commissioner on matters relating to electronic communication if requested. The request of the Commissioner must be a reasonable one.

Enforcement notices and monetary penalty notices

22–128   The Commissioner may serve an enforcement notice on any person who contravenes the requirements of the Regulations. In considering whether to serve a notice the Commissioner must have regard to whether the contravention has caused any individual damage but not distress. The provisions of s.41 of the DPA 98 under which those subject to enforcement notices may apply to the Commissioner to have the notice cancelled or varied by reason of a change of circumstances also apply. Notices may apply as a matter of urgency. The Commissioner may serve a notice requiring the service provider to notify subscribers or users of a personal data breach where the service provider has not done so but the Commissioner he considers that it is appropriate to do so given the likely adverse effect of the breach.[86] The provisions in relation to the service of monetary penalty notices of up to £500,000 for serious breaches apply subject to the procedural obligations and rights of appeal. In addition the Commissioner may serve a fixed penalty of up to £1,000 if the service provider has failed to notify of a personal data breach.

Information notices and audits

The power to serve information notices applies to breaches of the Regulations. A notice may be served where the Commissioner reasonably requires any information for the purpose of determining whether a person has complied or is complying with the relevant requirements of the Regulations. The notice may require him to furnish such information relating to compliance as is specified in the notice. The notice must contain a statement that the Commissioner regards the specified information as relevant for the purpose of determining whether the person has complied or is complying and his reason for regarding it as relevant. **22–129**

The Information Commissioner may audit the measures taken by a provider of a communications service to safeguard the security of that service[87] as well as more generally audit the compliance of service providers with their obligations in respect of personal data breaches.

Prosecutions and warrants

Failure to comply with an enforcement or information notice is an offence. The Commissioner's powers to apply for warrants will apply to breaches of the Regulations including power to apply for a warrant if a service provider fails to comply with an audit requirement imposed by the Commissioner. The warrant provisions are covered in Ch.21. **22–130**

Third party notices

The Commissioner may serve notices on service providers to divulge the identity of third party users of their services. **22–131**

---

[86] reg.5A(7).
[87] reg.5(6).

Pan European enforcement

22–132   Directive 2009/136 amended art.3 of 2002/58 to provide that breaches of these requirements can be tackled on a pan-European basis under Regulation (EC) No.2006/2004 on co-operation in the area of consumer protection. This should facilitate work in those cases where cross border co-operation is required.

TERRITORIAL APPLICATION

22–133   The impact of s.5(1)(b) based on art.4(1)(c) of the general Directive has given rise to significant debate in the area of electronic communication services. The UK provision follows art.4 very closely and provides that the Act will apply in cases where the data controller is not established in the UK or any other EEA state but "uses equipment in the United Kingdom for processing the data otherwise than for the purposes of transit through the UK". The wording in art.4(1)(c) is that the controller "makes use of equipment, automated or otherwise, situated on the territory of the Member State" "for purposes of processing personal data". The Article 29 WP has considered whether the insertion of a "cookie" or similar file on a user's browser and the subsequent collection of information when that cookie is read amounts to using equipment in the state where the user is situated. In Opinion 1/2008 it reiterated the view taken by the International Working Group on Data Protection in Telecommunications in April 1998 and reinforced in April 2006 that the insertion and use of a cookie or similar software on a user's browser amounts to making use of equipment on the territory of a Member State. It is difficult to fault this conclusion. The webserver makes use of the browser of the user to store the cookie and to collect information when it is recognised again. Cookies are not chosen or sought by users. They are delivered by the relevant webserver at the volition of whoever wishes to set them, unless of course the user rejects the cookies, in which case the question does not arise. If this is the correct view, and it has remained the view of the WP and of regulators since the Directive was passed, it follows that where the party that inserted the cookie processes personal data as a result of or in connection with the use of the cookie than they fall into the ambit of art.4(1).

Directive 2002/58 and the Regulations are silent on the issue of territorial application. The Regulations do not apply the territorial provisions of the DPA 98 and accordingly the general law will apply. In general terms therefore the Regulations will apply where actions are carried out in areas within the jurisdiction of the UK courts. In relation to control of traffic and billing data this is likely to be where the data are held. If a service or network provider is established in the United Kingdom then there is unlikely to be any problem. The issue becomes more cloudy in relation to obligations placed on those who use electronic communications services for example for marketing uses. If a person outside the United Kingdom uses an electronic communications network or service within the United Kingdom to send marketing material it is not clear whether the "use" takes place within the United Kingdom or outside it.

If a person such a network or service to transfer personal data overseas the usual rules in the DPA 98 will apply. There are no special rules for overseas transfers.

International review

The arts 29 and 31 Groups have a locus standi to consider and report on Directive   **22–134** 2002/58 as on the main Directive.

ADDITIONAL INFORMATION

Previous statutory instruments   **22–135**
SI 1998/3170 Telecommunications (Data Protection and Privacy)(Direct Marketing) Regulations 1998;
SI 199/2093 Telecommunications (Data Protection and Privacy) Regulations 1999;
SI 2000/157 Telecommunications (Data Protection and Privacy) (Amendmnet) Regulations 2000 (amended provisions relating to national security certificates in the main Regulations so as to be coherent with those in the DPA 98).

Derivations   **22–136**
Directives 2003/58 and 2009/136 on November 25, 2009.

ADDITIONAL INFORMATION

of a person such a network or service to transfer personal data overseas, the usual rules in the DPA 98 will apply. There are no special rules for overseas transfers.

International review

I heard 22 and 31 Groups have a joint remit to consider and report on Directive 2002/58 as on the main Directive   22-134

ADDITIONAL INFORMATION

Previous statutory instruments   22-135

SI 1999/2093 Telecommunications (Data Protection and Privacy) (Direct Marketing) Regulations 1999.

SI 1999/2093 telecommunications (Data Protection and Privacy) Regulations 1999.

SI 2000/157 Telecommunications (Data Protection and Privacy) (Amendment) Regulations 2000 (amended provisions relating to national security certificates to the main Regulations so as to be coherent with those in the DPA 98).

Derivations   22-136

Directives 2002/58 and 2002/136 on November 25, 2009.

CHAPTER 23

Monitoring Of Communications, Interception And Access To Encrypted Data

INTRODUCTION

Respect for the confidentiality of communication is a fundamental aspect of the right to privacy as set out in art.8 of the European Convention on Human Rights and Fundamental Freedoms ("the Human Rights Convention"). Article 8 requires the State to respect "private and family life, home and correspondence". Article 5 of Directive 2002/58/EC applies this right to the provision of electronic communications by public service providers. Crucially, art.5 restricts eavesdropping on electronic conversations or monitoring the use of communications systems in public electronic communications systems. In an era in which government security and policing are increasingly reliant on surveillance of all kinds, but particularly surveillance of communications, the scope of the restrictions imposed by art.5 and its predecessor in Directive 97/66 has been a matter of considerable controversy. The importance attached by the Government to surveillance and monitoring of communications for the purposes of tackling crime and terrorism has thrown the impact of these restrictions into sharp relief. The nature of digital surveillance and the proper approach to controlling such surveillance raises many challenging issues. The surveillance techniques to which we are now subject range from CCTV through ANRP to data collected as a result of purchases. In this chapter we only cover the specific areas of:

23 01

- the European legal background to the rules governing the monitoring of communications;
- the scope of the European legal instruments;
- the regulation of access to communications data and interception of communications on public telecommunications in the UK under the Regulation of Investigatory Powers Act (RIPA);
- the regulation of access to encryption keys in the UK under the RIPA; and
- the regulation of the interception of communications on private systems under the Telecommunications (Lawful Practice) (Interception of Communications) Regulations 2000 ("LBP Regulations") made under RIPA.

In addition to access to communications data and the interception of communications on public networks, RIPA covers covert surveillance, use of intelligence sources and related matters. Only Pt 1 of Ch.I—Unlawful and authorised interception, Ch.2—Acquisition and Disclosure of Communications Data, and Pt III—Investigation of electronic data protected by encryption, are covered in this chapter.

The scope of the European legal instruments is important in this context as it affects how much freedom the UK has to decide on its own rules in some of these areas. The relationship with the European legal instruments is therefore considered. Note that the overall scheme for the regulation of electronic communications is outlined in Ch.22.

BACKGROUND

23-02 The rules which govern this area are derived from supra-national legal instruments: the Human Rights Convention, Directive 2002/58 and its predecessor Directive 1997/66. There were deficiencies in the way that the UK implemented its obligations under these instruments which are noted in the text and action was taken in relation to deficiencies which came to the attention of the Commission as a result of the Phorm Webwise issue in 2008. This resulted in amendments to RIPA covered below. There are different rules for interception of communications and for access to communications data. Interception has a legal definition in the Regulation of Investigatory Powers Act 2000 (RIPA) but broadly covers any access to the content of communications. Interception may take place either by monitoring, that is listening into a conversation in the course of its transmission across a communications network[1] or viewing an e-mail exchange while it is taking place; or recording, that is accessing the communication message in the course of its transmission across a communications network and taking a copy to listen to or read later. Access to communications data means having access to the traffic data about the communication, including the service data and subscriber data.[2]

Communications data is the information generated as a result of electronic communications (such as the number called or the length of the call) rather than the content of the communication. There are special rules which allow businesses (which includes the public sector for these purposes) to intercept the contents of communications on their own systems subject to safeguards. These are found in the LBP Regulations. There are no provisions which specifically authorise businesses (including the public sector) to access or use the communications data on their systems.

---

[1] Note that monitoring one half (or even both halves) of a conversation via bugging devices would not constitute an interception: see, e.g., *R. v Smart* [2002] EWCA Crim 722 at para.68.

[2] See s.21(4)(b) and (c) of RIPA. Schs 1 and 2 of the Regulation of Investigatory Powers (Communications Data) Order 2010 (SI 2010/480) set out which public bodies have access to which types of communications data; many only have access to service data not traffic or subscriber data.

SUMMARY OF MAIN POINTS

23–03

(a) Interception of communications and access to communications data involve breaches of art.8 of the Convention rights and on public networks are subject to art.5 of Directive 2002/58.

(b) Interception, access to communications data and retention of communications data are covered by a number of intersecting provisions.

(c) Public bodies carrying out interception of content on private electronic communications systems which they control (e.g. internal government department systems) are subject to art.8 of the Convention and have a lawful basis for their interference with those rights as long as they comply with the LBP Regulations.

(d) Private bodies carrying out interception of content on private electronic communications systems (e.g. internal telephone systems) are not directly subject to art.8 of the Convention but in any event have a lawful basis for the interception as long as they comply with the LBP Regulations.

(e) Public or private bodies carrying out surveillance of or accessing communications data on private electronic communications systems which they control (e.g. internal systems) have no clear legal basis for the interference as the LBP regulations do not cover communications data and the legal position of such surveillance or access is uncertain.

(f) Public bodies carrying out interception or access to communications data on public telecommunications systems are subject to art.8 of the Convention and art.5 of Directive 2002/58 and have a lawful basis for their interference with those rights as long as they have proper authority under RIPA, e.g. warrants.

(g) There is no lawful basis for private organisations to be authorised to carry out interception or access communications data on or from public telecommunications systems. Any such interception or access carried out intentionally would be unlawful under RIPA unless those subject to the interception or access gave consent.

BACKGROUND

Article 8 of the Convention rights

The interception or surveillance of a communication is clearly an interference with the art.8 right of an individual.[3] Article 8 provides:

23–04

> "(1) Everyone has the right to respect for his private and family life, his home and his correspondence.
>
> (2) There shall be no interference by a public authority with the exercise of this right except such as is in accordance with law and is necessary in a democratic society in the interests of national security, public safety or he

---

[3] See Ch.2 for a full description of the impact of the HRA and the case law on art.8 since October 2000. Concerns about the impact of interception on private life were expressed by the Article 29 Working Party in its Recommendations in the Respect of Privacy in the Context of Interceptions of Telecommunications of May 3, 1999.

democratic well-being of the country, for the prevention of disorder or crime, for the protection of health or morals, or for the protection of the rights and freedoms of others".

This is now part of UK law by virtue of the Human Rights Act 1998. In the past the UK was found wanting before the European Court of Human Rights because of its failure to regulate comprehensively the interception of communications. The first statute to regulate the interception of communications was the Interception of Communications Act 1985 (IOCA), which was passed following an adverse finding against the UK in the case of *Malone v UK*.[4] UK practice had been for telephone taps to be carried out under administrative practices with no comprehensive statutory code governing surveillance activities. Thus the practice did not comply with the standards necessary to meet art.8(2) as it was not set out in a legal scheme which was sufficiently clear or transparent to enable the citizen to understand in what circumstances and in what conditions public authorities were empowered to carry out such activities.[5]

IOCA made it an offence to intentionally intercept a communication in the course of transmission by a public telecommunications system, unless either it was done with the authority of a warrant issued by the Secretary of State or the interceptor had reasonable grounds for believing that either the sender or the recipient had consented to the interception. However, the limited remit of IOCA meant that the UK continued to face adverse findings by the Court at Strasbourg in relation to interception. In the case of *Halford v United Kingdom*,[6] the Court found that the tapping of a telephone which was part of a private network was not covered by IOCA and thus without a proper legal basis. In a variety of cases the Court also found that the failure by the UK to regulate surveillance by electronic eavesdropping in other ways breached art.8.[7] In the UK courts in *R. v Effick*[8] it was held that calls from a cordless telephone which were intercepted between the base unit and the telephone were not covered by IOCA.

23–05   When the Convention rights were implemented in the United Kingdom by the HRA it was imperative that the entire area of surveillance was reviewed and put on to a proper statutory footing. The government decided that the appropriate approach was to deal with both art.5 of Directive 97/66 and art.8(2) of the Convention rights in the same legislation and did so in RIPA and the LBP Regulations.

Article 5 of Directive 97/66 and 2002/58

23–06   Article 5(1) of Directive 2002/58 requires Member States to ensure the confidentiality of

"... communications and the related traffic data by means of a public communications network and publicly available electronic communications services, through national legislation. In particular they shall prohibit listening, tapping, storage or

---

[4] (1985) E.H.R.R. 14.
[5] For a more detailed analysis see K. Starmer, *European Human Rights Law*.
[6] (1997) 24 E.H.R.R. 523.
[7] *Khan v United Kingdom* (2001) 31 E.H.R.R. 45; *PG v United Kingdom* [2002] Crim. L.R. 308.
[8] [1994] 3 All E.R. 458.

other kinds of interception or surveillance of communications and the related traffic data by persons other than users, except with the consent of the users concerned, except when legally authorised to do so in accordance with Article 15(1)."

In 2010 the UK was found to have failed to have implemented the requirement properly and made consequential amendments to RIPA in 2011, which are covered below. The provision largely re-states art.5 of Directive 1997/66; the difference is in the addition of the reference to "and related traffic data" which is dealt with below. However, in respect of the interception of the content of communications the provision is identical. It requires Member States to prohibit the interception of communications and access to communication data on public networks except either where users of the communication system have consented or the interception is legally authorised.

The scope of areas where legal authority may permit an interference is not in fact limited to the derogations provided for by art.15(1), as art.5(2) further provides that:

"(2)   Paragraph 1 shall not affect any legally authorised recording of communications and the related traffic data when carried out in the course of lawful business practice for the purposes of providing evidence of a commercial transaction or of any other business communication"

Recital 23 provides some further explanation of the scope of this derogation as follows:

"Confidentiality of communications should also be ensured in the course of lawful business practice. Where necessary and legally authorised, communications can be recorded for the purpose of providing evidence of a commercial transaction. Directive 95/46/EC applies to such processing. Parties to the communications should be informed prior to the recording about the recording, its purposes and the duration of its storage. The recorded communication should be erased as soon as possible and in any case at the latest by the end of the period during which the transaction can be lawfully challenged".

The derogations provided for by art.15(1) permit Member States to adopt legislative measures to restrict the scope of the rights and obligations where the restriction constitutes a necessary, appropriate and proportionate measure within a democratic society to safeguard   **23–07**

"... national security (i.e. State security), defence, public security, and the prevention, investigation, detection and prosecution of criminal offences or of unauthorised use of the electronic communication system."

The judgment of the Court of Justice of the European Union (CJEU) in *Productores de Música de España (Promusicae) v Telefónica de España SAU* (C-275/06) made clear that the grounds of exemption allowed in 95/46/EC should also be regarded as relevant to 2002/58. Article 15(1) makes it explicit that Member States may adopt laws to provide for the interception of communications including cases where the reasons fall outside community competence but the measures must be in limited to those allowed by the Article. Any abrogation of the confidentiality of communications must also be in accord with Community law including the principles in art.6(1) and (2) of the Treaty. The principles in art.6(1) and (2) enshrine the fact that the Union is founded on the principles of liberty, democracy, respect for human rights and fundamental freedoms.[9]

Directive 2002/58 does not apply to areas outside the scope of EU law and thus interception may take place for matters outside scope. Recital 11 of 2002/58 makes this point explicit but also makes it explicit that the Convention rights continue to apply to such interception. RIPA is primary legislation and its provisions apply to all interception which is within its scope.

Confidentiality of communications data

23–08   As noted above, Directive 97/66 did not impose any restriction on the access to communications data. It did impose restrictions on how such data can be used by those who provide public electronic services which have now been repeated in Directive 2002/58 and are implemented in the UK by the Privacy and Electronic Communications (EC Directive) Regulation 2003 (see Ch.22). Directive 2002/58 placed access to communications data arising from public electronic communications services on the same footing and subject to the same restrictions as interception. There has however been no subsequent change to the relevant statutory provisions in RIPA or the LBP Regulations.

RIPA covers the acquisition and disclosure of communications data by designated public authorities from public service providers and operators of private systems, such as those used internally in business and public offices. The LBP Regulations do not deal explicitly with communications data. The current situation therefore is that operators of private networks, both public and private sector, access and use communications data for their own purposes such as HR management without any general supervisory regime other than the data protection principles; specifically there is no legal basis for accessing such data. It can be assumed that the view of the UK Government was that operators of private systems, whether the system controller is in the public or the private sector, need no additional powers to access or use communications data. The case of *Copland*,[10] however, suggests that such use and access, by public bodies at least, engages art.8 of the Convention Rights

Copland v United Kingdom

23–09   Mrs Copland was employed by a Further Education College. During the course of her employment her telephone and internet useage were monitored by her employer. There was some dispute over whether interception of contents took place but the Court took the view that it did not have to decide that as the monitoring of the communications data amounted to a breach of art.8 in any event. Mrs Copland had not been told that her communications would be monitored. The UK government had argued that the monitoring of the communications data did not amount to an interference in private life but the Court held that it did. The Government also argued that, if there was an interference, it was on lawful grounds, being incidental to the powers of the

---

[9] art.15(1).
[10] Application No.62617/00.

college and was proportionate. The Court held that there was no lawful basis as there was no express power and therefore the question of proportionality did not arise. It found against the UK on art.8 and also art.13 in that Mrs Copland did not have an effective remedy for the breach of her art.8 rights. It appears that the UK Government dealt with the judgment by stating to the Joint Committee on Human Rights in 2007 that it had implemented the Court's judgment in Copland by virtue of Telecommunications (Lawful Business Practice) (Interception of Communications) Regulations 2000 and that this was accepted by the Committee of Ministers in March 2008.[11] However, the response did not deal specifically with communications data and although it has been accepted by the Committee of Ministers the result seems open to doubt as the Regulations do not cover communications data.

COVERAGE OF DIRECTIVES

Areas which are outside Community competence are outside the remit of Community law. Article 3(2) of Directive 95/46/EC specifically sets out those limits by providing that the Directive does not apply to the processing of personal data carried out in the course of activities which fall outside the scope of Community law and explicitly not to processing operations

23–10

> "concerning public security, defence, State security (including the economic well-being of the State when the processing operation relates to State security matters) and the activities of the State in the areas of criminal law".

A directive itself may also be limited in scope because of the basis on which it was made. Directives are secondary legislation of the Community. A legal basis for the making of a directive must be found in the Treaties.[12] Directive 95/46/EC was made as an internal market measure on the basis of art.95. Any purported action under the Directive must fall within the scope of art.95.

The limitations of the legal basis were emphasised by the ruling of the European Court of Justice in the cases heard on the transmission of Passenger Name records (PNR) to the United States.[13] Following the terrorist attacks of November 9, 2001 the United States had required airlines to disclose detailed passenger information relating to those who travelled to the country. In order to provide a lawful basis for the required disclosures the European Commission had adopted two decisions, the first holding that the US Bureau of Customs and Border Protection (CBP), part of the Department of Homeland Security, provided a sufficient level of protection for the personal data being transferred and the other embodying an agreement with the US authorising the transfers.[14] The

23–11

[11] *http://www.publications.parliament.uk/pa/jt200708/jtselect/jtrights/173/17317.htm* [Accessed October 5, 2012].
[12] For a fuller discussion of the scope of Community law, see Ch.1, paras 1–16 onwards.
[13] Joined Cases C-317/04 and C-318/04 of the European Court of Justice, May 30, 2006.
[14] Commission decision 2004/535/EC of May 14, 2004 on the adequate protection of personal data contained in Passenger Name Record of air passengers transferred to the United States Bureau of Customs and Border Protection ([2004]OJ L235 p.11) and Council Decision 2004/496/EC of May 17, 2004 on the conclusion of an Agreement between the European Community and the United States of America on the processing and transfer of PNR data by Air Carriers to the United States of America

European Parliament applied for the decisions to be annulled on the basis that the decisions were outwith the competence of the Council and the Commission.

Community competence

23–12   The institutions of the Community do not have competence to rule on matters that are not within the Treaties of the Union. Security is outside the scope of Community competence. The agreement with the US on PNR was for the purposes of security and thus the Commission and the Council were not able to make binding instruments in relation to it. The European Court agreed with the Parliament and the Decisions were annulled with effect from September 30, 2006.[15]

A Member State is not required by EU law to apply a provision of a Community instrument, such as a directive, to an activity outside an area of Community competence, although the Member State may chose to apply the standards required by a directive to all areas of relevant behaviour by national law. When implementing the data protection directives the UK had a choice as to how it would implement. It could have implemented by secondary legislation and made regulations under the European Communities Act 1972. Regulations can be made under this Act only in relation to areas falling within Community competence. Alternatively it could pass primary legislation. The United Kingdom elected to pass primary legislation, making the Data Protection Act 1998 generally applicable national law, including those areas which are not covered by Community competence.

Directives 1997/66 and 2002/58 however were implemented by regulations made under the European Communities Act 1972 and are therefore only applicable to areas covered by Community competence.

Directive 2002/58 applies, and will be relevant as an aid to interpretation, where the surveillance or interception falls within areas of Community competence, as with the monitoring of business calls, but does not apply, and is only persuasive, at best, when the surveillance or interception is carried out for purposes outside Community competence such as national security. It should be noted, however, that art.5 (see para.23-07, above) of the predecessor Directive was implemented by primary legislation, RIPA. The LBP Regulations are made under that primary legislation. RIPA will therefore apply irrespective of the rules relating to Community competence. The tortuous relationship between the two is recognised in reg.3(3) of the LBP Regulations, which provides that interception or monitoring falling within certain grounds (those in para.1(i)(a), that is those which relate to ordinary business use) are only authorised to the extent permitted by art.5. Implicitly, therefore, monitoring for other purposes, which cover areas such as national security which are outside Community competence, may exceed the remit of art.5 as Directive 2002/58 is irrelevant to those areas. Nevertheless, such activities will still be covered by RIPA 2000 and the DPA 98, which are both primary legislation of general application in the UK.

---

on the transfer and processing of PNR data by Air Carriers to the United States Department of Homeland security, Bureau of Customs and Border Protection ([2004] OJ L183 p.83).

[15] For a more detailed review, see Ch.1, paras 1-16 onwards.

This is relevant to the issues raised by the debate on the retention of traffic data as well as to the surveillance debate. Where art.8 of the Convention rights applies, however, interception, and now it appears following *Copland,* access to and use of communications data, must comply with art.8(2) of the Convention rights.

SCOPE OF CONVENTION RIGHTS

The Human Rights Convention and the HRA are only directly binding on public authorities. In some circumstances the ECtHR has held that the State has an obligation to ensure the protection of rights against the actions of another private person. The Court has said that this applies to art.8. The extent of the obligation is unclear. The courts in the UK have taken account of art.8 in the law as it is applied to private bodies such as the media in respect of the publication of information since the HRA came into effect in 2000.[16] It is possible, therefore, that the art.8 right could influence decisions in respect of private bodies, for example by influencing the interpretation of employment laws. In *McGowan v Scottish Water*[17] the EAT considered the application of art.8 in an employment case. The employer however was a public authority. In that case the EAT upheld the ruling of the Tribunal that covert surveillance of an employee's house was not a breach but if it was a breach it was justified.

23–13

As far as public bodies are concerned they are bound by art.8 of the Convention rights but they have no mechanism for obtaining authorisation for the monitoring of communications data generated by internal systems. Public bodies are only able to apply for authorisation for interception or access to communications data under the relevant provisions of RIPA for the purpose of their public functions. This point was made clear in the case of *C v Police and Secretary of State for the Home Department.*[18]

C v Police and Secretary of State for the Home Department[19]

The Investigatory Powers Tribunal has exclusive jurisdiction to hear complaints about the misuse of powers relating to surveillance authorised or carried out under RIPA. A retired police officer complained to the Tribunal that he had been subject to covert surveillance by private investigators acting for the police force. The complainant had taken early retirement on medical grounds. He had been awarded compensation and an "enhanced injury" award after tripping over a carpet in a police station. The force wished to check the extent of the injuries he had suffered. The complainant asserted that the surveillance should have been authorised under the provisions of s.26 of RIPA. This provides for the authorisation of planned covert surveillance which is not intrusive; is carried out "for the purpose of a specific investigation or specific operation", and will result in the obtaining of private information about a person.

23–14

---

[16] See Ch.2 for the cases on privacy and the media decided since October 2000.
[17] UKEAT/007/04
[18] Investigatory Powers Tribunal, No.IPT/03/32/H, November 14, 2006.
[19] Investigatory Powers Tribunal, No.IPT/03/32/H, November 14, 2006.

23–15   The case hinged on whether the surveillance by a public authority for a private law purpose such as employment-related matters was covered by s.26. The Tribunal held that it was not and that only surveillance for the purposes of the investigatory functions of public bodies can be authorised and carried out under RIPA. Accordingly the claimant had to bring his claim within the general law, applying art.8 and data protection and privacy rights, rather than having any remedy before the specialist tribunal.

As part of its judgment the Tribunal made some general comments on the nature of surveillance, the taking of photographs and the obtaining of information more generally:

"Surveillance by public authorities (or indeed anyone else) is not in itself unlawful at common law, nor does it necessarily engage Article 8 of the Convention. For example, general observation of members of the public by the police in the course of carrying out their routine public duties to detect crime and to enforce the law is lawful. It does not interfere with the privacy of the individual citizen in a way that requires specific justification; see, for example, Friedl v Austria (1995 21 EHRR)".

This should now be treated with some caution given the ECtHR and UK case law on the taking and use of photographs. In Wood v Commissioner for Police of the Metropolis,[2009] EWCA Civ 414. the Court of Appeal, by a two to one majority, decided that the Metropolitan Police had acted unlawfully when it retained photographs which it had taken of an anti-arms trade campaigner as he was leaving the AGM of Reed Elsevier Plc ("REP"). Although the police were justified in taking the photographs in the first instance the court said that they should have been destroyed after a short space of time once it was realised that they were not needed.[20]

REGULATION OF INVESTIGATORY POWERS ACT 2000

Communications data

23–16   Communications data under RIPA covers traffic data under Directive 2002/58 but is a wider definition. Chapter II makes provision for authorised persons to obtain communications data from telecommunication operators subject to service of appropriate notices and places operators under obligations to make disclosures. However, it imposes no obligation on operators to retain data for any specific length of time, a point which caused problems for both operators and authorities as the prohibition in Directives 97/66 and 2002/58 on the retention of traffic data was opposed to the wishes of the investigation and intelligence communities to have widespread access to such data accumulated over significant periods. This has now been addressed, at least in part, in the rules governing the retention of communications data (see Ch.24). It should be noted for completeness that access to communications data may not be sought exclusively under RIPA. There are

---

[20] See Ch.6 for the case law on photography.

numerous statutes which pre-date RIPA but which would also potentially allow for the relevant public body to seek such information for the purposes of their functions.[21]

Definition of communications data

This is defined as: 23–17

> "(a) any traffic data comprised in or attached to a communication (whether by the sender or otherwise) for the purposes of any postal service or telecommunications system by means of which it is being or may be transmitted;
>
> (b) any information which includes none of the contents of a communication (apart from any information falling within paragraph (a)) and is about the use made by any person—of any postal service or telecommunications service; or in connection with the provision to or use by any person of any telecommunications service, of any part of a telecommunications system;
>
> (c) any information not falling within paragraph (a) or (b) that is held or obtained, in relation to persons to whom he provides the service, by a person providing a postal service or telecommunications service".[22]

The contents of any communication are not included in the definition. Traffic data is defined in relation to any communication as:

> "(a) any data identifying, or purporting to identify, any person, apparatus or location to or from which the communication is or may be transmitted,
>
> (b) any data identifying or selecting, or purporting to identify or select, apparatus through which, or by means of which, the communication is or may be transmitted,
>
> (c) any data comprising signals for the actuation of apparatus used for the purposes of a telecommunication system for effecting (in whole or in part) the transmission of any communication, and
>
> (d) any data identifying the data or other data as data comprised in or attached to a particular communication, but that expression includes data identifying a computer file or computer programme access to which is obtained, or which is run, by means of the communication to the extent only that the file or program is identified by reference to the apparatus in which it is stored".[23]

It appears from the breadth of the definition that cookies would be capable of being communications data. If that is the case then, under Directive 2002/58, an employer who reviews the cookies on the system to see which websites have been visited by employees would be accessing communications data.

It is further provided that traffic data includes any references to the actual   23–18
apparatus through which it is transmitted.[24]

Chapter II applies to conduct in relation to a postal service or telecommunications service for obtaining communications data other than conduct consisting in

---

[21] See *Freedom from Suspicions—Surveillance reform for a digital age*, para.153, quoting Lord MacDonald in *Review of Counter Terrorism and Security Powers*(Com 8003, January 2011).
[22] s.21(4).
[23] s.21(5).
[24] s.21(7).

the interception of communications in the course of their transmission by means of such a service or system and the disclosure to any person of communications data.

It provides that conduct to which the Chapter applies shall be lawful where it is conducted by an authorised person in accordance with the authorisation.[25] As noted earlier however it makes no provision for establishing the lawfulness of access to and use of communications data other than under Ch.II.

It provides for designated persons to serve notice on postal or telecommunications service operators requiring the operator to disclose specified communications data[26] and places a duty on the service providers to comply with the requirements of the notice[27] as far as is reasonably practicable.[28] If the operator does not already have the data in his possession the notice may require him to obtain it, if the operator is capable of doing so. The obligation on the operator may be enforced by civil proceedings for an injunction by the Secretary of State "or other appropriate relief".[29]

The designated person must believe that it is necessary to obtain the communications data for one of the specified interests or purposes and that it is proportionate to the objective to be achieved that the data be obtained.

Specified interests or purposes

23–19   These are partially set out in reg.22(2), but the list is not exhaustive as it includes a provision for the Secretary of State to specify further purposes by order. There has been one order under this provision.[30] The purposes provided for in the sub-section are:

- the interests of national security;
- the purpose of preventing or detecting crime or of preventing disorder;
- the interests of the economic well-being of the United Kingdom;
- the purpose of protecting public health;
- the purpose of assessing or collecting any tax, duty, levy or other imposition, contribution or charge payable to a government department;
- the purpose, in an emergency, of preventing death or injury or any damage to a person's physical or mental health, or of mitigating any injury or damage to a person's physical or mental health;
- to assist in investigations into alleged miscarriages of justice; and
- to identify and notify the next of kin of a deceased or incapable person.

The categories of designated persons are officials or office holders for public authorities as listed or as prescribed by the Secretary of State.[31] Such persons are then entitled to authorise others of the same level or rank to exercise the powers.

---

[25] Regulation of Investigatory Powers Act 2000 s.21(1).

[26] s.22(4).

[27] s.22(6).

[28] s.22(7).

[29] s.22(8).

[30] The Regulation of Investigatory Powers (Communications Data) (Additional Functions and Amendment) Order 2006 (SI 2006/1878), replaced by SI 2010/480.

[31] Regulation of Investigatory Powers Act 2000 s.25(2).

All authorisations and notices must be given in writing and contain prescribed particulars.[32] A notice may have effect for a month but may be renewed. Notices may also be cancelled. The Secretary of State may make arrangements for contributing to the cost of complying with notices under these provisions.

These provisions potentially allow officials of public authorities widespread powers to serve notices requiring communications data with no other authorisation. The Home Secretary brought out a draft order under s.25(2) in June 2002, which listed a wide range of public authorities including government departments, local authorities, fire authorities and others as prescribed authorities. The draft met with stiff opposition and was withdrawn by the Government.[33] It was replaced by a narrower list under which access to all categories of communications data was restricted to broadly policing and associated organisations while other public bodies have access to only a sub-set of the possible categories of communications data. The number of bodies with access was extended by subsequent orders until in 2007[34] a total of 795 public bodies were able to request some level of communications data.[35] The use of communications data by some public bodies has been widely criticised, for example a local authority using the powers to check whether a family were using schools to which they were not entitled because they did not live in the catchment area.[36] As a result the Government issued a further consultation in April 2009. This resulted in the replacement of the previous Orders by one consolidated Order which sets out the additional purposes for which access to the data can be granted and lists the organisations and individual authorised to seek access.[37] The response did not satisfy critics. The criticisms of the provisions are not only directed at the number of bodies that may access communications data but the absence of an independent authorisation process. The Coalition programme for government included a commitment to address problems with RIPA and the Protection of Freedoms Act 2012 includes a provision requiring judicial sanction before allowing local authority access to communications data. This now appears as ss.23A and 23B of RIPA as inserted by s.37 of the 2012 Act.

The term operator simply means a person who provides a telecommunications service. Therefore notices can be served on those who provide services other than as a public telecommunications service, such as providers of private systems in hotels or businesses. **23–20**

Codes of practice

The provisions relating to codes are found in ss.71 and 72. Section 71 provides (inter alia) that the Secretary of State must issue one or more codes of practice relating to the exercise and performance of the powers and duties under Pts I–III **23–21**

---

[32] Regulation of Investigatory Powers Act 2000 s.23(1) and (2).

[33] See the website for the Foundation for Information Policy research (*www.fipr.org* [Accessed October 5, 2012]) for relevant press releases.

[34] The Regulation of Investigatory Powers (Communications Data) Order 2003 (SI 2003/3172) amended by the Regulation of Investigatory Powers (Communications Data) (Additional Functions and Amendment) Orders 2005 (SI 2007/1083) and 2006 (SI 2006/1878).

[35] Report of the Interception Commissioner.

[36] Poole Borough Council, reported by BBC, April 2010.

[37] The Regulation of Investigatory Powers (Communications Data) Order 2010 (SI 2010/480).

of RIPA. Before issuing a code the Secretary of State has to prepare and publish a draft and consider any representations made about the draft. The codes have to be laid before Parliament.

Under s.72 a person exercising or performing a power or duty in relation to which provision is made in a code shall in doing so have regard to every relevant code of practice. Failure to comply with a code results in no civil or criminal penalty but the code is admissible and may be taken into account by, inter alia, any court or tribunal conducting any civil or criminal proceedings (s.72(4)). Four codes came into force in July 2002; three impose obligations on public authorities in relation to the authorisation, disclosure and, copying of information. One code imposes obligations on service providers to maintain an intercept capacity.[38] A further code came into operation from October 1, 2007, the Acquisition and Disclosure of Communications Data Code of Practice which remains in force.[39] The Code covers the extent of the powers available in respect of communications data, the general rules on the granting of authorisations and giving of notices, contributions towards the costs incurred by service providers, special cases where disclosure is required for the public interest, records, data protection safeguards, oversight and complaints. The provisions of the Code are admissible in criminal or civil proceedings.

23–22   A distinction must be made between the *retention* of communications data and the right to access such data. As has been discussed in this section the Regulation of Investigatory Powers Act 2000 (RIPA) covers *access* to such data. However, after RIPA came into effect there was a period of uncertainty over the obligations on service providers to *retain* such data in the first place so that the rights of access could be exercised. The area is now covered by Directive 2006/24, which is examined in Ch.24.[40]

Public and private systems

23–23   The rules and provisions for interception and access to communications data vary depending on whether the system is part of the public system or a private one. A public system is one by which a public telecommunications service is provided. Private telecommunications system is defined in s.2 of RIPA and the LBP Regulations as a system which is not a public system but which is attached directly or indirectly to a public service and includes apparatus in the system located in the United Kingdom for making the connection to the public system.

INTERCEPTION OF COMMUNICATIONS

23–24   Interception of communications on the public telecommunication system is treated more seriously than interception of communications on private systems. It is a criminal offence for any person "intentionally and without lawful authority to

---

[38] The Regulation of Investigatory Powers (Interception of Communications: Code of Practice) Order 2002 (SI 2002/1693).

[39] The Regulation of Investigatory Power (Acquisition and Disclosure of Communications Data) Order 2007 (SI 2007/2197).

[40] The Regulation of Investigatory Power (Acquisition and Disclosure of Communications Data) Order 2007 (SI 2007/2197).

intercept at any place in the United Kingdom, any communication in the course of its transmission" if the transmission was by a public postal service or public telecommunication system.[41] (In this work we are only concerned with the interception of telecommunications and not postal services.)

The question of whether an interception has taken place on a public telecommunications system has been litigated several times in criminal cases. This may be because s.17 of RIPA precludes any material being adduced in evidence which discloses or suggests that interception under a warrant has taken place. Hence the tendency of accused who have been unfortunate enough to have incriminating calls recorded to claim that the evidence has been obtained by interception (and thus the incriminating material should be excluded). The courts have been correspondingly sceptical and tended to find that there is no interception. In *R. v Hardy* (October 2002) the Court of Appeal held that the tape recording of a telephone conversation by an undercover officer with the suspect did not amount to the interception of a communication in the course of its transmission by a telecommunications system within the meaning of s.2(2) of the RIPA. In *R v E*[42] the police obtained the necessary permission to place a surveillance device in E's car under provisions in the Police Act 1997 and RIPA. They recorded E speaking into a mobile telephone. E claimed that the recording was obtained as a result of an interception which was unlawful. The Court of Appeal considered the definition of "interception" in s.2(2) of RIPA under which an interception must take place "in the course of transmission". They held that the natural meaning was that this involved some interference with the signal in the course of transmission whereas the voices recorded in the car were recorded independently of the transmission system. This was consistent with *R. v Effick* and *Morgans v DPP*.[43] The decision was followed in *R. v Allsopp*.[44] In *Attorney General's Reference (No.5 of 2002) sub nom. R v W*(2003) the court held that a judge was entitled to hear evidence to decide whether a system was public or private in order to decide whether interceptions were of a public or private communication system.

23–25

The question of whether the deployment of a particular technology involves interception was an issue in the debate over the introduction of Phorm Webwise. The case demonstrates the challenges for regulators when faced with new technology in the area of interception. Phorm Webwise delivers advertising based on a user's interests as shown by the websites they visit, for example if an individual visits a golf equipment website and a fitness equipment website the technology will be used to deliver advertisements which reflect the individual's apparent interest in sports. Most behavioural advertising of this nature depends on the use of "cookies" dropped on to the browsers of the machines used. These are explained and covered in Ch.22. However, in the case of Phorm the cookies are used (in essence) to look at the traffic that takes place, and specifically the websites visited, during a browsing session. BT used Phorm without giving subscribers either notice of the trial or seeking consent. When the storm over the use without subscriber consent broke the privacy "techies" (among whom Dr

23–26

---

[41] Regulation of Investigatory Powers Act 2000 s.1(1).
[42] [2004] EWCA Crim 1243.
[43] (2001) 1 A.C. 315.
[44] [2005] EWCA Crim 703.

Richard Clayton of the Centre for Science and Policy University of Cambridge deserves honourable mention) made heroic efforts to explain the complex technology in an accessible manner to non-techies. The following is taken from one of Dr Clayton's papers:

> "The basic concept between the Phorm architecture is that they wish to take a copy of the traffic that passes between an end user and a website. This enable their systems to inspect what requests were made to the website and to determine what content comes back from that website. An understanding of the types of websites visited is used to target adverts and particular uses."

The process redirects a search three times within the system so that the cookies dropped can be inspected to: a) decide if the user has opted out of Phorm (which assumes that the user has been given notice and consent); b)set a unique ID for the user; and c) add a cookie that mimics the page the user wants to visit. The result is that the system "looks at" the search request and at the webpage that the user wants to visit and delivers advertising based on that information.

The system is applied by the ISP which is responsible for the cookies and the advertising delivered. The furore occurred in the UK because it came to attention in 2008 that BT had trialled the system without the consent of users in 2006.

23–27   The questions raised in relation to interception are clear. Do search requests to websites and the responses count as "communications" and is an automated system that looks at these an "interception"? When the story first broke there was uncertainty about how the system worked and hence the answer to those questions however it gradually became clear that it involved a monitoring of transmissions and an interference with the system because of the way that it redirects traffic.

No action was taken against Phorm in the UK. The Home Office had apparently given an earlier view and appeared to suggest that internet searches are not "communications" (although this would be a generous view). The CPS and the ICO decided to take no action against the parties, apparently influenced by the fact that the trials had caused no discernible harm to individuals and the technology was only used to deliver advertising.

An interesting facet of the debate was the polarisation between the responses from privacy campaigners, particularly those with an interest in technology, on the one hand, and the policy makers and regulators on the other hand. Those with an interest in privacy and technology pointed to the nature of the technology and its potential for misuse, intrusion and fraud. The policy makers and regulators appeared to focus on the outcomes and the use to which the technology was put.[45]

---

[45] As the author put it in a paper produced at the time: "It leaves us with the question posed in the regulation of all technology. Should regulation address the actual use of the technology or the potential for misuse? Should we worry if someone has a Kalashnikov if he only uses it to hang his washing on?"

Action by the European Commission

The European Commission took a less relaxed view than the UK regulators and, following on from its investigation of the Phorm issue, in September 2010 referred the UK to the Court of the European Union[46] for not fully implementing the EU Directive on privacy and electronic communications. There were four grounds for the referral:

(1)   Art.5 of the E Privacy Directive requires the confidentiality of communications such as email or Internet browsing to be protected by Member State unless the users consents to the breach. The E-Privacy Directive must be interpreted in accord with Directive 95/46/EC (the general directive), which requires that consent must be "freely given specific and informed" (art.2(h) of Directive 95/46/EC). In UK law under s.3(1) of RIPA the standard of consent did not meet this requirement; it was sufficient that the person had reasonable grounds for believing that consent applied;

(2)   the offence provision in s.1 only applied where the offence was committed intentionally, whereas art.5 requires all interception be controlled;

(3)   there was no independent authority to supervise the implementation of unintentional interception of communications as required by art.28 of the general directive; and

(4)   there were no appropriate sanctions for unintentional interception as required by art.24 of the general directive.

In response the Government passed the Regulation of Investigatory Powers (Monetary Penalty Notices and Consent to Interception) Regulations 2011,[47] which came into effect in June 2011. The Regulations amended s.3(1) of RIPA to restrict the consent provisions and omit the words "or which that person has reasonable grounds for believing" and imposed a new sanction against unintentional unlawful interception which is administered by the Interception of Communications Commissioner (ICC) who will hear complaints about such unlawful interception. Appeals against the penalties will be directed to the First Tier Tribunal (Information Rights). The ICC has published guidance with practical information on how it will exercise these new functions.

UNINTENTIONAL UNLAWFUL INTERCEPTION

The action by the Commission reflects a long-standing concern about the UK provisions. The fact that RIPA only covers intentional interception was implicitly criticised in the recitals to 2002/58. Recital 21 states:

"Measures should be taken to prevent unauthorised access to communications in order to protect the confidentiality of communications, including both the contents and any data relating to such communications, by means of public communications networks and publicly available electronic communications services. **National**

23–28

23–29

23–30

---

[46] IP 10 1225.
[47] SI 2011/1340.

legislation in some Member States only prohibits intentional unauthorised access to communications" [emphasis added].

A consultation on the proposed amendments to RIPA was conducted by the Home Office in November 2010. In the consultation it was explained that the Commission had received complaints alleging that some Communication Service Providers (CSPs) were deploying new value-added or advertising services which relied upon interception without seeking appropriate consent from users. The existing offence in s.1 of RIPA was confined to cases involving intentional interception but art.5(1) required that a sanction was needed to deter all unlawful interception by CSPs, whether intentional or not. The consultation suggested that art.5(1) of the E-Privacy Directive did not require any extension of the sanction beyond CSPs.

23–31   In the regulations, however, the penalty provisions have not been limited to CSPs. This must be the correct approach as art.5(1) requires that protections are imposed so that anyone "other than users" cannot access electronic communications or communications data. This is clearly not limited to CSPs. It is also clearly possible for non-CSPs to inadvertently intercept the content of communications. As an example it was widely reported in June 2010 that Google's Street View vehicles gathered MAC addresses (the unique device ID for WiFi hotspots) and network SSIDs (the user-assigned network ID name) tied to location information for private wireless networks as part of a programme to improve its location based services. At the same time it intercepted and stored data being transmitted by unprotected WiFi, some of which included discernible content. It was not clear from the reports whether the interceptions were of transmissions made on the public or private side of the services therefore they may have fallen outside these provisions of RIPA, but there was clearly interception. In the UK the Metropolitan Police, to whom a complaint was directed by Privacy International, determined that there would be no prosecution under RIPA, and the matter was dealt with by the Information Commissioner as a breach of the Act.

The Regulation of Investigatory Powers (Monetary Penalty Notices and Consents for Interceptions) Regulations 2011

23–32   The Regulations are made under the European Communities Act 1972 in order to fully implement Directive 2002/58. They are therefore only applicable to areas within Community competence. They insert a new s.1A and Sch.A1 to the Act. They also amend s.3(1) to RIPA to remove the words "or which that person has reasonable grounds to believe".[48]

Under s.1A the Interception of Communications Commissioner (ICC) may serve a monetary penalty notice on a person if he:

"(a)   considers that the person,
         (i)   has without lawful authority intercepted, at any place in the United Kingdom, any communication in the course of its transmission by means of a public telecommunications system, and

---

[48] SI 2011/1340 reg.3.

> (ii)   was not, at the time of the interception, making an attempt to act in accordance with an interception warrant which might, in the opinion of the Commissioner, explain the interception, and
>
> (b)   does not consider that the person has committed an offence under subsection (1)".[49]

The detailed provisions dealing with the monetary penalty notices are set out in a new Schedule A1.

Ofcom is under an obligation to assist the ICC if requested. If the ICC considers that there has been an intentional interception he will refer it to the police for investigation. Presumably if the police investigation finds that there was an interception but it was unintentional then the matter can be remitted to the ICC. However if it is found that the interception was intentional but the CPS decide, in accord with the Code for Crown Prosecutors, that prosecution would not be in the public interest the matter is closed. It cannot then be remitted to the ICC. The ICC must also consider whether the action results from an over-enthusiastic application of a warrant. Under s.65 of RIPA a complainant who is aggrieved by interception which he believes to have taken place "in challengeable circumstances" may complaint to the Investigatory Powers Tribunal (IPT).[50] It is assumed therefore that, in the event that the ICC determines that the interception was carried out as an attempt to act in accordance with a warrant, the ICC could direct the complainant to exercise his/her right to complain to the IPT.

Under Sch.A1 the ICC may:

23–33

- serve an information notice on any person on whom he is considering serving a monetary penalty notice to provide him with such information as he may reasonably require to decide whether to serve a monetary penalty notice;
- serve a Pt 2 monetary penalty notice of up £10,000 for failure to comply with the information notice;
- serve a Pt 1 monetary penalty notice of up to £50,000 for breach of s.1A; and
- include in a Pt 1 monetary penalty notice enforcement requirements which may require the person subject to the notice to cease conducting the interception or take or refrain from taking other specified steps connected with the breach.

Before serving a Pt 1 or 2 monetary penalty notice, the ICC must give notice of intent and consider representations. He must arrange an oral hearing if requested and hear representations including ones on any matter that could not be raised on an appeal to a court or tribunal because they would be excluded by virtue of s.17 of RIPA.[51] There are appeals to the First Tier Tribunal (Information Rights) against the service of an information notice, a monetary penalty notice or any provision in such a notice, or a refusal of a request to vary or cancel a Pt 1

---

[49] SI 2011/1340 reg.2.
[50] RIPA s.65(4).
[51] SI 2011/1340 reg.3(6)(b)(ii).

notice.[52] Monetary penalties are recoverable in the county court or High Court or Sheriff Court in Scotland and the enforcement obligations may be backed up by proceedings for an injunction.[53] The ICC must issue guidance on how he will exercise his functions.

The provisions came into effect in June 2011 and we have been unable to find any reported cases to date. The last available report from the ICC on the website at the date of writing[54] was published in July 2012 but the Commissioner makes no mention of his new powers.

There is no exemption for the withholding of material subject to legal professional privilege or which might be self-incriminatory in the information notice provisions. It raises the question of whether a response to a notice which showed that an interception was intentional could be passed to the police by the ICC. Presumably such an admission would not be admissible in a criminal prosecution but could be used to justify further enquiries.

23–34 There are only limited circumstances in which an interception will be protected by "lawful authority". On private systems it is an offence, intentionally and without lawful authority, to intercept a communication in the course of transmission unless the interceptor is a person with the right to control the operation of the system or he has the express or implied consent of such a person.[55]

The Court considered what amounted to the "right to control the operation or use" of a system in *R. v Clifford Stanford*.[56] In that case the court held that the right to control the operation and use meant more than mere rights to access and included a right to control how the system was used and operated by others. In the case an ousted director had persuaded an ex-colleague to divert e-mails to him. He had argued that, as the ex-colleague had legitimate access to the e-mail system, the ex-colleague was entitled to control its operation and there was therefore no offence of unauthorised interception. His contentions were not accepted by the Court. However if the interceptor is the person with the right to control the system or has been given consent by such a person the only penalties involved are civil penalties. The sender or recipient, or intended recipient, has a private right of action in tort unless the communication takes place with lawful authority.[57]

The limits of the public/private telecommunications system and the meaning of the terms "interception" and "in the course of transmission" are therefore significant.

Interception and the course of transmission

23–35 A person intercepts a communication in the course of transmission if he does any of the following acts:

> "(a)   so modifies or interferes with the system or its operation,

---

[52] SI 2011/1340 regs 5 and 10.
[53] SI 2011/1340 regs 6 and 11.
[54] April 2012.
[55] SI 2011/1340 s.1(6).
[56] [2006] EWCA Crim 258.
[57] SI 2011/1340 s.1(3).

(b)   so monitors transmissions made by means of the system, or

(c)   so monitors transmissions made by wireless telegraphy to or from some apparatus comprised in the system, as to make some or all of the contents of the communication available, while being transmitted, to a person other than the sender or intended recipient of the communication."

A communication broadcast for general reception cannot be intercepted and there is no interception involved in the operator ascertaining information to allow the communication to be sent, for example in cases where the postal service has to open a returned communication to find where it should be returned to. The contents of communication are distinguished from traffic data associated with a communication. The monitoring of communications data is not interception

The question of whether an activity amounts to an interception has sparked controversy in several areas notably in relation to the introduction of Phorm Webwise in 2006 and 2007 in the UK and the phone-hacking scandal in which the Metropolitan Police appear not to have acted against those who hacked voicemails under the view that such hacking did not amount to interception.

ACCESS TO STORED VOICEMAIL

The question of the whether access by a third party to voicemails which have previously been read by the recipient amounts to interception has been canvassed in previous editions of this text. We have consistently and staunchly adhered to the view that is an interception. It now appears that the DPP agrees and appropriate actions will be taken against those who transgress in this area in the future.

23–36

The question arises because of the provisions of s.2, which reads:

"(7)   For the purposes of this section the times while a communication is being transmitted by means of a telecommunications system shall be taken to include any time when the system by means of which the communication is being, or has been, transmitted is used for storing it in a manner that enables the intended recipient to collect it or otherwise to have access to it.

(8)   For the purposes of this section the cases in which any contents of a communication are to be taken as made available to a person while being transmitted shall include any case in which any of the contents of the communication, while being transmitted, are diverted or recorded so as to be available to a person subsequently."

This is an important definition in the context of email as email is not usually instantaneously received nor is it instantaneously erased on being read. It sits on servers waiting to be read and is stored by recipients in mailboxes after being read. On a straightforward reading of the definition in s.2(7) any reading of e-mail by another would be interception irrespective of whether it had already been opened by the recipient as long as the storage was in a manner that enabled the recipient to continue to access it.

However, the Information Commissioner in the code on monitoring employees in the workplace and the Home Office both expressed the view that once an email has been "collected" (and presumably read) by the recipient then s.2(7) no longer applied even though it is still stored in a manner that allows the recipient to have further access to it. This was on the basis that an "interception" must occur before the receipt of the material, and subsequent reading is not an "interception". In the previous editions of this text in 2004 and 2007 we said about this approach:

"It is suggested that this interpretation is wrong on both a straightforward reading of the words of the provision and as a matter of interpretation. If the provision is read in the light of the requirement in the HRA to interpret statutes so as to give effect to the Convention rights it is clear that the only interpretation that gives effect to the Art. 8 obligations of respect for private life and correspondence is to treat stored and opened emails as covered. As a matter of principle it is inconsistent to suggest that the right to respect disappears once the material has been opened by the intended recipient. Regrettably the point was not considered by the Court of Appeal in R. v Ipswich Crown Court Ex p. NTL Ltd.[58] The case was not on this particular point but in passing the Court commented that the effect of s. 2(7) was to extend the time within which an interception could be made until the intended recipient had collected it. They did not address whether there would still be an interception if the recipient left the read message on the server and it was subsequently read by another."

23–37   The issue came to light because the misguided interpretation was apparently part of the basis on which the Metropolitan Police decided not to launch criminal investigations of the records of phone hacking by private investigators. The position was clarified by the Director of Public Prosecutions in 2010 who made public his advice to the police that the narrow view should not be applied. As the hacking involved has given rise to a number of interesting cases we have covered the history and legal issues briefly here.

Actions for hacking of telephones against the *News of the World* journalists and others and Leveson

23–38   The demise of the *News of the World* followed the discovery of widespread hacking by and on behalf of journalists after the records kept by Glenn Mulcaire came to light. It should be noted of course that hacking was not the only murky method used by journalists from major newspaper as the results of Operation Motorman (covered in Ch.17 on the special purposes) demonstrates.

The matter came to light when a number of stories appeared in the *News of the World* which it seemed could only have been known to someone listening to voicemail records of members of the royal family. As a result of the investigation into the Royal Editor of the *News of the World* and the private investigator who he used, Mr Mulcaire, a very large number of records came into the possession of the Metropolitan Police. The records showed names, addresses, telephone numbers, PIN codes for mobile phones, pass words, call data and tapes for many people. It appeared that these had been used to access the voicemails of individuals. In 2006 Mr Goodman and Mr Mulcaire were convicted of conspiracy to intercept telephone calls in breach of s.1(1) of RIPA contrary to s.1(1) of the Criminal Law Act 1977 and Mr Mulcaire of a further five counts of unlawful interception in breach of s.1 RIPA in respect of the voicemails of five named individuals.

---

[58] [2002] EWHC 1585 (Admin).

Following the convictions several individuals took actions against or reached settlement with the *News of the World* for various claims including misuse of private information, breach of confidence and harassment. However, the Metropolitan Police did not notify many of the victims that their details had been found among the records. In July 2009, a journalist writing in the *Guardian* disclosed that the Metropolitan Police had taken that decision and that in fact several thousand people had been targeted by Mulcaire. The resulting series of revelations about the extent and nature of the hacking have been widely reported and resulted in the closure of the *News of the World* in July 2011.

In addition to the cases brought against the newspaper for misuse of private information, harassment and breach of confidence the events have given rise to some other interesting cases. In one set of actions a number of well-known figures brought action for judicial review of the decision of the Metropolitan Police not to notify them that there was information that their phones had been hacked. In *R. (on the application of Bryant) v the Commissioner of the Metropolitan Police*[59] the argument on behalf of the claimants was that the Metropolitan Police were under a duty to warn them of the risk to them on the basis of their art.8 rights which impose positive obligations on public authorities. Foskett J. gave permission for the application for judicial review to proceed. On February 7, 2012, the Metropolitan Police made a declaration effectively admitting that their failure to warn phone hacking victims in 2006 and 2007 constituted a breach of those individuals' art.8 rights and settled the case. In a separate action against NewsGroup and Glenn Mulcaire the High Court ruled that voicemails could be protected as a form of intellectual property if they contained commercial information, thus ruling that Mr Mulcaire was unable to claim privilege against self- incrimination to protect him against answering questions or providing material in response to orders in the proceedings as s.72(2)(a) of the Senior Courts Act 1981 provides that the privilege does not apply where proceedings are "for the infringement of rights pertaining to intellectual property".[60]

23–39

Public telecommunications service and system

There are interlocking definitions of "telecommunications service" and "telecommunications system". A system is:

23–40

"any system (including the apparatus included in it) which exists (whether wholly or partly in the United Kingdom or elsewhere) for the purpose of facilitating the transmission of communications by any means involving the use of electrical or electro-magnetic energy."

A service is:

"any service that consists in the provision of access to, and of facilities for making use of, any telecommunications system (whether or not one provided by the person providing the service)."

---

[59] [2011] EWHC 1314 (Admin).
[60] *Gray v NGN Ltd* [2011] EWHC 349 (Ch).

A public service is one offered or provided to the public or a substantial part of the public in the United Kingdom and a public system is one by which a public telecommunications service is provided. A private service is not defined but a private system is a system which is not a public system but which is attached directly or indirectly to a public service and includes apparatus in the system located in the United Kingdom for making the connection to the public system.

It follows from this that a telecommunications system which is entirely internal and has no connection with a public external network is entirely outside the province of these provisions.

Lawful authority

23-41   As interception with lawful authority will not attract civil or criminal penalties this is an important concept. What amounts to lawful authority varies depending on whether the communication is intercepted on a public or private system. It will also depend on whether the communication is a "stored communication".

Any communication may be intercepted with the authority of a warrant.[61] A stored communication may be intercepted by exercise of a statutory power to require the supply of information or the provision of any document or property.[62] There is no explanation of what amounts to a "stored communication". It would seem to cover any message in the possession of the person who controls the system. It appears that this conduct amounts to an interception and this gives added weight to the view that access to a read message is interception just as much as access to a message not yet read.

Interception may otherwise have lawful authority under ss.3 or 4 or regulations made under s.4(2).

Interceptions—overseas authorities

23-42   In the area of international co-operation in criminal and other matters of justice and security there are agreements for mutual assistance which may involve authorities in the United Kingdom making requests for assistance overseas and the Secretary of State must ensure than no such requests are made by officials in the United Kingdom without lawful authority.[63]

Interception will also be authorised where it is in relation to a person outside the United Kingdom, and carried out at the behest of an overseas authority which is subject to legal obligations to carry out the interception under the laws of the overseas territory. Such situations are subject to further conditions to be prescribed by the Secretary of State.[64]

---

[61] s.1(5)(b).
[62] s.1(5)(c).
[63] s.1(4).
[64] s.4(1).

Consent

An interception is lawful if it is an interception of a communication to which both parties to the communication have consented.[65] Recipient and sender are not defined in this Part. The assumption which has been made by commentators appears to be that the sender and recipient are the specific living individuals who compose and read the material respectively. Given the application of the definition of consent this would appear to be the correct view. Anyone relying on consent also must ensure that it is freely given and fully informed.

23–43

Interception and covert surveillance

Where the interception is part of a surveillance which has been authorised under Pt II of the RIPA and one party has consented the interception will be lawful.[66]

23–44

Service providers and wireless telegraphy

A service provider who intercepts in connection with the provision of the service or enforcement of legal requirements in connection with the service is authorised as is interception with the authority of a designated person under the Wireless Telegraphy Act 1949 for purposes under that Act.[67]

23–45

Prisons and other institutions

Interceptions in prisons or secure hospital units may be carried out under the specific rules governing such institutions.[68]

23–46

Relation with orders under the Police and Criminal Evidence Act 1984 (PACE)

In *R. v Ipswich Crown Court Ex p. NTL Ltd*[69] the court considered the relationship between the prohibition in s.1 of RIPA and the service of notices to preserve material under PACE. NTL were asked by the police to retain emails passing between suspects on their system pending an application by the police for a warrant under PACE to give them access to the e-mails. NTL queried whether they were entitled to do this before they received the order as the only method they had of retaining the material was to intercept and copy it. The Court decided that the notice of intent served by the police under PACE was sufficient lawful authority under RIPA to enable the service provider to preserve the material. The judge commented that in any event NTL would not be able to disclose the material until it was served with the court order.

23–47

---

[65] s.3(1).
[66] s.2 (2).
[67] s.4(4)–(6).
[68] s.4(4)–(6).
[69] See fn.63, above.

MONITORING FOR INTELLECTUAL PROPERTY RIGHT BREACHES

23–48   The topic of monitoring use of electronic communications, particularly Internet use, to investigate and then control breach of copyright has given rise to much discussion and has been the subject of litigation in the UK in the case of *R. (on the application of British Telecommunications Plc) v Secretary of State for Culture, Olympics, Media and Sport*.[70] The case arose from the obligations imposed by the Digital Economy Act 2010 (DEA). The DEA amended the Communications Act 2003 by inserting new provisions to deal with file sharing in breach of copyright. Under the new provisions copyright owners can pass ISPs notice of IP addresses which have been involved with the transfer of materials in breach of copyright. The ISPs then have to notify the subscribers who are associated with those IP addresses and warn them of the breach. Once a statutory code is put in place then the ISPs also have to provide the copyright owners with copyright infringement lists. The grounds of the judicial review challenge to the DEA were many but two of the grounds were that the contested provisions were incompatible with Directive 95/46/EC and 2002/58.Neither the first instance judgment by Parker J. nor the Court of Appeal judgment by Richards L.J. describe how the process would work but it is assumed that the copyright owners would trawl the Internet looking for peer to peer sharing operations (whether through their own staff or the use of third parties). They would then seek to obtain information about the IP addresses of those taking part. They would presumably also seek to ascertain the nature of the materials being downloaded or shared. These activities are clearly monitoring and involve the collection of data about the file sharers but, assuming that there is no actual unauthorised access to the content of what is being shared then there is no interception. The IP addresses would presumably be traffic data as the definition covers any information processed for the purposes of the communication. As noted earlier under the UK regime the only persons who are directly restricted in dealing with traffic data are communication service providers. However, under art.5 the State has an obligation to also restrict access to traffic data. The collection of the IP addresses therefore could engage Directive 2002/58 as well as 1995/46 even if it did not contravene UK law. If the nature of the films or other copyright material could be ascertained then the argument made in the case was that it could include sensitive personal data.

The IP addresses and other information would then be passed to the relevant ISP. The ISP would have to send the subscriber for that IP address a copyright infringement report, in effect notifying the subscriber that the infringement has been noticed and acting as a first warning to the subscriber. This would clearly involve the use of the personal data of the subscriber and it would involve the use of traffic and subscriber data by the ISP outside the uses allowed by 2002/58. The ISPs would also have to provide lists back to the copyright owners, if requested, showing that copyright infringement reports had been sent, although they would not identify the subscriber to the copyright owner. Among the many arguments raised by the appellants were that these activities would breach Directives 1995/46 and 2002/58.

---

[70]   [2012] EWCA Civ 232.

The appellants faced a difficult task because the European Court had already **23–49** held in *Productores de Música de España (Promusicae) v Telefónica de España SAU* (C-275/06) that the two data protection directives did not act as a barrier to national law requiring the disclosure of information about subscribers for the purpose of bringing civil proceedings for breach of copyright. In that case the Spanish communication service provider had sought a ruling on whether Directives dealing with copyright read in the light of arts 17 and 47 of the Charter, should be interpreted as requiring Member States to require the disclosure of personal data about subscribers to allow Promusicae to take civil proceedings. Before considering that question however the Court considered whether the data protection directives established a barrier to such disclosure.

It was not disputed that the communication sought by Promusicae involved the disclosure of the personal data of subscribers.

The Court considered the application of art.5(1) of Directive 2002/58, which provides that Member States must ensure the confidentiality of communications by means of a public communications network and publicly available electronic communications services, and of the related traffic data, and must inter alia prohibit, in principle, the storage of that data by persons other than users, without the consent of the users concerned. The only exceptions relate to persons lawfully authorised in accordance with art.15(1) of that directive and the technical storage necessary for conveyance of a communication.

Under art.15(1) Member States may adopt legislative measures to restrict the scope inter alia of the obligation to ensure the confidentiality of traffic data, where such a restriction constitutes a necessary, appropriate and proportionate measure within a democratic society to safeguard national security (i.e. State security), defence, public security, and the prevention, investigation, detection and prosecution of criminal offences or of unauthorised use of the electronic communications system, as referred to in art.13(1) of Directive 95/46.

While none of the exceptions in art.15(1) relate to civil proceedings, the article includes an express reference to art.13(1) of Directive 95/46. That provision also authorises the Member States to adopt legislative measures to restrict the obligation of confidentiality of personal data where that restriction is necessary inter alia for the protection of the rights and freedoms of others.

The Court held that, as art.13(1) does not specify the rights and freedoms concerned,

> "those provisions of Article 15(1) of Directive 2002/58 must be interpreted as expressing the Community legislature's intention not to exclude from their scope the protection of the right to property or situations in which authors seek to obtain that protection in civil proceedings.
>
> The conclusion must therefore be that Directive 2002/58 does not preclude the possibility for the Member States of laying down an obligation to disclose personal data in the context of civil proceedings."

The Court of Appeal agreed with the ruling in the Promusicae case that the **23–50** exemption in art.13(1) could be relied upon for the processing by the ISPs and rejected the contention that the decision in Promusicae should be read as relevant to civil proceedings only. In addition they found that, to the extent that sensitive personal data might could be processed by the copyright owners this would be permissible under ground 8(2)(c) that it was necessary for the establishment exercise or defence of legal claims.

The ruling did not address the processing of the traffic data by the copyright owners which is not directly mandated under the DEA and therefore still requires a legislative base as required by art.15(1) however that appears to be because such a basis will be provided under the code to be issued by Ofcom before the provisions are introduced.

The Court referred to an Opinion of the EDPS on the use of monitoring of Internet use to deal with breach of copyright[71] in which the EDPS raised concerns at the possibility of widespread monitoring of Internet use but disagreed with the EDPS on the application of the law and pointed out that, in any event, it was not binding on the Court. They also refered to but distinguished the case of *Scarlet Extended v SABAM*[72] in which the Advocate General had opined that a court order to an ISP to install a system for blocking and filtering all electronic communications to control breaches of copyright was not in accord with the Charter and that such a restriction on the privacy and freedom of speech rights of internet users would require a legislative base.

MONITORING OF BUSINESS COMMUNICATIONS

23–51   Directive 97/66 covered the use of public telecommunications networks, not wholly private ones. This is equally the case with 2002/58. Article 5(2) provides a "carve out" for the

> "legally authorised recording of communications and the related traffic data when carried out in the course of lawful business practice for the purpose of providing evidence of a commercial transaction or any other business communication",

made using such a network. It should be noted that the provision allows for the "recording" of calls in such circumstances. It should further be noted that the phrase "related traffic data" was not included in Directive 97/66. Traffic data are therefore not covered in the LBPs.

Section 4(2) of RIPA enables the Secretary of State to make regulations authorising such conduct

> "as appears to him to constitute a legitimate practice reasonably required for the purpose, in connection with the carrying on of any business, of monitoring or keeping a record of—
>
> (i)   communications by means of which transactions are entered into in the course of that business; or
>
> (ii)   other communications related to that business or taking place in the course of its being carried out."

---

[71] Opinion of the EDPS on the current negotiations by the European Union of an Anti-Counterfeiting Trade Agreement (IACTA) 2010/C 147/01.
[72] Opinion of the Advocate General Case C-70/10.

Although s.4(2) and the Regulations made under it primarily reflect art.5(2), it also implement aspects of art.15 which allows for derogation from the ban on interception as explained above. Thus they it permit interception for a wider range of purposes than would be permissible under art.5(2) alone (even taking a generous view of art.5(2)).

LAWFUL BUSINESS PRACTICE REGULATIONS 2000 (LBP)

The LBP Regulations are difficult to follow. To some extent this is caused by the use of the Regulations to deal, not only with the exemption in art.5(2), but with aspects of the derogation in art.15. The drafting adopted has conflated the two aspects. It therefore assists to "unpick" the two aspects to make sense of the Regulations. Article 5(2) only covers recording communications data in the course of business for providing evidence of commercial transactions; however the Regulations are not confined to this. They also cover the monitoring of electronic communications systems by public bodies for national security and crime prevention purposes. Section 4(7) provides that business includes references to activities of government departments, public authorities and those who hold office under statute. Regulation 3 provides that the purposes for which monitoring may be conducted includes crime-related matters and national security.

23–52

The use of the Regulations for this purpose has given rise to some stresses and ambiguities which only the courts will be able to resolve if the Regulations come before them. Oddly enough, even though it allows public bodies to monitor communications of those using their systems without oversight or the restrictions otherwise imposed by RIPA, this aspect of the Regulations does not appear to have attracted particular criticism on civil libertarian grounds, although it might have been expected to do so, particularly as it could be suggested that s.4(2) of RIPA does not authorise the use of the regulation-making power for this purpose.

Recording and monitoring

The terms are not defined but monitoring appear to mean contemporaneous monitoring, as in having a person actually listening to the conversations in real time, whereas recording would appear to allow a copy of the communication to be taken to listen to or read at another time.

23–53

The Regulations can only authorise interception of communications on the system used for the purposes of a business by, or on behalf of, the person carrying on the business.[73] In the Regulations any interception must take place by or with the consent of the system controller.[74] The provision previously included the possibility of relying on implied consent of the system controller but the words "or implied" were deleted from the end of reg.3(1) by the Privacy and Electronic Communications (EC Directive) (Amendment) Regulations 2011 with effect from May 2011. It is assumed that this was as a result of the Commission's action against the UK in relation to its rules on interception discussed earlier and

23–54

---

[73] s.4(3).
[74] reg.3(1).

ensures that the reference to consent reflects the definition in Directive 95/46/EC. The system controller is the one who, in relation to the particular telecommunications system, has the right to control the operation of the system[75]: *R. v Clifford Stanford*,[76] referred to earlier.

The system controller would usually be the data controller for any personal data held on the system.

The Regulations only cover interceptions and not the monitoring of communications data. As has been noted earlier the case of *Copland* suggests that access to communications data also engages art.8 and requires a lawful basis.

Conditions relevant to all interception under the LBP Regulations

23–55   Under reg.3(3) any interception:

- must be limited to the purpose of monitoring or keeping a record of communications relevant to the system controller's business;
- only take place on a telecommunication system provided for use wholly or partly in connection with that business; and
- the system controller must have made "all reasonable efforts" to inform everyone who may use the system that communications on it may be intercepted.

The first condition causes difficulty when dealing with the vexed issue of personal communications and is dealt with below. The last condition can give rise to practical difficulties in informing those who are sending in-coming communications for the first time and in respect of whom there is no obvious way of providing the information in every case. However, as the requirement is for the system controller to have made all reasonable efforts it appears that the practical difficulties have been appreciated.

Monitoring and keeping records of communications

23–56   Regulation 3(a) sets out the purposes for which communications may be both monitored and recorded. It lists five purposes as follows:

- monitoring for standards purposes;
- national security;
- the prevention or detection of crime;
- investigation or detection of unauthorised use of a telecommunications system; and
- ensuring the effective use of the system.

There are then two purposes for which the system controller may monitor but not record communications, which are:

---

[75] reg.2(d).
[76] [2006] EWCA Crim.

- deciding whether the communication is related to the system controller's business; or
- monitoring the use of confidential telephone lines.

Standards purposes

This is a messy provision. The relation between (aa) and the rest of the subsection is not as clear as it might be and it could be read as allowing the system controller to monitor or record in order to establish any set of facts for any purpose. This appears to be the view taken by the Commissioner's office; however, it is suggested that this would be wrong and the establishment of facts must be linked to ascertaining compliance with regulatory or self-regulatory practices. This is borne out by reg.3(3), which provides that conduct falling within this paragraph is only allowed to the extent permitted by art.5. **23–57**

Regulatory or self-regulatory practices or procedures

Monitoring is allowed in connection with regulatory or self-regulatory practices or procedures which are applicable to the system controller in the carrying on of his business or applicable to another person in the carrying on of his business where that person is supervised by the system controller in respect of those practices or procedures.[77] **23–58**

Regulatory or self-regulatory practices or procedures are defined as:

- any practices or procedures recommended or required by the law of any state within the EEA, or standards or codes of practice which meet certain criteria; or
- any practices or procedures applied for the purpose of reaching compliance with those laws or standards or codes of practice.

The standards or codes must meet certain criteria. Those are that the standard or code:

- published by or on behalf of a body which is established in a state in the EEA; and
- includes amongst its objectives the publication of standards or codes of practice for the conduct of business.

So under this heading a code or standard set by the Press Complaints Commission (PCC) or the Advertising Standards Authority (ASA) would qualify as would an in-house practice or procedure adopted in order to meet the requirements of the PCC or ASA code.

The system controller can monitor to:

- establish the existence of facts;
- ascertain compliance with the standards or codes; or

---

[77] reg.3(a)(i)(bb).

- ascertain or demonstrate standards applicable to users of the system for these purposes.

Effective use of the system

23–59   This permits monitoring and recording by the system controller to secure, or as an inherent part of, the effective operation of the system. It includes monitoring or recording by those who provide telecommunications services of their own services in relation to provision or enforcement under any enactment.

Prevention and detection of crime

23–60   There is no definition of these terms. There is no test of reasonableness or proportionality in the Regulations. The principles under the DPA will continue to apply, assuming that personal data are being processed as part of the interception. The ICO advises that in order for the processing to be fair the interception should be objectively justifiable and no more intrusive than necessary for the purpose. If the system controller is a public authority directly subject to the HRA then the intrusion would have to be justifiable in terms of art.8(2) of the Convention rights. It will be a matter of fact as to whether the particular interception was justified and proportionate for these purposes.

National security

23–61   There is no definition of national security imported into the Regulations.[78] In relation to oversight of the interception of communications the position is as described above in relation to the prevention or detection of crime. In circumstances where a system controller intercepts in the interests of national security it seems likely that the exemption under the DPA would also be claimed. This exemption involves no test of proportionality and a certificate under the DPA is conclusive proof of the application of the exemption.

Oversight of interception under the LBPR

23–62   There is no provision for oversight of such interceptions. If a system controller intercepts outside the protection given by the Regulations the individual whose communications have been intercepted could take private action in tort under s.1(3) of RIPA.

INTERCEPTION OR MONITORING OF "PERSONAL" COMMUNICATIONS

23–63   The question which has produced more comment than any other in relation to interception has been whether "personal" communications, usually telephone calls and emails, sent by employees can be intercepted by employers and if so in

---

[78] See Ch.15 for the meaning generally given to the term.

what circumstances. It has to be borne in mind that the EctHR has held that telephone calls from business premises are covered by art.8 as are e-mails.[79] The interception and monitoring of such calls must be justified within the LBPs. The question here is where the calls and e-mails are about personal matters rather than about work matters.

Do the Regulations apply to "personal" communications sent using an employer's electronic communications system?

By personal communications are meant any communications sent or received by an employee in a personal capacity, the contents of which are not related to work. It could be suggested that art.5 does not allow the monitoring or recording of such communications, unless they fall within the exceptions in art.14, as they are not a "business communication", on the other hand it can be argued that if they are sent in business hours using the business network system then they can validly be regarded as "business communications".

23–64

The exemptions in art.14 allow for circumstances where the interception is for the "prevention, investigation, detection or prosecution . . . of unauthorised use of the telecommunications system". If the employer has a rule that the employees must only use the communications systems for business or sets limits on the authorisation given to employees in the use of the system for private purposes, then it appears to follow that the employer may monitor in order to detect unauthorised use. Personal communications sent in business time using the business system could be regarded as being sent and received "in the course" of the business being carried on but the term is ambiguous. The Regulations use the phrase in reg.2(b)(ii), "a communication which otherwise takes place in the course of the carrying on of that business".

It is submitted that the phrase is sufficient to cover personal calls made in works time where employees are authorised to make some calls within limits. Regulation 3(1)(a)(iv) and (v) allow for monitoring for the purpose of investigating or detecting unauthorised use of the system (or any other telecommunications system) where the activity is undertaken in order to secure, or as an inherent part of, the effective operation of the system. Regulation 3(1)(b) allows for monitoring (but not recording) of in-coming communications for the purpose of determining whether they are communications relevant to the system controller's business which he is entitled to review for the purposes of facts, self-regulatory standards or business standards within reg.3(a)(i).

If the argument set out above is correct it would follow that an employer who sets a clear policy on what use may be made of the system would be entitled to monitor to ensure that the system is being used in accordance with the authorisation given as long as the monitoring was within the limits notified to the employees and was proportionate. It might be regarded as proportionate to carry out an initial review of communications data in those cases where there is some ground for concern and only to intercept messages marked as personal where there was good cause. In effect this is the approach adopted in the ICO's Employment Code of Practice. The position would be more difficult where the employer puts no limits at all on the private uses of the system and employees can

---

[79] See discussion of *Copland* above.

make any calls they wish from the employer's telecommunications system. In those circumstances, although reg.3(1)(b) would still provide for the monitoring of in-coming calls to check that they fall within reg.3(1)(a)(i), there would arguably be no basis for the monitoring of out-going personal calls by employees.

Right to private calls

23–65   Employees have no legal right to enjoy the benefit of using an employer's business facilities to send and receive personal communications during the course of employment. There do not appear to be any cases establishing a right to personal correspondence at work although the Article 29 Working Party in Opinion 2/2006 quotes an academic comment to the effect that "impeding" someone's right to initiate correspondence must be a breach. Cases before the ECtHR which deal with rights to correspondence and privacy of correspondence have been mainly in circumstances where the individual has had no opportunity, other than via the mechanism which has been intercepted, to communicate freely with others, for example in the case of mail from prisoners. Although the Home Office issued a recommendation to employers in the public sector that they should offer employees the use of a pay phone which could be available for private use there is no legal requirement for this. In the absence of such a positive right for employees the question hinges on what is in the contract between the parties.

While it might be arguable that an employer could make it a term of the employment contract that the employee would not use any of the employer's facilities for personal communication it would possibly be seen as unreasonable and unfair in today's environment. In practice it will depend on what is in the company policy and what has become practice or is accepted by the employer. In one case in France where an employee had used the employer's facilities with either agreement or acquiescence a court held that the employee was entitled to a degree of privacy in the communication.[80] It seems that once the employer allows some degree of personal use of work facilities the corollary is that, for reasons of fairness and respect for personal privacy and privacy of correspondence, he will also be expected to afford the individual a degree of privacy of that use.

Practical considerations in relation to private communications

23–66   If an employer is monitoring to check for other compliance matters there are practical problems in respecting employee privacy of correspondence. Unless the system has some method of allowing employees to mark private communications as such it is difficult to see how the employer can ensure that he never intercepts any such calls. The ICO advises that the employer should have regard to the "header" of messages to see whether they are likely to be personal in content and not intercept or monitor ones which appear to be unless it is necessary to do so to ensure that the system is not being used in an unauthorised manner. Even where messages are marked as private the employer may need to view them if there are grounds to suspect misuse of the system.

---

[80] See Ch.3 for a note of the case *Nikon v Frederic*, para.3-07.

Social media and employee privacy

The questions around the rights of employers to access social media sites and review them to check on the activities of employees or potential employees raises general privacy issues but does not amount to interception. The question has also been raised as to whether it is unlawful to require a potential employee to view the individual's social media site by handing over the password. Again, while this may raise broad questions of equity, it does not involve interception.

23–67

INTERCEPTION UNDER WARRANTS ISSUED UNDER RIPA

Warrants for the interception of communications on public telephone systems are dealt with under ss.5–20 of RIPA. Only a brief description of the arrangements is given here as such interceptions are not affected by the terms of Directive 2002/48. The interception will either relate to a matter which falls outside Community competence or will be covered by one of the exemptions in art.14.

23–68

Interception warrants may be issued by the Secretary of State, or in urgent or overseas cases by a senior official,[81] on the application of a limited number of public officials whose roles are connected with policing or security.[82] The Secretary of State may only issue a warrant if he is satisfied that it is necessary:

- in the interests of national security;
- to prevent or detect serious crime;
- to safeguard the economic well-being of the United Kingdom; or
- to give mutual assistance to an overseas authority in equivalent matters.

The Secretary must believe that the conduct authorised by the warrant is proportionate to the aim to be achieved.[83]

Warrants must identify either the person whose communications are to be intercepted or the premises in respect of which the interception is required.[84] They may be revoked, renewed or modified.

The Secretary of State may impose obligations on providers of telecommunications and postal services to ensure the intercept capability of systems and may contribute to the costs of establishing or maintaining such capability.[85]

There are restrictions on the disclosure of intercepted material[86] and restrictions on the disclosure of the existence of interceptions backed up by offence provisions for tipping off offences.[87]

---

[81] RIPA s.7(1).
[82] RIPA s.6.
[83] RIPA s.5.
[84] RIPA s.8(1).
[85] RIPA s.12.
[86] RIPA s.15.
[87] RIPA s.19.

Interception for the purposes of e-mail screening

23–69   The difficulties associated with the development of electronic communications, the way that a balance can be struck between the privacy rights of the individual, the legitimate business needs of employers and others and the needs of the State continue to be a source of debate and review. In 2006 the Article 29 Working Party commented on the interception of e mails for the purpose of detecting viruses, filtering spam and other mail related services in Opinion 2/2006.[88] It advised that the filtering of e mails for the purpose of detecting viruses and for removing spam can be justified under the obligations of the security requirements of Directive 2002/58, subject to notice to the users. However, it raised concerns at the screening of e-mail content for other reasons, for example to remove pre-determined content without the consent of the users of the system, and took the view that such activity amounts to an unlawful interception. The last area which it considered was other e mail related-services which involve an assessment by the service provider of the way that the recipient has handled to communication, for example by letting the sender know whether the e mail has been opened. It expressed "the strongest opposition" to this processing being carried out secretly and advised that these services should require the consent of the recipient.

ACCESS TO ENCRYPTION KEYS

23–70   Encryption is the action of scrambling messages into code so that the message can only be accessed by a person who has the key to unlock the code. Web browsers use a method called Secure Socket Layer (SSL). A web address that starts https:// uses SSL. However, all kinds of things can function as keys, from simple passwords through to biometrics such as fingerprints. As encrypted messages can only be read by those with the key to the message they are a secure way of sending data and are used on e-commerce sites and others where confidentiality is important. However, the use of encryption to secure messages is a concern for law enforcement agencies which fear that the extensive powers of retention and interception will be meaningless if they cannot access the content of communications because they are encrypted. Part III of RIPA allows for the compulsory disclosure of encryption keys in limited circumstances. The relevant provisions only came into effect in October 2007.[89] They were accompanied by a Code of Practice made under s.71 of the Act which sets out a helpful and clear exposition of the relevant provisions.

The provisions apply to "protected information", that is:

"any electronic data which, without the key to the data cannot or cannot readily be accessed or cannot or cannot readily be put into an accessible form".

---

[88] 00451/06/EN.
[89] Regulation of Investigatory Powers Act 2000 (Commencement No.4) Order 2007 (SI 2007/2196).

A "key" in relation to any electronic data means any key, code, password, algorithm or other data the use of which (with or without other keys) allows access to the electronic data or facilitates the putting of the data into an intelligible form.[90]

The provisions apply where protected information has come into the possession of "any person" under statutory powers or duties or by other lawful means has come into the possession of the intelligence services, police, SOCA or HMRC. The use of the term "any person" suggests that it could cover a person in the private sector but it seems highly unlikely that any organisation save a public body would come into the possession of protected material by the routes specified.[91] Once they have the protected material if they consider on reasonable grounds:

23–71

- that a disclosure of it is necessary in the interests of national security, the purpose of preventing or detecting crime, the economic well-being of the UK or necessary for the purpose of securing the effective exercise or proper performance by any public authority of any statutory power or statutory duty;
- that a key to the protected material is in the possession of any person;
- It is not reasonably practicable to obtain possession of the key without giving a notice; and
- the imposition of a notice to surrender the key is proportionate to the ends sought to be achieved.

Then a person "with appropriate permission" can serve a notice under the section imposing a disclosure requirement in respect of the key. A person "with appropriate permission" is one with judicial authorisation save for the police or intelligence service where information has been obtained other provisions.[92]

The disclosure requirement is complied with by the disclosure of the de-encrypted information in most cases although there is provision to require the key itself.[93] There is no appeal against the service of a notice and failure to comply is a criminal offence under s.53. Section 54 provides for the imposition of a gag on the person who has the key and an offence of "tipping off" if they reveal that the key has been the subject of a notice.

Under the Code of Practice the National Technical Assistance Centre is the lead for the use of these powers and all applications for notices must be cleared with the Centre.

---

[90] RIPA s.56.
[91] RIPA s.49(1).
[92] RIPA Sch.2.
[93] RIPA s.51(1).

ADDITIONAL INFORMATION

Extract employment practices code policy for the use of electronic communications

23–72   Employers should consider integrating the following data protection features into a policy for the use of electronic communications:

- Set out clearly to workers the circumstances in which they may or may not use the employer's telephone systems (including mobile phones), the e-mail system and the internet for private communications.

- Make clear the extent and type of private use that is allowed, for example restrictions on overseas phone calls or limits on the size and/or type of e-mail attachments that they can send or receive.

- In the case of internet access, specify clearly any restrictions on material that can be viewed or copied. A simple ban on "offensive material" is unlikely to be sufficiently clear for people to know what is and is not allowed. Employers may wish to consider giving examples of the sort of material that is considered offensive, for example material containing racist terminology or nudity.

- Advise workers about the general need to exercise care, about any relevant rules, and about what personal information they are allowed to include in particular types of communication.

- Make clear what alternatives can be used, e.g. the confidentiality of communications with the company doctor can only be ensured if they are sent by internal post, rather than by e-mail, and are suitably marked.

- Lay down clear rules for private use of the employer's communication equipment when used from home or away from the workplace, e.g. the use of facilities what enable external dialling into company networks.

- Explain the purposes for which any monitoring is conducted, the extent of the monitoring and the means used.

- Outline how the policy is enforced and penalties which exist for a breach.

CHAPTER 24

Retention Of Communications Data

INTRODUCTION

Retention of traffic data for the purposes of policing and security has been an area   24–01
of controversy in the EU for more than a decade. Access to traffic data is
regarded as critically important in combating crime and terrorism. In order for
policing organisations to obtain such access however it has to be retained for
periods of time. On the other hand, there are strong privacy arguments that such
data should not be retained: traffic data can provide much information about
individuals and retaining it is tantamount to holding a dossier on the private
communications of all citizens. Under Directive 2002/58 and its predecessor
1997/66, providers of electronic communications services were required to erase
traffic data once it was no longer required for the commercial purposes of the
providers in order to protect the privacy of individuals. The interplay between
these protective provisions, the boundaries of Community competence and the
use of such information for policing gave rise to deeply held differences of view
which were, if not resolved, at least dealt with in Directive 2006/24 of March 15,
2006 on the retention of data generated or processed in connection with the
provision of publicly available electronic communications services or of public
communications networks and amending Directive 2002/58 (the Data Retention
Directive). The Directive came into effect on May 3, 2006 and has been
implemented in the UK by the Data Retention (EC Directive) Regulations 2009.
The question of access to communications data however continues to be
controversial and in the UK the Government has proposed that retention
obligations be extended to other records of internet transactions in the draft
Communications Data Bill published in June 2012.[1] In this chapter the Data
Retention Directive, the EU and UK background to retention and the
implementing regulations are covered.[2]

SUMMARY OF MAIN POINTS   24–02

- Retention is mandated by Directive 2006/24 of March 15, 2006 on the
  retention of data generated or processed in connection with the provision of

---

[1] The bill was put forward in the Queen's speech in May 2012 and is undergoing pre-legislative
scrutiny at the time of writing.
[2] The law on access to communications data is covered in Ch.23.

publicly available electronic communications services or of public communications networks and amending Directive 2002/58 which came into effect on May 3, 2006.

- Directive 2006/24 not only deals with retention of communications data but also the grounds and procedures required for access to such data.
- The UK implemented the Directive in two stages with the first set of Regulations being adopted in July 2007 and coming into force on October 1, 2007. These excluded retention of records from internet communications but covered other forms of electronic communications data. They were replaced by the Data Retention (EC Directive) Regulations 2009 from April 2009. The current regulations cover specified traffic data from fixed and mobile telephony, internet access, internet e-mail and internet telephony.
- In addition some communication service providers retain additional date under the Code of Practice on Voluntary Retention of Communications Data made under s.102 of the Anti-Terrorism, Crime and Scurity Act 2001.
- Rights of access to such data are exercised under the Regulation of Investigatory Powers Act 2000.

BACKGROUND

24–03 Information which is used for the purposes of national security and policing will be outside Community competence and therefore outside the scope of Directives 1997/66 and 2002/58. It can therefore be retained irrespective of the restrictions imposed by those Directives. This is acknowledged in both Directives. Moreover, in art.15(1) of 2002/58 the rights of Member States to adopt measure to restrict the obligations to erase (in effect to require retention) are recognised where

> "such restriction constitutes a necessary, appropriate and proportionate measure within a democratic society to safeguard national security (i.e. State security) defence, public security, and the prevention, investigation , detection and prosecution of criminal offences or of unauthorised use of the electronic communication system as referred to in Article 13(1) of Directive 95/46/EC. To this end Member States may *inter alia* adopt legislative measures providing for the retention of data for a limited period justified on the grounds laid down by this paragraph".[3]

However, service providers cannot tell whether communications data will be required for those purposes at the point when they are generated. The only way that communications data can be preserved so that relevant data can be made available is for all data to be retained. It is therefore extremely difficult to be sure that the retention of data which is within scope fulfils the criteria required by art.15(1). Member States had very different responses to the question of requiring the retention of communications data and, even where it was retained, the length of time for which it should be kept.

24–04 The pressure for harmonised retention periods became more intense after the terrorist bombings in Madrid in March 2004. In April 2004 four countries

---

[3] The impact of this provision has been a matter of some debate which is dealt with at para.24–10, below.

(France, Ireland, Sweden and the UK) put forward a proposal for a third pillar Framework Decision for the retention of communications data. If taken forward, this would have led to a decision of the Council.[4] There was, however, considerable unease in the European Parliament and the Commission about the proposed use of a third pillar mechanism to legislate for matters of data protection and electronic communications which fall within the first pillar. One of the legal concerns expressed was that a Framework Decision could not legitimately alter or amend a directive.[5] Politically the privacy or data protection governance of matters covered by third pillar instruments have tended not to be as transparent or responsive as first pillar matters.[6] There were serious concerns at the impact on privacy which mandatory retention would entail.[7] The debate illustrates, not only the political difficulty of the issue, but the fact that the particular topic, the retention of data generated for communication so it can be accessed when required for purposes of crime and security, straddles the areas of Community and national competence.[8] The Parliament rejected the proposal for the framework decision.

In the same year the European Commission reported on the patchy state of retention obligations in the EU. Around 15 of the Member States did not have mandatory data retention requirements, in about half of those with mandatory retention laws in place the retention was not operational as the legislation had not been implemented, in those which had retention legislation in place the periods of retention and the scope of the obligations varied substantially.[9]

In September 2005, the Commission proposed a new Directive which would   **24-05** require retention and amend Directive 2002/58. The proposal was put forward as a harmonisation measure because retention requirements have an economic impact on service providers but also to meet the need for access for the purposes of policing and security. The justification for Directive 2006/24 falling within art.95 of the Treaties was not wholly satisfactory but it appears to have been accepted by the Parliament and the Commission, possibly because of a concern that the Council would press ahead with a Framework Decision if the Directive was not accepted. The legal basis of the Directive was challenged by Ireland in the European Court. In February 2009 the Court dismissed the action holding that the substantive content of the Directive related predominantly to the functioning of the internal market and its adoption on the basis of art.95 of the Treaties was justified.

Directive 2006/24 of March 15, 2006 on the retention of data generated or   **24-06** processed in connection with the provision of publicly available electronic

---

[4] For an explanation of the difference between first and third pillar areas, see Ch.1.

[5] art.47 Title VIII Final provisions (ex Article M).

[6] See Ch.1 for a note of the data protection supervisory regimes for third pillar matters. These were examined in detail in previous editions of this work but the detailed analysis has been omitted from this edition.

[7] See, for instance, Article 29 Data Protection Working Party Opinion of October 21, 2005, 1868/05/EN WP 113 on the proposed directive.

[8] On July 30, 2004, DG INFSO-DG JAI consultation document on traffic data retention was issued to seek "input from a broad range of stakeholders on a number of questions raised by the issue of traffic data retention".

[9] Commission Staff Working Document—Extended Impact Assessment. Annex to the proposal on the retention of data processed in connection with the provision of public electronic services and amending Directive 2002/58/EC (COM) (2005)438 (final) SEC (2005)1131.

communications services or of public communications networks and amending Directive 2002/58 came into effect on May 3, 2006. The Data Retention Directive not only deals with retention of communications data but also the grounds and procedures required for access to such data. It is dealt with in full below. The regulations implementing the Directive are then reviewed. It should be noted however that the regulations do not include any changes to the access regime which is dealt with under RIPA.

UK BACKGROUND

24–07   In the UK, the Government has evinced a long-standing aim to ensure the preservation of traffic data for the purpose of subsequent access if required for law enforcement. However, given the prohibitions on general retention in 1997/66 and 2002/58, until the Data Retention Directive came into effect it was reluctant to pass legislation requiring service providers to retain all communications data and instead sought to agree an industry standard for retention by setting up a procedure for the establishment of voluntary codes of practice under the Anti Terrorism, Crime and Security Act 2001 (ATCSA).

24–08   ATCSA includes provisions dealing with retention in Pt 11. The notes to the Act explain that:

> "This Part contains provisions to allow communications service providers to retain data about their customers' communications for national security purposes. Retained data can then be accessed by the security, intelligence and law enforcement agencies under the terms of a code of practice, which is being drawn up in consultation with industry and the Information Commissioner."

The notes go on to state that it provides for a:

> "voluntary code of practice defined in statute to ensure that service providers have a clear remit for retaining data which complements the powers given to public authorities under RIPA [to obtain access to such data] It also contains a reserve power to review these arrangements and issue directions under secondary legislation if necessary. The need to maintain a reserve power must be reviewed every two years and may be renewed by affirmative order. Once the power has been exercised, there is no need for further review".

And that:

> "RIPA sets out clear limits on the purposes for which the security intelligence and law enforcement agencies may request access to data relating to specific communications, i.e. relating to a particular customer or telephone line. Fishing expeditions are not permitted."

The reserve power in s.104 (the sunset clause) was reviewed twice and renewed until 2007.[10] In 2007 there was a consultation on a further renewal, ostensibly to deal with the implementation of the Data Retention Directive in relation to

---

[10] SI 2003/3173 and SI 2005/3335.

internet traffic data. However, in the event it was not renewed and the Data Retention Directive was implemented by regulations made under the European Communities Act 1972.

The UK Government never exercised the powers to issue directions but has proceeded by way of a voluntary code of practice. In March 2003 it conducted a consultation following which it issued the Code of Practice on Voluntary Retention of Communications Data under section 102 ATCSA.[11] The Code remains in force and provides for voluntary agreements with CSPs to retain certain types of communications data for the purposes of national security. The data retained and the retention periods are listed in the Annex to the Code and include some categories of information which are not mandated by the Retention Directive including date of birth of subscriber, account and credit card details if held and method of payment. Not all CSPs have entered into agreements under the Code. There does not appear to be a current published list of those that have done so. In May 2004 Baroness Scotland who was then Minister of State said in a Parliamentary statement on the Code that the Government did not intend to do so.[12]

DIRECTIVE 2006/24

Directive 2006/24 aimed to harmonise the different provisions in Member States dealing with the retention of communications data. It amended art.15 of 2002/58 by the insertion of the following paragraph:

24–09

> "1a. Paragraph 1 shall not apply to data specifically required by Directive 2006/24/EC of the European Parliament and of the Council of 15 March 2006 on the retention of data generated or processed in connection with the provision of publicly available electronic communications or of public communications networks to be retained for the purposes of Article 1(1) of that Directive".[13]

Article 3 provides that, by way of derogation from arts 5,6 and 9 of Directive 2002/58, Member States shall adopt measures to ensure that the data specified in art.5 are retained. This covers data described in six categories,[14]

> "generated or processed by providers of publicly available electronic communications services or of a public communications service within their jurisdiction in the process of supplying the communication services concerned".[15]

The categories are:

- data necessary to trace and identify the source of a communication;
- data necessary to identify the destination of a communication;
- data necessary to identify the date, time and duration of a communication;
- data necessary to identify the type of communication;

---

[11] SI 2003/3175.
[12] *Hansard*, May 17, 2004.
[13] art.11.
[14] art.5.
[15] art.3(1).

- data necessary to identify users' communication equipment or what purports to be their equipment; and
- data necessary to identify the location of mobile communication equipment.

For each category, art.5 specifies what the category comprises for telephones (both fixed and mobile) and for Internet use (including Internet telephony, e-mail and Internet access). The data to be retained are therefore specified in detail. As an example, under data necessary to identify the type of communication for mobile telephony six types of data must be retained, not only the calling and called numbers, the IMSI[16] of the calling and called party, the IMEI[17] of the calling and called party but also,

> "in the case of pre-paid anonymous services, the date and time of the initial activation of the service and the location label (Cell ID) from which the service was activated"

24–10   It is clear therefore that the specified data must be retained and that the obligation to erase traffic data within any of those categories is removed however there remains some lack of clarity as to the scope of Member States to require the retention of other categories of data beyond those set out in art.5 of Directive 2006/24. This has been noted by both the Commission and the Article 29 Working Party. The Article 29 group, not surprisingly, takes the strict view that the list of traffic data to be retained on a mandatory basis is to be regarded as exhaustive[18]; however, it also notes the aspirations in some States to retain more information and the debates that this has caused. In its Evaluation Report the Commission notes that the

> "complex legal relationship between the [retention] Directive and the e-Privacy Directive ... makes it difficult to distinguish, on the one hand, measures taken by Member States to transpose the retention obligations and on the other hand reliance on the general derogation under Article 15(1) of the e-Privacy Directive."

24–11   The Directive applies to data in the specified categories on both legal entities and natural persons and includes the related data necessary to identify the subscriber or user. It therefore covers some data which would not be covered by the data protection directives. Content is expressly excluded, including the content of material accessed during the use of the Internet. The retention obligation extends to "unsuccessful call attempts", that is calls that are connected but are not answered, but only to the extent that the service providers retains records of such calls. Not all providers keep such records. This was an issue of some dispute during the passage of the Directive. Some States were keen to have this information retained[19]; however, an obligation to retain such data would have had significant cost implications for service providers. Data about unconnected calls does not have to be retained. The term "unconnected calls" is not among the

---

[16] International Mobile Subscriber Identity.
[17] International Mobile Equipment Identity.
[18] Report 01/2010 on the second joint enforcement action 000068/10 WP 172.
[19] Data of this nature had been helpful in discovering those responsible for the bombings which killed 191 people and injured approximately 1,800 on March 11, 2004.

defined terms. There is no provision in the Directive to require Member States to compensate service providers for the costs involved in meeting the requirements.[20] The UK has funded the cost of providing additional facilities to allow for interception for relevant providers.

The Directive covers: **24–12**

- the obligation to retain data;
- procedures to provide access to data;
- the period of retention;
- data security and storage requirements;
- supervision, remedies, liabilities and penalties;
- evaluation, statistics and future measures; and
- implementation in national laws.

Definitions

Where terms defined in either of the data protection directives (1995/46 or **24–13** 2002/58) or the telecommunications directive (2001/21) are used the terms have the same meaning as in those directives. Accordingly, there are very few defined terms. The term "communications data" is not used and the Directive simply refers to "data" which means traffic data, location data (both defined in 2002/58: see Ch.22) and the related data necessary to identify the subscriber or user. A "user" is anyone who makes use of a "publicly available electronic communications service, whether for public or private use", and does not have to be a subscriber. "Telephone service" is widely defined and is distinct from other electronic communications services. A "user ID" is the unique identifier allocated to a person who registers with an Internet service, and a "cell ID" is the cell from which a call on a mobile was made or was received.

The obligation to retain data

The obligation to retain the data is set out in art.3. Member States must ensure **24–14** that the data are retained for a minimum period of six months after the communication up to a maximum of two years at which point they must be erased.[21] The only data which may be held after the maximum period are those records which have been accessed for the authorised purposes and in respect of which there is therefore a reason to retain them further.

Procedures to provide access to data

Article 4 deals with access to the stored data and provides that Member States **24–15** must adopt measures to ensure that the retained data are provided only to "the competent national authorities" in specific cases and in accordance with national law. The scope of this is not clear. It must presumably be read with art.1, which states that the purpose of the retention is to make the data available for the

---

[20] Such a provision was included by the Commission in the proposal but was removed by the Parliament. It will be a matter for Member States.
[21] arts 6 and 7(d).

purposes of the investigation, detection and prosecution of "serious crime as defined by each Member State in its national law". Member States clearly have some leeway as to what is defined as "serious crime" although the restriction to serious crime is intended to place a limitation on the types of illegal activity in respect of which communications data can be made available to investigators. The European Commission produced its first evaluation report on the implementation of 2006/24 in April 2011.[22] It noted that there are wide differences throughout the EU. Ten Member States have defined "serious crime" by reference to a minimum prison sentence, the possibility of a custodial sentence or a list of serious offences defined elsewhere in its law, four refer to "serious crime or serious offences" without further defining those terms, while eight require data to be retained for wider purposes that serious crime and include other criminal offences and investigations for them.

In its 2010 report, the Article 29 Working Party recommends the list of serious crimes should be laid down at domestic level in national law. Although the Report includes the UK as one of the jurisdictions in which serious crime is not defined it should be noted that this is not the case as there is a definition of serious crime in RIPA. Under s.5 of RIPA a warrant can only be sought where it is necessary in the interests of national security, for the purpose of preventing or detecting serious crime, for the purpose of safeguarding the economic well-being of the United Kingdom or an equivalent interest under a mutual assistance arrangements for an overseas entity. The interpretation provision at s.81 provides that references to crime are references to conduct which constitutes one or more criminal offences or is, or corresponds to, any conduct which, if it all took place in any one part of the United Kingdom would constitute one or more criminal offences; and reference to serious crime means:

- that the offence is one for which a person who has attained the age of twenty-one or eighteen in relation to England and Wales and has no previous convictions could reasonably be expected to be sentenced to imprisonment for a term of three years or more; or
- that the conduct involves the use of violence, results in substantial financial gain or is conduct by a large number of persons in pursuit of a common purpose.

Article 4 states the requirement that access procedures and conditions must be necessary and proportionate in accord with EU and Convention law. Moreover, individuals must be provided with remedies for breach of the Directive which are equivalent to the rights they have in respect of breaches of the Data Protection Act.[23] In the UK, the Information Commissioner has jurisdiction as far as the information constitutes personal data and a general role in relation to the storage obligations. It should be noted that individuals do not have a right to challenge access orders under RIPA in the normal courts but are restricted to the specialist Tribunal, the Investigatory Powers Tribunal which investigates complaints of misuse of data under RIPA.

---

[22] Evaluation Report on the Data Retention Directive COM (2011) 225.
[23] art.13(1).

Data storage and security requirements

Service providers must be required to retain the communications data and to ensure that it is of adequate quality and securely held. They must ensure that the retained data do not degrade during storage. The stored data must be of the same quality as the data on the network. In addition the data must be held securely to ensure that only authorised personnel can access them.[24] This is without prejudice to the existing obligations which apply to personal data. Article 13(2) requires Member States to impose penalties in respect of intentional and illegitimate access to the stored data.

24–16

Supervision, remedies and reports

Each Member State must designate a supervisory authority for the purpose of oversight of the storage obligation only. The authority is responsible for monitoring the security of storage and the compliance with the rules. It may be the data protection authority and in the UK the responsibility was placed with the Information Commissioner. Member States must provide the Commission with annual figures showing how many cases of access to communications data took place each year, the age of the data for each case and any cases where data could not be retrieved

24–17

Evaluation and future measures

Evaluation Report of the Commission 2011

The Directive imposed a duty on the Commission to evaluate the working of the Directive and report to Parliament and the Council on its economic impact within five years of the passage of the Directive, that is by September 2010. In doing so it had to consider the types of data retained, the length of retention and the statistics which it has garnered from Member States.[25] The Report was delivered in April 2011.[26] The Report covers the background to and aims of the Directive, its transposition in Member States, the role of retained data in criminal justice and law enforcement, the impact on operators and consumers and the human rights implications. It notes, in particular, that there are wide variations between Member States in the way that the Directive has been implemented and draws a number of conclusion and recommendations. The main areas of concern are:

24–18

● transposition has been uneven, three States are in breach of the Directive after their constitutional courts annulled the transposing legislation and two had yet to transpose[27];

---

[24] art.7.
[25] art.14.
[26] Evaluation Report on the Data Retention Directive COM(2011)225.
[27] In Romania, Germany and the Czech Republic the transposing laws were annulled as unconstitutional by the respective Constitutional Courts. Since the date of the report there has been a further notice of transposition. As at April 2012 only Sweden had not yet transposed the Directive.

- there is no common approach among States on purpose limitation or cost reimbursement and different countries have selected different retention periods; and
- there is no built-in mechanism for ensuring proportionality in the end to end process including in limiting access to the data retained, guidance on the use of data mining or consistency on the types of crimes that the data can be used to investigate.

It recognised this as an area for further harmonisation and proposed to start a programme leading to the revision of the Directive. It proposed further research, consultation and review before bringing forward any further proposals.

UK IMPLEMENTATION

Background[28]

24–19   The Directive had to be implemented by September 2007, but States could postpone the implementation in respect of Internet access, telephony and e-mail until March 2009. The UK declared that it would take advantage of this period of postponement as did 15 other Member States for varying lengths of time.[29] In the consultation paper before the initial implementation it was noted that the retention of traffic data from internet use "is a more complex issue involving much larger volumes of data and a considerably broader set of stakeholders within the industry" (para 2.10). However, such data was already retained by some service providers under the voluntary Code of Practice under the ATCSA and those arrangements were maintained and indeed continue to apply.

The first set of Regulations was adopted in July 2007 and came into force on 1 October 2007. These excluded retention of records from internet communications. They were eventually replaced by the Data Retention (EC Directive) Regulations 2009 from April 2009 after an somewhat tortuous process. In May 2008 the Government proposed to implement the outstanding elements of the Directive in primary legslation and included a proposal for a Communications Data Bill in its Draft Legislative Programme.[30] The proposal was linked to the Governement's Intercept Modernisation Programme and the Bill would have provided for the collection and retention of further communications data not required by the Directive or, it appears, by service providers for their own purposes. It would also have updated the legislative provisions for access to such data. The proposal sparked a significant controversy, largely because it was reported that part of the programme would be the creation of a central database of all electronic communications. In the face of the opposition that this generated the Government dropped the proposed Bill. The remaining provisions of Directive 2006/24 were implemented by regulations made under the European Communities Act 1972 while the proposals in respect of additional data retention were left to be taken forward under other auspicies.

---

[28]   SI 2009/ 859 replacing SI 2007/2199.
[29]   art.15.
[30]   Draft Legislative programme, Cm.7372, May 2008.

In April 2009 the Government published a separate consultation paper on extending the remit of interception, Protecting the Public in a Changing Communication Environment[31] in which it set out the rationale for further retention and its proposals. The position explained was that existing interception capabilities are declining because of the changes in industry. The challenges include the fact that there are more and more varied methods of communication and services, for example social networking sites and video messaging, combined with a growth of providers, many of whom may be overseas and providing services to users in the UK without having any physical networks of their own. This means that the proportion of communications data retained in the UK will decline and it will be more fragemeted as it crosses more boundaries and more difficult to match. The paper proposed that network infrastructure owners should collect and retain additional third party data relating to communications from services provided from overseas and for those service providers to process this data and match it with their own records where the two had "elements in common".

24–20

This was an ambitious proposal, although the central database had been abandoned it still met with opposition including a critical response from the Information Commissioner[32]. The last Government left office before it could take the proposal forward but the underlying concerns remain. The issue of interception modernisation was covered in the Conservative Administration's Strategic Defence and Security Review (SDSR) in 2010 and it remains a policy objective. One of the commitments from that review is to

24–21

> "introduce a programme to preserve the ability of the security, intelligence and law enforcement agencies to obtain communications data and intercept communications withnin the appropriate legal framework. This programme is required to keep up with changing technology and to maintain capabilities that are vital to the wok these agencies do to protect the public ... We will legislate to put in place the necessary regulations and safeguards to ensure that our response to thise technology challenge is compatible with the Government's approach to information storage and civil liberties".

The SDSR stated that legislaton would be announced in Parliament in due course. The possibility of extending the obligations to retain communications data was flagged in newspaper reports in early April and provoked some impassioned (although sometimes ill-informed) commentary. A legislative proposal was made in the Queen's Speech in May and a draft Communications Data Bill was published on June 14, 2012. It is to be submitted to pre-legislative scrunity by a Joint Committee of bothe Houses and considered by the Intelligence and Security Committee. The reports of both committees will be considered by the Government in formulating its final proposals which are expected to be submitted to Parliament later in 2012. The draft Bill has three parts. The meat of the proposal is in Pt 1, under which the Secretary of State will be empowered to make Orders under which further communications data not mandated by the Data Retention Directive is to be retained by operators. Part 11 of the ATCSA is to be

---

[31] Cm.7586, April 2009, Home Office.
[32] Information Commissioner's response to "Protecting the Public in a Changing Communication Environment", July 2009.

repealed so communications data would be retained under the replacement Order rather than the voluntary Code of Practice. The categories of data to be retained are not mandated by the Bill but the explanatory notes explain that the types of data in respect of which retention obligations are likely to be imposed are related to the operator's own services where there is currently no business reason to retain a record and records generated where individuals use the services of overseas operators and the UK operators only handle the transit of the calls and have no business reason to retain the communications data. The Bill would also replace Pt 2 of RIPA but largely replicate the current arrangements, including the changes made by the Protection of Freedoms Act, and the last part will remove a number of the legal provisions under which communications data can currently be accessed to ensure that all access falls under provisions offering safeguards equivalent to RIPA. The draft Bill has not given rise to much public controversy at the time of writing but is in very early stages. It will inevitable raise further questions about how far any Order made under it will be compatible with Directive 2006/24 and 2002/58 but those will only become clear once the details emerge.

Implementation

24–22   Having accepted that the provisions would be implemented under the European Communities Act 1972 the Government consulted on the draft regulations in August 2008 and published its response to the draft regulations in Febraury 2009 together with a revised draft. The Regulations were approved by Parliament in March 2009 and came into force in April 2009.

DATA RETENTION (EC DIRECTIVE) REGULATIONS 2009

Retention period and scope of data

24–23   The retention period under the Regulations is 12 months for all data, both from telephone records and internet use. Under the Code of Practice the period for retention of internet records was 6 months.[33] In its consultation before implementation of the 2007 Regulations, the Government set out the justification for the 12-month retention period. It stated that, while most requests for communications data are for data less than 6 months old, research carried out by the Association of Chief Police Officers (ACPO) in 2005 showed that there were a significant number of requests for older data and that these were in connection with more serious crimes. In the Regulatory Impact Assessment paper it explained that the period of 12 months was regarded as "the optimal trade-off" between law enforcement requirements and the intrusion into personal privacy. It explained that, in order to determine the appropriate length of time, the factors to be weighted were:

- the degree of intrusion in to personal life;
- the public policy need for the data; and

---

[33] reg.5.

- the adequacy of the safeguards to prevent abuse.

In the 2009 consultation, at least one of the same examples of cases in which communications data had been used in tackling crime was repeated and the Government maintained the position that 12 months is the optimum retention period.

The data to be retained are set out in the Schedule to the Regulations as follows. **24–24**

Fixed and mobile network telephony:

- the calling telephone number;
- the name and address of the subscriber or registered user of any such telephone;
- the telephone number dialled and, in cases involving supplementary services such as call forwarding or call transfer, the telephone number to which the call is forwarded or transferred;
- the name and address of the subscriber or registered user of any such telephone called;
- the date and time of the start and end of the call; and
- the telephone service used.

A telephone service is defined in reg.1 as: calls, including voice, voicemail and conference and data calls; supplementary services including call forwarding and call transfer; plus messaging and multi-media services including short message services, enhanced media services and multi-media services.

In relation to mobile telephony the following must also be retained: **24–25**

- the IMSI and the IMEI of the telephone which is used for the call[34];
- the IMSI and the IMEI of the telephone dialled;
- in the case of pre-paid services or anonymous services, the date and time of the initial activation of the service and the cell ID from which the service was activated;
- the cell ID at the start of the communication; and
- data identifying the geographic location of cells by reference to their cell ID.[35]

In relation to internet access, internet e-mail or internet telephony, the following must be retained: **24–26**

- the allocated user ID;
- the user ID and telephone number allocated to the communication entering the public telephone network;
- the name and address of the subscriber or registered user to whom and Internet Protocol (IP) address, user ID or telephone number was allocated at the time of the communication; in the case of internet telephony, the user ID or telephone number of the intended recipient of the call; in the case of

---

[34] IMSI—international mobile subscriber identity; IMEI—international mobile equipment identity.
[35] Pt 2 Sch. to the Regulations.

internet telephony, the user ID or telephone number of the intended recipient of the call; and in the case of internet access,

- the date and time of the log-in to and the log-off from the internet access service, based on a specified time zone,
- the IP address, whether dynamic or static, allocated by the internet access service provider to the communication, and
- the user ID of the subscriber or registered user of the internet access service; in the case of internet e-mail or internet telephony, the date and time of the log-in to and the log-off from the internet e-mail or internet telephony service, based on a specified time zone;
- in the case of internet e-mail or internet telephony, the internet service used;
- in the case of dial-up access the calling telephone number; and
- in any other case the digital subscriber line (DSL) or other end point of the originator of the communication.

These requirements cover those listed in art.5 of the Directive.

24–27 The cell ID is defined as "the identity or location of the cell from which a mobile telephony call started or in which it finished". All areas of the UK have a cell ID. The anonymous service provisions are included to allow for at least some information to be available to cover those users of Pay as You Go telephones who have never registered the identity of the user. There are a number of other definitions: "communications data" means traffic data and location data and the related data necessary to identify the subscriber or user; "location data" means data processed in a telecommunications network indicating the geographical position of the terminal equipment of a user of a public electronic communications service including data relating to the latitude, longitude or altitude of the terminal equipment of the user, the direction of travel of the user or the time the location information was recorded.

24–28 The obligation to retain is set out in reg.4 and applies to the data generated or processed by public communications providers in the process of supplying the communication services to the extent that the data are generated or processed in the UK.[36] Data derived from unsuccessful call attempts where such data are stored or logged in the UK are also covered. Unsuccessful call attempts are defined as communications where a telephone call has been successfully connected but not answered or there has been a network management intervention.[37] However, data relating to unconnected calls does not have to be retained.[38]

Application

24–29 The aim of the Regulations is to ensure that, where one public communications service provider retains the same data as another provider, the data will only be retained by one of them. The Regulatory Impact Assessment paper published before the 2007 Regulations explained that this approach ensures that the same data are only retained once; it reduces the burden on the private sector; and

---

[36] reg.3.
[37] reg.4.
[38] reg.4.

minimises the number of public communications service providers who are involved. It also reduces the number of organisations the public sector needs to deal with and encourage a "smaller pool of more experienced industry partners".[39] The mechanism can be utilised because of the structure of the industry, in which a significant number of providers provide services across networks owned by other service providers. Regulation 10 therefore provides that the Regulations do not apply to providers of public communication services unless the provider has received a notice to that effect from the Secretary of State. The Secretary of State is under an obligation to give such a notice to every provider unless the data concerned are retained by another provider.[40] Providers of public communication services are those who provide networks and those who provide services[41] and the definitions are as set out in the Communications Act 2003 s.151.[42] It follows that the vast bulk of the burden falls on to a few larger providers such as BT. If only part of one service providers' data is retained by another then the first provider must still retain the other parts independently. The notice must specify which public communications provider or category of providers it covers and the extent to which and the date from which the provisions apply. The notice must be given or published in an appropriate manner so it comes to the attention of the providers or relevant category of providers. It is the duty of a public communications services provider to comply with any notice given under the Regulations and the duty is enforceable by civil proceedings for an injunction or, in Scotland, specific performance of a statutory duty under the Court of Session Act 1988 or any other appropriate relief.[43]

Security

Regulations 6 and 7 deal with data security and access. They implement arts 7 and 8 of the Directive. The aim is not only for appropriate security to be maintained but also to ensure that the data are retained in such a way that they can be transmitted without undue delay in response to requests. In the Regulatory Impact Assessment, in the discussion of costs and reimbursement, the point is made that effective retention and effective retrieval mechanisms are part of the same solution. The terminology used in reg.6 in relation to the security obligation echoes closely the security obligation in principle 7 of the DPA. While the data are held the security requirements are as follows:

24–30

- the retained data must be the same quality and subject to the same security and protection as the data in the live service;
- the data must be subject to appropriate technical and organisational security to ensure that they can only be access by authorised personnel and protected against unlawful access, loss, destruction or disclosure; and
- except for data lawfully accessed and preserved, the data must be destroyed at the end of the period of retention.

---

[39] Regulatory impact assessment, para.4.12.1.
[40] reg.10(2).
[41] reg.2 interpretation.
[42] See Ch.22 for the relevant definitions.
[43] reg.10(6).

The Information Commissioner becomes the relevant Supervisory Authority for the security of the data.[44] The obligation of the Commissioner is to "monitor" the application of the regulations with respect to security. The term is used in art.9 of the Directive, to which reg.8 refers. The Commissioner is given no specific enforcement powers in respect of the stored data. Clearly where the data involve personal data then, if there is a security breach which would also be a breach of the Data Protection Act, he will be able to use his enforcement powers under that Act. Moreover, the provisions of s.55, which create the offence of unlawful procuring of personal data, will apply. The recitals to the Directive refer to the sanctions required by the Data Protection Directive (95/46) and to the rights of those who have suffered damage as a result of unlawful processing to redress and compensation. There are no specific provisions in UK law; however, the Data Protection Act and Computer Misuse Act provisions will apply.

Access and storage

24–31   Regulation 7 provides that access to data retained in accord with the regulations may be obtained only in specific cases and in circumstances in which the disclosure of the data is required or permitted by law. This imposes a specific prohibition and the data cannot be shared or used unless there is a specific legal basis. Regulation 8 requires that the data must be retained in such a way that it can be transmitted without undue delay in response to requests.

Statistics

24–32   Every 12 months, providers are required to supply the Secretary of State with statistics. The information must be provided as soon as practicable after March 31 in any year, and presumably the first statistics should have been provided to the Home Office after March 31, 2010. The Interception of Communications Commissioner is responsible for the compilation and publication of figures. A Parliamentary answer in October 2009 in response to a question by Willie Rennie MP showed that there were 504,073 access requests to CSPs in the calendar year 2008–2009.[45] The information to be supplied is:

- the number of times that retained data have been disclosed in response to a request;
- the time elapsed between the date the data were retained and the date of the request; and
- the number of occasions when a request for lawfully discloseable data could not be met.

Payments

24–33   There is no commitment in the Directive to make payments to service providers to assist with the cost of retention and retrieval system. However, the UK had already made that commitment in the ATCSA. Regulation 11 provides a power

---

[44] reg.6(2).
[45] *Hansard*, October 12, 2009, col.565W.

for the Secretary of State to reimburse any expenses incurred by a service provider in complying with the Regulations. The Secretary of State has a power and not a duty so he is free to determine how it is to be exercised. Where a service provider claims for reimbursement there is a concomitant power for the Secretary of State to require that the organisation complies with any audit that he may reasonably require in respect of the payments made. The Government has consistently maintained that efficient retrieval systems are essential to realise the benefits of the data. The reimbursement of costs is meant to be restricted to the cost of additional capacity provided for the purposes of RIPA access. The Government therefore maintained the arrangements in the UK to compensate CSPs. It has given the amount as £30.35 million between 2009 and 2014.

Public and private systems

The rules and provisions for interception and access to communications data vary depending on whether the system is part of the public system or a private one. A public system is one by which a public telecommunications service is provided. The only definition of a private telecommunications system appears to be in the Lawful Business Practice Regulation where it is defined as a system which is not a public system but which is attached directly or indirectly to a public service and includes apparatus in the system located in the United Kingdom for making the connection to the public system. Retention obligations are not currently imposed on those who supply private electronic communications systems. In a French case on a provision of the 1986 Liberty of Communications Act (*Loi relative a la liberte de communication*), as amended, in 2005 the Paris Court of Appeal found that there was no difference in the obligations in respect of data retention imposed on those who offer public services and those who run private networks where the private network provider allows staff access to the internet.[46] However, the case was on law which was prior to Directive 2006/24 and does not appear to have proved to be a precedent anywhere else in the EU.

24–34

FUTURE DEVELOPMENTS

The debates and differences of view over data retention and access to the information retained are on-going. The Commission lists a number of "Emerging Themes" on its website which it raises for discussion as part of its review of the retention rules. At the time of writing, it is still seeking feedback and comments on these to feed into its proposal which is to be put forward in 2012. The following are the key consultation questions taken from the document.

24–35

"

To what extent is data retention necessity?

- What is the **evidence** for the necessity of an EU obligation on operators to retain certain categories of telecommunications data?

---

[46] *BNP Paribas v World Press Online*, February 4, 2005: verdict of the Paris appeal court (in French).

- In relation to what **types of crime** should it be permissible to access and use stored telecommunications data?
- What precise **categories** of data should be retained in the light of evolutions in technology and criminal behaviour?
- For **how long** should these categories of data be stored?
- How can the EU **ensure that data is stored and used only where it is strictly necessary** to do so for the protection of the public against the harm of crime and terrorism?
- What rules at EU level would be **proportionate to the crimes** which the storage and use of telecommunications data is intended to help solve?
- Which **authorities** should be authorised to access and analyse these data?
- Are there any **alternatives** to data retention which could be equally effective in fighting crime? What could be the role at EU level of a form of data preservation or 'quick freeze'?

How could the data retention regime be better regulated?
- How should the **risks** of breaches of privacy and data protection be managed and minimised throughout the process of storage by providers, handover and use by authorities?
- How could the EU ensure **independent supervision** of requests for access and of the overall storage and use regimes applied in all Member States?
- How can particularly **confidential communications data** be protected?

How can we ensure appropriate standards of accountability?
- How can the EU ensure that service providers are **consistently reimbursed** and that the impact on consumers is minimised?
- What **metrics and reporting procedures** would enable assessment and comparison of how Member States apply the EU framework?
- How can the EU ensure that citizens and data protection authorities are able to **report abuses or seek information** on how data is being used?

Impact
- What would be the **impact** for security, criminal justice systems, for the work of law enforcement, for service providers and consumers of greater regulation at EU level in this area?"

The questions cover the range of concerns and issues which have provoked debate over this issue. The revision of Directive 2006/24 has been included in the 2012 Commission Work Programme,[47] which commits to bringing forward legislative proposals in 2012. No proposals have been made by the relevant Directorate General (Home Affairs) at the time of writing and, given the focus on the draft Regulation and Directive, it is possible that the timescale will slip. However, this is clearly an area in which further developments are to be anticipated. As noted earlier there are already proposals in the UK and it is clear that there will be continuing developments in the area of retention over the next few years.

---

[47] Commission Work Programme 15.11.2011 COM (2011) 777.

Additional information

Experts' Group on Data Retention

The Platform on Electronic Data Retention for the Investigation, Detection and **24–36** Prosecution of Serious Crime, also known as the Experts' Group on Data Protection, was set up in March 2008 as a forum for discussion on the application of the Directive and relevant technological developments. It is composed of experts from EU States' law enforcement authorities, the European Parliament, industry and data protection authorities, including the European Data Protection Supervisor. The group has published a number of papers providing technical guidance on the implementation of the directive, information on transposition of the directive and comments on the evaluation and review of the directive, listed below:

- Webmail and web-based messaging (Series A Document 1, December 3, 2009 and Annex).
- Obligation to retain e-mail logs—when can records of spam e-mails be retained? (Series A Document 2, July 16, 2009).
- Closer understanding of the term "transit providers" in relation to its application in Directive 2006/24/EC (Series A Document 3, December 3, 2009).
- Closer understanding of the term "third party networks and service providers" in relation to its application in Directive 2006/24/EC (Series A Position Paper 4, July 23, 2009).
- Closer understanding of the term "internet telephony" in relation to its application in Directive 2006/24/EC (Series A Position Paper 5 and Series B Position Paper 5A, December 3, 2009).
- Closer understanding of the possibilities of providers to store traffic data in a Member State other than the Member State of origin of the data ("Central data storage") in relation to its application in Directive 2006/24/EC (Series A Document 6, October 11, 2010).
- Closer understanding of the term "Data security" in relation to its application in Directive 2006/24/EC (Series A Document 7, October 11, 2010).

Documents concerning the Experts' Group are available on *http://ec.europa. eu/home-affairs/policies/police/police_data_en.htm*,[48] from which the information and list have been taken. Live links to the documents can also be found on that page.

---

[48] Accessed October 5, 2012.

CHAPTER 25

Data Sharing Code Of Practice, Database Policy And Governance

INTRODUCTION

The pervasive power of technology has allowed for the capture and use of personal information over the last 20 years in ways that were never envisaged when the Directive on which the current Act is based was formulated. The public sector has seen two linked developments as a result; the growth of massive databases of personal data to help deliver public services and the development of increased data-sharing between public bodies and to a lesser extent between the public and private sectors.

The Act applies to these databases and data sharing activities as to all other data processing. All of the legal areas covered in this text will be relevant to them. However the topic is of such significance that we consider that it merits a specific chapter, particularly in the light of the issue of the code of practice on data sharing. In this chapter we review the legal issues related to data sharing projects and the application of the code. Given the importance and topically of the issues we have also briefly reviewed the issues arising in the control of large public sector databases.

The twin topics of the growth of the "database state" as it is sometimes called and the development of data sharing are linked and there are significant synergies between the governance and control of large databases and the governance of data sharing. In many cases the two are linked as part of overall strategic initiatives, for example in the NHS. Oddly enough, although there has been a significant development in the rules addressing the governance of data sharing, this has been largely applied separately to the review of the governance of the large databases. In our view this is a missed opportunity and those responsible for the development, use and governance of the State's databases would benefit from having regard to the data sharing governance materials developed over the last few years including the Commissioner's Code of Practice.

Data sharing is the term used for the sharing or pooling of personal data in order to improve services or save money or achieve some other desirable aim. Data sharing is now defined in s.52A(4) of the Act, which provides that a reference to data-sharing is a reference to the disclosure of the data by transmission, dissemination or otherwise making it available. The wide definition echoes the way the term is generally used, not as a term of art, but rather loosely for a whole range of activities engaging the disclosure of personal data. In the Code the Commissioner has included reference to disclosure of personal data to

25–01

859

processors and "one-off" disclosures as well as longer term major decisions to share personal data between organisations or departments. In this chapter we use the term data sharing to apply to the disclosure of personal data between data controllers only and not disclosure to data processors. We take the view that disclosures to data processors raise wholly different legal points. We also focus primarily on projects in which a decision is made to share on a routine or regular basis as opposed to "one-off" disclosures in respect of which individual decisions can be made and in respect of which regard will often be had to relevant exemptions or appropriate consents.

The topic of data-sharing has been one of lively discussion since data protection laws came into force and in the UK for the last ten years or more. It was an area of particular interest for the Labour Government during its period of office, between 1997 and 2010; it proved to be a contentious issue. An attempt to legislate to provide public bodies with sweeping powers to disclose and use personal data for purposes other than those for which it had been obtained was included in the Coroners and Justice Bill in January 2009. The proposal sparked a strong response and was withdrawn by the then Home Secretary, Jack Straw, in the February to be replaced by provisions for a code of practice on data sharing to be drawn up by the Information Commissioner. Despite the last Government's enthusiasm for the sharing of data, therefore, there has been no general legislation in the area and the wider sharing of personal information has been encouraged by a mix of policy initiatives, legal advice and specific gateways in selected area. The process continues under the Conservative Government. At the time of writing there is draft legislation to empower wider sharing of information on welfare payments between the Department of Work and Pensions and local authorities.

Over the same period we have seen the development of large public sector IT projects involving the development of databases about particular groups, for example the ContactPoint database about children, plus the deployment of technologies such as Automatic Number Plate Recognition (ANPR) which have been used to amass large collections of data about individuals.

In this chapter we briefly review the policy and legal issues around the development of public sector databases and the legal challenges which this has posed; review the law which is relevant to the sharing of personal data for use for purposes other than those for which it was obtained, or by persons other than those notified to the data subject; explain the provisions of the Act and the code of practice; and examine the guidance provided by the Ministry of Justice and explain the background, issues and current position. There are particular constraints on the disclosure and sharing of conviction and criminal intelligence information and those are covered in more detail in Ch.27 on Criminal Records.

Although data is shared in the private sector the issue of data-sharing and the attendant legal challenges it presents have been seen as primarily public sector issues. However, commercial organisations sharing data should have regard to the Commissioner's Code as well as public bodies.

SUMMARY OF MAIN POINTS

25–02

(a)   There are no specific provisions in the Act dealing with the governance of large databases or data-sharing.

(b)   The Data Sharing Code of Practice drawn up under the Act provides guidance on the application of the Act and promotes good practice in the sharing of personal data.

(c)   The Code is admissible in any legal proceedings, not just proceedings under the Data Protection Act 1998.

(d)   The Code must be taken into account by the First Tier Tribunal, (Information Rights) or a court or tribunal considering matters in any legal proceedings in determining any question or the Commissioner in carrying out any function if any provision of the Code appears to be relevant to a question in those proceedings or in carrying out the function.[1]

(e)   Most public sector databases are based on specific legislation but there is no general legislation allowing the sharing of personal data although there are a number of statutory provisions allowing the disclosure of information in specific cases, usually referred to as "gateways".

(f)   In assessing whether it can share personal data the body involved (usually a public body) should review its powers and any constrains on those powers, such as the existence of an obligation of confidence, as well as the application of the Act.

(g)   The most influential guidance for the public sector is the Data Sharing Protocol published by the Ministry of Justice.

GOVERNANCE OF MAJOR DATABASES

Over the last decade there has been a move to develop shared information in every sector of public life. There is often a link between the development of core datasets or databases and an increase in sharing among related organisations. The National Health Service embarked on an ambitious project to produce an electronic health record for every patient in the UK with a core of data held in the "spine" as well as the capacity to share patient data around the entire health sector. The development of the Police National Database (PND) has allowed the police to share better and more information between forces as well as other sources. Police and criminality information was reviewed in 2008 by Sir Ian Magee,[2] resulting in the adoption by the National Criminal Justice Board of a policy setting the strategic direction for the sharing of information in England and Wales and the direction for sharing between the UK and other countries. In that review he developed the concept of the Public Protection Network as the network of organisations which contribute in one way or another to deliver public protection. The network includes the Border Agency, Courts, Policing bodies, HM Revenue and Customs, the Prison Service, Probation Service and Social

25–03

---

[1] s.52E(3).

[2] Sir Ian Magee, "Review of Criminality Information".

Services and others in local authorities. One of the strategic aims is to share criminality information in accordance with business needs subject to the requirements of law and proportionality.

In most cases, however, the issues raised by the development of databases and those raised by data sharing have been seen as separate; for example in March 2009 the Rowntree Trust published a report entitled *Database State*.[3] The report examined 46 major databases developed by the State but did not review the associated sharing of data. In 2008 the Walport/Thomas review focused on the control of data sharing but did not address the issues raised by the growth of major databases. In some cases the databases have a statutory basis and therefore the legal questions that can arise in relation to the powers to share data do not occur but in other cases the data is being collected under non-statutory powers. In any event the compliance and governance issues are very similar and we would strongly recommend that any practitioner asked to advise on or review the control or governance of a major database should have regard to the Commissioner's Code on Data Sharing and the advice on governance available from the Ministry of Justice.

Database policy

25–04 The significant growth of public sector databases is sometimes attributed to Tony Blair's enthusiasm for them during his tenure as Prime Minister, and sometimes to the eagerness of security interests in collecting information post 9/11. These were factors which speeded up some developments but actually there appears to be no one source of policy which gave rise to the growth of the database as a preferred tool to deliver public policies. The Cabinet Office document *Transformational Government* issued in 2005 re-stated and reaffirmed the commitment of Government to the use of IT in the public sector to deliver efficiencies and savings but the growth of the database culture had already taken root by then.

There are far too many massive sets of data held in the public sector to list but we can give some examples. In some cases the databases have always been held as one and the technology simply used to make them more effective, although the side effect of such increased effectiveness is make them easier to access, copy and use for other purposes, for example the Child Benefit Database and the DVLA databases are long standing central collections. In some cases the databases have been developed to bring together or link disparate silos of information within the public sector, for example the replacement of NHS systems with systems that would be able to share data in NPfIT announced in February 2002 and scaled back in 2010. In some cases the databases have developed as a result of available technology allowing greater collections of information, for example the records of Automatic Number Plate Recognition and the DNA Database. In some cases the databases have grown as a result of specific services, for example the TfL records of the use of Oystercards. As noted earlier there was also a clear policy objective during the Blair years to develop databases for specific purposes of social control, for example the National Childhood Obesity Database started in 2005 and ContactPoint, the database

---

[3] March 2009, published by the Joseph Rowntree Reform Trust Ltd.

aimed at collecting records of all interactions between children and the State. The most notable projects were NPfiT and the Identity Card Project supported by the national identity database.

Although all of these are subject to the Data Protection Act, and many of the ones with a statutory basis such as ContactPoint included at least some specific rules and some safeguards about the use of the data, there were deep-rooted concerns about many of the databases. One of these was the absence of proportionality, for example the genesis of the ContactPoint database can be traced to the death of Victoria Climbie where it was shown that information should have been shared between the professionals who had contact with her. However ContactPoint was planned to collect information on all children with widespread access to a vast number of health professionals. In addition there was not always a clear and transparent process before the collection of data began, no generally applicable guidance around how the Act was to be applied and no consistency in governance or transparency between the different collections of data.

Some statutory initiatives were clearly controversial and generated wide debate, such as ContactPoint and the ID scheme. In August 2004, interviewed by *The Times*, the Information Commissioner, Richard Thomas, warned in the context of these developments that the UK risked "sleepwalking into a surveillance society". The concept, and no doubt the phrase itself, struck a chord. In 2006 the Commissioner's Office sponsored a report into the issue, *A Report on the Surveillance Society*,[4] which was followed up by an action plan which included both awareness raising and practical measures. The practical measures included sponsoring the concept of Privacy by Design to ensure that any new database development takes account of privacy issues from the inception and the use of Privacy Impact Assessments to evaluate the intrusiveness and effect of new projects. The relevant materials can be found on the Commissioner's website.

ROWNTREE TRUST REPORT AND GOVERNMENT RESPONSE

There have been a number of further reports and enquiries, including a House of Lords Constitution Committee enquiry in 2008.[5] However, one of the most controversial was the report funded by the Rowntree Trust in 2009, *Database State*. The report was a very ambitious project. It sought to review 46 major state databases for compliance primarily with the Human Rights Act 2000 but also referencing the Data Protection Act and to carry out the project and produce the report within around 12 months. In view of the length and complexity of many of the laws involved and the procedural details around the use of the data it was clearly impossible for the team to do more than take a very high-level overview of the databases. The report was not accepted by the Government which regarded it as deeply flawed and came back with a strong rebuttal of the accusations raised. The documents, the report and in particular the Government rebuttal, are

25–05

---

[4] 2006, available from *www.ico.gov.uk*[Accessed October 5, 2012].

[5] *Surveillance, Citizens and the State*, 2nd Report of Session 2008–2009, Constitution Committee of the House of Lords, HL Paper January 18, 2009.

primarily interesting as an inventory of the main databases and the variety of the statutory bases on which they are founded.

25–06   Although the Government rejected the Rowntree report the growing unease about the explosion of the database culture had a result. When the Coalition Government came to power in 2010 it undertook to remove or roll back some of the data collections regarded as particularly intrusive. ContactPoint was closed down in August 2010, the ID scheme repealed and a promise made to regulate CCTV. The Protection of Freedoms Act 2012 brings in some further controls and restraints. These include a new framework for police retention of fingerprints and DNA data, a requirements that schools obtain parents' consent before processing children's biometric information, the introduction of a code of practice for surveillance camera systems, judicial approval of certain surveillance activities by local authorities and a restriction on the scope of the "vetting and barring" scheme for protecting vulnerable groups and changes to the system of criminal records checks.

In addition the Commissioner has been successful in obtaining new powers of compulsory audit of central Government and there is now a policy commitment to carry out PIAs before the adoption of any new major data development in the public sector.

There remains, however, no general guidance or code of practice on the establishment and governance of new databases and to that extent at least this area has not reached the standards that now apply to initiatives to specifically share data within the public sector. As an example of the absence of generally applicable standards it is instructive to consider the evidence given to the House of Commons Home Affairs Select Committee in March 2011 on the proposed changes to the structure of policing where the Commissioner made the following comments:

> "The Commissioner considers that the governance of national level policing systems could be improved and the NCA could potentially take on a national governance role.
>
> 10.   The Commissioner supports the government's aim of simplifying national policing arrangements to improve, rationalise and bring coherence to national level policing issues. The Commissioner also welcomes the Home Secretary's statement that the large scale devolution in power to local forces will be matched with a stronger, more streamlined approach to those issues that require national coordination. It is important to clarify which bodies are responsible for national level policing systems so that there is clear accountability for ensuring that information held on those systems complies with the law. The Commissioner's view is that information rights compliance would be greatly assisted by a clear national framework that achieves consistency of approach and clarity of responsibilities.
>
> 11.   The Commissioner recognises the challenges surrounding the relationships that underpin policing, in particular the relationship at a national level between central government, local forces, the professional leadership of the service and those responsible for its local accountability. As a regulator that deals with government, local police forces, police authorities and various national policing agencies and bodies, we recognise that the current arrangements could be improved.

12. The complex connections and interrelationships across police forces and national policing bodies is particularly apparent when it comes to the governance of, and accountability for, the police collection, storage and use of people's information. The picture becomes even more complex when we take into account the wider information sharing that takes place within 'the public protection network', for example, with the CRB, ISA and other parts of the criminal justice system.

13. Rapid advances in technology have resulted in vast amounts of personal data being collected and processed by the police at local and national level. This information is held in the Police National Computer, the new Police National Database and other national level policing databases such as the National DNA Database and the NADC. At present, responsibilities are fragmented across police forces and various national bodies (ACPO, ACRO, NPIA and various wider bodies such as the National DNA Database Strategy Board, National CCTV Strategy Board). At a basic level it is often challenging to identify who the data controllers are for the personal information held within those databases and very often all 43 forces are data controllers in common. This is further compounded by decisions as to funding, functionality and operational use being influenced by others such as the government, NPIA and various ACPO committees.

14. There is a danger that the fast pace of development can lead to lack of clarity about who is accountable for such databases. This can be evident, for example, in setting access procedures, retention periods and overseeing quality and security of the data. There is also a risk of a lack of transparency because the public may have little awareness of such systems, especially when information such as vehicle movements or CCTV images may have been obtained from third parties who collected the information for different purposes and hold it for much shorter periods. It is important that the development of such national systems should be subject to the fullest scrutiny and debate, with clear lines of responsibility and control.

15. These complex inter-relationships in local and national policing and connections between various databases pose significant challenges in terms of information governance. They also raise significant data protection and privacy concerns, especially with the large-scale collection of information about people who go about their lawful day to day business, for example through the NADC.

16. The Commissioner is also concerned about the lack of strategic management of, and accountability for, developments which engage wider surveillance concerns such as CCTV and ANPR. For example, the ICO sits as an observer on the relevant ACPO national working groups but they are looking at issues from a police perspective and there does not appear to be sufficient consideration of wider societal implications such as balancing public security and individual civil liberties.

17. It is important that there is clear accountability and leadership at a national level for the national policing databases so that they are managed in a more coherent and consistent way. This includes, for example, agreeing and setting national standards and coordinating responses to subject access requests".

DATA SHARING

The issue of sharing data between public authorities and the extent to which personal data can be shared and used raises several tricky question which raise wider areas of law than the DPA, namely: **25–07**

- the extent of the powers of a public authority to share data, particularly where data has been obtained for one purpose by the first body and is to be shared with another body for the purposes of that other body;
- the application of the common law of confidence and the circumstances under which that can be overridden; and
- The possible breach of art.8 rights if data is shared without due regard for the restrictions imposed by art.8.

These three issues are considered below.

Powers to share data

25–08   If a public body acts outside its powers in sharing data or in breaching legitimate rights of confidentiality or art.8, it will be acting unlawfully and will therefore be in breach of principle 1. This interpretation of the term "lawful" has been supported by the Tribunal in the case of *British Gas* and accepted by the courts (see *Murray v MGN Big Picture*[6] and *Law Society v Kordowsi*.[7] A full discussion of the impact of the term is to be found at Chapter 6. The first question facing any public body therefore is whether it has the legal power to share personal data with another body. The existence of a legal power is also crucial to ensure that art.8 of the HRA is met, as a use of personal data will often amount to an interference with the right to private life and requires a lawful basis for the activity.

Where a body is set up by statute, it can only do those things that the statute allows or those things that are incidental to it. The Crown has common law and prerogative powers so the Crown acting through its Ministers can do those things that an ordinary person can do. There are relatively few express powers to share data in statute.

There are some legislative provisions which may make disclosures mandatory, for example an obligation to provide information when required to another body, or permissive, which will give a public body a discretion to make disclosures for specific purposes. Public authorities established by statute or acting under statutory powers rely on implied powers to both disclose data for sharing and to receive it. The approach of the courts to the extent of implied powers has been to take a realistic and pragmatic view of incidental powers echoing the statement of the court in *Attorney General v Great Eastern Railway Co*,[8] in which Lord Selborne said:

> "whatever may fairly be regarded as incidental to or consequential upon those things that the legislature has authorized ought not, unless expressly prohibited to be held, by judicial construction to the ultra vires".

An activity carried out under incidental or implied powers must be incidental to the function of the body making the disclosure. In *Hazell v Hammersmith and Fulham London Borough*Council[9] the court held that interest rates swap transactions were not incidental to the borrowing functions of local authorities

---

[6] [2007] EWHC 1908.
[7] [2011] EWHC 3185 (QB).
[8] (1880) 5 App. Cas. 473.
[9] [1992] A.C. 1, HL.

but were being carried out for a separate reason. In *R. v Houdsham*[10] the Court of Appeal held that it was ultra vires the police under the Police Act 1996 to seek contributions to the cost of investigating fraud from insurance companies.

There are now a number of specific provisions in statute giving clear incidental powers and it may also be easier to imply powers as incidental where the duties of public bodies are set out in very general terms, such as the general duty in the Children Act for local authorities to provide services to meet children's needs.

Reliance on incidental powers

There are potential problems in relying on incidental powers or even common law powers of the Crown. The courts have consistently held that an interference with a fundamental right requires a power clearly given by legislation, whether expressly or by necessary implication.[11] In *Pierson*, Lord Browne Wilkinson said:

"A power conferred by Parliament in general terms is not to be taken to authorize the doing of acts by the donee of the power which adversely affect the legal rights of the citizen or the basic principles on which the law of the United Kingdom is based unless the statute conferring the power makes it clear that such was the intention of Parliament".

The difficulty is that the extent of the powers is unclear and the actions of the public body may not be sufficiently clearly known and forseeable to meet the standard of lawfulness required by the Human Rights Act 2000. The more serious an infringement of the right, the more carefully a court will scrutinize the legal basis for the infringement.[12]

There is relatively little case law around the extent that public authorities can use either incidental or general powers in order to use or disclose personal data obtained for one purpose for: a) a linked or similar purpose; and b) a wholly different purpose within the scope of their powers and without breach of art.8.

There is clear case law that, while the starting point is a general presumption that the police should not disclose information about convictions, individual disclosures can be made where the disclosure is for the purpose of preventing wrongdoing or protecting the public. In *R. v Chief Constable of the North Wales Police Ex p. AB*[13] the police were able to make a disclosure about an individual who was known to be a danger to children; and in *Woolgar v Chief Constable of Sussex Police*[14] a disclosure by the police to the regulatory body for nursing was accepted as being in the public interest and lawful. In a number of cases individuals have failed in a challenge to a disclosure where the court established that the disclosure served the purpose of protecting the public.[15] However, these were individual disclosures and a strong public interest can be seen in each case. There are also cases on the implied powers of the police and local authorities to

25–09

---

[10] [2005] EWCA Crim 1366.
[11] *R. v Secretary of State for the Home Department, Ex p. Simms* [2000] 2 A.C. 115; *R. v Secretary of State for the Home Department, Ex p. Pierson* [1998] A.C. 539.
[12] *Potter v Scottish Ministers* [2007] CSOH 56.
[13] [1999] Q.B. 396.
[14] [2001] W.L.R. 25.
[15] See, for example, *R. v Local Authority and Police Authority in the Midlands ex parte LM* [2000] 1 F.L.R. 612.

publicise the behaviour of offenders and notify people of the application of ASBOS.[16] In these cases the courts were considering the incidental or implied powers of the public bodies. The extent of the powers of the police to use information obtained for one purpose for another purpose was touched on in *R. (A) and B.*[17] The judgment focused on the application of art.8 to the question of whether the police would be justified in making a voluntary disclosure to employers. It held that the disclosure would not be justifiable under art.8 nor could it be justified if the court looked outside the Convention and took a common law view based which "begins with a restrictive approach to disclosure".

As noted earlier, the Crown also has common law powers, that is the power to do anything that an ordinary person can do. These may allow Government departments to share data. In the case of the Consultancy Index (the lists of those prohibited from working with children), before it was put on a statutory footing, the Court of Appeal held that the Index was lawful even though it was set up and conducted on the general powers of the Secretary of State. The court appeared to be influenced by the fact that the surrounding administrative scheme ensured that those affected were fully informed of their position and rights.[18]

ECtHR cases

25–10   The Court of Human Rights has considered the point to some extent in the cases of *Peck*[19] and *Copland*.[20] In *Peck* the local authority had a statutory power under the Crime and Disorder Act to run CCTV in public places. It photographed Mr Peck on the CCTV and publicised the images to show that the use of CCTV was a positive contribution to the reduction of problems. The Court held that the action of the authority in publishing the data was lawful because it was incidental to the function for which it had obtained the data. Accordingly the authority had a lawful basis for the processing. However, in *Copland* the authority monitored communications data relating to the calls and internet use of the applicant and argued that it had a lawful basis as this was incidental to its general powers to run the institution and its obligations to ensure that public funds were properly used. The Court did not accept that and said it found the argument "unpersuasive". The Court appeared to be influenced by the fact that the use was secret and the legal basis did not therefore meet the standards of being generally known and available law.

Sensitive personal data

25–11   The standards required for the use of sensitive information for new purposes are clearly higher than for ordinary information, although this may go more to a test of proportionality than whether the public body has legal powers to use the

---

[16] See *R. (on the application of Ellis) v Chief Constable of Essex* [2003] EWHC 1321; and *R. (on the application of Stanley) v Commissioner of Police of the Metropolis*[2004] EWHC 2229 (Admin).
[17] [2010] EWHC 2361 (Admin).
[18] *R. v Secretary of State for Health Ex p. C*[2000] 1 F.L.R. 627.
[19] Application no.44647/98 ECHR 2003-1.
[20] Application no.62617/00.

information. In *A Health Authority v X*[21] on appeal from a ruling of Mumby J.,[22] the Court of Appeal refused to discharge a condition that would have required the Health Authority to apply to the court for permission to use patient records outside the permitted area of investigating professional misconduct by medical practitioners. The Health Authority was unhappy at the limitations imposed on the use of information and appealed against them. The Authority submitted that the NHS depends on the free internal exchange of confidential information and would "grind to a halt" if the judgment of Mumby J. was "extensively construed and applied". The Court of Appeal dismissed the appeal and held that the conditions attached to the order should stand.

Information obtained under compulsion

In *R. (on the application of Ali) v Minister for the Cabinet Office and the Statistics Board*[23] the High Court followed the decision in *R. (on the application of Robertson) v Wakefield MDC* in holding that the disclosure of information which the individual has been compelled to impart under a statutory requirement requires a strong justification for disclosure in the absence of the consent of the individual. The judge noted that:

> "It is common ground that disclosure of personal data in a census form must comply with the DPA 1998. Secondly the defendants accept (as they have to in the light of *R (Robertson) v Wakefield MDC* and the Strasbourg authorities considered in it) that compulsory completion of a census is a prima facie interference with Article 8(1) and that disclosure of personal information provided on the census form requires very clear justification in view of the strong public interest in the confidentiality of census data."

Conclusions

The tentative conclusion that can be drawn from this is that there is a general power for the police to use and disclose information for the protection of the public and the prevention of crime and other public bodies may also have such powers. However, these are exceptions and such disclosures and uses should be made carefully and on a case by case basis, particularly where the information is sensitive and involve the private life of an individual. More generally implied or incidental powers or common law powers can provide a lawful basis for a use of personal data which would otherwise be ultra vires and in breach of art.8 as not having a lawful basis as long as the proposed uses are publicly acknowledged or set out in some proper way and the purpose is either closely associated with the original purpose for which the data were obtained or is clearly for the protection of the public. The use must be clearly incidental to the main function of the public body and forseeable by the person affected. The discussion in the cases on these points are distinctly brief but it appears therefore that the use of incidental

25–12

25–13

---

[21] [2001] EWCA Civ 2014.
[22] [2002] 2 All E.R. 780.
[23] [2012] EWHC 1943 (Admin).

powers is relatively constrained. Particular care should be taken where the information has been obtained under compulsory powers or includes sensitive personal data.

This approach, which links the consideration of the powers of public bodies with the impact of the Human Rights Act and results in a relatively cautious approach to reliance on incidental or implied powers for wide scale data sharing, was taken in the Guidance issued by the Commissioner and that issued by Department of Constitutional Affairs (issued 2003 and revised 2007). However, the more recent legal guidance from the Ministry of Justice (see below) separates the consideration of the impact of the HRA, which it suggests will be satisfied as long as the DPA is met, and places more reliance on the case law as authority for sharing. It is suggested that an authority considering a major project to share personal data without an express provision should carefully review its legal powers and may find it useful to review also the earlier Guidance which is still publicly available.

LAW OF CONFIDENCE

25–14   The law of confidence is examined in the context of the misuse of private information in Ch.2 and reference should be made to that chapter. In brief, however, it is clear that public bodies may be subject to obligations of confidence in relation to the personal data which they hold. Some of those obligations are imposed by common law or by statute, for example medical information is confidential. In some cases the nature of the information is clearly personal and confidential and in other cases the public authority will have given explicit undertakings of confidentiality.

The question of the extent of the obligation outside areas of particular sensitivity remains unanswered and it is suggested that public authorities should carefully review the nature of the information held and how it was obtained in advance of any exercise to share data where there is no specific statutory power.

An obligation of confidence can be set aside where the individual to whom it is owed consents to the disclosure, whether there is a legal obligation to disclose and where there is an overriding public interest in the disclosure. Interestingly in most if not all, of the cases described and referred to above the information was confidential and there was an overriding public interest in the disclosure made.

The problem often faced in data sharing arrangements where confidential information is engaged is that it is difficult to justify the disclosure in each individual case.

Article 8 of the HRA

25–15   The sharing of data will often be a breach of the individual's right to private and family life. In such a case it must meet the three tests of:

- having a legal basis for the sharing;
- being for one of the specified areas of public interest; and
- being proportionate.

The question of a lawful basis has been covered above in para.25-10. The question of whether a disclosure is in one of the specified interests i.e. national security, public safety, the economic well being of the country, the prevention of crime and disorder, the protection of health and morals or the protection of the rights and freedoms of others will be a question of fact for the particular exercise. The difficult area is the test of proportionality. In any data sharing exercise it must be established that the intrusion into privacy is both justified and appropriately safeguarded. It is in this aspect that the Commissioner's Code will be particularly useful.

The fact that a lawful basis for disclosure exists is not sufficient in itself and the tests of proportionality must be considered. In *Dental Health Council v Al-Naher*[24] the High Court held that the Dental Health Council was entitled to make internal disclosures of data about patients of a dentist to the relevant Practice Committee and Investigating Committee even if the patients did not consent and could do so without seeking a court order. The dentist in question was suspected of fraudulent activity in collusion with patients. The patients refused consent for records to be released to the various committees which were to investigate the matter. It was argued on behalf of the patients and the dentist that the GDC could not use the records without sanction of a court order. The High Court held that the public interest in investigating allegations of unfitness overrode the common law obligation of confidence to patients. The Court also held that there was no difficult presented by the Data Protection Act and the processing was justified under Schs 2 and 3. The Court then examined the HRA issues in relation to the disclosures proposed and held that the disclosure was proportionate to the importance of the professional proceedings. It took into account the safeguards which would apply, particularly that the information would be shared among a small group of professional people who would all be subject to obligations of confidence in relation to the data. It also took account of the procedure followed by the GDC in giving notice to the patients of the proposal.

Relation with the law of libel and qualified privilege

A further constraint which should be considered by public bodies operating data sharing is the possibility that information provided may be outside the area of qualified privilege and give rise to action in defamation. Such processing would also be unlawful under principle 1 of the Act. The issue arose in the case of *Jane Clift v Slough Borough Council*.[25] Ms Clift has complained to the Council after protesting against anti-social behaviour in a local park. When she contacted the Council to register her complaint, the member of staff who took the call, the Council's Anti-Social Behaviour Co-ordinator, ended up having a difficult call with Ms Clift. The evidence was that Ms Clift was left with the sense that she was the one in the wrong. Not unreasonably Ms Clift became cross and cut the call off with the member of staff. She then complained about the member of staff in strong terms and wrote a letter of complaint in which, in an apparent effort to make clear to the Council just how offensive the staff member's behaviour was,

25–16

---

[24] [2011] EWHC 3011 (Admin).
[25] [2010] EWCA Civ 1171.

she stated that she was so cross and affronted by the behaviour that she was certain that she would have physically attacked her if she had been anywhere near. As Ms Clift described herself as not being of such a disposition, the strength of the response should alert the Council to the behaviour of the member of staff. The Council instigated an investigation, the results of which did not appear (as far as is apparent from the case reports at least) to deal with Ms Clift's complaints at all or address the behaviour of the member of staff, but accused Ms Clift of "violent and threatening behaviour" towards the member of staff. As a result of this, the Council included Ms Clift's name and some inaccurate information on a Violent Persons Register, which was widely distributed among Council staff and other bodies associated with the Council. The evidence was that the Register was sent to around 150 people in total including a number of non-Council organisations. Ms Clift took issue with this and brought an action in defamation against the Council.

25–17   It is notable that Ms Clift did not take action under the DPA and in her action she did not as such address the fairness of the processing. It may be that she would have had further remedies had she done so.

In the High Court the jury found that the material was not justified and was defamatory. The Council defended itself on the basis that the dissemination was covered by qualified privilege.

In a case of defamation, even if the material is false and defamatory and therefore the person publishing the libel cannot justify it on those grounds, it may nevertheless be protected if the publisher can show that the communication was privileged. In some rare cases privilege is absolute, as with a statement made in Parliament, but in most cases it is qualified. This means that if the statement is malicious there is no defence but as long as it was made in good faith in circumstances to which qualified privilege applies then there is a defence to the libel.

Ms Clift had originally claimed that the publication was malicious and attributed the malice to the member of staff who had compiled the report on the investigation which had given rise to the entry on the Register. The jury in the High Court had found that the publication was not malicious so the Council was able to argue that qualified privilege applied.

25–18   The issue before the High Court and the Court of Appeal was on the extent of the publication. Put simply, the question was whether the Council was entitled to disseminate the information, which was admittedly defamatory, to everyone who fell into the class of persons with whom it had an established relationship covering the relevant area of interest, in this case a shared a common interest in the provision of public services or whether it had to constrain its disclosures to the circle of those who might potentially come into contact with Ms Clift and to whom therefore it owed duties of care to warn of and protect against violent individuals. The Council contended for the former and on this basis defended the dissemination to a very wide set of people which included staff in the Licensing, Food Safety, Education and Children's departments and four partner organisations plus trade union officials and community wardens none of whom were ever likely to come into contact with Ms Clift.

The Court of Appeal considered previous case law, as there was conflicting earlier authority on the point, and confirmed that qualified privilege only applied to those to whom the Council had an obligation to warn. In doing so it applied art.8. It reaffirmed that the protection of reputation is a right which as an element of private life falls within art.8 (*Guardian News and Media Ltd*); therefore the Council was under an obligation to respect Ms Clift's reputation unless the interference could be justified under art.8. It referred to the Commissioner's guidance on the use of violent warning markers which advises authorities that such information should only be disseminated to those to whom it was justified:

> "Ill considered and indiscriminate disclosure is bound to be disproportionate and no plea of administrative difficulty in verifying the information and limiting publication to those who truly have the need to know or those reasonably thought to be at risk can out-weight the substantial interference with the right to protect reputations. In my judgment the judge's ruling on proportionality is beyond challenge. To publish as widely as the Council did was to breach Ms Clift's Article 8 rights" (para.35, per Ward L.J.).

The lesson for public bodies that are sharing information about individuals which may be defamatory is twofold. It is critically important to ensure that the material shared in both accurate and includes only that required for the purpose. It is also important to ansure that it is not shared more widely that necessary and which sharing is proportionate.   **25–19**

In the case of Ms Clift, one of the reasons that the information was widely disseminated was that the Council's systems were not structured so as to allow for narrower dissemination. The court was deeply unsympathetic to this and made clear that it would not be regarded as an excuse.

Obligation to give notice of disclosures

In *Woolgar* it was indicated that in ordinary circumstances where confidential information is to be disclosed the person to whom the information relates should be informed in advance if possible. In the case of *General Dental Council v Al Naher* the issue of notice was considered. The judge recognised that such prior notice had not been said to be essential by the ECtHR in either *MS v Sweden* or *Z v Finland*, but commented that   **25–20**

> "there may be scope for development of the law in this area and for a greater focus on the safeguards for patients where confidential medical information about them is to be used for other purposes."

CODE OF DATA SHARING PRACTICE

A draft provision in the Coroners and Justice Bill to allow a designated authority to pass orders ("information-sharing orders") to enable any person to share information, including personal data, where it was considered necessary to achieve a policy objective, subject to the measure being proportionate was abandoned in favour of providing for the Commissioner to produce a Code of Practice on Data Sharing. The relevant provisions of the Coroners and Justice Act as they eventually reached the statute book are now incorporated as ss.52A–52E   **25–21** of the Act. They came into force on February 1, 2010.[26] The Commissioner issued a consultation document on the Data Sharing Code of Practice in October 2010 which ran until January 5, 2011. The code was submitted to the Secretary of State for approval and laid before the Houses of Parliament in February 2011. The approved version of the Code was launched by the Commissioner on May 11, 2011.

Definition

25–22   Section 52A requires the Commissioner to prepare a code of practice which contains practical guidance in relation to the sharing of data in accordance with the requirements of the Act plus "such other practice as the Commissioner considers appropriate to promote good practice in the sharing of personal data."[27] Section 52A(4) provides that a reference to data-sharing is a reference to the disclosure of the data by transmission, dissemination or otherwise making it available. The description of what is caught by data-sharing is therefore wide and is not limited to the use of personal data by the public sector but includes use by the private sector. There must be a disclosure before data sharing takes place, and before the code applies. It is not clear from the provision whether this must be a disclosure to the third party or whether a disclosure within the data controller's own organisation would be caught. The code however states that it covers internal disclosures such as those between different departments in one organisation.

Good practice means such practice in the sharing of personal data as appears to the Commissioner to be desirable having regard to the interests of data subjects and others and includes (but is not limited to) compliance with the requirements of the Act. This is a wide remit but if focuses on guidance on *practice* rather than legal considerations. This is reflected in the code in which most of the content is around how best and most safely to achieve sharing rather than other legal issues. As we have noted earlier some of the concerns around the increase in data sharing have focussed on the application of legal constraints however these are not areas covered in depth by the code and organisation are urged to take their own advice if they consider that it is necessary. The Commissioner is under an obligation to consult before preparing the code and must consult among trade associations (as defined in section 51), data subjects and persons who appear to the Commissioner to represent the interests of data subjects, as he considers appropriate.[28]

Procedure for approval

25–23   The Commissioner must consult the Secretary of State on the code and submit the final version to the Secretary of State to be laid before Parliament for approval.[29] The code is subject to negative resolution of the House and must be laid before both Houses of Parliament for a period of 40 days. The 40-day period ignores any period in which Parliament is dissolved or prorogued or adjourned for more than

---

[26] The Coroners and Justice 2009 (Commencement No.3 and Transitional Provisions) Order 2010 (SI 2010/145).

[27] s.52A.

[28] s.52A(3).

[29] s.52B(1) as amended by the Protection of Freedoms Act 2012.

four days. Otherwise the 40 days is calculated beginning of the day that the code is laid (or if not laid before both Houses on the same day the later date). If Parliament resolves not to approve it the Commissioner must prepare another version. Otherwise after the 40-day period it must be issued by the Commissioner and will come into effect 21 days after issue.[30] As noted above, the code was issued by the Commissioner at a launch on May 11, 2011. The Commissioner must keep the code under review and may prepare an alternative code or a replacement. This is a discretionary power save in the case where he becomes aware that a terms of the code could mean that the UK is in breach of any Community or other international obligation, in which case he must take action to alter the code so as to remedy the situation. If he does so he must follow the consultation process as described above and the same procedure for Parliamentary approval will be followed.[31] The code or any replacement must be issued by the Commissioner and published by him.[32]

Admissibility and impact

The code in of persuasive and advisory authority only. Section 52E(1) provides that a failure on the part of any person to act in accordance with any provision of the data sharing code does not of itself render any person liable to any legal proceedings in any court or tribunal. It cannot therefore be treated as hard law. However, it is admissible in any legal proceedings and is not limited to proceedings under the Data Protection Act. It may therefore be relevant in consumer cases or employment cases where information has been shared between parties. Moreover, whenever a court or tribunal is conducting any legal proceedings, including ones under the Data Protection Act, if the provisions of the code appear to the court or tribunal to be relevant to any question arising in those proceedings or in connection with the exercise of the jurisdiction in relation to the time when it was in force then the court or tribunal must take those provisions into account. The same obligation to take the code into account applies to the Commissioner in carrying out any function under the Act.[33]

25–24

Provisions of the code

The code has an introductory section on using the code, which explains the nature of the code and its non-statutory character and then covers the following topics:

25–25

- Definition of data sharing
- Data sharing and the law
- Deciding to share data
- Fairness and transparency
- Security
- Governance
- Individuals' rights

---

[30] s.52B.
[31] s.52C.
[32] s.52D.
[33] s. 52E.

- Things to avoid
- The Commissioner's powers and penalties
- Notification
- Freedom of Information
- Data sharing agreements

It includes data sharing checklists, one for systematic data sharing and the other for one-off requests, as well as a number of case studies.

Definition of data sharing

25–26   As noted above, the definition in s.52A(4) states that a reference to the sharing of data is a reference to the disclosure of the data by transmission, dissemination or otherwise making it available. The code defines data sharing as:

"the disclosure from one or more organisations to a third party organisation or organisations, or the sharing of data between different parts of an organisation".

It makes the point that data sharing essentially is about the sharing of personal data between data controllers and distinguishes that from sharing personal data with processors. It also distinguishes between two main types of data sharing, systematic routine sharing where the same data sets are shared between the same organisations for an established purpose or purposes and exceptional, one-off decisions to share data which may be urgent or unexpected and explains that different approaches apply to these two which is reflected in the code. It also distinguishes between sharing within organisations and sharing between separate bodies and notes that only some aspects of the code are likely to apply to internal disclosures.

Data sharing and the law

25–27   The code outlines the main areas relevant to the question of the lawfulness of data sharing although it does not link the question of lawfulness to the obligation to comply with principle 1 and uses non-technical terms throughout. In relation to public sector powers it explains that public bodies set up by statute are constrained by the powers in the statutes regulating their activities and that broadly speaking they should look for express obligations or powers to share or consider whether the sharing of data is conducive or incidental to the functions of the body. It also draws attention to the potentially limiting obligations which may restrict sharing such as obligations of confidence. The explanation is helpful and clear. The effort to simplify the section has meant that some of the legal complexities are not really rendered fully, for example it states that government departments headed by Ministers of the Crown will always have common law powers to share information, which appears to be an overly bold statement of the extent of inherent powers, given that the point does not appear to have been specifically litigated. In relation to the question of disclosure in the overriding public interest it the explanation is somewhat unclear and seems to suggest that a disclosure in the overriding public interest, for example to deal with serious crime, might be a justified breach of confidentiality but still be without a lawful basis whereas we would suggest that the better view is that a court would be likely to hold that all public bodies have an incidental power to make a disclosure in a real emergency in the public interest by nature of their inherent responsibilities as public bodies. However, these are quibbles rather than serious defects and the section clearly states that any organisations in doubt about the extent of powers should seek legal advice.

In relation to private sector bodies it explains that the legal situation is less difficult however it is prudent to check for any contractual or other restrictions that might apply.

In covering the effect of the Human Rights Act it explains the relevant of the art.8 right but takes the position that if the organisation is disclosing or sharing personal data only in ways that comply with the Data Protection Act then the sharing or disclosure of the data is likely to comply with the HRA. This reflects the statements in the Ministry of Justice Guidance on which we comment below. While it may well be fair to suggest that a data sharing project which complies with the principles is likely to be regarded as proportionate and appropriately safeguarded we would not agree that compliance with the DPA will necessarily satisfy the need to have a proper legal basis and be in defence of one or more of the specified interests and suggest that these points should be specifically addressed in any data sharing project.

Deciding to share data

This section deals with the points to review before deciding to share data and the possible grounds for processing. It advises controllers to carry out an assessment of the reasons for the sharing and the potential benefits and risks of sharing. In essence it advises an assessment of the proportionality of the exercise. The checklist of points to consider covers: the objective to be achieved and whether anonymised data could be used; the extent of the data to be shared; when and how it should be shared and who will have access with a view to ensuring security and minimising the level of intrusion engaged; whether other compliance issues are raised, such as transfer outside the EEA or a need to alter the notification of either party; the risks, although it does not explicitly refer to risks to the privacy of the individuals; and how the success of the project is to be measured.

25–28

In looking at the grounds for processing it makes the point that the use of sensitive personal data involves a stronger justification or a clear consent from the data subject. It makes clear that consent should not be considered where there is no real option for the data subject to object and other grounds should be considered. It accepts the balancing test in ground 6 as a legitimate basis for sharing and, although the example given is from a private sector case, implicitly accepts that the ground can be used by a public sector body.[34]

---

[34] The author remains of the view that this ground should not be acceptable as a basis for processing by a public body which should either be able to show that it has a duty to carry out specific processing or a power to do so and therefore should be restricted to grounds 3 and 5. Even though the Information Tribunal has found and the High Court accepted in cases under the Freedom of Information Act 2000 that ground 6 is the applicable ground the author continues to respectfully

The good practice points specifically recommended are to document the reason for the data sharing and the nature of the sharing. It also refers to a bad practice being to purport to offer individuals a "choice" if the data sharing is going to take place regardless of their wishes anyway.

Fairness and transparency

25–29 In this section the code deals with the provision of notices and the responsibility for providing those notices; the application of the exemption in s.29 to exempt from the obligation to give notice and deals with a couple of special situations, mergers and takeovers and emergency response planning. The advice on the provision of notice mirrors the advice in the Privacy Notices Code of Practice and explains how the organisation should assess the extent to which it requires an active communication with the data subject or can rely on existing notices or reasonably assumed knowledge. The disclosure without notice in reliance on an exemption is referred to and the example given of a disclosure to the police in which the disclosing organisation could rely on s.29; however other exemptions which might be relevant (that the notice would require disproportionate effort or the use of data for research are examples) are not mentioned specifically although reference is made to the guidance on exemptions in the Guide to data protection on the website.

In relation to mergers and takeovers the code focuses on information about customers or service users rather than employees, making the point that notice should be provided and information processed in line with the expectations of individuals. It also warns of the potential pitfalls in managing records once they have been merged from different systems.

The good practices specifically recommended are reviewing privacy notices regularly to ensure that they continue to reflect any data sharing that the organisation is engaged on; communicating a privacy notice actively in cases even where it is not a legal necessity to do so; cooperating with other organisations with whom data is shared to ensure that individuals remain informed throughout the process; explaining the disclosure of data even where there is a statutory basis such as money laundering obligations; notifying individual as soon as possible even if an exemption has been relied upon not to give notice in the first instance and documenting and retaining records of the reasons for making decisions on the provision of notices, particularly where the organisation has determined that notice is not required.

Security

25–30 This section includes two short checklists covering physical security and technical security respectively.

The basic good standards for security are reinforced. Two practical points are made; controller are alerted to the potential problems which can arise where organisations have different IT systems or security standards and advised that

---

disagree and remains of the view that, as a public body must be able to assert that it has either a duty or a power to carry out any action before it can lawfully carry out the action, a ground 6 should be irrelevant.

these be reviewed and dealt with before any sharing commences and reminded to put in place clear instructions about the transfer of data by phone, fax, e-mail, etc.

The good practices specifically recommended are ensuring that the organisation to which data is being disclosed has appropriate security measures and will apply them once the data comes into its possession; taking a series of measures before sharing consisting of:

- reviewing the information that the organisation receives from others and checking any conditions on its use;
- reviewing any information shared with others and ensuring that any access and use is known;
- assessing the sensitivity of data shared and ensuring appropriate security;
- identifying who has access to shared data in the organisation and restricting access as far as possible; and
- planning for a security breach.

Governance

The Governance section covers the use of data sharing protocols, accuracy and records management points, dealing with training needs and reviewing data sharing arrangements on a regular basis.

25–31

The contents of a data sharing agreement are outlined and this is a shortened version of the more detailed description at s.14 of the code.[35] The code notes that Privacy Impact Assessments are mandatory for UK central Government departments when introducing certain new processes involving personal data,[36] but also recommends their use by others for whom that are not mandated. In dealing with data quality and the matching of data the advice is practical and reflects common problems that are sometimes not anticipated by parties which agree to match in principle, such as the way that specific fields are recorded or the use of standard formats for particular information. It refers users to the data standards for government, local government and the NHS.[37] In covering the topic of data quality it also covers the importance of ensuring accuracy and sharing any corrections made to the data and the removal and destruction of the data after the exercise has finished, reminding controllers that there may also be associated hard copy personal data which will also require destruction.

In relation to training it distinguishes the training needs of those who are responsible for making decision about sharing from those who administer systems or those who make decision in one-off situations. It emphasises that serious decisions about sharing should be made be appropriately trained people at a senior level and not simply left to low grade staff without appropriate experience.

In relation to the review of data sharing arrangements it advises that these should cover:

---

[35] See below.
[36] See *www.justice.gov.uk* for the Ministry of Justice guidance for central Government departments on the use of PIAs.
[37] See *www.cabinetoffice.gov.uk* for the government data standards catalogue, *www.standards.esd. org.uk* for the equivalent for local government and *www.connectingforhealth.nhs.uk* for the NHS information standards.

- the continued justification for the sharing;
- the terms of the notices being used and any sharing protocol;
- the governance procedures and the data quality and retention safeguards; and
- individual access and complaints handling.

The good practices specifically recommended are the allocation of responsibility for information governance in respect of the data sharing to a senior responsible individual; the use of documented data sharing agreements; carrying out Privacy Impact Assessments before entering into data sharing agreements even where such Assessments are not mandatory (as they are for central Government departments); requiring common standards to allow interoperability between systems when procuring IT standards to ensure that sharing can take place; and checking on the quality of the data being shared from time to time.

Individuals' rights

25–32   In this section the code reminds controllers of the rights of subject access and objection in particular as these are the ones that arise particularly in the context of data sharing. It alerts controllers to the fact that they may be unable to make decisions on disclosure and the possible application of exemptions without the input of others and they should be prepared for this. It flags the need to be able to deal with queries or complaints and also encourages controllers who find that a proposal to share raises negative comments to respond in a positive manner and examine how far those are justified and whether other options can be considered.

The good practices specifically recommended are the provision of a single point for individuals to direct their access requests to allow them to access data shared across multiple organisations from one request; the provision of ways for individuals to see what data about them has been shared without a formal request for example by on line access; the adoption of a procedure to deal with queries or complaints and a process to analyse any comments to increase the understanding of public attitudes and the use of focus groups by large scale organisations to help them understand any concerns of individuals in relation to data sharing.

Things to avoid

25–33   This section summarises some of the bad practices which are warned against in the body of the code but reiterates that the adoption of these practices could lead to regulatory action against the controller. This is a clear warning from the Commissioner and for that reason controllers should review this list with particular care. The offending practices are:

- misleading individuals, for example not telling individuals of an intended sharing because objections are anticipated;
- sharing excessive or irrelevant information about people;
- sharing personal data where there is no need to do so for example where anonymised data could have been used;

- being careless or reckless about accuracy or the quality of the information shared;
- using incompatible information systems leading to corruption or degradation of the data; and
- having inadequate security leading to the loss or unauthorised disclosure of data.

The Commissioner's powers and penalties

In this section the powers of the Commissioner to take formal actions or conduct mandatory assessments of public sector organisations are set out.   25–34

Notification

There is a short section reminding organisations of their responsibilities to ensure that the register of notification is updated for any data sharing.   25–35

Freedom of information

The section notes that most, if not all, public sector bodies involved in data sharing are subject to freedom of information law and are therefore required to publish information in accord with their publication schemes and to respond to questions under the relevant access legislation. The Commissioner has introduced a model publication scheme for public authorities which is referenced. One of the classes of information to be published by public authorities covers policies and procedures (class 5). The code reminds public authorities that this should include policies and procedures relating to data sharing including details of those organisations with which information is shared.   25–36

The section also reminds organisations that any data shared with a public authority will be held by that authority and subject to requests under access legislation and points out that this should be drawn to the attention of private bodies which share with public bodies in particular.

Data sharing agreements

In this section organisations are advised to enter into data-sharing agreements as a matter of good practice and to contribute to the proper governance of the exercise. The Commissioner explains that he considers that an agreement should cover the following areas: 25–37

- purpose of the data sharing initiative;
- the identity of the organisations engaged in the sharing;
- the data items to be shared;
- the legal basis for sharing relied upon by public bodies;
- access and individual rights; and
- governance arrangements covering:
  (i)   limits on the datasets to be shared,
  (ii) safeguards to ensure accuracy,

(iii) ensuring that data is compatible,

(iv) common rules on retention and deletion,

(v) technical and security arrangments including for the transmission of the data,

(vi) procedures for handling DPA or FOIA requests,

(vii) review, and

(viii) termination.

It is also suggested that additional material such as guidance notes on the DPA or model forms should be included as appendices.

Other materials

25–38   The code also includes sample data sharing request and decision forms, a set of checklists and a number of case studies as well as a glossary and information on the Act.

MINISTRY OF JUSTICE GUIDANCE

25–39   In most areas relevant to data protection we have confined our commentary on guidance materials to that issued by the Commissioner. Exceptionally in this area we have commented on the Ministry of Justice materials as this set of materials provides the definitive Guidance on this topic.

Background

25–40   The first guidance on the impact of the requirement to process personal data lawfully in the public sector was given by the Data Protection Registrar in a publication called Private Lives and Public Powers issued in 1997. This examined the equivalent provisions of the 1984 and advised that public law restrictions on the powers of public authorities and obligations of confidentiality had a restrictive impact on the uses and disclosures that could legitimately be made of personal data in the public sector. In the Legal Guidance issued by the Commissioner under the 1998 Act in 2001 the analysis set out in Private Lives and Public Powers was largely repeated. However, in approximately 2000 the Commissioner agreed not to issue further guidance in this area, and that responsibility for such guidance should lie with the relevant government department. This was a response to the Government's focus on the data sharing agenda and an implicit acknowledgement that the advice of the Commissioner had acted as a brake on the rush to share more data among public bodies. The Commissioner also altered his approach in areas where he had previously taken a view that the law would be restrictive, for example, in December 2006, the Commissioner re-considered his long-standing advice that personal data derived from Council Tax functions could only be used for those functions, and any other use was unlawful; instead taking the stance that a decision on that point was not for the Commissioner but was for local authorities to make for themselves. The approach taken by the Commissioner's office is now that public authorities should take their own advice on issues of vires and more general public law issues and he will restrict his advice on data sharing to the effect of the Act itself. This is the line taken in the Code of Practice.

Detailed guidance on data sharing for public bodies is now issued by the Ministry of Justice as part of its role in overseeing the area of data protection and information law including the legislative and non-legislative framework for data sharing across Government. The guidance was re-issued in 2010 as part of the Ministry's "Data Sharing Protocol" (DSP). This is a set of guidance produced by the Ministry for any government department or other public sector body to provide "practical help when they start new projects which may involve the sharing of personal data".

It might have been anticipated that this Ministry guidance would have been subsumed into the statutory Data Sharing Code of Practice produced by the Commissioner in 2011 however it has not been and, as noted earlier, the Code scrupulously eschews any detailed discussion of the wider legal context for the public sector. It remains therefore that any Government department and indeed most public bodies considering a data sharing project will look for its primary legal guidance to the Ministry of Justice and the Code will presumably be of secondary importance in that area.

Guidance—overview

The first legal guidance, *Public Sector Data Sharing—Guidance on the Law*, was issued in November 2003 by the Department for Constitutional Affairs. It was updated, but little changed, in 2007. In the introduction to that Guidance the Secretary of State, Lord Falconer, made clear the view of the Government that public law restrictions did not impose constraints on the increased sharing of personal data:

25–41

> "Our view is that there is no inherent incompatibility between the increasingly ambitious scope of public service delivery and the legal and administrative conditions that have to be me in order to share data to help achieve that goal. The law, rightly, puts in place safeguards for the use of individuals' data and there are organizational costs in meeting those conditions. In a democratic society, it is important that those safeguards exist and are properly applied. This does not mean however that further and better uses of information should not be made in order to serve the best interests of the individual, of groups and of society more widely. An appropriate balance must be struck in he specific circumstances that surround each service or policy".[38]

Although there was a clear policy commitment to encourage wider sharing of data the legal advice given in 2003 and revised in 2007 was very similar to that given by the Commissioner. It included a detailed view of the impact of administrative law and other constraints and gave weight to the privacy interests of individuals.

In 2010 the legal guidance was reviewed by the Ministry of Justice and re-issued as part of the Data Sharing Protocol. The revised legal guidance takes a somewhat more generous view of the powers of public bodies to share data than

---

[38] Foreword by the Secretary of State, November 2003.

the Commissioner's original guidance. Overall we would agree with this approach; it can be argued that the original guidance from both the Registrar and the Department for Constitutional Affairs was overly prudent and overestimated the impact that the Human Rights Act would have in the UK. Nevertheless there are one or two areas in which, in our respectful submission, the guidance goes possibly too far and this is the subject of commentary below. There is also something less than comfortable about the lead role of the Ministry in providing the authoritative guidance on the topic.

The Commissioner's enforcement strategy has also been to refrain from taking action on data sharing although he reserves the possibility that the Commissioner would take action if there was real detriment to individuals. As far as we are able to ascertain no actions have been taken in this area.

Comment

25–42   Given the enthusiasm of successive Governments for the sharing of personal data among public bodies and the widening of its uses the fact that the Commissioner has nor taken the lead in providing guidance in this area seems less than satisfactory. Data sharing in the public sector involves the biggest area of disclosures of personal data in our society with the most potential to impact on individuals. While the Ministry of Justice's DSP is an excellent tool the Ministry not an independent regulator; the influential guidance and advice on this important topic is being given by a central Government Department which inevitably shares the policy agenda of the rest of Government.

Given the importance of the DSP, we have flagged its contents and specifically the legal guidance here as well as the Data Sharing Code issued by the Commissioner. The meaning of the term "unlawfully" is examined in Ch.6 and any practitioner considering a data-sharing exercise is also referred to that discussion.

The DSP consists of:

- a template—that is a guide to the factors that should be considered by those setting up data sharing projects;
- a flowchart about the process of sharing data;
- definitions of terms used in the Protocol;
- the Cabinet Office Guidance on Information Assurance and Information Security;
- information on when and how to complete a PIA;
- minimum mandatory measures for information security from the Data Handling Review 2008;
- guidance on establishing who is the data controller and the data processor when sharing data;
- guidance on the main responsibilities for Government Departments in their role as data controllers under the Data Protection Act 1998;
- data sharing legal guidance for use by lawyers, and other interested professionals working in the public sector (including those working for local authorities); and
- links to useful sites or sources of additional information.

Legal Guidance

The Guidance is written with reference to the laws of England and Wales, although certain statutes (the Human Rights Act 1998 and the Data Protection Act 1998) apply equally to Scotland. The aim of the Guidance is to clarify the legal circumstances in which data sharing powers of public bodies can be exercised and bring about a consistency of approach within the public sector on data sharing. It covers:

25–43

- an overview of the legal framework;
- powers to share;
- the Data Protection Act;
- the Human Rights Act;
- common law and statutory restrictions on the disclosure of data; and
- practical and other issues.

Unlike the earlier version of the Guidance, the current one footnotes case references but does not necessarily explain what the facts of the case. However, it gives examples of circumstances where particular rules would apply which is very helpful.

DATA SHARING IN OTHER AREAS OF THE PUBLIC SECTOR

Political background and proposals for statutory provisions

While this is not legally influential the development of policy and approaches in this area can be useful when making risk decisions on whether or not to share data and for that reason we have set out a brief history below.

25–44

In April 2003 the Cabinet Office issued a report on privacy and data-sharing which started from the presumption that any disclosures or uses for "new" purposes would be based on the consent of citizens.[39] In November 2003 the Department of Constitutional Affairs issued the first version of the legal guidance which set out a detailed exposition of the legal issues which are involved where information obtained for one purpose is intended to be used for another or disclosed for use by another public body. The Guidance applied largely the same legal analysis as the Commissioner had done in the earlier guidance materials.[40]

Over the same period however there was an increasing development of policy in Government to share more information as a way of transforming public services. In 2005 the Cabinet Office delivered Transformational Government enabled by technology[41] for consultation. The main focus of the paper was on the development of information technology solutions to streamline and improve

---

[39] PIU Report, Cabinet Office.
[40] See DCA Guidance and Toolkit on the DCA website.
[41] Cm.6683, November 2005.

public services while making savings from a more effective use of technology. It flagged data sharing as well as identity management as essential elements of the effective delivery of shared services:

> "Data sharing is integral to transforming services and reducing administrative burdens on citizens and businesses. But privacy rights and public trust must be retained. There will be a new Ministerial focus on finding and communicating the balance between maintaining the privacy of the individual and delivering more efficient, higher quality services with minimal bureaucracy".

This signalled a level of concern that the law had a restrictive impact on the potential sharing of information between public sector bodies. The position of Government appeared to have shifted considerably since the publication of the PIU Report and moved to the position that the consent of individuals should **not** be required before their information is shared (apart for some sensitive data categories) and there should be a presumption that personal data would be available for a wide range of public sector uses. The Ministerial focus on finding the correct balance gave rise to the next major policy document, somewhat grandiosely, entitled a Vision Statement for Data Sharing, issued in September 2006 by the Department of Constitutional Affairs. This committed Government to achieve more sharing of information including between public sector organisations and the public and private sectors. It made clear that some changes to the law were planned to facilitate this but no change to the Data Protection Act.

In June 2007 Gordon Brown replaced Tony Blair as Prime Minister. In a speech on Liberty at the start of the new Parliamentary session in October 2007 he announced a review of the legal framework for the sharing of information. The context of the review was a refreshed commitment to respect for private life. Among the liberties he listed as being ones in which "we can start immediately to make changes in our constitution and laws to safeguard and extend the liberties of our citizens" were:

> "in respecting privacy in the home, new rights against arbitrary intrusion; in a world of new technology, new rights to protect your private information and respecting the need for freedom from arbitrary treatment, new provision for independent judicial scrutiny and open parliamentary oversight."

He went on to announce the review in the following terms,

> "And it is the British way to insist that we do all we can to protect individual citizens and their rights.
> So we must always ensure that there is—as we have legislated on ID cards—proper accountability to Parliament, with limits to use of the data enshrined in parliamentary legislation, the exercise of responsibilities in this area subject to regular and open scrutiny by Parliament, with detailed reports on any new powers published and laid before it.
> These are issues not just for us but for others—and I know that similar debates are going on around the world.
> Jack Straw and I have asked the Information Commissioner, Richard Thomas and Doctor Mark Walport, Director of the Wellcome Trust, to undertake a review of the framework for the use of information—in both the private and public sector—to assess whether it is right for today's landscape and strikes the right balance—giving

people the protection they are entitled to, while allowing them to make the most of the opportunities which are being opened up by the new information age".

The review had the strange distinction of being concerned with a topic which was of little popular interest when it started but significant public interest by the time it finished. The catalyst for the topic reaching popular consciousness being the loss of two discs by HMRC in October 2007 which contained the entire child benefit database. As a result the whole issue of how data was being handled in Government and the public sector generally shot up the political agenda.

The review reported in July 2008 and made 19 recommendations, including a recommendation that there should be a specific power for the Secretary of State to remove barriers to information sharing. The relevant comment from the report was as follows:

"Legal barriers to information sharing are often in place for good reasons and serve to prevent inappropriate access or disclosure of people's personal details, such as HM Revenue and Customs strict statutory duty to maintain taxpayer confidentiality.

Nevertheless, we received evidence that necessary, proportionate and above all beneficial information sharing is at times frustrated, although there were few specific examples of situations where essential data sharing was being prevented by the legal framework. Indeed in its submission to the review the Welsh Assembly Government stated that 'We have always found a basis for sharing personal information where it is considered necessary'."[42]

Despite the absence of clear evidence of cases of information sharing being prevented by the legal framework the review recommended the creation of a new fast-track procedure to allow the Secretary of State to make an Order to be subject to affirmative resolution in both House to remove or modify any legal barrier to data sharing by:

- repealing or amending other primary legislation;
- changing any other rule of law, for example the application of the law of confidence; or
- creating a new power to share where that power is currently absent.[43]

The recommendation was then taken forward in the Coroners and Justice Bill 2009, which would have provided for a designated authority to make an "information-sharing order" which would enable any person to share information which consisted of or included personal data where necessary to achieve a policy objective. The draft clause included safeguards and required the order to be proportionate to the policy objective and strikes a fair balance between the public interest and the interests of any person affected by it. There were also provisions for the Commissioner to be involved and consultation with those affected. The clause had been agreed by the Commissioner before being included in the Bill however once it was made public it evoked a significant negative response from a range of civil society organisations. In the face of the response the Commissioner withdrew his support and the Home Secretary was placed in the difficult position

---

[42] Data Sharing Review, paras 6.20 and 6.21.
[43] Data Sharing Review report, Recommendation 8(a), para.8.41.

of losing the support of the Commissioner. The clause was withdrawn and replaced by the provisions enabling the Code of Practice described in this chapter.

ADDITIONAL MATERIALS

25–45   There are no additional materials for this chapter.

CHAPTER 26

Freedom Of Information And Personal Data

Sue Cullen

INTRODUCTION

Since coming into force on January 1, 2005, the Freedom of Information Act   26–01
2000 (FOIA) has had an impact on data protection which has gone well beyond
what was anticipated. Thanks to the FOIA, we now know far more about what
constitutes personal data, especially in relation to statistical information; about
fairness considerations under principle 1; and how the justification in condition 6
of Sch.2 works in detail. Furthermore, the detailed and robust procedures for
access under the FOIA contrast favourably with the regime for subject access
under the DPA and prefigure the new requirements for procedures for exercising
data subject rights contained in art.12 of the proposed General Data Protection
Regulation, which is at the time of writing being debated in Europe.

The right of subject access under the DPA swept up several existing rights of
individuals to their own information in specific areas, such as health records, and
introduced a general right of subject access to information. The FOIA similarly
followed earlier limited and specific rights of access to information held by some
public sector bodies, such as Local Government, and the non-statutory Code of
Practice on Access to Government Information, and introduced a general right of
access to all information held by all public authorities. This was more radical than
original introduction of the subject access right in 1984 because the aim of the
FOIA was to introduce more open government based on mutual trust, and so
change the balance between the institutions of the state and the public. Freedom
of information is a fast-developing area of law: not only is there a steady stream
of cases originating from decisions of the Commissioner, the Tribunals and the
courts, but it is also affected by the Government's transparency agenda and the
changes introduced by the Protection of Freedoms Act 2012. In its post-
legislative scrutiny of the FOIA published on July 26, 2012 (the FOIA Review)
the House of Commons justice committee has recommended some minor changes
to the FOIA regime.

The obvious impact of the FOIA on data protection is that in consequence of a   26–02
general right of access to all information held by a public authority there is now a
right of public access to all the personal data and other personal information
which it holds—whether relating to an applicant, or to anybody else. This has
huge implications for personal privacy. The balance between the DPA and the
FOIA is governed by an exemption for personal data in the FOIA, but in order to

achieve this balance it was necessary to amend the DPA to ensure that all personal information on record (that is, including all paper records) could be covered as personal data in the hands of a public authority.

In addition to the FOIA, there is a parallel access regime covering access to environmental information under the Environmental Information Regulations 2004 (EIR), which also came into force on January 1, 2005. Because freedom of information was a matter devolved to the Scottish Parliament, the FOIA extends only to England, Wales and Northern Ireland. The Scottish Parliament enacted the Freedom of Information (Scotland) Act 2002 (FOISA) which covers freedom of information in relation to Scottish public authorities in similar, but not identical, terms.

26–03   This chapter addresses the following:

- an overview of the FOIA and the EIR, referred to as the access regimes;
- consideration of the effect of the access regimes on subject access;
- treatment of requests for access to third party personal data, and detailed consideration of the exemptions from the duty to provide it in response; and
- key decisions of the Commissioner, the First Tier Tribunal (Information Rights) which is referred to as the Tribunal, the Upper Tribunal and the courts.

The extension of the definition of personal data and associated amendments to the DPA imposed by the FOIA are mentioned briefly, but are considered in Ch.11—Subject Access.

SUMMARY OF THE IMPACT OF THE ACCESS REGIMES ON
26–04 ## PERSONAL DATA

(a) In the hands of a public authority, *all recorded information counts as data* for the purposes of the DPA because of the new category (e) data added by the FOIA.

(b) An individual's right of access to his own information under the DPA is extended by the FOIA to include access to the new category (e) data, subject to some limitations.

(c) There is a general right of access by any person to all third party personal information on record with a public authority.

(d) The exemption for third party personal data in the FOIA at s.40 covers all third party personal information on record with a public authority as follows:

(i)   A disclosure to the public of any third party personal data which would breach any data protection principle is absolutely exempt.

(ii) Subject to a public interest test, if the third party has objected to disclosure by exercising his right in DPA s.10, it is exempt.

(iii) Subject to a public interest test, any third party personal data which the third party would not get under his subject access right because of a DPA exemption is also exempt under the FOIA.

There is no express obligation in the FOIA for a public authority to apply any FOIA exemption; the effective obligation to apply the s.40 exemption in derives from a data controller's obligation under s.4(4) of the DPA to apply the data protection principles to all processing of personal data, which obviously includes any disclosure of personal data under the FOIA by a public authority data controller. The s.40 exemption effectively dovetails the FOIA right with the DPA so that the application of the data protection principles determines the disclosure of personal data under the FOIA, but there is no express exemption for disclosures (whether or not of personal data) which would contravene art.8 of the European Convention on Human Rights and Fundamental Freedoms (ECHRFF).

26–05

RELATION BETWEEN THE FOIA AND THE EIR

The FOIA has no basis in European law and was voluntarily introduced by the Westminster Parliament to meet a growing demand for transparency in the public sector. The Scottish Parliament followed two years later with the FOISA. Nevertheless, there was EU law relating to public access to information under Directive 90/313/EEC, but this was confined to access to environmental information and took effect in the UK by the Environmental Information Regulations 1992. At the time of the passage of the FOIA in 2000 the UK was due to implement the rights of access in the Convention on Access to Information, Public Participation in Decision Making and Access to Justice in Environmental Matters of June 25, 1998 (the Aarhus Convention), and accordingly the Secretary of State was empowered to make new regulations for environmental information under s.74 of the FOIA. In the event, however, the EU dealt with Aarhus by replacing Directive 90/313/EEC with a new Directive 2003/4/EC, referred to as the 2003 Directive, on public access to environmental information, which meets this element of the requirements of Aarhus. The Government therefore implemented the 2003 Directive using the European Communities Act 1972 to create the EIR, and the old Environmental Information Regulations 1992 were repealed. The effect was to implement the relevant Convention obligations at the same time as those of the 2003 Directive, but the resulting production of the EIR at the last minute (they were made on December 21, 2004 and came into effect 11 days later) seems to be responsible for a number of drafting errors including at least one serious defect in the treatment of personal data—see paras 26-40—26-41, below.

26–06

The two access regimes operate side by side, and FOIA accommodates the EIR by the exemption for environmental information at s.39. Environmental information is very widely defined and access to any such information must be dealt with under the EIR, not under the FOIA. Although the EIR are in many ways similar to the FOIA there are a number of important differences arising both from their origin in a directive and because they relate only to a defined class of information. In relation to the treatment of requests for personal data the two regimes impose provisions which achieve largely the same practical result, mostly by way of identical clauses.

OVERVIEW OF THE FREEDOM OF INFORMATION ACT 2000[1]

26–07   Following gradual implementation of the provisions relating to publication schemes in the period between November 2002 and June 2004, the FOIA was brought fully into force on 1 January 2005.

Application of the FOIA

26–08   The FOIA applies in England, Wales and Northern Ireland but does not apply to bodies subject to the Scottish Government. The FOISA was passed by the Scottish Parliament on April 24, 2002 and received Royal Assent on May 28, 2002. It came into force at the same time as the FOIA and the EIR, on 1 January 2005. Although the FOIA and the FOISA are very similar in structure and general approach there are a number of differences between them. The FOISA provisions dealing with personal data are briefly outlined at para.28 below.

Who is a public authority under the FOIA?

26–09   The FOIA applies to public authorities. "Public authority" means a body listed in Sch.1, or designated by order of the Secretary of State under s.5, or a publicly-owned company as defined in s.6.[2] The bodies listed in Sch.1 cover: central government, which includes all government departments, the Houses of Parliament and National Assemblies, and the armed forces except the special forces; local government; the national health service; maintained schools and other educational establishments; the police; and a host of non-departmental public bodies listed in Pt VI of the Schedule. Courts and tribunals are not public authorities included within the FOIA, and records created for specific proceedings are exempt in the hands of FOIA public authorities. Some public bodies, such as the BBC and the Bank of England, are subject to the FOIA only in respect of part of their information; the implications of this are considered further at para.61 below. There are provisions enabling Sch.1 to be amended so that the list of bodies is kept up to date, and s.5 enables the Secretary of State to extend coverage to certain private sector bodies.[3] In November 2011 the Government extended the scope of FOIA for the first time, to include the Association of Chief Police Officers (ACPO), university admissions body UCAS, and the Financial Ombudsman Service and proposes to extend it further to a number of other bodies such as the Advertising Standards Authority and The Law Society. In addition the provisions covering publicly-owned companies under s.6 have been extended by the Protection of Freedoms Act 2012 (not yet in force at the time of writing) to include publicly-owned companies co-owned by two or more bodies

---

[1] More information can be found on the website of the Information Commissioner at *www.ico.gov.uk* [Accessed October 8, 2012] and the Ministry of Justice site at *www.justice.gov.uk* [Accessed October 8, 2012].

[2] FOIA s.3.

[3] FOIA s.5.

from the "wider public sector". All recorded information held by or on behalf of a public authority is available for access under the FOIA.[4]

How requests must be made

Any person may make a request for information. A request must be in writing, state the name of the applicant and an address for correspondence, and describe the information requested.[5] Since it is the accepted principle of freedom of information that it is applicant-blind, given that disclosure of information under the FOIA is to the public at large rather than to the particular requester, the name and address do not have to identify the person making the request as long as the particulars provided enable the authority to deal with the response. Nevertheless, the identity of the requester could be relevant in some circumstances, for example where personal data of the applicant might be involved, or where the request might be considered vexatious. Pseudonymous requests are therefore normally acceptable, unlike requests for subject access under the DPA. Writing includes electronic communication as long as it is legible and is capable of being used for subsequent reference. It is possible for requests and responses to be made using social media, such as Twitter and Facebook, as well as text messaging although email is the usual form of correspondence. The applicant does not have to refer to the FOIA in his request nor state that the request is made under the FOIA. It follows that public authorities must treat any written request for information as an FOIA request unless it is clear that it is not. A public authority cannot in any event ignore unsuccessful attempts to make a request since it has a duty to help applicants, discussed at para.19 below.[6]

26–10

Obligation to respond to requests for information

On receiving a valid request the public authority becomes subject to a twofold obligation:

26–11

(a) to inform the applicant in writing whether or not the authority holds information of the description specified in the request ("the duty to confirm or deny"); and

(b) if that is the case, to communicate the information to the applicant.[7]

These obligations are then qualified by any applicable exemptions. Where an authority releases information under the FOIA it must do so without constraint or conditions. A release is equivalent to placing the information into the public domain. The information will remain subject to any intellectual property rights which can be asserted by the authority or anyone else, so a requester who wishes to make a re-use of the information will have to apply to the owner of the intellectual property for a licence. In the case of a public authority which is subject to the Re-Use of Public Sector Information Regulations 2005, those

---

[4] FOIA ss.1 and 84.
[5] FOIA s.8.
[6] FOIA s.16.
[7] FOIA s.1.

regulations would apply to any request for re-use, and the official recommendation is that the authority should make use of the Open Government Licence provided by The National Archives.

Costs under the FOIA

26–12 The position in relation to costs incurred by public authorities under the FOIA has often been misunderstood, not least because the Freedom of Information and Data Protection (Appropriate Limit and Fees) Regulations 2004 (SI 2004/3244) (referred to as the Fees Regulations) were brought in only three weeks or so before the FOIA came into force—they were laid before Parliament on December 9, 2004. This was because until the autumn of 2004 it had been proposed that there should be provisions enabling public authorities to recover a proportion of the costs incurred in connection with responding to requests—indeed this is the model followed in Scotland. Then it was decided that although a fee could be still be charged for communication costs, no fee could be charged for supplying the information. Section 12 of the FOIA provides exemption where the cost of responding to a request would exceed a certain amount and the main function of the Fees Regulations is to provide a mechanism for determining whether this cap, called "the appropriate limit", would be reached.

The appropriate limit for public authorities listed in Pt 1 of Sch.1 (central government) is £600, and for any other public authority it is £450. The Fees Regulations stipulate at reg.4(3) that the only activities which may be taken into account in estimating whether the appropriate limit would be exceeded are: determining whether the information is held; locating it; retrieving it; and extracting it. "Extracting" does not include redacting exempt information (*Chief Constable of South Yorkshire Police v Information Commissioner*[8]) and staff time is to be costed at £25 per hour. No actual costs can be recovered under this element of the Fees Regulations; if the estimate exceeds the appropriate limit, then the authority is not obliged to supply the information and can apply the exemption in s.12, but if the estimate is below the appropriate limit then, in the absence of any other FOIA exemption, the authority must supply the information without charging for it. The only permitted charge for a response to a request is the recovery of communication costs under s.9 FOIA, and the Fees Regulations restrict these costs to postage and packing, including copying and putting the information into the form preferred by the applicant under s.11 but with the significant exclusion of any element to cover staff time. Consequently these costs are not usually worth recovering so in practice a fee is very rarely charged in FOIA requests. Where a charge is made, the authority serves a fees notice upon the applicant who must pay it within three months or the request lapses. The FOIA Review recommends a limited reduction in the amount of time an organisation has to spend on each request to reduce the burden on public bodies to allow them to take greater advantage of the costs exemption.

---

[8] (2011) EWHC 44 (Admin).

Time for compliance with requests

Public authorities must respond to requests within 20 working days following the date of receipt, but there is provision for the Secretary of State to set a longer the period of up to 60 working days, and a timescale of 60 working days has been set for the armed forces and schools. While the EIR allow a general extension of time for complex or voluminous requests, the FOIA makes no such general provision but does allow a longer period where a public authority is considering the application of the public interest test (PIT) to a qualified exemption (described at paras 26-16 and 26-17, below). Section 10(3) merely says that in these circumstances the authority need not comply until such time as is "reasonable in the circumstances", but note that there is of course no public interest test applicable to the main exemption for third party personal data (where disclosure under FOIA would breach any DPA principle) so this extension will not normally apply where release of personal data is being considered. Where an authority has served a fees notice (see above) the 20 working day clock stops until the fee is paid. The FOIA Review recommends that the Commissioner's guideline of another maximum 20 working days to consider the PIT should become statutory.

26–13

The exemptions regime in the FOIA

In comparison with the DPA exemptions, the FOIA exemptions are more numerous and generally wider. This is in part because the exemptions regime in the FOIA serves a number of different functions, only one of which is to afford secrecy for information which ought, in the public interest, not to be disclosed. The structure of the FOIA is that *all* information held by a public authority is available for access and the only justification for not complying with a request is the application of an FOIA exemption. This contrasts with the EIR, under which some environmental information is not covered in the first place (for example the EIR do not apply to an authority acting in a judicial or legislative capacity) or there is no duty to make it available on request (such as the personal data of the applicant).

26–14

As has been seen, under the FOIA an authority has a twofold obligation: to say whether or not requested information is held, and to communicate it to the applicant. If the authority wishes to refuse to comply with either duty then it must apply an exemption to justify that refusal, and from the point of view of the structure of the regime and the general procedure for handling requests and refusals it makes no difference whether the reason for refusal is because a response would be too costly (s.12), or the information is already in the public domain (s.21), or it is a state secret (s.23). It is apparent, therefore, that the exemptions regime in the FOIA covers not only disclosures which it would not be in the public interest to make public, such as those which would breach confidence (s.41), but also those which are already the subject of another access regime (public registers under s.21; personal data of the applicant under s.40(1)) and those with which a public authority ought not to have to deal as being too burdensome (such as repeat or vexatious requests under s.14).

The FOIA exemptions are, except for the exemptions at ss.12 and 14, further categorised into exemptions which require a preliminary harm test, as opposed to

26–15

class exemptions which are immediately engaged when information comes within them, and also as exemptions which require a PIT (these are called "qualified exemptions"), as opposed to absolute exemptions. While a "harm test" exemption will almost always require, additionally, a PIT, and an absolute exemption, besides not requiring a PIT, will hardly ever be subject to a harm test, there are some class exemptions which nevertheless require a PIT even though they have not been the subject of a preliminary harm test—examples are s.30 (criminal investigations); s.42 (legal privilege); and s.40(4) (third party personal data which are exempt from subject access under the DPA). A "harm test" exemption is usually identified by wording which states that information is exempt if disclosure would prejudice the particular interest specified, whereas a class exemption will merely describe the exempt information as information of a particular kind, such as constituting a trade secret (s.43(1)), or as relating to communications with the Sovereign (s.37(1)(a)), or as being contained in a court record (s.32). Where a harm test is required, the exemption cannot be engaged until a likely result of harm to the specified interest can be demonstrated; only then can the authority go on to apply the PIT in order to establish whether it can apply the exemption.

Except for the exemptions at ss.14 and 21 all the FOIA exemptions can be applied to the s.1(1)(a) duty to say whether information is held (duty to confirm or deny), as well as to the s.1(1)(b) duty to communicate it (disclosure). Note that while some of the exemptions in the DPA require a harm test, none of them require a PIT. The exemption for personal data at s.40 FOIA is summarised at para.26 below.

Qualified exemptions and the public interest test

26–16   There is a list of absolute exemptions at FOIA s.2(3), which include, among others, exemptions for information which is accessible to the requester by other means, information relating to the security services, personal information, information provided in confidence and information which the authority is barred from disclosing under other legislation or by order of a court. All of the other exemptions in Pt II (which excludes ss.12 and 14) are qualified, or non-absolute, because they require a PIT. The PIT, in relation to a specified qualified exemption, can be applied to the duty to confirm or deny holding the information as well as to the duty to disclose it. The requirement for a PIT means that even though the exemption can be engaged because the disclosure of the information would come within it (such as by causing prejudice to the economic interests of the United Kingdom, or merely by consisting of legally privileged information), the exemption cannot be applied unless the public interest in maintaining the exemption is greater than the public interest in disclosure. The test is whether:

> "in all the circumstances of the case the public interest in maintaining the exemption [or the exclusion of the duty to confirm or deny] outweighs the public interest in disclosing the information".[9]

---

[9] FOIA s.2.

and the starting point for the authority (although not expressly stated, as in the EIR) is the presumption that the public interest favours disclosure.

Most qualified exemptions also require a preliminary harm test, and very often   **26–17** the relevant factors which will demonstrate the likelihood of the harm which disclosure might cause to the interest specified in the exemption will also weigh in the public interest balance by showing that disclosure would additionally not be in the public interest. Nevertheless, the tests are different and must be conducted separately: first the harm test to engage the exemption, and, if successful, then the PIT in order to be able to apply the exemption. Therefore the PIT operates to ensure that disclosure is made where it is on balance in the public interest despite the fact that it has already been demonstrated that disclosure will likely harm the interest protected by the exemption. General public interest factors in favour of disclosure include accountability in spending public money, transparency in the decision-making process, and public health and safety. It is surprising that the exemption for environmental information at s.39 of the FOIA is subject to a PIT, given that its purpose is to ensure that such information is dealt with under the EIR in accordance with the 2003 Directive, and that reg.5(6) EIR expressly disapplies any law that would prevent disclosure of environmental information in accordance with the EIR. As will be seen, this is not the only peculiarity of the requirement to apply a PIT to some exemptions in the context of the EIR.

Refusals

Unlike the DPA regime for subject access, the FOIA prescribes a detailed   **26–18** procedure for refusals which applies to any withholding of requested information, on any ground permitted, and also to the duty to confirm or deny whether information is held. FOIA s.17 requires a written refusal notice to be given to the applicant within the 20 working day period, in which the authority must:

(a)   state the fact of refusal, which requires the authority to be clear about exactly what information is being refused;

(b)   specify the exemption(s) being applied (which means that it must be made clear what exemption applies to which information);

(c)   state (if that would not be otherwise apparent) why the exemption(s) applies;

(d)   if any of the exemptions being applied require a public interest test then state the reasons for claiming why the public interest in maintaining the exemption outweighs the public interest in disclosing the information; and

(e)   tell the requester of the authority's complaints procedure (if any) and of his right to appeal this refusal to the Commissioner for a decision under s.50.

A dissatisfied requester does not have to pay any fee to the authority for his complaint to be investigated, nor to the Commissioner for a decision notice, and this coupled with the rigorous refusal and appeals procedure has contributed to the torrent of ICO decisions on the FOIA, as well as to the numerous decisions of the Tribunal, and of the Upper Tribunal and the courts, in stark contrast to the outcomes under the DPA. The procedure for refusals under reg.14 of the EIR operates in the same way, apart from the authority's statutory duty to reconsider its decisions in reg.11. The FOIA Review considered, but rejected, suggestions that fees should be charged for internal reviews and for appeals to the Commissioner, but recommends that there should be a statutory time limit for internal reviews.

Duty to help requesters, and the s.45 Code of Practice on handling requests

26–19   The FOIA places public authorities under a duty to provide advice and assistance to those making or proposing to make requests for information. This duty, under s.16, is limited by what it would be reasonable to expect them to do and more specifically by the declaration at s.16(2) that an authority which conforms with the s.45 Code of Practice (the s.45 Code) is to be taken to have discharged this duty.

Section 45 of the FOIA requires the Secretary of State to issue a code of practice providing guidance to public authorities:

> "as to the practice which it would, in his opinion, be desirable for them to follow in connection with the discharge of the authority's functions under Part I".[10]

According to the Ministry of Justice, on whose website the code can be found, this code of practice

> "provides clear guidance on providing advice and assistance to applicants, transferring requests to other authorities, consulting third parties, the use of confidentiality clauses in contracts and the provision of internal complaints procedures."

There are practical suggestions for clarifying unclear requests, and advising applicants whose requests are likely to be refused on costs grounds, and a reminder that the provision of advice and assistance is also affected by the requirements of specified anti-discrimination legislation (now consolidated in the Equality Act 2010). The code was revised and re-issued in November 2004. At the time of writing we understand that the Government may be about to put out a revised code for public consultation.

The effect of the code may also be seen as bringing the FOIA into line with certain elements of the EIR enacted four years later, and also of the FOISA enacted two years later. For example, the FOIA does not require an authority to review its own decisions, although this is a requirement of the EIR and of the FOISA, but given that the s.45 Code says that each authority should have a complaints procedure and reconsider its decisions there is no difference in practice between the regimes. Similarly, the EIR (but not the FOIA or the FOISA) require an authority to transfer requests to other authorities that hold requested information, and the code contains detailed provisions regarding the transfer of such requests. The effect is to iron out some of the practical differences for

---

[10] FOIAs.45(1).

authorities operating (as practically all FOIA authorities must) both under the FOIA and the EIR. Detailed consideration of the contents of the s.45 Code is given at paras 26-143—26-145 below.

Obligations in relation to records keeping—the s.46 Code of Practice

The FOIA provides at s.46 for a further code of practice (the s.46 Code) to be issued by the Secretary of State providing guidance to relevant authorities as to

> "the practice which it would, in his opinion, be desirable for them to follow in connection with the keeping, management and destruction of their records."[11]

26–20

"Relevant authorities" include not only public authorities under the FOIA, but also bodies, such as GCHQ, excluded from the FOIA but subject to the Public Records Acts. This code was re-issued in July 2009, largely the production of The National Archives, and is available on the Ministry of Justice website. It brings together records standards for both paper and electronic records, and sets out standards for the handling of records from inception of the record to final destruction or long-term preservation. The s.46 code cites the importance of records management to the authority's discharge of its obligations under the FOIA and the EIR, but also stresses its importance in relation to compliance with the DPA. The standards cited as supporting the code are British Standards Institution standards, such as BS15489—records management, and BS 10008—legal admissibility of electronic information, which apply equally to records held by private sector bodies. For these reasons the s.46 Code can also be seen as relevant to the practices of private sector data controllers.

The s.46 code also describes, in Pt 2, the procedure to be followed for "timely and effective review and transfer of public records" to The National Archives or to the Public Record Office of Northern Ireland under the Public Records Act 1958 or the Public Records Act (Northern Ireland) 1923. In Pt VI of the FOIA the old rules for historical records, which delayed the opening of public records for three decades or more and, were swept away and all records, whenever created, are now subject to the same obligations of public access. The original reduction of the period after which a record becomes a historical record to 30 years is now to be further reduced to 20 years; the National Archives announced in July 2012 that this change will be gradually phased in, starting in 2013. There are no special exemptions for historical records and those exemptions that do apply gradually fall away with the years as the records age.[12]

Pro-active publication: publication schemes

Public authorities must, in addition to responding to requests for information, publish information proactively. The obligations contained in ss.19 and 20 require every public authority to adopt and maintain a publication scheme, in a form approved by the Commissioner, which sets out classes of information to be published, the manner of publication and whether there is any charge for the

26–21

---

[11] FOIA s.46(1).
[12] FOIA Pt VI, dealing with historical and public records.

information. Authorities must publish information in accordance with this scheme, although the FOIA says little about what information should be included—merely that the authority must have regard to the public interest in allowing public access to information it holds and in the publication of reasons for any decisions it makes.[13] It was thought that routine publication by the authority of most of its available information would have the effect of limiting requests for information under s.1, on the basis that enquirers would first search in the publication scheme, but that has not proved to be the case. Despite the Commissioner's extensive work with public sector bodies to produce newer standardised sector-specific models designed for easy accessibility, which became compulsory in January 2009 and are at the time of writing under review, the overwhelming majority of enquirers start by making a specific request. The FOIA Review heard evidence that this was partly because of the diverse subject matter of requests and also because the publication scheme was "bypassed by search engines on the web".

There is an exemption at s.21 for information which is reasonably accessible to the applicant by other means, and this refers, among other things, to information within the publication scheme (although if the requested information is not reasonably accessible to the particular applicant despite being available via the scheme the exemption would not apply). In practice authorities deal with requests for information which is published within their publication scheme by supplying the requester with a link to the relevant part of the authority's website, or other appropriate directions. It must be remembered that the s.16 duty to advise and assist requesters will apply in these circumstances.

Clearly there is bound to be some personal data which will be included in the publication scheme, such as details of senior office-holders, or of individuals who have a public-facing role, or who are the designated contact for enquiries. All such individuals should already be aware of the fact that some of their personal data relating to their official functions will be routinely published, but it might still be prudent to consider what information should be given to them at the outset, in the interests of fairness.

The Tribunal and the role of the Information Commissioner

26–22   The Data Protection Tribunal became the Information Tribunal following the implementation of the FOIA, but since November 2008 (following the Tribunals Courts and Enforcement Act 2007) its jurisdiction (now "Information Rights") has been within the General Regulatory Chamber which forms part of the First Tier Tribunal. The Tribunal is given detailed consideration in Ch.28.

The Data Protection Commissioner became the Information Commissioner in January 2002 with responsibility for both the FOIA and the DPA; he is here referred to as the Commissioner. He reports annually to Parliament on the exercise of his functions in relation to the access regimes as well as in relation to the DPA. His enforcement role is considered at para.26-23, below. In addition to approving publication schemes and dealing with complaints by requesters, the Information Commissioner has an obligation to promote the following of good practice by authorities and to arrange for the dissemination of information about

---

[13] FOIA s.19(3).

the Act.[14] He has produced very extensive guidance on all aspects of the access regimes, informed by his decisions and those of the Tribunal and the courts. Separate guidance has been produced by the Ministry of Justice on the procedural aspects of and exemptions in the FOIA, and by the Department of the Environment Food and Rural Affairs (DEFRA) in relation to the EIR. The Commissioner can also, with the consent of an authority, assess whether the authority is following good practice. This corresponds to the provisions for assessment in the DPA except that there is no power of compulsory audit in the access regimes, but in his published Regulatory Action Policy the Commissioner makes it clear that public authorities who refuse to co-operate can expect to have an information notice served upon them. In this policy the Commissioner also cites as options "negotiation", "monitoring" and "undertaking", which also feature in his regulatory policy in relation to DPA compliance.

The Scottish Information Commissioner (SIC) is the regulator for the FOISA, but there is no tribunal for FOISA in Scotland; appeal from a decision or other notice of the SIC is direct to the Court of Session.

Enforcement

The enforcement regime under the FOIA presents an interesting contrast to that under the DPA. On the one hand, while the Commissioner is armed with powers similar to those in the DPA to serve information and enforcement notices, failure to comply is not a criminal offence under the FOIA, although the Commissioner can ask the court to deal with the authority as if it had committed contempt of court. On the other hand, while an applicant has no direct right under the FOIA to take an authority to court, which appears to compare unfavourably with the many rights of action conferred upon data subjects by the DPA, anyone who is dissatisfied with the way in which a public authority has dealt with their request can ask the Commissioner to make a decision on the complaint and it is this right which has produced an avalanche of decisions over the past eight years. The Commissioner publishes all his decisions on his website, and in the year 2011/2012 alone the Commissioner issued 1,131 decision notices in respect of complaints made under the the access regimes, upholding (wholly or partly) 50 per cent. Many of these decisions are appealed to the Tribunal; no figure is given for the year 2011/2012, but in the previous year it was 25 per cent.

While the Commissioner handled a caseload of nearly 13,000 complaints in relation to the DPA in the same period, none of the outcomes was published, for obvious reasons, and in striking contrast to the high level of activity under the access regimes, the courts have proved so unfriendly to the exercise of a data subject's rights that published decisions in relation to actions founded in the DPA are rare. The peculiarly vague right of a person to ask the Commissioner "for an assessment" under DPA s.42 simply does not compare with the robust procedure under FOIA s.50, which entitles a party dissatisfied with the way a public authority has dealt with his request to complain to the Commissioner. The Commissioner will usually issue a decision notice, which if he upholds the complaint could require the authority to disclose information. Either party who is dissatisfied with the Commissioner's decision can appeal to the Tribunal, from

26–23

---

[14] FOIA s.47.

which there can be appeal on a point of law to the Upper Tribunal and from there to the Court of Appeal and the Supreme Court. An authority can also appeal to the Tribunal against an information or enforcement notice served by the Commissioner pursuant to his powers under the FOIA.

26–24   The Commissioner's enforcement powers apply to authorities' duties in respect of publication schemes as well as to those relating to requests, and include obtaining a warrant for entry and inspection, if he can satisfy a circuit judge of his grounds. His remit in respect of the two codes of practice includes not only his ability to assess good practice, mentioned at para.26-22 above, but also the power to serve a formal notice making recommendations as to good practice to authorities whose practice does not conform with the relevant code, but his only sanction is to "name and shame" defaulting authorities. In relation to decision or enforcement notices served on central government there is provision at FOIA s.53 for ministerial override of a requirement by the Commissioner to release information. At the time of writing, recent instances of the exercise of this override are on May 8, 2012 when the Secretary of State for Health vetoed disclosure of the Department of Health's Transition Risk Register, and on July 31, 2012 when the Attorney General issued another s.53 certificate preventing disclosure of Cabinet minutes relating to the March 2003 decision to take military action in Iraq, which had in 2009 been the subject of a previous veto by the Justice Secretary.

There is one criminal offence in the FOIA: at s.77 it is an offence to tamper with information which is the subject of a request for access with the intention of preventing disclosure, and this applies not only to requests made under the FOIA but also to a data subject access request made to a public authority data controller under DPA s.7.

Interface with data protection

26–25   The definition of personal data is extended for public authorities by the addition of category (e) to the definition of data at DPA s.1(1) so that all recorded information which relates to living individuals who can be identified is now covered. The amended definition reads:

> "'data' means information which—
> (a)   is being processed by means of equipment operating automatically in response to instructions given for that purpose,
> (b)   is recorded with the intention that it should be processed by means of such equipment,
> (c)   is recorded as part of a relevant filing system or with the intention that it should form part of a relevant filing system,
> (d)   does not fall within paragraphs (a) (b) or (c) but forms part of an accessible record as defined in section 68, or
> (e)   is recorded information held by a public authority and does not fall within any of paragraphs (a) to (d)."

It also provides that "public authority" has the same meaning in the DPA as in the FOIA. Rights of subject access and accuracy apply to all personal data within category (e), but the subject access provisions are modified in relation to part of it. Where requests are made for access to third party personal data (that is, personal data of a person other than the applicant) the FOIA provides extensive exemptions to ensure that there is no breach of privacy caused by the publication of such information. These changes are considered in greater detail below.

The exemption for personal data at FOIA s.40 has to do two jobs—first to ensure that the access rights in DPA s.7 prevail over those in the access regimes, and second to protect the privacy of individuals whose information would otherwise be made public. Because of the extension of the categories of "data" described above, the exemption for third party personal data in s.40(2)–(6) of the FOIA is effective to cover all personal information on record with a public authority which falls within the definition of "personal data" in the DPA. Section 40 has four limbs:

26–26

(i)   Personal data of the applicant are absolutely exempt (s.40(1)).
(ii) A disclosure of any third party personal data *to a member of the public otherwise than under this Act* which would breach any data protection principle is absolutely exempt (s.40(3)(a)(ii) and (b)).
(iii) A disclosure to the public of third party personal data within categories (a)–(d) of DPA s.1(1), which would contravene an objection made by the third party under DPA s.10, is exempt unless the public interest in disclosure is greater than the public interest in maintaining the s.10 objection (s.40(3)(a)(i)).
(iv) A disclosure to the public of third party personal data to which the third party would not himself be entitled to access because of an exemption in the DPA is exempt unless the public interest in disclosure is greater than the public interest in maintaining this exemption (s.40(4)).

There are, of course, numerous exemptions in the FOIA in addition to the exemption for personal data, and a requested disclosure of information which happens to be personal data may be exempt from disclosure under the FOIA by the application of any of the other FOIA exemptions. Of particular relevance are the exemption at s.41 for confidential information received from a third party, and the exemption for information the disclosure of which might endanger the health or safety of any individual at s.38, but there are also procedural exemptions for costly or vexatious requests which might sometimes be relevant to a request for disclosure of third party personal data. The application of the principles to disclosure becomes necessary only if the authority is minded to release the personal data; it will not arise if by virtue of other exemptions personal data are not to be disclosed.

26–27

It is has been pointed out that there is no express exemption for disclosures (whether or not of personal data) which would contravene art.8 of the ECHRFF. It has been argued, but with limited success, that such disclosures would effectively be prohibited by the operation of s.6 of the Human Rights Act 1998 (referred to as the HRA), which declares that it is unlawful for a public authority to act in a way which is incompatible with a Convention right. This would bring such disclosures within FOIA s.44, which grants an absolute exemption where there is a legal prohibition on disclosure but the Tribunal did not follow this route in *Bluck v Information Commissioner*,[15] considered in detail below at para.50.

---

[15] (2007) 98 B.M.L.R. 1.

The exemption for personal data in the FOISA

26–28   The exemptions in relation to personal data in the FOISA have the same effect as those in FOIA s.40 but they are worded slightly differently and include two further categories of information.

Section 38 provides that "information is exempt information if it constitutes" data within certain categories. These cover the categories covered by the FOIA (summarised at para.26 above) plus:

- personal census information; and
- a deceased person's health records.

Personal census information is defined at s.38(5) by reference to the census legislation. Had the FOIA contained a similar exemption for the health records of a deceased person the difficulties addressed in the *Bluck* litigation (see para.26-50, below) would not have arisen. Note that the Environmental Information (Scotland) Regulations 2004 (EISR) do not contain these additional exemptions. The exemption in FOISA s.38 does not extend to the duty to confirm or deny whether requested information is held, but the Freedom of Information (Amendment) (Scotland) Bill (at consultation stage at the time of writing) proposes to add s.38 to the exemptions at s.18 which qualify for a non-committal response so that a "neither confirm nor deny" response for personal data will then be allowed. That will certainly be an improvement in the protection of personal data in Scotland; generally the balance between protection of personal data and openness under the information access right has in Scotland tilted more noticeably in favour of openness and away from protection of personal data than in the rest of the UK under the FOIA, judging from the decisions of the SIC and the Court of Session. This was bought out at an early stage in the litigation *CSA v SIC* (discussed at para.26-48 below), which ended when the House of Lords firmly rejected the contention of the SIC and the court that personal data were not at risk in the disclosure that had been ordered. It is worth noting that the SIC, unlike her FOIA counterpart, has no regulatory role in relation to the protection of personal data.

OVERVIEW OF THE ENVIRONMENTAL INFORMATION REGULATIONS 2004

Application of the Regulations

26–29   The Environmental Information Regulations 2004 (SI 2004/3391) were made on December 21, 2004 and came into effect at the same time as the FOIA on January 1, 2005. The requirement was to implement the requirements of the 2003 Directive which applied throughout the UK but the approach taken was to draft them, as far as the directive would permit, by reference to the existing FOIA regime. This meant that there had to be a separate set of regulations for Scotland drafted by reference to the FOISA, so the EIR apply, broadly speaking, only to authorities in England, Wales and Northern Ireland and the EISR apply to

Scottish public authorities. The few differences between the two sets of regulations generally reflect the differences between the FOIA and the FOISA, except as mentioned below.

Who is covered?

The EIR apply to practically all the public authorities covered by the FOIA, but also cover some other bodies not subject to the FOIA. "Public authority" is defined in reg.2(2), and it includes the special forces and security bodies which are excluded from the list in Sch.1 to the FOIA. On the other hand, bodies, such as the BBC and the Bank of England, which are listed in Sch.1 to the FOIA as being included only in respect of certain information, and also bodies designated by order under FOIA s.5, are expressly excluded from the EIR. In addition, the EIR also apply to any other body or other person which carries out functions of public administration, such as utility companies; and also to any other body or other person under the control of a public authority which, in relation to the environment, has public responsibilities, or exercises functions of a public nature or provides public services—for example waste contractors performing waste collection on behalf of a local authority. There has been considerable debate concerning who is a public authority under reg.2. The finding of the UT in *Smartsource v IC and a Group of 19 additional water companies*[16] that water companies were not public authorities had been followed in subsequent decisions, but has now been referred to the ECJ by the UT in *Fish Legal v IC*[17] since it involves the interpretation of European legislation. The ECJ has published the questions it will be addressing, including the meaning of "performing public functions under national law"; "control" and the hybridity queston.

26–30

The EIR do not apply to a public authority acting in a judicial or legislative capacity, nor to either House of Parliament to the extent required for the purpose of avoiding an infringement of parliamentary privilege.

What is environmental information?

The EIR set out a wide definition of environmental information drawn from the 2003 Directive. Environmental information is any information in written, visual, aural, electronic or any other material form on:

26–31

(a)   the state of the elements of the environment including living things;

(b)   factors affecting the elements, e.g. noise, emissions;

(c)   measures affecting the elements and factors;

(d)   reports on implementation of environmental legislation;

(e)   cost benefit and other economic analyses used in connection with the measures; and

(f)   the state of human health and safety as affected by the above.

---

[16] [2010] UKUT 415 (AAC).
[17] [2012] UKUT 177 (AAC).

This wide scope of the definition of environmental information means that all public authorities are bound to hold some information which comes within it. The definition of what counts as held for the purposes of the EIR is different from that in the FOIA in that besides including, as the FOIA does, information held by another person on behalf of the authority, reg.3(2) says information is covered if it is in the possession of the authority and has been produced or received by the authority, unqualified by any stipulation corresponding to that in s.3(2) of the FOIA which excludes information held on behalf of another person. This appears to indicate that all environmental information which an authority happens to have is held for the purposes of the EIR but the wording, which closely follows the 2003 Directive, information which is "in its possession and has been produced or received by the authority" must preclude information which the authority holds (e.g. on its premises or in its computer systems) that was produced or received by a member of staff acting in his private capacity. It is less clear that information which an authority stores or looks after for someone else but does not use for its own purposes falls outside this definition.

The Commissioner, in his 2012 Guide to the EIR, expresses the view "that information is in your possession only if you hold it to any extent for your own purposes" and this is a helpful practical approach. It does not, of course, do away with the problem that an authority which has custody of someone else's information, such as by providing an archive service (e.g. where a county council looks after the records of a parish council), may properly be said to be in possession of environmental information that it has received. As will be seen, the EIR are riddled with defects which do appear to have caused much difficulty in practice, although in this case the relevant wording is imported wholesale from the 2003 Directive. Generally, the Commissioner's approach in his most recent series of practical guidance appears to be to smooth over such problems by indications that he will not take the point as regulator.

How requests can be made

26–32   The EIR give no definition of a request, unlike the FOIA, and no formalities are prescribed for making requests. The main practical difference is that there is no requirement for requests to be in writing, so it is possible to request environmental information by telephone, or in person.

Obligation to respond to requests for information

26–33   The EIR do not impose an explicit obligation on authorities to confirm or deny that information is held, but if an authority does not hold requested information then it is likely to issue a refusal for that reason, applying the exemption in reg.12(4)(a)—information not held. Therefore given that the authority must tell the applicant of the reasons for refusal, a refusal on the ground that the information is not held will achieve the same result as s.1(1)(a) of the FOIA. Accordingly, an authority is in effect obliged to tell the applicant that environmental information is not held, and unlike the FOIA it cannot generally apply any other reg.12 exemption to the duty to confirm or deny. The only exemption in reg.12 which can be applied to the duty to confirm or deny whether requested information is held is the exemption at reg.12(5)(a) protecting international relations, defence, national security and public safety—but note that this is not the case for the exemption for third party personal data because that comes under reg.13.[18]

The obligation to respond is set out in reg.5 under which a public authority that holds environmental information must make it available in response to a request. This is not the same as the duty to communicate the information to the applicant in s.1(1)(b) of the FOIA. Where the information is already publicly available and is easily accessible to the applicant then the authority may direct the applicant to the published version—this achieves a similar result to that achieved by the exemption in s.21 of the FOIA for information which is reasonably accessible to the applicant by other means.[19] Applicants can express a preference for the form and format in which the information is to be provided which the authority should accommodate unless it is reasonable to make the information available in another form.[20] Where the applicant requests it the authority must also direct them to the methods of sampling, analysis and measurement used in compiling the information.[21]

Costs of dealing with requests

There is no exemption for requests which would cost too much to deal with by reference to a fixed upper limit as in the FOIA, and the Fees Regulations do not apply to the EIR. Authorities can charge a "reasonable amount" for making environmental information available, but this does not apply to access to public registers nor to access by inspection of the authority's records. Schedules of charges must be published as well as the circumstances in which charges may be waived. If an authority wishes to impose a charge it must give a fees notice within 20 working days of the receipt of the request, and if not paid within 60 working days of the notice, the authority has no obligation to respond further. Both DEFRA and the ICO have produced guidance on charging which reflects the findings of the Tribunal in the leading decision *David Markinson v Information Commissioner*[22] that charges will comprise the cost of producing copies of the information, disregarding staff costs. Although there is no exemption specifically addressing requests which are very costly, as there is at s.12 of the FOIA, the exemption at reg.12(4)(b) for requests which are manifestly unreasonable could be applied to very expensive requests.

The DEFRA guidance to this exemption encourages its application to costly requests, but the Tribunal in *Kaye Little v Information Commissioner*[23] expressly disapproved of treating this exemption as a cap on costs along the lines of the appropriate limit in FOIA s.12. The effect of reg.5(6), which disapplies any law which would prevent disclosure of information in accordance with the EIR, has been demonstrated in relation to charges previously made by local authorities for

26–34

---

[18] reg.12(4)(a).
[19] reg.6(1).
[20] reg.6.
[21] reg.5(5).
[22] EA/2005/0014, March 28, 2006.
[23] EA/2010/0072.

planning and local search information. In *Kirklees Council v ICO*[24] the Tribunal put beyond doubt that that public authorities, such as in this case a council seeking to maintain standard charges for inspection of the register of Local Land Charges by commercial search companies, could not override the provisions of the EIR when giving access to environmental information. On the other hand, Government trading funds, such as the Ordnance Survey, are allowed by the 2003 Directive to make a market-based charge where the information is *supplied* on a commercial basis.

Time for compliance with requests

26–35   The time limit for response is 20 working days starting the day after receipt of the request, but this can be extended to 40 working days for complex and voluminous requests. Under the FOIA the only time extension is for consideration of the public interest in the context of the proposed application of a qualified exemption, but there is no corresponding extension for consideration of any EIR exemption. In *Kaye Little*, cited above, the Tribunal said that the fact that the EIR allow up to double the time to deal with complex and voluminous requests is an important consideration in the application of the exemption for requests which are manifestly unreasonable. In *Bragg v IC and Babergh Council*[25] the Tribunal generally supported the Commissioner's finding of request manifestly unreasonable by reference to his own guidance on vexatious requests.

Exceptions from the duty to disclose environmental information

26–36   The exemptions (called "exceptions") in the EIR are generally narrower than those in the FOIA and they are all subject to a PIT, in which there is an express presumption that the public interest favours disclosure. Although there are no absolute exemptions, the same effect is achieved by the carve-outs from the regime mentioned above, and by separate provisions for requests for personal data of third parties at reg.13. General exemptions at reg.12(4) enable refusal to be made where: information is not held; the request is manifestly unreasonable; description of the information is insufficient; the information is incomplete; or the request would involve the disclosure of internal communications.

"Information not held" is discussed above in the context of the duty to confirm or deny; it is however hard to envisage circumstances in which the public interest will favour disclosure of information that the authority does not hold, or what the authority should do in such a case, since under the access regimes there is no duty on an authority to acquire information for the purpose of satisfying a request. In his 2012 Guide to the EIR, the Commissioner acknowledges that in these circumstances it is not possible to consider the public interest in whether the information should be disclosed. The same point can be made in relation to reg.12(4)(c) where the operation of the PIT in relation to refusal of a request which is too vague to deal with is again hard to fathom. "Request manifestly unreasonable" is also discussed above. "Disclosure of internal communications" is a very wide exemption, which is perhaps why in the 2003 Directive there is an

[24] GI/258/2011, March 10, 2011.
[25] EA/2012/0107.

additional public interest consideration, not repeated in the regulations (presumably on grounds of redundancy). We have also noted earlier that s.39 of the FOIA, which provides exemption for environmental information under that regime so that the requirements of the 2003 Directive can be applied under the EIR, is itself subject to a PIT. If this were to be applied to cut out consideration of the request under the EIR then there would be a conflict with reg.5(6), which as has been pointed out, disapplies any law which would prevent disclosure of information in accordance with the EIR.

The exemptions protecting specific interests set out at reg.12(5) are all subject to a prior harm test, as well as a public interest test. This differs from the "would, or would be likely to, prejudice" test in the FOIA because it does not accommodate *likelihood* of harm, so these exemptions can be applied only where it is merely more probable than not that disclosure would adversely affect the interest protected. They cover broadly the same areas of interest as the FOIA exemptions, but are considerably shorter – international relations, defence, national security and public safety are all covered in just those brief terms, without the pages of additions and extensions in the corresponding FOIA exemptions. An authority seeking to refuse a request would usually be better off under the FOIA as the exemptions there tend to be not only easier to engage but broader in scope (not that the authority has a choice, given reg.5(6)). One exception to that is the EIR exemption at reg.12(5)(c) protecting intellectual property rights, which are limited in the FOIA to trade secrets. There is at reg.12(5)(b) an exemption covering the course of justice, fair trials, and the conduct of criminal or disciplinary enquiries. There are two very specific confidentiality exemptions at reg.12(5)(d) and (e), which are together narrower in effect than the general confidentiality exemption at FOIA s.41; and then at reg.12(5)(f) and (g) two exemptions not found in the FOIA—one to protect the environment itself and another to protect the interests of a person who volunteered information to the public body and who has not consented to its disclosure. Where the requested information relates to emissions it cannot be refused under any of the exemptions of reg.12(5)(d)–(g). As has previously been noted, apart from the exemption for personal data of a third party which is separately covered at reg.13, the only circumstances in which an authority may refuse to say whether or not requested information exists and is held are when it is applying the exemption at reg.12(5)(a).

26–37

Duty to help applicants, and Regulation 16 code of practice

As in the FOIA, public authorities must provide advice and assistance to applicants and prospective applicants, so far as it would be reasonable to expect them to do so, and compliance with a code of practice for handling requests discharges this duty. The code is produced by the Secretary of State and is available on the DEFRA website. It is in many ways similar to the s.45 Code under the FOIA, although it does not need to introduce as good practice transferring requests and dealing with complaints, since these are obligations imposed in the regulations themselves. The provisions under reg.9 for advice and assistance also specifically address an authority's obligations in relation to requests that are formulated in too general a manner (insufficient description)—

26–38

namely to ask the applicant for more particulars, and to assist the applicant in providing them. This is linked to the exemption at reg.12(4)(c).

Transferring requests, and complaints

26–39   Two procedural obligations contained in the regulations are not found in the FOIA, although they are contained in the s.45 Code. At reg.10, an authority which does not hold requested environmental information and which believes that it may be held by another public authority or by a Scottish public authority should either transfer the request to the other authority or supply the applicant with the relevant name and address in its refusal notice. At reg.11, applicants can complain to an authority if they think the authority has not dealt with their request in accordance with the regulations; they must make their written representations within 40 working days after the date on which they believe the authority failed to comply, which is likely to be the date of the authority's refusal. Authorities must reconsider their decisions and respond to the applicant within 40 working days after receipt of the representations. Refusals are dealt with under reg.14, which is similar in effect to FOIA s.17, described at para.26-18, above.

Proactive publication of information

26–40   Under reg.4, an authority is required to progressively make the environmental information which it holds available to the public by electronic means which are easily accessible. Most EIR public authorities are also subject to the FOIA and they are encouraged to integrate environmental information into their publication scheme under the FOIA. The minimum information which must be published is listed in art.7(2) of the 2003 Directive together with facts and analyses of facts considered relevant and important in framing major environmental policy proposals. Unlike the FOIA where an authority can choose what to publish, the EIR in effect require an authority to publish all the environmental information it holds. This is why it is necessary for the obligation to be qualified by the stipulation that it does not extend to publishing information which the authority would be entitled to refuse to disclose under reg.12. This does not work for personal data, because the exemption for third party personal data is not contained in reg.12 (otherwise it would be subject to a public interest test)—it is in reg.13. The problem is that although reg.13(1) imposes a prohibition on disclosure of third party personal data otherwise than in accordance with its terms (mainly, compliance with the data protection principles) it is expressed to apply to *information requested*, the "applicant" being specifically mentioned. There is no such request or applicant in the context of the dissemination obligation at reg.4, so the unfortunate consequence is that the obligation to publish information proactively is not qualified by any exemption for personal data and therefore obliges an authority to publish all personal data which comes within the definition of environmental information. This glaring defect in the drafting of the EIR is undoubtedly a consequence of a rushed job and does not reflect the requirements of the 2003 Directive, which says in art.7 (dissemination of environmental information) that "the exceptions in Article 4(1) and (2) may apply in relation to the duties imposed by this Article." The exceptions at art.4(2) include:

"(f) the confidentiality of personal data and/or files relating to a natural person where that person has not consented to the disclosure of the information to the public, where such confidentiality is provided for by national or Community law; and

Within this framework, and for the purposes of the application of subparagraph (f), Member States shall ensure that the requirements of Directive 95/46/EC of the European Parliament and of the Council of 24 October 1995 on the protection of individuals with regard to the processing of personal data and on the free movement of such data are complied with (1)."

In practice, even if an authority is, strictly speaking, in breach of EIR reg.4 by failing to publish all of its personal data which counts as environmental, the regulator (who is of course the Commissioner) is far more likely to take action against it for any breach of the DPA caused by publishing this information than for breach of the EIR by not doing so. Indeed the Commissioner, in his 2012 Guide to the EIR, ignores this technical difficulty and lists personal information subject to reg.13 in the category of information which an authority can refuse to publish.

26–41

In the EISR the obligation for "active dissemination of information" which, like reg.4 of the EIR, obliges an authority to publish all of its environmental information is not qualified by *any* of the exemptions in the EISR, whether relation to personal data exempted at reg.11 EISR or in relation to the general exemptions at EISR reg.10. This rather large defect in the EISR does not appear to have caused any reported problems so far.

Authorities are subject to an additional obligation in reg.4(1)(b) to organise their environmental information relevant to their functions with a view to its active and systematic dissemination which, along with data quality obligations mentioned below, is the nearest the regulations come to imposing records management obligations. The obligation to disseminate information in electronic form does not apply to non-electronic information collected before January 1, 2005. In relation to the requirement of easy accessibility, authorities will in any event be subject to the accessibility obligations of the Equality Act 2010.

Information quality obligations

Where information made available by the authority under reg.5(1) is compiled by the authority it must ensure that it is "up to date, accurate and comparable so far as the public authority reasonably believes".[26] This, together with the obligation in reg.4(1)(b) to organise environmental information relevant to an authority's functions with a view to its active and systematic dissemination, is a records management obligation. Note, however, that the regulations contain no code of practice for records management corresponding to FOIA s.46. Nevertheless, as the vast majority of public authorities subject to the EIR will also be subject to the FOIA their records management obligations under the s.46 Code will in any case apply to the environmental information which they hold.

26–42

---

[26] reg.5(4).

Enforcement

26–43   The EIR import from the FOIA the provisions as to the general functions of the Commissioner and the enforcement and appeal provisions, so the Commissioner is the regulator for the EIR and the enforcement provisions are the same as for the FOIA. There is also an offence of altering records with intent to prevent disclosure in the same terms as s.77 of the FOIA. An authority is obliged to consider any representations made by a dissatisfied applicant as detailed above at para.39, but as in the FOIA and in contrast to the DPA there are no rights conferred on applicants, or upon anybody else, to take direct action through the courts against an authority. While there is no express provision of the EIR corresponding to s.56 of the FOIA (which declares that there is no right of action in civil proceedings for any failure to comply with the FOIA) it seems very likely that a court would apply the same restriction in respect of the EIR.

Interface with data protection

26–44   The interface with data protection is, subject to the pro-active duty to disseminate all environmental information, in practice the same as that in the FOIA although achieved by different methods. If the information requested includes personal data of the applicant it is outside the EIR (in the FOIA it would be absolutely exempt under s.40(1)).[27] Where a request covers personal data which relates to another individual the provisions of reg.13 apply, and they impose a prohibition on disclosure which provides exemption in almost exactly the same terms as s.40 of the FOIA. Note that, for the purposes of the exemption in reg.13, the EIR take on board the extended meaning of "data" in DPA s.1(1) (to include category (e) data as held by a FOIA public authority) by declaring that "public authority" in this context means an EIR public authority.

OVERVIEW—HOW DEALING WITH PERSONAL INFORMATION IS AFFECTED BY THE ACCESS REGIMES

Exemption for third party personal data—section 40 and regulation 13

26–45   The exemptions apply only to the obligation to *disclose* information *requested* (apart from the obligation for pro-active dissemination of environmental information which is limited by reference to EIR reg.12). It follows that the other obligations under the access regimes continue to apply to information which constitutes personal data that is held by public authority data controllers. As has been seen in the overview of the access regimes these obligations cover record-keeping, the publication or dissemination of information, the provision of advice and assistance to inquirers and the handling of requests for information.

---

[27] reg.5(3).

RECORD-KEEPING AND PERSONAL DATA

As described above, under the FOIA a public authority has to establish and **26–46** maintain a system of record-keeping which meets the standards in the s.46 Code. The authority needs to be in a position to know what information it holds and to be in a position for find information requested so that a response can be given within 20 working days under the access regimes or 40 days under the DPA. It is worth remembering that public authorities subject to the access regimes now hold category (e) data, and for the purposes of any personal data which falls within it this category is subdivided to produce a subset of "unstructured personal data" for which there are special subject access rules. Data subjects who want access to these unstructured personal data must first describe the data, which poses less of a problem in terms of record-keeping, but authorities must also give subject access to all other personal data which falls within category (e) and so may wish to consider which of their manual records are subject to the access provisions in the DPA. The question of whether requested information falls within the definition of personal data is, however, the first issue which the controller has to consider and since this issue is of great importance both to requesters seeking disclosure from public bodies and to the public authority data controllers themselves seeking to protect personal privacy there have been numerous decisions on the personal data question arising out of the more rigorous appeal procedures of the FOIA.

Anonymisation of personal data

Anonymisation of personal information is the removal of identifying particulars **26–47** from personal information so that it is no longer identifiable with a unique individual. In data protection compliance work there is considerable emphasis on the adoption of Privacy Enhancing Technologies which are technologies which do not focus on individual identities but protect or remove them in different ways. Such technologies rarely achieve complete anonymisation as the data controller can usually reconstitute the data as personal data, but the data may be functionally anonymous because without the unique information available to the data controller, no third party will be able to reconstitute the data as personal data.

This gives rise to several questions in relation to the access regimes:

- Where data are functionally anonymous should they be disclosed even though technically they are personal data in the hands of the controller?
- Is there any obligation to process data so that identifiers are removed?
- Should this option be offered when a potential applicant seeks advice and assistance?

These issues were first considered by the Court of Session in the case of **26–48** *Common Services Agency v Scottish Information Commissioner*,[28] in which a requester had asked the Common Services Agency (CSA) for information on the incidence of childhood leukaemia in Dumfries and Galloway. The CSA was concerned that the numbers were so low that the release of the numbers could

---

[28] [2008] UKHL 47.

lead to the identification of specific individuals. They therefore declined to release the information. The SIC ordered the release at ward level after barnardisation. This is a technique used to disguise exact small figures by rounding them up or down. The CSA appealed to the Court of Session, which held that the barnardised data were not personal data and should be released. The CSA then appealed that judgment to the House of Lords, with a very different outcome. In *Common Services Agency v Scottish Information Commissioner*[29] Lord Hope of Craighead, delivering the leading judgment, commented on the earlier finding as follows:

> "There is much force in Lord Marnoch's observation in the Inner House that, as the whole purpose of FOISA is the release of information, it should be construed in as liberal a manner as possible. But that proposition must not be applied too widely, without regard to the way the Act was designed to operate in conjunction with DPA 1998. It is obvious that not all government can be completely open, and special consideration also had to be given to the release of personal information relating to individuals. So while the entitlement to information is expressed initially in the broadest terms that are imaginable, it is qualified in respects that are equally significant and to which appropriate weight must also be given."

He also said: "I do not think that the observations in *Durant v Financial Services Authority* on which the Lord President relied have any relevance to this issue."

26–49   The appeal was unanimously allowed, although their Lordships' reasoning did not always follow the same route. This difference of approach was brought out in *Department of Health v Information Commissioner* [30] in which the High Court overturned a decision of the Tribunal and upheld the original decision of the Commissioner in relation to the disclosure of abortion statistics for 2003, requested of the DoH by ProLife Alliance. The Department had withheld detailed statistics on the number of late-term abortions carried out on prescribed grounds because of the risk that, given the "low cell counts" in these categories, the relevant patients and/or doctors might be identified by those sufficiently motivated to do so. The Tribunal had agreed with DoH that they were personal data, but was not satisfied that s.40 exempted them as there was insufficient risk of identification, but the High Court upheld the original Commissioner decision that the requested information was not personal data on the basis that even though the DoH held additional information, which if disclosed would enable the identification of individuals who had had ground (e) abortions, the statistics alone could not amount to personal data. In the *DoH* case the court relied on Lord Hope's judgment in *CSA v SIC*, which had majority support, rather than Baroness Hale's which had been followed in an earlier decision of the Upper Tribunal in *All Party Parliamentary Group on Extraordinary Rendition v Information Commissioner*.[31] In this case, referred to as *APPGER,* the Tribunal had agreed that the disputed statistics constituted personal data, but concluded that there was insufficient risk of identification. In the *DoH* case, however, Cranston J. concluded:

---

[29] [2008] UKHL 47.
[30] [2011] EWHC 1430 (Admin).
[31] [2011] UKUT 15.

"In my view, the only interpretation open of Lord Hope's order is that it recognised that although the Agency held the information as to the identities of the children to whom the requested information related, it did not follow from that that the information, sufficiently anonymised, would still be personal data when publicly disclosed. All members of the House of Lords agreed with Lord Hope's order demonstrating, in my view, their shared understanding that anonymised data which does not lead to the identification of a living individual does not constitute personal data."

He also stated that to consider the requested data as personal data would establish a principle which would prevent any publication of medical statistics, however broad.

At the time of writing, the Commissioner's draft Anonymisation Code of Practice, published May 2012, is still subject to consultation but it cites the *DoH* case after noting the

"clear legal authority for the view that, where a data controller converts personal data into an anonymised form and publishes it, this will not amount to a disclosure of personal data—even though the disclosing organisation still holds the 'key' that would allow re-identification to take place. This means that the DPA no longer applies to the disclosed information".

Requests for information relating to deceased persons

Information about deceased persons cannot be protected by the exemption for personal data because personal data necessarily relate to a living individual, although it should be borne in mind that information about the dead could at the same time relate to those who are still living, and would have to be treated as personal data to that extent.

26-50

The question of how disclosures of information about the dead should be dealt with under the FOIA was considered by the Tribunal in *Bluck v Information Commissioner.*[32] The hospital had refused to volunteer disclosure of medical records to the mother of a deceased patient whose surviving husband had refused consent, but when she applied under the FOIA any disclosure to her would then have been to the public generally so it was important to find appropriate grounds to refuse to put medical records of a deceased patient into the public domain. This would not have been a problem for a Scottish public authority because s.38(1)(d) of the FOISA says that a deceased person's health record is absolutely exempt. Given the inapplicability of the s.40 exemption, the Commissioner had favoured the exemption at s.41 for confidential information obtained from another person over the argument that if disclosure would breach the art.8 rights of surviving family members, then s.6 of the HRA, which declares that it is unlawful for a public authority to act in a way which is incompatible with a Convention right, would amount to a legal prohibition for the purposes of the absolute exemption in s.44. The Tribunal followed the Commissioner's route.

---

[32] (2007) 98 B.M.L.R. 1.

There was much discussion as to whether the confidentiality of the medical records could survive the death of the confider and whether a breach would be actionable at the suit of her personal representatives, but the Tribunal claimed that:

> "such of the older authorities that suggest that personal representatives may not have a right to enforce a deceased's entitlement to confidentiality, should be regarded as having been overruled, at least in relation to medical records, by more recent decisions of the European Court of Human Rights on private information",

and also because

> "the basis of the duty of confidence in respect of private information lies in conscience; accordingly a duty of confidence is capable of surviving the death of the confider".

26–51   It is submitted that the problem with the application of the s.41 exemption is not whether there can be an action for a breach of confidence in these circumstances, but whether all the information contained in medical records can be said to come within the exemption in the first place since the exemption is limited to confidential information obtained from another person, and confidential information generated by the public authority itself is excluded. It is not enough simply to state, as the Commissioner does in his guidance to this exemption, that "information recorded by a doctor carrying out a physical examination of a patient is information obtained from that patient" and leave open the assumption that all medical records must therefore consist of information obtained from the patient or another third party. The Tribunal did not address this issue, merely stating that:

> "It is common ground between the parties that the Medical Records contain information obtained from a third person, namely Karen Davies, so that the requirement of section 41(1)(a) is satisfied."

The finding that medical records remain confidential does not entail that they were all obtained from another person for the purposes of s.41; in practice, much of the patient information held by hospitals will be generated by the hospital itself, such as test results, records of procedures carried out on the patient, case conferences, opinions and diagnoses based on information already held, and records of admission and discharge dates, to give a few examples. If it is to be assumed that because some information in a set of records legitimately comes within the s.41 exemption, all confidential information in those records should be treated in the same way regardless of whether it was generated by the authority itself, then a valuable protection for the right of public access to information will be lost. Clearly a great deal of information sought by requesters can be considered to be confidential in the hands of an authority, and unless the confidentiality exemption is limited to information which was obtained from someone else and which could also be the subject of an actionable breach of confidence it will be easy for public authorities to justify witholding a wide range of information, particularly as there is no public interest test to be applied in s.41.

For these reasons we are of the view that the application of the exemption at s.44 is to be preferred, but this is not a clear-cut option, and could not work for information requested under the EIR because instead of deferring to other legal prohibitions, as the FOIA does in s.44, the EIR expressly override any conflicting law at reg.5(6). The Tribunal in *Bluck* addressed the possibility of using s.44 but said

> "we do not believe that the effect of the Human Rights Act is to elevate to the level of a directly enforceable legal prohibition the general terms of Article 8".

The Commissioner expressly disapproves of the application of s.44 in these circumstances[33] (although he is prepared to find that a breach of art.8 will constitute unlawful processing in breach of the lawfulness requirement of principle 1) but it is noteworthy that the Ministry of Justice, which publishes guidance on the FOIA exemptions for use by government departments, has since 2008 adhered to the view that this is the effect of the HRA:

> "Some enactments can impose prohibitions of very general application. The most important of these is the Human Rights Act 1998. Section 6 of the Human Rights Act makes it unlawful for public authorities to act in a way that is incompatible with a Convention right. Disclosures that are incompatible with one of these Convention rights are therefore included within the scope of section 44",

adding that:

> "Section 44 might for example prohibit the disclosure of personal information that relates to deceased persons. This might interfere with the Article 8 rights of others—for example family members, or victims of the deceased's crimes, even where the data is not their own 'personal data' and therefore not exempt under section 40."

The fact is that the FOIA is deficient in its provision of protection of sensitive or confidential information about the dead, and express protection along the lines of the FOISA provision would have been preferable to the gymnastics required to make other exemptions fit the case. There is even less protection under the EIR because the exemptions for confidential information are narrower and there is no exemption accommodating other legal prohibitions.

Defence against action for defamation

Section 79 of the FOIA deals with the possibility that the authority may in response to an FOIA application provide information which is defamatory. The authority will have a privilege against an action based on such material as long as the material was provided by a third party (that is, not generated by the authority itself) and the publication was made without malice. There is no corresponding provision in the EIR.

26–52

26–53

---

[33] ICO Enforcement Notice to Southampton City Council, July 23, 2012.

Disclosures other than under the access regimes

26–54   The disclosure of personal data by public authorities to third parties is not a new phenomenon. Many disclosures are made under statutory obligations, for example by employers to HMRC for the purposes of tax and benefits. Disclosures are also made under settled arrangements or protocols, or disclosures to provide joint services, for example between Social Services Authorities and Health Trusts, and the Commissioner's statutory data sharing code of practice will also apply to such arrangements. There is, of course, no need for a specific statutory basis for disclosures of personal data by public authorities since there can sometimes be voluntary disclosures—for example, disclosures of information to the police to assist in the detection of crime. Data sharing is addressed in more detail in Ch.25.

Disclosures made under existing powers are not affected by the FOIA which expressly provides at s.78 that: "Nothing in this Act is to be taken to limit the powers of a public authority to disclose information held by it". The position is different under the EIR because reg.5(6) says that: "Any enactment or rule of law which would prevent disclosure of information in accordance with these Regulations shall not apply". As has been seen, the Tribunal has already applied this provision in *Markinson* and *Kirklees Council v PALI* where the charging provisions in the existing law would have produced a result different from that provided by reg.8. So wherever there is any conflict between the requirements of the EIR in relation to the disclosure of environmental information, and any other law, such as planning law or the rules under the Land Charges legislation, the EIR will override the conflicting law. This would, presumably, include the FOIA if the exemption at FOIA s.39 were to be overridden in the public interest as mentioned earlier.

Where information would be exempt from the rights of access but the public authority discloses under other powers there is nothing in the FOIA to prevent the authority from continuing to impose restrictions on the use or further disclosure of the information although the interface between disclosures under other powers and disclosures under the access regimes needs to be managed clearly and consistently.

Publication schemes and personal data

26–55   As outlined above, s.19 of the FOIA requires every public authority to adopt and maintain an approved scheme for the publication of its information. Authorities are required only to specify the classes of information which they publish or intend to publish, and to say whether there will be a charge for the information, but the Commissioner's model scheme stipulates considerably more detail concerning content and classification.

Personal information is highly likely to be included in the scheme—only consider the importance of giving out details of senior officials or of those in a public-facing role. The FOIA exemptions do not apply to the scheme because the authority can choose, within the confines of the model scheme, what to include and is unlikely to select anything which it would withhold under an access request. By contrast the EIR oblige an authority to disseminate all its environmental information but this obligation is subject to the exemptions in reg.12. As has been pointed out, that qualification does not extend to personal data, which is not covered in reg.12, so the regulations are deficient in that unlike the 2003 Directive they require the pro-active dissemination of any personal data which comes within the definition of environmental information. It is presumed that any authorities who are aware of this defect will nevertheless continue to apply the data protection principles to the inclusion of any personal data within the environmental information which they publish.

Applicant's duty to assist authority in locating the data requested

The DPA has always qualified the obligation to comply with a subject access request where the data controller reasonably requires further information to locate the information sought (and also to be sure of the identity of the requester). Unfortunately DPA s.7(3) as originally drafted imposed no obligation upon the controller to tell the requester that further information was needed before the request would be dealt with. This position was rectified in the DPA by an amendment contained in FOIA Sch.6, which substituted a new DPA s.7(3) as follows:

    "(3)   Where a data controller—
        (a)   reasonably requires further information in order to satisfy himself as to the identity of the person making a request under this section and to locate the information which that person seeks and
        (b)   has informed him of that requirement, the data controller is not obliged to comply with the request unless he is supplied with that further information."

The position under the DPA is now the same as in FOIA s.1(3) in that the controller must first tell the requester of the requirement for further information before his obligation to respond to the request is, at least temporarily, negatived. In relation to requests under the FOIA, s.1(3) provides that where a public authority:

    "(a)   reasonably requires further information in order to identify and locate the information requested and
    (b)   has informed the applicant of that requirement the authority is not obliged to comply with the request unless it is supplied with the further information."

The EIR, as ever, work differently and the corresponding provision for requests that are too vague to address without further information being supplied does not operate as a precondition of the authority's obligation to make information available. Under reg.9, where a public authority decides that an applicant has "formulated a request in too general a manner" it shall:

    "(a)   ask the applicant as soon as possible and in any event no later than 20 working days after the date of receipt of the request, to provide more particulars in relation to the request; and
    (b)   assist the applicant in providing those particulars".

26–56

26–57

Where the authority has been through this process and the request is still formulated in too general a manner for the authority to be able to deal with it then the authority may apply the exemption in reg.12(4)(c) and issue a refusal. But as has been pointed out this exemption, like all the exemptions in reg.12, is subject to a public interest test and it is interesting to speculate upon the public interest considerations which can operate upon the disclosure or withholding of requested information which cannot be clearly identified. It seems likely that the draftsman did not have time to think through the consequences of imposing a public interest test in relation to this exemption, and also in relation to that in reg.12(4)(a).[34] In this case, the Commissioner concedes in his 2012 Guide to the EIR that it may be difficult to carry out a meaningful public interest test and then proceeds to conflate the application of a PIT with the offer of advice and assistance, which seems to be an appropriate practical response.

Authority's duty to advise and assist applicants

26–58   Under the access regimes public authorities must advise and assist applicants and prospective applicants. This obligation to help applicants applies whether or not any information requested might be held by the authority or might be exempt. In contrast, the DPA imposes no obligation to assist data subjects with the framing of their subject access requests, nor to advise them of their entitlements once a request has been submitted. As a matter of good practice the Commissioner encourages data controllers to be helpful but they cannot be compelled. This obligation of public authorities is considered in detail above at para.26-19 in relation to the FOIA, and at para.26-38 in relation to the EIR.

Obtaining personal information and handling requests

26–59   Public authorities hold a great deal of information about living individuals, whether public figures, officials, other staff, clients or other services users, or members of the public. Access is frequently sought to such information. Moreover, even where a request is not specifically directed at obtaining personal information, the information produced to satisfy the request may often include personal information. Personal and non-personal information may be inextricably linked in records, whether in letters, reports, research papers, minutes or other documents, and of course in databases relating to staff and service users. It would certainly be good records management (and therefore in accordance with good practice under the s.46 Code) to bear in mind possible disclosure under the access regimes when considering methods of recording any information which may include some personal information in order to ensure that personal information is not opened to unnecessary disclosure in the future; indeed, this could be a data protection compliance issue under principle 7, when considering the organisational measures which it would be appropriate to take in relation to any personal information to which this principle applies.

26–60   The possibility that public access may be demanded affects the collection of personal information by public sector data controllers, and the fact that public disclosure may be made in response to an access request is likely to be relevant

---

[34] reg.12(4)(c).

information which should be notified to individuals at the point of collection; furthermore, any disclosures will need to be tested for fairness. Lest it be thought that fairness considerations under principle 1 will have already been taken into account it needs to be remembered that the personal information open to disclosure under the access regimes is wider than "personal data" as originally defined under the DPA (before the introduction of category (e) data), and in relation to personal data in category (e) that most of the principles (including principle 1) do not apply to it under the exemptions for category (e) data introduced via FOIA s.70. It is therefore important that public sector data controllers should consider applying the fair collection rules to all personal information which they hold, which is now all defined as "personal data" in their hands, thanks to category (e). Where a request under the access regimes involves personal information it will often be appropriate to notify the relevant individual and consult him or her before making a disclosure, particularly bearing in mind the good practice stipulations in the s.45 Code.

Organisations only partly covered by the FOIA

As mentioned above, there are a number of authorities which are covered by the FOIA only in relation to some of the information which they hold. Examples are public service broadcasters, such as the BBC and the Gaelic Media Service, which also hold information for the purposes of journalism, art or literature; bodies such as the Competition Commission and the Verderers of the New Forest which also hold information in relation to their tribunal functions; and the odd local authority, such as the Common Council of the City of London which also holds information in a private capacity outside its public functions. In these cases s.7 provides that nothing in Pts I–V of the FOIA applies to the information specified as not being held by the authority for the purposes of the FOIA. There is an amendment inserted into the DPA by FOIA s.68(3), which goes on to state that in these cases such information is not to be treated for the purposes of para.(e) of the definition of "data" in subsection 1 as held by a public authority. **26–61**

The boundaries of what information is covered by the FOIA and what is not were tested in litigation brought against the BBC by an applicant who wanted a copy of the Balen report created for the BBC about its Middle East news coverage. The BBC refused to entertain the request on the basis that they held this information for the purposes of journalism, so it was inaccessible via the FOIA. In *Sugar v British Broadcasting Commission*[35] the Supreme Court upheld a Court of Appeal decision that the report was outside the scope of the FOIA because it was held for the purposes of journalism. The court considered various possible approaches to the interpretation of the wording of the Act, ranging from information held exclusively for journalistic purposes to information held exclusively for non-journalistic purposes, with options in between for information held for mixed purposes which are either predominently journalistic or non-journalistic. In a majority decision (Lord Wilson dissenting) the court held that only information held *exclusively* for non-journalistic purposes could come within the scope of the FOIA, because the intention behind the exclusion was to protect the freedom of public service broadcasters to gather, edit and publish **26–62**

---

[35] [2012] UKSC 12.

news without the inhibition of disclosure obligations. Therefore if any part of the BBC's purpose in holding material was its broadcasting output, it would not be disclosable.

26–63   An interesting line of argument pursued on behalf of the applicant was that his rights under ECHRFF art.10 would be breached by the withholding of the information. Article 10, which confers the right of freedom of expression, adds that: "This right shall include freedom to … receive and impart information without interference by public authority". Lord Brown cited a passage from the unanimous Grand Chamber decision in *Roche v United Kingdom*[36] in which it was held:

> "that the freedom to receive information prohibits a Government from restricting a person from receiving information that others wish or may be willing to impart to him and that that freedom 'cannot be construed as imposing on a State, in circumstances such as those of the present case, positive obligations to … disseminate information of its own motion'".

He went on to say:

> "The appellant's difficulty to my mind is rather that article 10 creates no general right to freedom of information and where, as here, the legislation expressly limits such right to information held otherwise than for the purposes of journalism, it is not interfered with when access is refused to documents which *are* held for journalistic purposes."

He also found that even if there were any interference with art.10(1), a blanket exclusion for disclosure of information held for the purposes of journalism would be proportionate and therefore justified under art.10(2).

26–64   If the interpretation of information held for mixed purposes in *Sugar* can be applied in the case of all of the bodies which are subject to the FOIA only in respect of some of the information that they hold then, for example, bodies which also act as tribunals will have to make available under the FOIA only the information they hold for *exclusively* non-tribunal purposes. Given the focus of the *Sugar* litigation on information held for journalistic purposes by a public service broadcaster, however, it is not clear that this interpretation will necessarily apply to other bodies and other purposes. The effect on access to third party personal data is that the class of information potentially available from these bodies under the FOIA is narrower than might have been thought. The effect on subject access under the DPA is that since the class of "other information held by the authority" specified in s.7 is wider than might have been thought, and since it is this class of information which cannot qualify as data under category (e), then there is less information which can potentially be accessed via subject access under the DPA.

---

[36] (2006) 42 EHRR.

Section 34 exemption

Under s.34 of the DPA information which the data controller is obliged to make **26–65** available to the public, whether by publishing it or by some other mechanism, is exempt from the right of subject access, from the remedies for inaccuracy, and from the prohibitions on disclosure of information. Without more, this would have meant that where an authority was willing to give access to personal information to the public under the access regimes by publishing it in its publication scheme or providing it in response to a request for access, the data subject would as a consequence be deprived of both his individual rights of access and his remedies for wrongful disclosure and inaccuracy. While loss of the former would, unless there were disputes about the data covered, be of less moment because the individual would still be able to access the information as a member of the public, the latter deprivation would mean that the individual was also deprived of one of his rights guaranteed by Directive 95/46/EC. Section 72 of the FOIA deals with this by inserting the words "other than an enactment contained in the Freedom of Information Act" into s.34.

It is submitted that unfortunately this exclusion does not operate to exclude the EIR since the EIR are not contained in the FOIA. Had the EIR been made, as originally intended, pursuant to the power created for that purpose in FOIA s.74 then they would have been "an enactment contained in the FOIA", but in the event the EIR were made under s.2(2) of the European Communities Act 1972, not under s.74 of the FOIA. The fact that the exemption in FOIA s.39, as amended by EIR reg.20, refers to the EIR as they were actually made does not achieve the effect of containing the EIR in the FOIA any more than references to other regimes in some of the other FOIA exemptions have the effect of "containing" or perhaps incorporating those regimes into the FOIA. The consequence appears to be that once personal data are published under the EIR, as reg.4(1) obliges an authority to do without exemption for personal data, then the elements of the DPA regime excluded by DPA s.34 do not apply.

Extension of the definition of personal data and other amendments to the DPA

This section briefly examines the provisions which amend the DPA set out in Pt **26–66** VII of the FOIA. As has been explained above, the drafting approach adopted is to add a further category to the definition of "data" in s.1 of the DPA for the purposes of requests for access to public authorities. Category (e) data is recorded information held by a public authority which does not fall within any of paras (a)–(d), and "public authority" has the same meaning in the DPA as in the FOIA. The EIR adopt this amendment for the purposes of the exemption in reg.13 by declaring that "public authority" means an EIR public authority.

Where public authorities are concerned this amendment makes a massive extension to the range of personal information covered by the DPA. As long as the information is recorded in some form (s.84 of the FOIA defines "information" for the purposes of the FOIA as "information recorded in any form") then, if it falls within the definition of personal data (that is, it relates to a living individual who can be identified by those data or those data and other information in the possession of the data controller) it is covered by the DPA.

Effect of the extended definition on the rights of data subjects

26–67   The consequences of a vast increase in the DPA liability of public sector data controllers are immediately addressed by exemptions for the new category of data, which remove everything but the access and accuracy provisions and supporting provisions of the DPA. There are also special rules for subject access to some of this information.

By virtue of the exemption at s.33A(1) introduced via FOIA s.70 the new data will be covered only by the following provisions of the DPA:

- all of Pt I, that is preliminary definitions and territorial application;
- of Pt II, ss.7, 8, and 9 relating to subject access, s.13 as far as it relates to damage caused by contravention of s.7 or the principle 4 and to any distress caused as a result of that damage, s.14 which covers rectification, blocking erasure or destruction and s.15 which covers jurisdiction and procedure;
- Pt VI—all of the exemptions apply to the new sets of data, including the transitional exemptions (for details of which see below);
- Pt V—enforcement;
- Pt VI except for s.55 which deals with the unlawful obtaining of personal data. Section 55 is amended so that s.55(8) will read,

> "References in this section to personal data do not include references to personal data which by virtue of section 28 *or 33A* are exempt from this section"(s.70(2) of the FOIA).

Even the residual provisions which still apply to category (e) data are then expressed not to apply to employment and personnel records within this category by virtue of the further exemption inserted by FOIA s.70 as DPA s.33A(2). Detailed consideration of the treatment of personnel records, and of the effect of this exemption is given in Ch.16.

Duties of public authorities in relation to category (e) personal data

26–68   In respect of category (e) personal data, public authorities:

- must ensure that such data are accurate and, where necessary, kept up-to-date;
- must provide access in accordance with the subject access right (see Ch.11 for a full discussion of subject access rights);
- are liable to compensate data subjects for any damage caused by inaccuracy or failure to provide access and for any associated distress (see Ch.14 for a discussion of this);
- have a liability to comply with rectification, erasure, destruction or blocking orders made under s.14;
- are subject to the jurisdiction of the Commissioner and the Tribunal (see Chs 10 and 28 for these provisions).

EXTENDED RIGHT OF ACCESS IN RESPONSE TO REQUESTS FOR INFORMATION BY THE DATA SUBJECT

As noted above, where the applicant is the subject of any personal data requested, that information is exempt from the FOIA under s.40(1) and from the EIR under reg.5(3). Such applications will fall under the subject access provisions of the DPA. Given the extension in the scope of what can be included as personal data where public authorities are concerned this is a potentially very wide extension of the right of subject access. The obligations of authorities are, however, curtailed to make the exercise manageable by the introduction of the concepts of "structured" and "unstructured" category (e) data, and of the costs limitations applying to the latter. These terms are considered in full in Ch.4 on definitions but, broadly speaking, structured data is manual information which is part of a set of information relating to individuals to the extent that the set is structured by reference to individuals or criteria relating to individuals. Everything else then falls into the category of "unstructured" data. Where the category (e) data fall within the definition of structured data the public authority dealing with the subject access request must provide all of it, subject only to the usual DPA exemptions, for the usual DPA subject access fee (normally £10). Where the category (e) data fall within the unstructured category, the applicant must first describe it but even if he does the authority is not obliged to comply if it estimates that the cost of doing so would exceed the appropriate limit, which is by the provisions of DPA s.9A(5) and (6) determined by Fees Regulations, described above. The authority is not exempted from its obligation at s.7(1)(a), so must still say whether or not it holds the category (e) data described, unless the cost of doing that alone would exceed the appropriate limit; this is the element of "determining whether it holds the information" at para.4(3)(a) of the Fees Regulations.

Subject to those limitations, all of the requirements of s.7 of the DPA apply to category (e) personal data so the public authority must, except where the cost would exceed the appropriate limit for any unstructured data, be able to state:

- whether it holds any such personal data of the applicant;
- what information it holds, the purposes for which it holds the data and the recipients or classes of recipients; and
- whether it has any information available on the sources of the data;

in addition to providing access to the data. The usual DPA exemptions, and DPA fee for subject access, apply to requests for unstructured category (e) data.

Transitional exemptions

The transitional exemptions from the DPA for automated data came to an end on October 23, 2001, but the transitional exemptions for manual data applied to category (e) data until October 24, 2007. All those transitional provisions of the DPA are now exhausted.

26–69

26–70

Effect of the subject access exemptions under the DPA

26–71   These are to be taken into account in the usual way, but in respect of unstructured category (e) data they will arise only if the information is first described, and provided that the costs limitation does not then apply.

Provisions of the access regimes for requests involving personal data of the applicant

26–72   The access regimes do not allow applicants to request their own personal data because the access regimes cannot override or replace the provisions of the DPA, but they achieve this outcome by different routes. Under the EIR, reg.5(3) simply excludes personal data of which the applicant is the data subject from the obligation to make it available under the Regulations, but under the FOIA such data are covered by an exemption at s.40(1). The consequence is that under the FOIA the authority must serve a written refusal notice under s.17 which can then be tested via the authority's internal complaints procedure and appealed to the Commissioner for a decision, as described above. It follows that where a public authority receives an apparent FOIA request for information which relates to a living individual who seems to be the applicant then public authority is obliged, within 20 working days, to serve on the applicant a refusal notice on the grounds that the data are exempt under s.40(1). Although the public authority must tell the individual of his or her rights to complain and to appeal the decision there is no *specific* requirement in the FOIA for the public authority to tell the individual that he or she is entitled to make a subject access request for the same data. Given the authority's s.16 duty to help applicants, however, it is submitted that an authority ought to give the applicant this information in these circumstances. Under the EIR there appears to be no statutory requirement to respond at all but the corresponding duty at reg.9, which obliges authorities to give advice and assistance to applicants, will have the same effect. Therefore the access regimes do in practice impose an obligation on a public authority to inform an applicant under those regimes of his or her rights under the DPA.

The Commissioner's Guidance on the Exemption for Personal Information (version 4, issued March 2011, referred to as "the Commissioner's Guidance") states unequivocally that such a request will be a DPA subject access request and the authority will need to deal with it in accordance with the DPA.

Treating a request under the access regimes as a subject access

26–73   If the request is silent as to the legislation under which it is made the authority should consider whether it appears as a matter of fact to be a subject access request. The authority cannot automatically treat an ambiguous request as a subject access request because the requirements for subject access under the DPA are different from those in the access regimes. The identity of the applicant may not be clear, and under the access regimes the authority is not entitled to take the identity of the applicant into account, whereas under the DPA the data controller needs to ascertain the identity of the applicant before providing subject access. For example, an application for personal data could be made in the name of a specific individual but from an address other than the one the data controller has for that data subject so the public authority cannot be certain whether the application has been made by that data subject or not. The safest course is for the authority to provide (subject to any applicable exemptions) only such information as cannot be the personal data of the applicant and refuse the remainder of the request under s.40(1) of FOIA or EIR reg.5(3), while at the same time inviting the applicant to consider making an application for subject access. Relying on its right at DPA s.7(3) to ascertain the identity of the applicant for subject access it can then send the applicant an application form for subject access or ask for further identifying particulars. It can also ask for the fee for subject access, which is £10. If the authority refuses an FOIA or EIR request and does not notify the applicant of his or her rights to subject access then the individual may eventually complain to the Commissioner, who can serve an enforcement notice under FOIA s.52(1) requiring the public authority to comply with its s.16 (or reg.9) obligation to give an applicant in these circumstances information about rights to subject access and how to exercise them. The Commissioner cannot, however, treat the abortive access regimes request as a DPA subject access request unless it complies with the requirements for such a request under s.7 of the DPA, which means that it would have to be in writing and accompanied by a fee of £10.

APPLICATIONS FOR PERSONAL DATA BY THIRD PARTIES

The access regimes provide a right of access to all recorded information held in the public sector. Such recorded information will include information about living individuals, of which there is a considerable quantity held by public sector bodies. While authorities can refuse outright any request which is for the personal data of the applicant as explained above, they cannot do so if the request is for the personal data of a third party because the exemption for those data is not a simple absolute. The range of data which can be the subject of such requests is very wide, and even where a request is not specifically directed at obtaining personal information, the information produced to satisfy it may often involve third party personal data. The access regimes provide an exemption which allows public authorities to withhold access to such information unless they are satisfied that the disclosure will not interfere with the privacy of the individual by prescribing that the requested public disclosure of third party personal data must comply with the data protection principles. There are two further, but minor, elements of the exemption for third party data as described below, but the notorious complexities of the drafting of this exemption are mainly due to the torturous route by which all recorded information held by public authorities had to be brought into the exemption, and so can be said to stem ultimately from the limitations of the original scope of the DPA in its application to manual records.

26–74

Exemption of third party data from the access under the access regimes

26–75   A public authority is not obliged to release information where the exemption for personal data at FOIA s.41(2)–(7) applies, and is prohibited from releasing information where the conditions stipulated in EIR reg.13 apply. These are conditional exemptions, which apply only where specified conditions are satisfied. Although reg.13 is worded slightly differently it operates in exactly the same way as the FOIA provisions referred to, so to avoid confusion we refer in this section only to the relevant provisions of s.40 mentioned above, and not additionally to the corresponding provisions of the EIR.

There are, in effect, three possible conditions providing exemption. One of them, where disclosure would breach any data protection principle, confers an absolute exemption. The other two conditions provide a qualified exemption; in the case of non-category (e) personal data where a DPA s.10 notice would be breached, and in the case of any personal data where the information would not be provided in response to a subject access request made by the third party. Section 40(5) also provides an exemption from the FOIA s.1(1)(a) duty to confirm or deny that the information requested is held by the authority, and there is in EIR reg.13(5) a corresponding exemption from the implied duty under the EIR, considered further at paras 26–85—26–86, below.

Absolute and qualified exemptions

26–76   The difference between absolute and qualified exemptions in the access regimes has already been explained at para.26–15, above. The relevant provisions are set out in s.2 of the FOIA, which lists those sections which contain absolute exemptions and those which contain exemptions qualified by the requirement to apply a public interest test to the disclosure. Where a qualified exemption applies the authority must first engage the exemption (which in the case of many FOIA exemptions, and all the specific EIR exemptions requires a prior test of any harm to be caused by release) and then, before it can apply the exemption, it must balance the public interest arguments for and against release considering "all the circumstances of the case". The starting presumption is that the public interest is best served by disclosure and only if the authority is satisfied that, in all the circumstances of the case, the public interest is better served by maintaining the exemption is the authority exempt from the obligation to disclose the information.

In cases where an absolute exemption applies there is no public interest test to be applied and it is sufficient for the authority to be satisfied that the grounds of the exemption are made out. All of the exemptions in the EIR apart from reg.13 (third party personal data) are subject to a public interest test, although as has been pointed out the EIR achieve a similar result to many of the FOIA absolute exemptions by excluding information from the regime or just making separate provision as in reg.13.

Duty to confirm or deny that the authority holds information

The duty imposed on public authorities by the FOIA is twofold: once a valid   **26–77**
request has been received the authority must first give a written response as to
whether or not it holds the requested information, and if that is the case then the
authority must communicate the information to the applicant. The former
obligation is referred to in the FOIA as the duty to confirm or deny. The EIR are
differently constituted, although the effect is broadly the same. The authority's
duty under reg.5(1) is to make environmental information available on request,
and there is no express duty to say whether or not it is held. The EIR stipulate
only two instances in which an authority is entitled to respond by neither
confirming nor denying whether such information exists and is held by it—where
the exemption at reg.12(5)(a) applies to that disclosure, and at reg.13(5) where
that disclosure would breach any data protection principle. Under the access
regimes, just as information can be exempt from the obligation to disclose so it
can be exempt from the duty to confirm or deny that it is held by the authority, for
example in circumstances where the acknowledgment that information exists
would in itself damage the interest protected by the disclosure. As has already
been noted, there is an exemption at EIR reg.12(4)(a) where the authority does
not hold environmental information requested but this, like all reg.12 exemptions,
is subject to a public interest test.

Conditions for the application of the section 40(2) exemption

Condition applying to breach of principle

Section 40(2) states that where the requester is not the data subject then third   **26–78**
party personal data will be exempt if it fulfils either of two conditions. The first
condition varies depending on which category of data the requested information
falls within. If the data fall into ss.1(1)(a)–(d) of the DPA they are exempt if "the
disclosure of information to a member of the public other than under this Act"
would contravene either any of the data protection principles or s.10 of the DPA.
In any other case, that is if the data fall within s.1(1)(e) (referred to in this chapter
as "category (e) data"), the information will be exempt if the disclosure would
breach the standards in the data protection principles. It will be recalled that in
order to minimise the effects on the compliance obligations of public authorities,
category (e) data were subject to wide exemptions from the principles and rights
in the DPA by the new s.33A. This is why the exemption at s.40(3)(a)(ii) for
breach of a s.10 notice cannot apply to personal data of a third party which comes
within category (e)—there is no right under s.10 to object in respect of those data.
The exemption for category (e) third party personal data where disclosure would
breach any data protection principle is more problematic, because thanks to the
same provision, most of the principles do not apply to category (e) data in the
first place. That is why the exemption at s.40(3)(b) has to build them back in
again by expressly disregarding their disapplication, which gives the complexities
of this drafting a final twist. The category (e) third party personal data are for the
purposes of this exemption treated as though all the principles applied to them,

which has the effect of ensuring that disclosure of *any* personal information under the access regimes meets the standards required by the data protection principles.

Although complex, this drafting generally seems to work, subject to the reservations considered below, but it is unfortunate that in the condition at s.40(3)(a) the two exemptions—for contravention of the principles, and for contravention of a s.10 notice—are presented as if they are alternative options. It cannot be right to imply that application of the principles is optional, because DPA s.4(4) says that a controller must comply with them, subject to any DPA exemption. Some public authorities initially sought to advise staff to register objections, and would routinely consider this option as a mainstream exemption. The Commissioner had to issue repeated guidance that the principles must always be applied to any proposed disclosure under the access regimes, and that the two qualified exemptions in s.40 are "rarely used". These two qualified exemptions are considered in further detail at paras 26–116 and 26–140, below.

Disclosure of personal data "otherwise than under this Act"

26–79   The insertion of the words "to a member of the public otherwise than under this Act" in both limbs of the exemption at s.40(3) has caused considerable difficulty in the interpretation of exactly how the data protection principles apply to any disclosure of personal data under the access regimes. There are two elements:

(a)   disclosure to a member of the public; and
(b)   otherwise than under this Act.

The first element, that the disclosure should be treated as a disclosure to a member of the public, must mean that for the purpose of the application of the principles it is not to be treated as a disclosure to the particular applicant. This must be so because the access regimes are not there in order to accommodate particular private interests, but for general public interest purposes such as public transparency and accountability, and in principle the identity and purposes of the particular applicant should make no difference to the reasons for disclosing or withholding requested information. That is what is meant by saying that the access regimes are applicant-blind, and motive-blind. This element of the caveat to the application of the principles has clear implications for the purpose of considering the appropriate ground for disclosure under Schs 2 and 3 of principle 1, and furthermore for the application (or, as we maintain, non-application) of any of the DPA exemptions, both of which are considered in detail later on. By that we mean that, for instance, a Sch.2 ground should apply regardless of who makes the request and why they want the information, although this is contrary to a number of judicial findings as reported below, and also that a DPA exemption cannot apply to a disclosure under the access regimes because the exemptions in the DPA are directed to the accommodation of specified reasons for processing personal data for particular public interests and cannot be used to accommodate disclosures of personal data to the public at large.

26–80   The second element, that the disclosure should be considered otherwise than under the FOIA, is more problematic because of the inherent circularity of the result in the context of the appropriate Sch 2 and 3 grounds. It certainly does away with the difficulty that the exemption at DPA s.35(1) would disapply most of the principles to a disclosure under the access regimes on the basis that it is a disclosure required by an enactment; if it did not, the protection for personal privacy given by testing FOIA disclosures under the principles would be non-existent. The problem is that the attempts of the Tribunal and the courts to make sense of this caveat have produced some very odd readings of the DPA, as will be seen.

We cannot disagree with the opinion of the Tribunal in *House of Commons v Information Commissioner*[37] that there can be both ambiguity and absurdity in the application of the words "otherwise than under this Act". In that decision, after resorting to *Hansard*, the Tribunal said that once FOIA s.40(2) is engaged: **26–81**

> "Parliament intended that the request be considered under the DPA, without further consideration of FOIA. This means that information which is protected under the DPA may not be disclosed under FOIA."

There is nothing to suggest that any detailed consideration was given to what this means for the application of the conditions for processing in Schs 2 and 3, nor does it appear to contemplate the operation of the DPA exemptions.

The same phrase "otherwise than under this Act" is also employed in s.41 in the context of the exemption for confidential information. The wording in s.41 is slightly different , as highlighted by our italics:

> "(b) the disclosure of the information to the public (otherwise than under this Act) *by the public authority holding it*".

It may be significant that the whole of the wording of s.41(b) was contained in s.39 of the Freedom of Information Bill at the outset, whereas the qualification "otherwise than under this Act" in s.40(3) was put into the s.38 of the Bill at a late stage, which may account for the difference in the wording.

Much more recently in 2011 the Upper Tribunal considered the meaning of the phrase "otherwise than under this Act" in the *APPGER* case, and stated:

> "114. While it is true that disclosure under FOIA is effectively disclosure to the world, not simply to the information requester, so that there is good reason for s40(3) to require consideration of the effect of public disclosure, we consider that the MOD's submission goes too far. The test in s40(3) is not whether disclosure to the world under FOIA might contravene the data protection principles; the test is whether disclosure to a member of the public otherwise than under FOIA would contravene the data protection principles.
>
> 115. Whether a person is making the request as a member of the public in circumstances which satisfy a Schedule 2 or 3 condition and do not contravene the data protection principles, is a question to be considered in each case. It is right to say that there are some conditions which it will never be possible for a member of the public to fulfil, except in circumstances where the data controller is himself the person whose functions are referred to in the condition. Examples are Schedule 2 conditions 5(b) (exercise of functions conferred on a person by an enactment), 5(c) (exercise of functions of the Crown, a Minister or a government department) and 5(d) (exercise of functions of a public nature exercised in the public interest). By definition, a member of the public cannot have those particular functions. In

---

[37] [2011] 1 Info LR 935.

contrast, there are other conditions which can in suitable circumstances readily be fulfilled by a member of the public, even though they are not fulfilled by the public in general."

26–82   While s.40(3) does indeed say "the disclosure of the information *to a member of the public* otherwise than under this Act" (our italics) it is slightly odd that in para.115 the UT is saying that it falls to a disclosee of personal data, namely the requester as a member of the public, to fulfil the condition justifying the processing under Sch.2 or Sch.3. We have pointed out that s.41 talks of disclosure (otherwise than under this Act) by the public authority holding it, but the absence of that stipulation in s.40(3) should not be taken to mean that the purposes or motives of the disclosee are to be taken into account in any justification for processing under Schs 2 and 3 of the DPA. Those justifications simply do not operate in this way; the justification must be on the part of the data controller making the disclosure, not by the proposed disclosee producing reasons as to why the controller should disclose, although when it comes to data sharing those reasons will be very important.

Although the public functions accommodated in condition 5 are not in terms limited to the public functions of the data controller, the only case in which the disclosure to be justified can take into account the interests of the disclosee *specifically* is of course condition 6 of Sch.2, which was the route taken by the UT in the *APPGER* decision. If, however, the UT resorted to condition 6 of Sch.2 because it was thought that the other conditions required the member of the public making the request to fulfil them then it is respectfully submitted that the approach was misconceived. Even if it is appropriate to go to Sch.2(6) (as to which we express our reservations below) the legitimate interests to be taken onto account are usually those of the public authority data controller in making public the requested information, or if in the context of a disclosure under the FOIA the interests of the disclosee are to be taken into account then these are still public interests as opposed to particular personal interests of the requester.

The cases on this point are not especially clear or consistent, although the Tribunal said in *House of Commons v Information Commissioner* that the public interest in disclosure of official information is an interest which is relevant for the purposes of condition 6. The other slightly jarring note in para.115 is the clear implication that fulfilment of these conditions is a separate requirement from compliance with the data protection principles, of which those schedules form an integral part, although this is not the only instance of such an implication. These points will be considered in further detail in the context of the requirement for a Sch.2 condition addressed below at para.90 onwards.

It is helpful that in May 2012 these statements in *APPGER* received further consideration by the Tribunal, which in *A v Information Commissioner*[38] decided that paras 112–115 were obiter and particular to the facts of that case, so that the Tribunal was not bound to follow that reasoning; this element of *A v IC* is considered in further detail in the context of the exemption at DPA s.35 at para.26–114.

---

[38] EA/2011/0223.

Condition where section 10 notice would be contravened

There is a qualified exemption in s.40(3)(a)(ii) which applies only to data covered **26–83** by s.1(a)–(d) of the DPA. DPA s.10 provides that an individual may require a data controller to cease or not begin processing his personal data in a manner likely to cause substantial damage or distress to him or to someone else. This right does not apply where the data controller is relying on any of the grounds for processing set out in paras 1–4 of Sch.2. The data subject needs to give a written notice to the public authority, and there are various formalities to go through before a notice is accepted. Once accepted by the authority it can be enforced by the Commissioner or, where the individual applies to the court, by the court.[39] This exemption can, subject to a public interest test, be applied to disclosures of third party personal data under the access regimes, but as the Commissioner reminds practitioners in the Commissioner's Guidance a public authority is not thereby relieved of its obligation to apply the data protection principles. This exemption is considered in more detail at paras 26–116—26–118 below.

Condition where the third party would not get subject access

The public authority will not have to provide third party personal data requested **26–84** under the FOIA if that information would be exempt from subject access by virtue of any provision of Pt IV of the DPA. This is a qualified exemption. One effect of the FOIA amendments to the DPA is that subject access now extends to all manual data which qualifies under the definition of personal data in the hands of a public sector data controller, but this is then limited where the data are personnel data by the sweeping exemption at s.33A(2) of all category (e) data from any of the principles and rights under the DPA. This means that in the context of requested third party personal data, to the extent that they are category (e) personnel data of the third party, the third party would not be entitled to subject access because of the new exemption at s.33A(2) inserted in Pt IV of the DPA. Accordingly, the second condition for exemption, at s.40(4), will apply in those circumstances, as it does in the case of any of the other exemptions from the right of subject access contained in DPA Pt IV. These points are examined in more detail below at para.26–140 onwards.

Exemption from the duty to confirm or deny

There is an exemption from the duty to confirm or deny "if and to the extent" **26–85** that:

- where the information is data falling within s.1(1)(a)–(d) of the DPA, the provision of the confirmation or denial would contravene either the data protection principles or DPA s.10;
- where the information is data falling within s.1(1)(e) of the DPA, the provision of the confirmation or denial would contravene the standards set in the data protection principles; or

---

[39] See Ch.12 for a full discussion of s.10.

- the information is exempt under the DPA from the data subject's right to be informed whether personal data about the individual are being processed.

This element of the exemption for personal data in the FOIA is contained in s.40(5), but that subsection is not included in the parts of s.40 specifically designated in s.2(3)(f) as conferring an absolute exemption, so by default it would be a qualified exemption requiring a public interest test. This unfortunate result, which would require that a determination of the application of the data protection principles would then be subject to a public interest test, was addressed by the Tribunal in *A v IC*. The Tribunal, describing this result as "wholly unattractive" and noting that it would "likely bring the UK into breach of its obligations under the European Directive", adopted a purposive approach following *Department of Heath v Information Commissioner*[40] in finding that primacy can be given to the data protection principles on the basis that there was sufficient ambiguity in the meaning of "provision" in s.2(1) (as to whether it means a section of FOIA as a whole, or rather subsections). In *Heath v IC* the Tribunal had found that:

> "For the purpose of s.40(5)(b)(i), "the provision" conferring absolute exemption is s.40, which, by reason of s.40 (3)(a)(i) confers an absolute exemption for the purpose of s.2(1)(a)."

Presumably this would also apply for the purposes of s.40(3)(b), which is the exemption for breach of the principles in respect of a disclosure of category (e) personal data. The outcome, that no public interest test is required in respect of the elements of s.40(5) which confer exemption from the duty to confirm or deny where compliance would breach any data protection principle, is of course highly desirable. Is is not completely clear, however, given that the drafting of s.40(5) mixes these exemptions with the qualified elements of s.40, even within the same subparagraph at s.40(5)(b)(i), how this interpretation achieves the desired result, and for that reason it remains open to challenge.

26–86   The EIR also include at reg.13(5) an exemption from the duty to confirm or deny whether third party personal data are held, but this is also defective in so far as it was meant to reflect the position in relation to the three limbs of the personal data exemption at reg.13(2) and (3) (breach of principle, s.10 objection, and subject access exemption in the DPA). In this case, instead of rendering all three limbs subject to a PIT as the FOIA succeeded in doing, the EIR make the exemption from the duty to confirm or deny absolute in all cases by failing to insert a PIT in relation to the two qualified elements of the main exemption.

As observed earlier, the exemption for personal data in FOISA s.38 does not extend to the duty to confirm or deny whether requested information is held, but the Freedom of Information (Amendment) (Scotland) Bill (at consultation stage at the time of writing) proposes to add s.38 to the exemptions at s.18 which qualify for a non-committal response so that a 'neither confirm nor deny' response for personal data will then be allowed under the FOISA.

If there is to be consultation with the individual before a decision to disclose is made then the individual can be asked at the same time whether he or she objects

---

[40] EA/2009/0020.

to the authority confirming that data are held, which would also take into account questions of fairness to the data subject and afford an opportunity for him to consider the exercise of the s.10 right to object. There is no duty to confirm or deny where giving such confirmation or denial would contravene a s.10 notice, subject to the application of a PIT—because this limb of the s.40 exemption is definitely qualified.

Processing personal data in response to a request under the access regimes

If any conditions set out in the personal data exemption apply then third party personal data will be exempt from disclosure under the access regimes. Before examining the conditions in more depth consideration must first be given to the general application of the DPA to the processing of requests for third party personal data made via the access regimes.

26–87

No correspondence with DPA section 9A

It is important to be clear about the function of the new DPA s.9A, which is nothing to do with handling requests for information under the access regimes. This provision is made in order to minimise the DPA compliance burden which was imposed upon public authorities by the extension of the right of subject access to personal data within the new category (e). As has been explained, the s.9A limitations achieve this by classifying some category (e) data as unstructured personal data and then requiring an applicant to describe it, after which he still will not get access if complying with his request for those data would be too costly. Those provisions have no impact on the standard fee for subject access, which remains at £10, nor do they provide for any additional fee for subject access to unstructured category (e) data. A request under the access regimes for information which counts as third party personal data, on the other hand, is governed not by the subject access provisions in the DPA but by the provisions of the access regimes, which in the case of the FOIA includes at s.12 an exemption for requests which are too costly. That exemption can be applied in respect of any information requested under the FOIA whether or not it is personal data of a third party, and if it is third party personal data, then regardless of which category of data under DPA s.1(1) applies.

26–88

GROUNDS FOR PROCESSING IN RESPONSE TO A REQUEST UNDER THE ACCESS REGIMES

Every data controller must be able to show a basis for processing personal data which falls within one of the grounds set out in Sch.2 to the DPA. This applies as much to the processing required to deal with an application under the access regimes as to any other processing by a public authority data controller. There is nothing in the access regimes or in the DPA which specifically addresses the issue of exactly how processing of personal data in the context of a freedom of information request should be justified, nor was this consideration addressed in

26–89

detail or with any finality in the debates in Parliament on the passage of the Freedom of Information Bill. Furthermore, the justification for the processing required to consider, and possibly refuse, a request for third party personal data may not be the same as the justification for the disclosure of those data to the public in accordance with the request. When the access regimes first came into force on January 1, 2005 it was thought by some practitioners that the appropriate Sch.2 justification would be condition 3 (legal obligation) and by others that it was condition 5(b) (processing necessary for the exercise of statutory functions). What had not been anticipated was that the Sch.2 ground which was to be used in practice by the Commissioner and the courts would be condition 6 (necessary in legitimate interests), yet since 2005 this is the ground which has been routinely applied to test whether a disclosure of third party personal data to the public at large can be justified under this element of principle 1. On occasion, in decisions made by the Commissioner and by the Tribunal, there is also reference to the consent of the third party. Given this lack of clarity, it will be helpful to consider all the Sch.2 grounds available, and their potential for application in respect of disclosures under the access regimes.

26–90   Before doing so, however, it is necessary to address some of the differences between the range of justifications available for processing all personal data in Sch.2 and the more limited range of justifications for processing sensitive personal data in Sch.3. It has always been the case that the processing of sensitive data is hard to justify; indeed, that is the reason for the separate provisions in respect of this category of data. Whether it is still useful to maintain this separate provision is a moot point; in its response to the Council on the proposed General Data Protection Regulation (responses published on July 18, 2012) the UK said that it questions the need for special categories of personal data. The difficulty highlighted by the obligation of UK public sector data controllers to process personal data, including sensitive personal data, in response to a request under the access regimes is that some of the justifications utilised in this context under Sch.2 are not available under Sch.3. When it comes to the point at which a disclosure is taking place, the position will be that while disclosure of non-sensitive personal data might be justified under Sch.2, disclosure of any sensitive personal data might not be justifiable under Sch.3. There are problems with consistency of approach under the two schedules in terms of the different types of grounds for disclosure, as is evidenced by the varied approaches taken by the Tribunal and the courts (see our comments in relation to the *DoH* decision at para.26-101, below), but the resolution of the differences between availability of justifications under the two schedules is simply to refuse to disclose the sensitive personal data.

That approach cannot solve the problem of the need to justify the pre-disclosure processing of sensitive personal data which is necessary in order for a decision on disclosure to be reached. As noted, the generally accepted Sch.2 ground is condition 6 (necessary in legitimate interests), which is not available for sensitive data. We have previously argued for condition 3 (legal obligation) but again that is not available for sensitive data. Apart from data subject consent, and processing necessary for vital interests, neither of which is usually appropriate for processing in response to a request under the access regimes, the only ground for processing which is available in both Sch.2 and Sch.3 is that it is necessary for public functions (Schs 2(5) and 3(7)). This line has not generally been followed in decided cases, although the courts and Tribunal have usually been engaged in consideration of how a disclosure might be justified, rather than with the authority's grounds for processing personal data up to that point. Where ground 6 of Sch.2 is used we take the view that the only available ground in Sch.3 can be condition 5— that the data subject made the sensitive data public. Conversely, if ground 3(7) is used to justify processing of sensitive data, then the same Sch.2 ground—condition 5, probably 5(b) for reasons explained below— would have to be used. We will look at the application of the different conditions in turn, but have come to the conclusion that there is no right answer, given that this was not addressed when the Freedom of Information Bill was going through Parliament.

Schedule 2 conditions considered

Condition 1: data subject consent.   Although the consent of the third party to the proposed disclosure, or the lack of it, is sometimes mentioned as a factor in determining whether principle one would be complied with, it cannot be right that this is an appropriate justification for a disclosure under the access regimes. To allow disclosures to which the third party had consented and to refuse those with which he disagreed would be to render the disclosure of third party personal data under the access regimes at the whim of the data subject. As against this argument, it is noteworthy that in the debate on the Freedom of Information Bill (*Hansard*, col.245, November 14, 2000) that there was serious consideration given to the introduction of a statutory duty to seek the consent of the third party, which in the end was left as a prescribed good practice element of consultation with third parties "in some cases" in the s.45 Code. The data subject's views may well be relevant to consideration of whether disclosure would be lawful, where for example he consents to the release of his confidential personal information (although the barrier of confidentiality can be overridden in the public interest regardless of the consent of the confider, and in the context of a release of third party personal data under the access regimes this has on occasion been done) but they are most likely to be relevant to the other principle 1 consideration, which is fairness, considered below at paras 26-123—26-128. Note that consent is a ground which is also available under Sch.3 as a justification for processing sensitive personal data.

26-91

Condition 2: necessary for a contract.   We are not aware of any cases in which it had been argued that there can be a contractual basis for a disclosure under the access regimes—this ground seems to be obviously irrelevant. Nevertheless, it does seem to be possible, at least in theory, to set up a contractual arrangement with a data subject under which it would be necessary to disclose his personal data to the public. This is unattractive on the basis that disclosure under the access regimes should take place because it is in the general public interests of transparency and accountability which the access regimes are there to serve, rather than because there happens to be a specific contractual arrangement with the individual who is the subject of the information requested which accommodates such a disclosure, once all the other implications for the privacy

26-92

of that individual have been taken into account. This reasoning bears some similarity to the arguments against data subject consent under condition 1 but it also suggests the legitimate interests balance in condition 6, considered below at para.26-103 onwards. There is no contract justification in Sch.3.

26–93   **Condition 3: necessary to comply with a non-contractual legal obligation.** We have in previous editions of this book favoured this condition, and the arguments in its support are strong, but it is not a route which has ever been followed in practice in decided cases. The legal basis for an authority's processing of personal data is to be found in its obligations under the access regimes. The FOIA states at s.1(1) that any person making a request to a public authority is entitled to be informed in writing by the public authority whether it holds the information specified and if so to have it communicated to him. The EIR say at reg.5(1) that a public authority that holds environmental information shall make it available on request. Although the FOIA does not categorically state that an authority is obliged to consider every request and to determine what or what not to provide taking account of relevant considerations, clearly an authority does have such an obligation as a consequence of the s.1(1) declaration of entitlement, and if it failed to deliver then it could be forced by a mandatory order of the High Court to do so via the enforcement procedures at ss.52 and 54 of the FOIA, which are also incorporated into the EIR.

26–94   The entitlement at s.1(1) is immediately qualified by the provision at s.1(2) that it has effect subject to the provisions of ss.2, 9, 12 and 14, which cover all the exemptions (s.9 is about fees notices, but the s.1(1) obligation is deferred until any fee is paid). In respect of any information which is exempt the obligation to communicate it to the applicant will not apply if the exemption is absolute or, in the case of a qualified exemption, it will not apply to the extent that, "in all the circumstances of the case the public interest in maintaining the exemption outweighs the public interest in disclosing the information". The effect of the exemptions has been considered above at para.26–14. The entitlement of the requester at s.1(1) is therefore conditional, depending upon whether or not it is qualified by the application of any exemption. It follows that the legal obligation to disclose information in response to a request arises only in those cases where the exemptions do not apply. The public authority has to decide whether or not an exemption is engaged and if so whether it can or should be applied, and must make a decision on that before the legal obligation to disclose sets in.

This is not an argument that in practice an authority should upon receiving a request begin by checking all possible reasons to refuse; the accepted view which is, understandably, propounded by the Commissioner, is rather that an authority should in practice assume that information will be disclosed unless there seems to be a reason why not. Nevertheless, what this analysis of the legal effect of ss.1 and 2 reveals is that before making any FOIA disclosure—indeed before it is obliged to make any such disclosure—an authority must first take a view on its other obligations, such as its duties under the DPA, or its obligations of confidence, for example. This activity, plus the administration of the request, is what we have in mind when we talk about the pre-disclosure processing of any personal data involved.

Without more, then, it seems clear that, since the reason why an authority discloses personal data in response to a request under the access regimes is because it is subject to a legal obligation to do so, the appropriate Sch.2 justification for doing so must be condition 3: the processing is necessary for compliance with a legal obligation to which the data controller is subject. In respect of the pre-disclosure processing, considered below at para.26–111, this looks like the correct ground but for the problem that it will not justify the pre-disclosure processing of sensitive data. The question then arises as to whether this ground can apply to justify the disclosure itself, where the test stipulated at s.40(3) is:

26–95

> "would disclosure of the information to a member of the public otherwise than under this Act contravene any of the data protection principles".

We have seen in the earlier discussion of the effect of this caveat that the Tribunal and the courts have fairly consistently maintained that this means that the fact that the authority is obliged under the FOIA to disclose the information must be disregarded for the purposes of testing disclosures of personal data to the public. Hence the Commissioner's stance in the Commissioner's Guidance "otherwise than under this Act" has the effect that "the FOIA itself cannot be used to meet the third condition (that disclosure is necessary for compliance with a legal obligation)." We find it difficult to accept that this caveat was intended to close the statutory gateways for disclosure which were put into the Directive 95/46 EC, and therefore into the DPA; although as will be seen we think that the caveat is essential for the purpose of ruling out the application of the exemption at DPA s.35(1) to disclosures under the access regimes. Nevertheless, there are other difficulties in applying condition 3 to such disclosures, not least in relation to the applicability of the s.10 objection, considered below at para.26–116. For example, FOIA restrictions can still apply to voluntary disclosures when the obligation to disclose has been exhausted by the application of the costs exemption at.s12, but s.13 applies to limit what an authority can then charge for releasing information. Clearly a disclosure of personal data in these circumstances cannot be justified on the basis that the authority is legally obliged to make it, and another Sch.2 ground must be found. It is perhaps surprising that a legal obligation ground has never been available for sensitive data under Sch.3.

Condition 4: necessary in the vital interest of the data subject. Although it seems hard to envisage any circumstances in which it could be maintained that this condition could justify a disclosure of the data subject's personal data to the public under the access regimes, this contention was nevertheless argued (unsuccessfully) in *APPGER* with the following response by the UT:

26–96

> "In regard to condition 4, we have no reason to think that the vital interests of the few individuals whose detentions fall within the scope of the request and outside the protection of s23 were under threat such that disclosure of the details sought in respect of their detentions (which in nearly all cases were for a single day) would have protected them."

For what it is worth, this ground is, in a slightly wider form, available under Sch.3, but in the context of processing for the purposes of the access regimes, we do not think that it is worth much.

26–97 **Condition 5: necessary for official/statutory/public functions.** This condition, giving effect to the powers and functions which public authorities by their nature exercise, seems a particularly attractive candidate for the Sch.2 justification of a FOIA disclosure, since the FOIA in effect says that one of the things that public sector bodies must now do is deliver public transparency by responding to requests for information. Different limbs of this condition have been considered by the Tribunal and the courts, so the condition is here set out in full:

5. The processing is necessary
   (a)   for the administration of justice,
   (aa) for the exercise of any functions of either House of Parliament,
   (b)   for the exercise of any functions conferred on any person by or under any enactment,
   (c)   for the exercise of any functions of the Crown, a Minister of the Crown or a government department, or
   (d)   for the exercise of any other functions of a public nature exercised in the public interest by any person.

26–98 In the *APPGER* case the UT said: "In regard to condition 5, we do not consider that APG's request was made for the purpose of the administration of justice"; but we have earlier criticised the approach to Sch.2 justification on the basis of the applicant's purpose in requesting the disclosure, because the justification should properly be the data controller's purpose in, or reason for, disclosing the personal data. The approach focussing on the purpose of the applicant would also do violence to the general principle of freedom of information that it is not only applicant-blind, but also motive-blind. It is, nevertheless, noteworthy as a rare judicial comment about the applicability of condition 5(a). In the same decision, passing consideration was also given to conditions 5(b), 5(c) and 5(d), but as mentioned earlier, these options were dismissed on the similar ground that a member of the public cannot have the relevant functions:

"It is right to say that there are some conditions which it will never be possible for a member of the public to fulfil, except in circumstances where the data controller is himself the person whose functions are referred to in the condition. Examples are Schedule 2 conditions 5(b) (exercise of functions conferred on a person by an enactment), 5(c) (exercise of functions of the Crown, a Minister or a government department) and 5(d) (exercise of functions of a public nature exercised in the public interest). By definition, a member of the public cannot have those particular functions."

It is strange and puzzling that it should be thought that whenever a public body makes a disclosure of personal data the condition 5 justification for doing so has to be met by the disclosee. While this is not precluded by the language of condition 5(b) in that a data controller's disclosure to another public body might be necessary for the public functions of that other body, it is clear from the

Directive 95/46/EC (and from the current attempts to replace it) that the set of justifications in condition 5 is there to give a ground for processing that specifically accommodates data controllers who are public bodies—or, to use European terminology, processing that is necessary for their "public task". We discuss below the options open to a public authority, but we note that the Tribunal, in the subsequent decision in *A v IC*, did not follow it, as seen below at para.26–114.

In the litigation involving MP's expenses, the Tribunal in *Corporate Officer of the House of Commons v Information Commissioner* gave detailed consideration to justification under condition 5, and addressed whether disclosure under the FOIA was a function of the House of Commons, but said: **26–99**

> "If the argument is that it is a function of the House of Commons to administer the ACA scheme, simply on the basis that such administration is something that the House of Commons in fact undertakes, then we do not consider that this falls within the meaning of the term 'function' in condition 5."

Condition 5(d) was also argued before the Tribunal, but dismissed apparently for the same reasons as condition 5(aa):

> "We understand the functions of the House of Commons, in the sense intended in condition 5, as the specific functions of the House of Commons recognised in law."

Although this does not appear to recognise that the point of adding condition 5(d) is to confer another separate justification for processing in addition to the justifications listed at (a)–(c), in which the functions of the House of Commons are already accommodated. The question is, if the data controller who is attempting to justify disclosure happens to be the House of Commons, is condition 5(aa) the only option open to it under condition 5 or can it also have, for example, functions under any enactment (such as the FOIA) by reference to which the processing of personal data can be justified? Certainly a public body can have duties under other enactments, and of course an enactment may also confer new or additional functions upon a public authority, as when the Commissioner was made the regulator for freedom of information as well as for data protection under new provisions in the FOIA. Therefore the key consideration for condition 5(b) is whether the effect of access regimes can be said to be the imposition upon public authorities of, or the investing of public authorities with, new functions. Whether it does have such an effect is unclear.

In deciding the appeal against the Tribunal's decision in *House of Commons v Leapman*,[41] the High Court did not give any further consideration to the applicability of any limb of condition 5 but adopted the Tribunal's application of condition 6. Arguably, though, the only appropriate limb of condition 5 is (b), on the basis that it does not matter which public authority is trying to justify a FOIA disclosure, or what the particular role or functions of that authority might be, because the reason for the disclosure is that the FOIA requires it, and disclosure of information to the public is a function conferred on all public authorities by the enactment of the FOIA. Of course it follows that if this justification works under **26–100**

---

[41] [2008] EWHC 1084 (Admin).

Sch.2 then if the personal data are also sensitive within the definition at DPA s.2, Sch.3(7)(1)(b) is also automatically satisfied, as pointed out by Lord Roger in *CSA v SIC*:

> "59. So far as Schedule 2 is concerned, it seems clear that ISD needs to process personal data for the exercise of the functions - collecting and disseminating epidemiological data and participating in epidemiological investigations – conferred on it by the then Secretary of State under the predecessor to section 10(3) of the 1978 Act. So, prima facie, condition 5(b) would apply. Condition 6(1) also appears to be potentially relevant...
>
> 60. Assuming that any disclosure of sensitive personal data might satisfy one or other of these conditions, it could still not take place unless it met one or more of the conditions in Schedule 3. But, not surprisingly, para 7(1)(b) of Schedule 3 is in precisely the same terms as para 5(1)(b) of Schedule 2. So, if the processing of the data would prima facie meet the condition in para 5(1)(b) of Schedule 2, it would also prima facie meet the condition in para 7(1)(b) of Schedule 3."

Although Lord Roger is applying condition 5(b) to the disclosure under consideration, he does so by reference to the Department's specific functions, not by reference to any functions it may have under the FOIA, so his reasoning does not support the suggestion that disclosure under the access regimes amounts to a function which public authorities must now carry out.

26–101   In the *DoH* case the justification for disclosure of medical statistics under Sch.2 was ground 6—legitimate interests, but the justification under Sch.3 was ground 7—public functions. There it was argued by counsel for the public authority that the issues under Sch.2(6) and Sch.3(7), are different, and the Tribunal was wrong in transposing its reasoning on the first to the second, but Cranston J approved the transposition of Sch.2 justification across to Sch.3:

> "Although it may have been preferable for the Tribunal to spell out to a greater extent the Schedule 3 analysis, in my view there is no error in its reading across reasons set out in its Schedule 2 analysis across to justify disclosure under Schedule 3."

Given the difficulty of establishing a rational and consistent approach to justifying processing of personal data generally and sensitive data in particular under Schs 2 and 3 it is not surprising that the court did not re-open the arguments as to which grounds should have been used, but it cannot be right that the public functions justification under Sch.3(7) was not also used under Sch.2(5), or if it was not available under Sch.2(5) then how could it possibly work under Sch.3(7)? In any event it was held that the disclosure of the anonymised abortion statistics was not a disclosure of personal data so that no justification under Sch.2 was required, although if it had been then Cranston J said that condition 6 would be the appropriate condition:

> "In my view, the Tribunal was not flawed in concluding that the risk of individual identification is so remote that the right under Article 8.1 was not engaged. Even if it were wrong in that regard, any interference is prescribed by law under the Abortion Regulations. The reasons the Tribunal gave in relation to paragraph 6, Schedule 2, were a basis to conclude that any interference was both necessary and proportionate."

Clearly, none of the decided cases gives any significant support to arguments **26–102** in favour of one of the limbs of condition 5 as a Sch.2 ground for processing in disclosures under the access regimes, mainly on the basis that disclosure under the FOIA is not, apparently, thought to be a function of a public authority although that issue is not specifically addressed. The other principal argument which could be advanced against the applicability of condition 5 is the same as has been advanced against condition 3, namely that this ground would be displaced by the caveat in the test of the principles in s.40(3) that it has to be a test of "disclosure to a member of the public otherwise than under this Act". It does not appear in the cases cited above, except for the discussion in *APPGER* (considered above at para.98) where it is not applied to this precise effect. Earlier, however, in *House of Commons v Information Commissioner*[42] the Tribunal held:

> "..that once section 40(2) FOIA is engaged that Parliament intended that the request be considered under the DPA, without further consideration of FOIA. This means that information which is protected under the DPA may not be disclosed under FOIA."

Since the precise effect of the caveat "otherwise than under this Act" on the applicability of particular Sch.2 grounds for processing is not articulated in this or any of the other cases cited, it cannot be said that the application of condition 5(b) has been specifically disapproved for that reason, so if responding to FOIA requests can properly be considered to be a function of public authorities then this route remains open. Certainly if it can work under Sch.2(5) then it can also work under Sch.3(7) for sensitive data, and conversely if it can be successfully argued that it is not available for processing under the access regimes then the options for dealing with sensitive data are even more limited than may have been thought. Nevertheless, given the constant stream of decisions by the Commissioner, the Tribunal and the courts in relation to the personal data exemption in which this option under Sch.2(5) seldom, if ever, appears it seems unlikely that it will be the subject of much further consideration. As has already been noted, in just about every dispute the arguments about the applicability of a Sch.2 ground are always in relation to condition 6.

Condition 6: necessary in the legitimate interests of controller or disclosee. **26–103** This condition as a justification for disclosures under the access regimes first appeared in an early decision of the Commissioner in which he upheld a complaint against Corby Borough Council in respect of a requested disclosure relating to money paid to a former head of finance,[43] by applying condition 6. It provides:

> "The processing is necessary for the purposes of legitimate interests pursued by the data controller or by the third party or parties to whom the data are disclosed, except where the processing is unwarranted in any particular case by reason of prejudice to the rights and freedoms or legitimate interests of the data subject."

---

[42] [2011] 1 Info LR 935..
[43] FS50062124 25 August 2005.

This is the justification for disclosures under the access regimes that has consistently been applied by the Commissioner, the Tribunal and the courts, and most disputes between the requester and the public authority in respect of disclosures of third party personal data involve detailed arguments as to its application. For this reason there has been minute judicial consideration of its application in respect of a wide range of disclosures of personal data in a variety of circumstances, provided that the proposed disclosure is into the public domain in response to a request under the access regimes. As a result we now have very detailed case law from the Tribunal and the courts, which is implemented in the Commissioner's Guidance, as to exactly how condition 6 should be applied. For this we should be grateful, since it is in marked contrast to the paucity of jurisprudence on just about every other aspect of the application of the principles, with the exception of first principle fairness which is also regularly considered in cases brought under the access regimes. That does not, however, dispose of the arguments against using condition 6 of Sch.2 to justify FOIA disclosures in the first place.

26–104   Despite the de facto establishment of this ground as the appropriate justification for disclosure of personal data under the FOIA over the past eight years the problem remains that it is extremely questionable whether any public body ought to be able to rely on grounds other then conditions 3 and 5, considered in detail above. A public body must either have a legal obligation to process or must be exercising a discretionary power. In the case of *Rechnungshof v Osterreichischer Rundfunk* (C-465/00)[44] the European Court referred to the equivalent grounds in the Directive 95/46/EC as being the basis for processing by public authorities. It does seem that the adoption of the condition 6 ground was a last resort given the difficulties which arise when the attempt is made to apply the other more obvious grounds, and perhaps given the lack of understanding often displayed in the decisions of the Tribunal and the courts as to how these Sch.2 justifications work in practice. It is also noteworthy that in the first draft of the EC proposed General Data Protection Regulation published on January 25, 2012, public authorities were specifically debarred from using the legitimate interests justification, but in its revision published on June 22, 2012, and in response to criticisms from Member States, the Presidency removed this barrier saying:

> "The Presidency does not believe it can be assumed that all processing carried out by public authorities has a clear legal provision as its basis."

26–105   **Applying condition 6 to FOIA disclosures.**   The Commissioner's Guidance draws on the decision of the Tribunal in *HoC v IC and Leapman and ors* for the operation of condition 6 in the context of disclosures under the access regimes and states:

> "This requires a public authority to approach condition 6 as a three-part test:
>
> 1.   there must be a legitimate public interest in disclosure;
> 2.   the disclosure must be necessary to meet that public interest; and
> 3.   the disclosure must not cause unwarranted harm to the interests of the individual."

---

[44] May 20, 2003.

It goes on to say:

> "It is likely that the public authority will already have dealt with the first and third parts of the test in concluding that disclosure is fair. Legitimate interests, both in disclosure and of the individuals, will have been considered in the balancing exercise described in the previous section, and the unwarranted harm test dealt with when considering the possible consequences of disclosure on the individual."

While there is certainly a strong connection between fairness considerations and the first and third elements of this test, it must be remembered that the requirement to be fair to the data subject is a separate and two-stage obligation (addressed below at paras 26–120—26–128), and we remain of the view that the application of ground 6 in this way can lead to the conflation of the need to have an appropriate ground for processing with the application of the test of fairness and compatibility, which is what occurred in the decision of the Tribunal in *HoC v IC and Leapman and ors*. One important consequence of this three-stage test is that it clearly articulates the element of the necessity of the disclosure in the public interest. The Commissioner's Guidance notes:

> "... that the Tribunal, and later the High Court, said that 'necessary' in Condition 6 implies the existence of a pressing social need, reflecting the European Convention on Human Rights (in particular Article 8, the right to private life). However, there will be circumstances where relatively innocuous information is under consideration where the need for transparency will be sufficient to meet the test of necessity."

This introduces, by the back door, a quasi-public interest test into what is **26–106** supposed to be an absolute exemption. Of course, that is not the only instance of this kind in the FOIA; we have already mentioned that obligations of confidence, protected by the absolute exemption in s.41, can be overridden in the public interest. It is relevant that the exemption for legally privileged information at FOIA s.42, which does a similar job, is a qualified exemption. Nevertheless, a consideration of the general public interest is an alien element in the application of the data protection principles; the DPA is very specific about the particular public interests which are allowed to qualify the application of the principles. This is put into effect by the various exemptions of DPA Pt IV, which justify processing for particular public interest purposes such as crime prevention, and by the justifications for processing in conditions 2–5 of Sch.2, discussed above. On the other hand, the advantage of the test of necessity is that it does enable art.8 considerations to be taken into account, as described by the Commissioner above. This aspect is developed in the balancing of the necessity of the disclosure in the public interest against the impact on the data subject, as the Commissioner goes on to state:

> "This relates to the balancing of the interests of the individual against the collective weight of the public interest factors that have passed the necessity test. This is consistent with the approach to Article 8 of the European Convention on Human Rights (the right to respect for private and family life) in that interference with private life can only be justified where it is in accordance with the law, is necessary in a democratic society for the pursuit of legitimate aims, and is not disproportionate to the objective pursued (that is, whether a pressing public interest is involved and the measure employed is proportionate to the aim)."

The important difference between the public interest test in condition 6 and the general public interest test to be applied in exemptions under the access regimes is that there is no presumption that the public interest favours disclosure; instead, the interests of the data subject take precedence and can be overridden only if there is a stronger public interest in disclosure. Here again art.8 considerations can be taken into account in the balance because any interference with private life has to be proportionate to the aim of the disclosure, and this is certainly helpful given that, as we noted earlier, there is no gateway in the access regimes by way of a specific exemption which allows Art.8 considerations to be applied to a disclosure.

26–107   We have earlier observed with dismay that the Tribunal and the courts in applying this test under condition 6 often talk about whether the disclosure requested under the access regimes is necessary in the legitimate interests of the person who happens to be making the request, on the basis that the interests of the particular disclosee can, under condition 6, be used to justify disclosure, thus removing the element of applicant-blindness from a FOIA disclosure. We have already addressed this misconception; the Commissioner in the Commissioner's Guidance does not address it specifically in that he does not mention this element of condition 6 but he excludes the interests of the third party to whom the data are disclosed from his statement of the three-part test in which he confines the legitimate interests in disclosure to a legitimate public interest in disclosure. It is in our view unfortunate that the SIC's Guidance does not follow that of the Commissioner; instead, the SIC's guidance says:

> "1.   **Does the applicant have a legitimate interest in obtaining this personal data?** There is no definition within the DPA of the term "legitimate interest". When assessing whether an applicant has a legitimate interest, the Commissioner considers that it will be good practice for public authorities to ask the applicant why they want the information (unless it is already clear from the information request or from previous correspondence.) Authorities should remember, however, that applicants are not required to explain why they want the information if they do not wish to do so. In some cases, the legitimate interest might be personal to the applicant—e.g. he or she might want the information in order to bring legal proceedings. With most requests, however, there are likely to be wider legitimate interests, such as scrutiny of the actions of public bodies or public safety."

It is hard to tell from this advice whether the FOISA is meant to be applicant-blind, and motive blind, at least when it comes to requesting information about someone else. Unsurprisingly, perhaps, this guidance was followed in *South Lanarkshire Council v SIC*[45] in which, among other things, it was submitted that the SIC had misdirected himself in law by failing to identify clearly the nature of the requester's "legitimate interest" in obtaining the information sought. The court held that:

> "So far as the matter of specification of 'legitimate interest' is concerned, it is true that the Commissioner's findings in para 44 of his Decision leave something to be desired but, reading, as we must, the Decision as a whole, we are satisfied that as a

---

[45] [2012] CSIH 30XA45/11.

'freelance writer' who published a 'blog' specialising in, inter alia, issues of 'Equal Pay' the Requester did have such an interest."

It is difficult to see how the art.8 considerations of a pressing public interest in disclosure can properly be taken into account if the focus is on the requester's reasons for wanting the information, although the court then went on to broaden its reasoning by endorsing the SIC's finding

> "that the Requester's own interest coincided with a widespread public interest in the matter of gender equality and that it was important to achieve transparency on the subject of Equal Pay."

It seems that the data protection rules are operated differently in Scotland compared with the rest of the UK, although it is abundantly clear that the Tribunal and the courts south of the border can be similarly confused when it comes to consideration of identity and motives of the requester, of which the *APPGER* decision is one example.

Grounds for processing sensitive data under Schedule 3

Sometimes the third party personal data requested under the access regimes   **26–108** amount to sensitive personal data as defined in DPA s.2. The public authority must justify any disclosure by satisfying all the requirements of principle 1 which in these cases includes the requirement to satisfy a Sch.3 ground for processing. Since Sch.3 gives very limited justifications for processing—in particular there is no general legal obligation ground corresponding to Sch.2(3), nor is there any legitimate interests ground corresponding to Sch.2(6)—it was thought that in practice sensitive data would seldom if ever be released into the public domain under the access regimes. Certainly it does not happen often, but there are now a few cases in which consideration has been given to the treatment of sensitive data in the context of access requests.

Typically the sensitive data concerned will relate to an individual's alleged criminality or criminal convictions, or sexual life, but other sensitive data categories have arisen. In a decision upholding a complaint against the Ministry of Justice[46] who refused a request for the answers given by judges on the issue of Masonic membership on the ground that this was sensitive data, the Commissioner said that that Masonic membership is not similar to a religious belief. The Tribunal in *O'Connell*[47] ruled that a request relating to the Guildford bombings still involved sensitive data of the accused even though the conviction had been quashed. In the case of *Brett v Information Commissioner*[48] the request was for details relating the Gibraltar shootings of IRA members in 1998 on which the appellant was planning a book, and the Tribunal gave detailed consideration to the sensitive data conditions which were put forward. Condition 6(c) of Sch.3, which justifies processing necessary for defending legal rights, did not apply because the quality of the information was doubtful and it had not been demonstrated that disclosure was necessary for the defence of such rights, if

---

[46] February 8, 2010, FS50227348.
[47] EA 2009/0010.
[48] EA/2008/009821.

indeed there were any at stake. Of particular interest is the raising of two of the sensitive data conditions introduced into Sch.3(10) by the Data Protection (Processing of Sensitive Personal Data) Order 2000 (SI 200/417). Consideration was given to para.3, which provides a ground where the disclosure is in the substantial public interest, in connection with any unlawful act, and is made for the special purposes with a view to publication which is reasonably believed to be in the public interest. Note that in this condition the processing operation to be justified can only be disclosure and there is no test of necessity, but here the condition was not met because the material was merely additional speculation. The appellant also tried para.9, that the processing was in the substantial public interest and necessary for research purposes, but this ground was not met either.

26–109   There then followed two Tribunal decisions in which para.3 of SI 200/417 was considered again, but not applied. In *Ferguson v Information Commissioner*[49] the request concerned an unlawful political donation to an MSP, and the investigation by the Electoral Commission. Grounds 3, 6, and 7(1)(a) of Sch.3 were argued unsuccessfully, and although para.3 of SI 2000/417 was not put forward, the Tribunal commented that:

> "There are some cases in which the applicant's identity and motives may shed light on the public interests involved. More significantly, the applicant's identity and motives can be of direct relevance to the exemption in FOIA s40(2) because of the provisions of DPA Schedules 2 and 3, which contain a number of references to the purpose of the disclosure and to the interests pursued by the persons to whom disclosure would be made. For example, a journalist or author may be able to outflank the s40(2) exemption by reliance upon DPA Schedule 3 condition 10 and paragraph 3 of the Schedule to the Data Protection (Processing of Sensitive Personal Data) Order 2000, where it is in the substantial public interest that wrongdoing should be publicised."

These comments are relevant to other elements of the test of disclosure of personal data under the access regimes, as required to satisfy the principles on the basis that it is "a disclosure to a member of the public otherwise than under this Act", and illustrate that the motive and applicant blindness of the access regimes is by no means absolute. We cannot, however, agree with the assertion that Sch 2 and 3 "contain a number of references to the purpose of disclosure and to the interests of the persons to whom disclosure would be made", since the only specific references to the interests of a disclosee are in Sch.2(6) and Sch.3(10) para.3; there are no other references to disclosure or disclosees. In *Smith v Information Commissioner and Devon & Cornwall Constabulary*[50] the Tribunal held that there were public interest factors in favour of a disclosure relating to the level of activity by sexual offenders, in particular localities and transparency and accountability in what the police were doing about it, but it did not amount to "substantial public interest" as required by para.3 of SI 2000/417. Finally in *Cobain v Information Commissioner and Crown Prosecution Service*[51] this ground justifying disclosure was applied by the Tribunal in respect of certain information requested by a *Guardian* journalist from the CPS concerning the 1998 prosecution of Nick Griffin, the British National Party leader, under the

---

[49] EA/2010/0085.
[50] EA/2011/0006.
[51] EA/2011/0112 and EA/2011/0113.

Public Order Act 1986. The Tribunal said that it was necessary for CPS to disclose in order to fulfil a legitimate journalistic purpose, because it was in the substantial public interest for the information to be published and because that information was likely to be published. It said Griffin's rights, freedoms and legitimate interests would not be unfairly prejudiced by its decision: "Given his marked preference for publicity, not least as to the trial, and his prominent and sensitive political role". The Tribunal made a point of explaining why PACE-obtained evidence did not have to be handed over, and it is likely that this decision will prove a rare exception to the usual rule that disclosure of sensitive data to the public via the access regimes is unlikely to be justified.

In the *DoH* case, discussed earlier, the request was for statistics in relation to **26–110** abortions carried out. Clearly if these data had been personal data then some of them would certainly have been sensitive health data of the women concerned. It would have been a very surprising outcome if the court had found that a public disclosure of such information was justified, and in fact the disclosure was ordered on the basis that the statistics as disclosed were not personal data. The slightly disturbing element of this decision is the finding of the court that if those statistics had been personal data—that is, if it would have been possible to identify the women who had had abortions – then there would have been no difficulty in justifying the disclosure under Sch.2(6), and for the sensitive data, under Sch.3(7)—the publication of such statistics was necessary for the functions of the Department. This seems to be derived from the notion that the publication of statistical information which would *not*lead to the identification of individuals still needs to be justified under Schs 2 and 3 where the statistics are compilations of data which relate to individuals.

We have earlier expressed reservations about the possible justifications for the pre-disclosure processing of sensitive personal data, and we will consider the problem in more detail in the following section.

Justifying the pre-disclosure processing

When a request for third party data is received the authority will usually need to **26–111** process some personal data in order to locate the information requested and consider whether it should be disclosed. This looks like processing under a legal obligation, because as explained above, the authority is obliged to consider all requests. Applying this logic it would follow that the Sch.2 ground for this processing must be condition 3—that the processing is necessary for compliance with a legal obligation to which the data controller is subject, namely the obligation to deal with a request under the access regimes. Unfortunately, as has already been pointed out, that will not work for the pre-disclosure processing of any sensitive personal data because there is no condition in Sch.3 corresponding to the legal obligation ground in Sch.2(3). Schedule 3 offers very little to assist public authorities with their compliance with their responsibilities under the DPA at this stage, and in relation to sensitive data; the argument that in practice very little sensitive data will be disclosed under the access regimes, so this should not be a problem, overlooks the fact that a public authority must first give consideration to a request for sensitive data and that this will often involve the processing of such data before any decision on non-disclosure can properly be reached. In that context it should be remembered that s.1(2)(b) of the DPA stipulates that "using" or "disclosing", in relation to personal data, includes using or disclosing the information contained in the data, so taking a quick peek at sensitive data in file for these purposes counts as a processing operation under the DPA.

26–112   If ground (3) of Sch.2 works for the pre-disclosure processing of non-sensitive data then it does so regardless of the outcome of the debate about whether its operation in relation to disclosures is precluded by the caveat "otherwise than under this Act". Given that it is not available for sensitive data, however, other justifications in Sch.3 must be found for the pre-disclosure processing of sensitive data. For the reasons already mentioned above, the only sensitive data conditions which can generally be appropriate to this processing are condition 5—information made public by the data subject and condition 7—necessary for public functions. Condition 5 is dependent upon the particular sensitive data requested already being in the public domain so it is not going to operate as a gateway to further disclosures and is therefore likely to be of very little use in relation to requests under the access regimes. Condition 7 has been discussed above at paras 26–100—26–102 and is in our view the only general justification for the pre-disclosure processing of sensitive data in response to these requests, despite the question marks over its use in this context. We maintain, though, that if this is the chosen route under Sch.3, then consistency demands that it is also used to justify the same processing operation under Sch.2, which means that Sch.2(5) should be used rather than Sch.2(3) or Sch.2(6). For if processing sensitive data is necessary for public functions under Sch.3(7), then the same processing must be equally necessary for the same functions for the purposes of Sch.2(5), or if Sch.2(5) is not chosen then how can the justification under Sch.3(7) be made out? Other Sch.3 justifications which have been considered are paragraphs 3 and 9 of the additional justifications added at condition 10 by SI 2000/417 discussed above at paras 26–108—26–109, but these are extremely limited in their potential application to consideration of general public disclosures under the access regimes; similar reservations would apply to condition 6—necessary for legal proceedings.

PUBLIC DISCLOSURES AND OTHER ASPECTS OF THE DPA

Relation with section 35 and other exemptions in the DPA

26–113   At s.35, the DPA gives exemption for disclosures required by law, by providing at subs.(1) that personal data are exempt from any prohibition on disclosure imposed by the application of the principles and of some of the rights in cases where the disclosure is required by or under any enactment, rule of law or order of the court. Without the caveat in s.40(3) that the disclosure to be tested by the principles is "to a member of the public otherwise than under this Act", the exemption at s.35(1) would operate to exempt from the non-disclosure provisions, which include most of the principles, a disclosure made under the access regimes. This is because such a disclosure would qualify as being required "under any enactment", and the effect of applying the s.35(1) exemption would accordingly be to remove all the privacy protection intended to be provided by the exemption for third party data at s.40 of the FOIA in its requirement to apply the principles. This is most clearly the problem that the insertion of the caveat was made to solve, but whether it was also intended to have the effect of removing the statutory and other public function gateways for processing provided in Sch.2 and Sch.3 to accommodate public authorities performing their public task is, however, another matter.

Arguably the caveat also works to ensure that none of the other DPA exemptions can have the effect of removing any part of the test of the principles to a proposed disclosure under the access regimes because the DPA exemptions are provided in order to accommodate disclosures for specified public interest purposes, and it follows that a disclosure to "a member of the public" for no specified purpose (bearing in mind that as well as being applicant–blind, the access regimes are motive-blind) cannot come within them.

This view was not supported in the *APPGER* case in which it was contended that the exemption in DPA s.35(2) would apply to accommodate the disclosure requested because it was necessary for legal proceedings, with the effect that the operation of the principles to inhibit this disclosure would be removed by the application of that exemption. Neither the UT nor the Commissioner argued that a DPA exemption cannot be applied to a proposed disclosure under the access regimes, as we have stated above; instead, tacitly accepting that it did apply, all parties immediately proceeded to address the question of whether the disclosure requested under the FOIA was in fact necessary for legal proceedings. The UT said:

26–114

"The 'non-disclosure provisions' are defined in DPA s27(3)-(4). The effect of the definition in the present context is that, where s35(2) applies, the disclosure does not have to comply with the first data protection principle except to the extent that the principle requires compliance with a Schedule 2 condition. We have found above that condition 6 of Schedule 2 would be satisfied",

and concluded that the DPA s35(2) was not applicable on the facts. Since that judgment, however, the position of s.35(2) in relation to FOIA disclosures has been revisited in *A v IC,* already cited in relation to s.40(5). In this decision the Tribunal judge distinguished that element of *APPGER*. She first of all did not consider that disclosure under FOIA, further to the request, could be said to be "necessary" for "exercising or defending legal rights", and did not see why those rights could not have been pursued through the ordinary rights of appeal in court proceedings or possibly judicial review. Then the assumption in *APPGER* that s.35(2) could in principle apply was dealt with as follows:

"Counsel for HPC pointed out that subsection (1) of section 40 made reference to 'the applicant'. He submitted that had Parliament intended subsection (5) when referring to 'a member of the public' to mean the applicant or requester, then the provision would have expressly referred to 'the applicant' as it had done earlier on in the section. Moreover to introduce the specific position of the requester in this way would be to undermine the overwhelming thrust of FOIA which was that requests were to be treated as 'motive blind' and that, when considering the implications of disclosure, disclosure to the public at large is the test, not just disclosure to the person who has made the request. The Tribunal found both these arguments to be highly persuasive and concluded that the appropriate test was to ask whether HPC confirming or denying that it held the information requested to any member of the public, ie: the public in general, would breach the Data Protection Principles. In this regard the Tribunal did consider the Upper Tribunal case of All Party Parliamentary Group on Extraordinary Rendition v Information Commissioner [2011] UKUT 153 (AAC) case and what appeared, on the face of it to be a contrary view. Its views on this matter, contained in paragraphs 112 to 115, were however obiter and particular to the facts of that case. This Tribunal was not therefore bound to follow the Upper Tribunal's reasoning in this regard."

26–115   In view of our arguments above that disclosures must be considered as being made to the public at large, not to the individual requester, we respectfully endorse this finding as being the correct approach, and it applies equally to the treatment of Sch.2 and Sch.3 grounds as it does to the application of the exemptions in the DPA, subject to the peculiar features of the justification in SI 2000/417 para.3 described above. What is not completely clear is whether the s.35(1) exemption could possibly apply to protect the public authority from the consequences of a disclosure under the access regimes after the disclosure has taken place in circumstances where the data subject claims, successfully, that the principles were in fact breached. There seems to be no reason why a data subject should not be able to take action against the public authority by, for example, exercising his right to compensation under s.13 of the DPA because the principles did in fact apply to the disclosure, given that it was not exempt from the non-disclosure provisions by virtue of s.35(1).

Relation with the right in section 10 of the DPA

26–116   Analysis of the relation between s.10 notices and the access regimes can be particularly challenging, in part because the right can be exercised only in respect of data in DPA s.1(a)–(d), and not for any category (e) data, and also because there are severe limitations placed upon the exercise of this right by s.10(2). A notice under the s.10 right to object to processing which would cause substantial damage or distress cannot be served to prevent processing which is carried out in compliance with a legal obligation; this is one reason why the argument that disclosures made under the access regimes ought to be justified under Sch.2(3) cannot work because FOIA s.40(3)(a)(ii) specifically allows exemption in a case where the s.10 right has been exercised. Clearly, if the justification for the processing under the access regimes was that the authority was subject to a legal obligation to do it, as accommodated by condition 3 of Sch.2, then no data subject would be able to object to it by exercising the right under DPA s.10. The only grounds which can be challenged by objectors are conditions 5 and 6 of Sch.2, so it must follow from the ability of data subjects to raise objections to disclosure under the access regimes that such disclosure is being justified on one or other of those two grounds.

26–117   The accommodation of the s.10 right within the personal data exemption was necessary in order to ensure that the FOIA would not deprive individuals of their rights conferred under Directive 95/46/EC, but it is a qualified exemption so it can be overridden in the public interest. As with the other qualified exemption in FOIA s.40 (in relation to the third party's position on his subject access rights), it does not displace the test of the proposed disclosure by reference to the data protection principles but it means that a s.10 notice must be considered and taken into account in any decision concerning a disclosure under the access regimes. Section 10 notices were considered in *Greenwood v IC and Bolton MBC*[52] where the request was for disclosure of declaration of interests of senior officers of the Council, which included associations or membership of organisations such as Common Purpose and the Freemasons. A number of potentially affected council staff had been contacted for their views and many of them had in response served objections under s.10. The Tribunal said it was satisfied that disclosure of home addresses of council officers would be unfair and unwarranted because from the open parts of the s.10 statements it was clear that many officers would feel vulnerable, threatened and exposed if this information were to be made public. It went on to acknowledge that the Council made unpopular decisions at times and officers might be targeted by those who disagreed, and that while the public could raise matters with specific employees through their work contact details, the employees were entitled to prevent their employment intruding into their private time and life. From this decision it is apparent that consideration of the service of a s.10 notice will not take place independently of the mainstream fairness requirements of principle 1; the Tribunal did not specifically address the public interest arguments for the purpose of applying the s.40(3)(a)(ii) exemption. Of course, the requirement at s.40(3)(a)(i) that a disclosure under the FOIA must not breach any data protection principle means that, inter alia, principle 6 (processing must be in accordance with the rights of data subjects) must be complied with and this will not be the case if disclosure takes place despite a valid s.10 objection. For that reason, there is an inherent conflict between the potential for a public interest override of a s.10 objection and the requirement not to breach principle 6—this is most acute under the EIR which expressly prohibit a disclosure which would breach any of the data protection principles. In practice, on the few occasions when the exercise of the s.10 right is in play, the issue will likely be resolved on the mainstream first principle ground of fairness to the data subject as was the case in *Greenwood* above; see also the discussion below of the possibility that the data subject takes action to enforce his right.

We do not think that a s.10 notice could be used to restrict the processing **26–118** necessary to find information and to review whether it should be disclosed (pre-disclosure processing). It is suggested that, as s.40(3) and reg.13 specifically relate to the "disclosure of information" to a member of the public, only the disclosure and not the prior processing to locate and retrieve the relevant data can be restricted by a s.10 notice. This is consistent with the view that the pre-disclosure processing can be justified under Sch.2(3), in respect of which the data subject cannot raise any objection. Of course, if the data are sensitive then other grounds must be found, and if, as we have suggested, the public functions justification at Sch.2(5) is used then it will be vulnerable to objection under s.10, although it does not seem likely that this pre-disclosure processing could be successfully prevented by an attempt to object. Where, however, a s.10 notice already applies at the time a request is received the authority cannot regard it as a binding restriction on disclosure because it is subject to override in the public interest, so the authority has to decide whether it should disclose the information in the circumstances at the time of the request, applying the principles as well as

---

[52] EA/2011/0131 and 0137.

considering the notice. If, however, if the authority is considering disclosing in contravention of the notice then bearing in mind considerations of natural justice, the individual is arguably entitled to notice of the proposed disclosure so he can refresh and revisit the argument. If the authority then proposes to disclose, the individual will have the right to make an application to the court under s.10(4) of the DPA, although it is not clear what the position of the authority would be if the court ordered compliance with the notice in circumstances where the authority considered that it should be overridden because disclosure was in the public interest. In the context of considering an application under s.10(4) there is nothing to indicate that the court can take the public authority's position under the FOIA into account, although if the finding of the Court of Appeal in *Durant* is followed then at least as far as the UK is concerned the court has an unfettered discretion in applications by data subjects for specific performance of their rights.

In the vast majority of cases there is no existing s.10 notice given by the third party, and the question arises as to whether authority should consider not only giving the individual notice of the request but perhaps also alerting him to the s.10 right, although there is no requirement to do so. It is suggested that an authority contemplating a disclosure would have difficulty complying with principle 1 in terms of fairness to the data subject, and also with making out the grounds for disclosure via the three-stage test in Sch.2(6) if that data subject could show that disclosure would cause unwarranted damage or distress. For this reason we do not consider that it will usually be either necessary or appropriate to encourage the data subject to make a s.10 objection.

Penalties for wrongful disclosure of personal data under the access regimes

26–119   The question of remedies for wrongful disclosure of personal data under the access regimes does not so far appear to have been addressed by the Tribunal or the courts. We have suggested above that the exemption at s.35(1) is unlikely to operate post-disclosure to protect the authority from a claim. Clearly the principles do apply, and will have been applied, to the disclosure and it is certainly possible that an authority will sometimes get it wrong. Can the data subject rely on his remedies in the DPA and will the Commissioner be able to take action against the public authority data controller?

In respect of personal data falling within s.1(a)–(d) there will be remedies under the DPA, and in respect of category (e) data the aggrieved data subject will have to look to remedies under general law. Section 56 of the FOIA states that the FOIA does not

> "confer any right of action in any civil proceedings in respect of any failure to comply with any duty imposed by or under this Act".

Accordingly, there can be no action for breach of statutory duty under the FOIA but this does not have the effect of removing any right to take action under other Acts or for breach of other legal duties. The EIR do not contain an equivalent explicit prohibition, but it is suggested that the position in relation to remedies is as in the FOIA. There is a limited protection in s.79 against an action for defamation where the information was supplied to the authority by a third person, but other legal actions are not barred. It can be argued that an individual will be able to bring an action for negligence if an authority makes a disclosure without proper care and it causes loss. This could be argued both for the s.1(1)(a)–(d) data and category (e) data. Equally such an action might face the counter-argument that this was merely an action for breach of statutory duty under another name and was thus barred by s.56.

There must also be a strong possibility that a disclosure of any information, falling into either category, which breached individual privacy, would be open to action by the individual against the public body for breach of art.8 of ECHRFF, on the basis that the public authority is just as obliged to comply with the art.8 right to respect for private and family life, home and correspondence in respect of manual information, whether structured or unstructured, as it is for automated data or that held in manual filing systems.   **26–120**

The concerned public authority data controller should take comfort from the reasonable care defence to a compensation claim under DPA s.13, and consider that the Commissioner can issue a monetary penalty notice only for a serious breach of the principles. This does not seem especially likely to happen to a public authority which has given anxious consideration to its duties under the access regimes where they collide with its duties under the DPA, although of course the latter duties remain paramount.

APPLICATION OF THE PRINCIPLES TO PROPOSED DISCLOSURES

As noted above, one of the conditions for disclosure of personal information is that the disclosure must not breach the data protection principles. In this section we consider how a disclosure made under the access regimes might be a breach of the principles. In this context the distinction between s.1(1)(a)–(d) data and category (e) data is irrelevant because the principles are applied to all personal data for the purpose of assessing possible disclosure under the access regimes.   **26–121**

The incorporation of the principles so that they can bear on disclosures under the access regimes is dealt with at FOIA s.40(7), which provides that the data protection principles referred to in that section means:

> "the Principles set out in Part I of Schedule I to the Data Protection Act 1998 as read subject to Part II of that Schedule and section 27(1) of that Act".

Pt II contains the provisions for the interpretation of the principles which are, where appropriate, referred to below. Section 27(1) incorporates into the definition of the principles any exemptions which apply to them under the DPA. The wording of s.27(1) is:

> "References in any of the data protection principles or any provision of Parts II or III to personal data or to the processing of personal data do not include references to data or processing which by virtue of this Part are exempt from that principle or other provision".

26–122   This means that the exemptions from the principles must apply as well as the principles themselves. It might be argued that the result is that where a request for personal data is made to a public authority and a non-disclosure exemption applies under the DPA then the test of applying the principles is modified by the non-disclosure exemption which has the effect of taking most of the principles away. This would mean that, for example, the only remaining requirements of the test under principle 1 would be finding grounds for disclosure under Schs 2 and 3, and that disclosures under the access regimes would not have to be fair or lawful. The reason why this cannot happen is because, as has already been explained, the non-disclosure exemptions in the DPA all require the purpose of the recipient to be considered, but the access regimes are purpose blind so these exemptions cannot apply. That is one reason why the occasional pronouncements of the courts and Tribunals which take into account the identity, status or motivation of the particular applicant are particularly unhelpful when the interface between the DPA and the access regimes is under consideration.

Principle 1

26–123   In this discussion of the application of each principle to a disclosure under the FOIA, references are to the DPA unless otherwise stated. Part I of Sch.1 sets out the first principle as follows:

> "Personal data shall be processed fairly and lawfully and, in particular, shall not be processed unless:
>
> (a)   at least one of the conditions in Schedule 2 is met; and
> (b)   in the case of sensitive personal data, at least one of the conditions in Schedule 3 is also met."

There are then further interpretative provisions for principle 1 found in Sch.1 Pt II paras 1–4. Together these add up to an entire code by reference to which any the disclosure of personal data must be considered. The various aspects of this code are addressed under the following headings: grounds for processing; fair obtaining; fair processing; disproportionate effort; fairness; and lawfulness. The grounds for processing under Schs 2 and 3 have already received detailed attention.

26–124   **Fair obtaining by the applicant.**   There is a specific provision in para.1(1) of Pt II that personal data are treated as obtained fairly if they are supplied by a person who is authorised or required by an enactment to supply the data. That means a person who obtains personal data via a request under the access regimes will, from the point of view of his own liability as data controller, have obtained the data fairly. They will still be under an obligation to notify the data subject that they hold the data, and of course their further processing of the data is still required to be fair. Where, however, the acquirer is a private individual who has obtained the data for their personal reasons which come within the s.36 exemption then the principles will not apply.

Specific obligations for fair processing.   Paragraphs 2 and 3 of Pt II of Sch.1   **26–125**
set out formal requirements which must be met before processing can be regarded
as being fair. They require among other things that the data subject is alerted
beforehand to the purposes for which the data will be used and disclosed. It is the
responsibility of the data controller to ensure that the data subject knows, or has a
realistic opportunity of informing himself about, specified information before any
processing or disclosure. That information is:

- the identity of the data controller, and any nominated representative (for the
  purposes of s.5(2));
- the purpose or purposes for which the data are intended to be processed;
  and
- any further information which, having regard to the circumstances, is
  necessary to enable the processing to be fair.

Before disclosing third party personal data in response to a request under the
access regimes, the authority may need to consider any fair collection notice
which was provided to the data subject. The public authority should consider
whether the notice alerted the data subject to the possibility that his personal data
could be publicly disclosed in response to an access request, when the notice was
given, and whether it covered all the potentially discloseable information. In
practice, looking at the published decisions of the Commissioner and the
Tribunal, not much attention is paid to this aspect of first principle fairness and
they generally take the line that individuals in particular circumstances should
reasonably expect a certain amount of information about themselves to be put in
the public domain.

The Commissioner's Guidance says that authorities will need to carry out an
objective assessment of whether the expectation of the data subject is reasonable,
and that :

> "The Tribunal in the Norman Baker case came to the view that 'where data subjects
> carry out public functions, hold elective office or spend public funds they must have
> the expectation that their public actions will be subject to greater scrutiny than
> would be the case in respect of their private lives.' This means that it is more likely
> to be fair to release information that relates to the professional life of the individual.
> It will still be a matter of degree as, for example, there may be an expectation that
> information relating to personnel matters would not be disclosed. Other factors to
> take into account when considering the fairness of disclosure in this context will
> include:
> the seniority of the role,
> whether the role is public facing, and
> whether the position involves responsibility for making decisions on how public
> money is spent."

How is an access request to be handled where disclosure under the access   **26–126**
regimes has not been included in the collection notice? If no notice has been
given then the possibility of giving a notice before disclosure should be
considered and the question of whether the provision of the notice would involve
disproportionate effort should be taken into account. In para.3 of Pt II of Sch.1 it

is provided that the fair processing notice will not apply where either, the provision of the information would involve a disproportionate effort or where:

"... the disclosure of the data by the data controller is necessary for compliance with any legal obligation to which the data controller is subject other than an obligation imposed by a contract".

As with the s.10 objection and the effect of s.35, this provision once more raises the question of how the obligation to disclose under the FOIA should be treated in the interface with the protection of personal data under the DPA, bearing in mind that the DPA specifically accommodates legal obligations to process personal data. The DPA s.35(1) exemption does not apply to potential disclosures made under the access regimes because of the phrase "otherwise than under this Act" in FOIA s.40(3)(a), but as has been seen there is a specific exemption at s.40(3)(a)(ii) where the right at s.10 to object has been exercised.

Even if the disproportionate effort qualification to the obligation to give a fair processing notice does apply (and we are by no means certain that it does), the combination of the fair processing requirement, the s.10 right and the general obligation of fairness results in a strong argument that individuals who have not been given notice of possible disclosures as part of the collection process, and thus have not been able to raise legitimate objections to such disclosures, should be informed before a disclosure is made. This is further strengthened by guidance in the s.45 Code that "in some cases is will be necessary to consult, directly and individually, with such persons", but it should be remembered that this is not a legal duty, nor does it mean that there is a requirement to consult every time third party personal data are to be disclosed.

The Commissioner's Guidance makes this point in relation to fair processing notices to be given by public authorities in relation to possible disclosures under the access regimes:

"However, as disclosure under the FOIA is not a business purpose, it is not necessary to mention potential disclosure in such a [fair collection] notice in order for the disclosure to be fair. Whilst the notice may give an indication of a public authority's general intentions regarding the use of personal information, it does not mean that disclosures that fall outside this are automatically unfair. If it did, a public authority could then manipulate the fair processing notices such that disclosures under the FOIA would not be possible."

In the many decisions published by the Commissioner and the Tribunal fairness considerations do not tend to focus on what, if anything, was said beforehand to the data subject about possible disclosures under the access regimes but rather on general fairness considerations and the reasonable expectations of the data subject, which are now examined.

26–127 **General obligation to be fair.** In addition to the specific rules in the fair processing code the authority must consider the general issue of the fairness of any processing. In this part of the assessment the relevant considerations would usually be the nature of the data, the identity of the disclosee, the purpose or purposes to which the disclosee intends to put the data and the possible implications for the individual. In the case of a disclosure under the access regimes, however, the authority must look at it in a different way. Under the access regimes the authority is not to take account of the purpose for which the applicant wishes to have or use the information, nor can the authority place any limits on the subsequent use or disclosure of personal data released. Section 40(3) states that the disclosure must be considered as being made to "a member of the public"; in practice the purpose of such disclosure should be regarded as the publication of information under an access regime. Any personal motive of the particular applicant must be ignored. In *Blake v Wiltshire CC*[53] the request was for information relating to a disciplinary hearing about a head teacher, made by a strongly motivated parent. The Tribunal said:

> "The use of the expression 'in particular' in the first principle, means that there is a general obligation to process data fairly, in addition to the requirement to comply with the detailed conditions listed in Schedule 2. The general obligation to process data fairly does not involve a consideration of the interests of the requester or third parties; however, certain of the conditions set out in Schedule 2, do. What this means is that disclosure may amount to unfair or unlawful processing and therefore not permitted, regardless of what the interest in disclosure may be."

The conclusion of the Tribunal makes it very clear that the interests of a particular applicant in a disclosure cannot operate to make the disclosure fair, if otherwise it would not be so regarded, although for the reasons explained earlier we do not generally agree that these interests can properly taken into account in considering the application of a Sch.2 justification.

The Commissioner's Guidance on the fairness of disclosures of personal data **26–128** under the access regimes says that it will usually mean considering:

- the possible consequences of disclosure on the individual;
- the reasonable expectations of the individual, taking into account expectations both at the time the information was collected and at the time of the request;
- the nature of the information itself;
- the circumstances in which the information was obtained;
- whether the information has been or remains in the public domain;
- the 'freedom of information' principles of transparency and accountability; and
- any legitimate interests in the public having access to the information relevant to the specific case.

It is apparent from the last item that the considerations of legitimate interests in disclosure, which would be expected to be within the province of the test at Sch.2(6), are also relevant to the fairness of the disclosure. This is sometimes conflated with consideration of the applicant's motives in making the access request and may be regarded as one of the sources of the confusion about the relevance of those motives, which is apparent in some published decisions, including *Blake*. Indeed in some other cases it is not always clear whether, for example, the Tribunal is looking at fairness considerations or applying the

---

[53] EA/2009/0026.

Sch.2(6) test. In *Greenwood v Bolton* the Tribunal said that despite the requirement to consider FOIA disclosures as if they were made "otherwise than under this Act" it:

> "... does consider that the existence of FOIA and the climate of transparency encapsulated in the Nolan reforms, the trend towards publication of senior government salaries and awareness of the 10 Standards in public life are material in assessing the reasonable expectation of an Officer even in the context of a statement purporting to limit the dissemination of personal data."

26–129　**Lawfulness.**　The disclosure of the personal data must be lawful. Clearly all public authorities will have the vires or powers to make disclosures under the access regimes, because public authorities are obliged to disclose information under the legislation. There are however a number of legal prohibitions on the disclosure of personal information by public authorities which are considered relevant to the question of whether personal data are being processed lawfully. For example, if the information is protected by an obligation of confidence or by another legal barrier to disclosure, then the disclosure would be prohibited by the operation of principle 1.

Some information will be subject to obligations of confidence in the hands of the authority. These obligations may derive from specific arrangements between the individual and the authority, as where undertakings to treat information in confidence may have been given in particular cases, such as when an individual makes a whistle-blowing disclosure or a particular complaint. They may also derive from the nature of the relationship or the nature of the data, for example medical information that is disclosed by patients to doctors and statements taken under caution are protected by obligations of confidence.[54] There is also a range of statutory rules which prohibit the disclosure of information, including the Official Secrets Act 1989. It has already been noted that the EIR stipulate at reg.5(6) that no prohibition in any other enactment or rule of law can restrict disclosure under those regulations, and this raises an issue when considering how the concept of lawfulness applies under principle 1 of the DPA when the personal data requested come within the definition of environmental information. As with other aspects of the EIR noted earlier, the interplay is not entirely clear, but of course we also have at reg.13(1) a prohibition on disclosure unless either of the conditions set out in that regulation is satisfied. We take the view that first principle lawfulness is incorporated into the requirements of the EIR via the provisions at reg.13 of the conditions requiring the application of the data protection principles, which are themselves incorporated into the EIR at reg.2(4). The prohibition in reg.13(1) therefore allows first principle lawfulness to operate to inhibit disclosures of third party personal data by reason of other legal prohibitions, but the relevant prohibition is within the regulations themselves at reg.13(1), not in any other enactment or rule of law, and so reg.5(6) does not operate to prevent the usual lawfulness considerations being taken into account. In decisions by the Commissioner and the Tribunal the issue of lawfulness does not generally receive separate attention, but it is noteworthy in this context that

---

[54] See Ch.2 for the law of confidence.

the Commissioner is prepared to find that this requirement of principle 1 is contravened where there is a breach of art.8 rights, as mentioned above at para.26-52.

Principle 2

Principle 2 requires that personal data shall be obtained only for one or more specified and lawful purposes and shall not be further processed in any manner incompatible with those purposes. According to the interpretation provision at para.5 of Pt II of Sch.1 the purposes may be specified either in a fair processing notice given to the data subject or in the entry on the register of notifications. If disclosure under the access regimes is thought to be a separate purpose for which the public authority processes personal data the purpose could be described as "a disclosure to the public under the FOIA or the EIR", but in practice, and as has been seen to be the case in the many published decisions of the Commissioner and the Tribunal, it does not appear to be considered as a separate purpose. Public authority data controllers are in any event now required to state that they are public authorities in the register of data controllers maintained by the Commissioner, because FOIA s.71 inserted an amendment to s.16(1) of the DPA adding this item to the registrable particulars. Therefore concerned data subjects are in a position to ascertain that their personal data might be subject to disclosure under the access regimes.

The Commissioner has always maintained that disclosures under the access regimes only require consideration of principle 1, and says that a FOIA disclosure which complies with the DPA in other respects will not breach the second principle. Arguments based on the second principle do not arise very often in reported decisions in relation to FOIA disclosures, but have been considered in three cases.

It was argued in *HoC v Baker* that the widening of the purpose to require the disclosure of details of MPs' travel expenditure could amount to a new purpose, but the Tribunal found that the specified purpose of the House was to publish data on allowances in order to comply with FOIA, and that a breakdown of these allowances was set out in its publication scheme. The Tribunal found that publishing the details of mode of travel or other breakdown was not a new purpose nor was it incompatible with the purpose specified.

In *Greenwood v Bolton* the Council argued that the data were collected for the operation of a register of declared interests accessible only to a small number of authorised Council officers, and that public disclosure would constitute further processing incompatible with the purposes for which it was obtained and would therefore breach the second data protection principle. The Tribunal noted that the Council's constitution identified the following purpose, "for the purposes of ensuring that proper standards of conduct are maintained" and was satisfied that the data were gathered in order to ensure probity in public office and that disclosure under the FOIA would further the same purpose. The Tribunal clarified that defining those who would have access to the data was not the same as defining the purpose of the scheme; it just showed the way that the scheme was intended to be managed by the Council.

26–130

26–131

In *Camden LBC v Information Commissioner*[55] the Tribunal, while finding it unnecessary to reach a firm conclusion on the alleged infringement of the second data protection principle, commented,

> "though we are inclined to doubt whether the purpose of processing would be incompatible with the purposes for which the data were obtained. Whilst disclosure would be to the world at large, compatibility can only be judged against Mr. Leigh's intended purpose, when compliance with condition 6 is in issue."

26–132   We suggest that given that disclosures under the access regimes are applicant-blind and motive-blind the purposes of the particular applicant are not the ones against which compatibility ought to be judged; this is consistent with the view of the Tribunal in *A v IC & HPC* which endorsed the following argument:

> "to introduce the specific position of the requester in this way would be to undermine the overwhelming thrust of FOIA which was that requests were to be treated as 'motive blind' and that, when considering the implications of disclosure, disclosure to the public at large is the test, not just disclosure to the person who has made the request."

This point was made in relation to judging whether, for the purposes of s.40(5), confirmation or denial would breach any of the data protection principles, but in our view it must apply equally to the purposes of the requester in the context of second principle compatibility.

Principles 3–5

26–133   The next three principles deal with data quality. They require that data are adequate, relevant and not excessive for the purposes for which they are processed, are accurate and kept up-to-date, and are only retained for as long as is necessary for the purpose for which they are held. They do not have a direct impact on disclosure under the access regimes, although retaining bad or unnecessary data is something which will be exposed by public disclosure and will also demonstrate non-compliance with the s.46 Code.

Principle 6

26–134   This provides as follows:

> "Personal data shall be processed in accordance with the rights of data subjects under this Act."

The rights of data subjects are conferred in Pt II of the DPA, but the rights which are relevant to the data controller's obligation under principle 6 are only those rights which require some action or response from the data controller. They are specified in the interpretation provision in para.8 of Pt II of Sch.1 which provides that a person is to be regarded as contravening the sixth principle only if:

---

[55] [2011] 1 Info LR.

"(a)   he contravenes section 7 by failing to supply information in accordance with that section;

(b)   he contravenes section 10 by failing to comply with a notice given under subsection (1) of that section to the extent that the notice is justified or by failing to give a notice under subsection (3) of that section;

(c)   he contravenes section 11 by failing to comply with a notice given under subsection (1) of that section; or

(d)   he contravenes section 12 by failing to comply with a notice given under subsection (1) or (2)(b) of that section or failing to give a notification under subsection (2)(a) of that section or a notice under subsection (3) of that section".

The obligation placed upon public authority data controllers in dealing with access requests for third party personal data is to test the proposed public disclosure against all the data protection principles, to see whether such disclosure would breach any principle. In relation to principle 6 this appears to suggest that all four rights have to be considered. Clearly, though, three of the rights must in the overwhelming majority of cases be irrelevant to public disclosures of personal data. These are the subject access right at s.7, the right to object to direct marketing at s.11, and the rights in relation to automated decision-making at s.12, although disclosure under the access regimes could in theory engage ss.11 and 12, as considered below.

    The right under s.10 to object to processing causing substantial damage or distress is, however, different, and can obviously be relevant to the disclosure of the data subject's personal data to the public. Without more, then, it would already be relevant to consideration of whether public disclosure of the data subject's personal data would breach any principle, namely principle 6. In addition this right is specifically added to the exemption for third party personal data in FOIA s.40(3), at subpara.(a)(ii), so principle 6 will be engaged whenever the data subject has exercised this right to object. The implications of this have already been considered at above at para.26–117.

26–135

Application of the rights at sections 11 and 12 to disclosures under the access regimes

The right to object at s.10 has already been given detailed attention, and the subject access right at DPA s.7 must always be completely irrelevant given the absolute exemption for requests for personal data of the applicant at FOIA s.40(1). Although it seems unlikely that the rights at ss.11 and 12 could be engaged in the context of a general public disclosure under the access regimes, nevertheless some further consideration needs to be given to these rights.

26–136

    Section 11 gives the right to object to processing for direct marketing, which does not seem to have any obvious application to disclosures under the access regimes. That does not, however, take account of the decision in the case of *Robertson v Wakefield DC*.[56] Here, the court held that any s.11 objection of which the public authority is aware must be honoured, and that the public authority should specifically take account of objections to disclosures of names and addresses from the electoral register where the Electoral Registration Officer

---

[56] Case CO/284/2001 see Ch.2 for a full discussion of the case.

knew that the data disclosed would be used for marketing or other commercial uses by others. This decision is difficult to reconcile with the approach under the access regimes because it obliges the public authority, when making a disclosure under a statutory provision, to take account of the intentions of others. If it can be applied in cases other than disclosures of the electoral register it potentially impacts on whole areas of disclosure of information drawn from public sources. It is arguable that a public authority could be precluded from making any disclosure of personal data that might be used for marketing unless the authority has a method of accepting and honouring opt-out notices which would prevent the authority passing on the data, but we do not think that a disclosure of personal data in response to a request under the access regimes would be very likely to amount to processing by the authority for a marketing purpose, in contrast to the sale of the electoral register.

26–137   At the time of writing the specific point has not been tested before the Tribunal, although if it arose then the impact of the Re-use of Public Sector Information Regulations, mentioned earlier, would be a relevant consideration. Nevertheless, we consider that it would be extremely unlikely that this argument could be successfully used to block disclosures under the access regimes since all disclosures made are tested under the exemptions contained in those regimes, and not by reference to any other considerations. Generally it is considered that a public authority cannot control or take responsibility for what happens to the information once it has been publicly disclosed, and any remedies available to, for example, aggrieved data subjects would be available as against the disclosee data controller in respect of his processing. These concerns are not confined to disclosures of personal data; they apply equally to, for example, disclosures of information which constitutes intellectual property, for which there is limited protection under the access regimes.

26–138   The right in s.12 relates to the objection to automated decision-making, and it is mentioned here because it is conceivable that access under the access regimes could be delivered by wholly automated means. It would be possible for an authority to set up an automated response to requests for certain information, which could include some personal data, and although we are not aware of an authority having done so the possibility cannot be dismissed given the volume of requests that many authorities have to deal with and the pressures on time and other resources. We suspect, however, that the release of any personal data in such a way would be unlikely to qualify as decision-making of the significant kind required to trigger the s.12 right.

Principles 7 and 8

26–139   Principles 7 and 8 have not so far been regarded as having any particular resonance in the context of a disclosure of personal data under the access regimes. Principle 7 relates mainly to the security of personal data and to its misuse, and principle 8 concerns adequate protection when transferring personal data outside the EEA. The Commissioner's Guidance says that

"... consideration of these principles is unlikely to add anything where it is fair to release the information to the public at large under the first principle".

The question of release to an applicant based outside the EEA has not been addressed in any reported decisions, although conceivably the authority could circumvent tricky questions of compliance with principle 8 by publishing any information to be released in its publication scheme, via its website, rather than by communicating it to the applicant, as required under s.1(1)(b) of the FOIA. This view is not wholly consistent with the Commissioner's current (2010) guidance on international transfers, which appears to contemplate that the subsequent downloading of personal data by a third party can amount to an act of transferral on the part of the data controller who earlier posted it on a website, but the implications of such a view for personal data available via the internet are much wider than the scope of this chapter. The same problem does not arise under the EIR since there is no duty to communicate the information to the applicant, merely to make the requested information available.

Subject access exemption

The exemption at s.40(4) of the FOIA provides that the authority will not have to disclose third party personal data which is requested under the FOIA if the data subject would be denied access to it himself by way of an exemption from the right of subject access in the DPA. The subject access exemptions are covered in Chs 15–19. There are some similarities between the subject access exemptions in the DPA and the exemptions in the access regimes but there are also some important differences. The scope of the subject access right is set out in s.7(1) of the DPA which gives the data subject separate rights to receive: **26–140**

- a statement as to whether the data controller holds information about the individual;
- a description of the data, of the purposes for which it is processed and of any recipients;
- communication of the data, and of its sources, if available; and
- information about the logic of any relevant automated decision making.

Some of the exemptions from subject access are set out in full in Pt IV of the DPA, and others are contained in the miscellaneous exemptions set out in Sch.7. In most cases they are expressed to apply to the rights contained in s.7 to the extent to which the application of those rights would prejudice the interest protected by the exemption. This is a harm test, just like the prejudice and adverse affect tests which apply to many of the exemptions under the access regimes. There is no separate exemption from the duty to state whether data are held, as in the access regimes, but the effect is the same, given that the right to be told whether the data are held is part of the entitlement under s.7 to which all the subject access exemptions apply.

If a subject access exemption would apply to the disclosure of the information to the data subject, then the authority has a qualified exemption from the obligation to disclose under the access regimes. It does not, however, follow that the authority should in every case consider the application of the exemptions from subject access in the DPA to see if this exemption would be engaged. In practice the test for disclosure under the access regimes is always whether it   **26–141** would be compatible with the principles, but there may, very rarely, be a case in which this test would be satisfied but the third party would not himself get subject access. In such cases this limb of s.40 will need to be considered, and the public interest arguments, both for and against disclosure, will be of particular interest.

Such an argument was raised by the Cabinet Office in correspondence with the Commissioner following a complaint about the withholding of requested information relating to the award of a peerage to Lord Ashcroft. In his decision *FS50197502* issued March 16, 2010, the Commissioner upheld the complaint against the Cabinet Office in its application of a number of more mainstream exemptions, but also gave a detailed analysis of the proposed application of s.40(4). He accepted that the requested information concerned the conferring by the Crown of a dignity in March 2000 and that it was therefore exempt from the provisions of s.7(1)(c) of the DPA by virtue of the exemption provided by DPA Sch.7(3)(b), and went on to consider the public interest arguments for and against disclosure as required in respect of s.40(4) of the FOIA. The Commissioner said that there is an inherent public interest consideration in maintaining the s.40(4) exemption that personal data which cannot be accessed by the data subject should not be accessible to a wider audience through the provisions of the FOIA, but he found that, in the particular circumstances of the case, disclosure of some of the requested information would serve the public interest in providing a necessary degree of openness and transparency of the honours system operating at the time of Lord Ashcroft's ennoblement. He also took account of the controversial nature of Lord Ashcroft's nomination and subsequent award of his peerage, which provided sufficient weight to favour disclosure when balanced against any detriment or harm to Lord Ashcroft or to the honours system that would flow from such disclosure.

Subject access exemptions in the DPA

26–142   For a detailed discussion of each of the exemptions see Chs 15–19:

- national security;
- prejudice to the prevention or detection of crime, apprehension or prosecution of offenders, assessment or collection of any tax or duty;
- in the interests of the operation of a classification as part of a risk assessment by a relevant authority;
- prejudice to the physical or mental health of the data subject;
- prejudice to the carrying out of social work;
- certain educational data held by schools;
- prejudice to specified regulatory functions;
- incompatibility with journalism, literature or art where the publication is in the public interest;
- research purposes where the data are not made available in an identifiable manner;
- data made public under any other enactment other than the FOIA;
- confidential references in the hands of the data controller;
- prejudice to the effectiveness of the armed forces of the Crown;
- judicial office, honours, QC appointments;

- Crown employment or office;
- personnel information which is category (e) data and relates to employment by a public authority;
- prejudice to management forecasts or planning;
- price sensitive information;
- prejudice to negotiations with the data subject;
- premature revelation of examination results;
- examination scripts;
- legal professional privilege; and
- privilege against self incrimination.

GUIDANCE AVAILABLE ON DISCLOSURES OF PERSONAL DATA UNDER THE ACCESS REGIMES

Guidance on third party disclosures in the s.45 Code

Public authorities must provide advice and assistance to requesters and those proposing to make requests as required under s.16 of the FOIA, and they discharge this duty by conforming with the s.45 Code (which describes itself as a Code of Practice on the discharge of public authorities' functions under Pt I of the FOIA). It is issued by the Secretary of State who is now the Minister of Justice. There is a corresponding duty to help requesters under reg.9 of the EIR and a corresponding code of practice issued under reg.16 of the EIR by the Secretary of State for DEFRA. For the purposes of this section we will refer to the s.45 Code, but it should be borne in mind that where the request is for environmental information the relevant code of practice is that issued by DEFRA, to be found on the DEFRA website. The provisions of the s.45 Code apply to requests involving personal data as they do to all other requests or attempts to make requests, and in summary they say that a public authority should: **26–143**

- publish its procedures for dealing with requests for information;
- draw the FOIA to the attention of potential applicants;
- help potential applicants make requests in writing;
- help potential applicants frame their requests;
- consider what can be provided free of charge if applicant does not want to pay;
- consider what can be provided within the upper limit if the request exceeds the costs appropriate limit;
- advise on procedures for the transfer of requests from one public authority to another (but transfer is mandatory under the EIR, unlike the FOIA);
- consider consultation with persons affected by an FOI request;
- consider what confidentiality contract clauses should be used; and
- have a procedure for dealing with complaints by requesters (mandatory under the EIR).

Of particular relevance to requests for personal data will be the giving of appropriate advice to applicants who ask for information about themselves,   **26–144** which is absolutely exempt under FOIA s.40(1). This is not specifically addressed in the s.45 Code, but it is expected that authorities will direct such applicants to their procedures for making subject access requests under the DPA. The other especially relevant item is Pt IV of the s.45 Code—consultation with third parties. This is expressed to cover circumstances in which:

- requests for information may relate to persons other than the applicant and the authority; or
- disclosure of information is likely to affect the interests of persons other than the applicant or the authority

The consultation need not be restricted to an individual who is the subject of the requested information but may be with others, particularly if they are able to contribute to the decision as to the applicability of relevant exemptions. The most important recommendations are:

> "26. It is highly recommended that public authorities take appropriate steps to ensure that such third parties, and those who supply public authorities with information, are aware of the public authority's duty to comply with the Freedom of Information Act, and that therefore information will have to be disclosed upon request unless an exemption applies.
> 27. In some cases is will be necessary to consult, directly and individually, with such persons in order to determine whether or not an exemption applies to the information requested, or in order to reach a view on whether the obligations in section 1 of the Act arise in relation to that information. But in a range of other circumstances it will be good practice to do so; for example where a public authority proposes to disclose information relating to third parties, or information which is likely to affect their interests, reasonable steps should, where appropriate, be taken to give them advance notice, or failing that, to draw it to their attention afterwards."

There is no specific requirement to obtain the consent of a third party to disclosure of his personal data, either in the DPA (given that only one of the six options for justification of the processing in Sch.2 is consent) or in the FOIA, which just requires that the principles are complied with. The s.45 Code does not say that consent ought to be obtained—indeed, it could not do so because there is no provision in the access regimes which would enable any such third party to veto a proposed disclosure. What it does suggest is that consultation may well be very important, and in particular that third parties affected need to be made aware of the possibility of disclosure under the FOIA, which in the case of personal data is no more than what is already required by first principle fairness.

26–145   The s.45 Code is a supplement to the legislation, not a substitute for it, but under FOIA s.48 the Commissioner can serve a practice recommendation upon an authority whose practice appears not to be in conformity with the s.45 Code, specifying the steps which ought in the Commissioner's opinion to be taken by the authority for promoting such conformity. There is no sanction other than "name and shame"—the Commissioner publishes on his website details of the regulatory action taken, naming the defaulting public authorities. Note, however, that if a public authority fails in its statutory duty to advise and assist under s.16, then the Commissioner may issue a decision notice under s.50 or an enforcement notice under s.52. The s.45 Code has not been revised since it was issued in November 2004, unlike the s.46 Code (for records management) which was re-issued in July 2009, and it is overdue for updating in the light of the experience of the past eight years, and of the changes made in the Protection of Freedoms Act 2012, which among other things imposes new rules for the release and publication of datasets held by public authorities. At the time of writing we understand that the Government may be considering a revised code.

Guidance and decisions published by the Commissioner and other sources

The Commissioner produces and regularly updates fairly detailed guidance covering all aspects of the operation of the access regimes; these are published on his webite, and many are available in hard copy. This guidance is informed by decisions made by the Commissioner himself, and by decisions of the Tribunal and the courts. We have frequently referred in this chapter to his guidance in relation to the personal data exemption (the Commissioner's Guidance), currently in version 4. In addition the Commissioner publishes in full on his website all the decisions he makes under s.50 FOIA, in a form searchable by reference to the relevant section or regulation of the regime referred to. This is a useful resource, but there are so many decisions which relate to the personal data exemption that it is difficult to keep track of them, and they are not searchable by topic, as is the case with online law reports. It will always be helpful to see if the Commissioner has made a decision relating to a particular point at issue, and the brief summary of his decision will usually say whether the decision was appealed to the Tribunal, and the outcome if it is known.   26–146

Other sources of guidance are the two government departments with responsibility for the access regimes. The Ministry of Justice has responsibility for the FOIA, and makes available on its website some general guidance to the regime and specific guidance for each exemption. These are directed towards the practice of government departments, but are both relevant and useful for all public authorities although in comparison with the Commissioner's series of guidance they tend to be more technical in discussing applicable law. DEFRA has responsibility for the EIR, and in addition to producing the reg.16 Code of Practice has also produced guidance to the regulations, which is all available on the department's website. All this information was, however, archived in July 2010; it is still accessible via the departmental website but has not been updated for over two years. If a new s.45 code is issued then we would expect a corresponding update of the reg.16 code to follow. The Commissioner's output has been prolific; at the time of writing in August 2012 he had just published a comprehensive new Guide to the EIR (referred to above as his 2012 Guide to the EIR), which runs to 53 pages and contains links to his other specific guidance where relevant.   26–147

The SIC also publishes detailed guidance to the FOISA and the EISR on her website, as well as her decisions; we have referred earlier to her guidance in relation to the personal data exemption.

RELATION BETWEEN RIGHTS OF ACCESS TO INFORMATION AND THE EUROPEAN CONVENTION ON HUMAN RIGHTS AND FUNDAMENTAL FREEDOMS

26–148   The Convention does not include a right of access to information. Article 10 covers the right of freedom of expression, and has been used in the UK since October 2000 in a number of cases. Those dealing specifically with personal privacy and the rights of the media have been covered in Ch.2. In the cases in which the ECtHR has decided that applicants do have rights to access information held by the State the rights have been founded on art.8 rather than art.10.[57] The Court has held that individuals may need to have access to information held by the State in order to protect their private or family lives. The effect of art.10 in the context of access to information was addressed in *Sugar v BBC*, considered at para.26–62 above.

26–149   Although the right of access is not supported by the ECHRFF there have been moves in Europe to enforce greater openness on governments. The Treaty of Amsterdam in 1997 included a provision committing the EU to openness:

> "Article 255
>
> 1.   Any citizen of the Union, and any natural or legal person residing or having its registered office in a Member State, shall have a right of access to European Parliament, Council and Commission documents, subject to the principles and the conditions to be defined in accordance with paragraphs 2 and 3
>
> 2.   General principles and limits on grounds of public or private interest governing this right of access to documents shall be determined by the Council... within two years of the entry into force of the Treaty of Amsterdam
>
> 3.   Each institution referred to above shall elaborate in its own Rules of Procedure specific provisions regarding access to its documents."

This policy, aimed at making actions and decisions of the Community more transparent, has been applied. It has not been wholly successful as the criticism by the European Ombudsman that officials have used data protection as a reason not to comply with the principles of openness evidences. The Commission has enacted a Regulation providing rights of access to commission and institution materials.[58] Despite the admirably liberal regime introduced in relation to access to environmental information, it has to be accepted that there is a long way to go at European level before the concept of open information becomes a core value of the Community.

---

[57] [2002] 2 All E.R. 756.
[58] 1049/2001.

CONCLUSION

Despite initial concerns that the new access rights might not be successful with   26–150
the public, or that authorities might be reluctant to apply the access regimes or
might not know what their duties were, it is fair to say that public rights of access
to information held by public bodies have now become part of the political
culture of the UK. The FOIA Review states that the Act has achieved its principal
objectives. The public appetite for information on a wide range of topics, but
especially for information about other people, has exceeded all expectations and
there are regular news items in the media about information obtained "in
response to a freedom of information request". Before the access regimes came
into effect it was thought that although third party personal data could of course
be requested under the FOIA, in practice very little would be released, but that
has not turned out to be the case. As a result of the frequent battles between
requesters and public authorities, arbitrated by the Commissioner, the Tribunal
and in the courts the provisions of the DPA have received a more thorough-going
scrutiny than ever they did by virtue of the DPA alone. Certainly access to
personal data via the access regimes has shown up some shortcomings in the
understanding of data protection, as when the Metropolitan Police turned down a
request for "all Special Branch information relating to John Lennon" by applying
the personal data exemption (*FS5015439*). The Cabinet Office also adopted an
innovative approach in its Open Data White Paper published in June 2012, where
the definition of personal data is:

> "Personal data: As defined by the Data Protection Act 1998, data relating to a
> specific individual where the individual is identified or identifiable in the hands of a
> recipient of the data".

If this were indeed the definition in the DPA then there would have been no
problem in applying the personal data exemption to information about the late
John Lennon; of course this is not as defined by the DPA for the additional reason
that the Act specifically refers to identification from other information which
comes into possession of the data controller, and does not mention any recipient,
let alone a hands-on method of identification of the individual concerned.
Changing the identification criteria to introduce a test by recipient may be an
attempt to ensure that personal privacy does not stand in the way of greater public
openness; if it is then we can look forward to more debates about striking the
right balance which should also contribute to a better understanding of how the
access regimes and the DPA actually work.

Privacy and access

As is explained in Ch.1, the Data Protection Act 1998 derives from Directive   26–151
95/46. Prima facie, where a conflict occurs between privacy and openness, the
right to privacy of personal information might be expected to carry more weight
than the right to access information. The access regimes incorporate an
exemption for personal information which defers to the rules laid down in the
DPA—that is to the statutory duty of public sector data controllers to comply with
the data protection principles, which are intended to deliver privacy. They cannot,

however, finally determine all questions. In some circumstances the right under art.8 of the ECHRFF to respect for private and family life can be used to support disclosure of information[59]; equally, it has been argued that this right justifies non-disclosure in cases where the data protection principles do not apply, although there are difficulties in finding a gateway in the FOIA through which art.8 considerations can be taken into account (see the discussion of *Bluck* at para.26–50, above, and of Sch.2(6) at paras 26–103—26–107, above). It had been thought that the balance between privacy and openness might swing in favour of openness where the freedom of the press is involved but that was before the press abuses of personal privacy unfolded to general public condemnation in the Leveson enquiry into the role of the press and police in the phone-hacking scandal, which opened on November 14, 2011 and at the time of writing still continues. Furthermore, in February 2012 the Supreme Court (following rulings in the ECtHR) ruled against an interpretation of art.10 as imposing a positive obligation to disseminate information in *Sugar v BBC* (considered at para.26–62 above). One thing is certain: since the introduction of the FOIA, the field of information access law has been the subject of such rapid development in the Tribunal and the courts that its future direction cannot be safely predicted.

---

[59] See Ch.2 for an explanation of the recent cases on privacy. *Gaskin v UK* (1987) 9 E.H.R.R. CD279; see Ch.2 for a discussion of the *Gaskin* case.

CHAPTER 27

Access To Criminal Records And Enforced Subject Access

INTRODUCTION

Section 56 of the DPA makes enforced subject access to certain records a criminal offence. The provision does not derive from the Directive or from earlier legislation. It was inserted in response to a problem which developed in the United Kingdom under the 1984 Act. Enforced subject access occurs where a person, often a prospective employer, makes the offer of a benefit, such as employment or the provision of services, conditional on sight of the material given in response to a subject access request made by the individual to a third party. The requests have usually been for criminal records. The use of enforced subject access provides the prospective employer with information about the individual, usually the contents of any criminal record. The section has still not been brought fully into force at the time of publication. It was brought partially into force from May 2008[1] as far as access to the lists of those barred from working with vulnerable adults and children is concerned[2] and from March 3, 2011[3] in relation to the same information in Scotland under the Scottish Ministers' functions under Pts 1 and 2 of the Protection of Vulnerable Groups (Scotland) Act 2007(3); however, it has not otherwise been implemented in respect of England, Wales and Northern Ireland. The provision can only be understood in the context of the schemes for access to criminal records and we have set out that background in this chapter.

27–01

Over the last 25 years there has been a significant change in attitudes to access to criminal records. Gradually the number of instances where prospective employers and others are expected or required to check the antecedents of employees or volunteers has risen. Opposition to the disclosure of records has been replaced with a recognition of its importance. In England, Wales and Northern Ireland under the previous Government an ambitious scheme for monitoring those working with children or vulnerable adults under the Safeguarding Vulnerable Groups Act 2006 would have brought even wider use and disclosure of such records under the proposed vetting and barring scheme. That has now been scaled back by changes made by the Protection of Freedoms Act 2012. The revised scheme has not yet been implemented, although the lists of those barred from working with children and vulnerable adults are available

27–02

---

[1] Safeguarding Vulnerable Groups (Commencement No) Order 2008.
[2] Provisions inserted into the DPA by paragraph 15 of the Safeguarding Vulnerable Groups Act 2006.
[3] Data Protection Act 1998 (Commencement No.3) Order 2011 (SI 2011/601).

under that Act. In Scotland a vetting and barring scheme was set up by the Protection of Vulnerable Groups (Scotland) Act 2007. It should be noted that the Protection of Freedoms Act made some further changes to access to criminal records which are covered later in the chapter. In England and Wales access to criminal records is provided by the Criminal Records Bureau (CRB). The CRB was established in March 2002 under Pt V of the Police Act 1997. It became an Executive Agency of the Home Office in 2003. The CRB obtains records from the Police National Computer (PNC), the 43 forces in England and Wales, police forces in Guernsey, Jersey and Northern Ireland, and Scottish police forces via a cross-border police intelligence system. It has the power under the Serious Organised Crime and Police Act 2005 to obtain information from a range of other sources including other policing bodies in the UK, such as the British Transport Police. It also receives information from the lists of those registered as unsuitable to work with vulnerable people and children from the Independent Safeguarding Authority. It has been announced that the CRB and the Independent Safeguarding Authority are to be merged into a single non-departmental public body called the Disclosure and Barring Service. The planned operational date is December 2012.

One of the CRB's primary functions is to disclose information drawn from these records to Registered Bodies acting for employers and others for vetting purposes. The disclosures are made under specific provisions in the Police Act 1997, taking account of the Rehabilitation of Offenders Act 1974 (ROA). In Northern Ireland access to criminal records is provided by Access NI which is a part of the Department of Justice NI. In Scotland access to criminal records is via Disclosure Scotland which is an Executive Agency of the Scottish Government and which fulfils the same function, providing access to criminal records under the Police Act 1997. The chapter covers the reasons for and the context of s.56, that is the nature of criminal records, the background to the protection and disclosure of criminal records, the relevant provisions of the ROA and the Police Act 1997.

27–03 SUMMARY OF MAIN POINTS

(a)   Criminal records are retained both nationally and within individual police forces in England and Wales.

(b)   The Report of the Bichard Enquiry which was held after the murder of two children made a number of recommendations for improvements in records and extension of access for vetting. These have been carried forward and over the last decade there has been significant development in the way that criminal records are managed.

(c)   Access to criminal records is currently provided in England Wales and Northern Ireland under Pt V of the Police Act 1997. In England and Wales it is at two levels: Standard and Enhanced Disclosure. Basic Disclosure is provided by Access NI but not by the CRB.

(d)   Scotland has its own system and Basic Disclosure is also available as well as Standard and Enhanced Disclosure.

(e)   Enforced subject access is made an offence of strict liability in s.56 of the DPA. It has been brought partially into force as far as the lists of those who are barred from working with children and vulnerable adults is concerned. It is anticipated that the section will be brought fully into force after arrangements for the issue of Basic Certificates in England and Wales, although there is as yet no date for the introduction of the section.

(f) The prohibition on enforced subject access extends to information associated with criminal convictions, barring records and National Insurance records, and there is a power to extend the provision to other records.[4]

THE NATURE OF CRIMINAL RECORDS

Criminal records include both intelligence and conviction records. Conviction information is very powerful personal data. The existence of a conviction can make it more difficult to find employment, accommodation or services. There is a strong public interest in conviction information being available to those with a need to know and an equally strong public interest in encouraging those who have been convicted in the past to rehabilitate themselves in society. Since convictions are declared in open court they are not generally treated as confidential information,[5] certainly while they can still be researched from public domain information. Nevertheless there are restrictions on their use and dissemination. In *R. v Chief Constable of North Wales Police*[6] a police officer had shown the owner of a caravan site cuttings from a newspaper covering the criminal convictions of two persons who were resident on the site.

27–04

The Court of Appeal held that there was no breach of confidence as the material was from a publication but endorsed the fact that the force was required to treat disclosure seriously and only make disclosures in appropriate circumstances. Criminal records are sensitive data under the Data Protection Act and a disclosure will be a breach of an individual's right to respect for private life, accordingly it must be lawful, justifiable under one of the exemptions in Art. 8.2, and be proportionate to the aim served by the breach.[7] In the case of *R. (on the application of Ellis) v Chief Constable of Essex Police*,[8] the Court held that the disclosure of the identifying of an individual convicted of offences by displaying posters showing photographs of the offender and details of his offence risked breaching the HRA. The Court held that the scheme could not be assessed in principle but a judgment would have to be made on the facts of the case. In the particular case the Claimant was withdrawn from the scheme. The Court expressed concerns as to whether the intrusion into art.8 rights was proportionate to the benefits claimed.

---

[4] In her response to the post-implementation appraisal of the DPA in December 2000, the Information Commissioner noted that enforced subject access might also be sought to health records and gave notice that she would seek an extension to cover such records if the practice spread.

[5] See *Re Attorney General's Reference (No.3 of 1999)*[2009] UKHL 34; see 17-20 for a discussion of the case.

[6] 6 [1999] Q.B. 396.

[7] See Ch.2 for a full treatment of the effect of art.8.

[8] [2003] F.L.R. 566. The Chief Constable of Essex introduced an offender-naming scheme with a view to reducing burglary and car crime. The claimant was selected to be the first offender used in the scheme.

27–05   Before the Police Act came into force criminal records were disclosed on non-statutory grounds under administrative arrangements set out in Home Office Circulars. The statutory basis for disclosure in the Police Act clearly provided a firmer footing for the wide disclosures made for employment vetting. Nevertheless, the common law power of the police to make disclosures has not been replaced and is relied upon for a range of disclosures, including those proposed under "Clare's law". This is emphasised by the Explanatory Notes to the Protection of Freedoms Act which, in relation to the repeal of a specific enabling power in respect of disclosures, state that police forces will still be able to make such disclosures under their common law powers. This use of discretionary disclosures is considered further later in the chapter.

27–06   The primary source of records available are those held on the Police National Computer (PNC). Records of reportable offences are held on the PNC. The PNC is run as a common policing service involving chief police officers, the Home Office and the National Policing Improvement Agency (NPIA). In effect the PNC acts as a vast pool of data. All police forces have access to it, all add information to it and there are rules allocating responsibility for the inclusion of inaccurate data. In addition to the PNC records, every force holds its own databases of information and intelligence covering for example stolen property, intelligence and protection of children. Access is shared to much of this locally-held operational information under the Police National Database (PND). The PND has been in operation since June 2011. It replaced an interim system the IMPACT Nominal Index which operated between 2005 and 2011. The PND programme has vastly improved the extent and quality of the data available to be shared between police forces by providing increased access to many policing databases.

27–07   The more recent the record of a conviction the more likely it is that it will be held on the PNC. The first criminal records database, Phoenix, became operational in 1995 and some older records which had previously been held on microfiche were transferred to it when it started. One of the tasks being undertaken by the ACPO Criminal Records Office is to continue to transfer microfiche records on to the PNC. However, even if the record was generated after 1995, if the punishment was of a minor nature it might not have been recorded centrally. All convictions for recordable offences are now centrally recorded. Recordable offences are those designated by the Secretary of State under regulations made under s.27(4) of the Police and Criminal Evidence Act 1984. Cautions are to be treated as convictions and included under an amendment made by the Protection of Freedoms Act 2012.[9] Previously cautions were sometimes recorded and sometimes not.

GOVERNANCE AND MANAGEMENT OF CRIMINAL RECORDS

27–08   The current management and governance arrangements for criminal records is provided by the Home Office, the Association of Chief Police Officeers (ACPO) Criminal Records Office (ACRO) and the UK Central Authority for the Exchange of Criminal Records. The Government is advised by the Independent Adviser on

---

[9] s.85 not in force at the time of writing.

Criminality Information and appeals against inaccuracy or the inclusion of information on certificates can be made to an Independent Monitor. The criminal records system did not always deliver the current level of quality, availablity and governance. However, following the recommendations of the Bichard Report to improve the arrangements for retrieval of and disclosure of intelligence information between forces, and the concerns raised by the disclovery in in late 2006 that the records of thousands of British residents who had been convicted of crimes abroad had never been added to the PNC, there has been a clear commitment by Government to improve the criminal record and intelligence system.

There are a number of strategy boards which oversee specific records in the policing area, for example the DNA Database Board. There also appears to be a Police Databases Board which is referred to in the ICO's 2012 Annual Report.

The police forces themselves have an active role in the management of records. ACRO was formed in 2006 and provides the police forces of England and Wales with a number of services. It operates as a central point of expertise in respect of criminal records and also handles subject access requests on behalf of many of the forces; it works with the UK Central Authority for the Exchange of Criminal Records and it provides "Police Certificates" to individuals wanting proof that they have no criminal convictions for the purposes of emigration.

Independent adviser for criminality information

In 2008 the Government commissioned a review of police and criminality information by Sir Ian Magee.[10]   27–09

The Magee Review looked widely at the use of information covering far more than conviction information or disclosure. His review resulted in the adoption by the National Criminal Justice Board of a policy setting the strategic direction for the sharing of criminality information in England and Wales and the direction for sharing between the UK and other countries. One of the outcomes was the specific consideration of criminal records and this led to the appointment of the first Independent Adviser for Criminality Information in 2009. In October 2010 she was asked to conduct a review of the Criminal Records Regime (CRR) and in particular to consider whether the regime achieved "the right balance between respecting civil liberties and protecting the public and what actions were needed to rebalance the system". The report was delivered in two phases: phase one focussed on improvements to the CRB processes and the Vetting and Barring arrangements and most if not all of the recommendations have been implemented in the Protection of Freedoms Act. Phase two looked at improvements in the wider criminal records regime.[11] The response of the Government to that part of the report was to accept the need for a more integrated approach to the administration of criminal records and for more clarity around what is included in the records. It recognises the need to make long-term arrangements for the management and delivery of the PNC services and the exchange of international

---

[10] Review of Criminality Information, Sir Ian Magee.
[11] A Common Sense Approach—report of the Independent Adviser, March 2011.

criminal records.[12] It is therefore likely that there will be further changes to the arrangements for, and the management of, the databases over the next few years.

Weeding of criminal records

27–10   One of the recommendations from the Independent Adviser is for a system of weeding of old records:

> "I recommend that, at the earliest opportunity, the Government introduces a filter to remove, where appropriate, old and minor conviction information (which includes caution, warning and reprimand information) from criminal records."

The Government response recognises the problem around old and minor disposals and notes that it will try to find "an appropriate and workable filtering mechanism". The recommendation reflects the long-standing problems of achieving proper data protection compliance in relation to the retention of police records of minor convictions. Originally the ACPO Code of Practice for Data Protection accepted that records would be weeded to remove old minor convictions. However, the code of practice produced after the Bichard Enquiry, the Management of Police Information (MoPI) did not include an obligation to weed and the view was taken by senior officers that conviction information should generally not be deleted. The Information Commissioner took issue with this and served enforcement notices requiring the erasure or removal of old records of spent convictions on the basis that the records were excessive and being retained for longer than was necessary for the purpose.

The case came before the Information Tribunal in 2005 as *Chief Constable of West Yorkshire, South Yorkshire and North Wales v Information Commissioner*.[13] The case is examined in Ch.6 in relation to retention. In essence the Tribunal held that the records could be retained for policing purposes and the administration of justice but should not be used or disclosed for any other purposes such as vetting. The Tribunal and the parties appeared to believe that such "stepped down" records would not be available to the CRB and therefore would not be revealed on a CRB disclosure. In fact it became clear that under Pt V of the Police Act all conviction information should be provided on a CRB disclosure certificate. In 2008 the ICO issued a further set of enforcement notices against five chief constables requiring the deletion of a number of old and minor conviction records on the basis that they were no longer of utility to the core purpose of operational policing. The case was appealed to the Court of Appeal which held that the purposes for which the conviction information was held included operational policing, vetting, disclosure to the CPS and the courts and multi-agency work by the police and that accordingly the information remained relevant for those purposes.[14] The current situation, therefore, is that all convictions and cautions are retained.

---

[12] Government Response to the independent review of criminal records, December 6, 2011, Home Office.

[13] In the Information Tribunal 2006.

[14] *Chief Constable of Humberside v Information Commissioner* [2009] EWCA Civ 1079.

BACKGROUND TO THE PROTECTION AND DISCLOSURE OF CRIMINAL RECORDS

Conflicting pressures

Originally criminal records were kept for use by the police in investigating crime and for the purposes of the criminal justice system, for example use by the courts in sentencing offenders. Apart from these uses the policy was that police information (including criminal records) should not be disclosed "unless there are important considerations of public interest to justify departure from the general rule of confidentiality".[15]

27–11

The three areas of exception where disclosure was traditionally regarded as being in the public interest were:

- for the purposes of national security;
- to ensure probity in the administration of law; and
- for the protection of vulnerable members of society.

Those who were considered to fall within the exceptions were listed in Home Office circulars. The circulars also listed the persons authorised to make such searches. However, they only provided for access to a limited number of persons and in a limited number of circumstances.

In 1993, the Home Office issued a consultation paper on the Disclosure of Criminal Records for Employment Vetting Purposes.[16] The paper considered the then current arrangements in England and Wales, outlined the pressures on the system and explored the options for making new arrangements. The consultation paper described a situation in which access to criminal records for vetting varied across different police areas and was haphazard in effect. It also listed the Home Office circulars which dealt with disclosure of criminal records. It described the existing arrangements as "obviously muddled". One of the options it considered as part of the remedy for the situation was the establishment of a central unit to deal with handling access to criminal records.

In responding to the consultation paper the then Data Protection Registrar, Eric Howe, explained the growing problem with the use of subject access to obtain copies of records and commented:

> "It is undoubtedly true that, over the last few years, pressure has increased to make available details of an individual's criminal records in a wide variety of circumstances. From my position as Data Protection Registrar I see particularly the escalating use of enforced subject access whereby individuals are obliged to use their right of access under the Data Protection Act 1984 to obtain a copy of their criminal record from the police and pass it on to the prospective employer. I have argued frequently that this is an abuse of individual's rights and should be prevented by criminal sanctions.
>
> The growth of the use of enforced subject access highlights the need to review the current arrangements for disclosure. ..."

---

[15] Home Office Circular No.45/1986, dated July 17, 1986, para.2.
[16] Cmnd.2319.

> If wider access is to be permitted it is important that a proper framework is established within which such access can take place and that access outside that framework is effectively restricted."[17]

As a result of these concerns the Government determined that a proper and more generous framework for legitimate access coupled with the criminalisation of enforced subject access was the most effective solution. In order to achieve this it created the offence of enforced subject access in s.56 coupled with the provisions for criminal certificates in the Police Act 1997. It has always been intended that the two legal provisions would be implemented in tandem, with s.56 delayed until ss.112, 113A and 113B (formerly 113 and 115) of the Police Act are working. Section 56 has not yet been brought fully into force but most of the relevant provisions of the Police Act were brought into force on March 1, 2002.[18] Section 115 was amended by the Criminal Justice Act 2003 and then ss.113 and 115 were repealed with effect from April 2006 and replaced by ss.113A and 113B by s.163(2) of the Serious Organised Crime and Police Act 2005. The provisions were re-enacted in virtually the same terms. Access to the lists of those barred from working with children and vulnerable adults was added by the Safeguarding Vulnerable Groups Act 2006.[19] Subsequent changes have been made by the Protection of Freedoms Act 2012.

It should be noted that the offence provisions in s.56 in the DPA 98 do not cover enforced subject access to all data: only those highlighted as being particular problems. Initially this covered criminal records and National Insurance records. However, the formula adopted allows the Secretary of State to add further categories of records if problems should arise in other areas and the lists of those barred from working with children and vulnerable adults have been added as noted above.

The provisions of Pt V of the Police Act were intended to strike a balance between rights to legitimate access and the protection of those who are rehabilitated.

REHABILITATION OF OFFENDERS ACT 1974 (ROA)

27–12 The ROA is predicated on the basis that an individual who has paid the penalty for a crime committed should be able to rehabilitate himself and build a new life. The Act allows for certain convictions to be "spent" and s.4(1) provides that, in respect of spent convictions, the offender

> "shall be treated for all purposes in law as a person who has not committed or been charged with or prosecuted for or convicted of or sentenced for the offence or offences which were the subject of that conviction."

Convictions for serious crimes which result in lengthy periods of imprisonment are excluded from the Act and will never be spent. Broadly speaking convictions are spent at between six months and ten years after conviction, depending on the

---

[17] *Annual Report of the Data Protection Registrar*(June 1994).
[18] Police Act 1997 (Commencement No.9) Order 2002 (SI 2002/413).
[19] Sch.9 para.14 adding ss.113BA, 113BB and 113BC.

gravity of the offence as reflected in the sentence passed. Since December 2008 the Act has covered warnings, cautions and reprimands. The Secretary of State has power to exclude the application of s.4(1) by Order.

Exemptions

The Rehabilitation of Offenders Act 1974 (Exceptions) Order 1975 as amended[20] sets out a wide range of circumstances in which convictions will not be treated as spent. They cover appointments in the criminal justice system, appointment to posts concerned with the provision of care to children and young persons, and appointments in social or medical services where the carer is concerned with looking after vulnerable persons. The Order also contains a list of excepted professions where members of the profession must disclose any convictions where appropriate and a list of licences and permits, applications for which also require the disclosure of convictions which would otherwise be spent. Further amends have been made to the Exceptions Order statutory instruments which (inter alia):

27–13

- provide for exceptions where the suitability of persons with permission under the Financial Services and Markets Act 2000 are involved[21];
- add justices' chief executive to the excepted offices and employment and extend the definition of "working with children"[22];
- add a range of further professions and offices and employment such as the Crown Prosecution Service and receivers for the Court of Protection.[23]

The number of exceptions to the Order has grown over the years and given rise to concerns at the widespread access to criminal records. In the judgment of Lord Justice Hughes in case of the chief constable of Humberside and others, he commented that he would respectfully agree with the Information Commissioner that the time may well have come to review the accretions to the Order.[24]

Access to criminal records

Since March 2002 the CRB has been responsible for handling requests for disclosures from criminal records in England Wales and Northern Ireland. In broad terms, individuals can obtain certificates showing their own records for the purposes of supplying information to a third party, but will only obtain limited information. There is no limitation on the use that an individual can make of these records. Wider legitimate access to criminal records is available to employers of those concerned with the care of children and the vulnerable, those who work in the criminal justice system, and those concerned with granting various applications for licences and permits. Access is also available for national security vetting. Organisations which employ staff who will work with children

27–14

---

[20] SI 1975/1023.
[21] Rehabilitation of Offenders (Exceptions) (Amendment) (No.2) Order 2001 (SI 2001/3816).
[22] Rehabilitation of Offenders (Exceptions) (Amendment) Order 2001 (SI 2001/192).
[23] Rehabilitation of Offenders (Exceptions) (Amendment) Order 2002 (SI 2001/441).
[24] See fn.14, paragraph 112

or vulnerable adults must also request a check be carried out on the barred lists, that is the lists of those who have been barred from working is such posts.

CERTIFICATES UNDER THE POLICE ACT 1997

27–15   Part V of the Police Act 1997 provides for three types of certificates of criminal records to be provided. The certificates are:

(a)   Criminal Convictions Certificates (Basic Disclosures);
(b)   Criminal Records Certificates (Standard Disclosures); and
(c)   Enhanced Criminal Records Certificates (Enhanced Disclosures).

As the names suggest there is a gradation in the range and depth of information available under each one.

Arrangements for Standard and Enhanced Disclosure have been made. The rules governing these are set out in the Police Act (Criminal Records) Regulations 2002 (SI 2002/233).[25] The Regulations make detailed provisions for the matters which are to appear on the certificates. As well as criminal records these include information about those prohibited from working with children or disqualified from working with children or vulnerable adults. The criminal records included on the certificates include cautions, and reprimands or warnings given to children or young persons under s.65 of the Crime and Disorder Act 1998. The Regulations define what is covered by the term "recorded in central records" in s.II3(3) of the Police Act 1997. Accordingly a CRB search will show all convictions, cautions or warnings recorded in central records.

Criminal Convictions Certificates or Basic Disclosures

27–16   The CRB has not yet made arrangements for the issue of the Basic Disclosure In England and Wales.[26] However, Basic Disclosure can be obtained from Disclosure Scotland and Access NI. Basic Disclosure is available to any individual and will show the records relating to that individual. They must be applied for in the prescribed form and a fee may be prescribed. The individual will obtain a certificate which will show any conviction recorded against him in central records or state that there is no such conviction. It will show offences kept on central records, which means such records held for the use of police forces as may be prescribed.[27] It will not show spent offences. This is the basic form of certificate available to allow individuals to prove their bona fides in certain circumstances.

There is no limitation on the uses to which the certificates may be put. It is possible therefore that in the future insurance companies, hire car companies and a range of other service providers may require sight of the certificates before being prepared to enter into contracts. This has not however occurred to date.

---

[25] As amended by the Police Act 1997 (Criminal Records) (Amendment) Regulations 2007 from April 1, 2007.
[26] Police Act 1997 s.112.
[27] Police Act 1997 s.112(3).

Criminal Records Certificates or Standard Disclosures[28]

These certificates are available in respect of persons over the age of 16[29] where the applicant produces:

27–17

(a) an application countersigned by a registered person; and
(b) a statement that the certificate is required in connection with "an exempted question", that is a question excluded from the effect of the ROA under an order made by the Secretary of State.

Such a certificate will show convictions recorded in the central records including spent convictions and any cautions, reprimands or warnings held in central records.[30] If the employer has asked a relevant question it will also show whether the individual appears on any of the lists maintained by the Independent Safeguarding Authority. A caution is not a conviction but is a record of an admitted offence in respect of which a prosecution could have been brought. Cautions, reprimands and final warnings are brought within the scope of central records by reg.9. A fee is payable for the certificate. Such a certificate will still not be a full record of all data held in the criminal justice system.

Enhanced Criminal Records Certificates or Enhanced Disclosures (ECRC)[31]

These are available where the applicant produces:

27–18

(a) an application countersigned by a registered person; and
(b) a statement by the registered person that the certificate:
  (i) is required in connection with an "exempted question" that is a question excluded from the effect of ROA by an order of the Secretary of State made under s.4(4) of the Rehabilitation of Offenders Act 1974; and
  (ii) is in relation to one of the specified range of activities (being broadly those concerned with betting and gaming or the care of children) listed in s.115(6).

The provision of an enhanced criminal record certificate will produce the fullest search of the three possibilities. This will show all convictions including spent convictions, cautions, reprimands and warnings, where relevant, whether the individual appears on lists maintained by the Independent safeguarding Authority plus information from local police force records. The extent of such information is left to the discretion of the local force. The duty on the chief officer is to disclose information that "might be relevant". The extent of that duty and the question of whether chief officers have any discretion in respect of what they disclose has been the subject of a number of cases. In *R. (X) v Chief*

---

[28] Police Act 1997 s.113.
[29] Inserted by the Protection of Freedoms Act 2012 s.80 but not in force at the time of writing.
[30] Police Act 1997 s.113(5).
[31] Police Act 1997 s.115.

Constable of the West Midlands Police[32] the applicant challenged the wide disclosure of information and the Court held that the Chief Constable was justified in making the disclosure and in effect should disclose all information held on a record. Lord Woolf said that, having regard to the language of s.115(7) the Chief Constable was under a duty to disclose if the information might be relevant, unless there was good reason for not making such disclosure. He said that, as long as the Chief Constable was entitled to form an opinion that the information might be relevant, it was difficult to see that there could be any reason why the information that might not be relevant ought not to be included in the certificate. However in *R. (on the application of L) v Commissioner of the Metropolis*[33] it was argued that this approach goes too far and involved an disproportionate interference with art.8. The Supreme Court accepted this argument and made clear that the police must undertake a balancing act when deciding whether to disclose non-conviction information on an ECRC and must give proper weight to the privacy rights of the individuals. Lord Hope gave the leading judgment stating that the correct approach, as in other cases where competing Convention rights are at issue, is that neither consideration has precedence over the other (para.45). The court held that the approach set out in *R. v X* had struck the wrong balance. On the facts they dismissed the appeal from the Appellant who had challenged the Commissioner's decision to disclose information about her on an ECRC, holding that the facts were relevant and should be disclosed.

Discretion in making disclosures ECRC

27–19   It is clear that there is no discretion where the information concerns a conviction, caution or warning. This fact, coupled with the fact that old conviction information is never removed from the records, means that minor convictions from juvenile behaviour can be revealed on a certificate. In *T v Greater Manchester Police*[34] the court accepted that there was no discretion available to the Chief Constable to remove a record of a warning. In *T* the claimant had received a warning under the Crime and Disorder Act 1998 from the police in 2002 when he was 11 years old. The warning was given in relation to a bicycle theft. The warning appeared to have worked as the young man had kept out of trouble thereafter. At the age of 20 he applied to take a sports studies course and was obliged to obtain an Enhanced Criminal Records Certificate (ECRC), presumably because he would be working with children in carrying out sports studies. This showed the warning in 2002. The Claimant challenged the lawfulness of the disclosure arguing that the disclosure was an unlawful act under the Human Rights Act as it breached his art.8 rights, being disproportionate, and also sought to challenge the lawfulness of the Rehabilitation of Offenders Act (Exceptions) Order 1975 which removes the protection for spent convictions in certain circumstances. He argued that the inflexible requirement of the Police Act to disclose all warnings, cautions and convictions was disproportionate and incompatible with art.8. The court was sympathetic to the Claimant but held that

---

[32] [2005] 1 W.L.R. 65.
[33] [2009] UKSC 3.
[34] [2002] EW.

it was bound by the ruling in *L* that the requirement to disclose all convictions, cautions and warnings did not violate art.8 nor did the Exceptions Order.

The position in relation to the disclosure of conviction information has not altered but the test for the disclosure of additional information from local force databases has been changed by the Protection of Freedoms Act. The revised test provides that information should be disclosed where the chief officer "reasonably believes" the information to be relevant. In addition the Secretary of State will be able to issue guidance on the provision of relevant non-conviction information which Chief Constables must take into account.

Disclosures to registered persons

Section 113B(5) also provided that, where additional information was held   **27–20**
locally which it would not be appropriate to put into the certificate itself, because it is not in the interest of the prevention or detection of crime that the individual should see such information, this could be sent directly to the counter-signatory. The guidance issued to police forces both by the Association of Chief Police Officers (ACPO) and the Home Office was that information be provided to the Registered Body instead of being shown on the face of the CRB disclosure itself only in very exceptional circumstances.[35] The provision allowing for the disclosure of such information to the counter-signatory has now been repealed by s.79(2) of the Protection of Freedoms Act. There may still however be disclosures which the requester does not see. The Explanatory Notes to the Act state that police forces will still be able to make such disclosures under their common law powers. This use of discretionary disclosures is considered below.

The registered persons who act as counter-signatories for both Standard   **27–21**
Disclosure and Enhanced Disclosure have to abide by a Code of Practice drawn up by the Secretary of State (revised version April 2009). The Code is intended to ensure that the information released will be used fairly and that the information is handled and stored appropriately and kept for only as long as is necessary. The Code does not apply to Basic Disclosures. A person who obtains access to conviction information under a Standard or Enhanced Disclosure will be guilty of an offence under s.124 of the Police Act 1997 if he makes an unauthorised disclosure of that information.

The Act sets out those who may be approved to countersign applications and contains provisions to deal with disputes about the identity of applicants and the accuracy of records. It is an offence, under s.124 of the Police Act 1997, to pass Disclosure information to those who do not need to have access to it in the course of their duties. There is provision for umbrella bodies to act as registered persons for smaller organisations and thus provide a conduit for the disclosure of information, particularly for the voluntary sector.

---

[35] Home Office Circular No.5/2005, "Criminal Records Bureau: Local checks for the purpose of enhanced disclosures".

Legal use of enforced subject access

27–22   Although the stated policy of the Government has consistently been that it wishes to stop the use of enforced subject access as a backdoor way of obtaining access to criminal records attention has to be drawn to the fact that it has been sanctioned in some legislation. In the Licensing Act 2003 (Personal License) Regulations 2005[36] an applicant for a grant or renewal of a personal licence must supply either:

(i)   a criminal conviction certificate issued under s.112 of the Police Act 1997(1);
(ii)   a criminal record certificate issued under s.113A of the Police Act 1997; or
(iii) the results of a subject access search of the Police National Computer by the National Identification Service under the Data Protection Act 1998,

in addition to a declaration that the applicant has not been convicted of a relevant offence or a foreign offence or if he has details of any such offence. This is the only provision of this type of which we are aware.

VOLUNTARY DISCLOSURE OF CRIMINALITY INFORMATION

27–23   The practice of discretionary "limited disclosure" by police to employers and others where information is known about an individual which the police consider should be disclosed is done on a non-statutory basis using common law powers. The circumstances where the police will report convictions to particular types of employer or professional bodies (and also cautions where the job involves substantial access to children) are set out in Home Office Circular 6/2006—The Notifiable Occupations Scheme: Revised Guidance for Police Forces. This guidance distinguishes between two different categories of cases.

The first category is where an individual is working in a profession or occupation (whether as an employee or volunteer) bearing special trust and responsibility, and specifically in jobs or activities relating to:

●   protection of the vulnerable, including children;
●   national security; and
●   probity in the administration of justice.

In such cases, the Government's policy is that there is a presumption that the police force should notify the appropriate Government department, professional regulatory or disciplinary body, and/or the employer of all recordable convictions, cautions, reprimands, and final warnings unless there are exceptional reasons which make it inappropriate to do so. The Guidance states that:

"Exceptional reasons might, in a given case, include a conviction for a relatively minor offence which clearly has no bearing on the person's employment. But

---

[36] SI 2005/41.

exceptional reasons are highly sensitive to the context of the case: for example, the police would usually be expected to disclose such a caution where the relevant person is, or is applying to become, a magistrate or judge."

The second category of cases applies to less sensitive professions or occupations where probity and integrity may nevertheless be an important factor in preventing crime. For example, this applies to those with particular financial responsibilities. In these cases, a conviction or other information should only be shared with the relevant interested person or body if it is relevant to do so. In *W v Chief Constable of Northumbria*[37] the Court held that a disclosure of allegations of child abuse to an employer was justified.

Child Sex Offender disclosure scheme

The disclosure arrangements have been formalised under two specific disclosure schemes; one relating to sex offenders who target children and the other to perpetrators of domestic violence. Under the Child Sex Offenders Scheme anyone can ask the police in England and Wales to check whether people who have contact with children pose a risk. If the individual has convictions for sexual offences against children or poses a risk of causing harm then the police can choose to disclose this information to a relevant parent, carer or guardian. This provides a formal mechanism for a person to make an application for information about a particular individual who has contact with a child or children. A pilot scheme was run by four police authorities ending in September 2009, followed by a phased introduction beginning in August 2010. By April 4, 2011, all 43 police forces were running the scheme. The formal nature of the scheme is accompanied by appropriate guidance. In an earlier case serious concern about the way that such disclosures were being made was expressed in the case of *A v B*.[38] In that case the Metropolitan Police Child Abuse Investigation Command (CACI) contacted the employer of a senior member of staff to disclose the existence of intelligence and accusations against a senior employee concerned with alleged child abuse in Cambodia. The EAT case arose because after various investigations the employer dismissed the employee and the dismissal was appealed to the EAT.

27–24

While the EAT upheld the dismissal they expressed concern at the very nature of the disclosures and the way that they had been made in the particular case:

> "We have found this a worrying case....If he is indeed innocent he has suffered a grave injustice. But the risk of such injustice is inherent in a system where the police are permitted to make apparently authoritative 'disclosures' of the kind made here, unsupported by any finding of a court; and it will no doubt be said that that risk is the price that has to be paid for the protection of children. ...
>
> Having said that and acknowledging that our concern is with the Respondent's conduct and not that of CAIC, we feel bound to record that the evidence before the Tribunal raises a concern that the CAIC officers acted with the scrupulous care and judgment which is essential in these cases".

---

[37] [2009] EWHC 747 (Admin).
[38] EAT Appeal UK EAT /0206/09/SM.

Domestic Violence Disclosure Scheme (Clare's Law)

27–25   The second scheme is to cover the disclosure of information about individuals with previous history of violence against partners, usually women. This follows a Home Office commissioned report in 2009, "Tackling Perpetrators of Violence against Women and Girls". The proposal to make disclosures in response to enquiries was the subject of a consultation in 2011. A one year pilot involving four police forces has been launched from July 2012. The scheme will set up a recognised and consistent process which will enable the police to alert women who have concerns about the possibility that their partner has a history of violence. In all of these cases the need for accurate information and care in making disclosures will clearly be paramount.

Duty of care

27–26   In *Desmond v Chief Constable of Nottingham Police*[39] the Court of Appeal held that the police owe no common law duty of care to individuals who have been damaged by failures by the police to provide careful and accurate information on the ECRCs but pointed out that individuals may have remedies under the DPA or the HRA for such failures. Some of the potential problems have been ameliorated by changes brought by the Protection of Freedoms Act.[40] The copies of certificates were previously to be sent at the same time to the registered persons who acted as counter-signatories and the applicant. Even if the applicant disputed the accuracy of the information it had already been seen by the potential employer. The requirement to send the copy to the registered bodies was removed by the Act. Applicants will now have an opportunity to review the content and if they dispute it to have the matter resolved before the potential employer sees the document.

Comments

27–27   As will be appreciated from this brief outline, there is a complex regime for making disclosures of criminal records and intelligence both under the Police Act and various discretionary schemes. While these provisions may appear to provide fully for any reasonable need to access conviction information, it must be recognised that they will not provide the same range and detail as a subject access response. The concern was therefore that the abuse of subject access might continue despite the availability of certificates under the Police Act. Accordingly the Government made enforced subject access an offence, although the provisions are still not fully in effect.

---

[39] [2011] EWCA Civ 3.
[40] s.79 repealing ss.113A(4) and 113B(5) and (6) not in force at the time of writing.

ENFORCED SUBJECT ACCESS

The pressure to use the subject access right to obtain details about prospective employees' previous convictions was foreseen during the passage of the 1984 Act. The response of Ministers was to reassure Parliament that if there proved to be a problem it would be dealt with by the police by "administrative measures". In due course the problem occurred as had been foreseen but, despite the best attempts of police forces, no administrative remedy for it could be found. Gradually the practice of requiring individuals to provide subject access searches in order to vet for previous criminal records became widespread among employers. In a debate on the Data Protection Bill in June 1998 Mr George Howarth outlined the problem which the clause was intended to tackle in the following terms:

27–28

> "That term covers the circumstances when one person forces another to hand over his data protection subject access record as a condition of being considered for, or obtaining, some form of benefit, such as a job.
>   This happens mainly with criminal records. Some employers tell job applicants to hand over a data protection subject access printout obtained from the police if they want to be considered for a job. Sometimes they ask for Department of Social Security contributions records, believing that gaps in contributions show a period in custody. The police and the DSS believe that of the approximately 100,000 subject access applications they receive each year, the vast majority are enforced. Often the letters come in standard form, for example, as prescribed by employees."

The efforts to find administrative solutions continue and the police now offer a Police Certificate which can be purchased by those who are seeking to provide information about good character to overseas governments in relation to immigration. Nevertheless police forces continue to receive many thousands of subject access requests every year.

Types of record covered by section 56

In general terms, s.56 makes it an offence for a prospective employer to require an individual to produce a subject access search as a condition of employment. The offence is, however, rather technical and only applies to "relevant records". These are defined in s.56(6), being those containing the particular information specified in respect of particular data controllers as set out in an accompanying table. This method of describing the information means that further categories can be added if and when necessary.

27–29

Convictions and cautions

The information specified includes information relating to convictions and cautions obtained by a data subject from a chief officer of police in England, Wales, Scotland or Northern Ireland; or the Director General of the Serious Organised Crime Agency Information "relating to" convictions or cautions may be wider than simply a record of a conviction or a caution and would be wide enough to embrace a record of a decision not to give a caution or a record of a

27–30

989

conviction which had been overturned on appeal. It would not cover criminal intelligence, although it seems unlikely such information would be forthcoming on a subject access request in any event, as it would be more than likely to be withheld under the exemption for crime prevention.

"Relevant Record" is described as one which, "has been or is to be obtained by a data subject from [one of the specified data controllers]". It follows that the data do not have to be retained or processed by the data controller to whom the request is made or who supplies the data in response to the request. This reflects the somewhat diffuse nature of control over records of convictions and cautions as described above. Cautions and convictions are defined in s.56(7). In England and Wales a caution may be given instead of a prosecution where there is evidence of guilt sufficient to give a reasonable prospect of conviction and there is an unequivocal admission. Under s.56(7) a caution means a caution given in England or Wales in respect of an admitted offence. The concept of a caution does not exist in Scotland. In Scotland the Procurator Fiscal may issue an admonition which is of a similar nature and which may be recorded on the Scottish Criminal Records Office System. Conviction has the same meaning as in the Rehabilitation of an Offenders Act 1974. The Secretary of State may amend these definitions and may therefore add to or alter the categories of caution and conviction. In the Rehabilitation of Offenders Act conviction is defined in s.1. A further four sets of information controlled by the Secretary of State are in the prohibited list.

Records relating to young persons

27–31   Records relating to the functions of the Lord Chancellor under the Powers of the Criminal Courts (Sentencing) Act 2000 s.92 and the equivalent provisions for Scotland and Northern Ireland in respect of any young person sentenced to detention are covered. This Act makes provision for the detention of children and young persons between the ages of 10 and 18 who are sentenced for offences the sentence for which is fixed by law as life imprisonment, such as manslaughter or murder. It should be noted that such records will largely duplicate information held in the register of criminal convictions and cautions.

Prison information

27–32   A further category of prohibited information is that relating to the functions of the Lord Chancellor under the Prison Act 1952 and its equivalents in Scotland and Northern Ireland. The 1952 Act was a consolidating statute bringing together provisions governing, inter alia, the central administration of prisons, the consignment and treatment of prisoners and various offence provisions connected to the prison service.

National Insurance records

27–33   National Insurance records may be a target for employers because a certain category of National Insurance record contributions indicate that a person has spent time in custody. The data also show gaps in continuity of employment to check against an applicant's declared job history. The functions of the Lord Chancellor under the Social Security Contributions and Benefits Act 1992 and other benefits legislation and the Department of Health and Social Services for Northern Ireland for equivalent legislation for Northern Ireland have therefore been included.

Police Act 1997

The Lord Chancellor's functions under Pt V of the Police Act 1997, which deals with the provision of criminal records (dealt with above) are included.

27–34

Safeguarding Vulnerable Groups Act 2006

The Secretary of State's functions and the functions of the Independent Safeguarding Authority under the Safeguarding Vulnerable Groups Act 2006 have been added to the list as far as the lists of those who are barred from working with children or vulnerable adults are concerned. The criminal provisions of s.56 have been implemented as far as these lists are concerned but we are not aware of any cases brought under the section.

27–35

Prohibited circumstances

A person is prohibited on pain of criminal penalties from requiring another to exercise his subject access right in respect of any of the prohibited data categories in three circumstances. These are:

27–36

(a)   employment;
(b)   a contract for services; and
(c)   the provision of goods, facilities and services.

Employment

By s.5(10) the term "employee" is given an extended definition. It not only covers those who would be regarded as employees for most legal and employment purposes but also any individual who works under a contract of employment as designated by s.230(2) of the Employment Rights Act 1996. This is the definition applied in employment law in relation to employment rights but this definition excludes those who hold office under other arrangements, for example, police officers or those who provide services as independent contractors. However, for the purposes of s.56 office holders are included as employees by s.56(10)(b).

27–37

In the case of either employees, or those treated as employees by virtue of this provision, it is immaterial whether the individual is entitled to any remuneration. The term remuneration is a wide term sufficient to cover payment in kind or honoraria. Thus a scout leader or a church choir master who holds office would be covered even though these are voluntary organisations and the individuals would not normally be regarded as employees and do not receive any payment.

The employment prohibition applies in connection with both the recruitment of any person or the continued employment of any person (s.56(1)(a) and (b)).

Contract for services

27–38   A contract for services is distinguished from an employment relationship as the parties are not master and servant. There are a number of tests to ascertain whether a relationship is one of employee/employer or independent contractor, such as the degree of control exercised[41] and whether the individual has a choice when and how to carry out the work.[42] Such distinctions are immaterial in the case of enforced subject access. The offence extends to any contract for the provision of services. Thus, any service from providing window-cleaning to an engineering consultancy would be within its scope.

A person must not, in connection with either employment or any contract for the provision of services, require another person or a third party to supply him with a relevant record. The requirement need not be a condition of the employment offer or the contract to fall foul of the prohibition; it needs simply to be made "in connection with" it.

The provision of goods or services

27–39   In respect of the provision of goods or services it is prohibited to make the provision conditional on the supply of a relevant record, under s.56(2):

> "A person concerned with the provision (for payment or not) of goods, facilities or services to the public or a section of the public must not, as a condition of providing or offering to provide any goods facilities or services to another person, require that other person or a third party to supply him with a relevant record or to produce a relevant record to him."

The prohibition applies to voluntary groups, clubs, churches and other non-profit making bodies as well as to commercial relationships such as those of landlord and tenant. "Goods, facilities or services" is a broad phrase and capable of covering anything from the sale of consumer goods on credit terms through to financial services, property transactions and legal services. The person must, however, be concerned with the provision of such services to the public or a section of the public. The public means any person who may be interested; a section of the public will be relevant where a service is offered to a number of persons of a particular class but there is no selection to enter that class. An employer who offers discounted goods to his employees would possibly not be covered by the prohibition, therefore, and could make it a condition of their claiming a staff discount that individuals should supply a subject access search.

---

[41] *Yewens v Noakes* (1880) 6 Q.B.D. 530.
[42] *Ready Mixed Concrete (South East) Ltd v Minster of Pensions and National Insurance* [1968] 1 All E.R. 433.

Empty records

A record which shows no data will still be caught by the prohibition as s.56(9)   **27–40**
provides that for the purposes of this section an "empty" record is to be taken as
a record containing information relating to that matter.

Mens rea

The requirement to produce a relevant record in the prohibited circumstances is   **27–41**
the actus reus of the offence. It is an offence of strict liability.[43] Section 56(5)
states that "a person who contravencs sub-section (1) or (2) is guilty of an
offence." It is immaterial that the person requiring the search neither knew it was
wrong nor intended to break the law. However, there are two defences to the
offence.

Defences

The prohibitions in s.56(1) and (2) will not bite in two sets of circumstances. In   **27–42**
each case, the person who requires the data subject to obtain his records will
carry the burden of proof and must show that those circumstances apply. In any
proceedings for an offence in which one of the defences is raised, the burden of
proof on the defence will be to prove it to the civil standard.[44]

Compulsion of law

An enforced subject access requirement will not be prohibited if the person who   **27–43**
demanded it shows that it was required or authorised under any enactment by any
rule of law or by the order of a court. To the best of the writer's knowledge, the
only enactment which requires an individual to obtain subject access is the
licensing provision descibed at para.27-22 above. Possibly a person under a duty
of care or due diligence who required an employee or contractor to obtain subject
access might seek to argue that the imposition was "required" so they could
comply with their legal obligations of care. However, as certificates of criminal
conviction are available lawfully it may be anticipated that absent a specific
statutory provision any requirement or authorisation to obtain a criminal record
information will be interpreted as a requirement or authority which applies to
those records which may be lawfully obtained, as opposed to those which may
not. The circumstances under which a court might make such an order are left at
large but it is difficult to envisage a court ordering an individual to commit what
would otherwise be a criminal offence.

Public interest

Public interest makes a further appearance in the Act in this context. Enforced   **27–44**
subject access will not be prohibited if the person requiring it can show that "in

---

[43] In other words, the prosecution do not have to show that the accused knew that the act was wrong.
[44] *R. v Carr-Briant* [1943] K.B. 607.

the particular circumstances" the imposition of the requirement "was justified as being in the public interest". In this case, public interest is partially defined by exclusion. Section 54(4) states that:

> "having regard to the provisions of Part V of the Police Act 1997 (certificates of criminal records etc), the imposition of the requirement referred to in sub-section (1) or (2) is not to be regarded as being justified as being in the public interest on the grounds that it would assist in the prevention or detection of crime."

Although this removes one, and probably the most often asserted, public interest justification, it leaves other aspects at large.

PROSECUTIONS

Prosecutors

27–45   As with all offences under the Act, there can be no private prosecutions. Any proceedings must be brought either by the Commissioner or by or with the consent of the Director of Public Prosecutions, or in Northern Ireland the Director of the Public Prosecution for Northern Ireland (s.60(1)).

Courts

27–46   The offence is triable either way and accordingly a prosecution may be brought in any magistrates' court, although usually proceedings will be brought in the court for the area in which the offence was committed.

Proceedings

27–47   The power to charge any director or other person treated as a directing mind of a body in appropriate circumstances where the offence is committed other than by an individual applies to the enforced subject access offence.[45] The court's power to order the forfeiture or destruction of any data connected with the commission of the offence also applies.[46] For a full discussion of the criminal regimes, see Ch.21.

Immunity from prosecution

27–48   Diplomatic immunity is available to the staff of foreign embassies and consulates under international conventions. Enforced subject access has been used in the past by overseas governments via the embassy or consulate in the United Kingdom in connection with the grant of visa and work or entry permits.

---

[45] DPA s.61.
[46] DPA s.60(4).

Health records

Section 57 contains a provision aimed at dealing with the problem of enforced subject access to health records. This provision makes void any contractual requirement that an individual shall seek subject access to a health record. It does not provide for any criminal sanction. The reason for the two different approaches appears to be historical. Section 57 derives from the Access to Health Records Act. It repeats a provision of the earlier Act. There does not appear to be a problem of enforced subject access to health records and at this stage there are no plans to extend the provisions of s.56 to such records.

27–49

Section 56 was amended by the Freedom of Information Act 2000 to make it explicit that the prohibition on enforced subject access does not extend to the new category of data falling within s.1(e). The reasoning behind this is very difficult to follow. The effect is that enforced subject access to recorded information not falling within the original definition in the DPA, will not be an offence when s.56 comes fully into effect. The abuse of subject access can threfore continue in respect of such information. It may not prove to be a practical problem as the provisions in respect of the need for the applicant to describe unstructured data will possibly cut down that which will be potentially available under this anyway but as a matter of principle one might have expected the protection to be afforded to all the relevant personal information.

27–50

Future challenges

There is an ongoing move to "open data" and "data portability" in which individuals would be provided with access on line to their records from various sources, such as health data or provided with electronic copies of records of accounts to help move suppliers. These records will be potentially attractive to employers, landlords and others and may face the same threat of enforced access as criminal records have done. It remains to be seen whether the protection of s.56 will need to be extended even further to ensure the privacy of such records in a new environment.

27–51

ADDITIONAL INFORMATION

27–52

- 14th Report of the Data Protection Registrar, June 1998, p.22 (report on *R. v Director of "B" County Constabulary and the Director of National Identification Services Ex p. R*, November 25, 1997), p.46.

    Website: *www.crb.gov.uk*

Directive

Although it is accurate to say that the provision does not derive from the Directive it has been suggested that the ban on enforced subject access is required by art.12, which requires "Member States shall guarantee every data subject to the right of subject access 'without constraint'."

27–53

27–54   *Hansard* **references**

Commons Standing Committee D, June 2, 1998, cols 270–272:

Enforced subject access.

Vol.591, No.184, col.1502, Lords consideration of Commons amendments, July 10, 1998:

Enforced subject access.

Previous case law

27–55   *R. v Chief Constable of B County Constabulary; Director of the National Identification Services Ex p. R* Unreported November 1997: see Ch.11, Subject Access for an analysis of this case.

CHAPTER 28

First-Tier Tribunal (Information Rights) And Upper Tribunal

INTRODUCTION

Appeals against decisions, notices and orders of the Information Commissioner lie to the First-tier Tribunal (Information Rights),[1] which is a part of the First-tier Tribunal in the General Regulatory Chamber. Appeals from the First-tier Tribunal and hearings involving national security certificates are dealt with by the Administrative Appeals Tribunal of the Upper Tribunal. In addition, the Upper Tribunal can hear appeals at first instance which are directed to it but will not usually do so.

28–01

This chapter explains the constitution, jurisdiction, and procedure of the First-tier Tribunal (Information Rights) and the Upper Tribunal (together referred to for ease as "the tribunals"). In considering the role and powers of the tribunals, practitioners must bear in mind that the tribunals are part of a statutory tribunal system and therefore their powers must be found in the governing statute or the statutory instrument setting out its rules of procedure. Neither the First-tier nor the Upper Tribunal have any inherent powers.

SUMMARY OF MAIN POINTS

28–02

(a) The First-tier Tribunal (Information Rights) and the Upper Tribunal are part of the tribunal structure established under the Tribunals, Courts and Enforcement Act 2007.

(b) The First-tier Tribunal (Information Rights) is a chamber of the First-tier Tribunal General Regulatory Chamber.

(c) Cases, apart from those dealing with national security certificates, all start in the First-tier but may be allocated to the Upper Tribunal.

(d) Appeals from decisions of the First-tier Tribunal (Information Rights) may be made on points of law only to the Administrative Appeals Chamber of the Upper Tribunal. Appeals from the Upper Tribunal are made to the Court of Appeal.

(e) The tribunals hear appeals against regulatory actions taken by the Information Commissioner under the:
  •   Data Protection Act 1998;

---

[1] The Transfer of Tribunal Functions Order 2010 (SI 2010/22) art.3.

- Data Protection (Monetary Penalty) Order 2010;
- Privacy and Electronic Communications (EC Directive) Regulations 2003;
- Freedom of Information Act 2000;
- Environmental Information Regulations 2004; and
- Environmental Protection Public Sector (INSPIRE) Regulations 2009,

against decision notices and enforcement, assessment and information notices, including third party information notices under PECR and the issue or amount of monetary penalty notices including fixed monetary penalty notices under PECR and notices served under the INSPIRE Regulations.

(f)   The Upper Tribunal hears appeals which are directed to it, appeals from decisions of the First-tier Tribunal and appeals in relation to the application of the national security exemptions under the DPA and FOIA.

(g)   The Upper Tribunal may hear related applications for judicial review subject to the rules.

(h)   Administrative support is provided as part of the administrative system to support the work of all the tribunals subject to the Tribunals, Courts and Enforcement Act 2007.

HISTORY AND ESTABLISHMENT

28–03   A specialist Tribunal was first established under the 1984 Act to hear appeals against orders made under that Act. The functions of the Tribunal were retained under the 1998 Act. It was then renamed the Information Tribunal under the Freedom of Information Act 2000,[2] which also made a number of consequential amendments related to the change.[3] The rules of procedure, made under statutory instruments under the Data Protection Act 1998[4] were amended in 2000 and 2002 to make the technical changes necessary to enable the Tribunal to deal with appeals under the Freedom of Information Act (FOIA) and then replaced entirely in 2005.

The Information Tribunal was one of the many statutory tribunals with specific remit established in the last 30 years. Over that period there has been a significant expansion in the role of such tribunals. Many were established under specific pieces of legislation. Although the procedures and processes have had much in common nevertheless there were separate provisions for appointment of members, different rules of procedure and separate administrative arrangements. The Tribunals Courts and Enforcement Act 2007 (TCEA) addressed this fragmented and often inefficient system. Many smaller tribunals, such as the Information Tribunal, were abolished and brought into the new unified system with one set of rules for the appointment of members, the establishment of a unified core set of rules of procedure and a unified administrative system to support the tribunal system. The Information Tribunal was abolished from

---

[2] Freedom of Information Act 2000 s.18(2).

[3] s.18(3) and Sch.4.

[4] Information Tribunal (Enforcement Appeals) Rules 2005 (SI 2005/14); Information Tribunal (Enforcement Appeals) (Amendment) Rules 2005 (SI 2005/450); Information Tribunal (National Security Appeals) Rules 2005 (SI 2005/13).

January 2010. Its functions were incorporated into the tribunal structure established under the Tribunals Courts and Enforcement Act 2007. All the tribunals brought into this system as well as the functions of the employment tribunals, the Employment Appeals Tribunal and the Asylum and Immigration Tribunal have been brought under the supervision of a senior member of the judiciary, the Senior President of Tribunals.[5] The changes brought to the many administrative tribunals were extensive. A full schedule of the relevant legislation and secondary legislation can be found on the Ministry of Justice website at *www.justice.gov.uk/guidance/courts-and-tribunals/tribunals/rules.htm*.[6]

The TCEA makes it clear that the aim of the tribunal system is to ensure that tribunals should be accessible, proceedings should be fair and handled quickly and efficiently and aim to achieve appropriate resolution of the issues before them.[7] This is echoed in the overriding objectives of the rules of procedure for the First-tier Tribunal which state that the overriding objective of the rules is to deal with cases fairly and justly which includes:

28–04

- dealing with cases in ways which are proportionate to the importance of the case, the complexity of issues and the anticipated costs and resources of the parties;
- avoiding unnecessary formality and seeking flexibility in the proceedings;
- ensuring so far as practicable that the parties are able to participate fully in the proceedings;
- using any special expertise of the Tribunal effectively; and
- avoiding delay so far as compatible with the proper consideration of the issues.[8]

CONSTITUTION

Section 3 of the TCEA provides that there are to be two tribunals, one to be known as the First-tier Tribunal and the other to be known as the Upper Tribunal. Both are to consist of judges and other members and both are to deal with any functions conferred on them by statute. The Senior President of Tribunals presides over both tribunals. The Upper Tribunal becomes a superior court of record[9] and has the powers of the High Court to require attendance of witnesses and production of documents and all other matters incidental to the Tribunal's functions.[10] Accordingly these are two separate judicial bodies. The fact that the Upper Tribunal becomes a court of record means that, while the decisions of the First-Tier remain persuasive only, judgments of the Upper Tribunal are binding precedents.

28–05

---

[5] Tribunals, Courts and Enforcement Act 2007 s.2.
[6] Accessed October 7, 2012.
[7] Tribunals, Courts and Enforcement Act 2007 s.2(3) setting out the matters to which the President must have regard and s.22(4) on rules of procedure.
[8] The Tribunal Procedure (First-tier Tribunal) (General Regulatory Chamber) Rules 2009 (SI 2009/1976) art.2.
[9] Tribunals, Courts and Enforcement Act 2007 s.3(1)–(5).
[10] Tribunals, Courts and Enforcement Act 2007 s.25.

Section 7 TCEA provides that the Lord Chancellor may make provision for the tribunals to be organised into chambers with an appointed person to be the Chambers President. Although the same person cannot preside over two chambers he or she can preside over the same chamber of both the First-Tier and Upper Tribunal. The Lord Chancellor may also make provision for the allocation of the functions of the tribunals to appropriate chambers.[11] The tribunals have been organised into six chambers for the First-Tier and four chambers of the Upper Tribunal.[12] Five of the chambers of the First-Tier are specialist jurisdictions such as tax, with the functions of the former Information Tribunal being allocated to the General Regulatory Chamber, which covers all functions relating to

> "proceedings in respect of the decisions and actions of regulatory bodies which are not allocated to the Health, Education and Social Care Chamber by article 4 or the Tax Chamber by article 7".[13]

28–06   Four of the chambers of the Upper Tribunal are specialist with one general, the Administrative Appeals Chamber. The functions allotted to the Administrative Appeals Chamber are all functions related to the following matters:

- an appeal against a decision made by the First-tier Tribunal of any chamber with an exception for appeals allocated to the Tax and Chancery Chamber or the Immigration and Asylum Chamber of the Upper Tribunal;
- appeals against decsions of some specialist tribunals for Northern Ireland, Scotand and Wales;
- appeals transferred to the Upper Tribunal from the First-tier Tribunal under Tribunal Procedure Rules, except an appeal allocated to the Tax and Chancery Chamber;
- appeals under s.4 of the Safeguarding Vulnerable Groups Act 2006;
- appeals against decisions of traffic commissioner;
- applications for "judical review" relief[14];
- reviews of decisions of First-tier Tribunals referred by those Tribunals under s.9(5)(b) (under which a First-tier Tribunal is enabled to refer to the Upper Tribunal) unless the proceedings must go to another chamber;
- cases where there has been non-compliance with a requirement of a First-tier Tribunal and the matter should be referred to the Upper Tribunal under the Rules unless the proceedings must go to another chamber;
- a determination or decision under s.4 of the Forfeiture Act 1982;
- proceedings, or a preliminary issue, transferred under Tribunal Procedure Rules to the Upper Tribunal from the First-tier Tribunal, except those allocated to the Tax and Chancery Chamber by art.13(1)(e).

Article 14 provides that, if there is any doubt or dispute as to the chamber in which a particular matter is to be dealt with, the Senior President of Tribunals

---

[11] Tribunals, Courts and Enforcement Act 2007 s.7(9).
[12] First-tier Tribunal and Upper Tribunal (Chambers) Order 2010 (SI 2010/2655).
[13] SI 2010/2655 art.3(a).
[14] See s.15(1) of the Tribunals, Courts and Enforcement Act 2007 (Upper Tribunal's "judicial review" jurisdiction) and s.21(2) of that Act (Upper Tribunal's "judicial review" jurisdiction: Scotland).

may allocate that matter to the chamber which appears to him or her to be most appropriate. There is also provision for a case to be re-allocated to another chamber where the Chamber President of the chamber to which a case or any issue has been allocated agrees with the corresponding Chamber President that this should happen.[15]

Unified rules of procedure

The TCEA establishes a Tribunal Procedure Rules Committee[16] responsible for making the rules governing the procedures to be followed by all First-tier and Upper Tribunals. The rules must reflect the aims of the tribunal system.

28–07

Review and appellate functions

The First-tier Tribunal has a power to review its own decisions and may correct accidental errors in decisions, amend reasons given for decisions and even set decisions aside. If it does set a decision aside it must either re-decide the matter or remit it to the Upper Tribunal to decide.[17] The Upper Tribunal may exercise the same power.[18] Rights of appeal lie to the Upper Tribunal on points of law only and an appeal may only be brought with leave. Leave can be granted by the First-tier Tribunal or the Upper Tribunal unless it is an excluded decision within s.11. Excluded decisions include appeals against the issue or extent of national security certificates under the DPA or the FOIA. Where the Upper Tribunal finds that a decision of the First-tier Tribunal involved an error of law it may set aside the decision and either make its own decision or remit it to the First tier for re-hearing by a differently constituted tribunal.[19]

28–08

Appeals from the Upper Tribunal to the Court of Appeal

Appeals from the Upper Tribunal may be made to the Court of Appeal on points of law only and with leave of either the Upper Tribunal or the appellate court. Appeals may not be made in respect of excluded decisions and decisions of the Upper Tribunal in respect of the issue or extent of national security certificates are excluded decisions.[20] The Lord Chancellor may by order make permission for leave to be granted only on a limited basis. The relevant order is SI 2008/2834, The Appeals from the Upper Tribunal to the Court of Appeal Order 2008. This provides that permission to appeal to the Court of Appeal in England and Wales or leave to appeal to the Court of Appeal in Northern Ireland shall not be granted unless the Upper Tribunal or, where the Upper Tribunal refuses permission, the relevant appellate court, considers that:

28–09

---

[15] SI 2010/2655 arts 14 and 15.
[16] TCEA s.22(3) and Sch.5 Pt 2.
[17] TCEA s.9.
[18] TCEA s.10.
[19] TCEA s.122.
[20] TCEA s.13.

(a)   the proposed appeal would raise some important point of principle or practice; or

(b)   there is some other compelling reason for the relevant appellate court to hear the appeal.

Judicial review functions of Upper Tribunal

28–10   The Upper Tribunal is empowered to issue relief relating to judicial review being mandatory orders, prohibiting orders, quashing orders, declarations and injunctions. In deciding whether to grant such relief the Upper Tribunal must apply the principles that the High Court would do in a judicial review case. The applicant must have a sufficient interest in the case and must obtain leave of the Tribunal to make the application. The limits of the jurisdiction of the Tribunal are set out in s.18 of the TCEA and any case must be able to meet the four conditions set out in that section. If these cannot be met the case must be transferred to the High Court. Equally cases started in the High Court must be transferred to the Upper Tribunal where all four of the relevant conditions are met.

Membership

28–11   The First-tier Tribunal and Upper Tribunal continues to consist of judges and other members.[21] The judges are legally qualified and the members are individuals with special expertise in the areas covered by the tribunals.

New appointments

28–12   The provisions for the appointment of judges and members to the First-tier Tribunal, their terms of appointment, remuneration, training and other matters are set out in Sch.2 TCEA. Judges are appointed by the Lord Chancellor and must satisfy the eligibility criteria of having relevant qualifications plus five years' experience. Members are eligible for appointment if they satisfy the qualifications prescribed in an order made by the Lord Chancellor.

The appointment of judges of the Upper Tribunal, their terms of appointment, remuneration, training and other matters are covered in TCEA Sch.3. A person may only sit as a judge of the Upper Tribunal where they satisfy the eligibility criteria and have seven years relevant experience. The Lord Chancellor may also appoint members of the Upper Chamber if they satisfy the qualifications prescribed in an order made by the Lord Chancellor.

The relevant order covering the appointment of members was made in 2008[22] and covers membership of both chambers. The order lists a number of qualifications which would be relevant to a range of tribunals, for example medical experience. A range of general experience is set out at para.(4), including substantial experience:

●   of educational, child care, health, or social care matters;

---

[21] TCEA s.3(3).

[22] Qualifications for Appointment of Members to the First-tier Tribunal and Upper Tribunal Order 2008 (SI 2008/2692).

- in the regulatory field;
- in consumer affairs;
- in an industry, trade or business sector and the matters that are likely to arise as issues in the course of disputes with regulators of such industries, trades or businesses; or
- in a business, trade or not-for-profit organisation.

It must be assumed that these categories are wide enough to cover those with relevant experience in the matters covered by the First-tier Tribunal (Information Rights) and the Upper Chamber.

Transferred judges and members

Section 30 of the TCEA provides for the Lord Chancellor to provide for a function of a tribunal listed in Sch.6 to that Act to be transferred to the new system. The Lord Chancellor was empowered to make appropriate determinations as to transfer to the First-tier or Upper Tribunal or arrangements for the allocation of functions of existing tribunals to be appropriately divided between the two. The Information Rights Tribunal was one of those listed in Sch.6. Under s.31, where such functions were transferred, the Lord Chancellor could by order make provision for existing judges and members of such tribunals to become holders of appropriate offices in the new system and become transferred-in judges of the First-tier Tribunal or Upper Tribunal or transferred-in members of the First-tier Tribunal or Upper Tribunal.[23]

28–13

Transfer of functions

The functions of the Information Rights Tribunal were formally transferred by the Transfer of Tribunal Functions Order 2010 (SI 2010/22), which came into effect on January 18, 2010. The Order also dealt with the transfer of existing judges and members to the new structure. The Information Tribunal was abolished and its functions were transferred to the First-tier Tribunal and the Upper Tribunal with the question as to which one of them is to exercise the functions in a particular case being determined by, or under, Tribunal Procedure Rules. The Chairman and Deputy Chairs of the Information Tribunal became deputy judges in the Upper Tribunal. The Deputy chairs and all other legally qualified chairs became judges in the First-tier Tribunal. All the lay members became transferred-in members of the Upper Tribunal and the First-tier Tribunal.

28–14

The Order amended the Data Protection Act 1998 as follows:

- removing all the references to the Tribunal from s.6 and Sch.5;
- amending the fees provision in s.26 so that the cost of running the Tribunal is no longer taken into account in setting the fees for notification;
- removing the provision for appeals on points of law to the High Court from s.49, as such appeals are now to be made to the Upper Chamber;
- altered other references to the Tribunal to references to the Upper or First-tier Tribunal; and

---

[23] TCEA s.31.

- repealed most of Sch.6 dealing with the hearing of appeals but retained provision to make specific rules dealing with cases under the DPA and the FOIA for the purposes of securing the production of documents and material used for the purposes of processing personal data, for the inspection, examination, operation and testing of any equipment or material used in connection with the processing of personal data and for hearing an appeal in the absence of the appellant or for determining an appeal without a hearing. The provisions relating to obstruction in paragraph 8 are also retained.

Any provisions in the Act that refer to "the Tribunal" are to be treated after January 2010 as applying to the Upper Tribunal in a case where it is determined that the Upper Tribunal shall hear the case and the First-tier Tribunal in any other case. The provision that no enactment or rule of law prohibiting or restricting the disclosure of information shall preclude a person from furnishing information necessary for the discharge of functions applies to the tribunals as it does to the Commissioner.[24] Equivalent changes are also made to the Freedom of Information Act 2000 and the Privacy and Electronic Communications (EC Directive) Regulations 2003.[25]

Transitional provisions

28–15   The transitional provisions are set out in Sch.5 of SI 2010/22. Cases which were pending under the old system were treated as cases brought under the new system. Cases which had started under the old tribunal system but had not been concluded were allocated to the judge and members already dealing with the case and the new tribunal was empowered to apply the old procedural rules or waive the new ones as required in order to achieve a fair hearing. Directions or orders made under the old rules were treated as though made under the new rules. The transition appeared to run smoothly and there were no reported problems.

SECRETARIAT

28–16   The Secretariat to both chambers of the tribunal is provided by an administrative office which is part of HM Courts and Tribunals Service. The Ministry of Justice website describes the Service as an agency of the Ministry of Justice which and was created on April 1, 2011 and operates as a partnership between the Lord Chancellor, the Lord Chief Justice and the Senior President of Tribunals. The administrative arrangements are set out in a Framework Document. The Service is responsible for the administration of the criminal, civil and family courts and tribunals in England and Wales and non-devolved tribunals in Scotland and Northern Ireland. The First-tier Tribunal (Information Rights) administrative officers are based in Leicester and the contact details are: Arnhem House Support Centre, PO Box 9300, Leicester LEI 8DJ. The First-tier Tribunal (Information

---

[24] DPA s.58 as amended by Sch.2 para.18 of the FOIA. Definition of "the Tribunal" in s.70(1) amended by SI 2010/22 art.29.
[25] SI 2010/22 art.40.

Rights) has no dedicated premises but sits at a number of venues around the UK which it uses in common with other First-tier Tribunals.

MEMBERS

The number of members who sit in the First-tier is not set but is determined by the Senior President of Tribunals. However, where the matter which falls to be decided by the tribunal fell to a tribunal in a list in Sch.6 to the Tribunals, Courts and Enforcement Act 2007 before its functions were transferred by order under s.30(1) of that Act, the President must have regard to any provision made by or under any enactment for determining the number of members of that tribunal.[26] The Information Tribunal is listed in Pt 1 of Sch.6 to the TCEA therefore the President must have regard to the relevant repealed provisions of the Data Protection Act 1998. Schedule 6 of the Act provided that, subject to the special cases in which the rules of procedure for the Tribunal allowed for the chair or deputy to sit alone, for example in handling preliminary or incidental matters, or appeals against information notices, a Tribunal should consist of a chair or deputy who presides over the proceedings and an equal number of the lay members who are appointed to represent the relevant interests on each side. In making nominations account must be taken of the desirability of having lay members with specialist knowledge of a particular subject. Under the current provisions the President must have regard to the need for members of tribunals to have particular expertise, skills or knowledge.[27]

28–17

Number of members of the Upper Tribunal

The number of members of the tribunal who are to decide any matter that falls to be decided by the Upper Tribunal is one unless determined otherwise under para.(2). Under that paragraph the tribunal may consist of two or three members if the Senior President of Tribunals so determines. Where a matter is to be decided by a single member of a tribunal, it must be decided by a judge of the tribunal unless if the Senior President of Tribunals determines that it may be decided by one of the other members of the tribunal.[28]

28–18

Where a matter is to be decided by two or more members of a tribunal the number of members who are to be judges of the tribunal and the number of members who are to be other members of the tribunal must be determined by the Senior President of Tribunals who must select one of the members (the "presiding member") to chair the tribunal. If the decision of the tribunal is not unanimous, the decision of the majority is the decision of the tribunal; and the presiding member has a casting vote if the votes are equally divided.

---

[26] First-tier Tribunals and Upper Tribunal (Composition of Tribunal) Order 2008 (SI 2008/2835).
[27] SI 2008/2835.
[28] SI 2008/2835.

JURISDICTION

28–19   The Commissioner can serve a range of notices, decisions and orders. In each case, the Commissioner must inform the controller of the extent of any rights of appeal available and the time within which such appeals must be brought. Appeals can be brought on various grounds primarily on matters of fact and law although in cases where the discretion of the Commissioner is involved an appeal may also be brought against the exercise of the discretion. In all cases save national security ones the appeal must be brought with 28 days of the disputed decision. Although there is provision for the tribunals to hear appeals brought out of time they will only do so where the applicant can show a strong justification.

Appeals under the Data Protection Act

28–20   Section 48 sets out the other matters which may be appealed to the Tribunal under the DPA. They are:

(i)   appeals against enforcement, assessment, information or special information notices (s.48(1));

(ii)   appeals against refusals of the Commissioner to cancel or vary existing enforcement notices (s.48(2));

(iii) appeals against the inclusion of urgency provisions in any notices (s.48(3));

(iv)   appeals against a determination by the Commissioner under s.45 (s.48(4)); and

(v)   appeals against the issue or amount of a monetary penalty notice under s.55B DPA.

Appeals under the Privacy and Electronic Communications (EC Directive) Regulations 2003

28–21   Regulation 31 of PECR applies the enforcement and appeal provisions of the DPA subject to the changes in Sch.1. There are no provisions in PECR covering the special purposes but the Commissioner has additional powers in respect of personal data breaches. Therefore the following appeals can be brought in respect of actions taken under PECR:

(i)   appeals against enforcement, or information notices (s.48(1));

(ii)   appeals against refusals of the Commissioner to cancel or vary existing enforcement notices (s.48(2));

(iii) appeals against the inclusion of urgency provisions in any notices (s.48(3));

(iv)   appeals against the issue or amount of a monetary penalty notice under s.55B DPA; and

(v)   appeals against the issue of fixed monetary penalty notices and third party information notices.

Appeals under the Data Protection (Monetary Penalty) Regulations 2010 (DPMPR)

28–22

(i)   Appeals against the variation of a monetary penalty notice under reg.7 of the Regulations applying DPA s.49.

(ii) Where appeals are brought under the DPA, PECR or the DPMPR they may only be brought by data controllers. Individuals have no route by which to appeal to the Tribunal apart from under the national security certificate provisions. By contract individuals or others affected by a refusal of information have the right to appeal under the FOIA and EIRs.

Appeals under the Freedom of Information Act 2000

Section 57 of the FOIA sets out the other matters which may be appealed. They are:

28–23

(i)   appeals by public authorities against enforcement notices (s.57(2));
(ii) appeals by public authorities against information notices (s.57(2));
(iii) appeals public authorities against decision notices (s.57(1)); or
(iv) appeals by individuals against decision notices (s.57(1)).

There are no urgency provisions under the FOIA.

Appeals under the Environmental Information Regulations 2005

The Environmental Information Regulations provide for a specific regime to access such information. Under reg.18, the enforcement and appeals provisions of the Freedom of Information Act 2000 are applied. The Commissioner can serve decision notices, information notices and enforcement notices for failure to comply with the Regulations as he can do under the FOIA. The following appeals can therefore be made to the Tribunals:

28–24

(i)   appeals by public authorities against enforcement notices (s.57(2));
(ii) appeals by public authorities against information notices (s.57(2));
(iii) appeals public authorities against decision notices (s.57(1)); or
(iv) appeals by individuals against decision notices (s.57(1)).

Appeals under the INSPIRE Regulations 2009[29]

The INSPIRE Regulations implement Directive 2007/2/EC establishing an Infrastructure for Spatial Information in the European Community. They place public authorities under obligations to make spatial data sets available to the public over the internet or otherwise electronically and to provide facilities to view, download and manipulate the data. The duty does not apply where certain exemptions, such as an exemption to protect personal data, apply. Under reg.11, the enforcement and appeals provisions of the Freedom of Information Act 2000

28–25

---

[29] SI 2009/3157.

apply with appropriate amendments. The Commissioner can serve information notices and enforcement notices in respect of the INSPIRE regulations. The following appeals can therefore be made to the Tribunals:

(i)   appeals against information notices served under s.50 of the FOIA as applied by reg.11 of the INSPIRE regulations; and

(ii)   appeals against enforcement notices served under s.52 of the FOIA as applied by reg.11 of the INSPIRE regulations.

Decisions of the Tribunals

28–26   The tribunals have different powers to deal with different types of appeal before it. The powers vary with the pieces of legislation.

All appeals

28–27   The tribunals have wide powers in respect of considering appeals. In respect of any notice or determination they may decide:

(a)   that the action is invalid because formalities required have not been complied with, for example a notice has not been properly addressed or served;

(b)   that the Commissioner failed to consider a relevant issue which would have altered his judgment;

(c)   that the Commissioner was mistaken in his understanding of the facts on which the decision was based; or

(d)   that the Commissioner was wrong in his view of the meaning or effect of the relevant law.

The tribunals may review any determination of fact on which a decision is based. This means that the tribunal will proceed by re-hearing in any case where the facts are in dispute, unless the hearing is an Upper Tribunal appeal on a point of law only. Even if the tribunal decides that the disputed decision was correct in law it may overturn or vary the Commissioner's decision if that decision involved the exercise of a discretion and it is the tribunal's view that the discretion should have been exercised differently. The tribunals may allow an appeal in full and quash the notice or order involved or may substitute such other order or determination as could have been made by the Commissioner. They may not make a determination broader than that which could have been made by the Commissioner when considering the original matter.

Specific provisions

Application for cancellation or change of an enforcement notice under the DPA or PECR

28–28   Under s.49(3) of the DPA, the tribunals have a narrower power when hearing these cases. They may vary or cancel an existing enforcement notice only where there has been a change of circumstances. The tribunal must consider that there is something in that change of circumstances which means that the notice ought to be altered or revoked. Any alterations to the notice must be in response to the change. The tribunal cannot make changes to the notice unconnected to the change in circumstances.

Appeal against inclusion of an urgency provisions under the DPA or PECR

Supervisory notices generally do not take effect for 28 days after service and if an appeal is lodged the effect of the notice is suspended until the appeal is decided. However, any notice may include an urgency provision stating that, because of special circumstances, the notice should be complied with as a matter of urgency and giving the reasons why the Commissioner has reached that conclusion. In such a case a notice can take effect within seven days. This applies to enforcement notices (s.40(7)), information notices including third party information notices under PECR (s.43(6)) and special information notices (s.44(7)).

28–29

A controller can appeal against the inclusion of an urgency provision even if he does not appeal against the rest of the notice. On such an appeal the tribunal can either strike out the urgency provision in whole, so the entire notice no longer takes effect in the seven days, or it can strike it out in part so that some of the notice provisions might come in as a matter of urgency and others not. The tribunal might also make associated modifications to give effect to its decision on the urgency provisions. The most usual modification would be to replace the seven-day period for the notice taking effect with a 28-day or longer period.

Special purpose determination under the DPA

A s.45 determination is made by the Commissioner where he decides that personal data are not being processed only for the special purposes or are not being processed with a view to publication of materials which has not previously been published by the data controller for the special purposes. Such a determination will be a matter of both fact and law. The appeal against such a determination may be on either fact or law. Where an appeal against such a determination is brought the tribunal may either dismiss the appeal or cancel the determination. The tribunal has a narrower power to deal with such appeals than with other matters of appeal. It has no power to vary or modify the determination even if it finds as a matter of fact that part of the data are being processed for the special purposes.

28–30

Appeals against service of assessment notices under the DPA

Assessment notices are subject to a specific code of practice under section 41C. The code must specify the factors to be considered in determining whether to serve an assessment notice on a data controller. A controller could therefore appeal on the grounds that the Commissioner had failed to take proper account of the specified factors or give appropriate weight to them.

28–31

Appeals against decision notices under the FOIA or EIRs

28–32   Where the exemption relied upon is an absolute exemption the grounds of an appeal, apart from technical ones in respect of the nature or service of a notice, can only relate to the question of whether the information requested falls within the terms of the exemption. Where the exemption is subject to the test of public interest an appeal can also be raised on the application of the public interest.

Appeals against monetary penalty notices under the DPA and PECR

28–33   Appeals may be brought under s.55B against issue of a monetary penalty notice or the amount of a monetary penalty notice. Appeals can therefore be brought challenging the facts on which the Commissioner has determined to issue the notice, arguing that the grounds for the notice were not made out including that the breach was not sufficiently serious to warrant the service of a notice or other that the Commissioner should have exercised his discretion differently. No appeals have been brought under this section at the time of writing.

Appeals against fixed monetary penalty notices under PECR

28–34   Fixed monetary penalty notices may be served when the Commissioner has ordered an entity to notify individuals of a personal data breach and the entity has failed to do so. It is not clear whether the appellant will be able to use such an appeal to challenge the substantive decision. The point is discussed at para.xx. It would seem, however, to be a breach of fundamental principles for the entity served with an order to give such notice to be left without an appeal on the substantive decision and the tribunals may be prepared to allow such an appeal be used as an opportunity to review the substantive decision.

Appeals against third party notices under PECR

28–35   The appeal under this provision would be brought by the communications service provider under reg.31B when served with a notice to disclose the information requested by the Commissioner.

Appeals against the variation of a monetary penalty notice under the DPMPR

28–36   The Regulations include a specific provision under which the Commissioner may vary the penalty to a lower sum only and a linked appeal provision.

National Security Certificates—Data Protection Act

28–37   Appeals may be brought under s.28(4) and (6). These are explained in Ch.15 on regulation, crime and taxation. To recap briefly here, s.28 exempts personal data from data protection control if the exemption is required in order to safeguard national security. "Conclusive evidence" of the fact that the exemption is required for that purpose is to be provided by a certificate signed by a Minister of the

Crown. The certificate must identify the personal data to which it applies. Where such a certificate has been issued there are two possibilities of appeal:

(i)   Under s.28(4), a person directly affected by a certificate may appeal on the ground that the Minister who issued it did not have reasonable grounds for doing so. The test to be applied will be that employed in judicial review cases. The decision may only be overruled if it was "Wednesbury" unreasonable, that is following the principle in *Associated Provincial Picture Houses v Wednesbury Corp*[30] that it was so unreasonable that no reasonable authority could have reached it taking account of proper considerations. On hearing such a case the tribunal can either allow the appeal or quash the certificate or dismiss the appeal. The tribunal does not appear to have any power to vary the certificate, unlike the powers in respect of enforcement notices. The applicant in the case of *Baker v Secretary of State* appealed successfully on this ground and the certificate was revoked.

(ii) Under s.28(6) the possibility of appeal is only open to someone who is a party to other proceedings under the Data Protection Act. If such a litigant is confronted by a national security certificate which describes personal data by a general description and which the defendant data controller claims covers personal data which are the subject of those proceedings then the litigant can refer the question of whether or not it properly does so by way of an appeal. Presumably, under general principles, the other proceedings will have to be stayed pending the determination of the tribunal on the matter of the certificate. The tribunal's powers in such a case are limited to determining that the certificate does or does not apply to the personal data in question.

In the case of *R. (on the application of SSHD) v Information Tribunal and the Information Commissioner*[31] the High Court held that the Information Tribunal was correct to allow the Information Commissioner to appeal where there was a question as to whether a s.28 certificate had been properly applied. The facts of the case were that the data subject made a subject access request to the Immigration and Nationality Directorate of the Home Office (IND). The subject was not satisfied with the response he received and made an application to the Commissioner for an assessment. The ICO contacted the IND and was informed that the IND considered that s.28, the national security exemption was applicable. The ICO asked the IND to allow the Commissioner to have sight of the data in question, to supply a s.28 certificate and queried whether the subject had been informed of the IND's reliance on s.28. The IND responded that it did not intend to inform the data subject and would not allow the Commissioner to see the data in question. The Commissioner then served an Information Notice under s.43 seeking access to the information which had been withheld and the IND served a certificate under s.28 stating, not that the personal data was exempt from the subject access right for the purpose of safeguarding antional security, but that the personal data was exempt from the power of the Information Commissioner to

28–38

---

[30] [1948] 1 K.B. 223.
[31] [2002] EWHC 2958 Admin.

service the Information Notice under s.43. This was based on the argument that, as s.28(11) states that the Commissioner cannot exercise any of his regulatory functions in relation to any personal data to which a s.28 certificate applies, this effectively ousted his powers entirely where the exemption was claimed. .

28–39   Section 28(4) states that any person directly affected by the issuing of a certificate may appeal to the tribunal against the certificate. The Information Commissioner appealed to the Tribunal as a person "directly affected". The IND also appealed against the service of the Information Notice but that was deferred pending the hearing of the Commissioner's application. Where the tribunal finds, applying the principles applied by a court on an application for judicial review, that the Minister did not have reasonable grounds for issuing the certificate, it may quash the certificate. The Tribunal considered the IND's arguments that the effect of s.28(11) was to remove the Commissioner's powers to the extent that he was not even able to lodge the appeal in question and took the view that the IND could not purport to remove the Commissioner's right to appeal the certificate and quashed the certificate. The IND appealed to the High Court which upheld the decision of the Tribunal.

National Security Certificates—Freedom of Information Act and Environmental Information Regulations 2005

28–40   Appeals may be brought under s.60 by the Commissioner or an applicant whose request for information has been affected where a certificate under ss.23(2) or 24(3) has been issued.

Section 23 allows for a Minister of the Crown to issue a certificate that the information applied for under the FOIA is exempt because it relates to or was supplied by one of the listed national security bodies. Such a certificate is conclusive evidence of such a fact. Nevertheless an appeal may be made on the grounds that the information is not entitled to the exemption and if the tribunal makes a finding that it was not so entitled the tribunal may allow the appeal and quash the certificate.

Section 24 allows a Minister of the Crown to issue a certificate that the information applied for under the FOIA is exempt because the exemption is necessary for the purpose of safeguarding national security. Such a certificate is conclusive evidence of such a fact. Neverthelesss an appeal may be made on the ground that the Minister who issued it did not have reasonable grounds for doing so. The test to be applied will be that applied in judicial review cases (see below, para.28-44).

Section 60(4) also allows appeals on the ground that a certificate issued under s.24(3) which identifies information in general terms does not in fact cover the information which is being withheld. The tribunal may determine whether the certificate covers the information.

28–41   Requests for environmental information may be refused under reg.12(1) of the EIRs on the basis that the disclosure would adversely affect national security and that in all the circumstances of the case the public interest in maintaining the exemption out weights the public interest in disclosing it, Unlike the equivalent exemption in the FOIA the EIR provision is subject to the test of public interest. Under reg.15, a Minister of the Crown may certify that the grounds of the exemption apply to particular information. As with the DPA, such a certificate is conclusive evidence of the application of the exemption and the certificate may be expressed in general terms to describe the information. As with the FOIA, an appeal may be brought on the grounds that the Minister who issued the certificate did not have reasonable grounds to do so (reg.18(7)) or that the certificate does not cover the information in question.

PROCEDURE

The rules of procedure are set out in the Tribunal Procedure (First-tier Tribunal)(General Regulatory Chamber) Rules 2009[32] and the Tribunal Procedure (Upper Tribunal) Rules 2008.[33] The two sets of rules are largely the same with necessary additions or changes to cover the judicial review powers of the Upper Tribunal and other specialist or appellate functions. In relation to the specific jurisdiction to hear Information Rights cases provision is made for all cases under the Data Protection Act or the Freedom of Information Act 2000 which concern national security certificates to be transferred to the Upper Tribunal.[34] The Information Tribunal (National Security Appeals) Rules 2005 were repealed by SI 2010/22. Such appeals are now heard by the Upper Tribunal under the rules of procedure for the Upper Tribunal. There is a specific provision that in a case involving national security the Tribunal must ensure that information is not disclosed contrary to the interests of national security,[35] which is presumably especially relevant to cases involving the issue of national security certificates.   **28–42**

All appeals must be brought within 28 days of the disputed decision or ruling save that an appeal under s.28(4) of the DPA or s.60(1) to the FOIA may be brought at any time during the currency of the disputed certificate to which the appeal relates.   **28–43**

The First-tier Tribunal is also empowered to make an entry direction in cases where an appeal is lodged against a decision or notice issued by the Information Commissioner.[36] This may require the occupier of premises to permit entry to specified persons in order to allow such persons to inspect, examine, operate or test relevant equipment and to inspect, examine or test relevant materials. The direction must state the time and date of the entry and be given at least seven days in advance. Relevant equipment is equipment on the premises used or intended to be used to process personal data or the storage, recording or deletion of other information. Relevant materials means any documents and other materials on the premises connected with the processing of personal data or the storage, recording or deletion of other information. The direction cannot compel a person to produce anything that they could not be compelled to produce in a court of law. The First-tier Tribunal does not have the enforcement powers of the Upper Tribunal and therefor the rules provide that any person who has failed to comply with a ruling of the First-tier Tribunal to attend to give evidence or produce documents   **28–44**

---

[32] SI 2009/1976.
[33] SI 2008/2698.
[34] r.19.
[35] SI 2009/1976 r.14(9).
[36] SI 2009/1976 r.18.

may be referred to the Upper Tribunal to exercise its powers.[37] It would appear that a person who failed to comply with an entry direction could be referred to the Upper Tribunal under this provision.

There is also a specific provision in the First-tier rules to enable the Tribunal to select a lead case where it appears that there are a number of cases dealing with the same matters. Otherwise the procedural rules are the same for the two levels.

28–45   The rules cover general management powers, procedure at hearings, decisions and procedures for review and appeals. The provisions covering case management powers including giving directions, striking out, addition or removal of parties, representatives, evidence and submissions are straightforward. In both tiers the general rule is that hearing are to be held in public subject to provisions to prevent the disclosure of documents or specified information or to remove persons who are causing disruption.

Forms for application to the Tribunal and guidance on how to appeal are available at *http://www.justice.gov.uk/global/forms/hmcts/tribunals/information-rights/index.htm*.[38]

Costs

28–46   Costs may be awarded in any proceedings of the First-tier or Upper Tribunal but are at the discretion of the Tribunal. Costs are not usually awarded, but there are provisions allowing for their award in specific cases where the tribunal considers that the appeal was manifestly unreasonable, or against the Commissioner where it considers that the disputed decision was manifestly unreasonable. Where the tribunal is considering awarding costs against a party it must give that party an opportunity to make representations on the point.

---

[37] SI 2009/1976 r.7.
[38] Accessed October 7, 2012.

CHAPTER 29

Data Protection Law In The Channel Islands And The Isle Of Man

Many organisations work closely with associated or other entities based in the Channel Islands and the Isle of Man. The Channel Islands and the Isle of Man are Crown dependencies. They are possessions of the British Crown but are neither part of the United Kingdom nor colonies. They enjoy full independence in government, except for international relations and defence which are the responsibility of the UK. The States of Jersey, the Bailiwick of Guernsey and the Isle of Man are therefore each a separate jurisdiction. The UK Data Protection Act does not apply in any of these jurisdictions and therefore each of the jurisdictions has had to pass its own legislation. Neither the Channel Islands nor the Isle of Man belong to the European Economic Area (EEA). If dealing with a specific problem in one of the islands the practitioner should check the specific legislation for that jurisdiction. Although the wording and import of most of the provisions are in most instances identical to the UK Act there are differences. Each Act is arranged slightly differently and therefore the section numbers may differ, even where the content is the same. Some of the differences are significant, for example in the Isle of Man, on the application of an aggrieved data subject, the High Court can order a data controller who has not dealt with a subject access request properly to pay a penalty of up to £5,000. In addition each jurisdiction has an independent regulator whose approach may not be the same as the one taken by the Information Commissioner in the UK.

29–01

SUMMARY OF MAIN POINTS

29–02

(a) In order to apply to the European Commission for a finding that each jurisdiction affords adequate protection, the legislature of each of the islands has had to pass data protection law which meets the requirements of the Directive.

(b) In Jersey the law is the Data Protection (Jersey) Law 2005, which came in to effect on December 1, 2005 and replaced the Data Protection (Jersey) Law 1987.

(c) In Guernsey this is the Data Protection (Bailiwick of Guernsey) Law 2001, which came into effect on August 1, 2002 and replaced the Data Protection (Bailiwick of Guernsey) Law 1986.

(d) In the Isle of Man the law is the Data Protection Act 2002, which came into effect on April 1, 2003 and replaced the Data Protection Act 1986.

(e) The EU made findings of adequacy in respect of Guernsey on November 21, 2003, the Isle of Man on April 28, 2004 and the States of Jersey on May 8, 2008 (see Ch.8 for a full discussion of the implications of a finding of adequacy).

(f) Each of the regimes follows closely the UK Act, but there are some areas of difference.

RELATION WITH THE DIRECTIVE

29–03 As the islands are not part of the EU, the Data Protection Directive does not apply nor are the courts under any obligation to take account of the Directive as a matter of general law. This is dealt with by the inclusion of specific interpretative provisions in the Isle of Man Act but not in the other two laws. In the Isle of Man law s.62(3) provides that:

> "in construing any provision of this Act any court or tribunal shall have regard to any provision of the Convention or of the Data Protection directive which appears to the court or tribunal to be relevant".

The reference to the Convention is a reference to the European Convention on Human Rights.

SUPERVISORY AUTHORITIES

29–04 As each jurisdiction has its own legislation which implements the Directive, it follows that each Act sets up an independent supervisory body. In the Isle of Man this is the role of the Isle of Man Data Protection Supervisor; in the States of Jersey, the Data Protection Commissioner; and in the Bailiwick of Guernsey, the Data Protection Commissioner. The Bailiwick of Guernsey also covers Alderney and Sark, although there are slightly different provisions for the courts on Alderney and Sark.

29–05 Each of the supervisory authorities is the relevant designated authority for the purposes of art.13 of the Convention for the Protection of Individuals with regard to the Automatic Processing of Personal Data (Treaty 108). The islands do not directly ratify treaties, instead treaties are extended to the islands by the UK, which formally notifies the Council of the ratification.

INTER-ISLANDS CO-OPERATION

29–06 The posts of Data Protection Commissioner in Jersey and Guernsey are currently held by the same official so that the Offices can share resources. The regulatory authorities of the UK, the islands and Ireland hold regular meetings to discuss matters of common interest. In many cases the guidance issued by the regulators follows the same lines; however, this is not universally the case and reference should be made to the websites for specific guidance (see *www.gov.im/odps*, *www.dataprotection.gov.je* and *www.gov.gg/dataprotection*).

Overview of differences

There are inevitable differences arising simply from the difference in jurisdic-   29–07
tions. The UK DPA amends the Consumer Credit Act 1974 (s.62) and deals with
the exercise of rights by children in Scotland (s.66) while none of the other pieces
of legislation make similar amends. There are provisions in the UK Act which
deal with educational records and accessible records but which are not covered
by the Jersey or Guernsey acts, although the Isle of Man does cover accessible
records.

Jersey

In the UK Act and the Jersey Law, the section numbers and topics are the same up   29–08
to s.60 of the Jersey Law. The Jersey Law adds a specific provision which deals
with the provision of false information as s.60. It also has a specific provision
excluding civil liability by the Commissioner or Tribunal in s.66. The UK's s.62
is omitted and thereafter the sections differ slightly as the Jersey provisions for
definitions are contained in the initial definition section rather than separated as
in the UK Act. The schedule numbers are the same up until Schs 11 and 12,
which in the UK deal with educational records and accessible records which have
no counterpart in the Jersey Law.

Isle of Man

In the UK Act and the Isle of Man law the section numbers diverge at s.3 as the   29–09
Isle of Man deals with sensitive personal data and special purposes in the first
section containing the interpretative provisions. There are further differences and
the section numbers never converge. The schedule numbers are the same until
Sch.9 as the Isle of Man Act includes specific provisions dealing with the register
of electors, notification of concerns about specific registrations to the Tribunal
and there is no provision for assistance in cases where the special purposes are
relevant.

Guernsey

The section references in the Guernsey Law are the same up to s.62 where the   29–10
UK provision which covers the amendments to the Consumer Credit Act does not
apply. However, in Guernsey SI 2002/12 includes an analogous statement of
rights. The schedule numbers are the same up to Sch.6, which in the Guernsey
Law covers miscellaneous exemptions.

Freedom of Information Act 2000 (FOIA)

The amendments to the UK DPA made by the FOIA are not applicable in any of   29–11
the islands. Jersey has passed a Freedom of Information (Jersey) Law 2011 but it
is not yet in force. Moreover, the provisions covering personal data are
considerably more straightforward and even when implemented it will not change
the data protection law.

OTHER AMENDMENTS TO THE LAWS

29–12   The Jersey Law was amended by the Data Protection (Amendment) Jersey Law 2005 in April 2005 to clarify the powers of the States to provide for exemptions which would apply where enactments or rules of law outside the jurisdiction prohibited or restricted the disclosure of information or authorised a person to withhold it. The fee for notification has been amended so it is the same in all of the islands, being £50. It was most recently altered in the Isle of Man from October 2011. None of the changes to the UK law made in respect of assessment notices or the powers of the Commissioner to impose monetary penalty notices have been brought forward in any of the islands.

COMPARATIVE ANALYSIS

Definition

29–13   Inevitably there are some technical differences in definitions: for example the courts are different through the jurisdictions. The definitions are also dealt with rather differently. In the Jersey Law all the interpretation provisions are included in s.1, whereas in the other laws the main definitions are in s.1 but with further lists of defined terms at the end of the law. There are no significant alterations in the definitions between the legislation however user should check whether specific terms are defined terms as not all the same defined terms are covered in each law.

Individual rights

Subject access

29–14   The subject access provisions in ss.7, 8 and 9 of the UK Act are mirrored by almost identical provisions in the other three sets of provisions. There are some minor drafting differences but only one major difference, which is found in the Isle of Man provisions. In drafting terms the Jersey Law makes it explicit that the data controller responding to a subject access request is only required to describe the purposes for which that data controller processes the data, and not the purposes of others and the same is true in respect of the descriptions of recipients. The Jersey Law also includes the 40-day timescale as a default provision in the section itself rather than in secondary legislation. The provisions that deal with making a request of the data subject for further identifying information are now the same following the amendment to the UK Act brought about by the Freedom of Information Act. The Isle of Man and the Guernsey laws include the powers of the court to view information in the procedural provisions for subject access rather than under the powers of the court but the effect of the provisions is the same. In Guernsey the statutory period for responding to a subject access request is 60 days.

29–15   The substantive difference lies in the Isle of Man law, which provides that where an individual succeeds on an application to the High Court in obtaining an order that a data controller has failed to comply with a subject access request served in accord with the relevant provisions then:

> "(9)(b) if the court is satisfied that the failure was unjustified and that the data controller knew or ought to have known that it was unjustified, [the court may] impose on him a penalty of such amount (not exceeding £5000) as the court thinks fit".

The penalty is treated as a fine imposed by the criminal court. This affords a strong incentive to data controllers in the Isle of Man to comply with their subject access obligations.

Rights to object to processing

The rights to object to processing and to processing for the purposes of direct marketing are identical in all four laws.   **29–16**

Rights of rectification and correction

Here the Guernsey Law follows the UK Act in full, but both the Isle of Man and Jersey provide stronger rights to compensation. While in the UK and Guernsey an individual may only claim compensation for distress where the distress is either caused by the same contravention for which the individual has been able to recover damage or there has been a contravention of the Act in connection with processing for the special purposes. However, the Jersey Law provides that an individual who suffers distress by reason of any contravention by a data controller of any requirement imposed by or under the law may recover compensation for that distress. The Isle of Man is not so generous but does allow for recovery for distress caused by a failure to deal properly with a subject access request where the High Court has imposed a penalty.   **29–17**

Rectification and other remedies

The provisions are identical to the UK law as are the provisions which provide that a court may view personal data which is the subject of a disputed access application but must not disclose the data to the individual of its own volition. The Guernsey Act sets out which cases are to go to which courts in the islands as between Guernsey, Alderney and Sark.   **29–18**

Notification

The provisions for notification in all the laws follow the UK model. There are some slight differences in wording in the Jersey law but there are only one or two substantive differences throughout the sections of the laws that deal with notification. The substantive difference of significance is the provision in the Isle of Man law which enables the Supervisor to refer an application for notification to the Tribunal. This breaks the mould of notification as merely an administrative function.   **29–19**

Section 20 of the Isle of Man Act provides that if it appears to the Supervisor that a notification of processing made shows that the processing would contravene any of the principles he may refer the notification to the Tribunal. He must, at the same time, specify the principle or principles that he considers would be contravened and why he is making the reference. The Supervisor is not expected to refer merely technical breaches. The section provides that, in deciding whether to make the reference he must consider whether the processing in question has caused or would cause any person damage or distress.

Where the Tribunal are satisfied that the processing would cause such a breach it may direct the Supervisor to either cancel the entry in the register or vary it to such an extent as the Tribunal directs. Schedule 6 sets out the procedures to be followed and there is an appeal to the High Court for a party who is affected by the reference to the Tribunal.

The effect of the provision is to make the process of notification capable of being used as a supervisory regime. To the best of our knowledge there have been no references to the Tribunal however the power has been helpful to the Supervisor who has been able to query notifications and ensure that amendments are made.

29–20 All of the regimes provide for the State authorities to determine particular types of processing as assessable processing but none has done so; nor has the power to provide for data protection officers as independent overseers been used.

29–21 In relation to overseas transfers all the islands provide that the notification must be of transfers outside the particular jurisdiction, rather than outside the EEA as the UK Act requires.

29–22 Only Jersey follows s.16(1)(g) in requiring that the controller include a statement on the register of notifications that the data controller also holds personal data which are exempt from the obligation to notify.

Exemptions

29–23 The basic definition of the nature of exemptions, that is non-disclosure exemptions or subject information exemptions, are common to all the laws. The exemption for public or national security works the same way although the bodies which issue the certificates and hear appeals are distinct for each jurisdiction. The appeals provisions in Jersey and Guernsey which cover those appeals which may be made by a person directly affected by a certificate against the issue thereof do not refer to the application of the principles of judicial review but merely to the question of whether the issue of the certificate was reasonable.

29–24 In relation to the exemption for crime and security the substantive provisions are the same for all the laws, apart from the references to the administrative units which are relevant public authorities for the purposes of the risk classification aspect of the exemption. However, the Guernsey and Jersey Laws both make it explicit that the investigations may take place in other places and may cover offences may have been committed either in or outside the jurisdiction. The Jersey Law refers to the investigation "anywhere of crime" and the Guernsey Law to crime "within or outside the Bailiwick".

29–25 In relation to health, education and social work each law includes enabling provisions which allow exemptions from the right of subject access to be made by order and is the same (apart from a slight difference in wording in the last paragraph of the Jersey Law) in each provisions. We have not examined the substantive orders and if a data controller wishes to rely on any of those orders the specific wording of the order should be consulted.

In relation to regulatory activity the main provisions are the same for all the laws however this is an exemption which has been differently drafted in the detail of the materials covered. In the UK provision s.31(4) lists a number of regulatory authorities and provides for a subject information exemption in respect of the functions which they carry out for a list of purposes which are for the protection of the public. This is not repeated in the Guernsey or Isle of Man laws. In the Jersey Law there is provision for the relevant authorities or be designated by order and the protective functions listed are more widely drawn to cover cases where the protective function relates to various business activities. In the Guernsey Law, the designated functions include those designed to protect the reputation and standing of the Bailiwick.   29–26

In relation to the special purposes of journalism art and literature the exemption is identical in each case apart from some slight drafting alterations (for example using one paragraph instead of two) and the administrative provisions for the designation of relevant codes of practice.   29–27

In relation to research, history and statistics, the terms of this exemption are identical in all the laws.   29–28

In relation to information available to the public, the exemptions are the same, apart from a provision in art.34(2) (b) of the Guernsey Law. In the Guernsey Law "public information" is defined not only as that which a data controller is obliged by or under an enactment to make public, but as including also: 29–29

> "(b) information or any type or class of information held by any person or body designated by the Committee for the purposes of this section".

In relation to legal proceedings, domestic purposes and the power to make further exemptions by order the provisions are the same in each law.   29–30

The Isle of Man has an exemption for the privileges of Tynwald. If it is required for the purpose of avoiding an infringement of the privileges of Tynwald (the Isle of Man parliament) the Council (the Isle of Man Cabinet) or the Keys (the Isle of Man Upper house) then there is a very wide exemption. This allows for exemption from: 29–31

- the first principle, except for Schs 2 and 3; and
- the second, third, fourth and fifth principles, s.5 (that is the right of subject access) and ss.8 and 12(1)–(3) (that is rights of rectification).

Miscellaneous exemptions

The miscellaneous exemptions from subject access or the subject information provisions are the same as the UK in all the laws, apart from some technical and necessary differences in dealing with corporate finance. Anyone seeking to rely on that exemption would need to consider the specific definitions in the individual law. In the Guernsey law there is an additional exemption from subject access in para.12 of Sch.6. Paragraph 12 covers personal data which consist of   29–32 records of criminal convictions or cautions of data subjects who are not ordinarily resident in the Bailiwick. Where such persons are able to obtain access to such records "under and subject to the law of a jurisdiction other than the Bailiwick" then the records are exempt from the subject information provisions under the Guernsey Law. The intention of this provision was to prevent "back-door" enforced subject access to criminal records from the UK via Guernsey. It is notable that the data are not merely exempt from the subject access provisions but from the subject information provisions. The effect of this is that a data controller subject to the Guernsey Law may not have to provided notice of processing of such data to the data subjects. The exemption, however, only applies where the subject would be able to obtain access under the law of another jurisdiction. The access presumably need not be obtained under a data protection law but could be any legal basis. It is not clear whether the individual must simply have the right to apply for access (and implicitly may fail in an access request if an exemption applies) or the data controller must be satisfied that the individual would actually succeed in obtaining access to the information.

ENFORCEMENT

29–33 The enforcement provisions, including provisions in relation to the special purposes and appeals follow exactly the same approach. The only difference in substance between all four jurisdictions is that in Jersey information notices and special information notices may be served on data processors and processors are obliged to respond. If notices are served on such processors a copy must, at the same time, be served on the data controller and both parties are entitled to appeal against the service of the notices.

MISCELLANEOUS AND GENERAL PROVISIONS

29–34 The provisions are again largely the same although, unexpectedly given that the law is in other ways more supportive of individual rights than the others, the Isle of Man does not provide for the Supervisor to assist individuals in cases involving the special purposes. There is no equivalent of s.53 in the UK Act in the Isle of Man. Jersey includes a specific offence provision covering the provision of false information which, in effect, not only criminalises the act of lying to the Commissioner, but appears to also criminalise the provision of false information in response to a subject access request. The drafting of s.60 is not easy to follow. It provides that any person who, knowingly or recklessly, provides the Commissioner *or any other person entitled to information under this Law or under Regulations made under this Law,* with information that is false or misleading in a material particular shall be guilty of an offence. The provision applies where the information is provided either directly in meeting the legal requirement to provide information or indirectly where information is provided

"... in circumstances in which the person providing the information intends, or could reasonably have been expected to know, that the information would be used by the Commissioner for the purpose of carrying out the Commissioner's functions under this Law".

It would appear therefore that a person who makes a false report of non-compliance with the Law could fall foul of this provision. The section goes on to provide that a person who knowingly or recklessly provides the Commissioner or any other person entitled to information under the Law with information in connection with an application under the Law that is false or misleading in a material particular shall be guilty of an offence. The offence carries a term of imprisonment of up to five years.   **29–35**

The general duties of the regulatory authorities are the same in all the jurisdictions save that, in the Isle of Man, the Supervisor has no obligation to promulgate Community Findings or Commission decisions on adequacy. In Guernsey, the obligation to lay an annual report before the legislature is found in Sch.5 and, like the other, simply requires a report every 12 months; whereas in Jersey, the obligation is not only imposed but is specific as to the timescale within which such a report must be laid.   **29–36**

The provisions in relation to international co-operation vary slightly between the laws. None of the islands have the equivalent of s.54(5) of the UK Act which provides that the Commissioner shall assist with data protection in any specified colony.   **29–37**

The criminal offences of procuring and selling personal data without the consent of the data controller appear in all the laws even thought they would not be required for the purpose of achieving a finding of adequacy from the Commission. The only difference, again apart from some minor drafting changes, is that in the Jersey Law the prohibition applies even where the obtaining was in relation to national security. The UK and the other laws preserve the right of those dealing with national security to use surreptitious methods where it is necessary for the purposes of national security but this is not the case with the Jersey regime.   **29–38**

The remaining provisions which deal with enforced subject access, access to health records, disclosure of information by the supervisory authority, obligations of confidentiality and prosecutions are identical in effect.   **29–39**

There remain the administrative and technical provisions including definitions but again the only differences are either minor drafting ones or ones that reflect the different composition of the government in the particular jurisdiction.

SCHEDULES 1–4

In view of their significance we have considered Schs 1–4 and Sch.7 (exemptions) in detail; however, we have not carried out the equivalent detailed assessment of all of the others. In this section, therefore, we provide only an overview. There are no significant differences in the schedules, although they are not numbered the same in each case. The Guernsey Law does not include a schedule dealing with appeals, however, as appeals are made the courts this is   **29–40** because the relevant provisions are found in procedural rules of the courts. Rules of court have been drafted which are similar to the UK rules which applied to the Information Tribunal.

The principles and the interpretative provisions

29–41   All of these are identical apart from a small drafting addition in the Jersey Law and the fact that the additional safeguards which are applied where the disproportionate effort provision is relied upon where personal data are obtained from a third party appear on the face of the Act in the Isle of Man provisions rather than in secondary legislation.

Schedule 2

29–42   Apart from one omission from the Jersey Law and the most minor drafting differences (the movement of "for" into the first part of a phrase in principle 2 in the Jersey Law) the provisions are identical throughout. In the Jersey Law "prospective legal proceedings" is omitted. It is difficult to assess whether this could make a material difference but clearly it could be used to base an argument that the provision in Jersey is narrower than in the other jurisdictions.

Schedule 3

29–43   The provisions of Sch.3 are identical, again apart from the most minor drafting differences, until one comes to grounds 10 onward of the Isle of Man Act. The Isle of Man has included in the Schedule the grounds set out in the UK in the Data Protection (Processing of Sensitive Personal Data) Order 2000 (SI 2000/417). The only omission is ground 8 in SI 2000/417, which relates to information held by political parties for the purposes of legitimate political activities.

Schedule 4

29–44   The provisions of Sch.4 are identical apart from some slightly different wording in the Jersey Law and again the omission of the reference to "prospective" legal proceedings.

REGISTER OF ELECTORS—ISLE OF MAN

29–45   The Isle of Man used the opportunity of the passage of its Data Protection Act to insert primary legislation authorising the passage of regulations to deal with the use of the electoral roll for marketing and the rights of electors to opt-out of the full register for that purpose. Schedule 9 of the Act amends the Jury Act 1980 to allow the Council of Ministers to make the appropriate regulations.

SECONDARY LEGISLATION

The secondary legislation for all of the islands follows the pattern of the UK with **29–46** amendments to reflect the local situation or differences in the primary legislation highlighted in this chapter. Guernsey SI 2002/19 provides a specific exemption from the subject information provisions in the following terms. The disclosure to a relevant body of personal data, consisting of information relating to any person, is exempt from the non-disclosure provisions where the disclosure is necessary for the purpose of protecting that person or any other person from suffering serious harm.

TRANSITIONAL ARRANGEMENTS

These have now ended in all the jurisdictions.   **29–47**

Implementation of Directive 2002/58

The Isle of Man has Regulations which cover e-mail and telephone marketing— **29–48** the Unsolicited Communications Regulations 2005, which implement the provisions of Directive 2002/58 and are the equivalent of the Privacy and Electronic Communications (EC Directive) 2003.

Further information

Data Protection Supervisor Isle of Man

Iain McDonald
PO Box 69
Douglas
Isle of Man
IM99 1EQ
Tel: +44 (0) 1624 693260
E-mail: enquiries@odps.gov.im
Website: *www.gov.im/odps*

Data Protection Commissioner Jersey

Emma Martins
Office of the Data Protection Commissioner
Morier House
Halkett Place
St. Helier
Jersey
JE1 1DD
Tel: +44 (0)1534 441064
Fax: +44 (0)1534 441065
E-mail: dataprotection@gov.je
Website: *www.dataprotection.gov.je*

Data Protection Commissioner Guernsey

Emma Martins
Data Protection Office
PO Box 642
Frances House
Sir William Place
St Peter Port
GY1 3JE
Guernsey
Tel: +44 1481 742074
Fax: +44 1481 742077
E-mail: dataprotection@gov.gg
Website: *www.dpr.gov.gg*

APPENDIX A

Implementation of Directive 95/46/EC in the United Kingdom

Introduction in the United Kingdom

1 While Directive 95/46/EC allowed Member States some room for manoeuvre in certain areas it required harmonisation of national laws at a high level. The Home Office published a consultation paper in March 1996 setting out a number of questions as to how the Directive should be implemented in the United Kingdom. Although that document was published and responses to it were received under the Conservative Government the Data Protection Bill which followed did not see the light of day until some nine months after the May 1997 election, which had returned a substantial Labour majority.

The general approach to the implementation of the Directive had been set out under the Conservative Government and was summarised in Ch.1 of the Consultation Paper as follows:

> "*Over-elaborate data protection threatens competitiveness and does not necessarily bring additional benefit for individuals. It follows that the Government intends to go no further in implementing the Directive than is absolutely necessary to satisfy the U.K.'s obligations in European law. It will also consider whether any additional changes to the current data protection regime are needed so as to ensure that it does not go beyond what is required by the Directive and the Council of Europe Convention.*"[1]

This approach to implementation remained a starting-point for the legislation despite the change of government between consultation and introduction of the Bill. However, as the Bill moved through Parliament the Labour Government indicated a willingness to alter its position and provide some stronger regulatory protection for individuals than appeared in the first draft. In particular, it accepted the inclusion of an offence provision outlawing the practice of enforced subject access.

Following the consultation, the Government decided to implement the Directive by primary legislation. This had not been a foregone conclusion. It might have been possible to implement it by regulations under the European Communities Act 1972. However, this possibility was the cause of considerable concern among those potentially affected by the Directive. There were worries that it would give rise to two parallel legal regimes governing the use of personal data in the United Kingdom with concomitant difficulties for data users in deciding which regime applied to particular data used for particular functions. There was considerable lobbying by those concerned to persuade the Government to proceed by primary legislation and the decision to do so was generally welcomed. It also provided the Government with an

---

[1] Chapter 1, para.1.2.

opportunity to deal with some outstanding matters of concern which did not arise directly from the Directive and which could therefore not have been dealt with under the European Community regulations.

Passage of the Act through Parliament

2 At the end of each chapter, reference is made to relevant *Hansard* materials to enable practitioners to consider material which may be admissible under the rules in *Pepper v Hart* [1993] A.C. 593.[2] It may be worth noting that on some occasions, particularly as the Bill neared its final stages, a conscious attempt to insert *Pepper v Hart* materials appears to have been made. It was treated by all parties as a technical piece of legislation. When it was first introduced it was missing some important provisions which were added in as it progressed through both Houses.

The Bill was introduced to the House of Lords on January 14, 1998 and the Second Reading took place on February 2. It was considered in Standing Committee D on February 23, 24 and 25 and went to Report on March 16 with the Third Reading in the Lords on March 24.

It went through the House of Commons between April 20 and July 2 with Committee Stages on May 5, 12, 14, 19 and 21 and June 2 and 4.

The Commons amendments were considered and agreed in the Lords on July 10 with Royal Assent following on July 16, 1998.

Passage of the Act through Parliament

3 In order to ensure that the summary makes sense without having to go back to early versions of the Bill, the clause references used are those to the clauses as they appear in the final version, even if the clause had a different number at the time of the debate.

OVERVIEW

The Bill was treated by both parties as a technical and largely non-partisan matter. The Government was under pressure to have the Act implementing the main Directive on the statute book by October 24, 1998. To achieve that end, it had to receive Royal Assent by the end of the summer session 1999. Pressure of time to get it before the House meant that it was still missing some important elements when it was introduced into the Lords in February 1998. These were gradually added as the Bill progressed. However, even with the addition of further provisions, some important matters were left to be dealt with in regulations, notably the detail of the notification scheme.

Speeches in the main debates on the Bill tended to focus on a number of particular elements:

(a) the exemption for journalistic, literary and artistic purposes;

(b) the coverage of manual records;

(c) the powers of the Commissioner to conduct audits and serve notices;

(d) the exemptions available to the Inland Revenue and others;

(e) the effect of the enhanced individual rights on those dealing with automated decision-making;

---

[2] See Ch.3 for the role of *Hansard* material.

(f) the control of data matching by government departments;

(g) the effect of the Bill on overseas transfers of personal data;

(h) the prohibition on the processing of sensitive personal data; and

(i) the replacement of registration with a simplified form of notification.

House of Lords

4 Second Reading. The Data Protection Bill was introduced in the House of Lords on January 14, 1998. The Second Reading in the Lords took place on February 2, 1998 when it was introduced by Lord Williams for the Government in the following terms:

> "*I recognise that data protection does not sound like a subject to attract obsessive interest; witness the general exodus from your Lordship's House as I start to introduce this Second Reading. Data protection is redolent in many ways of computers and electronic processing; necessary but essentially technical providers of services. In fact it affects our well-being in a much more general way. It shares common ground to that extent with the Human Rights Bill. That Bill will improve the position of citizens of this country by enabling them to rely on the wide range of civil and political rights contained in the European Convention on Human Rights. Those rights include the right to respect for private and family life. The Data Protection Bill also concerns privacy, albeit a specific form of privacy: personal information privacy. The subject matter of the Bill is, therefore, inherently important to our general social welfare.*"[3]

During Lord Williams' brief tour of the main provisions he referred particularly to some of the exemptions, including that for journalistic, artistic and literary purposes:

> "*It is not the intention of the Government for the Directive to be used to inhibit programme makers from making the programmes they have up to now. The Government believes that both privacy and freedom of expression are important rights and that the directive is not intended to alter the balance, which is a fine one and always should be, that currently exist between these rights and responsibilities. I believe that the Bill does strike the right note in that respect. It was not until after a great deal of consultation and discussion, and perhaps cross-fertilisation of ideas, that we came to our conclusion.*"

He also referred to the new powers of the Commissioner and the rules for overseas transfers.

Viscount Astor speaking for the Opposition raised concerns about the cost of implementing the Directive and the possible burdens for business. He highlighted concerns brought to him by the CBI about the restrictions on the holding of sensitive data and the problems those could cause for employers who might find it necessary to hold criminal records. He queried the application of the new law to the internet and its effects on the use of processors based overseas, as well as raising the interface with freedom of information. Other contributors to the debate were Baroness Nicholson of Winterbourne, who took a wide-ranging overview of the bill, and Lord Wakeham, who dealt exclusively with the media exemption in clause 32 which he welcomed warmly. Lord Norton raised some detailed points on the effect on fraud prevention, in which he expressed an interest, and a number of points on the individual rights. Some criticisms were made by the Earl of Northesk who described the Bill as being,

---

[3] *Hansard*, HL Vol. 585, No. 95, col 436.

"almost a quarter of a century past its sell-by date" and highlighted the absence of a code to deal with data matching.

The Bill was referred to the Grand Committee for consideration by motion of February 19. It was considered by Standing Committee D on February 23, 24 and 25.

The motion for consideration of the amendments tabled for Report stage was moved on March 11 and Report took place on March 16.

5 Report Stage. At Report, Lord Williams explained the Government's position on the nature and extent of the manual records covered by the definition of the term "relevant filing system". Soon after publication of the Bill, the Registrar issued a statement setting out her opinion that the definition of "relevant filing system" as it appeared in the Bill did not achieve the Government's stated intention to exclude personnel records. At Second Reading, Lord Williams had made clear the Government's intention to focus the definition on highly structured files and by amendment at Report altered the word "particular" to "specific" in the definition. Lord Williams spoke to the effect of the amendment in the following terms:

> "We intend that 'particular' information should mean 'specific' information. That is what our amendment provides. The search for unambiguous language can sometimes be exhausting. I do not say that 'specific' admits of no shades of meaning; it does. Information may be more or less specific in different degrees of detail. Very much may depend on context. But if there is any significant ambiguity in the introduction of 'specific' into the definition of 'relevant filing system', it is not capable of admitting into that definition the sort of general, unindexed personnel files that we have been talking about. All the information in those files may conceivably be though 'particular' but not 'specific'. 'Specific' information is intended to mean and does mean distinct information within the file which can be distinguished from other information in the file and separately accessed. It means information of a distinct identity which sets it apart from the rest of the generality of personal information held. That is what our amendment intends to pin down."

Viscount Astor returned to the potential problems caused to business by the rules governing overseas transfers, especially in relation to trade with the United States. Lord Dholakia moved an amendment to include the purpose of ethnic monitoring among the categories of permitted processing of sensitive data which was sympathetically received by the Government and subsequently incorporated into Sch.3.

The provisions bringing the rights of access to consumer credit reference files, previously exercised under the Consumer Credit Act 1974, into the Bill were inserted by Government amendment and gave rise to some expressions of concern that this might affect the position of third-party credit information on an individual's credit file. A concern which the Government dismissed. Credit industry concerns were also aired in discussions on the meaning of the term "trade secret" in relation to automated decision making and whether it was wide enough to cover all the interests which would merit protection. The Government was firm in the view that it would.

An amendment originally proposed by Lord Norton in Committee to require controllers who receive individual rights notices to respond to them and in writing was moved by the Government (although this was later removed in the case of the direct marketing notices).

The Government also put forward a complete re-draft of cl.12 dealing with the right to object to automated decision-making. In the new formulation, the individual must activate the objection rather than there being an outright ban on such processing.

Other government amendments were used to introduce the first elements of the transitional relief provisions. Amendment was also made allowing the Commissioner to assist her opposite number in a colony, altering the confidentiality clause binding the Commissioner and making the provision for consultation on Codes of Practice mandatory.

Lord Norton argued that the term "substantial damage and distress" as used in cl.10

to describe the basis on which an individual could object to the processing of personal data about him should be replaced by the words of the Directive, "compelling legitimate grounds", but his argument was not accepted.

In relation to the Commissioner's power, Lord Norton spoke for giving the Commissioner stronger audit powers to carry out audits without the consent of the controller. Lord Astor suggested procedural restrictions on the exercise of her powers under which she would be bound to try to resolve matters by informal methods before moving to formal action. Neither proposal found favour with the Government.

There was further debate on the need to control data matching by imposition of a statutory code but expressions of concern were met by resolute government refusal to move on the issue.

6 Third Reading. The Third Reading took place in the Lords on March 24 and saw the only division forced during the Bill's passage through Parliament. The division resulted in a government defeat on cl.28(4). This clause would have given the Secretary of State wide-ranging powers to allow exemptions for the purposes of tax collection. The provision had been inserted, explained Lord Falconer, speaking for the Government, to deal with particular problems faced by the Inland Revenue:

"I remind the House that without the clause 28(4) general exemption, as opposed to case by case exemptions, the Inland Revenue and hence honest taxpayers would suffer losses with information being revealed to suspect taxpayers about the nature and origin of material passed to the Inland revenue by third parties such as banks and retail businesses and about the revenue's risk rules and scores under the new self assessment tax system."[4]

The clause allowed for class exemptions whereas other exemptions in the Bill were to be applied on a case-by-case basis. The clause had already been criticised by the Delegated Powers and Deregulation Select Committee in its consideration of the Bill on February 4 in the following terms:

"Of far greater concern is the wide ranging power under clause 28(4) to grant exemptions from the requirement to process personal data fairly and lawfully (the first data protection principle). This principle goes to the heart of the Bill and the Committee views with the greatest concern the scope of this provision. If the power remains in the Bill as it is currently drafted, there will be no limits to the inroads which could be made into the fundamental requirement that personal data be processed fairly and lawfully—a power which in the Committee's view it would be impossible to justify. The House will no doubt wish to consider these issues with the greatest care during the Bill's subsequent passage and may wish to amend the Bill to remove the general power to grant exemption from the first data protection principle."[5]

Despite attempts by the Government to head off the division by expressing a willingness to hold further talks with the Registrar over the issue it was moved and the Government defeated. In the Commons the Government returned with a limited exemption related specifically to the risk assessment system adopted by the Revenue. In respect of which Lord Falconer subsequently said in the Lords' closing debate:

". . . we have decided not to pursue further in this Bill the non-disclosure exemption. On reflection we accept that, where systematic disclosure of information to government departments is appropriate, we should seek specific statutory powers within the relevant departmental legislation. On risk assessment we have concluded that we can

---

[4] *Hansard,* HL Vol.587, col.1101 March 24, 1998.
[5] Select Committee on Delegated Powers and Deregulation (199798 HL 66), para.8.

deal with this on the face of the Bill in a way that should reassure the House about our intentions".[6]

7 Government amendments were moved to alter the category of those able to claim compensation for breaches of the law to "individuals" rather than "persons" as the latter term would have covered companies and other legal entities; to extend the powers of the Commissioner; to serve information notices in those cases where information is required to determine if there has been a breach of principle; and to deal with a number of technical and drafting points, particularly on transition.

The other amendments moved and defeated related to cl.32. Lord Lester argued that the clause as it stood did not comply with the ECHR. It did not provide for the appropriate balance to be struck between the rights to private life and freedom of expression in particular cases, nor did it import the tests of proportionality or necessity but simply required that the journalist should hold a reasonable belief that the technical grounds to claim the exemption were made out. When it became clear that a wider attempt to amend the clause was going to be resisted by the Government, he proposed a more modest amendment. His proposal was to insert the word "necessary" in relation to the public interest, so the journalist would not only have to show that publication was in the public interest but it was "necessary" in the public interest, saying:

"in other words, the amendment requires the data controller to have a reasonable belief that the obtaining, storing or publishing of personal data is necessary in the interests of free expression and does not involve a disproportionate interference in the right to private life".[7]

He also commented on the unsatisfactory nature of the discretionary power given to the courts to consider codes of practice under this clause, arguing that, in the interests of legal certainty, such reference should be mandatory.

The refusal of the Government to heed neither the proposed amendment nor the comments on the role of the codes of practice led Lord Lester to prophesy a litigious future for cl.32.[8]

Commons Stages

8 Second Reading. In the Commons, the Bill had its Second Reading on April 20 when it was introduced by the Home Secretary Jack Straw. He drew attention to the limitation of the coverage of manual records to structured records; the approach being taken to deal with adequacy requirements for overseas transfers; the continuing commitment of the Government to deal with the problems of enforced subject access; the amendments made in the Lords to cl.28 and the resolution of the concerns of the media in cl.32.

The Conservative spokesman supported the aims of the Directive but vented concerns that the Bill should implement at the minimum level necessary to achieve compliance and raised the question of the suggested costs of compliance to business. There were also queries over the controls on sensitive data and the regulatory powers of the supervisory body.

The Liberal Democrats generally welcomed the Bill but raised the absence of provisions to deal with enforced subject access, to allow for the holding of sensitive data for ethnic monitoring purposes or to control data matching by government depart-

---

[6] *Hansard,* HL Vol.591, No.184, col.1494.
[7] *Hansard,* HL Vol.587, No.127, col.1114.
[8] A prophecy only partially fulfilled so far in the case of *Naomi Campbell v Mirror Group Newspapers* above.

ments. Concerns about the interrelationship of cl.32 and the Human Rights Bill were also raised. The other main issue of concern to the House was the removal of cl.28(4) and the question of whether it should be replaced and if so by what, a point which the Government was still considering at that stage.

9 Committee Stages. The Bill went to Standing Committee D and was considered on May 5, 12, 14, 19 and 21 and June 2 and 4. Government amendments continued to be added as the Bill passed through the Committee Stage. As well as dealing with a considerable number of drafting and technical points, many of them revising the detail of notification, Government amendments during the passage through the Commons covered:

- the introduction of the access rights given under other legislation (the Access to the Personal Files Act 1987, the Access to Health Records Act 1990 and the Education (School records) Regulations 1989 and corresponding Northern Ireland and Scotland provisions) to the DPA in order to consolidate the rights and incorporate the *Gaskin* ECHR ruling;
- the removal of the requirement (which had been inserted during the passage through the Lords) for direct marketers who received notice of objection to respond to individuals in writing;
- provision for individuals serving notices under the Act to do so electronically;
- insertion of the court's power to require notification to third parties of a finding of inaccuracy;
- the insertion of the offence provisions in respect of enforced subject access;
- the addition of ethnic monitoring as a ground for holding sensitive personal data;
- the addition of the exemption for corporate finance from the subject information provisions;
- the insertion of a number of the transitional provisions; and
- the replacement of a revised cl.28(4) containing a limited exemption.

10 Third Reading. It was read for the third time in the Commons on July 2. In contrast to the Third Reading in the Lords, which had dwelt on issues of principle, the debate was largely on technical points. Government amendments were still being inserted. The Government deleted provisions which had been included to deal with the geographical scope of the Bill and clarify what amounted to a transfer of data. The provisions had been much criticised and the Government decided to withdraw them. There were various drafting amends, for example to tidy up the provisions dealing with prior checking, and to allow exemptions to the rights of subject access to educational records.

Mr Harry Cohen moved several amendments aimed at strengthening the protection given by the Bill, none of which were successful. He sought to reduce the breadth of the exemption for national security purposes and "introduce some element of accountability to the processing of personal data for the purpose of national security"[9] by making some aspects subject to external review. He pressed for some restrictions to be introduced on the potential uses of information available on public registers, such as registers of shareholders. He asked for the definition of "relevant filing system" to be extended to ensure that private bodies like the Economic League could not use paper files to remain outside the scope of the data protection regime. In response, Mr Hoon reiterated the Government's determination to cover manual records to the extent required by the Directive but not an iota more.

---

[9] *Hansard,* HC Vol.315, No.198, col.583.

An amendment was unsuccessfully sought to allow third-party credit reference information to be kept confidential.

Mr Greenway asked the Government to extend the reach of the crime prevention exemption by adding the term "investigation of crime " to the list of activities, and the phrase "safeguarding public security" to the list of purposes, for which the exemption could be claimed. He explained the particular aim was to enable information sharing between the police and other concerned parties about football hooligans. In response, the Government spokesman explained that the problems encountered in making disclosures relating to convictions of football supporters was not attributable to data protection problems but to the general law and practical problems of correct identification.

Mr Richard Shephard proposed that the Commissioner should be enabled to keep a register of enforcement action taken and that the restrictions on disclosure of information by her should be lessened. This was met by some easing of the position on both points by the Government in the form of allowing for notification regulations to include additional information on the register and slightly widening the grounds for disclosure by the Commissioner.

Another proposed amendment which met with some sympathy from the Government was one to include political canvassing in the list of permitted activities for which sensitive data could be held without individual consent. The preference of the Government, however, was to deal with it by subordinate legislation which they undertook to do.

An amendment aimed at making millennium compliance a specific statutory obligation for data controllers met with less success and was rejected.

In summing up spokesmen on all sides (as well as expressing relief at having concluded work on the Bill), expressed some satisfaction with the changes made during its passage through the House, although Mr Greenway concluded with some lingering concerns at the failure to revisit cl.32 and to tackle the potential problems which the Lords had described.

At the conclusion of the debate Mr Howarth announced that implementation would not be possible by October 24, 1998 in view of the substantial amounts of secondary legislation still to be put into place.

Final Stages

11 The Bill returned to the Lords where the Commons amendments were considered and agreed on July 10. The Lords' consideration gave rise to some final efforts to insert potential *Pepper v Hart* material. On the incorporation of the access rights to some kinds of manual information Lord Williams said:

> "*Gaskin is to do with refusal of subject access. It says that where access is refused because of the risk of identifying third parties who have not consented there must be a mechanism for independent review of that refusal. The Bill deals with this in two ways. Where access has been refused data subjects may seek a court order requiring access to be given or they may request an assessment to be made by the data protection commissioner who has the power to take the necessary enforcement action.*"[10]

There was also discussion on the meaning of the term "trade secret" in cl.8(5) in which Lord Williams expressed the Government view that the term carried its ordinary meaning but was probably wide enough to allow the withholding of algorithms:

---

[10]   *Hansard,* HL Vol.591, No.184, col.1477, July 10.

"which some organisations use to determine whether to meet individual's requests for a service of some kind; for instance a credit scoring system used to determine whether or not to give people credit."[11]

Baroness Nicholson of Winterbourne asked a final question of the Government on cl.32:

"Will the Minister confirm that as his Written Answer of April 8 to my noble friend Lord Lester of Herne Hill indicates, the Data Protection Bill interpretation of clause 31 will be applied by the courts and interpreted in accordance with the European legal principles of proportionality and legal certainty."

The response of Lord Williams for the Government was:

"The noble Baroness gave me notice of this matter and I affirm that what I said in the Written Answer remains correct".[12]

The written answer was:
"Yes: According to the consistent case law of the European Court of Justice, in the application of Community law the guiding principles, which include proportionality and legal certainty, must be observed by the courts."

Implementation timetable

12 Some technical measures to allow preparatory work for the full introduction of the Act came into force on Royal Assent being:

    (a) s.75 (commencement);

    (b) ss.1–3 (definitions of data, data controller, data processor, data subject, personal data, processing, relevant filing system, sensitive data and special purposes);

    (c) ss.25(1) and (4) (provisions for submission of proposals for a notification scheme by the Commissioner to the Secretary of State and duty on the Secretary of State to consider any such proposals after consultation of the Commissioner);

    (d) s.26 (fees regulations, provision for different fees to be prescribed for different types of notification cases and those matters to which the Secretary of State must have regard in making fees regulations);

    (e) ss.67–71 (s.67 contains the order making powers, ss.68, 69, 70 and 71 further definitions and a table of defined terms);

    (f) s.75(2)(g) (powers to make subordinate legislation).

There was some delay before implementation of the substantive provisions. This was announced in the House of Commons by George Howarth, the Minister of State in the Home Office, on July 3, 1998. In the event the Act, together with supporting secondary legislation, but excluding the provisions dealing with enforced subject access, did not come into force until March 1, 2000. The delay meant that the Government did not implement by October 24, 1998 in accordance with the requirements of the Directive.

---

[11] *Hansard,* HL Vol.591, No.184, col.1482, July 10.
[12] *Hansard,* HL Vol.591, No.184, col.1499.

Statutory Instruments

13 Section 67 sets out the powers of the Secretary of State to make secondary legislation.

Nine of the instruments which may be made under the Act require the positive approval of Parliament. The draft instrument must be laid before each House of Parliament and approved by positive resolution of each House. The instruments subject to this procedure are primarily those which deal with exemptions; prior checking and the extension of the enforced subject access offence to further organisations would also require affirmative resolution.

Most orders are subject to negative resolution, that is they require laying before Parliament subject to annulment in pursuance of resolution of either House. It should be noted that if an instrument contains a mixture of provisions some of which would require positive and some simply negative procedure, they must be treated as requiring positive affirmation.

Orders which prescribe fees for the purposes of the Data Protection Act 1998 or of the Consumer Credit Act 1974 need only follow the procedure for laying before Parliament after being made in order to be valid.

Consultation on subordinate legislation

14 In August 1998 the Home Office published a Consultation Paper on subordinate legislation inviting comments by the end of September 1998. A number of orders were proposed for initial implementation. In the event, implementation was delayed in order to allow for the orders to be ready. In all cases, except the proposals in respect of prior checking, the consultation resulted in the passage of the appropriate secondary legislation and is dealt with in the text. The proposal for prior checking has not been taken further to date and there is no indication that it will be.

Prior checking

15 This term is used in the Directive but in the Act it has become "preliminary assessment". A number of categories of processing were proposed to be subject to preliminary assessment in the White Paper in July 1997. They covered data matching, processing involving genetic data, processing by private investigators and the processing of sensitive data. However no orders dealing preliminary assessment have been forthcoming and it is understood that at the time of writing none are under consideration.

Repeals

16 These are set out in s.74(2) and Sch.15, Pt I. The Data Protection Act 1984 was repealed in its entirety, as has the Access to Personal Files Act 1987. The remainder of repeals in the Schedule consists largely of technical amendments to tidy up the legal provisions where the old provision has been replaced by one in the 1998 Act.

Revocations

17 These are found in Pt II of Sch.15. Revocations apply to statutory instruments and regulations. Only one statutory instrument was revoked in whole, the Data Protection Registration Fees Order 1991. Other orders made under the Data Protection Act 1984 simply died with the repeal of the 1984 Act.

The other orders listed in this part of the Schedule are those made under other legislation which have been revoked in part where the relevant provisions in the order have now been covered by the new law.

Consequential amendments

18 These are set out in Sch.14, under s.74(1). Amendments have been made to 10 pieces of primary legislation and two statutory instruments. The amendments in paras 1, 2, 3, 4, 5, 6, 7, 9, 10, 14, 16 and 18 simply reproduce the same legal effect as the current law by replacing references to the 1984 Act and associated elements, such as replacing the Registrar with references to the Commissioner. The others substitute the definitions of health professional in the new Act for the one found in earlier Acts or make consequential changes to the access to health information provisions

APPENDIX B

Data Protection Act 1998

(1998, c.29)

PART I

PRELIMINARY

1. *Basic interpretative provisions*

(1) In this Act, unless the context otherwise requires—

"data" means information which—

(a) is being processed by means of equipment operating automatically in response to instructions given for that purpose,

(b) is recorded with the intention that it should be processed by means of such equipment,

(c) is recorded as part of a relevant filing system or with the intention that it should form part of a relevant filing system, [. . .]¹

(d) does not fall within paragraph (a), (b) or (c) but forms part of an accessible record as defined by section 68; [or] ²

[(e) is recorded information held by a public authority and does not fall within any of paragraphs (a) to (d);] ²

"data controller" means, subject to subsection (4), a person who (either alone or jointly or in common with other persons) determines the purposes for which and the manner in which any personal data are, or are to be, processed;

"data processor", in relation to personal data, means any person (other than an employee of the data controller) who processes the data on behalf of the data controller;

"data subject" means an individual who is the subject of personal data;

"personal data" means data which relate to a living individual who can be identified—

(a) from those data, or

(b) from those data and other information which is in the possession of, or is likely to come into the possession of, the data controller,

and includes any expression of opinion about the individual and any indication of the intentions of the data controller or any other person in respect of the individual;

"processing", in relation to information or data, means obtaining, recording or holding the information or data or carrying out any operation or set of operations on the information or data, including—

(a) organisation, adaptation or alteration of the information or data,

(b) retrieval, consultation or use of the information or data,

(c) disclosure of the information or data by transmission, dissemination or otherwise making available, or

(d) alignment, combination, blocking, erasure or destruction of the information or data;

["public authority" means a public authority as defined by the Freedom of Information Act 2000 or a Scottish public authority as defined by the Freedom of Information (Scotland) Act 2002;][3]

"relevant filing system" means any set of information relating to individuals to the extent that, although the information is not processed by means of equipment operating automatically in response to instructions given for that purpose, the set is structured, either by reference to individuals or by reference to criteria relating to individuals, in such a way that specific information relating to a particular individual is readily accessible.

(2) In this Act, unless the context otherwise requires—

(a) "obtaining" or "recording", in relation to personal data, includes obtaining or recording the information to be contained in the data, and

(b) "using" or "disclosing", in relation to personal data, includes using or disclosing the information contained in the data.

(3) In determining for the purposes of this Act whether any information is recorded with the intention—

(a) that it should be processed by means of equipment operating automatically in response to instructions given for that purpose, or

(b) that it should form part of a relevant filing system,

it is immaterial that it is intended to be so processed or to form part of such a system only after being transferred to a country or territory outside the European Economic Area.

(4) Where personal data are processed only for purposes for which they are required by or under any enactment to be processed, the person on whom the obligation to process the data is imposed by or under that enactment is for the purposes of this Act the data controller.

[(5) In paragraph (e) of the definition of "data" in subsection (1), the reference to information "held" by a public authority shall be construed in accordance with section 3(2) of the Freedom of Information Act 2000 [or section 3(2), (4) and (5) of the Freedom of Information (Scotland) Act 2002][5] .

[(6) Where

(a) section 7 of the Freedom of Information Act 2000 prevents Parts I to V of that Act or

(b) section 7(1) of the Freedom of Information (Scotland) Act 2002 prevents that Act

from applying to certain information held by a public authority, that information is not to be treated for the purposes of paragraph (e) of the definition of "data" in subsection (1) as held by a public authority.

‖⁶
‖⁴

Notes

1   Words repealed by Freedom of Information Act 2000 c. 36 Sch.8(III) para.1 (January 1, 2005)
2   Added by Freedom of Information Act 2000 c. 36 Pt VII s.68(2)(a) (January 1, 2005 for purposes specified in SI 2004/1909 art.2(1); January 1, 2005 otherwise)
3   Definition substituted by Freedom of Information (Scotland) Act 2002 (Consequential Modifications) Order 2004/3089 art.2(2)(a) (January 1, 2005)
4   Added by Freedom of Information Act 2000 c. 36 Pt VII s.68(3) (January 1, 2005 for purposes specified in SI 2004/1909 art.2(1); January 1, 2005 otherwise)
5   Words inserted by Freedom of Information (Scotland) Act 2002 (Consequential Modifications) Order 2004/3089 art.2(2)(b) (January 1, 2005)
6   Existing text renumbered as s.1(6)(a) and s.1(6)(b) inserted by Freedom of Information (Scotland) Act 2002 (Consequential Modifications) Order 2004/3089 art.2(2)(c) (January 1, 2005)

Commencement

Pt I s. 1(1)–(1) definition of "data", (1) definition of "data" (b)–(4): July 16, 1998 (1998 c. 29 Pt VI s. 75(2)(a)) Pt I s. 1(1) definition of "data" (a): July 16, 1999

Extent

Pt I s. 1(1)–(1) definition of "data", (1) definition of "data" (b)–(1) definition of "data" (d), (1) definition of "data controller"-(1) definition of "processing" (d), (1) definition of "relevant filing system"-(4): United Kingdom (subject to s.75(6))
Pt I s. 1(1) definition of "data" (a), (1) definition of "data" (e), (1) definition of "public authority", (5)–(6)(b): United Kingdom

2. *Sensitive personal data.*

In this Act "sensitive personal data" means personal data consisting of information as to—

(a) the racial or ethnic origin of the data subject,

(b) his political opinions,

(c) his religious beliefs or other beliefs of a similar nature,

(d) whether he is a member of a trade union (within the meaning of the Trade Union and Labour Relations (Consolidation) Act 1992), (e) his physical or mental health or condition, (f) his sexual life,

(g) the commission or alleged commission by him of any offence, or

(h) any proceedings for any offence committed or alleged to have been committed by him, the disposal of such proceedings or the sentence of any court in such proceedings.

Commencement

Pt I s. 2(a)–(h): July 16, 1998 (1998 c. 29 Pt VI s. 75(2)(a))

Extent

Pt I s. 2(a)–(h): United Kingdom (subject to s.75(6))

3. *The special purposes.*

In this Act "the special purposes" means any one or more of the following—

    (a) the purposes of journalism,

    (b) artistic purposes, and

    (c) literary purposes.

Commencement

Pt I s. 3(a)–(c): July 16, 1998 (1998 c. 29 Pt VI s. 75(2)(a))

Extent

Pt I s. 3(a)–(c): United Kingdom (subject to s.75(6))

4. *The data protection principles.*

(1) References in this Act to the data protection principles are to the principles set out in Part I of Schedule 1.

(2) Those principles are to be interpreted in accordance with Part II of Schedule 1.

(3) Schedule 2 (which applies to all personal data) and Schedule 3 (which applies only to sensitive personal data) set out conditions applying for the purposes of the first principle; and Schedule 4 sets out cases in which the eighth principle does not apply.

(4) Subject to section 27(1), it shall be the duty of a data controller to comply with the data protection principles in relation to all personal data with respect to which he is the data controller.

Commencement

Pt I s. 4(1)–(4): March 1, 2000 (SI 2000/183 art. 2(1))

Extent

Pt I s. 4(1)–(4): United Kingdom (subject to s.75(6))

5. *Application of Act.*

(1) Except as otherwise provided by or under section 54, this Act applies to a data controller in respect of any data only if—

    (a) the data controller is established in the United Kingdom and the data are processed in the context of that establishment, or

    (b) the data controller is established neither in the United Kingdom nor in any other EEA State but uses equipment in the United Kingdom for processing the data otherwise than for the purposes of transit through the United Kingdom.

(2) A data controller falling within subsection (1)(b) must nominate for the purposes of this Act a representative established in the United Kingdom.

(3) For the purposes of subsections (1) and (2), each of the following is to be treated as established in the United Kingdom—

(a) an individual who is ordinarily resident in the United Kingdom,

(b) a body incorporated under the law of, or of any part of, the United Kingdom,

(c) a partnership or other unincorporated association formed under the law of any part of the United Kingdom, and

(d) any person who does not fall within paragraph (a), (b) or (c) but maintains in the United Kingdom—

(i) an office, branch or agency through which he carries on any activity, or
(ii) a regular practice;

and the reference to establishment in any other EEA State has a corresponding meaning.

Commencement

Pt I s. 5(1)–(3)(d)(ii): March 1, 2000 (SI 2000/183 art. 2(1))

Extent

Pt I s. 5(1)–(3)(d)(ii): United Kingdom (subject to s.75(6))

6. *The Commissioner [. . .]*[1].

[(1) For the purposes of this Act and of the Freedom of Information Act 2000 there shall be an officer known as the Information Commissioner (in this Act referred to as "the Commissioner").][2]

(2) The Commissioner shall be appointed by Her Majesty by Letters Patent.

(3)–(6) [. . .][3]

(7) Schedule 5 has effect in relation to the Commissioner [. . .][4].

Notes

[1] Words repealed by Transfer of Tribunal Functions Order 2010/22 Sch.2 para.25(a) (January 18, 2010)
[2] Substituted by Freedom of Information Act 2000 c. 36 Sch.2(I) para.13(2) (January 30, 2001)
[3] Repealed by Transfer of Tribunal Functions Order 2010/22 Sch.2 para.25(b) (January 18, 2010)
[4] Words repealed by Transfer of Tribunal Functions Order 2010/22 Sch.2 para.25(c) (January 18, 2010)

Commencement

Pt I s. 6(1)–(7): March 1, 2000 (SI 2000/183 art. 2(1))

Extent

Pt I s. 6(1)–(6)(a), (6)(b), (7): United Kingdom (subject to s.75(6)) Pt I s. 6(6)(aa), (6)(bb): United Kingdom

7. *Right of access to personal data.*

(1) Subject to the following provisions of this section and to [sections 8, 9 and 9A][1], an individual is entitled—

(a) to be informed by any data controller whether personal data of which that individual is the data subject are being processed by or on behalf of that data controller,

(b) if that is the case, to be given by the data controller a description of—

    (i) the personal data of which that individual is the data subject,

    (ii) the purposes for which they are being or are to be processed, and

    (iii) the recipients or classes of recipients to whom they are or may be disclosed,

(c) to have communicated to him in an intelligible form—

    (i) the information constituting any personal data of which that individual is the data subject, and

    (ii) any information available to the data controller as to the source of those data, and

(d) where the processing by automatic means of personal data of which that individual is the data subject for the purpose of evaluating matters relating to him such as, for example, his performance at work, his credit worthiness, his reliability or his conduct, has constituted or is likely to constitute the sole basis for any decision significantly affecting him, to be informed by the data controller of the logic involved in that decision-taking.

(2) A data controller is not obliged to supply any information under subsection (1) unless he has received—

(a) a request in writing, and

(b) except in prescribed cases, such fee (not exceeding the prescribed maximum) as he may require.

[(3) Where a data controller—

(a) reasonably requires further information in order to satisfy himself as to the identity of the person making a request under this section and to locate the information which that person seeks, and

(b) has informed him of that requirement,

the data controller is not obliged to comply with the request unless he is supplied with that further information.

][2]

(4) Where a data controller cannot comply with the request without disclosing information relating to another individual who can be identified from that information, he is not obliged to comply with the request unless—

(a) the other individual has consented to the disclosure of the information to the person making the request, or

(b) it is reasonable in all the circumstances to comply with the request without the consent of the other individual.

(5) In subsection (4) the reference to information relating to another individual includes a reference to information identifying that individual as the source of the information sought by the request; and that subsection is not to be construed as excusing a data controller from communicating so much of the information sought by the request as can be communicated without disclosing the identity of the other individual concerned, whether by the omission of names or other identifying particulars or otherwise.

(6) In determining for the purposes of subsection (4)(b) whether it is reasonable in all the circumstances to comply with the request without the consent of the other individual concerned, regard shall be had, in particular, to—

(a) any duty of confidentiality owed to the other individual,

(b) any steps taken by the data controller with a view to seeking the consent of the other individual,

(c) whether the other individual is capable of giving consent, and

(d) any express refusal of consent by the other individual.

(7) An individual making a request under this section may, in such cases as may be prescribed, specify that his request is limited to personal data of any prescribed description.

(8) Subject to subsection (4), a data controller shall comply with a request under this section promptly and in any event before the end of the prescribed period beginning with the relevant day.

(9) If a court is satisfied on the application of any person who has made a request under the foregoing provisions of this section that the data controller in question has failed to comply with the request in contravention of those provisions, the court may order him to comply with the request.

(10) In this section—

"prescribed" means prescribed by the [Secretary of State] 3 by regulations ; "the prescribed maximum" means such amount as may be prescribed;

"the prescribed period" means forty days or such other period as may be prescribed;

"the relevant day", in relation to a request under this section, means the day on which the data controller receives the request or, if later, the first day on which the data controller has both the required fee and the information referred to in subsection (3).

(11) Different amounts or periods may be prescribed under this section in relation to different cases.

Notes

1   Words substituted by Freedom of Information Act 2000 c. 36 Pt VII s.69(1) (November 30, 2000 for conferring powers to make any order, regulations or code of practice; January 1, 2005 for purposes specified in SI 2004/1909 art.2(1); January 1, 2005 otherwise)
2   Substituted by Freedom of Information Act 2000 c. 36 Sch.6 para.1 (May 14, 2001)
3   Words substituted by Secretary of State for Constitutional Affairs Order 2003/1887 Sch.2 para.9(1)(a) (August19, 2003)

Commencement

Pt II s. 7(1)–(6)(d), (8)–(11): March 1, 2000 (SI 2000/183 art. 2(1))
Pt II s. 7(7): July 16, 1998 for the purpose of conferring power to make subordinate legislation; March 1, 2000 otherwise (SI 2000/183 art. 2(1); 1998 c. 29 Pt VI s. 75(2))

Extent

Pt II s. 7(1)–(3), (4)–(11): United Kingdom (subject to s.75(6)) Pt II s. 7(3)(a)–(3)(b): United Kingdom

8. *Provisions supplementary to section 7.*

(1) The [Secretary of State] **1** may by regulations provide that, in such cases as may be prescribed, a request for information under any provision of subsection (1) of section 7 is to be treated as extending also to information under other provisions of that subsection.

(2) The obligation imposed by section 7(1)(c)(i) must be complied with by supplying the data subject with a copy of the information in permanent form unless—

    (a) the supply of such a copy is not possible or would involve disproportionate effort, or

    (b) the data subject agrees otherwise;

and where any of the information referred to in section 7(1)(c)(i) is expressed in terms which are not intelligible without explanation the copy must be accompanied by an explanation of those terms.

(3) Where a data controller has previously complied with a request made under section 7 by an individual, the data controller is not obliged to comply with a subsequent identical or similar request under that section by that individual unless a reasonable interval has elapsed between compliance with the previous request and the making of the current request.

(4) In determining for the purposes of subsection (3) whether requests under section 7 are made at reasonable intervals, regard shall be had to the nature of the data, the purposes for which the data are processed and the frequency with which the data are altered.

(5) Section 7(1)(d) is not to be regarded as requiring the provision of information as to the logic involved in any decision-taking if, and to the extent that, the information constitutes a trade secret.

(6) The information to be supplied pursuant to a request under section 7 must be supplied by reference to the data in question at the time when the request is received, except that it may take account of any amendment or deletion made between that time and the time when the information is supplied, being an amendment or deletion that would have been made regardless of the receipt of the request.

(7) For the purposes of section 7(4) and (5) another individual can be identified from the information being disclosed if he can be identified from that information, or from that and any other information which, in the reasonable belief of the data controller, is likely to be in, or to come into, the possession of the data subject making the request.

Notes

1   Words substituted by Secretary of State for Constitutional Affairs Order 2003/1887 Sch.2 para.9(1)(a) (August 19, 2003)

Commencement

Pt II s. 8(1): July 16, 1998 for the purpose of conferring power to make subordinate legislation; March 1, 2000 otherwise (SI 2000/183 art. 2(1); 1998 c. 29 Pt VI s. 75(2))
Pt II s. 8(2)–(7): March 1, 2000 (SI 2000/183 art. 2(1))

Extent

Pt II s. 8(1)–(7): United Kingdom (subject to s.75(6))

9. *Application of section 7 where data controller is credit reference agency.*

(1) Where the data controller is a credit reference agency, section 7 has effect subject to the provisions of this section.

(2) An individual making a request under section 7 may limit his request to personal data relevant to his financial standing, and shall be taken to have so limited his request unless the request shows a contrary intention.

(3) Where the data controller receives a request under section 7 in a case where personal data of which the individual making the request is the data subject are being processed by or on behalf of the data controller, the obligation to supply information under that section includes an obligation to give the individual making the request a statement, in such form as may be prescribed by the [Secretary of State] [1] by regulations, of the individual's rights—

(a) under section 159 of the Consumer Credit Act 1974, and

(b) to the extent required by the prescribed form, under this Act.

Notes

[1] Words substituted by Secretary of State for Constitutional Affairs Order 2003/1887 Sch.2 para.9(1)(a) (August 19, 2003)

Commencement

Pt II s. 9(1)–(2): March 1, 2000 (SI 2000/183 art. 2(1))
Pt II s. 9(3)–(3)(b): July 16, 1998 for the purpose of conferring power to make subordinate legislation; March 1, 2000 otherwise (SI 2000/183 art. 2(1); 1998 c. 29 Pt VI s. 75(2))

Extent

Pt II s. 9(1)–(3)(b): United Kingdom (subject to s.75(6))

[9A. *Unstructured personal data held by public authorities.*

(1) In this section "unstructured personal data" means any personal data falling within paragraph (e) of the definition of "data" in section 1(1), other than information which is recorded as part of, or with the intention that it should form part of, any set of information relating to individuals to the extent that the set is structured by reference to individuals or by reference to criteria relating to individuals.

(2) A public authority is not obliged to comply with subsection (1) of section 7 in relation to any unstructured personal data unless the request under that section contains a description of the data.

(3) Even if the data are described by the data subject in his request, a public authority is not obliged to comply with subsection (1) of section 7 in relation to unstructured personal data if the authority estimates that the cost of complying with the request so far as relating to those data would exceed the appropriate limit.

(4) Subsection (3) does not exempt the public authority from its obligation to

comply with paragraph (a) of section 7(1) in relation to the unstructured personal data unless the estimated cost of complying with that paragraph alone in relation to those data would exceed the appropriate limit.

(5) In subsections (3) and (4) "the appropriate limit" means such amount as may be prescribed by the [Secretary of State] [2] by regulations, and different amounts may be prescribed in relation to different cases .

(6) Any estimate for the purposes of this section must be made in accordance with regulations under section 12(5) of the Freedom of Information Act 2000.

][1]

Notes

[1]   Added by Freedom of Information Act 2000 c. 36 Pt VII s.69(2) (November 30, 2000 for conferring powers to make any order, regulations or code of practice; January 1, 2005 for purposes specified in SI 2004/1909 art.2(1); January 1, 2005 otherwise)
[2]   Words substituted by Freedom of Information Act 2000 c. 36 Pt VII s.69 (August 19, 2003: commenced by an amendment)

Extent

Pt II s. 9A(1)–(6): United Kingdom

10. *Right to prevent processing likely to cause damage or distress.*

(1) Subject to subsection (2), an individual is entitled at any time by notice in writing to a data controller to require the data controller at the end of such period as is reasonable in the circumstances to cease, or not to begin, processing, or processing for a specified purpose or in a specified manner, any personal data in respect of which he is the data subject, on the ground that, for specified reasons—

(a) the processing of those data or their processing for that purpose or in that manner is causing or is likely to cause substantial damage or substantial distress to him or to another, and

(b) that damage or distress is or would be unwarranted.

(2) Subsection (1) does not apply—

(a) in a case where any of the conditions in paragraphs 1 to 4 of Schedule 2 is met, or

(b) in such other cases as may be prescribed by the [Secretary of State] 1 by order.

(3) The data controller must within twenty-one days of receiving a notice under subsection (1) ("the data subject notice") give the individual who gave it a written notice—

(a) stating that he has complied or intends to comply with the data subject notice, or

(b) stating his reasons for regarding the data subject notice as to any extent unjustified and the extent (if any) to which he has complied or intends to comply with it.

(4) If a court is satisfied, on the application of any person who has given a notice under subsection (1) which appears to the court to be justified (or to be justified to any extent), that the data controller in question has failed to comply with the notice, the

court may order him to take such steps for complying with the notice (or for complying with it to that extent) as the court thinks fit.

(5) The failure by a data subject to exercise the right conferred by subsection (1) or section 11(1) does not affect any other right conferred on him by this Part.

Notes

[1] Words substituted by Secretary of State for Constitutional Affairs Order 2003/1887 Sch.2 para.9(1)(a) (August 19, 2003)

Commencement

Pt II s. 10(1)–(1)(b), (3)–(5): March 1, 2000 (SI 2000/183 art. 2(1))
Pt II s. 10(2)–(2)(b): July 16, 1998 for the purpose of conferring power to make subordinate legislation; March 1, 2000 otherwise (SI 2000/183 art. 2(1); 1998 c. 29 Pt VI s. 75(2))

Extent

Pt II s. 10(1)–(5): United Kingdom (subject to s.75(6))

11. *Right to prevent processing for purposes of direct marketing.*

(1) An individual is entitled at any time by notice in writing to a data controller to require the data controller at the end of such period as is reasonable in the circumstances to cease, or not to begin, processing for the purposes of direct marketing personal data in respect of which he is the data subject.

(2) If the court is satisfied, on the application of any person who has given a notice under subsection (1), that the data controller has failed to comply with the notice, the court may order him to take such steps for complying with the notice as the court thinks fit.

[(2A) This section shall not apply in relation to the processing of such data as are mentioned in paragraph (1) of regulation 8 of the Telecommunications (Data Protection and Privacy) Regulations 1999 (processing of telecommunications billing data for certain marketing purposes) for the purposes mentioned in paragraph (2) of that regulation.] [1]

(3) In this section "direct marketing" means the communication (by whatever means) of any advertising or marketing material which is directed to particular individuals.

Notes

[1] Added by Telecommunications (Data Protection and Privacy) Regulations 1999/2093 Sch.1(II) para.3 (March 1, 2000)

Commencement

Pt II s. 11(1)–(3): March 1, 2000 (SI 2000/183 art. 2(1))

Extent

Pt II s. 11(1)–(3): United Kingdom (subject to s.75(6))

12. *Rights in relation to automated decision-taking.*

(1) An individual is entitled at any time, by notice in writing to any data controller, to require the data controller to ensure that no decision taken by or on behalf of the data controller which significantly affects that individual is based solely on the processing by automatic means of personal data in respect of which that individual is the data subject for the purpose of evaluating matters relating to him such as, for example, his performance at work, his credit worthiness, his reliability or his conduct.

(2) Where, in a case where no notice under subsection (1) has effect, a decision which significantly affects an individual is based solely on such processing as is mentioned in subsection (1)—

(a) the data controller must as soon as reasonably practicable notify the individual that the decision was taken on that basis, and

(b) the individual is entitled, within twenty-one days of receiving that notification from the data controller, by notice in writing to require the data controller to reconsider the decision or to take a new decision otherwise than on that basis.

(3) The data controller must, within twenty-one days of receiving a notice under subsection (2)(b) ("the data subject notice") give the individual a written notice specifying the steps that he intends to take to comply with the data subject notice.

(4) A notice under subsection (1) does not have effect in relation to an exempt decision; and nothing in subsection (2) applies to an exempt decision.

(5) In subsection (4) "exempt decision" means any decision—

(a) in respect of which the condition in subsection (6) and the condition in subsection (7) are met, or

(b) which is made in such other circumstances as may be prescribed by the [Secretary of State]¹ by order.

(6) The condition in this subsection is that the decision—

(a) is taken in the course of steps taken—

    (i) for the purpose of considering whether to enter into a contract with the data subject,
    (ii) with a view to entering into such a contract, or
    (iii) in the course of performing such a contract, or

(b) is authorised or required by or under any enactment.

(7) The condition in this subsection is that either—

(a) the effect of the decision is to grant a request of the data subject, or

(b) steps have been taken to safeguard the legitimate interests of the data subject (for example, by allowing him to make representations).

(8) If a court is satisfied on the application of a data subject that a person taking a decision in respect of him ("the responsible person") has failed to comply with subsection (1) or (2)(b), the court may order the responsible person to reconsider the decision, or to take a new decision which is not based solely on such processing as is mentioned in subsection (1).

(9) An order under subsection (8) shall not affect the rights of any person other than the data subject and the responsible person.

Notes

[1] Words substituted by Secretary of State for Constitutional Affairs Order 2003/1887 Sch.2 para.9(1)(a) (August 19, 2003)

Commencement

Pt II s. 12(1)–(4), (6)–(9): March 1, 2000 (SI 2000/183 art. 2(1))
Pt II s. 12(5)–(5)(b): July 16, 1998 for the purpose of conferring power to make subordinate legislation; March 1, 2000 otherwise (SI 2000/183 art. 2(1); 1998 c. 29 Pt VI s. 75(2))

Extent

Pt II s. 12(1)–(9): United Kingdom (subject to s.75(6))

12A. *[. . .]¹*

Notes

[1] Repealed by Data Protection Act 1998 c. 29 Sch.13 para.1 (October 23, 2007)

13. *Compensation for failure to comply with certain requirements.*

(1) An individual who suffers damage by reason of any contravention by a data controller of any of the requirements of this Act is entitled to compensation from the data controller for that damage.

(2) An individual who suffers distress by reason of any contravention by a data controller of any of the requirements of this Act is entitled to compensation from the data controller for that distress if—

    (a) the individual also suffers damage by reason of the contravention, or

    (b) the contravention relates to the processing of personal data for the special purposes.

(3) In proceedings brought against a person by virtue of this section it is a defence to prove that he had taken such care as in all the circumstances was reasonably required to comply with the requirement concerned.

Commencement

Pt II s. 13(1)–(3): March 1, 2000 (SI 2000/183 art. 2(1))

Extent

Pt II s. 13(1)–(3): United Kingdom (subject to s.75(6))

14. *Rectification, blocking, erasure and destruction.*

(1) If a court is satisfied on the application of a data subject that personal data of which the applicant is the subject are inaccurate, the court may order the data controller to rectify, block, erase or destroy those data and any other personal data in respect of which he is the data controller and which contain an expression of opinion which appears to the court to be based on the inaccurate data.

(2) Subsection (1) applies whether or not the data accurately record information received or obtained by the data controller from the data subject or a third party but where the data accurately record such information, then—

(a) if the requirements mentioned in paragraph 7 of Part II of Schedule 1 have been complied with, the court may, instead of making an order under subsection (1), make an order requiring the data to be supplemented by such statement of the true facts relating to the matters dealt with by the data as the court may approve, and

(b) if all or any of those requirements have not been complied with, the court may, instead of making an order under that subsection, make such order as it thinks fit for securing compliance with those requirements with or without a further order requiring the data to be supplemented by such a statement as is mentioned in paragraph (a).

(3) Where the court—

(a) makes an order under subsection (1), or

(b) is satisfied on the application of a data subject that personal data of which he was the data subject and which have been rectified, blocked, erased or destroyed were inaccurate,

it may, where it considers it reasonably practicable, order the data controller to notify third parties to whom the data have been disclosed of the rectification, blocking, erasure or destruction.

(4) If a court is satisfied on the application of a data subject—

(a) that he has suffered damage by reason of any contravention by a data controller of any of the requirements of this Act in respect of any personal data, in circumstances entitling him to compensation under section 13, and

(b) that there is a substantial risk of further contravention in respect of those data in such circumstances,

the court may order the rectification, blocking, erasure or destruction of any of those data.

(5) Where the court makes an order under subsection (4) it may, where it considers it reasonably practicable, order the data controller to notify third parties to whom the data have been disclosed of the rectification, blocking, erasure or destruction.

(6) In determining whether it is reasonably practicable to require such notification as is mentioned in subsection (3) or (5) the court shall have regard, in particular, to the number of persons who would have to be notified.

Commencement

Pt II s. 14(1)–(6): March 1, 2000 (SI 2000/183 art. 2(1))

Extent

Pt II s. 14(1)–(6): United Kingdom (subject to s.75(6))

15. *Jurisdiction and procedure.*

(1) The jurisdiction conferred by sections 7 to 14 is exercisable by the High Court or a county court or, in Scotland, by the Court of Session or the sheriff.

(2) For the purpose of determining any question whether an applicant under subsection (9) of section 7 is entitled to the information which he seeks (including any question whether any relevant data are exempt from that section by virtue of Part IV) a court may require the information constituting any data processed by or on behalf of the data controller and any information as to the logic involved in any decision-taking as mentioned in section 7(1)(d) to be made available for its own inspection but shall not, pending the determination of that question in the applicant's favour, require the information sought by the applicant to be disclosed to him or his representatives whether by discovery (or, in Scotland, recovery) or otherwise.

Commencement

Pt II s. 15(1)–(2): March 1, 2000 (SI 2000/183 art. 2(1))

Extent

Pt II s. 15(1)–(2): United Kingdom (subject to s.75(6))

PART III

NOTIFICATION BY DATA CONTROLLERS

16. *Preliminary*

(1) In this Part "the registrable particulars", in relation to a data controller, means—

(a) his name and address,

(b) if he has nominated a representative for the purposes of this Act, the name and address of the representative,

(c) a description of the personal data being or to be processed by or on behalf of the data controller and of the category or categories of data subject to which they relate,

(d) a description of the purpose or purposes for which the data are being or are to be processed,

(e) a description of any recipient or recipients to whom the data controller intends or may wish to disclose the data,

(f) the names, or a description of, any countries or territories outside the European Economic Area to which the data controller directly or indirectly transfers, or intends or may wish directly or indirectly to transfer, the data, [. . .]¹

(ff) where the data controller is a public authority, a statement of that fact, [. . .]²]¹

(g) in any case where—

(i) personal data are being, or are intended to be, processed in circumstances in which the prohibition in subsection (1) of section 17 is excluded by subsection (2) or (3) of that section, and

(ii) the notification does not extend to those data, a statement of that fact [, and]³

[(h) such information about the data controller as may be prescribed under section 18(5A).]³

DATA PROTECTION ACT 1998

(2) In this Part—

"fees regulations" means regulations made by the [Secretary of State] 4 under section 18(5) or 19(4) or (7);

"notification regulations" means regulations made by the [Secretary of State]⁴ under the other provisions of this Part ;

"prescribed", except where used in relation to fees regulations, means prescribed by notification regulations.

(3) For the purposes of this Part, so far as it relates to the addresses of data controllers—

(a) the address of a registered company is that of its registered office, and

(b) the address of a person (other than a registered company) carrying on a business is that of his principal place of business in the United Kingdom.

Notes

1 Added by Freedom of Information Act 2000 c. 36 Pt VII s.71 (January 1, 2005 for purposes specified in SI 2004/1909 art.2(1); January 1, 2005 otherwise)
2 Word repealed by Coroners and Justice Act 2009 c. 25 Sch.20(1) para.1(a) (February 1, 2010: repeal comes into force on February 1, 2010 as SI 2010/145 art.2 and Sch.1 para.24 and is also purportedly brought into force on April 6, 2010 by SI 2010/816 art.2 and Sch.1 para.22(d))
3 Added by Coroners and Justice Act 2009 c. 25 Sch.20(1) para.1(b) (February 1, 2010)
4 Words substituted by Secretary of State for Constitutional Affairs Order 2003/1887 Sch.2 para.9(1)(a) (August 19, 2003)

Commencement

Pt III s. 16(1)–(3)(b): March 1, 2000 (SI 2000/183 art. 2(1))

Extent

Pt III s. 16(1)–(1)(f), (1)(g)–(1)(g)(ii), (2)–(3)(b): United Kingdom (subject to s.75(6)) Pt III s. 16(1)(ff), (1)(h): United Kingdom

17. *Prohibition on processing without registration.*

(1) Subject to the following provisions of this section, personal data must not be processed unless an entry in respect of the data controller is included in the register maintained by the Commissioner under section 19 (or is treated by notification regulations made by virtue of section 19(3) as being so included).

(2) Except where the processing is assessable processing for the purposes of section 22, subsection (1) does not apply in relation to personal data consisting of information which falls neither within paragraph (a) of the definition of "data" in section 1(1) nor within paragraph (b) of that definition.

(3) If it appears to the [Secretary of State] ¹ that processing of a particular description is unlikely to prejudice the rights and freedoms of data subjects, notification regulations may provide that, in such cases as may be prescribed, subsection (1) is not to apply in relation to processing of that description.

(4) Subsection (1) does not apply in relation to any processing whose sole purpose is the maintenance of a public register.

Notes

¹ Words substituted by Secretary of State for Constitutional Affairs Order 2003/1887 Sch.2 para.9(1)(a) (August 19, 2003)

Commencement

Pt III s. 17(1)–(2), (4): March 1, 2000 (SI 2000/183 art. 2(1))
Pt III s. 17(3): July 16, 1998 for the purpose of conferring power to make subordinate legislation; March 1, 2000 otherwise (SI 2000/183 art. 2(1); 1998 c. 29 Pt VI s. 75(2))

Extent

Pt III s. 17(1)–(4): United Kingdom (subject to s.75(6))

18. *Notification by data controllers.*

(1) Any data controller who wishes to be included in the register maintained under section 19 shall give a notification to the Commissioner under this section.

(2) A notification under this section must specify in accordance with notification regulations—

(a) the registrable particulars, and

(b) a general description of measures to be taken for the purpose of complying with the seventh data protection principle.

(3) Notification regulations made by virtue of subsection (2) may provide for the determination by the Commissioner, in accordance with any requirements of the regulations, of the form in which the registrable particulars and the description mentioned in subsection (2)(b) are to be specified, including in particular the detail required for the purposes of section 16(1)(c), (d), (e) and (f) and subsection (2)(b).

(4) Notification regulations may make provision as to the giving of notification—

(a) by partnerships, or

(b) in other cases where two or more persons are the data controllers in respect of any personal data.

(5) The notification must be accompanied by such fee as may be prescribed by fees regulations.

[(5A) Notification regulations may prescribe the information about the data controller which is required for the purpose of verifying the fee payable under subsection (5).]¹

(6) Notification regulations may provide for any fee paid under subsection (5) or section 19(4) to be refunded in prescribed circumstances.

Notes

¹ Added by Coroners and Justice Act 2009 c. 25 Sch.20(1) para.2 (February 1, 2010)

Commencement

Pt III s. 18(1), (3): March 1, 2000 (SI 2000/183 art. 2(1))
Pt III s. 18(2)–(2)(b), (4)–(6): July 16, 1998 for the purpose of conferring power to make subordinate legislation; March 1, 2000 otherwise (SI 2000/183 art. 2(1); 1998 c. 29 Pt VI s. 75(2))

Pt III s. 18(1)–(5), (6): United Kingdom (subject to s.75(6)) Pt III s. 18(5A): United Kingdom

19. *Register of notifications.*

(1) The Commissioner shall—

  (a) maintain a register of persons who have given notification under section 18, and

  (b) make an entry in the register in pursuance of each notification received by him under that section from a person in respect of whom no entry as data controller was for the time being included in the register.

(2) Each entry in the register shall consist of—

  (a) the registrable particulars notified under section 18 or, as the case requires, those particulars as amended in pursuance of section 20(4), and

  (b) such other information as the Commissioner may be authorised or required by notification regulations to include in the register.

(3) Notification regulations may make provision as to the time as from which any entry in respect of a data controller is to be treated for the purposes of section 17 as having been made in the register.

(4) No entry shall be retained in the register for more than the relevant time except on payment of such fee as may be prescribed by fees regulations.

(5) In subsection (4) "the relevant time" means twelve months or such other period as may be prescribed by notification regulations; and different periods may be prescribed in relation to different cases.

(6) The Commissioner—

  (a) shall provide facilities for making the information contained in the entries in the register available for inspection (in visible and legible form) by members of the public at all reasonable hours and free of charge, and

  (b) may provide such other facilities for making the information contained in those entries available to the public free of charge as he considers appropriate.

(7) The Commissioner shall, on payment of such fee, if any, as may be prescribed by fees regulations, supply any member of the public with a duly certified copy in writing of the particulars contained in any entry made in the register.

[(8) Nothing in subsection (6) or (7) applies to information which is included in an entry in the register only by reason of it falling within section 16(1)(h).] [1]

Notes
[1] Added by Coroners and Justice Act 2009 c. 25 Sch.20(1) para.3 (February 1, 2010)

Commencement
Pt III s. 19(1)–(2)(b), (5)–(6)(b): March 1, 2000 (SI 2000/183 art. 2(1))
Pt III s. 19(3)–(4), (7): July 16, 1998 for the purpose of conferring power to make subordinate legislation; March 1, 2000 otherwise (SI 2000/183 art. 2(1); 1998 c. 29 Pt VI s. 75(2))

Extent
Pt III s. 19(1)–(7): United Kingdom (subject to s.75(6)) Pt III s. 19(8): United Kingdom

20. *Duty to notify changes.*

(1) For the purpose specified in subsection (2), notification regulations shall include provision imposing on every person in respect of whom an entry as a data controller is for the time being included in the register maintained under section 19 a duty to notify to the Commissioner, in such circumstances and at such time or times and in such form as may be prescribed, such matters relating to the registrable particulars and measures taken as mentioned in section 18(2)(b) as may be prescribed.

(2) The purpose referred to in subsection (1) is that of ensuring, so far as practicable, that at any time—

    (a) the entries in the register maintained under section 19 contain current names and addresses and describe the current practice or intentions of the data controller with respect to the processing of personal data, and

    (b) the Commissioner is provided with a general description of measures currently being taken as mentioned in section 18(2)(b).

(3) Subsection (3) of section 18 has effect in relation to notification regulations made by virtue of subsection (1) as it has effect in relation to notification regulations made by virtue of subsection (2) of that section.

(4) On receiving any notification under notification regulations made by virtue of subsection (1), the Commissioner shall make such amendments of the relevant entry in the register maintained under section 19 as are necessary to take account of the notification.

Amendments Pending

Pt III s. 20(2): words repealed by Coroners and Justice Act 2009 c. 25, Sch. 23(8) para. 1 (date to be appointed)
Pt III s. 20(2)(b): words inserted by Coroners and Justice Act 2009 c. 25, Sch. 20(1) para. 4(d) (date to be appointed) Pt III s. 20(2)(aa): added by Coroners and Justice Act 2009 c. 25, Sch. 20(1) para. 4(c) (date to be appointed)
Pt III s. 20(2)(a): words inserted by Coroners and Justice Act 2009 c. 25, Sch. 20(1) para. 4(b) (date to be appointed)

Commencement

Pt III s. 20(1): July 16, 1998 for the purpose of conferring power to make subordinate legislation; March 1, 2000 otherwise (SI 2000/183 art. 2(1); 1998 c. 29 Pt VI s. 75(2))
Pt III s. 20(2)–(4): March 1, 2000 (SI 2000/183 art. 2(1))

Extent

Pt III s. 20(1)–(2)(a), (2)(b)–(4): United Kingdom (subject to s.75(6)) Pt III s. 20(2)(aa): United Kingdom

21. *Offences.*

(1) If section 17(1) is contravened, the data controller is guilty of an offence.

(2) Any person who fails to comply with the duty imposed by notification regulations made by virtue of section 20(1) is guilty of an offence.

(3) It shall be a defence for a person charged with an offence under subsection (2) to show that he exercised all due diligence to comply with the duty.

Commencement

Pt III s. 21(1)–(3): March 1, 2000 (SI 2000/183 art. 2(1))

Extent

Pt III s. 21(1)–(3): United Kingdom (subject to s.75(6))

22. *Preliminary assessment by Commissioner.*

(1) In this section "assessable processing" means processing which is of a description specified in an order made by the [Secretary of State] 1 as appearing to him to be particularly likely—

    (a) to cause substantial damage or substantial distress to data subjects, or

    (b) otherwise significantly to prejudice the rights and freedoms of data subjects.

(2) On receiving notification from any data controller under section 18 or under notification regulations made by virtue of section 20 the Commissioner shall consider—

    (a) whether any of the processing to which the notification relates is assessable processing, and

    (b) if so, whether the assessable processing is likely to comply with the provisions of this Act.

(3) Subject to subsection (4), the Commissioner shall, within the period of twenty-eight days beginning with the day on which he receives a notification which relates to assessable processing, give a notice to the data controller stating the **extent** to which the Commissioner is of the opinion that the processing is likely or unlikely to comply with the provisions of this Act.

(4) Before the end of the period referred to in subsection (3) the Commissioner may, by reason of special circumstances, extend that period on one occasion only by notice to the data controller by such further period not exceeding fourteen days as the Commissioner may specify in the notice.

(5) No assessable processing in respect of which a notification has been given to the Commissioner as mentioned in subsection (2) shall be carried on unless either—

    (a) the period of twenty-eight days beginning with the day on which the notification is received by the Commissioner (or, in a case falling within subsection (4), that period as extended under that subsection) has elapsed, or

    (b) before the end of that period (or that period as so extended) the data controller has received a notice from the Commissioner under subsection (3) in respect of the processing.

(6) Where subsection (5) is contravened, the data controller is guilty of an offence.

(7) The [Secretary of State] [1] may by order amend subsections (3), (4) and (5) by substituting for the number of days for the time being specified there a different number specified in the order.

Notes

[1] Words substituted by Secretary of State for Constitutional Affairs Order 2003/1887 Sch.2 para.9(1)(a) (August 19, 2003)

Commencement

Pt III s. 22(1)–(1)(b), (7): July 16, 1998 for the purpose of conferring power to make subordinate legislation; March 1, 2000 otherwise (SI 2000/183 art. 2(1); 1998 c. 29 Pt VI s. 75(2)) Pt III s. 22(2)–(6): March 1, 2000 (SI 2000/183 art. 2(1))

Extent

Pt III s. 22(1)–(7): United Kingdom (subject to s.75(6))

23. *Power to make provision for appointment of data protection supervisors.*

(1) The [Secretary of State] 1 may by order—

(a) make provision under which a data controller may appoint a person to act as a data protection supervisor responsible in particular for monitoring in an independent manner the data controller's compliance with the provisions of this Act, and

(b) provide that, in relation to any data controller who has appointed a data protection supervisor in accordance with the provisions of the order and who complies with such conditions as may be specified in the order, the provisions of this Part are to have effect subject to such exemptions or other modifications as may be specified in the order.

(2) An order under this section may—

(a) impose duties on data protection supervisors in relation to the Commissioner, and

(b) confer functions on the Commissioner in relation to data protection supervisors.

Notes

1 Words substituted by Secretary of State for Constitutional Affairs Order 2003/1887 Sch.2 para.9(1)(a) (August 19, 2003)

Commencement

Pt III s. 23(1)–(1)(b): July 16, 1998 for the purpose of conferring power to make subordinate legislation; March 1, 2000 otherwise (SI 2000/183 art. 2(1); 1998 c. 29 Pt VI s. 75(2)) Pt III s. 23(2)–(2)(b): March 1, 2000 (SI 2000/183 art. 2(1))

Extent

Pt III s. 23(1)–(2)(b): United Kingdom (subject to s.75(6))

24. *Duty of certain data controllers to make certain information available.*

(1) Subject to subsection (3), where personal data are processed in a case where—

(a) by virtue of subsection (2) or (3) of section 17, subsection (1) of that section does not apply to the processing, and

(b) the data controller has not notified the relevant particulars in respect of that processing under section 18,

the data controller must, within twenty-one days of receiving a written request from any person, make the relevant particulars available to that person in writing free of charge.

(2) In this section "the relevant particulars" means the particulars referred to in paragraphs (a) to (f) of section 16(1).

(3) This section has effect subject to any exemption conferred for the purposes of this section by notification regulations.

(4) Any data controller who fails to comply with the duty imposed by subsection (1) is guilty of an offence.

(5) It shall be a defence for a person charged with an offence under subsection (4) to show that he exercised all due diligence to comply with the duty.

Commencement

Pt III s. 24(1)–(2), (4)–(5): March 1, 2000 (SI 2000/183 art. 2(1))
Pt III s. 24(3): July 16, 1998 for the purpose of conferring power to make subordinate legislation; March 1, 2000 otherwise (SI 2000/183 art. 2(1); 1998 c. 29 Pt VI s. 75(2))

Extent

Pt III s. 24(1)–(5): United Kingdom (subject to s.75(6))

25. *Functions of Commissioner in relation to making of notification regulations.*

(1) As soon as practicable after the passing of this Act, the Commissioner shall submit to the Secretary of State proposals as to the provisions to be included in the first notification regulations.

(2) The Commissioner shall keep under review the working of notification regulations and may from time to time submit to the [Secretary of State] [1] proposals as to amendments to be made to the regulations.

(3) The [Secretary of State] [1] may from time to time require the Commissioner to consider any matter relating to notification regulations and to submit to him proposals as to amendments to be made to the regulations in connection with that matter.

(4) Before making any notification regulations, the [Secretary of State] [1] shall—

(a) consider any proposals made to him by the Commissioner under [subsection (2) or (3)] [2] , and

(b) consult the Commissioner.

Notes

[1] Words substituted by Secretary of State for Constitutional Affairs Order 2003/1887 Sch.2 para.9(1)(a) (August 19, 2003)
[2] Words substituted by Transfer of Functions (Miscellaneous) Order 2001/3500 Sch.2(I) para.6(2) (November 26, 2001)

Commencement

Pt III s. 25(1), (4)–(4)(b): July 16, 1998 (1998 c. 29 Pt VI s. 75(2)(b)) Pt III s. 25(2)–(3): March 1, 2000 (SI 2000/183 art. 2(1))

Extent

Pt III s. 25(1)–(4)(b): United Kingdom (subject to s.75(6))

26. *Fees regulations.*

(1) Fees regulations prescribing fees for the purposes of any provision of this Part may provide for different fees to be payable in different cases.

(2) In making any fees regulations, the [Secretary of State] [1] shall have regard to the desirability of securing that the fees payable to the Commissioner are sufficient to offset—

[(a) the expenses incurred by the Commissioner in discharging his functions under this Act and any expenses of the Secretary of State in respect of the Commissioner so far as attributable to those functions; and] 2

(b)   to the **extent** that the [Secretary of State] 1 considers appropriate—

(i) any deficit previously incurred (whether before or after the passing of this Act) in respect of the expenses mentioned in paragraph (a), and

(ii) expenses incurred or to be incurred by the [Secretary of State] 1 in respect of the inclusion of any officers or staff of the Commissioner in any scheme under section 1 of the Superannuation Act 1972.

Notes

[1]   Words substituted by Secretary of State for Constitutional Affairs Order 2003/1887 Sch.2 para.9(1)(a) (August 19, 2003)

[2]   Substituted by Transfer of Tribunal Functions Order 2010/22 Sch.2 para.26 (January 18, 2010)

Commencement

Pt III s. 26(1)–(2)(b)(ii): July 16, 1998 (1998 c. 29 Pt VI s. 75(2))

Extent

Pt III s. 26(1)–(2)(b)(ii): United Kingdom (subject to s.75(6))

PART IV

EXEMPTIONS

27. *Preliminary.*

(1) References in any of the data protection principles or any provision of Parts II and III to personal data or to the processing of personal data do not include references to data or processing which by virtue of this Part are exempt from that principle or other provision.

(2) In this Part "the subject information provisions" means —

(a) the first data protection principle to the extent to which it requires compliance with paragraph 2 of Part II of Schedule 1, and

(b) section 7.

(3) In this Part "the non-disclosure provisions" means the provisions specified in subsection (4) to the extent to which they are inconsistent with the disclosure in question.

(4) The provisions referred to in subsection (3) are—

(a) the first data protection principle, except to the extent to which it requires compliance with the conditions in Schedules 2 and 3,

(b) the second, third, fourth and fifth data protection principles, and

(c) sections 10 and 14(1) to (3).

(5) Except as provided by this Part, the subject information provisions shall have effect notwithstanding any enactment or rule of law prohibiting or restricting the disclosure, or authorising the withholding, of information.

Commencement

Pt IV s. 27(1)–(5): March 1, 2000 (SI 2000/183 art. 2(1))

Extent

Pt IV s. 27(1)–(5): United Kingdom (subject to s.75(6))

28. *National security.*

(1) Personal data are exempt from any of the provisions of—

(a) the data protection principles,

(b) Parts II, III and V, and

(c) [sections 54A and section 55] 1 ,

if the exemption from that provision is required for the purpose of safeguarding national security.

(2) Subject to subsection (4), a certificate signed by a Minister of the Crown certifying that exemption from all or any of the provisions mentioned in subsection (1) is or at any time was required for the purpose there mentioned in respect of any personal data shall be conclusive evidence of that fact.

(3) A certificate under subsection (2) may identify the personal data to which it applies by means of a general description and may be expressed to have prospective effect.

(4) Any person directly affected by the issuing of a certificate under subsection (2) may appeal to the Tribunal against the certificate.

(5) If on an appeal under subsection (4), the Tribunal finds that, applying the principles applied by the court on an application for judicial review, the Minister did not have reasonable grounds for issuing the certificate, the Tribunal may allow the appeal and quash the certificate.

(6) Where in any proceedings under or by virtue of this Act it is claimed by a data controller that a certificate under subsection (2) which identifies the personal data to which it applies by means of a general description applies to any personal data, any other party to the proceedings may appeal to the Tribunal on the ground that the certificate does not apply to the personal data in question and, subject to any determination under subsection (7), the certificate shall be conclusively presumed so to apply.

(7) On any appeal under subsection (6), the Tribunal may determine that the certificate does not so apply.

(8) A document purporting to be a certificate under subsection (2) shall be received in evidence and deemed to be such a certificate unless the contrary is proved.

(9) A document which purports to be certified by or on behalf of a Minister of the Crown as a true copy of a certificate issued by that Minister under subsection (2) shall in any legal proceedings be evidence (or, in Scotland, sufficient evidence) of that certificate.

(10) The power conferred by subsection (2) on a Minister of the Crown shall not be exercisable except by a Minister who is a member of the Cabinet or by the Attorney General or the [Advocate General] [2] .

(11) No power conferred by any provision of Part V may be exercised in relation to personal data which by virtue of this section are exempt from that provision.

(12) Schedule 6 shall have effect in relation to appeals under subsection (4) or (6) and the proceedings of the Tribunal in respect of any such appeal.

Notes

[1] Word substituted by Crime (International Co-operation) Act 2003 c. 32 Sch.5 para.69 (April 26, 2004)
[2] Words substituted by Transfer of Functions (Lord Advocate and Advocate General for Scotland) Order 1999/679 Sch.1 para.1 (March 1, 2000: substitution came into force on May 20, 1999 but could not take effect until the commencement of 1998 c.29 s.28(10) on March 1, 2000)

Commencement

Pt IV s. 28(1)–(12): March 1, 2000 (SI 2000/183 art. 2(1))

Extent

Pt IV s. 28(1)–(12): United Kingdom (subject to s.75(6))

29. *Crime and taxation.*

(1) Personal data processed for any of the following purposes—

(a) the prevention or detection of crime,

(b) the apprehension or prosecution of offenders, or

(c) the assessment or collection of any tax or duty or of any imposition of a similar nature, are exempt from the first data protection principle (except to the extent to which it requires compliance with the conditions in Schedules 2 and 3) and section 7 in any case to the extent to which the application of those provisions to the data would be likely to prejudice any of the matters mentioned in this subsection.

(2) Personal data which—

(a) are processed for the purpose of discharging statutory functions, and

(b) consist of information obtained for such a purpose from a person who had it in his possession for any of the purposes mentioned in subsection (1),

are exempt from the subject information provisions to the same extent as personal data processed for any of the purposes mentioned in that subsection.

(3) Personal data are exempt from the non-disclosure provisions in any case in which—

(a) the disclosure is for any of the purposes mentioned in subsection (1), and

(b) the application of those provisions in relation to the disclosure would be likely to prejudice any of the matters mentioned in that subsection.

(4) Personal data in respect of which the data controller is a relevant authority and which—

    (a) consist of a classification applied to the data subject as part of a system of risk assessment which is operated by that authority for either of the following purposes—

        (i) the assessment or collection of any tax or duty or any imposition of a similar nature, or

        (ii) the prevention or detection of crime, or apprehension or prosecution of offenders, where the offence concerned involves any unlawful claim for any payment out of, or any unlawful application of, public funds, and

    (b) are processed for either of those purposes,

are exempt from section 7 to the extent to which the exemption is required in the interests of the operation of the system.

(5) In subsection (4)—

    "public funds" includes funds provided by any [EU] 1 institution ; "relevant authority" means—

    (a) a government department,

    (b) a local authority, or

    (c) any other authority administering housing benefit or council tax benefit.

Notes

1 Word substituted by Treaty of Lisbon (Changes in Terminology) Order 2011/1043 Pt 2 art.6(1)(c) (April 22, 2011)

Commencement

Pt IV s. 29(1)–(5) definition of "relevant authority" (c): March 1, 2000 (SI 2000/183 art. 2(1))

Extent

Pt IV s. 29(1)–(5) definition of "relevant authority" (c): United Kingdom (subject to s.75(6))

30. *Health, education and social work.*

(1) The [Secretary of State] 1 may by order exempt from the subject information provisions, or modify those provisions in relation to, personal data consisting of information as to the physical or mental health or condition of the data subject.

(2) The [Secretary of State] ¹ may by order exempt from the subject information provisions, or modify those provisions in relation to—

    (a) personal data in respect of which the data controller is the proprietor of, or a teacher at, a school, and which consist of information relating to persons who are or have been pupils at the school, or

    (b) personal data in respect of which the data controller is an education authority in Scotland, and which consist of information relating to persons who are receiving, or have received, further education provided by the authority.

(3) The [Secretary of State] 1 may by order exempt from the subject information provisions, or modify those provisions in relation to, personal data of such other descriptions as may be specified in the order, being information—

(a) processed by government departments or local authorities or by voluntary organisations or other bodies designated by or under the order, and

(b) appearing to him to be processed in the course of, or for the purposes of, carrying out social work in relation to the data subject or other individuals;

but the [Secretary of State]¹ shall not under this subsection confer any exemption or make any modification except so far as he considers that the application to the data of those provisions (or of those provisions without modification) would be likely to prejudice the carrying out of social work.

(4) An order under this section may make different provision in relation to data consisting of information of different descriptions.

(5) In this section—

"education authority" and "further education"have the same meaning as in the Education (Scotland) Act 1980 ("the 1980 Act"), and

"proprietor"—

(a) in relation to a school in England or Wales, has the same meaning as in the Education Act 1996,

(b) in relation to a school in Scotland, means—

(i) [. . .]²
(ii) in the case of an independent school, the proprietor within the meaning of the 1980 Act,
(iii) in the case of a grant-aided school, the managers within the meaning of the 1980 Act, and
(iv) in the case of a public school, the education authority within the meaning of the 1980 Act, and

(c) in relation to a school in Northern Ireland, has the same meaning as in the Education and Libraries (Northern Ireland) Order 1986 and includes, in the case of a controlled school, the Board of Governors of the school.

Notes

1. Words substituted by Secretary of State for Constitutional Affairs Order 2003/1887 Sch.2 para.9(1)(a) (August 19, 2003)
2. Repealed by Standards in Scotland's Schools etc. Act 2000 asp 6 (Scottish Act) Sch.3 para. (December 31, 2004: as SSI 2004/528)

Commencement

Pt IV s. 30(1)–(3)(b): July 16, 1998 for the purpose of conferring power to make subordinate legislation; March 1, 2000 otherwise (SI 2000/183 art. 2(1); 1998 c. 29 Pt VI s. 75(2))
Pt IV s. 30(4)–(5) definition of "proprietor" (c): March 1, 2000 (SI 2000/183 art. 2(1))

Extent

Pt IV s. 30(1)–(5) definition of "proprietor" (c): United Kingdom (subject to s.75(6))

31. *Regulatory activity.*

(1) Personal data processed for the purposes of discharging functions to which this subsection applies are exempt from the subject information provisions in any case to the extent to which the application of those provisions to the data would be likely to prejudice the proper discharge of those functions.

(2) Subsection (1) applies to any relevant function which is designed—

    (a) for protecting members of the public against—

        (i) financial loss due to dishonesty, malpractice or other seriously improper conduct by, or the unfitness or incompetence of, persons concerned in the provision of banking, insurance, investment or other financial services or in the management of bodies corporate,

        (ii) financial loss due to the conduct of discharged or undischarged bankrupts, or

        (iii) dishonesty, malpractice or other seriously improper conduct by, or the unfitness or incompetence of, persons authorised to carry on any profession or other activity,

    (b) for protecting charities [or community interest companies]¹ against misconduct or mismanagement (whether by trustees [, directors]² or other persons) in their administration,

    (c) for protecting the property of charities [or community interest companies] ¹ from loss or misapplication,

    (d) for the recovery of the property of charities [or community interest companies] 1 ,

    (e) for securing the health, safety and welfare of persons at work, or

    (f) for protecting persons other than persons at work against risk to health or safety arising out of or in connection with the actions of persons at work.

(3) In subsection (2) "relevant function" means—

    (a) any function conferred on any person by or under any enactment,

    (b) any function of the Crown, a Minister of the Crown or a government department, or

    (c) any other function which is of a public nature and is exercised in the public interest.

(4) Personal data processed for the purpose of discharging any function which—

    (a) is conferred by or under any enactment on—

        (i) the Parliamentary Commissioner for Administration,

        (ii) the Commission for Local Administration in England [. . .]3 [. . .]4 ,

        (iii) the Health Service Commissioner for England [. . .]3 [. . .]5 ,

    [(iv) the Public Services Ombudsman for Wales,] 6

        (v) the Assembly Ombudsman for Northern Ireland, [. . .]7

        (vi) the Northern Ireland Commissioner for Complaints, [or] 8

    [(vii) the Scottish Public Services Ombudsman, and] 9

    (b) is designed for protecting members of the public against—

        (i) maladministration by public bodies,

        (ii) failures in services provided by public bodies, or

(iii) a failure of a public body to provide a service which it was a function of the body to provide,

are exempt from the subject information provisions in any case to the extent to which the application of those provisions to the data would be likely to prejudice the proper discharge of that function.

[(4A) Personal data processed for the purpose of discharging any function which is conferred by or under Part XVI of the Financial Services and Markets Act 2000 on the body established by the Financial Services Authority for the purposes of that Part are exempt from the subject information provisions in any case to the extent to which the application of those provisions to the data would be likely to prejudice the proper discharge of the function.] [10]

[(4B) Personal data processed for the purposes of discharging any function of the Legal Services Board are exempt from the subject information provisions in any case to the extent to which the application of those provisions to the data would be likely to prejudice the proper discharge of the function.] [11]

[(4C) Personal data processed for the purposes of the function of considering a complaint under the scheme established under Part 6 of the Legal Services Act 2007 (legal complaints) are exempt from the subject information provisions in any case to the extent to which the application of those provisions to the data would be likely to prejudice the proper discharge of the function.] [12]

(5) Personal data processed for the purpose of discharging any function which—

(a) is conferred by or under any enactment on [the Office of Fair Trading] [13] , and

(b) is designed—

(i) for protecting members of the public against conduct which may adversely affect their interests by persons carrying on a business,
(ii) for regulating agreements or conduct which have as their object or effect the prevention, restriction or distortion of competition in connection with any commercial activity, or
(iii) for regulating conduct on the part of one or more undertakings which amounts to the abuse of a dominant position in a market,

are exempt from the subject information provisions in any case to the extent to which the application of those provisions to the data would be likely to prejudice the proper discharge of that function.

[(5A) Personal data processed by a CPC enforcer for the purpose of discharging any function conferred on such a body by or under the CPC Regulation are exempt from the subject information provisions in any case to the extent to which the application of those provisions to the data would be likely to prejudice the proper discharge of that function.

(5B) In subsection (5A)—

(a) "CPC enforcer" has the meaning given to it in section 213(5A) of the Enterprise Act 2002 but does not include the Office of Fair Trading;

(b) "CPC Regulation" has the meaning given to it in section 235A of that Act.

] [14]

[(6) Personal data processed for the purpose of the function of considering a complaint under section 113(1) or (2) or 114(1) or (3) of the Health and Social Care (Community Health and Standards) Act 2003, or [section 24D, 26 or 26ZB of the Children Act 1989] [16] , are exempt from the subject information provisions in any case to the extent to which the application of those provisions to the data would be likely to prejudice the proper discharge of that function.] [15]

[(7) Personal data processed for the purpose of discharging any function which is conferred by or under Part 3 of the Local Government Act 2000 on–

(a) the monitoring officer of a relevant authority, [or] [18]

(b) [. . .] [18]

(c) ˙the Public Services Ombudsman for Wales,

are exempt from the subject information provisions in any case to the extent to which the application of those provisions to the data would be likely to prejudice the proper discharge of that function.

(8) In subsection (7)–

(a) "relevant authority"has the meaning given by section 49(6) of the Local Government Act 2000, and

(b) any reference to the monitoring officer of a relevant authority [. . .]19 has the same meaning as in Part 3 of that Act.

] [17]

Notes

[1] Words inserted by Companies (Audit, Investigations and Community Enterprise) Act 2004 c. 27 Pt 2 s.59(3)(a) (July 1, 2005)

[2] Word inserted by Companies (Audit, Investigations and Community Enterprise) Act 2004 c. 27 Pt 2 s.59(3)(b) (July 1, 2005)

[3] Words repealed by Public Services Ombudsman (Wales) Act 2005 c. 10 Sch.7 para.1 (April 1, 2006 as SI 2005/2800)

[4] Words repealed by Scottish Public Services Ombudsman Act 2002 (Consequential Provisions and Modifications) Order 2004/1823 art.19(a)(ii) (July 14, 2004)

[5] Words repealed by Scottish Public Services Ombudsman Act 2002 (Consequential Provisions and Modifications) Order 2004/1823 art.19(b)(ii) (July 14, 2004)

[6] Substituted by Public Services Ombudsman (Wales) Act 2005 c. 10 Sch.6 para.60(c) (April 1, 2006)

[7] Word repealed by Scottish Public Services Ombudsman Act 2002 (Consequential Provisions and Modifications) Order 2004/1823 art.19(c) (July 14, 2004)

[8] Word substituted by Scottish Public Services Ombudsman Act 2002 (Consequential Provisions and Modifications) Order 2004/1823 art.19(d) (July 14, 2004)

[9] Added by Scottish Public Services Ombudsman Act 2002 (Consequential Provisions and Modifications) Order 2004/1823 art.19(e) (July 14, 2004)

[10] Added by Financial Services and Markets Act 2000 c. 8 Pt XVI s.233 (December 1, 2001 as SI 2001/3538)

[11] Added by Legal Services Act 2007 c. 29 Pt 7 s.170 (January 1, 2010)

[12] Added by Legal Services Act 2007 c. 29 Pt 6 s.153 (October 6, 2010)

[13] Words substituted by Enterprise Act 2002 c. 40 Sch.25 para.37(2) (April 1, 2003)

[14] Added by Enterprise Act 2002 (Amendment) Regulations 2006/3363 reg.29 (January 8, 2007)

[15] Added by Health and Social Care (Community Health and Standards) Act 2003 c. 43 Pt 2 c.9 s.119 (June 1, 2004)

[16] Word repealed by Education and Inspections Act 2006 c. 40 Sch.18(5) para.1 (April 1, 2007 as SI 2007/935)

[17] Added by Local Government and Public Involvement in Health Act 2007 c. 28 Pt 10 c.1 s.200 (April 1, 2008)

[18] Repealed by Localism Act 2011 c. 20 Sch.25(5) para.1 (January 31, 2012: repeal has effect as SI 2012/57 subject to transitional and savings provisions specified in SI 2012/57 arts 6 and 8)

[19] Words repealed by Localism Act 2011 c. 20 Sch.25(5) para.1 (January 31, 2012: repeal has effect as SI 2012/57 subject to transitional and savings provisions specified in SI 2012/57 arts 6 and 8)

Amendments Pending

Pt IV s. 31(6): words inserted by NHS Redress Act 2006 c. 44, s. 14(10) (date to be appointed)

Commencement

Pt IV s. 31(1)–(5)(b)(iii): March 1, 2000 (SI 2000/183 art. 2(1))

Extent

Pt IV s. 31(1)–(4)(a)(vi), (4)(b)–(4)(b)(iii), (5)–(5)(b)(iii): United Kingdom (subject to s.75(6)) Pt IV s. 31(4)(a)(vii), (4A)–(4C), (5A)–(8)(b): United Kingdom

32. *Journalism, literature and art.*

(1) Personal data which are processed only for the special purposes are exempt from any provision to which this subsection relates if—

   (a) the processing is undertaken with a view to the publication by any person of any journalistic, literary or artistic material,

   (b) the data controller reasonably believes that, having regard in particular to the special importance of the public interest in freedom of expression, publication would be in the public interest, and

   (c) the data controller reasonably believes that, in all the circumstances, compliance with that provision is incompatible with the special purposes.

(2) Subsection (1) relates to the provisions of—

   (a) the data protection principles except the seventh data protection principle,

   (b) section 7,

   (c) section 10,

   (d) section 12, and

   (dd) [. . .]1

   (e) section 14(1) to (3).

(3) In considering for the purposes of subsection (1)(b) whether the belief of a data controller that publication would be in the public interest was or is a reasonable one, regard may be had to his compliance with any code of practice which—

   (a) is relevant to the publication in question, and

   (b) is designated by the [Secretary of State] 2 by order for the purposes of this subsection.

(4) Where at any time ("the relevant time") in any proceedings against a data controller under [section 7(9), 10(4), 12(8) or 14] 3 or by virtue of section 13 the data controller claims, or it appears to the court, that any personal data to which the proceedings relate are being processed—

   (a) only for the special purposes, and

   (b) with a view to the publication by any person of any journalistic, literary or artistic material which, at the time twenty-four hours immediately before the relevant time, had not previously been published by the data controller,

the court shall stay the proceedings until either of the conditions in subsection (5) is met.

(5) Those conditions are—

   (a) that a determination of the Commissioner under section 45 with respect to the data in question takes effect, or

(b) in a case where the proceedings were stayed on the making of a claim, that the claim is withdrawn.

(6) For the purposes of this Act "publish", in relation to journalistic, literary or artistic material, means make available to the public or any section of the public.

Notes

1 Words repealed by Data Protection Act 1998 c. 29 Sch.13 para.2(a) (October 23, 2007)
2 Words substituted by Secretary of State for Constitutional Affairs Order 2003/1887 Sch.2 para.9(1)(a) (August 19, 2003)
3 Words repealed by Data Protection Act 1998 c. 29 Sch.13 para.2(b) (October 23, 2007)

Commencement

Pt IV s. 32(1)–(2)(e), (4)–(6): March 1, 2000 (SI 2000/183 art. 2(1))
Pt IV s. 32(3)–(3)(b): July 16, 1998 for the purpose of conferring power to make subordinate legislation; March 1, 2000 otherwise (SI 2000/183 art. 2(1); 1998 c. 29 Pt VI s. 75(2))

Extent

Pt IV s. 32(1)–(2)(d), (2)(e)–(6): United Kingdom (subject to s.75(6)) Pt IV s. 32(2)(dd): United Kingdom

33. *Research, history and statistics.*

(1) In this section—

"research purposes"includes statistical or historical purposes;

"the relevant conditions", in relation to any processing of personal data, means the conditions—

(a) that the data are not processed to support measures or decisions with respect to particular individuals, and

(b) that the data are not processed in such a way that substantial damage or substantial distress is, or is likely to be, caused to any data subject.

(2) For the purposes of the second data protection principle, the further processing of personal data only for research purposes in compliance with the relevant conditions is not to be regarded as incompatible with the purposes for which they were obtained.

(3) Personal data which are processed only for research purposes in compliance with the relevant conditions may, notwithstanding the fifth data protection principle, be kept indefinitely.

(4) Personal data which are processed only for research purposes are exempt from section 7 if—

(a) they are processed in compliance with the relevant conditions, and

(b) the results of the research or any resulting statistics are not made available in a form which identifies data subjects or any of them.

(5) For the purposes of subsections (2) to (4) personal data are not to be treated as processed otherwise than for research purposes merely because the data are disclosed—

(a) to any person, for research purposes only,

(b) to the data subject or a person acting on his behalf,

(c) at the request, or with the consent, of the data subject or a person acting on his behalf, or

(d) in circumstances in which the person making the disclosure has reasonable grounds for believing that the disclosure falls within paragraph (a), (b) or (c).

Commencement

Pt IV s. 33(1)–(5)(d): March 1, 2000 (SI 2000/183 art. 2(1))

Extent

Pt IV s. 33(1)–(5)(d): United Kingdom (subject to s.75(6))

[33A. *Manual data held by public authorities.*

(1) Personal data falling within paragraph (e) of the definition of "data" in section 1(1) are exempt from—

(a) the first, second, third, fifth, seventh and eighth data protection principles,

(b) the sixth data protection principle except so far as it relates to the rights conferred on data subjects by sections 7 and 14,

(c) sections 10 to 12,

(d) section 13, except so far as it relates to damage caused by a contravention of section 7 or of the fourth data protection principle and to any distress which is also suffered by reason of that contravention,

(e) Part III, and

(f) section 55.

(2) Personal data which fall within paragraph (e) of the definition of "data" in section 1(1) and relate to appointments or removals, pay, discipline, superannuation or other personnel matters, in relation to—

(a) service in any of the armed forces of the Crown,

(b) service in any office or employment under the Crown or under any public authority, or

(c) service in any office or employment, or under any contract for services, in respect of which power to take action, or to determine or approve the action taken, in such matters is vested in Her Majesty, any Minister of the Crown, the National Assembly for Wales, any Northern Ireland Minister (within the meaning of the Freedom of Information Act 2000) or any public authority,

are also exempt from the remaining data protection principles and the remaining provisions of Part II.

] [1]

Notes

[1]   Added by Freedom of Information Act 2000 c. 36 Pt VII s.70(1) (January 1, 2005 for purposes specified in SI 2004/1909 art.2(1); January 1, 2005 otherwise)

Extent

Pt IV s. 33A(1)–(2)(c): United Kingdom

34. *Information available to the public by or under enactment.*

Personal data are exempt from—

(a) the subject information provisions,

(b) the fourth data protection principle and [section 14(1) to (3)] **1** , and

(c) the non-disclosure provisions,

if the data consist of information which the data controller is obliged by or under any enactment [other than an enactment contained in the Freedom of Information Act 2000] **2** to make available to the public, whether by publishing it, by making it available for inspection, or otherwise and whether gratuitously or on payment of a fee.

Notes

1   Words substituted by Data Protection Act 1998 c. 29 Sch.13 para.3 (October 23, 2007)
2   Words inserted by Freedom of Information Act 2000 c. 36 Pt VII s.72 (November 30, 2002)

Commencement

Pt IV s. 34(a)–(c): March 1, 2000 (SI 2000/183 art. 2(1))

Extent

Pt IV s. 34(a)–(c): United Kingdom (subject to s.75(6))

35. *Disclosures required by law or made in connection with legal proceedings etc.*

(1) Personal data are exempt from the non-disclosure provisions where the disclosure is required by or under any enactment, by any rule of law or by the order of a court.

(2) Personal data are exempt from the non-disclosure provisions where the disclosure is necessary—

(a) for the purpose of, or in connection with, any legal proceedings (including prospective legal proceedings), or

(b) for the purpose of obtaining legal advice,

or is otherwise necessary for the purposes of establishing, exercising or defending legal rights.

Commencement

Pt IV s. 35(1)–(2)(b): March 1, 2000 (SI 2000/183 art. 2(1))

Extent

Pt IV s. 35(1)–(2)(b): United Kingdom (subject to s.75(6))

[**35A.** *Parliamentary privilege.*

Personal data are exempt from—

(a) the first data protection principle, except to the extent to which it requires compliance with the conditions in Schedules 2 and 3,

(b) the second, third, fourth and fifth data protection principles,

(c) section 7, and

(d) sections 10 and 14(1) to (3),

if the exemption is required for the purpose of avoiding an infringement of the privileges of either House of Parliament.

] [1]

Notes

[1] Added by Freedom of Information Act 2000 c. 36 Sch.6 para.2 (January 1, 2005 for purposes specified in SI 2004/1909 art.2(1); January 1, 2005 otherwise)

Extent

Pt IV s. 35A(a)–(d): United Kingdom

36. *Domestic purposes.*

Personal data processed by an individual only for the purposes of that individual's personal, family or household affairs (including recreational purposes) are exempt from the data protection principles and the provisions of Parts II and III.

Commencement

Pt IV s. 36: March 1, 2000 (SI 2000/183 art. 2(1))

Extent

Pt IV s. 36: United Kingdom (subject to s.75(6))

37. *Miscellaneous exemptions.*

Schedule 7 (which confers further miscellaneous exemptions) has effect.

Commencement

Pt IV s. 37: March 1, 2000 (SI 2000/183 art. 2(1))

Extent

Pt IV s. 37: United Kingdom (subject to s.75(6))

38. *Powers to make further exemptions by order.*

(1) The [Secretary of State] 1 may by order exempt from the subject information provisions personal data consisting of information the disclosure of which is prohibited or restricted by or under any enactment if and to the extent that he considers it necessary for the safeguarding of the interests of the data subject or the rights and freedoms of any other individual that the prohibition or restriction ought to prevail over those provisions.

(2) The [Secretary of State] [1] may by order exempt from the non-disclosure provi-

sions any disclosures of personal data made in circumstances specified in the order, if he considers the exemption is necessary for the safeguarding of the interests of the data subject or the rights and freedoms of any other individual.

Notes

1   Words substituted by Secretary of State for Constitutional Affairs Order 2003/1887 Sch.2 para.9(1)(a) (August 19, 2003)

Commencement

Pt IV s. 38(1)–(2): July 16, 1998 for the purpose of conferring power to make subordinate legislation; March 1, 2000 otherwise (SI 2000/183 art. 2(1))

Extent

Pt IV s. 38(1)–(2): United Kingdom (subject to s.75(6))

39. *Transitional relief.*

Schedule 8 (which confers transitional exemptions) has effect.

Commencement

Pt IV s. 39: March 1, 2000 (SI 2000/183 art. 2(1))

Extent

Pt IV s. 39: United Kingdom (subject to s.75(6))

PART V

ENFORCEMENT

40. *Enforcement notices.*

(1) If the Commissioner is satisfied that a data controller has contravened or is contravening any of the data protection principles, the Commissioner may serve him with a notice (in this Act referred to as "an enforcement notice") requiring him, for complying with the principle or principles in question, to do either or both of the following—

    (a) to take within such time as may be specified in the notice, or to refrain from taking after such time as may be so specified, such steps as are so specified, or

    (b) to refrain from processing any personal data, or any personal data of a description specified in the notice, or to refrain from processing them for a purpose so specified or in a manner so specified, after such time as may be so specified.

(2) In deciding whether to serve an enforcement notice, the Commissioner shall consider whether the contravention has caused or is likely to cause any person damage or distress.

(3) An enforcement notice in respect of a contravention of the fourth data protection principle which requires the data controller to rectify, block, erase or destroy any

inaccurate data may also require the data controller to rectify, block, erase or destroy any other data held by him and containing an expression of opinion which appears to the Commissioner to be based on the inaccurate data.

(4) An enforcement notice in respect of a contravention of the fourth data protection principle, in the case of data which accurately record information received or obtained by the data controller from the data subject or a third party, may require the data controller either—

    (a) to rectify, block, erase or destroy any inaccurate data and any other data held by him and containing an expression of opinion as mentioned in subsection (3), or

    (b) to take such steps as are specified in the notice for securing compliance with the requirements specified in paragraph 7 of Part II of Schedule 1 and, if the Commissioner thinks fit, for supplementing the data with such statement of the true facts relating to the matters dealt with by the data as the Commissioner may approve.

(5) Where—

    (a) an enforcement notice requires the data controller to rectify, block, erase or destroy any personal data, or

    (b) the Commissioner is satisfied that personal data which have been rectified, blocked, erased or destroyed had been processed in contravention of any of the data protection principles,

an enforcement notice may, if reasonably practicable, require the data controller to notify third parties to whom the data have been disclosed of the rectification, blocking, erasure or destruction; and in determining whether it is reasonably practicable to require such notification regard shall be had, in particular, to the number of persons who would have to be notified.

(6) An enforcement notice must contain—

    (a) a statement of the data protection principle or principles which the Commissioner is satisfied have been or are being contravened and his reasons for reaching that conclusion, and

    (b) particulars of the rights of appeal conferred by section 48.

(7) Subject to subsection (8), an enforcement notice must not require any of the provisions of the notice to be complied with before the end of the period within which an appeal can be brought against the notice and, if such an appeal is brought, the notice need not be complied with pending the determination or withdrawal of the appeal.

(8) If by reason of special circumstances the Commissioner considers that an enforcement notice should be complied with as a matter of urgency he may include in the notice a statement to that effect and a statement of his reasons for reaching that conclusion; and in that event subsection (7) shall not apply but the notice must not require the provisions of the notice to be complied with before the end of the period of seven days beginning with the day on which the notice is served.

(9) Notification regulations (as defined by section 16(2)) may make provision as to the effect of the service of an enforcement notice on any entry in the register maintained under section 19 which relates to the person on whom the notice is served.

(10) This section has effect subject to section 46(1).

Commencement

Pt V s. 40(1)–(8), (10): March 1, 2000 (SI 2000/183 art. 2(1))
Pt V s. 40(9): July 16, 1998 for the purpose of conferring power to make subordinate legislation; March 1, 2000 otherwise (SI 2000/183 art. 2(1); 1998 c. 29 Pt VI s. 75(2))

Extent

Pt V s. 40(1)–(10): United Kingdom (subject to s.75(6))

41. *Cancellation of enforcement notice.*

(1) If the Commissioner considers that all or any of the provisions of an enforcement notice need not be complied with in order to ensure compliance with the data protection principle or principles to which it relates, he may cancel or vary the notice by written notice to the person on whom it was served.

(2) A person on whom an enforcement notice has been served may, at any time after the expiry of the period during which an appeal can be brought against that notice, apply in writing to the Commissioner for the cancellation or variation of that notice on the ground that, by reason of a change of circumstances, all or any of the provisions of that notice need not be complied with in order to ensure compliance with the data protection principle or principles to which that notice relates.

Commencement

Pt V s. 41(1)–(2): March 1, 2000 (SI 2000/183 art. 2(1))

Extent

Pt V s. 41(1)–(2): United Kingdom (subject to s.75(6))

[41A *Assessment notices*

(1) The Commissioner may serve a data controller within subsection (2) with a notice (in this Act referred to as an "assessment notice") for the purpose of enabling the Commissioner to determine whether the data controller has complied or is complying with the data protection principles.

(2) A data controller is within this subsection if the data controller is—

   (a) a government department,

   (b) a public authority designated for the purposes of this section by an order made by the Secretary of State, or

   (c) a person of a description designated for the purposes of this section by such an order.

(3) An assessment notice is a notice which requires the data controller to do all or any of the following—

   (a) permit the Commissioner to enter any specified premises;

   (b) direct the Commissioner to any documents on the premises that are of a specified description;

   (c) assist the Commissioner to view any information of a specified description that is capable of being viewed using equipment on the premises;

(d) comply with any request from the Commissioner for—

    (i) a copy of any of the documents to which the Commissioner is directed;

    (ii) a copy (in such form as may be requested) of any of the information which the Commissioner is assisted to view;

(e) direct the Commissioner to any equipment or other material on the premises which is of a specified description;

(f) permit the Commissioner to inspect or examine any of the documents, information, equipment or material to which the Commissioner is directed or which the Commissioner is assisted to view;

(g) permit the Commissioner to observe the processing of any personal data that takes place on the premises;

(h) make available for interview by the Commissioner a specified number of persons of a specified description who process personal data on behalf of the data controller (or such number as are willing to be interviewed).

(4) In subsection (3) references to the Commissioner include references to the Commissioner's officers and staff.

(5) An assessment notice must, in relation to each requirement imposed by the notice, specify—

(a) the time at which the requirement is to be complied with, or

(b) the period during which the requirement is to be complied with.

(6) An assessment notice must also contain particulars of the rights of appeal conferred by section 48.

(7) The Commissioner may cancel an assessment notice by written notice to the data controller on whom it was served.

(8) Where a public authority has been designated by an order under subsection (2)(b) the Secretary of State must reconsider, at intervals of no greater than 5 years, whether it continues to be appropriate for the authority to be designated.

(9) The Secretary of State may not make an order under subsection (2)(c) which designates a description of persons unless—

(a) the Commissioner has made a recommendation that the description be designated, and

(b) the Secretary of State has consulted—

    (i) such persons as appear to the Secretary of State to represent the interests of those that meet the description;

    (ii) such other persons as the Secretary of State considers appropriate.

(10) The Secretary of State may not make an order under subsection (2)(c), and the Commissioner may not make a recommendation under subsection (9)(a), unless the Secretary of State or (as the case may be) the Commissioner is satisfied that it is necessary for the description of persons in question to be designated having regard to—

(a) the nature and quantity of data under the control of such persons, and

(b) any damage or distress which may be caused by a contravention by such persons of the data protection principles.

(11) Where a description of persons has been designated by an order under subsection (2)(c) the Secretary of State must reconsider, at intervals of no greater than 5 years, whether it continues to be necessary for the description to be designated having regard to the matters mentioned in subsection (10).

(12) In this section—

"public authority"includes any body, office-holder or other person in respect of which—

(a) an order may be made under section 4 or 5 of the Freedom of Information Act 2000, or

(b) an order may be made under section 4 or 5 of the Freedom of Information (Scotland) Act 2002;

"specified" means specified in an assessment notice.

]¹

Notes

¹ Added by Coroners and Justice Act 2009 c. 25 Pt 8 s.173 (April 6, 2010 as SI 2010/816)

Extent

Pt V s. 41A(1)–(12) definition of "specified": England, Wales

[41B Assessment notices: limitations

(1) A time specified in an assessment notice under section 41A(5) in relation to a requirement must not fall, and a period so specified must not begin, before the end of the period within which an appeal can be brought against the notice, and if such an appeal is brought the requirement need not be complied with pending the determination or withdrawal of the appeal.

(2) If by reason of special circumstances the Commissioner considers that it is necessary for the data controller to comply with a requirement in an assessment notice as a matter of urgency, the Commissioner may include in the notice a statement to that effect and a statement of the reasons for that conclusion; and in that event subsection (1) applies in relation to the requirement as if for the words from "within" to the end there were substituted "of 7 days beginning with the day on which the notice is served".

(3) A requirement imposed by an assessment notice does not have effect in so far as compliance with it would result in the disclosure of—

(a) any communication between a professional legal adviser and the adviser's client in connection with the giving of legal advice with respect to the client's obligations, liabilities or rights under this Act, or

(b) any communication between a professional legal adviser and the adviser's client, or between such an adviser or the adviser's client and any other person, made in connection with or in contemplation of proceedings under or arising out of this Act (including proceedings before the Tribunal) and for the purposes of such proceedings.

(4) In subsection (3) references to the client of a professional legal adviser include references to any person representing such a client.

(5) Nothing in section 41A authorises the Commissioner to serve an assessment notice on—

(a) a judge,

(b) a body specified in section 23(3) of the Freedom of Information Act 2000 (bodies dealing with security matters), or

(c) the Office for Standards in Education, Children's Services and Skills in so far as it is a data controller in respect of information processed for the purposes of functions exercisable by Her Majesty's Chief Inspector of Eduction, Children's Services and Skills by virtue of section 5(1)(a) of the Care Standards Act 2000.

(6) In this section "judge"includes—

(a) a justice of the peace (or, in Northern Ireland, a lay magistrate),

(b) a member of a tribunal, and

(c) a clerk or other officer entitled to exercise the jurisdiction of a court or tribunal;

and in this subsection "tribunal" means any tribunal in which legal proceedings may be brought.

] [1]

Notes

[1] Added by Coroners and Justice Act 2009 c. 25 Pt 8 s.173 (April 6, 2010 as SI 2010/816)

Extent

Pt V s. 41B(1)–(6)(c): England, Wales

[41C *Code of practice about assessment notices*

(1) The Commissioner must prepare and issue a code of practice as to the manner in which the Commissioner's functions under and in connection with section 41A are to be exercised.

(2) The code must in particular—

(a) specify factors to be considered in determining whether to serve an assessment notice on a data controller;

(b) specify descriptions of documents and information that—

(i) are not to be examined or inspected in pursuance of an assessment notice, or

(ii) are to be so examined or inspected only by persons of a description specified in the code;

(c) deal with the nature of inspections and examinations carried out in pursuance of an assessment notice;

(d) deal with the nature of interviews carried out in pursuance of an assessment notice;

(e) deal with the preparation, issuing and publication by the Commissioner of assessment reports in respect of data controllers that have been served with assessment notices.

(3) The provisions of the code made by virtue of subsection (2)(b) must, in particular, include provisions that relate to—

(a) documents and information concerning an individual's physical or mental health;

(b) documents and information concerning the provision of social care for an individual.

(4) An assessment report is a report which contains—

    (a) a determination as to whether a data controller has complied or is complying with the data protection principles,

    (b) recommendations as to any steps which the data controller ought to take, or refrain from taking, to ensure compliance with any of those principles, and

    (c) such other matters as are specified in the code. (5) The Commissioner may alter or replace the code.

(6) If the code is altered or replaced, the Commissioner must issue the altered or replacement code.

(7) The Commissioner may not issue the code (or an altered or replacement code) without the approval of the Secretary of State.

(8) The Commissioner must arrange for the publication of the code (and any altered or replacement code) issued under this section in such form and manner as the Commissioner considers appropriate.

(9) In this section "social care"has the same meaning as in Part 1 of the Health and Social Care Act 2008 (see section 9(3) of that Act).

] [1]

Notes

[1]   Added by Coroners and Justice Act 2009 c. 25 Pt 8 s.173 (February 1, 2010 as SI 2010/145)

Amendments Pending

Pt V s. 41C(7): substituted by Protection of Freedoms Act 2012 c. 9, Pt 6 s. 106(1) (date to be appointed)

Extent

Pt V s. 41C(1)–(9): England, Wales

42. *Request for assessment.*

(1) A request may be made to the Commissioner by or on behalf of any person who is, or believes himself to be, directly affected by any processing of personal data for an assessment as to whether it is likely or unlikely that the processing has been or is being carried out in compliance with the provisions of this Act.

(2) On receiving a request under this section, the Commissioner shall make an assessment in such manner as appears to him to be appropriate, unless he has not been supplied with such information as he may reasonably require in order to—

    (a) satisfy himself as to the identity of the person making the request, and

    (b) enable him to identify the processing in question.

(3) The matters to which the Commissioner may have regard in determining in what manner it is appropriate to make an assessment include—

    (a) the extent to which the request appears to him to raise a matter of substance,

    (b) any undue delay in making the request, and

    (c) whether or not the person making the request is entitled to make an application under section 7 in respect of the personal data in question.

(4) Where the Commissioner has received a request under this section he shall notify the person who made the request—

    (a) whether he has made an assessment as a result of the request, and

    (b) to the extent that he considers appropriate, having regard in particular to any exemption from section 7 applying in relation to the personal data concerned, of any view formed or action taken as a result of the request.

Commencement

Pt V s. 42(1)–(4)(b): March 1, 2000 (SI 2000/183 art. 2(1))

Extent

Pt V s. 42(1)–(4)(b): United Kingdom (subject to s.75(6))

43. *Information notices.*

(1) If the Commissioner—

    (a) has received a request under section 42 in respect of any processing of personal data, or

    (b) reasonably requires any information for the purpose of determining whether the data controller has complied or is complying with the data protection principles,

he may serve the data controller with a notice (in this Act referred to as "an information notice") requiring the data controller [to furnish the Commissioner with specified information relating to the request or to compliance with the principles] 1 .

[(1A) In subsection (1) "specified information" means information—

    (a) specified, or described, in the information notice, or

    (b) falling within a category which is specified, or described, in the information notice.

(1B) The Commissioner may also specify in the information notice—

    (a) the form in which the information must be furnished;

    (b) the period within which, or the time and place at which, the information must be furnished.

] 2

(2) An information notice must contain—

    (a) in a case falling within subsection (1)(a), a statement that the Commissioner has received a request under section 42 in relation to the specified processing, or

    (b) in a case falling within subsection (1)(b), a statement that the Commissioner regards the specified information as relevant for the purpose of determining whether the data controller has complied, or is complying, with the data protection principles and his reasons for regarding it as relevant for that purpose.

(3) An information notice must also contain particulars of the rights of appeal conferred by section 48.

(4) Subject to subsection (5), [a period specified in an information notice under subsection (1B)(b) must not end, and a time so specified must not fall,] 3 before the end of the period within which an appeal can be brought against the notice and, if such an

appeal is brought, the information need not be furnished pending the determination or withdrawal of the appeal.

(5) If by reason of special circumstances the Commissioner considers that the information is required as a matter of urgency, he may include in the notice a statement to that effect and a statement of his reasons for reaching that conclusion; and in that event subsection (4) shall not apply, but the notice shall not require the information to be furnished before the end of the period of seven days beginning with the day on which the notice is served.

(6) A person shall not be required by virtue of this section to furnish the Commissioner with any information in respect of—

(a) any communication between a professional legal adviser and his client in connection with the giving of legal advice to the client with respect to his obligations, liabilities or rights under this Act, or

(b) any communication between a professional legal adviser and his client, or between such an adviser or his client and any other person, made in connection with or in contemplation of proceedings under or arising out of this Act (including proceedings before the Tribunal) and for the purposes of such proceedings.

(7) In subsection (6) references to the client of a professional legal adviser include references to any person representing such a client.

(8) A person shall not be required by virtue of this section to furnish the Commissioner with any information if the furnishing of that information would, by revealing evidence of the commission of any offence [, other than an offence under this Act or an offence within subsection (8A),] [4] expose him to proceedings for that offence.

[(8A) The offences mentioned in subsection (8) are —

(a) an offence under section 5 of the Perjury Act 1911 (false statements made otherwise than on oath),

(b) an offence under section 44(2) of the Criminal Law (Consolidation) (Scotland) Act 1995 (false statements made otherwise than on oath), or

(c) an offence under Article 10 of the Perjury (Northern Ireland) Order 1979 (false statutory declarations and other false unsworn statements).

(8B) Any relevant statement provided by a person in response to a requirement under this section may not be used in evidence against that person on a prosecution for any offence under this Act (other than an offence under section 47) unless in the proceedings—

(a) in giving evidence the person provides information inconsistent with it, and

(b) evidence relating to it is adduced, or a question relating to it is asked, by that person or on that person's behalf.

(8C) In subsection (8B) "relevant statement", in relation to a requirement under this section, means—

(a) an oral statement, or

(b) a written statement made for the purposes of the requirement.

] [5]

(9) The Commissioner may cancel an information notice by written notice to the person on whom it was served.

(10) This section has effect subject to section 46(3).

Notes

1 Words substituted by Coroners and Justice Act 2009 c. 25 Sch.20(3) para.8(2) (April 6, 2010)
2 Added by Coroners and Justice Act 2009 c. 25 Sch.20(3) para.8(3) (April 6, 2010)
3 Words substituted by Coroners and Justice Act 2009 c. 25 Sch.20(3) para.8(4) (April 6, 2010)
4 Words substituted by Coroners and Justice Act 2009 c. 25 Sch.20(4) para.10(2) (April 6, 2010)
5 Added by Coroners and Justice Act 2009 c. 25 Sch.20(4) para.10(3) (April 6, 2010)

Commencement

Pt V s. 43(1)–(10): March 1, 2000 (SI 2000/183 art. 2(1))

Extent

Pt V s. 43(1)–(1)(b), (2)–(8), (9)–(10): United Kingdom (subject to s.75(6)) Pt V s. 43(1A)–(1B)(b), (8A)–(8C)(b): United Kingdom

44. *Special information notices.*

(1) If the Commissioner—

(a) has received a request under section 42 in respect of any processing of personal data, or

(b) has reasonable grounds for suspecting that, in a case in which proceedings have been stayed under section 32, the personal data to which the proceedings relate—

(i) are not being processed only for the special purposes, or
(ii) are not being processed with a view to the publication by any person of any journalistic, literary or artistic material which has not previously been published by the data controller,

he may serve the data controller with a notice (in this Act referred to as a "special information notice") requiring the data controller [to furnish the Commissioner with specified information for the purpose specified in subsection (2).] 1

[(1A) In subsection (1) "specified information" means information—

(a) specified, or described, in the special information notice, or

(b) falling within a category which is specified, or described, in the special information notice.

(1B) The Commissioner may also specify in the special information notice—

(a) the form in which the information must be furnished;

(b) the period within which, or the time and place at which, the information must be furnished.

]2

(2) That purpose is the purpose of ascertaining—

(a) whether the personal data are being processed only for the special purposes, or

(b) whether they are being processed with a view to the publication by any person of any journalistic, literary or artistic material which has not previously been published by the data controller.

(3) A special information notice must contain—

(a) in a case falling within paragraph (a) of subsection (1), a statement that the Commissioner has received a request under section 42 in relation to the specified processing, or

(b) in a case falling within paragraph (b) of that subsection, a statement of the Commissioner's grounds for suspecting that the personal data are not being processed as mentioned in that paragraph.

(4) A special information notice must also contain particulars of the rights of appeal conferred by section 48.

(5) Subject to subsection (6), [a period specified in a special information notice under subsection (1B)(b) must not end, and a time so specified must not fall,]³ before the end of the period within which an appeal can be brought against the notice and, if such an appeal is brought, the information need not be furnished pending the determination or withdrawal of the appeal.

(6) If by reason of special circumstances the Commissioner considers that the information is required as a matter of urgency, he may include in the notice a statement to that effect and a statement of his reasons for reaching that conclusion; and in that event subsection (5) shall not apply, but the notice shall not require the information to be furnished before the end of the period of seven days beginning with the day on which the notice is served.

(7) A person shall not be required by virtue of this section to furnish the Commissioner with any information in respect of—

(a) any communication between a professional legal adviser and his client in connection with the giving of legal advice to the client with respect to his obligations, liabilities or rights under this Act, or

(b) any communication between a professional legal adviser and his client, or between such an adviser or his client and any other person, made in connection with or in contemplation of proceedings under or arising out of this Act (including proceedings before the Tribunal) and for the purposes of such proceedings.

(8) In subsection (7) references to the client of a professional legal adviser include references to any person representing such a client.

(9) A person shall not be required by virtue of this section to furnish the Commissioner with any information if the furnishing of that information would, by revealing evidence of the commission of any offence [, other than an offence under this Act or an offence within subsection (9A),]⁴ expose him to proceedings for that offence.

[(9A) The offences mentioned in subsection (9) are—

(a) an offence under section 5 of the Perjury Act 1911 (false statements made otherwise than on oath),

(b) an offence under section 44(2) of the Criminal Law (Consolidation) (Scotland) Act 1995 (false statements made otherwise than on oath), or

(c) an offence under Article 10 of the Perjury (Northern Ireland) Order 1979 (false statutory declarations and other false unsworn statements).

(9B) Any relevant statement provided by a person in response to a requirement under this section may not be used in evidence against that person on a prosecution for any offence under this Act (other than an offence under section 47) unless in the proceedings—

(a) in giving evidence the person provides information inconsistent with it, and

(b) evidence relating to it is adduced, or a question relating to it is asked, by that person or on that person's behalf.

(9C) In subsection (9B) "relevant statement", in relation to a requirement under this section, means—

(a) an oral statement, or

(b) a written statement made for the purposes of the requirement.

] [5]

(10) The Commissioner may cancel a special information notice by written notice to the person on whom it was served.

Notes

[1] Words substituted by Coroners and Justice Act 2009 c. 25 Sch.20(3) para.9(2) (April 6, 2010)
[2] Added by Coroners and Justice Act 2009 c. 25 Sch.20(3) para.9(3) (April 6, 2010)
[3] Words substituted by Coroners and Justice Act 2009 c. 25 Sch.20(3) para.9(4) (April 6, 2010)
[4] Words substituted by Coroners and Justice Act 2009 c. 25 Sch.20(4) para.11(2) (April 6, 2010)
[5] Added by Coroners and Justice Act 2009 c. 25 Sch.20(4) para.11(3) (April 6, 2010)

Commencement

Pt V s. 44(1)–(10): March 1, 2000 (SI 2000/183 art. 2(1))

Extent

Pt V s. 44(1)–(1)(b)(ii), (2)–(9), (10): United Kingdom (subject to s.75(6)) Pt V s. 44(1A)–(1B)(b), (9A)–(9C)(b): United Kingdom

45. *Determination by Commissioner as to the special purposes.*

(1) Where at any time it appears to the Commissioner (whether as a result of the service of a special information notice or otherwise) that any personal data—

(a) are not being processed only for the special purposes, or

(b) are not being processed with a view to the publication by any person of any journalistic, literary or artistic material which has not previously been published by the data controller,

he may make a determination in writing to that effect.

(2) Notice of the determination shall be given to the data controller; and the notice must contain particulars of the right of appeal conferred by section 48.

(3) A determination under subsection (1) shall not take effect until the end of the period within which an appeal can be brought and, where an appeal is brought, shall not take effect pending the determination or withdrawal of the appeal.

Commencement

Pt V s. 45(1)–(3): March 1, 2000 (SI 2000/183 art. 2(1))

Extent

Pt V s. 45(1)–(3): United Kingdom (subject to s.75(6))

46. *Restriction on enforcement in case of processing for the special purposes.*

(1) The Commissioner may not at any time serve an enforcement notice on a data controller with respect to the processing of personal data for the special purposes unless—

(a) a determination under section 45(1) with respect to those data has taken effect, and

(b) the court has granted leave for the notice to be served.

(2) The court shall not grant leave for the purposes of subsection (1)(b) unless it is satisfied—

(a) that the Commissioner has reason to suspect a contravention of the data protection principles which is of substantial public importance, and

(b) except where the case is one of urgency, that the data controller has been given notice, in accordance with rules of court, of the application for leave.

(3) The Commissioner may not serve an information notice on a data controller with respect to the processing of personal data for the special purposes unless a determination under section 45(1) with respect to those data has taken effect.

Commencement

Pt V s. 46(1)–(3): March 1, 2000 (SI 2000/183 art. 2(1))

Extent

Pt V s. 46(1)–(3): United Kingdom (subject to s.75(6))

47. *Failure to comply with notice.*

(1) A person who fails to comply with an enforcement notice, an information notice or a special information notice is guilty of an offence.

(2) A person who, in purported compliance with an information notice or a special information notice—

(a) makes a statement which he knows to be false in a material respect, or

(b) recklessly makes a statement which is false in a material respect, is guilty of an offence.

(3) It is a defence for a person charged with an offence under subsection (1) to prove that he exercised all due diligence to comply with the notice in question.

Commencement

Pt V s. 47(1)–(3): March 1, 2000 (SI 2000/183 art. 2(1))

Extent

Pt V s. 47(1)–(3): United Kingdom (subject to s.75(6))

48. *Rights of appeal.*

(1) A person on whom an enforcement notice [, an assessment notice] 1 , an information notice or a special information notice has been served may appeal to the Tribunal against the notice.

(2) A person on whom an enforcement notice has been served may appeal to the Tribunal against the refusal of an application under section 41(2) for cancellation or variation of the notice.

(3) Where an enforcement notice [, an assessment notice] 2 , an information notice or a special information notice contains a statement by the Commissioner in accordance with [section 40(8),

41B(2), 43(5) or 44(6)] 3 then, whether or not the person appeals against the notice, he may appeal against—

(a) the Commissioner's decision to include the statement in the notice, or

(b) the effect of the inclusion of the statement as respects any part of the notice.

(4) A data controller in respect of whom a determination has been made under section 45 may appeal to the Tribunal against the determination.

(5) Schedule 6 has effect in relation to appeals under this section and the proceedings of the Tribunal in respect of any such appeal.

Notes

1 Words inserted by Coroners and Justice Act 2009 c. 25 Sch.20(2) para.5(2) (April 6, 2010)
2 Words inserted by Coroners and Justice Act 2009 c. 25 Sch.20(2) para.5(3)(a) (April 6, 2010)
3 Word inserted by Coroners and Justice Act 2009 c. 25 Sch.20(2) para.5(3)(b) (April 6, 2010)

Commencement

Pt V s. 48(1)–(5): March 1, 2000 (SI 2000/183 art. 2(1))

Extent

Pt V s. 48(1)–(5): United Kingdom (subject to s.75(6))

49. *Determination of appeals.*

(1) If on an appeal under section 48(1) the Tribunal considers—

(a) that the notice against which the appeal is brought is not in accordance with the law, or

(b) to the extent that the notice involved an exercise of discretion by the Commissioner, that he ought to have exercised his discretion differently,

the Tribunal shall allow the appeal or substitute such other notice or decision as could have been served or made by the Commissioner; and in any other case the Tribunal shall dismiss the appeal.

(2) On such an appeal, the Tribunal may review any determination of fact on which the notice in question was based.

(3) If on an appeal under section 48(2) the Tribunal considers that the enforcement notice ought to be cancelled or varied by reason of a change in circumstances, the Tribunal shall cancel or vary the notice.

(4) On an appeal under subsection (3) of section 48 the Tribunal may direct—

(a) that the notice in question shall have effect as if it did not contain any such statement as is mentioned in that subsection, or

(b) that the inclusion of the statement shall not have effect in relation to any part of the notice,

and may make such modifications in the notice as may be required for giving effect to the direction.

(5) On an appeal under section 48(4), the Tribunal may cancel the determination of the Commissioner.

(6)–(7) [. . .]¹

Notes

¹   Repealed by Transfer of Tribunal Functions Order 2010/22 Sch.2 para.27 (January 18, 2010)

Commencement

Pt V s. 49(1)–(7)(b): March 1, 2000 (SI 2000/183 art. 2(1))

Extent

Pt V s. 49(1)–(7)(b): United Kingdom (subject to s.75(6))

50.*Powers of entry and inspection.*

Schedule 9 (powers of entry and inspection) has effect.

Commencement

Pt V s. 50: March 1, 2000 (SI 2000/183 art. 2(1))

Extent

Pt V s. 50: United Kingdom (subject to s.75(6))

PART VI

MISCELLANEOUS AND GENERAL

Functions of Commissioner

51.— *General duties of Commissioner.*

(1) It shall be the duty of the Commissioner to promote the following of good practice by data controllers and, in particular, so to perform his functions under this Act as to promote the observance of the requirements of this Act by data controllers.

(2) The Commissioner shall arrange for the dissemination in such form and manner as he considers appropriate of such information as it may appear to him expedient to give to the public about the operation of this Act, about good practice, and about

other matters within the scope of his functions under this Act, and may give advice to any person as to any of those matters.

(3) Where—

(a) the [Secretary of State] 1 so directs by order, or

(b) the Commissioner considers it appropriate to do so,

the Commissioner shall, after such consultation with trade associations, data subjects or persons representing data subjects as appears to him to be appropriate, prepare and disseminate to such persons as he considers appropriate codes of practice for guidance as to good practice.

(4) The Commissioner shall also—

(a) where he considers it appropriate to do so, encourage trade associations to prepare, and to disseminate to their members, such codes of practice, and

(b) where any trade association submits a code of practice to him for his consideration, consider the code and, after such consultation with data subjects or persons representing data subjects as appears to him to be appropriate, notify the trade association whether in his opinion the code promotes the following of good practice.

(5) An order under subsection (3) shall describe the personal data or processing to which the code of practice is to relate, and may also describe the persons or classes of persons to whom it is to relate.

[(5A) In determining the action required to discharge the duties imposed by subsections (1) to (4), the Commissioner may take account of any action taken to discharge the duty imposed by section 52A (data-sharing code).] 2

(6) The Commissioner shall arrange for the dissemination in such form and manner as he considers appropriate of—

(a) any Community finding as defined by paragraph 15(2) of Part II of Schedule 1,

(b) any decision of the European Commission, under the procedure provided for in Article 31(2) of the Data Protection Directive, which is made for the purposes of Article 26(3) or (4) of the Directive, and

(c) such other information as it may appear to him to be expedient to give to data controllers in relation to any personal data about the protection of the rights and freedoms of data subjects in relation to the processing of personal data in countries and territories outside the European Economic Area.

(7) The Commissioner may, with the consent of the data controller, assess any processing of personal data for the following of good practice and shall inform the data controller of the results of the assessment.

(8) The Commissioner may charge such sums as he may with the consent of the [Secretary of State] 1 determine for any services provided by the Commissioner by virtue of this Part.

(9) In this section—

"good practice" means such practice in the processing of personal data as appears to the Commissioner to be desirable having regard to the interests of data subjects and others, and includes (but is not limited to) compliance with the requirements of this Act;

"trade association"includes any body representing data controllers.

Notes

1   Words substituted by Secretary of State for Constitutional Affairs Order 2003/1887 Sch.2 para.9(1)(a) (August 19, 2003)
2   Added by Coroners and Justice Act 2009 c. 25 Pt 8 s.174(2) (February 1, 2010)

Amendments Pending

Pt VI s. 51(8A)–(8B): added by Protection of Freedoms Act 2012 c. 9, Pt 6 s. 107(1)(b) (date to be appointed)
Pt VI s. 51(8): words repealed by Protection of Freedoms Act 2012 c. 9, Sch. 10(8) para. 1 (date to be appointed) Pt VI s. 51(8): word inserted by Protection of Freedoms Act 2012 c. 9, Pt 6 s. 107(1) (a)(ii) (date to be appointed)

Commencement

Pt VI s. 51(1)–(2), (4)–(9) definition of "trade association": March 1, 2000 (SI 2000/183 art. 2(1))
Pt VI s. 51(3)–(3)(b): July 16, 1998 for the purpose of conferring power to make subordinate legislation; March 1, 2000 otherwise (SI 2000/183 art. 2(1); 1998 c. 29 Pt VI s. 75(2))

Extent

Pt VI s. 51(1)–(5), (6)–(8), (9)–(9) definition of "trade association": United Kingdom (subject to s.75(6)) Pt VI s. 51(5A), (8A)–(8B): United Kingdom

52. *Reports and codes of practice to be laid before Parliament.*

(1) The Commissioner shall lay annually before each House of Parliament a general report on the exercise of his functions under this Act.

(2) The Commissioner may from time to time lay before each House of Parliament such other reports with respect to those functions as he thinks fit.

(3) The Commissioner shall lay before each House of Parliament any code of practice prepared under section 51(3) for complying with a direction of the [Secretary of State] [1] , unless the code is included in any report laid under subsection (1) or (2).

Notes

1   Words substituted by Secretary of State for Constitutional Affairs Order 2003/1887 Sch.2 para.9(1)(a) (August 19, 2003)

Commencement

Pt VI s. 52(1)–(3): March 1, 2000 (SI 2000/183 art. 2(1))

Extent

Pt VI s. 52(1)–(3): United Kingdom (subject to s.75(6))

[52A *Data-sharing code*

(1) The Commissioner must prepare a code of practice which contains—

(a) practical guidance in relation to the sharing of personal data in accordance with the requirements of this Act, and

(b) such other guidance as the Commissioner considers appropriate to promote good practice in the sharing of personal data.

(2) For this purpose "good practice" means such practice in the sharing of personal data as appears to the Commissioner to be desirable having regard to the interests of data subjects and others, and includes (but is not limited to) compliance with the requirements of this Act.

(3) Before a code is prepared under this section, the Commissioner must consult such of the following as the Commissioner considers appropriate—

(a) trade associations (within the meaning of section 51);

(b) data subjects;

(c) persons who appear to the Commissioner to represent the interests of data subjects.

(4) In this section a reference to the sharing of personal data is to the disclosure of the data by transmission, dissemination or otherwise making it available.

]¹

Notes

¹ Added by Coroners and Justice Act 2009 c. 25 Pt 8 s.174(1) (February 1, 2010)

Extent

Pt VI s. 52A(1)–(4): England, Wales

[52B *Data-sharing code: procedure*

(1) When a code is prepared under section 52A, it must be submitted to the Secretary of State for approval.

(2) Approval may be withheld only if it appears to the Secretary of State that the terms of the code could result in the United Kingdom being in breach of any of its [EU]² obligations or any other international obligation.

(3) The Secretary of State must—

(a) if approval is withheld, publish details of the reasons for withholding it;

(b) if approval is granted, lay the code before Parliament.

(4) If, within the 40-day period, either House of Parliament resolves not to approve the code, the code is not to be issued by the Commissioner.

(5) If no such resolution is made within that period, the Commissioner must issue the code. (6) Where—

(a) the Secretary of State withholds approval, or

(b) such a resolution is passed, the Commissioner must prepare another code of practice under section 52A.

(7) Subsection (4) does not prevent a new code being laid before Parliament.

(8) A code comes into force at the end of the period of 21 days beginning with the day on which it is issued.

(9) A code may include transitional provision or savings.

(10) In this section "the 40-day period" means the period of 40 days beginning with the day on which the code is laid before Parliament (or, if it is not laid before each House of Parliament on the same day, the later of the 2 days on which it is laid).

(11) In calculating the 40-day period, no account is to be taken of any period during which Parliament is dissolved or prorogued or during which both Houses are adjourned for more than 4 days.

]¹

Notes

¹ Added by Coroners and Justice Act 2009 c. 25 Pt 8 s.174(1) (February 1, 2010)
² Word substituted by Treaty of Lisbon (Changes in Terminology) Order 2011/1043 Pt 2 art.6(1)(e) (April 22, 2011)

Amendments Pending

Pt VI s. 52B(6): words substituted by Protection of Freedoms Act 2012 c. 9, Pt 6 s. 106(2)(b) (date to be appointed) Pt VI s. 52B(1)–(3): s.52B(1) and (2) substituted for s.52B(1)–(3) by Protection of Freedoms Act 2012 c. 9, Pt 6 s.106(2)(a) (date to be appointed)

Extent

Pt VI s. 52B(1)–(11): England, Wales

[52C *Alteration or replacement of data-sharing code*

(1) The Commissioner—

(a) must keep the data-sharing code under review, and

(b) may prepare an alteration to that code or a replacement code.

(2) Where, by virtue of a review under subsection (1)(a) or otherwise, the Commissioner becomes aware that the terms of the code could result in the United Kingdom being in breach of any of its [EU] 2 obligations or any other international obligation, the Commissioner must exercise the power under subsection (1)(b) with a view to remedying the situation.

(3) Before an alteration or replacement code is prepared under subsection (1), the Commissioner must consult such of the following as the Commissioner considers appropriate—

(a) trade associations (within the meaning of section 51);

(b) data subjects;

(c) persons who appear to the Commissioner to represent the interests of data subjects.

(4) Section 52B (other than subsection (6)) applies to an alteration or replacement code prepared under this section as it applies to the code as first prepared under section 52A.

(5) In this section "the data-sharing code" means the code issued under section 52B(5) (as altered or replaced from time to time).

]¹

Notes

¹ Added by Coroners and Justice Act 2009 c. 25 Pt 8 s.174(1) (February 1, 2010)
² Substituted by Treaty of Lisbon (Changes in Terminology) Order 2011/1043 Pt 2 art.6(1)(e) (April 22, 2011)

Extent

Pt VI s. 52C(1)–(5): England, Wales

[52D *Publication of data-sharing code*

(1) The Commissioner must publish the code (and any replacement code) issued under section 52B(5).

(2) Where an alteration is so issued, the Commissioner must publish either—

(a) the alteration, or

(b) the code or replacement code as altered by it.

]1

Notes

1 Added by Coroners and Justice Act 2009 c. 25 Pt 8 s.174(1) (February 1, 2010)

Extent

Pt VI s. 52D(1)–(2)(b): England, Wales

[52E *Effect of data-sharing code*

(1) A failure on the part of any person to act in accordance with any provision of the data-sharing code does not of itself render that person liable to any legal proceedings in any court or tribunal.

(2) The data-sharing code is admissible in evidence in any legal proceedings. (3) If any provision of the data-sharing code appears to—

(a) the Tribunal or a court conducting any proceedings under this Act,

(b) a court or tribunal conducting any other legal proceedings, or

(c) the Commissioner carrying out any function under this Act, to be relevant to any question arising in the proceedings, or in connection with the exercise of that jurisdiction or the carrying out of those functions, in relation to any time when it was in force, that provision of the code must be taken into account in determining that question.

(4) In this section "the data-sharing code" means the code issued under section 52B(5) (as altered or replaced from time to time).

]1

Notes

1 Added by Coroners and Justice Act 2009 c. 25 Pt 8 s.174(1) (February 1, 2010)

Extent

Pt VI s. 52E(1)–(4): England, Wales

53. *Assistance by Commissioner in cases involving processing for the special purposes.*

(1) An individual who is an actual or prospective party to any proceedings under [section 7(9), 10(4), 12(8) or 14] 1 or by virtue of section 13 which relate to personal data processed for the special purposes may apply to the Commissioner for assistance in relation to those proceedings.

(2) The Commissioner shall, as soon as reasonably practicable after receiving an application under subsection (1), consider it and decide whether and to what extent to grant it, but he shall not grant the application unless, in his opinion, the case involves a matter of substantial public importance.

(3) If the Commissioner decides to provide assistance, he shall, as soon as reasonably practicable after making the decision, notify the applicant, stating the extent of the assistance to be provided.

(4) If the Commissioner decides not to provide assistance, he shall, as soon as reasonably practicable after making the decision, notify the applicant of his decision and, if he thinks fit, the reasons for it.

(5) In this section—

(a) references to "proceedings"include references to prospective proceedings, and

(b) "applicant", in relation to assistance under this section, means an individual who applies for assistance.

(6) Schedule 10 has effect for supplementing this section.

Notes

1   Words repealed by Data Protection Act 1998 c. 29 Sch.13 para.4 (October 23, 2007)

Commencement

Pt VI s. 53(1)–(6): March 1, 2000 (SI 2000/183 art. 2(1))

Extent

Pt VI s. 53(1)–(6): United Kingdom (subject to s.75(6))

54. *International co-operation.*

(1) The Commissioner—

(a) shall continue to be the designated authority in the United Kingdom for the purposes of Article 13 of the Convention, and

(b) shall be the supervisory authority in the United Kingdom for the purposes of the Data Protection Directive.

(2) The [Secretary of State] 1 may by order make provision as to the functions to be discharged by the Commissioner as the designated authority in the United Kingdom for the purposes of Article 13 of the Convention.

(3) The [Secretary of State] 1 may by order make provision as to co-operation by the Commissioner with the European Commission and with supervisory authorities in other EEA States in connection with the performance of their respective duties and, in particular, as to—

(a) the exchange of information with supervisory authorities in other EEA States or with the European Commission, and

(b) the exercise within the United Kingdom at the request of a supervisory authority in another EEA State, in cases excluded by section 5 from the application of the other provisions of this Act, of functions of the Commissioner specified in the order.

(4) The Commissioner shall also carry out any data protection functions which the [Secretary of State] 1 may by order direct him to carry out for the purpose of enabling Her Majesty's Government in the United Kingdom to give effect to any international obligations of the United Kingdom.

(5) The Commissioner shall, if so directed by the [Secretary of State]¹, provide any authority exercising data protection functions under the law of a colony specified in the direction with such assistance in connection with the discharge of those functions as the [Secretary of State]¹ may direct or approve, on such terms (including terms as to payment) as the [Secretary of State]¹ may direct or approve.

(6) Where the European Commission makes a decision for the purposes of Article 26(3) or (4) of the Data Protection Directive under the procedure provided for in Article 31(2) of the Directive, the Commissioner shall comply with that decision in exercising his functions under paragraph 9 of Schedule 4 or, as the case may be, paragraph 8 of that Schedule.

(7) The Commissioner shall inform the European Commission and the supervisory authorities in other EEA States—

(a) of any approvals granted for the purposes of paragraph 8 of Schedule 4, and

(b) of any authorisations granted for the purposes of paragraph 9 of that Schedule.

(8) In this section—

"the Convention" means the Convention for the Protection of Individuals with regard to Automatic Processing of Personal Data which was opened for signature on 28th January 1981;

"data protection functions" means functions relating to the protection of individuals with respect to the processing of personal information.

Notes

1 Words substituted by Secretary of State for Constitutional Affairs Order 2003/1887 Sch.2 para.9(1)(a) (August 19, 2003)

Commencement

Pt VI s. 54(1)–(1)(b), (5)–(8) definition of "data protection functions": March 1, 2000 (SI 2000/183 art. 2(1))
Pt VI s. 54(2)–(4): July 16, 1998 for the purpose of conferring power to make subordinate legislation; March 1, 2000 otherwise (SI 2000/183 art. 2(1); 1998 c. 29 Pt VI s. 75(2))

Extent

Pt VI s. 54(1)–(8) definition of "data protection functions": United Kingdom (subject to s.75(6))

[54A *Inspection of overseas information systems*

(1) The Commissioner may inspect any personal data recorded in–

(a) the Schengen information system,

(b) the Europol information system,

(c) the Customs information system.

(2) The power conferred by subsection (1) is exercisable only for the purpose of assessing whether or not any processing of the data has been or is being carried out in compliance with this Act.

(3) The power includes power to inspect, operate and test equipment which is used for the processing of personal data.

(4) Before exercising the power, the Commissioner must give notice in writing of his intention to do so to the data controller.

(5) But subsection (4) does not apply if the Commissioner considers that the case is one of urgency.

(6) Any person who–

(a) intentionally obstructs a person exercising the power conferred by subsection (1), or

(b) fails without reasonable excuse to give any person exercising the power any assistance he may reasonably require,

is guilty of an offence.

(7) In this section–

"the Customs information system" means the information system established under Chapter II of the Convention on the Use of Information Technology for Customs Purposes,

"the Europol information system" means the information system established under Title II of the Convention on the Establishment of a European Police Office,

"the Schengen information system" means the information system established under Title IV of the Convention implementing the Schengen Agreement of 14th June 1985 , or any system established in its place in pursuance of any [EU] 2 obligation .

]¹

Notes

¹ Added by Crime (International Co-operation) Act 2003 c. 32 Pt 4 s.81 (April 26, 2004)
² Substituted by Treaty of Lisbon (Changes in Terminology) Order 2011/1043 Pt 2 art.6(1)(e) (April 22, 2011)

Extent

Pt VI s. 54A(1)–(7) definition of "the Schengen information system": United Kingdom

Unlawful obtaining etc. of personal data

55. *Unlawful obtaining etc. of personal data.*

(1) A person must not knowingly or recklessly, without the consent of the data controller—

(a) obtain or disclose personal data or the information contained in personal data, or

(b) procure the disclosure to another person of the information contained in personal data.

(2) Subsection (1) does not apply to a person who shows—

(a) that the obtaining, disclosing or procuring—

(i) was necessary for the purpose of preventing or detecting crime, or

(ii) was required or authorised by or under any enactment, by any rule of law or by the order of a court,

(b) that he acted in the reasonable belief that he had in law the right to obtain or disclose the data or information or, as the case may be, to procure the disclosure of the information to the other person,

(c) that he acted in the reasonable belief that he would have had the consent of the data controller if the data controller had known of the obtaining, disclosing or procuring and the circumstances of it, or

(d) that in the particular circumstances the obtaining, disclosing or procuring was justified as being in the public interest.

(3) A person who contravenes subsection (1) is guilty of an offence.

(4) A person who sells personal data is guilty of an offence if he has obtained the data in contravention of subsection (1).

(5) A person who offers to sell personal data is guilty of an offence if—

(a) he has obtained the data in contravention of subsection (1), or

(b) he subsequently obtains the data in contravention of that subsection.

(6) For the purposes of subsection (5), an advertisement indicating that personal data are or may be for sale is an offer to sell the data.

(7) Section 1(2) does not apply for the purposes of this section; and for the purposes of subsections (4) to (6), "personal data" includes information extracted from personal data.

(8) References in this section to personal data do not include references to personal data which by virtue of [section 28 or 33A] [1] are exempt from this section.

Notes

[1] Words added by Freedom of Information Act 2000 c. 36 Pt VII s.70(2) (January 1, 2005 for purposes specified in
SI 2004/1909 art.2(1); January 1, 2005 otherwise)

Amendments Pending

Pt VI s. 55(2)(ca): added by Criminal Justice and Immigration Act 2008 c. 4, Pt 5 s. 78 (date to be appointed)

Commencement

Pt VI s. 55(1)–(8): March 1, 2000 (SI 2000/183 art. 2(1))

Extent

Pt VI s. 55(1)–(2)(c), (2)(d)–(8): United Kingdom (subject to s.75(6)) Pt VI s. 55(2)(ca)–(2)(ca) (iii): United Kingdom

[Monetary penalties] [1]

Notes

[1] Added by Criminal Justice and Immigration Act 2008 c. 4 Pt 11 s.144(1) (October 1, 2009 as SI 2009/2606)

[55A *Power of Commissioner to impose monetary penalty*

[(1) The Commissioner may serve a data controller with a monetary penalty notice if the Commissioner is satisfied that—

  (a) there has been a serious contravention of section 4(4) by the data controller,

  (b) the contravention was of a kind likely to cause substantial damage or substantial distress, and

  (c) subsection (2) or (3) applies.

(2) This subsection applies if the contravention was deliberate. (3) This subsection applies if the data controller—

  (a) knew or ought to have known

    (i) that there was a risk that the contravention would occur, and

    (ii) that such a contravention would be of a kind likely to cause substantial damage or substantial distress, but

  (b) failed to take reasonable steps to prevent the contravention.

] [2]

[(3A) The Commissioner may not be satisfied as mentioned in subsection (1) by virtue of any matter which comes to the Commissioner's attention as a result of anything done in pursuance of—

  (a) an assessment notice;

  (b) an assessment under section 51(7).

] [3]

(4) A monetary penalty notice is a notice requiring the data controller to pay to the Commissioner a monetary penalty of an amount determined by the Commissioner and specified in the notice.

(5) The amount determined by the Commissioner must not exceed the prescribed amount.

[(6) The monetary penalty must be paid to the Commissioner within the period specified in the notice.] [2]

(7) The notice must contain such information as may be prescribed.

[(8) Any sum received by the Commissioner by virtue of this section must be paid into the Consolidated Fund.]²

(9) In this section—

"data controller"does not include the Crown Estate Commissioners or a person who is a data controller by virtue of section 63(3);
"prescribed" means prescribed by regulations made by the Secretary of State.

]¹

Notes

¹ Added by Criminal Justice and Immigration Act 2008 c. 4 Pt 11 s.144(1) (October 1, 2009 as SI 2009/2606)
² Added by Criminal Justice and Immigration Act 2008 c. 4 Pt 11 s.144(1) (April 6, 2010 as SI 2010/712)
³ Added by Coroners and Justice Act 2009 c. 25 Sch.20(5) para.13 (April 6, 2010 as SI 2010/816)

Extent

Pt VI s. 55A(1)–(9) definition of "prescribed": United Kingdom

[55B *Monetary penalty notices: procedural rights*

[(1) Before serving a monetary penalty notice, the Commissioner must serve the data controller with a notice of intent.] ²

(2) A notice of intent is a notice that the Commissioner proposes to serve a monetary penalty notice.

(3) A notice of intent must—

[(a) inform the data controller that he may make written representations in relation to the Commissioner's proposal within a period specified in the notice, and] ²

(b) contain such other information as may be prescribed.

[(4) The Commissioner may not serve a monetary penalty notice until the time within which the data controller may make representations has expired.

(5) A person on whom a monetary penalty notice is served may appeal to the Tribunal against—

(a) the issue of the monetary penalty notice;

(b) the amount of the penalty specified in the notice.

] ²

(6) In this section, "prescribed" means prescribed by regulations made by the Secretary of State.

]¹

Notes

¹ Added by Criminal Justice and Immigration Act 2008 c. 4 Pt 11 s.144(1) (October 1, 2009 as SI 2009/2606)
² Added by Criminal Justice and Immigration Act 2008 c. 4 Pt 11 s.144(1) (April 6, 2010 as SI 2010/712)

Extent

Pt VI s. 55B(1)–(6): United Kingdom

[55C *Guidance about monetary penalty notices*

(1) The Commissioner must prepare and issue guidance on how he proposes to exercise his functions under sections 55A and 55B.

(2) The guidance must, in particular, deal with—

(a) the circumstances in which he would consider it appropriate to issue a monetary penalty notice, and

(b) how he will determine the amount of the penalty.

(3) The Commissioner may alter or replace the guidance.

(4) If the guidance is altered or replaced, the Commissioner must issue the altered or replacement guidance.

(5) The Commissioner may not issue guidance under this section without the approval of the Secretary of State.

(6) The Commissioner must lay any guidance issued under this section before each House of Parliament.

(7) The Commissioner must arrange for the publication of any guidance issued under this section in such form and manner as he considers appropriate.

(8) In subsections (5) to (7), "guidance"includes altered or replacement guidance.

] [1]

Notes

[1] Added by Criminal Justice and Immigration Act 2008 c. 4 Pt 11 s.144(1) (October 1, 2009 as SI 2009/2606)

Amendments Pending

Pt VI s. 55C(5): substituted by Protection of Freedoms Act 2012 c. 9, Pt 6 s. 106(3) (date to be appointed)

Extent

Pt VI s. 55C(1)–(8): United Kingdom

[55D *Monetary penalty notices: enforcement*

(1) This section applies in relation to any penalty payable to the Commissioner by virtue of section 55A.

(2) In England and Wales, the penalty is recoverable—

(a) if a county court so orders, as if it were payable under an order of that court;

(b) if the High Court so orders, as if it were payable under an order of that court.

(3) In Scotland, the penalty may be enforced in the same manner as an extract regis-

tered decree arbitral bearing a warrant for execution issued by the sheriff court of any sheriffdom in Scotland.

(4) In Northern Ireland, the penalty is recoverable—

(a) if a county court so orders, as if it were payable under an order of that court;

(b) if the High Court so orders, as if it were payable under an order of that court.

] [1]

Note

[1]   Added by Criminal Justice and Immigration Act 2008 c. 4 Pt 11 s.144(1) (April 6, 2010 as SI 2010/712)

Extent

Pt VI s. 55D(1)–(4)(b): United Kingdom

[55E *Notices under sections 55A and 55B: supplemental*

(1) The Secretary of State may by order make further provision in connection with monetary penalty notices and notices of intent.

(2) An order under this section may in particular—

(a) provide that a monetary penalty notice may not be served on a data controller with respect to the processing of personal data for the special purposes except in circumstances specified in the order;

(b) make provision for the cancellation or variation of monetary penalty notices;

(c) confer rights of appeal to the Tribunal against decisions of the Commissioner in relation to the cancellation or variation of such notices;

(d) [. . .][2]

(e) make provision for the determination of [appeals made by virtue of paragraph (c)] [3] [.] [4]

(f) [. . .]4

(3) An order under this section may apply any provision of this Act with such modifications as may be specified in the order.

(4) An order under this section may amend this Act.

] [1]

Notes

[1]   Added by Criminal Justice and Immigration Act 2008 c. 4 Pt 11 s.144(1) (October 1, 2009 as SI 2009/2606)
[2]   Repealed by Transfer of Tribunal Functions Order 2010/22 Sch.2 para.28(a) (January 18, 2010)
[3]   Words substituted by Transfer of Tribunal Functions Order 2010/22 Sch.2 para.28(b) (January 18, 2010)
[4]   Repealed by Transfer of Tribunal Functions Order 2010/22 Sch.2 para.28(c) (January 18, 2010)

Extent

Pt VI s. 55E(1)–(4): United Kingdom

Records obtained under data subject's right of access

56.— *Prohibition of requirement as to production of certain records.*

(1) A person must not, in connection with—

(a) the recruitment of another person as an employee,

(b) the continued employment of another person, or

(c) any contract for the provision of services to him by another person,

require that other person or a third party to supply him with a relevant record or to produce a relevant record to him.

(2) A person concerned with the provision (for payment or not) of goods, facilities or services to the public or a section of the public must not, as a condition of providing or offering to provide any goods, facilities or services to another person, require that other person or a third party to supply him with a relevant record or to produce a relevant record to him.

(3) Subsections (1) and (2) do not apply to a person who shows—

(a) that the imposition of the requirement was required or authorised by or under any enactment, by any rule of law or by the order of a court, or

(b) that in the particular circumstances the imposition of the requirement was justified as being in the public interest.

(4) Having regard to the provisions of Part V of the Police Act 1997 (certificates of criminal records etc.), the imposition of the requirement referred to in subsection (1) or (2) is not to be regarded as being justified as being in the public interest on the ground that it would assist in the prevention or detection of crime.

(5) A person who contravenes subsection (1) or (2) is guilty of an offence. (6) In this section "a relevant record" means any record which—

(a) has been or is to be obtained by a data subject from any data controller specified in the first column of the Table below in the exercise of the right conferred by section 7, and

(b) contains information relating to any matter specified in relation to that data controller in the second column,

and includes a copy of such a record or a part of such a record.

TABLE

Data controller	Subject-matter
1. Any of the following persons—	(a) Convictions.
(a) a chief officer of police of a police force in England and Wales.	(b) Cautions.
	]¹
(b) a chief constable of a police force in Scotland.	1953 in relation to any person imprisoned or detained.
(c) the Chief Constable of the Royal Ulster Constabulary.	

1101

Data controller	Subject-matter
(c) the Chief Constable of the Royal Ulster Constabulary. [(d) the Director General of the Serious Organised Crime Agency.	
2. The Secretary of State.	(a) Convictions. (b) Cautions. (c) His functions under [section 92 of the Powers of Criminal Courts (Sentencing) Act 2000]² , section 205(2) or 208 of the Criminal Procedure (Scotland) Act 1995 or section 73 of the Children and Young Persons Act (Northern Ireland) 1968 in relation to any person sentenced to detention. (d) His functions under the Prison Act 1952, the Prisons (Scotland) Act 1989 or the Prison Act (Northern Ireland) (e) His functions under the Social Security Contributions and Benefits Act 1992, the Social Security Administration Act 1992 [, the Jobseekers Act 1995 or Part 1 of the Welfare Reform Act 2007] ³ . (f) His functions under Part V of the Police Act 1997. (g) His functions under the Safeguarding Vulnerable Groups Act 2006 [or the Safeguarding Vulnerable Groups (Northern Ireland) Order 2007] ⁵ .]⁴
3. The Department of Health and Social Services for Northern Ireland.	Its functions under the Social Security Contributions and Benefits (Northern Ireland) Act 1992, the Social Security Administration (Northern Ireland) Act 1992 [, the Jobseekers (Northern Ireland) Order 1995 or Part 1 of the Welfare Reform Act (Northern Ireland) 2007.] ⁶
[4. The [Independent Safeguarding Authority] 8 [5. The Scottish Ministers.	Its functions under the Safeguarding Vulnerable Groups Act 2006 [or the Safeguarding Vulnerable Groups (Northern Ireland) Order 2007] ⁵ .]⁷ Their functions under Parts 1 and 2 of the Protection of Vulnerable Groups (Scotland) Act 2007 (asp 14).]⁹

[(6A) A record is not a relevant record to the extent that it relates, or is to relate, only to personal data falling within paragraph (e) of the definition of "data" in section 1(1).] ¹⁰

(7) In the Table in subsection (6)—

"caution" means a caution given to any person in England and Wales or Northern Ireland in respect of an offence which, at the time when the caution is given, is admitted; "conviction"has the same meaning as in the Rehabilitation of Offenders Act 1974 or the Rehabilitation of Offenders (Northern Ireland) Order 1978.

(8) The [Secretary of State] [11] may by order amend— (a) the Table in subsection (6), and (b) subsection (7).

(9) For the purposes of this section a record which states that a data controller is not processing any personal data relating to a particular matter shall be taken to be a record containing information relating to that matter.

(10) In this section "employee" means an individual who—

(a) works under a contract of employment, as defined by section 230(2) of the Employment Rights Act 1996, or

(b) holds any office,

whether or not he is entitled to remuneration; and "employment"shall be construed accordingly.

Notes

[1] Words substituted by Serious Organised Crime and Police Act 2005 c. 15 Sch.4 para.112 (April 1, 2006)
[2] Words substituted by Powers of Criminal Courts (Sentencing) Act 2000 c. 6 Sch.9 para.191 (August 25, 2000)
[3] Words substituted by Social Security (Miscellaneous Amendments) (No. 3) Regulations 2011/2425 Pt 2 reg.4(a) (October 31, 2011)
[4] Entry inserted by Safeguarding Vulnerable Groups Act 2006 c. 47 Sch.9(2) para.15(2)(a) (May 19, 2008)
[5] Words inserted by Safeguarding Vulnerable Groups (Northern Ireland) Order 2007/1351 Sch.7 para.4(1) (May 29, 2008)
[6] Words substituted by Social Security (Miscellaneous Amendments No. 2) Regulations (Northern Ireland) 2011/357 Pt 2 reg.4 (October 31, 2011)
[7] Entries inserted by Safeguarding Vulnerable Groups Act 2006 c. 47 Sch.9(2) para.15(2)(b) (May 19, 2008)
[8] Words substituted by Policing and Crime Act 2009 c. 26 Pt 8 c.1 s.81(3)(i) (November 12, 2009)
[9] Entry inserted by Protection of Vulnerable Groups (Scotland) Act 2007 (Consequential Modifications) Order 2011/565 art.3(2) (March 1, 2011)
[10] Added by Freedom of Information Act 2000 c. 36 Pt VII s.68(4) (January 1, 2005 for purposes specified in SI 2004/1909 art.2(1); January 1, 2005 otherwise)
[11] Words substituted by Secretary of State for Constitutional Affairs Order 2003/1887 Sch.2 para.9(1)(a) (August 19, 2003)

Commencement

Pt VI s. 56(1)–(7) definition of "conviction", (9)–(10)(b): July 7, 2008 for purposes specified in SI 2008/1592 art.2; March 3, 2011 for purposes specified in SI 2011/601 art.2; not yet in force otherwise (SI 2008/1592 art. 2; SI 2011/601 art. 2)
Pt VI s. 56(8)–(8)(b): July 16, 1998 for the purpose of conferring power to make subordinate legislation; July 7, 2008 for purposes specified in SI 2008/1592 art.2; March 3, 2011 for purposes specified in SI 2011/601 art.2; not yet in force otherwise (SI 2008/1592 art. 2; SI 2011/601 art. 2; 1998 c. 29 Pt VI s. 75(2))

Extent

Pt VI s. 56(1)–(6)(b), (7)–(10)(b): United Kingdom (subject to s.75(6)) Pt VI s. 56(6A): United Kingdom

57. *Avoidance of certain contractual terms relating to health records.*

(1) Any term or condition of a contract is void in so far as it purports to require an individual—

    (a) to supply any other person with a record to which this section applies, or with a copy of such a record or a part of such a record, or

    (b) to produce to any other person such a record, copy or part.

(2) This section applies to any record which—

    (a) has been or is to be obtained by a data subject in the exercise of the right conferred by section 7, and

    (b) consists of the information contained in any health record as defined by section 68(2).

Commencement

Pt VI s. 57(1)–(2)(b): March 1, 2000 (SI 2000/183 art. 2(1))

Extent

Pt VI s. 57(1)–(2)(b): United Kingdom (subject to s.75(6))

Information provided to Commissioner or Tribunal

58. *Disclosure of information.*

No enactment or rule of law prohibiting or restricting the disclosure of information shall preclude a person from furnishing the Commissioner or the Tribunal with any information necessary for the discharge of their functions under this Act [or the Freedom of Information Act 2000] [1] .

Notes

[1] Words added by Freedom of Information Act 2000 c. 36 Sch.2(II) para.18 (November 30, 2000)

Commencement

Pt VI s. 58: March 1, 2000 (SI 2000/183 art. 2(1))

Extent

Pt VI s. 58: United Kingdom (subject to s.75(6))

59. *Confidentiality of information.*

(1) No person who is or has been the Commissioner, a member of the Commissioner's staff or an agent of the Commissioner shall disclose any information which—

    (a) has been obtained by, or furnished to, the Commissioner under or for the purposes of [the information Acts] 1 ,

(b) relates to an identified or identifiable individual or business, and

(c) is not at the time of the disclosure, and has not previously been, available to the public from other sources,

unless the disclosure is made with lawful authority.

(2) For the purposes of subsection (1) a disclosure of information is made with lawful authority only if, and to the extent that—

(a) the disclosure is made with the consent of the individual or of the person for the time being carrying on the business,

(b) the information was provided for the purpose of its being made available to the public (in whatever manner) under any provision of [the information Acts] [1] ,

(c) the disclosure is made for the purposes of, and is necessary for, the discharge of—

(i) any functions under [the information Acts] [1] , or
(ii) any [EU] [2] obligation,

(d) the disclosure is made for the purposes of any proceedings, whether criminal or civil and whether arising under, or by virtue of, [the information Acts] [1] or otherwise, or

(e) having regard to the rights and freedoms or legitimate interests of any person, the disclosure is necessary in the public interest.

(3) Any person who knowingly or recklessly discloses information in contravention of subsection (1) is guilty of an offence.

[(4) In this section "the information Acts" means this Act and the Freedom of Information Act 2000.] [3]

Notes

[1] Words substituted by Freedom of Information Act 2000 c. 36 Sch.2(II) para.19(2) (November 30, 2000)
[2] Word substituted by Treaty of Lisbon (Changes in Terminology) Order 2011/1043 Pt 2 art.6(1)(e) (April 22, 2011)
[3] Added by Freedom of Information Act 2000 c. 36 Sch.2(II) para.19(3) (November 30, 2000)

Commencement

Pt VI s. 59(1)–(3): March 1, 2000 (SI 2000/183 art. 2(1))

Extent

Pt VI s. 59(1)–(3): United Kingdom (subject to s.75(6)) Pt VI s. 59(4): United Kingdom

General provisions relating to offences

60. Prosecutions and penalties.

(1) No proceedings for an offence under this Act shall be instituted—

(a) in England or Wales, except by the Commissioner or by or with the consent of the Director of Public Prosecutions;

(b) in Northern Ireland, except by the Commissioner or by or with the consent of the Director of Public Prosecutions for Northern Ireland.

(2) A person guilty of an offence under any provision of this Act other than [section 54A and paragraph 12 of Schedule 9] 1 is liable—

(a) on summary conviction, to a fine not exceeding the statutory maximum, or

(b) on conviction on indictment, to a fine.

(3) A person guilty of an offence under [section 54A and paragraph 12 of Schedule 9] 1 is liable on summary conviction to a fine not exceeding level 5 on the standard scale.

(4) Subject to subsection (5), the court by or before which a person is convicted of—

(a) an offence under section 21(1), 22(6), 55 or 56,

(b) an offence under section 21(2) relating to processing which is assessable processing for the purposes of section 22, or

(c) an offence under section 47(1) relating to an enforcement notice,

may order any document or other material used in connection with the processing of personal data and appearing to the court to be connected with the commission of the offence to be forfeited, destroyed or erased.

(5) The court shall not make an order under subsection (4) in relation to any material where a person (other than the offender) claiming to be the owner of or otherwise interested in the material applies to be heard by the court, unless an opportunity is given to him to show cause why the order should not be made.

Note

1   Words inserted by Crime (International Co-operation) Act 2003 c. 32 Sch.5 para.70 (April 26, 2004)

Commencement

Pt VI s. 60(1)–(5): March 1, 2000 (SI 2000/183 art. 2(1))

Extent

Pt VI s. 60(1)–(5): United Kingdom (subject to s.75(6))

61. *Liability of directors etc.*

(1) Where an offence under this Act has been committed by a body corporate and is proved to have been committed with the consent or connivance of or to be attributable to any neglect on the part of any director, manager, secretary or similar officer of the body corporate or any person who was purporting to act in any such capacity, he as well as the body corporate shall be guilty of that offence and be liable to be proceeded against and punished accordingly.

(2) Where the affairs of a body corporate are managed by its members subsection (1) shall apply in relation to the acts and defaults of a member in connection with his functions of management as if he were a director of the body corporate.

(3) Where an offence under this Act has been committed by a Scottish partnership and the contravention in question is proved to have occurred with the consent or connivance of, or to be attributable to any neglect on the part of, a partner, he as well as the partnership shall be guilty of that offence and shall be liable to be proceeded against and punished accordingly.

Commencement

Pt VI s. 61(1)–(3): March 1, 2000 (SI 2000/183 art. 2(1))

Extent

Pt VI s. 61(1)–(3): United Kingdom (subject to s.75(6))

Amendments of Consumer Credit Act 1974

62.— *Amendments of Consumer Credit Act 1974.*

(1) In section 158 of the Consumer Credit Act 1974 (duty of agency to disclose filed information)—

    (a) in subsection (1)—

        (i) in paragraph (a) for "individual" there is substituted "partnership or other unincorporated body of persons not consisting entirely of bodies corporate", and

        (ii) for "him" there is substituted "it",

    (b) in subsection (2), for "his" there is substituted "the consumer's", and

    (c) in subsection (3), for "him" there is substituted "the consumer".

(2) In section 159 of that Act (correction of wrong information) for subsection (1) there is substituted—

    "(1) Any individual (the "objector") given—

    (a) information under section 7 of the Data Protection Act 1998 by a credit reference agency, or

    (b) information under section 158,

who considers that an entry in his file is incorrect, and that if it is not corrected he is likely to be prejudiced, may give notice to the agency requiring it either to remove the entry from the file or amend it."

(3) In subsections (2) to (6) of that section—

    (a) for "consumer", wherever occurring, there is substituted "objector", and

    (b) for "Director", wherever occurring, there is substituted "the relevant authority". (4) After subsection (6) of that section there is inserted—

"(7) The Data Protection Commissioner may vary or revoke any order made by him under this section.

(8) In this section "the relevant authority" means—

    (a) where the objector is a partnership or other unincorporated body of persons, the Director, and

    (b) in any other case, the Data Protection Commissioner."

(5) In section 160 of that Act (alternative procedure for business consumers)—

    (a) in subsection (4)—

        (i) for "him" there is substituted "to the consumer", and

        (ii) in paragraphs (a) and (b) for "he" there is substituted "the consumer", and for "his" there is substituted "the consumer's", and

(b) after subsection (6) there is inserted—

"(7) In this section "consumer"has the same meaning as in section 158."

Commencement

Pt VI s. 62(1)–(5)(b): March 1, 2000 subject to transitional provisions specified in SI 2000/183 art.2(2) (SI 2000/183 art. 2(1), art. 2(2))

Extent

Pt VI s. 62(1)–(5)(b): United Kingdom (subject to s.75(6))

General

63. *Application to Crown.*

(1) This Act binds the Crown.

(2) For the purposes of this Act each government department shall be treated as a person separate from any other government department.

(3) Where the purposes for which and the manner in which any personal data are, or are to be, processed are determined by any person acting on behalf of the Royal Household, the Duchy of Lancaster or the Duchy of Cornwall, the data controller in respect of those data for the purposes of this Act shall be—

(a) in relation to the Royal Household, the Keeper of the Privy Purse,

(b) in relation to the Duchy of Lancaster, such person as the Chancellor of the Duchy appoints, and

(c) in relation to the Duchy of Cornwall, such person as the Duke of Cornwall, or the possessor for the time being of the Duchy of Cornwall, appoints.

(4) Different persons may be appointed under subsection (3)(b) or (c) for different purposes.

(5) Neither a government department nor a person who is a data controller by virtue of subsection (3) shall be liable to prosecution under this Act, but [sections 54A and 55 and paragraph 12 of Schedule 9] [1] shall apply to a person in the service of the Crown as they apply to any other person.

Note

[1]   Word substituted by Crime (International Co-operation) Act 2003 c. 32 Sch.5 para.71 (April 26, 2004)

Commencement

Pt VI s. 63(1)–(5): March 1, 2000 (SI 2000/183 art. 2(1))

Extent

Pt VI s. 63(1)–(5): United Kingdom (subject to s.75(6))

[63A. *Application to Parliament.*

(1) Subject to the following provisions of this section and to section 35A, this Act applies to the processing of personal data by or on behalf of either House of Parliament as it applies to the processing of personal data by other persons.

(2) Where the purposes for which and the manner in which any personal data are, or are to be, processed are determined by or on behalf of the House of Commons, the data controller in respect of those data for the purposes of this Act shall be the Corporate Officer of that House.

(3) Where the purposes for which and the manner in which any personal data are, or are to be, processed are determined by or on behalf of the House of Lords, the data controller in respect of those data for the purposes of this Act shall be the Corporate Officer of that House.

(4) Nothing in subsection (2) or (3) is to be taken to render the Corporate Officer of the House of Commons or the Corporate Officer of the House of Lords liable to prosecution under this Act, but section 55 and paragraph 12 of Schedule 9 shall apply to a person acting on behalf of either House as they apply to any other person.

]¹

Note

¹ Added by Freedom of Information Act 2000 c. 36 Sch.6 para.3 (January 1, 2005 for purposes specified in SI 2004/1909 art.2(1); January 1, 2005 otherwise)

Extent

Pt VI s. 63A(1)–(4): United Kingdom

64. *Transmission of notices etc. by electronic or other means.*

(1) This section applies to—

    (a) a notice or request under any provision of Part II,

    (b) a notice under subsection (1) of section 24 or particulars made available under that subsection, or

    (c) an application under section 41(2),

but does not apply to anything which is required to be served in accordance with rules of court.

(2) The requirement that any notice, request, particulars or application to which this section applies should be in writing is satisfied where the text of the notice, request, particulars or application—

    (a) is transmitted by electronic means,

    (b) is received in legible form, and

    (c) is capable of being used for subsequent reference.

(3) The [Secretary of State] 1 may by regulations provide that any requirement that any notice, request, particulars or application to which this section applies should be in writing is not to apply in such circumstances as may be prescribed by the regulations.

Note

¹ Words substituted by Secretary of State for Constitutional Affairs Order 2003/1887 Sch.2 para.9(1)(a) (August 19, 2003)

Commencement

Pt VI s. 64(1)–(2)(c): March 1, 2000 (SI 2000/183 art. 2(1))
Pt VI s. 64(3): July 16, 1998 for the purpose of conferring power to make subordinate legislation; March 1, 2000 otherwise (SI 2000/183 art. 2(1); 1998 c. 29 Pt VI s. 75(2))

Extent

Pt VI s. 64(1)–(3): United Kingdom (subject to s.75(6))

65. *Service of notices by Commissioner.*

(1) Any notice authorised or required by this Act to be served on or given to any person by the Commissioner may—

    (a) if that person is an individual, be served on him—

        (i) by delivering it to him, or
        (ii) by sending it to him by post addressed to him at his usual or last-known place of residence or business, or
        (iii) by leaving it for him at that place;

    (b) if that person is a body corporate or unincorporate, be served on that body—

        (i) by sending it by post to the proper officer of the body at its principal office, or
        (ii) by addressing it to the proper officer of the body and leaving it at that office;

    (c) if that person is a partnership in Scotland, be served on that partnership—

        (i) by sending it by post to the principal office of the partnership, or
        (ii) by addressing it to that partnership and leaving it at that office.

(2) In subsection (1)(b) "principal office", in relation to a registered company, means its registered office and "proper officer", in relation to any body, means the secretary or other executive officer charged with the conduct of its general affairs.

(3) This section is without prejudice to any other lawful method of serving or giving a notice.

Commencement

Pt VI s. 65(1)–(3): March 1, 2000 (SI 2000/183 art. 2(1))

Extent

Pt VI s. 65(1)–(3): United Kingdom (subject to s.75(6))

66. *Exercise of rights in Scotland by children.*

(1) Where a question falls to be determined in Scotland as to the legal capacity of a person under the age of sixteen years to exercise any right conferred by any provision of this Act, that person shall be taken to have that capacity where he has a general understanding of what it means to exercise that right.

(2) Without prejudice to the generality of subsection (1), a person of twelve years of age or more shall be presumed to be of sufficient age and maturity to have such understanding as is mentioned in that subsection.

Commencement

Pt VI s. 66(1)–(2): March 1, 2000 (SI 2000/183 art. 2(1))

Extent

Pt VI s. 66(1)–(2): United Kingdom (subject to s.75(6))

67. *Orders, regulations and rules.*

(1) Any power conferred by this Act on the [Secretary of State] 1 to make an order, regulations or rules shall be exercisable by statutory instrument.

(2) Any order, regulations or rules made by the [Secretary of State] 1 under this Act may—

    (a) make different provision for different cases, and

    (b) make such supplemental, incidental, consequential or transitional provision or savings as the [Secretary of State] 1 considers appropriate;

and nothing in section 7(11), 19(5), 26(1) or 30(4) limits the generality of paragraph (a).

(3) Before making—

    (a) an order under any provision of this Act other than section 75(3),

    (b) any regulations under this Act other than notification regulations (as defined by section 16(2)),

the [Secretary of State] 1 shall consult the Commissioner.

(4) A statutory instrument containing (whether alone or with other provisions) an order under—

    section 10(2)(b),

    section 12(5)(b),

    section 22(1),

    section 30,

    section 32(3),

    section 38,

    [section 41A(2)(c),] 2

    [section 55E(1),] 3

    section 56(8),

    paragraph 10 of Schedule 3,

    or paragraph 4 of Schedule 7,

shall not be made unless a draft of the instrument has been laid before and approved by a resolution of each House of Parliament.

(5) A statutory instrument which contains (whether alone or with other provisions)—

   (a) an order under—

        section 22(7),
        section 23,
        [section 41A(2)(b),] **4**
        section 51(3),
        section 54(2), (3) or (4),
        paragraph 3, 4 or 14 of Part II of Schedule 1,
        paragraph 6 of Schedule 2,
        paragraph 2, 7 or 9 of Schedule 3,
        paragraph 4 of Schedule 4,
        paragraph 6 of Schedule 7,

   (b) regulations under section 7 which—

      (i) prescribe cases for the purposes of subsection (2)(b),
     (ii) are made by virtue of subsection (7), or
    (iii) relate to the definition of "the prescribed period", (c) regulations under [
       section 8(1), 9(3) or 9A(5)] **5** ,

  [(ca) regulations under section 55A(5) or (7) or 55B(3)(b),] **6**

   (d) regulations under section 64,

   (e) notification regulations (as defined by section 16(2)), or

   (f) rules under paragraph 7 of Schedule 6,

and which is not subject to the requirement in subsection (4) that a draft of the instrument be laid before and approved by a resolution of each House of Parliament, shall be subject to annulment in pursuance of a resolution of either House of Parliament.

   (6) A statutory instrument which contains only—

   (a) regulations prescribing fees for the purposes of any provision of this Act, or

   (b) regulations under section 7 prescribing fees for the purposes of any other enactment, shall be laid before Parliament after being made.

Notes

1 Words substituted by Secretary of State for Constitutional Affairs Order 2003/1887 Sch.2 para.9(1)(a) (August 19, 2003)
2 Words inserted by Coroners and Justice Act 2009 c. 25 Sch.20(2) para.6(a) (April 6, 2010)
3 Words inserted by Criminal Justice and Immigration Act 2008 c. 4 Pt 11 s.144(2)(a) (October 1, 2009)
4 Words inserted by Coroners and Justice Act 2009 c. 25 Sch.20(2) para.6(b) (April 6, 2010)
5 Words substituted by Freedom of Information Act 2000 c. 36 Pt VII s.69(3) (November 30, 2000 for conferring powers to make any order, regulations or code of practice; January 1, 2005 for purposes specified in SI 2004/1909 art.2(1); January 1, 2005 otherwise)
6 Added by Criminal Justice and Immigration Act 2008 c. 4 Pt 11 s.144(2)(b) (October 1, 2009)

Amendments Pending

Pt VI s. 67(5)(a): words inserted by Protection of Freedoms Act 2012 c. 9, Pt 6 s. 107(2) (date to be appointed)

Commencement

Pt VI s. 67(1)–(6)(b): July 16, 1998 (1998 c. 29 Pt VI s. 75(2))

Extent

Pt VI s. 67(1)–(5)(c), (5)(d)–(6)(b): United Kingdom (subject to s.75(6)) Pt VI s. 67(5)(ca): United Kingdom

68. *Meaning of "accessible record".*

(1) In this Act "accessible record" means —

(a) a health record as defined by subsection (2),

(b) an educational record as defined by Schedule 11, or

(c) an accessible public record as defined by Schedule 12.

(2) In subsection (1)(a) "health record" means any record which—

(a) consists of information relating to the physical or mental health or condition of an individual, and

(b) has been made by or on behalf of a health professional in connection with the care of that individual.

Commencement

Pt VI s. 68(1)–(2)(b): July 16, 1998 (1998 c. 29 Pt VI s. 75(2)(d))

Extent

Pt VI s. 68(1)–(2)(b): United Kingdom (subject to s.75(6))

69. *Meaning of "health professional".*

(1) [. . .]¹ In this Act "health professional" means any of the following–

(a) a registered medical practitioner,

(b) a registered dentist as defined by section 53(1) of the Dentists Act 1984,

[(c) a registered dispensing optician or a registered optometrist within the meaning of the Opticians Act 1989,]²

(d) [a registered pharmacist or a registered pharmacy technician within the meaning of article 3(1) of the Pharmacy Order 2010]3 or a registered person as defined by Article 2(2) of the Pharmacy (Northern Ireland) Order 1976,

[(e) a registered nurse or midwife,]⁴

(f) a registered osteopath as defined by section 41 of the Osteopaths Act 1993,

(g) a registered chiropractor as defined by section 43 of the Chiropractors Act 1994,

(h) any person who is registered as a member of a profession to which [the Health and Social Work Professions Order 2001]5 for the time being extends [, except in so far as the person is registered as a social worker in England (within the meaning of that Order)]⁶,

(i) a [. . .]⁷ [child psychotherapist]⁸ , [and]⁹

(j) [. . .]⁹

(k) a scientist employed by such a body as head of a department.

(2) In subsection (1)(a) "registered medical practitioner"includes any person who is provisionally registered under section 15 or 21 of the Medical Act 1983 and is engaged in such employment as is mentioned in subsection (3) of that section.

(3) In subsection (1) "health service body" means —

(a) a [Strategic Health Authority] [10] [established under section 13 of the National Health Service Act 2006][11] ,

(b) a Special Health Authority established under [section 28 of that Act, or section 22 of the National Health Service (Wales) Act 2006] [12] ,

[(bb) a Primary Care Trust established under [section 18 of the National Health Service Act 2006] [14] ,] [13]

[(bbb) a Local Health Board established under [section 11 of the National Health Service (Wales) Act 2006] [15] ,] [1]

(c) a Health Board within the meaning of the National Health Service (Scotland) Act 1978, (d) a Special Health Board within the meaning of that Act,

(e) the managers of a State Hospital provided under section 102 of that Act,

(f) a National Health Service trust first established under section 5 of the National Health Service and Community Care Act 1990 [, section 25 of the National Health Service Act 2006, section 18 of the National Health Service (Wales) Act 2006] [16] or section 12A of the National Health Service (Scotland) Act 1978,

[(fa) an NHS foundation trust,] [17]

(g) a Health and Social Services Board established under Article 16 of the Health and Personal Social Services (Northern Ireland) Order 1972,

(h) a special health and social services agency established under the Health and Personal Social Services (Special Agencies) (Northern Ireland) Order 1990, or

(i) a Health and Social Services trust established under Article 10 of the Health and Personal Social Services (Northern Ireland) Order 1991.

Notes

[1] Added by National Health Service Reform and Health Care Professions Act 2002 c. 17 Sch.5 para.41 (March 1, 2007 as SI 2006/1407)

[2] Substituted by Opticians Act 1989 (Amendment) Order 2005/848 Sch.1(2) para.12 (March 22, 2005 for the purposes of those provisions which confer powers enabling rules, regulations or orders to be made, but for the purpose only of the exercise of those powers; June 30, 2005 as specified in the London Gazette dated June 3, 2005 otherwise)

[3] Words substituted by Pharmacy Order 2010/231 Sch.4(1) para.6 (September 27, 2010)

[4] Substituted by Nursing and Midwifery Order (2001) 2002/253 Sch.5 para.14 (August 1, 2004 as specified in the London Gazette dated July 21, 2004)

[5] Words substituted by Health and Social Care Act 2012 c. 7 Pt 7 s.213(7)(h) (August 1, 2012)

[6] Words inserted by Health and Social Care Act 2012 c. 7 Pt 7 s.220(5) (August 1, 2012)

[7] Words repealed by Health Care and Associated Professions (Miscellaneous Amendments and Practitioner Psychologists) Order 2009/1182 Sch.5(1) para.4 (July 1, 2009)

[8] Words substituted by Health Professions Order 2001 (Consequential Amendments) Order 2003/1590 Sch.1(1) para.1(a) (July 9, 2003)

[9] Repealed by Health Professions Order 2001 (Consequential Amendments) Order 2003/1590 Sch.1(1) para.1(b) (July 9, 2003)

[10] Words inserted by National Health Service Reform and Health Care Professions Act 2002 (Supplementary, Consequential etc. Provisions) Regulations 2002/2469 Sch.1(1) para.24 (October 1, 2002)

[11] Words substituted by National Health Service (Consequential Provisions) Act 2006 c. 43 Sch.1 para.191(a) (March 1, 2007)

[12] Words substituted by National Health Service (Consequential Provisions) Act 2006 c. 43 Sch.1 para.191(b) (March 1, 2007)

[13] Added by Health Act 1999 (Supplementary, Consequential etc. Provisions) Order 2000/90 Sch.1 para.33 (February 8, 2000)

14 Words substituted by National Health Service (Consequential Provisions) Act 2006 c. 43 Sch.1 para.191(c) (March 1, 2007)
15 Words substituted by National Health Service (Consequential Provisions) Act 2006 c. 43 Sch.1 para.191(d) (March 1, 2007)
16 Words inserted by National Health Service (Consequential Provisions) Act 2006 c. 43 Sch.1 para.191(e) (March 1, 2007)
17 Added by Health and Social Care (Community Health and Standards) Act 2003 c. 43 Sch.4 para.107 (April 1, 2004: November 20, 2003 for the purpose of making regulations or orders as specified in 2003 c.43 s.199(4); April 1, 2004 otherwise)

Amendments Pending

Pt VI s. 69(3)(fc): added by Health and Social Care Act 2012 c. 7, Sch. 19 para. 7 (date to be appointed) Pt VI s. 69(3)(fb): added by Health and Social Care Act 2012 c. 7, Sch. 17 para. 7 (date to be appointed)
Pt VI s. 69(3)(f): words repealed by Health and Social Care Act 2012 c. 7, Sch. 14(2) para. 74 (date to be appointed) Pt VI s. 69(3)(bb): repealed by Health and Social Care Act 2012 c. 7, Sch. 5 para. 82(d) (date to be appointed)
Pt VI s. 69(3)(aa)–(ab): added by Health and Social Care Act 2012 c. 7, Sch. 5 para. 82(c) (date to be appointed) Pt VI s. 69(3)(a): repealed by Health and Social Care Act 2012 c. 7, Sch. 5 para. 82(b) (date to be appointed)
Pt VI s. 69(1)(k): words substituted by Health and Social Care Act 2012 c. 7, Sch. 5 para. 82(a) (date to be appointed)

Commencement

Pt VI s. 69(1)–(3)(i): July 16, 1998 (1998 c. 29 Pt VI s. 75(2)(d))

Extent

Pt VI s. 69(1)–(3)(a), (3)(b), (3)(c)–(3)(f), (3)(g)–(3)(i): United Kingdom (subject to s.75(6)) Pt VI s. 69(3)(aa)–(3)(ab), (3)(bb)–(3)(bbb), (3)(fa)–(3)(fc): United Kingdom

70. *Supplementary definitions.*

(1) In this Act, unless the context otherwise requires—

"business"includes any trade or profession;

"the Commissioner" means [the Information Commissioner] 1 ;

"credit reference agency"has the same meaning as in the Consumer Credit Act 1974;

"the Data Protection Directive" means Directive 95/46/EC on the protection of individuals with regard to the processing of personal data and on the free movement of such data; "EEA State" means a State which is a contracting party to the Agreement on the European Economic Area signed at Oporto on 2nd May 1992 as adjusted by the Protocol signed at Brussels on 17th March 1993;

"enactment"includes an enactment passed after this Act [and any enactment comprised in, or in any instrument made under, an Act of the Scottish Parliament] 2 ;

["government department"includes—

(a) any part of the Scottish Administration;
(b) a Northern Ireland department;
(c) the Welsh Assembly Government;
(d) any body or authority exercising statutory functions on behalf of the Crown;

] [3]

"Minister of the Crown"has the same meaning as in the Ministers of the Crown Act 1975;

"public register" means any register which pursuant to a requirement imposed—

(a) by or under any enactment, or

(b) in pursuance of any international agreement,

is open to public inspection or open to inspection by any person having a legitimate interest; "pupil"—

(a) in relation to a school in England and Wales, means a registered pupil within the meaning of the Education Act 1996,

(b) in relation to a school in Scotland, means a pupil within the meaning of the Education (Scotland) Act 1980, and

(c) in relation to a school in Northern Ireland, means a registered pupil within the meaning of the Education and Libraries (Northern Ireland) Order 1986;

"recipient", in relation to any personal data, means any person to whom the data are disclosed, including any person (such as an employee or agent of the data controller, a data processor or an employee or agent of a data processor) to whom they are disclosed in the course of processing the data for the data controller, but does not include any person to whom disclosure is or may be made as a result of, or with a view to, a particular inquiry by or on behalf of that person made in the exercise of any power conferred by law;

"registered company" means a company registered under the enactments relating to companies for the time being in force in the United Kingdom;

"school"—

(a) in relation to England and Wales, has the same meaning as in the Education Act 1996,

(b) in relation to Scotland, has the same meaning as in the Education (Scotland) Act 1980, and

(c) in relation to Northern Ireland, has the same meaning as in the Education and Libraries (Northern Ireland) Order 1986;

"teacher"includes—

(a) in Great Britain, head teacher, and

(b) in Northern Ireland, the principal of a school;

"third party", in relation to personal data, means any person other than—

(a) the data subject,

(b) the data controller, or

(c) any data processor or other person authorised to process data for the data controller or processor;

["the Tribunal", in relation to any appeal under this Act, means—

(a) the Upper Tribunal, in any case where it is determined by or under Tribunal Procedure Rules that the Upper Tribunal is to hear the appeal; or

(b) the First-tier Tribunal, in any other case.

] [4]

(2) For the purposes of this Act data are inaccurate if they are incorrect or misleading as to any matter of fact.

Notes

1 Words substituted by Freedom of Information Act 2000 c. 36 Sch.2(I) para.14(a) (January 30, 2001)
2 Words inserted by Scotland Act 1998 (Consequential Modifications) (No.2) Order 1999/1820 Sch.2(I) para.133 (July 1, 1999 the principal appointed day for 1998 c.46)
3 Definition substituted by Coroners and Justice Act 2009 c. 25 Sch.20(2) para.7 (April 6, 2010)
4 Definition substituted by Transfer of Tribunal Functions Order 2010/22 Sch.2 para.29 (January 18, 2010)

Commencement

Pt VI s. 70(1)–(2): July 16, 1998 (1998 c. 29 Pt VI s. 75(2)(d))

Extent

Pt VI s. 70(1)–(1) definition of "government department", (1) definition of "Minister of the Crown"-(1) definition of
"the Tribunal", (2): United Kingdom (subject to s.75(6))
Pt VI s. 70(1) definition of "government department" (a)–(1) definition of "government department" (d), (1) definition of "the Tribunal" (a)–(1) definition of "the Tribunal" (b): United Kingdom

71. *Index of defined expressions.*

The following Table shows provisions defining or otherwise explaining expressions used in this Act (other than provisions defining or explaining an expression only used in the same section or Schedule)—

cessible record	section 68
address (in Part III)	section 16(3)
business	section 70(1)
the Commissioner	section 70(1)
credit reference agency	section 70(1)
data	section 1(1)
data controller	sections 1(1) and (4) and 63(3)
data processor	section 1(1)
the Data Protection Directive	section 70(1)
data protection principles	section 4 and Schedule 1
data subject	section 1(1)
disclosing (of personal data)	section 1(2)(b)
EEA State	section 70(1)
enactment	section 70(1)
enforcement notice	section 40(1)
fees regulations (in Part III)	section 16(2)
government department	section 70(1)
health professional	section 69
inaccurate (in relation to data)	section 70(2)
information notice	section 43(1)
Minister of the Crown	section 70(1)
the non-disclosure provisions (in Part IV)	section 27(3)
notification regulations (in Part III)	section 16(2)
obtaining (of personal data)	section 1(2)(a)
personal data	section 1(1)

prescribed (in Part III)	section 16(2)
processing (of information or data)	section 1(1) and paragraph 5 of Schedule 8
[public authority	section 1(1)][1]
public register	section 70(1)
publish (in relation to journalistic, literary or artistic material)	section 32(6)
pupil (in relation to a school)	section 70(1)
recipient (in relation to personal data)	section 70(1)
recording (of personal data)	section 1(2)(a)
registered company	section 70(1)
registrable particulars (in Part III)	section 16(1)
relevant filing system	section 1(1)
school	section 70(1)
sensitive personal data	section 2
special information notice	section 44(1)
the special purposes	section 3
the subject information provisions (in Part IV)	section 27(2)
teacher	section 70(1)
third party (in relation to processing of personal data)	section 70(1)
the Tribunal	section 70(1)
using (of personal data)	section 1(2)(b).

Notes

[1] Entry added to table by Freedom of Information Act 2000 c. 36 Pt VII s.68(5) (January 1, 2005 for purposes specified in SI 2004/1909 art.2(1); January 1, 2005 otherwise)

Commencement

Pt VI s. 71: July 16, 1998 (1998 c. 29 Pt VI s. 75(2)(d))

Extent

Pt VI s. 71: United Kingdom (subject to s.75(6))

72. *Modifications of Act.*

During the period beginning with the commencement of this section and ending with 23rd October 2007, the provisions of this Act shall have effect subject to the modifications set out in Schedule 13.

Commencement

Pt VI s. 72: March 1, 2000 (SI 2000/183 art. 2(1))

Extent

Pt VI s. 72: United Kingdom (subject to s.75(6))

73. *Transitional provisions and savings.*

Schedule 14 (which contains transitional provisions and savings) has effect.

Commencement

Pt VI s. 73: March 1, 2000 (SI 2000/183 art. 2(1))

Extent

Pt VI s. 73: United Kingdom (subject to s.75(6))

74. *Minor and consequential amendments and repeals and revocations.*

(1) Schedule 15 (which contains minor and consequential amendments) has effect.

(2) The enactments and instruments specified in Schedule 16 are repealed or revoked to the extent specified.

Commencement

Pt VI s. 74(1)–(2): March 1, 2000 (SI 2000/183 art. 2(1))

Extent

Pt VI s. 74(1)–(2): United Kingdom (subject to s.75(6))

75. *Short title, commencement and extent.*

(1) This Act may be cited as the Data Protection Act 1998. (2) The following provisions of this Act—

(a) sections 1 to 3,

(b) section 25(1) and (4), (c) section 26,

(d) sections 67 to 71, (e) this section,

(f) paragraph 17 of Schedule 5, (g) Schedule 11,

(h) Schedule 12, and

(i) so much of any other provision of this Act as confers any power to make subordinate legislation,

shall come into force on the day on which this Act is passed.

(3) The remaining provisions of this Act shall come into force on such day as the [Secretary of State] [1] may by order appoint; and different days may be appointed for different purposes.

(4) The day appointed under subsection (3) for the coming into force of section 56 must not be earlier than the first day on which [sections 112, 113A and 113B of the Police Act 1997] [2] (which provide for the issue by the Secretary of State of criminal conviction certificates, criminal record certificates and enhanced criminal record certificates) are all in force.

[(4A) Subsection (4) does not apply to section 56 so far as that section relates to a record containing information relating to–

(a) the Secretary of State's functions under the Safeguarding Vulnerable Groups Act 2006 [or the Safeguarding Vulnerable Groups (Northern Ireland) Order 2007] [4] , [. . .][5]

(b) the [Independent Safeguarding Authority's] [6] functions under that Act [or that Order] [7] [, or] [8]

[(c) the Scottish Ministers' functions under Parts 1 and 2 of the Protection of Vulnerable Groups (Scotland) Act 2007 (asp 14).] [8]

] [3]

(5) Subject to [subsections (5A) and (6)] [9] , this Act extends to Northern Ireland.

[(5A) In section 56(6) (prohibition of requirement as to production of certain records), paragraph (2)(e) of the Table in that section, insofar as it relates to Part 1 of the Welfare Reform Act 2007, extends to England and Wales and Scotland only.] [9]

(6) Any amendment, repeal or revocation made by Schedule 15 or 16 has the same extent as that of the enactment or instrument to which it relates.

Notes

[1] Words substituted by Secretary of State for Constitutional Affairs Order 2003/1887 Sch.2 para.9(1)(a) (August 19, 2003)
[2] Words substituted by Protection of Freedoms Act 2012 c. 9 Pt 5 c.2 s.86 (September 10, 2012 immediately after the coming into force of SI 2012/2157)
[3] Added by Safeguarding Vulnerable Groups Act 2006 c. 47 Sch.9(2) para.15(3) (May 19, 2008)
[4] Words inserted by Safeguarding Vulnerable Groups (Northern Ireland) Order 2007/1351 Sch.7 para.4(2)(a) (May 29, 2008)
[5] Word repealed by Protection of Vulnerable Groups (Scotland) Act 2007 (Consequential Modifications) Order 2011/565 art.3(3)(a) (March 1, 2011)
[6] Words substituted by Policing and Crime Act 2009 c. 26 Pt 8 c.1 s.81(3)(i) (November 12, 2009)
[7] Words inserted by Safeguarding Vulnerable Groups (Northern Ireland) Order 2007/1351 Sch.7 para.4(2)(b) (May 29, 2008)
[8] Added by Protection of Vulnerable Groups (Scotland) Act 2007 (Consequential Modifications) Order 2011/565 art.3(3)(b) (March 1, 2011)
[9] Amended by Social Security (Miscellaneous Amendments) (No. 3) Regulations 2011/2425 Pt 2 reg.4(b) (October 31, 2011)

Commencement

Pt VI s. 75(1)–(6): July 16, 1998 (1998 c. 29 Pt VI s. 75(2)(e))

Extent

Pt VI s. 75(1)–(4), (5), (6): United Kingdom (subject to s.75(6)) Pt VI s. 75(4A)–(4A)(c), (5A): United Kingdom

SCHEDULE 1—THE DATA PROTECTION PRINCIPLES

SECTION 4(1) AND (2)

PART I

THE PRINCIPLES

1. Personal data shall be processed fairly and lawfully and, in particular, shall not be processed unless—

    (a) at least one of the conditions in Schedule 2 is met, and

    (b) in the case of sensitive personal data, at least one of the conditions in Schedule 3 is also met.

Commencement

Sch. 1(I) para. 1(a) (b): March 1, 2000 (SI 2000/183 art. 2(1))

Extent

Sch. 1(I) para. 1(a)–(b): United Kingdom (subject to s.75(6))

2. Personal data shall be obtained only for one or more specified and lawful purposes, and shall not be further processed in any manner incompatible with that purpose or those purposes.

Commencement

Sch. 1(I) para. 2: March 1, 2000 (SI 2000/183 art. 2(1))

Extent

Sch. 1(I) para. 2: United Kingdom (subject to s.75(6))

3. Personal data shall be adequate, relevant and not excessive in relation to the purpose or purposes for which they are processed.

Commencement

Sch. 1(I) para. 3: March 1, 2000 (SI 2000/183 art. 2(1))

Extent

Sch. 1(I) para. 3: United Kingdom (subject to s.75(6))

4. Personal data shall be accurate and, where necessary, kept up to date.

Commencement

Sch. 1(I) para. 4: March 1, 2000 (SI 2000/183 art. 2(1))

Extent

Sch. 1(I) para. 4: United Kingdom (subject to s.75(6))

5. Personal data processed for any purpose or purposes shall not be kept for longer than is necessary for that purpose or those purposes.

Commencement

Sch. 1(I) para. 5: March 1, 2000 (SI 2000/183 art. 2(1))

Extent

Sch. 1(I) para. 5: United Kingdom (subject to s.75(6))

6. Personal data shall be processed in accordance with the rights of data subjects under this Act.

Commencement

Sch. 1(I) para. 6: March 1, 2000 (SI 2000/183 art. 2(1))

Extent

Sch. 1(I) para. 6: United Kingdom (subject to s.75(6))

7. Appropriate technical and organisational measures shall be taken against unauthorised or unlawful processing of personal data and against accidental loss or destruction of, or damage to, personal data.

Commencement

Sch. 1(I) para. 7: March 1, 2000 (SI 2000/183 art. 2(1))

Extent

Sch. 1(I) para. 7: United Kingdom (subject to s.75(6))

8. Personal data shall not be transferred to a country or territory outside the European Economic Area unless that country or territory ensures an adequate level of protection for the rights and freedoms of data subjects in relation to the processing of personal data.

Commencement

Sch. 1(I) para. 8: March 1, 2000 (SI 2000/183 art. 2(1))

Extent

Sch. 1(I) para. 8: United Kingdom (subject to s.75(6))

PART II

INTERPRETATION OF THE PRINCIPLES IN PART I

The first principle

1.—(1) In determining for the purposes of the first principle whether personal data are processed fairly, regard is to be had to the method by which they are obtained, including in particular whether any person from whom they are obtained is deceived or misled as to the purpose or purposes for which they are to be processed.

(2) Subject to paragraph 2, for the purposes of the first principle data are to be treated as obtained fairly if they consist of information obtained from a person who—

    (a) is authorised by or under any enactment to supply it, or

(b) is required to supply it by or under any enactment or by any convention or other instrument imposing an international obligation on the United Kingdom.

Commencement

Sch. 1(II) para. 1(1)–(2)(b): March 1, 2000 (SI 2000/183 art. 2(1))

Extent

Sch. 1(II) para. 1(1)–(2)(b): United Kingdom (subject to s.75(6))

2.—(1) Subject to paragraph 3, for the purposes of the first principle personal data are not to be treated as processed fairly unless—

(a) in the case of data obtained from the data subject, the data controller ensures so far as practicable that the data subject has, is provided with, or has made readily available to him, the information specified in sub-paragraph (3), and

(b) in any other case, the data controller ensures so far as practicable that, before the relevant time or as soon as practicable after that time, the data subject has, is provided with, or has made readily available to him, the information specified in sub-paragraph (3).

(2) In sub-paragraph (1)(b) "the relevant time" means—

(a) the time when the data controller first processes the data, or

(b) in a case where at that time disclosure to a third party within a reasonable period is envisaged—

(i) if the data are in fact disclosed to such a person within that period, the time when the data are first disclosed,

(ii) if within that period the data controller becomes, or ought to become, aware that the data are unlikely to be disclosed to such a person within that period, the time when the data controller does become, or ought to become, so aware, or

(iii) in any other case, the end of that period.

(3) The information referred to in sub-paragraph (1) is as follows, namely—

(a) the identity of the data controller,

(b) if he has nominated a representative for the purposes of this Act, the identity of that representative,

(c) the purpose or purposes for which the data are intended to be processed, and

(d) any further information which is necessary, having regard to the specific circumstances in which the data are or are to be processed, to enable processing in respect of the data subject to be fair.

Commencement

Sch. 1(II) para. 2(1)–(3)(d): March 1, 2000 (SI 2000/183 art. 2(1))

Extent

Sch. 1(II) para. 2(1)–(3)(d): United Kingdom (subject to s.75(6))

3.—(1) Paragraph 2(1)(b) does not apply where either of the primary conditions in sub-paragraph (2), together with such further conditions as may be prescribed by the [Secretary of State] [1] by order, are met.

(2) The primary conditions referred to in sub-paragraph (1) are—

(a) that the provision of that information would involve a disproportionate effort, or

(b) that the recording of the information to be contained in the data by, or the disclosure of the data by, the data controller is necessary for compliance with any legal obligation to which the data controller is subject, other than an obligation imposed by contract.

Note

¹   Words substituted by Secretary of State for Constitutional Affairs Order 2003/1887 Sch.2 para.9(1)(b) (August 19, 2003)

Commencement

Sch. 1(II) para. 3(1)–(2)(b): March 1, 2000 (SI 2000/183 art. 2(1))

Extent

Sch. 1(II) para. 3(1)–(2)(b): United Kingdom (subject to s.75(6))

4.—(1) Personal data which contain a general identifier falling within a description prescribed by the [Secretary of State] ¹ by order are not to be treated as processed fairly and lawfully unless they are processed in compliance with any conditions so prescribed in relation to general identifiers of that description.

(2) In sub-paragraph (1) "a general identifier" means any identifier (such as, for example, a number or code used for identification purposes) which—

(a) relates to an individual, and

(b) forms part of a set of similar identifiers which is of general application.

Note

¹   Words substituted by Secretary of State for Constitutional Affairs Order 2003/1887 Sch.2 para.9(1)(b) (August 19, 2003)

Commencement

Sch. 1(II) para. 4(1)–(2)(b): March 1, 2000 (SI 2000/183 art. 2(1))

Extent

Sch. 1(II) para. 4(1)–(2)(b): United Kingdom (subject to s.75(6))

The second principle

5. The purpose or purposes for which personal data are obtained may in particular be specified—

(a) in a notice given for the purposes of paragraph 2 by the data controller to the data subject, or

(b) in a notification given to the Commissioner under Part III of this Act.

Commencement

Sch. 1(II) para. 5(a)–(b): March 1, 2000 (SI 2000/183 art. 2(1))

Extent

Sch. 1(II) para. 5(a)–(b): United Kingdom (subject to s.75(6))

6. In determining whether any disclosure of personal data is compatible with the purpose or purposes for which the data were obtained, regard is to be had to the purpose or purposes for which the personal data are intended to be processed by any person to whom they are disclosed.

Commencement

Sch. 1(II) para. 6: March 1, 2000 (SI 2000/183 art. 2(1))

Extent

Sch. 1(II) para. 6: United Kingdom (subject to s.75(6))

The fourth principle

7. The fourth principle is not to be regarded as being contravened by reason of any inaccuracy in personal data which accurately record information obtained by the data controller from the data subject or a third party in a case where—

   (a) having regard to the purpose or purposes for which the data were obtained and further processed, the data controller has taken reasonable steps to ensure the accuracy of the data, and

   (b) if the data subject has notified the data controller of the data subject's view that the data are inaccurate, the data indicate that fact.

Commencement

Sch. 1(II) para. 7(a)–(b): March 1, 2000 (SI 2000/183 art. 2(1))

Extent

Sch. 1(II) para. 7(a)–(b): United Kingdom (subject to s.75(6))

The sixth principle

8. A person is to be regarded as contravening the sixth principle if, but only if—

   (a) he contravenes section 7 by failing to supply information in accordance with that section,

   (b) he contravenes section 10 by failing to comply with a notice given under sub-section (1) of that section to the extent that the notice is justified or by failing to give a notice under subsection (3) of that section,

   (c) he contravenes section 11 by failing to comply with a notice given under sub-section (1) of that section, [or] [1] [. . .][2]

   (d) he contravenes section 12 by failing to comply with a notice given under sub-section (1) or (2)(b) of that section or by failing to give a notification under subsection (2)(a) of that section or a notice under subsection (3) of that section [.] [3]

   (e) [. . .][3]

Notes

1 Word inserted by Data Protection Act 1998 c. 29 Sch.13 para.5 (October 23, 2007)
2 Word repealed by Data Protection Act 1998 c. 29 Sch.13 para.5 (March 1, 2000)
3 Repealed by Data Protection Act 1998 c. 29 Sch.13 para.5 (October 23, 2007)

Commencement

Sch. 1(II) para. 8(a)–(d): March 1, 2000 (SI 2000/183 art. 2(1))

Extent

Sch. 1(II) para. 8(a)–(d): United Kingdom (subject to s.75(6)) Sch. 1(II) para. 8(e): United Kingdom

The seventh principle

9. Having regard to the state of technological development and the cost of implementing any measures, the measures must ensure a level of security appropriate to—

    (a) the harm that might result from such unauthorised or unlawful processing or accidental loss, destruction or damage as are mentioned in the seventh principle, and

    (b) the nature of the data to be protected.

Commencement

Sch. 1(II) para. 9(a)–(b): March 1, 2000 (SI 2000/183 art. 2(1))

Extent

Sch. 1(II) para. 9(a)–(b): United Kingdom (subject to s.75(6))

10. The data controller must take reasonable steps to ensure the reliability of any employees of his who have access to the personal data.

Commencement

Sch. 1(II) para. 10: March 1, 2000 (SI 2000/183 art. 2(1))

Extent

Sch. 1(II) para. 10: United Kingdom (subject to s.75(6))

11. Where processing of personal data is carried out by a data processor on behalf of a data controller, the data controller must in order to comply with the seventh principle—

    (a) choose a data processor providing sufficient guarantees in respect of the technical and organisational security measures governing the processing to be carried out, and

    (b) take reasonable steps to ensure compliance with those measures.

Commencement

Sch. 1(II) para. 11(a)–(b): March 1, 2000 (SI 2000/183 art. 2(1))

Extent

Sch. 1(II) para. 11(a)–(b): United Kingdom (subject to s.75(6))

12. Where processing of personal data is carried out by a data processor on behalf of a data controller, the data controller is not to be regarded as complying with the seventh principle unless—

    (a) the processing is carried out under a contract—

        (i) which is made or evidenced in writing, and
        (ii) under which the data processor is to act only on instructions from the data controller, and

    (b) the contract requires the data processor to comply with obligations equivalent to those imposed on a data controller by the seventh principle.

Commencement

Sch. 1(II) para. 12(a)–(b): March 1, 2000 (SI 2000/183 art. 2(1))

Extent

Sch. 1(II) para. 12(a)–(b): United Kingdom (subject to s.75(6))

The eighth principle

13. An adequate level of protection is one which is adequate in all the circumstances of the case, having regard in particular to—

    (a) the nature of the personal data,

    (b) the country or territory of origin of the information contained in the data,

    (c) the country or territory of final destination of that information,

    (d) the purposes for which and period during which the data are intended to be processed, (e) the law in force in the country or territory in question,

    (f) the international obligations of that country or territory,

    (g) any relevant codes of conduct or other rules which are enforceable in that country or territory (whether generally or by arrangement in particular cases), and

    (h) any security measures taken in respect of the data in that country or territory.

Commencement

Sch. 1(II) para. 13(a)–(h): March 1, 2000 (SI 2000/183 art. 2(1))

Extent

Sch. 1(II) para. 13(a)–(h): United Kingdom (subject to s.75(6))

14. The eighth principle does not apply to a transfer falling within any paragraph of Schedule 4 , except in such circumstances and to such extent as the [Secretary of State] [1] may by order provide.

Notes

[1] Words substituted by Secretary of State for Constitutional Affairs Order 2003/1887 Sch.2 para.9(1)(b) (August 19, 2003)

Commencement

Sch. 1(II) para. 14: March 1, 2000 (SI 2000/183 art. 2(1))

Extent

Sch. 1(II) para. 14: United Kingdom (subject to s.75(6))

15.— (1) Where—

(a) in any proceedings under this Act any question arises as to whether the requirement of the eighth principle as to an adequate level of protection is met in relation to the transfer of any personal data to a country or territory outside the European Economic Area, and

(b) a Community finding has been made in relation to transfers of the kind in question, that question is to be determined in accordance with that finding.

(2) In sub-paragraph (1) "Community finding" means a finding of the European Commission, under the procedure provided for in Article 31(2) of the Data Protection Directive, that a country or territory outside the European Economic Area does, or does not, ensure an adequate level of protection within the meaning of Article 25(2) of the Directive.

Commencement

Sch. 1(II) para. 15(1)–(2): March 1, 2000 (SI 2000/183 art. 2(1))

Extent

Sch. 1(II) para. 15(1)–(2): United Kingdom (subject to s.75(6))

SCHEDULE 2—CONDITIONS RELEVANT FOR PURPOSES OF THE FIRST PRINCIPLE: PROCESSING OF ANY PERSONAL DATA

SECTION 4(3)

1. The data subject has given his consent to the processing.

Commencement

Sch. 2 para. 1: March 1, 2000 (SI 2000/183 art. 2(1))

Extent

Sch. 2 para. 1: United Kingdom (subject to s.75(6))

2. The processing is necessary—

(a) for the performance of a contract to which the data subject is a party, or

(b) for the taking of steps at the request of the data subject with a view to entering into a contract.

Commencement

Sch. 2 para. 2(a)–(b): March 1, 2000 (SI 2000/183 art. 2(1))

Extent

Sch. 2 para. 2(a)–(b): United Kingdom (subject to s.75(6))

3. The processing is necessary for compliance with any legal obligation to which the data controller is subject, other than an obligation imposed by contract.

Commencement

Sch. 2 para. 3: March 1, 2000 (SI 2000/183 art. 2(1))

Extent

Sch. 2 para. 3: United Kingdom (subject to s.75(6))

4. The processing is necessary in order to protect the vital interests of the data subject.

Commencement

Sch. 2 para. 4: March 1, 2000 (SI 2000/183 art. 2(1))

Extent

Sch. 2 para. 4: United Kingdom (subject to s.75(6))

5. The processing is necessary—

    (a) for the administration of justice,

[(aa) for the exercise of any functions of either House of Parliament,] 1

    (b) for the exercise of any functions conferred on any person by or under any enactment,

    (c) for the exercise of any functions of the Crown, a Minister of the Crown or a government department, or

    (d) for the exercise of any other functions of a public nature exercised in the public interest by any person.

Notes

1   Added by Freedom of Information Act 2000 c. 36 Sch.6 para.4 (January 1, 2005 for purposes specified in SI 2004/1909 art.2(1); January 1, 2005 otherwise)

Commencement

Sch. 2 para. 5(a)–(d): March 1, 2000 (SI 2000/183 art. 2(1))

Extent

Sch. 2 para. 5(a), (b)–(d): United Kingdom (subject to s.75(6)) Sch. 2 para. 5(aa): United Kingdom

6.— (1) The processing is necessary for the purposes of legitimate interests pursued by the data controller or by the third party or parties to whom the data are disclosed, except where the processing is unwarranted in any particular case by reason of prejudice to the rights and freedoms or legitimate interests of the data subject.

(2) The [Secretary of State] 1 may by order specify particular circumstances in which this condition is, or is not, to be taken to be satisfied.

Notes

1   Words substituted by Secretary of State for Constitutional Affairs Order 2003/1887 Sch.2 para.9(1)(b) (August 19, 2003)

Commencement

Sch. 2 para. 6(1): March 1, 2000 (SI 2000/183 art. 2(1))
Sch. 2 para. 6(2): July 16, 1998 for the purpose of conferring power to make subordinate legislation; March 1, 2000 otherwise (SI 2000/183 art. 2(1); 1998 c. 29 Pt VI s. 75(2))

Extent

Sch. 2 para. 6(1)–(2): United Kingdom (subject to s.75(6))

SCHEDULE 3—CONDITIONS RELEVANT FOR PURPOSES OF THE FIRST PRINCIPLE: PROCESSING OF SENSITIVE PERSONAL DATA

SECTION 4(3)

1. The data subject has given his explicit consent to the processing of the personal data.

Commencement

Sch. 3 para. 1: March 1, 2000 (SI 2000/183 art. 2(1))

Extent

Sch. 3 para. 1: United Kingdom (subject to s.75(6))

2.—(1) The processing is necessary for the purposes of exercising or performing any right or obligation which is conferred or imposed by law on the data controller in connection with employment.

(2) The [Secretary of State]¹ may by order—

    (a) exclude the application of sub-paragraph (1) in such cases as may be specified, or

    (b) provide that, in such cases as may be specified, the condition in sub-paragraph (1) is not to be regarded as satisfied unless such further conditions as may be specified in the order are also satisfied.

Notes

¹ Words substituted by Secretary of State for Constitutional Affairs Order 2003/1887 Sch.2 para.9(1)(b) (August 19, 2003)

Commencement

Sch. 3 para. 2(1): March 1, 2000 (SI 2000/183 art. 2(1))
Sch. 3 para. 2(2)–(2)(b): July 16, 1998 for the purpose of conferring power to make subordinate legislation; March 1, 2000 otherwise (SI 2000/183 art. 2(1); 1998 c. 29 Pt VI s. 75(2))

Extent

Sch. 3 para. 2(1)–(2)(b): United Kingdom (subject to s.75(6))

3. The processing is necessary—

    (a) in order to protect the vital interests of the data subject or another person, in a case where—

        (i) consent cannot be given by or on behalf of the data subject, or

        (ii) the data controller cannot reasonably be expected to obtain the consent of the data subject, or

(b) in order to protect the vital interests of another person, in a case where consent by or on behalf of the data subject has been unreasonably withheld.

Commencement

Sch. 3 para. 3(a)–(b): March 1, 2000 (SI 2000/183 art. 2(1))

Extent

Sch. 3 para. 3(a)–(b): United Kingdom (subject to s.75(6))

4. The processing—

(a) is carried out in the course of its legitimate activities by any body or association which—

(i) is not established or conducted for profit, and
(ii) exists for political, philosophical, religious or trade-union purposes,

(b) is carried out with appropriate safeguards for the rights and freedoms of data subjects,

(c) relates only to individuals who either are members of the body or association or have regular contact with it in connection with its purposes, and

(d) does not involve disclosure of the personal data to a third party without the consent of the data subject.

Commencement

Sch. 3 para. 4(a)–(d): March 1, 2000 (SI 2000/183 art. 2(1))

Extent

Sch. 3 para. 4(a)–(d): United Kingdom (subject to s.75(6))

5. The information contained in the personal data has been made public as a result of steps deliberately taken by the data subject.

Commencement

Sch. 3 para. 5: March 1, 2000 (SI 2000/183 art. 2(1))

Extent

Sch. 3 para. 5: United Kingdom (subject to s.75(6))

6. The processing—

(a) is necessary for the purpose of, or in connection with, any legal proceedings (including prospective legal proceedings),

(b) is necessary for the purpose of obtaining legal advice, or

(c) is otherwise necessary for the purposes of establishing, exercising or defending legal rights.

Commencement

Sch. 3 para. 6(a)–(c): March 1, 2000 (SI 2000/183 art. 2(1))

Extent

Sch. 3 para. 6(a)–(c): United Kingdom (subject to s.75(6))

7.—(1) The processing is necessary—

(a) for the administration of justice,

[(aa) for the exercise of any functions of either House of Parliament,] 1

(b) for the exercise of any functions conferred on any person by or under an enactment, or

(c) for the exercise of any functions of the Crown, a Minister of the Crown or a government department.

(2) The [Secretary of State] 2 may by order—

(a) exclude the application of sub-paragraph (1) in such cases as may be specified, or

(b) provide that, in such cases as may be specified, the condition in sub-paragraph (1) is not to be regarded as satisfied unless such further conditions as may be specified in the order are also satisfied.

Notes

[1] Added by Freedom of Information Act 2000 c. 36 Sch.6 para.5 (January 1, 2005 for purposes specified in SI 2004/1909 art.2(1); January 1, 2005 otherwise)

[2] Words substituted by Secretary of State for Constitutional Affairs Order 2003/1887 Sch.2 para.9(1)(b) (August 19, 2003)

Commencement

Sch. 3 para. 7(1)–(1)(c): March 1, 2000 (SI 2000/183 art. 2(1))
Sch. 3 para. 7(2)–(2)(b): July 16, 1998 for the purpose of conferring power to make subordinate legislation; March 1, 2000 otherwise (SI 2000/183 art. 2(1); 1998 c. 29 Pt VI s. 75(2))

Extent

Sch. 3 para. 7(1)–(1)(a), (1)(b)–(2)(b): United Kingdom (subject to s.75(6)) Sch. 3 para. 7(1)(aa): United Kingdom

[7A (1) The processing–

(a) is either–

(i) the disclosure of sensitive personal data by a person as a member of an anti-fraud organisation or otherwise in accordance with any arrangements made by such an organisation; or

(ii) any other processing by that person or another person of sensitive personal data so disclosed; and

(b) is necessary for the purposes of preventing fraud or a particular kind of fraud.

(2) In this paragraph "an anti-fraud organisation" means any unincorporated association, body corporate or other person which enables or facilitates any sharing of information to prevent fraud or a particular kind of fraud or which has any of these functions as its purpose or one of its purposes.

] 1

Notes

[1] Added by Serious Crime Act 2007 c. 27 Pt 3 c.1 s.72 (October 1, 2008)

Extent

Sch. 3 para. 7A(1)–(2): United Kingdom

8.—(1) The processing is necessary for medical purposes and is undertaken by—

(a) a health professional, or

(b) a person who in the circumstances owes a duty of confidentiality which is equivalent to that which would arise if that person were a health professional.

(2) In this paragraph "medical purposes" includes the purposes of preventative medicine, medical diagnosis, medical research, the provision of care and treatment and the management of health care services.

Commencement

Sch. 3 para. 8(1)–(2): March 1, 2000 (SI 2000/183 art. 2(1))

Extent

Sch. 3 para. 8(1)–(2): United Kingdom (subject to s.75(6))

9.—(1) The processing—

(a) is of sensitive personal data consisting of information as to racial or ethnic origin,

(b) is necessary for the purpose of identifying or keeping under review the existence or absence of equality of opportunity or treatment between persons of different racial or ethnic origins, with a view to enabling such equality to be promoted or maintained, and

(c) is carried out with appropriate safeguards for the rights and freedoms of data subjects.

(2) The [Secretary of State] 1 may by order specify circumstances in which processing falling within sub-paragraph (1)(a) and (b) is, or is not, to be taken for the purposes of sub-paragraph (1)(c) to be carried out with appropriate safeguards for the rights and freedoms of data subjects.

Notes

1   Words substituted by Secretary of State for Constitutional Affairs Order 2003/1887 Sch.2 para.9(1)(b) (August 19, 2003)

Commencement

Sch. 3 para. 9(1)–(1)(c): March 1, 2000 (SI 2000/183 art. 2(1))
Sch. 3 para. 9(2): July 16, 1998 for the purpose of conferring power to make subordinate legislation; March 1, 2000 otherwise (SI 2000/183 art. 2(1); 1998 c. 29 Pt VI s. 75(2))

Extent

Sch. 3 para. 9(1)–(2): United Kingdom (subject to s.75(6))

10. The personal data are processed in circumstances specified in an order made by the [Secretary of State] 1 for the purposes of this paragraph.

Notes

1   Words substituted by Secretary of State for Constitutional Affairs Order 2003/1887 Sch.2 para.9(1)(b) (August 19, 2003)

Commencement

Sch. 3 para. 10: July 16, 1998 for the purpose of conferring power to make subordinate legislation; March 1, 2000 otherwise (SI 2000/183 art. 2(1); 1998 c. 29 Pt VI s. 75(2))

Extent

Sch. 3 para. 10: United Kingdom (subject to s.75(6))

SCHEDULE 4—CASES WHERE THE EIGHTH PRINCIPLE DOES NOT APPLY

SECTION 4(3)

1. The data subject has given his consent to the transfer.

Commencement

Sch. 4 para. 1: March 1, 2000 (SI 2000/183 art. 2(1))

Extent

Sch. 4 para. 1: United Kingdom (subject to s.75(6))

2. The transfer is necessary—

(a) for the performance of a contract between the data subject and the data controller, or

(b) for the taking of steps at the request of the data subject with a view to his entering into a contract with the data controller.

Commencement

Sch. 4 para. 2(a)–(b): March 1, 2000 (SI 2000/183 art. 2(1))

Extent

Sch. 4 para. 2(a)–(b): United Kingdom (subject to s.75(6))

3. The transfer is necessary—

(a) for the conclusion of a contract between the data controller and a person other than the data subject which—

(i) is entered into at the request of the data subject, or

(ii) is in the interests of the data subject, or

(b) for the performance of such a contract.

Commencement

Sch. 4 para. 3(a)–(b): March 1, 2000 (SI 2000/183 art. 2(1))

Extent

Sch. 4 para. 3(a)–(b): United Kingdom (subject to s.75(6))

4.—(1) The transfer is necessary for reasons of substantial public interest.

(2) The [Secretary of State] [1] may by order specify—

(a) circumstances in which a transfer is to be taken for the purposes of sub- paragraph (1) to be necessary for reasons of substantial public interest, and

(b) circumstances in which a transfer which is not required by or under an enactment is not to be taken for the purpose of sub-paragraph (1) to be necessary for reasons of substantial public interest.

Note

[1] Words substituted by Secretary of State for Constitutional Affairs Order 2003/1887 Sch.2 para.9(1)(b) (August 19, 2003)

Commencement

Sch. 4 para. 4(1): March 1, 2000 (SI 2000/183 art. 2(1))
Sch. 4 para. 4(2)–(2)(b): July 16, 1998 for the purpose of conferring power to make subordinate legislation; March 1, 2000 otherwise (SI 2000/183 art. 2(1); 1998 c. 29 Pt VI s. 75(2))

Extent

Sch. 4 para. 4(1)–(2)(b): United Kingdom (subject to s.75(6))

5. The transfer—

(a) is necessary for the purpose of, or in connection with, any legal proceedings (including prospective legal proceedings),

(b) is necessary for the purpose of obtaining legal advice, or

(c) is otherwise necessary for the purposes of establishing, exercising or defending legal rights.

Commencement

Sch. 4 para. 5(a)–(c): March 1, 2000 (SI 2000/183 art. 2(1))

Extent

Sch. 4 para. 5(a)–(c): United Kingdom (subject to s.75(6))

6. The transfer is necessary in order to protect the vital interests of the data subject.

Commencement

Sch. 4 para. 6: March 1, 2000 (SI 2000/183 art. 2(1))

Extent

Sch. 4 para. 6: United Kingdom (subject to s.75(6))

7. The transfer is of part of the personal data on a public register and any conditions subject to which the register is open to inspection are complied with by any person to whom the data are or may be disclosed after the transfer.

Commencement

Sch. 4 para. 7: March 1, 2000 (SI 2000/183 art. 2(1))

Extent

Sch. 4 para. 7: United Kingdom (subject to s.75(6))

8. The transfer is made on terms which are of a kind approved by the Commissioner as ensuring adequate safeguards for the rights and freedoms of data subjects.

Commencement

Sch. 4 para. 8: March 1, 2000 (SI 2000/183 art. 2(1))

Extent

Sch. 4 para. 8: United Kingdom (subject to s.75(6))

9. The transfer has been authorised by the Commissioner as being made in such a manner as to ensure adequate safeguards for the rights and freedoms of data subjects.

Commencement

Sch. 4 para. 9: March 1, 2000 (SI 2000/183 art. 2(1))

Extent

Sch. 4 para. 9: United Kingdom (subject to s.75(6))

SCHEDULE 5—THE [INFORMATION COMMISSIONER][1] [INFORMATION TRIBUNAL][-1]

SECTION 6(7)

Note

[1]   Words substituted by Freedom of Information Act 2000 c. 36 Sch.2(I) para.1(1) (January 30, 2001)

PART I

THE COMMISSIONER

Status and capacity

1.— (1) The corporation sole by the name of the Data Protection Registrar established by the Data Protection Act 1984 shall continue in existence by the name of the [Information Commissioner][1].

(2) The Commissioner and his officers and staff are not to be regarded as servants or agents of the Crown.

Note

[1]   Words substituted by Freedom of Information Act 2000 c. 36 Sch.2(I) para.15(2) (January 30, 2001)

Commencement

Sch. 5(I) para. 1(1)–(2): March 1, 2000 (SI 2000/183 art. 2(1))

Extent

Sch. 5(I) para. 1(1)–(2): United Kingdom (subject to s.75(6))

Tenure of office

2.—(1) Subject to the provisions of this paragraph, the Commissioner shall hold office for such term not exceeding five years as may be determined at the time of his appointment.

(2) The Commissioner may be relieved of his office by Her Majesty at his own request.

(3) The Commissioner may be removed from office by Her Majesty in pursuance of an Address from both Houses of Parliament.

(4) The Commissioner shall in any case vacate his office—

(a) on completing the year of service in which he attains the age of sixty-five years, or

(b) if earlier, on completing his fifteenth year of service.

(5) Subject to sub-paragraph (4), a person who ceases to be Commissioner on the expiration of his term of office shall be eligible for re-appointment, but a person may not be re-appointed for a third or subsequent term as Commissioner unless, by reason of special circumstances, the person's re-appointment for such a term is desirable in the public interest.

Amendments Pending

Sch. 5(I) para. 2(4)–(5): repealed by Protection of Freedoms Act 2012 c. 9, Sch. 10(8) para. 1 (date to be appointed)
Sch. 5(I) para. 2(3A)–(3C): added by Protection of Freedoms Act 2012 c. 9, Pt 6 s. 105(2) (date to be appointed)
Sch. 5(I) para. 2(1): words substituted by Protection of Freedoms Act 2012 c. 9, Pt 6 s. 105(1) (date to be appointed)

Commencement

Sch. 5(I) para. 2(1)–(5): March 1, 2000 (SI 2000/183 art. 2(1))

Extent

Sch. 5(I) para. 2(1)–(3), (4)–(5): United Kingdom (subject to s.75(6))
Sch. 5(I) para. 2(3A)–(3C): United Kingdom

Salary etc.

3.—(1) There shall be paid—

(a) to the Commissioner such salary, and

(b) to or in respect of the Commissioner such pension, as may be specified by a resolution of the House of Commons.

(2) A resolution for the purposes of this paragraph may—

(a) specify the salary or pension,

(b) provide that the salary or pension is to be the same as, or calculated on the same basis as, that payable to, or to or in respect of, a person employed in a specified office under, or in a specified capacity in the service of, the Crown, or

(c) specify the salary or pension and provide for it to be increased by reference to such variables as may be specified in the resolution.

(3) A resolution for the purposes of this paragraph may take effect from the date on which it is passed or from any earlier or later date specified in the resolution.

(4) A resolution for the purposes of this paragraph may make different provision in relation to the pension payable to or in respect of different holders of the office of Commissioner.

(5) Any salary or pension payable under this paragraph shall be charged on and issued out of the Consolidated Fund.

(6) In this paragraph "pension" includes an allowance or gratuity and any reference to the payment of a pension includes a reference to the making of payments towards the provision of a pension.

Commencement

Sch. 5(I) para. 3(1)–(6): March 1, 2000 (SI 2000/183 art. 2(1))

Extent

Sch. 5(I) para. 3(1)–(6): United Kingdom (subject to s.75(6))

Officers and staff

4.—(1) The Commissioner—

(a) shall appoint a deputy commissioner [or two deputy commissioners] [1] , and

(b) may appoint such number of other officers and staff as he may determine.

[(1A) The Commissioner shall, when appointing any second deputy commissioner, specify which of the Commissioner's functions are to be performed, in the circumstances referred to in paragraph 5(1), by each of the deputy commissioners.] [2]

(2) The remuneration and other conditions of service of the persons appointed under this paragraph shall be determined by the Commissioner.

(3) The Commissioner may pay such pensions, allowances or gratuities to or in respect of the persons appointed under this paragraph, or make such payments towards the provision of such pensions, allowances or gratuities, as he may determine.

(4) The references in sub-paragraph (3) to pensions, allowances or gratuities to or in respect of the persons appointed under this paragraph include references to pensions, allowances or gratuities by way of compensation to or in respect of any of those persons who suffer loss of office or employment.

(5) Any determination under sub-paragraph (1)(b), (2) or (3) shall require the approval of the [Secretary of State] [3] .

(6) The Employers' Liability (Compulsory Insurance) Act 1969 shall not require insurance to be effected by the Commissioner.

Notes

[1]   Words added by Freedom of Information Act 2000 c. 36 Sch.2(II) para.20(2) (November 30, 2000)
[2]   Added by Freedom of Information Act 2000 c. 36 Sch.2(II) para.20(3) (November 30, 2000)
[3]   Words substituted by Secretary of State for Constitutional Affairs Order 2003/1887 Sch.2 para.9(1)(c) (August 19, 2003)

Amendments Pending

Sch. 5(I) para. 4(5): repealed by Protection of Freedoms Act 2012 c. 9, Sch. 10(8) para. 1 (date to be appointed)
Sch. 5(I) para. 4(4A): added by Protection of Freedoms Act 2012 c. 9, Pt 6 s. 108(2) (date to be appointed)

Commencement

Sch. 5(I) para. 4(1)–(6): March 1, 2000 (SI 2000/183 art. 2(1))

Extent

Sch. 5(I) para. 4(1)–(1)(b), (2)–(4), (5)–(6): United Kingdom (subject to s.75(6))
Sch. 5(I) para. 4(1A), (4A): United Kingdom

5.—(1) The deputy commissioner [or deputy commissioners] [1] shall perform the functions conferred by this Act [or the Freedom of Information Act 2000] [2] on the Commissioner during any vacancy in that office or at any time when the Commissioner is for any reason unable to act.

(2) Without prejudice to sub-paragraph (1), any functions of the Commissioner under this Act [or the Freedom of Information Act 2000] [3] may, to the extent authorised by him, be performed by any of his officers or staff.

Notes

[1] Words added by Freedom of Information Act 2000 c. 36 Sch.2(II) para.21(2)(a) (November 30, 2000)
[2] Words added by Freedom of Information Act 2000 c. 36 Sch.2(II) para.21(2)(b) (November 30, 2000)
[3] Words added by Freedom of Information Act 2000 c. 36 Sch.2(II) para.21(3) (November 30, 2000)

Commencement

Sch. 5(I) para. 5(1)–(2): March 1, 2000 (SI 2000/183 art. 2(1))

Extent

Sch. 5(I) para. 5(1)–(2): United Kingdom (subject to s.75(6))

Authentication of seal of the Commissioner

6. The application of the seal of the Commissioner shall be authenticated by his signature or by the signature of some other person authorised for the purpose.

Commencement

Sch. 5(I) para. 6: March 1, 2000 (SI 2000/183 art. 2(1))

Extent

Sch. 5(I) para. 6: United Kingdom (subject to s.75(6))

Presumption of authenticity of documents issued by the Commissioner

7. Any document purporting to be an instrument issued by the Commissioner and to be duly executed under the Commissioner's seal or to be signed by or on behalf of the Commissioner shall be received in evidence and shall be deemed to be such an instrument unless the contrary is shown.

Commencement

Sch. 5(I) para. 7: March 1, 2000 (SI 2000/183 art. 2(1))

Extent

Sch. 5(I) para. 7: United Kingdom (subject to s.75(6))

Money

8. The [Secretary of State] 1 may make payments to the Commissioner out of money provided by Parliament.

Note

1   Words substituted by Secretary of State for Constitutional Affairs Order 2003/1887 Sch.2 para.9(1)(c) (August 19, 2003)

Commencement

Sch. 5(I) para. 8: March 1, 2000 (SI 2000/183 art. 2(1))

Extent

Sch. 5(I) para. 8: United Kingdom (subject to s.75(6))

9.—(1) All fees and other sums received by the Commissioner in the exercise of his functions under this Act [, under section 159 of the Consumer Credit Act 1974 or under the Freedom of Information Act 2000] 1 shall be paid by him to the [Secretary of State] 2 .

(2) Sub-paragraph (1) shall not apply where the [Secretary of State] 2 , with the consent of the Treasury, otherwise directs.

(3) Any sums received by the [Secretary of State] 2 under sub-paragraph (1) shall be paid into the Consolidated Fund.

Notes

1   Words substituted by Freedom of Information Act 2000 c. 36 Sch.2(II) para.22 (November 30, 2000)
2   Words substituted by Secretary of State for Constitutional Affairs Order 2003/1887 Sch.2 para.9(1)(c) (August 19, 2003)

Commencement

Sch. 5(I) para. 9(1)–(3): March 1, 2000 (SI 2000/183 art. 2(1))

Extent

Sch. 5(I) para. 9(1)–(3): United Kingdom (subject to s.75(6))

Accounts

10.—(1) It shall be the duty of the Commissioner—

(a) to keep proper accounts and other records in relation to the accounts,

(b) to prepare in respect of each financial year a statement of account in such form as the [Secretary of State] 1 may direct, and

(c) to send copies of that statement to the Comptroller and Auditor General on or before 31st August next following the end of the year to which the statement relates or on or before such earlier date after the end of that year as the Treasury may direct.

(2) The Comptroller and Auditor General shall examine and certify any statement sent to him under this paragraph and lay copies of it together with his report thereon before each House of Parliament.

(3) In this paragraph "financial year" means a period of twelve months beginning with 1st April.

Note

¹ Words substituted by Secretary of State for Constitutional Affairs Order 2003/1887 Sch.2 para.9(1)(c) (August 19, 2003)

Commencement

Sch. 5(I) para. 10(1)–(3): March 1, 2000 (SI 2000/183 art. 2(1))

Extent

Sch. 5(I) para. 10(1)–(3): United Kingdom (subject to s.75(6))

Application of Part I in Scotland

11. Paragraphs 1(1), 6 and 7 do not extend to Scotland.

Commencement

Sch. 5(I) para. 11: March 1, 2000 (SI 2000/183 art. 2(1))

Extent

Sch. 5(I) para. 11: United Kingdom (subject to s.75(6))

PART II

THE TRIBUNAL

Tenure of office

12.— [. . .]¹

Note

1 Repealed by Transfer of Tribunal Functions Order 2010/22 Sch.2 para.30(b) (January 18, 2010)

Salary etc.

13. [. . .]¹

Note

¹ Repealed by Transfer of Tribunal Functions Order 2010/22 Sch.2 para.30(b) (January 18, 2010)

Officers and staff

14. [. . .]¹

Note

¹ Repealed by Transfer of Tribunal Functions Order 2010/22 Sch.2 para.30(b) (January 18, 2010)

Expenses

15. [. . .]¹

Note

¹ Repealed by Transfer of Tribunal Functions Order 2010/22 Sch.2 para.30(b) (January 18, 2010)

PART III

TRANSITIONAL PROVISIONS

16. [. . .]¹

Note

¹ Repealed by Freedom of Information Act 2000 c. 36 Sch.8(II) para.1 (January 30, 2001)

17. [. . .]¹

Note

¹ Repealed by Freedom of Information Act 2000 c. 36 Sch.8(II) para.1 (January 30, 2001)

SCHEDULE 6—APPEAL PROCEEDINGS

SECTIONS 28(12), 48(5)

Hearing of appeals

1. [. . .]¹

Note

¹ Repealed by Transfer of Tribunal Functions Order 2010/22 Sch.2 para.31(a) (January 18, 2010)

Constitution of Tribunal in national security cases

2.— [. . .]¹

Note

¹ Repealed by Transfer of Tribunal Functions Order 2010/22 Sch.2 para.31(a) (January 18, 2010)

3. [. . .]¹

Note

1 Repealed by Transfer of Tribunal Functions Order 2010/22 Sch.2 para.31(a) (January 18, 2010)

Constitution of Tribunal in other cases

4.— [. . .]¹

Note

¹ Repealed by Transfer of Tribunal Functions Order 2010/22 Sch.2 para.31(a) (January 18, 2010)

Determination of questions by full Tribunal

5. [. . .]¹

Note

¹ Repealed by Transfer of Tribunal Functions Order 2010/22 Sch.2 para.31(a) (January 18, 2010)

Ex parte proceedings

6.— [. . .]¹

Note

¹ Repealed by Transfer of Tribunal Functions Order 2010/22 Sch.2 para.31(a) (January 18, 2010)

[Tribunal Procedure Rules]¹

Note

¹ Words substituted by Transfer of Tribunal Functions Order 2010/22 Sch.2 para.31(b)(i) (January 18, 2010)

7.—[(1) Tribunal Procedure Rules may make provision for regulating the exercise of the rights of appeal conferred—

(a) by sections 28(4) and (6) and 48 of this Act, and

(b) by sections 47(1) and (2) and 60(1) and (4) of the Freedom of Information Act 2000.

(2) In the case of appeals under this Act and the Freedom of Information Act 2000, Tribunal Procedure Rules may make provision—

(a) for securing the production of material used for the processing of personal data;

(b) for the inspection, examination, operation and testing of any equipment or material used in connection with the processing of personal data;

(c) for hearing an appeal in the absence of the appellant or for determining an appeal without a hearing.

]¹

(3) [. . .]²

Notes

¹ Substituted by Transfer of Tribunal Functions Order 2010/22 Sch.2 para.31(b)(ii) (January 18, 2010)
² Repealed by Transfer of Tribunal Functions Order 2010/22 Sch.2 para.31(b)(iii) (January 18, 2010)

Commencement

Sch. 6 para. 7(1)–(3): July 16, 1998 for the purpose of conferring power to make subordinate legislation; March 1, 2000 otherwise (SI 2000/183 art. 2(1); 1998 c. 29 Pt VI s. 75(2))

Extent

Sch. 6 para. 7(1), (2)–(2)(a), (2)(b)–(3): United Kingdom (subject to s.75(6))
Sch. 6 para. 7(1)(a)–(1)(b), (2)(aa)–(2)(ab): United Kingdom

Obstruction etc.

8.—(1) If any person is guilty of any act or omission in relation to proceedings before the Tribunal which, if those proceedings were proceedings before a court having power to commit for contempt, would constitute contempt of court, the Tribunal may certify the offence to the High Court or, in Scotland, the Court of Session.

(2) Where an offence is so certified, the court may inquire into the matter and, after hearing any witness who may be produced against or on behalf of the person charged with the offence, and after hearing any statement that may be offered in defence, deal with him in any manner in which it could deal with him if he had committed the like offence in relation to the court.

Commencement

Sch. 6 para. 8(1)–(2): March 1, 2000 (SI 2000/183 art. 2(1))

Extent

Sch. 6 para. 8(1)–(2): United Kingdom (subject to s.75(6))

SCHEDULE 7—MISCELLANEOUS EXEMPTIONS

Confidential references given by the data controller

1. Personal data are exempt from section 7 if they consist of a reference given or to be given in confidence by the data controller for the purposes of—

(a) the education, training or employment, or prospective education, training or employment, of the data subject,

(b) the appointment, or prospective appointment, of the data subject to any office, or

(c) the provision, or prospective provision, by the data subject of any service.

Commencement

Sch. 7 para. 1(a)–(c): March 1, 2000 (SI 2000/183 art. 2(1))

Extent

Sch. 7 para. 1(a)–(c): United Kingdom (subject to s.75(6))

Armed forces

2. Personal data are exempt from the subject information provisions in any case to the extent to which the application of those provisions would be likely to prejudice the combat effectiveness of any of the armed forces of the Crown.

Commencement

Sch. 7 para. 2: March 1, 2000 (SI 2000/183 art. 2(1))

Extent

Sch. 7 para. 2: United Kingdom (subject to s.75(6))

Judicial appointments and honours

3. Personal data processed for the purposes of—

(a) assessing any person's suitability for judicial office or the office of Queen's Counsel, or

(b) the conferring by the Crown of any honour [or dignity] [1] ,are exempt from the subject information provisions.

Note

[1]   Words added by Freedom of Information Act 2000 c. 36 Sch.6 para.6 (May 14, 2001)

Commencement

Sch. 7 para. 3(a)–(b): March 1, 2000 (SI 2000/183 art. 2(1))

Extent

Sch. 7 para. 3(a)–(b): United Kingdom (subject to s.75(6))

[[4]. (1) The [Secretary of State] [2] may by order exempt from the subject information provisions personal data processed for the purposes of assessing any person's suitability for—

(a) employment by or under the Crown, or

(b) any office to which appointments are made by Her Majesty, by a Minister of the Crown or by a Northern Ireland authority.

(2) In this paragraph "Northern Ireland authority" means the First Minister, the deputy First Minister, a Northern Ireland Minister or a Northern Ireland department.

] [1]

Notes

[1] Existing Sch.7 para.4 renumbered as Sch.7 para.4(1) and Sch.7 para.4(2) is inserted by Northern Ireland Act 1998 c. 47 Sch.13 para.21(2) (December 2, 1999)

[2] Words substituted by Secretary of State for Constitutional Affairs Order 2003/1887 Sch.2 para.9(1)(e) (August 19, 2003)

Commencement

Sch. 7 para. 4(a)–(b): July 16, 1998 for the purpose of conferring power to make subordinate legislation; March 1, 2000 otherwise (SI 2000/183 art. 2(1); 1998 c. 29 Pt VI s. 75(2))

Extent

Sch. 7 para. 4(1)–(2): United Kingdom
Sch. 7 para. 4(a)–(b): United Kingdom (subject to s.75(6))

Management forecasts etc.

5. Personal data processed for the purposes of management forecasting or management planning to assist the data controller in the conduct of any business or other activity are exempt from the subject information provisions in any case to the extent to which the application of those provisions would be likely to prejudice the conduct of that business or other activity.

Commencement

Sch. 7 para. 5: March 1, 2000 (SI 2000/183 art. 2(1))

Extent

Sch. 7 para. 5: United Kingdom (subject to s.75(6))

6.—(1) Where personal data are processed for the purposes of, or in connection with, a corporate finance service provided by a relevant person—

(a) the data are exempt from the subject information provisions in any case to the extent to which either—

(i) the application of those provisions to the data could affect the price of any instrument which is already in existence or is to be or may be created, or

(ii) the data controller reasonably believes that the application of those provisions to the data could affect the price of any such instrument, and

(b) to the extent that the data are not exempt from the subject information provisions by virtue of paragraph (a), they are exempt from those provisions if the exemption is required for the purpose of safeguarding an important economic or financial interest of the United Kingdom.

(2) For the purposes of sub-paragraph (1)(b) the [Secretary of State] [1] may by order specify—

(a) matters to be taken into account in determining whether exemption from the subject information provisions is required for the purpose of safeguarding an important economic or financial interest of the United Kingdom, or

(b) circumstances in which exemption from those provisions is, or is not, to be taken to be required for that purpose.

(3) In this paragraph—

"corporate finance service" means a service consisting in—

(a) underwriting in respect of issues of, or the placing of issues of, any instrument,

(b) advice to undertakings on capital structure, industrial strategy and related matters and advice and service relating to mergers and the purchase of undertakings, or

(c) services relating to such underwriting as is mentioned in paragraph (a); "instrument" means any instrument listed in [section C of Annex I to Directive 2004/39/EC of the European Parliament and of the Council of 21 April 2004 on markets in financial instruments] [2] [. . .] [3];

"price" includes value; "relevant person" means—

[(a) any person who, by reason of any permission he has under Part IV of the Financial Services and Markets Act 2000, is able to carry on a corporate finance service without contravening the general prohibition, within the meaning of section 19 of that Act,

(b) an EEA firm of the kind mentioned in paragraph 5(a) or (b) of Schedule 3 to that Act which has qualified for authorisation under paragraph 12 of that Schedule, and may lawfully carry on a corporate finance service,

(c) any person who is exempt from the general prohibition in respect of any corporate finance service—

(i) as a result of an exemption order made under section 38(1) of that Act, or

(ii) by reason of section 39(1) of that Act (appointed representatives), (cc) any person, not falling within paragraph (a), (b) or (c) who may lawfully carry on a corporate finance service without contravening the general prohibition,] [4]

(d) any person who, in the course of his employment, provides to his employer a service falling within paragraph (b) or (c) of the definition of "corporate finance service", or

(e) any partner who provides to other partners in the partnership a service falling within either of those paragraphs.

Notes

1 Words substituted by Secretary of State for Constitutional Affairs Order 2003/1887 Sch.2 para.9(1)(e) (August 19, 2003)
2 Words substituted by Financial Services and Markets Act 2000 (Markets in Financial Instruments) Regulations 2007/126 Sch.6(1) para.12 (April 1, 2007 for the purposes specified in SI 2007/126 reg.1(2); November 1, 2007 otherwise)
3 Words repealed by Financial Services and Markets Act 2000 (Consequential Amendments) Order 2002/1555 Pt 2 art.25(2) (July 3, 2002)
4 Subparas.(a)–(cc) substituted for subparas.(a)–(c) by Financial Services and Markets Act 2000 (Consequential Amendments) Order 2002/1555 Pt 2 art.25(3) (July 3, 2002)

Commencement

Sch. 7 para. 6(1)–(1)(b), (3)–(3) definition of "relevant person" (e): March 1, 2000 (SI 2000/183 art. 2(1))
Sch. 7 para. 6(2)–(2)(b): July 16, 1998 for the purpose of conferring power to make subordinate legislation; March 1, 2000 otherwise (SI 2000/183 art. 2(1); 1998 c. 29 Pt VI s. 75(2))

Extent

Sch. 7 para. 6(1)–(3) definition of "relevant person" (c), (3) definition of "relevant person" (d)–(3) definition of "relevant person" (e): United Kingdom (subject to s.75(6))
Sch. 7 para. 6(3) definition of "relevant person" (c)(i)–(3) definition of "relevant person" (cc): United Kingdom

Negotiations

7. Personal data which consist of records of the intentions of the data controller in relation to any negotiations with the data subject are exempt from the subject information provisions in any case to the extent to which the application of those provisions would be likely to prejudice those negotiations.

Commencement

Sch. 7 para. 7: March 1, 2000 (SI 2000/183 art. 2(1))

Extent

Sch. 7 para. 7: United Kingdom (subject to s.75(6))

Examination marks

8.—(1) Section 7 shall have effect subject to the provisions of sub-paragraphs (2) to (4) in the case of personal data consisting of marks or other information processed by a data controller—

    (a) for the purpose of determining the results of an academic, professional or other examination or of enabling the results of any such examination to be determined, or

    (b) in consequence of the determination of any such results.

(2) Where the relevant day falls before the day on which the results of the examination are announced, the period mentioned in section 7(8) shall be extended until—

    (a) the end of five months beginning with the relevant day, or

(b) the end of forty days beginning with the date of the announcement, whichever is the earlier.

(3) Where by virtue of sub-paragraph (2) a period longer than the prescribed period elapses after the relevant day before the request is complied with, the information to be supplied pursuant to the request shall be supplied both by reference to the data in question at the time when the request is received and (if different) by reference to the data as from time to time held in the period beginning when the request is received and ending when it is complied with.

(4) For the purposes of this paragraph the results of an examination shall be treated as announced when they are first published or (if not published) when they are first made available or communicated to the candidate in question.

(5) In this paragraph—

"examination"includes any process for determining the knowledge, intelligence, skill or ability of a candidate by reference to his performance in any test, work or other activity; "the prescribed period" means forty days or such other period as is for the time being prescribed under section 7 in relation to the personal data in question;

"relevant day"has the same meaning as in section 7.

Commencement

Sch. 7 para. 8(1)–(5) definition of "relevant day": March 1, 2000 (SI 2000/183 art. 2(1))

Extent

Sch. 7 para. 8(1)–(5) definition of "relevant day": United Kingdom (subject to s.75(6))

Examination scripts etc.

9.—(1) Personal data consisting of information recorded by candidates during an academic, professional or other examination are exempt from section 7.

(2) In this paragraph "examination"has the same meaning as in paragraph 8.

Commencement

Sch. 7 para. 9(1)–(2): March 1, 2000 (SI 2000/183 art. 2(1))

Extent

Sch. 7 para. 9(1)–(2): United Kingdom (subject to s.75(6))

Legal professional privilege

10. Personal data are exempt from the subject information provisions if the data consist of information in respect of which a claim to legal professional privilege [or, in Scotland, to confidentiality of communications] 1 could be maintained in legal proceedings.

Note

1 Words substituted by Freedom of Information Act 2000 c. 36 Sch.6 para.7 (May 14, 2001)

Commencement

Sch. 7 para. 10: March 1, 2000 (SI 2000/183 art. 2(1))

Extent

Sch. 7 para. 10: United Kingdom (subject to s.75(6))

Self-incrimination

11.—(1) A person need not comply with any request or order under section 7 to the extent that compliance would, by revealing evidence of the commission of any offence [, other than an offence under this Act or an offence within sub-paragraph (1A),] [3] expose him to proceedings for that offence.

[(1A) The offences mentioned in sub-paragraph (1) are—

(a) an offence under section 5 of the Perjury Act 1911 (false statements made otherwise than on oath),

(b) an offence under section 44(2) of the Criminal Law (Consolidation) (Scotland) Act 1995 (false statements made otherwise than on oath), or

(c) an offence under Article 10 of the Perjury (Northern Ireland) Order 1979 (false statutory declarations and other false unsworn statements).

][2]

(2) Information disclosed by any person in compliance with any request or order under section 7 shall not be admissible against him in proceedings for an offence under this Act.

Notes

[1]   Words substituted by Coroners and Justice Act 2009 c. 25 Sch.20(4) para.12(2) (April 6, 2010)
[2]   Added by Coroners and Justice Act 2009 c. 25 Sch.20(4) para.12(3) (April 6, 2010)

Commencement

Sch. 7 para. 11(1)–(2): March 1, 2000 (SI 2000/183 art. 2(1))

Extent

Sch. 7 para. 11(1), (2): United Kingdom (subject to s.75(6))
Sch. 7 para. 11(1A)–(1A)(c): United Kingdom

SCHEDULE 8—TRANSITIONAL RELIEF

SECTION 39

PART I

INTERPRETATION OF SCHEDULE

1.—(1) For the purposes of this Schedule, personal data are "eligible data" at any time if, and to the extent that, they are at that time subject to processing which was already under way immediately before 24th October 1998.

(2) In this Schedule—

"eligible automated data" means eligible data which fall within paragraph (a) or (b) of the definition of "data" in section 1(1);

"eligible manual data" means eligible data which are not eligible automated data;

"the first transitional period" means the period beginning with the commencement of this Schedule and ending with 23rd October 2001;

"the second transitional period" means the period beginning with 24th October 2001 and ending with 23rd October 2007.

Commencement

Sch. 8(I) para. 1(1)–(2) definition of "the second transitional period": March 1, 2000 (SI 2000/183 art. 2(1))

Extent

Sch. 8(I) para. 1(1)–(2) definition of "the second transitional period": United Kingdom (subject to s.75(6))

PART II

EXEMPTIONS AVAILABLE BEFORE 24TH OCTOBER 2001

Manual data

2.—(1) Eligible manual data, other than data forming part of an accessible record, are exempt from the data protection principles and Parts II and III of this Act during the first transitional period.

(2) This paragraph does not apply to eligible manual data to which paragraph 4 applies.

Commencement

Sch. 8(II) para. 2(1)–(2): March 1, 2000 (SI 2000/183 art. 2(1))

Extent

Sch. 8(II) para. 2(1)–(2): United Kingdom (subject to s.75(6))

3.—(1) This paragraph applies to—

(a) eligible manual data forming part of an accessible record, and

(b) personal data which fall within paragraph (d) of the definition of "data" in section 1(1) but which, because they are not subject to processing which was already under way immediately before 24th October 1998, are not eligible data for the purposes of this Schedule.

(2) During the first transitional period, data to which this paragraph applies are exempt from—

(a) the data protection principles, except the sixth principle so far as relating to sections 7 and 12A,

1151

(b) Part II of this Act, except—

    (i) section 7 (as it has effect subject to section 8) and section 12A, and

    (ii) section 15 so far as relating to those sections, and

(c) Part III of this Act.

Commencement

Sch. 8(II) para. 3(1)–(2)(c): March 1, 2000 (SI 2000/183 art. 2(1))

Extent

Sch. 8(II) para. 3(1)–(2)(c): United Kingdom (subject to s.75(6))

4.—(1) This paragraph applies to eligible manual data which consist of information relevant to the financial standing of the data subject and in respect of which the data controller is a credit reference agency.

(2) During the first transitional period, data to which this paragraph applies are exempt from—

(a) the data protection principles, except the sixth principle so far as relating to sections 7 and 12A,

(b) Part II of this Act, except—

    (i) section 7 (as it has effect subject to sections 8 and 9) and section 12A, and

    (ii) section 15 so far as relating to those sections, and

(c) Part III of this Act.

Commencement

Sch. 8(II) para. 4(1)–(2)(c): March 1, 2000 (SI 2000/183 art. 2(1))

Extent

Sch. 8(II) para. 4(1)–(2)(c): United Kingdom (subject to s.75(6))

Processing otherwise than by reference to the data subject

5. During the first transitional period, for the purposes of this Act (apart from paragraph 1), eligible automated data are not to be regarded as being "processed" unless the processing is by reference to the data subject.

Commencement

Sch. 8(II) para. 5: March 1, 2000 (SI 2000/183 art. 2(1))

Extent

Sch. 8(II) para. 5: United Kingdom (subject to s.75(6))

Payrolls and accounts

6.—(1) Subject to sub-paragraph (2), eligible automated data processed by a data controller for one or more of the following purposes—

(a) calculating amounts payable by way of remuneration or pensions in respect of service in any employment or office or making payments of, or of sums deducted from, such remuneration or pensions, or

(b) keeping accounts relating to any business or other activity carried on by the data controller or keeping records of purchases, sales or other transactions for the purpose of ensuring that the requisite payments are made by or to him in respect of those transactions or for the purpose of making financial or management forecasts to assist him in the conduct of any such business or activity,

are exempt from the data protection principles and Parts II and III of this Act during the first transitional period.

(2) It shall be a condition of the exemption of any eligible automated data under this paragraph that the data are not processed for any other purpose, but the exemption is not lost by any processing of the eligible data for any other purpose if the data controller shows that he had taken such care to prevent it as in all the circumstances was reasonably required.

(3) Data processed only for one or more of the purposes mentioned in sub-paragraph (1)(a) may be disclosed—

(a) to any person, other than the data controller, by whom the remuneration or pensions in question are payable,

(b) for the purpose of obtaining actuarial advice,

(c) for the purpose of giving information as to the persons in any employment or office for use in medical research into the health of, or injuries suffered by, persons engaged in particular occupations or working in particular places or areas,

(d) if the data subject (or a person acting on his behalf) has requested or consented to the disclosure of the data either generally or in the circumstances in which the disclosure in question is made, or

(e) if the person making the disclosure has reasonable grounds for believing that the disclosure falls within paragraph (d).

(4) Data processed for any of the purposes mentioned in sub-paragraph (1) may be disclosed—

(a) for the purpose of audit or where the disclosure is for the purpose only of giving information about the data controller's financial affairs, or

(b) in any case in which disclosure would be permitted by any other provision of this Part of this Act if sub-paragraph (2) were included among the non-disclosure provisions.

(5) In this paragraph "remuneration" includes remuneration in kind and "pensions" includes gratuities or similar benefits.

Commencement

Sch. 8(II) para. 6(1)–(5): March 1, 2000 (SI 2000/183 art. 2(1))

Extent

Sch. 8(II) para. 6(1)–(5): United Kingdom (subject to s.75(6))

Unincorporated members' clubs and mailing lists

7. Eligible automated data processed by an unincorporated members' club and relating only to the members of the club are exempt from the data protection principles and Parts II and III of this Act during the first transitional period.

Commencement

Sch. 8(II) para. 7: March 1, 2000 (SI 2000/183 art. 2(1))

Extent

Sch. 8(II) para. 7: United Kingdom (subject to s.75(6))

8. Eligible automated data processed by a data controller only for the purposes of distributing, or recording the distribution of, articles or information to the data subjects and consisting only of their names, addresses or other particulars necessary for effecting the distribution, are exempt from the data protection principles and Parts II and III of this Act during the first transitional period.

Commencement

Sch. 8(II) para. 8: March 1, 2000 (SI 2000/183 art. 2(1))

Extent

Sch. 8(II) para. 8: United Kingdom (subject to s.75(6))

9. Neither paragraph 7 nor paragraph 8 applies to personal data relating to any data subject unless he has been asked by the club or data controller whether he objects to the data relating to him being processed as mentioned in that paragraph and has not objected.

Commencement

Sch. 8(II) para. 9: March 1, 2000 (SI 2000/183 art. 2(1))

Extent

Sch. 8(II) para. 9: United Kingdom (subject to s.75(6))

10. It shall be a condition of the exemption of any data under paragraph 7 that the data are not disclosed except as permitted by paragraph 11 and of the exemption under paragraph 8 that the data are not processed for any purpose other than that mentioned in that paragraph or as permitted by paragraph

11, but—

    (a) the exemption under paragraph 7 shall not be lost by any disclosure in breach of that condition, and

    (b) the exemption under paragraph 8 shall not be lost by any processing in breach of that condition,

if the data controller shows that he had taken such care to prevent it as in all the circumstances was reasonably required.

Commencement

Sch. 8(II) para. 10(a)–(b): March 1, 2000 (SI 2000/183 art. 2(1))

Extent

Sch. 8(II) para. 10(a)–(b): United Kingdom (subject to s.75(6))

11.Data to which paragraph 10 applies may be disclosed—

(a) if the data subject (or a person acting on his behalf) has requested or consented to the disclosure of the data either generally or in the circumstances in which the disclosure in question is made,

(b) if the person making the disclosure has reasonable grounds for believing that the disclosure falls within paragraph (a), or

(c) in any case in which disclosure would be permitted by any other provision of this Part of this Act if paragraph 10 were included among the non-disclosure provisions.

Commencement

Sch. 8(II) para. 11(a)–(c): March 1, 2000 (SI 2000/183 art. 2(1))

Extent

Sch. 8(II) para. 11(a)–(c): United Kingdom (subject to s.75(6))

Back-up data

12. Eligible automated data which are processed only for the purpose of replacing other data in the event of the latter being lost, destroyed or impaired are exempt from section 7 during the first transitional period.

Commencement

Sch. 8(II) para. 12: March 1, 2000 (SI 2000/183 art. 2(1))

Extent

Sch. 8(II) para. 12: United Kingdom (subject to s.75(6))

Exemption of all eligible automated data from certain requirements

13.—(1) During the first transitional period, eligible automated data are exempt from the following provisions—

(a) the first data protection principle to the extent to which it requires compliance with—

(i) paragraph 2 of Part II of Schedule 1,
(ii) the conditions in Schedule 2, and
(iii) the conditions in Schedule 3,

(b) the seventh data protection principle to the extent to which it requires compliance with paragraph 12 of Part II of Schedule 1;

(c) the eighth data protection principle,

(d) in section 7(1), paragraphs (b), (c)(ii) and (d),

(e) sections 10 and 11,

(f) section 12, and

(g) section 13, except so far as relating to—

(i) any contravention of the fourth data protection principle,

(ii) any disclosure without the consent of the data controller,

(iii) loss or destruction of data without the consent of the data controller, or

(iv) processing for the special purposes.

(2) The specific exemptions conferred by sub-paragraph (1)(a), (c) and (e) do not limit the data controller's general duty under the first data protection principle to ensure that processing is fair.

Commencement

Sch. 8(II) para. 13(1)–(2): March 1, 2000 (SI 2000/183 art. 2(1))

Extent

Sch. 8(II) para. 13(1)–(2): United Kingdom (subject to s.75(6))

PART III

EXEMPTIONS AVAILABLE AFTER 23RD OCTOBER 2001 BUT BEFORE 24TH OCTOBER 2007

14.— (1) This paragraph applies to—

(a) eligible manual data which were held immediately before 24th October 1998, and

(b) personal data which fall within paragraph (d) of the definition of "data" in section 1(1)

but do not fall within paragraph (a) of this sub-paragraph.
but does not apply to eligible manual data to which the exemption in paragraph 16 applies.

(2) During the second transitional period, data to which this paragraph applies are exempt from the following provisions—

(a) the first data protection principle except to the extent to which it requires compliance with paragraph 2 of Part II of Schedule 1,

(b) the second, third, fourth and fifth data protection principles, and

(c) section 14(1) to (3).

Commencement

Sch. 8(III) para. 14(1)–(2)(c): March 1, 2000 (SI 2000/183 art. 2(1))

Extent

Sch. 8(III) para. 14(1)–(2)(c): United Kingdom (subject to s.75(6))

[**14A.**— (1) This paragraph applies to personal data which fall within paragraph (e) of the definition of "data" in section 1(1) and do not fall within paragraph 14(1)(a), but does not apply to eligible manual data to which the exemption in paragraph 16 applies.

(2) During the second transitional period, data to which this paragraph applies are exempt from—

    (a) the fourth data protection principle, and

    (b) section 14(1) to (3).

] [1]

Note

[1]   Added by Freedom of Information Act 2000 c. 36 Pt VII s.70(3) (January 1, 2005 for purposes specified in SI 2004/1909 art.2(1); January 1, 2005 otherwise)

Extent

Sch. 8(III) para. 14A(1)–(2)(b): United Kingdom

PART IV

EXEMPTIONS AFTER 23RD OCTOBER 2001 FOR HISTORICAL RESEARCH

15. In this Part of this Schedule "the relevant conditions"has the same meaning as in section 33.

Commencement

Sch. 8(IV) para. 15: March 1, 2000 (SI 2000/183 art. 2(1))

Extent

Sch. 8(IV) para. 15: United Kingdom (subject to s.75(6))

16.— (1) Eligible manual data which are processed only for the purpose of historical research in compliance with the relevant conditions are exempt from the provisions specified in sub-paragraph (2) after 23rd October 2001.

(2) The provisions referred to in sub-paragraph (1) are—

    (a) the first data protection principle except in so far as it requires compliance with paragraph 2 of Part II of Schedule 1,

    (b) the second, third, fourth and fifth data protection principles, and

    (c) section 14(1) to (3).

Commencement

Sch. 8(IV) para. 16(1)–(2)(c): March 1, 2000 (SI 2000/183 art. 2(1))

Extent

Sch. 8(IV) para. 16(1)–(2)(c): United Kingdom (subject to s.75(6))

17.— (1) After 23rd October 2001 eligible automated data which are processed only for the purpose of historical research in compliance with the relevant conditions are exempt from the first data protection principle to the extent to which it requires compliance with the conditions in Schedules 2 and 3.

(2) Eligible automated data which are processed—

(a) only for the purpose of historical research,

(b) in compliance with the relevant conditions, and

(c) otherwise than by reference to the data subject,

are also exempt from the provisions referred to in sub-paragraph (3) after 23rd October 2001.

(3) The provisions referred to in sub-paragraph (2) are—

(a) the first data protection principle except in so far as it requires compliance with paragraph 2 of Part II of Schedule 1,

(b) the second, third, fourth and fifth data protection principles, and

(c) section 14(1) to (3).

Commencement

Sch. 8(IV) para. 17(1)–(3)(c): March 1, 2000 (SI 2000/183 art. 2(1))

Extent

Sch. 8(IV) para. 17(1)–(3)(c): United Kingdom (subject to s.75(6))

18. For the purposes of this Part of this Schedule personal data are not to be treated as processed otherwise than for the purpose of historical research merely because the data are disclosed—

(a) to any person, for the purpose of historical research only,

(b) to the data subject or a person acting on his behalf,

(c) at the request, or with the consent, of the data subject or a person acting on his behalf, or

(d) in circumstances in which the person making the disclosure has reasonable grounds for believing that the disclosure falls within paragraph (a), (b) or (c).

Commencement

Sch. 8(IV) para. 18(a)–(d): March 1, 2000 (SI 2000/183 art. 2(1))

Extent

Sch. 8(IV) para. 18(a)–(d): United Kingdom (subject to s.75(6))

PART V

EXEMPTION FROM SECTION 22

19. Processing which was already under way immediately before 24th October 1998 is not assessable processing for the purposes of section 22.

Commencement

Sch. 8(V) para. 19: March 1, 2000 (SI 2000/183 art. 2(1))

Extent

Sch. 8(V) para. 19: United Kingdom (subject to s.75(6))

SCHEDULE 9—POWERS OF ENTRY AND INSPECTION

Section 50

Issue of warrants

! Amendment(s) Pending

1.— (1) If a circuit judge is satisfied by information on oath supplied by the Commissioner that there are reasonable grounds for suspecting—

(a) that a data controller has contravened or is contravening any of the data protection principles, or

(b) that an offence under this Act has been or is being committed,

and that evidence of the contravention or of the commission of the offence is to be found on any premises specified in the information, he may, subject to sub-paragraph (2) and paragraph 2, grant a warrant to the Commissioner.

[(1A) Sub-paragraph (1B) applies if a circuit judge or a District Judge (Magistrates' Courts) is satisfied by information on oath supplied by the Commissioner that a data controller has failed to comply with a requirement imposed by an assessment notice.

(1B) The judge may, for the purpose of enabling the Commissioner to determine whether the data controller has complied or is complying with the data protection principles, grant a warrant to the Commissioner in relation to any premises that were specified in the assessment notice; but this is subject to sub-paragraph (2) and paragraph 2.] [1]

(2) A judge shall not issue a warrant under this Schedule in respect of any personal data processed for the special purposes unless a determination by the Commissioner under section 45 with respect to those data has taken effect.

(3) A warrant issued under [this Schedule] [2] shall authorise the Commissioner or any of his officers or staff at any time within seven days of the date of the warrant [—] [3]

[(a) to enter the premises;

(b) to search the premises;

(c) to inspect, examine, operate and test any equipment found on the premises which is used or intended to be used for the processing of personal data;

(d) to inspect and seize any documents or other material found on the premises which—

(i) in the case of a warrant issued under subparagraph (1), may be such evidence as is mentioned in that paragraph;

(ii) in the case of a warrant issued under subparagraph (1B), may enable the Commissioner to determine whether the data controller has complied or is complying with the data protection principles;

(e) to require any person on the premises to provide an explanation of any document or other material found on the premises;

(f) to require any person on the premises to provide such other information as may reasonably be required for the purpose of determining whether the data controller has contravened, or is contravening, the data protection principles.] [3]

Notes

[1] Added by Coroners and Justice Act 2009 c. 25 Sch.20(6) para.14(2) (April 6, 2010: insertion has effect subject to transitional provisions specified in 2009 c.25, Sch.22, para.46)

² Words substituted by Coroners and Justice Act 2009 c. 25 Sch.20(6) para.14(3)(a) (April 6, 2010)
³ Para.1(3)(a)–(f) substituted for words by Coroners and Justice Act 2009 c. 25 Sch.20(6) para.14(3)(b) (April 6,2010)

Amendments Pending

Sch. 9 para. 1(1): words inserted by Courts Act 2003 c. 39, Sch. 4 para. 8 (date to be appointed)

Commencement

Sch. 9 para. 1(1)–(3): March 1, 2000 (SI 2000/183 art. 2(1))

Extent

Sch. 9 para. 1(1)–(1)(b), (2)–(3): United Kingdom (subject to s.75(6))
Sch. 9 para. 1(1A)–(1B), (3)(a)–(3)(f): United Kingdom

2.—(1) A judge shall not issue a warrant under this Schedule unless he is satisfied—

(a) that the Commissioner has given seven days' notice in writing to the occupier of the premises in question demanding access to the premises, and

(b) that either—

(i) access was demanded at a reasonable hour and was unreasonably refused, or

(ii) although entry to the premises was granted, the occupier unreasonably refused to comply with a request by the Commissioner or any of the Commissioner's officers or staff to permit the Commissioner or the officer or member of staff to do any of the things referred to in paragraph 1(3), and

(c) that the occupier, has, after the refusal, been notified by the Commissioner of the application for the warrant and has had an opportunity of being heard by the judge on the question whether or not it should be issued.

[(1A) In determining whether the Commissioner has given an occupier the seven days' notice referred to in sub-paragraph (1)(a) any assessment notice served on the occupier is to be disregarded.]¹

(2) Sub-paragraph (1) shall not apply if the judge is satisfied that the case is one of urgency or that compliance with those provisions would defeat the object of the entry.

Note

¹ Added by Coroners and Justice Act 2009 c. 25 Sch.20(6) para.14(4) (April 6, 2010)

Commencement

Sch. 9 para. 2(1)–(2): March 1, 2000 (SI 2000/183 art. 2(1))

Extent

Sch. 9 para. 2(1)–(1)(c), (2): United Kingdom (subject to s.75(6))
Sch. 9 para. 2(1A): United Kingdom

3. A judge who issues a warrant under this Schedule shall also issue two copies of it and certify them clearly as copies.

Commencement

Sch. 9 para. 3: March 1, 2000 (SI 2000/183 art. 2(1))

Extent

Sch. 9 para. 3: United Kingdom (subject to s.75(6))

Execution of warrants

4. A person executing a warrant issued under this Schedule may use such reasonable force as may be necessary.

Commencement

Sch. 9 para. 4: March 1, 2000 (SI 2000/183 art. 2(1))

Extent

Sch. 9 para. 4: United Kingdom (subject to s.75(6))

5. A warrant issued under this Schedule shall be executed at a reasonable hour unless it appears to the person executing it that there are grounds for suspecting that the [object of the warrant would be defeated] 1 if it were so executed.

Note

1   Words substituted by Coroners and Justice Act 2009 c. 25 Sch.20(6) para.14(5) (April 6, 2010)

Commencement

Sch. 9 para. 5: March 1, 2000 (SI 2000/183 art. 2(1))

Extent

Sch. 9 para. 5: United Kingdom (subject to s.75(6))

6. If the person who occupies the premises in respect of which a warrant is issued under this Schedule is present when the warrant is executed, he shall be shown the warrant and supplied with a copy of it; and if that person is not present a copy of the warrant shall be left in a prominent place on the premises.

Commencement

Sch. 9 para. 6: March 1, 2000 (SI 2000/183 art. 2(1))

Extent

Sch. 9 para. 6: United Kingdom (subject to s.75(6))

7.— (1) A person seizing anything in pursuance of a warrant under this Schedule shall give a receipt for it if asked to do so.

(2) Anything so seized may be retained for so long as is necessary in all the circumstances but the person in occupation of the premises in question shall be given a copy of anything that is seized if he so requests and the person executing the warrant considers that it can be done without undue delay.

Commencement

Sch. 9 para. 7(1)–(2): March 1, 2000 (SI 2000/183 art. 2(1))

Extent

Sch. 9 para. 7(1)–(2): United Kingdom (subject to s.75(6))

Matters exempt from inspection and seizure

8. The powers of inspection and seizure conferred by a warrant issued under this Schedule shall not be exercisable in respect of personal data which by virtue of section 28 are exempt from any of the provisions of this Act.

Commencement

Sch. 9 para. 8: March 1, 2000 (SI 2000/183 art. 2(1))

Extent

Sch. 9 para. 8: United Kingdom (subject to s.75(6))

9.— (1) Subject to the provisions of this paragraph, the powers of inspection and seizure conferred by a warrant issued under this Schedule shall not be exercisable in respect of—

    (a) any communication between a professional legal adviser and his client in connection with the giving of legal advice to the client with respect to his obligations, liabilities or rights under this Act, or

    (b) any communication between a professional legal adviser and his client, or between such an adviser or his client and any other person, made in connection with or in contemplation of proceedings under or arising out of this Act (including proceedings before the Tribunal) and for the purposes of such proceedings.

(2) Sub-paragraph (1) applies also to—

    (a) any copy or other record of any such communication as is there mentioned, and

    (b) any document or article enclosed with or referred to in any such communication if made in connection with the giving of any advice or, as the case may be, in connection with or in contemplation of and for the purposes of such proceedings as are there mentioned.

(3) This paragraph does not apply to anything in the possession of any person other than the professional legal adviser or his client or to anything held with the intention of furthering a criminal purpose.

(4) In this paragraph references to the client of a professional legal adviser include references to any person representing such a client.

Commencement

Sch. 9 para. 9(1)–(4): March 1, 2000 (SI 2000/183 art. 2(1))

Extent

Sch. 9 para. 9(1)–(4): United Kingdom (subject to s.75(6))

10. If the person in occupation of any premises in respect of which a warrant is issued under this Schedule objects to the inspection or seizure under the warrant of any material on the grounds that it consists partly of matters in respect of which those powers are not exercisable, he shall, if the person executing the warrant so requests, furnish that person with a copy of so much of the material as is not exempt from those powers.

Commencement

Sch. 9 para. 10: March 1, 2000 (SI 2000/183 art. 2(1))

Extent

Sch. 9 para. 10: United Kingdom (subject to s.75(6))

Return of warrants

11. A warrant issued under this Schedule shall be returned to the court from which it was issued—

    (a) after being executed, or

    (b) if not executed within the time authorised for its execution;

and the person by whom any such warrant is executed shall make an endorsement on it stating what powers have been exercised by him under the warrant.

Commencement

Sch. 9 para. 11(a)–(b). March 1, 2000 (SI 2000/183 art. 2(1))

Extent

Sch. 9 para. 11(a)–(b): United Kingdom (subject to s.75(6))

Offences

12. Any person who—

    (a) intentionally obstructs a person in the execution of a warrant issued under this Schedule, [. . .]¹

    (b) fails without reasonable excuse to give any person executing such a warrant such assistance as he may reasonably require for the execution of the warrant,

    [(c) makes a statement in response to a requirement under paragraph (e) or (f) of paragraph

    1(3) which that person knows to be false in a material respect, or

    (d) recklessly makes a statement in response to such a requirement which is false in a material respect,] ²

is guilty of an offence.

Notes

¹ Word repealed by Coroners and Justice Act 2009 c. 25 Sch.23(8) para.1 (April 6, 2010 as SI 2010/816)

² Added by Coroners and Justice Act 2009 c. 25 Sch.20(6) para.14(6) (April 6, 2010)

Commencement

Sch. 9 para. 12(a)–(b): March 1, 2000 (SI 2000/183 art. 2(1))

Extent

Sch. 9 para. 12(a)–(b): United Kingdom (subject to s.75(6))
Sch. 9 para. 12(c)–(d): United Kingdom

Vessels, vehicles etc.

13. In this Schedule "premises"includes any vessel, vehicle, aircraft or hovercraft, and references to the occupier of any premises include references to the person in charge of any vessel, vehicle, aircraft or hovercraft.

Commencement

Sch. 9 para. 13: March 1, 2000 (SI 2000/183 art. 2(1))

Extent

Sch. 9 para. 13: United Kingdom (subject to s.75(6))

Scotland and Northern Ireland

14. In the application of this Schedule to Scotland—

(a) for any reference to a circuit judge there is substituted a reference to the sheriff,

(b) for any reference to information on oath there is substituted a reference to evidence on oath, and

(c) for the reference to the court from which the warrant was issued there is substituted a reference to the sheriff clerk.

Commencement

Sch. 9 para. 14(a)–(c): March 1, 2000 (SI 2000/183 art. 2(1))

Extent

Sch. 9 para. 14(a)–(c): United Kingdom (subject to s.75(6))

15. In the application of this Schedule to Northern Ireland—

(a) for any reference to a circuit judge there is substituted a reference to a county court judge, and

(b) for any reference to information on oath there is substituted a reference to a complaint on oath.

Commencement

Sch. 9 para. 15(a)–(b): March 1, 2000 (SI 2000/183 art. 2(1))

Extent

Sch. 9 para. 15(a)–(b): United Kingdom (subject to s.75(6))

[*Self-incrimination* **]** *[1]*

Note

[1] Added by Coroners and Justice Act 2009 c. 25 Sch.20(6) para.14(7) (April 6, 2010)

[16 An explanation given, or information provided, by a person in response to a requirement under paragraph (e) or (f) of paragraph 1(3) may only be used in evidence against that person—

    (a) on a prosecution for an offence under—

        (i) paragraph 12,

        (ii) section 5 of the Perjury Act 1911 (false statements made otherwise than on oath),

        (iii) section 44(2) of the Criminal Law (Consolidation) (Scotland) Act 1995 (false statements made otherwise than on oath), or

        (iv) Article 10 of the Perjury (Northern Ireland) Order 1979 (false statutory declarations and other false unsworn statements), or

    (b) on a prosecution for any other offence where—

        (i) in giving evidence that person makes a statement inconsistent with that explanation or information, and

        (ii) evidence relating to that explanation or information is adduced, or a question relating to it is asked, by that person or on that person's behalf.

] *[1]*

Note

[1] Added by Coroners and Justice Act 2009 c. 25 Sch.20(6) para.14(7) (April 6, 2010)

Extent

Sch. 9 para. 16(a)–(b)(ii): United Kingdom

SCHEDULE 10—FURTHER PROVISIONS RELATING TO ASSISTANCE UNDER SECTION 53

Section 53(6)

1. In this Schedule "applicant" and "proceedings"have the same meaning as in section 53.

Commencement

Sch. 10 para. 1: March 1, 2000 (SI 2000/183 art. 2(1))

Extent

Sch. 10 para. 1: United Kingdom (subject to s.75(6))

2. The assistance provided under section 53 may include the making of arrangements for, or for the Commissioner to bear the costs of—

    (a) the giving of advice or assistance by a solicitor or counsel, and

    (b) the representation of the applicant, or the provision to him of such assistance as is usually given by a solicitor or counsel—

(i) in steps preliminary or incidental to the proceedings, or

(ii) in arriving at or giving effect to a compromise to avoid or bring an end to the proceedings.

Commencement

Sch. 10 para. 2(a)–(b)(ii): March 1, 2000 (SI 2000/183 art. 2(1))

Extent

Sch. 10 para. 2(a)–(b)(ii): United Kingdom (subject to s.75(6))

3. Where assistance is provided with respect to the conduct of proceedings—

(a) it shall include an agreement by the Commissioner to indemnify the applicant (subject only to any exceptions specified in the notification) in respect of any liability to pay costs or expenses arising by virtue of any judgment or order of the court in the proceedings,

(b) it may include an agreement by the Commissioner to indemnify the applicant in respect of any liability to pay costs or expenses arising by virtue of any compromise or settlement arrived at in order to avoid the proceedings or bring the proceedings to an end, and

(c) it may include an agreement by the Commissioner to indemnify the applicant in respect of any liability to pay damages pursuant to an undertaking given on the grant of interlocutory relief (in Scotland, an interim order) to the applicant.

Commencement

Sch. 10 para. 3(a)–(c): March 1, 2000 (SI 2000/183 art. 2(1))

Extent

Sch. 10 para. 3(a)–(c): United Kingdom (subject to s.75(6))

4. Where the Commissioner provides assistance in relation to any proceedings, he shall do so on such terms, or make such other arrangements, as will secure that a person against whom the proceedings have been or are commenced is informed that assistance has been or is being provided by the Commissioner in relation to them.

Commencement

Sch. 10 para. 4: March 1, 2000 (SI 2000/183 art. 2(1))

Extent

Sch. 10 para. 4: United Kingdom (subject to s.75(6))

5. In England and Wales or Northern Ireland, the recovery of expenses incurred by the Commissioner in providing an applicant with assistance (as taxed or assessed in such manner as may be prescribed by rules of court) shall constitute a first charge for the benefit of the Commissioner—

(a) on any costs which, by virtue of any judgment or order of the court, are payable to the applicant by any other person in respect of the matter in connection with which the assistance is provided, and

(b) on any sum payable to the applicant under a compromise or settlement arrived at in connection with that matter to avoid or bring to an end any proceedings.

Commencement

Sch. 10 para. 5(a)–(b): March 1, 2000 (SI 2000/183 art. 2(1))

Extent

Sch. 10 para. 5(a)–(b): United Kingdom (subject to s.75(6))

6. In Scotland, the recovery of such expenses (as taxed or assessed in such manner as may be prescribed by rules of court) shall be paid to the Commissioner, in priority to other debts—

(a) out of any expenses which, by virtue of any judgment or order of the court, are payable to the applicant by any other person in respect of the matter in connection with which the assistance is provided, and

(b) out of any sum payable to the applicant under a compromise or settlement arrived at in connection with that matter to avoid or bring to an end any proceedings.

Commencement

Sch. 10 para. 6(a)–(b): March 1, 2000 (SI 2000/183 art. 2(1))

Extent

Sch. 10 para. 6(a)–(b): United Kingdom (subject to s.75(6))

SCHEDULE 11—EDUCATIONAL RECORDS

Section 68(1)(b)

Meaning of "educational record"

1. For the purposes of section 68"educational record" means any record to which paragraph 2, 5 or 7 applies.

Commencement

Sch. 11 para. 1: July 16, 1998 (1998 c. 29 Pt VI s. 75(2)(g))

Extent

Sch. 11 para. 1: United Kingdom (subject to s.75(6))

England and Wales

2. This paragraph applies to any record of information which—

(a) is processed by or on behalf of the governing body of, or a teacher at, any school in England and Wales specified in paragraph 3,

(b) relates to any person who is or has been a pupil at the school, and

(c) originated from or was supplied by or on behalf of any of the persons specified in paragraph 4,

other than information which is processed by a teacher solely for the teacher's own use.

Commencement

Sch. 11 para. 2(a)–(c): July 16, 1998 (1998 c. 29 Pt VI s. 75(2)(g))

Extent

Sch. 11 para. 2(a)–(c): United Kingdom (subject to s.75(6))

3. The schools referred to in paragraph 2(a) are—

    (a) a school maintained by a [local authority] [1] , and

    (b) a special school, as defined by section 6(2) of the Education Act 1996, which is not so maintained.

Note

[1] Words substituted by Local Education Authorities and Children's Services Authorities (Integration of Functions) Order 2010/1158 Sch.2(2) para.42(2) (May 5, 2010)

Commencement

Sch. 11 para. 3(a)–(b): July 16, 1998 (1998 c. 29 Pt VI s. 75(2)(g))

Extent

Sch. 11 para. 3(a)–(b): United Kingdom (subject to s.75(6))

4. The persons referred to in paragraph 2(c) are—

    (a) an employee of the [local authority] [1] which maintains the school, (b) in the case of—

        (i) a voluntary aided, foundation or foundation special school (within the meaning of the School Standards and Framework Act 1998), or

        (ii) a special school which is not maintained by a [local authority] [1] ,

    a teacher or other employee at the school (including an educational psychologist engaged by the governing body under a contract for services),

    (c) the pupil to whom the record relates, and

    (d) a parent, as defined by section 576(1) of the Education Act 1996, of that pupil.

Note

[1] Words substituted by Local Education Authorities and Children's Services Authorities (Integration of Functions) Order 2010/1158 Sch.2(2) para.42(2) (May 5, 2010)

Commencement

Sch. 11 para. 4(a)–(d): July 16, 1998 (1998 c. 29 Pt VI s. 75(2)(g))

Extent

Sch. 11 para. 4(a)–(d): United Kingdom (subject to s.75(6))

[**4A.** In paragraphs 3 and 4"local authority"has the meaning given by section 579(1) of the Education Act 1996.

] [1]

Note

¹ Added by Local Education Authorities and Children's Services Authorities (Integration of Functions) Order 2010/1158 Sch.2(2) para.42(3) (May 5, 2010)

Extent

Sch. 11 para. 4A: United Kingdom

Scotland

5. This paragraph applies to any record of information which is processed—

(a) by an education authority in Scotland, and

(b) for the purpose of the relevant function of the authority,

other than information which is processed by a teacher solely for the teacher's own use.

Commencement

Sch. 11 para. 5(a)–(b): July 16, 1998 (1998 c. 29 Pt VI s. 75(2)(g))

Extent

Sch. 11 para. 5(a)–(b): United Kingdom (subject to s.75(6))

6. For the purposes of paragraph 5—

(a) "education authority" means an education authority within the meaning of the Education (Scotland) Act 1980 ("the 1980 Act") [. . .]¹ ,

(b) "the relevant function" means, in relation to each of those authorities, their function under section 1 of the 1980 Act and section 7(1) of the 1989 Act, and

(c) information processed by an education authority is processed for the purpose of the relevant function of the authority if the processing relates to the discharge of that function in respect of a person—

(i) who is or has been a pupil in a school provided by the authority, or
(ii) who receives, or has received, further education (within the meaning of the 1980 Act) so provided.

Note

¹ Words repealed by Standards in Scotland's Schools etc. Act 2000 asp 6 (Scottish Act) Sch.3 para. (December 31, 2004: as SSI 2004/528)

Commencement

Sch. 11 para. 6(a)–(c)(ii): July 16, 1998 (1998 c. 29 Pt VI s. 75(2)(g))

Extent

Sch. 11 para. 6(a)–(c)(ii): United Kingdom (subject to s.75(6))

Northern Ireland

7.— (1) This paragraph applies to any record of information which—

(a) is processed by or on behalf of the Board of Governors of, or a teacher at, any grant-aided school in Northern Ireland,

(b) relates to any person who is or has been a pupil at the school, and

(c) originated from or was supplied by or on behalf of any of the persons specified in paragraph 8,

other than information which is processed by a teacher solely for the teacher's own use.

(2) In sub-paragraph (1) "grant-aided school"has the same meaning as in the Education and Libraries (Northern Ireland) Order 1986.

Commencement

Sch. 11 para. 7(1)–(2): July 16, 1998 (1998 c. 29 Pt VI s. 75(2)(g))

Extent

Sch. 11 para. 7(1)–(2): United Kingdom (subject to s.75(6))

8. The persons referred to in paragraph 7(1) are—

(a) a teacher at the school,

(b) an employee of an education and library board, other than such a teacher,

(c) the pupil to whom the record relates, and

(d) a parent (as defined by Article 2(2) of the Education and Libraries (Northern Ireland) Order 1986) of that pupil.

Commencement

Sch. 11 para. 8(a)–(d): July 16, 1998 (1998 c. 29 Pt VI s. 75(2)(g))

Extent

Sch. 11 para. 8(a)–(d): United Kingdom (subject to s.75(6))

England and Wales: transitory provisions

9.— (1) Until the appointed day within the meaning of section 20 of the School Standards and Framework Act 1998, this Schedule shall have effect subject to the following modifications.

(2) Paragraph 3 shall have effect as if for paragraph (b) and the "and" immediately preceding it there were substituted—
"(aa) a grant-maintained school, as defined by section 183(1) of the Education Act 1996,
(ab) a grant-maintained special school, as defined by section 337(4) of that Act, and
(b) a special school, as defined by section 6(2) of that Act, which is neither a maintained special school, as defined by section 337(3) of that Act, nor a grant-maintained special school."

(3) Paragraph 4(b)(i) shall have effect as if for the words from "foundation", in the first place where it occurs, to "1998)" there were substituted "or grant-maintained school".

Commencement

Sch. 11 para. 9(1)–(3): July 16, 1998 (1998 c. 29 Pt VI s. 75(2)(g))

Extent

Sch. 11 para. 9(1)–(3): United Kingdom (subject to s.75(6))

SCHEDULE 12—ACCESSIBLE PUBLIC RECORDS

Section 68(1)(c)

Meaning of "accessible public record"

1. For the purposes of section 68"accessible public record" means any record which is kept by an authority specified—

(a) as respects England and Wales, in the Table in paragraph 2,

(b) as respects Scotland, in the Table in paragraph 4, or

(c) as respects Northern Ireland, in the Table in paragraph 6,

and is a record of information of a description specified in that Table in relation to that authority.

Commencement

Sch. 12 para. 1(a)–(c): July 16, 1998 (1998 c. 29 Pt VI s. 75(2)(h))

Extent

Sch. 12 para. 1(a)–(c): United Kingdom (subject to s.75(6))

Housing and social services records: England and Wales:

2. The following is the Table referred to in paragraph 1(a).

TABLE OF AUTHORITIES AND INFORMATION

The authorities	*The accessible information*
Housing Act local authority.	Information held for the purpose of any of the authority's tenancies.
Local social services authority.	Information held for any purpose of the authority's social services functions.

Commencement

Sch. 12 para. 2: July 16, 1998 (1998 c. 29 Pt VI s. 75(2)(h))

Extent

Sch. 12 para. 2: United Kingdom (subject to s.75(6))

3.— (1) The following provisions apply for the interpretation of the Table in paragraph 2.

(2) Any authority which, by virtue of section 4(e) of the Housing Act 1985, is a local

authority for the purpose of any provision of that Act is a "Housing Act local authority" for the purposes of this Schedule, and so is any housing action trust established under Part III of the Housing Act 1988.

(3) Information contained in records kept by a Housing Act local authority is "held for the purpose of any of the authority's tenancies" if it is held for any purpose of the relationship of landlord and tenant of a dwelling which subsists, has subsisted or may subsist between the authority and any individual who is, has been or, as the case may be, has applied to be, a tenant of the authority.

(4) Any authority which, by virtue of section 1 or 12 of the Local Authority Social Services Act 1970, is or is treated as a local authority for the purposes of that Act is a "local social services authority" for the purposes of this Schedule; and information contained in records kept by such an authority is "held for any purpose of the authority's social services functions" if it is held for the purpose of any past, current or proposed exercise of such a function in any case.

(5) Any expression used in paragraph 2 or this paragraph and in Part II of the Housing Act 1985 or the Local Authority Social Services Act 1970 has the same meaning as in that Act.

Commencement

Sch. 12 para. 3(1)–(5): July 16, 1998 (1998 c. 29 Pt VI s. 75(2)(h))

Extent

Sch. 12 para. 3(1)–(5): United Kingdom (subject to s.75(6))

Housing and social services records: Scotland

! Amendment(s) Pending
4. The following is the Table referred to in paragraph 1(b).

TABLE OF AUTHORITIES AND INFORMATION

The authorities	*The accessible information*
Local authority. Scottish Homes.	Information held for the purpose of any of the body's tenancies.
Social work authority.	Information held for any purpose of the authority's functions under the Social Work (Scotland) Act 1968 and the enactments referred to in section 5(1B) of that Act.

Amendments Pending

Sch. 12 para. 4: entry repealed by Housing (Scotland) Act 2001 asp 10 (Scottish Act), Sch. 10 para. 26(a) (date to be appointed)

Commencement

Sch. 12 para. 4: July 16, 1998 (1998 c. 29 Pt VI s. 75(2)(h))

Extent

Sch. 12 para. 4: United Kingdom (subject to s.75(6))

! Amendment(s) Pending
5.— (1) The following provisions apply for the interpretation of the Table in paragraph 4.

(2) "Local authority" means —

(a) a council constituted under section 2 of the Local Government etc. (Scotland) Act 1994,

(b) a joint board or joint committee of two or more of those councils, or

(c) any trust under the control of such a council.

(3) Information contained in records kept by a local authority or Scottish Homes is held for the purpose of any of their tenancies if it is held for any purpose of the relationship of landlord and tenant of a dwelling-house which subsists, has subsisted or may subsist between the authority or, as the case may be, Scottish Homes and any individual who is, has been or, as the case may be, has applied to be a tenant of theirs.

(4) "Social work authority" means a local authority for the purposes of the Social Work (Scotland) Act 1968; and information contained in records kept by such an authority is held for any purpose of their functions if it is held for the purpose of any past, current or proposed exercise of such a function in any case.

Amendments Pending

Sch. 12 para. 5(3): repealed by Housing (Scotland) Act 2001 asp 10 (Scottish Act), Sch. 10 para. 26(b) (date to be appointed)

Commencement

Sch. 12 para. 5(1) (4): July 16, 1998 (1998 c. 29 Pt VI s. 75(2)(h))

Extent

Sch. 12 para. 5(1)–(4): United Kingdom (subject to s.75(6))

Housing and social services records: Northern Ireland

6. The following is the Table referred to in paragraph 1(c).

TABLE OF AUTHORITIES AND INFORMATION

The authorities	*The accessible information*
The Northern Ireland Housing Executive.	Information held for the purpose of any of the Executive's tenancies.
A Health and Social Services Board.	Information held for the purpose of any past, current or proposed exercise by the Board of any function exercisable, by virtue of directions under Article 17(1) of the Health and Personal Social Services (Northern Ireland) Order

The authorities	The accessible information
	1972, by the Board on behalf of the Department of Health and Social Services with respect to the administration of personal social services under— (a) the Children and Young Persons Act (Northern Ireland) 1968; (b) the Health and Personal Social Services (Northern Ireland) Order 1972; (c) Article 47 of the Matrimonial Causes (Northern Ireland) Order 1978; (d) Article 11 of the Domestic Proceedings (Northern Ireland) Order 1980; (e) the Adoption (Northern Ireland) Order 1987; or (f) the Children (Northern Ireland) Order 1995.
An HSS trust	Information held for the purpose of any past, current or proposed exercise by the trust of any function exercisable, by virtue of an authorisation under Article 3(1) of the Health and Personal Social Services (Northern Ireland) Order 1994, by the trust on behalf of a Health and Social Services Board with respect to the administration of personal social services under any statutory provision mentioned in the last preceding entry.

Commencement

Sch. 12 para. 6: July 16, 1998 (1998 c. 29 Pt VI s. 75(2)(h))

Extent

Sch. 12 para. 6: United Kingdom (subject to s.75(6))

7.— (1) This paragraph applies for the interpretation of the Table in paragraph 6.

(2) Information contained in records kept by the Northern Ireland Housing Executive is "held for the purpose of any of the Executive's tenancies" if it is held for any purpose of the relationship of landlord and tenant of a dwelling which subsists, has subsisted or may subsist between the Executive and any individual who is, has been or, as the case may be, has applied to be, a tenant of the Executive.

Commencement

Sch. 12 para. 7(1)–(2): July 16, 1998 (1998 c. 29 Pt VI s. 75(2)(h))

Extent

Sch. 12 para. 7(1)–(2): United Kingdom (subject to s.75(6))

SCHEDULE 13—MODIFICATIONS OF ACT HAVING EFFECT BEFORE 24TH OCTOBER 2007

Section 72

1. After section 12 there is inserted—

"12A.— Rights of data subjects in relation to exempt manual data.

(1) A data subject is entitled at any time by notice in writing—

    (a) to require the data controller to rectify, block, erase or destroy exempt manual data which are inaccurate or incomplete, or

    (b) to require the data controller to cease holding exempt manual data in a way incompatible with the legitimate purposes pursued by the data controller.

(2) A notice under subsection (1)(a) or (b) must state the data subject's reasons for believing that the data are inaccurate "or incomplete or, as the case may be, his reasons for believing that they are held in a way incompatible with the legitimate purposes pursued by the data controller.

(3) If the court is satisfied, on the application of any person who has given a notice under subsection (1) which appears to the court to be justified (or to be justified to any extent) that the data controller in question has failed to comply with the notice, the court may order him to take such steps for complying with the notice (or for complying with it to that extent) as the court thinks fit.

(4) In this section "exempt manual data" means —

    (a) in relation to the first transitional period, as defined by paragraph 1(2) of Schedule 8, data to which paragraph 3 or 4 of that Schedule applies, and

    (b) in relation to the second transitional period, as so defined, data to which [paragraph 14 or 14A] [1] of that Schedule applies.

(5) For the purposes of this section personal data are incomplete if, and only if, the data, although not inaccurate, are such that their incompleteness would constitute a contravention of the third or fourth data protection principles, if those principles applied to the data."

Note

[1] Words added by Freedom of Information Act 2000 c. 36 Pt VII s.70(4) (January 1, 2005 for purposes specified in SI 2004/1909 art.2(1); January 1, 2005 otherwise)

Commencement

Sch. 13 para. 1: March 1, 2000 (SI 2000/183 art. 2(1))

Extent

Sch. 13 para. 1: United Kingdom (subject to s.75(6))

2. In section 32—

    (a) in subsection (2) after "section 12" there is inserted—

        "(dd) section 12A," and

    (b) in subsection (4) after "12(8)" there is inserted ", 12A(3)".

Commencement

Sch. 13 para. 2(a)–(b): March 1, 2000 (SI 2000/183 art. 2(1))

Extent

Sch. 13 para. 2(a)–(b): United Kingdom (subject to s.75(6))

3. In section 34 for "section 14(1) to (3)" there is substituted "sections 12A and 14(1) to (3)."

Commencement

Sch. 13 para. 3: March 1, 2000 (SI 2000/183 art. 2(1))

Extent

Sch. 13 para. 3: United Kingdom (subject to s.75(6))

4. In section 53(1) after "12(8)" there is inserted ", 12A(3)".

Commencement

Sch. 13 para. 4: March 1, 2000 (SI 2000/183 art. 2(1))

Extent

Sch. 13 para. 4: United Kingdom (subject to s.75(6))

5. In paragraph 8 of Part II of Schedule 1, the word "or" at the end of paragraph (c) is omitted and after paragraph (d) there is inserted
"or
  (e) he contravenes section 12A by failing to comply with a notice given under
      subsection (1) of that section to the extent that the notice is justified."

Commencement

Sch. 13 para. 5: March 1, 2000 (SI 2000/183 art. 2(1))

Extent

Sch. 13 para. 5: United Kingdom (subject to s.75(6))

SCHEDULE 14—TRANSITIONAL PROVISIONS AND SAVINGS

Section 73

Interpretation

1. In this Schedule—

"the 1984 Act" means the Data Protection Act 1984;

"the old principles" means the data protection principles within the meaning of the 1984 Act;

"the new principles" means the data protection principles within the meaning of this Act.

Commencement

Sch. 14 para. 1 definition of "the 1984 Act"– definition of "the new principles": March 1, 2000 (SI 2000/183 art. 2(1))

Extent

Sch. 14 para. 1 definition of "the 1984 Act"– definition of "the new principles": United Kingdom (subject to s.75(6))

Effect of registration under Part II of 1984 Act

2. – (1) Subject to sub-paragraphs (4) and (5) any person who, immediately before the commencement of Part III of this Act—

(a) is registered as a data user under Part II of the 1984 Act, or

(b) is treated by virtue of section 7(6) of the 1984 Act as so registered, is exempt from section 17(1) of this Act until the end of the registration period [. . .]¹.

(2) In sub-paragraph (1) "the registration period", in relation to a person, means —

(a) where there is a single entry in respect of that person as a data user, the period at the end of which, if section 8 of the 1984 Act had remained in force, that entry would have fallen to be removed unless renewed, and

(b) where there are two or more entries in respect of that person as a data user, the period at the end of which, if that section had remained in force, the last of those entries to expire would have fallen to be removed unless renewed.

(3) Any application for registration as a data user under Part II of the 1984 Act which is received by the Commissioner before the commencement of Part III of this Act (including any appeal against a refusal of registration) shall be determined in accordance with the old principles and the provisions of the 1984 Act.

(4) If a person falling within paragraph (b) of sub-paragraph (1) receives a notification under section 7(1) of the 1984 Act of the refusal of his application, sub-paragraph (1) shall cease to apply to him—

(a) if no appeal is brought, at the end of the period within which an appeal can be brought against the refusal, or

(b) on the withdrawal or dismissal of the appeal.

(5) If a data controller gives a notification under section 18(1) at a time when he is exempt from section 17(1) by virtue of sub-paragraph (1), he shall cease to be so exempt.

(6) The Commissioner shall include in the register maintained under section 19 an entry in respect of each person who is exempt from section 17(1) by virtue of sub-paragraph (1); and each entry shall consist of the particulars which, immediately before the commencement of Part III of this Act, were included (or treated as included) in respect of that person in the register maintained under section 4 of the 1984 Act.

(7) Notification regulations under Part III of this Act may make provision modifying the duty referred to in section 20(1) in its application to any person in respect of whom an entry in the register maintained under section 19 has been made under sub-paragraph (6).

(8) Notification regulations under Part III of this Act may make further transitional provision in connection with the substitution of Part III of this Act for Part II of the

1984 Act (registration), including provision modifying the application of provisions of Part III in transitional cases.

Note

[1] Words repealed by Freedom of Information Act 2000 c. 36 Sch.8(I) para.1 (November 30, 2000)

Commencement

Sch. 14 para. 2(1)–(8): March 1, 2000 (SI 2000/183 art. 2(1))

Extent

Sch. 14 para. 2(1)–(8): United Kingdom (subject to s.75(6))

Rights of data subjects

3.— (1) The repeal of section 21 of the 1984 Act (right of access to personal data) does not affect the application of that section in any case in which the request (together with the information referred to in paragraph (a) of subsection (4) of that section and, in a case where it is required, the consent referred to in paragraph (b) of that subsection) was received before the day on which the repeal comes into force.

(2) Sub-paragraph (1) does not apply where the request is made by reference to this Act.

(3) Any fee paid for the purposes of section 21 of the 1984 Act before the commencement of section 7 in a case not falling within sub-paragraph (1) shall be taken to have been paid for the purposes of section 7.

Commencement

Sch. 14 para. 3(1)–(3): March 1, 2000 (SI 2000/183 art. 2(1))

Extent

Sch. 14 para. 3(1)–(3): United Kingdom (subject to s.75(6))

4. The repeal of section 22 of the 1984 Act (compensation for inaccuracy) and the repeal of section 23 of that Act (compensation for loss or unauthorised disclosure) do not affect the application of those sections in relation to damage or distress suffered at any time by reason of anything done or omitted to be done before the commencement of the repeals.

Commencement

Sch. 14 para. 4: March 1, 2000 (SI 2000/183 art. 2(1))

Extent

Sch. 14 para. 4: United Kingdom (subject to s.75(6))

5. The repeal of section 24 of the 1984 Act (rectification and erasure) does not affect any case in which the application to the court was made before the day on which the repeal comes into force.

Commencement

Sch. 14 para. 5: March 1, 2000 (SI 2000/183 art. 2(1))

Extent

Sch. 14 para. 5: United Kingdom (subject to s.75(6))

6. Subsection (3)(b) of section 14 does not apply where the rectification, blocking, erasure or destruction occurred before the commencement of that section.

Commencement

Sch. 14 para. 6: March 1, 2000 (SI 2000/183 art. 2(1))

Extent

Sch. 14 para. 6: United Kingdom (subject to s.75(6))

Enforcement and transfer prohibition notices served under Part V of 1984 Act

7.— (1) If, immediately before the commencement of section 40—

(a) an enforcement notice under section 10 of the 1984 Act has effect, and

(b) either the time for appealing against the notice has expired or any appeal has been determined,

then, after that commencement, to the extent mentioned in sub-paragraph (3), the notice shall have effect for the purposes of sections 41 and 47 as if it were an enforcement notice under section 40.

(2) Where an enforcement notice has been served under section 10 of the 1984 Act before the commencement of section 40 and immediately before that commencement either—

(a) the time for appealing against the notice has not expired, or

(b) an appeal has not been determined,

the appeal shall be determined in accordance with the provisions of the 1984 Act and the old principles and, unless the notice is quashed on appeal, to the extent mentioned in sub-paragraph (3) the notice shall have effect for the purposes of sections 41 and 47 as if it were an enforcement notice under section 40.

(3) An enforcement notice under section 10 of the 1984 Act has the effect described in sub-paragraph (1) or (2) only to the extent that the steps specified in the notice for complying with the old principle or principles in question are steps which the data controller could be required by an enforcement notice under section 40 to take for complying with the new principles or any of them.

Commencement

Sch. 14 para. 7(1)–(3): March 1, 2000 (SI 2000/183 art. 2(1))

Extent

Sch. 14 para. 7(1)–(3): United Kingdom (subject to s.75(6))

8.— (1) If, immediately before the commencement of section 40—

(a) a transfer prohibition notice under section 12 of the 1984 Act has effect, and

(b) either the time for appealing against the notice has expired or any appeal has been determined,

then, on and after that commencement, to the extent specified in sub-paragraph (3), the notice shall have effect for the purposes of sections 41 and 47 as if it were an enforcement notice under section 40.

(2) Where a transfer prohibition notice has been served under section 12 of the 1984 Act and immediately before the commencement of section 40 either—

(a) the time for appealing against the notice has not expired, or

(b) an appeal has not been determined,

the appeal shall be determined in accordance with the provisions of the 1984 Act and the old principles and, unless the notice is quashed on appeal, to the extent mentioned in sub-paragraph (3) the notice shall have effect for the purposes of sections 41 and 47 as if it were an enforcement notice under section 40.

(3) A transfer prohibition notice under section 12 of the 1984 Act has the effect described in sub-paragraph (1) or (2) only to the extent that the prohibition imposed by the notice is one which could be imposed by an enforcement notice under section 40 for complying with the new principles or any of them.

Commencement

Sch. 14 para. 8(1)–(3): March 1, 2000 (SI 2000/183 art. 2(1))

Extent

Sch. 14 para. 8(1)–(3): United Kingdom (subject to s.75(6))

Notices under new law relating to matters in relation to which 1984 Act had effect

9. The Commissioner may serve an enforcement notice under section 40 on or after the day on which that section comes into force if he is satisfied that, before that day, the data controller contravened the old principles by reason of any act or omission which would also have constituted a contravention of the new principles if they had applied before that day.

Commencement

Sch. 14 para. 9: March 1, 2000 (SI 2000/183 art. 2(1))

Extent

Sch. 14 para. 9: United Kingdom (subject to s.75(6))

10. Subsection (5)(b) of section 40 does not apply where the rectification, blocking, erasure or destruction occurred before the commencement of that section.

Commencement

Sch. 14 para. 10: March 1, 2000 (SI 2000/183 art. 2(1))

Extent

Sch. 14 para. 10: United Kingdom (subject to s.75(6))

11. The Commissioner may serve an information notice under section 43 on or after the day on which that section comes into force if he has reasonable grounds for suspecting that, before that day, the data controller contravened the old principles by reason of any act or omission which would also have constituted a contravention of the new principles if they had applied before that day.

Commencement

Sch. 14 para. 11: March 1, 2000 (SI 2000/183 art. 2(1))

Extent

Sch. 14 para. 11: United Kingdom (subject to s.75(6))

12. Where by virtue of paragraph 11 an information notice is served on the basis of anything done or omitted to be done before the day on which section 43 comes into force, subsection (2)(b) of that section shall have effect as if the reference to the data controller having complied, or complying, with the new principles were a reference to the data controller having contravened the old principles by reason of any such act or omission as is mentioned in paragraph 11.

Commencement

Sch. 14 para. 12: March 1, 2000 (SI 2000/183 art. 2(1))

Extent

Sch. 14 para. 12: United Kingdom (subject to s.75(6))

Self-incrimination, etc.

13.— (1) In section 43(8), section 44(9) and paragraph 11 of Schedule 7, any reference to an offence under this Act includes a reference to an offence under the 1984 Act.

(2) In section 34(9) of the 1984 Act, any reference to an offence under that Act includes a reference to an offence under this Act.

Commencement

Sch. 14 para. 13(1)–(2): March 1, 2000 (SI 2000/183 art. 2(1))

Extent

Sch. 14 para. 13(1)–(2): United Kingdom (subject to s.75(6))

Warrants issued under 1984 Act

14. The repeal of Schedule 4 to the 1984 Act does not affect the application of that Schedule in any case where a warrant was issued under that Schedule before the commencement of the repeal.

Commencement

Sch. 14 para. 14: March 1, 2000 (SI 2000/183 art. 2(1))

Extent

Sch. 14 para. 14: United Kingdom (subject to s.75(6))

Complaints under section 36(2) of 1984 Act and requests for assessment under section 42

15. The repeal of section 36(2) of the 1984 Act does not affect the application of that provision in any case where the complaint was received by the Commissioner before the commencement of the repeal.

Commencement

Sch. 14 para. 15: March 1, 2000 (SI 2000/183 art. 2(1))

Extent

Sch. 14 para. 15: United Kingdom (subject to s.75(6))

16. In dealing with a complaint under section 36(2) of the 1984 Act or a request for an assessment under section 42 of this Act, the Commissioner shall have regard to the provisions from time to time applicable to the processing, and accordingly—

(a) in section 36(2) of the 1984 Act, the reference to the old principles and the provisions of that Act includes, in relation to any time when the new principles and the provisions of this Act have effect, those principles and provisions, and

(b) in section 42 of this Act, the reference to the provisions of this Act includes, in relation to any time when the old principles and the provisions of the 1984 Act had effect, those principles and provisions.

Commencement

Sch. 14 para. 16(a)–(b): March 1, 2000 (SI 2000/183 art. 2(1))

Extent

Sch. 14 para. 16(a)–(b): United Kingdom (subject to s.75(6))

Applications under Access to Health Records Act 1990 or corresponding Northern Ireland legislation

17.— (1) The repeal of any provision of the Access to Health Records Act 1990 does not affect—

(a) the application of section 3 or 6 of that Act in any case in which the application under that section was received before the day on which the repeal comes into force, or

(b) the application of section 8 of that Act in any case in which the application to the court was made before the day on which the repeal comes into force.

(2) Sub-paragraph (1)(a) does not apply in relation to an application for access to information which was made by reference to this Act.

Commencement

Sch. 14 para. 17(1)–(2): March 1, 2000 (SI 2000/183 art. 2(1))

Extent

Sch. 14 para. 17(1)–(2): United Kingdom (subject to s.75(6))

18.— (1) The revocation of any provision of the Access to Health Records (Northern Ireland) Order 1993 does not affect—

(a) the application of Article 5 or 8 of that Order in any case in which the application under that Article was received before the day on which the repeal comes into force, or

(b) the application of Article 10 of that Order in any case in which the application to the court was made before the day on which the repeal comes into force.

(2) Sub-paragraph (1)(a) does not apply in relation to an application for access to information which was made by reference to this Act.

Commencement

Sch. 14 para. 18(1)–(2): March 1, 2000 (SI 2000/183 art. 2(1))

Extent

Sch. 14 para. 18(1)–(2): United Kingdom (subject to s.75(6))

Applications under regulations under Access to Personal Files Act 1987 or corresponding Northern Ireland legislation

19.— (1) The repeal of the personal files enactments does not affect the application of regulations under those enactments in relation to—

(a) any request for information,

(b) any application for rectification or erasure, or

(c) any application for review of a decision,

which was made before the day on which the repeal comes into force.

(2) Sub-paragraph (1)(a) does not apply in relation to a request for information which was made by reference to this Act.

(3) In sub-paragraph (1) "the personal files enactments" means —

(a) in relation to Great Britain, the Access to Personal Files Act 1987, and

(b) in relation to Northern Ireland, Part II of the Access to Personal Files and Medical Reports (Northern Ireland) Order 1991.

Commencement

Sch. 14 para. 19(1)–(3)(b): March 1, 2000 (SI 2000/183 art. 2(1))

Extent

Sch. 14 para. 19(1)–(3)(b): United Kingdom (subject to s.75(6))

Applications under section 158 of Consumer Credit Act 1974

20. Section 62 does not affect the application of section 158 of the Consumer Credit Act 1974 in any case where the request was received before the commencement of section 62, unless the request is made by reference to this Act.

Commencement

Sch. 14 para. 20: March 1, 2000 (SI 2000/183 art. 2(1))

Extent

Sch. 14 para. 20: United Kingdom (subject to s.75(6))

SCHEDULE 15—MINOR AND CONSEQUENTIAL AMENDMENTS

Section 74(1)

Public Records Act 1958 (c. 51)

1.— [. . .]¹

Notes

¹ Repealed by Freedom of Information Act 2000 c. 36 Sch.8(III) para.1 (January 1, 2005)

Parliamentary Commissioner Act 1967 (c. 13)

2. [. . .]¹

Notes

¹ Repealed by Freedom of Information Act 2000 c. 36 Sch.8(II) para.1 (January 30, 2001)

3. [. . .]¹

Notes

¹ Repealed by Freedom of Information Act 2000 c. 36 Sch.8(III) para.1 (January 1, 2005)

Superannuation Act 1972 (c. 11)

4. [. . .]¹

Notes

¹ Repealed by Freedom of Information Act 2000 c. 36 Sch.8(II) para.1 (January 30, 2001)

House of Commons Disqualification Act 1975 (c. 24)

5.— [. . .]¹

Notes

¹ Repealed by Freedom of Information Act 2000 c. 36 Sch.8(III) para.1 (January 1, 2005)

Northern Ireland Assembly Disqualification Act 1975 (c. 25)

6.— [. . .]¹

Note

¹ Repealed by Freedom of Information Act 2000 c. 36 Sch.8(III) para.1 (January 1, 2005)

Representation of the People Act 1983 (c. 2)

7. In Schedule 2 of the Representation of the People Act 1983 (provisions which may be included in regulations as to registration etc), in paragraph 11A(2)—

(a) for "data user" there is substituted "data controller", and

(b) for "the Data Protection Act 1984" there is substituted "the Data Protection Act 1998".

Commencement

Sch. 15 para. 7(a)–(b): March 1, 2000 (SI 2000/183 art. 2(1))

Extent

Sch. 15 para. 7(a)–(b): United Kingdom (subject to s.75(6))

Access to Medical Reports Act 1988 (c. 28)

8. In section 2(1) of the Access to Medical Reports Act 1988 (interpretation), in the definition of "health professional", for "the Data Protection (Subject Access Modification) Order 1987" there is substituted "the Data Protection Act 1998".

Commencement

Sch. 15 para. 8: March 1, 2000 (SI 2000/183 art. 2(1))

Extent

Sch. 15 para. 8: United Kingdom (subject to s.75(6))

Football Spectators Act 1989 (c. 37)

9.— [. . .]¹

Note

¹ Repealed by Violent Crime Reduction Act 2006 c. 38 Sch.5 para.1 (April 6, 2007 as SI 2007/858)

Education (Student Loans) Act 1990 (c. 6)

10. Schedule 2 to the Education (Student Loans) Act 1990 (loans for students) so far as that Schedule continues in force shall have effect as if the reference in paragraph 4(2) to the Data Protection Act 1984 were a reference to this Act.

Commencement

Sch. 15 para. 10: March 1, 2000 (SI 2000/183 art. 2(1))

Extent

Sch. 15 para. 10: United Kingdom (subject to s.75(6))

Access to Health Records Act 1990 (c. 23)

11. For section 2 of the Access to Health Records Act 1990 there is substituted—

"2. Health professionals.
In this Act "health professional"has the same meaning as in the Data Protection Act 1998."

Commencement

Sch. 15 para. 11: March 1, 2000 (SI 2000/183 art. 2(1))

Extent

Sch. 15 para. 11: United Kingdom (subject to s.75(6))

12. In section 3(4) of that Act (cases where fee may be required) in paragraph (a), for "the maximum prescribed under section 21 of the Data Protection Act 1984" there is substituted "such maximum as may be prescribed for the purposes of this section by regulations under section 7 of the Data Protection Act 1998".

Commencement

Sch. 15 para. 12: March 1, 2000 (SI 2000/183 art. 2(1))

Extent

Sch. 15 para. 12: United Kingdom (subject to s.75(6))

13. In section 5(3) of that Act (cases where right of access may be partially excluded) for the words from the beginning to "record" in the first place where it occurs there is substituted "Access shall not be given under section 3(2) to any part of a health record".

Commencement

Sch. 15 para. 13: March 1, 2000 (SI 2000/183 art. 2(1))

Extent

Sch. 15 para. 13: United Kingdom (subject to s.75(6))

Access to Personal Files and Medical Reports (Northern Ireland) Order 1991
(1991/1707 (N.I. 14))

14. In Article 4 of the Access to Personal Files and Medical Reports (Northern Ireland) Order 1991 (obligation to give access), in paragraph (2) (exclusion of information to which individual entitled under section 21 of the Data Protection Act 1984) for "section 21 of the Data Protection Act 1984" there is substituted "section 7 of the Data Protection Act 1998".

Commencement

Sch. 15 para. 14: March 1, 2000 (SI 2000/183 art. 2(1))

Extent

Sch. 15 para. 14: United Kingdom (subject to s.75(6))

15. In Article 6(1) of that Order (interpretation), in the definition of "health professional", for "the Data Protection (Subject Access Modification) (Health) Order 1987" there is substituted "the Data Protection Act 1998".

Commencement

Sch. 15 para. 15: March 1, 2000 (SI 2000/183 art. 2(1))

Extent

Sch. 15 para. 15: United Kingdom (subject to s.75(6))

Tribunals and Inquiries Act 1992 (c. 53)

16. In Part 1 of Schedule 1 to the Tribunals and Inquiries Act 1992 (tribunals under direct supervision of Council on Tribunals), for paragraph 14 there is substituted—

"Data protection 14.(a) The Data Protection Commissioner appointed under section 6 of the Data Protection Act 1998;

(b) the Data Protection Tribunal constituted under that section, in respect of its jurisdiction under section 48 of that Act."

Commencement

Sch. 15 para. 16: March 1, 2000 (SI 2000/183 art. 2(1))

Extent

Sch. 15 para. 16: United Kingdom (subject to s.75(6))

Access to Health Records (Northern Ireland) Order 1993 (1993/1250 (N.I. 4))

17. For paragraphs (1) and (2) of Article 4 of the Access to Health Records (Northern Ireland) Order 1993 there is substituted—

"(1) In this Order "health professional"has the same meaning as in the Data Protection Act 1998.""

Commencement

Sch. 15 para. 17: March 1, 2000 (SI 2000/183 art. 2(1))

Extent

Sch. 15 para. 17: United Kingdom (subject to s.75(6))

18. In Article 5(4) of that Order (cases where fee may be required) in sub-paragraph (a), for "the maximum prescribed under section 21 of the Data Protection Act 1984" there is substituted "such maximum as may be prescribed for the purposes of this Article by regulations under section 7 of the Data Protection Act 1998".

Commencement

Sch. 15 para. 18: March 1, 2000 (SI 2000/183 art. 2(1))

Extent

Sch. 15 para. 18: United Kingdom (subject to s.75(6))

19. In Article 7 of that Order (cases where right of access may be partially excluded) for the words from the beginning to "record" in the first place where it occurs there is substituted "Access shall not be given under Article 5(2) to any part of a health record".

Commencement

Sch. 15 para. 19: March 1, 2000 (SI 2000/183 art. 2(1))

Extent

Sch. 15 para. 19: United Kingdom (subject to s.75(6))

SCHEDULE 16 REPEALS AND REVOCATIONS

Section 74(2)

PART I

REPEALS

Chapter	Short title	Extent of repeal
1984 c. 35.	The Data Protection Act 1984.	The whole Act.
1986 c. 60.	The Financial Services Act 1986.	Section 190.
1987 c. 37.	The Access to Personal Files Act 1987.	The whole Act. Section 223.
1988 c. 40.	The Education Reform Act 1988.	In Schedule 17, paragraph 80.
1988 c. 50.	The Housing Act 1988.	In section 1(1), the words from "but does not" to the end.

Chapter	Short title	Extent of repeal
1990 c. 23.	The Access to Health Records Act 1990.	In section 3, subsection (1)(a) to (e) and, in subsection (6)(a), the words "in the case of an application made otherwise than by the patient".
		Section 4(1) and (2).
		In section 5(1)(a)(i), the words "of the patient or" and the word "other".
		In section 10, in subsection (2) the words "or orders" and in subsection (3) the words "or an order under section 2(3) above".
		In section 11, the definitions of "child" and "parental responsibility".
1990 c. 37.	The Human Fertilisation and Embryology Act 1990.	Section 33(8).
1990 c. 41.	The Courts and Legal Services Act 1990.	In Schedule 10, paragraph 58.
1992 c. 13.	The Further and Higher Education Act 1992.	Section 86.
1992 c. 37.	The Further and Higher Education (Scotland) Act 1992.	Section 59.
1993 c. 8.	The Judicial Pensions and Retirement Act 1993.	In Schedule 6, paragraph 50.
		Section 59.
		In Schedule 6, paragraph 50.
1993 c. 10.	The Charities Act 1993	Section 12.
1993 c. 21.	The Osteopaths Act 1993.	Section 38.
1994 c. 17.	The Chiropractors Act 1994.	Section 38.
1994 c. 19.	The Local Government (Wales) Act 1994.	In Schedule 13, paragraph 30.
1994 c. 33.	The Criminal Justice and Public Order Act 1994.	Section 161.
1994 c. 39.	The Local Government etc. (Scotland) Act 1994.	In Schedule 13, paragraph 154.

Commencement

Sch. 16(I) para. 1: March 1, 2000 (SI 2000/183 art. 2(1))

Extent

Sch. 16(I) para. 1: United Kingdom (subject to s.75(6))

PART II

REVOCATIONS

Number	Title	Extent of revocation
S.I. 1991/1142.	The Data Protection Registration Fee Order 1991.	The whole Order.
S.I. 1991/1707 (N.I. 14).	The Access to Personal Files and Medical Reports (Northern Ireland) Order 1991.	Part II.
S.I. 1992/3218.	The Banking Co-ordination (Second Council Directive) Regulations 1992.	The Schedule.
S.I. 1993/1250 (N.I. 4).	The Access to Health Records (Northern Ireland) Order 1993.	In Schedule 10, paragraphs 15 and 40.
		In Article 2(2), the definitions of "child" and "parental responsibility".
		In Article 3(1), the words from "but does not include" to the end.
		In Article 5, paragraph (1)(a) to (d) and, in paragraph (6)(a), the words "in the case of an application made otherwise than by the patient".
		Article 6(1) and (2).
		In Article 7(1)(a)(i), the words "of the patient or" and the word "other".
S.I. 1994/429 (N.I. 2).	The Health and Personal Social Services (Northern Ireland) Order 1994.	In Schedule 1, the entries relating to the Access to Personal Files and Medical Reports (Northern Ireland) Order 1991.
S.I. 1994/1696.	The Insurance Companies (Third Insurance Directives) Regulations 1994.	In Schedule 8, paragraph 8.
S.I. 1995/755 (N.I. 2).	The Children (Northern Ireland) Order 1995.	In Schedule 9, paragraphs 177 and 191.
S.I. 1995/3275.	The Investment Services Regulations 1995.	In Schedule 10, paragraphs 3 and 15.
S.I. 1996/2827.	The Open-Ended Investment Companies (Investment Companies with Variable Capital) Regulations 1996.	In Schedule 8, paragraphs 3 and 26.

DATA PROTECTION ACT 1998

Commencement

Sch. 16(II) para. 1: March 1, 2000 (SI 2000/183 art. 2(1))

Extent

Sch. 16(II) para. 1: United Kingdom (subject to s.75(6))

MODIFICATIONS

Whole Document	Nationality, Immigration and Asylum Act 2002 (Juxtaposed Controls) Order 2003/2818, Pt 3 art. 11(4) Scotland Act 1998 c. 46, Sch. 5(II)(002) para. B2
Pt I s. 6(4)(a)	Transfer of Functions (Lord Advocate and Secretary of State) Order 1999/678, art. 7(4)
Pt II s. 7	Data Protection (Subject Access Modification) (Education) Order 2000/414, art. 6 Data Protection (Subject Access Modification) (Education) Order 2000/414, art. 7 Data Protection (Subject Access Modification) (Health) Order 2000/413, art. 6(1) Data Protection (Subject Access Modification) (Health) Order 2000/413, art. 8 Data Protection (Subject Access Modification) (Social Work) Order 2000/415, art. 6 Data Protection (Subject Access Modification) (Social Work) Order 2000/415, art. 7 Data Protection Act 1998 c. 29, Sch. 7 para. 8(1)
Pt II s. 7(1)	Data Protection Act 1998 c. 29, Pt II s. 8(1)
Pt II s. 7(8)	Data Protection Act 1998 c. 29, Sch. 7 para. 8(2)
Pt II s. 7(9)	Data Protection (Subject Access Modification) (Education) Order 2000/414, art. 7(1)(b)(ii) Data Protection (Subject Access Modification) (Health) Order 2000/413, art. 8(b)(ii) Data Protection (Subject Access Modification) (Social Work) Order 2000/415, art. 7(1)(b)(ii)
Pt III	Data Protection Act 1998 c. 29, Sch. 14 para. 2(7) Data Protection Act 1998 c. 29, Sch. 14 para. 2(8)
Pt III s. 18(1)	Data Protection Act 1998 c. 29, Sch. 14 para. 2(5)
Pt III s. 19(4)–(5)	Data Protection (Notification and Notification Fees) Regulations 2000/188, reg. 15(3)
Pt III s. 25	Nationality, Immigration and Asylum Act 2002 (Juxtaposed Controls) Order 2003/2818, Pt 3 art. 12(1)(b)
Pt IV s. 28(4)	Data Protection Act 1998 c. 29, Sch. 6 para. 6(1)
Pt IV s. 28(6)	Data Protection Act 1998 c. 29, Sch. 6 para. 6(1)

Pt IV s. 30	National Assembly for Wales (Transfer of Functions) Order 1999/672, Sch. 1 para. 1
Pt V	Privacy and Electronic Communications (EC Directive) Regulations 2003/2426, reg. 31 Telecommunications (Data Protection and Privacy) Regulations 1999/2093, Pt VII reg. 36(1)
Pt V s. 40	Data Protection Act 1998 c. 29, Sch. 14 para. 7(1) Data Protection Act 1998 c. 29, Sch. 14 para. 7(2) Data Protection Act 1998 c. 29, Sch. 14 para. 8(1) Data Protection Act 1998 c. 29, Sch. 14 para. 8(2) Data Protection Act 1998 c. 29, Sch. 14 para. 9 Privacy and Electronic Communications (EC Directive) Regulations 2003/2426, Sch. 1 para. 1 Telecommunications (Data Protection and Privacy) Regulations 1999/2093, Sch. 3 para. 5 Telecommunications (Data Protection and Privacy) Regulations 1999/2093, Sch.4 para. 1
Pt V s. 41	Telecommunications (Data Protection and Privacy) Regulations 1999/2093, Sch.3 para. 5 Telecommunications (Data Protection and Privacy) Regulations 1999/2093, Sch.4 para. 2
Pt V s. 41(1)–(2)	Privacy and Electronic Communications (EC Directive) Regulations 2003/2426, Sch. 1 para. 2
Pt V s. 41A-41C	Privacy and Electronic Communications (EC Directive) Regulations 2003/2426, Sch. 1 para. 2A
Pt V s. 42	Data Protection Act 1998 c. 29, Sch. 14 para. 16 Data Protection Act 1998 c. 29, Sch. 14 para. 16(b) Privacy and Electronic Communications (EC Directive) Regulations 2003/2426, Sch. 1 para. 3 Telecommunications (Data Protection and Privacy) Regulations 1999/2093, Sch. 4 para. 3
Pt V s. 43	Privacy and Electronic Communications (EC Directive) Regulations 2003/2426, Sch. 1 para. 4 Telecommunications (Data Protection and Privacy) Regulations 1999/2093, Sch. 3 para. 5 Telecommunications (Data Protection and Privacy) Regulations 1999/2093, Sch. 4 para. 4 Telecommunications (Data Protection and Privacy) Regulations 1999/2093, Sch. 4 para. 5
Pt V s. 43(2)(b)	Data Protection Act 1998 c. 29, Sch. 14 para. 12
Pt V s. 43(8)	Data Protection Act 1998 c. 29, Sch. 14 para. 13(1)
Pt V s. 44–46	Privacy and Electronic Communications (EC Directive) Regulations 2003/2426, Sch. 1 para. 5 Telecommunications (Data Protection and Privacy) Regulations 1999/2093, Sch. 4 para. 6
Pt V s. 44(9)	Data Protection Act 1998 c. 29, Sch. 14 para. 13(1)

Pt V s. 47	Privacy and Electronic Communications (EC Directive) Regulations 2003/2426, Sch. 1 para. 6
Pt V s. 48	Privacy and Electronic Communications (EC Directive) Regulations 2003/2426, Sch. 1 para. 7 Telecommunications (Data Protection and Privacy) Regulations 1999/2093, Sch. 4 para. 7
Pt V s. 48(3)	Data Protection Act 1998 c. 29, Sch. 6 para. 6(2)
Pt V s. 48(5)	Telecommunications (Data Protection and Privacy) Regulations 1999/2093, Sch. 4 para. 8
Pt V s. 49	Data Protection (Monetary Penalties) Order 2010/910, art. 7 Privacy and Electronic Communications (EC Directive) Regulations 2003/2426, Sch. 1 para. 8
Pt VI s. 55A	Privacy and Electronic Communications (EC Directive) Regulations 2003/2426, Sch. 1 para. 8A
Pt VI s. 55B	Privacy and Electronic Communications (EC Directive) Regulations 2003/2426, Sch. 1 para. 8B
Pt VI s. 58	Privacy and Electronic Communications (EC Directive) Regulations 2003/2426, reg. 28(8)(c)
Sch. 6	Data Protection (Monetary Penalties) Order 2010/910, art. 7 Privacy and Electronic Communications (EC Directive) Regulations 2003/2426, reg. 31 Telecommunications (Data Protection and Privacy) Regulations 1999/2093, Pt VII reg. 36(1)
Sch. 6 para. 2(1)	Data Protection Act 1998 c. 29, Sch. 6 para. 2(2)
Sch. 6 para. 4(1)	Privacy and Electronic Communications (EC Directive) Regulations 2003/2426, Sch. 1 para. 9 Telecommunications (Data Protection and Privacy) Regulations 1999/2093, Sch. 4 para. 9
Sch. 7 para. 11	Data Protection Act 1998 c. 29, Sch. 14 para. 13(1)
Sch. 9	Data Protection Act 1998 c. 29, Sch. 9 para. 14(a) Data Protection Act 1998 c. 29, Sch. 9 para. 14(b) Data Protection Act 1998 c. 29, Sch. 9 para. 14(c) Data Protection Act 1998 c. 29, Sch. 9 para. 15(a) Data Protection Act 1998 c. 29, Sch. 9 para. 15(b) Privacy and Electronic Communications (EC Directive) Regulations 2003/2426, reg. 31 Telecommunications (Data Protection and Privacy) Regulations 1999/2093, Pt VII reg. 36(1) Telecommunications (Data Protection and Privacy) Regulations 1999/2093, Sch. 3 para. 5
Sch. 9 para. 1	Privacy and Electronic Communications (EC Directive) Regulations 2003/2426, Sch. 1 para. 10 Telecommunications (Data Protection and Privacy) Regulations 1999/2093, Sch. 4 para. 10

Sch. 9 para. 1(1A)	Coroners and Justice Act 2009 c. 25, Sch. 22(5) para. 46
Sch. 9 para. 2(1A)	Privacy and Electronic Communications (EC Directive) Regulations 2003/2426, Sch. 1 para. 10A
Sch. 9 para. 9	Privacy and Electronic Communications (EC Directive) Regulations 2003/2426, Sch. 1 para. 11 Telecommunications (Data Protection and Privacy) Regulations 1999/2093, Sch. 4 para. 11
Sch. 11 para. 3(b)	Data Protection Act 1998 c. 29, Sch. 11 para. 9(2)
Sch. 11 para. 4(b)(i)	Data Protection Act 1998 c. 29, Sch. 11 para. 9(3)

APPENDIX C

Directive 95/46/EC of the European Parliament and of the Council of 24 October 1995 on the protection of individuals with regard to the processing of personal data and on the free movement of such data

DIRECTIVE 95/46/EC OF THE EUROPEAN PARLIAMENT AND OF THE COUNCIL of 24 October 1995

on the protection of individuals with regard to the processing of personal data and on the free movement of such data

THE EUROPEAN PARLIAMENT AND THE COUNCIL OF THE EUROPEAN UNION,

Having regard to the Treaty establishing the European Community, and in particular Article 100a thereof,

Having regard to the proposal from the Commission,[1]

Having regard to the opinion of the Economic and Social Committee,[2]

Acting in accordance with the procedure referred to in Article 189b of the Treaty,[3]

(1) Whereas the objectives of the Community, as laid down in the Treaty, as amended by the Treaty on European Union, include creating an ever closer union among the peoples of Europe, fostering closer relations between the States belonging to the Community, ensuring economic and social progress by common action to eliminate the barriers which divide Europe, encouraging the constant improvement of the living conditions of its peoples, preserving and strengthening peace and liberty and promoting democracy on the basis of the fundamental rights recognized in the constitution and laws of the Member States and in the

---

[1] OJ No C 277, 5.11.1990, p. 3 and OJ No C 311, 27.11.1992, p. 30.
[2] OJ No C 159, 17.6.1991, p. 38. (3) Opinion of the European Parliament of 11 March (OJ No C 94, 13.4.1992, p. 198), comfirmed on 2 December 1993 (OJ No C 342, 20.12.1993, p. 30); Council common position of 20 february 1995 (OJ No C 93, 13.4.1995, p. 1) and decision of the European Parliament of 15 June 1995 (OJ No C 166, 3.7.1995).
[3] OJ No L 197, 18.7.1987, p.33.

European Convention for the Protection of Human Rights and Fundamental Freedoms;

(2) Whereas data-processing systems are designed to serve man whereas they must, whatever the nationality or residence of natural persons, respect their fundamental rights and freedoms, notably the right to privacy, and contribute to economic and social progress, trade expansion and the well-being of individuals;

(3) Whereas the establishment and functioning of an internal market in which, in accordance with Article 7a of the Treaty, the free movement of goods, persons, services and capital is ensured require not only that personal data should be able to flow freely from one Member State to another, but also that the fundamental rights of individuals should be safeguarded;

(4) Whereas increasingly frequent recourse is being had in the Community to the processing of personal data in the various spheres of economic and social activity whereas the progress made in information technology is making the processing and exchange of such data considerably easier;

(5) Whereas the economic and social integration resulting from the establishment and functioning of the internal market within the meaning of Article 7a of the Treaty will necessarily lead to a substantial increase in cross-border flows of personal data between all those involved in a private or public capacity in economic and social activity in the Member States whereas the exchange of personal data between undertakings in different Member States is set to increase whereas the national authorities in the various Member States are being called upon by virtue of Community law to collaborate and exchange personal data so as to be able to perform their duties or carry out tasks on behalf of an authority in another Member State within the context of the area without internal frontiers as constituted by the internal market;

(6) Whereas, furthermore, the increase in scientific and technical cooperation and the coordinated introduction of new telecommunications networks in the Community necessitate and facilitate cross-border flows of personal data;

(7) Whereas the difference in levels of protection of the rights and freedoms of individuals, notably the right to privacy, with regard to the processing of personal data afforded in the Member States may prevent the transmission of such data from the territory of one Member State to that of another Member State whereas this difference may therefore constitute an obstacle to the pursuit of a number of economic activities at Community level, distort competition and impede authorities in the discharge of their responsibilities under Community law whereas this difference in levels of protection is due to the existence of a wide variety of national laws, regulations and administrative provisions;

(8) Whereas, in order to remove the obstacles to flows of personal data, the level of protection of the rights and freedoms of individuals with regard to the processing of such data must be equivalent in all Member States whereas this objective is vital to the internal market but cannot be achieved by the Member States alone, especially in view of the scale of the divergences which currently exist between the relevant laws in the Member States and the need to coordinate the laws of the Member States so as to ensure that the cross-border flow of personal data is regulated in a consistent manner that is in keeping with the objective of the internal market as provided for in Article 7a of the Treaty whereas Community action to approximate those laws is therefore needed;

(9) Whereas, given the equivalent protection resulting from the approximation of

national laws, the Member States will no longer be able to inhibit the free movement between them of personal data on grounds relating to protection of the rights and freedoms of individuals, and in particular the right to privacy whereas Member States will be left a margin for manoeuvre, which may, in the context of implementation of the Directive, also be exercised by the business and social partners whereas Member States will therefore be able to specify in their national law the general conditions governing the lawfulness of data processing whereas in doing so the Member States shall strive to improve the protection currently provided by their legislation whereas, within the limits of this margin for manoeuvre and in accordance with Community law, disparities could arise in the implementation of the Directive, and this could have an effect on the movement of data within a Member State as well as within the Community;

(10) Whereas the object of the national laws on the processing of personal data is to protect fundamental rights and freedoms, notably the right to privacy, which is recognized both in Article 8 of the European Convention for the Protection of Human Rights and Fundamental Freedoms and in the general principles of Community law whereas, for that reason, the approximation of those laws must not result in any lessening of the protection they afford but must, on the contrary, seek to ensure a high level of protection in the Community;

(11) Whereas the principles of the protection of the rights and freedoms of individuals, notably the right to privacy, which are contained in this Directive, give substance to and amplify those contained in the Council of Europe Convention of 28 January 1981 for the Protection of Individuals with regard to Automatic Processing of Personal Data;

(12) Whereas the protection principles must apply to all processing of personal data by any person whose activities are governed by Community law whereas there should be excluded the processing of data carried out by a natural person in the exercise of activities which are exclusively personal or domestic, such as correspondence and the holding of records of addresses;

(13) Whereas the acitivities referred to in Titles V and VI of the Treaty on European Union regarding public safety, defence, State security or the acitivities of the State in the area of criminal laws fall outside the scope of Community law, without prejudice to the obligations incumbent upon Member States under Article 56 (2), Article 57 or Article 100a of the Treaty establishing the European Community whereas the processing of personal data that is necessary to safeguard the economic well-being of the State does not fall within the scope of this Directive where such processing relates to State security matters;

(14) Whereas, given the importance of the developments under way, in the framework of the information society, of the techniques used to capture, transmit, manipulate, record, store or communicate sound and image data relating to natural persons, this Directive should be applicable to processing involving such data;

(15) Whereas the processing of such data is covered by this Directive only if it is automated or if the data processed are contained or are intended to be contained in a filing system structured according to specific criteria relating to individuals, so as to permit easy access to the personal data in question;

(16) Whereas the processing of sound and image data, such as in cases of video surveillance, does not come within the scope of this Directive if it is carried out for the purposes of public security, defence, national security or in the course of State activities relating to the area of criminal law or of other activities which do not come within the scope of Community law;

(17) Whereas, as far as the processing of sound and image data carried out for purposes of journalism or the purposes of literary or artistic expression is concerned, in particular in the audiovisual field, the principles of the Directive are to apply in a restricted manner according to the provisions laid down in Article 9;

(18) Whereas, in order to ensure that individuals are not deprived of the protection to which they are entitled under this Directive, any processing of personal data in the Community must be carried out in accordance with the law of one of the Member States whereas, in this connection, processing carried out under the responsibility of a controller who is established in a Member State should be governed by the law of that State;

(19) Whereas establishment on the territory of a Member State implies the effective and real exercise of activity through stable arrangements whereas the legal form of such an establishment, whether simply branch or a subsidiary with a legal personality, is not the determining factor in this respect whereas, when a single controller is established on the territory of several Member States, particularly by means of subsidiaries, he must ensure, in order to avoid any circumvention of national rules, that each of the establishments fulfils the obligations imposed by the national law applicable to its activities;

(20) Whereas the fact that the processing of data is carried out by a person established in a third country must not stand in the way of the protection of individuals provided for in this Directive whereas in these cases, the processing should be governed by the law of the Member State in which the means used are located, and there should be guarantees to ensure that the rights and obligations provided for in this Directive are respected in practice;

(21) Whereas this Directive is without prejudice to the rules of territoriality applicable in criminal matters;

(22) Whereas Member States shall more precisely define in the laws they enact or when bringing into force the measures taken under this Directive the general circumstances in which processing is lawful whereas in particular Article 5, in conjunction with Articles 7 and 8, allows Member States, independently of general rules, to provide for special processing conditions for specific sectors and for the various categories of data covered by Article 8;

(23) Whereas Member States are empowered to ensure the implementation of the protection of individuals both by means of a general law on the protection of individuals as regards the processing of personal data and by sectorial laws such as those relating, for example, to statistical institutes;

(24) Whereas the legislation concerning the protection of legal persons with regard to the processing data which concerns them is not affected by this Directive;

(25) Whereas the principles of protection must be reflected, on the one hand, in the obligations imposed on persons, public authorities, enterprises, agencies or other bodies responsible for processing, in particular regarding data quality, technical security, notification to the supervisory authority, and the circumstances under which processing can be carried out, and, on the other hand, in the right conferred on individuals, the data on whom are the subject of processing, to be informed that processing is taking place, to consult the data, to request corrections and even to object to processing in certain circumstances;

(26) Whereas the principles of protection must apply to any information concerning

an identified or identifiable person whereas, to determine whether a person is identifiable, account should be taken of all the means likely reasonably to be used either by the controller or by any other person to identify the said person whereas the principles of protection shall not apply to data rendered anonymous in such a way that the data subject is no longer identifiable whereas codes of conduct within the meaning of Article 27 may be a useful instrument for providing guidance as to the ways in which data may be rendered anonymous and retained in a form in which identification of the data subject is no longer possible;

(27) Whereas the protection of individuals must apply as much to automatic processing of data as to manual processing whereas the scope of this protection must not in effect depend on the techniques used, otherwise this would create a serious risk of circumvention whereas, nonetheless, as regards manual processing, this Directive covers only filing systems, not unstructured files whereas, in particular, the content of a filing system must be structured according to specific criteria relating to individuals allowing easy access to the personal data whereas, in line with the definition in Article 2(c), the different criteria for determining the constituents of a structured set of personal data, and the different criteria governing access to such a set, may be laid down by each Member State whereas files or sets of files as well as their cover pages, which are not structured according to specific criteria, shall under no circumstances fall within the scope of this Directive;

(28) Whereas any processing of personal data must be lawful and fair to the individuals concerned whereas, in particular, the data must be adequate, relevant and not excessive in relation to the purposes for which they are processed whereas such purposes must be explicit and legitimate and must be determined at the time of collection of the data whereas the purposes of processing further to collection shall not be incompatible with the purposes as they were originally specified;

(29) Whereas the further processing of personal data for historical, statistical or scientific purposes is not generally to be considered incompatible with the purposes for which the data have previously been collected provided that Member States furnish suitable safeguards whereas these safeguards must in particular rule out the use of the data in support of measures or decisions regarding any particular individual;

(30) Whereas, in order to be lawful, the processing of personal data must in addition be carried out with the consent of the data subject or be necessary for the conclusion or performance of a contract binding on the data subject, or as a legal requirement, or for the performance of a task carried out in the public interest or in the exercise of official authority, or in the legitimate interests of a natural or legal person, provided that the interests or the rights and freedoms of the data subject are not overriding whereas, in particular, in order to maintain a balance between the interests involved while guaranteeing effective competition, Member States may determine the circumstances in which personal data may be used or disclosed to a third party in the context of the legitimate ordinary business activities of companies and other bodies whereas Member States may similarly specify the conditions under which personal data may be disclosed to a third party for the purposes of marketing whether carried out commercially or by a charitable organization or by any other association or foundation, of a political nature for example, subject to the provisions allowing a data subject to object to the processing of data regarding him, at no cost and without having to state his reasons;

(31) Whereas the processing of personal data must equally be regarded as lawful where it is carried out in order to protect an interest which is essential for the data subject's life;

(32) Whereas it is for national legislation to determine whether the controller per-

forming a task carried out in the public interest or in the exercise of official authority should be a public administration or another natural or legal person governed by public law, or by private law such as a professional association;

(33) Whereas data which are capable by their nature of infringing fundamental freedoms or privacy should not be processed unless the data subject gives his explicit consent whereas, however, derogations from this prohibition must be explicitly provided for in respect of specific needs, in particular where the processing of these data is carried out for certain health-related purposes by persons subject to a legal obligation of professional secrecy or in the course of legitimate activities by certain associations or foundations the purpose of which is to permit the exercise of fundamental freedoms;

(34) Whereas Member States must also be authorized, when justified by grounds of important public interest, to derogate from the prohibition on processing sensitive categories of data where important reasons of public interest so justify in areas such as public health and social protection — especially in order to ensure the quality and cost-effectiveness of the procedures used for settling claims for benefits and services in the health insurance system—scientific research and government statistics whereas it is incumbent on them, however, to provide specific and suitable safeguards so as to protect the fundamental rights and the privacy of individuals;

(35) Whereas, moreover, the processing of personal data by official authorities for achieving aims, laid down in constitutional law or international public law, of officially recognized religious associations is carried out on important grounds of public interest;

(36) Whereas where, in the course of electoral activities, the operation of the democratic system requires in certain Member States that political parties compile data on people's political opinion, the processing of such data may be permitted for reasons of important public interest, provided that appropriate safeguards are established;

(37) Whereas the processing of personal data for purposes of journalism or for purposes of literary of artistic expression, in particular in the audiovisual field, should qualify for exemption from the requirements of certain provisions of this Directive in so far as this is necessary to reconcile the fundamental rights of individuals with freedom of information and notably the right to receive and impart information, as guaranteed in particular in Article 10 of the European Convention for the Protection of Human Rights and Fundamental Freedoms whereas Member States should therefore lay down exemptions and derogations necessary for the purpose of balance between fundamental rights as regards general measures on the legitimacy of data processing, measures on the transfer of data to third countries and the power of the supervisory authority whereas this should not, however, lead Member States to lay down exemptions from the measures to ensure security of processing whereas at least the supervisory authority responsible for this sector should also be provided with certain ex-post powers, e.g. to publish a regular report or to refer matters to the judicial authorities;

(38) Whereas, if the processing of data is to be fair, the data subject must be in a position to learn of the existence of a processing operation and, where data are collected from him, must be given accurate and full information, bearing in mind the circumstances of the collection;

(39) Whereas certain processing operations involve data which the controller has not collected directly from the data subject whereas, furthermore, data can be legitimately disclosed to a third party, even if the disclosure was not anticipated at the time the data were collected from the data subject whereas, in all these cases, the data subject

should be informed when the data are recorded or at the latest when the data are first disclosed to a third party;

(40) Whereas, however, it is not necessary to impose this obligation of the data subject already has the information whereas, moreover, there will be no such obligation if the recording or disclosure are expressly provided for by law or if the provision of information to the data subject proves impossible or would involve disproportionate efforts, which could be the case where processing is for historical, statistical or scientific purposes whereas, in this regard, the number of data subjects, the age of the data, and any compensatory measures adopted may be taken into consideration;

(41) Whereas any person must be able to exercise the right of access to data relating to him which are being processed, in order to verify in particular the accuracy of the data and the lawfulness of the processing whereas, for the same reasons, every data subject must also have the right to know the logic involved in the automatic processing of data concerning him, at least in the case of the automated decisions referred to in Article 15(1); whereas this right must not adversely affect trade secrets or intellectual property and in particular the copyright protecting the software whereas these considerations must not, however, result in the data subject being refused all information;

(42) Whereas Member States may, in the interest of the data subject or so as to protect the rights and freedoms of others, restrict rights of access and information whereas they may, for example, specify that access to medical data may be obtained only through a health professional;

(43) Whereas restrictions on the rights of access and information and on certain obligations of the controller may similarly be imposed by Member States in so far as they are necessary to safeguard, for example, national security, defence, public safety, or important economic or financial interests of a Member State or the Union, as well as criminal investigations and prosecutions and action in respect of breaches of ethics in the regulated professions whereas the list of exceptions and limitations should include the tasks of monitoring, inspection or regulation necessary in the three last-mentioned areas concerning public security, economic or financial interests and crime prevention whereas the listing of tasks in these three areas does not affect the legitimacy of exceptions or restrictions for reasons of State security or defence;

(44) Whereas Member States may also be led, by virtue of the provisions of Community law, to derogate from the provisions of this Directive concerning the right of access, the obligation to inform individuals, and the quality of data, in order to secure certain of the purposes referred to above;

(45) Whereas, in cases where data might lawfully be processed on grounds of public interest, official authority or the legitimate interests of a natural or legal person, any data subject should nevertheless be entitled, on legitimate and compelling grounds relating to his particular situation, to object to the processing of any data relating to himself whereas Member States may nevertheless lay down national provisions to the contrary;

(46) Whereas the protection of the rights and freedoms of data subjects with regard to the processing of personal data requires that appropriate technical and organizational measures be taken, both at the time of the design of the processing system and at the time of the processing itself, particularly in order to maintain security and thereby to prevent any unauthorized processing whereas it is incumbent on the Member States to ensure that controllers comply with these measures whereas these measures must ensure an appropriate level of security, taking into account the state of the art and the costs of their implementation in relation to the risks inherent in the processing and the nature of the data to be protected;

(47) Whereas where a message containing personal data is transmitted by means of a telecommunications or electronic mail service, the sole purpose of which is the transmission of such messages, the controller in respect of the personal data contained in the message will normally be considered to be the person from whom the message originates, rather than the person offering the transmission services whereas, nevertheless, those offering such services will normally be considered controllers in respect of the processing of the additional personal data necessary for the operation of the service;

(48) Whereas the procedures for notifying the supervisory authority are designed to ensure disclosure of the purposes and main features of any processing operation for the purpose of verification that the operation is in accordance with the national measures taken under this Directive;

(49) Whereas, in order to avoid unsuitable administrative formalities, exemptions from the obligation to notify and simplification of the notification required may be provided for by Member States in cases where processing is unlikely adversely to affect the rights and freedoms of data subjects, provided that it is in accordance with a measure taken by a Member State specifying its limits whereas exemption or simplification may similarly be provided for by Member States where a person appointed by the controller ensures that the processing carried out is not likely adversely to affect the rights and freedoms of data subjects whereas such a data protection official, whether or not an employee of the controller, must be in a position to exercise his functions in complete independence;

(50) Whereas exemption or simplification could be provided for in cases of processing operations whose sole purpose is the keeping of a register intended, according to national law, to provide information to the public and open to consultation by the public or by any person demonstrating a legitimate interest;

(51) Whereas, nevertheless, simplification or exemption from the obligation to notify shall not release the controller from any of the other obligations resulting from this Directive;

(52) Whereas, in this context, ex post facto verification by the competent authorities must in general be considered a sufficient measure;

(53) Whereas, however, certain processing operation are likely to pose specific risks to the rights and freedoms of data subjects by virtue of their nature, their scope or their purposes, such as that of excluding individuals from a right, benefit or a contract, or by virtue of the specific use of new technologies whereas it is for Member States, if they so wish, to specify such risks in their legislation;

(54) Whereas with regard to all the processing undertaken in society, the amount posing such specific risks should be very limited whereas Member States must provide that the supervisory authority, or the data protection official in cooperation with the authority, check such processing prior to it being carried out whereas following this prior check, the supervisory authority may, according to its national law, give an opinion or an authorization regarding the processing whereas such checking may equally take place in the course of the preparation either of a measure of the national parliament or of a measure based on such a legislative measure, which defines the nature of the processing and lays down appropriate safeguards;

(55) Whereas, if the controller fails to respect the rights of data subjects, national legislation must provide for a judicial remedy whereas any damage which a person may suffer as a result of unlawful processing must be compensated for by the control-

ler, who may be exempted from liability if he proves that he is not responsible for the damage, in particular in cases where he establishes fault on the part of the data subject or in case of force majeure whereas sanctions must be imposed on any person, whether governed by private of public law, who fails to comply with the national measures taken under this Directive;

(56) Whereas cross-border flows of personal data are necessary to the expansion of international trade whereas the protection of individuals guaranteed in the Community by this Directive does not stand in the way of transfers of personal data to third countries which ensure an adequate level of protection whereas the adequacy of the level of protection afforded by a third country must be assessed in the light of all the circumstances surrounding the transfer operation or set of transfer operations;

(57) Whereas, on the other hand, the transfer of personal data to a third country which does not ensure an adequate level of protection must be prohibited;

(58) Whereas provisions should be made for exemptions from this prohibition in certain circumstances where the data subject has given his consent, where the transfer is necessary in relation to a contract or a legal claim, where protection of an important public interest so requires, for example in cases of international transfers of data between tax or customs administrations or between services competent for social security matters, or where the transfer is made from a register established by law and intended for consultation by the public or persons having a legitimate interest whereas in this case such a transfer should not involve the entirety of the data or entire categories of the data contained in the register and, when the register is intended for consultation by persons having a legitimate interest, the transfer should be made only at the request of those persons or if they are to be the recipients;

(59) Whereas particular measures may be taken to compensate for the lack of protection in a third country in cases where the controller offers appropriate safeguards whereas, moreover, provision must be made for procedures for negotiations between the Community and such third countries;

(60) Whereas, in any event, transfers to third countries may be effected only in full compliance with the provisions adopted by the Member States pursuant to this Directive, and in particular Article 8 thereof;

(61) Whereas Member States and the Commission, in their respective spheres of competence, must encourage the trade associations and other representative organizations concerned to draw up codes of conduct so as to facilitate the application of this Directive, taking account of the specific characteristics of the processing carried out in certain sectors, and respecting the national provisions adopted for its implementation;

(62) Whereas the establishment in Member States of supervisory authorities, exercising their functions with complete independence, is an essential component of the protection of individuals with regard to the processing of personal data;

(63) Whereas such authorities must have the necessary means to perform their duties, including powers of investigation and intervention, particularly in cases of complaints from individuals, and powers to engage in legal proceedings whereas such authorities must help to ensure transparency of processing in the Member States within whose jurisdiction they fall;

(64) Whereas the authorities in the different Member States will need to assist one another in performing their duties so as to ensure that the rules of protection are properly respected throughout the European Union;

(65) Whereas, at Community level, a Working Party on the Protection of Individuals with regard to the Processing of Personal Data must be set up and be completely independent in the performance of its functions whereas, having regard to its specific nature, it must advise the Commission and, in particular, contribute to the uniform application of the national rules adopted pursuant to this Directive;

(66) Whereas, with regard to the transfer of data to third countries, the application of this Directive calls for the conferment of powers of implementation on the Commission and the establishment of a procedure as laid down in Council Decision 87/373/EEC (1);

(67) Whereas an agreement on a modus vivendi between the European Parliament, the Council and the Commission concerning the implementing measures for acts adopted in accordance with the procedure laid down in Article 189b of the EC Treaty was reached on 20 December 1994;

(68) Whereas the principles set out in this Directive regarding the protection of the rights and freedoms of individuals, notably their right to privacy, with regard to the processing of personal data may be supplemented or clarified, in particular as far as certain sectors are concerned, by specific rules based on those principles;

(69) Whereas Member States should be allowed a period of not more than three years from the entry into force of the national measures transposing this Directive in which to apply such new national rules progressively to all processing operations already under way whereas, in order to facilitate their cost-effective implementation, a further period expiring 12 years after the date on which this Directive is adopted will be allowed to Member States to ensure the conformity of existing manual filing systems with certain of the Directive's provisions whereas, where data contained in such filing systems are manually processed during this extended transition period, those systems must be brought into conformity with these provisions at the time of such processing;

(70) Whereas it is not necessary for the data subject to give his consent again so as to allow the controller to continue to process, after the national provisions taken pursuant to this Directive enter into force, any sensitive data necessary for the performance of a contract concluded on the basis of free and informed consent before the entry into force of these provisions;

(71) Whereas this Directive does not stand in the way of a Member State's regulating marketing activities aimed at consumers residing in territory in so far as such regulation does not concern the protection of individuals with regard to the processing of personal data;

(72) Whereas this Directive allows the principle of public access to official documents to be taken into account when implementing the principles set out in this Directive,

DIRECTIVE 95/46/EC OF THE EUROPEAN PARLIAMENT

HAVE ADOPTED THIS DIRECTIVE:

CHAPTER I

GENERAL PROVISIONS

Article 1

Object of the Directive

1. In accordance with this Directive, Member States shall protect the fundamental rights and freedoms of natural persons, and in particular their right to privacy with respect to the processing of personal data.

2. Member States shall neither restrict nor prohibit the free flow of personal data between Member States for reasons connected with the protection afforded under paragraph 1.

Article 2

Definitions

For the purposes of this Directive:

(a) "personal data" shall mean any information relating to an identified or identifiable natural person ("data subject"); an identifiable person is one who can be identified, directly or indirectly, in particular by reference to an identification number or to one or more factors specific to his physical, physiological, mental, economic, cultural or social identity;

(b) "processing of personal data" ("processing") shall mean any operation or set of operations which is performed upon personal data, whether or not by automatic means, such as collection, recording, organization, storage, adaptation or alteration, retrieval, consultation, use, disclosure by transmission, dissemination or otherwise making available, alignment or combination, blocking, erasure or destruction;

(c) "personal data filing system" ("filing system") shall mean any structured set of personal data which are accessible according to specific criteria, whether centralized, decentralized or dispersed on a functional or geographical basis;

(d) "controller" shall mean the natural or legal person, public authority, agency or any other body which alone or jointly with others determines the purposes and means of the processing of personal data where the purposes and means of processing are determined by national or Community laws or regulations, the controller or the specific criteria for his nomination may be designated by national or Community law;

(e) "processor" shall mean a natural or legal person, public authority, agency or any other body which processes personal data on behalf of the controller;

(f) "third party" shall mean any natural or legal person, public authority, agency or any other body other than the data subject, the controller, the processor and the persons who, under the direct authority of the controller or the processor, are authorized to process the data;

(g) "recipient" shall mean a natural or legal person, public authority, agency or any other body to whom data are disclosed, whether a third party or not however, authorities which may receive data in the framework of a particular inquiry shall not be regarded as recipients;

(h) "the data subject's consent" shall mean any freely given specific and informed indication of his wishes by which the data subject signifies his agreement to personal data relating to him being processed.

Article 3

Scope

1. This Directive shall apply to the processing of personal data wholly or partly by automatic means, and to the processing otherwise than by automatic means of personal data which form part of a filing system or are intended to form part of a filing system.

2. This Directive shall not apply to the processing of personal data:

— in the course of an activity which falls outside the scope of Community law, such as those provided for by Titles V and VI of the Treaty on European Union and in any case to processing operations concerning public security, defence, State security (including the economic well-being of the State when the processing operation relates to State security matters) and the activities of the State in areas of criminal law,

— by a natural person in the course of a purely personal or household activity.

Article 4

National law applicable

1. Each Member State shall apply the national provisions it adopts pursuant to this Directive to the processing of personal data where:

(a) the processing is carried out in the context of the activities of an establishment of the controller on the territory of the Member State when the same controller is established on the territory of several Member States, he must take the necessary measures to ensure that each of these establishments complies with the obligations laid down by the national law applicable;

(b) the controller is not established on the Member State's territory, but in a place where its national law applies by virtue of international public law;

(c) the controller is not established on Community territory and, for purposes of processing personal data makes use of equipment, automated or otherwise, situated on the territory of the said Member State, unless such equipment is used only for purposes of transit through the territory of the Community.

2. In the circumstances referred to in paragraph 1 (c), the controller must designate a representative established in the territory of that Member State, without prejudice to legal actions which could be initiated against the controller himself.

DIRECTIVE 95/46/EC OF THE EUROPEAN PARLIAMENT

CHAPTER II

GENERAL RULES ON THE LAWFULNESS OF THE PROCESSING OF PERSONAL DATA

Article 5

Member States shall, within the limits of the provisions of this Chapter, determine more precisely the conditions under which the processing of personal data is lawful.

SECTION I

PRINCIPLES RELATING TO DATA QUALITY

Article 6

1. Member States shall provide that personal data must be:

   (a) processed fairly and lawfully;

   (b) collected for specified, explicit and legitimate purposes and not further processed in a way incompatible with those purposes. Further processing of data for historical, statistical or scientific purposes shall not be considered as incompatible provided that Member States provide appropriate safeguards;

   (c) adequate, relevant and not excessive in relation to the purposes for which they are collected and/or further processed;

   (d) accurate and, where necessary, kept up to date every reasonable step must be taken to ensure that data which are inaccurate or incomplete, having regard to the purposes for which they were collected or for which they are further processed, are erased or rectified;

   (e) kept in a form which permits identification of data subjects for no longer than is necessary for the purposes for which the data were collected or for which they are further processed. Member States shall lay down appropriate safeguards for personal data stored for longer periods for historical, statistical or scientific use.

2. It shall be for the controller to ensure that paragraph 1 is complied with.

SECTION II

CRITERIA FOR MAKING DATA PROCESSING LEGITIMATE

Article 7

Member States shall provide that personal data may be processed only if:

   (a) the data subject has unambiguously given his consent; or

(b) processing is necessary for the performance of a contract to which the data subject is party or in order to take steps at the request of the data subject prior to entering into a contract; or

(c) processing is necessary for compliance with a legal obligation to which the controller is subject; or

(d) processing is necessary in order to protect the vital interests of the data subject; or

(e) processing is necessary for the performance of a task carried out in the public interest or in the exercise of official authority vested in the controller or in a third party to whom the data are disclosed; or

(f) processing is necessary for the purposes of the legitimate interests pursued by the controller or by the third party or parties to whom the data are disclosed, except where such interests are overridden by the interests for fundamental rights and freedoms of the data subject which require protection under Article 1(1).

SECTION III

SPECIAL CATEGORIES OF PROCESSING

Article 8

The processing of special categories of data

1. Member States shall prohibit the processing of personal data revealing racial or ethnic origin, political opinions, religious or philosophical beliefs, trade-union membership, and the processing of data concerning health or sex life.

2. Paragraph 1 shall not apply where:

(a) the data subject has given his explicit consent to the processing of those data, except where the laws of the Member State provide that the prohibition referred to in paragraph 1 may not be lifted by the data subject's giving his consent; or

(b) processing is necessary for the purposes of carrying out the obligations and specific rights of the controller in the field of employment law in so far as it is authorized by national law providing for adequate safeguards; or

(c) processing is necessary to protect the vital interests of the data subject or of another person where the data subject is physically or legally incapable of giving his consent; or

(d) processing is carried out in the course of its legitimate activities with appropriate guarantees by a foundation, association or any other non-profit-seeking body with a political, philosophical, religious or trade-union aim and on condition that the processing relates solely to the members of the body or to persons who have regular contact with it in connection with its purposes and that the data are not disclosed to a third party without the consent of the data subjects; or

(e) the processing relates to data which are manifestly made public by the data subject or is necessary for the establishment, exercise or defence of legal claims.

3. Paragraph 1 shall not apply where processing of the data is required for the purposes of preventive medicine, medical diagnosis, the provision of care or treatment or the management of health-care services, and where those data are processed by a health professional subject under national law or rules established by national competent bodies to the obligation of professional secrecy or by another person also subject to an equivalent obligation of secrecy.

4. Subject to the provision of suitable safeguards, Member States may, for reasons of substantial public interest, lay down exemptions in addition to those laid down in paragraph 2 either by national law or by decision of the supervisory authority.

5. Processing of data relating to offences, criminal convictions or security measures may be carried out only under the control of official authority, or if suitable specific safeguards are provided under national law, subject to derogations which may be granted by the Member State under national provisions providing suitable specific safeguards. However, a complete register of criminal convictions may be kept only under the control of official authority.

Member States may provide that data relating to administrative sanctions or judgements in civil cases shall also be processed under the control of official authority.

6. Derogations from paragraph 1 provided for in paragraphs 4 and 5 shall be notified to the Commission.

7. Member States shall determine the conditions under which a national identification number or any other identifier of general application may be processed.

Article 9

Processing of personal data and freedom of expression

Member States shall provide for exemptions or derogations from the provisions of this Chapter, Chapter IV and Chapter VI for the processing of personal data carried out solely for journalistic purposes or the purpose of artistic or literary expression only if they are necessary to reconcile the right to privacy with the rules governing freedom of expression.

SECTION IV

INFORMATION TO BE GIVEN TO THE DATA SUBJECT

Article 10

Information in cases of collection of data from the data subject

Member States shall provide that the controller or his representative must provide a data subject from whom data relating to himself are collected with at least the following information, except where he already has it:

    (a) the identity of the controller and of his representative, if any;

    (b) the purposes of the processing for which the data are intended;

(c) any further information such as

— the recipients or categories of recipients of the data,
— whether replies to the questions are obligatory or voluntary, as well as the possible consequences of failure to reply,
— the existence of the right of access to and the right to rectify the data concerning him in so far as such further information is necessary, having regard to the specific circumstances in which the data are collected, to guarantee fair processing in respect of the data subject.

Article 11

Information where the data have not been obtained from the data subject

1. Where the data have not been obtained from the data subject, Member States shall provide that the controller or his representative must at the time of undertaking the recording of personal data or if a disclosure to a third party is envisaged, no later than the time when the data are first disclosed provide the data subject with at least the following information, except where he already has it:

(a) the identity of the controller and of his representative, if any;

(b) the purposes of the processing;

(c) any further information such as

— the categories of data concerned,
— the recipients or categories of recipients,
— the existence of the right of access to and the right to rectify the data concerning him in so far as such further information is necessary, having regard to the specific circumstances in which the data are processed, to guarantee fair processing in respect of the data subject.

2. Paragraph 1 shall not apply where, in particular for processing for statistical purposes or for the purposes of historical or scientific research, the provision of such information proves impossible or would involve a disproportionate effort or if recording or disclosure is expressly laid down by law. In these cases Member States shall provide appropriate safeguards.

SECTION V

THE DATA SUBJECT'S RIGHT OF ACCESS TO DATA

Article 12

Right of access

Member States shall guarantee every data subject the right to obtain from the controller:

(a) without constraint at reasonable intervals and without excessive delay or expense:

— confirmation as to whether or not data relating to him are being processed and information at least as to the purposes of the processing, the categories of data concerned, and the recipients or categories of recipients to whom the data are disclosed,

— communication to him in an intelligible form of the data undergoing processing and of any available information as to their source,

— knowledge of the logic involved in any automatic processing of data concerning him at least in the case of the automated decisions referred to in Article 15(1);

(b) as appropriate the rectification, erasure or blocking of data the processing of which does not comply with the provisions of this Directive, in particular because of the incomplete or inaccurate nature of the data;

(c) notification to third parties to whom the data have been disclosed of any rectification, erasure or blocking carried out in compliance with (b), unless this proves impossible or involves a disproportionate effort.

SECTION VI

EXEMPTIONS AND RESTRICTIONS

Article 13

Exemptions and restrictions

1. Member States may adopt legislative measures to restrict the scope of the obligations and rights provided for in Articles 6(1), 10, 11(1), 12 and 21 when such a restriction constitutes a necessary measures to safeguard:

(a) national security;

(b) defence;

(c) public security;

(d) the prevention, investigation, detection and prosecution of criminal offences, or of breaches of ethics for regulated professions;

(e) an important economic or financial interest of a Member State or of the European Union, including monetary, budgetary and taxation matters;

(f) a monitoring, inspection or regulatory function connected, even occasionally, with the exercise of official authority in cases referred to in (c), (d) and (e);

(g) the protection of the data subject or of the rights and freedoms of others.

2. Subject to adequate legal safeguards, in particular that the data are not used for taking measures or decisions regarding any particular individual, Member States may, where there is clearly no risk of breaching the privacy of the data subject, restrict by a legislative measure the rights provided for in Article 12 when data are processed solely for purposes of scientific research or are kept in personal form for a period which does not exceed the period necessary for the sole purpose of creating statistics.

THE DATA SUBJECT'S RIGHT TO OBJECT

Article 14

The data subject's right to object

Member States shall grant the data subject the right:

(a) at least in the cases referred to in Article 7(e) and (f), to object at any time on compelling legitimate grounds relating to his particular situation to the processing of data relating to him, save where otherwise provided by national legislation. Where there is a justified objection, the processing instigated by the controller may no longer involve those data;

(b) to object, on request and free of charge, to the processing of personal data relating to him which the controller anticipates being processed for the purposes of direct marketing, or to be informed before personal data are disclosed for the first time to third parties or used on their behalf for the purposes of direct marketing, and to be expressly offered the right to object free of charge to such disclosures or uses.

Member States shall take the necessary measures to ensure that data subjects are aware of the existence of the right referred to in the first subparagraph of (b).

Article 15

Automated individual decisions

1. Member States shall grant the right to every person not to be subject to a decision which produces legal effects concerning him or significantly affects him and which is based solely on automated processing of data intended to evaluate certain personal aspects relating to him, such as his performance at work, creditworthiness, reliability, conduct, etc.

2. Subject to the other Articles of this Directive, Member States shall provide that a person may be subjected to a decision of the kind referred to in paragraph 1 if that decision:

(a) is taken in the course of the entering into or performance of a contract, provided the request for the entering into or the performance of the contract, lodged by the data subject, has been satisfied or that there are suitable measures to safeguard his legitimate interests, such as arrangements allowing him to put his point of view; or

(b) is authorized by a law which also lays down measures to safeguard the data subject's legitimate interests.

Article 16

Confidentiality of processing

Any person acting under the authority of the controller or of the processor, including the processor himself, who has access to personal data must not process them except on instructions from the controller, unless he is required to do so by law.

Article 17

Security of processing

1. Member States shall provide that the controller must implement appropriate technical and organizational measures to protect personal data against accidental or unlawful destruction or accidental loss, alteration, unauthorized disclosure or access, in particular where the processing involves the transmission of data over a network, and against all other unlawful forms of processing.

Having regard to the state of the art and the cost of their implementation, such measures shall ensure a level of security appropriate to the risks represented by the processing and the nature of the data to be protected.

2. The Member States shall provide that the controller must, where processing is carried out on his behalf, choose a processor providing sufficient guarantees in respect of the technical security measures and organizational measures governing the processing to be carried out, and must ensure compliance with those measures.

3. The carrying out of processing by way of a processor must be governed by a contract or legal act binding the processor to the controller and stipulating in particular that:

— the processor shall act only on instructions from the controller,

— the obligations set out in paragraph 1, as defined by the law of the Member State in which the processor is established, shall also be incumbent on the processor.

4. For the purposes of keeping proof, the parts of the contract or the legal act relating to data protection and the requirements relating to the measures referred to in paragraph 1 shall be in writing or in another equivalent form.

SECTION IX

NOTIFICATION

Article 18

Obligation to notify the supervisory authority

1. Member States shall provide that the controller or his representative, if any,

must notify the supervisory authority referred to in Article 28 before carrying out any wholly or partly automatic processing operation or set of such operations intended to serve a single purpose or several related purposes.

2. Member States may provide for the simplification of or exemption from notification only in the following cases and under the following conditions:

— where, for categories of processing operations which are unlikely, taking account of the data to be processed, to affect adversely the rights and freedoms of data subjects, they specify the purposes of the processing, the data or categories of data undergoing processing, the category or categories of data subject, the recipients or categories of recipient to whom the data are to be disclosed and the length of time the data are to be stored, and/or

— where the controller, in compliance with the national law which governs him, appoints a personal data protection official, responsible in particular:

— for ensuring in an independent manner the internal application of the national provisions taken pursuant to this Directive
— for keeping the register of processing operations carried out by the controller, containing the items of information referred to in Article 21(2),

thereby ensuring that the rights and freedoms of the data subjects are unlikely to be adversely affected by the processing operations.

3. Member States may provide that paragraph 1 does not apply to processing whose sole purpose is the keeping of a register which according to laws or regulations is intended to provide information to the public and which is open to consultation either by the public in general or by any person demonstrating a legitimate interest.

4. Member States may provide for an exemption from the obligation to notify or a simplification of the notification in the case of processing operations referred to in Article 8(2)(d).

5. Member States may stipulate that certain or all non-automatic processing operations involving personal data shall be notified, or provide for these processing operations to be subject to simplified notification.

Article 19

Contents of notification

1. Member States shall specify the information to be given in the notification. It shall include at least:

(a) the name and address of the controller and of his representative, if any;

(b) the purpose or purposes of the processing;

(c) a description of the category or categories of data subject and of the data or categories of data relating to them;

(d) the recipients or categories of recipient to whom the data might be disclosed;

(e) proposed transfers of data to third countries;

(f) a general description allowing a preliminary assessment to be made of the appropriateness of the measures taken pursuant to Article 17 to ensure security of processing.

2. Member States shall specify the procedures under which any change affecting the information referred to in paragraph 1 must be notified to the supervisory authority.

Article 20

Prior checking

1. Member States shall determine the processing operations likely to present specific risks to the rights and freedoms of data subjects and shall check that these processing operations are examined prior to the start thereof.

2. Such prior checks shall be carried out by the supervisory authority following receipt of a notification from the controller or by the data protection official, who, in cases of doubt, must consult the supervisory authority.

3. Member States may also carry out such checks in the context of preparation either of a measure of the national parliament or of a measure based on such a legislative measure, which define the nature of the processing and lay down appropriate safeguards.

Article 21

Publicizing of processing operations

1. Member States shall take measures to ensure that processing operations are publicized.

2. Member States shall provide that a register of processing operations notified in accordance with Article 18 shall be kept by the supervisory authority.

The register shall contain at least the information listed in Article 19(1)(a) to (e).
The register may be inspected by any person.

3. Member States shall provide, in relation to processing operations not subject to notification, that controllers or another body appointed by the Member States make available at least the information referred to in Article 19(1)(a) to (e) in an appropriate form to any person on request.
Member States may provide that this provision does not apply to processing whose sole purpose is the keeping of a register which according to laws or regulations is intended to provide information to the public and which is open to consultation either by the public in general or by any person who can provide proof of a legitimate interest.

CHAPTER III

JUDICIAL REMEDIES, LIABILITY AND SANCTIONS

Article 22

Remedies

Without prejudice to any administrative remedy for which provision may be made, inter alia before the supervisory authority referred to in Article 28, prior to referral to the judicial authority, Member States shall provide for the right of every person to a judicial remedy for any breach of the rights guaranteed him by the national law applicable to the processing in question.

Article 23

Liability

1. Member States shall provide that any person who has suffered damage as a result of an unlawful processing operation or of any act incompatible with the national provisions adopted pursuant to this Directive is entitled to receive compensation from the controller for the damage suffered.

2. The controller may be exempted from this liability, in whole or in part, if he proves that he is not responsible for the event giving rise to the damage.

Article 24

Sanctions

The Member States shall adopt suitable measures to ensure the full implementation of the provisions of this Directive and shall in particular lay down the sanctions to be imposed in case of infringement of the provisions adopted pursuant to this Directive.

CHAPTER IV

TRANSFER OF PERSONAL DATA TO THIRD COUNTRIES

Article 25

Principles

1. The Member States shall provide that the transfer to a third country of personal data which are undergoing processing or are intended for processing after transfer

may take place only if, without prejudice to compliance with the national provisions adopted pursuant to the other provisions of this Directive, the third country in question ensures an adequate level of protection.

2. The adequacy of the level of protection afforded by a third country shall be assessed in the light of all the circumstances surrounding a data transfer operation or set of data transfer operations particular consideration shall be given to the nature of the data, the purpose and duration of the proposed processing operation or operations, the country of origin and country of final destination, the rules of law, both general and sectoral, in force in the third country in question and the professional rules and security measures which are complied with in that country.

3. The Member States and the Commission shall inform each other of cases where they consider that a third country does not ensure an adequate level of protection within the meaning of paragraph 2.

4. Where the Commission finds, under the procedure provided for in Article 31(2), that a third country does not ensure an adequate level of protection within the meaning of paragraph 2 of this Article, Member States shall take the measures necessary to prevent any transfer of data of the same type to the third country in question.

5. At the appropriate time, the Commission shall enter into negotiations with a view to remedying the situation resulting from the finding made pursuant to paragraph 4.

6. The Commission may find, in accordance with the procedure referred to in Article 31(2), that a third country ensures an adequate level of protection within the meaning of paragraph 2 of this Article, by reason of its domestic law or of the international commitments it has entered into, particularly upon conclusion of the negotiations referred to in paragraph 5, for the protection of the private lives and basic freedoms and rights of individuals.

Member States shall take the measures necessary to comply with the Commission's decision.

Article 26

Derogations

1. By way of derogation from Article 25 and save where otherwise provided by domestic law governing particular cases, Member States shall provide that a transfer or a set of transfers of personal data to a third country which does not ensure an adequate level of protection within the meaning of Article 25(2) may take place on condition that:

(a) the data subject has given his consent unambiguously to the proposed transfer; or

(b) the transfer is necessary for the performance of a contract between the data subject and the controller or the implementation of precontractual measures taken in response to the data subject's request; or

(c) the transfer is necessary for the conclusion or performance of a contract concluded in the interest of the data subject between the controller and a third party; or

(d) the transfer is necessary or legally required on important public interest grounds, or for the establishment, exercise or defence of legal claims; or

(e) the transfer is necessary in order to protect the vital interests of the data subject or (f) the transfer is made from a register which according to laws or regulations is intended to provide information to the public and which is open to consultation either by the public in general or by any person who can demonstrate legitimate interest, to the extent that the conditions laid down in law for consultation are fulfilled in the particular case.

2. Without prejudice to paragraph 1, a Member State may authorize a transfer or a set of transfers of personal data to a third country which does not ensure an adequate level of protection within the meaning of Article 25(2), where the controller adduces adequate safeguards with respect to the protection of the privacy and fundamental rights and freedoms of individuals and as regards the exercise of the corresponding rights such safeguards may in particular result from appropriate contractual clauses.

3. The Member State shall inform the Commission and the other Member States of the authorizations it grants pursuant to paragraph 2.

If a Member State or the Commission objects on justified grounds involving the protection of the privacy and fundamental rights and freedoms of individuals, the Commission shall take appropriate measures in accordance with the procedure laid down in Article 31(2).

Member States shall take the necessary measures to comply with the Commission's decision.

4. Where the Commission decides, in accordance with the procedure referred to in Article 31(2), that certain standard contractual clauses offer sufficient safeguards as required by paragraph 2, Member States shall take the necessary measures to comply with the Commission's decision.

CHAPTER V

CODES OF CONDUCT

Article 27

1. The Member States and the Commission shall encourage the drawing up of codes of conduct intended to contribute to the proper implementation of the national provisions adopted by the Member States pursuant to this Directive, taking account of the specific features of the various sectors.

2. Member States shall make provision for trade associations and other bodies representing other categories of controllers which have drawn up draft national codes or which have the intention of amending or extending existing national codes to be able to submit them to the opinion of the national authority.

Member States shall make provision for this authority to ascertain, among other things, whether the drafts submitted to it are in accordance with the national provisions adopted pursuant to this Directive. If it sees fit, the authority shall seek the views of data subjects or their representatives.

3. Draft Community codes, and amendments or extensions to existing Community codes, may be submitted to the Working Party referred to in Article 29. This Working Party shall determine, among other things, whether the drafts submitted to it are

in accordance with the national provisions adopted pursuant to this Directive. If it sees fit, the authority shall seek the views of data subjects or their representatives. The Commission may ensure appropriate publicity for the codes which have been approved by the Working Party.

CHAPTER VI

SUPERVISORY AUTHORITY AND WORKING PARTY ON THE PROTECTION OF INDIVIDUALS WITH REGARD TO THE PROCESSING OF PERSONAL DATA

Article 28

Supervisory authority

1. Each Member State shall provide that one or more public authorities are responsible for monitoring the application within its territory of the provisions adopted by the Member States pursuant to this Directive.

These authorities shall act with complete independence in exercising the functions entrusted to them.

2. Each Member State shall provide that the supervisory authorities are consulted when drawing up administrative measures or regulations relating to the protection of individuals' rights and freedoms with regard to the processing of personal data.

3. Each authority shall in particular be endowed with:

— investigative powers, such as powers of access to data forming the subject-matter of processing operations and powers to collect all the information necessary for the performance of its supervisory duties,

— effective powers of intervention, such as, for example, that of delivering opinions before processing operations are carried out, in accordance with Article 20, and ensuring appropriate publication of such opinions, of ordering the blocking, erasure or destruction of data, of imposing a temporary or definitive ban on processing, of warning or admonishing the controller, or that of referring the matter to national parliaments or other political institutions,

— the power to engage in legal proceedings where the national provisions adopted pursuant to this Directive have been violated or to bring these violations to the attention of the judicial authorities.

Decisions by the supervisory authority which give rise to complaints may be appealed against through the courts.

4. Each supervisory authority shall hear claims lodged by any person, or by an association representing that person, concerning the protection of his rights and freedoms in regard to the processing of personal data. The person concerned shall be informed of the outcome of the claim.

Each supervisory authority shall, in particular, hear claims for checks on the lawfulness of data processing lodged by any person when the national provisions adopted pursuant to Article 13 of this Directive apply. The person shall at any rate be informed that a check has taken place.

5. Each supervisory authority shall draw up a report on its activities at regular intervals. The report shall be made public.

6. Each supervisory authority is competent, whatever the national law applicable to the processing in question, to exercise, on the territory of its own Member State, the powers conferred on it in accordance with paragraph 3. Each authority may be requested to exercise its powers by an authority of another Member State.

The supervisory authorities shall cooperate with one another to the extent necessary for the performance of their duties, in particular by exchanging all useful information.

7. Member States shall provide that the members and staff of the supervisory authority, even after their employment has ended, are to be subject to a duty of professional secrecy with regard to confidential information to which they have access.

Article 29

Working Party on the Protection of Individuals with regard to the Processing of Personal Data

1. A Working Party on the Protection of Individuals with regard to the Processing of Personal Data, hereinafter referred to as "the Working Party", is hereby set up.

It shall have advisory status and act independently.

2. The Working Party shall be composed of a representative of the supervisory authority or authorities designated by each Member State and of a representative of the authority or authorities established for the Community institutions and bodies, and of a representative of the Commission.

Each member of the Working Party shall be designated by the institution, authority or authorities which he represents. Where a Member State has designated more than one supervisory authority, they shall nominate a joint representative. The same shall apply to the authorities established for Community institutions and bodies.

3. The Working Party shall take decisions by a simple majority of the representatives of the supervisory authorities.

4. The Working Party shall elect its chairman. The chairman's term of office shall be two years. His appointment shall be renewable.

5. The Working Party's secretariat shall be provided by the Commission.

6. The Working Party shall adopt its own rules of procedure.

7. The Working Party shall consider items placed on its agenda by its chairman, either on his own initiative or at the request of a representative of the supervisory authorities or at the Commission's request.

Article 30

1. The Working Party shall:

(a) examine any question covering the application of the national measures adopted under this Directive in order to contribute to the uniform application of such measures;

(b) give the Commission an opinion on the level of protection in the Community and in third countries;

(c) advise the Commission on any proposed amendment of this Directive, on any additional or specific measures to safeguard the rights and freedoms of natural persons with regard to the processing of personal data and on any other proposed Community measures affecting such rights and freedoms;

(d) give an opinion on codes of conduct drawn up at Community level.

2. If the Working Party finds that divergences likely to affect the equivalence of protection for persons with regard to the processing of personal data in the Community are arising between the laws or practices of Member States, it shall inform the Commission accordingly.

3. The Working Party may, on its own initiative, make recommendations on all matters relating to the protection of persons with regard to the processing of personal data in the Community.

4. The Working Party's opinions and recommendations shall be forwarded to the Commission and to the committee referred to in Article 31.

5. The Commission shall inform the Working Party of the action it has taken in response to its opinions and recommendations. It shall do so in a report which shall also be forwarded to the European Parliament and the Council. The report shall be made public.

6. The Working Party shall draw up an annual report on the situation regarding the protection of natural persons with regard to the processing of personal data in the Community and in third countries, which it shall transmit to the Commission, the European Parliament and the Council. The report shall be made public.

CHAPTER VII

COMMUNITY IMPLEMENTING MEASURES

Article 31

The Committee

1. The Commission shall be assisted by a committee composed of the representatives of the Member States and chaired by the representative of the Commission.

2. The representative of the Commission shall submit to the committee a draft of the measures to be taken. The committee shall deliver its opinion on the draft within a time limit which the chairman may lay down according to the urgency of the matter.

The opinion shall be delivered by the majority laid down in Article 148(2) of the Treaty. The votes of the representatives of the Member States within the committee shall be weighted in the manner set out in that Article. The chairman shall not vote.

The Commission shall adopt measures which shall apply immediately. However, if these measures are not in accordance with the opinion of the committee, they shall be communicated by the Commission to the Council forthwith. It that event:

— the Commission shall defer application of the measures which it has decided for a period of three months from the date of communication,

— the Council, acting by a qualified majority, may take a different decision within the time limit referred to in the first indent.

FINAL PROVISIONS

Article 32

1. Member States shall bring into force the laws, regulations and administrative provisions necessary to comply with this Directive at the latest at the end of a period of three years from the date of its adoption.

When Member States adopt these measures, they shall contain a reference to this Directive or be accompanied by such reference on the occasion of their official publication. The methods of making such reference shall be laid down by the Member States.

2. Member States shall ensure that processing already under way on the date the national provisions adopted pursuant to this Directive enter into force, is brought into conformity with these provisions within three years of this date.

By way of derogation from the preceding subparagraph, Member States may provide that the processing of data already held in manual filing systems on the date of entry into force of the national provisions adopted in implementation of this Directive shall be brought into conformity with Articles 6, 7 and 8 of this Directive within 12 years of the date on which it is adopted. Member States shall, however, grant the data subject the right to obtain, at his request and in particular at the time of exercising his right of access, the rectification, erasure or blocking of data which are incomplete, inaccurate or stored in a way incompatible with the legitimate purposes pursued by the controller.

3. By way of derogation from paragraph 2, Member States may provide, subject to suitable safeguards, that data kept for the sole purpose of historical research need not be brought into conformity with Articles 6, 7 and 8 of this Directive.

4. Member States shall communicate to the Commission the text of the provisions of domestic law which they adopt in the field covered by this Directive.

Article 33

The Commission shall report to the Council and the European Parliament at regular intervals, starting not later than three years after the date referred to in Article 32(1), on the implementation of this Directive, attaching to its report, if necessary, suitable proposals for amendments. The report shall be made public.

The Commission shall examine, in particular, the application of this Directive to the data processing of sound and image data relating to natural persons and shall submit any appropriate proposals which prove to be necessary, taking account of developments in information technology and in the light of the state of progress in the information society.

Article 34

This Directive is addressed to the Member States.

Done at Luxembourg, 24 October 1995.
For the European Parliament
The President
K. HAENSCH

For the Council
The President
L. ATIENZA SERNA

APPENDIX D

Privacy and Electronic Communications (EC Directive) Regulations

(2003/2426)

Made: 18 September 2003

Laid before Parliament: 18 September 2003

Coming into force: 11 December 2003

The Secretary of State, being a Minister designated[1] for the purposes of section 2(2) of the European Communities Act 1972 in respect of matters relating to electronic communications, in exercise of the powers conferred upon her by that section, hereby makes the following Regulations:

1. *Citation and commencement*

These Regulations may be cited as the Privacy and Electronic Communications (EC Directive) Regulations 2003 and shall come into force on 11th December 2003.

2. *Interpretation*

(1) In these Regulations—

"bill" includes an invoice, account, statement or other document of similar character and "billing" shall be construed accordingly;

"call" means a connection established by means of a telephone service available to the public allowing two-way communication in real time;

"communication" means any information exchanged or conveyed between a finite number of parties by means of a public electronic communications service, but does not include information conveyed as part of a programme service, except to the extent that such information can be related to the identifiable subscriber or user receiving the information;

"communications provider" has the meaning given by section 405 of the Communications Act 2003[2];

"corporate subscriber" means a subscriber who is—

---

[1] S.I.2001/3495.

[2] For the commencement of section 405, see section 411(2) and (3) of the same Act.

(a) a company within the meaning of section 735(1) of the Companies Act 1985;

(b) a company incorporated in pursuance of a royal charter or letters patent;

(c) a partnership in Scotland;

(d) a corporation sole; or

(e) any other body corporate or entity which is a legal person distinct from its members;

"the Directive" means Directive 2002/58/EC of the European Parliament and of the Council of 12 July 2002 concerning the processing of personal data and the protection of privacy in the electronic communications sector (Directive on privacy and electronic communications);

"electronic communications network" has the meaning given by section 32 of the Communications Act 2003[3];

"electronic communications service" has the meaning given by section 32 of the Communications Act 2003;

"electronic mail" means any text, voice, sound or image message sent over a public electronic communications network which can be stored in the network or in the recipient's terminal equipment until it is collected by the recipient and includes messages sent using a short message service;

"enactment" includes an enactment comprised in, or in an instrument made under, an Act of the Scottish Parliament;

"individual" means a living individual and includes an unincorporated body of such individuals;

"the Information Commissioner" and "the Commissioner" both mean the Commissioner appointed under section 6 of the Data Protection Act 1998[4];

"information society service" has the meaning given in regulation 2(1) of the Electronic Commerce (EC Directive) Regulations 2002;

"location data" means any data processed in an electronic communications network indicating the geographical position of the terminal equipment of a user of a public electronic communications service, including data relating to—

(f) the latitude, longitude or altitude of the terminal equipment;

(g) the direction of travel of the user; or

(h) the time the location information was recorded;

"OFCOM" means the Office of Communications as established by section 1 of the Office of Communications Act 2002;

"programme service" has the meaning given in section 201 of the Broadcasting Act 1990[5];

"public communications provider" means a provider of a public electronic communications network or a public electronic communications service;

"public electronic communications network" has the meaning given in section 151 of the Communications Act 2003[6];

---

[3] For the commencement fo section 32, see article 2(1) of S.I. 2003/1900 (C. 77)

[4] Section 6 was amended by section 18(4) of and paragraph 13(1) and (2) of Part 1 of Schedule 2 to the freedom of Information Act 2000 (c. 36).

[5] Section 201 was amended by section 148(1) of and paragraph 11 of Schedule 10 to the Broadcasting Act 1996 (c. 55).

[6] For the commencement of section 151, see article 2(1) of S.I. 2003/1900 (C. 77).

"public electronic communications service" has the meaning given in section 151 of the Communications Act 2003;

"subscriber" means a person who is a party to a contract with a provider of public electronic communications services for the supply of such services;

"traffic data" means any data processed for the purpose of the conveyance of a communication on an electronic communications network or for the billing in respect of that communication and includes data relating to the routing, duration or time of a communication;

"user" means any individual using a public electronic communications service; and

"value added service" means any service which requires the processing of traffic data or location data beyond that which is necessary for the transmission of a communication or the billing in respect of that communication.

(2) Expressions used in these Regulations that are not defined in paragraph (1) and are defined in the Data Protection Act 1998 shall have the same meaning as in that Act.

(3) Expressions used in these Regulations that are not defined in paragraph (1) or the Data Protection Act 1998 and are defined in the Directive shall have the same meaning as in the Directive.

(4) Any reference in these Regulations to a line shall, without prejudice to paragraph (3), be construed as including a reference to anything that performs the function of a line, and "connected", in relation to a line, is to be construed accordingly.

3. *Revocation of the Telecommunications (Data Protection and Privacy) Regulations 1999*

The Telecommunications (Data Protection and Privacy) Regulations 1999 and the Telecommunications (Data Protection and Privacy) (Amendment) Regulations 2000 are hereby revoked.

4. *Relationship between these Regulations and the Data Protection Act 1998*

Nothing in these Regulations shall relieve a person of his obligations under the Data Protection Act 1998 in relation to the processing of personal data.

5. *Security of public electronic communications services*

(1) Subject to paragraph (2), a provider of a public electronic communications service ("the service provider") shall take appropriate technical and organisational measures to safeguard the security of that service.

(2) If necessary, the measures required by paragraph (1) may be taken by the service provider in conjunction with the provider of the electronic communications network by means of which the service is provided, and that network provider shall comply with any reasonable requests made by the service provider for these purposes.

(3) Where, notwithstanding the taking of measures as required by paragraph (1),

there remains a significant risk to the security of the public electronic communications service, the service provider shall inform the subscribers concerned of—

(a) the nature of that risk;

(b) any appropriate measures that the subscriber may take to safeguard against that risk; and

(c) the likely costs to the subscriber involved in the taking of such measures.

(4) For the purposes of paragraph (1), a measure shall only be taken to be appropriate if, having regard to—

(a) the state of technological developments, and

(b) the cost of implementing it,

it is proportionate to the risks against which it would safeguard.

(5) Information provided for the purposes of paragraph (3) shall be provided to the subscriber free of any charge other than the cost to the subscriber of receiving or collecting the information.

6. Confidentiality of communications

(1) Subject to paragraph (4), a person shall not use an electronic communications network to store information, or to gain access to information stored, in the terminal equipment of a subscriber or user unless the requirements of paragraph (2) are met.

(2) The requirements are that the subscriber or user of that terminal equipment—

(a) is provided with clear and comprehensive information about the purposes of the storage of, or access to, that information; and

(b) is given the opportunity to refuse the storage of or access to that information.

(3) Where an electronic communications network is used by the same person to store or access information in the terminal equipment of a subscriber or user on more than one occasion, it is sufficient for the purposes of this regulation that the requirements of paragraph (2) are met in respect of the initial use.

(4) Paragraph (1) shall not apply to the technical storage of, or access to, information—

(a) for the sole purpose of carrying out or facilitating the transmission of a communication over an electronic communications network; or

(b) where such storage or access is strictly necessary for the provision of an information society service requested by the subscriber or user.

7. Restrictions on the processing of certain traffic data

(1) Subject to paragraphs (2) and (3), traffic data relating to subscribers or users which are processed and stored by a public communications provider shall, when no longer required for the purpose of the transmission of a communication, be—

(a) erased;

(b) in the case of an individual, modified so that they cease to constitute personal data of that subscriber or user; or

(c) in the case of a corporate subscriber, modified so that they cease to be data that would be personal data if that subscriber was an individual.

(2) Traffic data held by a public communications provider for purposes connected with the payment of charges by a subscriber or in respect of interconnection payments may be processed and stored by that provider until the time specified in paragraph (5).

(3) Traffic data relating to a subscriber or user may be processed and stored by a provider of a public electronic communications service if—

(a) such processing and storage are for the purpose of marketing electronic communications services, or for the provision of value added services to that subscriber or user; and

(b) the subscriber or user to whom the traffic data relate has given his consent to such processing or storage; and

(c) such processing and storage are undertaken only for the duration necessary for the purposes specified in subparagraph (a).

(4) Where a user or subscriber has given his consent in accordance with paragraph (3), he shall be able to withdraw it at any time.

(5) The time referred to in paragraph (2) is the end of the period during which legal proceedings may be brought in respect of payments due or alleged to be due or, where such proceedings are brought within that period, the time when those proceedings are finally determined.

(6) Legal proceedings shall not be taken to be finally determined—

(a) until the conclusion of the ordinary period during which an appeal may be brought by either party (excluding any possibility of an extension of that period, whether by order of a court or otherwise), if no appeal is brought within that period; or

(b) if an appeal is brought, until the conclusion of that appeal.

(7) References in paragraph (6) to an appeal include references to an application for permission to appeal.

8. *Further provisions relating to the processing of traffic data under regulation 7*

(1) Processing of traffic data in accordance with regulation 7(2) or (3) shall not be undertaken by a public communications provider unless the subscriber or user to whom the data relate has been provided with information regarding the types of traffic data which are to be processed and the duration of such processing and, in the case of processing in accordance with regulation 7(3), he has been provided with that information before his consent has been obtained.

(2) Processing of traffic data in accordance with regulation 7 shall be restricted to what is required for the purposes of one or more of the activities listed in paragraph (3) and shall be carried out only by the public communications provider or by a person acting under his authority.

(3) The activities referred to in paragraph (2) are activities relating to—

(a) the management of billing or traffic;

(b) customer enquiries;

(c) the prevention or detection of fraud;

(d) the marketing of electronic communications services; or

(e) the provision of a value added service.

(4) Nothing in these Regulations shall prevent the furnishing of traffic data to a person who is a competent authority for the purposes of any provision relating to the settling of disputes (by way of legal proceedings or otherwise) which is contained in, or made by virtue of, any enactment.

9. *Itemised billing and privacy*

(1) At the request of a subscriber, a provider of a public electronic communications service shall provide that subscriber with bills that are not itemised.

(2) OFCOM shall have a duty, when exercising their functions under Chapter 1 of Part 2 of the Communications Act 2003, to have regard to the need to reconcile the rights of subscribers receiving itemised bills with the rights to privacy of calling users and called subscribers, including the need for sufficient alternative privacy-enhancing methods of communications or payments to be available to such users and subscribers.

10. *Prevention of calling line identification—outgoing calls*

(1) This regulation applies, subject to regulations 15 and 16, to outgoing calls where a facility enabling the presentation of calling line identification is available.

(2) The provider of a public electronic communications service shall provide users originating a call by means of that service with a simple means to prevent presentation of the identity of the calling line on the connected line as respects that call.

(3) The provider of a public electronic communications service shall provide subscribers to the service, as respects their line and all calls originating from that line, with a simple means of preventing presentation of the identity of that subscriber's line on any connected line.

(4) The measures to be provided under paragraphs (2) and (3) shall be provided free of charge.

11. *Prevention of calling or connected line identification—incoming calls*

(1) This regulation applies to incoming calls.

(2) Where a facility enabling the presentation of calling line identification is available, the provider of a public electronic communications service shall provide the called subscriber with a simple means to prevent, free of charge for reasonable use of the facility, presentation of the identity of the calling line on the connected line.

(3) Where a facility enabling the presentation of calling line identification prior to the call being established is available, the provider of a public electronic communications service shall provide the called subscriber with a simple means of rejecting incoming calls where the presentation of the calling line identification has been prevented by the calling user or subscriber.

(4) Where a facility enabling the presentation of connected line identification is available, the provider of a public electronic communications service shall provide the

called subscriber with a simple means to prevent, without charge, presentation of the identity of the connected line on any calling line.

(5) In this regulation "called subscriber" means the subscriber receiving a call by means of the service in question whose line is the called line (whether or not it is also the connected line).

12. Publication of information for the purposes of regulations 10 and 11

Where a provider of a public electronic communications service provides facilities for calling or connected line identification, he shall provide information to the public regarding the availability of such facilities, including information regarding the options to be made available for the purposes of regulations 10 and 11.

13. Co-operation of communications providers for the purposes of regulations 10 and 11

For the purposes of regulations 10 and 11, a communications provider shall comply with any reasonable requests made by the provider of the public electronic communications service by means of which facilities for calling or connected line identification are provided.

14. Restrictions on the processing of location data

(1) This regulation shall not apply to the processing of traffic data.

(2) Location data relating to a user or subscriber of a public electronic communications network or a public electronic communications service may only be processed—

(a) where that user or subscriber cannot be identified from such data; or

(b) where necessary for the provision of a value added service, with the consent of that user or subscriber.

(3) Prior to obtaining the consent of the user or subscriber under paragraph (2)(b), the public communications provider in question must provide the following information to the user or subscriber to whom the data relate—

(a) the types of location data that will be processed;

(b) the purposes and duration of the processing of those data; and

(c) whether the data will be transmitted to a third party for the purpose of providing the value added service.

(4) A user or subscriber who has given his consent to the processing of data under paragraph (2)(b) shall—

(a) be able to withdraw such consent at any time, and

(b) in respect of each connection to the public electronic communications network in question or each transmission of a communication, be given the opportunity to withdraw such consent, using a simple means and free of charge.

(5) Processing of location data in accordance with this regulation shall—

(a) only be carried out by—

    (i) the public communications provider in question;

    (ii) the third party providing the value added service in question; or

    (iii) a person acting under the authority of a person falling within (i) or (ii); and

(b) where the processing is carried out for the purposes of the provision of a value added service, be restricted to what is necessary for those purposes.

15. Tracing of malicious or nuisance calls

(1) A communications provider may override anything done to prevent the presentation of the identity of a calling line where—

(a) a subscriber has requested the tracing of malicious or nuisance calls received on his line; and

(b) the provider is satisfied that such action is necessary and expedient for the purposes of tracing such calls.

(2) Any term of a contract for the provision of public electronic communications services which relates to such prevention shall have effect subject to the provisions of paragraph (1).

(3) Nothing in these Regulations shall prevent a communications provider, for the purposes of any action relating to the tracing of malicious or nuisance calls, from storing and making available to a person with a legitimate interest data containing the identity of a calling subscriber which were obtained while paragraph (1) applied.

16. Emergency calls

(1) For the purposes of this regulation, "emergency calls" means calls to either the national emergency call number 999 or the single European emergency call number 112.

(2) In order to facilitate responses to emergency calls—

(a) all such calls shall be excluded from the requirements of regulation 10;

(b) no person shall be entitled to prevent the presentation on the connected line of the identity of the calling line; and

(c) the restriction on the processing of location data under regulation 14(2) shall be disregarded.

17. Termination of automatic call forwarding

(1) Where—

(a) calls originally directed to another line are being automatically forwarded to a subscriber's line as a result of action taken by a third party, and

(b) the subscriber requests his provider of electronic communications services ("the subscriber's provider") to stop the forwarding of those calls,

the subscriber's provider shall ensure, free of charge, that the forwarding is stopped without any avoidable delay.

(2) For the purposes of paragraph (1), every other communications provider shall comply with any reasonable requests made by the subscriber's provider to assist in the prevention of that forwarding.

18. *Directories of subscribers*

(1) This regulation applies in relation to a directory of subscribers, whether in printed or electronic form, which is made available to members of the public or a section of the public, including by means of a directory enquiry service.

(2) The personal data of an individual subscriber shall not be included in a directory unless that subscriber has, free of charge, been—

    (a) informed by the collector of the personal data of the purposes of the directory in which his personal data are to be included, and

    (b) given the opportunity to determine whether such of his personal data as are considered relevant by the producer of the directory should be included in the directory.

(3) Where personal data of an individual subscriber are to be included in a directory with facilities which enable users of that directory to obtain access to that data solely on the basis of a telephone number—

    (a) the information to be provided under paragraph (2)(a) shall include information about those facilities; and

    (b) for the purposes of paragraph (2)(b), the express consent of the subscriber to the inclusion of his data in a directory with such facilities must be obtained.

(4) Data relating to a corporate subscriber shall not be included in a directory where that subscriber has advised the producer of the directory that it does not want its data to be included in that directory.

(5) Where the data of an individual subscriber have been included in a directory, that subscriber shall, without charge, be able to verify, correct or withdraw those data at any time.

(6) Where a request has been made under paragraph (5) for data to be withdrawn from or corrected in a directory, that request shall be treated as having no application in relation to an edition of a directory that was produced before the producer of the directory received the request.

(7) For the purposes of paragraph (6), an edition of a directory which is revised after it was first produced shall be treated as a new edition.

(8) In this regulation, "telephone number" has the same meaning as in section 56(5) of the Communications Act 2003[7] but does not include any number which is used as an internet domain name, an internet address or an address or identifier incorporating either an internet domain name or an internet address, including an electronic mail address.

19. *Use of automated calling systems*

(1) A person shall neither transmit, nor instigate the transmission of, communications comprising recorded matter for direct marketing purposes by means of an automated calling system except in the circumstances referred to in paragraph (2).

---

[7] For the commencement of section 56(5), see article 2(1) of S.I. 2003/1900 (C. 77).

(2) Those circumstances are where the called line is that of a subscriber who has previously notified the caller that for the time being he consents to such communications being sent by, or at the instigation of, the caller on that line.

(3) A subscriber shall not permit his line to be used in contravention of paragraph (1).

(4) For the purposes of this regulation, an automated calling system is a system which is capable of—

(a) automatically initiating a sequence of calls to more than one destination in accordance with instructions stored in that system; and

(b) transmitting sounds which are not live speech for reception by persons at some or all of the destinations so called.

20. *Use of facsimile machines for direct marketing purposes*

(1) A person shall neither transmit, nor instigate the transmission of, unsolicited communications for direct marketing purposes by means of a facsimile machine where the called line is that of—

(a) an individual subscriber, except in the circumstances referred to in paragraph (2);

(b) a corporate subscriber who has previously notified the caller that such communications should not be sent on that line; or

(c) a subscriber and the number allocated to that line is listed in the register kept under regulation 25.

(2) The circumstances referred to in paragraph (1)(a) are that the individual subscriber has previously notified the caller that he consents for the time being to such communications being sent by, or at the instigation of, the caller.

(3) A subscriber shall not permit his line to be used in contravention of paragraph (1).

(4) A person shall not be held to have contravened paragraph (1)(c) where the number allocated to the called line has been listed on the register for less than 28 days preceding that on which the communication is made.

(5) Where a subscriber who has caused a number allocated to a line of his to be listed in the register kept under regulation 25 has notified a caller that he does not, for the time being, object to such communications being sent on that line by that caller, such communications may be sent by that caller on that line, notwithstanding that the number allocated to that line is listed in the said register.

(6) Where a subscriber has given a caller notification pursuant to paragraph (5) in relation to a line of his—

(a) the subscriber shall be free to withdraw that notification at any time, and

(b) where such notification is withdrawn, the caller shall not send such communications on that line.

(7) The provisions of this regulation are without prejudice to the provisions of regulation 19.

21. *Unsolicited calls for direct marketing purposes*

(1) A person shall neither use, nor instigate the use of, a public electronic communications service for the purposes of making unsolicited calls for direct marketing purposes where—

    (a) the called line is that of a subscriber who has previously notified the caller that such calls should not for the time being be made on that line; or

    (b) the number allocated to a subscriber in respect of the called line is one listed in the register kept under regulation 26.

(2) A subscriber shall not permit his line to be used in contravention of paragraph (1).

(3) A person shall not be held to have contravened paragraph (1)(b) where the number allocated to the called line has been listed on the register for less than 28 days preceding that on which the call is made.

(4) Where a subscriber who has caused a number allocated to a line of his to be listed in the register kept under regulation 26 has notified a caller that he does not, for the time being, object to such calls being made on that line by that caller, such calls may be made by that caller on that line, notwithstanding that the number allocated to that line is listed in the said register.

(5) Where a subscriber has given a caller notification pursuant to paragraph (4) in relation to a line of his—

    (a) the subscriber shall be free to withdraw that notification at any time, and

    (b) where such notification is withdrawn, the caller shall not make such calls on that line.

22. *Use of electronic mail for direct marketing purposes*

(1) This regulation applies to the transmission of unsolicited communications by means of electronic mail to individual subscribers.

(2) Except in the circumstances referred to in paragraph (3), a person shall neither transmit, nor instigate the transmission of, unsolicited communications for the purposes of direct marketing by means of electronic mail unless the recipient of the electronic mail has previously notified the sender that he consents for the time being to such communications being sent by, or at the instigation of, the sender.

(3) A person may send or instigate the sending of electronic mail for the purposes of direct marketing where—

    (a) that person has obtained the contact details of the recipient of that electronic mail in the course of the sale or negotiations for the sale of a product or service to that recipient;

    (b) the direct marketing is in respect of that person's similar products and services only; and

    (c) the recipient has been given a simple means of refusing (free of charge except for the costs of the transmission of the refusal) the use of his contact details for the purposes of such direct marketing, at the time that the details were initially collected, and, where he did not initially refuse the use of the details, at the time of each subsequent communication.

(4) A subscriber shall not permit his line to be used in contravention of paragraph (2).

23. *Use of electronic mail for direct marketing purposes where the identity or address of the sender is concealed*

A person shall neither transmit, nor instigate the transmission of, a communication for the purposes of direct marketing by means of electronic mail—

(a) where the identity of the person on whose behalf the communication has been sent has been disguised or concealed; or

(b) where a valid address to which the recipient of the communication may send a request that such communications cease has not been provided.

24. *Information to be provided for the purposes of regulations 19, 20 and 21*

(1) Where a public electronic communications service is used for the transmission of a communication for direct marketing purposes the person using, or instigating the use of, the service shall ensure that the following information is provided with that communication—

(a) in relation to a communication to which regulations 19 (automated calling systems) and *20* (facsimile machines) apply, the particulars mentioned in paragraph (2)(a) and (b);

(b) in relation to a communication to which regulation 21 (telephone calls) applies, the particulars mentioned in paragraph (2)(a) and, if the recipient of the call so requests, those mentioned in paragraph (2)(b).

(2) The particulars referred to in paragraph (1) are—

(a) the name of the person;

(b) either the address of the person or a telephone number on which he can be reached free of charge.

25. *Register to be kept for the purposes of regulation 20*

(1) For the purposes of *regulation 20* OFCOM shall maintain and keep up-to-date, in printed or electronic form, a register of the numbers allocated to subscribers, in respect of particular lines, who have notified them (notwithstanding, in the case of individual subscribers, that they enjoy the benefit of regulation 20(1)(a) and (2)) that they do not for the time being wish to receive unsolicited communications for direct marketing purposes by means of facsimile machine on the lines in question.

(2) OFCOM shall remove a number from the register maintained under paragraph (1) where they have reason to believe that it has ceased to be allocated to the subscriber by whom they were notified pursuant to paragraph (1).

(3) On the request of—

(a) a person wishing to send, or instigate the sending of, such communications as are mentioned in paragraph (1), or

(b) a subscriber wishing to permit the use of his line for the sending of such communications,

for information derived from the register kept under paragraph (1), OFCOM shall, unless it is not reasonably practicable so to do, on the payment to them of such fee as is, subject to paragraph (4), required by them, make the information requested available to that person or that subscriber.

(4) For the purposes of paragraph (3) OFCOM may require different fees—

    (a) for making available information derived from the register in different forms or manners, or

    (b) for making available information derived from the whole or from different parts of the register,

but the fees required by them shall be ones in relation to which the Secretary of State has notified OFCOM that he is satisfied that they are designed to secure, as nearly as may be and taking one year with another, that the aggregate fees received, or reasonably expected to be received, equal the costs incurred, or reasonably expected to be incurred, by OFCOM in discharging their duties under paragraphs (1), (2) and (3).

(5) The functions of OFCOM under paragraphs (1), (2) and (3), other than the function of determining the fees to be required for the purposes of paragraph (3), may be discharged on their behalf by some other person in pursuance of arrangements made by OFCOM with that other person.

26. Register to be kept for the purposes of regulation 21

(1) For the purposes of regulation 21 OFCOM shall maintain and keep up-to-date, in printed or electronic form, a register of the numbers allocated to subscribers, in respect of particular lines, who have notified them that they do not for the time being wish to receive unsolicited calls for direct marketing purposes on the lines in question.

(1A) Notifications to OFCOM made for the purposes of paragraph (1) by corporate subscribers shall be in writing.

(2) OFCOM shall remove a number from the register maintained under paragraph (1) where they have reason to believe that it has ceased to be allocated to the subscriber by whom they were notified pursuant to paragraph (1).

(2A) Where a number allocated to a corporate subscriber is listed in the register maintained under paragraph (1), OFCOM shall, within the period of 28 days following each anniversary of the date of that number being first listed in the register, send to the subscriber a written reminder that the number is listed in the register.

(3) On the request of—

    (a) a person wishing to make, or instigate the making of, such calls as are mentioned in paragraph (1), or

    (b) a subscriber wishing to permit the use of his line for the making of such calls, for information derived from the register kept under paragraph (1), OFCOM shall, unless it is not reasonably practicable so to do, on the payment to them of such fee as is, subject to paragraph (4), required by them, make the information requested available to that person or that subscriber.

(4) For the purposes of paragraph (3) OFCOM may require different fees—

(a) for making available information derived from the register in different forms or manners, or

(b) for making available information derived from the whole or from different parts of the register,

but the fees required by them shall be ones in relation to which the Secretary of State has notified OFCOM that he is satisfied that they are designed to secure, as nearly as may be and taking one year with another, that the aggregate fees received, or reasonably expected to be received, equal the costs incurred, or reasonably expected to be incurred, by OFCOM in discharging their duties under paragraphs (1), (2) and (3).

(5) The functions of OFCOM under paragraphs (1), (2)[, (2A)][8] and (3), other than the function of determining the fees to be required for the purposes of paragraph (3), may be discharged on their behalf by some other person in pursuance of arrangements made by OFCOM with that other person.

27. *Modification of contracts*

To the extent that any term in a contract between a subscriber to and the provider of a public electronic communications service or such a provider and the provider of an electronic communications network would be inconsistent with a requirement of these Regulations, that term shall be void.

28. *National security*

(1) Nothing in these Regulations shall require a communications provider to do, or refrain from doing, anything (including the processing of data) if exemption from the requirement in question is required for the purpose of safeguarding national security.

(2) Subject to paragraph (4), a certificate signed by a Minister of the Crown certifying that exemption from any requirement of these Regulations is or at any time was required for the purpose of safeguarding national security shall be conclusive evidence of that fact.

(3) A certificate under paragraph (2) may identify the circumstances in which it applies by means of a general description and may be expressed to have prospective effect.

(4) Any person directly affected by the issuing of a certificate under paragraph (2) may appeal to the Tribunal against the issuing of the certificate.

(5) If, on an appeal under paragraph (4), the Tribunal finds that, applying the principles applied by a court on an application for judicial review, the Minister did not have reasonable grounds for issuing the certificate, the Tribunal may allow the appeal and quash the certificate.

(6) Where, in any proceedings under or by virtue of these Regulations, it is claimed by a communications provider that a certificate under paragraph (2) which identifies the circumstances in which it applies by means of a general description applies in the circumstances in question, any other party to the proceedings may appeal to the Tribunal on the ground that the certificate does not apply in those circumstances and,

---

[8] word inserted by Privacy and Electronic Communications (EC Directive) (Amendment) Regulations 2004/1039 Reg. 2(5).

subject to any determination under paragraph (7), the certificate shall be conclusively presumed so to apply.

(7) On any appeal under paragraph (6), the Tribunal may determine that the certificate does not so apply.

(8) In this regulation—

(a) "the Tribunal" means the Information Tribunal referred to in section 6 of the Data Protection Act 1998;

(b) Subsections (8), (9), (10) and (12) of section 28 of and Schedule 6 to that Act apply for the purposes of this regulation as they apply for the purposes of section 28;

(c) section 58 of that Act shall apply for the purposes of this regulation as if the reference in that section to the functions of the Tribunal under that Act included a reference to the functions of the Tribunal under paragraphs (4) to (7) of this regulation; and

(d) subsections (1), (2) and (5)(f) of section 67 of that Act shall apply in respect of the making of rules relating to the functions of the Tribunal under this regulation.

29. *Legal requirements, law enforcement etc.*

(1) Nothing in these Regulations shall require a communications provider to do, or refrain from doing, anything (including the processing of data)—

(a) if compliance with the requirement in question—

(i) would be inconsistent with any requirement imposed by or under an enactment or by a court order; or
(ii) would be likely to prejudice the prevention or detection of crime or the apprehension or prosecution of offenders; or

(b) if exemption from the requirement in question—

(i) is required for the purposes of, or in connection with, any legal proceedings (including prospective legal proceedings);
(ii) is necessary for the purposes of obtaining legal advice; or
(iii) is otherwise necessary for the purposes of establishing, exercising or defending legal rights.

30. *Proceedings for compensation for failure to comply with requirements of the Regulations*

(1) A person who suffers damage by reason of any contravention of any of the requirements of these Regulations by any other person shall be entitled to bring proceedings for compensation from that other person for that damage.

(2) In proceedings brought against a person by virtue of this regulation it shall be a defence to prove that he had taken such care as in all the circumstances was reasonably required to comply with the relevant requirement.

(3) The provisions of this regulation are without prejudice to those of regulation 31.

31. *Enforcement—extension of Part V of the Data Protection Act 1998*

(1) The provisions of Part V of the Data Protection Act 1998 and of Schedules 6 and 9 to that Act are extended for the purposes of these Regulations and, for those purposes, shall have effect subject to the modifications set out in Schedule 1.

(2) In regulations 32 and 33, "enforcement functions" means the functions of the Information Commissioner under the provisions referred to in paragraph (1) as extended by that paragraph.

(3) The provisions of this regulation are without prejudice to those of regulation 30.

32. *Request that the Commissioner exercise his enforcement functions*

Where it is alleged that there has been a contravention of any of the requirements of these Regulations either OFCOM or a person aggrieved by the alleged contravention may request the Commissioner to exercise his enforcement functions in respect of that contravention, but those functions shall be exercisable by the Commissioner whether or not he has been so requested.

33. *Technical advice to the Commissioner*

OFCOM shall comply with any reasonable request made by the Commissioner, in connection with his enforcement functions, for advice on technical and similar matters relating to electronic communications.

34. *Amendment to the Telecommunications (Lawful Business Practice) (Interception of Communications) Regulations 2000*

In regulation 3 of the Telecommunications (Lawful Business Practice) (Interception of Communications) Regulations 2000, for paragraph (3), there shall be substituted—

"(3) Conduct falling within paragraph (1)(a)(i) above is authorised only to the extent that Article 5 of Directive 2002/58/EC of the European Parliament and of the Council of 12 July 2002 concerning the processing of personal data and the protection of privacy in the electronic communications sector so permits."

35. *Amendment to the Electronic Communications (Universal Service) Order 2003*

(1) In paragraphs 2(2) and 3(2) of the Schedule to the Electronic Communications (Universal Service) Order 2003, for the words "Telecommunications (Data Protection and Privacy) Regulations 1999" there shall be substituted "Privacy and Electronic Communications (EC Directive) Regulations 2003".

(2) Paragraph (1) shall have effect notwithstanding the provisions of section 65 of the Communications Act 2003[9] (which provides for the modification of the Universal Service Order made under that section).

---

[9] For the commencement of section 65, see article 2(1) of S.I. 2003/1900 (C. 77).

36. *Transitional provisions*

The provisions in Schedule 2 shall have effect.

SCHEDULE 1—MODIFICATIONS FOR THE PURPOSES OF THESE REGULATIONS TO PART V OF THE DATA PROTECTION ACT 1998 AND SCHEDULES 6 AND 9 TO THAT ACT AS EXTENDED BY REGULATION 31

1. In section 40—

    (a) in subsection (1), for the words "data controller" there shall be substituted the word "person", for the words "data protection principles" there shall be substituted the words "requirements of the Privacy and Electronic Communications (EC Directive) Regulations 2003 (in this Part referred to as "the relevant requirements") and for the words "principle or principles" there shall be substituted the words "requirement or requirements";

    (b) in subsection (2), the words "or distress" shall be omitted;

    (c) subsections (3), (4), (5), (9) and (10) shall be omitted; and

    (d) in subsection (6)(a), for the words "data protection principle or principles" there shall be substituted the words "relevant requirement or requirements."

2. In section 41(1) and (2), for the words "data protection principle or principles", in both places where they occur, there shall be substituted the words "relevant requirement or requirements".

3. Section 42 shall be omitted.

4. In section 43—

    (a) for subsections (1) and (2) there shall be substituted the following provisions—

"(1) If the Commissioner reasonably requires any information for the purpose of determining whether a person has complied or is complying with the relevant requirements, he may serve that person with a notice (in this Act referred to as "an information notice") requiring him, within such time as is specified in the notice, to furnish the Commissioner, in such form as may be so specified, with such information relating to compliance with the relevant requirements as is so specified.

(2) An information notice must contain a statement that the Commissioner regards the specified information as relevant for the purpose of determining whether the person has complied or is complying with the relevant requirements and his reason for regarding it as relevant for that purpose."

    (b) in subsection (6)(a), after the word "under" there shall be inserted the words "the Privacy and Electronic Communications (EC Directive) Regulations 2003 or";

    (c) in subsection (6)(b), after the words "arising out of" there shall be inserted the words "the said Regulations or"; and

    (d) subsection (10) shall be omitted.

5. Sections 44, 45 and 46 shall be omitted.

6. In section 47—

(a) in subsection (1), for the words "an information notice or special information notice" there shall be substituted the words "or an information notice"; and

(b) in subsection (2) the words "or a special information notice" shall be omitted.

7. In section 48—

(a) in subsections (1) and (3), for the words "an information notice or a special information notice", in both places where they occur, there shall be substituted the words "or an information notice";

(b) in subsection (3) for the words "43(5) or 44(6)" there shall be substituted the words "or 43(5)"; and

(c) subsection (4) shall be omitted.

8. In section 49 subsection (5) shall be omitted.

9. In paragraph 4(1) of Schedule (6), for the words "(2) or (4)" there shall be substituted the words "or (2)".

10. In paragraph 1 of Schedule 9—

(a) for subparagraph (1)(a) there shall be substituted the following provision—

"(a) that a person has contravened or is contravening any of the requirements of the Privacy and Electronic Communications (EC Directive) Regulations 2003 (in this Schedule referred to as "the 2003 Regulations") or";

and

(b) subparagraph (2) shall be omitted.

11. In paragraph 9 of Schedule 9—

(a) in subparagraph (1)(a) after the words "rights under" there shall be inserted the words "the 2003 Regulations or"; and

(b) in subparagraph (1)(b) after the words "arising out of" there shall be inserted the words "the 2003 Regulations or".

SCHEDULE 2—TRANSITIONAL PROVISIONS

Interpretation

1. In this Schedule "the 1999 Regulations" means the Telecommunications (Data Protection and Privacy) Regulations 1999 and "caller" has the same meaning as in regulation 21 of the 1999 Regulations.

2.—(1) Regulation 18 of these Regulations shall not apply in relation to editions of directories first published before 11th December 2003.

(2) Where the personal data of a subscriber have been included in a directory in accordance with Part IV of the 1999 Regulations, the personal data of that subscriber may remain included in that directory provided that the subscriber—

(a) has been provided with information in accordance with regulation 18 of these Regulations; and

(b) has not requested that his data be withdrawn from that directory.

(3) Where a request has been made under subparagraph (2) for data to be withdrawn from a directory, that request shall be treated as having no application in relation to an edition of a directory that was produced before the producer of the directory received the request.

(4) For the purposes of subparagraph (3), an edition of a directory, which is revised after it was first produced, shall be treated as a new edition.

3.—(1) A notification of consent given to a caller by a subscriber for the purposes of regulation 22(2) of the 1999 Regulations is to have effect on and after 11th December 2003 as a notification given by that subscriber for the purposes of *regulation 19(2)* of these Regulations.

(2) A notification given to a caller by a corporate subscriber for the purposes of regulation 23(2)(a) of the 1999 Regulations is to have effect on and after 11th December 2003 as a notification given by that subscriber for the purposes of regulation 20(1)(b) of these Regulations.

(3) A notification of consent given to a caller by an individual subscriber for the purposes of regulation 24(2) of the 1999 Regulations is to have effect on and after 11th December 2003 as a notification given by that subscriber for the purposes of regulation 20(2) of these Regulations.

(4) A notification given to a caller by an individual subscriber for the purposes of regulation 25(2)(a) of the 1999 Regulations is to have effect on and after the 11th December 2003 as a notification given by that subscriber for the purposes of regulation 21(1) of these Regulations.

4.—(1) A notification given by a subscriber pursuant to regulation 23(4)(a) of the 1999 Regulations to the Director General of Telecommunications (or to such other person as is discharging his functions under regulation 23(4) of the 1999 Regulations on his behalf by virtue of an arrangement made under *regulation 23(6)* of those Regulations) is to have effect on or after 11th December 2003 as a notification given pursuant to regulation 25(1) of these Regulations.

(2) A notification given by a subscriber who is an individual pursuant to regulation 25(4)(a) of the 1999 Regulations to the Director General of Telecommunications (or to such other person as is discharging his functions under regulation 25(4) of the 1999 Regulations on his behalf by virtue of an arrangement made under regulation 25(6) of those Regulations) is to have effect on or after 11th December 2003 as a notification given pursuant to regulation 26(1) of these Regulations.

5. In relation to times before an order made under section 411[10] of the Communications Act 2003 brings any of the provisions of Part 2 of Chapter 1 of that Act into force for the purpose of conferring on OFCOM the functions contained in those provisions, references to OFCOM in these Regulations are to be treated as references to the Director General of Telecommunications.

Explanatory Note

These Regulations implement Articles 2, 4, 5(3), 6 to 13, 15 and 16 of Directive 2002/58/EC of the European Parliament and of the Council of 12 July 2002 concerning the processing of personal data and the protection of privacy in the electronic communications sector (Directive on privacy and electronic communications) ("the Directive").

---

[10] For the commencement of section 411, see article 411(2) and (3) of the Communications Act 2003 (C. 21).

The Directive repeals and replaces Directive 97/66/EC of the European Parliament and of the Council of 15 December 1997 concerning the processing of personal data and the protection of privacy in the telecommunications sector which was implemented in the UK by the Telecommunications (Data Protection and Privacy) Regulations 1999. Those Regulations are revoked by regulation 3 of these Regulations.

Regulation 2 sets out the definitions which apply for the purposes of the Regulations.

Regulation 4 provides that nothing in these Regulations relieves a person of any of his obligations under the Data Protection Act 1998.

Regulation 5 imposes a duty on a provider of a public electronic communications service to take measures, if necessary in conjunction with the provider of the electronic communications network by means of which the service is provided, to safeguard the security of the service, and requires the provider of the electronic communications network to comply with the service provider's reasonable requests made for the purposes of taking the measures ("public electronic communications service" has the meaning given by section 151 of the Communications Act 2003 and "electronic communications network" has the meaning given by section 32 of that Act). Regulation 5 further requires the service provider, where there remains a significant risk to the security of the service, to provide subscribers to that service with certain information ("subscriber" is defined as "a person who is a party to a contract with a provider of public electronic communications services for the supply of such services").

Regulation 6 provides that an electronic communications network may not be used to store or gain access to information in the terminal equipment of a subscriber or user ("user" is defined as "any individual using a public electronic communications service") unless the subscriber or user is provided with certain information and is given the opportunity to refuse the storage of or access to the information in his terminal equipment.

Regulations 7 and 8 set out certain restrictions on the processing of traffic data relating to a subscriber or user by a public communications provider. "Traffic data" is defined as "any data processed for the purpose of the conveyance of a communication on an electronic communications network or for the billing in respect of that communication". "Public communications provider" is defined as "a provider of a public electronic communications network or a public electronic communications service".

Regulation 9 requires providers of public electronic communications services to provide subscribers with non-itemised bills on request and requires OFCOM to have regard to certain matters when exercising their functions under Chapter 1 of Part 2 of the Communications Act 2003.

Regulation 10 requires a provider of a public electronic communications service to provide users of the service with a means of preventing the presentation of calling line identification on a call-by-call basis, and to provide subscribers to the service with a means of preventing the presentation of such identification on a per-line basis. This regulation is subject to regulations 15 and 16. Regulation 11 requires the provider of a public electronic communications service to provide subscribers to that service with certain facilities where facilities enabling the presentation of connected line identification or calling line identification are available.

Regulation 12 requires a public electronic communications service provider to provide certain information to the public for the purposes of regulations 10 and 11, and regulation 13 requires communications providers (the term "communications provider" has the meaning given by section 405 of the Communications Act 2003) to co-operate with reasonable requests made by providers of public electronic communications services for the purposes of those regulations.

Regulation 14 imposes certain restrictions on the processing of location data, which is defined as "any data processed in an electronic communications network indicating the geographical position of the terminal equipment of a user of a public electronic communications service, including data relating to the latitude, longitude or altitude of the terminal equipment; the direction of travel of the user; or the time the location information was recorded."

Regulation 15 makes provision in relation to the tracing of malicious or nuisance calls and *regulation 16* makes provision in relation to emergency calls, which are defined in regulation 16(1) as calls to the national emergency number 999 or the European emergency call number 112.

Regulation 17 requires the provider of an electronic communications service to a subscriber to stop, on request, the automatic forwarding of calls to that subscriber's line and also requires other communications providers to comply with reasonable requests made by the subscriber's provider to assist in the prevention of that forwarding.

Regulation 18 applies to directories of subscribers, and sets out requirements that must be satisfied where data relating to subscribers is included in such directories. It also gives subscribers the right to verify, correct or withdraw their data in directories.

Regulation 19 provides that a person may not transmit communications comprising recorded matter for direct marketing purposes by an automated calling system unless the line called is that of a subscriber who has notified the caller that he consents to such communications being made.

Regulations 20, 21 and 22 set out the circumstances in which persons may transmit, or instigate the transmission of, unsolicited communications for the purposes of direct marketing by means of facsimile machine, make unsolicited calls for those purposes, or transmit unsolicited communications by means of electronic mail for those purposes. Regulation 22 (electronic mail) applies only to transmissions to individual subscribers (the term "individual" means "a living individual" and includes "an unincorporated body of such individuals").

Regulation 23 prohibits the sending of communications by means of electronic mail for the purposes of direct marketing where the identity of the person on whose behalf the communication is made has been disguised or concealed or an address to which requests for such communications to cease may be sent has not been provided.

Regulation 24 sets out certain information that must be provided for the purposes of *regulations 19, 20 and 21*.

Regulation 25 imposes a duty on OFCOM, for the purposes of regulation 20, to maintain and keep up-to-date a register of numbers allocated to subscribers who do not wish to receive unsolicited communications by means of facsimile machine for the purposes of direct marketing. Regulation 26 imposes a similar obligation for the purposes of regulation 21 in respect of individual subscribers who do not wish to receive calls for the purposes of direct marketing.

Regulation 27 provides that terms in certain contracts which are inconsistent with these Regulations shall be void.

Regulation 28 exempts communications providers from the requirements of these Regulations where exemption is required for the purpose of safeguarding national security and further provides that a certificate signed by a Minister of the Crown to the effect that exemption from a requirement is necessary for the purpose of safeguarding national security shall be conclusive evidence of that fact. It also provides for certain questions relating to such certificates to be determined by the Information Tribunal referred to in section 6 of the Data Protection Act 1998.

Regulation 29 provides that a communications provider shall not be required by these Regulations to do, or refrain from doing, anything if complying with the requirement in question would be inconsistent with a requirement imposed by or under an enactment or by a court order, or if exemption from the requirement is necessary in connection with legal proceedings, for the purposes of obtaining legal advice or is otherwise necessary to establish, exercise or defend legal rights.

Regulation 30 allows a claim for damages to be brought in respect of contraventions of the Regulations. Regulations 31 and 32 make provision in connection with the enforcement of the Regulations by the Information Commissioner (who is the Commissioner appointed under *section 6* of the Data Protection Act 1998).

Regulation 33 imposes a duty on OFCOM to comply with any reasonable request made by the Commissioner for advice on technical matters relating to electronic communications.

Regulation 34 amends the Telecommunications (Lawful Business Practice) (Interception of Communications) Regulations 2000 and regulation 35 amends the Electronic Communications (Universal Service) Order 2003.

Regulation 36 provides for the transitional provisions in Schedule 2 to have effect.

A transposition note setting out how the main elements of the Directive are transposed into law and a regulatory impact assessment have been placed in the libraries of both Houses of Parliament. Copies are also available from the Department of Trade and Industry, Bay 202, 151 Buckingham Palace Road, London SW1W 9SS and can also be found on *www.dti.gov.uk*.

APPENDIX E

The Privacy and Electronic Communications (EC Directive) (Amendment) Regulations 2011

2011 No. 1208

Made -	*4th May 2011*
Laid before Parliament -	*5th May 2011*
Coming into force -	*26th May 2011*

The Secretary of State, being a Minister designated[1] for the purposes of section 2(2) of the European Communities Act 1972[2] in respect of matters relating to electronic communications, in exercise of the powers conferred by that section makes the following Regulations:

Citation, commencement and interpretation

1.— (1) These Regulations may be cited as the Privacy and Electronic Communications (EC Directive) (Amendment) Regulations 2011 and shall come into force on 26th May 2011.

(2)   In these Regulations "the 2003 Regulations" means the Privacy and Electronic Communications (EC Directive) Regulations 2003[3].

Amendment of the 2003 Regulations

2. The 2003 Regulations are amended as set out in the following regulations.

3. In regulation 2—

    (a) in the definition of "location data" after "electronic communications network" insert "or by an electronic communications service";

---

[1]   S.I. 2001/3495: which has been amended, but those amendments are not relevant to these regulations.

[2]   1972 c.68. Section 2(2) was amended by section 27 of the Legislative and Regulatory Reform Act 2006 (c.51) and section 3 of, and Part 1 of the Schedule to, the European Union (Amendment) Act 2008 (c.7).

[3]   S.I. 2003/2426; which have been amended, but those amendments are not relevant to these regulations.

(b) after the definition of "OFCOM", insert ""personal data breach" means a breach of security leading to the accidental or unlawful destruction, loss, alteration, unauthorised disclosure of, or access to, personal data transmitted, stored or otherwise processed in connection with the provision of a public electronic communications service;".

4.—(1) In regulation 5, after paragraph (1) insert—

"(1A) The measures referred to in paragraph (1) shall at least—

(a) ensure that personal data can be accessed only by authorised personnel for legally authorised purposes;

(b) protect personal data stored or transmitted against accidental or unlawful destruction, accidental loss or alteration, and unauthorised or unlawful storage, processing, access or disclosure; and

(c) ensure the implementation of a security policy with respect to the processing of personal data."

(2) After paragraph (5) insert—

"(6) The Information Commissioner may audit the measures taken by a provider of a public electronic communications service to safeguard the security of that service.".

5. After regulation 5, insert—

"Personal data breach

5A.—(1) In this regulation and in regulations 5B and 5C, "service provider" has the meaning given in regulation 5(1).

(2) If a personal data breach occurs, the service provider shall, without undue delay, notify that breach to the Information Commissioner.

(3) Subject to paragraph (6), if a personal data breach is likely to adversely affect the personal data or privacy of a subscriber or user, the service provider shall also, without undue delay, notify that breach to the subscriber or user concerned.

(4) The notification referred to in paragraph (2) shall contain at least a description of—

(a) the nature of the breach;

(b) the consequences of the breach; and

(c) the measures taken or proposed to be taken by the provider to address the breach.

(5) The notification referred to the paragraph (3) shall contain at least—

(a) a description of the nature of the breach;

(b) information about contact points within the service provider's organisation from which more information may be obtained; and

(c) recommendations of measures to allow the subscriber to mitigate the possible adverse impacts of the breach.

(6) The notification referred to in paragraph (3) is not required if the service provider has demonstrated, to the satisfaction of the Information Commissioner that—

(a) it has implemented appropriate technological protection measures which render the data unintelligible to any person who is not authorised to access it, and

(b) that those measures were applied to the data concerned in that breach.

(7) If the service provider has not notified the subscriber or user in compliance with paragraph (3), the Information Commissioner may, having considered the likely adverse effects of the breach, require it to do so.

(8) Service providers shall maintain an inventory of personal data breaches comprising —

    (a) the facts surrounding the breach,

    (b) the effects of that breach, and

    (c) remedial action taken

which shall be sufficient to enable the Information Commissioner to verify compliance with the provisions of this regulation. The inventory shall only include information necessary for this purpose.

Personal data breach: audit

5B. The Information Commissioner may audit the compliance of service providers with the provisions of regulation 5A.

Personal data breach: enforcement

5C.—(1) If a service provider fails to comply with the notification requirements of regulation 5A, the Information Commissioner may issue a fixed monetary penalty notice in respect of that failure.

(2) The amount of a fixed monetary penalty under this regulation shall be £1,000.

(3) Before serving such a notice, the Information Commissioner must serve the service provider with a notice of intent.

(4) The notice of intent must—

    (a) state the name and address of the service provider;

    (b) state the nature of the breach;

    (c) indicate the amount of the fixed monetary penalty;

    (d) include a statement informing the service provider of the opportunity to discharge liability for the fixed monetary penalty;

    (e) indicate the date on which the Information Commissioner proposes to serve the fixed monetary penalty notice; and

    (f) inform the service provider that he may make written representations in relation to the proposal to serve a fixed monetary penalty notice within the period of 21 days from the service of the notice of intent.

(5) A service provider may discharge liability for the fixed monetary penalty if he pays to the Information Commissioner the amount of £800 within 21 days of receipt of the notice of intent.

(6) The Information Commissioner may not serve a fixed monetary penalty notice until the time within which representations may be made has expired.

(7) The fixed monetary penalty notice must state—

    (a) the name and address of the service provider;

    (b) details of the notice of intent served on the service provider;

    (c) whether there have been any written representations;

    (d) details of any early payment discounts;

(e) the grounds on which the Information Commissioner imposes the fixed monetary penalty;

(f) the date by which the fixed monetary penalty is to be paid; and

(g) details of, including the time limit for, the service provider's right of appeal against the imposition of the fixed monetary penalty.

(8) A service provider on whom a fixed monetary penalty is served may appeal to the Tribunal against the issue of the fixed monetary penalty notice.

(9) Any sum received by the Information Commissioner by virtue of this regulation must be paid into the Consolidated Fund.

(10) In England and Wales and Northern Ireland, the penalty is recoverable—

(a) if a county court so orders, as if it were payable under an order of that court;

(b) if the High Court so orders, as if it were payable under an order of that court.

(11) In Scotland, the penalty may be enforced in the same manner as an extract registered decree arbitral bearing a warrant for execution issued by the sheriff court of any sheriffdom in Scotland."

6.—(1) In regulation 6—

(2) In paragraph (1) for "use an electronic communications network to store information, or to", substitute "store or".

(3) For paragraph (2)(b) substitute "(b) has given his or her consent".

(4) After paragraph (3) insert—

"(3A) For the purposes of paragraph (2), consent may be signified by a subscriber who amends or sets controls on the internet browser which the subscriber uses or by using another application or programme to signify consent."

(5) In paragraph (4)(a) omit "or facilitating".

7. In regulation 7(3)(b) for "given his consent" substitute "previously notified the provider that he consents".

8. In regulation 19(1) after "automated calling" insert "or communication".

9.—(1) In regulation 23, at the end of paragraph (a) omit "or".

(2) After paragraph (b) insert—

"(c) where that electronic mail would contravene regulation 7 of the Electronic Commerce (EC Directive) Regulations 2002[4]; or

(d) where that electronic mail encourages recipients to visit websites which contravene that regulation."

10. After regulation 29 insert—

"**29A.**—(1) Where regulations 28 and 29 apply, communications providers must establish and maintain internal procedures for responding to requests for access to users' personal data.

(2) Communications providers shall on demand provide the Information Commissioner with information about—

---

[4]   S.I. 2002/2013; which has been amended but those amendments are not relevant.

(a) those procedures;

(b) the number of requests received;

(c) the legal justification for the request; and

(d) the communications provider's response."

11. In regulation 31—

(a) in paragraph (1) after "provisions of Part V" insert "and sections 55A to 55E".

(b) at the end of paragraph (2) insert "and the functions set out in regulations 31A and 31B".

12. After regulation 31 insert—

"Enforcement: third party information notices

31A.—(1) The Information Commissioner may require a communications provider (A) to provide information to the Information Commissioner by serving on A a notice ("a third party information notice").

(2) The third party information notice may require A to release information held by A about another person's use of an electronic communications network or an electronic communications service where the Information Commissioner believes that the information requested is relevant information.

(3) Relevant information is information which the Information Commissioner considers is necessary to investigate the compliance of any person with these Regulations.

(4) The notice shall set out—

(a) the information requested,

(b) the form in which the information must be provided;

(c) the time limit within which the information must be provided; and

(d) information about the rights of appeal conferred by these Regulations.

(5) The time limit referred to in paragraph (4)(c) shall not expire before the end of the period in which an appeal may be brought. If an appeal is brought, the information requested need not be provided pending the determination or withdrawal of the appeal.

(6) In an urgent case, the Commissioner may include in the notice—

(a) a statement that the case is urgent; and

(b) a statement of his reasons for reaching that conclusion,

in which case paragraph (5) shall not apply.

(7) Where paragraph (6) applies, the communications provider shall have a minimum of 7 days (beginning on the day on which the notice is served) to provide the information requested.

(8) A person shall not be required by virtue of this regulation to disclose any information in respect of—

(a) any communication between a professional legal adviser and the adviser's client in connection with the giving of legal advice with respect to the client's obligations, liabilities or rights under these Regulations, or

(b) any communication between a professional legal adviser and the adviser's client, or between such an adviser or the adviser's client and any other person, made in connection with or in contemplation of proceedings under or arising out of these Regulations (including proceedings before the Tribunal) and for the purposes of such proceedings.

Enforcement: appeals

31B.—(1) A communications provider on whom a third party information notice has been served may appeal to the Tribunal against the notice.

(2) Appeals shall be determined in accordance with section 49 of and Schedule 6 to the Data Protection Act 1998 as modified by Schedule 1 to these Regulations."

13. After regulation 36 insert—

"Review of implementation

37.—(1) Before the end of each review period, the Secretary of State must—

(a) carry out a review of the implementation in the United Kingdom of the Directive;

(b) set out the conclusions of the review in a report; and

(c) publish the report.

(2) In carrying out the review the Secretary of State must, so far as is reasonable, have regard to how the Directive is implemented in other member States.

(3) The report must in particular—

(a) set out the objectives intended to be achieved by the implementation in the United Kingdom of the Directive;

(b) assess the extent to which those objectives are achieved; and

(c) assess whether those objectives remain appropriate and, if so, the extent to which they could be achieved with a system that imposes less regulation.

(4) "Review period" means—

(a) the period of five years beginning with the 26th May 2011; and

(b) subject to paragraph (5), each successive period of 5 years.

(5) If a report under this regulation is published before the last day of the review period to which it relates, the following review period is to being with the day on which that report is published."

14. Schedule 1 to the 2003 Regulations is amended as follows—

(a) In the title of the Schedule, after "Part V" insert "and sections 55A to 55E";

(b) After paragraph 2 insert "2A. Sections 41A to 41C shall be omitted.";

(c) In paragraph 4, at the end of the substituted subparagraph (c) for "; and" and paragraph (d) there shall be substituted—

"(d) in subsection (8), for "under this Act" there shall be substituted "under the Privacy and Electronic Communications (EC Directive) Regulations 2003";

(e) in subsection (8B), for "under this Act (other than an offence under section 47)" there shall be substituted "under the Privacy and Electronic Communications (EC Directive) Regulations 2003"; and

(f) subsection (10) shall be omitted.";

(d) For paragraph 6 there shall be substituted—

"**6.** In section 47—

(a) in subsection (1), "special information notice" there shall be substituted "third party information notice"; and

(b) in subsection (2), for "special information notice" there shall be substituted "third party information notice".";

(e) After paragraph 8, insert—

"**8A.** In section 55A—

(a) in subsection (1)—

(i) for "data controller" there shall be substituted "person", and

(ii) for "of section 4(4) by the data controller" there shall be substituted "of the requirements of the Privacy and Electronic Communications (EC Directive) Regulations 2003";

(b) in subsection (3), for "data controller" there shall be substituted "person";

(c) subsection (3A) shall be omitted;

(d) in subsection (4), for "data controller" there shall be substituted "person";

(e) in subsection (9), the definition of "data controller" shall be omitted.

8B. In section 55B, for the words "data controller" (in subsections (1), (3) and (4)), there shall be substituted the word "person".";

(f) In paragraph 9, for "Schedule (6)" substitute "Schedule 6";

(g) In paragraph 10 at the end of subparagraph (a) omit "; and" and subparagraph (b) and replace with—

"(b) in subparagraph (1A) for "data controller" there shall be substituted "person", and for "requirement imposed by an assessment notice" there shall be substituted "the audit provisions in regulations 5 and 5B of the 2003 Regulations";

(c) in subparagraph (1B)—

(i) for "data controller" there shall be substituted "person";

(ii) for "data protection principles" there shall be substituted "the requirements of the 2003 Regulations";

(iii) for "assessment notice" there shall be substituted "audit notice"; and

(iv) the words "subparagraph (2) and" shall be omitted;

(d) subparagraph (2) shall be omitted;

(e) in subparagraphs (3)(d)(ii) and (3)(f) for the words "data controller" there shall be substituted "person", and for the words "the data protection principles" there shall be substituted "the requirements of the 2003 Regulations".";

(h) After paragraph 10 insert—

"**10A.** In paragraph 2(1A) of Schedule 9 for "assessment notice" there shall be substituted "audit notice".."

Amendment of the Telecommunications (Lawful Business Practice) (Interception of Communications) Regulations 2000

15. The Telecommunications (Lawful Business Practice) (Interception of Communications) Regulations 2000[5] are amended as follows—

(a) in regulation 3(1) omit "or implied";

---

[5] S.I. 2000/2699; which was amended by S.I. 2003/2426. (6) O.J. L 337, 18.12.2009, p.11.

(b) at the end of regulation 3(3) insert "as amended by Directive 2009/136/EC of the European Parliament and of the Council of 25 November 2009 amending Directive 2002/22/EC on universal service and users' rights relating to electronic communications networks and services, Directive 2002/58/EC concerning the processing of personal data and the protection of privacy in the electronic communications sector and Regulation (EC) No 2006/2004 on cooperation between national authorities responsible for the enforcement of consumer protection laws[6].".

Amendment of the Enterprise Act 2002

16. The Enterprise Act 2002[7] is amended as follows—

(a) in section 213(5A), after paragraph (i) insert "(j) the Information Commissioner";

(b) in Schedule 13, after paragraph 11 insert—

"**12.** Article 13 of Directive 2002/58/EC of the European Parliament and of the Council of 12 July 2002 concerning the processing of personal data and the protection of privacy in the electronic communications sector (Directive on privacy and electronic communications).".

Amendment of the Enterprise Act 2002 (Part 8 Community Infringements Specified UK Laws) Order 2003

17. At the end of the Schedule to the Enterprise Act 2002 (Part 8 Community Infringements Specified UK Laws) Order 2003(8)[8] insert—

"Article 13 of Directive 2002/58/EC of the European Parliament and of the Council of 12 July 2002 concerning the processing of personal data and the protection of privacy in the electronic communications sector (Directive on privacy and electronic communications)	Regulations 19 to 26 and 30 and 32 of the Privacy and Electronic Communications (EC Directive) Regulations 2003"

Ed Vaizey
Parliamentary Under Secretary of State
Department for Culture, Media and Sport

4thMay 2011

---

[6] O.J. L 337, 18.12.2009, p.11
[7] 2002 c.40. Section 213(5A) was inserted by S.I. 2006/3363. Schedule 13 has been amended by S.I. 2004/2095, 2006/3363, 2008/1277, 2009/2999 and 2010/2960.
[8] S.I. 2003/1374; which has been amended but those amendments are not relevant.

PRIVACY AND ELECTRONIC COMMUNICATIONS

Explanatory Note

(This note is not part of the Order)

These Regulations implement Articles 2 and 3 of Directive 2009/136/EC of the European Parliament and of the Council of 25 November 2009 amending Directive 2002/22/EC on universal service and users' rights relating to electronic communications networks and services, Directive 2002/58/ EC concerning the processing of personal data and the protection of privacy in the electronic communications sector and Regulation (EC) No 2006/2004 on cooperation between national authorities responsible for the enforcement of consumer protection laws by making amendments to the Privacy and Electronic Communications (EC Directive) Regulations 2003 ("the 2003 Regulations").

Regulation 3 amends the definition of "location data" and inserts a new definition of "personal data breach" into the 2003 Regulations.

Regulation 4 makes provision in relation to the required measures to be taken by communications providers in ensuring that the processing of personal data is secure. Regulation 4 also gives the Information Commissioner the power to audit compliance with these requirements.

Regulation 5 inserts a new provision into the 2003 Regulations which relates to the notification of personal data breaches. In all cases, the Information Commissioner must be notified. In some cases, the subscriber or user must also be notified where there is a risk that the breach would adversely affect the personal data or privacy of that user.

Regulation 5 also inserts provision into the 2003 Regulations for the auditing and enforcement of the notification provisions. In the event of failure to comply, the Information Commissioner will be able to impose a fixed civil monetary penalty on a service provider.

Regulation 6 amends the provisions in the 2003 Regulations on the storage of or access to information on the terminal equipment of end users. It also makes provision as to the signification of consent which must be sought as a result of the changes to the Directive.

Regulation 7 makes a minor textual amendment to regulation 7 of the 2003 Regulations.

Regulation 8 makes a minor textual amendment to regulation 19(1) of the 2003 Regulations. Regulation 9 amends regulation 23 of the 2003 Regulations, by providing for the prohibition of sending electronic mail which contravenes the information requirements in regulation 7 of the Electronic Commerce (EC Directive) Regulations 2002, or sending an e-mail which encourages recipients to visit websites which contravene that regulation.

Regulation 10 makes provision to allow police and the security services to have access to personal data of users of public electronic communications networks and services. It also makes provision to compel service providers to establish and maintain procedures to allow access to that data.

Regulation 11 makes minor amendments to regulation 31 of the 2003 Regulations. The amendments extend section 55A to 55E of the Data Protection Act 1998 to the 2003 Regulations which will allow the Information Commissioner to issue civil monetary penalties for non-compliance with the Regulations of up to £500,000.

Regulation 12 inserts new regulations 31A and 31B which make provision for third party information notices. The Information Commissioner may request information from a communications provider which relates to the use of that provider's network or service by a third party which is in contravention of any part of the Regulations. New regulation 31B makes provision for appeals against third party information notices.

Regulation 13 inserts a new regulation 37 into the 2003 Regulations which requires the Secretary of State to conduct a review of the implementation of the Directive in the United Kingdom at least every 5 years and lay a report of that review before Parliament.

Regulation 14 amends Schedule 1 to the 2003 Regulations.

Regulation 15 amends the Telecommunications (Lawful Business Practice) (Interception of Communications) Regulations 2000.

Regulation 16 amends the Enterprise Act 2002 to include reference to the Information Commissioner, and Article 13 of the 2002 Directive for the purposes of the enforcement of the provisions of that Article as a Community Infringement under Part 8 of the Enterprise Act 2002.

Regulation 17 inserts article 13 of the 2002 Directive into the Schedule to the Enterprise Act 2002 (Part 8 Community Infringements Specified UK Laws) Order 2003, which lists Community infringements for the purposes of the Enterprise Act 2002.

A transposition and a full impact assessment of the effect that this instrument will have on the costs of business and the voluntary sector are available from the Department for Culture, Media and Sport, 2–4 Cockspur Street, London, SW1Y 5DH and are published with the Explanatory Memorandum alongside the instrument on www.legislation.gov.uk.

APPENDIX F

Regulation of Investigatory Powers Act 2000

(2000 c.23)

PART I

COMMUNICATIONS

CHAPTER I

INTERCEPTION

Unlawful and authorised interception

1. *Unlawful interception*

(1) It shall be an offence for a person intentionally and without lawful authority to intercept, at any place in the United Kingdom, any communication in the course of its transmission by means of—

(a) a public postal service; or

(b) a public telecommunication system.

(2) It shall be an offence for a person—

(a) intentionally and without lawful authority, and

(b) otherwise than in circumstances in which his conduct is excluded by subsection (6) from criminal liability under this subsection,

to intercept, at any place in the United Kingdom, any communication in the course of its transmission by means of a private telecommunication system.

(3) Any interception of a communication which is carried out at any place in the United Kingdom by, or with the express or implied consent of, a person having the right to control the operation or the use of a private telecommunication system shall be actionable at the suit or instance of the sender or recipient, or intended recipient, of the communication if it is without lawful authority and is either—

    (a) an interception of that communication in the course of its transmission by means of that private system; or

    (b) an interception of that communication in the course of its transmission, by means of a public telecommunication system, to or from apparatus comprised in that private telecommunication system.

(4) Where the United Kingdom is a party to an international agreement which—

    (a) relates to the provision of mutual assistance in connection with, or in the form of, the interception of communications,

    (b) requires the issue of a warrant, order or equivalent instrument in cases in which assistance is given, and

    (c) is designated for the purposes of this subsection by an order made by the Secretary of State,

it shall be the duty of the Secretary of State to secure that no request for assistance in accordance with the agreement is made on behalf of a person in the United Kingdom to the competent authorities of a country or territory outside the United Kingdom except with lawful authority.

(5) Conduct has lawful authority for the purposes of this section if, and only if—

    (a) it is authorised by or under section 3 or 4;

    (b) it takes place in accordance with a warrant under section 5 ("an interception warrant"); or

    (c) it is in exercise, in relation to any stored communication, of any statutory power that is exercised (apart from this section) for the purpose of obtaining information or of taking possession of any document or other property;

and conduct (whether or not prohibited by this section) which has lawful authority for the purposes of this section by virtue of paragraph (a) or (b) shall also be taken to be lawful for all other purposes.

(6) The circumstances in which a person makes an interception of a communication in the course of its transmission by means of a private telecommunication system are such that his conduct is excluded from criminal liability under subsection (2) if—

    (a) he is a person with a right to control the operation or the use of the system; or

    (b) he has the express or implied consent of such a person to make the interception.

(7) A person who is guilty of an offence under subsection (1) or (2) shall be liable—

    (a) on conviction on indictment, to imprisonment for a term not exceeding two years or to a fine, or to both;

    (b) on summary conviction, to a fine not exceeding the statutory maximum.

(8) No proceedings for any offence which is an offence by virtue of this section shall be instituted—

    (a) in England and Wales, except by or with the consent of the Director of Public Prosecutions;

    (b) in Northern Ireland, except by or with the consent of the Director of Public Prosecutions for Northern Ireland.

2. *Meaning and location of "interception" etc*

(1) In this Act—

"postal service" means any service which—

(a) consists in the following, or in any one or more of them, namely, the collection, sorting, conveyance, distribution and delivery (whether in the United Kingdom or elsewhere) of postal items; and

(b) is offered or provided as a service the main purpose of which, or one of the main purposes of which, is to make available, or to facilitate, a means of transmission from place to place of postal items containing communications;

"private telecommunication system" means any telecommunication system which, without itself being a public telecommunication system, is a system in relation to which the following conditions are satisfied—

(a) it is attached, directly or indirectly and whether or not for the purposes of the communication in question, to a public telecommunication system; and

(b) there is apparatus comprised in the system which is both located in the United Kingdom and used (with or without other apparatus) for making the attachment to the public telecommunication system;

"public postal service" means any postal service which is offered or provided to, or to a substantial section of, the public in any one or more parts of the United Kingdom;

"public telecommunications service" means any telecommunications service which is offered or provided to, or to a substantial section of, the public in any one or more parts of the United Kingdom;

"public telecommunication system" means any such parts of a telecommunication system by means of which any public telecommunications service is provided as are located in the United Kingdom;

"telecommunications service" means any service that consists in the provision of access to, and of facilities for making use of, any telecommunication system (whether or not one provided by the person providing the service); and

"telecommunication system" means any system (including the apparatus comprised in it) which exists (whether wholly or partly in the United Kingdom or elsewhere) for the purpose of facilitating the transmission of communications by any means involving the use of electrical or electro-magnetic energy.

(2) For the purposes of this Act, but subject to the following provisions of this section, a person intercepts a communication in the course of its transmission by means of a telecommunication system if, and only if, he—

(a) so modifies or interferes with the system, or its operation,

(b) so monitors transmissions made by means of the system, or

(c) so monitors transmissions made by wireless telegraphy to or from apparatus comprised in the system,

as to make some or all of the contents of the communication available, while being transmitted, to a person other than the sender or intended recipient of the communication.

(3) References in this Act to the interception of a communication do not include references to the interception of any communication broadcast for general reception.

(4) For the purposes of this Act the interception of a communication takes place in the United Kingdom if, and only if, the modification, interference or monitoring or, in the case of a postal item, the interception is effected by conduct within the United Kingdom and the communication is either—

(a) intercepted in the course of its transmission by means of a public postal service or public telecommunication system; or

(b) intercepted in the course of its transmission by means of a private telecommunication system in a case in which the sender or intended recipient of the communication is in the United Kingdom.

(5) References in this Act to the interception of a communication in the course of its transmission by means of a postal service or telecommunication system do not include references to—

(a) any conduct that takes place in relation only to so much of the communication as consists in any traffic data comprised in or attached to a communication (whether by the sender or otherwise) for the purposes of any postal service or telecommunication system by means of which it is being or may be transmitted; or

(b) any such conduct, in connection with conduct falling within paragraph (a), as gives a person who is neither the sender nor the intended recipient only so much access to a communication as is necessary for the purpose of identifying traffic data so comprised or attached.

(6) For the purposes of this section references to the modification of a telecommunication system include references to the attachment of any apparatus to, or other modification of or interference with—

(a) any part of the system; or

(b) any wireless telegraphy apparatus used for making transmissions to or from apparatus comprised in the system.

(7) For the purposes of this section the times while a communication is being transmitted by means of a telecommunication system shall be taken to include any time when the system by means of which the communication is being, or has been, transmitted is used for storing it in a manner that enables the intended recipient to collect it or otherwise to have access to it.

(8) For the purposes of this section the cases in which any contents of a communication are to be taken to be made available to a person while being transmitted shall include any case in which any of the contents of the communication, while being transmitted, are diverted or recorded so as to be available to a person subsequently.

(9) In this section "traffic data", in relation to any communication, means—

(a) any data identifying, or purporting to identify, any person, apparatus or location to or from which the communication is or may be transmitted,

(b) any data identifying or selecting, or purporting to identify or select, apparatus through which, or by means of which, the communication is or may be transmitted,

(c) any data comprising signals for the actuation of apparatus used for the purposes of a telecommunication system for effecting (in whole or in part) the transmission of any communication, and

(d) any data identifying the data or other data as data comprised in or attached to a particular communication, but that expression includes data identifying a computer file or computer program access to which is obtained, or which is run, by means of the communication to the extent only that the file or program is identified by reference to the apparatus in which it is stored.

(10) In this section—

(a) references, in relation to traffic data comprising signals for the actuation of apparatus, to a telecommunication system by means of which a communication is being or may be transmitted include references to any telecommunication system in which that apparatus is comprised; and

(b) references to traffic data being attached to a communication include references to the data and the communication being logically associated with each other;

and in this section "data", in relation to a postal item, means anything written on the outside of the item.

(11) In this section "postal item" means any letter, postcard or other such thing in writing as may be used by the sender for imparting information to the recipient, or any packet or parcel.

3. *Lawful interception without an interception warrant*

(1) Conduct by any person consisting in the interception of a communication is authorised by this section if the communication is one which, or which that person has reasonable grounds for believing, is both—

(a) a communication sent by a person who has consented to the interception; and

(b) a communication the intended recipient of which has so consented.

(2) Conduct by any person consisting in the interception of a communication is authorised by this section if—

(a) the communication is one sent by, or intended for, a person who has consented to the interception; and

(b) surveillance by means of that interception has been authorised under Part II.

(3) Conduct consisting in the interception of a communication is authorised by this section if—

(a) it is conduct by or on behalf of a person who provides a postal service or a telecommunications service; and

(b) it takes place for purposes connected with the provision or operation of that service or with the enforcement, in relation to that service, of any enactment relating to the use of postal services or telecommunications services.

(4) Conduct by any person consisting in the interception of a communication in the course of its transmission by means of wireless telegraphy is authorised by this section if it takes place—

(a) with the authority of a designated person under section 48 of the Wireless Telegraphy Act 2006 (interception and disclosure of wireless telegraphy messages); and

(b) for purposes connected with anything falling within subsection (5).

(5) Each of the following falls within this subsection—

(a) the grant of wireless telegraphy licences under the Wireless Telegraphy Act 2006;

(b) the prevention or detection of anything which constitutes interference with wireless telegraphy; and

[(c) the enforcement of—

(i) any provision of Part 2 (other than Chapter 2 and sections 27 to 31) or Part 3 of that Act, or

(ii) any enactment not falling within subparagraph (i);

that relates to such interference.]¹

4. *Power to provide for lawful interception*

(1) Conduct by any person ("the interceptor") consisting in the interception of a communication in the course of its transmission by means of a telecommunication system is authorised by this section if—

(a) the interception is carried out for the purpose of obtaining information about the communications of a person who, or who the interceptor has reasonable grounds for believing, is in a country or territory outside the United Kingdom;

(b) the interception relates to the use of a telecommunications service provided to persons in that country or territory which is either—

(i) a public telecommunications service; or

(ii) a telecommunications service that would be a public telecommunications service if the persons to whom it is offered or provided were members of the public in a part of the United Kingdom;

(c) the person who provides that service (whether the interceptor or another person) is required by the law of that country or territory to carry out, secure or facilitate the interception in question;

(d) the situation is one in relation to which such further conditions as may be prescribed by regulations made by the Secretary of State are required to be satisfied before conduct may be treated as authorised by virtue of this subsection; and

(e) the conditions so prescribed are satisfied in relation to that situation.

(2) Subject to subsection (3), the Secretary of State may by regulations authorise any such conduct described in the regulations as appears to him to constitute a legitimate practice reasonably required for the purpose, in connection with the carrying on of any business, of monitoring or keeping a record of—

(a) communications by means of which transactions are entered into in the course of that business; or

(b) other communications relating to that business or taking place in the course of its being carried on.

(3) Nothing in any regulations under subsection (2) shall authorise the interception of any communication except in the course of its transmission using apparatus or services provided by or to the person carrying on the business for use wholly or partly in connection with that business.

(4) conduct taking place in a prison is authorised by this section if it is conduct in exercise of any power conferred by or under any rules made under section 47 of the Prison Act 1952, section 39 of the Prisons (Scotland) Act 1989 or section 13 of the Prison Act (Northern Ireland) 1953 (prison rules).

(5) Conduct taking place in any hospital premises where high security psychiatric services are provided is authorised by this section if it is conduct in pursuance of, and in accordance with, any direction given under section 8 of the National Health Service Act 2006, or section 19 or 23 of the National Health Service (Wales) Act 2006 (directions as to the carrying out of their functions by health bodies) to the body providing those services at those premises.

(6) Conduct taking place in a state hospital is authorised by this section if it is conduct in pursuance of, and in accordance with, any direction given to the State Hospitals Board for Scotland under section 2(5) of the National Health Service (Scotland) Act 1978 (regulations and directions as to the exercise of their functions by health boards) as applied by Article 5(1) of and the Schedule to The State Hospitals Board for Scotland Order 1995 (which applies certain provisions of that Act of 1978 to the State Hospitals Board).

(7) In this section references to a business include references to any activities of a government department, of any public authority or of any person or office holder on whom functions are conferred by or under any enactment.

(8) In this section—

"government department" includes any part of the Scottish Administration, a Northern Ireland department and [the Welsh Assembly Government][2];

"high security psychiatric services" has the same meaning as in the section 4 of the National Health Service Act 2006;

"hospital premises" has the same meaning as in *section 4(3)* of that Act; and

"state hospital" has the same meaning as in the National Health Service (Scotland) Act 1978.

(9) In this section "prison" means—

(a) any prison, young offender institution, young offenders centre or remand centre which is under the general superintendence of, or is provided by, the Secretary of State under the Prison Act 1952 or the Prison Act (Northern Ireland) 1953, or

(b) any prison, young offenders institution or remand centre which is under the general superintendence of the Scottish Ministers under the Prisons (Scotland) Act 1989, and includes any contracted out prison, within the meaning of Part IV of the Criminal Justice Act 1991 or section 106(4) of the Criminal Justice and Public Order Act 1994, and any legalised police cells within the meaning of section 14 of the Prisons (Scotland) Act 1989.

[. . .]

CHAPTER II

ACQUISITION AND DISCLOSURE OF COMMUNICATIONS DATA

21. *Lawful acquisition and disclosure of communications data*

(1) This Chapter applies to—

(a) any conduct in relation to a postal service or telecommunication system for obtaining communications data, other than conduct consisting in the interception of communications in the course of their transmission by means of such a service or system; and

(b) the disclosure to any person of communications data.

(2) Conduct to which this Chapter applies shall be lawful for all purposes if—

(a) it is conduct in which any person is authorised or required to engage by an authorisation or notice granted or given under this Chapter; and

(b) the conduct is in accordance with, or in pursuance of, the authorisation or requirement.

(3) A person shall not be subject to any civil liability in respect of any conduct of his which—

(a) is incidental to any conduct that is lawful by virtue of subsection (2); and

(b) is not itself conduct an authorisation or warrant for which is capable of being granted under a relevant enactment and might reasonably have been expected to have been sought in the case in question.

(4) In this Chapter "communications data" means any of the following—

(a) any traffic data comprised in or attached to a communication (whether by the sender or otherwise) for the purposes of any postal service or telecommunication system by means of which it is being or may be transmitted;

(b) any information which includes none of the contents of a communication (apart from any information falling within paragraph (a)) and is about the use made by any person—

(i) of any postal service or telecommunications service; or
(ii) in connection with the provision to or use by any person of any telecommunications service, of any part of a telecommunication system;

(c) any information not falling within paragraph (a) or (b) that is held or obtained, in relation to persons to whom he provides the service, by a person providing a postal service or telecommunications service.

(5) In this section "relevant enactment" means—

(a) an enactment contained in this Act;

(b) section 5 of the Intelligence Services Act 1994 (warrants for the intelligence services); or

(c) an enactment contained in Part III of the Police Act 1997 (powers of the police and of customs officers).

(6) In this section "traffic data", in relation to any communication, means—

(a) any data identifying, or purporting to identify, any person, apparatus or location to or from which the communication is or may be transmitted,

(b) any data identifying or selecting, or purporting to identify or select, apparatus through which, or by means of which, the communication is or may be transmitted,

(c) any data comprising signals for the actuation of apparatus used for the purposes of a telecommunication system for effecting (in whole or in part) the transmission of any communication, and

(d) any data identifying the data or other data as data comprised in or attached to a particular communication.

but that expression includes data identifying a computer file or computer program access to which is obtained, or which is run, by means of the communication to the extent only that the file or program is identified by reference to the apparatus in which it is stored.

(7) In this section—

(a) references, in relation to traffic data comprising signals for the actuation of apparatus, to a telecommunication system by means of which a communication is being or may be transmitted include references to any telecommunication system in which that apparatus is comprised; and

(b) references to traffic data being attached to a communication include references to the data and the communication being logically associated with each other;

and in this section "data", in relation to a postal item, means anything written on the outside of the item.

22. *Obtaining and disclosing communications data*

(1) This section applies where a person designated for the purposes of this Chapter believes that it is necessary on grounds falling within subsection (2) to obtain any communications data.

(2) It is necessary on grounds falling within this subsection to obtain communications data if it is necessary—

(a) in the interests of national security;

(b) for the purpose of preventing or detecting crime or of preventing disorder;

(c) in the interests of the economic well-being of the United Kingdom;

(d) in the interests of public safety;

(e) for the purpose of protecting public health;

(f) for the purpose of assessing or collecting any tax, duty, levy or other imposition, contribution or charge payable to a government department;

(g) for the purpose, in an emergency, of preventing death or injury or any damage to a person's physical or mental health, or of mitigating any injury or damage to a person's physical or mental health; or

(h) for any purpose (not falling within paragraphs (a) to (g)) which is specified for the purposes of this subsection by an order made by the Secretary of State.

(3) Subject to subsection (5), the designated person may grant an authorisation for persons holding offices, ranks or positions with the same relevant public authority as the designated person to engage in any conduct to which this Chapter applies.

(4) Subject to subsection (5), where it appears to the designated person that a postal or telecommunications operator is or may be in possession of, or be capable of obtaining, any communications data, the designated person may, by notice to the postal or telecommunications operator, require the operator—

(a) if the operator is not already in possession of the data, to obtain the data; and

(b) in any case, to disclose all of the data in his possession or subsequently obtained by him.

(5) The designated person shall not grant an authorisation under subsection (3), or give a notice under subsection (4), unless he believes that obtaining the data in question

by the conduct authorised or required by the authorisation or notice is proportionate to what is sought to be achieved by so obtaining the data.

(6) It shall be the duty of the postal or telecommunications operator to comply with the requirements of any notice given to him under subsection (4).

(7) A person who is under a duty by virtue of subsection (6) shall not be required to do anything in pursuance of that duty which it is not reasonably practicable for him to do.

(8) The duty imposed by subsection (6) shall be enforceable by civil proceedings by the Secretary of State for an injunction, or for specific performance of a statutory duty under section 45 of the Court of Session Act 1988, or for any other appropriate relief.

(9) The Secretary of State shall not make an order under subsection (2)(h) unless a draft of the order has been laid before Parliament and approved by a resolution of each House.

23. *Form and duration of authorisation and notices*

(1) An authorisation under section 22(3)—

    (a) must be granted in writing or (if not in writing) in a manner that produces a record of its having been granted;

    (b) must describe the conduct to which this Chapter applies that is authorised and the communications data in relation to which it is authorised;

    (c) must specify the matters falling within section 22(2) by reference to which it is granted; and

    (d) must specify the office, rank or position held by the person granting the authorisation.

(2) A notice under section 22(4) requiring communications data to be disclosed or to be obtained and disclosed—

    (a) must be given in writing or (if not in writing) must be given in a manner that produces a record of its having been given;

    (b) must describe the communications data to be obtained or disclosed under the notice;

    (c) must specify the matters falling within section 22(2) by reference to which the notice is given;

    (d) must specify the office, rank or position held by the person giving it; and

    (e) must specify the manner in which any disclosure required by the notice is to be made.

(3) A notice under section 22(4) shall not require the disclosure of data to any person other than—

    (a) the person giving the notice; or

    (b) such other person as may be specified in or otherwise identified by, or in accordance with, the provisions of the notice;

but the provisions of the notice shall not specify or otherwise identify a person for the purposes of paragraph (b) unless he holds an office, rank or position with the same relevant public authority as the person giving the notice.

(4) An authorisation under section 22(3) or notice under section 22(4)—

(a) shall not authorise or require any data to be obtained after the end of the period of one month beginning with the date on which the authorisation is granted or the notice given; and

(b) in the case of a notice, shall not authorise or require any disclosure after the end of that period of any data not in the possession of, or obtained by, the postal or telecommunications operator at a time during that period.

(5) An authorisation under section 22(3) or notice under section 22(4) may be renewed at any time before the end of the period of one month applying (in accordance with subsection (4) or subsection (7)) to that authorisation or notice.

(6) A renewal of an authorisation under section 22(3) or of a notice under section 22(4) shall be by the grant or giving, in accordance with this section, of a further authorisation or notice.

(7) Subsection (4) shall have effect in relation to a renewed authorisation or renewal notice as if the period of one month mentioned in that subsection did not begin until the end of the period of one month applicable to the authorisation or notice that is current at the time of the renewal.

(8) Where a person who has given a notice under subsection (4) of section 22 is satisfied—

(a) that it is no longer necessary on grounds falling within subsection (2) of that section for the requirements of the notice to be complied with, or

(b) that the conduct required by the notice is no longer proportionate to what is sought to be achieved by obtaining communications data to which the notice relates,

he shall cancel the notice.

(9) The Secretary of State may by regulations provide for the person by whom any duty imposed by subsection (8) is to be performed in a case in which it would otherwise fall on a person who is no longer available to perform it; and regulations under this subsection may provide for the person on whom the duty is to fall to be a person appointed in accordance with the regulations.

24. *Arrangements for payments*

(1) It shall be the duty of the Secretary of State to ensure that such arrangements are in force as he thinks appropriate for requiring or authorising, in such cases as he thinks fit, the making to postal and telecommunications operators of appropriate contributions towards the costs incurred by them in complying with notices under section 22(4).

(2) For the purpose of complying with his duty under this section, the Secretary of State may make arrangements for payments to be made out of money provided by Parliament.

25. *Interpretation of Chapter II*

(1) In this Chapter—

"communications data" has the meaning given by section 21(4);

"designated" shall be construed in accordance with subsection (2);

"postal or telecommunications operator" means a person who provides a postal service or telecommunications service;

"relevant public authority" means (subject to subsection (4)) any of the following—

  (a) a police force;

  (b) the Serious Organised Crime Agency;

  [(ca) the Scottish Crime and Drug Enforcement Agency;][3]

  (d) the Commissioners of Customs and Excise;

  (e) the Commissioners of Inland Revenue;

  (f) any of the intelligence services;

  (g) any such public authority not falling within paragraphs (a) to (f) as may be specified for the purposes of this subsection by an order made by the Secretary of State.

(2) Subject to subsection (3), the persons designated for the purposes of this Chapter are the individuals holding such offices, ranks or positions with relevant public authorities as are prescribed for the purposes of this subsection by an order made by the Secretary of State.

(3) The Secretary of State may by order impose restrictions—

  (a) on the authorisations and notices under this Chapter that may be granted or given by any individual holding an office, rank or position with a specified public authority; and

  (b) on the circumstances in which, or the purposes for which, such authorisations may be granted or notices given by any such individual.

(3A) References in this Chapter to an individual holding an office or position with the Serious Organised Crime Agency include references to any member of the staff of that Agency.

(4) The Secretary of State may by order—

  (a) remove any person from the list of persons who are for the time being relevant public authorities for the purposes of this Chapter; and

  (b) make such consequential amendments, repeals or revocations in this or any other enactment as appear to him to be necessary or expedient.

(5) The Secretary of State shall not make an order under this section—

  (a) that adds any person to the list of persons who are for the time being relevant public authorities for the purposes of this Chapter, or

  (b) that by virtue of subsection (4)(b) amends or repeals any provision of an Act, unless a draft of the order has been laid before Parliament and approved by a resolution of each House.

APPENDIX G

Telecommunications (Lawful Business Practice) (Interception of Communications) Regulations

2000/2699

1. *Citation and commencement*

These Regulations may be cited as the Telecommunications (Lawful Business Practice) (Interception of Communications) Regulations 2000 and shall come into force on 24th October 2000.

2. *Interpretation*

In these Regulations—

(a) references to a business include references to activities of a government department, of any public authority or of any person or office holder on whom functions are conferred by or under any enactment;

(b) a reference to a communication as relevant to a business is a reference to—

    (i) a communication—

        (aa) by means of which a transaction is entered into in the course of that business, or

        (bb) which otherwise relates to that business, or

    (ii) a communication which otherwise takes place in the course of the carrying on of that business;

(c) "regulatory or self-regulatory practices or procedures" means practices or procedures—

    (i) compliance with which is required or recommended by, under or by virtue of—

        (aa) any provision of the law of a member state or other state within the European Economic Area, or

        (bb) any standard or code of practice published by or on behalf of a body established in a member state or other state within the European

Economic Area which includes amongst its objectives the publication of standards or codes of practice for the conduct of business, or

(ii) which are otherwise applied for the purpose of ensuring compliance with anything so required or recommended;

(d) "system controller" means, in relation to a particular telecommunication system, a person with a right to control its operation or use.

3. *Lawful interception of a communication*

(1) For the purpose of section 1(5)(a) of the Act, conduct is authorised, subject to paragraphs (2) and (3) below, if it consists of interception of a communication, in the course of its transmission by means of a telecommunication system, which is effected by or with the express or implied consent of the system controller for the purpose of—

(a) monitoring or keeping a record of communications—

(i) in order to—

(aa) establish the existence of facts, or
(bb) ascertain compliance with regulatory or self-regulatory practices or procedures which are—

applicable to the system controller in the carrying on of his business or

applicable to another person in the carrying on of his business where that person is supervised by the system controller in respect of those practices or procedures, or

(cc) ascertain or demonstrate the standards which are achieved or ought to be achieved by persons using the system in the course of their duties, or

(ii) in the interests of national security, or
(iii) for the purpose of preventing or detecting crime, or
(iv) for the purpose of investigating or detecting the unauthorised use of that or any other telecommunication system, or
(v) where that is undertaken—

(aa) in order to secure, or
(bb) as an inherent part of,

the effective operation of the system (including any monitoring or keeping of a record which would be authorised by section 3(3) of the Act if the conditions in paragraphs (a) and (b) thereof were satisfied); or

(b) monitoring communications for the purpose of determining whether they are communications relevant to the system controller's business which fall within regulation 2(b)(i) above; or

(c) monitoring communications made to a confidential voice-telephony counselling or support service which is free of charge (other than the cost, if any, of making a telephone call) and operated in such a way that users may remain anonymous if they so choose.

(2) Conduct is authorised by paragraph (1) of this regulation only if—(a) the interception in question is effected solely for the purpose of monitoring or (where appropriate) keeping a record of communications relevant to the system controller's business;

(b) the telecommunication system in question is provided for use wholly or partly in connection with that business;

(c) the system controller has made all reasonable efforts to inform every person who may use the telecommunication system in question that communications transmitted by means thereof may be intercepted; and

(d) in a case falling within—

(i) paragraph (1)(a)(ii) above, the person by or on whose behalf the interception is effected is a person specified in section 6(2)(a) to (i) of the Act;

(ii) paragraph (1)(b) above, the communication is one which is intended to be received (whether or not it has been actually received) by a person using the telecommunication system in question.

(3) Conduct falling within paragraph (1)(a)(i) above is authorised only to the extent that Article 5 of Directive 2002/58/EC of the European Parliament and of the Council of 12 July 2002 concerning the processing of personal data and the protection of privacy in the electronic communications sector so permits.[1]

---

[1] substituted by Privacy and Electronic Communications (EC Directive) Regulations 2003/2426 reg. 34

INDEX

This index has been prepared using Sweet and Maxwell's Legal Taxonomy. Main index entries conform to keywords provided by the Legal Taxonomy except where references to specific documents or non-standard terms (denoted by quotation marks) have been included. These keywords provide a means of identifying similar concepts in other Sweet and Maxwell publications and online services to which keywords from the Legal Taxonomy have been applied. Readers may find some minor differences between terms used in the text and those which appear in the index. Suggestions to *sweetandmaxwell.taxonomy@thomson.com*.

All references are to paragraph number

INDEX